Winner's Electoral College Vote %	Winner's Popular Vote %	Congress	House		Senate	
			Majority Party	Minority Party	Majority Party	Minority Party
**	No popular vote	1st	38 Admin †	26 Opp	17 Admin	9 Opp
		2nd	37 Fed ††	33 Dem-R	16 Fed	13 Dem-R
**	No popular vote	3rd	57 Dem-R	48 Fed	17 Fed	13 Dem-R
		4th	54 Fed	52 Dem-R	19 Fed	13 Dem-R
**	No popular vote	5th	58 Fed	48 Dem-R	20 Fed	12 Dem-R
		6th	64 Fed	42 Dem-R	19 Fed	13 Dem-R
HR**	No popular vote	7th	69 Dem-R	36 Fed	18 Dem-R	13 Fed
		8th	402 Dem-R	39 Fed	25 Dem-R	9 Fed
92.0	No popular vote	9th	116 Dem-R	25 Fed	27 Dem-R	7 Fed
		10th	118 Dem-R	24 Fed	28 Dem-R	6 Fed
69.7	No popular vote	11th	94 Dem-R	48 Fed	28 Dem-R	6 Fed
		12th	108 Dem-R	36 Fed	30 Dem-R	6 Fed
59.0	No popular vote	13th	112 Dem-R	68 Fed	27 Dem-R	9 Fed
		14th	117 Dem-R	65 Fed	25 Dem-R	11 Fed
84.3	No popular vote	15th	141 Dem-R	42 Fed	34 Dem-R	10 Fed
		16th	156 Dem-R	27 Fed	35 Dem-R	7 Fed
99.5	No popular vote	17th	158 Dem-R	25 Fed	44 Dem-R	4 Fed
		18th	187 Dem-R	26 Fed	44 Dem-R	4 Fed
HR	39.1 †††	19th	105 Admin	97 Dem-J	26 Admin	20 Dem-J
		20th	119 Dem-J	94 Admin	28 Dem-J	20 Admin
68.2	56.0	21st	139 Dem	74 Nat R	26 Dem	22 Nat R
		22nd	141 Dem	58 Nat R	25 Dem	21 Nat R
76.6	54.5	23rd	147 Dem	53 AntiMas	20 Dem	20 Nat R
		24th	145 Dem	98 Whig	27 Dem	25 Whig
57.8	50.9	25th	108 Dem	107 Whig	30 Dem	18 Whig
		26th	124 Dem	118 Whig	28 Dem	22 Whig
79.6	52.9					
–	52.9	27th	133 Whig	102 Dem	28 Whig	22 Dem
		28th	142 Dem	79 Whig	28 Whig	25 Dem
61.8	49.6	29th	143 Dem	77 Whig	31 Dem	25 Whig
		30th	115 Whig	108 Dem	36 Dem	21 Whig
56.2	47.3	31st	112 Dem	109 Whig	35 Dem	25 Whig
–	–	32nd	140 Dem	88 Whig	35 Dem	24 Whig
85.8	50.9	33rd	159 Dem	71 Whig	38 Dem	22 Whig
		34th	108 Rep	83 Dem	40 Dem	15 Rep
58.8	45.6	35th	118 Dem	92 Rep	36 Dem	20 Rep
		36th	114 Rep	92 Dem	36 Dem	26 Rep
59.4	39.8	37th	105 Rep	43 Dem	31 Rep	10 Dem
		38th	102 Rep	75 Dem	36 Rep	9 Dem
91.0	55.2					
–	–	39th	149 Union	42 Dem	42 Union	10 Dem
		40th	143 Rep	49 Dem	42 Rep	11 Dem
72.8	52.7	41st	149 Rep	63 Dem	56 Rep	11 Dem
		42nd	134 Rep	104 Dem	52 Rep	17 Dem
81.9	55.6	43rd	194 Rep	92 Dem	49 Rep	19 Dem
		44th	169 Rep	109 Dem	45 Rep	29 Dem
50.1	47.9 †††	45th	153 Dem	140 Rep	39 Rep	36 Dem
		46th	149 Dem	130 Rep	42 Dem	33 Rep
58.0	48.3	47th	147 Rep	135 Dem	37 Rep	37 Dem
–	–	48th	197 Dem	118 Rep	38 Rep	36 Dem
54.6	48.5	49th	183 Dem	140 Rep	43 Rep	34 Dem
		50th	169 Dem	152 Rep	39 Rep	37 Dem

Source for election data: Svend Peterson, *A Statistical History of American Presidential Elections.* New York: Frederick Ungar Publishing, 1963. Updates: Richard Scammon, *America Votes* 19. Washington D.C.: Congressional Quarterly, 1991; *Congressional Quarterly Weekly Report*, Nov. 7, 1992, p. 3552.

Abbreviations:

Admin = Administration supporters
AntiMas = Anti-Masonic
Dem = Democratic
Dem-R = Democratic-Republican
Fed = Federalist

Dem-J = Jacksonian Democrats
Nat R = National Republican
Opp = Opponents of administration
Rep = Republican
Union = Unionist

Current, award-winning coverage . . . Interactive text and online links!

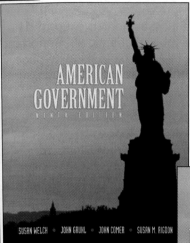

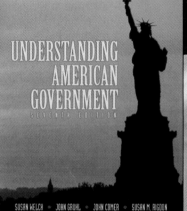

American Government,
Ninth Edition
Casebound. 736 pages.
Nineteen chapters.

Understanding American Government,
Seventh Edition
Paperbound. 592 pages.
Fifteen chapters.

Students experience the **excitement** of today's political debate . . .

the intriguing **diversity** of our citizenry . . .

and see the great difference that **participation** really makes!

Whether you select *American Government* with its four additional chapters devoted to public policy issues or the briefer *Understanding American Government* (without the policy chapters), you'll find that these best-sellers excel in their ability to light the spark of active citizenship in today's student. Authors Susan Welch, John Gruhl, John Comer, and Susan Rigdon infuse the text with current, authoritative scholarship and award-winning coverage of how diverse opinions and interests drive America's government and political climate.

Interacting at every turn with a NEW information-packed **Companion Web Site** and the NEW **American Government Resource Center,** designed specifically to encourage student participation, these new editions of *American Government* and *Understanding American Government* are exemplary choices for your course.

Innovative Web, CD-ROM, and video tools that make course preparation easier than ever
For details, see pages 7–11 of this Preview.

Not only is this the most extensive selection that you'll find with any text, we offer an added bonus: the *Resource Integration Guide*. This essential tool links every chapter's outline—topic by topic—to instructional ideas and corresponding supplement resources. At a glance, you see which specific slides, videos, and other resources for instructors and students are appropriate for each key chapter topic. The *Resource Integration Guide* begins on page 14, following this PREVIEW.

Engaging, current scholarship is at the cornerstone of these authors' success with your students. Welch, Gruhl, Comer, and Rigdon include the most authoritative, up-to-date sources—more than 1,000 in all—bringing students relevance that intrigues, important debate that clarifies, and current news that involves. In this meticulous page-by-page revision, you'll find engaging discussions and analysis of the most hotly debated issues facing the nation today. A few examples:

- **The 2002 elections . . . analysis and aftermath**— Coverage of the 2002 elections is integrated where relevant throughout, including attention to the impact of Iraq and the war on terrorism on the elections' outcome, the difficulties of the Democratic Party and its leadership issues, congressional campaigns, and much more.

- **A new look at the 2000 elections**—The authors discuss the role of the media in the Florida recount (Chapter 5), aspects of election laws that affected the Florida outcome (Chapter 8), the Gore and Bush post-election strategies (Chapter 8), and the role of the Supreme Court in the election outcome (Chapter 13).

- **The role of government in the corporate scandals of 2002**—A completely updated Chapter 9, "Money and Politics," includes new sections on reforms in 2002, secret spending, and the role that campaign finance played in corporate scandals.

- **New discussion of the Bush administration**— Incorporated into Chapter 11, "The Presidency," and throughout this edition, is material on the organization, operation, and policies of the Bush administration. Also included in Chapter 11 is a new section, "Office of the First Lady."

- **A completely rewritten Chapter 12, "The Bureaucracy,"** opens with a new **You Are There** vignette that takes students back to the summer of 2002, asking them to role-play as FBI Director Robert Mueller as he makes critical decisions about the FBI's future.

- **"A Day in the Life of a U.S. Representative,"** a new boxed feature in Chapter 10, "The Congress," offers a fascinating inside account of a day in the life of Illinois Congressman Timothy Johnson, showing students how very "untypical" a typical day for an elected official can really be.

A Day in the Life of a U.S. Representative

There is no such thing as a "typical" day for a member of Congress. But this is one of those ordinary workdays for Representative Timothy V. Johnson, who represents Illinois's Fifteenth District. His newly redistricted constituency will be 350 miles long and will include twenty-two counties. Much of the district is occupied by thousand-plus acre farms, but it also includes the University of Illinois and Illinois State University.

Johnson shares a Washington apartment with staff and flies home at the weekend. Those days are spent traveling the district, making rounds of coffee shops and visiting schools, and, in the summer months, visiting fairs and local celebrations. He also works with his press secretary to prepare a weekly radio spot to update constituents and makes many calls to local TV and radio stations.

Face time with constituents: Representative Timothy Johnson talks to customers of the Edgar, Illinois, County Farm Credit Services agency at an annual gathering in a nearby state park.

Photo by Matt Bisbee. Used with permission.

6:00 A.M.–8:00 A.M. Johnson begins every day with a workout, either on the stationary bike or swimming at the House gym. While he bikes, he reads *Roll Call* and the major daily newspapers.

8:00 Johnson walks a few short blocks to speak at a breakfast fundraiser for Speaker of the House Dennis Hastert. Johnson is not fund-raising himself, but it is an occasion to make contacts with representatives of business and labor interest groups as well as to pay tribute to a powerful member of his state delegation.

9:30 Johnson returns to the House office building for a meeting of the Agriculture Committee. Today it is re-

New boxes that link September 11 issues to chapter topics

Each of the books' new **After 9/11** boxes highlights an issue posed by the September 11 terrorist attacks, helping students understand the event's important connections to specific chapter topics. **After 9/11** topics include:

- Immigration: Is the Door Still Open?
- Interrogating Terrorists
- Media Coverage of International Affairs and War
- The CNN of the Middle East (Al-Jazeera)
- Feeding-Frenzy Lobbying
- Bipartisanship for a While
- Patriotism and Partisanship
- Continuity in Government
- Surveillance Court
- Civil Liberties at Risk
- Profiling of Arabs

AFTER 9/11
INTERROGATING TERRORISTS

The war on terrorism, like past wars, raises questions about the viability of constitutional rights: Can we wage effective war and still maintain civil liberties? Americans have accepted restricted access to government buildings and national monuments and heightened screening at airports, but these policies are more of an inconvenience than a threat to civil liberties. Would Americans accept other policies that would pose a risk to civil liberties? Should they?

Consider the problem of interrogating captured terrorist suspects. Under our law, when police interrogate criminal suspects, they must advise the suspects of their rights to remain silent and have counsel, and they must stop the questioning whenever the suspects express a desire to exercise those

physical harm, including bringing a weapon into the interrogation room, are contrary to international law.[1] So are depriving suspects of food or water or injecting them with drugs to coerce information.[2]

In addition to philosophical objections to these tactics, there are practical objections. Officials might get the wrong person and force him to say what they want to hear even if it is not true. Then they have unreliable information. Or officials might use brutal methods that damage or kill him.

Despite these restrictions, police interrogation of suspected criminals is often successful (as Chapter 14 explains). Military officials, like police officers, try to put their suspects at a disadvantage. In the war on terrorism, military officials sometimes isolate a suspect from other

it as a reward for talking.[3] But these methods do not work on all suspects.

Officials have tried to use inducements, including money, jobs, lenient sentences, and new identities in the witness protection program, but these offers have been spurned. The terrorists are committed to their cause and steeled to their death, even seeking "martyrdom." In addition, an FBI agent involved in the investigation noted, "We are known for humanitarian treatment, so basically we are stuck."[4]

Middle Eastern governments threatened by Islamic extremists, from Israel to the "moderate" Arab states, have found that torture and threats to harm their family are the only methods that prod suspected terrorists into talking. Today torture may involve a combination of

AFTER 9/11
IMMIGRATION: IS THE DOOR STILL OPEN?

After the terrorist attacks on the World Trade Center and the Pentagon on September 11, 2001, newscasters and analysts often observed that our system had been changed "profoundly" or "forever." Now, with some distance from the events, we are better able to evaluate the impact of those events. In this edition's "After 9/11" boxes, we discuss ways in which the events of that day have affected government and politics in the United States. We begin by asking if the door to immigrants is as open as it was before 9/11.

We see ourselves as a community of people joined by a common commitment to the pursuit of opportunity, individual liberty, and government of, by, and for the people. But who, other than those born into it, can join this community? We think of ourselves as a refuge for al and religious dissidents and the mically downtrodden, just as it says Emma Lazarus poem engraved on tue of Liberty: "Give me your our poor, your huddled masses g to breathe free." By this stan-he "golden door" would be open dreds of millions of people, when y only a small fraction of refugees pportunity seekers can settle in the States. Thus, rules must be estab-o determine who qualifies for an ration visa, who is entitled to e status, and how many people allowed to take up residency in ited States each year. r time, the "golden door" has ed and narrowed depending on shes of Congress (immigration

law is then implemented and enforced by the Immigration and Naturalization Service [INS]). Few Americans argue with the proposition that the government has the right to police its borders, but there are always disagreements over the standards regulating admission. These standards often come under scrutiny during hard times, such as war or recession, so it is not surprising that the laws governing entry into the United States were reviewed after 9/11.

One of the many unhappy findings about the perpetrators of the 9/11 attacks was that some had entered the country legally on tourist or student visas and overstayed their departure dates. The knowledge that a tiny fraction of foreigners living in our midst came for the express purpose of doing harm led to immediate changes in immigration enforcement. Hundreds of Arab and/or Muslim men who had violated their visas were detained for questioning and some were deported. Overstaying visas is an everyday occurrence in the United States, where an estimated 5 to 8 million people live illegally, only about 100,000 of whom are of Middle Eastern descent.[1] A hold was placed on immigration and visa applications from Middle Eastern and other predominantly Muslim countries while they could be subjected to extensive background checks.

Immigration applications from Arab and Muslim countries are not the first to be singled out for special handling. The United States has been restricting immigration since 1798, when Congress gave the president power to deport people he deemed "dangerous to the peace and

safety" of the country. An 1807 law prohibited the migration or "importation" of people for purposes of slavery. Immigration within the western hemisphere remained open, but immigration from East Asia was virtually shut down by an 1882 law prohibiting further immigration from China and the 1907 "Gentleman's Agreement" with the Japanese government, which limited new Japanese to the Hawaiian Islands. Between the 1920s and 1960s, immigration was open mainly to the European countries represented in the American population at the time of the 1910 census, thus favoring British, German and northern Europeans, while penalizing southern and eastern Europeans. Laws passed up through the end of World War II added new categories of people prohibited entry, including anarchists and revolutionaries, members of communist parties, alcoholics, those with contagious diseases, and others deemed undesirable.

After the 1960s civil rights movement led to the removal of the old quota system, the door opened to people of every race, religion, and nationality. To ensure that people from all parts of the world have a chance to apply, the INS divides the world into regions and assigns annual quotas to countries within each region. Fifty thousand slots per year are set aside for people in countries where a low number of visa requests had been granted in the previous five years. Political categories were created and assigned preferential treatment. During the Cold War, virtually everyone fleeing a communist country was pretty much guaranteed refugee or

CHAPTER 19
FOREIGN POLICY

An extensively updated Chapter 19, "Foreign Policy"

Included only in *American Government* (which contains four policy chapters), this current chapter discusses whether or not we should give the President a "blank check" to invade Iraq and includes these new sections: "Homeland Security and Preemption," "Instruments of Foreign Policy" (which features material on diplomacy, intelligence gathering, and economic instruments), and an **After 9/11** box, "Fighting War at Home."

YOU ARE THERE

Should the President Get a New Cabinet Department?

ou are California congresswoman Jane Harman, the most senior Democrat on the House Intelligence Committee's Subcommittee on Terrorism and Homeland Security. Over the past few years, your committee work has made you one of the House's leading experts on counterterrorism.[1] It is July 2002, and you must decide whether to support President Bush's proposal to create a new cabinet department for homeland security.

This bill would authorize the most massive reorganization ever attempted in the executive branch. The president described the new agency as having "clear and efficient organizational structure" divided into four responsibilities: Border and Transportation Security; Emergency Preparedness and Response; Chemical, Biological, Radiological and Nuclear Countermeasures; and Information Analysis and Infrastructure Protection. But the proposed $38 billion agency seems to have an organizational structure that is anything but "clear and efficient." It involves reshuffling departments within twenty-two different agencies and reassigning as many as 170,000 employees. The responsibilities of the new department would extend to border security, coastal patrols, immigration, biological and nuclear weaponry, public health, airport security, disaster management, police work and firefighting, domestic surveillance, and other intelligence gathering and

analysis, to name just a few. The department would assume responsibility for the United States Coast Guard, the United States Customs Service, the Immigration and Naturalization Service (including the Border Patrol), the Animal and Plant Health Inspection Service, the Federal Emergency Management Agen
other
cracy,
tice t
and H
segm
would
that y
comm

Y
any n
this p
couns
fense
Since
you h
and A
devel
both
spend
you d
Calife
in the
You h
engag
health
practi
that n
to me

I
the H

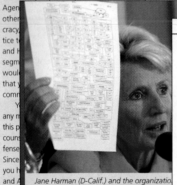
Jane Harman (D-Calif.) and the organizatio[n] chart of the Office of Homeland Security.

the Intelligence Committee. You are also a member of the powerful Energy and Commerce Committee, where you deal with telecommunications, the Internet, trade, and some environmental issues, including hazardous materials. You were cochairing an investigation into terrorism and homeland security needs when 9/11 happened and were subsequently asked to submit a report on intelligence lapses prior to the attacks.

Most are NEW!

By placing students in challenging real-life situations and asking them to make decisions and consider the ramifications, these engaging **You Are There** scenarios not only draw students into chapter topics, but also help them use critical thinking skills to analyze the issues presented. Each **You Are There** scenario is linked to a corresponding **Epilogue** found at the end of the chapter where the authors reveal the actual decision and discuss it in light of ideas presented in the chapter. Instructors often use **You Are There** scenarios to encourage lively class discussion.

EPILOGUE

Harman Votes with the President

arman voted for the president's proposal to establish a new cabinet office, even though just six weeks earlier she had been touting her own legislation as providing the strategy and the organizational plan the president had failed to produce.

As the Homeland Security Act of 2002 moved through the House, members of both parties looked skeptically at the provisions calling for Congress to cede some of its budgetary authority to the executive branch. The House Appropriations Committee was reluctant to grant the president independent authority over any part of the new department's budget. The committee chair said what he was asking for was "overly broad and unprecedented" and "would constitute a major erosion of the separation of powers abrogating the central role of the Congress—the direction and oversight of public expenditures."

the president this authority, the Department of Homeland Security "would become a $30 billion slush fund for the executive branch."[94] But the provisions ceding some budgetary authority to the executive branch and to waive workers' rights remained in the House bill over the objections of many Democrats.

From the beginning of the legislative process, Bush had courted Harman, knowing that, because she was the ra[nking minority member] on the Terro[
curity Subc[
of competi[
was crucia[
three Dem[
vited to the[
tation and p[
the new off[
support was[
trist, a defe[
election in v[
close contes[

A Web icon at the end of the Epilogue box prompts students to go online to the books' Companion Web Sites to participate in a variety of activities.

Linked to interactive Internet activities at the books' robust NEW Companion Web Sites:

http://politicalscience.wadsworth.com/welch9/
http://politicalscience.wadsworth.com/welch7/

Designed exclusively for the Ninth Edition of *American Government* and the Seventh Edition of *Understanding American Government,* the Companion Web Sites include:

- **You Are There simulations** that place students in a variety of roles (Expanded and customized from the American Government Web Site, these simulations include unique critical thinking questions.)
- **Tutorial quizzing** for every chapter
- **Outlines/learning objectives** for every chapter
- **Interactive timelines**
- **Web links for every chapter**
- **InfoTrac College Edition** and Internet activities
- **Flash cards**

- **Many password-protected resources for instructors,** including lecture outlines in PowerPoint®, an *Instructor's Manual*, and *Test Bank*—all available for download
- **PLUS** *NewsEdge*, an authoritative news service for instructors that brings the latest developments from the field into your classroom! *NewsEdge* offers up-to-the-minute news stories in daily feeds that you can customize to reflect your particular course focus.

4

Three-time winners of the *American Government Textbook Award* for coverage of women's issues from the Women's Caucus of the American Political Science Association, both *Understanding American Government* and *American Government* weave diversity topics and issues throughout. Many chapters also include "American Diversity" boxes offering specific examples of how America's diversity of backgrounds and attitudes shapes views of politics and positions on issues.

The authors address the impact of various diversity issues on course topics. As students read about each key topic, they discover the relationship between how government operates and government's impact on the diverse groups living in America.

AMERICAN DIVERSITY
WOMEN AND MINORITIES IN THE CIVIL SERVICE

Americans expect their public bureaucracies to be open and responsive. Andrew Jackson recognized this when he opened the civil service to frontiersmen of "common" origins. He hoped to make the bureaucracy more responsive and more representative by putting his frontier supporters in office. In the twentieth century, the expectation that public agencies should be open to all qualified applicants gave some groups, such as the Irish, Jews, and African Americans, more job opportunities than in the more restricted private corporate world.

In the past decade, significant progress has been made in making the federal bureaucracy more reflective of American diversity. Thirty-one percent of Americans identified as minorities in the 2000 census, and today 30 percent of federal workers are minorities.[1] African Americans are particularly well represented, being a substantially larger portion of the federal workforce (almost 18 percent) than of the general population.[2] Both Asian Americans and

American Indians have a slightly larger share of federal jobs than population share. Hispanics, on the other hand, are underrepresented in the federal workforce despite an aggressive Hispanic recruitment program.[3] Women are slightly underrepresented, too, filling 44 percent of federal positions compared with 46 percent of private sector jobs.

The relatively good news about the overall profile of the bureaucracy fades as we move up the pay scale (see the table). Women and minority men have not yet broken completely through the "glass ceiling" that has kept them out of top management positions. Even after passage of civil rights and equal opportunity legislation, barriers did not fall because often those who enforced the new regulations were white men opposed to the policies. Indeed, the Justice Department backed white males who sued the government for reverse discrimination.

There is progress, however. Women now fill about 24 percent of all positions at senior pay grade, tripling their proportion of 1985. Collectively, minorities hold about 14 percent of all senior positions.[4]

Federal court rulings and out-of-court settlements in discrimination cases account for some of the improvement in upward mobility. African Americans won a suit against the Education Department charging management abuse of a system designed to promote those who took on extra work. The additional responsibilities were usually given to whites, putting them on a faster promotion track.[5] Women agents charged the FBI with a similar tactic to restrict their promotion. They were prohibited or discouraged from joining SWAT teams, even

Federal employment has historically opened opportunity for African Americans. Shown here are two Bureau of Engraving and Printing employees checking the quality of $20 bills (the woman at right is holding $8,000 in printing mistakes).

though service on them was crucial to advancement. When they threatened to sue, the FBI changed its promotion procedures.[6]

1. Office of Personnel Management, *The Fact Book, 2001 Edition*, Table 11 (www.opm.gov).
2. The comparison of public and private sector employment is from "Diversity Trickles Up in Government," *Champaign-Urbana News-Gazette*, July 17, 2001, A3.
3. "Hispanics Sought for Federal Work Force," *Champaign-Urbana News-Gazette*, February 3, 2002, A6; "Diversity Trickles Up."
4. *The Fact Book*, Table 46.
5. "Diversity Trickles Up."
6. Katherine C. Naff, "Through the Glass Ceiling: Prospects for the Advancement of Women in the Federal Civil Service," *Public Administration Review*, November/December 1994, 513.

Percentage of Senior Federal Civil Service Who Are Women and Minorities

	1985	1990	2000
Women	8	12	24
African Americans	4	5	7
Hispanics	1	2	3
Asians and Pacific Islanders	1	1	2

Data are for those at senior pay levels. Overall, about 1 percent of all federal employees are in this grade.
SOURCE: Office of Personnel Management, *The Fact Book: Federal Civilian Workforce Statistics*, 2001 (www.opm.gov).

Elitism

The failure of pluralist theory to acknowledge the limited power of citizens with average or below-average incomes has led some political scientists to argue that American democracy is much less democratic than pluralists believed. One set of counterarguments to pluralism explanation comes from elite theory, an explanation of how government works that focuses on the roles of a relatively small number of individuals in key positions. The modern statement of this idea began with Robert Michels who, in 1915, formulated the "iron law of oligarchy."[42] This "law" says that effective power in a group or organization, no matter what its size, usually gravitates to a few—an oligarchy or an elite. In fact, interest groups do create their own elites by establishing permanent organizations with paid staff and leadership; this arrangement creates the potential for an issue gap between leaders and the rank and file. As the professional staff spend more time with decision makers and develop ties to public officials, they may come to see group interests differently than does the rank-and-file membership. When this happens, group membership is no longer a guarantee that one's interests will be accurately represented to decision makers.

One group of elite theorists argue that a power elite, the holders of a few top jobs in major corporations, universities, foundations, media outlets, and the most powerful agencies of government, such as the Defense Department, dominate governmental decision making.[43] One political scientist identified 5,416 key decision makers in major organizations such as these.[44] They included 3,572 elite business leaders who controlled 50 percent of America's corporate wealth, and almost 40 percent of whom had once held a government post. According to the power elite explanation, relatively few people share the most powerful jobs and make the most important

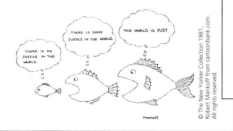

THERE IS SOME JUSTICE IN THE WORLD.

THE WORLD IS JUST.

THERE IS NO JUSTICE IN THE WORLD.

MANKOFF

Religious Diversity

We know that many of our earliest settlers came here to escape religious intolerance in Europe: French Huguenots, German Anabaptists, British Methodists, Catholics, and Quakers. Nevertheless, few who emigrated to the Americas expected to live in an areligious state. Once here, however, many found it necessary to establish separate communities to ensure freedom for their form of religious practice. "New Jersey, Pennsylvania, and Maryland were conceived and established as 'plantations of religion,'" that gave state protection to specific religious groups.[17] Rhode Island was founded by the religious dissident Roger Williams who, after

Chapter 1 has been extensively rewritten, featuring completely new sections on religious diversity and elitism. The authors discuss American government and politics in terms of the diverse cultural nature of our population.

Resources to help students understand the larger picture . . . and *retain* what they study

CHAPTER 10

CONGRESS

Chapter-opening Outlines that preview and guide students' reading

Bold-faced Key Terms within the text, at the ends of chapters, and in the end-of-book glossary

Committees

Most of the work of Congress is done in committees. Observers of American politics take this for granted; yet the power of legislative committees is rather rare among Western democracies. In Britain, for example, committees cannot offer amendments that change the substance of a bill.

Standing Committees

Today there are nineteen **standing committees** in the House and sixteen in the Senate. Each deals with a different subject matter, such as finance or education or agriculture. Each has a number of subcommittees, totaling seventy-five in the House and sixty-eight in the Senate.[60] Nearly all legislation introduced in Congress is referred to a standing committee and then to a subcommittee. Subcommittees hold public hearings to give interested parties a chance to speak for or against a bill. They also hold **markup** sessions to provide an opportunity for the committee to rewrite the bill. Following markup, the bill is sent to the full committee, which also may hold hearings. If approved there, it goes to the full House or Senate.

Standing committees vary in size from nine to

Further Reading

Michael Barone et al., *The Almanac of American Politics* (Washington, D.C.: National Journal, since 1980). Offers background on each member, his or her district, and voting record. Revised every two years since 1980. A volume similar in format and publication schedule is *Congressional Quarterly's Politics in America,* compiled by CQ staff. The most recent edition is for the 107th Congress (Washington, D.C.: CQ Press, 2001).

Robert A. Caro, *Master of the Senate* (New York: Knopf, 2002). When you have some time on your hands, check out this monumental study of a master legislator at work. This is the second in a projected three-volume study that tracks the House and Senate career of former president Lyndon B. Johnson, arguably the most powerful Senate majority leader in U.S. history.

Timothy Cook, *Making Laws and Making News* (Washington, D.C.: Brookings Institution, 1989). A revealing account of how media coverage affects the legislative process in the U.S. House.

Roger H. Davidson and Walter J. Oleszek, *Congress and Its Members,* 7th ed. (Washington, D.C.: CQ Press, 2000). Now a classic general reference work on Congress, revised every few years.

Marjorie Margolies-Mezvinsky, *A Woman's Place: The Freshmen Women Who Changed the Face of Congress* (New York: Crown, 1994). Representative Margolies-Mezvinsky reflects on the changes brought about in Congress by the largest group of women representatives ever.

Timothy Phelps and Helen Winternitz, *Capitol Games: Clarence Thomas, Anita Hill and the Story of a Supreme Court Nomination* (New York: Hyperion, 1992). A close look at the Senate hearings on Clarence Thomas's nomination to the Supreme Court.

Pat Schroeder, *24 Years of House Work and the Place Is Still a Mess: My Life in Politics* (Kansas City, Mo.: McMeel, 1998). One of the most outspoken women in Congress from 1973 to 1995, Schroeder tells how a woman succeeded in this male-dominated institution.

Steven Waldman, *The Bill: How the Adventures of Clinton's National Service Bill Reveal What Is Corrupt, Comic,*

Further Reading sections that enrich chapter topics

InfoTrac College Edition references that guide students to this extensive online library

Electronic Resources that feature chapter-related Web URLs

InfoTrac College Edition

Search for the following articles in the InfoTrac database:

Adler, David Gray. "Virtues of the War Clause," *Presidential Studies Quarterly* (December 2000).

Crowley, Michael. "On the Hill: Switch Hit (Jim Jeffords)," *New Republic* (December 31, 2001).

Devins, Neal. "Congress as Culprit: How Lawmakers

Electronic Resources

thomas.loc.gov/
Links to texts of bills, the Congressional Record (reporting entire floor debates), and committee hearings and reports. It is also a good site for congressional history and information about individual members. Want to know how many Asian Americans are in Congress and who they are? How much members of Congress make? Who the leadership is? This page links to all kinds of statistics about Congress, along with links to the home pages and e-mail addresses of members.

www.c-span.org/
The Web site of the two cable stations that cover congressional proceedings. It is a treasure trove of information on congressional history as well as current affairs. It also has an archive of frequently asked questions about Congress and resources for students of American government.

www.washingtonpost.com/
This is the Web site of the Washington Post, *whose news coverage of Congress is unrivaled.*

www.cq.com/
The Web site of Congressional Quarterly, *publisher of the most authoritative weekly review of congressional affairs.*

InfoTrac® College Edition . . .
FREE access!

A four-month subscription to this extensive online library is FREE with every new copy of the book. **InfoTrac College Edition** includes innumerable articles from thousands of magazines, newsletters, and such respected journals and popular periodicals as *American Political Science Review, Foreign Policy, Newsweek,* and *Political Science Quarterly.* These full-length articles (not just excerpts) are updated daily, expertly indexed, and ready to use—24 hours a day, seven days a week! Suggested searches at the ends of chapters in *American Government* and *Understanding American Government* guide students to current articles online.

WebTutor™ Advantage . . .
Online course management and student tutorials
Available on WebCT and Blackboard

"Out of the box" or customizable, this versatile online tool is filled with pre-loaded, text-specific content, including diagrams and illustrations, as well as Microsoft® PowerPoint® files, organized by text chapter. For students, **WebTutor Advantage** offers access to a full array of study tools, including glossary flashcards, practice quizzes, online tutorials, and Web links. Instructors can use **WebTutor Advantage** to provide virtual office hours, post syllabi, set up threaded discussions, and track student progress with the quizzing material. And now, you can bring the latest news right into your classroom with **NewsEdge!** WebTutor's newest feature, **NewsEdge** is an authoritative news service that delivers customized news feeds daily. You can even customize the feeds to reflect your particular course focus! **WebTutor Advantage** is now available on **eCollege!** Ask your Thomson/ Wadsworth representative for more information or visit **http://webtutor.thomsonlearning.com** and click on **eCollege.**

To package **WebTutor Advantage** with every student copy, go to the back cover of this book for ordering information.

MyCourse 2.1 . . .
Our online course builder!
Newly improved! FREE!

Whether you want only the easy-to-use tools to build your site or the content to furnish it, **MyCourse 2.1** offers you the simple solution for a custom course Web site that allows you to assign, track, and report on student progress, attach or load your syllabus, and more. Version 2.1 includes new features that let you import your class roster and gradebook, see assignments as students will see them using the "Student Preview Mode," create individual performance gradebooks, and copy content from an existing course to a new course! Contact your Thomson/ Wadsworth representative for details. You can demo **MyCourse 2.1** at **http://mycourse.thomsonlearning.com.**

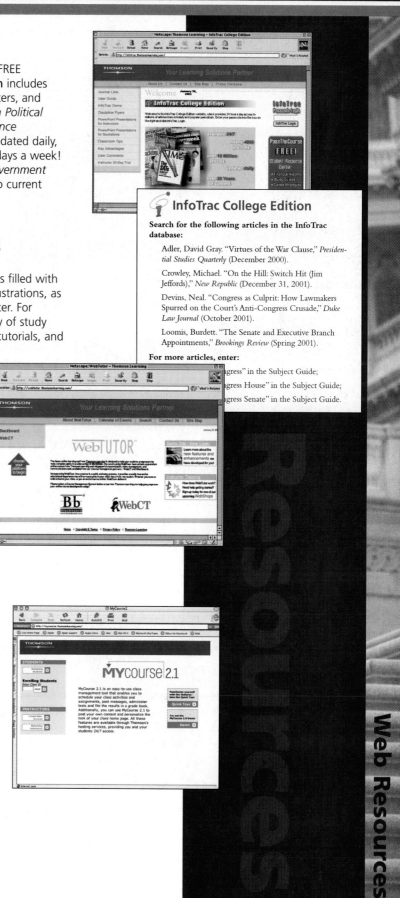

InfoTrac College Edition

Search for the following articles in the InfoTrac database:

Adler, David Gray. "Virtues of the War Clause," *Presidential Studies Quarterly* (December 2000).

Crowley, Michael. "On the Hill: Switch Hit (Jim Jeffords)," *New Republic* (December 31, 2001).

Devins, Neal. "Congress as Culprit: How Lawmakers Spurred on the Court's Anti-Congress Crusade," *Duke Law Journal* (October 2001).

Loomis, Burdett. "The Senate and Executive Branch Appointments," *Brookings Review* (Spring 2001).

For more articles, enter:

...gress" in the Subject Guide;

...gress House" in the Subject Guide;

...gress Senate" in the Subject Guide.

http://politicalscience.wadsworth.com/amgov/

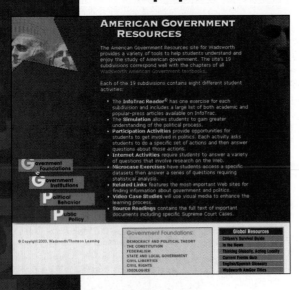

With the tools included on this exceptional class-tested site, students experience the excitement and satisfaction of participating in government and politics. By linking each of nineteen core American government topics to eight engaging types of activities, this new site actively involves students in your course—and in civic participation at the grassroots level!

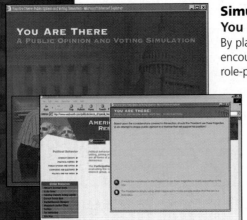

Simulations . . .
You are there!

By placing the student in a variety of roles, these **Simulations** encourage critical thinking and decision-making skills. The student role-plays as a state senator, an adviser to a president who must appoint a new member of the Supreme Court, a lawyer who must determine his clients' rights, an adviser to a presidential candidate, and other political roles. The **Simulations** are appropriate for individual and group work.

Participation Activities . . .
Getting involved

Students work on a political campaign, help an interest group, lobby Congress, and become activists as they participate in these activities. Once the activity is completed, a series of questions about the experience asks students how they feel they "made a difference."

Video Clips . . .
Observing and making decisions

Using visual media to enhance the learning process, these video excerpts—featuring contemporary policy issues—conclude with provocative questions that encourage decision making.

MicroCase® Exercises . . .
Analyzing by the numbers

Students analyze actual real-world data with these **MicroCase** **Exercises.** Written specifically for the American Government Resource Center, each exercise presents an issue in American government and directs students to pertinent information through data sets. Accompanying questions help students to consider and understand how to interpret data.

The NEW American Government Resource Center
enriches course content with current online material

http://politicalscience.wadsworth.com/amgov/

InfoTrac® College Edition Reader
This reader is updated every semester and organized by core American government topics—featuring exercises that guide students to current articles in the **InfoTrac College Edition** online library (Access to the library is FREE with this text. *See page 7 of this PREVIEW for details.*)

Source Readings
This section of the Web site contains the full text of Supreme Court cases, as well as other important primary and secondary source documents. Political and historical contexts are explained.

Internet Activities
Divided into three groups—"Just the Facts, Please," "Compare and Contrast," and "Exploration"—these activities ask students to answer a variety of questions that involve research on the Web.

Related Links
These useful links for each core topic include the most important informational Web sites for government and politics.

Plus these important resources ▶

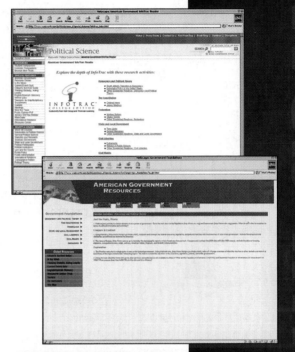

Global Resources
- Citizen's Survival Guide
- In the News
- Thinking Globally, Acting Locally
- Current Events Quiz
- English/Spanish Glossary
- Wadsworth AmGov Titles
- Toolbox
- For Instructors
- Site Map

Also available . . .
the NEW Companion Web Sites
http://politicalscience.wadsworth.com/welch9
http://politicalscience.wadsworth.com/welch7
Designed exclusively for the Ninth Edition of *American Government* and the Seventh Edition of *Understanding American Government,* the Companion Web Sites include: additional activites with critical thinking questions, interactive timelines, tutorial quizzes, hypercontent for each chapter, additional **InfoTrac College Edition** and Internet Activities, Flash Cards, and Learning Objectives, as well as a selection of password-protected instructor resources. *Turn back to page 4 of this PREVIEW for details.*

Instructor's Edition . . .
Featuring the *Resource Integration Guide!*
This Instructor's Edition includes the *Resource Integration Guide*—an essential tool for instructors. The guide provides grids that link each chapter's outline—topic by topic—to instructional ideas and corresponding supplement resources. At a glance, you'll see which specific transparencies, **CNN® Today** video clips, and relevant **InfoTrac® College Edition** articles are appropriate for each key chapter topic.

Instructor's Manual . . .
Comprehensive in scope
by Lauren Holland, University of Utah
Correlated chapter by chapter with both *American Government* and *Understanding American Government,* the *Instructor's Manual* contains chapter outlines, suggested assignments, and recommended Internet sites, as well as the *Resource Integration Guide.*
0-534-59639-8

Instructor's Resource CD-ROM . . .
With PowerPoint® images and ExamView® testing
This new, all-inclusive resource contains PowerPoint images, featuring important new figures from each chapter of *American Government* and *Understanding American Government,* as well as the *Instructor's Manual* and *Resource Integration Guide.* Also included is **ExamView,** an easy-to-use assessment and tutorial program that allows you to edit and import your own questions and graphics, edit and maneuver existing questions, and change test layouts. Tests appear on screen just as they will when printed. **ExamView** offers flexible delivery and the ability to test and grade online.
0-534-59642-8

Test Bank . . .
An extensive selection
by John Soares
The *Test Bank* includes a variety of well-conceived multiple-choice, fill-in-the-blank, and long- and short-essay questions for each chapter in *American Government* and *Understanding American Government.* **0-534-59640-1**

American Government Transparency Acetate Package, 2004 Edition

Illustrate and enhance your lectures with these colorful diagrams, charts, tables, and figures from the text and additional sources. The set contains more than 165 full-color acetates in all.
0-534-61685-2 (Also available—2003 Edition: **0-534-58657-9**)

CNN® Today: American Government Video Series

Now you can integrate the up-to-the-minute programming power of CNN and its affiliate networks right into your course. Organized by topics covered in the typical American government course, these 45- to 60-minute videos are divided into clips of three to six minutes in length. As students watch each clip, they'll learn to make connections between everyday events and their relationship to the core concepts you cover in class.

Volume I: 0-534-51944-X   **Volume II: 0-534-55362-1**

Volume III: 0-534-56957-9   **Volume IV: 0-534-58661-9**

America's New War: CNN® Looks at Terrorism

Free to qualified adopters, this great discussion starter includes 16 two- to five-minute segments featuring CNN news footage, commentator remarks, and speeches dealing with terrorist attacks on U.S. targets throughout the world. Topics include: anthrax and biological warfare, new security measures, Osama bin Laden, al Qaeda, asset freezing, homeland defense, new weapons of terrorism, and the Arab American response to recent events. Ask your Thomson/Wadsworth representative about our video policy by adoption size.
0-534-16805-1

NEW! Video Case Studies in American Government

Free to adopters, this award-winning video contains 12 video case studies, addressing recent developments in the debate on such policy issues as "Affirmative Action" and "Show Me the Money: Money and the Presidential Campaign." Each case study concludes with questions designed to spark classroom discussion. **0-15-504160-6**

An accompanying *Instructor's Manual* (**0-15-504244-0**) offers suggestions for use and activities for each case.

Wadsworth Political Science Video Library

Choose from this library's varied selection of videos to enrich your lectures and extend discussions of text material. Available FREE to qualified adopters. Policy based on adoption size.

All of the items listed below are available for packaging with each copy of *American Government* and *Understanding American Government.* Please refer to the back cover for package order numbers.

Study Guide
by John Soares
Includes the following for each chapter in *American Government* and *Understanding American Government:* a summary; outline; key terms, concepts, events, and people; multiple-choice questions; essay topics; and critical thinking questions. **0-534-59637-1**

Practice Tests
by John Soares
Contains a 25-item practice test for each chapter in *American Government* and *Understanding American Government.*
0-534-59651-7

America at Odds CD-ROM
This dynamic CD-ROM for the introduction to American government course enables students to research issues, discuss ideas, formulate opinions, and interpret data in an interactive format. The CD-ROM's 20 interactive modules cover enduring, multidimensional issues, presented within a rich mix of media, including digital video and audio, photos, graphics, and Internet technology. **0-534-57644-3**

InfoTrac® College Edition Student Guide for Political Science
Contains 24 pages of guidance to help students get the most benefit from the **InfoTrac® College Edition** database—including log-in help, search tips, a search tips cheat sheet, and a topic list of suggested keyword search terms for political science. **0-534-24728-8**

American Government: Readings and Responses
by Monica Bauer, Metropolitan State College of Denver
A wonderful collection of readings from prominent writers, plus "Chat Room" conversations with students who debate the topics in the readings. **0-534-52804-X**

Point/Counterpoint: Readings in American Government, Seventh Edition
by Herbert M. Levine
A diverse collection of articles on many hotly contested issues! Sure to stimulate critical thinking and lively debate about the foundations of the American political system. **0-534-61416-7**

Readings in American Government, Fourth Edition
edited by Mack C. Shelley, Jamie Swift, and Steffen W. Schmidt, all of Iowa State University
Updated articles covering the latest issues in American political debate, as well as classic topics such as race relations, Social Security, the environment, and education. **0-534-59269-4**

Critical Thinking and American Government, Second Edition
by Kent M. Brudney, Cuesta College; John H. Carver, California Polytechnic University; and Mark E. Weber, Cuesta College
Provides information and exercises that help students hone the skills necessary for interpreting and analyzing American government issues. The exercises correspond to chapter topics in American government texts. **0-15-505848-7**

Election 2002: An American Government Supplement
by John A. Clark and Brian F. Schaffner, both of Western Michigan University
This unique 32-page booklet uses many engaging real-life examples—as well as maps, charts, and graphs—to discuss and clarify the unpredictable nature of America's national political climate after September 11, 2001. Factors discussed include the post–September 11 economic slowdown, congressional redistricting that has affected election outcomes, and the potential ramifications of the 2002 gubernatorial elections. **0-534-59273-2**

9-11: The Giant Awakens
by Jeremy Mayer, Georgetown University
Focuses on how the American political system, its institutions, and its system of civil liberties and rights are responding to the challenges posed by the September 11 terrorist attacks. **0-534-61659-3**

American Government: Using MicroCase® ExplorIt®, Eighth Edition
by Michael Corbett, Ball State University and Barbara Norrander, University of Arizona
Featuring a Windows version of MicroCase Student ExplorIt, this user-friendly workbook/CD-ROM combo makes it easy for students to manipulate and learn from real data without getting bogged down in complicated statistical software. **0-534-58785-2**

Thinking Globally, Acting Locally
by John Soares
A concise book offering specific guidance for getting involved as an active citizen. Topics include writing letters to the editor, volunteering, how to change laws, and registering to vote. **0-534-55329-X**

American Government Internet Activities, Third Edition
Contains activities for all major topics in the text. Students are asked to surf the Web to obtain answers to thought-provoking questions. **0-534-57098-4**

The Handbook of Selected Court Cases
Includes more than 30 Supreme Court cases. **0-534-53613-1**

The Handbook of Selected Legislation and Other Documents
Features excerpts from 12 laws passed by the U.S. Congress that have had a significant impact on American politics. **0-534-53614-X**

An Introduction to Critical Thinking and Writing in American Politics
Presents a number of critical thinking and writing techniques, helping students make better use of the information they receive in class and in the text.
0-534-53634-4

Student Tools

Chapter Outline	Ideas for Instruction	Print Resources	Media & Internet Resources
The American People	**Instructor's Manual** Lecture Ideas Suggested Student Activities **American Government Transparency Acetate Package, 2003 Edition** D-1, D-2, D-3, D-4, D-5, D-6, D-7, D-8	**Test Bank** Chapter 1 **Study Guide** Chapter 1 ***Bauer's* American Government: Readings & Responses** **9-11: The Giant Awakens** Introduction **Handbook of Selected Legislation & Other Documents** The Magna Carta (p. 53) The Mayflower Compact (p. 57)	**Instructor's Resource CD-ROM** **American Government: Using MicroCase® ExplorIt®, 8th Edition** Exercise 1: One Nation **Chapter 1 Web site** Online quiz and Web links at http://politicalscience.wadsworth.com/welch9/ **American Government Resource Center** http://politicalscience.wadsworth.com/amgov/ **WebTutor™ Advantage** Chapter 1
Political Culture	**Instructor's Manual** Lecture Ideas Suggested Student Activities	**Test Bank** Chapter 1	
American Democracy: The Core Values	**Instructor's Manual** Lecture Ideas Suggested Student Activities	**Test Bank** Chapter 1	**InfoTrac® College Edition** "The Human Rights Blame Game" *Keyword:* ideology
American Democracy in Practice	**Instructor's Manual** Lecture Ideas Suggested Student Activities	**Test Bank** Chapter 1	**InfoTrac® College Edition** *Keywords:* direct democracy and pluralism
Conclusion: Is Government Responsive?	**Instructor's Manual** Lecture Ideas	**Test Bank** Chapter 1 **Practice Tests** Chapter 1	

Chapter Outline	Ideas for Instruction	Print Resources	Media & Internet Resources
The Articles of Confederation	**Instructor's Manual** Lecture Ideas Suggested Student Activities **American Government Transparency Acetate Package, 2003 Edition** C-2, C-4	**Test Bank** Chapter 2 **Study Guide** Chapter 2 ***Bauer's* American Government: Readings & Responses** **Handbook of Selected Court Cases** *U.S. Term Limits Inc. v. Thornton (p. 157)* **Handbook of Selected Legislation & Other Documents** The Articles of Confederation (p. 59)	**Instructor's Resource CD-ROM** **Chapter 2 Web site** Online quiz and Web links at http://politicalscience.wadsworth.com/welch9/ **American Government Resource Center** http://politicalscience.wadsworth.com/amgov/ **CNN® Today Video, American Government, Vol. 2** "Gun Control" **CNN® Today Video, American Government, Vol. 3** "Gun Control" **InfoTrac® College Edition** *Keywords:* slavery, checks and balances, electoral college **WebTutor™ Advantage** Chapter 2
The Constitution	**Instructor's Manual** Lecture Ideas Suggested Student Activities **American Government Transparency Acetate Package, 2003 Edition** C-1, C-3, C-6, C-7, C-8, C-9	**Test Bank** Chapter 2	**Video Case Studies in American Government** "Constitutional Foundations: Impeaching the President"
Impact of the Civil War and Great Depression	**Instructor's Manual** Lecture Ideas **American Government Transparency Acetate Package, 2003 Edition** C-10	**Test Bank** Chapter 2	
Conclusion: Does the Constitution Allow Government to Be Responsive?	**Instructor's Manual** Lecture Ideas Suggested Student Activities	**Test Bank** Chapter 2 **Practice Tests** Chapter 2	

Chapter Outline	Ideas for Instruction	Print Resources	Media & Internet Resources
Federal and Unitary Systems	**Instructor's Manual** Lecture Ideas Suggested Student Activities	**Test Bank** Chapter 3 **Study Guide** Chapter 3 ***Bauer's* American Government: Readings & Responses** **Handbook of Selected Court Cases** *Gibbons v. Ogden* (p. 53) **Handbook of Selected Legislation & Other Documents** The Preamble to the Charter of the United Nations (p. 83)	**Instructor's Resource CD-ROM** **Chapter 3 Web site** Online quiz and Web links at http://politicalscience. wadsworth.com/welch9/ **American Government Resource Center** http://politicalscience.wadsworth. com/amgov/ **American Government: Using MicroCase® ExplorIt®, 8th Edition** Exercise 2: A More Perfect Union **WebTutor™ Advantage** Chapter 3
The Political Bases of American Federalism	**Instructor's Manual** Lecture Ideas Suggested Student Activities	**Test Bank** Chapter 3	**Video Case Studies in American Government** "Federalism: Deciding Who Decides"
The Constitutional Bases of Federalism	**Instructor's Manual** Lecture Ideas Suggested Student Activities **American Government Transparency Acetate Package, 2003 Edition** F-1, F-3, F-4	**Test Bank** Chapter 3	
Federalism and the Growth of Government	**Instructor's Manual** Lecture Ideas Suggested Student Activities **American Government Transparency Acetate Package, 2003 Edition** F-5, F-6, F-7, F-8, F-9	**Test Bank** Chapter 3 **Handbook of Selected Court Cases** *McCulloch v. Maryland* (p. 83)	
The Practice of Federalism	**Instructor's Manual** Lecture Ideas	**Test Bank** Chapter 3 **Handbook of Selected Court Cases** *Printz v. U.S.* (p. 113)	
Conclusion: Is Federalism Responsive?	**Instructor's Manual** Lecture Ideas	**Test Bank** Chapter 3 **Practice Tests** Chapter 3	

Resource Integration Guide

Chapter Outline	Ideas for Instruction	Print Resources	Media & Internet Resources
Nature of Public Opinion	**Instructor's Manual** Lecture Ideas **American Government Transparency Acetate Package, 2003 Edition** PO-1, PO-2, PO-3	**Test Bank** Chapter 4 **Study Guide** Chapter 4 *Bauer's* **American Government: Readings & Responses** **9-11: The Giant Awakens** Chapter 4	**Instructor's Resource CD-ROM** **Chapter 4 Web site** Online quiz and Web links at http://politicalscience.wadsworth.com/welch9/ **American Government Resource Center** http://politicalscience.wadsworth.com/amgov/ **American Government: Using MicroCase® ExplorIt®, 8th Edition** Exercise 3: Of the People Exercise 6: Public Opinion & Political Socialization
Formation of Public Opinion	**Instructor's Manual** Lecture Ideas Suggested Student Activities	**Test Bank** Chapter 4	**WebTutor™ Advantage** Chapter 4
Measuring Public Opinion	**Instructor's Manual** Lecture Ideas	**Test Bank** Chapter 4	**Video Case Studies in American Government** "Public Opinion and Socialization: Measuring Public Opinion" **InfoTrac® College Edition** *Keywords:* Internet polling, public opinion polls
How Informed Is Public Opinion?	**Instructor's Manual** Lecture Ideas **American Government Transparency Acetate Package, 2003 Edition** PO-8, PO-9 **Instructor's Manual** Lecture Ideas	**Test Bank** Chapter 4	**InfoTrac® College Edition** *Keyword:* political trust
Public Opinion	**American Government Transparency Acetate Package, 2003 Edition** PO-4, PO-5, PO-6, PO-7, PO-10, PO-11	**Test Bank** Chapter 4	
Conclusion: Is Government Responsive to Public Opinion?	**Instructor's Manual** Lecture Ideas	**Test Bank** Chapter 4 **Practice Tests** Chapter 4	

Resource Integration Guide

Chapter Outline	Ideas for Instruction	Print Resources	Media & Internet Resources
The Media State	**Instructor's Manual** Lecture Ideas Suggested Student Activities **American Government Transparency Acetate Package, 2003 Edition** M-1, M-2, M-3, M-5	**Test Bank** Chapter 5 **Study Guide** Chapter 5 *Bauer's* **American Government: Readings & Responses** **Handbook of Selected Court Cases** *New York Times v. United States* (p. 73) *Zurcher v. Stanford Daily* (p. 169)	**Instructor's Resource CD-ROM** **Chapter 5 Web site** Online quiz and Web links at http://politicalscience. wadsworth.com/welch9/ **American Government Resource Center** http://politicalscience.wadsworth. com/amgov/ **American Government: Using MicroCase® ExplorIt®, 8th Edition** Exercise 7: The Media **WebTutor™ Advantage** Chapter 5
Relationship between Media and Politicians	**Instructor's Manual** Lecture Ideas Suggested Student Activities	**Test Bank** Chapter 5	**InfoTrac® College Edition** *Keywords:* media and political campaigns, television broadcasting
Bias of the Media	**Instructor's Manual** Lecture Ideas Suggested Student Activities **American Government Transparency Acetate Package, 2003 Edition** M-8	**Test Bank** Chapter 5	
Impact of the Media on Politics	**Instructor's Manual** Lecture Ideas Suggested Student Activities **American Government Transparency Acetate Package, 2003 Edition** M-6, M-7	**Test Bank** Chapter 5	**InfoTrac® College Edition** *Keywords:* spin doctor, campaign debates, television broadcasting of news, narrowcasting
Conclusion: Are the Media Responsive?	**Instructor's Manual** Lecture Ideas	**Test Bank** Chapter 5 **Practice Tests** Chapter 5	

Chapter Outline	Ideas for Instruction	Print Resources	Media & Internet Resources
Group Formation	**Instructor's Manual** Lecture Ideas Suggested Student Activities **American Government Transparency Acetate Package, 2003 Edition** I-1	**Test Bank** Chapter 6 **Study Guide** Chapter 6 ***Bauer's* American Government: Readings & Responses** **Handbook of Selected Court Cases** *Austin v. Michigan Chamber of Commerce* (p. 7) *United States v. Harriss* (p. 137)	**Instructor's Resource CD-ROM** **Chapter 6 Web site** Online quiz and Web links at http://politicalscience.wadsworth.com/welch9/ **American Government Resource Center** http://politicalscience.wadsworth.com/amgov/ **American Government: Using MicroCase® ExplorIt®, 8th Edition** Exercise 11: Interest Groups and PACs **InfoTrac® College Edition** *Keywords:* lobbying, political action committee, lobbying reform
Types of Interest Groups	**Instructor's Manual** Lecture Ideas Suggested Student Activities **American Government Transparency Acetate Package, 2003 Edition** I-2, I-3, I-4	**Test Bank** Chapter 6	**WebTutor™ Advantage** Chapter 6
Tactics of Interest Groups	**Instructor's Manual** Lecture Ideas Suggested Student Activities	**Test Bank** Chapter 6 **Handbook of Selected Legislation & Other Documents** The Federal Regulation of Lobbying Act of 1946 The Federal Election Campaign Act of 1971 **Handbook of Selected Court Cases** *Austin v. Michigan Chamber of Commerce* (p. 7) *United States v. Harriss* (p. 137)	
Success of Interest Groups	**Instructor's Manual** Lecture Ideas Suggested Student Activities **American Government Transparency Acetate Package, 2003 Edition**, I-5	**Test Bank** Chapter 6	
Conclusion: Do Interest Groups Help Make Government Responsive?	**Instructor's Manual** Lecture Ideas Suggested Student Activities	**Test Bank** Chapter 6 **Practice Tests** Chapter 6	

Chapter Outline	Ideas for Instruction	Print Resources	Media & Internet Resources
What Are Political Parties?	**Instructor's Manual** Lecture Ideas Suggested Student Activities **American Government Transparency Acetate Package, 2003 Edition**, PP-1, PP-3	**Test Bank** Chapter 7 **Study Guide** Chapter 7 *Bauer's* **American Government: Readings & Responses** **Handbook of Selected Legislation & Other Documents** The Hatch Act of 1939 (p. 1)	**Instructor's Resource CD-ROM** **Chapter 7 Web site**–Online quiz and Web links at http://political science.wadsworth.com/welch9/ **American Government Resource Center** http://politicalscience.wadsworth.com/amgov/ **American Government: Using MicroCase® ExplorIt®, 8th Edition** Exercise 9: Political Parties **CNN® Today Video, American Government, Vol. 3,** "Green Party" **Video Case Studies in American Government,** "Political Parties: The National Conventions" **InfoTrac® College Edition** *Keyword:* political party platforms **WebTutor™ Advantage** Chapter 7
Development and Change in the Party System	**Instructor's Manual** Lecture Ideas **American Government Transparency Acetate Package, 2003 Edition**, PP-2, PP-4, PP-10 Instructor's Manual, Lecture Ideas Suggested Student Activities	**Test Bank** Chapter 7	**InfoTrac® College Edition** *Keywords:* ticket splitting, political activists, and party identification
Characteristics of the Party System	**Instructor's Manual**, Lecture Ideas Suggested Student Activities **American Government Transparency Acetate Package, 2003 Edition**, PP-5, PP-6, PP-8, PP-9, PP-13, PP-15, PP-16, PP-17	**Test Bank** Chapter 7	**CNN® Today Video, American Government, Vol. 3** "Reform Party Split" "Nader Protests" "Debate Wrap-up"
Party in the Electorate	**Instructor's Manual**, Lecture Ideas Suggested Student Activities	**Test Bank** Chapter 7	**InfoTrac® College Edition** *Keyword:* party identification
Party in the Government	**Instructor's Manual**, Lecture Ideas Suggested Student Activities **American Government Transparency Acetate Package, 2003 Edition**, PP-7	**Test Bank** Chapter 7	**CNN® Today Video, American Government, Vol. 3** "What's the Difference?"
Party Organization	**Instructor's Manual**, Lecture Ideas **American Government Transparency Acetate Package, 2003 Edition**, PP-11	**Test Bank** Chapter 7	
The Nominating Process	**Instructor's Manual** Lecture Ideas Suggested Student Activities	**Test Bank** Chapter 7	
Conclusion: Do Political Parties Make Government More Responsive?	**Instructor's Manual** Lecture Ideas	**Test Bank** Chapter 7 **Practice Tests** Chapter 7	

Chapter Outline	Ideas for Instruction	Print Resources	Media & Internet Resources
The American Electorate	**Instructor's Manual** Lecture Ideas Suggested Student Activities **American Government Transparency Acetate Package, 2003 Edition** CEV-8	**Test Bank** Chapter 8 **Study Guide** Chapter 8 *Bauer's* **American Government: Readings & Responses** **Handbook of Selected Court Cases** *Baker v. Carr* (p. 13) *Reynolds v. Sims* (p. 95) **Handbook of Selected Legislation & Other Documents** The Hatch Act of 1939 (p. 1)	**Instructor's Resource CD-ROM** **Chapter 8 Web site** Online quiz and Web links at http://politicalscience. wadsworth.com/welch9/ **American Government Resource Center** http://politicalscience.wadsworth. com/amgov/ **American Government: Using MicroCase® ExplorIt®, 8th Edition** Exercise 10: Elections Exercise 8: Political Participation **WebTutor™ Advantage** Chapter 8
Voter Turnout	**Instructor's Manual** Lecture Ideas Suggested Student Activities **American Government Transparency Acetate Package, 2003 Edition** CEV-9, CEV-10, CEV13	**Test Bank** Chapter 8	**InfoTrac® College Edition** *Keywords:* political consultants, voter registration
Other Campaign Participation	**Instructor's Manual** Lecture Ideas Suggested Student Activities	**Test Bank** Chapter 8	**Video Case Studies in American Government** "Political Participation: Voting Behavior and Youth"
Presidential Nominating Campaigns	**Instructor's Manual** Lecture Ideas **American Government Transparency Acetate Package, 2003 Edition** CEV-1, CEV-2, CEV-3, CEV-4	**Test Bank** Chapter 8	**Video Case Studies in American Government** "Campaigns and Elections: Close Calls in Presidential Contests" **CNN® Today Video, American Government, Vol. 3** "The Debates"
The General Election Campaign	**Instructor's Manual** Lecture Ideas Suggested Student Activities **American Government Transparency Acetate Package, 2003 Edition** CEV-6, CEV-16	**Test Bank** Chapter 8	**InfoTrac® College Edition** *Keyword:* electoral college **CNN® Today Video, American Government, Vol. 3** "Democratic Dogfight," "Republican Stances," "Bradley Quits," "McCain Bows Out," "Nader Factor," "Gore Story So Far"
The Permanent Campaign **Voting Choices**	**Instructor's Manual** Lecture Ideas **American Government Transparency Acetate Package, 2003 Edition** CEV-12, CEV-15	**Test Bank** Chapter 8	
Conclusion: Do Elections Make Government Responsive?	**Instructor's Manual** Lecture Ideas	**Test Bank** Chapter 8 **Practice Tests** Chapter 8	

Resource Integration Guide

21

Chapter Outline	Ideas for Instruction	Print Resources	Media & Internet Resources
Money and Politics in Earlier America	**Instructor's Manual** Lecture Ideas Suggested Student Activities	**Test Bank** Chapter 9 **Study Guide** Chapter 9 *Bauer's* **American Government: Readings & Responses** **9-11: The Giant Awakens** **Handbook of Selected Court Cases** *Austin v. Michigan Chamber of Commerce* (p. 7) **Handbook of Selected Legislation & Other Documents** The Federal Election Campaign Act of 1971 (p. 21)	**Instructor's Resource CD-ROM** **Chapter 9 Web site** Online quiz and Web links at http://politicalscience.wadsworth.com/welch9/ **American Government Resource Center** http://politicalscience.wadsworth.com/amgov/ **CNN® Today Video, American Government, Vol. 2** "Political Action Committee" **InfoTrac® College Edition** *Keywords:* campaign funds, soft money, Bipartisan Campaign Finance Reform Act
Regulating Money in Modern Campaigns	**Instructor's Manual** Lecture Ideas Suggested Student Activities **American Government Transparency Acetate Package, 2003 Edition** I-6, I-7	**Test Bank** Chapter 9 **Handbook of Selected Legislation & Other Documents** The Federal Regulation of Lobbying Act of 1946 (p. 5)	**WebTutor™ Advantage** Chapter 9
The Impact of Campaign Money	**Instructor's Manual** Lecture Ideas Suggested Student Activities	**Test Bank** Chapter 9	
Conflicts of Interest	**Instructor's Manual** Lecture Ideas Suggested Student Activities	**Test Bank** Chapter 9	**CNN® Today Video, American Government, Vol. 2** "Negative Campaign Ads"
Conclusion: Does the Influence of Money Make Government Less Responsive?	**Instructor's Manual** Lecture Ideas	**Test Bank** Chapter 9 **Practice Tests** Chapter 9	

Chapter Outline	Ideas for Instruction	Print Resources	Media & Internet Resources
Members and Constituencies	Instructor's Manual Lecture Ideas Suggested Student Activities	Test Bank Chapter 10 Study Guide Chapter 10 Bauer's American Government: Readings & Responses 9-11: The Giant Awakens Chapter 2 Handbook of Selected Court Cases Baker v. Carr (p. 13) Reynolds v. Sims (p. 95) U.S. Term Limits Inc. v. Thornton (p. 127) Handbook of Selected Legislation & Other Documents The Federal Election Campaign Act of 1971 (p. 21)	Instructor's Resource CD-ROM Chapter 10 Web site Online quiz and Web links at http://politicalscience.wadsworth.com/welch9/ American Government Resource Center http://politicalscience.wadsworth.com/amgov/ American Government: Using MicroCase® ExplorIt®, 8th Edition Exercise 12: Congress InfoTrac® College Edition Keyword: reapportionment WebTutor™ Advantage Chapter 10
The Representative on the Job	Instructor's Manual Lecture Ideas Suggested Student Activities	Test Bank Chapter 10	InfoTrac® College Edition Keywords: U.S. Congress, representation
How Congress Is Organized	Instructor's Manual Lecture Ideas Suggested Student Activities American Government Transparency Acetate Package, 2003 Edition CO-1, CO-2	Test Bank Chapter 10	InfoTrac® College Edition Keywords: U.S. Congress, committees
What Congress Does	Instructor's Manual Lecture Ideas Suggested Student Activities American Government Transparency Acetate Package, 2003 Edition CO-3, CO-4, CO-5, CO-6, CO-7, CO-8, CO-9	Test Bank Chapter 10	InfoTrac® College Edition Keyword: filibuster
Congress and the Public	Instructor's Manual Lecture Ideas	Test Bank Chapter 10	Video Case Studies in American Government "Congress: The Cost of Campaigning"
Conclusion: Is Congress Responsive?	Instructor's Manual Lecture Ideas	Test Bank Chapter 10 Practice Tests Chapter 10	

Resource Integration Guide

Chapter Outline	Ideas for Instruction	Print Resources	Media & Internet Resources
The Growth of the Presidency	**Instructor's Manual** Lecture Ideas	**Test Bank** Chapter 11 **Study Guide** Chapter 11 ***Bauer's* American Government: Readings & Responses** **9-11: The Giant Awakens** Chapter 1 **Handbook of Selected Court Cases** *Austin v. Michigan Chamber of Commerce* (p. 7) **Handbook of Selected Legislation & Other Documents** The Federal Regulation of Lobbying Act of 1946 (p. 5), The Federal Campaign Act of 1971 (p. 21)	**Instructor's Resource CD-ROM** **Chapter 11 Web site** Online quiz and Web links at http://politicalscience. wadsworth.com/welch9/ **American Government Resource Center** http://politicalscience.wadsworth. com/amgov/ **American Government: Using MicroCase® ExploreIt®, 8th Edition** Exercise 13: The Presidency **Video Case Studies in American Government** "The Presidency: Presidential Style" **WebTutor™ Advantage** Chapter 11
Terms of Office	**Instructor's Manual** Lecture Ideas Suggested Student Activities **American Government Transparency Acetate Package, 2003 Edition** P-1	**Test Bank** Chapter 11	
Duties and Powers of Office	**Instructor's Manual** Lecture Ideas Suggested Student Activities **American Government Transparency Acetate Package, 2003 Edition** P-10	**Test Bank** Chapter 11	**InfoTrac® College Edition** *Keywords:* executive orders, executive privilege, line item veto **CNN® Today Video, American Government, Vol. 2** "Executive Privilege"
Presidential Staff and Advisors	**Instructor's Manual** Lecture Ideas **American Government Transparency Acetate Package, 2003 Edition** P-2, P-3	**Test Bank** Chapter 11	
The President and the People	**Instructor's Manual** Lecture Ideas Suggested Student Activities **American Government Transparency Acetate Package, 2003 Edition** P-4, P-5, P-6, P-7, P-11	**Test Bank** Chapter 11	**InfoTrac® College Edition** *Keyword:* civil service
The President and Congress	**Instructor's Manual** Lecture Ideas **American Government Transparency Acetate Package, 2003 Edition,** P-8	**Test Bank** Chapter 11	
Limits on Presidential Power	**Instructor's Manual** Lecture Ideas Suggested Student Activities	**Test Bank** Chapter 11	
What Makes an Effective President?	**Instructor's Manual** Lecture Ideas Suggested Student Activities	**Test Bank** Chapter 11	
Conclusion: Is the Presidency Responsive?	**Instructor's Manual** Lecture Ideas	**Test Bank** Chapter 11 **Practice Tests** Chapter 11	

Resource Integration Guide

Chapter Outline	Ideas for Instruction	Print Resources	Media & Internet Resources
The Nature of Bureaucracies	**Instructor's Manual** Lecture Ideas Suggested Student Activities	**Test Bank** Chapter 12 **Study Guide** Chapter 12 ***Bauer's* American Government: Readings & Responses** **Handbook of Selected Court Cases** *United States Civil Service Commission v. National Association of Letter Carriers* (p. 147) **Handbook of Selected Legislation & Other Documents** The Hatch Act of 1939	**Instructor's Resource CD-ROM** **Chapter 12 Web site** Online quiz and Web links at http://politicalscience. wadsworth.com/welch9/ **American Government Resource Center** http://politicalscience.wadsworth. com/amgov/ **American Government: Using MicroCase® ExplorIt®, 8th Edition** Exercise 14: The Bureaucracy **WebTutor™ Advantage** Chapter 12
Growth of the Federal Bureaucracy	**Instructor's Manual** Lecture Ideas Suggested Student Activities	**Test Bank** Chapter 12	**Video Case Studies in American Government** "The Power of Rule Making"
What Bureaucracies Do	**Instructor's Manual** Lecture Ideas Suggested Student Activities	**Test Bank** Chapter 12	
Politics and Professional Standards	**Instructor's Manual** Lecture Ideas Suggested Student Activities	**Test Bank** Chapter 12	
Overseeing the Bureaucracy	**Instructor's Manual** Lecture Ideas Suggested Student Activities	**Test Bank** Chapter 12	
Conclusion: Is the Bureaucracy Responsive?	**Instructor's Manual** Lecture Ideas Suggested Student Activities	**Test Bank** Chapter 12 **Practice Tests** Chapter 12	

Resource Integration Guide

Chapter Outline	Ideas for Instruction	Print Resources	Media & Internet Resources
Development of the Courts' Role in Government	**Instructor's Manual** Lecture Ideas Suggested Student Activities	**Test Bank** Chapter 13 **Study Guide** Chapter 13 ***Bauer's* American Government: Readings & Responses** **Handbook of Selected Court Cases** All cases would be informative.	**Instructor's Resource CD-ROM** **Chapter 13 Web site** Online quiz and Web links at http://politicalscience.wadsworth.com/welch9/ **American Government Resource Center** http://politicalscience.wadsworth.com/amgov/ **American Government: Using MicroCase® ExplorIt®, 8th Edition** Exercise 15: The Courts **InfoTrac® College Edition** *Keywords:* common law, briefs
Courts	**Instructor's Manual** Lecture Ideas **American Government Transparency Acetate Package, 2003 Edition** CT-1, CT-2, CT-3	**Test Bank** Chapter 13	**WebTutor™ Advantage** Chapter 13
Judges	**Instructor's Manual** Lecture Ideas Suggested Student Activities **American Government Transparency Acetate Package, 2003 Edition** CT-4	**Test Bank** Chapter 13	**Video Case Studies in American Government** "The Judiciary: Appointments to the Bench—A Conversation with Senator Joseph Biden" **InfoTrac® College Edition** *Keyword:* judicial appointments
Access to the Courts	**Instructor's Manual** Lecture Ideas	**Test Bank** Chapter 13	
Deciding Cases	**Instructor's Manual** Lecture Ideas Suggested Student Activities **American Government Transparency Acetate Package, 2003 Edition** CT-5, CT-9	**Test Bank** Chapter 13	
The Power of the Courts	**Instructor's Manual** Lecture Ideas	**Test Bank** Chapter 13	
Conclusion: Are the Courts Responsive?	**Instructor's Manual** Lecture Ideas	**Test Bank** Chapter 13 **Practice Tests** Chapter 13	

Chapter Outline	Ideas for Instruction	Print Resources	Media & Internet Resources
The Constitution and the Bill of Rights	**Instructor's Manual** Lecture Ideas **American Government Transparency Acetate Package, 2003 Edition** CRL-1	**Test Bank** Chapter 14 **Study Guide** Chapter 14 *Bauer's* **American Government: Readings & Responses** **9-11: The Giant Awakens** Chapter 3 **Handbook of Selected Legislation & Other Documents** The Privacy Act of 1974 (p. 25)	**Instructor's Resource CD-ROM** **Chapter 14 Web site** Online quiz and Web links at http://politicalscience. wadsworth.com/welch9/ **American Government Resource Center** http://politicalscience.wadsworth. com/amgov/ **American Government: Using MicroCase® ExploreIt®, 8th Edition** Exercise 4: Civil Liberties: Free Speech **CNN® Today Video, American Government, Vol. 4** "Stem Cell Research" "Music and Video Internet Policy" "Child Pornography on the Internet" "School Vouchers" **InfoTrac® College Edition** *Keywords:* freedom of religion, prayer in public schools **WebTutor™ Advantage** Chapter 14
Freedom of Expression	**Instructor's Manual** Lecture Ideas Suggested Student Activities	**Test Bank** Chapter 14 **Handbook of Selected Court Cases** *Miller v. California* (p. 63) *New York Times v. United States"* (p. 73) *Zurcher v. Stanford Daily* (p. 169)	**InfoTrac® College Edition** *Keywords:* freedom of speech, libel & slander **CNN® Today Video, American Government, Vol. 2** "The Internet and Free Speech" **CNN® Today Video, American Government, Vol. 4** "Writers' Rights"
Rights of Criminal Defendants	**Instructor's Manual** Lecture Ideas Suggested Student Activities **American Government Transparency Acetate Package, 2003 Edition** CRL-2	**Test Bank** Chapter 14 **Handbook of Selected Court Cases** *DeJonge v. Oregon* (p. 25) *Ford v. Wainwright* (p. 35) *Gideon v. Wainwright* (p. 47) *Gitlow v. New York* (p. 53) *Miranda v. Arizona* (p. 67) *Powell v. Alabama* (p. 83)	**InfoTrac® College Edition** *Keyword:* exclusionary rule **CNN® Today Video, American Government, Vol. 2** "Death Penalty in the U.S."
Right to Privacy	**Instructor's Manual** Lecture Ideas **American Government Transparency Acetate Package, 2003 Edition** D-2	**Test Bank** Chapter 14 *Roe v. Wade* (p. 101)	**CNN® Today Video, American Government, Vol. 3** "RNC Status Abortion"
Conclusion: Are the Courts Responsive in Interpreting Civil Liberties?	**Instructor's Manual** Lecture Ideas	**Test Bank** Chapter 14 **Practice Tests** Chapter 14	

Chapter Outline	Ideas for Instruction	Print Resources	Media & Internet Resources
Race Discrimination	**Instructor's Manual** Lecture Ideas Suggested Student Activities **American Government Transparency Acetate Package, 2003 Edition** CRL-3, CRL-4	**Test Bank** Chapter 15 **Study Guide** Chapter 15 ***Bauer's* American Government: Readings & Responses** **Handbook of Selected Court Cases** *Brown v. Board of Education in Topeka* (p. 19) *Loving v. Commonwealth of Virginia* (p. 59) *Plessy v. Ferguson* (p. 79) *Smith v. Allwright* (p. 121) **Handbook of Selected Legislation & Other Documents** Title VII of the Civil Rights Act of 1964 (p. 9) The Voting Rights Act of 1965 (p. 13) The Civil Rights Act of 1964 (p. 17) The Native American Languages Act of 1990 (p. 29) The Americans with Disabilities Act of 1990 (p. 33) The Civil Rights Act of 1991 (p. 37)	**Instructor's Resource CD-ROM** **Chapter 15 Web site** Online quiz and Web links at http://politicalscience. wadsworth.com/welch9/ **American Government Resource Center** http://politicalscience.wadsworth. com/amgov/ **American Government: Using MicroCase® ExplorIt®, 8th Edition** Exercise 5: Civil Rights: Equality **InfoTrac® College Edition** *Keywords:* bilingual education, segregation, Rosa Parks, slavery **WebTutor™ Advantage** Chapter 15
Sex Discrimination	**Instructor's Manual** Lecture Ideas Suggested Student Activities	**Test Bank** Chapter 15 **Handbook of Selected Court Cases** *Romer v. Evans* (p. 107) **Handbook of Selected Legislation & Other Documents** Seneca Falls Declaration (p. 73) Emancipation Proclamation (p. 75)	**InfoTrac® College Edition** *Keywords:* gender gap, feminism
Affirmative Action	**Instructor's Manual** Lecture Ideas Suggested Student Activities **American Government Transparency Acetate Package, 2003 Edition** D-7	**Test Bank** Chapter 15 **Handbook of Selected Court Cases** *Adarand Constructors Inc. v. Pena* (p. 1) *United Steelworkers of America v. Weber* (p. 153) *Regents of the University of California v. Bakke* (p. 89) *United Automobile Workers v. Johnson Controls, Inc.* (p. 133)	**Video Case Studies in American Government** "Civil Rights: Affirmative Action in Higher Education"
Conclusion: Is Government Responsive in Granting Civil Rights?	**Instructor's Manual** Lecture Ideas	**Test Bank** Chapter 15 **Practice Tests** Chapter 15	

Resource Integration Guide

28

Chapter Outline	Ideas for Instruction	Print Resources	Media & Internet Resources
Types of Economic Systems	**Instructor's Manual** Lecture Ideas Suggested Student Activities	**Test Bank** Chapter 16 **Study Guide** Chapter 16 ***Bauer's* American Government: Readings & Responses** **Handbook of Selected Legislation & Other Documents** The North American Free Trade of 1993 (p. 41) The General Agreement on Tariffs and Trade of 1994 (p. 45)	**Instructor's Resource CD-ROM** **Chapter 16 Web site** Online quiz and Web links at http://politicalscience.wadsworth.com/welch9/ **American Government Resource Center** http://politicalscience.wadsworth.com/amgov/ **WebTutor™ Advantage** Chapter 16
Regulating the Economy	**Instructor's Manual** Lecture Ideas Suggested Student Activities **American Government Transparency Acetate Package, 2003 Edition** DEP-9	**Test Bank** Chapter 16	
The Budget in the Economy	**Instructor's Manual** Lecture Ideas Suggested Student Activities **American Government Transparency Acetate Package, 2003 Edition** DEP-1, DEP-5, DEP-6, DEP-7, DEP-8	**Test Bank** Chapter 16	
Postwar Boom and Bust	**Instructor's Manual** Lecture Ideas	**Test Bank** Chapter 16	
The American Economy in the Twenty-First Century	**Instructor's Manual** Lecture Ideas Suggested Student Activities	**Test Bank** Chapter 16	**CNN® Today American Government, Vol. 4** "Profit Recession" "DotCom Business Discussion" "401K Year-end Analysis"
Conclusion: Is Our Economic Policy Responsive?	**Instructor's Manual** Lecture Ideas	**Test Bank** Chapter 16 **Practice Tests** Chapter 16	

* This chapter appears only in *American Government.*

Chapter Outline	Ideas for Instruction	Print Resources	Media & Internet Resources
The Political and Legal Bases of Social Welfare Policies	**Instructor's Manual** Lecture Ideas Suggested Student Activities **American Government Transparency Acetate Package, 2003 Edition** DEP-18	**Test Bank** Chapter 17 **Study Guide** Chapter 17 *Bauer's* **American Government: Readings & Responses**	**Instructor's Resource CD-ROM** **Chapter 17 Web site** Online quiz and Web links at http://politicalscience. wadsworth.com/welch9/ **American Government Resource Center** http://politicalscience.wadsworth. com/amgov/ **CNN® Today American Government, Vol. 2** "Welfare Reform" **CNN® Today American Government, Vol. 4** "Why Hate the Rich?"
The Evolution of Social Welfare Policies	**Instructor's Manual** Lecture Ideas	**Test Bank** Chapter 17	**WebTutor™ Advantage** Chapter 17
Income Support Programs	**Instructor's Manual** Lecture Ideas Suggested Student Activities **American Government Transparency Acetate Package, 2003 Edition** DEP-10, DEP-11, DEP-12, DEP-14, DEP-15, DEP-16, DEP-17	**Test Bank** Chapter 17	
Health Care Programs	**Instructor's Manual** Lecture Ideas Suggested Student Activities **American Government Transparency Acetate Package, 2003 Edition** DEP-13	**Test Bank** Chapter 17	
Other Subsidized Services	**Instructor's Manual** Lecture Ideas **American Government Transparency Acetate Package, 2003 Edition** DEP-19	**Test Bank** Chapter 17	
Tax Subsidies	**Instructor's Manual** Lecture Ideas Suggested Student Activities	**Test Bank** Chapter 17	
The Future of Social Welfare Policies	**Instructor's Manual** Lecture Ideas Suggested Student Activities	**Test Bank** Chapter 17	
Conclusion: Are Social Welfare Programs Responsive?	**Instructor's Manual** Lecture Ideas	**Test Bank** Chapter 17 **Practice Tests** Chapter 17	

* This chapter appears only in *American Government*.

Chapter Outline	Ideas for Instruction	Print Resources	Media & Internet Resources
Reasons for Regulation **Kinds of Regulation**	**Instructor's Manual** Lecture Ideas Suggested Student Activities	**Test Bank** Chapter 18 **Study Guide** Chapter 18 *Bauer's* **American Government: Readings & Responses**	**Instructor's Resource CD-ROM** **Chapter 18 Web site** Online quiz and Web links at http://politicalscience.wadsworth.com/welch9/ **American Government Resource Center** http://politicalscience.wadsworth.com/amgov/ **CNN® Today: American Government, Vol. 3** "The Environment"
The Regulatory Process	**Instructor's Manual** Lecture Ideas Suggested Student Activities	**Test Bank** Chapter 18	**WebTutor™ Advantage** Chapter 18
Cycles of Regulation	**Instructor's Manual** Lecture Ideas Suggested Student Activities	**Test Bank** Chapter 18	
Regulatory Politics and Environmental Protection	**Instructor's Manual** Lecture Ideas Suggested Student Activities**s** **American Government Transparency Acetate Package, 2003 Edition** DEP-20, DEP-21	**Test Bank** Chapter 18	**InfoTrac® College Edition** *Keyword:* environmental policy **CNN® Today American Government, Vol. 2** "Environmental Protection"
Benefits and Costs of Regulation	**Instructor's Manual** Lecture Ideas	**Test Bank** Chapter 18	
Conclusion: Is Regulatory Policy Responsive?	**Instructor's Manual** Lecture Ideas	**Test Bank** Chapter 18 **Practice Tests** Chapter 18	

* This chapter appears only in
American Government.

Resource Integration Guides

Chapter Outline	Ideas for Instruction	Print Resources	Media & Internet Resources
Foreign Policy Goals	**Instructor's Manual** Lecture Ideas Suggested Student Activities	**Test Bank** Chapter 19 **Study Guide** Chapter 19 ***Bauer's* American Government: Readings & Responses** **9-11: The Giant Awakens** Chapter 5 **Handbook of Selected Legislation & Other Documents** The Preamble to the Charter of the United Nations (p. 81) The North American Free Trade Agreement of 1993 (p. 41) The General Agreement on Tariffs and Trade of 1994 (p. 45)	**Instructor's Resource CD-ROM** **Chapter 19 Web site** Online quiz and Web links at http://politicalscience. wadsworth.com/welch9/ **American Government Resource Center** http://politicalscience.wadsworth. com/amgov/ **CNN® Today American Government, Vol. 2** "Foreign Policy" **CNN® Today American Government, Vol. 4** "Arafat—Hero or Foe?" "The American Empire" "Afghan Offensive"
Making Foreign Policy in a Democracy	**Instructor's Manual** Lecture Ideas Suggested Student Activities	**Test Bank** Chapter 19	**WebTutor™ Advantage** Chapter 19
Changing Approaches to U.S. Foreign Policy	**Instructor's Manual** Lecture Ideas Suggested Student Activities **American Government Transparency Acetate Package, 2003 Edition** FP-2, FP-3, FP-4, FP-5, FP-6, FP-7	**Test Bank** Chapter 19 **Handbook of Selected Legislation & Other Documents** The Monroe Doctrine (p. 69)	
Instruments of Foreign Policy	**Instructor's Manual** Lecture Ideas Suggested Student Activities **American Government Transparency Acetate Package, 2003 Edition** FP-1	**Test Bank** Chapter 19 **Test Bank** Chapter 19	
Defining Security in the Global Age	**Instructor's Manual** Lecture Ideas		
Conclusion: Is Our Foreign Policy Responsive?	**Instructor's Manual** Lecture Ideas	**Test Bank** Chapter 19 **Practice Tests** Chapter 19	

* This chapter appears only in
American Government.

NINTH EDITION

AMERICAN GOVERNMENT

SUSAN WELCH
The Pennsylvania State University

JOHN GRUHL
University of Nebraska—Lincoln

JOHN COMER
University of Nebraska—Lincoln

SUSAN M. RIGDON
University of Illinois at Urbana-Champaign

THOMSON

WADSWORTH

Australia • Canada • Mexico • Singapore • Spain
United Kingdom • United States

Executive Editor: *David Tatum*
Development Editor: *Sue Gleason*
Assistant Editor: *Heather Hogan*
Technology Project Manager: *Melinda Newfarmer*
Marketing Manager: *Janise Fry*
Marketing Assistant: *Mary Ho*
Advertising Project Manager: *Nathaniel Bergson-Michelson*
Project Manager, Editorial Production: *Ray Crawford*
Print/Media Buyer: *Barbara Britton*
Permissions Editor: *Joohee Lee*
Production Service: *Penmarin Books*

Text Designer: *Carolyn Deacy*
Art Editor: *Hal Lockwood*
Photo Researcher: *Connie Hathaway*
Copy Editor: *Laura Larson*
Illustrator: *Carlisle Communications, Joe VanDerBos (boxes)*
Cover Designer: *Sue Hart*
Cover Image: *Joseph Pobereskin / Getty Images*
Cover Printer: *Transcontinental / Interglobe*
Compositor: *Carlisle Communications*
Printer: *Transcontinental / Interglobe*

Printed in Canada
1 2 3 4 5 6 7 06 05 04 03 02

For more information about our products, contact us at:
Thomson Learning Academic Resource Center
1-800-423-0563
For permission to use material from this text, contact us by:
Phone: 1-800-730-2214   **Fax:** 1-800-730-2215
Web: http://www.thomsonrights.com

Library of Congress Control Number: 2003100398

Student Edition with InfoTrac: ISBN 0-534-59634-7
Student Edition without InfoTrac: ISBN 0534-59635-5
Instructor's Edition: ISBN 0534-59636-3

Wadsworth/Thomson Learning
10 Davis Drive
Belmont, CA 94002-3098
USA

Asia
Thomson Learning
5 Shenton Way #01-01
UIC Building
Singapore 068808

Australia
Nelson Thomson Learning
102 Dodds Street
South Melbourne, Victoria 3205
Australia

Canada
Nelson Thomson Learning
1120 Birchmount Road
Toronto, Ontario M1K 5G4
Canada

Europe/Middle East/Africa
Thomson Learning
High Holborn House
50/51 Bedford Row
London WC1R 4LR
United Kingdom

Latin America
Thomson Learning
Seneca, 53
Colonia Polanco
11560 Mexico D.F.
Mexico

Spain
Paraninfo Thomson Learning
Calle Magallanes, 25
28015 Madrid
Spain

BRIEF CONTENTS

CONTENTS

PART TWO

Links between People and Government

Institutions

a great deal has happened in American politics since our last edition. The attack on the World Trade Center and the Pentagon dramatically affected the politics and the psyche of the nation. The reaction to 9/11 gave the administration new stature and popularity at home and thus has shaped both domestic and foreign politics since then.

The fiasco over the 2000 presidential election is another major event that had immediate as well as longer-term effects on American politics. This series of events offers an opportunity to understand not just the role of the Electoral College but also the importance of the judiciary and the role of the states in our federal system.

A third major set of events since our last edition is the widespread corruption and looting of stockholders uncovered in several of America's major corporations. Though the focus of most news coverage has been on private corruption, these crises have implications for campaign finance laws, the federal government's role in regulation of the economy, and the government's ability to protect unsuspecting shareholders and employees of major corporations.

But despite these striking events, not all has changed. Much of American politics has reverted to its pre-9/11 form. Popular esteem for American political institutions grew after 9/11 but then dropped to pre-9/11 levels as months went by. Sales of flags boomed, and the national anthem was played at every occasion. But despite this surge in the manifestation of patriotic sentiment, the public remains suspicious of, if not outright negative toward, politics and politicians. Yet the role of government in our lives remains crucial, as 9/11 and the later corporate scandals so starkly demonstrated.

The ninth edition of our text, *American Government,* tries, as did the previous editions, to demonstrate to students why government is important and to interest students in learning about the exciting, important, and controversial issues in American public life. We believe an introductory course succeeds if most students develop an understanding of major ideas, an interest in learning more about American government, and an ability to begin to understand and evaluate the news they hear about American political issues. Although a firm grounding in the essential "nuts and bolts" of American government is crucial, other approaches are helpful in motivating students' interest in government.

We offer the essentials of American government, but we also want the student to understand why (and sometimes how) these important features have evolved, their impact on government and individuals, and why they are controversial (if they are) and worth learning about.

For example, we prefer students to leave the course remembering why government tries to regulate corporations, how it does so, and the political factors that lead to stronger or weaker regulations rather than specific regulatory acts. The latter will change or soon be forgotten, but understanding the "whys" will help the student understand the issues long after the course is over.

We have also tried to interest students by describing and discussing the impact of various features of government. For example, students who do not understand why learning about voter registration laws is important may "see the light" when they understand the link between such laws and low voter turnout. Therefore, a particular emphasis throughout the book is on the *impact* of government: how individual features of government affect its responsiveness to different groups (in Lasswell's terms, "Who gets what and why?"). We realize that nothing in American politics is simple; rarely does one feature of government produce, by itself, a clear outcome. Nevertheless, we think that students will be more willing to learn about government if they see some relationships between how government operates and the impact it has on them as American citizens.

The Organization and Contents of the Book

While the basic organization of American government books is fairly standard, our text has a unique chapter on money and politics and a half-chapter on environmental politics. Other features include a civil rights chapter that integrates a thorough treatment of constitutional issues concerning minorities and women, a discussion of the civil rights and women's rights movements, and contemporary research on the political status of these groups. We include in this chapter the special legal problems of Hispanics and Native Americans.

Substantive policy chapters reinforce the emphasis on the impact of government action. The chapter on social welfare and health policy now includes major sections on types of policies: income support programs, health care programs, other subsidized services (including education, insurance, mortgages, and agriculture), and tax subsidies. A chapter on economic policymaking complements the section on budgeting found in the chapter on Congress. The treatment of economic policy highlights the relationship between politics and the economy, and it should help the student better understand issues such as the deficit, inflation, and unemployment. The chapter on regulation emphasizes the underlying rationale for regulation and its problems and benefits, with special emphasis on environmental regulation. The chapter on foreign policy places current foreign policy issues in the context of the history of our foreign policy aims, especially since World War II, and features new issues arising in the post–Cold War world.

Some instructors will prefer not to use any of the policy chapters. The book stands as a whole without them, as many policy examples are integrated into the rest of the text. Different combinations of the policy chapters may also be used, as each chapter is independent.

The organization of the book is straightforward. After material on democracy, the Constitution, and federalism, the book covers linkages, including money and politics, then institutions, and finally policy. Civil liberties and rights are treated after the chapter on the judiciary.

But the book is flexible enough that instructors can modify the order of the chapters. Some instructors will prefer to cover institutions before process. Others may prefer to discuss civil liberties and rights when discussing the Constitution.

Changes in the Ninth Edition

The attack on 9/11, the 2000 election fiasco, the Bush administration, and now the recapture of the U.S. Senate by the Republicans have created many new issues for analysts of American government. We explore these recent phenomena in light of the fundamentals about American government that students should learn.

We highlight the effect of 9/11 by adding a new feature in most chapters: "After 9/11," described below under "Special Features." Other revisions also allow us to explore the impact of 9/11. For example, the controversies over the president's Homeland Security Department are featured in the bureaucracy and foreign policy chapters.

The 2000 election and especially its aftermath are treated extensively through an analysis of the role of the media in the Florida recount in the media chapter, exploration of the Gore and Bush postelection strategies in the elections chapter, and the role of the Supreme Court in the election outcome in the judiciary chapter. In the elections chapter, we also explore several aspects of election laws that affected the Florida outcome.

The role of government in the corporate scandals of 2002 is featured in the chapter on money and politics as well as in the regulation and environmental policy chapter. We explore the influence of the accounting lobby and other major corporate lobbies on campaign funding, and in turn, the impact of that funding on the way members of Congress seek to influence regulatory agencies.

The text of every chapter has been substantially revised. Throughout we have also replaced photos and cartoons to complement the new material and to give students a chance to learn through graphic as well as textual material. Discussions of the Bush administration, its organization, operation, and policies are integrated into relevant portions throughout the book. As always, we have updated the judiciary, civil liberties, and civil rights chapters to incorporate new Supreme Court decisions. Chapter 15, "Civil Rights," also includes a new treatment of how Arabs and Arab Americans have been scrutinized in the post-9/11 environment and a focus on discrimination against homosexuals.

Of course, all the policy chapters have been revised to reflect new public policy developments. The economic policy chapter covers the economic downturn of the past two years and how government policy is or is not coping with it. The social welfare chapter has been reorganized to reflect economic changes, too. The foreign policy chapter contains a substantial discussion of U.S. policy toward Iraq in the context of presidential foreign policy decision making.

We are delighted to have the opportunity to write this ninth edition and to improve the text further in ways suggested by our students and readers. We have been extremely pleased by the reaction of instructors and students to our first eight editions. We were especially gratified to have won three times the American Government Textbook Award from the Women's Caucus for Political Science of the American Political Science Association.

Special Features

Student interest and analytic abilities grow when confronted with a clash of views about important issues. Today there is much discussion about how to stimulate the critical thinking abilities of students. Beginning with the first edition, our text has provided features especially designed to do this by involving students in the controversies—and excitement—of American politics.

You Are There

Each chapter opens with a scenario called "You Are There." In a page or two, the student reads about a real-life political dilemma faced by a public official or a private citizen involved in a controversial issue. Students are asked to put themselves in that individual's shoes, to weigh the pros and cons, and to decide what should be done. The instructor may want to poll the entire class and use the "You Are There" as a basis for class discussion. In the "Epilogue" at the end of the chapter, we reveal the actual decision and discuss it in light of the ideas presented in the chapter.

Nearly two-thirds of the "You Are There" features in this edition are new. They focus on contemporary topics such as, for example, the controversy over the party switch of Senator Jeffords (Chapter 7), the Florida election strategies of the presidential candidates (Chapter 8), the impeachment controversy in Congress (Chapter 10), whether the FBI should be part of a homeland security department (Chapter 12), whether the Boy Scouts can discriminate against homosexuals (Chapter 14), and whether Congress should give the president a blank check to invade Iraq (Chapter 19).

After 9/11

Each of these new features highlights an issue posed by 9/11 and its aftermath that is relevant to the chapter's subject. For example, in the introductory chapter, we feature the impact of 9/11 on immigration policy; in the interest group chapter, we discuss how lobbyists used 9/11 to further their existing agendas; in the bureaucracy chapter, we explore government's new emphasis on secrecy; in the civil liberties chapter, we examine how 9/11 fears have affected the civil liberties of Americans.

American Diversity

In many chapters, "American Diversity" boxes illustrate the impact of the social diversity of the American population on political life. These boxes help students understand how a variety of backgrounds and attitudes shapes views of politics and positions on issues.

Boxes

In each chapter, several boxes highlighting interesting aspects of American politics draw the students into the material. Many illustrate how government and politics really work in a particular situation—how a corporation lobbies for government benefits, how a seemingly powerless group is able to organize for political action, how interest groups solicit money by mail, and how political polls are done—while others highlight features of government that may be of particular interest to students—how ethnicity shapes voting behavior and how teen pregnancies and abortions affect the abortion debate.

Other Features

Several other features also help students organize their study.

Outline

Each chapter begins with an outline of its contents.

Key Terms

Key terms are boldfaced within the text and listed at the end of each chapter and in the glossary.

Further Reading

A brief, annotated list of further readings contains works that might be useful to a student doing research or looking for additional material.

Electronic Resources

Each chapter lists addresses of particularly interesting or useful sites on the Internet that relate directly to the topics covered in the chapter.

InfoTrac College Edition®

At the end of each chapter are lists of suggested topic-related articles that they can access in InfoTrac College Edition's extensive online library of important political science and other popular sources.

American Government Resources

A reminder for students to visit the Wadsworth American Government Resources Web site, with its many helpful tools, appears at the end of each chapter.

Ancillaries for Instructors

NEW!

Instructor's Resource Guide CD-ROM

This instructor's resource provides a wealth of materials available electronically, including the full Instructor's Manual, ExamView, a Video Case Study Instructor's Manual, PowerPoint images of new graphics in the text, a resource integration guide, interactive timelines, and InfoTrac activities.

Instructor's Manual

Corresponding to each text chapter, every chapter in the manual contains chapter outlines, suggested assignments, recommended Internet sites, and an extensive section correlating the chapter's content to other components of the complete ancillary package for this text, including relevant InfoTrac articles, transparencies, PowerPoint slides, and clips from the Political Science Video Library (including CNN). One version of the Instructor's Manual accompanies both versions of this text.

Test Bank

A large selection of test items appears here, including multiple-choice, fill-in-the-blank, short-answer, and essay questions. One version of the Test Bank accompanies both versions of the text.

ExamView® Computerized Testing for Windows and Macintosh

Create, deliver, and customize tests and study guides (both print and online) in minutes with this easy-to-use assessment and tutorial system. ExamView offers both a Quick Test Wizard and an Online Test Wizard that guide instructors step by step through the process of creating tests, while its unique "WYSIWYG" capability allows users to see the test they are creating on the screen exactly as it will print or display online. You can build tests of up to 250 questions using up to twelve question types. Using ExamView's complete word-processing capabilities, users can enter an unlimited number of new questions or edit existing questions. ExamView is available on the *Instructor's Resource Guide* CD-ROM.

American Government Transparency Acetate Package, 2004 Edition

Includes more than 165 full-color acetates (tables, charts, and figures from the text and additional sources).

Multimedia Manager for Political Science: A Microsoft PowerPoint Link Tool

An advanced PowerPoint presentation tool containing text-specific lecture outlines, figures, and images that allows instructors to deliver dynamic lectures quickly. In addition, it provides the flexibility to customize each presentation by editing what we have provided or by adding a personal collection of slides, videos, and animations. All of the acetates and selected photos have also been incorporated into each of the lectures.

CNN Today Videos for American Government

Four volumes of three- to six-minute video clips on relevant political issues. They serve as great lecture or discussion launchers.

NEW!

America's New War: CNN Looks at Terrorism

Free to qualified adopters, this great discussion starter includes sixteen two- to five-minute segments on terrorist attacks on U.S. targets around the world.

NEW!

Video Case Studies for American Government

Free to adopters, this award-winning video contains twelve case studies on the debate on recent policy issues, such as affirmative action. Each case ends with questions designed to spark classroom discussion.

Wadsworth Political Science Video Library

So many exciting new videos . . . so many great ways to enrich your lectures and spark discussion of the material in this text. Your Wadsworth/Thomson representative will be happy to provide details on our video policy by adoption size.

Ancillaries for Instructors and Students

Book-Specific Web Site

Easily accessible from the Wadsworth Political Science Resource Center at http://politicalscience.wadsworth.com, this site is the ultimate in interactive learning. Linking online material to the text at every opportunity, it includes the following:

- Interactive quizzes for each chapter where students can self-assess and review their knowledge
- Interactive timelines
- Hypercontents for each chapter—an extensive hypertext list of sites that provide reviews of related material, supplemental media, and chapter-related news and research
- Simulations that encourage students to role-play various political actors
- Video case studies
- Flashcards
- InfoTrac exercises
- Internet exercises based on the "You Are There" features in the text
- The instructor's resource integration guide
- Learning objectives

NEW!

Wadsworth American Government Resource Center

By linking each of eighteen American government topic areas to eight different types of activities, this site actively involves students in the course and in civic participation. The activities include simulations, participation activities, MicroCase exercises, video clips, the InfoTrac College Edition Reader, primary and secondary source documents, Internet activities, and more links.

InfoTrac® College Edition

Free access to an extensive online library of current articles! Available exclusively from Wadsworth/Thomson Learning, four months of access to the InfoTrac College Edition library is included *free* to adopters and their students. Featuring thousands of full-length articles (not abstracts) from such publications as *National*

Review, Washington Monthly, and many others, this online resource opens new worlds of information for your students.

WebTutor™

Takes your course beyond classroom boundaries! Rich with content for your American government course, this Web-based teaching and learning tool includes course management, study/mastery, and communication tools. Use WebTutor to provide virtual office hours, post your syllabus, and track student progress with WebTutor's quizzing material. For students, WebTutor offers real-time access to interactive online tutorials and simulations, practice quizzes, and Web links—all correlated to *American Government* and *Understanding American Government.* Available in WebCT and Blackboard.

NEW!

MyCourse 2.0

Whether easy-to-use tools to build a course Web site or the content to fill it, MyCourse 2.0 offers a simple solution for custom Web site design that allows instructors to assign, track, and report on student progress; load a syllabus; and more.

Student Resources

NEW!

American Government: Using MicroCase ExplorIt, Eighth Edition

Windows-compatible package that Includes a CD-ROM and workbook. Students make their own decisions about the issues as they analyze and interpret current NES and GSS data.

America at Odds CD-ROM

Your students actually participate in American politics with the twenty interactive modules in this CD-ROM as they research the issues, discuss ideas, formulate opinions, and interpret data! Features a rich mix of media, including digital video and audio, photos, graphics, and Internet technology.

American Government: Readings and Responses

By Monica Bauer. A wonderful collection of readings from prominent writers, plus "Chat Room" conversations with students who debate the topics in the readings.

Study Guide

Features (in each chapter) a chapter summary; key terms, and fill-in-the blank, true/false, multiple-choice, and short essay questions.

NEW!

Practice Tests

Twenty-five multiple-choice items for each chapter of the text allow students to prepare for tests using items similar to those instructors may use.

NEW!

9/11: The Giant Awakens

By Jeremy Meyer. Focuses on how the American political system is responding to the challenges posed by the 9/11 attacks.

Critical Thinking and American Government, Second Edition

By Kent M. Brudney, John H. Carver, and Mark E. Weber. Provides information and exercises that help students hone the skills necessary for interpreting and analyzing American government issues.

Thinking Globally, Acting Locally

By John Soares. Designed to help students get involved and become active citizens. Topics include tips for writing letters to the editor, volunteering, how to change laws, and registering to vote.

American Government Internet Activities, Third Edition

Contains activities for all major topics in the text. Students are asked to surf the Web to obtain answers to thought-provoking questions.

An Introduction to Critical Thinking and Writing in American Politics

Introduces a number of critical thinking and writing techniques, helping students make better use of the information they receive in class and in the text.

InfoTrac College Edition Student Guide for Political Science

Helps students make the most of the InfoTrac database available with their textbook, including suggested keyword search terms for political science.

The Handbook of Selected Court Cases

Includes more than thirty Supreme Court cases.

The Handbook of Selected Legislation and Other Documents

Features excerpts from twelve laws passed by the U.S. Congress that have had a significant impact on American politics.

Acknowledgments

We would like to thank the many people who have aided and sustained us during the lengthy course of this project.

We first acknowledge the work of Margery Ambrosius, the coauthor of earlier editions of Chapters 12 and 17, for her intellectual contribution to this book. Our current and former University of Nebraska and Penn State colleagues have been most tolerant and helpful. We thank them all. In particular, we appreciate the assistance of John Hibbing, Philip Dyer, Robert Miewald, Beth Theiss-Morse, Louis Picard, John Peters, David Rapkin, Peter Maslowski, David Forsythe, W. Randy Newell, and Steven Daniels, who provided us with data, bibliographic information, and other insights that we have used here. We are especially grateful to Philip Dyer, Alan Booth, Louis Picard, Robert Miewald, and John Hibbing, who read one or more chapters and saved us from a variety of errors.

We are also grateful to the many other readers of our draft manuscript, as listed here. Without their assistance the book would have been less accurate, less complete, and less lively.

We are also grateful to those instructors who have used the book and relayed their comments and suggestions to us. Our students at the University of Nebraska have also provided invaluable reactions to the previous editions.

Others, too, have been of great assistance to us. John Soares and Lauren Holland provided essential service and help in producing the ancillary materials for the book.

Several people at Wadsworth Publishing also deserve our thanks. Clark Baxter has been a continual source of encouragement and optimism from the beginning of the first edition through the beginning of the ninth, David Tatom has been his able replacement. We are greatly in debt to Carolyn Deacy, who designed this edition of the book, and to Ray Crawford and Hal Lockwood, who produced it.

Reviewers

REVIEWERS OF THE NEW EDITION

James Benze
Washington and Jefferson College

Rhodell J. Fields
St. Petersburg College

Jeff Fox
Catawba College

Stephen I. Frank
St. Cloud State University

Sonia R. Garcia
St. Mary's University

Kay Hofer
Southwest Texas State University

Michael K. Moore
University of Texas at Arlington

Glen Sussman
Old Dominion University

David Van Heemst
Olivet Nazarene University

James Matthew Wilson
Southern Methodist University

John H. Wilson Jr.
Itawamba Community College

REVIEWERS OF PREVIOUS EDITIONS

Alan Abramowitz
State University of New York at Stony Brook

Larry Adams
Baruch College–City University of New York

Danny M. Adkison
Oklahoma State University

James Alt
Harvard University

Margery Marzahn Ambrosius
Kansas State University

Kevin Bailey
North Harris Community College

Kennette M. Benedict
Northwestern University

Timothy Bledsoe
Wayne State University

Jon Bond
Texas A&M University

Paul R. Brace
New York University

Joseph V. Brogan
La Salle University

James R. Brown Jr.
Central Washington University

Chalmers Brumbaugh
Elon College

Alan D. Buckley
Santa Monica College

Richard G. Buckner Jr.
Santa Fe Community College

Ronald Busch
Cleveland State University

Carl D. Cavalli
Memphis State University

Richard A. Champagne
University of Wisconsin, Madison

Michael Connelly
Southwestern Oklahoma State University

Gary Copeland
University of Oklahoma

George H. Cox Jr.
Georgia Southern College

Paige Cubbison
Miami-Dade University

Landon Curry
Southwest Texas State University

Jack DeSario
Case Western Reserve University

Robert E. DiClerico
West Virginia University

Ernest A. Dover Jr.
Midwestern State University

Georgia Duerst-Lahti
Beloit College

Ann H. Elder
Illinois State University

Ghassan E. El-Eid
Butler University

C. Lawrence Evans
College of William and Mary

Murray Fischel
Kent State University

Bobbe Fitzhugh
Eastern Wyoming College

Marianne Fraser
University of Utah

Jarvis Gamble
Owens Community College

David Garrison
Collin County Community College

Phillip L. Gianos
California State University–Fullerton

Doris A. Graber
University of Illinois–Chicago

Ruth M. Grubel
University of Wisconsin–Whitewater

Stefan D. Haag
Austin Community College

Larry M. Hall
Belmont University

Edward Harpham
University of Texas–Dallas

Peter O. Haslund
Santa Barbara City College

Richard P. Heil
Fort Hays State University

Peggy Heilig
University of Illinois at Urbana

Craig Hendricks
Long Beach City College

Marjorie Hershey
Indiana University

Kay Hofer
Southwest Texas State University

Samuel B. Hoff
Delaware State College

Robert D. Holsworth
Virginia Commonwealth University

Jesse C. Horton
San Antonio College

Gerald Houseman
Indiana University

Peter G. Howse
American River College

David W. Hunt
Triton College

Pamela Imperato
University of North Dakota

Jerald Johnson
University of Vermont

Loch Johnson
University of Georgia

Evan M. Jones
St. Cloud State University

Joseph F. Jozwiak Jr.
Texas A & M University–Kingsville

Henry C. Kenski
University of Arizona

Matt Kerbel
Villanova University

Marshall R. King
Maryville College

Orma Lindford
Kansas State University

Peter J. Longo
University of Nebraska–Kearney

Roger C. Lowery
University of North Carolina–Wilmington

H. R. Mahood
Memphis State University

Jarol B. Manheim
The George Washington University

Kenneth M. Mash
East Stroudsburg University

A. Nick Minton
University of Massachusetts–Lowell

Matthew Moen
University of Maine

Michael K. Moore
University of Texas at Arlington

Michael Nelson
Vanderbilt University

Bruce Nesmith
Coe College

Walter Noelke
Angelo State University

Thomas Payette
Henry Ford Community College

Theodore B. Pedeliski
University of North Dakota

Jerry Perkins
Texas Tech University

Toni Phillips
University of Arkansas

C. Herman Pritchett
University of California–Santa Barbara

Charles Prysby
University of North Carolina–Greensboro

Sandra L. Quinn-Musgrove
Our Lady of the Lake University

Donald R. Ranish
Antelope Valley Community College

Linda Richter
Kansas State University

Jerry Sandvick
North Hennepin Community College

James Richard Sauder
University of New Mexico

Eleanor A. Schwab
South Dakota State University

Earl Sheridan
University of North Carolina–Wilmington

Edward Sidlow
Northwestern University

Cynthia Slaughter
Angelo State University

John Squibb
Lincolnland Community College

M. H. Tajalli-Tehrani
Southwest Texas State University

Kristine A. Thompson
Moorehead State University

R. Mark Tiller
Austin Community College

Gordon J. Tolle
South Dakota State University

Susan Tolleson-Rinehart
Texas Tech University

Bernadyne Weatherford
Rowan College of New Jersey

Richard Unruh
Fresno Pacific College

Jay Van Bruggen
Clarion University of Pennsylvania

Kenny Whitby
University of South Carolina

Donald C. Williams
Western New England College

Clifford J. Wirth
University of New Hampshire

Ann Wynia
North Hennepin Community College

Mary D. Young
Southwestern Michigan College

SUSAN WELCH received her A.B. and Ph.D. degrees from the University of Illinois at Urbana-Champaign. She is currently Dean of the College of the Liberal Arts and Professor of Political Science at The Pennsylvania State University. Her teaching and research areas include legislatures, state and urban politics, and women and minorities in politics. She has edited the *American Politics Quarterly.*

JOHN GRUHL, a Professor of Political Science, received his A.B. from DePauw University in Greencastle, Indiana, and his Ph.D. from the University of California at Santa Barbara. Since joining the University of Nebraska faculty in 1976, he has taught and researched in the areas of judicial process, criminal justice, and civil rights and liberties. He won University of Nebraska campus-wide and system-wide distinguished teaching awards and has become a charter member of the University's Academy of Distinguished Teachers.

JOHN COMER is a Professor of Political Science at the University of Nebraska. He received his A.B. in political science from Miami University of Ohio in 1965 and his Ph.D. from the Ohio State University in 1971. His teaching and research focus on interest groups, public opinion, voting behavior, and political parties.

SUSAN RIGDON received A.B. and Ph.D. degrees in political science from the University of Illinois in 1966 and 1971. She has taught American Government at several institutions in the U.S. and China, and has other teaching and research interests in foreign policy, comparative government, and political development. She is a Research Associate in Anthropology at the University of Illinois at Urbana-Champaign.

CHAPTER 1

AMERICAN DEMOCRACY

World Financial Center, New York City, late September 2001.

Joel Meyerowitz/Courtesy of the Ariel Meyerowitz Gallery, New York

Who, Me?

In the opening section of this and all following chapters, you will be asked to step into the shoes of decision makers and analyze how and why they made certain key decisions. The epilogue to each chapter provides an outcome for the decision-maker's dilemma.

The first decision maker you are asked to be is, well, *you.* You are sitting there reading your American government text but wondering how much you are really interested in government or politics. You know that every two years there is a national election, every four years one to elect a president, and that, on or between these dates, there are a host of state and local elections for governors, mayors, city councils, and school, library, and county board members. Perhaps in the next election you will be a first-time voter, or maybe you already have several campaigns under your belt. Yet each time an election approaches, you ask yourself whether it is worth the effort. Maybe you are one of those people who shares Groucho Marx's observation that "politics is the art of finding trouble everywhere, diagnosing it incorrectly, and applying the wrong remedy."

If you are going to vote, you will have to make decisions on dozens of candidates. Do you have the time to get to know something about each of them and to read up on the issues? Maybe you should vote only for those candidates whose positions you know and only in those elections you think will have a significant impact on your life. And what about the campaigns leading up to election day? Should you become active in a political party, write letters in support of an issue, make campaign contributions, attend rallies, or campaign for candidates? And what about all the other efforts to influence policy outcomes that do not involve electoral politics? Should you join one or more of the many interest groups that lobby unelected officials such as bureaucrats, political appointees, and federal judges?

You are a busy person, so why bother to get involved in politics? You look at the news and see dog-eat-dog, negative campaigning, character attacks, investigations into the most intimate aspects of the lives of public figures, gridlock caused by party conflict in Congress and state legislatures, and huge campaign donations buying access to candidates or officials. You sometimes get the impression that interest groups and legislators spend years debating issues only to achieve a standoff. Who needs it? After all, government works: your mail comes, your grandparents' Social Security checks arrive on time, your state issued you a driver's license, the roads are paved, the bridges and dams hold up, the schools are open, and we have a large military establishment, local law enforcement, a great-looking capital city, and a massive infrastructure.

America has social stability and a well-functioning economy. Government is doing the basics. Why should you get involved in politics?

One obvious argument is that if you do not, others will, and they may not agree with your idea of what government should be doing to solve the country's problems and prepare for the future. This is a huge country—it is economically, ethnically, and religiously diverse and becoming more so every year. There will always be divergent views and therefore competing interests trying to shape government policy. If you opt out, and candidates are elected and policies made that you disagree with, quite frankly, you will not have much basis for complaint. Furthermore, you know that participation is integral to the concept on which our form of government is founded. Americans have fought for generations to expand rights to the point where virtually every citizen eighteen or older who is not a convicted felon has full rights of participation. Why did they make the effort? Now, in the aftermath of the terrorist attacks, we hear there has been a resurgence of patriotic feeling, a new pride in being American. What is more American than helping to choose the men and women who govern us?

What will you do? Are you going to vote in some, all, or none of the upcoming local, state, and federal elections? Do you believe the major parties and candidates differ sufficiently on the issues or philosophically to make your vote worth casting? If your candidates are elected, do you think they will be able to move government in the direction you want it to go? Do you care enough about some issues that you might be willing to invest time and effort, beyond voting, to influence policy? Do you think that if you do get involved, you as an ordinary citizen will have any chance of reaching policymakers with your views? What would it take to get you involved in government and the political process?

The epilogues to this and succeeding chapters explain how and why the You Are There decision makers made their choices.

There may be conflict in our political life, but Americans are members of one community. We are parties to a single legal contract, the Constitution, and are all equally subject to the protections and obligations of a common set of laws. We also share an economic system, and although the Constitution has little to say about its nature, our government is deeply implicated in its successes and failures. In fact, government's role in managing the economy is sufficient to link the level of confidence we have in government to how well the economy is doing, or at minimum to how well we are doing. Our economic well-being also affects how much we participate and how much access we have to policymakers.

It is part of the American political character to fear any concentration of power that threatens individual liberty and hence to be suspicious of government for its potential to concentrate and misuse power. Yet in arguing for the ratification of the Constitution in 1789, John Jay wrote "Nothing is more certain than the indispensable necessity of Government."[1] Why is government indispensable? Because even though government *can* be a threat to individual liberty, there is no way to guarantee liberty without the protections and constraints that government and the rule of law can provide. The Preamble of the Constitution identifies other governmental functions—to form a union among the disparate states, establish a system of justice, maintain social order, promote the general welfare of the people, and provide a defense against external threats. How far its authority extends in fulfilling any of these tasks is the topic of an eternal debate about the proper role of government in a system of constitutionally restricted powers. This debate in turn encompasses much of what is at stake in the political process.

If government is the instrument for forging one interest out of many in order to legislate and to speak for the country as a whole in matters of national interest, then **politics** is a means through which individual and group interests compete to shape government's impact on society's problems and goals. These interests compete through political parties and many other extragovernmental organizations. But the institutions of government also were created to represent competing interests, not just to mediate among them. So politics is also the art of governing.

More than two thousand years ago, Aristotle wrote that politics is the most noble endeavor in which people can engage, partly because it helps them know themselves and partly because it forces them to relate to others. Through political participation, individuals pursue their own needs and interests, but not without consideration for the needs of other citizens. In other words, it is through politics that we learn to balance our own needs and interests against the good of the political community as a whole. Today Americans are less inclined to share Aristotle's conception of politics than the cynical view of novelist Gore Vidal that "who collects what money from whom in order to spend on what is all there is to politics."[2]

Even while taking pride in their form of government, Americans express ambivalence toward the political process. We cherish the Declaration of Independence and the Constitution and love the symbols of democracy. We visit Washington, D.C., to marvel at the Washington Monument, the Jefferson and Lincoln Memorials, the Capitol, and the White House. We show these symbols of our democracy to our children, hop-

Immigrants crowd a New York City neighborhood in 1900.

ing they will learn to revere them, too. At the same time that we point with pride to the documents and symbols of American democracy, we often seem unwilling to accept the realities of democratic practice.[3] Many of us are unwilling to spend the time it takes to familiarize ourselves with candidates and issues. We are impatient with the slow pace at which government deals with the nation's problems. "Yet many of us are unwilling to spend the time it takes to familiarize ourselves with candidates and issues." We refer to debates over issues as quarrels or "bickering"; we call compromises "selling out"; we too readily label conflict as mere self-interest and tag interest groups and political parties as "*special* interests." In other words, we love the concept of democracy but hate the rough and tumble, the give and take, and the conflict of democracy in action.[4]

How do people, politics, government, and the economy come together to form the "American system"? How might these relationships change as we move through the twenty-first century? Have they been permanently changed by the events of September 11, 2001? This chapter provides short answers to these questions by profiling the American people, identifying the political values we share, and describing how they are expressed in our form of government. It also briefly describes how democracy, when practiced by people who

are ethnically, economically, and religiously diverse and scattered across a vast and varied landscape, is destined to be characterized as much by competition and conflict as by cooperation and community. All of these topics will be developed in greater detail in later chapters.

The American People

When the poet Walt Whitman wrote, "Here is not merely a nation but a teeming Nation of nations," he said a lot about our country and its politics.[5] It is a cliché, yet true, that the United States is a land of immigrants, peopled by individuals from all over the world. Americans are a conglomeration of religions, races, ethnicities, cultural traditions, and socioeconomic groups, or what one historian calls "a collision of histories."[6]

Immigration and Ethnic Diversity

Long before Europeans arrived, the population of North America was characterized by cultural diversity. Anthropologists are still debating the timing and points of origin of the first inhabitants, but many probably arrived after crossing a land bridge from Asia thousands of

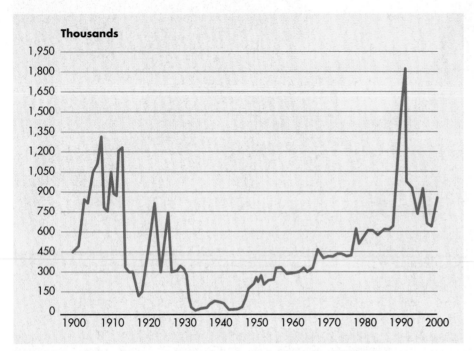

FIGURE 1 ■ Immigrants Admitted to the United States, 1900–2000

SOURCE: *2000 Statistical Yearbook of the Immigration and Naturalization Service*, Table 1 (www.ins.gov).

years ago. Although sometimes characterized by a single term such as Indians or Native Americans, they went on to found many different civilizations, both agricultural and hunting/gathering. Their nations were competitive and at times at war, and their differences substantial enough to doom eighteenth-century efforts to form pan-Indian alliances against European colonization.[7] Today the Census Bureau recognizes 562 different tribes, many fewer than three hundred years ago, but still suggestive of the wide array of cultures that predated European settlement.

The umbrella term *European* is itself somewhat deceptive in that European settlers emigrated from countries that not only differed linguistically, religiously, and politically but also had often been at war with one another. Migrants carried some of these conflicts with them to America. Because the colonies were ruled from England and its language and culture were dominant, we tend to think of early Americans as Anglos and Protestants. But the earliest European settlers of the southeastern and southwestern territories were more likely to be Roman Catholics from France and Spain than Anglo-Protestants. And over time, Germany, a distinctly non-Anglo country and one evenly split between Catholics and Protestants, provided more immigrants to America than England. By preference, or to avoid discrimination by earlier-arriving or more dominant settlers, immigrants often self-segregated into territories (Puritans in Massachusetts, Quakers in Pennsylvania and Rhode Island, Catholics in Maryland), which later became states. These different beliefs and traditions con-

tributed to the rise of distinctive local cultures and to the varying character of state governments and politics.

Like Europeans, Africans, too, came from a huge continent that encompassed many languages, cultures, and religions. Even though the European slave trade was concentrated in coastal areas of Africa, the men and women forcibly removed to the Americas did not share a common tradition. But their experience in the American colonies united most in a common condition as noncitizens lacking all political and economic rights.

The ethnic and racial composition of the American population broadened further in the mid- to late nineteenth century as new waves of settlers came from southern and eastern Europe, China, and Japan, as well as Ireland and Germany. They included large numbers of Roman, Eastern and Russian Orthodox Catholics, Jews, and some Buddhists. Immigration continued at high levels into the twentieth century before peaking in the decade 1905–1914, when more than ten million immigrants entered the country.

Not all immigrants who came, stayed. In addition to deportations, 31 percent of those who arrived between 1900 to 1990 returned voluntarily to their home countries (compared to about 21 percent of today's arrivals).[8] For a few years during the Great Depression of the 1930s, more people left the United States than entered.[9] Then, following the peak years of the second decade through the end of World War II, a deliberate effort was made to slow the rate of new arrivals. It was not until the decade 1987–1996 that immigration reached its peak level to date (Figure 1).

In 2000, 10.4 percent of all residents of the United States were foreign-born, less than the 14.8 percent in the peak year 1910, but three times as many as in 1970.[10] These new Americans are far more varied in national origin than those who emigrated prior to the 1970s. In 1910, the overwhelming majority of foreign-born in the United States had emigrated from Canada and Europe, whereas in 2000 over half of all foreign-borns had emigrated from Central and South America and another one-quarter from Asian countries. More of the new arrivals were born in Mexico than any other country.[11] This shift in nationality of immigrants was the result of a change in immigration law in 1965 that ended nationality restrictions that had been in place since the 1920s. (See the box "After 9/11.") They were replaced with a preference system that targets family reunification and specific job skills. During the past thirty years, this system has undergone considerable tinkering, including an amnesty that gave permanent residency to 2.6 million illegal residents between 1989 and 1992, but the priority system remains in place.

When permanent residents become citizens—and one-third of all foreign-borns are naturalized U.S. citizens—all immediate members of their families living outside the United States automatically qualify for residency visas. In 2000, family-sponsored individuals accounted for almost 70 percent of all legal immigrants admitted.[12] This insures that current trends in the ethnic diversification of the American population will continue and explains why Hispanics, who accounted for less than 7 percent of the population in the 1990 census, are now, at 13 percent of the population, America's largest minority.

The Census Bureau predicts that, if current trends continue, the 72 percent population share held by white non-Hispanics in 1999 will fall to 53 percent by the middle of the century. This prediction is increasingly challenged for its failure to take into account the rising rate of intermarriage: in 1999, more than 5 percent of all marriages were interracial or mixed Hispanic/non-Hispanic. A third of all Hispanic and Asian marriages were mixed.[13] Should this pattern continue, the only majority in the United States by 2050 would be white/mixed race.[14]

Immigration and Political Cleavage

There have always been some native-born Americans who fear economic competition from newcomers or perceive non-English-speaking people or anyone with different traditions and religious practices as a cultural threat. So throughout our history there has been antiforeign, or nativist, sentiment, even by first-generation immigrants, but the political impact of antiforeign sentiment is typically greatest when immigration levels are high. Hence, strong nativist sentiments influenced the politics of the mid-1800s, the 1920s, and the 1990s. Some of the most intense political cleavages have arisen between older and new immigrants.

The wave of immigration produced by Ireland's potato famine in the 1840s created a fever of anti-Irish and anti-Catholic sentiment, which found expression in the Know-Nothing Party. Patriotic fervor during World War I produced hostility toward Americans of German ancestry, and the Russian Revolution led to the "Red Scare" of the 1920s and the deportation of many Russian and Eastern European immigrants. During World War II, Japanese Americans were targeted as potential

collaborators with Japan, had their property confiscated, and were interned in camps under military guard (discussed further in Chapter 14).

After the high tide of immigration from Latin American and Asia in the 1990s, Republican presidential candidate Patrick Buchanan argued that the arrival of so many non-Europeans would "submerge" and dilute our "predominantly Caucasian Western society" and our European heritage.[15] In the same period, a newspaper criticized immigrants who "bring with them their non-Christian Third World cultures, poverty-mindedness and a tendency toward crime."[16] These characterizations are little different from those made against earlier waves of Eastern European, Irish, and Jewish immigrants. But they also obscure certain demographic truths. The country that is the single biggest contributor of new Americans—Mexico—is Western, Christian, and of mixed European heritage, as were most earlier arrivals. The majority of Muslims in the United States are African Americans, whereas three-quarters of all Arab Americans, much more recent arrivals, are Christians, not Muslims.

Although each generation of immigrants has faced resentment from preceding generations, each has contributed to the building of America. Early European immigrants settled the eastern seaboard and pushed west to open the frontier. Africans' slave labor helped build the South's economy. Germans helped develop the Midwest into an agricultural heartland, while Irish, Italian, Polish, and Russian newcomers provided labor for America's industrial revolution and turned many cities into huge metropolises. Chinese immigrants helped build the transcontinental railroad linking East and West, and Japanese and Hispanics helped California become our top food producer. More recently, young Chinese and Indian immigrants have figured prominently in high-tech industries, while older Indian immigrants dominate the motel business in the United States. All immigrant groups have gone on from their initial roles to play a fuller part in American life.

Religious Diversity

We know that many of our earliest settlers came here to escape religious intolerance in Europe: French Huguenots, German Anabaptists, British Methodists, Catholics, and Quakers. Nevertheless, few who emigrated to the Americas expected to live in an areligious state. Once here, however, many found it necessary to establish separate communities to ensure freedom for their form of religious practice. "New Jersey, Pennsylvania, and Maryland were conceived and established as 'plantations of religion,'" that gave state protection to specific religious groups.[17] Rhode Island was founded by the religious dissident Roger Williams who, after

AFTER 9/11

IMMIGRATION: IS THE DOOR STILL OPEN?

After the terrorist attacks on the World Trade Center and the Pentagon on September 11, 2001, newscasters and analysts often observed that our system had been changed "profoundly" or "forever." Now, with some distance from the events, we are better able to evaluate the impact of those events. In this edition's "After 9/11" boxes, we discuss ways in which the events of that day have affected government and politics in the United States. We begin by asking if the door to immigrants is as open as it was before 9/11.

We see ourselves as a community of people joined by a common commitment to the pursuit of opportunity, individual liberty, and government of, by, and for the people. But who, other than those born into it, can join this community? We like to think of ourselves as a refuge for political and religious dissidents and the economically downtrodden, just as it says in the Emma Lazarus poem engraved on the Statue of Liberty: "Give me your tired, your poor, your huddled masses yearning to breathe free." By this standard, the "golden door" would be open to hundreds of millions of people, when in reality only a small fraction of refugees and opportunity seekers can settle in the United States. Thus, rules must be established to determine who qualifies for an immigration visa, who is entitled to refugee status, and how many people will be allowed to take up residency in the United States each year.

Over time, the "golden door" has widened and narrowed depending on the wishes of Congress (immigration

law is then implemented and enforced by the Immigration and Naturalization Service [INS]). Few Americans argue with the proposition that the government has the right to police its borders, but there are always disagreements over the standards regulating admission. These standards often come under scrutiny during hard times, such as war or recession, so it is not surprising that the laws governing entry into the United States were reviewed after 9/11.

One of the many unhappy findings about the perpetrators of the 9/11 attacks was that some had entered the country legally on tourist or student visas and overstayed their departure dates. The knowledge that a tiny fraction of foreigners living in our midst came for the express purpose of doing harm led to immediate changes in immigration enforcement. Hundreds of Arab and/or Muslim men who had violated their visas were detained for questioning and some were deported. Overstaying visas is an every-day occurrence in the United States, where an estimated 5 to 8 million people live illegally, only about 100,000 of whom are of Middle Eastern descent.[1] A hold was placed on immigration and visa applications from Middle Eastern and other predominantly Muslim countries while they could be subjected to extensive background checks.

Immigration applications from Arab and Muslim countries are not the first to be singled out for special handling. The United States has been restricting immigration since 1798, when Congress gave the president power to deport people he deemed "dangerous to the peace and

safety" of the country. An 1807 law prohibited the migration or "importation" of people for purposes of slavery. Immigration within the western hemisphere remained open, but immigration from East Asia was virtually shut down by an 1882 law prohibiting further immigration from China and the 1907 "Gentleman's Agreement" with the Japanese government, which limited new Japanese to the Hawaiian Islands. Between the 1920s and 1960s, immigration was open mainly to the European countries represented in the American population at the time of the 1910 census, thus favoring British, German and northern Europeans, while penalizing southern and eastern Europeans. Laws passed up through the end of World War II added new categories of people prohibited entry, including anarchists and revolutionaries, members of communist parties, alcoholics, those with contagious diseases, and others deemed undesirable.

After the 1960s civil rights movement led to the removal of the old quota system, the door opened to people of every race, religion, and nationality. To ensure that people from all parts of the world have a chance to apply, the INS divides the world into regions and assigns annual quotas to countries within each region. Fifty thousand slots per year are set aside for people in countries where a low number of visa requests had been granted in the previous five years. Political categories were created and assigned preferential treatment. During the Cold War, virtually everyone fleeing a communist country was pretty much guaranteed refugee or

being expelled from Massachusetts Puritan society, bought land from the Naragansett Indians and founded a colony for other religious outcasts.[18]

With Independence, the United States disassociated itself not just from the government of England but from its state religion, the Anglican Church, which was (and is) headed by the monarch. Some at the Constitutional convention wanted to name the Episcopalian Church, the newly independent Anglican Church in the United States, as the state religion but most knew that in a country of such religious diversity, the Constitution would never be ratified. But six of the thirteen states did establish an official religion, and some levied a religious tax, while leaving it to the individual taxpayer to desig-

asylee status. In this way several million Cubans, Russians, Eastern Europeans, Vietnamese, Cambodians, and Laotians emigrated, and thousands of Chinese students were granted permanent residency under an amnesty following the 1989 Tiananmen Square massacre.

The door was opened so wide that by 1991 immigration surpassed the peak period at the beginning of the twentieth century. But then immigration policy took a turn toward tighter control.Changes came in reaction to the high levels of new arrivals in the preceding decade, the recession of the early 1990s, the increasing fear of terrorism after the first attack on the World Trade Center in 1993, and to a wave of bad publicity about abuses of the lax admission policies for asylees. In 1996, Congress passed laws that made the detention and deportation of illegal entrants without judicial review much easier—paving the way for the crackdown of 2002—and the federal courts ruled the INS can, on its own authority, revoke the citizenship of any naturalized American who has lied about a criminal record on an immigration application.[2] In 1997 and 1998, the INS set new records for deportations, while apprehending and turning back roughly 1.5 million people, virtually all from Mexico.[3] The Coast Guard even began picking up Cubans in international waters and returning them to the island.

In 2001 it appeared that the door would be opened wider as the Bush administration, in an effort to improve relations with Mexico, proposed a new amnesty for an estimated 3 million undocumented Mexicans living here ille-

gally. (Nationals from all other countries were excluded from the proposal.) Before the policy could be adopted, terrorists attacked New York and Washington, and talk of the amnesty and more open borders with Mexico was put on hold.

Thus far since 9/11 there has been no similar groundswell of anti-immigration policy among the American public. Polls show Americans giving strong support to the detention of Arab and Muslim men living in the country *illegally* and even for the questioning of thousands of those with legal residence, including college students. Yet in multiple polls conducted in consecutive months after the attack that asked respondents to identify the country's most pressing problems, only 1 to 3 percent of those polled mentioned immigration. There is, however, support for tighter border security and better enforcement of immigration law.

To achieve this, the INS was split up, with its enforcement offices and personnel moved to a new cabinet office for Homeland Security in 2003. The INS entered into an agreement with Canada for stricter review of asylee claims, and it is requiring new biometric identity cards (laser visas) for those who cross the U.S.–Mexico border frequently. In addition, the INS now requires all men entering the country from certain North African and Middle Eastern countries on any kind of visa to be fingerprinted and photographed. Some of the most stringent new rules are for those entering the United States on student visas because some never show up for their classes, while many overstay their visas or use them as a first step to permanent resi-

dence. Extensive background checks and verification of student records kept thousands of foreign students from beginning their classes in the fall of 2002. After their arrival, their universities will be required to verify their enrollments and report on their academic status to the INS.

All of these new measures are significant changes for people who enter the United States on nonimmigrant visas. But if effective, they could reduce de facto immigration levels because, according to INS estimates, almost 275,000 people enter the country illegally annually (a number equal to about one-third of the legal immigrants admitted in an average year).[4] Despite their support for heightened security measures, including those that target special religious or nationality groups, there is no evidence yet that Americans want to shut down immigration or return to the era of restricting immigration on the basis of national origin.

1. Immigration and Naturalization Service, Office of Policy and Planning, "Legal Immigration, Fiscal Year 1997," *Annual Report,* no. 1, January 1999, 4.
2. The 1995 changes in asylum law can be found at www.ins.usdoj.gov/graphics/aboutins/history/jan95.html.
3. In 1998, the INS deported 171,154 illegal residents, one-third of whom had criminal records. This was a 50 percent increase over the 1997 record of 114,383. Mexican nationals accounted for 81 percent of all removals. "Illegal Aliens Deported in Record Numbers in 1998," *Champaign-Urbana News-Gazette,* January 9, 1999, A-5.
4. "Illegal Alien Resident Population;" "Immigrants," *2000 INS Statistical Abstract* (www.ins.gov).

nate which church would receive his tax payment. State religions were not disestablished in Connecticut, Massachusetts or New Jersey until the nineteenth century and even then some courts still considered Christian teachings part of common law.[19]

Despite the diversity in religious practice, instruction and textbooks in public schools drew much of

their content from the Protestant Bible. School officials maintained instruction was "nonsectarian," but their reluctance to remove blatantly anti-Catholic material led to the creation of Catholic church-run schools, which remain today the major alternative to public schools. Occasionally religious differences led to violence, as in Philadelphia's Bible riots of 1844

Photography Collection, Miriam and Ira D. Wallach Division of Art, Prints and Photographs, The New York Public Library, Astor, Lenox and Tilden Foundations

Celebration of Christian holidays was an integral part of the public school year in the nineteenth and early twentieth centuries, even when many students were Jewish, as in New York City, where this photo was taken.

when Protestants burned down a Catholic school and thirteen people were killed.[20]

The Know-Nothing Party won popularity during this period by spreading fear of a Catholic takeover. Catholic-Protestant conflict lasted well into the twentieth century, could be intense, and sometimes trumped ethnicity. In the small farm community of Carroll, Iowa, for example, German and other Protestants joined forces against allied German and Irish Catholics, passing "puritan Sunday" laws that prohibited Catholic church dances, singing parties, and serving alcohol on the Sabbath.[21]

These anecdotes from the distant past are a reminder that being "all white and all Christian" did not spare communities from exclusionary or repressive assimilationist tactics or violence against those of a different ancestry or religion. Claims that our political unity is being undermined by ethnic and religious diversity are hardly new phenomena.

Today, America's religious profile is changing along with its ethnic makeup. Although a large majority (87 percent) still identify as Christians, Americans now claim affiliation with an estimated 1,600 different religions and denominations, including 5.5 million Jews, 750,000 to 1 million Buddhists, about the same number of Hindus, and at least as many Muslims as Presbyterians (3.5 million).[22] To some, these figures may represent the potential for social fragmentation; in fact, a proliferation of religious affiliations may both bolster liberty and serve as its measure. A nation with one church, Voltaire wrote, will have oppression; with two, civil war; with a hundred, freedom.[23]

Economic and Demographic Diversity

Diversity involves more than differences in national origin and religious affiliation. Where people settle, what they do for a living, how much they earn, when they were born, and how long they have been here are all potential bases for political difference, and over time these factors are probably more important than religion or country of origin.

Although racial and ethnic cleavages have garnered much of the attention throughout our history, economic diversity is at least as important. We may think of America as a land of opportunity, but most people who are born poor in the United States stay poor. Opportunities knock harder and more often for those who are born into the upper and middle classes. And, although our society is not as class-conscious as many others, our personal economic situations play an important part in shaping our views toward politics and our role in the process. Most people who are poor, for example, do not vote, but those who do tend to vote Democratic. Most well-off Americans do vote, and they vote in larger numbers for Republicans than for Democrats.

Regional and residential differences can also be important, especially since they often intertwine with economic interests. Farmers in California and the Midwest, for example, are more likely than city dwellers to be supportive of farm subsidy legislation. City dwellers may be far more enthusiastic about federal laws creating national parks or wilderness areas than the western ranchers who use the land to graze their livestock. The classic and most costly example of regional conflict in our history was the division between South and North over the right of southern states to secede from the Union in order to maintain a regional economic system rooted in slavery. Although in that case economic and political disparities led to the bloodiest conflict in our history, regional diversity usually results in no more than political difference. However, in the face of growing income inequality and the residential segregation of gated communities, there is the danger that residential separation will lead to the political indifference of the well-off to the needs of poor neighborhoods.

Age difference, too, can affect political orientation. The needs and interests of older citizens are on average substantially different from those of young adults. The United States, like Canada and Western Europe, has an aging population; in 2002, twelve of every one hundred Americans was sixty-five or older. This fact has led to a focus on economic security for senior citizens and less focus on similar security for children.

Diversity and Identity Politics

There is nothing new or strange about organizing around difference. Up to a point, it is common sense. How we are situated in the world in terms of power, money, geography, race, ethnicity, age, and religion affects our perceptions of the world. As a result, people tend to define society's problems differently and have conflicting views about what government should do about them. Reconciling differences is what the political process is for.

Why, when the American population has always been so heterogeneous, does diversity seem to have so much more meaning in contemporary political life? The reason in part is that, while society was diverse in the early decades of the republic, the political spectrum was narrow. The majority were excluded from participation. Those granted full rights of participation varied from state to state, but two groups—women and African American men, with the exception of a small number of free black men living in the North—were comprehensively shut out after the ratification of the Constitution, as were some unpropertied white men.

Diversity's scope for expression has been greatly broadened through the slow expansion of the electorate and the opening up of the political system. This process (discussed in Chapter 8) included the extension of voting rights to African American men and, almost fifty years later, to all women. About the same time, citizenship was granted to American Indians and to residents of Puerto Rico, whose country had been incorporated as a U.S. territory after the Spanish-American War. Although full black suffrage was not effectively achieved until the 1960s, the voting and politically active public has been becoming gradually more heterogeneous since the 1920s.

Two later developments—the adoption by the federal government, beginning in the Nixon administration, of race, gender, and ethnic preference programs, and the wave of immigration from Asia and Latin America in the 1980s and 1990s—have increased the importance of diversity in American politics.

As government adopted affirmative action policies to compensate for historical discrimination (Chapter 15), an individual's race, gender, or ethnicity took on added political importance. Their use as factors influencing the division of public resources has given rise to **identity politics.** This is the practice of organizing on the basis of one's ethnic or racial identity, sex, or sexual orientation to compete for public resources and to influence public policy.[24]

Paradoxically, identity politics has intensified during a period in which racial and ethnic boundaries are beginning to blur. (See the box "Census and Sensibility.") Among white ethnic groups, so much intermarriage has occurred that many people cannot identify their ancestry. By the 1990 census, 100 million Americans could name no specific ancestry or reported multiple ancestries.[25]

Political Culture

In recent years, diversity has become a political catchword and has been raised to the level of a civic virtue. Yet our motto is "E Pluribus Unum"—"Out of Many, One"—referring to the union of many states and the molding of one people from many traditions. There is a popular saying that Americans are people of many cultures united by a single idea. But what is that single idea, and is it, however fundamental, sufficient to form a political culture? A **political culture** is a shared body of values and beliefs that shapes perception and attitudes toward politics and government and, in turn, influences political behavior.

The Significance of Political Culture

Governments rely for their stability and vitality on the support of citizens: their identity with the country and its method of governing, and adoption of political values and behavior necessary to sustain the system. The alternatives are for government to be ineffective or to gain obedience through force or coercion.

In a democracy, sharing a political culture does not mean that citizens must agree on specific issues or even generally on what government's role should be in dealing with the country's problems. Democracy embraces conflict and competition just as it requires cooperation and a sense of community. A basic function of government is to establish the rules under which interests can compete. So the essence of political culture is not agreement on issues but on fundamental principles and on a common perception of the *rights* and *obligations* of citizenship and the rules for participating in the political process. These shared values reduce the strains produced by our differences and allow us to compete intensely on some issues while cooperating on others.

Learning Political Culture

Whether the newly created United States of America came about by "design of Providence," was a "lucky accident," or the result of the Founders' skill in shaping a workable Constitution, it faced a problem common to all political systems: how to create a national identity among the citizenry.[26] While American society has often been characterized as a melting pot, it has been a slow melt, and it has not happened by luck or accident.

CENSUS AND SENSIBILITY

Every ten years the U.S. government takes a census of the American population. This should be a fairly straightforward statistical procedure, but it has often been a contentious political issue. This is largely because the census does much more than establish the size and geographic distribution of the population; its findings have important political and economic consequences. Of special significance are the figures that establish the racial and ethnic breakdown of the population. These data have become essential for implementation of the Voting Rights Act and court rulings stemming from the modern civil rights movement, as well as for "a smorgasbord of set-asides and entitlements and affirmative-action programs."[1] Thus, today, unlike the past, the collection of information on the racial heritage of Americans has greater significance for inclusion than for exclusion.

Racial categories have been used since the first census was taken in 1790, when Americans were identified as white males, white females, other (free blacks, and Indians living off reservations, for example), and slaves (obviously not a racial category, but since only people of African descent were enslaved, *slave* became synonymous with *black*). Some states classified as "black" people with as little as 1/32 African ancestry, thereby consigning them to political and economic exclusion. "Chinese" and "American Indian" became census categories in 1860; Japanese was added in 1870, and other Asian "races" in 1910. Mexicans were "whites" in the 1920 census, a separate racial category in 1930, and by the 1950 census reabsorbed into the whites category.

From this it should be apparent that over time little has been fixed about how race and color classifications have been used. They reflect "common or social usage" rather than scientifically determined biological differences. Through the 1950 census, race was established solely by the census taker's observation, which usually resulted in people of mixed white and other heritage being counted as "other." One government study showed that 6 percent of people considering themselves black, one-third who considered themselves Asian, and 70 percent of those who considered themselves American Indian were thought to be white by survey researchers. A study of infant deaths showed that many infants were classified by a different race at death than on their birth certificates.

The 1980 census was the first in which an individual's ethnicity and race were established entirely by self-classification.[2] But in the 1990 census, each person had to choose from one of four racial groups: black; white; American Indian or Native Alaskan; Asian or Pacific Islander; and, where applicable, also to claim a Hispanic/Latino ethnic heritage. Complaints about this classificatory scheme intensified as immigration and interracial marriage increased the number of multiracial Americans, many of whom now object to defining their heritage by a single census category. The archetypal representative of this dilemma is golf pro Tiger Woods, who describes himself as a "Cablinasian," a person of white, African, American Indian, and Asian ancestry. Why, Woods asks, should he be asked to identify himself with only one part of his ancestry, and how would he decide which one to choose?[3]

In response to these considerations, Census 2000 offered five racial categories (Native Hawaiians and Pacific Islanders were split off from Asians), while retaining the Hispanic ethnic designation. A "multiracial" category was rejected in favor of letting each person check more than one box—even if that meant, as in the case of Tiger Woods, selecting four. The new method permits up to sixty-three variations in reporting race and ethnicity. While allowing more Americans to identify their ancestry ac-

---

The Founders spoke of a united country, a people with common ancestry, a shared language, the same religion, and a commitment to the same political principles. From what you have read earlier in this chapter, you know this view was in some part wishful thinking. One of the most significant challenges to establishing a national political culture was the division of Americans among nearly sovereign states. It is easy to forget that not long ago people's identity as Virginians or Pennsylvanians was much more important to them than being an American. And it was not until the Civil War, under the influence of Abraham Lincoln's powerful reference at Gettysburg to the "unfinished work" of preserving the Union, that Americans began referring to the United States with the singular *is* rather than the plural *are*.[27]

Most of the Founders believed that an educated citizenry was essential to the survival of the new republic, and advocates of public education like Daniel Webster and Thomas Jefferson argued that *only* educated citizens would be able to understand public issues, elect virtuous leaders, and "sustain the delicate balance between liberty and order in the new political system."[28] Over time it became widely accepted that "schooling was a public good essential to the health of the nation . . .[because] civic society depended on instilling common values."[29] As the public school system emerged, increasing emphasis was placed on "training of citizens in patriotism, political knowledge and public affairs."[30] Although schools were then (as they are now) under local control, there was some common content in civic

curately, it created new problems. In the analysis of the 2000 census data someone had to decide whether to count multiple box-checkers like Tiger Woods more than once, divide them into fractions, or just assign them to a single racial category. This may sound ridiculous, but it is a very real problem to the Census Bureau. Laws guaranteeing equal access and representation have meant, in practice, that the racial or ethnic composition of the population affects who is admitted to universities, how the boundaries of legislative districts are drawn, whether school districts need to submit desegregation plans, and whether minorities are adequately represented among workers hired on federally funded projects and among business owners receiving federal contracts.

The new categories are therefore of great concern to interest groups representing American minorities. The National Association for the Advancement of Colored People (NAACP), for example, worried that an undercount of African Americans would lead to a decrease of the opportunities it worked decades to win because people who would have been classified as black under the old "one-drop-of-blood" standard could be counted as white or Asian

if they self-identified as multiracial on their census form. One NAACP official said, "Let those mixed race people check all the boxes they want—but *count* them as black."[4] A Hispanic American organization asked that "Hispanic" be categorized as a race rather than an ethnicity, and the Arab American Institute requested that a special protected category be created for people of Middle Eastern ancestry. An official of an Asian American interest group said she opposed the multiple-choice approach because racial and ethnic data are collected for a reason, and "If you can't tabulate it, you've undermined the ability of the federal government to provide information that will help set policy and help ensure that the civil rights laws are effectively enforced. That is the bottom line."[5] Or, as more bluntly put by a member of the House committee that oversees the Census Bureau, "The numbers drive the dollars."[6]

In the end, only 6.8 million, or 2.4 percent, of all Americans self-identified as multiracial in the 2000 census, slightly higher than predicted but way below the actual numbers of Americans with multiracial heritage.[7] Many Hispanics have mixed race ancestry: white and African, Asian or Native American, while by some estimates as many as 75 per-

cent of all African Americans are mixed white-black.[8] Once seemingly clear notions of "race" as African, Caucasian or Asian are becoming confused as we become an increasingly multiracial society. One survey showed that one-third of African Americans believe that blacks are not a single race, and almost half of both black and white respondents believed that our census, like Canada's, should not collect information on race at all.[9]

1. Lawrence Wright, "One Drop of Blood," *New Yorker,* July 25, 1994, 47.
2. Campbell J. Gibson and Emily Lennon, "Historical Census Statistics on the Foreign-born Population of the United States: 1850–1990," Census Bureau, Population Division Working Paper, no.29 (February 1999), p. 9. This report can be found at www.census.gov/population/www/documentation/twps0029/twps0029.html.
3. Rochelle L. Stanfield, "Multiple Choice," *National Journal,* November 22, 1997, 2352–2355.
4. Ibid., 2355.
5. Ibid.
6. Representative Thomas C. Sawyer (D-Ohio) quoted in Wright, "One Drop of Blood," 47.
7. "Politics of Identity Resurface with Census," *Champaign-Urbana News-Gazette,* March 25, 2001, B8.
8. "Politics of Identity Resurface with Census," *The Champaign-Urbana News-Gazette,* March 25, 2001, B8.
9. Reported in Tom Morganthau, "What Color Is Black?" *Newsweek,* February 13, 1995, 64.
OTHER SOURCES: Jack E. White, "I'm Just Who I Am," *Time,* May 5, 1997, 30–36.

education around the country. By mid-twentieth century, most elementary school children were studying current events in their *Weekly Reader* and beginning each day by reciting the Pledge of Allegiance to the flag. Many high school students are required to pass an exam on the U.S. Constitution, and perhaps their state's as well, to graduate.

Elementary and secondary schools are not the only purveyors of political culture. Much is absorbed simply by living in the country and participating in the political process. Television and newspapers also transmit a great deal of information on the rules of the game and how government and politics work in the United States.

Today one of the most controversial issues in the debate over what is required to sustain a political culture is

whether all citizens should speak a common language. But the Founders took it for granted that English would be the national language, and Daniel Webster's 1783 textbook promoting "a new national language to be spelled and pronounced differently from British English" was one of the first attempts to create an American national identity.[31] Fear of German-speaking immigrants in the early part of the twentieth century led Iowa to pass a law requiring all groups of two or more people to speak in English, even when using the telephone.[32] In the current era, when most immigration has come from non-English-speaking countries and some urban school districts teach in a hundred or more languages, twenty-seven states have passed laws establishing English as the official language.

The significance of political culture—even its definition—has long been and will continue to be a topic of debate. Some argue that Americans are too diverse to share a common set of political values and that every country in the world, regardless of its level of development, is composed of "competing political cultures, not a single political culture."[33] But unless there is some overarching commitment, some principles that take precedence over group interests, there will be no basis for political unity. While government provides rules and venues for group competition, this is not the reason government exists.

American Democracy: The Core Values

Our "nation of nations" is crosscut with cultural, political, and economic cleavages, but despite our sometimes overwhelming diversity, most Americans do share some basic goals and values. The words Americans use to characterize their form of government are less likely to come from the Constitution than from the second paragraph of the Declaration of Independence: "We hold these Truths to be self-evident, that all Men are created equal, that they are endowed by the Creator with certain unalienable Rights, that among these are Life, Liberty, and the Pursuit of Happiness."

These words suggest the basic assumptions, or core beliefs, on which the American system was founded: universal truths that can be known and acted upon, equality before the law, belief in a higher power that transcends human law, and rights that are entitlements at birth and therefore can be neither granted nor taken away by government. The fundamental concept is liberty, especially the freedom to pursue one's livelihood and other personal goals that lead to a "happy" life.

The Declaration was primarily a political argument for separation from Great Britain and, as such, was concerned with the basic principles and philosophy of government.[34] Guaranteeing the rights of individuals, the Declaration postulated, was the primary reason for government to exist. The Constitution reinforced the Declaration's emphasis on equality while specifying other core principles of American democracy: majority rule exercised through elected representatives and minority rights (a reference to political or religious minorities, not to racial or ethnic minorities). But unlike the Declaration, the Constitution had to deal with the practical problems of governing and of creating institutions that would protect the rights and pursuits of the individual while balancing them against the public interest. Thus, while the Declaration is all principle, the Constitution, of necessity, is founded on political compromise.

In this section, we look briefly at each of the core principles of American democracy. A more detailed description of their legal expression in the Constitution is provided in Chapter 2.

Individual Liberty

Our belief in individual liberty has roots in the Judeo-Christian belief that every individual is equal and has worth before God. It has also been shaped by the works of the English philosophers Thomas Hobbes and John Locke. Briefly, they wrote that individuals give some of their rights to government so it can protect them from each other. Individuals then use their remaining liberties to pursue their individually defined visions of the good life. These ideas are part of social contract theory, which we discuss in Chapter 2.

Influenced by these ideas, early Americans emphasized individual liberty over other goals of government. James Madison, for example, justified the Constitution by writing that government's job is to protect the "diversity" of interests and abilities that exists among individuals. Liberty is also reflected in our long tradition of rights, deriving from Great Britain's. Usually, these rights are framed as powers *denied* to government—for example, government shall not deny freedom of assembly or engage in unreasonable searches and seizures. Essentially, this means the overall right to be left alone by the government. Such individualistic values have molded popular expectations. Immigrants often came and still come to America to be their own bosses. The other side of this coin is that we are also at liberty to fail and accept the consequences. Although the opportunities for many individuals to get ahead in America are limited by prejudice and poverty, living in a society with an explicit commitment to individual liberty can be exciting and liberating.

The commitment to liberty is not absolute however; that is, it cannot be exercised free of restrictions. This is what it means to live under constitutional government and in society with other citizens; we give up some rights for the good of all and to achieve the purpose for which government was created in the first place. At what point restrictions can be placed on our exercise of individual rights and liberties is another of those ongoing debates about what American democracy should be, and what it was intended to be.

One of the liveliest debates in the past few decades has been that between advocates of broadening individual liberty and those who believe there has been an overemphasis on individual freedom at the expense of community interests. A number of observers of American society believe that our fixation on individual rights has led to declining community consciousness and a general lack of civility. They advocate revitalizing the concept of citizenship, including the responsibilities to

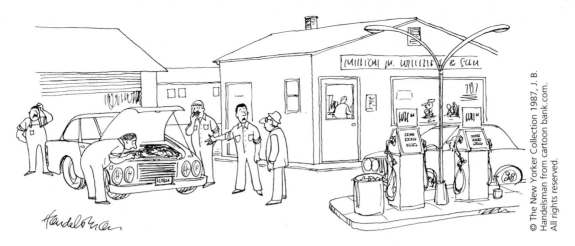

"We can't come to an agreement about how to fix your car, Mr. Simons. Sometimes that's the way things happen in a democracy."

participate in public life and renewed emphasis on "shaping the qualities of character that self-government requires."[35] They call their program communitarianism and claim it is much closer to the Founders' republican conception of freedom than is the modern liberal celebration of the unencumbered individual.

Political Equality

The Judeo-Christian belief that all people are equal in the eyes of God reflects one type of equality, but it led logically to other types, such as political equality. The ancient Greek emphasis on the opportunity and responsibility of all citizens to participate in ruling their city-states also contributed to our notion of political equality. Thus, the Declaration of Independence proclaims that "all Men are created equal." This does not mean that all people are born with equal talents or abilities. It means that all citizens are born with equal standing before government and are entitled to equal rights.

In the early years of our country, however, as in the ancient Greek city-states, full rights of citizenship were conferred only on those thought to have the intellectual and moral judgment to act in the public interest. This wisdom could be acquired from experience in the public arena, such as through one's work, not just by formal education. In both Greece and the United States, such thinking denied political rights to slaves, who were believed incapable of independent judgment, and women, whose knowledge was seen as limited to the private or domestic sphere. This left a deep tension between the value of the individual conferred by religious belief and the secular concept of political rights rooted in circumstances of birth or acquired experience. Over time, this conflict was resolved in favor of the inherent worth of every individual and hence the political equality of all.

Americans have long considered themselves relatively equal politically and socially if not economically.

Or, at minimum, they believe they are inherently equal, even when that condition cannot be realized in the political arena. Alexis de Tocqueville, a perceptive Frenchman who traveled through the United States in the 1830s, observed that Americans felt more equal than Europeans did. He attributed this feeling to the absence of a hereditary monarchy and aristocracy in this country. There was no tradition in America of looking up to kings and queens and aristocrats as one's "betters."[36]

A belief in political equality leads to **popular sovereignty,** or rule by the people. Lincoln expressed this concept when he spoke of "government of the people, by the people and for the people." If individuals are equal, no one person or small group has the right to rule others. Instead, the people collectively rule themselves. And so we arrive at our form of government, a **democracy.** The word *democracy,* derived from the Greek, means "authority of the people." If all political authority resides in the people, then the people have the right to govern themselves.

Majority Rule

If political authority rests in the people collectively, and if all people are equal, then the majority should rule. That is, when there are disagreements over policies, majorities rather than minorities should decide. If individuals are equal, then policies should be determined according to the desires of the greater number. Otherwise, some individuals would be bestowed with more authority than others.

Majority rule helps provide the support necessary to control the governed. Those in the minority go along because they accept this principle and expect to be in the majority on other issues. At a minimum, the minority expects those in the majority to respect their basic rights. If these expectations are not fulfilled, the minority is less likely to accept majority rule and tolerate majority decisions. Thus, majority rule necessarily entails minority rights.

Minority Rights

While majority rule is important, it sometimes conflicts with minority rights. Majorities make decisions *for* "the people" but in doing so do not *become* "the people." "The people" includes members of the majority *and* members of the minority. As a result, majorities that harm minority rights diminish everyone's rights.

Sadly, as James Madison and other writers of the Constitution feared, majorities in the United States have sometimes forgotten this principle, the most egregious example being the enslavement of African Americans. At various times in our history, women and ethnic, political, and religious minorities have been denied basic rights. The idea that everyone loses when minority rights are trampled is a lesson that does not stay learned.

Economic Rights

Everyone is familiar with the idea that the American Revolution was triggered by what the colonists saw as unfair taxation and other economic burdens placed on them by the British Parliament. To a certain extent, Americans fought the Revolution to be left alone to pursue their livelihoods and to ensure that they would not have to give up any part of their wealth without their consent.

Economic freedom, specifically the right to own property, is an adjunct to our concepts of individual liberty and the "pursuit of happiness." But just as tension exists between majority and minority rights and between individual liberty and the good of all, so also there is potential conflict between the political equality the Declaration avows and the property rights the Constitution protects. Inevitably, some people, through inheritance, luck, or initiative, amass more wealth and power than others and come to exercise more influence over government. The ancient Greeks feared that democracy could not tolerate extremes of wealth and poverty. They thought a wealthy minority, out of smugness, and an impoverished minority, out of desperation, would try to act independently of the rest of the people and consequently would disregard the public interest.

Early Americans worried less about this. They thought they could create a government that would protect individual diversity, including economic disparity, and still survive. But the pursuit of political equality in a real world of great economic inequities has led government to a much greater role in regulating economic activity than the Founders anticipated.

By now it should be clear that democratic principles sometimes contradict each other. Americans have struggled for more than two centuries to reconcile practice with democratic aims and to perfect a system of government that was revolutionary for its time.

American Democracy in Practice

Democratic principles come alive only when people participate in government. But the principle of rule by the people can be implemented in various forms. In a large and complex society, as ours already was in 1789, direct democracy is not practical.

A **direct democracy** permits citizens to vote on most issues. The best example of a direct democracy is the town meeting, which has been the form of governance of many New England towns for over 350 years. Although town meetings today are often attended by relatively small numbers of citizens, they still offer one of the few opportunities people have to govern themselves directly. Citizens attending town meetings make their own decisions (for example, whether to put parking meters on the main street) and elect officers to enforce them (such as the police chief and city clerk).

Our national government is an **indirect democracy**, or a **republic.** Citizens have an indirect impact on government because they select policymakers to make decisions for them. Members of Congress, not rank-and-file citizens, vote bills into law. But these officials are not rulers; they are the representatives of the people and draw their authority from law sanctioned by the people.

Classical Democracy

The Greek philosopher Aristotle's definition of democracy emphasized the importance of citizen participation in government through debating, voting, and holding office. We call this vision **classical democracy.** In a classical democracy, citizens are committed to learning about and participating in government. They are well informed, discuss public affairs regularly, tell public officials what they think, and they vote. Some political theorists think that, compared to individuals who do not take their roles as democratic citizens seriously, those who do are more likely to see the complexities in issues and, while disagreeing with each other, still share common goals and work together to accomplish them.[37]

Political scientists initially accepted the classical democratic view as a fairly accurate picture of the American political process. By the 1940s, however, as they used information from surveys and voter turnout records, they discovered that far fewer citizens take advantage of their democratic rights than classical democratic theory predicts. For example, voting is the easiest way to participate in politics and the least costly in terms of time and energy. Yet only one-half of Americans vote in presidential elections, and only one-third have voted in recent nonpresidential-year congressional elections. Even fewer vote in local elections. Instead of being motivated to participate in politics as in a classical democracy, most Americans are little involved. In fact, one-fifth of the electorate does nothing at all political; they do not even discuss politics.[38]

Only about one-tenth of the population takes full advantage of the opportunities to participate. These activists vote, give money to candidates, make phone calls, distribute leaflets, write letters to legislators, attend meetings, or join neighbors to work for a common end (such as improving local schools).

Why does the reality of political participation fall short of classical democratic expectations? One recent analysis argues that many Americans do not participate because they are turned off by, among other things, long political campaigns in which sound bites and negative campaigning replace meaningful dialogue about issues.[39] Another, better-substantiated explanation is that political participation is class based: Those who participate tend to be better educated and to have more money. The working class and America's poorest, unlike their counterparts in many European countries, lack strong trade unions and political parties to represent them. American trade unions represent less than 14 percent of civilian employees, and most of their members are middle-class and better-off workers. American political parties, too, appeal more to middle-class than working-class interests.

The poor tend to belong to fewer organizations of any kind (civic groups, labor unions, or issue-oriented groups) than do the middle or upper classes. Political participation requires both time and money. Many poor adults are single heads of families with little spare time for political activity or money for transportation and baby-sitters. As a result, they have fewer opportunities to be drawn into political action through such associations and in turn have no strong organizations to promote their political participation.

Race and ethnicity explain political participation, too, but not as well. Overall, blacks and Hispanics participate less than others, but this is due primarily to average lower education and income levels. At each education and income level, African Americans and Hispanics participate at about the same rates as whites.

Age also explains participation in politics. Young people participate much less than their elders. The middle-aged, who have the highest participation rate, are more likely to be established in a career and family life and have more time and money to devote to political activities. They are also likely to be in better health than older people. Yet older Americans are more politically active than young adults.

Thus, American government is not a classical democracy. Only a small minority of citizens fully participate in politics. Majorities cannot rule when most people do not take advantage of their right to vote or try to influence government by other means.[40] Furthermore, those who do participate are not representative of the whole population in income and other social characteristics. This can have an important impact on the kind of public policy we have. Elected officials chosen by wealthier and better-educated Americans are more likely to share the perspectives of those who elect them than those of the less well-off and less educated who do not vote.

Pluralism

In the 1950s, many political scientists sought to reconcile democratic principles with the evidence that most people do not participate actively in politics. They thought they had an alternate explanation of how American democracy operated. In a theory called **pluralism,** they argued that enough people belong to interest groups to ensure that government ultimately hears everyone.[41] Individuals who share a position on an issue or range of issues join organizations whose leaders and paid staff carry the membership's views to decision makers. According to pluralist theory, this process produces a kind of balance in which no group loses so often that it stops competing. As a result, no group or small number of groups can dominate government.

Believing that while they may not have won this round, they might win the next, encourages people to continue participating and to accept compromise. It also leads government to avoid major policy changes to maintain the existing balance of interests and the popular support that comes with it.

Pluralist theory is compelling because it says democracy can still work even when many do not participate. And there is evidence to support this explanation. Thousands of interest groups in Washington, D.C., do employ experts to represent them in congressional corridors, bureaucratic agencies, and courtrooms, and they clearly can influence legislative outcomes and other decision making. The pluralist explanation of American democracy has parallels in the theory that capitalism works because an "invisible hand" is continuously readjusting the market and moving it toward the greatest efficiencies in production and consumption. Similarly, in a pluralist system, groups are seen as competing in a marketplace of ideas, interests, and political objectives under rules that allow for the distribution of policy victories across the great majority of the electorate while preventing any one group from becoming permanent losers. This allows the greater good to be served with an economy of participation.

As Chapter 6 will show, however, many people and issues do fall through the cracks of interest group representation. The poor are especially unlikely to be organized or to have sufficient resources to fight political battles. In addition, there is no guarantee that every issue can be resolved through competition to influence decision makers. If competition is between well-organized groups with intensely held issue positions—such as on abortion and gun control—it may be difficult or impossible to reach a policy outcome that satisfies anyone.

Elitism

The failure of pluralist theory to acknowledge the limited power of citizens with average or below-average incomes has led some political scientists to argue that American democracy is much less democratic than pluralists believed. One set of counterarguments to pluralism explanation comes from elite theory, an explanation of how government works that focuses on the roles of a relatively small number of individuals in key positions. The modern statement of this idea began with Robert Michels who, in 1915, formulated the "iron law of oligarchy."[42] This "law" says that effective power in a group or organization, no matter what its size, usually gravitates to a few—an oligarchy or an elite. In fact, interest groups do create their own elites by establishing permanent organizations with paid staff and leadership; this arrangement creates the potential for an issue gap between leaders and the rank and file. As the professional staff spend more time with decision makers and develop ties to public officials, they may come to see group interests differently than does the rank-and-file membership. When this happens, group membership is no longer a guarantee that one's interests will be accurately represented to decision makers.

One group of elite theorists argue that a power elite, the holders of a few top jobs in major corporations, universities, foundations, media outlets, and the most powerful agencies of government, such as the Defense Department, dominate governmental decision making.[43] One political scientist identified 5,416 key decision makers in major organizations such as these.[44] They included 3,572 elite business leaders who controlled 50 percent of America's corporate wealth, and almost 40 percent of whom had once held a government post. According to the power elite explanation, relatively few people share the most powerful jobs and make the most important economic and political decisions, decisions that favor their interests and help retain their grip on power.

A more complex version of elite theory says pluralism falls short because it focuses only on the public sector where there is, undeniably, a wide array of competing interest groups. The problem is, this theory contends, that we have a dual system, with a parallel private sector that includes many of the country's most important decisions makers, such as heads of major corporations and media moguls. Students of government read little about the private sector power structure, according to this argument, because most textbooks assume that most decisions about how our system functions are made in the highly visible public sector where interest group competition is evident and often intense. But, out of pubic view, business forms a system unto itself, where elites make decisions that affect the welfare of all Americans and use their vast resources to influence the outcome of public policy as well.[45] Basically this argument is saying that the great majority of interest groups are competing for only part of the pie, and a small part at that. In this view of how American democracy works, there are groups and classes of individuals—those with little or no access to decision makers in the public or private sector—who are permanent losers.

There is another, very different version of elitism. In contrast to the conception of a malignant power elite who conspire against reform and in support of policies keeping economic and political power in their hands, others argue that throughout the twentieth century there have been groups of elites who acted primarily to promote the general welfare rather than their own interests. This view holds that without the academics and intellectuals from the Ivy League, think tanks, and foundations like the Brookings Institution and Ford Foundation, we would not have had the sweeping social welfare and redistributive policies of Franklin Roosevelt's New Deal or the War on Poverty legislation of the Kennedy and Johnson administrations. Elites are often best situated to win these battles, the argument maintains, because they occupy "A position of independence, between the wealthy and the people . . . prepared to curb the excesses of either."[46]

The argument that government is run by the few rather than the many continues to find credibility with the public. When asked in a recent poll whether government was "run by a few big interests looking out for themselves or . . . run for the benefit of all," only 38 percent agreed that it was being run for the benefit of all.[47]

Pluralism Reconsidered

It is often hard to know what is *really* going on in Washington and easy to be frustrated when the process yields outcomes we do not like. It is misleading, however, to think that a few powerful people determine everything.

THERE IS NO JUSTICE IN THE WORLD.

THERE IS SOME JUSTICE IN THE WORLD.

THE WORLD IS JUST.

MANKOFF

America's diversity produces too many different interests and opinions to permit this. And political power is dispersed among local, state, and federal decision makers as well as across the private sector in corporate boardrooms and the leadership councils of interest groups and trade unions. There is abundant evidence that these decision makers are often in conflict or competition with one another so that getting legislation passed requires the compromise of competing interests. Nevertheless, theories of power elites are useful because they remind us that tremendous inequalities of resources exist, enabling some individuals and groups to influence government more than others. But gradually, most political scientists have come to agree that interest groups do not represent everyone, especially the poor, the working class, and the politically disinterested.

Current perspectives on how government works stress the "veto" many interest groups can exercise on issues affecting them. Some political scientists have labeled this **hyperpluralism,** suggesting a pluralist system run wild. With so many interests, it is difficult to find common ground to work out solutions to problems. The close ties of many interests to congressional committees and subcommittees considering legislation allow them to stop policy ideas they dislike. And modern technology heightens their impact. A witness to congressional hearings on tax reform reported that lobbyists used cellular phones to produce floods of protest by phone or fax the instant anyone "even *thought*" about something they opposed.[48] So many powerful groups with clout exist that attempts to alter the status quo or change national priorities are extremely difficult. Presidents Carter, Reagan, and Clinton found this out when they tried to make major changes in energy, budget, and health care policy, respectively. The Clinton White House tried to work with over 1,100 interest groups on health care reform, to no avail.[49] Efforts to bring about major changes in national domestic priorities are extremely difficult. It is telling that one of the most sweeping changes in entrenched policy was the overhaul of the welfare system, a reform whose impact will be felt primarily by the poorest and least politically active Americans.

The difficulties created by interest group vetoes often contribute to gridlock and what one observer calls the "blame game."[50] Gridlock occurs when policies are not enacted or administered effectively because the president and Congress cannot agree on what to do. Politicians representing different interests often blame each other for this inaction, or play the blame game, when they see that gridlock is likely to keep them from getting what they want. The blame game encourages elected officials to distrust each other and furthers public cynicism about government's responsiveness and effectiveness.

Given the presence of many strong groups and their veto opportunities, passing a law means fashioning com-

"Remember when people had only themselves to blame?"

promises out of competing group views.[51] In addition to being slow, the process often leads to vaguely worded laws giving actual policymaking authority to bureaucrats who work less visibly with interest group help. In effect, agencies and interest groups, not Congress, often legislate. Thus, chemical industry lobbyists help write regulations on hazardous waste, oil companies help write energy policy, and military contractors help the Pentagon write weapons contracts.

The growth of bureaucratic policymaking makes our democracy more indirect than the writers of the Constitution intended. Most citizens cannot monitor the actions of the president and 535 members of Congress organized into almost two hundred committees and subcommittees *and,* in addition, more than one hundred federal agencies. The leaders of major interest groups can, and this gives them considerable power. The possibility that these leaders may be relatively independent of their rank-and-file memberships makes them even more important.

These views challenge the pluralist explanation by concluding that government responds to many but not all groups. This suggests a hybrid explanation of American government stressing the clout of more powerful groups, whose leaders may belong to a larger, more diversified elite.

Conclusion: Is Government Responsive?

America has a split political personality. Most people have a low opinion of Congress, yet they reelect most of its members. We love the idea that the average person has a say in government, yet half of us do not vote, even in presidential elections. We criticize big government while complaining that it does not do very much. As one newspaper columnist put it, "All the evidence suggests that when Americans look at Washington they see a conniving bunch of hustlers playing an insider's game at the expense of the nation."[52]

As they rallied behind the war on terrorism, however, Americans did express less cynicism about government; 69 percent said they had a "much more" or "somewhat more favorable" view of government after 9/11. But there was little more interest in participation, nor did our leaders ask for any sacrifice from most Americans. Almost 60 percent of respondents thought it was possible to be patriotic without getting involved in political or civic life.[53] Flag waving and support for military efforts abroad may be essential to national survival, but they have little to do with what makes the country a democracy.

Why do we act as if we dislike democracy in action? Has government failed? Are the laws it enacts not what the people want? Is it the fault of the media, emphasizing mostly the negative side of government? Are average citizens actually shut out of the process? Or is the problem really the fault of citizens and not government at all? In a 1999 poll asking "What's wrong with government?" 38 percent of respondents named special interests, 29 percent said the media, while elected officials and political parties were each tabbed by 24 percent.[54] No one blamed the voters. The same poll had eight out of ten respondents saying they believed government will be as or more important in improving people's lives in this century as it has been in the past. If this is what we believe, then dropping out of the political process because we think it is futile or controlled by special interests is like cutting off our noses to spite our faces.

Although each person is not equally well situated to influence policymakers, more avenues for political participation are available now than ever before. The number of organized interests and their effectiveness in making their views known have multiplied so dramatically that government officials are besieged by a cacophony of views. We have argued that this is a necessary component of a democratic system in a large and diverse nation. American government is characterized by conflict and compromise because Americans do not agree on either the nature of the problems that confront us or their solutions. If we all agreed, there would be no need for debate, bargaining, compromise, or delays. Nonetheless, to say we must live with debate, compromise, and slowness in our system does not mean we cannot improve and speed the workings of government. In the coming chapters we will examine the major institutions and processes of our democracy, describe their evolution since the Founding and take up some of the arguments on how they might be reformed to make government more efficient, more just, and more democratic.

EPILOGUE

Who, Me?

is is the only epilogue in which we authors cannot provide the outcome of the decision-making process. But we can speculate. Based on present evidence, there is only about one chance in three that you cast your vote in the 2002 midterm election—that chance is much less if you are under twenty-five years of age. The probability that you will vote in a local election is from only 10 percent to 20 percent and that you will become politically active beyond voting, only 20 percent. Where do you fit into this pattern?

Collectively, Americans have been accused of practicing "couch potato politics," refusing to accept the responsibilities of national citizenship.[55] Most of us, even those highly dissatisfied with the way government works, do not want a king, a dictator, or an emperor to make decisions for us. Indeed, democracy assumes that majorities control government and indirect democracy assumes that citizens control their representatives. This means that people need to get up off their couches and participate. The razor-thin 2000 election margin illustrated that the participation and vote of every citizen can be crucial.

Even after 9/11, when Americans were talking about a new kind of patriotism, only 48 percent believed that Americans were now more willing to "put themselves on the line to improve politics."[56]

About their unwillingness to get involved in issue debates or the electoral process, Americans often say, "It's all politics." Of course! Issue debates and elections are political because the competition to determine what policy will be is essential to government. Politics is inescapable because divergence of interests is unavoidable. Politics is necessary to govern a democratic society. Ignoring politics and the institutions that represent the people to government, such as political parties and interest groups, will not eliminate politics. Rather, it would eliminate the most effective way yet developed for the public to influence government's decisions.

Key Terms

politics	indirect democracy
identity politics	republic
political culture	classical democracy
popular sovereignty	pluralism
democracy	hyperpluralism
direct democracy	

Further Reading

Joyce Appleby, *Inheriting the Revolution* (Cambridge, Mass.: Harvard University Press, 2000). A historian looks at what the first generation of Americans made of their new government and how they invented a new culture and identity. Special emphasis is given to the rise of a community of free black Americans.

Edward Countryman, *Americans: A Collision of Histories* (New York: Hill & Wang, 1996). A historian traces the history of the dominant ethnic groups in America from 1600 to 1900. He argues that the very different experiences of Native, African, and European Americans mean that there is no unified American history and no one "type" who can be identified as American.

Robert S. Dahl, *How Democratic Is the American Constitution?* (New Haven, Conn.: Yale University Press, 2001). A slim, wonderfully written book drawn from lectures delivered at Yale by one of the country's leading political scientists. He discusses how little the framers knew—and how little there was to know at the time from historical experience—about real democracies and republics. Then he looks at major features of the U.S. Constitution and discusses the limitations they place on achieving full democracy.

John B. Judis, *The Paradox of American Democracy: Elites, Special Interests and the Betrayal of Public Trust* (New York: Pantheon, 1999). A counterargument to the malignant interpretation of elitism, this book attributes the twentieth century's great waves of reform and social welfare legislation to small groups of Ivy League and think tank elites.

Harold Lasswell, *Politics: Who Gets What, When, How* (New York: New World, 1958). A classic treatment of some very practical political problems.

Pauline Maier, *American Scripture: The Making of the Declaration of Independence* (New York: Knopf, 1997). A historian offers a revisionist view of the importance of the Declaration by arguing that its language was not original but rather was almost identical in content to that of ninety other declarations written in the colonies at the same time. Given the widespread agreement on language and principles in all these documents, she judges the Declaration "an expression of the American mind."

Michael J. Sandel, *Democracy's Discontent: America in Search of a Public Philosophy* (Cambridge, Mass.: Belknap, Harvard University Press, 1996). A political theorist argues that American politics is "ill-equipped to allay discontent" over the unravelling moral fabric of the country and suggests that one reason is the supremacy of individual rights over community interests.

 Electronic Resources

In each chapter, we will provide a few Internet addresses for particularly useful or interesting sites relevant to the chapter. Today, you can access information, including statistics and information about public officials, that was formerly accessible only in libraries. Unlike library call numbers, however, Internet addresses sometimes change.

www.firstgov.gov/
This is a central federal government site providing links to 27 million government Web pages, including all branches of government, federal agencies and commissions, and important policy areas.

www.fedstats.gov/
The primary link to all federal statistics.

www.census.gov/
The primary source for results of the 2000 census.

www.ins.gov/
This site of the Immigration and Naturalization Service leads you to the text of immigration law, official statistics on immigration flows to the United States, and analytical reports on immigration trends.

lcweb.loc.gov/exhibits/religion
A rich source on the role of religion in the founding of the American republic and on the relationship between organized religion and the state governments. Contains many original documents on the relationship between church and state.

InfoTrac College Edition

Search for the following articles in the InfoTrac database:

Barber, Benjamin R. "Three Scenarios for the Future of Technology and Strong Democracy," *Political Science Quarterly* (Winter 1998).

Elgin, Duane. "Revitalizing Democracy through Electronic Town Meetings," *Spectrum: the Journal of State Government* (Spring 1993).

Grosswiler, Paul. "Historical Hopes, Media Fears, and the Electronic Town Meeting Concept: Where Technology Meets Democracy or Demagogy?" *Journal of Communication Inquiry* (April 1998).

McWilliams, Wilson C. "Democracy as Means and End," *Social Policy* (Summer 2002).

For more articles, enter:

"democracy" in the Subject Guide.

"direct democracy" in Keywords.

 American Government Resources

Visit the Government Foundations section of the Wadsworth American Government Resources Web site (politicalscience.wadsworth.com/amgov/) for a variety of tools to help you explore American democracy further. Included are simulations, video clips, Microcase exercises, and a wealth of other activities.

CHAPTER 2

THE CONSTITUTION

Soon after their deaths, the founders were venerated by the people. Here George Washington is pictured ascending to heaven.

The Case of the Confidential Tapes

n June 1972, a security guard for the Watergate building in Washington, D.C., noticed that tape had been placed across the latch of a door to keep it from locking. The guard peeled off the tape. When he made his rounds later, he noticed that more tape had been placed across the latch. He called the police.

The police encountered five burglars in the headquarters of the Democratic National Committee. Wearing surgical gloves and carrying tear gas guns, photographic equipment, and electronic gear, they had been installing wiretaps on the Democratic Party's phones.

No one expected this break-in to lead to the White House. The *Washington Post* assigned two young reporters who usually covered local matters to the story. But the unlikely pair of Bob Woodward, a Yale graduate, and Carl Bernstein, a college dropout, were ambitious, and they uncovered a series of bizarre connections. The burglars had links to President Richard Nixon's Committee to Reelect the President (CREEP).

The administration dismissed the break-in as the work of overzealous underlings. Even the press called it a "caper." Indeed, it was hard to imagine that high officials in the administration could be responsible. In public opinion polls, Nixon enjoyed an enormous lead, almost 20 percent, over the various Democrats vying for their party's nomination to challenge him in the fall

election. Risky tactics seemed unnecessary.

But Woodward and Bernstein discovered that White House staff members had engaged in other criminal and unethical actions to sabotage the Democrats' campaign. They had forged letters accusing some of the Democrats' candidates of homosexual acts. Later they had obtained and publicized psychiatric records, causing the Democrats' vice presidential nominee to resign.

In the November election, Nixon won handily, but the revelations forced his two top aides to resign and prompted the Senate to establish a special committee to investigate what was being called the **Watergate scandal.** When investigators happened to ask a lower-level aide to the president whether there was a taping device in the Oval Office, he said, "I was hoping you fellows wouldn't ask me about that." Then he revealed what only a handful of aides had known—that Nixon had secretly tape-recorded conversations in nine locations in the White House, the Executive Office Building across the street, and Camp David in Maryland. Nixon had intended to create a comprehensive record of his presidency to demonstrate his greatness.[1]

The tapes could confirm or refute charges of White House complicity in the break-in and cover-up, but Nixon refused to release them. The special prosecutor filed suit to

Washington Post *reporters Carl Bernstein (left) and Bob Woodward uncovered the Watergate scandal.*

Dennis Brack Ltd./Black Star

force Nixon to do so, and a federal trial court ordered him to do so. After the federal appeals court affirmed the trial court's decision, Nixon demanded that his attorney general fire the special prosecutor. The attorney general and deputy attorney general both refused and resigned in protest. Then the third-ranking official in the Justice Department, Robert Bork, fired the special prosecutor. (Bork later would be nominated to the Supreme Court by President Reagan.)

The public furor over this "Saturday Night Massacre" was so intense that Nixon finally did release some tapes. But one crucial tape contained a mysterious eighteen-minute gap that a presidential aide speculated was caused by "some sinister force."

To mollify critics, Nixon appointed a new special prosecutor, Leon Jaworski. After his investigation, Jaworski presented evidence to a grand jury that indicted seven of the president's aides for the cover-up, specifically for obstruction of justice,

and even named the president as an "unindicted coconspirator."

The House Judiciary Committee considered impeaching the president, and Jaworski subpoenaed more tapes. Nixon issued edited transcripts of the conversations but not the tapes themselves. As a compromise, he proposed that one person listen to the tapes—a senator who was seventy-two years old and hard of hearing. Frustrated, Jaworski went to the court, which ordered Nixon to release the tapes. When Nixon refused, Jaworski appealed directly to the Supreme Court.

You are Chief Justice Warren Burger, appointed to the Court by President Nixon in 1969 partly because of your calls for more law and order. Three of your brethren also were appointed by Nixon. In the case of *United States* v. *Nixon,* you are faced with a question that could lead to a grave constitutional showdown with the president. Special Prosecutor Jaworski claims he needs the tapes because they contain evidence pertaining to the

upcoming trial of the president's aides indicted for the cover-up. Without all relevant evidence, which possibly could vindicate the aides, the trial court might not convict them.

President Nixon claims he has executive privilege—authority to withhold information from the courts and Congress. Although the Constitution does not mention such a privilege, Nixon claims the privilege is inherent in the powers of the presidency. Without it, presidents could not guarantee confidentiality in conversations with other officials or even foreign leaders. This could make it difficult for them to govern.

You have few precedents to guide you. Many past presidents exercised executive privilege when pressed for information by Congress. In these instances, Congress ordinarily acquiesced rather than sued for the information, so the courts did not rule on the existence of the privilege. Once, in 1953, the Eisenhower administration invoked the privilege, and the Supreme Court upheld the claim. However, that case involved national security.[2]

In addition to considering the merits of the opposing sides, you also need to consider the extent of the Supreme Court's power. The Court lacks strong means to enforce its rulings. It has to rely on its authority as the highest interpreter of the law in the country. Therefore, if the Court orders Nixon to relinquish the tapes and Nixon refuses, there would be little the Court could do. His refusal would show future officials they could disregard your orders with impunity.

In this high-stakes contest, do you and your brethren on the Court order Nixon to turn over the tapes, or do you accept his claim of executive privilege?

Early settlers came to America for different reasons. Some came to escape religious persecution, others to establish their own religious orthodoxy. Some came to get rich, others to avoid debtors' prison. Some came to make money for their families or employers in the Old World, others to flee the closed society of that world.

Some came as free persons, others as indentured servants or slaves. Few came to practice self-government. Yet the desire for self-government was evident from the beginning.[3] The settlers who arrived in Jamestown in 1607 established the first representative assembly in America. The pilgrims who reached Plymouth in 1620 drew up the Mayflower Compact in which they vowed to "solemnly & mutually in the presence of God, and one of another, covenant and combine our selves together into a civill body politick." They pledged to establish laws for "the generall good of the colonie" and in return promised "all due submission and obedience."[4]

During the next century and a half, the colonies adopted constitutions and elected representative assemblies. Of course, the colonies lived under British rule; they had to accept the appointment of royal governors and the presence of British troops. But a vast ocean separated the two continents. At such a distance, Britain could not wield the control it might at closer reach. Consequently, it granted the colonies a measure of autonomy, with which they practiced a degree of self-government.

These early efforts toward self-government led to conflict with the mother government. In 1774, the colonies established the Continental Congress to coordinate their actions. Within months, the conflict reached flashpoint, and the Congress urged the colonies to form their own governments. In 1776, the Congress adopted the Declaration of Independence.

After six years of war, the Americans accepted the British surrender. At the time it seemed they had met their biggest test. Yet they would find fomenting a revolution easier than fashioning a government and drafting a declaration of independence easier than crafting a constitution.

Although the Articles gave the federal government authority to print money, the states circulated their own currencies as well.

The Articles of Confederation

Even before the war ended, the Continental Congress passed a constitution, and in 1781 the states ratified it. This first constitution, the **Articles of Confederation,** formed a "league of friendship" among the states. As a confederation, it allowed each state to retain its "sovereignty" and "independence." That is, it made the states supreme over the federal government.

Under the Articles, however, Americans would face problems with both their national and state governments.

National Government Problems

The Articles of Confederation established a Congress, with one house in which each state had one vote. But they strictly limited the powers that Congress could exercise, and they provided no executive or judicial branch.

The Articles reflected the colonial experience under the British government. The leaders feared a powerful central government with a powerful executive like a king. They thought such a government would be too

strong and too distant to guarantee individual liberty. Additionally, the Articles reflected a lack of national identity among the people. Most did not view themselves as Americans yet. As Edmund Randolph remarked, "I am not really an American, I am a Virginian."[5] (And George Washington worried that Kentuckians would join Spain.[6]) Consequently, the leaders established a very decentralized government that left most authority to the states.

The Articles satisfied many people. Most people were small farmers, and although many of them sank into debt during the depression that followed the war, they felt they could influence the state governments to help them. They realized they could not influence a distant central government as readily.

But the Articles frustrated bankers, merchants, manufacturers, and others in the upper classes. They envisioned a great commercial empire replacing the agricultural society that existed in the late eighteenth century. More than local trade, they wanted national and even international trade. For this they needed uniform laws, stable money, sound credit, and enforceable debt collection. They needed a strong central government that could protect them against debtors and against state governments sympathetic to debtors. The Articles provided neither the foreign security nor the domestic climate necessary to nourish these requisites of a commercial empire.

After the war, the army disbanded, leaving the country vulnerable to hostile forces surrounding it. Britain maintained outposts with troops in the Northwest Territory (now the Midwest), in violation of the peace treaty, and an army in Canada. Spain, which had occupied Florida and California for a long time and had claimed the Mississippi River valley as a result of a treaty before the war, posed a threat. Barbary pirates from North Africa seized American ships and sailors.

Congress could not raise an army, because it could not draft individuals directly, or finance an army, because it could not tax individuals directly. Instead, it had to ask the states for soldiers and money. The states, however, were not always sympathetic to the problems of the distant government. And although Congress could make treaties with foreign countries, the states made (or broke) treaties independently of Congress. Without the ability to establish a credible army or negotiate a binding treaty, the government could not get the British troops out of the country. Nor could it get the British government to ease restrictions on shipping or the Spanish government to permit navigation on the Mississippi River.[7]

In addition to an inability to confront foreign threats, the Articles demonstrated an inability to cope with domestic crises. The country bore a heavy war debt that brought the government close to bankruptcy. Since Congress could not tax individuals directly, it could not shore up the shaky government.

The states competed with each other for commercial advantage. As independent governments, they imposed tariffs on goods from other states. The tariffs slowed the growth of businesses.

In short, the government under the Articles of Confederation seemed too decentralized to ensure either peace or prosperity. The Articles, one leader concluded, gave Congress the privilege of asking for everything, while reserving to each state the prerogative of granting nothing.[8] A similar situation exists today in the United Nations, which must rely on member countries to furnish troops for its peacekeeping forces and dues for its operating expenses.[9]

State Government Problems

Other conflicts arose closer to home. State constitutions adopted during the American Revolution made the state legislatures more representative than the colonial legislatures had been. Most state legislatures also began to hold elections every year. The result was heightened interest among candidates and turnover among legislators. In the eyes of national leaders, there was much pandering to voters and horse trading by politicians as various factions vied for control. The process seemed up for grabs. According to the Vermont Council of Censors, laws were "altered—realtered—made better—made worse; and kept in such a fluctuating position that persons in civil commission scarce know what is law."[10] In short, state governments were experiencing more democracy than any other governments in the world at the time. National leaders, stunned by the changes in the few years since the Revolution, considered this development an "excess of democracy."

Moreover, state constitutions made the legislative branch the most powerful. Some state legislatures began to dominate the other branches, and national leaders called them "tyrannical."

The national leaders, most of whom were wealthy and many of whom were creditors, pointed to the laws passed in some states that relieved debtors of some of their obligations. The farmers who were in debt pressed the legislatures for relief that would slow or shrink the payments owed to their creditors. Some legislatures granted such relief.

While these laws worried the leaders, **Shays's Rebellion** in western Massachusetts in 1786 and 1787 scared them. Boston merchants who had loaned Massachusetts money during the war insisted on being repaid in full so they could trade with foreign merchants. The state levied steep taxes that many farmers could not pay during the hard times. The law authorized foreclosure—sale of the farmers' property for the taxes—and jail for the debtors. The law essentially transferred wealth from the farmers to the merchants. The farmers protested the legislature's refusal to grant any relief from the law. Bands of farmers blocked entrances to courthouses where judges were scheduled to hear cases calling for foreclosure and jail. Led by Daniel Shays, some marched to the Springfield arsenal to seize weapons. Although they were defeated by the militia, their sympathizers were victorious in the next election, and the legislature did provide some relief from the law.

Both the revolt and the legislature's change in policy frightened the wealthy. To them it raised the specter of "mob rule." Nathaniel Gorham, the president of the Continental Congress and a prominent merchant, wrote Prince Henry of Prussia, announcing "the failure of our free institutions" and asking whether the prince would agree to become king of America (the prince declined).[11] Just months after the uprising, Congress approved a convention for "the sole and express purpose of revising the Articles of Confederation."

To a significant extent, then, the debate at the time reflected a conflict between two competing visions of the future American political economy—agricultural or

Charles Francis Adams, a grandson of President John Adams and Abigail Adams, declared in 1840, "The heroism of the females of the Revolution has gone from memory with the generation that witnessed it, and nothing, absolutely nothing remains upon the ear of the young of the present day."[1] That statement is still true today; in the volumes written about the revolutionary and Constitution-making eras, much is said of the "Founding Fathers" and very little about the "Founding Mothers." Although no women were at the Constitutional Convention, in many other ways women contributed significantly to the political ferment of the time. The political role of women during the Constitution-making era was probably greater than it would be again for a century.

Before the Revolutionary War, women were active in encouraging opposition to the British. Groups of women, some called the "daughters of liberty," led boycotts of British goods as part of the protest campaign against taxation without representation. A few women were political pamphleteers, helping increase public sentiment for independence. One of those pamphlet writers, Mercy Otis Warren, of Massachusetts, was thought to be the first person to urge the Massachusetts delegates to the Continental Congress to vote for separation from

This English political cartoon satirizes a gathering of leading women in North Carolina who drew up a resolution to boycott taxed English goods and tea.

(The Metropolitan Museum of Art, Bequest of Charles Allen Munn, 1924 (24-90-35))

A SOCIETY of PATRIOTIC LADIES,
AT
EDENTON in NORTH CAROLINA.
Plate V.

Britain.[2] Throughout the period before and after the Revolution, Warren shared her political ideas in personal correspondence with leading statesmen of the time, such as John Adams and Thomas Jefferson. Later she wrote a three-volume history of the American Revolution.

Many women were part of the American army during the battles for independence. Most filled traditional women's roles as cooks, seamstresses, and nurses, but some disguised themselves as men (this was before a military bureaucracy mandated preenlistment physical exams) and fought in battle. One such woman, wounded in action in 1776, is the only Revolutionary War veteran buried at West Point. Still other women fought to defend their homes using hatchets, farm implements, and pots of boiling lye in addition to muskets.

Following independence, some women continued an active political role. Mercy Warren, for example, campaigned against the proposed Constitution because she felt it was not democratic enough.

Independence did not bring an improvement in the political rights of women. In fact, after adoption of the Constitution, some women lost the right to vote. It would be another century before the rights of women would become a full-fledged part of our national political agenda.

1. Quoted in Linda Grant DePauw and Conover Hunt, *Remember the Ladies* (New York: Viking, 1976), 9.
2. Alice Felt Tyler, *Freedom's Ferment* (New York: Harper & Row, 1962).

commercial.[12] Most leaders espoused the latter, and the combination of national problems and state problems prompted them to push for a new government.[13]

The Constitution

The Constitutional Convention

The Setting

The **Constitutional Convention** convened in Philadelphia, then the country's largest city, in 1787.

That year the Industrial Revolution was continuing to sweep Europe and beginning to reach this continent. The first American cotton mill opened in Massachusetts, and the first American steamboat plied the Delaware River.

State legislatures chose seventy-four delegates to the convention; fifty-five attended. They met at the Pennsylvania State House—now Independence Hall—in the same room where some of them had signed the Declaration of Independence eleven years before. (See the box "Founding Mothers.")

Delegates came from every state except Rhode Island. That state was controlled by farmers and debtors who feared that the convention would weaken states' powers to relieve debtors of their debts.

The delegates were distinguished by their education, experience, and enlightenment. Benjamin Franklin, of Pennsylvania, was the best-known American in the world. He had been a printer, scientist, and diplomat. At eighty-one he was also the oldest delegate. George Washington, of Virginia, was the most respected American in the country. As the commander of the revolutionary army, he was a national hero. He was chosen to preside over the convention. The presence of men like Franklin and Washington gave the convention legitimacy.

The delegates quickly determined that the Articles were hopeless. Rather than revise them, as instructed by Congress, the delegates decided to start over and draft a new constitution.[14]

The Predicament

The delegates came to the convention because they complained about a government that was too weak. Yet previously Americans had fought a revolution because they chafed under a government that was too strong. "The nation lived in a nearly constant alternation of fears that it would cease being a nation altogether or become too much of one."[15] People feared both anarchy and tyranny.

This predicament was made clear by the diversity of opinions among the leaders. At one extreme was Patrick Henry, of Virginia, who had been a firebrand of the Revolution. He felt the government would become too strong, perhaps even become a monarchy, in reaction to the current problems with the Articles. He said he "smelt a rat" and did not attend the convention. At the other extreme was Alexander Hamilton, of New York, who had been an aide to General Washington during the war and had seen the government's inability to supply and pay its own troops. Since then he had called for a stronger national government. He wanted one that could veto the laws of the state governments. He also wanted one person to serve as chief executive for life and others to serve as senators for life. He did attend the convention but, finding little agreement with his proposals, participated infrequently.

In between were those like James Madison, of Virginia. Small and frail, timid and self-conscious as a speaker, he was nonetheless intelligent and savvy as a politician. He had operated behind the scenes to convene the convention and to secure Washington's attendance. (He publicized that Washington would attend without asking Washington first. Washington, who was in retirement, did not plan to attend and only reluctantly agreed to do so because of the expectation that he would.[16]) Madison had secretly drafted a plan for a new government, one that was a total departure from the government under the Articles and one that would set the agenda for the convention. During the convention, Madison was "up to his ears in politics, advising, persuading, softening the harsh word, playing down this difficulty and exaggerating that, engaging in debate, harsh controversy, polemics, and sly maneuver."[17] In the end, his views more than anyone else's would prevail, and he would be called the Father of the Constitution.

Consensus

Despite disagreements, the delegates did see eye to eye on the most fundamental issues. They agreed that the government should be a republic—an indirect democracy—in which people could vote for at least some of the officials who would represent them. They did not seriously consider any other form of government. They also agreed that the national government should be stronger than before. At the same time, they thought the government should be limited, with checks to prevent it from exercising too much power.

They agreed that the national government should have three separate branches—legislative, executive, and judicial—to exercise separate powers. They thought both the legislative and executive branches should be strong.

Conflict

Although there was considerable agreement over the fundamental principles and elemental structure of the new government, the delegates quarreled about the specific provisions concerning representation, slavery, and trade.

Representation Sharp conflict was expressed between delegates from large states and those from small states over representation. Large states sought a strong central government that they could control; small states feared a government that would control them.

When the convention began, Edmund Randolph introduced the Virginia Plan drafted by Madison. According to this plan, the central government would be strong. The legislature would have more power than under the Articles of Confederation, and a national executive and national judiciary also would have considerable power. The legislature would be divided into two houses, with representation based on population in each.

But delegates from the small states calculated that the three largest states—Pennsylvania, Virginia, and Massachusetts—would have a majority of the representatives and could control the legislature. These delegates countered with the New Jersey Plan, introduced by William Paterson. According to this plan, the legislature would consist of one house, with representation by states, which would have one vote each. This was exactly the

This plan of a slave ship shows the overcrowding that led to inhumane conditions, rampant disease, and high mortality.

same as the structure of Congress under the Articles, also designed to prevent the largest states from controlling the legislature.

To complicate matters, some states claimed vast territory to their west, while other states feared that such expansion would make frontier states even larger.

The convention deadlocked. George Washington wrote that he almost despaired of reaching agreement. To ease tensions, Benjamin Franklin suggested that the delegates begin each day with a prayer, but they could not agree on this either; Alexander Hamilton insisted they did not need "foreign aid."

Faced with the possibility that the convention would disband without a constitution, the delegates compromised. Delegates from Connecticut and other states proposed a plan in which the legislature would have two houses. In one, representation would be based on population, and members would be elected by voters. In the other, representation would be by states, and members would be selected by state legislatures. Presumably, the large states would dominate the former, the small states the latter. The delegates narrowly approved this **Great Compromise,** or Connecticut Compromise. Delegates from the large states still objected, but those from the small states made it clear that such a compromise was necessary for their agreement and, in turn, their states' ratification. The large states, though, did extract a concession that all taxing and spending bills must originate in the house in which representation was based on population. This provision would allow the large states to take the initiative on these important measures. The compromise was "great" in that it not only resolved this critical issue but paved the way for resolution of other issues.

This decision began a pattern that continues to this day. When officials face implacable differences, they try to compromise, but the process is not easy and a resolution is not inevitable. It is an apt choice of words to say that officials "hammer out" a compromise; it is not a coincidence that we use *hammer* rather than a softer metaphor.

Slavery In addition to conflict between large states and small states over representation, conflict emerged between northern states and southern states over slavery, trade, and taxation.

With representation in one house based on population, the delegates had to decide how to apportion the seats. They agreed that Indians would not count as part of the population but differed about slaves. Delegates from the South, where slaves were one-third of the population, wanted slaves to count fully in order to boost the number of their representatives. They argued that their use of slaves produced wealth that benefited the entire nation. Delegates from the North, where most states had outlawed slavery or at least the slave trade after the Revolution, did not want slaves to count at all. Gouverneur Morris, of Pennsylvania, said the southerners' position

> comes to this: that the inhabitant of Georgia and South Carolina who goes to the coast of Africa, and in defiance of the most sacred laws of humanity tears away his fellow creatures from their dearest connections and damns them to the most cruel bondages, shall have more votes in a government instituted for the protection of the rights of mankind than the citizen of Pennsylvania or New Jersey who views with a laudable horror so nefarious a practice.[18]

Others pointed out that slaves were not considered persons when it came to rights such as voting. Nevertheless, southerners asserted that they would not support a constitution if slaves were not counted at least partially. In the **Three-fifths Compromise,** the delegates agreed that three-fifths of the slaves would be counted in apportioning the seats.

As a result, the votes of southern whites would be worth more than those of northerners in electing members to the House of Representatives and presidents (because the Electoral College would be based on membership in Congress). Between 1788 and 1860, nine of the fifteen presidents, including all five who served two terms, were slaveowners.[19]

Southerners pushed through two other provisions addressing slavery. One forbade Congress from banning the importation of slaves before 1808; another required free states to return escaped slaves to their owners in slave states. In these provisions, southerners won most of what they wanted; even the provision permitting Congress to ban the importation of slaves in 1808 was little limitation because by then planters would have enough slaves to fulfill their needs by natural population increases rather than importation. In return, northerners, who represented shippers, got authority for Congress to regulate commerce by a simple majority rather than a two-thirds majority. Thus, northerners conceded these two provisions reinforcing slavery in order to benefit shippers.[20]

Yet the framers were embarrassed by the hypocrisy of claiming to have been enslaved by the British while allowing enslavement of blacks. Their embarrassment is reflected in their language. The three provisions reinforcing slavery never mention "slavery" or "slaves"; one gingerly refers to "free persons" and "other persons."

Slavery was the most divisive issue at the convention. As Madison noted, "the real difference of interests lay, not between the large and small, but between the northern and southern states. The institution of slavery and its consequences formed the line of discrimination."[21] The unwillingness to tackle the slavery issue more directly has been called the "Greatest Compromise" by one political scientist.[22] But an attempt to abolish slavery would have caused the five southern states to refuse to ratify the Constitution.

Trade and Taxation Slavery also underlay a compromise on trade and taxation. With a manufacturing economy, northerners sought protection for their businesses. In particular, they wanted a tax on manufactured goods imported from Britain. Without a tax, these goods would be cheaper than northern goods; but with a tax, northern goods would be more competitive—and prices for southern consumers more expensive. With an agricultural economy, southerners sought free trade for their plantations. They wanted a guarantee that no tax would be levied on agricultural products exported to Britain. Such a tax would make their products less competitive abroad and, they worried, amount to an indirect

tax on slavery—the labor responsible for the products. The delegates compromised by allowing Congress to tax imported goods but not exported ones. Tariffs on imported goods would become a point of controversy between the North and South in the years leading up to the Civil War.

After seventeen weeks of debate, the Constitution was ready. On September 17, 1787, thirty-nine of the original fifty-five delegates signed it. Some delegates had left when they saw the direction the convention was taking, and three others refused to sign, feeling that the Constitution gave too much authority to the national government. Most of the rest were not entirely happy with the result (even Madison, who was most responsible for the content of the document, was despondent that his plan for a national legislature was compromised by having one house with representation by states), but they thought it was the best they could do. Benjamin Franklin was more optimistic. Referring to the sun painted on the back of George Washington's chair, he remarked that throughout the proceedings he had wondered whether it was a rising or a setting sun. "But now . . . I have the happiness to know that it is a rising and not a setting sun."

Features of the Constitution

William Gladstone, a British prime minister in the nineteenth century, said the American Constitution was "the most wonderful work ever struck off at a given time by the brain and purpose of man."[23] To see why it was unique, it is necessary to examine its major features.

A Republic

The Founders distinguished between a democracy and a republic. For them a "democracy" meant a **direct democracy,** which permits citizens to vote on most issues, and a "republic" meant an **indirect democracy,** which allows citizens to vote for their representatives who make governmental policies.

The Founders opposed a direct democracy for the whole country. Many individual towns in New England had a direct democracy (and some still do), but these communities were small and manageable. Some city-states of ancient Greece and medieval Europe had a direct democracy, but they could not sustain it. The Founders thought a large country would have even less ability to do so because people could not be brought together in one place in order to act. They also believed human nature was such that people could not withstand the passions of the moment and would be swayed by a demagogue to take unwise action. Eventually, democracy would collapse into tyranny. "Remember," John Adams wrote, "democracy never lasts long. It soon wastes, exhausts, and murders itself. There never was a democracy yet that did not commit suicide."[24]

The Founders favored an indirect democracy—a republic—because they firmly believed the people should have some voice in the government because the government should be based on the consent of the governed. So the Founders provided that the people could elect representatives to the House and that the state legislators, themselves elected by the people, could select senators and members of the Electoral College, who would choose the president. In this way, the people would have a voice but one partially filtered through their presumably wiser representatives.

The Founders' views reflect their ambivalence about the people. Rationally they believed in popular sovereignty, but emotionally they feared it. New England clergyman Jeremy Belknap voiced their ambivalence when he declared, "Let it stand as a principle that government originates from the people; but let the people be taught . . . that they are not able to govern themselves."

The Founders considered a democracy radical and a republic only slightly less radical. Because they believed the country could not maintain a democracy, they worried that it might not be able to maintain a republic either. When the Constitutional Convention closed, Benjamin Franklin was approached by a woman who asked, "Well, Doctor, what have we got, a republic or a monarchy?" Franklin responded, "A republic, madam, if you can keep it."

Fragmentation of Power

Other countries assumed that government must have a concentration of power to be strong enough to govern. However, when the Founders made our national government more powerful than it had been under the Articles of Confederation, they feared they also had made it more capable of oppression, and therefore they fragmented its power.

The Founders believed people were selfish, coveting more and more property, and that leaders lusted after more and more power. They assumed such human nature was unchangeable. Madison speculated, "If men were angels, no government would be necessary." But, alas, he added, men are not angels. Therefore, "In framing a government which is to be administered by men over men, the great difficulty lies in this: you must first enable the government to control the governed; and in the next place oblige it to control itself."[25] (Madison's views are reflected in two of the Federalist Papers included in the appendix.) The Founders decided the way to oblige government to control itself was to structure it to prevent any one leader, group of leaders, or factions of people from exercising power over more than a small part of it. Thus, the Founders fragmented government's

Tom Myer, San Francisco Chronicle

power. This is reflected in three concepts they built into the structure of government: federalism, separation of powers, and checks and balances.

Federalism The first division of power was between the national government and the state governments. This division of power is called **federalism.** Foreign governments had been "unitary"; that is, the central government wielded all authority. At the other extreme, the U.S. government under the Articles had been "confederal"; the state governments wielded almost all authority. The Founders wanted a strong national government, but they also wanted, or at least realized they would have to accept, reasonably strong state governments as well. They invented a federal system as a compromise between the unitary and confederal systems. (Chapter 3 explains these types of government further.)

They even incorporated federalism into the national government by stipulating that one house of Congress, the Senate, would be based on the states. It would have two senators from each state regardless of the population of any state. This would protect the interests of the states—in particular, the small states that would be dwarfed in a house based on population. Thus, this would give power to small states disproportionate to their population.

Separation of Powers The second division of power was within the national government. The power to make, administer, and judge the laws was split into three branches: legislative, executive, and judicial (see Figure 1). In the legislative branch, the power was split further into two houses. This **separation of powers** contrasts with the parliamentary system in most developed democracies in which the legislature is supreme. Both executive and judicial officials are drawn from it and responsible to it. There is no separation of powers. (If the United States had a parliamentary system in the mid-1990s, consider the possibility: Newt Gingrich [R-Ga.]

Branch:	Legislative Congress		Executive Presidency	Judicial Federal Courts
	House	Senate	President	Judges
Officials chosen by:	People	People, (originally, state legislatures)	Electoral College, whose members are chosen by the people (originally, by state legislatures)	President, with advice and consent of Senate
For term of:	2 years	6 years	4 years	Life
To represent primarily:	Common people	Wealthy people	All people	Constitution
	Large states	Small states		

FIGURE 1 ■ Separation of Powers

Separation of powers, as envisioned by the Founders, means not only that government functions are to be performed by different branches but also that officials of these branches are to be chosen by different people, for different terms, and to represent different constituencies.

would have been our head of state.) Madison expressed the American view of such an arrangement when he said that "the accumulation of all powers, legislative, executive, and judiciary, in the same hands . . . may justly be pronounced the very definition of tyranny."[26] (However, the parliamentary systems today are no more tyrannous than other systems.)

To reinforce the separation of powers, officials of the three branches were chosen by different means. Representatives were elected by the people (at that time mostly white men who owned property), senators were selected by the state legislatures, and the president was selected by the Electoral College, whose members were selected by the states. Only federal judges were chosen by officials in the other branches. They were nominated by the president and confirmed by the Senate. Once appointed, however, they were allowed to serve for "good behavior"—essentially life—so they had much independence. (Since the Constitution was written, the Seventeenth Amendment has provided for election of senators by the people, and the state legislatures have provided for election of members of the Electoral College by the people.)

Officials of the branches were also chosen at different times. Representatives were given a two-year term, senators a six-year term (with one-third of them up for reelection every two years), and the president a four-year term. These staggered terms would make it less likely that temporary passions in society would bring about a massive switch of officials or policies.

The Senate was designed to act as a conservative brake on the House, due to senators' selection by state legislatures and their longer terms. After returning from France, Thomas Jefferson met with George Washington

over breakfast. Jefferson protested the establishment of a legislature with two houses. Washington supposedly asked, "Why did you pour that coffee into your saucer?" "To cool it," Jefferson replied. Similarly, Washington explained, "We pour legislation into the senatorial saucer to cool it."[27]

Checks and Balances To guarantee separation of powers, the Founders built in overlapping powers called **checks and balances** (see Figure 2). Madison suggested that "the great security against a gradual concentration of the several powers in the same department consists in giving those who administer each department the necessary constitutional means and personal motives to resist encroachments by the others. . . . *Ambition must be made to counteract ambition*."[28] To that end, each branch was given some authority over the others. If one branch abused its power, the others could use their checks to thwart it.

Thus, rather than a simple system of separation of powers, ours is a complex, even contradictory, system of both separation of powers and checks and balances. The principle of separation of powers gives each branch its own sphere of authority, but the system of checks and balances allows each branch to intrude into the other branches' spheres. For example, because of separation of powers, Congress makes the laws; but due to checks and balances, the president can veto them, and the courts can rule them unconstitutional. In these ways all three branches are involved in legislating. One political scientist calls ours "a government of separated institutions sharing powers."[29]

With federalism, separation of powers, and checks and balances, the Founders expected conflict. They invited the parts of government to struggle against each other to limit any part's ability to dominate the rest. The Founders hoped for "balanced government." The national and state governments would represent different interests, and the branches within the national government would represent different interests. The House would represent the "common" people and the large states; the Senate, the wealthy people and the small states; the president, all the people; and the Supreme Court, the Constitution. The parts of government would have to compromise to get anything accomplished. Although each part would struggle for more power, it could not accumulate enough to dominate the others. Eventually, it would have to compromise and accept policies that would be in the interest of all of the parts and their constituencies. Paradoxically, then, the Founders expected narrow conflict to produce broader harmony.

Motives of the Founders

To understand the Constitution better, it is useful to consider the motives of the Founders. Were they selfless patriots, sharing their wisdom and experience? Or were they selfish property owners, protecting their interests?

First consider the people who migrated to America. Some came for religious reasons. Their religious beliefs put them at odds with many in their native country. They were denied privileges or penalized or, occasionally, persecuted. Usually they were adherents of Protestant sects rather than members of established churches like the Church of England or the Roman Catholic Church. As such, they were more suspicious of governmental authority and religious authority than those who remained in the old world. They were "runaways from authority."[30] Others came for economic reasons. Whether poor or well-to-do, they saw America as the land of economic opportunity. They sought to improve their status, acquiring property and perhaps even becoming wealthy. Although they were not as suspicious of established authority, they were opposed to active government. More government meant more taxes, which meant less money in their pockets. So both groups of people who migrated to America had reasons to prefer limited government.[31] They passed down their beliefs to their descendants.

Now consider the philosophical ideas, political experience, and economic interests that more directly influenced the Founders.

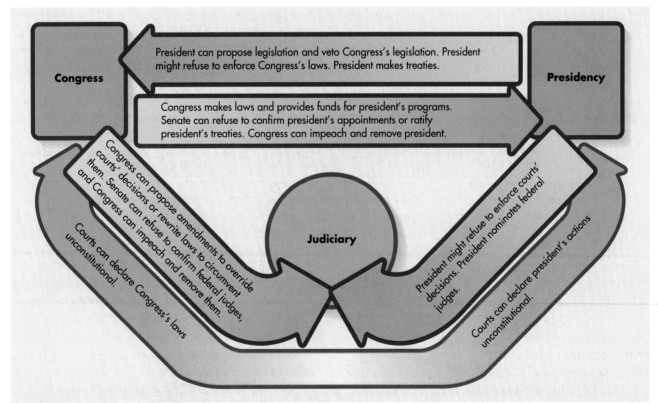

FIGURE 2 ■ Checks and Balances

Most of the major checks and balances between the three branches are explicit in the Constitution, though some are not. For example, the courts' power to declare congressional laws or presidential actions unconstitutional—their power of "judicial review"—is not mentioned. The president's power to refuse to enforce congressional laws or judicial decisions is also not mentioned or even implied. In fact, it contradicts the Constitution, but sometimes it is asserted by the president nonetheless.

DID THE IROQUOIS INFLUENCE THE FOUNDERS?

For many years, popular writers portrayed Native Americans as simple savages. To some they were "bloodthirsty savages." To others they were "noble savages." But to almost all writers, Indians were so preoccupied by surviving that they had little time for anything but hunting and fighting. Yet these Native Americans had far more sophisticated societies than most writers, until recently, gave them credit for.

Although most Americans are aware that the colonists adopted the tactics of Indian warfare—the forerunner of modern guerrilla warfare—to defeat the British in the Revolutionary War, few Americans realize that the colonists mirrored several other Indian practices in founding the country. In fact, the colonists used some concepts similar to those of the Iroquois in the Declaration of Independence, Articles of Confederation, and Constitution.

The Iroquois, who inhabited what is now New York State, included the Cayugas, Mohawks, Oneidas, Onondagas, and Senecas. (After the early 1700s, they also included the Tuscaroras, who migrated from the Carolinas.) After generations of bloody warfare, the "Five Nations" formed the **Iroquois Confederacy** sometime between 1000 and 1450, according to various estimates.[1]

Iroquois Government

The Confederacy adopted a constitution called the "Great Law of Peace." Although some provisions were not written, others were recorded on "wampum belts," constructed of shells sewn in intricate patterns on hides. Few white Americans realized that the Iroquois constitution was partly written until it was transcribed into English in the late nineteenth century.

The Great Law provided for a union with federalism, checks and balances, restrictions on the power of the leaders, opportunities for participation by the people, and some natural rights and equality for the people.

Federalism was most apparent. Each of the Five Nations was essentially a state within a state. Each was allowed to govern its internal affairs. (Even non-Iroquois nations conquered by the Iroquois were allowed to keep their form of government as long as they did not make war on other nations.)

Checks and balances were incorporated in several ways. The Confederacy established a system of clans that overlapped the boundaries of the nations. Members of clans were considered relatives despite living in different nations. Thus, the system of clans was designed to operate like the system of checks and balances in the U.S. Constitution: Where checks and balances were intended to prevent the dominance of one branch of government or one faction that got control of a branch of government, clans were intended to prevent the dominance of one nation in the Confederacy.

The Confederacy used governing procedures that also entailed checks and balances.

The "older brothers"—Mohawks and Senecas—were on "one side of the house." The "younger brothers"—Cayugas and Oneidas—were on the "opposite side of the house." The "firekeepers"—Onondagas—would break the tie if the two sides disagreed. If the two sides agreed, the firekeepers could veto the measure, but then the two sides could override the veto. Thus, the governing council was analogous to a two-house legislature and an executive with a limited veto.

The Great Law had elaborate provisions for the selection and obligations of the chiefs who sat on the governing council. Most chiefs were selected by women from extended families that had hereditary power. Thus, these women were permitted to participate in making these important political decisions, although they themselves were not permitted to serve on the council.

The chiefs were obligated to communicate with the people—send messages to them and consider requests from them. The chiefs were expected to tolerate anger and criticism by the people and to reflect "endless patience" and "calm deliberation." The chiefs were to be the people's servants rather than their masters. As such, they were not supposed to accumulate more wealth than the people. (In fact, there was some pressure to give away their material possessions, so they would be poorer than the people.) If the chiefs failed to follow these rules, they could be recalled or impeached.

Philosophical Ideas

The Founders were exceptionally well-educated intellectuals who incorporated philosophical ideas into the Constitution. At a time when the average person did not dream of going to college, a majority of the Founders graduated from college. As learned men, they shared a common library of writers and philosophers.

The framers of the Constitution reflected the ideals of the Enlightenment, a pattern of thought emphasizing the use of reason, rather than tradition or religion, to solve problems; they studied past governments to determine why they had failed in the hope they could apply these lessons to the present.

From all accounts, the framers engaged in a level of debate at the convention that was rare in politics, citing

The Great Law also provided for some natural rights and equality. There was significant separation of church and state. There was no state religion, and the duties of the civil chiefs were distinct from those of the religious leaders. The Great Law upheld freedom of expression in religious and political matters, and it reflected tolerance of different races and national origins. For example, its adoption rules included no restrictions on the basis of race or national origin. Even some Anglo-Americans received full citizenship in the Confederacy.

Thus, in various ways the Iroquois government, unlike the Indian civilizations in Central and South America, reflected characteristics we consider democratic.[2] As one historian concludes, "all these things were part of the American way of life before Columbus landed."[3]

Iroquois Influence on American Government?

In colonial times, the Iroquois occupied land between the English on the Atlantic coast and the French in what is now southern Canada. The Iroquois controlled the only level mountain pass and the best communication and trade route between the English and the French. The Iroquois were the balance of power between these settlers, whose nations were at war with each other.

Britain tried to forge an alliance with the Iroquois. Colonial envoys and Indian chiefs held treaty councils to establish the alliance. As early as 1744 one chief, Canassatego, advised the colonies to

unite, as the Iroquois had, for the colonists' protection (and for the Indians' convenience—to reduce the confusion of dealing with separate colonies). Benjamin Franklin, who served as an envoy and as the printer of the proceedings of the councils, was fascinated by the Iroquois and seemed influenced by Canassatego's advice. He, too, urged the colonies to unite, and he proposed a plan very similar to the Iroquois Confederacy. But the plan was not adopted by the colonies, which fretted that it would deny their individual independence. It was not accepted by the Crown, either, which feared that it would establish the colonies' joint independence from the mother country. The colonies would not unite until the Crown imposed the Stamp Act and other measures two decades later.

Many colonists were intrigued by Iroquois ways. Franklin found a market eager for his accounts of the treaty councils. He printed accounts of thirteen councils in twenty-six years. An official in New York's colonial government published a systematic description of Iroquois government in 1727 and expanded it in 1747. Other officials asked the Iroquois for information about their confederacy's structure.

Over the years, much intermingling between European and Native American cultures took place. (At least one colonial official was adopted by the Mohawks, and another was allowed to serve on their councils and even lead their war parties at times.) Some

Founders admired certain Indian practices and ideas. Besides Franklin, Thomas Jefferson and Thomas Paine, for example, were attracted to the Iroquois' emphasis on natural rights and their restrictions on their leaders' power and wealth. Thus, "the American frontier became a laboratory for democracy precisely at a time when colonial leaders were searching for alternatives to what they regarded as European tyranny and class stratification."[4]

Historians debate whether the Iroquois actually influenced the Founders. The parallels between the Iroquois government and our Declaration of Independence, Articles of Confederation, and Constitution could be coincidental. Political ideas can take root in more than one society simultaneously. But the parallels are striking, and the possibilities are intriguing. The roots of our political ideas might be more numerous and complex than we have assumed.[5]

SOURCE: Bruce E. Johansen, *Forgotten Founders* (Ipswich, Mass.: Gambit, 1982). Additional sources are cited, especially in Chapter 1.
1. Bruce E. Johansen, *Forgotten Founders* (Ipswich, Mass.: Gambit, 1982), 22.
2. Johansen, *Forgotten Founders*, 17–18.
3. Felix Cohen, quoted in ibid., 13.
4. Ibid., xv.
5. At least fragments of evidence suggest that Native Americans influenced European philosophers, such as Locke, Montesquieu, and Rousseau, who in turn influenced the colonists. Some Iroquois chiefs had been to Europe, and the Europeans were as intrigued by their ways as the colonists were. Ibid., 14, 52.

philosophers ranging from the ancient Greeks to the modern British and French. Even when they did not mention them explicitly, their comments seemed to reflect the writings of particular philosophers.

The views of John Locke, a seventeenth-century English philosopher, underlay many of the ideas of the Founders. In fact, his views permeate the Declaration of Independence and Constitution more than those of any

other single person. Locke believed people had **natural rights.** These rights were inherent; they existed from the moment people were born. They were inalienable; they were given by God so they could not be taken away.

The right to property, according to Locke, was one of the most important natural rights. When people worked the land, clearing it and planting it, they mixed their labor with it. This act made the land their property. Although

Numerous constitutional provisions, some obvious and others not, were designed to protect property:

"The Times, Places and Manner of holding Elections for Senators and Representatives, shall be prescribed in each State by the Legislature thereof."	Allows state to set property qualifications to vote.
"The Congress shall have Power . . . To coin Money."	Centralizes currency.
"No State shall . . . emit bills of credit."	Prevents states from printing paper money.
"Congress shall have Power . . . To establish uniform Laws on the subject of Bankruptcies."	Allows Congress to prevent states from relieving debtors of obligation to pay.
"No State shall . . . pass any . . . Law impairing the Obligation of Contracts."	Prevents states from relieving debtors of obligation to pay.
"The United States shall guarantee to every State [protection] against domestic Violence."	Protects states from debtor uprisings.
"Congress shall have Power . . . To provide for calling forth the Militia to execute the Laws of the Union, suppress insurrections."	Protects creditors from debtor uprisings.

Americans had gotten their land through theft from the Indians and through luck from their ancestors, who had gotten it for little or nothing by a royal grant in colonial times, the important thing in this view was what they did with their land. For example, farmers would start with trees and dirt and create wealth from it. Some, due to more work or better luck, would accumulate more property and create more wealth than others. Thus, the right to property would result in significant inequality of wealth. Yet Locke thought it would lead to great productivity for society.[32] This view of property appealed to Americans who saw an abundance of land in the new country.

Locke wrote that people came together to form government through a social contract—an implied agreement between the people and their government—that established a **limited government,** strong enough to protect their rights but not too strong to threaten these rights. This government should not act without the consent of the governed. To make its decisions, this government should follow majority rule. (Locke never resolved the conflict between majority rule and natural rights—that is, between majority rule and some rights for those who disagree with the majority.)

The views of Charles de Montesquieu, an eighteenth-century French philosopher, also influenced the debate at the convention and the provisions of the Constitution. Others had suggested separation of powers before, but Montesquieu refined the concept and added that of checks and balances. Referring to him as "the celebrated Montesquieu," the Founders cited him more than any other thinker.[33] (Presumably, they cited him more than Locke because by this time Locke's views had

so permeated American society that the Founders considered them just "common sense."[34])

The principles of the system of mechanics formulated by Isaac Newton, a British mathematician of the late seventeenth and early eighteenth centuries, also pervaded the provisions of the Constitution. As Newton viewed nature as a machine, so the Founders saw the constitutional structure as a machine, with different parts having different functions and balancing each other. Newton's principle of action and reaction is manifested in the Founders' system of checks and balances. Both the natural environment and the constitutional structure were viewed as self-regulating systems.[35]

Political Experience

Although the Founders were intellectuals, they were also practical politicians. According to one interpretation, they were "first and foremost superb democratic politicians," and the convention was "a nationalist reform caucus which had to operate with great delicacy and skill in a political cosmos full of enemies."[36]

The Founders brought extensive political experience to the convention: Eight had signed the Declaration of Independence; thirty-nine had served in Congress; seven had been governors; many had held other state offices; some had helped write their state constitutions. The framers drew on this experience. For example, while they cited Montesquieu in discussing separation of powers, they also referred to the experience of colonial and state governments that already had some separation of powers.[37] (See also the box "Did the Iroquois Influence the Founders?")

As practical politicians, "no matter what their private dreams might be, they had to take home an acceptable package and defend it—and their own political futures—against predictable attack."[38] So they compromised the difficult issues and ducked the stickiest ones. Ultimately, they pieced together a document that allowed each delegate to return home and announce that his state had won something.

Economic Interests

Historian Charles Beard sparked a lively debate when he published *An Economic Interpretation of the Constitution* in 1913.[39] Beard argued that those with money and investments in manufacturing and shipping dominated the Constitutional Convention and state ratification conventions and that they produced a document that would increase their wealth. (After Beard published his conclusions, an Ohio newspaper proclaimed, "Scavengers, hyena-like, desecrate the graves of the dead patriots we revere."[40]) Later scholars questioned Beard's facts and interpretations, pointing out that support for the Constitution was not based strictly on wealth.[41]

Although some of Beard's specific points do not hold up, his underlying position that the Founders represented an elite that sought to protect its property from the masses seems more valid. The delegates to the Constitutional Convention were an elite. They included prosperous planters, manufacturers, shippers, and lawyers. About one-third were slave owners. Most came from families of prominence and married into other families of prominence. Not all were wealthy, but most were at least well-to-do. Only one, a delegate from Georgia, was a yeoman farmer like most men in the country. In short, "this was a convention of the well-bred, the well-fed, the well-read, and the well-wed."[42]

The Founders supported the right to property. The promise of land and perhaps riches enticed most immigrants to come to America.[43] A desire for freedom from arbitrary taxes and trade restrictions spurred some colonists to fight in the Revolution.[44] And the inability of the government under the Articles of Confederation to provide a healthy economy prompted the Founders to convene the Constitutional Convention. They apparently agreed with Madison that "the first object of government" is to protect property.[45]

The Founders' emphasis on property was not as elitist as it might seem, however. Land was plentiful, and, with westward expansion, even more would be available. Already most men were middle-class farmers who owned some property. Many who owned no property could foresee the day when they would, so most wanted to protect property.

The Founders diverged from the farmers in their desire to protect other property in addition to land, such as wealth and credit. Of the fifty-five delegates, forty

"Religious freedom is my immediate goal, but my long range plan is to go into real estate"

were owners of government bonds that had depreciated under the Articles, and twenty-four were moneylenders.[46] So the delegates included provisions to protect commerce, including imports and exports, contracts, and debts, and provisions to regulate currency, bankruptcy, and taxes. (See the box "Constitutional Provisions Protecting Property.")

Political scientists and historians disagree about which of these three influences on the Founders—philosophical, political, or economic—was most important. Actually, the influences are difficult to separate because they reinforce each other; the framers' ideas point to the same sort of constitution that their political experience and economic interests do.[47]

Ratification of the Constitution

The Constitution specified that ratification would occur through conventions in the states and that the document would take effect with approval of just nine states. These procedures were illegal. According to the Articles of Confederation, which was still in effect, any changes had to be approved by all thirteen states. However, the framers feared that the Constitution would not be supported in some states.

Indeed, ratification was uncertain. Many people opposed the Constitution, and a lively campaign against it appeared in newspapers, pamphlets, and mass meetings.

Knowing opponents would charge them with setting up a national government to dominate the state governments, those who supported the Constitution ingeniously adopted the name **Federalists** to emphasize a real division of power between the national and state governments.

They dubbed their opponents **Anti-Federalists** to imply that they did not want a division of power between the governments. (See the box "The Federalist Papers.")

The Anti-Federalists faulted the Constitution for lacking a bill of rights. The Constitution did contain some protection for individual rights, such as the provision that the writ of habeas corpus, which protects against arbitrary arrest and detention, cannot be suspended except during rebellion or invasion, and the provision that a criminal defendant has a right to a jury trial. But the framers made no effort to include most of the rights people believed they had, because most states already had a bill of rights in their own constitutions. The framers also thought that by fragmenting power no branch could become strong enough to deny individual rights. Yet critics demanded provisions protecting various rights of criminal defendants and freedom of the press. In response, the Federalists promised to propose amendments guaranteeing these rights as soon as the government began.

The Anti-Federalists also criticized the Constitution for other reasons. Localists at heart, they were wary of entrusting power to officials far away. They correctly claimed that republics historically worked only in small geographic areas where the population was more homogeneous and the officials were closer to the people. They worried that the central government, to function effectively, would accumulate too much power and the presidency would become a monarchy or Congress an aristocracy. One delegate to the Massachusetts convention blasted the Federalists:

These lawyers, and men of learning and moneyed men, that talk so finely, and gloss over matters so smoothly, to make us poor illiterate people swallow down the pill, expect to get into Congress themselves; they expect to . . . get all the power and all the money into their own hands, and then they will swallow up all us little folks . . . just as the whale swallowed up Jonah![48]

But the Anti-Federalists had no alternative plan. They were divided; some wanted to amend the Articles of Confederation, while others wanted to reject both the Articles and the Constitution in favor of some yet undetermined form of government. Their lack of unity on an alternative was instrumental in their inability to win support.[49]

Within six months, nine states ratified the new Constitution, allowing the new government, with George Washington as president, to begin in 1788. Within one year the remaining states approved the Constitution.

Changing the Constitution

The framers expected their document to last; Madison wrote, "We have framed a constitution that will probably be still around when there are 196 million people."[50] Yet because the framers realized it would need some changes, they drafted a Constitution that can be changed either formally by constitutional amendment or informally by judicial interpretation or political practice. In doing so, they left a legacy for later governments. "The example of changing a Constitution, by assembling the wise men of the state, instead of assembling armies," Jefferson noted, "will be worth as much to the world as the former examples we had given them."[51]

By Constitutional Amendment

That the Articles of Confederation could be amended only by a unanimous vote of the states posed an almost insurmountable barrier to any amendment at all. The framers of the Constitution made sure this experience would not repeat itself. Yet they did not make amendment easy; the procedures, while not requiring unanimity, do require widespread agreement.

Procedures The procedures for amendment entail action by both the national government and the state governments. Amendments can be proposed in either of two ways: by a two-thirds vote of both houses of Congress or by a national convention called by Congress at the request of two-thirds of the state legislatures. Congress then specifies which way amendments must be ratified—either by three-fourths of the state legislatures or by ratifying conventions in three-fourths of the states. Among these avenues, the usual route has been proposal by Congress and ratification by state legislatures.

Amendments In the first Congress under the Constitution, the Federalists fulfilled their promise to support a bill of rights. Madison drafted the amendments, Congress proposed them, and the states ratified ten of them in 1791. This **Bill of Rights** includes freedom of expression—speech, press, assembly, and religion (First Amendment). It also includes numerous rights for those accused of crimes—protection against unreasonable searches and seizures (Fourth), protection against compulsory self-incrimination (Fifth), guarantee of due process of law (Fifth), the right to counsel and a jury trial in criminal cases (Sixth), and protection against excessive bail and fines, and cruel and unusual punishment (Eighth). It also includes a jury trial in civil cases (Seventh).

In addition to these major rights, the Bill of Rights includes two amendments that grew out of the colonial experience with Great Britain—the right to bear arms for a militia (Second) and the right not to have soldiers quartered in homes during peacetime (Third). The Bill of Rights also includes two general amendments—a statement that the listing of these rights does not mean these are the only ones people have (Ninth) and a statement that the powers not given to the national government are reserved to the states (Tenth).

Among the other seventeen amendments to the Constitution, the strongest theme is the expansion of citizenship rights:[52]

- Abolition of slavery (Thirteenth, 1865)
- Equal protection, due process of law (Fourteenth, 1868)
- Right to vote for black men (Fifteenth, 1870)
- Direct election of senators (Seventeenth, 1913)
- Right to vote for women (Nineteenth, 1920)
- Right to vote in presidential elections for District of Columbia residents (Twenty-third, 1960)
- Abolition of poll tax in federal elections (Twenty-fourth, 1964)
- Right to vote for persons eighteen and older (Twenty-sixth, 1971)

Recently, two amendments proposed by Congress were not ratified by the states. One would have provided equal rights for women (this amendment will be discussed in Chapter 15), and the other would have given congressional representation to the District of Columbia, as though it were a state.

These and other recent amendments have had time limits for ratification—usually seven years—set by Congress. But an amendment preventing members of Congress from giving themselves a midterm pay raise, written by Madison and passed by Congress in 1789, had no time limit. Once Michigan ratified it in 1992, it reached the three-fourths mark and became the Twenty-seventh Amendment.

Although the Constitution expressly provides for change by amendment, its ambiguity about some subjects and silence about others virtually guarantee change by interpretation and practice as well.

By Judicial Interpretation

If there is disagreement about what the Constitution means, who is to interpret it? Although the Constitution does not say, the judicial branch has taken on this role. To decide disputes before them, the courts must determine what the relevant provisions of the Constitution mean. By saying the provisions mean one thing rather than another, the courts can, in effect, change the Constitution. Woodrow Wilson called the Supreme Court "a constitutional convention in continuous session." The Court has interpreted the Constitution in ways that bring about the same results as new amendments. (Chapters 13, 14, and 15 provide many examples.)

By Political Practice

Political practice has accounted for some very important changes. These include the rise of political parties and the demise of the Electoral College as an independent body. They also include the development of the cabinet to advise the president and the development of the committee system to operate the two houses of Congress. (Chapters 7, 8, and 10 explain these changes.)

The Founders would be surprised to learn that only seventeen amendments, aside from the Bill of Rights,

INTERROGATING TERRORISTS

The war on terrorism, like past wars, raises questions about the viability of constitutional rights: Can we wage effective war and still maintain civil liberties? Americans have accepted restricted access to government buildings and national monuments and heightened screening at airports, but these policies are more of an inconvenience than a threat to civil liberties. Would Americans accept other policies that would pose a risk to civil liberties? Should they?

Consider the problem of interrogating captured terrorist suspects. Under our law, when police interrogate criminal suspects, they must advise the suspects of their rights to remain silent and have counsel, and they must stop the questioning whenever the suspects express a desire to exercise these rights. Any statements by the suspects are supposed to be voluntary rather than coerced. Torture and threats of physical harm to the suspects or their relatives are forbidden. No matter how heinous the crime or depraved the criminal, we believe that torture and threats of physical harm violate human dignity. In fact, torture and threats of

physical harm, including bringing a weapon into the interrogation room, are contrary to international law.[1] So are depriving suspects of food or water or injecting them with drugs to coerce information.[2]

In addition to philosophical objections to these tactics, there are practical objections. Officials might get the wrong person and force him to say what they want to hear even if it is not true. Then they have unreliable information. Or officials might use brutal methods that damage or kill him.

Despite these restrictions, police interrogation of suspected criminals is often successful (as Chapter 14 explains). Military officials, like police officers, try to put their suspects at a disadvantage. In the war on terrorism, military officials sometimes isolate a suspect from other detainees until the suspect becomes dependent on his interrogator for human contact. Then being kind or offering a cigarette to a smoker can produce a bit of useful information. Officials sometimes use more extreme methods, such as lowering the temperature of the suspect's cell and depriving him of sleep. They reduce his food and later increase

it as a reward for talking.[3] But these methods do not work on all suspects.

Officials have tried to use inducements, including money, jobs, lenient sentences, and new identities in the witness protection program, but these offers have been spurned. The terrorists are committed to their cause and steeled to their death, even seeking "martyrdom." In addition, an FBI agent involved in the investigation noted, "We are known for humanitarian treatment, so basically we are stuck."[4]

Middle Eastern governments threatened by Islamic extremists, from Israel to the "moderate" Arab states, have found that torture and threats to harm their family are the only methods that prod suspected terrorists into talking. Today torture may involve a combination of drug injections and sleep deprivation. "It's not pulling out fingernails," an American military official said, "but it's pretty brutal."[5]

So what should the United States do when officials want to interrogate al Qaeda suspects? Bring the suspects to the United States and do whatever is necessary? Bring the suspects to an American military base or prison camp

---

have been adopted in over two hundred years. In part this is due to their wisdom, but in part it is due to changes in judicial interpretation and political practice, which have combined to create a "living Constitution."

Impact of the Civil War and the Great Depression

The two most significant events in American history, following the Founding of the country, were the Civil War in the 1860s and the Great Depression in the 1930s. These two events had such an important impact on the Constitution that it would be inadequate, even inaccurate, for us to refer only to the Founders when we explain the Constitution.[53]

Here we will briefly sketch the impact of the Civil War and the Great Depression on the Constitution. Later chapters will further elaborate on these developments.

The Civil War and Reconstruction

The Civil War, from 1861 through 1865, and Reconstruction, from the end of the war through 1876, constituted a "second American Revolution."[54] After all the bullets and bayonets, the bloodletting and scorched earth, more than six hundred thousand blue and gray soldiers lay in graves—one of every seven men between fifteen and thirty—and parts of the South lay in waste. The North's victory preserved the Union, but it did far more than this: It also altered the Constitution—in the minds of the people and in formal amendments to the document.

outside of the United States, such as Guantanamo Bay, Cuba, and do whatever is necessary? Either way would involve American agents engaging in unsavory practices, although the latter would not be on American soil. Does this matter? Even if it does, should we forsake our principles and violate international law? Would we risk a step backward in the progress of Western civilization? Would we risk becoming like the people, who disregard law and devalue life, who are our enemies?

In addition to the legal and ethical concerns, one American military official said, "We've been out of that business for so long that it's best handled by others."[6]

In fact, since 1993, the United States has arranged with other countries to interrogate suspected terrorists for us. In a procedure called "rendition," the United States seizes suspects in foreign countries and whisks them away to other countries whose intelligence services have ties with the Central Intelligence Agency (CIA). Islamic extremists have been seized from countries in Africa, Asia, and the Balkans and taken to countries such as Egypt and Jordan.

The transfers have been made in secret, with unmarked planes in remote corners of airports, at night. The process ignores legal formalities, such as extradition procedures. Sometimes it defies national laws; six suspects were taken from Bosnia even though the Bosnian Supreme Court ordered them released. The secrecy reduces court battles and minimizes the publicity that could tip off suspects' comrades or inflame public opinion, especially where the government feels threatened by rebellious groups with numerous sympathizers. An official of Indonesia, which has a huge Muslim population, said, "We can't be seen cooperating too closely with the United States."[7] Since September 11, the United States has employed this procedure for "dozens" of suspects. According to one American official, it is happening "all the time" now.[8]

Is this procedure of rendition more acceptable than having American agents use torture and make threats? Does it reduce our culpability because it gets other countries to do our dirty work? Or does it just let us pretend, to ourselves and the world, that we have clean hands?

Or are all of these concerns beside the point in a time of war? Despite the restrictions of domestic law and international law, should the existence of war justify the use of extreme methods? Supreme Court Justice Robert Jackson said, "The Constitution is not a suicide pact." He could have said the same about international law. But does this mean the government should set aside these inconvenient interrogation limitations anytime there is a national security threat? Once we cross the line, where do we stop?

1. According to both treaty law, to which the United States is a party, and customary law, which is binding on all states. A permanent International Criminal Court to try persons for war crimes was established in 2002.
2. Eric Schmitt, "There Are Ways to Make Them Talk," New York Times, June 16, 2002, WK1.
3. Michael Elliott, "The Next Wave," Time, June 24, 2002, 25.
4. Walter Pincus, "How Can We Make Them Talk?" Washington Post National Weekly Edition, October 29–November 4, 2001, 31.
5. Jodie Morse, "How Do We Make Him Talk?" Time, April 15, 2002, 92.
6. Ibid.
7. Rajiv Chandrasekaran and Peter Finn, "Interrogating Terrorist Suspects, 'in a Way We Can't Do on U.S. Soil,'" Lincoln Journal-Star, March 12, 2002.
8. Ibid.

Although the North's leader, President Abraham Lincoln, a Republican, held views that would be considered racist today (he believed that black people were inherently inferior and that they should emigrate from the United States[55]), he despised slavery, because it deprived persons of their inalienable rights to life, liberty, and the pursuit of happiness promised by the Declaration of Independence. But efforts to abolish slavery were constrained by the political climate, and Lincoln was a practical politician. Before the war, he seemed willing to allow slavery to continue in the southern states, though not to extend into any new state; and at the beginning of the war, he seemed concerned only to preserve the Union. But after one year of the war, he decided that this goal was not enough.[56] Abolitionist sentiment was spreading in the North, providing Lincoln with the opportunity to lead efforts to abolish slavery as well as preserve the Union. In the process, he helped reinvent America.

Emancipation Proclamation

The **Emancipation Proclamation** offered the promise of a new constitution. President Lincoln announced it in September 1862 and ordered it to take effect in January 1863. The document proclaimed that the slaves "shall be . . . forever free" in the Confederate states where the Union army was not in control. Its language limited its sweep, for it exempted those parts of the Confederate states where the Union army was in control and also the slave states that remained loyal to the Union (Delaware, Kentucky, Maryland, and Missouri). And, despite its language, it could not be enforced in the parts of the Confederate states where the Union army was not in control. Thus, as a legal document, the proclamation was problematic. However, as a symbolic measure, it was successful. The proclamation made clear that the war was not just to preserve the Union anymore but to abolish slavery as well. The announcement captured people's imagination. Between the announcement and the date it was to take effect, the proclamation created so much suspense, according to one historian, that "it had assumed the significance of one of the great documents of all times."[57] When slaves heard about it, many left their plantation, and some joined the Union army. The result sowed confusion in the South and denied a reliable labor force for the region.[58]

Gettysburg Address

President Lincoln's **Gettysburg Address** became the preamble of the new constitution.[59] The battle at Gettysburg, Pennsylvania, in 1863, was a Union victory and the turning point in the Civil War. Lincoln was invited to deliver "a few appropriate remarks" during the dedication of the battlefield where many had fallen. Lincoln was not the main speaker, and his speech was not long. While the main speaker took two hours, explaining the battle and reciting the names of the leaders and even some of their soldiers, Lincoln took two minutes to give a 268-word speech. (He spoke so briefly that the photographer, with his clumsy equipment and its slow exposure, failed to get a single photograph.) Lincoln used the occasion to advance his ideal of equality.

He began: "Four score and seven [eighty-seven] years ago our fathers brought forth on this continent, a new nation, conceived in liberty and dedicated to the proposition that all men are created equal." Here Lincoln referred not to the Constitution of 1787 but to the Declaration of Independence of 1776. For Lincoln, the Constitution had abandoned the principle of equality that the Declaration had promised. He sought to resurrect this principle.

Lincoln did not mention slavery or the Emancipation Proclamation, which were divisive. A shrewd politician, he wanted people to focus on the Declaration, which was revered.

Lincoln concluded by addressing "the great task remaining before us . . . that we here highly resolve that these dead shall not have died in vain, that this nation, under God, shall have a new birth of freedom, and that government of the people, by the people, for the people shall not perish from the earth." This phrase, which Lincoln made famous, was borrowed from a speaker at an antislavery convention.[60] It meant government elected by all the people, to serve all the people.[61] Lincoln's conclusion reinforced his introduction; both emphasized equality.

Although he gave a brief speech, Lincoln used the word *nation* five times, including the phrase "a new nation" once. His purpose was not to encourage support for the Union but to urge people to think of the nation as a whole, its identity now forged in a bloody war of brother against brother, rather than as simply a collection of individual states with their own interests.[62]

Thus, the president essentially added the Declaration's promise of equality to the Constitution, and he substituted his vision of a unified nation for the Founders' precarious arrangement of a balance of power between the nation and the states. According to one his-

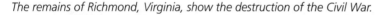

The remains of Richmond, Virginia, show the destruction of the Civil War.

Corbis-Bettmann

torian, "he performed one of the most daring acts of open-air sleight-of-hand ever witnessed by the unsuspecting. . . . The crowd departed with a new thing in its ideological luggage, that new constitution Lincoln had substituted for the one they brought with them."[63]

The Gettysburg Address was heard by an audience of perhaps fifteen thousand, but its language was spread through word of mouth and newspapers, and eventually by politicians and teachers. It was read and repeated, and sometimes memorized, by generations of schoolchildren. Although some critics at the time perceived what Lincoln was attempting—the *Chicago Times* quoted the Constitution to the president and charged him with betraying the document he swore to uphold—most citizens came to accept Lincoln's addition. His speech, which has been called "the best political address" in the country's history, thus became "the secular prayer of the postbellum American Republic."[64] (The speech is included in the appendix.)

The Reconstruction Amendments

If the Gettysburg Address became the preamble of the new constitution, the **Reconstruction Amendments** became the body of this new constitution. These three amendments, adopted from 1865 through 1870, began to implement the promise of equality and the vision of a unified nation rather than a collection of individual states.

The Thirteenth Amendment abolished slavery, essentially constitutionalizing the Emancipation Proclamation. This amendment focused on the wrongs committed by private persons. As such, it reflected a new perspective toward government—not as a threat to peoples' liberties, as the original Constitution and the Bill of Rights did, but as a guarantor of peoples' freedom. Whereas the original Constitution and the Bill of Rights are preoccupied with freedom from government, the Thirteenth Amendment is concerned with freedom from exploitation by other persons.

The Fourteenth Amendment declared that all persons born or naturalized in the United States are citizens, overturning the Supreme Court's ruling before the Civil War that blacks, whether slave or free, could not be citizens.[65] The Fourteenth Amendment also included the equal protection clause, which requires states to treat persons equally, and the due process clause, which requires states to treat persons fairly. The equal protection clause would become the primary legal means to end discrimination, while the due process clause would become the primary legal means to give persons the full benefit of the Bill of Rights.[66] This amendment, one legal scholar observes, was "a revolutionary change. The states were no longer the autonomous sovereigns that they thought they were when they claimed the right of secession. They were now, in

fact, servants of their people. [They] existed to guarantee due process and equal justice for all."[67]

The Fifteenth Amendment provided the right to vote to blacks. Because women could not vote at the time, the amendment essentially provided the right to vote to black men. This amendment initiated a trend of democratizing the Constitution by extending the right to vote. Of the ten succeeding amendments added after this one (not counting the Eighteenth, which established Prohibition, or the Twenty-first, which repealed the Eighteenth), five expanded the right to vote.

As important as the substantive content of these amendments was a procedural provision authorizing Congress to have the power to enforce them. That is, the amendments gave Congress broad power, beyond the power the original Constitution granted Congress, to pass new laws to reach the goals of the amendments. Consequently, the federal government would come to oversee, even intervene in, the policies of state and local governments to make sure these governments did not disregard the guarantees of the amendments. These amendments initiated a trend of federalizing the Constitution by increasing the power of Congress.[68] Of the ten succeeding amendments added after these three, five included this provision.

President Lincoln initiated the Thirteenth Amendment, and the Radical Republicans who controlled Congress after Lincoln's assassination initiated the Fourteenth and Fifteenth Amendments. There was a passionate national debate. Ultimately, the public supported the amendments. Although most Americans, northerners as well as southerners, were racists, many were inspired by Lincoln or propelled by the war to support greater equality. They elected, and reelected, supporters of the amendments to Congress.[69]

The net results of the Reconstruction Amendments were to promote equality and to shift power from the states to the federal government.

During Reconstruction, the Union army occupied the South and enforced the amendments and congressional laws implementing them. But white southerners resisted, and eventually white northerners grew weary of the struggle. At the same time, there was a desire for healing between the two regions and lingering feelings for continuity with the past. In 1876, the two parties struck a deal to withdraw the Union army and to allow the southern states to govern themselves again. The entrenched attitudes of white southerners prompted them to establish segregation and discrimination in place of slavery, thus preventing blacks from enjoying their new rights. Therefore, the new constitution would not really be enforced until the 1950s and 1960s, when the civil rights movement, Supreme Court rulings, presidential initiatives, and congressional acts would converge to give effect to the ideal of racial equality. In the meantime, the new constitution would lay, in our collective conscious, as an unfulfilled constitution, occasionally emerging to foster greater equality.[70]

The Great Depression and New Deal

The Great Depression began when the stock market crashed in 1929. Wealthy people lost their investments, and business activity declined. Ordinary people lost their jobs, with a quarter of them becoming unemployed. Investors lost their savings when many banks collapsed. President Franklin Roosevelt, a Democrat, was elected in 1932. He initiated an ambitious program, heralded as "a new deal for the American people," to stimulate the economy and to help the people who were suffering. His program and his administration came to be known as the **New Deal.**

This era also altered the Constitution—not by formal amendments but through Supreme Court rulings and political practice. In the process, it changed the minds of the people.[71] As a result, we replaced our small, limited government, as envisioned by the Founders, with a big, activist government.

Supreme Court Rulings

In the late nineteenth and early twentieth centuries, a laissez-faire economic philosophy was popular in the country and reflected in governmental policies. According to this philosophy, government should not interfere in the economy. Although government could *aid* businesses, at least it should not *regulate* them.[72] People who believed this philosophy thought it would create a robust and efficient economy. The industrialization of the time, producing an array of new products for consumers and an increase in personal wealth for owners, seemed to confirm their expectations. But it also led to negative consequences especially for employees, who were forced to labor in harsh, even dangerous, conditions for long hours and little pay. Many pressed government to address these problems. But when Congress and state legislatures passed laws to regulate child labor, maximum hours of work, and minimum wages for work, the Supreme Court, following the traditional philosophy, usually declared the laws unconstitutional. Then when Congress passed laws to implement President Roosevelt's recovery program, a majority of the Court often declared these laws unconstitutional as well. The impasse reached a climax in 1935 and 1936 when the Court invalidated twelve laws that had been proposed by the president and passed by Congress. The Court's resistance made clear that the New Deal reforms were not simply fine-tuning governmental policy toward the economy but were overhauling it.[73] In response to the Court's resistance, members of Congress introduced thirty-nine constitutional amendments to reverse the Court's rulings.

After Roosevelt was resoundingly reelected in 1936, intense pressure from the president, Congress, and the public prompted two justices who had voted against government regulation of business to switch sides and vote for such regulation in 1937.[74] One case clearly illustrates the Court's about-face. Farmers had produced crop surpluses, which drove down the prices. The government sought to reduce the surpluses in order to drive up the prices. One small farmer in Ohio was allowed by the Department of Agriculture, under a law passed by Congress, to plant eleven acres of wheat, but he chose to plant twenty-three acres. When he was cited for violating the law, he said it should not apply to him because his farm was very small. He did not sell any of the wheat—his family and farm animals consumed all of it—so he said he did not affect market prices. But now, after the switch in 1937, the Court ruled unanimously against him.[75] Thus, the Court allowed the government to extend its reach far beyond what was thought permissible just a few years before.

These transformative rulings created a "constitutional revolution."[76] They took the place of formal amendments to the Constitution, which were no longer necessary once the Court acquiesced to the policies of the president and Congress. As a result, government could regulate businesses when the public believed that regulation would be beneficial.

Political Practice

Before the Depression, Washington had been "a sleepy southern town," in the eyes of reporters.[77] When Roosevelt took office, he was uncertain exactly what to do, but he was willing to experiment, and he did believe he had a mandate from the people, who had rejected the incumbent president, Herbert Hoover, and his administration. Roosevelt's personality and his ambitious ideas attracted many more people—hundreds of thousands of people—some simply relieved to find a job, but others excited to work for the government. These reformers brought new ideas, even radical ideas, that would receive consideration and perhaps acceptance in the depths of the Depression. As federal efforts to provide relief and regulation spread through the country, many other people got jobs in federal offices outside Washington.

Within six years of Roosevelt's taking office, the number of federal workers in the District of Columbia had more than doubled,[78] the number of federal workers in the country had almost doubled, and the size of the federal budget had almost doubled.[79] In the process, the scope of the federal government had expanded tremendously. In short, we got big government and activist government in just a handful of years. These changes were so dramatic that one political scientist has said they created a "second American republic."[80]

Roosevelt's exuberance and experimentation had given people hope. As the country gradually pulled out of the Depression (though the country would not fully recover until the economic activity generated by World War II would provide the final boost), people gave Roosevelt credit, electing him to an unprecedented four terms and returning Democrats to Congress to support him.[81] Ever since, Americans, albeit to different degrees, have expected the government to tackle society's problems. While sometimes mouthing the language of the Founders—for example, Thomas Jefferson's assertion, "That government is best which governs least"—they usually have accepted the reality of the government that was expanded during the Depression.[82]

These changes during the Depression would lay the foundation for the government of the 1960s, which would promote the equality advanced during the Civil War. Without a powerful government pushing for change, the entrenched attitudes supporting segregation and discrimination would not have been overcome.

National Archives, Courtesy of the Franklin D. Roosevelt Library (NLR-PHOCO-A-64371)

During the Depression, many people who lost their job lost their ability to put food on the table. Breadlines and soup kitchens were common.

A Combination of Constitutions

As a result of President Lincoln and the Radical Republicans in the 1860s and 1870s, and President Roosevelt and the New Deal Democrats in the 1930s and 1940s, our government is very different than the one the Founders bequeathed us.[83] Later generations of Americans made the eighteenth-century Constitution work in the nineteenth century and then they made it work in the twentieth century—by remaking that Constitution. Changes in the nineteenth century added the concept of equality and elevated the national government over the state governments. Changes in the twentieth century transformed a relatively small, limited government into a very large, activist government.

The original Constitution and the remade Constitution reflect competing visions. Should we emphasize liberty or equality? Should we demand individuals to solve their own problems or ask government to help them? Americans have not reconciled these visions. Sometimes we cling to the Founders' Constitution; other times we embrace the post–Civil War and post-Depression Constitution. In political debates, politicians, commentators, or citizens take positions without articulating, perhaps without even realizing, that these positions hearken to the Founders' Constitution, while opponents espouse views that rely on the post–Civil War and post-Depression Constitution. Thus, the two constitutions coexist, sometimes uneasily, in our minds and in government policies.[84] As a consequence of our history, then, we actually have a combination of constitutions.

Conclusion: Does the Constitution Allow Government to Be Responsive?

The Constitution established a government that has survived for over two centuries. In this document, the Founders set forth a mechanism to govern a vast territory and to provide for majority rule while allowing minority rights. This government has enabled more people to live in liberty and in prosperity than the people of any nation before or since.[85]

Americans have been grateful, venerating the Founders and embracing the Constitution as a secular Bible. Citizens consult it for guidance and cite it for support at the same time they debate the meaning of its provisions.

The Constitution has proved so popular that many countries have copied parts of it. The Kenyan constitution speaks of "freedom of expression," the Costa Rican gives the "right to petition," and the German says that "all persons shall be equal before the law." Officials and groups in Eastern European countries, emerging from communist governments, and South Africa, transforming its apartheid regime, considered provisions in our Constitution as they changed theirs.[86]

The brevity of our Constitution remains unique. With just eighty-nine sentences, it is far shorter than those of other countries. Because it is short, it is necessarily general; because it is general, it is necessarily ambiguous; because it is ambiguous, it is necessarily open to interpretation. This allows the Constitution to be changed not only through formal amendments, which are time-consuming and difficult, but through judicial rulings and political practices as well.

Although it is common to consider the Founders geniuses and later Americans merely followers, Thomas Jefferson at least had a more balanced view. Late in life, he observed:

> Some men look at constitutions with sanctimonious reverence, and deem them like the ark of the covenant, too sacred to be touched. They ascribe to the men of the preceding age a wisdom more than human, and suppose what they did to be beyond amendment. I knew that age well; I belonged to it, and labored with it. It deserved well of its country. It was very like the present, but without the experience of the present; and forty years of experience in government is worth a century of book-reading; and this they would say themselves, were they to rise from the dead.[87]

Indeed, the Founders left important problems unresolved for succeeding generations. Most notable was slavery and the treatment of African Americans. Also troublesome was the uncertain relationship between the nation and the states.

Later Americans would have to resolve these problems, and in the process they, too, would contribute to the Constitution. As we have seen, succeeding generations remade the Constitution especially in the wake of the Civil War and the Great Depression, and they remade it more than many realize.

But most of the original Constitution remains. We have kept the basic structure of government and the underlying fragmentation of power. Although most of the original Constitution has been responsive enough to survive, is it responsive enough to allow us to solve our problems?

Intended to construct a government responsive to the masses of people to a limited extent, the Constitution set up a republic, which granted the people the right to elect some representatives who would make their laws. This gave the people more say in government than people in other countries enjoyed at the time.

But the Constitution was intended to construct a government unresponsive to the masses of people to a large extent. It was expected to filter the public's passions and purify their selfish desires. Consequently, the Founders limited participation in government, allowing people to vote only for members of the House of Representatives—not for members of the Senate or the president.

Moreover, the Founders fragmented the power of government. Federalism, separation of powers, and checks and balances combine to make it difficult for any one group to capture all of government. Instead, one faction might control one branch, another faction another branch, and so on, with the result a standoff. Then the factions must compromise to accomplish anything.

Since the time of the Founding, changes in the Constitution, whether by amendment, interpretation, or practice, have expanded opportunities for participation in government. But the changes have done little to modify the fragmentation of power, which remains the primary legacy of the Founders.

This structure has prevented many abuses of power, though it has not always worked. During the Vietnam War, for example, one branch—the presidency—exercised vast power while the others acquiesced.

This structure also has provided the opportunity for one branch to pick up the slack when the others became sluggish. The overlapping of powers ensured by checks and balances allows every branch to act on virtually every issue it wants to. In the 1950s, President Eisenhower and Congress were reluctant to push for civil rights, but the Supreme Court did so by declaring segregation unconstitutional.

But the system's very advantage has become its primary disadvantage. In their efforts to fragment power so that no branch could accumulate too much, the Founders divided power to the point where the branches sometimes cannot wield enough. In their efforts to build a government that requires a national majority to act, they built one that allows a small minority to block action. This problem has become increasingly acute as society has become increasingly complex. Like a mechanical device that operates only when all of its parts function in harmony, the system moves only when there is consensus or compromise. Consensus is rare in a large heterogeneous society; compromise is common, but it requires a long time as well as the realization by competing interests that they cannot achieve much of what they want without compromise. Even then, compromise often results in only a partial solution.

At best, the system moves inefficiently and incrementally. At worst it moves hardly at all; the Constitution has established a government that is slow to respond to change. One political scientist characterizes it as a "negative, do-nothing system."[88] Although other political scientists consider this characterization an exaggeration, virtually all agree that the system is structured to preserve the status quo and to respond to the groups that want to maintain it.

Although the changes made in the wake of the Depression brought us big, activist government, they did not negate all of our historical aversion to such government. We still have more limited government than other advanced industrialized countries. Our taxes are lower, contrary to what many Americans think, and governmental policies in numerous areas, such as health care, welfare, and transportation, are less ambitious.[89] This, of course, limits our ability to address our problems.

Yet some political scientists believe the American people actually prefer a system that is hard to move. Because the people are suspicious of government, they may be reluctant to let one party dominate it and use it to advance that party's policies. In surveys, many people—a quarter to a third of those polled—say they think it is good for one party to control the presidency and the other to control Congress.[90] In presidential and congressional elections, more than a quarter of the voters split their ticket between the two parties.[91] As a result, between 1968 and 2002, opposing parties controlled the executive branch and at least one house in the legislative branch for all but six years.

Another disadvantage of the fragmentation of power is that it makes it difficult, if not impossible, for citizens to pin responsibility on particular officials and parties for the decisions and policies of government. "If no individual or institution possesses the authority to act without the consent of everybody else in the room, then nobody is ever at fault if anything goes wrong. Congress can blame the president, the president can blame the Congress or the Supreme Court, the Supreme Court can blame the Mexicans or the weather in Ohio."[92] If citizens cannot determine who is responsible for what, they cannot hold them accountable and make them responsive. In this way, the fragmentation of power reduces the responsiveness of government.

Era of confrontation . . . at home

© 1974 Engelhardt in the *St. Louis Post-Dispatch*

EPILOGUE

The President Complies in the Case of the Confidential Tapes

hief Justice Warren Burger announced the unanimous decision in the case of *United States v. Nixon:* The president must turn over the tapes.[93] The Court acknowledged the existence of executive privilege in general but rejected it in this situation because another court needed the information for an upcoming trial and because the information did not relate to national security.

The Court emphasized that courts would determine the legitimacy of claims of executive privilege, not presidents, as Nixon wanted. Because of separation of powers, Nixon argued, neither the judicial nor legislative branch should involve itself in this executive decision.

However, this president, who as a high school student in Whittier, California, had won a prize from the Kiwanis Club for the best oration on the Constitution, ignored the system of checks and balances, which limits separation of powers. In this case, checks and balances authorized the courts to conduct criminal trials of the president's aides and Congress to conduct impeachment proceedings against the president. To do so, the courts and Congress needed the information on the tapes.

Within days of the Court's decision, the House Judiciary Committee passed three articles of impeachment. These charged Nixon with obstruction of justice, by covering up a crime; defiance of the committee's

subpoenas for the tapes; and abuse of power. (The committee also considered an article of impeachment for cheating on his income taxes, but members decided that this was a personal matter, rather than a governmental matter, and as such not appropriate for impeachment.[94])

Despite the charges, some Republicans maintained there was no "smoking gun"—that is, no clear evidence of crimes. They said the impeachment effort was strictly political.

Regardless, Nixon's support in Congress dwindled, and he found himself caught between a rock and a hard place: Releasing the tapes would furnish more evidence for impeachment, but not releasing them would spur impeachment. He reportedly considered disregarding the decision but, after twelve days of weighing his options, complied with the order.

Releasing the tapes did reveal a smoking gun. Although the tapes did not show that Nixon had participated in planning the break-in, they did show that he had participated in covering it up. When the burglars blackmailed the administration, Nixon approved paying them hush money. He ordered the head of his reelection committee to "stonewall it" and "cover up." He and an aide formulated a plan to have the CIA thwart the FBI in its investigation of the scandal. When his top aides were subpoenaed to appear before the grand jury, he encouraged them to lie.

In addition to this evidence of crimes, the tapes revealed profanity, vulgarity, and derogatory remarks about women, Catholics, Jews, blacks, Hispanics, and various ethnic groups. ("The Italians . . . they're not like us . . . they smell different, they look different, act different. . . . Of course, the trouble is . . . you can't find one that is honest."[95]) Such language repelled the public and undercut the image Nixon had tried to project.

As his presidency came collapsing all around him, White House insiders began telling people privately that Nixon was dazed, like a "wind-up doll" or a "madman." They said that he was drinking heavily, "going bananas," talking to portraits of past presidents, and showing other signs of cracking under the strain. Some worried that he was considering suicide. One day he said to his chief of staff, General Alexander Haig, "You fellows, in your business [the army], you have a way of handling problems like this. Somebody leaves a pistol in the drawer." He paused, then added sadly, "I don't have a pistol." Afterward, Haig notified Nixon's doctors and had Nixon's sleeping pills and tranquilizers taken away.[96]

When it became clear that public opinion would force the House to impeach him and the Senate to remove him, Nixon decided to resign. On August 9, 1974—just seventeen days after the Supreme Court's ruling—he became the first American president to do so. Vice President Gerald Ford became the new president.

Although the smoking gun had been found, some people thought Nixon should not have been driven from office. But Watergate was not just a break-in. It was a series of acts, more than can be detailed here, to subvert the Constitution and democratic elections. As the magnitude of these acts came to light, Nixon lost some support. Then, as the cover-up of these acts came to light, he lost even more support. He had campaigned for president on a platform calling for "law and order" and had sworn an oath promising to "take care that the laws be faithfully executed." When Watergate revelations appeared in the media, he had proclaimed his innocence. Ultimately, the hypocrisy and the lying became too much for the public to stomach. Nixon no longer could lead the public he had misled for so long.

Despite depression and cynicism about the scandal, many people saw that the system had worked as it was supposed to. The Founders had divided power to make it difficult for any one branch to amass too much power. In the face of the president's efforts to exercise vast power, the courts, with their orders to turn over the tapes, and Congress, with its Senate Watergate Committee hearings and House Judiciary Committee impeachment proceedings, checked the president's abuse of power. In addition, the media, with its extensive publicity, first prompted and then reinforced the actions of the courts and Congress.

However, although the system worked, it worked slowly. More than two years lapsed between the break-in and the resignation. For more than half the length of a presidential term, the president and many of his aides were so preoccupied with Watergate they could not devote sufficient attention to other problems facing the country.

When the affair was over, twenty-one of the president's men were convicted and sentenced to prison for their Watergate crimes. Except for one, a burglar who was most uncooperative and who served fifty-two months (G. Gordon Liddy, who now hosts a radio talk show), the men served from four to twelve months. Nixon, who could have and probably would have been prosecuted after leaving office, received a pardon from President Ford before any prosecution could begin.

Nine years after the resignation, the security guard who had discovered the break-in was convicted for shoplifting in Augusta, Georgia. Unemployed, he had stolen a pair of shoes for his son. Unlike the president's men, he received the maximum sentence—twelve months for the $12 shoes.

Congress passed a law mandating that other, unreleased tapes and documents be turned over to the National Archives, which was to make public any that related to Watergate or had "general historic significance." The archives has slowly released these materials. On one tape, Nixon is heard remarking to his chief of staff, "I always wondered about that taping equipment, but I'm damn glad we have it, aren't you?"[97]

Not only does Nixon's voice remain, but the effects of Watergate linger. The public has become less trustful of government officials, and the media have become more suspicious of them. The parties have become more aware of the benefits of a scandal involving their opponents. In the wake of Watergate, the Democrats captured the White House and gained many seats in Congress. These results have prompted both parties to point accusing fingers and to launch congressional investigations—though only against members of the other party—even when the alleged transgressions have been far less serious than those in Watergate. Thus, Watergate contributed to the culture of scandal that afflicts American politics today.

 To learn more about executive privilege and *United States v. Nixon,* go to this chapter's "You Are There" exercises on the text Web site.

Key Terms

Watergate scandal	limited government
Articles of Confederation	Iroquois Confederacy
Shays's Rebellion	Federalists
Constitutional Convention	Anti-Federalists
Great Compromise	*Federalist Papers*
Three-fifths Compromise	Bill of Rights
direct democracy	Emancipation Proclamation
indirect democracy	Gettysburg Address
federalism	Reconstruction
separation of powers	Amendments
checks and balances	New Deal
natural rights	

Further Reading

Leonard W. Levy, ed., *Essays on the Making of the Constitution* (New York: Oxford University Press, 1969). These essays address the question "Was the Constitution an undemocratic document framed and ratified by an undemocratic minority for an undemocratic society?"

David McCullough, *John Adams* (New York: Simon & Schuster, 2001). A readable biography of the revolutionary stalwart and our second president.

Clinton Rossiter, *1787: The Grand Convention* (New York: Macmillan, 1966). A lively account of the Constitutional Convention and the ratification campaign.

Theodore H. White, *Breach of Faith* (New York: Atheneum, 1975). A chronicle of the Watergate scandal as a Greek tragedy in which actors on both sides behaved in such ways as to fulfill their destinies.

Bob Woodward and Carl Bernstein, *All the President's Men* (New York: Simon & Schuster, 1974). A riveting account of journalistic sleuthing by the two reporters who broke the Watergate story.

Electronic Resources

lcweb.loc.gov/exhibits/declara/declara4.html
At this site, you can learn more about how the Declaration of Independence was written and see a special Library of Congress exhibit on the Declaration.

www.nwbuildnet.com/nwbn/usconstitutionsearch. html
Even the Constitution has a home page. Here it is, with links to other historical documents and to PBS Project Democracy.

Another Constitution page with interesting links is www. usconstitution.net/, a site originally set up by a political science student as a class project.

InfoTrac College Edition

Search for the following articles in the InfoTrac database:

Cornell, Saul. "Commonplace or Anachronism: The Standard Model, the Second Amendment, and the Problem of History in Contemporary Constitutional Theory," *Constitutional Commentary* (Summer 1999).

Ferguson, Robert A. "The Forgotten Publius," *Early American Literature* (Fall 1999).

Hammons, Christopher W. "Was James Madison Wrong? Rethinking the American Preference for Short, Framework-Oriented Constitutions," *American Political Science Review* (December 1999).

Rakove, Jack N. "Judicial Power in the Constitutional Theory of James Madison," *William and Mary Law Review* (March 2002).

For more articles, enter:

"James Madison" in the Subject Guide.

"United States Constitution" in the Subject Guide.

"Articles of Confederation in Keywords.

American Government Resources

Visit the Government Foundations section of the Wadsworth American Government Resources Web site (politicalscience.wadsworth.com/amgov/) for a variety of tools to help you explore the constitution further. Included are simulations, video clips, Microcase exercises, and a wealth of other activities.

CHAPTER 3

FEDERALISM AND THE GROWTH OF GOVERNMENT

During disasters, federal and state agencies come to the aid of local rescue agencies.

Dave Martin/AP

Should the President Expand Federal Lands?

ou are Bill Clinton, the lame duck president of the United States. It is 2000, and in this your last year in office you are facing a legacy problem. You will leave behind eight years of prosperity, balanced budgets, and the reform of welfare and entitlement programs. But the economy runs in cycles, prosperity is not forever, and the outcome of your welfare reform is still unknown. You want to leave something permanent for the American people as part of your legacy. Having served during one of the most partisan eras of the twentieth century, you have found it impossible to get most of your legislative program through Congress. So you have to look elsewhere, to areas where you can act on executive authority.

In your first term you discovered, as did many presidents before you, how to use the 1906 Antiquities Act to further your environmental goals without congressional approval.[1] The act allows presidents to safeguard objects or lands of historic, scientific, or archaeological significance by declaring them national monuments. Conferring this status on land or natural wonders limits access to them and prohibits their sale or development. Only three presidents since Teddy Roosevelt—Richard Nixon, Ronald Reagan, and George H. Bush—have chosen not to use the act to set aside some spectacular piece of publicly held land for posterity. Jimmy Carter, another president

famously frustrated by Congress, used the act to conserve 54 million acres of wilderness in Alaska, making him the all-time champion of land set-asides.

You have used the act four times since 1996: to create the Grand Staircase Escalante National Monument in Utah, the Grand Canyon Parashant and Agua Fria national monuments in Arizona, and the California Coastal National Monument, thousands of offshore rocks and tiny islands that run the length of the California coast. All of these are in western states where the federal government already owns and manages huge tracts of land, to the consternation of governors, legislators, and local business interests.

Now your agriculture secretary is recommending that you use your executive powers to confer national monument status on 355,000 acres of the Sequoia National Forest in California that contain seventy-five groves of giant sequoias.

You do not have to consult state or local officials. All you have to do is issue an executive order. There are good reasons to do it. Giant sequoias, the world's largest trees, used to grow as far east as Colorado but now are found only on the west slope of the Sierra Nevadas. About half are already protected because they are inside national parkland, but the trees in national forests are subject to fewer restrictions. And these trees are in an area with a history of fires.

Politically, making this declaration would improve your image with environmentalists. Although your environmental record has not been bad, you can point to few specific actions that would endear you to ecology-minded citizens. On the other hand, many residents of the communities surrounding the sequoia groves will resent your action. Declaring the area a national monument would put an end to further development and limit recreational use. More important, many will see your action as another example of the federal government using its power to impose its will on the states. The federal government already owns almost 45 percent of California land. Indeed, in other western states (Idaho, Oregon, Utah), the federal government owns well over 50 percent of the land. In Nevada, it owns more than 80 percent.[2]

A state government has little control over how federally owned land within its boundaries is used. Through the Bureau of Land Management and the Forest Service, the federal government limits the number of cattle that can graze the land, the amount of timber that can be cut from forested lands, and, in some areas, the kind of vehicles that can drive on the land. Although the bureau tries to balance the interests of farmers, ranchers, loggers, and miners with environmental concerns, any regulation arouses angry protests. As one irate state legislator noted, "The federal government has a stranglehold on the rural West."[3]

The antagonism of many westerners to federal regulation is growing. At least thirty-five counties in the West have claimed jurisdiction over the federally owned lands lying within their boundaries.[4] Such claims strike at the heart of federal authority and our federalist structure.

Even if there are good reasons for declaring the area a national monument, opponents are likely to criticize your motives. You worry that you will be accused of political opportunism. If people believe that you acted only to beef up your legacy, you will have saved the trees but undermined your political goal. But maybe this is a time when political motives coincide with genuine policy concerns. You know that kind of convergence occurs much more frequently than cynics would admit.

On the other hand, you recall that when you were governor of Arkansas, you would have deeply resented a president shutting you out of a decision so important to your state. A middle ground might be to ask Congress to preserve the sequoias. Although this would still be a federal action, at least California's representatives and senators could help make the decision. If you make the declaration alone, the state and the affected communities will be kept out of the decision-making process.

Your time in office is running out. What do you do? Do you declare the giant sequoias a national monument, or, to avoid antagonizing local interests, do you pass up this opportunity to make a gift to the American people?

Since Independence, the states and the national government have wrangled over how power should be divided between them. The victory of the Union over secessionist states in the Civil War (1861–1865) determined that the Union was indivisible and that the states could not nullify federal law or the Constitution. But the war settled little else about the federal relationship.

Today, because of the sheer size and complexity of our country, its role in world affairs, and our expanded expectations of government, we live in a nation with a strong central government. Yet we continue to disagree about just how strong it should be. Most Americans say they want small government, but they also want a government powerful enough to keep the peace abroad and able to meet their needs at home. So, over the past seventy years, when states could not or would not respond to calls for government action, Americans have turned to Washington to legislate across a broad spectrum of policy, all the while claiming to believe that state governments are more responsive to them than the federal government. Because Americans are predisposed to suspect big government, it is easy for critics to decry its growth and accuse Congress of creating programs that are too large, too expensive, and too intrusive on the rights of the states. These critics, however, never mention that over the past twenty-five years, the size of state governments has doubled while the number of federal employees has fallen (Figure 1). These contradictions are perhaps inevitable in a government created, run, and elected by people who have never agreed on the proper distribution of power within a federal system.

In this chapter, we will look at the politics behind the choice of federalism as our form of government, the constitutional provisions that define it, and how the federal distribution of power has changed over time through federal court rulings and through practice. Finally, we look at some of the day-to-day mechanics of state and national cooperation in our federal republic.

Federal and Unitary Systems

Federal Systems

The term **federalism** describes a system in which power is constitutionally divided between a central government and subnational or local governments (in the United States the subnational governments are the states). Nations that have federal systems—Germany, Canada, India, Brazil, and Mexico, for example—vary greatly in their basic economic and political characteristics. They are similar only in that each has a written constitution allocating some powers to the national and some to the subnational governments.

In American federalism, both levels of government receive their grants of power from a higher authority—the will of the people (popular sovereignty) as expressed in the Constitution. In other words, federalism divides something—sovereignty—that is theoretically indivisible. This is the source of some of the conflict over jurisdiction that inevitably arises between levels of government. Making arrangements even more complex, the powers granted to each level are not necessarily exclusive. Both national and state governments have the power to tax, regulate, and provide benefits. And because each level of government is sovereign in its own right, neither can dissolve the other.

In contrast, in a **confederal system** the central government has only those powers given to it by the subnational governments; it cannot act directly on citizens and it can be dissolved by the states that created it. The first American government, established by the Articles of Confederation, was a confederal system in which all sovereignty was vested in the states. The national government was the creation of the states—not the people—and it existed only at their pleasure. In addition to the first government of the United States, the United Nations is an example of a confederal system. The lack of central authority in such systems makes them basically unworkable as governmental arrangements for modern nations.

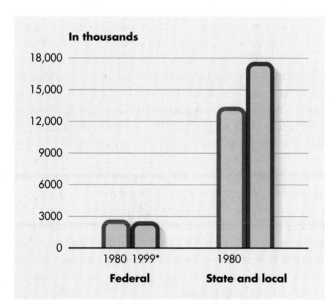

FIGURE 1 ■ Federal, State, and Local Civilian Employees
Number of Full- and Part-Time Civilian Employees in the Federal and State Governments, 1980–1999
*Latest figures available.
SOURCE: *Statistical Abstract of the United States, 2001* (Washington, D.C.: U.S. Government Printing Office, 2001), Table 449.

Unitary Systems

In contrast to federalism, in a **unitary system** the national government creates subnational governments and gives them only those powers it wants them to have. Thus, the national government is supreme. In Britain, for example, the national government can give or take away any power previously delegated to the subnational governments, and it can even abolish them, as it did with some city governments in the 1980s. In unitary Sweden, the national parliament abolished 90 percent of its local governments between 1952 to 1975.

In the United States, the fifty states are each unitary with respect to their local governments; cities, counties, townships, and school districts can be altered or even eliminated by state governments. Yet every state is (and is required to be by the U.S. Constitution) a republic—that is, a representative democracy. So clearly the difference between unitary and federal systems is not at all related to the distinction between democracy and authoritarianism. Some unitary systems are among the most democratic in the world (Britain and Sweden); others are authoritarian (Egypt and China). And while some federal systems are democracies (Canada, Mexico, Germany, and India), others are authoritarian (the former Soviet Union and Yugoslavia).

It is also not accurate simply to classify federal systems as decentralized and unitary systems as centralized. All modern governments have to delegate some power because a central government, even in a unitary system, cannot run every local service or deal directly with every local problem.

Why Choose Federalism?

Except for a few loosely organized leagues or confederations of states, there were no federal governments before the United States was created. Yet by the 1960s, as much as half the world's territory was governed by federalism.[5] Some new nations created after World War II chose federalism because they, like the American colonies, were trying to unite diverse states or territories into a single country. Federal systems are often ethnically, linguistically, religiously, or racially diverse (though not always—Germany is relatively homogeneous, for example). Agreeing to divide power among levels of government may be the only way to unite people who have strong motivation to live apart.

The power-sharing arrangements in federal governments often do not work, and many have failed. In some cases, there were not enough shared values to hold a nation together. Sometimes too much power was invested in the central government, and sometimes too little. Pakistan split from India and Bangladesh from Pakistan; there have been secessionist movements in Nigeria, Canada, Mexico, and the Congo, among many others.

Yugoslavia, the Soviet Union, and Czechoslovakia ceased to exist, and their constituent republics became independent countries.

The Political Bases of American Federalism

The Founders of the United States did not chose federalism as an ideal form of government or as a principle in itself; the few historical examples held little to recommend it as a form appropriate to the American situation. They had to write from scratch a document that would accommodate the political reality of their loose compact of states. Although at least one delegate to the Constitutional Convention proposed abolishing the states to create a unitary system, few took this option seriously.[6] This required finding a compromise that could satisfy those who thought only strong central government could work and those who thought the union could be preserved only if the individual state governments retained most of the authority they had under the Articles of Confederation. The Founders proposed a dual form of government, a compromise between the *national* form (a strong central government) favored by some delegates and the *confederal* form (a league of states) favored by others. In arguing for its ratification, James Madison defended the Constitution in just this way, saying it would create a government that was partly national and partly federal.[7] Although today we refer to the government in Washington as the "federal" government, the Founders referred to the government they created by the type of democracy it was—a republic. The word *federalism* does not appear in the Constitution.

Political Benefits of Federalism

The division of power between the national and state governments was one politically attractive feature of federalism for those delegates who worried about the center gaining advantage over the states. But with federalism's provisions for accommodating national diversity also came a means for limiting the authority of government in general. Madison explained how this would work. In *Federalist 10*, he asserted that it is inevitable that factions—groups of citizens seeking some goal contrary to the rights of other citizens or to the well-being of the whole country—would threaten the national stability. To cure the **"mischiefs of faction,"** Madison said, government has either to remove the causes of factionalism or to control its effects. The first option, Madison believed, was unrealistic because it would require the impossible: changing human nature. It also would require taking away freedom by outlawing opinions and strictly regulating behavior. People

James Madison.

The Granger Collection, New York

inevitably have different ideas and beliefs, and government, he thought, should not try to prevent this.

Because the causes of faction could not be removed without placing too many restrictions on freedom, its effects had to be controlled by a properly constructed government. If a faction were less than a majority, Madison believed it could be controlled through majority rule, the majority defeating the minority faction. If the faction were a majority, however, a greater problem arose, but one for which Madison had an answer.

To control a majority faction, one had only to limit the ability of a majority to carry out its wishes. Madison believed this was impossible in a small democracy, where there is little to check a majority determined to do something. But in a large federalist system, there are many checks on a majority faction—more interests competing with each other and large distances to separate those who might scheme to deprive others of liberty. As Madison noted, "The influence of factious leaders may kindle a flame within their particular States, but will be unable to spread a general conflagration through the other States." Having many states and having them spread over a large territory would serve as major checks against majority tyranny. (Madison's argument in *Federalist 10* remains among the most influential works of American political theory and is reprinted in the appendix.)

Perhaps the benefit of the federal arrangement can be best understood by the adage "politics is the art of the possible." The division of power made the Union possible. It allowed states their differences, ceded control over local affairs, and in the process protected against both an abusive central government and the tyranny of factions.

Political Costs of Federalism

If the division of power made the union possible, what are the drawbacks of such division? One disadvantage is that allegiance to the union can falter if too much value is placed on accommodation of state or regional differences. The union can also erode if the differences among the states become more important than their commitment to common principles. The United States faced secessionist threats almost immediately after its creation—by southern states when the Federalists (John Adams) were in power and by New England states when the Republicans (Jefferson) were in power. Secession was averted in part by the fear of external threats, but mainly by key political leaders' commitment to make the Union work.

The constitutional provisions protecting the rights and individuality of the states were meant to accommodate what has been called our "psychology of localism."[8] Although we are now a more mobile and a more nation-oriented people than we were in the eighteenth and nineteenth centuries, we retain enough local allegiance to tilt our federal system toward decentralization and fragmentation. Indeed, federalism "creates separate, self-sustaining centers of power, privilege and profit which may be sought and defended as desirable in themselves."[9] In part, federalism is *intended* to do this, but if taken too far, it can prevent coherence and unity on major policy issues. Even when there is need for national policy—whether on energy, the environment, health care, or even national defense—members of Congress may still base their votes primarily on local interests (see Chapter 10).

Political Culture and Federalism

Despite a national media, franchises and chains bringing the same products to all parts of the country, and transportation systems that can carry us across the nation in a few hours, there are still significant differences among the states—that is, something more than Texans preferring chili and New Englanders clam chowder. States *want* to be different from one another. Each has its own constitution, flag, motto, symbols of state, not to mention its very own official state bird and flower. Each state is basically a political actor competing for a share of the nation's resources. Just as individuals organize around identity issues, states compete with one another on the basis of their distinctive profiles.

When we refer to the Midwest, the Southwest, New England, or the Deep South, certain images immediately come to mind, not just of geographic areas but of life styles and political orientations. Partisan preferences, ideology, and political style continue to vary along regional lines. Individual states have developed sufficiently different political styles and attitudes that

Republican strategists, for example, would never run the same kind of election campaign for a candidate in New York as they would for one in Idaho. For the same reason, candidates for national office change the points of emphasis in their stump speeches as they move from state to state.

We have defined *political culture* as a shared body of values and beliefs that shapes perceptions and attitudes toward politics and government and, in turn, influences behavior. For much of the twentieth century, the United States was said to have three geographically based political subcultures—that is, three distinctive ways of looking at and participating in politics.[10] The *moralistic* political culture characterized the New England and the Upper Midwest view of politics as a way of improving life and the strong belief they should participate. In the *individualistic* political culture, said to be typical of the industrial Midwest and the East, the ultimate objective of politics was not to create a better life for all but to get benefits for oneself and one's group. In the *traditionalistic* political culture, associated with the states of the Deep South, politics was seen not as a way to further the public good but as a way to maintain the status quo, and little value was placed on participation.

Today, traces of these patterns remain though much has changed. The economic transformation of the United States from an industry- and agriculture-based economy to a high-tech and service economy has had an inevitable impact on political culture. Mass communication, especially television and the spread of Internet access, has radically altered political style. The Deep South, having been the site of intense political mobilization during the modern civil rights movement, is now a center of considerable grassroots activity among religious conservatives. Also, the mobility of the American population means that fewer people are likely to have a political orientation as strongly rooted in a state or regional identity as in earlier decades.

This is not to suggest that the three archetypal political subcultures have been completely homogenized. The country is just as diverse as ever; indeed, it is ethnically and racially more diverse. The fact that immigrants tend to settle in clusters in a handful of states and big cities helps shape regional differences. Patterns of dispersion of blacks, Hispanics, and Asians also overlay regional differences and shape distinctive state profiles. In New Mexico, for instance, 42 percent of the population is of Hispanic origin, while in Maine Hispanics make up less than 1 percent of the population. In Mississippi, African Americans make up over 36 percent of the population and in Vermont 0.5 percent. In Florida, almost as many people are over age sixty-five (18 percent of the population) as are under seventeen (22 percent), but in Utah, young people outnumber senior citizens by more than four to one. And in Mississippi, annual per capita income is only 51 percent of what it is in Connecticut ($20,993 versus $40,640).[11]

These disparities make for different politics in the states. The priorities of older people (health care, for instance) are different than those of younger people (financial aid for education, for example). In states with larger numbers of Hispanics and African Americans, civil rights issues are more salient than in states with predominantly white populations. And states such as Mississippi, West Virginia, and Arkansas, whose citizens are poorer than those in the rest of the country, face greater demands for services and have correspondingly fewer resources to provide them.

States also vary in where they fit on the conservative-liberal continuum. One way to measure this is to look at how much a state spends on education and health care and how restrictive or lenient its policies are toward gambling and crime.[12] The map in Figure 2 illustrates the results of one such analysis. The differences among the states can be explained by the kind of political culture the state has and by how "liberal" or "conservative" (see Chapter 4) each state's citizens are. Policies and laws enacted by state legislatures reflect the different views and social and economic circumstances of their citizens.

Thus, state boundaries mean something beyond identifying the place where you register to vote. In policy areas as diverse as economic development, taxation, welfare, and regulation of personal morality (gambling and prostitution, for example), states vary widely. Federalism, even with a strong national government, provides sufficient autonomy for states to adopt and maintain policies consistent with their own political cultures.

Key

■ Most conservative policies

■ Most liberal policies

■ Somewhat conservative policies

■ Somewhat liberal policies

■ Middle-of-the-road policies

F I G U R E 2 ■ States Vary in How Liberal or Conservative Their Policies Are

SOURCE: Robert S. Erikson, Gerald C. Wright, and John P. McIver, *Statehouse Democracy: Public Opinion and Policy in the American States* (New York: Cambridge University Press, 1993), 77, Table 4.2.

The Constitutional Bases of Federalism

Major Features of American Federalism

As we saw in Chapter 2, the Founders were unsure how to solve the problem of national versus state powers. Although they saw federalism as one way to limit government power by dividing it, they were creating an untried form of federalism.

One thing almost all delegates could agree on was the need for a central government that was stronger than that provided for in the Articles of Confederation. But they never agreed on how much of their sovereignty the individual states would have to surrender to achieve a national government. The Constitution assigned some powers, set limits on the exercise of others, but did so with an ambiguity and economy of wording that made the document acceptable both to advocates of a strong national government and supporters of states' rights.

Strengthening National Government

Two powers the Founders knew were necessary to the creation of a stronger national government were the right to tax without the permission of the states and the authority to make foreign and domestic policies without the states' consent. Granting Congress the authority to tax and to regulate interstate commerce gave tremendous power to the national government and made it far more independent of the will of the state governments than it had been under the Articles. But the Constitution also assigned Congress many general duties, granting it authority to make all laws **"necessary and proper"** for carrying out its specific powers. This is sometimes called the **implied powers clause** because the federal courts soon interpreted its vague wording to mean that Congress could legislate in almost any area it wished. This greatly expanded the reach of the national government.

The Founders' decision to make the president independent of Congress and the state legislatures also strengthened the federal government by giving the occupant a base from which to exercise independent national leadership. The president's role as commander in chief and principal executor of the laws of the United States further enlarged national powers.

Finally, the **supremacy clause** established the predominance of the national government over the states. It says that treaties, the Constitution, and "laws made in pursuance thereof" are to be the supreme law of the land whenever they come into conflict with state laws or state actions. Furthermore, when there is a difference of opinion on whether state actions are in conflict with the

Constitution or federal law, the matter is to be decided at the national level.[13] The Constitution did not specify the individual or institution that would make these decisions, but, as discussed in Chapter 2, the federal courts assumed that role during the tenure of Chief Justice Marshall.

The significance of the supremacy clause took some time to emerge. This was because the delegates to the Constitutional Convention were not in agreement on whether they were there as representatives of their states (the view of John Calhoun and many southerners) or whether they were there as representatives of the people of their states (the view of John Adams and many New Englanders).[14] This meant there was no initial consensus on who created, and therefore who could abolish or withdraw from, the new government. Was government simply the creation of the states, as the wording of Article VII makes it seem, or was it the creation of the people, as the Preamble seems to say? Individuals may continue to disagree over what the Founders intended, but the primacy of the supremacy clause was fixed by the Union victory in the Civil War.

Restricting Powers of State Governments

In addition to the categorical limitation placed on state rule making by the supremacy clause, the Constitution also identifies specific actions that states cannot take because they are reserved for the national government. States cannot enter into treaties, keep standing armies or navies, make war, print or coin money, or levy import or export taxes. These prohibitions reaffirmed that with respect to foreign policy and interstate commerce, sovereignty was vested in the national government.

The Constitution also prohibits states from infringing on certain rights of individuals. For example, a state cannot pass a law making an action a crime and then punish citizens who committed the "crime" before it was made illegal (an *ex post facto* or after-the-fact law).

Limiting Powers of the National Government

The most important general restriction on the power of the national government with respect to the states is contained in the **Tenth Amendment.** It reserves to the states and to the people those powers not granted by the Constitution to the national government. At the time it was written, the understanding of this wording was that the national government would have only those powers specifically assigned to it in the Constitution. It was added as a separate amendment in the Bill of Rights just in case this point was not clear in the body of the Constitution. But the broad construction of Congress's "necessary and proper" powers, established by many federal court rulings over the decades, weakened the Tenth Amendment. Yet the wording remains open to

more restrictive interpretations, and since the 1990s, the federal courts have breathed new life into this amendment.[15] (See the section "A Return to State-Centered Federalism?")

The Ninth Amendment extends similar assurance to the people; it states that the enumeration of certain individual rights in the Constitution and the Bill of Rights cannot be read to mean the people do not retain other rights.

Article IV of the Constitution specifically prohibits the national government from altering or abolishing existing states. No agency or branch of the national government has the power to create new states within existing states, to combine states, or to alter existing state boundaries without the approval of the legislatures of the affected states.

The creation of a presidency independent of Congress, the assignment of potentially broad legislative authority to Congress, and the supremacy clause, in combination with the provisions for restricting the powers of both the state and national governments, ensured a strong national government as well as a significant role for the states.

Interpretations of the Constitutional Provisions

Having reached agreement on a division of powers, the Founders left vague the details of how the nation–state relationship would work. Given the disagreements among its authors, the Constitution may never have been ratified if it *had* contained specifics on the practice of federalism. In fact, agreement may not even have been reached on a final document, so great was the gulf between those who thought they were creating a nation—an indivisible union—and those who thought they were writing a contract between states. These competing views are the source of what still today is the biggest disagreement about our constitutional system.[16]

Political Interpretations

Those who saw the Constitution as written by representatives of the people, and ratified by the people, were inclined to view the national government as the supreme power in the federal relationship. Alexander Hamilton clearly articulated this view of **nation-centered federalism** in the *Federalist Papers.* This interpretation accepts that the Constitution grants many powers to the states and recognizes they existed before the Union and are sovereign in the sense that they cannot be dissolved by the national government. But the national government's sovereignty is seen as supreme in that its ultimate responsibility is to preserve the Union and its indivisibility.[17] Nation-centered federalism was the view used by northerners to justify a war to prevent the southern states from seceding in 1861.

Opponents of the Hamiltonian interpretation, including many from the South, argued that because the Constitution recognized the states' existence as sovereign entities before the creation of the Union, the form our system was to take was **state-centered federalism,** giving precedence to state sovereignty over that of the national government or the Union. They cited the Tenth Amendment limiting the powers granted to Congress to those specifically mentioned in Article I and to Madison's words in *Federalist Paper* 45: "The powers delegated . . . to the federal government are few and defined. Those which are to remain in the state governments are numerous and indefinite." In this view, any attempt by Congress to go beyond these explicitly listed powers violated state authority.

In justifying their secession from the Union, southerners held to the extreme version of state-centered federalism: that the Constitution had been written by representatives of the states, not the people. In their view, if the states had created the union, they could dissolve it.

The Constitution can also be interpreted as having created a government in which the division of power leaves neither level dominant over the other. In this view—**dual federalism**—the Constitution created a system in which the national government and the states each have separate grants of power, with each supreme in its own sphere. In this interpretation of the division of powers, sovereignty is not just divided but divided in such a way as to leave both levels of government essentially equal. The differences between levels derive from their separate jurisdictions, not from inequality of power. Madison's description of the government created by the Constitution as a hybrid of national and federal forms (in *Federalist Paper* 39) provides one basis for this interpretation.

Over the years, the dominant interpretations of power sharing in our form of federalism have shifted among the nation-centered, state-centered, and dual views. Interpretations reflect changing federal court composition, economic conditions, the philosophies of those in the executive and legislative branches, and changing public demands. Overall, there has been a general trend away from state-centered and toward nation-centered federalism, but significant shorter-term shifts have occurred back toward the states.

Early Judicial Interpretations

Very soon after the Constitution was ratified, the federal courts became the arbiters of the Constitution. John Marshall, chief justice of the United States from 1801 to 1835, was a Federalist, a firm believer in the need for a strong national government, and the decisions of his Court supported this view.

The Marshall-led Supreme Court established early the legal bases for the supremacy of national authority over the states. Among the Court's most important rulings were that decisions of the state courts could be overturned by the federal courts and, in the case of **McCulloch v. Maryland,** that the implied powers given Congress in the Constitution could be broadly interpreted. The *McCulloch* decision said that the "necessary and proper" clause in Article I implied that Congress has the right to make all laws necessary to carry out its Constitutional powers.

The *McCulloch* case grew out of a dispute over the establishment of a national bank. Because the Constitution does not explicitly grant Congress the authority to charter banks, many people thought Congress may have been infringing on rights the Constitution left to the states. Ironically, it was John Calhoun, later to become the leading states' rights advocate, who introduced a bill to charter a Bank of the United States.

Once established, the bank was immediately unpopular because it competed with smaller banks operating under state laws and because some of its branches engaged in reckless and even fraudulent practices. When the government of Maryland levied a tax on the notes, or currency, issued by the Baltimore branch of the bank, the constitutionality of the bank was called into question, and a case was brought to the Supreme Court.

Marshall's ruling in *McCulloch v. Maryland* in 1819 was one of the most influential of any Supreme Court decision for the fate of the federal relationship.[18] Pronouncing the tax unconstitutional, Marshall wrote that "the power to tax involves the power to destroy." The states should not have the power to destroy the bank, he stated, because the bank was "necessary and proper" to carry out Congress's powers to collect taxes, borrow money, regulate commerce, and raise an army. Marshall argued that if the goal of the legislation is legitimate and constitutional, "all means which are appropriate, which are plainly adapted to that end, which are not prohibited, but consistent with the letter and spirit of the Constitution, are constitutional."

Thus, Marshall interpreted "necessary" quite loosely. The bank was probably not necessary, but it was "useful." This interpretation of the implied powers clause allowed Congress, and thus the national government, to wield much more authority than the Constitution gave it explicitly. Although there was some negative reaction—"a deadly blow has been struck at the sovereignty of the states," cried one Baltimore newspaper—the Court maintained its strong nation-centered position as long as Marshall was chief justice.

In 1836, with a new chief justice, the Court began to interpret the Tenth Amendment as a strict limitation on federal powers, holding that powers to provide for public health, safety, and order were *exclusively* powers of the state governments, not of the national government. This dual federalism interpretation eroded some of the nation-centered federal interpretations of the Marshall Court while continuing to uphold the rights of the federal courts to interpret the Constitution.

There have since been many Court rulings on the division of power between Washington and the States, but these early rulings set the pattern for what would be shifting interpretations of how the Constitution distributes power between levels of government.

Federalism and the Growth of Government

One indication of how dominant the national government has become in the public consciousness is the conflation of "federal" with "national." It is a confusing but now common usage to say "federal government" when we refer to the "national government." In just over two hundred years, the national government has grown from a few hundred people with relatively limited impact on the residents of thirteen small states to a government employing several millions, affecting the daily lives of 282 million people in fifty states and billions of people beyond our borders. The transformation to a large complex nation inevitably changed the way our federal system functions. Territorial expansion, war, economic crises, the growth of government, and the political philosophies of presidents have changed federalism.

Small-Scale Government

At the same time the courts were interpreting national powers broadly, the national government was exercising its powers on a rather small scale. The federal government had only one thousand employees in the administration of George Washington, and this number had increased only to thirty-three thousand by the presidency of James Buchanan seventy years later. The national government also raised relatively little revenue, most of it from import-export and excise taxes. But state governments were also small and had limited functions. There were only a few federal-state cooperative activities. For example, the federal government gave land to the states to support education and participated in joint federal-state-private ventures, such as canal-building projects initiated by the states.

Thus, the first fifty years were characterized by the growth of nation-centered federalism in legal doctrine, by small-scale state and national government, and by a few intergovernmental cooperative activities responding to the needs of an expanding nation. But the groundwork for the growth of government was laid by Jefferson's purchase of the Louisiana Territory. Once the country decided to expand its borders from the Atlantic to the Pacific, bigger government and more units of government were inevitable.

In a spirit of optimism amid the turmoil of the Civil War, Congress in 1862 established federal support for the land grant colleges, a striking example of intergovernmental cooperation in the nineteenth century. Today many of these institutions are among our finest universities. Here, students plow on the campus of The Pennsylvania State University, one of the first land grant colleges. U.S.

Department of Agriculture

The Civil War

The next great impetus to the growth of government came with the Civil War; wartime almost always expands the power of the national over lower levels of government. Lincoln assumed extraordinary powers for the presidency during the war, and its outcome, of course, reaffirmed the supremacy clause and guaranteed that there would be only one national government in the continental United States. Northerners saw their Civil War victory as a severe blow to state-centered federalism, but for southerners, the setback for this constitutional interpretation was limited to their forced inclusion in the Union.

Government as a "Bully Pulpit"

In the decades following the war, vast urbanization and industrialization took place throughout the United States. Living and working conditions for many city dwellers were appalling. Adults as well as children who moved into the cities often took jobs in sweatshops—factories where they worked long hours in unsafe conditions for low pay.

Spurred by revelations of these unsafe and degrading conditions, states and sometimes Congress tried to regulate working conditions, working hours, and pay through such means as child labor and industrial safety laws. Beginning in the 1880s, a conservative Supreme Court used the dual federalism doctrine to rule unconstitutional many federal attempts to regulate. But it often ruled that the states had overstepped their powers as

well, displaying more of an antigovernment, probusiness stance than a commitment to dual federalism. From 1874 to 1937, the Supreme Court found fifty federal and four hundred state laws unconstitutional.[19] Before the Civil War, in contrast, the Court overturned only two congressional and sixty state laws.

At the same time that the Court was limiting both state and national action in regulating business and industry, both levels of government were slowly expanding. Theodore Roosevelt's presidency (1901–1909) was a time of tremendous government activism. He saw his office as a "bully pulpit" to advocate for the improvement of living and working conditions of average Americans and for environmental protection, and to press for the regulation of big business, especially its corrupting influence on state legislatures. These years saw a flood of new legislation and regulatory activity, and Roosevelt's concept of government as advocate for the average citizen changed the direction and purpose of government at the beginning of the twentieth century.

During this period, the revenues of both the national and state governments grew—the United States through an income tax, made legal by an amendment to the Constitution ratified in 1913. States and localities levied gasoline and cigarette taxes, higher property taxes, and some states adopted income taxes. Federal support for state programs also grew through land and cash grants given by the federal government to the states.[20] By the late 1920s, however, most governmental functions still rested primarily in state and local hands. The states were clearly

Underwood & Underwood/Corbis

AP/Wide World Photos

Theodore (Teddy) Roosevelt (left) rode into the presidency determined to use government to improve working conditions, regulate business corruption, and preserve national resources. Thirty-two years later, his cousin President Franklin Delano Roosevelt's confidence, along with the hopes people had in his New Deal programs, led to public support for a new expansion of the role of the federal government.

the dominant partner in providing most services, from health and sanitation to police and fire protection; the federal government provided few direct services to individuals. The Great Depression caused a dramatic shift in this arrangement.

The New Deal and World War II

To grasp the scope of the changes that have taken place in our federal structure between 1930 and today, consider the report of a sociologist who studied community life in Muncie, Indiana.[21] In 1924, the federal government in Muncie was symbolized by little more than the post office and the American flag. Now, two-thirds of the households in Muncie depend in part on federal funds—federal employment, Social Security and other income support, veterans benefits, student scholarships and loans, Medicare and Medicaid, and many other smaller programs.

In large part, the Great Depression brought about these changes. During the stock market crash of 1929, wealthy people became poor overnight. In the depths of the Depression, one-fourth of the workforce was unemployed, and banks failed daily. Unlike today, there was no systematic national program of relief for the unemployed then—no unemployment compensation, no food stamps, no welfare, nothing to help put food on the table and pay the rent. Millions were hungry, homeless, and hopeless. States and localities, which had the responsibility for providing relief to the poor, were overwhelmed; they did not have the funds or organizational resources to cope with the millions needing help. And private charities did not have enough resources to assume the burden.

The magnitude of the economic crisis led to the election of Franklin Delano Roosevelt in 1932. He formulated, and Congress passed, a program called the **New Deal.** Its purpose was to stimulate economic recovery and aid those who were unemployed, hungry, and in ill health. New Deal legislation regulated many activities of business and labor, set up a welfare system for the first time, and began large-scale federal-state cooperation in funding and administering programs through federal grants-in-aid. Grants-in-aid provided federal money to states (and occasionally to local governments) to set up programs to help people—for example, the aged poor or the unemployed.

These measures had strong popular support, although they were opposed by many business and conservative groups and initially by the Supreme Court. But after the reelection of Roosevelt in 1936, the Court became more favorable toward New Deal legislation, and later resignations of two conservative judges ensured that the Court would be sympathetic

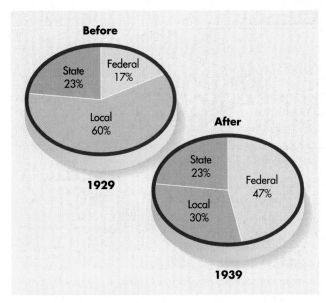

FIGURE 3 ■ The New Deal Increased Federal Share of Government Spending
Share of nonmilitary spending by each level of government, before and after New Deal legislation.
SOURCE: "Significant Features of Fiscal Federalism," *Advisory Commission on Intergovernmental Relations* (Washington, D.C.: U.S. Government Printing Office, 1979), 7.

to the New Deal (see Chapter 13 for more on the Court and the New Deal).

The Court decisions approving New Deal legislation were, in a sense, a return to the nation-centered federalism of John Marshall's day. But although the Supreme Court upheld much of the New Deal, it also approved more sweeping *state* regulations of business and labor than had the more conservative pre–New Deal Court. Thus, the change in Court philosophy did not enlarge the federal role at the expense of the powers of the states. *It enlarged the powers of both state and federal government.* In doing so, the Court responded to preferences on the part of taxpayers for a more active government to cope with the tragedy of the Great Depression. The limited government desired by the Founders became less limited as both state and national government grew.

Changes in patterns of taxing and spending soon reflected the green light given to federal involvement with the states and localities. As Figure 3 indicates, the federal share of spending for domestic needs (exclusive of military spending) nearly tripled, from 17 percent in 1929, before the New Deal, to 47 percent in 1939, a decade later. Due to this huge growth, the state share of overall spending stayed constant, while increasing dramatically in absolute terms. Local governments' share of total spending also dropped dramatically. The federal government raised more revenue and in turn gave much of it to the states and localities in the form of grants-in-aid to

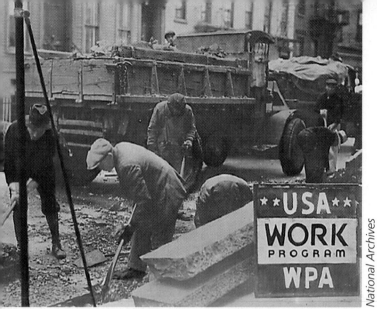

Franklin Roosevelt took office on March 4, 1933. He immediately sent to Congress a group of legislative proposals, many of which Congress passed within one hundred days. Roosevelt's program, known as the New Deal, enlarged the role of the federal government. Shown in the photo are civilians employed in the Works Progress Administration (WPA), a New Deal agency that built schools, roads, airports, and post offices in many towns in the late 1930s. Though the term boondoggle *was coined in reference to some WPA projects, the agency was successful in putting millions to work and improving the nation's public buildings, roads, and bridges.*

National Archives

carry out programs such as unemployment compensation, free school lunches, emergency welfare relief, farm surpluses to the needy, and other programs.

The New Deal brought a dramatic change in the relationship of the national government to its citizens. Before this, when the national government directly touched the lives of citizens, it usually was to give or sell them something, such as land for settlers or subsidies for businesses helping develop the frontier.[22] With New Deal programs, the federal government directly affected the lives of its citizens through its regulations (of banks and working conditions, for example) and its redistributive policies designed to protect the poor (such as Social Security and Aid to Dependent Children).

During the years that followed the initiation of the New Deal, federal aid to states increased steadily but not dramatically. But federal support to the states carried conditions. For example, local administrators of Aid to Dependent Children programs had to be hired through a merit system, not because of political or personal connections. Construction funds for highways could be spent only on highways whose designs met professional standards. Thus, federal "strings" accompanied federal money.

The other major event influencing the growth of the national government during this era was World War II. As the war brought the United States out of the Depression, Congress rolled back many of FDR's aid programs, but this could not stop the growth of government. As Lincoln had during the Civil War, FDR assumed extraordinary powers to meet the emergencies of wartime, including price controls and rationing, and suspension of some civil liberties. Spending on armaments and the military gave a tremendous boost to the economy, and defense spending has remained an important element of many states' economies ever since.

Social Justice and the Great Society

By the 1950s, some public officials became uneasy about the growing size of the federal government and its involvement in so many state and local programs. Yet under President Dwight D. Eisenhower, a Republican concerned about the growth of federal involvement, many new federal grants-in-aid to the states were added, ranging from the massively expensive interstate highway program to collegiate programs in science, engineering, and languages. Federal grants-in-aid spending nearly tripled during his administration (1952–1960). Although worried about the impact of military expenditures on the economy, Eisenhower accepted the United States' post–World War II role in world affairs and did little to reduce spending.

The size of federal programs exploded in the 1960s. The momentum for change came from the growing number of movements for social justice and racial equality, especially the civil rights movement. Most of the new programs adopted were initiated by President Lyndon Johnson's (1963–1968) massive social welfare program called the Great Society. The federal government began supporting areas that were formerly state and local preserves, such as law enforcement, urban mass transit, public education, and fire protection. Johnson's concept of federalism was born in the New Deal era; his was a centralizing approach in which program areas were identified by, funded from, and monitored at the national level while allowing states and localities a say on which projects got funded. A new feature of the Great Society era was the increasing number of grants that went directly to localities, bypassing states. Urban and other local officials, believing the state legislatures were unresponsive to their interests, now demanded, and got, direct federal support.

From 1960 to 1968, as the number of federal programs grew from 132 to 379 and federal aid more than tripled, state and local governments became increasingly dependent on federal funding.[23] The vast increase in programs and the multiplying requirements and conditions of the grants made federal aid ever more complex.

State and local officials soon felt hamstrung by the increasingly burdensome regulations.

New Federalism

When Richard Nixon (1969–1974) came into office, he wanted to make government "more effective as well as more efficient." Nixon took a managerial rather than ideological approach to streamlining the cumbersome structure created by the profusion of Great Society programs. He saw a messy bureaucratic problem and an overconcentration of decision making at the federal level, and he tried to find a solution through more efficient management.[24]

Nixon's plan had two primary elements. One was to consolidate the several hundred grant programs into six major functional areas. Instead of trying to micromanage hundreds of types of grants from the federal level, Washington would make block grants to the states and localities and leave it to them to determine how to fund programs in these functional areas. This greater leeway in how to spend grant money gave local officials more opportunity to target projects to local needs. It also meant administrative streamlining at the federal level.

The second major aspect of Nixon's **new federalism** was general revenue sharing. Under this program, tax money paid into the federal government was returned to the states to fund local projects and services. It was a way of encouraging state activism in the hope that it would decrease the need for federal programs. The main restriction on use was that money had to be spent consistently with federal civil rights and equal opportunity laws.

In contrast to Nixon's managerial approach, Ronald Reagan's (1981–1988) new federalism had a more ideological purpose, as he made clear when he declared in his first inaugural address: "Government is not the solution to our problems. Government is the problem." Reagan said he was seeking a "quiet revolution" to bring people closer to government. Thus, his new federalism was aimed at reducing the power and influence of government rather than at improving intergovernmental management and effectiveness. Instead of seeing block grants as a way to encourage states to provide services the federal government would fund, Reagan saw them as a step toward ending all federal involvement in these program areas. He opposed general revenue sharing and ended that program.

Reagan's critics have a more pragmatic explanation for his new federalism; they said it was driven as much or more by fiscal as ideological considerations. They say he chose to cut federal funding for state and local programs to reduce the size of the budget deficits created by his increased military spending. While this may well

have been a factor, it is hard to deny that Reagan's federalism was much more ideologically driven than Nixon's managerial approach to reform. It is also true that Reagan's new federalism was rooted not so much in state-centered or dual federalism as it was in his opposition to government in general. Reagan's ultimate goal was to reduce the role of government at all levels (except for national defense) and increase reliance on private markets and institutions.[25] This approach—cutting federal spending on local and state programs to downsize government at all levels—has been called *instrumental federalism* in contrast with Nixon's "rationalizing" approach, in which making government more efficient and effective was an end in itself.

While Reagan had an ideological commitment to smaller government, he had no significant programmatic approach to achieve it, and he was often more preoccupied with the Cold War than with his domestic program. In fact, the size and expenditures of the federal government grew during his administration, and states gained few new powers. Reagan took a more indirect approach to rolling back government power by slowing enforcement or blocking implementation of rules he thought were an abuse of federal power.

The New New Federalism

Like Reagan, Bill Clinton (1993–2000) came to office with a wary view of Washington and a commitment to working in partnership with governors. Clinton was a multiterm governor from a southern state where the states' rights tradition held sway. Reforming state-federal relations had been a special interest when he chaired both the national organization of governors and a reform group within the Democratic Party. Except in the area of civil rights policy, Clinton claimed to be a supporter of state activism.

During most of Clinton's term, Republicans held a majority in Congress. In an address to the American people in 1995, Republican former House Speaker Newt Gingrich said, "This country is too big and too diverse for Washington to have the knowledge to make the right decisions on local matters; we've got to return the power back to you—to your families, your neighborhoods, your local and state governments."[26] The goal, he said, was "to rethink the entire structure of American society, and . . . American government. . . . This is a real revolution."[27]

Unlike the Gingrich Republicans, Clinton was not an advocate of state-centered federalism or smaller government for its own sake. But he was committed to the idea of the states as laboratories (earlier articulated by Justice Louis Brandeis)—that is, as places for policy experimentation. He used the phrase frequently, wrote

Former president Ronald Reagan, whose preference for small government was well known, liked to say that the ten scariest words in the English language were, "Hello, I'm from the government, and I'm here to help." This is funny when things are going well and states and localities have no urgent need for government intervention. In times of crisis however, such as the Great Depression, a war, or a natural disaster, the words "I'm here to help" may sound more reassuring than scary.

Sometimes problems are just too big for a city, county, or state to manage with local resources. The destruction of the World Trade Center provides an exceptional example of a locality calling for federal help to rebuild a disaster area. But even the more "ordinary" destruction caused by a hurricane, flood, tornado, or earthquake may be so severe and widespread that the resources of the affected states and localities are overwhelmed. And if the damage is not quickly repaired, the local economy slows, people lose jobs, and recovery is difficult. When people can't work, no income taxes are withheld; when people can't shop because stores are destroyed, sales taxes are not collected. Just when a state or city needs to spend money to rebuild roads, bridges, buildings, and houses, their tax revenues fall and local resources are stretched to the breaking point. When a state decides it cannot deal with a natural disaster on its own, it can ask the president to declare it a federal disaster area.

The national government helps out in these situations through the Federal Emergency Management Agency (FEMA). The agency was created in 1979 to cope with the effects of a nuclear attack,[1] but before 9/11, it was called on mainly to provide financial help, temporary shelters, and other emergency aid to areas struck by natural disasters.

Created for one purpose and diverted to another, the agency got off to a rough start. It was especially criticized for an inadequate response to Hurricane Andrew in south Florida in 1992. It took three days for the agency to begin distributing emergency food and water, and medical help was delayed, too. The widespread criticism FEMA received from both Republicans and Democrats led to some major changes. The agency got new appointees with significant disaster relief experience. FEMA also changed its approach, from reactive ("Let's see whether they ask for help") to proactive ("Let's see what we can do right now"). Red tape was cut, and agency response time was drastically reduced. For instance, a FEMA advance team arrived in Oklahoma City about five hours after the bombing of the Alfred P. Murrah Federal Office Building in 1995, and a search and rescue team was on the scene by 2:30 A.M. the following morning.[2]

The agency responded with similar success to the devastating floods in the Midwest in 1993. When the Des Moines (Iowa) Water Works was on the verge of collapse, FEMA set up water distribution centers and water purification systems within a day. It provided clean water to Des Moines residents for over two weeks. In the first nine months after September 11, FEMA sent almost $1 billion to state, local, and nonprofit agencies to clear debris and repair the damaged roads and sidewalks in the vicinity of the World Trade Center (WTC), provide crisis counseling, and help pay for a ferry service into Manhattan to replace the subway stations destroyed by the collapse of the towers.[3] In addition, Congress committed $20 billion overall to the first year of rebuilding New York City's economy.

The collaboration of FEMA and other federal agencies with city and state offices, and the help of nonprofits and volunteers from around the country, resulted in one of the most remarkable intergovernmental responses to disaster the country has ever seen. The WTC site was cleaned up six months ahead of schedule at one-tenth of the estimated cost.

With the United States now planning for the possibility of multiple terrorist attacks, FEMA staff are training to handle new categories of disasters. In 2003 the agency was moved to the new cabinet department of Homeland Security where, in addition to its usual work responding to natural disasters, it will provide support to first responders to terrorist attacks, such as fire fighters and police officers, especially by getting all types of federal aid to the places it is most needed. After the space shuttle *Columbia* disintegrated during reentry into the earth's atmosphere in 2003, President Bush assigned

it into executive orders, and eventually based his welfare, health care, and education policies around it.[28] During the period from 1994 through the end of his administration, Clinton and congressional Republicans supported policies that delegated more powers to the states. Overall, Clinton's federalism policies were much closer to Nixon's than to Reagan's in that both

Clinton and Nixon were primarily interested in "rationalizing intergovernmental relations" and making government more efficient.

The Gingrich Republicans, on the other hand, shared Reagan's view of government and put forward a legislative program for downsizing the federal government. The return of, or delegation of powers to,

State and federal disaster workers and specialists joined New York City fire fighters and police in the lengthy rescue and cleanup operations at the World Trade Center.

FEMA another job that was beyond the capacity of any local or state agency: coordinating the search for the shuttle debris that fell over states from California to Louisiana. Working with its local partner agencies, FEMA recovered debris and human remains from four states, tested debris sites for toxic contamination, and processed claims of personal injury and damage to property caused by falling debris. When all levels of government cooperate to meet the needs of an emergency situation, we are reminded that we are all part of the same nation, sharing its benefits and helping to carry one another's burdens no matter which state we live in.

1. Ted Gup, "How FEMA Learned to Stop Worrying about Civilians and Love the Bomb," *Mother Jones* (January/February 1994): 28.
2. Ibid., 32.
3. FEMA press release, June 3, 2002 (www.fema.gov/).

subunits or lower levels of government from a higher level is called **devolution.** Here we use it to refer to the delegation, by the national to state and local governments, of the authority to make and implement policy in specific areas. In contrast to Nixon's new federalism, which was a piecemeal attempt to give states sharply restricted areas of decision-making authority, devolution meant the return of functional areas of policymaking to subnational units of government. Yet what happened to welfare, for example, during the Clinton years was by no means a wholesale surrender of policymaking authority because the federal government still told the states that they had to provide services. But Clinton did embrace the devolutionary trend by adopting a more deferential stance toward the states in implementation of federal rules and regulations, especially regulation of business and the environment. (See the discussion on unfunded mandates in the later "Conflict" section.)

A Return to State-Centered Federalism?

The fervid support of the Gingrich Republicans for a smaller national government and more power to the states, Clinton's qualified acceptance of both, and a series of Supreme Court rulings that favored state immunity from federal rules suggested that, by the time the Bush administration took office, the country was headed toward a more state-centered form of federalism. In this final section on the growth of government, we look at current views of the federal relationship.

President

George W. Bush, like Clinton, came to the presidency from the governorship of a southern state. Unlike Clinton, who opposed state-centered federalism, while targeting specific policy areas for decentralization, Bush presented himself as an advocate in principle of returning power to the states. Clinton favored delegating rule implementation to state agencies, but he insisted on the right of federal agencies to set national standards, such as for clean air and water, and consumer and worker safety. During his last months in office, Clinton imposed a number of such standards by executive order. Within months of taking office, Bush reversed many of these, including standards for arsenic levels in water, pollutants in the air, and health and safety in the workplace. In addition, he issued a new order making it harder for federal officials to overrule state decisions. In explaining Bush's actions, the White House press secretary said, "it will reflect that state and local governments are closer to the people and are often better able to solve problems . . . than the federal government."[29]

But the Bush administration has sent mixed signals on state-centered federalism. While being an advocate for devolution in domestic policymaking, especially regulatory policy, Bush believed in greatly strengthening the office of the president and the national armed forces. He also wanted a less open government and issued orders limiting public access to information about the workings of the national government. His support for expanding the role of the states in making and implementing welfare policy was countered by his intervention in public education to impose mandatory national testing on local school systems. (See the "Providing a Spare" box.) Even in the area of business regulation, Bush butted heads with governors, most of whom want to regulate the distribution of electric power in their states. Bush argued that state regulation was inefficient and called for the construction of a national distribution system for electrical power.

Supreme Court

For a decade, the rulings of the Supreme Court have shown a trend toward empowering the states at the expense of the national government. Between 1992 and 2002, it handed down seven key decisions that restrict Congress's ability to impose rules and regulations on state governments and prevent litigants from bypassing state courts to seek remedies in federal courts. In a 1995 decision, the Court ruled for the first time since the New Deal that Congress had exceeded its authority to regulate interstate commerce. While the rulings do not try to reinterpret or limit the areas in which Congress can legislate, the Court has overturned a number of obligations Congress had placed on the states to implement federal laws. Now that the direction of the thinking of the Court's majority is known, dozens of other federalism suits are being filed.

The current Court's interpretation of federal relations has been summarized as "Rights without Remedies," or one that permits Congress to confer rights on citizens but not to tell the states how to enforce them.[30] The four dissenting justices say that recent decisions giving states immunity from federal rules are the "result of a fundamentally flawed understanding of the role of the states within the federal system" and that they intend to go on dissenting in all cases where this principle of state immunity is applied by the Court's majority. Describing the bitter division among the "Federalism Five" and the four dissenting justices in these cases, one reporter said, "These days, federalism means war."[31] In other words, it is business as usual in American government.

But the Supreme Court, like the White House and Congress, vacillates between support for states' rights and the exercise of federal authority. In 2000, during a high tide of rulings in defense of states' rights, the Court intervened in the recount of votes cast by Floridians in the presidential election, overruling the State Supreme Court. (Elections, whether for national, state, or local office, are the jurisdiction of the states, not the federal government.) This federal intervention, in a partisan 5–4 ruling that was applied to a single election, determined who would get the state's electoral votes and effectively decided the outcome of the presidential election. (See the Chapter 13 "You Are There" section.)

Congress

Despite its support for devolution, Congress appears to have few advocates of pure state-centered federalism. While willing to delegate some authority, Congress continues to supersede the states in rule making whenever it thinks necessary. In recent years, bills have been introduced to supplant state laws on drunk driving with a national standard; allow property owners to bypass state courts and go directly to federal courts to protest local zoning laws; and override state laws on late-term abortions, medical use of marijuana, and assisted suicides.[32] In 1998, Congress used its power to regulate interstate commerce to impose a three-year moratorium on state taxation of e-commerce and other Internet activity. States claimed it would cost them $20 billion in lost revenue.[33] Even after twenty states had negotiated interstate tax collection agreements and lobbied hard for lifting the ban, Congress renewed it in 2002, a time when most states were facing serious declines in revenue and budget deficits.

One congressman said of his colleagues that they "don't really believe in states' rights; they believe in deciding the issue at whatever level of government they think will do it their way. They want to be Thomas Jefferson on Monday, Wednesday and Friday and Alexander Hamilton on Tuesday and Thursday and Saturday."[34] All branches of government find it convenient to support federal power when it supports their policy goals and state power when that supports their policy goals. That is why there is no sustained momentum toward giving power to the states.

The States

States are key players, not just entities acted upon, in the federal relationship. All states make important policies affecting their citizens' lives, and the policy preferences of each state's citizens and officials influence the balance of power between Washington and the state capitals. For example, some states have been very supportive of publicly funded social insurance and mass transit programs and the taxes needed to pay for them, while others are committed to limited state action and no income taxes.

The past two decades have been a period of increased state activism, in part *because* of the public's expectations of government and Washington's refusal or inability to satisfy them. During the Reagan years, there was an ideological commitment to reducing the scope of government in every area but national security. Yet those years of tax cutting and increased spending on defense left spiraling budget deficits and imposed fiscal restraints that made it difficult for the Clinton administration or Congress to propose new initiatives or to fund existing programs. At the same time, the Vietnam War and the Watergate, Iran-Contra, and Clinton scandals all contributed to increased partisanship and gridlock at the federal level and to declining trust among the public. State governments began looking less often to Washington, instead launching their own policy initiatives.

In the 1990s, the states experimented with charter schools and vouchers for private schools, rolled back affirmative action and bilingual programs, looked at new ways to try to teach religion in schools, and adopted a variety of crime laws such as mandatory sentencing, three-strikes laws, and victims' compensation. A few states adopted term limits and tax caps and passed their own campaign financing laws. Some placed restrictions on gay rights, while a few passed laws strengthening them and supporting health benefits for gay partners. After gaining control over welfare, the states experimented with many different job training and work programs.[35] In addition, they became more bold in challenging or refusing to enforce federal regulations affecting business and the environment and in one case refused to implement federal gun laws.

State activism increased during the second Bush administration as Washington continued its retreat from many policy areas and became preoccupied with the war on terrorism. While Congress was stalemated on how to handle the cloning issue, twenty-two state legislatures took up their own anticloning bills.[36] As the Bush administration was rolling back regulation, the states began reregulating, especially in the areas of consumer and worker safety. Some state legislatures passed "no call" laws limiting telemarketing; some outlawed predatory lending.[37] One lawyer called the amount of new state legislation on workplace conditions—electronic monitoring of workers, child labor laws, right to breast-feed—"mind-boggling."[38] On the use of genetic testing in hiring, for example, twenty-one states had already passed laws protecting workers from use of such tests by their employer before Congress even held hearings.[39] Thirty-four states enacted some form of equal-pay legislation, and almost half of all states in 2002 were considering laws to raise the minimum wage above the national level. Interest groups, seeing the trend, are shifting their effort toward the states. Some of the largest have lobbying operations in all fifty states.

It is important to remember that through all these policy changes, nothing has changed in the constitutional relationship between the national and state governments. Authority delegated can be taken back by the center. This is where the divergence of views occurs among contemporary supporters of devolution. Advocates of state-centered and dual federalism believe Washington has only surrendered powers that by right belong to the states, whereas the nonideological supporters of devolution see it as a practical measure to bring more efficiency to policymaking and implementation.

But devolution carries no guarantee of greater efficiency or responsiveness. States are not bureaucracy-free. Collectively, state and local governments account for 86 percent of all civilian governmental employees, 33 percent of all governmental spending, and about 12 percent of the gross domestic product.[40]

Few people argue that the states could do a better job than Washington providing for the national defense. But there is sharp disagreement over which level of government can make other policies more efficiently and effectively. In practice, this issue is rarely decided on principle. Sometimes one level of government fails at a certain task and it gets reassigned to another level. Or, as one cynic put it, for those times when "we have wrecked one level of government, the Founding Fathers had the foresight to provide a spare."[1]

Here we look at two policy areas: the much-maligned federal welfare program, whose administration has been put in the hands of the states; and state- and local-managed public education, for which the federal government is assuming increasing responsibility. These examples illustrate how, for political and pragmatic reasons, state and national levels shift the burden for policymaking and implementation.

Welfare: The Feds Step Back

By the 1990s, many Americans saw welfare policy as a bungled federal program that was pouring billions of dollars annually into subsidized income and health support programs while doing little to help decrease recipients' need for them. In fact, those programs were always jointly funded and implemented by Washington and the states and localities, with much of the administration at the county level. But the federal government got all the criticism because it was Congress that authorized the programs. Americans wanted a major change.

Governors, including Bill Clinton in Arkansas, wanted control over welfare because they were sick of rising costs and the increasing number of services mandated from Washington. Clinton made this an issue in his 1992 presidential campaign. When elected, he found a Congress sympathetic to re-

form although for somewhat different reasons than his. But if advocates of devolution wanted to hand over to the states primary responsibility for welfare, he was willing to support that as long as the federal government still mandated the basic services they had to provide.

So, in 1996, as the federal government was setting caps on spending and trying to eliminate budget deficits, Congress, with Clinton's approval, devolved welfare programs on the states. The federal government would identify services and provide grants to pay for them, but the states would decide how to provide the services and how to meet the time limits set on eligibility. Clinton's approach to devolving welfare rationalized the administrative process. It was also smart politics to put accountability at the level where most decisions are made.

A major feature of the reform was that all able-bodied applicants for welfare were supposed to work full- or part-time to remain eligible for benefits. The booming economy of the late 1990s gave all states a leg up in making welfare reform work. The millions of new jobs created helped many welfare recipients leave the rolls for full-time employment as employers scram-

bled to find workers and were willing to provide training for those who didn't have it.

But it is arguable whether state administration of welfare has made it more efficient, inexpensive, or responsive to local needs. In Wisconsin, one of the pioneers in moving to "workfare," the initial costs actually rose because of that state's intensive approach to reintegrating the unemployed in the job market. So many new programs were created they were described as a mini–New Deal.[2] But in other states, many qualified children and poor families have gone without health insurance or food stamps since welfare reform was enacted, because their governments did not spend money allocated by Congress, or they diverted it to other programs favored by the middle class.[3]

Five years after the reform, the average number of welfare recipients who were working ranged from 20 to 30 percent, depending on the state. Most of those workers had high school diplomas or some additional education. Now the states face the difficulty of training the less skilled to find jobs at a time when unemployment is rising, state revenues are in freefall, and most new jobs are for the well educated.

Education: The Feds Step In

Americans often regard public schools as a neighborhood institution to which they entrust their children and which, therefore, should be subject to their influence and oversight. In fact, elementary and secondary education have been locally controlled since the earliest days of the Republic. In those early days, when communities were often segregated by religious or other sectarian beliefs, people in rural districts especially feared government interference. They wanted to be free "to shape the curriculum of local schools with their distinctive beliefs."[4]

The common school movement eventually put most public school education in the hands of professionals, but policymaking remained with local school boards and state officials.[5] Fifty years ago, we had over one hundred thousand school districts; today we still have close to fourteen thousand, each making its own decisions on what students need to know and how to test them on it. There has never been an attempt to organize these thousands of districts into a national system; in fact, just the creation of a cabinet-level Office of Education by the Carter administration in 1979 led to an immediate movement to abolish it. Republican opponents saw it as one more power grab by the national government, another step toward co-opting this quintessential local responsibility.

But during the 1990s, a general rumbling about the failure of public schools grew to a roar. American schoolchildren consistently scored well below their peers in other industrialized countries in science and math skills. Employers believed that the level and type of training offered in high schools was inappropriate for a labor market transformed by globalization, high technology, and the perennial need to communicate clearly. In addition, there was a general feeling in the public that schools were lax in teaching character

and too tolerant of misbehavior, drug use, truancy, and even violence.

Washington began to take notice and for more than a decade tinkered with various kinds of reforms: a voluntary national curriculum, an idea from the first Bush administration; a voluntary national testing system, a proposal of the Clinton administration; and a Republican-backed school choice program, which was enacted by Congress.[6] The main element in school choice was a voucher program that allowed children to leave public schools for privately run schools and take their tax dollars with them to help pay their tuition. This encouraged the creation of new private, or charter, schools to compete with the public schools (some assumed that competition would force public schools to improve in order to retain their students). Almost all school districts responded to the growing criticism, trying to improve performance and develop their own systems of standards-based testing. But there appeared to be waning public confidence that localities could fix the broken system.

George W. Bush decided the federal government should intervene, proposing a system of mandatory national testing under his "Leave No Child Behind" program; it became law in 2001. Instead of pushing for national standards or a standardized curriculum, Bush recommended mandatory testing in basic skills for every child, beginning in the third grade. Every state must develop its own system of standards-based reform within five years, and within twelve years all students must meet these standards. The measure of success will be whether students can pass a standards-based test devised by their school districts. There is no national standard.

Thus, the Bush program imposes a national rule but allows localities considerable flexibility in how they meet the federal requirement. Yet from the standpoint of local control over education, a good deal has been surrendered. The school districts can set their

curricula and devise their own tests, but they will have far less autonomy in deciding how the school day is spent. A large part of every teacher's effort now will be devoted to test preparation. Should sufficient numbers of students fail to pass the school's standards-based test, federal dollars for running the testing program could be lost, and schools could even be closed through loss of pupils.

It is far too early to know what impact the national testing system will have on quality of education. But public acceptance, even eagerness, to have the national government step into this area, and to have the states assume responsibility for welfare policy, illustrates the politics of policymaking in a federal system. Our system is paradoxical in that Clinton, an advocate of nation-centered federalism, devolved welfare policy to the states, and Bush, an advocate of state-centered federalism, intervened in education, the most localized of all policy areas. But in both cases, action was taken for political, not philosophical or ideological, reasons. There was a public demand for action, and policymakers wanted to be responsive. But people are not clamoring for either centralization or devolution. People want policy that works, by whatever level of government can make it work.

1. John D. Donahue, "The Disunited States," *Atlantic Monthly,* May 1997, 20.
2. Gary Wills, "The War between the States . . . and Washington," *New York Times Magazine,* July 5, 1998, 27.
3. "States Sitting on Unspent Welfare Funds, Group Says," *Champaign-Urbana News-Gazette,* February 24, 2000, A-4; "Audit: States Denying Medicaid," *Champaign-Urbana News-Gazette,* December 15, 1999; Robert Pear, "Cash to Ensure Health Coverage for the Poor Goes Unused," *New York Times,* May 21, 2000, 18, A6.
4. Carl F. Kaestle, "Introduction," in *School: The Story of American Public Education,* ed. Sarah Mondale and Sarah B. Patton (Boston: Beacon, 2001), 15.
5. David Tyack, in *School,* 4.
6. James Traub, "The Test Mess," *New York Times Magazine,* April 7, 2002, 48.

The Practice of Federalism

Today's federalism is a mixture of cooperation and conflict. One expert calls it "competitive federalism," because states and the federal government are competing for leadership of the nation's domestic policy.[41] At the same time, Washington and the fifty states cooperate to carry out the day-to-day work of government.

Federal-State Relations

Given the large number of governments in the United States (Table 1), cooperation is essential. The term *cooperative federalism* describes the day-to-day joint activities and continuing cooperation among federal, state, and local officials in carrying out the business of government: distributing payments to farmers, providing welfare services, planning highways, organizing centers for the elderly, and carrying out all the functions that the national and state governments jointly fund and organize. It also refers to informal cooperation in locating criminals, tracking down the source of contagious diseases, and many other activities.

One example of informal but intensive cooperation is the Centers for Disease Control in Atlanta, which helps state and local governments meet health emergencies and prevent the spread of contagious diseases. National and state police and other crime-fighting agencies share data on crimes and criminals. The federal government and the states also jointly regulate in several areas, including occupational safety and the environment. Since the 2001 terrorist attacks, there is increased reliance on state resources to help with national defense. (See the box "The States' Role in National Defense.")

To help pay for essential services provided by state and local governments, the federal government returns tax revenues to states (Figure 4). Mass transit, community development, and unemployment compensation are good examples. Despite some inefficiency, federal funding has succeeded in helping state and local governments meet real needs. Along the way, the performance standards and regulations attached to the grants have increased the professionalism of state and local bureaucrats.

The federal government also considers certain tax deductions as aid to the states. When reporting income to the IRS, residents of all states are allowed to deduct the amount that they paid in tax—income, property, and sales—to their states and localities. This is counted as aid to the states because it lowers federal revenue by billions of dollars each year, while leaving more money to be spent in the states.

Conflict

Current federal-state relations are also characterized by conflict. One of the sharpest clashes concerns so-called **unfunded mandates.** A law or regulation imposed on the states unaccompanied by sufficient funding to implement it is an unfunded mandate. For example, the federal government requires the states to deduct child support from the wages of parents who fall behind on payments and from the paychecks of fathers of children whose mothers are on welfare.[42] The administrative costs incurred in carrying out such mandates are substantial, yet states that fail to enforce them risk losing federal contributions to their welfare funds.

Other mandates order states and localities to educate the children of illegal immigrants and to make public buildings, sidewalks, and transportation accessible to people with disabilities. Environmental regulations are the most expensive of all federal mandates, costing billions annually.

The fiscal burden of unfunded mandates led to state and local officials joining together to mount a national campaign to restrict their use. Congress passed a bill reforming procedures under which unfunded or underfunded mandates, especially regulatory mandates, are sent to the states, but it stopped short of prohibiting them. The federal government is required to provide information on the costs of implementing laws and rules before Congress or an executive branch agency, such as the Environmental Protection Agency, can adopt them. Federal agencies are required to consult with states and localities before imposing mandates and to adopt regulations that impose the smallest burden for implementation.[43]

Another source of national-state friction is the management of federally owned land—military bases,

---

TABLE 1	Number of Government Units in the United States

Part of the reason that intergovernmental relations in the United States are so complex is that there are so many units of government. Though the number of school districts has decreased dramatically in the last fifty years, and the number of townships has declined slowly, the number of "special districts"—created for a single purpose, such as parks, airports, or flood control management—continues to grow.

	States	Counties	Municipalities	Townships and Towns	School Districts	Special Districts
1942	48	3,050	16,220	18,919	108,579	8,299
1997*	50	3,043	19,372	16,629	13,726	34,683

*Latest figures available. The Census Bureau takes a count of governmental units every five years, in years ending in 2 and 7.
SOURCE: *Statistical Abstract of the United States, 2001* (Washington, D.C.: U.S. Government Printing Office, 2001), Table 414.

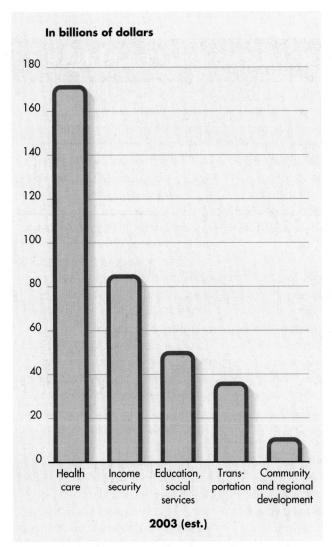

In billions of dollars

FIGURE 4 ■ What Does the Federal Government Give the States Money to Do?
Ninety-two percent of the $376.4 billion the federal government is sending back to the states in 2003 is for programs in these areas.

SOURCE: *Budget of the United States, Fiscal Year 2003, Analytical Perspectives* (Washington, D.C.: U.S. Government Printing Office, 2002), 237–243.

proved a nuclear waste storage facility in Nevada (just 90 miles from Las Vegas) over the vigorous protests of the governor and many citizens. The governor threatened civil disobedience, and, in fact, he had few other options to prevent opening of the facility.

States and Localities as Lobbyists
Lobbying is a crucial part of the relationship between the states and the federal government. The importance of federal money to states and localities and the need for coordination between federal and state bureaucracies have stimulated the organization of groups of state and local officials, such as the National Conference of State Legislatures, the National League of Cities, and the American Public Welfare Association. These groups lobby for favorable legislation for states and localities and work with federal agencies to ensure that new regulations are implemented in a way acceptable to the states. Most of these organizations have multimillion-dollar budgets and employ sizable staffs. Many individual states and cities have their own Washington lobbyists, who appear to have some positive effect on increasing federal aid.[44]

But why should states lobby when they are all represented by their elected representatives in the House and Senate? One advantage that lobbying organizations offer is the capability to contact large numbers of members at the same time. Moreover, the members of a state's congressional delegation may belong to different parties than state leaders, or they may not agree with state leaders—as, for example, when Congress waived state sales tax on e-commerce. Or a state may have an urban majority while its congressional delegation is closer in views to rural and suburban residents. But mainly states hire lobbyists because there is a lot at stake.

The Assembly on Federal Issues, the group that coordinates the lobbying of the Conference of State Legislatures, monitors bills under consideration by every major committee in Congress. They look especially for any new provisions that would undercut state laws or have an impact on state revenue, or tie the hands of state officials in some policy area. For example, some states are concerned about the free trade agreements Congress has approved. Many states are big exporters, and if Congress says that certain countries are exempt from paying import taxes, it could affect the competitiveness of a state's businesses and ultimately of state revenues. So states lobby in large part to maintain maximum control over their legislative, regulatory, and taxing authority.

Interstate Relations

Constitutional Relationship
Dealing with Washington is not the only problem in intergovernmental relations faced by the states. State

weapons facilities, and national park and wilderness areas (see the "You Are There" that opened this chapter). Twenty-seven percent of all land within the United States is held by the federal government, the majority in western states. Few Americans are against national parks or national defense, but in those states where half or more of the land is federally owned, state governments often do not have the control they would like to have over the state's natural resources. Usually the friction is over economic exploitation of resources in park land, but sometimes states object to activities they believe put their populations at risk—radioactivity from weapons production or the testing and storage of nuclear waste. In 2002, the Bush administration and Congress ap-

THE STATES' ROLE IN NATIONAL DEFENSE

Responding to the destruction in New York and Virginia on 9/11, and the anthrax attacks that followed, required the cooperation of dozens of federal, state, and local law enforcement, public safety, and health agencies. It was not only buildings that came down but "decades-old divisions of labor between the various parts of American government."[1] After Tom Ridge, director of the new Office of Homeland Security, assigned governors the responsibility for coordinating security planning at state and local levels, every governor appointed a state director of homeland security.

With this new mandate came the promise of new money—a 1,000 percent increase in funding for the "first responders," police, firefighters, and emergency medical teams.[2] New money also flowed to airport safety and security and FEMA. Funding was proposed to help states prepare for bioterrorism and to establish a Citizen Corps to train people at the community level to deal with terrorist attacks.[3]

While the money is new, a role for the states in national security is not. Each state has a militia provided for by Article I and the Second Amendment of the U.S. Constitution, as well as by each state's constitution. In the early days of the Republic when there was no large standing army, the state militia provided most of the troops for the Revolution, the Indian frontier wars, and the War of 1812. In fact, the militia were the recipients of the first grant-in-aid ever given by Congress to the states.[4]

Known as the National Guard since 1933, the militia are still jointly funded by Washington and the states; the president serves as commander in chief of any units activated for national duty. When not in national service (which is most of the time), state militia are under the command of their governors, who also appoint guard officers. Each state determines how militia troops are recruited. The Illinois Constitution states

that the "State militia consists of all able-bodied persons residing in the State," unless they have been exempted by law. (You may want to look at your state constitution to see what your obligations are.) The United States is the only advanced industrial country with a military establishment that has dual national and state sources of command and loyalty.

Governors can call on their militia to help manage natural disasters, such as floods and forest fires, or to assist local and state police forces at times of social unrest. Occasionally a governor refuses to call out the National Guard to help with enforcement because there is strong or perhaps violent local opposition to a federal law, as was the case in many southern areas fighting racial integration in the 1950s and 1960s. Then the president of the United States can nationalize (or threaten to nationalize) state troops and put them under his command, as Dwight Eisenhower did to enforce integration in Little Rock, Arkansas, schools and John Kennedy did to enforce integration at the University of Mississippi.

The president can also call up National Guard units to supplement U.S. armed forces when there are not enough active-duty or reserve troops to meet national defense needs. Thousands of men and women from National Guard units served in the Gulf War and afterward policed the no-fly zones in Iraq. In combination with other reserve units, National Guard troops outnumber regular army personnel in peacekeeping missions in the Balkans.[5]

Already making a crucial contribution to the overextended national armed forces, the state militia took on additional responsibilities after 9/11. National Guard and Air National Guard units from New York City, Virginia, and Pennsylvania were part of the immediate response to the airplane hijackings, but militia from all states were soon involved. Guard troops under the com-

mand of New York's governor, and drawing their pay from the state, provided local security and logistical support during the cleanup of the World Trade Center. Other Guard units, operating under presidential orders and paid for with federal funds, flew patrols over U.S. cities; still others, paid by Washington but under state command, provided security at local airports. Guard units are often expected "to switch from one master and one mission to another without losing track of who is currently in charge."[6]

Governors are not altogether happy that their National Guard units, for which they have new needs at home, have been serving for the past decade as de facto reserves for the U.S. armed forces. In addition, some are already worried that the president and Congress may be mandating new areas of responsibility in national security work without providing enough funding to do the work.[7] In turn, members of Congress are skeptical as states ask for money to do non-defense-related projects that governors and mayors had been unable to get funding for prior to 9/11.

In the federal relationship, the more things change, the more they stay the same.

1. Sydney J. Freedberg Jr., "Shoring Up America," *National Journal,* online edition, October 19, 2001.
2. Homeland security budget provisions, including funding for the Citizen Corps, are available at www.whitehouse.gov/homeland/.
3. Funding for bioterrorism preparedness and response and other grants to the states can be found in *The United States Budget for Fiscal Year 2003: Analytical Perspectives* (Washington, D.C.: U.S. Government Printing Office, 2002), 237–240.
4. On the creation and evolution of state militia, see William H. Riker, *Soldiers of the States* (Washington, D.C.: Public Affairs Press, 1957).
5. Sydney J. Freedberg, "Weekend Warriors No More," *National Journal,* June 8, 2002, 1690–1698.
6. Freedberg, "Shoring Up America."
7. Pat Towell, "Armed Forces' New Workload Heats Defense Funding Debate," *Congressional Quarterly,* November 17, 2001, 2749; "Security Costs Skyrocket," *Congressional Quarterly,* April 13, 2002, 972.

governments must also work with one another. The Constitution established rules governing some aspects of interstate relationships. One important provision is the **full faith and credit clause,** which requires states to recognize contracts. No matter in which state you contract your marriage, every state must recognize it. The Constitution also provides that if a fugitive from justice flees from one state to another, he or she is supposed to be extradited—that is, sent back to the state with jurisdiction.

Normally, meeting full faith and credit requirements is rather routine. However, politics vary sufficiently from state to state so that occasionally honoring the laws of another state can be controversial. A historical example is the Fugitive Slave Act, which required the authorities in every state to return escaped slaves to their owners. This is something abolitionists living in free states were loathe to do yet bound to do by the Constitution. More recently, when Vermont became the first state to register unions between gays, it set off a controversy in other states worried about having to recognize the unions and extend to these partners the same legal status and rights (health and retirement benefits, inheritance) as married heterosexual couples.

Voluntary Cooperation

Most state-to-state interaction is informal and voluntary, with state officials consulting with officials in other states about common problems and states borrowing ideas from one another. Sometimes states enter into formal agreements, called *interstate compacts,* to deal with a common problem—operating a port or allocating water from a river basin, for example. Some states have agreements exempting citizens of neighboring states who have taken up temporary residence from paying local income taxes. But access to water supplies, for residential and industrial use, is one of the most common areas of state cooperation and conflict.

Interstate Competition

Changing economic patterns and an overall loss of economic competitiveness by the United States in the world market have stimulated vigorous competition among the states to attract new businesses and jobs. They market their states to prospective new businesses by touting lower taxes, a better climate, a more skilled, better educated workforce, and less government regulation than other states competing for the same business. Most states are willing to give tax subsidies and other financial incentives to businesses willing to relocate.

Critics believe that these offers erode a state's tax base and have little impact on most business relocation decisions. Evidence indicates that low taxes are not the primary reason why businesses relocate.[45] Nevertheless, without offering some special break, some states feel at a competitive disadvantage in recruiting new businesses.

The absence of an income tax is a benefit trumpeted by nine states. The tax burden may be one factor in where people decide to settle. One estimate is that during the 1990s, almost 3 million people relocated to states without income taxes. And between 1990 and 2000, the overall population growth in the forty-one states that have income taxes was 11 percent, while in the nine states that have none, it was 22 percent.[46] But this relationship is not consistent for every state. Furthermore, if taxes are so low that the quality of schools and public services are affected, they will almost certainly be a disincentive to both population growth and business relocation.

One certain prerequisite for business and population growth is an ample water supply, and, given our shrinking resources, maintaining or increasing water flow into and out of states is a very high-priority issue, especially for states that do not have large bodies of water within their boundaries. These are the everyday issues governors and other state officials are continuously negotiating. How much water should New York state officials agree to be taken from upstate farmers for urban dwellers or for use in New Jersey and Connecticut? The waters of the Upper Colorado are shared by four states and those of the Lower Colorado by three others. So rural residents of Colorado constantly struggle to keep ever more water from being channeled from the Colorado River to meet the needs of fast-growing metropolitan areas in other states.

All governors have to deal with a set of common problems such as resource management, education, ways to foster economic growth, taxation, crime, and prison systems, in addition to managing their relationships with Washington. The Governors Conference, which meets annually, was formed to facilitate information sharing and cooperation among the governors of all states. Three of our last four presidents were governors, and governors with presidential ambitions can use the Conference as a platform to build political networks and national reputations.

State-Local Relations

The relationship of states to their localities—counties, cities, and special districts—is another important feature of contemporary federalism. All but fifty-one of 87,504 government units in the United States exist below the level of state government (see Table 1). These relationships are defined by state constitutions; they are not dealt with in the federal Constitution, and states

Fighting large-scale forest fires often involves both federal and interstate cooperation. Here a Montana crew helps combat a fire on an Apache Indian reservation in Arizona during the summer of 2002, when 6 million square miles of forest burned.

differ in the autonomy they grant to their localities. In some states, **home rule** charters give local governments considerable autonomy in such matters as setting tax rates, regulating land use, and choosing their form of local government. In many states, cities of different sizes have different degrees of autonomy. And in some states, counties are given the power to create levels of government below them. In Illinois, for example, each county can decide whether to establish township governments or do without them.

Although states exist independently of the national government while localities are creatures of the states, some of the same problems that affect national-state relations also affect state-local relations. City and county officials often wish for more authority and fewer mandates from the state.

People, States, and the Federal Government

One of the most important elements in the federal relationship is the people. In a system with responsibilities divided among thousands of governmental units and power divided among levels of government, where do the people fit? How do they elect and communicate with all these officials and get them to be responsive?

It is often claimed that people feel closer to their state than to the national government. At the state level, the argument goes, government and its decision makers are nearby and more accessible to the voters, more likely to have a sense of the public mood and be more responsive to their specific preferences. This is important because economic conditions and political culture vary from state to state, resulting in different policy preferences. Moreover, local officials may have a better grasp of local conditions and therefore be better situated to shape policy to fit these preferences.

Are state governments more responsive to the people? State governments *are* undeniably smaller than the national government. While the United States has 282 million residents, nine states have populations under a million. (On the other end of the spectrum, 42 percent of all Americans live in states with more than 10 million residents.) But smaller does not make for greater familiarity; the average person is not necessarily better informed about state and local officials than national ones. Most local candidates get far less media exposure than national candidates, partly because there are so many of them. Voter turnout rates for local and state elections suggest that there is less interest in state and local than in national government. And if the basic premise is correct, then people should be even closer to local government than to state government. There is no evidence that this is true. There are layers of local government (some with taxing authority), such as townships, special districts, or planning agencies, that Americans know little about. And though most Americans know about school districts and city councils, voter turnout is much lower in those elections than in state and federal elections, and public knowledge about most of these officials is very low.

One indication that Americans do not feel especially close to state and local government was the increasing use of the ballot initiative throughout the 1990s. Interest groups tried to bypass not only Congress but state legislatures by getting policy questions placed on state ballots and having them directly decided by voters. Doing an end run around their elected representatives, voters approved initiatives that killed state laws on affirmative action, sanctioned medical use of marijuana, imposed limits on campaign spending and contributions, expanded casino gambling, and gave adopted children the right to know the names of their biological parents. About 40 percent of all initiatives became law, while only a tiny percentage of bills submitted to legislatures get passed into law.[47] But these laws can be confusing. One year California's citizens had to wade through a 222-page pamphlet outlining ballot choices.

In San Francisco, facing a ballot with more than one hundred items, voters passed one proposition for public financing of campaigns while simultaneously passing another measure outlawing it.[48]

Moreover, lobbyists have substantial clout in most state legislatures because these bodies operate far out of the media spotlight in most states. An estimated 18 to 25 percent of all state legislators do not abide by conflict-of-interest laws.[49] They regulate businesses in which they have an interest, and they have financial ties to lobbyists. Forty-five percent of Louisianans thought the state was so corrupt that a vote for change would not make a difference. On a scale of 1 to 10 for trustworthiness, Louisianans gave their state leaders a 5.5.[50]

Big interests influence voting on initiatives, too. Huge sums of money flow into states from outside organizations to support or defeat initiatives. When an initiative to undo a gay rights law was put on the ballot in Maine, for example, money from national antigay rights poured in to defeat it.

Still, some see the move toward greater state autonomy and more direct democracy as taking us nearer to the Founders' ideal of a government closer to the people. But the increasing use of grassroots initiatives is not a move toward the kind of government the Founders envisioned. The Founders established a system of checks on popular passions.[51] Indeed, the Founders feared policymaking getting too close to the people and government being too responsive to popular demands. They saw the potential for overheating the political process through too much direct democracy, which is why they chose an indirect or republican form of democracy and a federal division of power. The issue is how to keep a balance in these divisions sufficient to prevent a tyranny of factions while maintaining a sense of national unity and purpose.

Conclusion: Is Federalism Responsive?

Our Founders probably did not foresee a national government that would surpass the states in power and scope of action in domestic policy. Yet one of the paradoxes of our system is that as the national government has gained extraordinary power, so have the states and localities. All levels of government are stronger than in the eighteenth century. Federal power *and* state power have grown hand in hand.

It is probably foolish to pretend to know how the Founders might deal with our complex federal system. However, many of them were astute politicians who would undoubtedly recognize that our system had to evolve along with population and territorial growth and social and economic change. Yet we continue to believe in local control and grassroots government. This is a paradox built into our form of government, one that Thomas Jefferson discovered very early. He called his election a revolution, abolished all internal taxes, and set about making government as small, simple, and informal as possible. He tried to keep the United States out of war in Europe and closed down ports and foreign trade but soon found he needed federal policing to enforce his policy.[52] He also had an expansionist vision and, with or without formal authority, purchased the Louisiana Territory, instantly setting the country down the road from a small coastal agrarian republic to a vast continental empire where his idea of small government would no longer be possible.

Today, across the United States, our beliefs in democracy, freedom, and equality bind us together. In many ways we are becoming more alike, as rapid transportation, television and other forms of instant communication, fast-food franchises, hotel chains, and other nationwide businesses bring about increasing similarity. But to say that Alabama is more like New York than it used to be is certainly not to say they are alike. Our federal system helps us accommodate this diversity by allowing both state and federal governments a role in policymaking.

Is such a complex system responsive? It is very responsive in that groups and individuals whose demands are rejected at one level of government can go to another level. The federal system creates multiple points of access, each with power to satisfy political demands by making policy rejected at another level.

Yet many Americans still believe government cannot be trusted and is not sufficiently responsive. In late 1997, only 39 percent of Americans polled said they trusted the federal government, and 74 percent said the federal government should be running only those things that cannot be run at the local level.[53] Yet Americans are not that enamored of state governments, either, as indicated by the increasing use of ballot initiatives to bypass both national and local legislators.

In polls conducted in the months immediately following the 2001 terrorist attacks, Americans viewed government more favorably, especially its ability to deal with foreign policy issues.[54] Most still preferred "smaller government" but there was an increase in those favoring larger government with many services.[55] But by summer 2002, the polls reflected a return to higher levels of mistrust.[56] In some ways, that should make the Founders happy: There must be enough confidence in government for it to function and the Union to hold, yet there must be enough suspicion of government to prevent the abuse of power.

Clinton Expands Federal Lands

n April 2000, ninety-two years to the day after Teddy Roosevelt designated the Grand Canyon a national monument, Bill Clinton used his authority under the Antiquities Act to protect virtually all remaining sequoia groves not already lying within national parkland. By changing their designation from "national forest" to "national monument," Clinton protected the giant sequoias "for eternity." The agriculture secretary recommended creation of a science advisory panel to draw up guidelines for management of the area. Existing logging agreements and property owners' water and grazing rights will be honored, but hunting is banned, recreational access restricted, and further development prohibited.

Three members of California's congressional delegation introduced a bill to block the action, but Clinton acted before it came to a vote. One of the bill's sponsors accused Clinton of "declaring war" on the communities surrounding the forest. Local officials said the new designation would cost their communities millions of dollars in lost logging jobs. In addition, they argued, the protection was not needed. Thinning the areas around the groves through logging had helped protect the sequoias from fires and pest infection.

With nine months still remaining in his term, Clinton had committed 3.1 million acres to his "land

legacy," the most land set aside in the lower forty-eight states by any president since Teddy Roosevelt. The Antiquities Act gained sufficient celebrity to serve as a plot line in the popular *West Wing* television series.

But Clinton was not finished: He ordered a study of 50 million additional acres in thirty-eight states for possible designation as wilderness areas. A reporter said Clinton's resolve to use the act was "like a golfer who has just discovered the power of a titanium driver."[57] By the time he left office, he had created twenty national monuments on federal land.

There is no way for us to know exactly the reasons for Clinton's decision. The political costs to him were probably small since he would not stand again for election to national office, and opposition to land set-asides is greatest in the affected areas. It did improve his stature with environmental groups. As he was leaving office, this president who had not been seen as "a bird-watcher" was being touted by the Wilderness Society as "one of the top conservation presidents of all time."[58]

States will never be equally affected by the creation of federal parks because wilderness areas and spectacular land formations are not evenly distributed across the country. Yet Clinton's actions illustrate well the political dynamics of our federal system. The national government can override the wishes of

President Clinton looks over seeds from sequoia trees while touring Sequoia National Park.

a state when there is a national majority supporting its actions. Willing to face opposition from western governors, ranchers, and others, the president was responding to a broader national constituency of those who love their national parks and believe more should be done to conserve wilderness areas and natural landmarks. No one but the president, or the president and Congress acting together, could have saved the giant sequoias for all the people for eternity.

To learn more about the Antiquities Act and the controversy surrounding it, go to this chapter's "You Are There" exercises on the text Web site.

Key Terms

federalism

confederal system

unitary system

"mischiefs of faction"

"necessary and proper"
implied powers clause
supremacy clause
Tenth Amendment
nation-centered federalism
state-centered federalism
dual federalism
McCulloch v. Maryland

New Deal
new federalism
devolution
cooperative federalism
unfunded mandates
full faith and credit clause
home rule

Further Reading

David S. Broder, *Democracy Derailed: Initiative Campaigns and the Power of Money* (New York: Harcourt Brace, 2000). A senior Washington correspondent and nationally syndicated columnist takes a look at the rise in use of the ballot initiative to legislate and explains why he believes it is a threat to our republican form of government.

Joseph Ellis, *The Founding Brothers* (New York: Knopf, 2001). A wonderfully readable account of the personal and philosophical conflict between the proponents of a strong national government and the defenders of states rights and how their differences played out through the first years of the Republic.

The Federalist Papers, 39 and 23–25 (any edition). Read Madison's description of the relation between state and national governments in Paper 39; then compare it to Alexander Hamilton's arguments for a strong national government in Papers 23–25. You will see why we are still arguing over federalism.

John Ferejohn and Barry R. Weingast, eds., *The New Federalism: Can the States Be Trusted?* (Stanford, Calif.: Hoover Institution Press, 1997). Seven scholars of federalism look at interstate competition to attract new business and how the states are handling welfare reform and environmental regulation.

John W. Kingdon, *America the Unusual* (New York: St. Martin's/Worth, 1999). A slim volume, several extended essays, summarizing what American federalism looks like today and how it got that way.

Forrest McDonald, *States' Rights and the Union: Imperium in Imperio, 1776–1876* (Lawrence: University Press of Kansas, 2000). An historian's account of how the states' right concept evolved through the post–Civil War years.

John T. Noonan Jr., *Narrowing the Nation's Power: The Supreme Court Sides with the States* (Berkeley: University of California Press, 2002). A former federal judge and law and philosophy professor examines recent federalism rulings and explains why he thinks the Supreme Court has taken a mistakenly narrow view of congressional authority.

Jeffrey Pressman and Aaron Wildavsky, *Implementation* (Berkeley: University of California Press, 1973). A classic look at the difficulties of translating federal laws into working programs when dealing with a multiplicity of state and local governments.

John Steinbeck, *The Grapes of Wrath* (New York: Viking, 1939). A novel ■ portraying the conditions facing the country that set the stage for the New Deal.

 ## Electronic Resources

www.ncsl.org/
The home page of the National Council of State Legislatures. The council promotes reform and increased efficiency in state legislatures, helps facilitate interstate cooperation, and lobbies for state issues. Its home page also provides information about current issues of relevance to states and links to the home pages of all state legislatures.

www.fema.gov
The home page of the Federal Emergency Management Agency contains reports on cooperation with states and localities to manage current and past natural disasters and other emergencies. It provides a summary of FEMA's involvement in the response to the terrorist attacks of September 11, 2001.

www.dhs.gov
The Web site for the new Department of Homeland Security. At this site you can read about the division of responsibility for Homeland Security among national, state, and local governments.

InfoTrac College Edition

Search for the following articles in the InfoTrac database:

Cherminsky, Erwin. "Shrinking Federal Powers," *Trial* (January 2001).

Conlan, Timothy J., and Francois Vergniole de Chantal. "The Rehnquist Court and Contemporary American Federalism," *Political Science Quarterly* (Summer 2001).

Elazar, Daniel J. "International and Comparative Federalism," *PS: Political Science & Politics* (June 1993).

Stuntz, William J. "Terrorism, Federalism, and Police Misconduct," *Harvard Journal of Law & Public Policy* (Spring 2002).

For more articles, enter:

"federalism" in the Subject Guide."

"states' rights" in the Subject Guide.

 ## American Government Resources

Visit the Government Foundations section of the Wadsworth American Government Resources Web site (politicalscience.wadsworth.com/amgov/) for a variety of tools to help you explore federalism and the growth of government further. Included are simulations, video clips, Microcase exercises, and a wealth of other activities.

CHAPTER 4

PUBLIC OPINION

Neighbors built an impromptu shrine to the fifteen dead firefighters at Engine Company 54.

Photo by Jonathan Saunders, www.saundersjonathan.com

How Can the President Maintain Popularity and Help Republican Candidates?

t is January 2002 and you are George W. Bush, planning your upcoming State of the Union address. The address is part of a political strategy to maintain your popularity, help your party in the fall election, position yourself for your own reelection in 2004, and secure your favored domestic policies from the Congress where the Senate is controlled by the Democrats. This is your first major speech to Congress and the nation since you addressed both shortly after the terrorist attacks on September 11.

In the months since, events have seemed to go well for you. While Osama bin Laden has avoided capture, the war in Afghanistan has at least temporarily succeeded in routing the Taliban and al Qaeda. The war has showcased American military power and discredited those who warned against the dangers of military action in that part of the world. While it will take the continued presence of the U.S. and other military forces to ensure its survival, a new government has been established. Some European allies would have preferred a nonmilitary response to September 11, but several countries in the region have supported your efforts, allowing the U.S. military to launch attacks from within their borders.

While diminished somewhat since the weeks following September 11, patriotic feelings continue to run high, and the nation seems united more than it has been in a long time. Polls show that the overwhelming majority of Americans believe the war is going well and approve of your actions taken at home to combat terrorism.[1] Your job ratings, reflected in the polls, were in the mid-50s prior to September 11 and then jumped to the high 80s immediately and reached 92 percent in October, the highest ever recorded by a president.[2] Since September, your job approval has been higher for a longer period of time than for any president since Franklin Roosevelt.[3] At the moment, your popularity remains at an amazing 83 percent.

Your success in combating terrorism has also helped you and your party on domestic issues even though a significant number of Americans are worried. For example, only three in ten think the economy is healthy. Seven out of ten believe that the collapse of the Enron Corporation, a major institution whose value plunged to almost zero after revelations of phony bookkeeping, is a sign of deeper problems with American financial and economic institutions. There are calls for you and Vice President Dick Cheney to disclose meetings and correspondence the vice president and others had with Enron officials, a major bankroller of your campaign. At the same time, majorities approve of your handling of the economy, environment, and education. Sixty-two percent trust you over the Democrats in Congress to do a better job with the problems facing the nation. More voters say they will vote Republican in the 2002 congressional elections than Democratic.[4]

The war has also helped increase support among groups of voters that supported Al Gore in the last election.[5] American women have been drawn by your message of hardship and discrimination facing Afghan women. Minorities have responded positively to your calls for tolerance toward Muslims. Republicans who supported John McCain for president over you in the Republican primaries are impressed with your call for humanitarian aid as part of the battle plan in war-torn Afghanistan. The highly divisive 2000 election is a distant memory for most Americans.

Your call for national unity in the face of September 11 has also put Democrats on the defensive. Not wishing to appear unpatriotic, the Democrats in Congress have supported you on the war and are reluctant to challenge you on domestic issues. For the moment, you have the advantage. You realize, however, that things can change quickly as the terrorism threat recedes and other issues come to the fore. You recall the very strong job ratings of your father, George H. Bush, in January 1991, when as president he approved a military strike against Iraq (the Gulf War). Even though the military action was largely successful, by that June his perceived slowness in dealing with a sagging economy led to a dramatic drop in his popularity. The following year he lost reelection to Bill Clinton. Friends have noticed that this experience made a deep impression on you. Obviously, you hope to avoid a similar fate. What can you do to maintain the support of the American people?

Recognizing the increasing concern of Americans with the economy, one strategy is to make it the major focus of your address. If it does not improve, it will be an issue in the November elections. You certainly want to be seen as someone who cares about the struggles of average Americans. However, the strategy has risks. Should you focus on the economy, and it does not improve, you will give the Democrats an issue to use against you. The Democrats will become more critical as the 2002 election approaches, even if the economy improves, and they will take you to task if it does not. Your standing in the polls is likely to drop, inviting still more criticism and reducing prospects of winning support in Congress for your domestic policy goals. You and the party are likely to suffer, perhaps losing control of the nearly evenly divided House of Representatives, losing seats in the Senate, as well as reducing your reelection prospects in 2004.

Another tactic is to remain focused on terrorism. Concern for safety may keep Americans fixated on security. You have told them many times to prepare for a long war. You have identified an international terrorist network with operatives in dozens of countries, including the United States. Your approval ratings to date are based on your success in Afghanistan and dealing with terrorism. Why shift from an issue that has brought success? If Americans are worried about terrorism, they may forget about their economic woes. Besides, you may be able to play on patriotic sentiments that will cut you some slack on the economy, particularly if you can link the economy to the war. You are likely to be no worse off should the strategy fail then if you shift attention to the economy. And if you succeed, it may provide the popular support for your other domestic initiatives. You are also likely to keep the Democrats off-balance, concerned that they appear unpatriotic if they are too critical.

But this approach, too, has risks. The tendency of Americans to "rally around the flag" and support the president in military crises is generally temporary, decreasing as the conflict continues. Your father learned this in the Gulf War. Nor do you want to be accused of ignoring the domestic needs of the country, and surely you will, if the economy continues its slide. The public's attention may be largely focused on terrorism, but economic woes strike personally and are unlikely to be overlooked by those who lose jobs or whose employers' financial situations seem shaky.

What do you do? Do you draw attention to the economic needs of the nation or keep the nation focused on war and defeating terrorism?

Public opinion is often contradictory. The public is often hostile toward political leaders for failing to respond to their needs, yet at the same time complain that leaders simply follow the latest public opinion polls rather than lead. Many are angry with government. They do not trust it; they think it is too big and spends too much money. Yet, they like the services government provides, and very few are willing to cut spending to eliminate their favorite services or programs.

This chapter explores public opinion to better understand these contradictions. It describes how public opinion is formed and measured, discusses the pattern of public opinion on some important issues, and assesses the extent to which government is responsive to public opinion. Because political science is primarily interested in opinions that affect government, the focus is opinions on political issues, personalities, institutions, and events.

Nature of Public Opinion

Public opinion can be defined as the collection of individual opinions toward issues or objects of general interest—that is, those that concern a significant number of people. Public opinion can be positive or negative. That is, people can have positive feelings about something, or they can have negative feelings about it. This is the property of direction. Generally, public opinion is mixed. Some are positive, others negative. Intensity reflects the strength of public opinion. The public may have rather weak feelings about an issue or feel quite strongly about it. Intense opinions often drive behavior. The very strong opinions of prolife and prochoice advocates lead them to lobby and demonstrate for their positions.

When it comes to most public issues, public opinion is not very intense. A small minority may feel intensely about an issue, but rarely will a majority. With the exception of the racial and states' rights issues that almost destroyed the nation in the 1860s, there has been nothing in the United States like the long-standing and highly divisive class and religious conflicts in Europe that often resulted in wars.

Opinions also vary in stability. Some constantly change, while others never change. Stable opinions are often intense. They are also likely to be grounded in information, some accurate, some inaccurate. Opinions on abortion tend to be stable and intense, more so than opinions of candidates for public office, especially at the beginning of a campaign when voters know little about them. For example, opinion polls following the party nominating conventions in 1992 showed challenger Bill Clinton's margins over George Bush seesawing back and forth from day to day (Figure 1). Most voters did not know enough about Clinton to form a stable opinion.

They would see something on television or read something in the press favorable to Clinton and report a preference for him, and then see something unfavorable and shift back to Bush.[6] In 2000, voters knew more about Al Gore, as he had served as Clinton's vice president for eight years, and about George W. Bush, who was the son of the former president. Their opinions were less variable than in 1992.[7]

Formation of Public Opinion

People have opinions about issues, individuals, and institutions because they learn them in a process called **political socialization.**

As with other types of learning, individuals learn about politics by being exposed to new information from parents, peers, schools, the media, political leaders, and the community. These are **agents of political socialization.** Individuals also learn about politics through personal experience.

Political learning begins at an early age and continues throughout life. In young children, learning is influenced by reasoning capacity and expectations of parents.[8] Where parents push, learning begins earlier and proceeds more quickly. Preschoolers are unable to distinguish political from nonpolitical objects. Some are unable to separate political figures from cartoon characters, and some confuse religion with politics. A

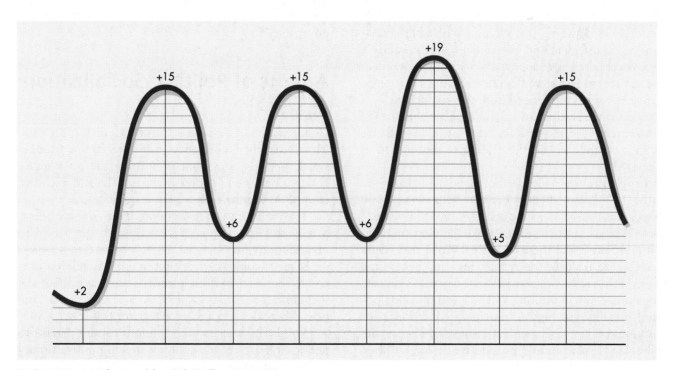

FIGURE 1 ■ The Presidential "Poller Coaster"
Clinton's margins over Bush rose and fell dramatically early in the 1992 campaign.
SOURCE: *USA Today,* October 3, 1992. Polls taken August 20 to September 2, 1992. The term *poller coaster* was coined by Richard Morin, "The Ups and Downs of Political Poll-Taking," *Washington Post National Weekly Edition,* October 5, 1992, 37.

significant number of five- and six-year-olds report that the president takes his orders from God.[9] By first grade, these confusions are resolved, and children begin to see government as distinct and unique.[10]

However, the inability to understand abstract concepts or complex institutions means children's conception of government is limited. Most identify government with the president.[11] Children can recognize the president—they see him on television—and understand that he is the leader of the nation much like the parent is the leader of the family. Experiences with parents and other adults provide children with a basis for understanding their relationship with authority figures such as the president with whom they have no contact.[12] Feelings toward parents are generalized to the president. Typically, children describe the president as good and helpful[13] and view him as more powerful than he really is.[14]

Older children are introduced to political ideas and political institutions in school and through the media. Their conception of government broadens to include Congress, the act of voting, and ideas such as freedom and democracy. The positive view of government reflected in feelings toward the president gives way to more complex and realistic images. The process can be accelerated by political events and the reaction of others to them. Children were much less positive toward the president and government in the 1970s than in the 1960s. The Watergate scandal in 1973 lowered both adults' and children's evaluations of the president.[15] The Clinton sexual scandals and the impeachment proceedings of 1998, however, had no impact on adult evaluations of the president and government, and presumably none on children. The approval ratings of the president reached record levels, and confidence in the executive branch remained unchanged from the year before.[16]

Even when scandal lowers children's evaluations of government, the effect does not last. The negative feelings of children during Watergate diminished as they aged.[17]

In adolescence, political understanding expands still further. Children discuss politics with family and friends. By middle teens, positions on issues develop.[18] Some fifteen- and sixteen-year-olds develop opinions that look much like those of adults'. While they begin to recognize faults in the system, they still believe the United States is the best country in the world. They rate the country low in limiting violence and fostering political morality but high in providing educational opportunities, a good standard of living, and science and technology.[19] For most, the positive feelings toward government learned earlier are reinforced.

In adulthood, opinions toward specific policies and personalities develop, and political activity becomes more serious. Most Americans revere their democracy

in the abstract and do not want to change the system, but they tend to be cynical and distrustful of political leaders. Some of the negative feeling about politics grows out of Americans' dislike of the conflict, partisanship, and the give-and-take characteristic of political decisions in an open and free society.[20] And some of the negative feeling develops from media coverage, which not only highlights conflict, partisanship, and give and take but also exaggerates the extent of these characteristics in our politics. Occasionally, anger boils over, but it is temporary and rarely leads to major political change. Despite specific criticisms, the media, like schools, lay the foundation for overall acceptance of the American system.[21]

While critical comments about government and political leaders sharply declined after September 11, much of this effect was short-lived. Americans "rallied around the flag" and suspended most partisan debate. Most Americans felt gratitude toward the government agencies and institutions that responded to the attacks so valiantly. But except for those who were called to serve in the armed forces or who were able to volunteer to help in the World Trade Center cleanup, Americans were not asked to translate their newly positive feelings into action. Though commentators on September 11 and immediately afterward predicted that nothing would ever be the same, in fact for most people (with the obvious exception of those who survived the attacks, lost loved ones in the attacks, and troops sent abroad), life did return to normal relatively quickly, including a return of skepticism toward government.

Agents of Political Socialization

Family

Children are not born little Democrats or Republicans. Most learn these allegiances from the family. Families are particularly important in shaping the opinions of children because of strong emotional ties and exclusive control during the early years.

The family influences opinions in several ways. First, parents share their opinions directly with children, who may adopt them.

Second, parents say or do things that children imitate. They may overhear parents' comments about the Republican or Democratic Parties and repeat what they hear. Many develop a party allegiance this way.

Third, children transfer opinions toward parents to political objects. When children are less positive toward parents, they are less positive toward the president.[22]

Fourth, the family shapes the personality of the child, which influences political opinions and behavior. For example, the family shapes self-esteem, and self-

This boy, at a white supremacist rally, likely was socialized in these views by his parents.

esteem is linked to the development of political opinions and a willingness to share them in public.

Fifth, children inherit their social and economic position in society from parents, and this influences how they view themselves, the world they live in, and how the world views them. Those reared in a middle-class suburb have a different view of themselves and the world around them than children reared in poor inner-city areas.

Research shows that a child is more likely to reflect the opinions of parents when the parents' opinion is clearly perceived and the opinion is important to the parents. With party allegiance, cues are frequent and unambiguous. Other opinions are less likely to be picked up. Seventy-percent of high school seniors were able to correctly identify the party of their parents, while no more than 36 percent could identify their parents' opinion on other issues.[23]

Even where parental influence is strong, it is not immutable. As young adults leave their parents' circle, agreement between their opinions, including party allegiance, and those of their parents declines. New agents and experiences come into play.[24] Even among

younger children, parental influence may not be as strong as in the past. Parents no longer have exclusive control during a child's preschool years, and the number of households with both parents working or with a single parent who works means contact with parents is less. Others can be expected to fill this void. Today, schools often deal with problems the family dealt with in the past. While parental influence may be declining, whether or not one is raised in the traditional two-parent family or one with a single parent has little or no impact on important political opinions and political behavior.[25]

School

A child of our acquaintance who came to the United States at the age of five could not speak English and did not know the name of his new country. After a few months of kindergarten, he knew that George Washington and Abraham Lincoln were good presidents, he was able to recount stories of the Pilgrims, he could draw the flag, and he felt strongly that the United States was the best country in the world. This child illustrates the importance of the school in political socialization and how values and symbols of government are explicitly taught in American schools, as they are in schools in every nation.[26]

While we do not understand exactly which aspects of formal schooling influence political opinions, there is little doubt that education, years of formal schooling—the skills it provides and experiences it represents—make a difference. People who have more education are more interested in and knowledgeable about politics.[27] They are also more likely to participate in politics and to be politically tolerant.[28] Perceptions that school administrators and teachers are fair are associated with trust in other people.[29] Education does not, however, lead to a greater appreciation of democracy as an arena where there are disagreements typically resolved through bargaining and compromise.[30]

How does school make a difference? Schools promote patriotic rituals, such as beginning each day with the Pledge of Allegiance, and include patriotic songs and programs in many activities. In the lower grades, children celebrate national holidays such as Presidents' Day and Thanksgiving and learn the history and symbols associated with them. Such exercises foster love and respect of country.

In the upper grades, mock conventions, elections, and student government introduce students to the operation of government. School clubs often operate with democratic procedures and reinforce the concepts of voting and majority rule. The state of Illinois let the state's elementary school children vote to select the official state animal, fish, and tree, conveying the message that voting is the way issues are decided.

Issues that involve moral questions have the greatest potential to be divisive. Slavery was a moral issue that almost destroyed the nation. In the first decades of this century, prohibition—banning the sale of alcoholic beverages—was a divisive moral issue. In the 1990s and early 2000s, the rights of gays and lesbians has become a moral issue.

Abortion emerged as a moral issue in the 1970s and continues today. There are two dimensions to public opinion on this issue. One involves the health and safety of the mother or child. The vast majority of Americans endorse legal abortion when the mother's health may be endangered, the child is likely to have a serious defect, or the pregnancy is the result of rape or incest. This pattern of opinion has been reasonably stable over the past decade.

The other dimension relates to the personal preferences of the mother. Americans are divided on whether a legal abortion is acceptable when the family has a low income and does not want any more children or when the mother is unmarried and does not want to marry the father.

Although the graphs do not reveal intensity, the patterns in boxes a, b, and c show agreement, or consensus, whereas boxes d, e, and f reveal disagreement, or conflict.

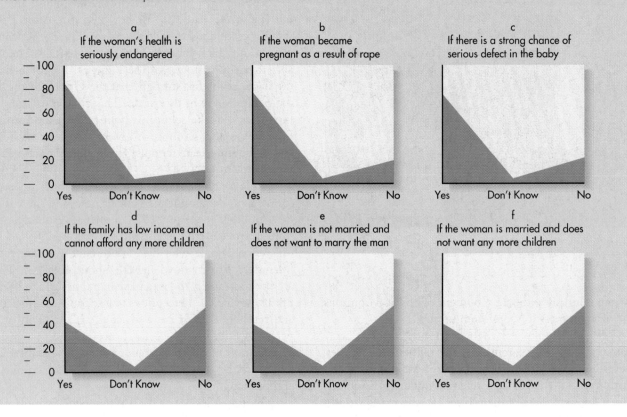

Textbooks often foster commitment to government and the status quo. Those used in elementary grades emphasize compliance with authority and the need to be a "good" citizen. Even textbooks in advanced grades present idealized versions of the way government works and exaggerate the role of citizens in holding public officials accountable and in shaping public policy.

Textbooks are less likely, however, to emphasize the need for citizens to uphold democratic values such as participating in politics and tolerating others' views about politics. Nor do they help students understand that conflicts and differences of opinion are inevitable in a large and diverse society and that the role of politics is to address and resolve these disagreements.

But the number of civics courses taken in high school does improve students' knowledge of government and politics and foster beliefs that government pays attention to people and that elections are important in holding government responsible. Courses during the senior year, when students are ready to make the transition to adulthood and when government and politics are likely to be more meaningful, are particularly important.[31] Honors and advanced placement (AP) programs, along with active learning, can improve student understanding and achievement in American history.[32]

Reading habits and language skills are also important to democratic citizenship. Reading, a skill learned in school but often nurtured in the home, is related to interest in politics, knowledge of public affairs, political participation, and political tolerance. Those who spend time reading are more likely to reflect these attributes of democratic citizenship than whose who do not.[33] Proficiency with language is important, too, as language is the mechanism for communicating and assessing information. Those with the skill are able to digest, organize, and make sense of and evaluate new ideas and arguments.[34]

In sum, the major impact of kindergarten through high school seems to be that it creates "good" citizens, citizens who accept political authority and the institutions of government and limit their political activities to the conventional and routine such as voting in elections. In this way, elementary and secondary education serve government in ways that most leaders prefer. Schools are not as good at fostering political participation and commitment to democratic values. The overall limitation of schools helping foster participating citizens who understand the role of dissent and argument over politics is sometimes attributed to the "hidden curriculum."[35] Schools are not democratic institutions in which students are encouraged to participate in a meaningful way. Indeed, most schools foster a climate averse to controversy. In such an environment, the value attached to participation and democracy is likely to remain underdeveloped.

The impact of college often moves students toward support for activist government directed at reducing income inequality and greater individual freedom with respect to civil liberties. (Civil liberties are discussed in Chapter 14.) Many go to college to get a job that pays well. Some go to expand their knowledge and understanding of the world. Others attend because parents insist or simply because everyone else does. No one goes to become more liberal, but this is often the result.[36] College students are more liberal than the population as a whole, and the longer they are in college, the more liberal they become. Seniors are more liberal than freshmen, and graduate students are more liberal than undergraduates.

Some argue that college professors indoctrinate students. A Carnegie Commission survey showed that 64 percent of the social science faculty in the nation's colleges identify themselves as liberal, and only 20 percent regard themselves as conservative. However, faculty in other fields are less liberal. For example, only 30 percent of the business faculty identify themselves as liberal.

During the height of the Vietnam War (1968–1971), students were more likely to identify themselves as liberal than students before or after the war. During the same period, the outlook of college faculty changed very little. Students are not simply a reflection of their college teachers. At large universities, where the largest percentage of students attend, the environment is sufficiently diverse to reinforce many points of view. Moreover, it is college that provides students with the self-confidence and independence that enable them to resist indoctrination.

It is possible that college students are liberal because college attracts those who are more liberal in the first place. Although this may have been true in the early 1970s when many more college freshmen identified themselves as liberal than did members of the public generally, more recently, college freshman were only about as liberal as the rest of society.[37] Today, most college freshmen are moderates.[38]

On issues, college freshmen look much like the population as a whole, liberal on some issues but conservative on others. They are liberal in wanting the government to do more to control pollution and the sale of handguns and provide national health care to cover everyone's medical costs. They are conservative in wishing to retain the death penalty, believing that the courts show too much concern for the rights of criminals, and asserting that racial discrimination is no longer a problem. They are divided on abortion and affirmative action in college admissions (Table 1).

TABLE 1	Opinions of College Freshmen
	Percentage Who Agree
Federal government is not doing enough to control pollution (1997).	81
Federal government needs to do more to control sale of handguns.	81
National health care is needed to cover everyone's medical costs (1997).	72
Affirmative action in college admissions should be abolished.	49
Abortion should be abolished.	45
Courts show too much concern for rights of criminals.	64
The death penalty should be abolished.	32
Racial discrimination is no longer a problem.	20

SOURCE: Thomas Bartlett, "Evaluating Student Attitudes Is More Difficult This Year," *Chronicle of Higher Education*, February 1, 2002, A35–A38. See also Alexander W. Astin, W. S. Korn, and Linda Sax, *The American Freshman: Thirty Year Trends* (Los Angeles: Higher Education Research Institute, Graduate School of Education and Information Studies, 1997), and Linda Sax, Alexander Astin, William Korn, and Kathryn Mahoney, *The American Freshman: National Norms for Fall 1999* (Los Angeles: Higher Education Research Institute, Graduate School of Education and Information Studies, 1999).

During the past few years, freshmen have become slightly more liberal in their opinions even if not in their self-identification.[39]

The most distinctive characteristic of college freshmen in recent years has been their declining interest in politics. In 1999, only 15 percent said that they had discussed politics in the past year, and only 21 percent voted in a school election. Only 26 percent of college freshmen considered it very important to keep up with politics. These figures represented all-time lows.[40] In many respects, the political apathy that has gripped adults was also reflected in college freshmen. However, 2001 showed an increase in interest, with 34 percent judging that it is important to keep up with political events, the largest one-year increase in that response in thirty years.[41] Perhaps this reflects a long-term upward trend in the attention of college students toward politics, but it may only represent a short-lived bump, attributable to the excitement and suspense associated with the resolution of the presidential election in 2000.

In spite of declining political interest, recent college freshmen have increased their participation in organized demonstrations and volunteer work. In 2001, nearly half reported participating in a demonstration during the year, and most reported volunteering. Increased volunteerism reflects the growing tendency of community service requirements for high school graduation. Rising levels of activism and involvement bode well for democratic participation in the future.

Peers

In many instances, peers simply reinforce the opinions of the family or school. When there is a conflict between peer and parental socialization, peers sometimes win but only on issues of special relevance to youth. For example, peer influence is more important than family influence on the issue of whether eighteen-year-olds should be allowed to vote, but parental influence appears to be more significant with respect to partisanship and vote choice.[42] Peers have the most influence when the peer group is attractive to the individual and when the individual spends more time with the group. With growing numbers of single-parent families and working parents, parental influence may be diminishing. Friends and associates, of course, take on greater importance for adults.

Mass Media

The primary effect of the media on children is to increase their level of information about politics. The primary effect on adults is to influence what they think about—that is, the issues, events, and personalities they pay attention to.[43] The media also influence opinions about issues and individuals; in recent years, many parts of the media have tended to display a high degree of cynicism and negativism about political leaders. Research shows that changes in public opinion tend to follow sentiments expressed by television news commentators.[44] The impact of the media is explored in more detail in Chapter 5.

Adult Socialization

Not all political socialization occurs in childhood. It is a lifelong process; opinions change with new experiences. For example, marriage, divorce, unemployment, a new job, or a move to a new location can affect political opinions.[45]

Economic, political, and social events have the potential to change the way Americans think about politics. Many hard hit by the Great Depression were drawn to politics seeking help. Most, voting for the first time, cast their ballot for the Democrats in 1932 and have voted Democratic ever since. World War II and the attack on Pearl Harbor shaped the opinions of a generation of Americans. The war in Vietnam moved many college students to the streets in protest and some to reject their country and travel to Canada to avoid the draft. In contrast, terrorist attacks on the Pentagon and World Trade Center have pushed the public closer to government (see the "After 9/11" box), but many of these effects dissipated within a few months.[46]

Impact of Political Socialization

Each new generation of Americans is socialized to a large extent by the preceding generations. In many ways each new generation will look and act much like the one that came before. In this sense, political socialization is biased against change. Typically, it leads to support for and compliance with government and the social order. Although many disagree with particular government policies, few question the basic structure of government.

Yet the impact of political socialization is not the same for all groups of people. For example, the socialization experiences of poor rural children are different from those of rich suburban ones. In the 1970s and the 1980s, children from low-income families were more cynical about government; black children felt less able to influence government and were less inclined to trust it.[47] These differences, especially racial differences, are reflected in the slightly greater trust in government by white adults today.

ATTACKS AFFECT OPINION ABOUT GOVERNMENT

Nothing since World War II has moved public opinion more dramatically than the events of 9/11. Before the terrorist attacks, many Americans considered government unimportant and irrelevant to their lives. Some disaffected Americans even considered it dangerous to their liberties. With the fall of the Soviet Union, the nation's principal antagonist for nearly four decades, a booming economy and surging stock market during the 1990s, and a constant barrage of negative commentary about the government from the media and critical politicians, many Americans felt that government was not necessary to their security and well-being. In 2000, one-third felt it unimportant who was elected president, and over 80 percent believed it unimportant to listen to the president's State of the Union address. But the attacks altered people's perceptions. From the ashes of the World Trade Center and Pentagon sprang a new feeling of patriotism and an increased level of trust and favorable feelings toward the national government.

Flag sales soared, and millions of people bought flag pins, ties, bumper stickers, and other objects displaying the flag. Athletes wore flags on their uniforms, and audiences sang the national anthem more frequently.

Attitudes also changed in less demonstrable ways. Suddenly what the president had to say was important. Fifty-four percent, more than twice as many as the year before, found the president's address to the nation in January 2002 especially important. Eighty-two percent, compared with just 50 percent the year before, had a favorable view of the national government. Trust in government, hovering at 30 percent

"But first our national anthem."

for most of the decade, nearly doubled following the attacks.[1] The public standing of the president and Congress similarly surged. The approval rating of the president was at the highest levels ever recorded (there was no polling at the time of Pearl Harbor). There was an elevated sense that citizens needed the national government, at least to provide protection at home and wage war abroad. As someone remarked, "The only persons going up the stairs of the World Trade Center while everyone else was going down were government officials. The events brought home the fact that the government does important work."[2]

Along with renewed feelings of the importance of government, support for increased spending on the military

tripled. Not since the end of World War II has the public been more eager to use military force abroad; majorities supported military action against nations linked to the struggle against terrorism.

Already some (though not all) of the public's views have returned to pre-9/11 levels, but immediately after the attacks, these opinion changes gave the Bush administration the public support it needed to retaliate against terrorism.

1. Alexander Stille, "Suddenly, Americans Trust Uncle Sam," *New York Times,* November 3, 2001, from the Web.
2. "Public Opinion Six Months Later," Pew Research Center for the People and the Press, news release, March 7, 2002.

Measuring Public Opinion

Public opinion is typically measured by asking individuals to answer questions in a survey or poll. Before polls, other techniques were employed that are still used today along with polls. Elected officials listen to opinions of people who write or talk to them; journalists gauge public opinion by talking selectively to individuals; letters written to newspaper editors or newspaper editorials are a measure of public opinion. Protests and demonstrations also are reflections of public opinion.

All of these techniques provide an incomplete picture, however. Letters to public officials and newspapers are more likely to come from people with extreme opinions[48] or from those with writing skills—that is, people with more education. Nor will opinions culled from a few conversations match the pattern of opinion for the nation as a whole. Editorial opinion is even less likely to provide an accurate picture of public opinion because most newspaper publishers tend to be conservative, and this view is often reflected in their editorials. For example, in most presidential elections in the twentieth century, newspapers favored the Republican candidate by about three to one.[49]

On the other hand, using polls to measure public opinion may shift public opinion from being an expression of the public to being a creation of the pollsters.[50] Prior to the use of polls, people who wanted to be heard had to write letters, deliver speeches, or organize protests. Today, pollsters initiate the expression of public opinion by conducting a poll. Rather than focusing on what the public is exercised about, polls concentrate on what pollsters and their sponsors are most interested in. Many issues of importance to the public may never become the subject of a poll.

Polling remains, however, the only accurate way to assess what the nation as a whole thinks about political issues and personalities. In this sense, polls are the best measure of public opinion, but they are not without problems.

Early Polling Efforts

The first attempts to measure popular sentiments on a large scale were the **straw polls** (or unscientific polls) developed by newspapers in the nineteenth century.[51] In 1824, the *Harrisburg Pennsylvanian,* in perhaps the first poll assessing candidate preferences, sent reporters to check on support for the four presidential contenders that year. In July, the paper reported that Andrew Jackson was the popular choice over John Quincy Adams, Henry Clay, and William H. Crawford. Jackson also received the most votes in the election, but John Quincy Adams was elected president after the contest was decided in the House of Representatives. Toward the end of the nineteenth century, the *New York Herald* regularly tried to forecast election outcomes in local, state, and national races. During presidential election years, the paper collected estimates from reporters and political leaders across the country and predicted the Electoral College vote by state.

Straw polls are still employed today. Some newspapers have interviewers who ask adults at shopping malls and other locations their voting preferences. Some have readers return coupons printed in the papers. Television and radio stations often ask questions and provide two telephone numbers for listeners to call—one for yes, one for no. Some television networks ask viewers to indicate their preferences on the Web. The votes are then electronically recorded and tabulated.

No straw poll is scientifically valid, though such polls may spark interest in the subject being discussed. The major problem with straw polls is that there is no way to ensure that the sample of individuals giving opinions is representative of the larger population. Generally, they are not.

The famed *Literary Digest* poll is a good example. This magazine conducted polls of presidential preferences between 1916 and 1936. As many as 18 million ballots were mailed out to persons drawn from telephone directories and automobile registration lists. Although the purpose was less to measure public opinion than to boost subscriptions, the *Digest* did have a pretty good record. It had predicted the winners in 1924, 1928, and 1932. In 1936, however, the magazine predicted Alfred Landon would win, but Franklin Delano Roosevelt won by a landslide. The erroneous prediction ended the magazine's polling, and in 1938 the *Digest* went out of business.

A bias in the *Digest*'s polling procedure that the editors failed to consider led to an erroneous prediction. At the time, owners of telephones and automobiles were disproportionately middle- and high-income individuals who could afford a telephone or car in the depths of the Great Depression; these people were much more likely to vote for Landon (a Republican) than were lower-income people.[52] Since the sample was drawn from telephone directories and auto registrations, lower-income people were disproportionately excluded from the poll.

Emergence of Scientific Polling

Scientific polling began after World War I, inspired by the new field of business known as marketing research. After the war, demand for consumer goods rose, and American business, no longer engaged in the production of war materials, turned to satisfying consumer demand. Businesses used marketing research to identify what consumers wanted and, perhaps more important,

A major problem for public opinion pollsters is designing questions that accurately measure what the public believes about issues. "It's not the case that a few words don't make a lot of difference in a poll question." What? Poorly worded questions, such as those with double negatives, can confuse the public and lead pollsters to draw the wrong conclusions.

This point was illustrated in a poll sponsored by the American Jewish Committee to find out the proportion of Americans who doubt that the Holocaust (the mass murder of millions of Jews by the Nazis in World War II) happened. The survey asked the following question: "As you know, the term *Holocaust* usually refers to the killing of millions of Jews in Nazi death camps during World War II. Does it seem possible or does it seem impossible to you that the Nazi extermination of the Jews never happened?" The results: Twenty-two percent said it was possible that the Holocaust never happened; another 12 percent were not sure. The conclusion: About one-third of the country either doubted the truth of the Holocaust or was uncertain.

Since no reputable historian or anyone with the slightest knowledge of world affairs denies that the Holocaust happened, this "finding" was shocking. Commentators reflected on how the public could be so ignorant of one of the major events, not just of twentieth-century history but of all recorded history. On further investigation, however, it seems that the wording of the question influenced the responses.

Another version of the question asked, "Does it seem possible to you that the Nazi extermination of Jews never happened, or do you feel certain that it happened?" This time only 1 percent said it was possible the Holocaust never happened. Eight percent were unsure, and 90 percent said they were certain the Holocaust happened.

Why the difference? A study of thirteen polls with estimates of Holocaust doubters from 1 percent to 46 percent found that studies with high estimates used double-negative wording. For example, to express that the Holocaust happened, one had to respond "impossible" that it "never happened." Such wording often results in a response that is exactly the opposite of what is intended.

What do Americans really know about the Holocaust? Nine of ten have heard of the Holocaust; however, only two-thirds are able to identify the Holocaust correctly. In 1992, knowledge of the Holocaust increased with publicity surrounding the opening of the Holocaust Museum in Washington and the release of the Academy Award–winning movie *Schindler's List*.

Even when questions are worded properly, the wording can lead to different conclusions. For example, when asked whether or not the budget surplus should be used to cut taxes or fund new programs, 60 percent say cut taxes. When, however, the option is cut taxes or fund programs for education, the environment, health care, crime fighting, and military defense, only 22 percent opt for tax cuts. Apparently, reminding the public of real needs stimulates a propensity to want to deal with those needs.

SOURCE: Richard Morin, "From Confusing Questions, Confusing Answers," *Washington Post National Weekly Edition*, July 18–24, 1994, 37.

---

how products should be packaged so consumers would buy them. For example, the American Tobacco Company changed from a green to a white package during World War II because it found that a white package was more attractive to women smokers.[53]

The application of mathematical principles of probability was also important to the development of scientific polling. To determine the frequency of defects in manufactured products, random or spot inspections of a few items, called a *sample,* were conducted. From these, projections of defects for the entire group of items were made. From this use of sampling, it was a small step to conclude that sampling a small number of individuals could provide information about a larger population.

In the early 1930s, George Gallup and several others, using probability-based sampling techniques, began polling opinions on a wide scale. In 1936, Gallup predicted that the *Literary Digest* would be wrong and that Roosevelt would be reelected with 55.7 percent of the vote. Though Gallup underestimated Roosevelt's actual vote (he won 62.5 percent), his correct prediction of a landslide lent credibility to probability-based polls.

Increasingly, government used polls. In 1940, Roosevelt became the first president to use polls on a regular basis, employing a social scientist to measure trends in public opinion about the war in Europe.

Polls and Politics

Most major American universities have a unit that does survey research, and there are hundreds of commercial marketing research firms, private pollsters, and newspaper polls. For politicians, polls have become what the oracle of Delphi was to the ancient Greeks and

Although an interesting gimmick to attract customers, this is not a very scientific way of measuring public opinion.

Todd Yates/The Facts, Clute, Texas

Merlin was to King Arthur: a divine source of wisdom. During the budget debate between President Clinton and congressional Republicans, Republicans used polls that told them that promising to "put the government on a diet" would be popular in the upcoming 1996 election. Polls directed Clinton to counter by accusing the Republicans of trying to cut Medicare. When the media wanted to make sense out of the debate, they conducted still more polls.[54]

Beginning in the 1960s, presidents increasingly turned to polls to assess the public's thinking on issues.[55] None, however, can match the extent to which President Clinton relied on polls during his presidency. He rarely made a move without consulting his pollster. Following the 1994 elections in which Democrats lost control of both the House and Senate, Clinton vowed never again to be out of step with the public.[56] Weekly polls shaped his centrist message, leading to his reelection in 1996. If polls showed a position to be popular, Clinton was likely to adopt it as his own. He embraced welfare reform, a Republican idea opposed by Democrats in Congress and liberals in his administration, partly because it was popular.[57] A White House poll in 1997 suggested that Americans preferred using the surplus to bolster Social Security rather than a Republican-preferred tax cut. In his State of the Union address, he called on Congress to "save Social Security first." Clinton would also quickly withdraw when polls showed an issue to be unpopular. For example, a proposal allowing needle exchanges to check the spread of AIDS was pulled an hour before it was to be announced because a poll revealed it to be politically risky. Polls directed the administration on V-chips to block inappropriate TV programs directed at children, Food and Drug Administration authority to regulate tobacco, and subsidies for college tuition. Clinton even used polls to select a vacation spot.[58] Rather than vacation on Martha's Vineyard and play golf, Clinton went hiking in the Rockies instead, having been told by a consultant that golf was a Republican sport and that the voters he needed to win were campers.

Of course, Clinton did not adopt positions only because they were popular or go against his own instincts about what the right policy choices were. He bucked public opinion and many leaders of his own party in his support for NAFTA (the North American Free Trade Agreement) and was again out of step with public opinion in his support for a multibillion-dollar bailout when the Mexican peso collapsed. He also defied public opinion in sending troops to Bosnia. To his surprise, his standing in the polls rose.[59]

Mindful of the negative publicity Clinton received as one who would not move without a poll, George W. Bush leaves the impression that he doesn't do polls.[60] When asked by a former Clinton press secretary at an informal luncheon what polls showed regarding public warnings of nonspecific terrorist threats, Bush responded, "In this White House, we don't poll on something as important as national security."[61]

But, of course, the Bush administration does use polls. While Bush's spending on polls during his first year did not match Clinton's, Bush's pollster, lower profile than Clinton's, toils in the background to find the words and phrases to sell Bush's policies to the public. In a speech pushing privatizing Social Security, Bush avoided that phrase, opting instead for terms such as "retirement security," "choice," and "opportunity." The goal is to find poll-tested phrases that can be used to sell the public on the idea of privatizing Social Security. Similarly, Bush's energy plan was described as "balanced" and "comprehensive" and one that relies on "modern" methods to prevent environmental damage. "School choice," "death tax," and "wealth-generating private accounts" are other poll-tested phrases designed to push an agenda with limited appeal. While Clinton relied on polls to find policies with broad public support, Bush relies on them to package and camouflage policies favored by his conservative base to make them more attractive to mainstream voters.[62] "Crafted-talk," as it is called, enables politicians to move away from the center and cater to the somewhat more extremist views of their base yet at the same time appear mainstream.[63]

Polls by news organizations have also increased. The number of network-sponsored tracking polls, in which a small number are polled on successive evenings throughout a campaign in order to assess changes in the level of voter support, exploded in 2000. Originally used in campaigns to assess the effectiveness of political ads, ABC was the first to use tracking polls in the New Hampshire presidential primary in 1984 to assess the growing strength of candidate Gary Hart. Based on small samples, no more than two hundred, networks were reluctant to air their results until CNN did so in 1988. In 2000, virtually every news organization of any size featured daily tracking polls.[64] Tracking polls monitor the movement of the candidates during the campaign, who is rising and who is falling behind. This horse race aspect of the campaign makes a good news story, and such polls are designed to attract an audience.

The ease of conducting polls explains, in part, their increasing use. Pollsters can conduct a poll at a moment's notice and have the results within a few hours. Not all polls are, however, equally useful or accurate. On clearly defined issues that the public has thought about carefully and on which it holds strong views, such as the vote in tomorrow's election, a well-designed poll is usually fairly accurate. All eight of the election eve polls in the 1996 presidential election predicted the winner. One got it exactly right, finding Clinton with a 9 percent advantage over Dole. The president's actual margin of victory was 8.4 percent. The average error of these polls was a remarkably low 1.7 percent.[65] In 2000, each candidate received 48 percent, with Gore, a half million votes ahead. This election proved too close to call, but all election eve polls predicted the candidates' totals within each poll's margin of error.

On issues that the public has not thought much about and on which choices are less clearly defined, polls rarely provide a meaningful guide to what the public thinks. Poll results reflecting support for candidates seeking office for the first time often jump up and down simply because voters do not know much about the candidates.

Even when issues are well defined and opinions are fairly stable, it is increasingly difficult to obtain a sample that provides a representative picture of public opinion. Many respondents refuse to be interviewed,[66] some because they do not want to be bothered, others because they fear they will be asked to buy something or contribute money. Nonrespondents, those who refuse or cannot be reached, number from 50 to 80 percent of those called, and these people are more likely to be better educated, more affluent, and live in suburbs rather than cities and rural areas.[67]

Another problem for pollsters is the tendency of some respondents to express an opinion when they do not have one. No one wants to appear ignorant. Some

SLOP Surveys Are Sloppy Surveys

SLOP is an acronym for self-selected listener opinion polls. SLOP surveys are telephone call-in or Web-based polls, which are being used increasingly by radio and television stations and even by newspapers. Why attach such a negative label to call-in polls? The answer is simple: The results are meaningless because those who call in do not reflect the views of the general public.

Of course, some of these polls are harmless, such as when sports Web sites invite fans to vote for their favorite athlete or play of the week or predict the outcome of the next week's big matchup. But as a guide to public opinion on important issues, these polls are worthless.

An example was CBS's survey to gauge public reaction to President Bush's 1992 State of the Union address. The program allowed viewers to dial and then respond to a series of recorded questions by pushing buttons on their telephone. CBS recorded the views of more than three hundred thousand respondents. In an effort to measure representativeness, at the same time CBS also conducted a survey of 1,241 adults. A comparison of the two polls revealed that the results differed by 10 percent or more on seven of the nine questions. One question asked whether respondents were better off or worse off than four years ago. In the call-in poll, 54 percent said they were worse off, compared to 32 percent in the scientific survey. In other words, viewers who are angrier or more concerned may be more likely to call to express their opinions.

Nonetheless, SLOP surveys are likely to continue. As one pollster put it, "It's a good show. And who's going to give up a good show just for the truth?"

SOURCES: Richard Morin, "Another Contribution to SLOPpy Journalism," *Washington Post National Weekly Edition*, February 10–17, 1992, 38; Richard Morin, "Numbers from Nowhere: The Hoax of the Call-in 'Polls,'" *Washington Post*, February 9, 1992, B3.

respondents volunteer an answer even though they know little or nothing about a subject. The problem is getting worse as pollsters increasingly probe topics on which the public has no opinion and on which there is little reason to believe it should. For instance, pollsters asked whether the public thought President Reagan's colon cancer was serious and whether the bloody glove originally fit O. J. Simpson.[68]

Although polls can unintentionally be biased because of these problems, some pollsters and politicians

At 7:50 P.M. election night, the television networks declared Al Gore the winner in Florida. While the election was far from over, a win in Florida made it more likely that Gore would be elected president. About 9:30 the call went out from Voter News Service (VNS), the consortium that conducts exit polls for the networks, to pull back. Florida was "too close to call." At 2:15 the next morning, George W. Bush was pronounced the winner in Florida and the next president of the United States with 271 electoral votes, one more than needed. The nation waited for Gore's concession. It didn't come. Bush's lead in Florida began to erode. Sometime after 3:30, Gore's campaign manager issued a statement: "Without being certain of Florida, we cannot be certain about the election. Until the results in Florida are official, the Gore campaign continues."[1] At nearly the same moment, the networks pulled back again. Florida was too close to call.

Exit polls, a part of American elections since the 1960s, are used by television networks to project winners before all votes are counted. Voting precincts throughout a state are se-

lected at random. As voters leave polling places in these precincts throughout the day, they are asked how they voted. These results, coupled with early but incomplete election returns and an analysis of how precincts voted in the past, are used to project winners. While each network decides for itself when to call a race, they jointly contract with VNS to poll for all of them to reduce their costs. So the networks receive the same information at the same time. Usually, then, they declare a winner within a few minutes of each other. Even so, each tries to be the first to declare the winner. In the competitive news business, they scramble for bragging rights and for more viewers who might be lured by faster calls.

Exit polls worked well in 1992 and 1996, but 2000 was a disaster. How did it happen? Early in the day, exit poll information seemed suspect.[2] Precincts were out of step with past performance. There was still time, however, to make adjustments, and VNS rushed to alter its statistical models. While the networks were concerned with the last-minute changes, this was not shared with viewers.[3]

As the day wore on, it was apparent to all who were mulling over the data that this election was going to be very close. Shortly before the election polls closed in Florida, exit polls showed less than a 1 in 200 chance that a Gore prediction would prove wrong, even though only a fraction of the actual votes was counted at that point. A few minutes before eight, the networks declared Gore the winner.

The uncertainty and error were due to several factors. In a close race, a very large sample size is necessary. VNS did not have a very large sample size. In fact, no sample could predict a race this close. A second problem was that those polled were not representative of all who cast ballots. For example, a Tampa precinct, which weighed heavily in the initial projections, overrepresented the Gore vote.[4] Also, absentee ballots cast before the election, which tend to be Republican, were not sampled at all. Excluding absentee ballots from exit polls will become more critical now that states make it easier to vote before election day. A third problem is that VNS relies on past voting history in particular

---

consciously distort poll results. Today, many pollsters come from political consulting backgrounds and poll exclusively for members of one political party. Rather than provide accurate information about public opinion, their goal is to present their client in the most favorable light.[69]

An egregious example of misuse is the "push poll." A pollster for Jones asks whether the person called is for John Jones, Mary Smith, or undecided in the upcoming congressional election. If the answer is Smith or undecided, the voter is asked, "If you were told that Smith's hobby is driving a high-powered sports car at dangerous speeds through residential neighborhoods to see how many children and pets she can run over, would it make a difference in your vote?" The voter is then asked her preference again. The idea is to see whether certain "information" can "push" voters away from a candidate or

a neutral opinion toward the candidate favored by those doing the poll.[70] Learning the weaknesses of the opposition has always been a part of politics, but push polls seek to manipulate opinion, rarely focus on a candidate's issue positions, and often distort a candidate's record and the facts.

An even more vicious tactic is to pump thousands of calls into a district or state under the guise of conducting a poll but with the intent of spreading false information about a candidate. John McCain accused the Bush campaign of spreading false information in the guise of a poll in the 2000 South Carolina primary when both were seeking the Republican presidential nomination. Similarly, Bush chided McCain for using a push poll in the Michigan presidential primary. Both the push poll and the phony poll are corruptions of the political process as well as violations of polling ethics.

precincts to help interpret current votes. That is, compared to its history, is the current vote in a particular precinct more Democratic or Republican? Voting history is a reliable guide during periods of stability but not when states are undergoing change. In Florida, a major influx of northerners along with a growing Hispanic population has altered Florida's political makeup, making elections less predictable.

Another problem goes to the heart of the controversy in Florida. A significant number of voters in one large county intended to vote for Gore but marked their ballots in ways that led them to be counted for another candidate. They, of course, did not realize this mix-up, and they told the pollsters that they had voted for Gore. So they were counted as Gore voters in the exit polls but not in the election itself.

Despite these problems, the networks might not have made incorrect projections if they had not been so preoccupied with cost cutting. Networks have been taken over by conglomerates such as Disney and General Electric, which focus on the bottom line. The reason that the networks jointly contracted with VNS was to save money. Then they reduced the budget for VNS, so it apparently sampled too few precincts.[5] Thus, cost cutting made the networks vulnerable. If their single source of exit polls got it wrong, they all would get it wrong. If there had been multiple sources with separate polls and different samples, probably some would have suggested a Gore win, others a Bush win, and others that it was too close to call. Then the networks would have exercised more caution and the public would have received a more realistic picture.

The wrong calls were not merely an embarrassment to the networks. Because the networks initially called Florida for Gore ten minutes before polling places in the state's western panhandle closed, it is possible that a few Republicans on their way to vote might have turned around and gone home without voting. Because the networks later called Florida for Bush, proclaiming him our "forty-third president," it is likely that many people around the country considered Bush the legitimate winner even when the networks decided the election was too close to call after all. Then in the post-election contest, when the two sides were struggling for public support, Gore was put in the position of seeming to try to take Bush's victory, and his presidency, away from him.

While the disaster in 2000 is unlikely to deter networks from exit polling and projecting winners permanently, they are likely to be more cautious. In 2002, the networks did not use exit polling to project winners and VNS is currently trying to improve its methods.

1. Seth Mnookin, "It Happened One Night," *Brill's Content* (February 2001): 152.
2. Marvin Kalb, "TV Pays Big Price: Credibility," *Lincoln Journal-Star,* December 3, 2000, 7D; Tom Wolzien, "The Bottom Line," *Brill's Content* (February 2001): 97.
3. Mnookin, "It Happened One Night," 98.
4. Diana Owen, "Media Mayhem: Performance of the Press in Election 2000," in *Overtime! The Election 2000 Thriller,* ed. Larry J. Sabato (New York: Longman, 2002), 144.
5. Richard Morin and Claudia Deane, "Why the Florida Exit Polls Were Wrong," *Washington Post,* November 8, 2000.

Even reputable polls have their downside in politics. Poor standing in the polls may discourage otherwise viable candidates from entering a race, leaving the field to others who have less chance of winning or who lack the skills necessary to govern effectively. In 2000, several potential Republican candidates passed up the presidential race when early polls suggested that George W. Bush was the odds-on favorite to win the Republican nomination. And, in an unprecedented move, in 2002, Robert Torricelli (D-N.J.) withdrew from his Senate race thirty-six days before the election when polls showed that he could not win the election (he had been censured by the Senate for his unethical conduct).

Polls also can have a negative effect on political campaigns. Prior to polling, the purpose of campaigns was to reveal the candidates' views on the issues and their solutions to the pressing problems of the day. Instead, polls

Harry Truman exults in incorrect headlines, based on poll results and early returns, the morning after the 1948 election.

From the collection of the St. Louis Mercantile Library

focus attention on the electorate and what they think. Polls find out what the voters want, and the candidates develop images to suit the market.

The ease of polling also means that judgment and leadership often give way to the sentiments expressed in public opinion polls. Politicians rarely make a decision without one. Rather than educate the public regarding the merits of particular policies, many politicians seem to follow the polls blindly or use polls to package unpopular policies in a way that the public will find appealing.

Former senator Daniel Patrick Moynihan (D-N.Y.) decried politicians' addiction to poll results, suggesting that it had caused Congress to adopt popular causes, such as the line item veto, that were later found by the Supreme Court to be unconstitutional. "We've lost our sense of ideas that we stand by, principles that are important to us."[71]

As the number of polls, both good and bad, increases, their importance for the public and perhaps politicians may decline. The sheer number of polls may lead everyone to take them less seriously. Moreover, if politicians allow themselves to be driven by poll results and use them to manipulate the public, no one will gain an advantage from the information they provide.[72] Still, it is unlikely that ambitious politicians bent on winning at all costs will abandon something that may help them win.

In spite of problems and abuses, polls still provide a valuable service to the nation. If direct democracy, like the New England town meeting, is the ideal, the use of public opinion polls is about as close as the modern state is likely to get to it. Polls help interpret the meaning of elections. When voters cast their ballots for one candidate over another, all anyone knows for sure is that a majority preferred one candidate. Polls can help reveal what elections mean in terms of policy preferences and thus help make the government more responsive to voters. For example, the Republicans claimed their victory in the 1994 congressional elections was an indication that voters supported the party's Contract with America. However, polls showed that most Americans had never heard of it.

How Informed Is Public Opinion?

Many Americans are uninformed or misinformed concerning government and politics. Only one-fourth can name their two senators,[73] and only one-third can name their U.S. representative.[74] More than one-third do not know the party of their representative,[75] and 40 percent do not know which party controls Congress.[76]

TABLE 2	Large Proportions of the Public Are Ignorant of Politics
	Percentage Unable to Identify
Who is in Washington?	
Vice president	40
Speaker of the House	46
Their Senate representative	54
Majority leader in Senate	66
Their House representative	67
What goes on in Washington?	
That the number of federal employees decreased in last three years	72
That the government spends more on Medicare than on foreign aid	73
That the House passed a plan to balance federal budget	75
That the Senate passed a plan to balance the budget	78

SOURCE: Richard Morin, "Tuned Out, Turned Off," *Washington Post National Weekly Edition,* February 5–11, 1996, 6–8.

Many Americans are unable to identify prominent political personalities (see Table 2). Six years after he was elected vice president, 24 percent could not identify George H. Bush. More people can identify the judge on the television show *The People's Court* than can identify the chief justice of the United States.[77] In spite of increases in education, levels of knowledge regarding politics have not changed much since the 1940s.[78]

Although Americans revere the Constitution and see it as a blueprint for democracy, many do not know what is in it. One-third think it established English as the country's official language, and one in six thinks it established America as a Christian nation. One-fourth cannot name a single First Amendment right, and only 6 percent can name all four.[79]

Only a small percentage of Americans can identify a single piece of legislation passed by Congress.[80] Nearly 60 percent were ignorant of a widely discussed plan passed by the House of Representatives in 1995 to balance the federal budget.[81]

Misperception regarding government policies is widespread. While polls show Americans in favor of reducing the size of the federal government, more than 70 percent are unaware that the number of federal employees has decreased in recent years.[82] Most Americans feel that the country spends too much on foreign aid and think we should cut the amount we do spend, but one-half estimate foreign aid to be about fifteen times greater than it is. Asked what an appropriate spending level would be, the average answer is eight times more than the country actually spends.[83]

Nearly half of the public had an opinion on whether the Public Affairs Act of 1975 should be repealed. The act does not exist; the question was a ploy to see how many would volunteer an answer when they have no opinion. The problem is that they offered an opinion on something that does not exist.[84]

Most Americans do not think much about politics. Their major concerns are family, work, and friends. Lack of concern for government means that politicians can sometimes ignore what the public wants and what it needs. That is, politicians can be less responsive to the public. Although the public may not pay much attention to politics and is uninformed on many things, some political scientists argue that average citizens know what they need to know to make sound political judgments.[85] Most do take an active interest in politics when their personal stake is affected. For example, 80 percent know that Congress passed a law requiring employers to provide family leave following the birth of a child or a family emergency. Family leave touches people directly.

Lack of knowledge is an impediment to holding government accountable. Polls show that those who are less politically knowledgeable find it difficult to sort through the claims and counterclaims of politicians. Some support candidates and policies that work against their self-interest.[86]

Sometimes public officials prefer that voters lack knowledge on issues. Politicians often do not like to discuss issues, especially controversial ones. When they do, public awareness increases. After President Reagan made an issue of American support for the Nicaraguan Contras, for example, awareness of the issue and the side the United States was supporting jumped from 25 percent to 59 percent.[87] There are also politicians who try to deceive the public by packaging their proposals and ideas in language the public finds appealing.[88]

Public Opinion

Public opinion polls cover virtually every aspect of American life. Polls have reported the number of California drivers with paraphernalia hanging from their rearview mirrors and Iowans with ornaments on their lawns. Political polls examine opinions about political issues and political candidates, whether the American people are liberal or conservative, and whether this influences their positions on issues and preferences for political candidates. Although it is important to know how Americans stand on current issues and how they feel about political candidates, it is also important to know what they think about government: its founding principles, political institutions, and political leaders. This is

especially true when large numbers of Americans see government and politics as unimportant or even feel hostile toward them.

This section begins with a discussion of ideology—what it is, what the labels liberal and conservative mean, and whether Americans are liberal or conservative. Next it looks at how liberals and conservatives stand on specific issues such as social welfare, social issues, and race. Finally, it explores how liberals and conservatives feel about extending rights and liberties to individuals who do not share their opinions and whether they trust the government to do the right thing.

Ideology

The term *ideology* refers to a highly organized and coherent set of opinions. In the extreme, one who is ideological takes a position on all issues consistent with his or her ideology. *Liberalism* and *conservatism* are terms used to describe the current major ideologies in American politics. Liberals are sometimes identified by the label "left" or "left wing" and conservatives by the label "right" or "right wing." These terms date from the French National Assembly of the early nineteenth century in which conservative parties occupied the right side of the chamber and liberal parties occupied the left side.

Liberalism, as a set of ideas, endorses the notion that government has an obligation to help individuals, groups, and communities that are economically disadvantaged by providing them with such things as health care, education, and income. In the New Deal era, liberal ideas were the justification for using government to expand opportunities and improve the quality of life for all. With this view as their platform, the Democrats came to power in the 1930s and dominated American politics through the 1960s. During the 1960s, liberalism came to be identified with the civil rights policies of the Democrats. These policies threatened the white-dominated social order in the South and white ethnic communities in the North. Blacks increasingly turned to the Democratic Party, and many whites, especially in the South, turned to the Republican Party. Liberalism was also linked to anti–Vietnam War protests and to Supreme Court decisions that expanded the rights of persons accused of crimes, legalized abortion, and barred mandatory prayer in schools. These less popular policies led to attacks on liberalism and government activism by conservatives.

Today, liberals continue to believe that the free market does not always produce acceptable outcomes and that sometimes government must intervene. Liberalism is therefore associated with support for Social Security; a progressive income tax; government assistance for the poor and, in different forms, working- and middle- class Americans; and regulation to protect the environment. Liberals also tend to believe that government should not be involved in personal moral decisions and so favor abortion rights. Liberals tend to oppose expansion of military spending except in times of crisis. But liberals range from Clinton's very middle-of-the-road beliefs that combined beliefs in racial jus-tice, keeping government at arm's length from personal moral decisions such as abortion, and an opposition to too much government, to those much more support-ive of government intervention into a great variety of policy areas.

Conservatism, on the other hand, identifies a set of ideas emphasizing that individuals are responsible for their own well-being and that the government has

Focus Groups: Measuring or Manipulating Public Opinion?

Few are so naive to assume that a pres-ident writes his own speeches, but most accept that his speechwriters use their own words. Not so. Increasingly, presidents, candidates, and political parties use language that is tested in focus groups before it is included in a presidential address, featured in a cam-paign ad, or incorporated into a party platform. A *focus group* is a dozen or so average men and women who are brought together to share feelings and reactions to any one of a number of things, including language. For political consultants, the task is to find words and phrases that will produce the de-sired reaction on the part of the public toward particular policies and political candidates. There are dozens of "word labs," but one of the more elaborate is run by Republican pollster Frank Luntz. In 2000, he produced a pocket-size pamphlet called "Right Words" and a four-hundred-page loose-leaf binder called "A Conversation with America" for the Republican Party.

Based on his focus groups, Luntz counseled Republicans that "Depart-ment of Defense" is preferred to "Pen-tagon," "opportunity scholarships" to "vouchers," "tax relief" to "tax cuts," and "climate change" to "global warming." If the goal is to turn people away from a policy, he recommends linking it with the supernegatives "Washington" and "IRS."

Unlike public opinion polls, partici-pants are not selected because they are representative of a group or popula-tion, nor is a great deal of time spent ensuring that questions are fair and un-biased. The only requirement is that participants feel comfortable enough with each other to share their feelings. This often means a degree of similarity with respect to race, income, educa-tion, and ideology. For example, com-bining blacks and whites or liberals and conservatives may limit the willingness of participants to share and restrict the give and take that characterizes focus groups.

The objective is to identify feelings that lie below the surface, which indi-viduals may not be aware of them-selves, are seldom voiced in public, and thus are not likely to be captured in a public opinion poll. Public opinion polls rarely reveal the depth or nuance of feeling that often rises to the surface in focus groups. These feelings are likely to come into play when people vote, and political consultants want to know which will activate a positive response to their candidates or issues.

In a typical session, Luntz begins with "I want to give you a word, and I want you to tell me how you define it. If someone said 'quality of life,' what would it mean to you?"[1] Responses come from around the room: "A com-fortable living." "Health care." "Secu-rity." "Safety." After some discussion, he throws out, "When I say 'govern-ment,' what comes to mind?"[2] He then points a finger at participants who volunteer, "The president," "Control-ling," "Providing security for people," "Laws," "Bureaucracy," "Wasteful," and "Liars." Another speaks up, "They could leave me alone. My company would be bigger if I had a little less law and a little more help."[3] A little less law and a little more help—interesting phrase, Luntz thinks. He asks the group, "What do you think?"[4]

Focus group participants invariably come away with a sense of empower-ment, a feeling that someone is gen-uinely interested in how they feel. Most forget what they suspected going in—that they are being used for the mod-est fee they are given to participate. Political handlers and consultants are interested in how participants feel, not to make the system more responsive but to produce potent messages that will color how they react and feel to-ward political issues and candidates. It makes one wonder whether the phrase "Real Plans for Real People" just popped into George Bush's head or was this the brain child of a word lab? Did President Clinton "build the bridge to the twenty-first century" or did he have help?

1. Nicholas LeMann, "The World Lab," *New Yorker,* October 16 and 23, 2000, 107.
2. Ibid.
3. Ibid., 108.
4. Ibid.
Sources: Elizabeth Kolbert, "Test-Marketing a President," *New York Times Magazine,* Au-gust 30, 1992; Nicholas LeMann, "The World Lab," *New Yorker,* October 16 and 23, 2000.

little or no obligation to help or improve individuals or communities. Whereas liberalism turns to government to solve social and economic problems, conservatism relies on the "invisible hand" of the economic marketplace. Conservatives would, for example, scale back or eliminate welfare payments to the poor and create incentives for the private sector to employ them and reduce government regulation of the environment and financial systems. They would place restrictions on labor's right to organize and bargain collectively, opt for a flat income tax, and look to the market to deal with issues of health care, public education, and Social Security.

However, since the 1960s, some strains of conservatism, particularly those rooted in the religious right, have called for more government intervention in certain moral issues. These conservatives endorse government-imposed solutions in the realm of social behavior, and they would outlaw abortion, require prayer in school, and legislate against homosexuality whenever possible. However, as with liberalism, the term *conservative* covers quite a variety of opinion. Some conservatives are strongly supportive of individual choice in abortion and oppose government intervention into other personal moral decisions such as sexual orientation.

How do Americans identify on the liberal–conservative continuum? One way to find out is to ask them. Slightly more Americans identify themselves as conservative than liberal, and this pattern has changed very little in the past fifteen years. Most Americans, however, identify themselves as moderate or in the middle. Moderates can be those who fall in the middle on most issues—that is, those who are neither liberal nor conservative, or those who are liberal on some issues and conservative on others.

Self-identifications reflected in asking Americans whether they are liberal or conservative are helpful, but they do not reveal whether those who claim to be liberal or conservative actually hold liberal or conservative issue positions. In fact, although self-identified liberals and conservatives do take different positions on a number of issues, on most issues a majority of liberals and conservatives take the same position. On social welfare issues, for example, most liberals and conservatives endorse increased spending for health care, education, the environment, and antidrug policies. Majorities of liberals and conservatives have similar feelings on issues of race and are supportive of civil liberties for all Americans whatever their views. Both tend to agree on the failings of the government. Findings such as these mean that most Americans are not very ideological. While many call themselves liberals or conservatives, they do not constitute cohesive blocs of citizens with opposing issue positions seeking to control the government in order to enact their positions into law.

Why aren't Americans more ideological? First, Americans are not very interested in politics. Much of what is important to average men and women in life falls outside politics. Most are concerned about family and jobs, which for the most part are not directly and immediately affected by government. Lack of interest leads to lack of intensity. Even where majorities of liberals and conservatives disagree—as, for example, on abortion and prayer in school—the feelings of most are not very intense, perhaps because most are not touched by these issues, either.

Second, political candidates and parties do not usually mobilize their followings with ideological or issue appeals. Both candidates and parties try to be all things to all people, for reasons discussed in Chapter 7, and often blunt the ideological or issue content of their message to attract support from both liberals and conservatives as well as those in the middle. Evidence also shows that candidates, at least those running for president, are more successful the closer they are to the middle compared to their opponent. President Clinton received his highest approval ratings following movement to the center when he supported welfare reform, free trade, and a balanced budget. His ratings declined when he advocated removing restrictions on gays in the military and health care reform, policies more associated with the liberal wing of his party.[89] President Bush moved quickly to the middle once he secured the Republican nomination in 2000, for example, downplaying positions of the party's conservative wing, such as support for privatizing Social Security and opposition to government regulation of the environment.

In spite of their generally moderate campaign rhetoric and frequent centrist policies, political leaders of both parties are more ideological than the rank and file. They are more interested in politics, which contributes to a higher level of intensity. And whereas scholars once wrote of "the end of ideology" in American politics, today they remark on its increase.

Social Welfare and the Proper Role of Government

Government programs to help individuals deal with economic hardship started during the Great Depression in the 1930s. These included programs to provide aid for the elderly (Social Security), unemployed, and poor. Most Americans supported government assistance of this kind in the 1930s and support it today (see Figure 2).

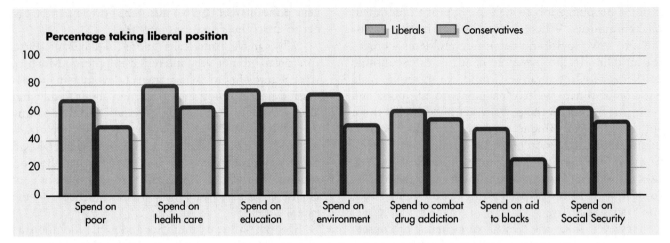

FIGURE 2 ■ Self-identified Liberals and Conservatives Differ Modestly on Spending for Social Services

SOURCE: 2000 General Social Survey.

Still, Americans have mixed feelings about social welfare spending. Support is high for keeping Social Security and for helping the poor. Nearly two-thirds feel that the nation is spending too little to assist the poor, and nearly the same number feel we spend too little on Social Security.[90] Nearly three-fourths favor additional government spending to improve and protect the nation's health.[91]

On the other hand, support for what is stigmatized as welfare, government spending for the "undeserving," is much lower.[92] Polls show most (60 to 80 percent) supported reforms that require persons on welfare to work and get off welfare after two years. Over 50 percent feel, however, that it is unfair for the government to cut off payments after two years if there is no other source of income. Most Americans (75 percent) believe the answer to welfare is job training and are willing to pay more in the short term to provide it. Americans appear to favor helping the poor, but they do not like "welfare," which for decades has been criticized by just about everyone, especially conservative politicians. They believe that requiring work and training for jobs are the keys to welfare reform.

Americans approve increased spending for education, the environment, drug rehabilitation, and crime and law enforcement.[93] Nearly 40 percent favor increases in spending for the nation's highways and bridges, mass transportation, and parks; and only one in ten oppose additional funding in these areas.[94]

In spite of these sentiments, two-thirds report that their federal income taxes are too high, and 84 percent indicate that taxes are very important when deciding among candidates for Congress. Other things equal, Americans want lower taxes and smaller government, but they are also concerned about the well-being of people in the country and caring for the disadvantaged.

Strong sentiment exists for state governments to assume many responsibilities of the national government.[95] Only 12 percent say that the national government does the best job of spending tax dollars in an efficient and constructive manner. Thirty-two percent say that state governments do the best job. While September 11 registered an improvement in Americans' level of confidence with the national government, more than half still believe the national government is wasteful and inefficient and controls too much of our daily lives.[96] It is possible (indeed, likely) that the greater visibility of the national government compared to state governments is responsible for the lower level of confidence. If state legislatures received the same level of publicity as Congress, evaluations by the public would likely be lower.

Since 9/11, Americans have a greater appreciation for the federal government. Few want to see the government made smaller by cutting spending and programs. They want it managed better and want to see better performance from government employees.

Social Issues

Beginning in the 1960s, so-called social issues, those relating to morality, became topics of political debate. Examples include abortion, prayer in schools, restrictions on pornography, tolerance of homosexuals, capital punishment, and the role of women in society. Not all surfaced at the same time, but by the 1990s all were included in what some described as the family values agenda.

Social issues represent a clash of values between those seeking to impose traditional moral standards on society and those who are less willing to do so. Many of these cleavages stem from the rapid social change in the 1960s and 1970s. Conventional ways of doing things were challenged by a number of social movements, including civil rights, women's, and environmental movements. Many people believed that government decisions, particularly court decisions, favored the agenda of these groups. The Supreme Court approved abortion, outlawed mandated prayer in school, extended rights to people accused of crimes, and raised questions about capital punishment. Women moved into the workforce in large numbers, aided by affirmative action policies. Homosexuals became more visible as a group and more outspoken regarding their civil rights. Some people, particularly Christian conservatives, believed (and continue to believe) that these developments were evidence of a decline in moral standards.

The division over values was reflected in opinions of Americans toward the impeachment of President Clinton. Some religious conservatives accused Clinton of subverting honesty and decency to such a degree that he should not be allowed to continue in office; on the other side, others accused the president's opponents of practicing "sexual McCarthyism" (see Chapter 14), trampling civil liberties and invading people's privacy.[97] While most found the president's relationship with Monica Lewinsky and his later denial of the relationship lacking in morality and ethics, nearly one-half felt it was unimportant as long as he was doing a good job running the country.

The position of liberals and conservatives on social issues is opposite of what it is on social welfare. On social welfare issues, liberals are likely to support government action, but on social issues, they reject government involvement. Liberals generally prefer to leave questions of religious belief and sexual morality to individuals to decide for themselves, while conservatives are more willing to call on government to enforce particular standards of behavior.

Conservatives, for example, are more likely to favor a ban on abortion and to require prayer in public schools (see Figure 3). They are more willing to support capital punishment and traditional roles for women. For example, conservatives are slightly more likely to feel that women should take care of the home and leave running the country to men. The vast majority of both liberals and conservatives, however, are open to men and women running the country and would support a woman for president.

Conservatives are considerably more likely than liberals to respond that homosexual relations are always

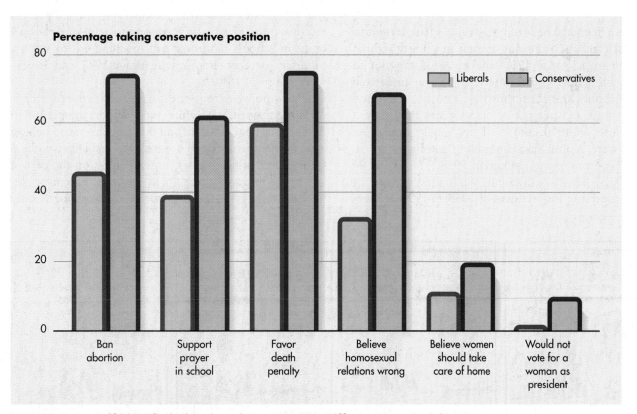

FIGURE 3 ■ Self-identified Liberals and Conservatives Differ on Many Social Issues
SOURCE: 1998, 2000 General Social Survey.

wrong. A significant generational divide suggests that society will become more tolerant in the future. Seven out of ten of those over sixty-five say homosexual behavior is wrong, but only five in ten of those eighteen to twenty-nine have this view.[98] Eight out of ten Americans, including both liberals and conservatives, think homosexuals should have equal rights in job opportunities and housing.

Race

Public opinion has influenced as well as responded to the progress of the black struggle for equality. Although the historical record of America's black–white relationships extends to colonial times, the polling record begins in the 1940s. Polls show white America increasingly opposed to discrimination and segregation, at least in principle.[99] In fact, the change might be characterized as revolutionary. For example, whereas only one-third of whites accepted the idea of black and white children going to the same schools in 1942, in the 1980s more than 90 percent approved. Today nearly everyone (98 percent) agrees. Over 80 percent respond that they have no objection to sending their children to schools where more than half of the students are black. Nearly two-thirds would not object to schools where most of the students are black.

The percentage believing that whites have a right to keep African Americans out of their neighborhood has been cut in half since 1963, and a 1996 survey found that two-thirds of white Americans live in integrated neighborhoods and claim they have a fairly close friend who is black (83 percent of blacks claim they have a fairly close white friend).[100] Thirty-eight percent of whites were against laws forbidding intermarriage in 1963; 85 percent were opposed in 1998.[101]

Only 37 percent expressed a willingness to vote for a black candidate for president in 1958; in 1996, 92 per-

cent expressed such willingness. These findings suggest that white America is becoming much more tolerant of racial diversity (see Figure 4). Although the North continues to be more supportive of black rights than the South, whites in both regions show increased acceptance of blacks.

Public opinion can change because individuals change or because older individuals with one set of opinions are replaced by a new generation with a different set. Changes in whites' racial opinions through 1960 occurred for both reasons. In the 1970s, most changes occurred because of replacement. Differences in socialization between those born in the 1920s and 1930s and those born in the 1950s and 1960s have led to much greater support for racial integration. More change can be expected in the future as white and black teens age and replace older Americans. A majority of white adults agree that the failure of blacks to take advantage of opportunities is more of a problem than discrimination by whites, while a large plurality of white teens consider discrimination by whites to be the bigger problem.[102]

While white Americans accept integration, they have been much slower to accept government initiatives to achieve it. In some issues, the direction of change has shifted from greater to lesser support. For example, 38 percent approved the federal government's ensuring fair treatment for blacks in jobs in 1964; only 28 percent endorsed the idea in 1996. Busing to achieve racial balance in schools has never had much appeal to whites. Thirteen percent endorsed the idea in 1972, and 33 percent did so in 1996.

How do we explain the discrepancy between the increasing majorities of whites who support integration in its various manifestations and the majorities who believe that government should not make special efforts to help minorities? In some cases, unwillingness on the part of whites to endorse government initiatives to end segregation reflects racist sentiments.[103] Although only

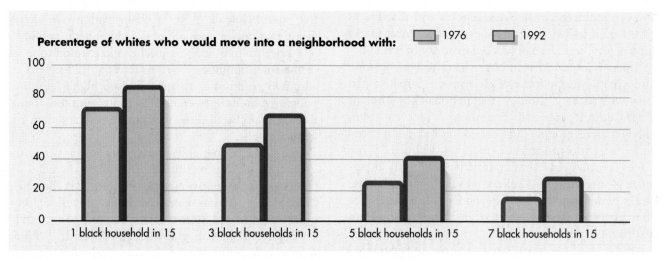

F I G U R E 4 ■ Whites Have Grown More Accepting of Neighborhood Integration
Residential segregation is the linchpin of racial separation in America. Such segregation influences the quality and nature of schools, employment opportunities, and the amenities of daily life. In the past twenty years, American cities have become somewhat less segregated, stimulated in part by whites' changing attitudes about residential segregation.
Source: Douglas Massey and Nancy Denton, *American Apartheid* (Cambridge, Mass.: Harvard University Press, 1993).

10 percent of white Americans respond that differences in jobs, housing, and income between whites and blacks are the result of biological differences,[104] 43 percent cling to the racist belief that it is lack of motivation and will power on the part of blacks.[105] Thus, anywhere from 10 to 40 percent of white Americans harbor racist beliefs in spite of their willingness to accept blacks, live in integrated neighborhoods, and have their children attend integrated schools.

However, some whites oppose government help for blacks on principle. They object to being told what to do by government or feel government assistance for blacks is discrimination against whites. For some, government help violates their sense that individuals have a responsibility to provide for themselves.

Another reason that some white Americans are reluctant to accept government intervention is that many do not see the need. African Americans and white Americans live in very different perceptual worlds. Anywhere from 40 to 60 percent of whites believe that the average African American is as well or better off than the average white American in terms of jobs, income, schooling, and health care.[106] This is in direct contradiction to the reality that blacks lag behind whites on virtually every social and economic indicator. But misperceptions such as these lead many whites to reject any government effort to equalize the social and economic standing of the races. When whites more accurately recognize the plight of black Americans, most are likely to accept the government's role in providing equal education for black and white children

and ensuring that blacks are treated equally by courts and police.[107]

Affirmative action has become a touchstone of racial issue polarization. A solid majority of white Americans reject affirmative action programs that give preferences to blacks.[108] It is not only Republicans and conservatives who oppose racial preferences but many Democrats and liberals as well.[109] (Affirmative action is discussed in Chapter 15.) However, a majority of African Americans favor various sorts of affirmative action giving preferences to blacks in education and employment.

The disconnect for many whites between perception and reality is linked to black success. As the black middle class increases, whites see blacks living in their communities with job skills and income comparable to their own. Some whites are in competition with blacks for jobs, promotion, and college admission. They are unlikely to accept that blacks are worse off than whites, and government programs targeted toward blacks are likely to breed resentment.

Blacks, not unexpectedly, see things differently. A majority view themselves trailing whites in education, income, jobs, and health care.[110] Forty-four percent indicate that they personally have been denied a job or promotion because of race.[111]

What do blacks believe should be done about race discrimination? Although the polling record for blacks does not extend as far back as it does for whites, blacks have overwhelmingly endorsed integration. Nearly all blacks have responded consistently that blacks and whites should go to the same schools and that blacks have a right to live anywhere they want to. Most blacks approve of intermarriage (as do a majority of whites).

Like whites, African Americans have become somewhat less supportive of government initiatives. In 1964, 92 percent thought the national government should ensure blacks fair treatment in jobs; by 1996, only 64 percent did. Support for government assistance in school integration has also declined. Some blacks fear that government initiatives will only antagonize whites. Others believe government aid hurts blacks by making them too dependent. Still others believe government is ineffective in bringing about an end to discrimination.

Differences on racial issues between self-identified liberals and conservatives are slight. Liberals are somewhat more likely to oppose laws that ban racial intermarriage, to disagree that whites have a right to keep blacks out of their neighborhood, and to be willing to send their children to a school where most are a different race. However, majorities of both liberals and conservatives take the proequality position on each issue.

One of the unexpected results of 9/11 has been at least a short-term increase in interracial harmony.[112] Whites appear to trust blacks more, blacks to trust whites more. Asians trust Hispanics more; Hispanics, Asians more; and so on. All of these groups registered an increase in trust toward each other after 9/11. The exception is the much lower degree of trust toward Arab Americans. Traditional taboos such as interracial marriage across ethnic and racial lines have also weakened in the wake of 9/11. Again with the exception of Arab Americans and immigrants, Americans also appear more tolerant of ethnic diversity than they were prior to 9/11.[113] The powerful images of devastation and suffering, and the horrified and stunned reaction to them that crossed racial lines, pulled Americans together across the racial and ethnic divide like no event since World War II. Of course, it is unlikely that these changes will be permanent.

Political Tolerance

Political tolerance is the willingness of individuals to extend procedural rights and liberties to people with whom they disagree. Tolerance is important because it embodies many elements essential to democratic government, such as freedom of speech and assembly.

J. William Fulbright, the former senator from Arkansas, once said, "Americans believe in the right to free speech until someone tries to exercise it." In other words, people are tolerant in the abstract but not when called upon to support speakers they disagree with. More than 85 percent of Americans claim to believe in free speech for all,[114] yet a classic nationwide survey found that only 37 percent of the respondents would allow a person opposed to churches and religion to speak in their communities.[115] Even fewer would permit an admitted communist to speak. More highly educated people were more tolerant than those with less education, and political elites were more tolerant than the general public.

The finding that elites were more tolerant than the general public was reassuring. After all, many elites are in a position to deprive people of rights, and elites help shape public opinion. Later studies have revealed, however, that elites are more tolerant than the general public largely because they are better educated.[116] Elites, however, do influence the opinions of the general public on civil liberties. When elites agree among themselves, the general public is more likely to reflect this consensus.[117]

More recent studies suggest that Americans have become substantially more tolerant of communists, socialists, and atheists.[118] However, overall levels of tolerance may not have increased that much. Today two-thirds or more think that members of their least-liked group should be banned from being president and from teaching in the public schools. Many think that the group should be outlawed, indicating a high degree of intolerance.

Economic insecurity in the 1980s and early 1990s helped promote intolerance toward minorities, immigrants, and others outside the mainstream. Long before September 11, more than 80 percent agreed that people coming to live in the United States should be restricted and controlled more than they are now.[119]

Certainly the war on terrorism in response to 9/11 has the potential to undermine public support for civil liberties and civil rights at least toward those persons of Middle Eastern descent. Periods of stress and threat embolden public officials to take action against suspected groups, and public opinion generally concurs. Polls show, for example, that a majority of Americans support the president's plan to try suspected terrorists in military courts, wiretap conversations between lawyers and suspected terrorists, and detain persons traveling in the United States from the Middle East.[120] Few Americans raise concerns about civil liberties and rights in the war on terrorism, though we can expect to see these concerns heighten as the distance from 9/11 increases.

Trust in Government

An important dimension of public opinion is the trust or support citizens have for their government, its insti-

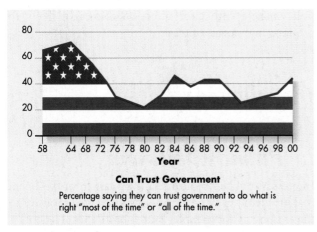

FIGURE 5 ■ Trust in Government Declined during the 1960s and 1970s

SOURCE: National Election Studies, the Center for Political Studies.

Can Trust Government

Percentage saying they can trust government to do what is right "most of the time" or "all of the time."

tutions and officials, and their fellow citizens. With high levels of trust, citizens might do everything government demands. They would pay their taxes and, if called upon to do so, defend the government. They might also gullibly accept anything officials tell them. At low levels of trust, citizens would be skeptical; they might even disobey the law. At the lowest levels, they might try to overthrow the government or commit violent acts against it, as with the Oklahoma City bombing. Thus, democratic government "depends on a fine balance between trust and distrust."[121]

Public trust of government has declined significantly in the last forty years. In the early 1960s, most Americans trusted the government. A comparison of five nations— the United States, Britain, West Germany, Italy, and Mexico—found Americans to be the most positive about the responsiveness and performance of government; 95 percent of the Americans sampled pointed to the government when asked what aspects of the nation they were proud of.[122] The picture that emerged was one of trust and confidence.

The pattern, however, changed sometime in the mid-1960s. Trust in government declined after 1964 and continued to decline through 1980 (see Figure 5). The pattern was characteristic not only of opinions toward government but of opinions toward all major institutions in society, including the medical profession, business, and the press.

Why did levels of trust and confidence in government decline? One answer is the performance of government itself. In the mid- to late 1960s, the nation was divided over many issues, including what to do about the war in Vietnam and the civil rights demands of blacks. Many people wanted the government to do everything possible to win the war in Vietnam, whereas others wanted an immediate withdrawal of U.S. forces; the Johnson and Nixon policies of limited and prolonged war were unresponsive to both sides.

The civil rights struggle also divided the nation. Some wanted government to do more to speed the progress of blacks and other minorities, whereas others thought government was moving too fast. Once more, government chose a middle course fully responsive to neither side.[123]

Following on the heels of these seemingly intractable problems, the early 1970s brought news of Watergate and corruption in government, and after 1973 the nation experienced economic problems, inflation, high interest rates, and unemployment. The government was little more successful in dealing with these than it was with the problems of the 1960s. Levels of trust again declined.

During the first Reagan administration (1981 to 1984), levels of trust and confidence in government increased modestly. People seemed to respond to what appeared to be an improved economy and a few foreign policy successes. President Reagan's personal popularity seemed to inspire confidence.

Reagan's involvement in the Iran–Contra scandal, a sense that his administration lacked compassion, and popular dissatisfaction with domestic and foreign policy diminished his appeal, however, and no doubt contributed to a decline in trust starting in his second term.[124] In the 1990s, trust remained low.[125] Following the 1994 election, President Clinton and the Republican majority deadlocked over health care reform, welfare, and the budget deficit. However, negative reaction to the Lewinsky scandal and impeachment process in Congress did not affect trust in government. In fact, the level just prior to the election in 1998 jumped.[126]

Trust in government continued to increase after 1998 and, as we mentioned, jumped after 9/11. Within weeks of the disaster, the number of Americans responding most of the time increased to 55 percent, its highest level in thirty years. Suddenly Americans felt the country was moving in the right direction, and both the president and Congress benefited from improved approval ratings. Bush topped out at 92 percent and Congress at 85 percent. As one observer noted, "Trauma and war remind people why we have government."[127]

Policy success and failure are predictors of trust. Citizens have become increasingly oriented to government in terms of the services (jobs and high standard of living) they expect government to provide. When performance falls short of expectations, trust in government falls.[128] Between 1966 and 1980, every percentage increase in unemployment lowered confidence in government by almost 3 percent.[129]

Partisan differences influence levels of trust. During Republican administrations, liberals tend to be less trusting; when Democrats hold office, liberals are more trusting.[130]

Societal problems may also cause decreasing trust. Trust in government is tied to public concern about declining morality and values, something over which government has limited control.[131]

Another explanation for declining trust focuses on the political process.[132] Declining trust is highly related to the increasing visibility of government. As Americans see more of their federal government on a day-to-day basis, through C-SPAN and newscasts, they like and trust it less. Talk radio and television interpret normal parts of the democratic process—lobbying, bargaining, negotiation, and compromise—as cynical acts done by self-interested individuals, groups, or political parties. However, compromise and negotiation are part of democracy at work, and self-interest pervades any human activity. Since most Americans seem neither to understand nor to like self-interest and compromise, the more exposure the process receives, the less the public likes it.

Both policy and process reinforce each other in contributing to declining trust in government. Policy deadlock contributes to negative reactions to process. Even when the process yields significant policies, the public visibility of the mechanics of the policy process, with its negotiations and deals, still contributes to cynicism and mistrust.

Expressions of trust in government involve more than evaluations of government performance or process, however. After all, 9/11 was hardly a policy success for the United States. It did, however, increase the importance of government to most people. And the dramatic, horrific events blotted out, for a few weeks, the kind of debate, discussion, and conflict that sours attitudes toward government.

What would it take to restore public trust? This is a very difficult question. Most of the public think the country would be better off if the nation's leaders followed public opinion more closely. Only 18 percent of Americans believe Congress would make the same decision they personally would most of the time. Most Americans believe that the decisions of five hundred Americans selected to represent the nation would be better than the decisions of Congress. Two out of three would like public officials to consult the polls to find out what Americans think.[133] However, following the polls, which often reveal a divided public, will not provide policymakers with clear direction. Nor is it likely to produce high levels of trust.

Conclusion: Is Government Responsive to Public Opinion?

Interest in public opinion stems in part from the belief that in a democracy government should be responsive to the wishes of the people. But is it? Political scientists have had only limited success answering this question because of the difficulty in measuring influence.

The most direct way to assess whether public policy is responsive to public opinion is to compare changes in policy with changes in opinion. The largest study of this type examined several hundred public opinion surveys done between 1935 and 1979. From these surveys, the researchers culled hundreds of questions, each of which dealt with a particular policy and had been asked more than once. On more than three hundred of these questions, public opinion had changed. The authors of the study compared changes in these three hundred opinions with changes, if any, in public policy. They found agreement between opinion changes and policy changes in more than two-thirds of the opinions. Agreement was most likely when the opinion change was large and stable and when the opinion moved in a liberal direction.

The authors acknowledged that in about one-half of the cases, the policy change may have caused the opinion change, but in the other half the opinion change probably caused the policy change, or they both affected each other. Although in many instances policy was not in agreement with public opinion, on important issues, when changes in public opinion were clear-cut, policy usually became consistent with opinion.[134]

Although policy usually changes with changes in opinions, sometimes it does not. One reason is that reelection does not rest with the entire public but with the voting public, and those who vote often differ in their policy preferences from those who do not.[135] To the extent that elected public officials are responsive to voters, and voters differ from nonvoters, public policy will not reflect public opinion.

Public officials must also pay attention to the intensity of public opinion. It may be advantageous for an elected official to vote in support of a minority opinion that is intensely held. A minority with intense feelings is more likely to vote against a candidate who does not support its position than is a group with weak preferences.

When elected officials are confronted with an intense minority, public policy may not reflect public opinion.

Moreover, public opinion is not the only influence on public policy, nor is it necessarily the most important. Interest groups, political parties, other institutions of government, and public officials' own preferences also influence policy, and they may or may not agree with public opinion. Where the preferences of the various influences do not agree, policy generally reflects a compromise among them.

Finally, there is nothing sacred about public opinion. Even when a majority of the public favors a course of action, this may not be the most desirable course. This possibility led the Founders to establish a government that is insulated from public opinion. There is not agreement between public opinion and public policy because the Founders wanted it that way. They established a federal system with separation of powers and many checks and balances to ensure that the majority could not work its will. Thus, one should not expect public policy to reflect public opinion perfectly. The fact that policy usually comes to reflect large and stable majorities does indicate, however, that government is eventually responsive on important issues. Indeed, some observers think politicians pay too much attention to public opinion, to the point that leaders are fearful of leading or of offending the competing groups pulling in opposite directions. The result is gridlock.

EPILOGUE

President Bush Ties the Economy to the War on Terrorism

rather than focus on one and ignore the other, the president dealt with both domestic and foreign policy as part of a "security package" devoted to dealing with the nation's economic woes and the threat of terror at home. He hoped to maintain popularity by keeping voters focused on his success in dealing with the continuing threat posed by terrorists around the world. He then hoped to use his standing with the public as leverage in pushing through a number of domestic policy initiatives to deal with the economy and win support for his party in November.

He opened his address with "Our nation is at war, our economy in recession and the civilized world faces unprecedented dangers."[136] He reviewed the nation's successes in combating terrorism since September 11 but cautioned that the war is just beginning. To keep terrorism central in the nation's consciousness, he warned that "thousands of dangerous killers, schooled in the methods of murder, often supported by outlaw regimes, are now spread throughout the world like ticking time bombs, set to go off without warning."[137]

You WOULDN'T DESECRATE THE FLAG, WOULD YOU?

CONGRESS

BUDGET

© 2002 The Washington Post. Reprinted by permission.

To al Qaeda and the Taliban as targets in the war on terrorism, he added the nations of Iraq, Iran, and North Korea, calling them the "axis of evil." While resonating with some Americans, reaction from abroad, including most of our allies, to the "axis" portrayal was quite hostile, and the president moderated his tone in the weeks following the State of the Union.

But foreign challenges were linked to domestic policies, too. At a cost of a billion dollars a month to fight the war, the president called for an increase in defense spending.

This may have happened without September 11 but now was more urgent and certainly less likely to be criticized. He pointed to an impending budget deficit but justified it in terms of the war. He called on Americans to show the same resolve in defeating the recession as they showed in defeating the Taliban. His economic security plan called for good jobs, and he linked good jobs to reliable and affordable energy, expanded trade, and tax cuts, all elements of the Bush domestic agenda. In his weekly radio address shortly after the State of the

Union, the president renewed his call for opening Alaska's Arctic National Wildlife refuge to oil exploration, contending that it was essential to national security and job creation.[138]

Mindful of criticism following September 11 that he did not take advantage of the desire of Americans to help in the war on terrorism, he called on them to devote two years over a lifetime to community and national service. He proposed a new USA Freedom Corps to respond to the crisis at home, rebuild communities, and extend American compassion abroad. He called for doubling the size of the Peace Corps in an effort to reach out to the Islamic world and standing firm for American values.

The speech was a success in terms of rallying the American people, but how long would the rally last? The president's popularity continued high through summer 2002, in the 70 percent range, but it did not lead to major domestic public policy success. He managed an increase in defense spending but failed to secure a permanent tax cut. Nor was the Arctic National Wildlife Refuge open to exploration. Thus, the president's tremendous popularity was clearly tied to his leadership in the war on terror but did not translate into domestic successes.

Indeed, as the 2002 elections grew closer, the president increased his focus on war—this time against Iraq—and decreased attention to domestic policy. Counseled by his close advisers to focus on Iraq, the president saw this as the best way to ensure Republican success in the congressional elections of 2002. As the election approached, it became increasingly a referendum on the president and his approach. He campaigned feverishly across the nation for Republicans, emphasizing the need to combat terror and take military action against Saddam. The strategy paid off. Republicans won control of both the House and Senate.

 To learn more about Bush's speech and its implications, go to this chapter's "You Are There" exercises on the text Web site.

Key Terms

public opinion

political socialization

agents of political socialization

straw polls

exit polls

ideology

liberalism

conservatism

political tolerance

Further Reading

Herbert Asher, *Polling and the Public: What Every Citizen Should Know* (Washington, D.C.: CQ Press, 1998). An introduction to polling methodology and the influence of polls on American politics as well as advice to citizens on how to evaluate polls. Paul Brace and Barbara Hinckley, *Follow the Leader: Opinion Polls and the Modern President* (New York: Basic Books, 1992). A survey of how recent presidents have allowed the results of public opinion polls to influence their position on issues.

Susan Herbst, *Numbered Voices: How Opinion Polling Has Shaped American Politics* (Chicago: University of Chicago Press, 1993). A historical review of the way public opinion has been measured and the way the evolution of measurement techniques has affected the definition of public opinion.

Lawrence R. Jacobs and Robert Y. Shapiro, *Politicians Don't Pander: Political Manipulation and the Loss of Democratic Responsiveness* (Chicago: University of Chicago Press, 2000). An examination of how politicians use polls to craft language that will make policies that the public would likely reject acceptable to the public.

Celinda Lake, *Public Opinion Polling: A Handbook for Public Interest and Citizen Advocacy Groups* (Washington, D.C.: Island, 1987). A step-by-step treatment for lay audiences on how to conduct a public opinion poll.

Thomas E. Mann and Gary R. Orren, eds., *Media Polls and American Politics* (Washington, D.C.: Brookings Institution, 1992). Several essays focusing on the influence of media-conducted polls on American political institutions and elections.

Benjamin I. Page and Robert Y. Shapiro, *The Rational Public: Fifty Years of Trends in American's Policy Preferences* (Chicago: University of Chicago Press, 1992). An examination of the influence of public opinion on public policy using public opinion polling information generated over the past fifty years.

Electronic Resources

Many polling firms and media polls have home pages. Here is a sampling of some of the more reputable ones.

www.ropercenter.uconn.edu

The Roper Center Web site contains information on the current and past presidents' job performance and a listing of current Roper surveys.

www.harrisinteractive.com/harris_poll/index.asp? PollYear=2002

The Louis Harris Center archive Web site links to current and past Harris surveys. Frequencies are available for all questions, and information can be downloaded and analyzed.

www.umich.edu/~nes/nesguide/nesguide.htm
The National Election Studies of the University of Michigan Web site provides access to the most recent national election study. This information can be analyzed online.

www.washingtonpost.com/wp-srv/politics/polls/vault/vault.htm
This site links to polls conducted by the Washington Post.

abcnews.go.com/sections/politics/PollVault/PollVault.html
The Web site links to ABC Television News surveys.

people-press.org/
The Pew Center Web site provides recent polling information.

InfoTrac College Edition

Search for the following articles in the InfoTrac database:

Edmondson, Brad. "How to Spot a Bogus Poll," *American Demographics* (October 1996).

Irwin, Galen A., and Joop J. M. Van Holsteyn. "According to the Polls: The Influence of Opinion Polls on Expectations," *Public Opinion Quarterly* (Spring 2002).

Simon Ropsenthal, Cindy, James A. Rosenthal, and Jocelyn Jones. "Preparing for Elite Political Participation: Simulations and the Political Socialization of Adolescents," *Social Science Quarterly* (September 2001).

Weissberg, Robert. "The Problem with Polling," *Public Interest* (Summer 2002).

For more articles, enter:

"public opinion polls" in the Subject Guide.
"political socialization" in the Subject Guide.

American Government Resources

Visit the Political Behavior section of the Wadsworth American Government Resources Web site (politicalscience.wadsworth.com/amgov/) for a variety of tools to help you explore public opinion further. Included are simulations, video clips, Microcase exercises, and a wealth of other activities.

NEWS MEDIA

Admiral Mike Boorda.

Should You Torpedo the Admiral?

You are Evan Thomas, the Washington bureau chief of *Newsweek* magazine, and it is 1996. One of your contributors is proposing an exposé about an admiral who has worn medals he is not authorized to wear. The story could make a big splash in military, political, and publishing circles. You have to decide whether to pursue it.[1]

Admiral Mike Boorda is chief of naval operations (CNO)—the highest-ranking admiral in the United States Navy. The son of Ukrainian immigrants, he enlisted as a seventeen-year-old in 1956, and almost four decades later he reached the top. His appointment by President Bill Clinton broke precedents. Boorda became the first CNO who had been an enlisted man, the first who had not graduated from the Naval Academy, and the first who was Jewish.

Boorda is devoted to his sailors. Every time he visits a ship or base, he holds a session to respond to the sailors' questions and complaints. He tries to show the sailors that he understands their jobs. He learned how to handle the ships, from small boats to battleships, even in choppy waters, and he learned how to fly helicopters and fighter planes.

Boorda also knows how to navigate the treacherous waters of politics. He has forged ties with members of Congress and has developed skills in negotiating. Before becoming CNO, he demonstrated his talent for diplomacy by persuading UN,

NATO, and U.S. commands to work together in Bosnia. (In Sarajevo, he once slipped away from UN officials and showed up in the trenches and buildings of the Serb and Muslim fighters. To their surprise, he explained, "It's the American way. We talk to each other.")

But the admiral has come under attack from traditionalists in the navy. In the aftermath of the Tailhook convention in 1991, when several dozen women were assaulted by drunken aviators, he was expected to improve the climate for women. But when he implemented new policies developed by civilians in Washington, such as allowing women to serve on combat ships and fly combat planes and encouraging toleration of homosexuals (under the "don't ask, don't tell" policy, which will be explained in Chapter 14), he was criticized for trying to make the policies work rather than trying to resist them.

He has been criticized by retired admirals, who wield clout like an interest group, and by current officers for helping enlisted sailors with their problems. They say he is usurping the authority of ship and base commanders. And he has even been criticized for driving his own car, rather than using a chauffeur as other admirals do. They say he is eroding the prestige of the admirals.

A former secretary of the navy in the Reagan administration who opposed women attending the

Naval Academy and serving in combat units gave a fiery speech at the academy accusing Boorda of sacrificing navy traditions for political correctness. Excerpts were printed in the *Washington Times*, a conservative newspaper, and the *San Diego Union-Tribune*, a prominent newspaper covering navy issues. Criticisms were also printed in the *Navy Times*, a newspaper circulating throughout the navy.

After two years as CNO, Boorda has been under so much pressure that he recently told his family he will not finish the two years remaining in his term.

Amid this controversy, a Washington correspondent for the National Security News Service, which, like similar organizations with a political agenda and foundation funding, locates specialized information that it passes on to bigger media, received a tip that Boorda had worn medals he might not have been authorized to wear. The correspondent contacted a friend, David Hackworth, a retired army officer who was highly decorated and who has sharply criticized the military's medal inflation (as some college professors have complained about grade inflation). After Hackworth had written a popular autobiography, he had been appointed a contributing editor of *Newsweek*. In competition with *Time* for readers, *Newsweek* had sought prominent peo-

ple, like Hackworth, who would contribute occasional articles.

Hackworth examined photos of Boorda in his uniform and concluded that the admiral should not have worn a small *V* on two ribbons from the Vietnam War. Although he was entitled to wear the ribbons, he might not have been entitled to wear the *V*, which stands for *valor* and is reserved for troops who face fire in combat. Yet later photos of Boorda show that he stopped wearing the *V*. Still, Hackworth, who is motivated by a desire to expose wrongdoing by generals and admirals, thinks he has a story. Researching regulations at the Pentagon, he confided to some officers that he is working on a story that will bring down an admiral.

Hackworth contacted the editor of *Newsweek*, informing him of the story and telling him that it could be "a real career ender" for the admiral. The editor referred the story to you, as Washington bureau chief of the magazine, and reserved a page in the next issue if you decide to run it. You met with the correspondent for the National Security News Service, who showed the photos and explained the navy's regulations to you.

You are uneasy, wary of both the correspondent for the National Security News Service and Hackworth. Neither is a regular reporter in your bureau. Nei-

ther, in fact, is an experienced reporter. You told a fellow editor, "There's something about this story that is too good to be true. Stories are never this neat." You consulted with a senior correspondent who specializes in national defense for the magazine. He noted that the navy's regulations concerning the *V* had changed during the war, perhaps reflecting the navy's confusion over its regulations, so perhaps Boorda had not worn the *V* improperly or had not done so intentionally.

Do you run Hackworth's article exposing Boorda?

Do you first seek clarification from the navy to determine whether the *V* was actually improper? Or do you question Boorda to determine whether he was honestly mistaken? If so, do you still run the article?

If you run the article, do you balance your findings of wrongdoing with information about Boorda's contributions to the navy in his forty years of service?

Or do you reject the article, because Boorda no longer wears the *V?*

You are mindful of the competition with *Time* and realize that this story would be a real scoop and could make a big splash for *Newsweek*. You also realize that the editor has reserved a page for this story, yet you do have discretion.

A *medium* transmits something. The mass media—which include newspapers, magazines, books, radio, television, movies, records, and the Internet—transmit communications to masses of people.

Although the media do not constitute a branch of government or even an organization established to influence government, such as a political party or interest group, they have an impact on government. In addition to providing entertainment, the media provide information about government and politics. This chapter focuses on the news media—the part of the media that delivers the news about government and politics.

The Media State

The media have developed and flourished to an extent the Founders could not have envisioned. As one po-

litical scientist noted, the media have become "pervasive . . . and atmospheric, an element of the air we breathe."[2] Without exaggeration, another observer concluded, "Ancient Sparta was a military state. John Calvin's Geneva was a religious state. Mid–nineteenth century England was Europe's first industrial state, and the contemporary United States is the world's first media state."[3]

Americans spend more time being exposed to the media than doing anything else. In a year, according to one calculation, the average full-time worker puts in 1,824 hours on the job, 2,737 hours in bed, and 3,256 hours exposed to the media (almost nine hours a day).[4] Seventy-seven percent of adults read newspapers; the average person does so for three and a half hours a week. The average person also reads two magazines for one and a half hours a week.[5] Ninety-eight percent of American homes have a radio, and the same percentage have a television. More homes have a television than have a toilet.[6] The average adult or child watches television three hours a day.[7] By the time the average child graduates from high school, he or she has spent more time in front of the tube than in class.[8] By the time the average American dies, he or she has spent one and a half years just watching television commercials.[9]

The rest of this section will examine three continuing trends in journalism: the shifting roles of the media, the increasing concentration of the media, and the increasing atomization of the media.

Roles of the Media

American newspapers originated in colonial times, and political magazines appeared in the 1800s, but there were no "mass media" until the advent of the broadcast media. Radio, which became popular in the 1920s, and television, which became popular in the 1950s, reached people who could not or would not read. Television would become so central and influential in American life that one scholar has speculated that the second half of the twentieth century will go down in history as "the age of television."[10]

Although people bought television sets to watch entertainment programs, they also began to watch newscasts. At first the newscasts, lasting only fifteen minutes and consisting solely of an anchor and a few correspondents reading news in front of a camera, were not compelling. In 1963, the networks expanded the time to thirty minutes and altered the format to emphasize visual interest. That year, for the first time, people said they got more political information from television than from any other source.

As television grew in popularity, newspapers waned. People did not need to read their headlines anymore, and some people did not care to read their more in-depth coverage. Newspapers have struggled for readers and advertisers, and some have folded. Since 1970, the number of adults and the number of households have increased significantly, but the circulation of daily newspapers has remained stagnant.[11] The percentage of regular readers has declined (from 78 percent of adults in 1970 to 59 percent in 1997).[12] The percentage of young adults who are regular readers has declined the most. (In 1966, 58 percent of first-year college students said "keeping up-to-date with political affairs" was an "essential" or "very important" goal. In 1998, only 26 percent held this view.[13]) Even after 9/11, which prompted a surge of interest in foreign affairs, readership continued to decline.[14]

Consequently, television has become the most important of the media for politics. According to surveys, people pay more attention to it and put more faith in it than in other media. This makes positive coverage on television essential for politicians.

Courtesy of the National Archives, 33-SC-4899

When radio was new in the 1920s, families such as this one in Oregon gathered around the set to listen.

While television offers more immediate and dramatic coverage, newspapers provide more thorough and thoughtful coverage. Because newspapers require more effort and provide more depth, they leave a longer-lasting impression. People remember the news they read in newspapers better than the news they watch on television.[15]

Moreover, national newspapers such as the *New York Times* and *Washington Post,* which blanket the country with in-depth international and national news, influence opinion leaders who, in turn, influence other persons.

Now the Internet is challenging the established media. It allows people to get the news when they want it around the clock, rather than at a specified schedule, and to get more news if they want it, rather than the brief newscasts on radio and television. Although the Internet is still in its infancy, already a significant number of adults, mostly young and well educated, get most of their news from this source (see Tables 1 and 2).

TABLE 1	Where Do You Get Most of Your News?

Source	Percentage
Television	50
Newspaper	25
Radio	11
News magazine	5
Internet	5
Other	4

SOURCE: Responses from a survey of randomly selected American adults, published in Frank Luntz, "Public to Press: Cool It," *Brill's Content* (March 2000): 76.

TABLE 2	Number of Years after Introduction to Attract 50 Million Users	
Medium		Years
Radio		38
Television		13
Internet		4

SOURCE: "Ticker," *Brill's Content* (March 1999): 128.

These trends will likely continue: Newspapers and radio will lose more readers and listeners, while television will lose its dominance, and the Internet will gain new users.[16]

Different media appeal to different groups. Seniors read the newspapers and watch the network newscasts, while the youngest adults are more likely to surf the Web for their news. The all-news cable networks attract the least educated, while the Internet attracts the most educated. Conservatives tend to watch Fox television and listen to talk radio, while liberals tend to watch the Public Broadcasting System (PBS) and listen to National Public Radio (NPR).[17]

Concentration of the Media

Journalism is a big business. The media industry is the nation's ninth largest, above the electronics industry and just below the aerospace industry.[18]

Journalism has become a bigger business in recent decades. First, small media organizations owned by local families or local companies were taken over by chains (owning multiple newspapers, radio stations, *or* television stations) or conglomerates (owning multiple newspapers, radio stations, *and* television stations). Then, large media organizations were taken over by chains or conglomerates. Finally, chains and conglomerates were bought out by larger chains and conglomerates.

The largest merger of media in history occurred when America Online (AOL) bought Time Warner in 2000. AOL was the dominant Internet corporation, with half the market for the services that link computer users to the Internet, and Time Warner was the largest media conglomerate. The new company has over eighty thousand employees and $30 billion in annual revenues. It boasts 50 percent of the online business, 20 percent of the cable television business, 18 percent of the movie business, and 16 percent of the record business in the country. It also has 160 magazines, five publishing houses, and "Looney Tunes" cartoons.[19]

In addition, other large corporations—telecommunications companies, such as AT&T, and computer software companies, such as Microsoft—established alliances with the media conglomerates. Microsoft

formed an alliance with General Electric, which owns NBC, to launch a twenty-four-hour cable news channel (MSNBC) and an interactive online news service. This will enable Microsoft, which has already conquered the software industry, to extend its reach into the news business.

The long-range goal of the mergers and alliances is to control the information and entertainment markets of the future. Media conglomerates want to offer all types of media—newspapers, radio stations, television stations, magazines, books, movies, records, and computer services—in various formats, including through such devices as Palm Pilots, at all times of the day. Each conglomerate seeks to become *the* source of all of your news and entertainment.

An early expectation for the Internet—that it would provide unlimited diversity and offer an alternative to established media—is already being dashed, as powerful conglomerates are racing to swallow their competitors and influence the government to adopt policies that will lock in their advantage.[20]

This trend toward concentration of the media is certain to continue. It will provide much more convenience, allowing much easier access, at somewhat more cost for consumers, but it will pose problems for a democracy that relies on the media to inform its citizens. Already this trend toward concentration makes these problems apparent.

The news comes from fewer sources than it used to. Although there are many media in the United States,[21] the numbers are misleading. Chains and conglomerates own the newspapers and magazines with most of the readers, the radio stations with most of the listeners, and the television stations with most of the viewers.[22] One media analyst, referring to the chains and conglomerates that dominate the industry now, observed, "These two dozen profit-driven companies, owned and managed by billionaires operating in barely competitive markets, account for nearly the entirety of the U.S. media culture."[23] Yet media observers predict a shakeout will further reduce this small number.

Moreover, just one wire service—AP—supplies the international and national news for most of the newspapers. Only four radio networks—ABC, CBS, NBC, and Mutual—furnish the news for most of the radio stations, and only four television networks—ABC, CBS, NBC, and CNN—furnish the news for most of the television stations.

With fewer sources of news, there is less of a range of views—less of a marketplace of ideas—than is healthy for a democracy. A small number of powerful people provide information—essentially, define reality—for all the rest of the people.

Another problem resulting from concentration of the media is corporate pressure to avoid some topics if the

"That's all for Competition, Folks!"

AOL TIME WARNER

Steven Benson. Reprinted by permission of United Features Syndicate, Inc.

coverage would affect corporate interests. ABC killed a story that Disney, its owner, followed employment practices that allowed the hiring of convicted pedophiles at its parks. (Apparently ABC, as a small division of the huge company, got mouseke*fear*.[24]) There is also corporate pressure to slant the coverage. NBC aired a documentary that advocated more use of nuclear power. NBC's owner, General Electric, is a builder of nuclear power plants. NBC broadcast a report about defective bolts used in airplanes and bridges built by GE and other companies, but the references to GE were removed. When the president of NBC News complained about interference in their newscasts, the boss of GE poked a finger in his chest and shouted, "You work for GE!"[25]

Although other media might pick up a story killed by one organization, what if some story affects the interests of many organizations? In 1996, Congress passed the Telecommunications Act, which set aside a portion of the nation's airwaves for new digital television broadcasts. Although the frequencies were valued at $70 billion, the act handed them to broadcasters for free. When the bill was proposed, Senator John McCain (R-Ariz.) predicted, "You will not see this story on any television or hear it on any radio broadcast because it directly affects them."[26] Indeed, during the nine months in which the bill was pending, there was little coverage of the bill or the lobbying by the broadcasters. ABC, CBS, and NBC television news shows devoted an average of just six and a half minutes to the bill and virtually none to this provision.[27] If citizens had been more aware of this legislation, they might have demanded that Congress, rather than giving the broadcasters a windfall, charge the market value for the frequencies and use the $70 billion to bolster popular governmental programs.

Another problem resulting from concentration of the media is financial pressure to reduce the quality of news coverage. Media organizations are under pressure to show sizable profits each year; some are under pressure to show expanding profits each year. Media organizations are expected to match other divisions in their corporations. Corporate officers feel pressure from Wall Street analysts and major stockholders, such as managers of mutual funds, retirement funds, and insurance companies, who are more concerned with the value of the stock than the quality of the journalism. As a result, costs are cut and profits are not reinvested in more staff training or investigative reports. A reporter for a midsize newspaper in Illinois learned, "If a story needs a real investment of time and money, we don't do it anymore." He lamented, "Who the hell cares about corruption in city government, anyway?"[28]

The trend toward concentration of the media is potentially harmful for everyone but stockholders. Some observers foresee "the free-enterprise equivalent of a Ministry of Culture"[29]—the government office that regulates the media in small countries that lack a free press. In fact, the financial value of some American conglomerates is greater than the entire economy of some foreign countries whose monopolistic policies we condemn as hostile to a democratic society.

Atomization of the Media

Despite the growing concentration of the media, a contrary trend—an atomization of the media—has also developed in recent decades. Whereas concentration has led to a national media, atomization has fragmented the influence of this national media. The major newspapers and broadcast networks have lost their dominance, while other media, some not even considered news organizations, have started to play a significant role in politics.

This trend is partly the result of technological changes. First the national networks lost viewers to the local stations, as the local stations linked with other local stations, via satellite, to share coverage of national and international events. Then the traditional stations lost viewers to cable television. With its multiplicity of channels, cable can offer competing newscasts and more specialized programs. It can provide "narrowcasting" to appeal to small segments of the audience in contrast to the networks' broadcasting to appeal to the overall audience. For example, C-SPAN covers Congress on three channels and, unlike the networks, lingers on members' speeches and committees' hearings. Even MTV covers presidential campaigns in formats to attract young viewers.

Other national cable networks cater to blacks and Hispanics. A cable system in Los Angeles and New York caters to Jews. A cable channel in California broadcasts in Chinese, one in Hawaii broadcasts in Japanese, and one in Connecticut and Massachusetts broadcasts in Portuguese. Stations in New York also provide programs in Greek, Hindi, Korean, and Russian.

Cable has led to twenty-four-hour news. CNN, created as a twenty-four-hour news network, has a large audience. Now it is being challenged by Fox and MSNBC.

The Internet has led to additional news sites. Major newspapers post their articles on Web sites before the papers themselves are delivered. Online "magazines" also address politics. During the congressional impeachment of President Clinton, one online magazine—*Salon*—revealed that the Republican representative spearheading the effort (Henry Hyde of Illinois) had had an adulterous relationship. Self-styled "journalists" even post their "news" as well. Matt Drudge offers political gossip on his own Web site, the Drudge Report, from his one-bedroom apartment in Hollywood.[30]

With such proliferation of newscasts, the audience for the traditional nightly news has sunk to its lowest level since 1961[31]—two years before the networks attracted a mass audience by expanding the newscast and emphasizing visual interest.

The trend toward atomization of the media is also partly the result of the populist backlash against government officials and established journalists, perceived as "Washington insiders," that characterized American politics in the 1980s and 1990s. This is reflected in the popularity of radio talk shows. Many stations have such programs, and many people tune in.[32] Their numbers make talk radio a force in politics. Its middle-class audience acts as a national jury on governmental controversies.

The populist backlash is also reflected in the increasing attention paid to fringe media by the public. In the 1992 presidential campaign, the *Star,* a supermarket tabloid, published allegations by Gennifer Flowers, a former nightclub singer, that she had had a twelve-year affair with Bill Clinton while he was governor of Arkansas. The major media hesitated to repeat the *Star's* story—they had nothing but scorn for the tabloids, which, they insisted, did not practice true journalism—but within days most gave in, under the pretense of debating the propriety of reporting personal matters. Flowers then appeared on *A Current Affair,* a syndicated television show, rated Clinton as a lover on a scale from 1 to 10, and sang "Stand by Your Man." Thus, Flowers did not need to take her story to the major media; she got the tabloid media to tell it and pay her for it ($150,000 from the *Star* and $25,000 from *A Current Affair*).[33]

During the impeachment of President Clinton, Larry Flynt, the publisher of *Hustler* magazine, was offended by the hypocrisy of some of the president's adversaries. Seeking information about affairs they had, he ran an ad in the *Washington Post* offering to pay for such information. He published an article about an affair involving the Speaker of the House–designate, Robert Livingston (R–La.). Although the article appeared in a magazine read by relatively few men, the revelation received publicity in other media and caused Livingston to resign.

Because the public pays attention to the fringe media more than it used to, politicians have begun to use these media now. Instead of announcing their candidacy at a press conference, as politicians traditionally did, some have announced their candidacy on television talk shows. During the campaign, they have appeared on other television shows. Clinton fielded questions on the *Phil Donahue Show* and played the saxophone on the *Arsenio Hall Show.* Bush appeared on the *Oprah Winfrey Show.* Candidates swapped jokes with Jay Leno and David Letterman—and prayed they would not end up looking silly. Candidates have used these shows to reach people who do not follow the major media and to communicate their messages without having them "filtered"—that is, condensed, simplified, distorted, or challenged—by professional reporters.

All this blurs the line between politics and entertainment. When Senator Bill Bradley (D–N.J.) appeared at a Houston radio station, ranked number one among men in the area, he expected to discuss his new book. Instead, the disc jockeys had two women disrobe from the waist up to report his reaction.[34]

Because of the expanding role of fringe media, mainstream journalists envision a shrinking role for themselves. They no longer monopolize the market of political information; they no longer control the gates through which such information must pass.

When candidates buy television time for "electronic town halls," shows in which they take questions from voters in several cities without journalists present, the shrinking role is apparent. "Max in Seattle feels as well represented by Julie's question from Houston as he would be by Sam Donaldson's inquiry from New York." (Actually, Max might prefer Julie's to Sam Donaldson's. Many citizens are annoyed by the "cult of toughness" among journalists that leads them to challenge public figures with "a level of shamelessness and aggression that ordinary people cannot manage."[35])

This trend toward atomization of the media has significant implications beyond its impact on the established media and their professional journalists. Although this trend makes the news more accessible to more people, it also makes the news less factual and less analytical.

The proliferation of news outlets, including fringe media, and newscasts around the clock, from cable channels and Internet sites, creates intense competition for news stories. The media have more space or time to fill than information to fill it. So they feel pressure to locate new stories or identify new angles of old stories. In addition, they use talk shows that blend news, opinion, gossip, rumor, and speculation, because these shows are cheap to produce and, if the hosts and guests are provocative, entertaining for viewers. The media can fill their time and attract an audience. But the result is a commingling of facts and nonfacts. Then these facts and nonfacts are repeated by other organizations making sure they are not left behind. In the rush to broadcast and publish, the media put less emphasis on assessing the accuracy of the content they disseminate than they used to. "The great new sin . . . is not to be inaccurate," a veteran reporter observed. Rather, "it is to be boring."[36]

Interest groups eager to exploit the competition among the media add to the problem. When Vince Foster, deputy counsel for President Clinton, apparently committed suicide in a park, a right-wing group sent a fax to news organizations linking the suicide to the Whitewater land deal. The group passed the rumor that Foster died at an administration "safe house" and later was moved to the park. Talk show host Rush Limbaugh reported the rumor. Other talk show hosts repeated it, while some added the rumor that Foster was murdered. A few financial speculators spread the rumors as a way to manipulate the stock market, and the next day newspaper business sections repeated the rumors in articles about their effect on the stock market. Thus, through announcement and repetition by the media, the rumors came to seem true to many people—yet they remained just rumors[37] (and false ones, according to three independent counsels).

A similar pattern occurred when a conservative magazine, *Insight,* charged that the Clinton administration was "selling" burial plots in Arlington National Cemetery to "dozens of big-time political donors or friends of the Clintons." Because the cemetery is reserved for military veterans, anonymous officials were quoted as saying this was "corruption of the worst kind." The charge was repeated on talk radio and then aired in Congress when some members demanded an investigation. Within forty-eight hours, it was reported by the mainstream media. Yet there was no truth to it.[38]

The mainstream media have been uncertain how to act in such situations. They are reluctant to report rumors they are unable to verify. But they fear they will lose their audience if they fail to report stories other media report. Usually, they decide to report the stories but in a different context—under the guise of addressing the political ramifications of the accusation or the journalistic ethics of publicizing it. Nevertheless, the effect is nearly the same: The accusation winds up in the mainstream media, and the public believes it. As a result, unscrupulous groups realize they can use the fringe media to manipulate the mainstream media into publicizing bogus charges. Thus, they can drag the mainstream media down to their level. President Clinton's lawyer said it reminds him of when he lived with a

bunch of guys in college: Four were neat and one was a slob; by the end of the year, they were all slobs.[39]

The fringe media aggravate the problem. Their goal is entertainment and their audience is politically unsophisticated, so the fringe media are less careful about the accuracy of the information they disseminate. Some pay for stories, possibly encouraging people to lie for the money; many sensationalize stories, possibly distorting the truth. Of course, the mainstream media also are commercial enterprises subject to the pressures of the marketplace. Yet these established media are subject to the pressures of tradition. Reporters at major newspapers and broadcast networks often speak of their responsibility to follow certain journalistic norms, while members of the fringe media sometimes reflect the views of radio talk show host Don Imus, who asserts, "The news isn't sacred to me. It's entertainment . . . designed to revel in the agony of others."[40]

The Internet aggravates the problem even more. With no editors, any person with a computer and a phone line can deliver any "fact," however erroneous, to the whole world. In 1997, Pierre Salinger, the respected press secretary to President John F. Kennedy and then correspondent for ABC, announced in a speech to an airline association that the TWA flight that crashed off the coast of Long Island had been accidentally shot down by a navy missile and that this fact was being covered up by the U.S. government. At the time, the cause of the crash had been listed as "unknown," so Salinger's speech was reported prominently worldwide. When doubters asked how he had learned this, Salinger replied that he received the information from a top intelligence agent in France. Salinger was hoodwinked. The information originated in the fertile imagination of a retired pilot in Florida who hypothesized this scenario and posted it on the Internet, where it eventually reached the intelligence agent in France.[41] (The government has since concluded that the crash was due to mechanical failure.)

Meanwhile, the public is lost in this factual free-for-all. Most citizens are not well versed in the issues or very knowledgeable about the politicians. Without the help of professional journalists, many are not able to separate the blarney from the gospel truth when candidates and officials speak.

In sum, two opposite trends—concentration of the media and atomization of the media—are occurring. It is not clear how they are going to interact. Now they are developing side by side. But strong financial pressures persist, and very powerful corporations are working to dominate the media business. In the future, the huge conglomerates probably will dominate more than they do now. Independent voices from the Internet occasionally may break through on issues that have a human interest angle.

Relationship between the Media and Politicians

"Politicians live—and sometimes die—by the press. The press lives by politicians," according to a former presidential aide. "This relationship is at the center of our national life."[42]

This relationship was not always so close. President Herbert Hoover once refused to tell a reporter whether he enjoyed a baseball game he attended.[43]

But now politicians and journalists realize that they need each other. Politicians need journalists to reach the public and to receive feedback from the public. They scan the major newspapers in the morning and the network newscasts in the evening. President Lyndon Johnson watched three network newscasts on three televisions simultaneously. Journalists need politicians to cover government. They seek a steady stream of fresh information to fill their news columns and newscasts.

The close relationship between the media and politicians is both a **symbiotic relationship,** meaning they use each other for their mutual advantage, and an **adversarial relationship,** meaning they fight each other.

Symbiotic Relationship

President Johnson told individual reporters, "You help me, and I'll help make you a big man in your profession." He gave exclusive interviews, told outrageous tales, and invited reporters to bunk overnight at his Texas ranch.[44] In return, he expected favorable coverage.

Reporters get information from politicians in various ways. Some reporters are assigned to monitor beats. Washington beats include the White House, Congress, Supreme Court, State Department, Defense Department, and some other departments and agencies. Other reporters are assigned to cover specialized subjects, such as economics, energy issues, and environmental problems, which are addressed by several branches, departments, or agencies.

The government has press secretaries and public information officers who provide reporters with ideas and information for stories. The number of these officials is significant; one year the Defense Department employed almost 1,500 people just to handle press relations.[45]

The government supplies reporters with a variety of news sources, including copies of speeches, summaries of committee meetings, news releases, and news briefings about current events. Officials also grant interviews, hold press conferences, and stage "media events." The vast majority of reporters rely on these sources rather than engage in more difficult and time-consuming investigative reporting.

Interviews

Interviews show the symbiotic nature of the relationship between reporters and politicians. During the early months of the Reagan presidency, *Washington Post* writer William Greider had a series of eighteen off-the-record meetings with budget director David Stockman. Greider recounted:

> *Stockman and I were participating in a fairly routine transaction of Washington, a form of submerged communication which takes place regularly between selected members of the press and the highest officials of government. Our mutual motivation, despite our different interests, was crassly self-serving. It did not need to be spelled out between us. I would use him and he would use me. . . . I had established a valuable peephole on the inner policy debates of the new administration. And the young budget director had established a valuable connection with an important newspaper. I would get a jump on the unfolding strategies and decisions. He would be able to prod and influence the focus of our coverage, to communicate his views and positions under the cover of our "off the record" arrangement, to make known harsh assessments that a public official would not dare to voice in the more formal setting of a press conference, speech, or "on the record" interview.*[46]

Leaks

Interviews can result in **leaks**—disclosures of information some officials want to keep secret. Other officials in the administration or the bureaucracy and members of Congress use leaks for many reasons. Officials might leak to make competing officials or opposing policies look bad. Officials who feel slighted

Politicians must expect to be "captured" by reporters and photographers any time. A New Hampshire journalist on the campaign trail caught this glimpse of Clinton removing television makeup but looking haggard.

might leak to call attention to their ideas or to force public debates instead of closed-door decisions. After Congress's investigation of the intelligence failures leading up to the terrorist attacks on September 11, someone leaked the information that the National Security Agency—the ultrasecret agency that engages in electronic surveillance around the world—had intercepted al Qaeda messages on September 10 saying, "Tomorrow is zero day" and "The match begins tomorrow," but had not translated the messages from Arabic until September 12.

Officials also leak for strategic reasons. Officials in the administration might leak information about a proposed policy to test the water for it, without committing themselves or their offices to it, in case intense opposition surfaces. Or they might leak to prod the president to do what they think he should do.[47]

Officials in the administration might leak even embarrassing information but do so at a less damaging time or in a less damaging way than when or how this information otherwise would come out. Officials leak information during holidays or, if these are not near, weekends, when the news receives less attention. They also leak to newspapers other than the *New York Times* or *Washington Post* because these influential papers dislike giving prominent play to stories broken by less prestigious papers.[48] After President George H. Bush nominated Clarence Thomas to the Supreme Court, an official in the Bush administration leaked the fact that Thomas had experimented with marijuana in college. The official's purpose was to inoculate Thomas from the greater controversy that could have occurred if the press had discovered and revealed this fact closer to the confirmation vote.[49]

Most presidents get enraged by leaks. Reagan said he was "up to my keister" in leaks, and Nixon established a "plumbers" unit to wiretap aides and plug leaks once they learned who was responsible. Nevertheless, despite accusations that leaks are from low-level employees in the opposite party, most are from high-ranking officials in the same party. "The ship of state," one experienced reporter noted, "is the only kind of ship that leaks mainly from the top."[50] During the Vietnam War, President Johnson himself ordered an aide to leak the charge that steel companies were "profiteering" from the war. After an executive complained, Johnson assured him that "if I find out some damn fool aide did it, I'll fire the sonuvabitch!"[51]

Officials outside the administration might leak information about those inside the administration. Prosecutors in the independent counsel's office frequently leaked tidbits uncovered during their investigations of President Clinton. They even leaked information from grand jury testimony, which is supposed to remain secret.[52] The prosecutors' goal was to sway public opinion—

create a presumption of guilt and generate a sense of momentum—against the president as his impeachment approached. Although the prosecutors apparently broke the law—a felony—the press paid little attention to this fact because the reporters were grateful for the information.[53]

Reporters value leaks because leaks enable them to break a story before other media can report it. Then, reporters are said to **scoop** their competitors.

Hence the rush among the networks to "call" elections. In 2000, CBS's Dan Rather announced, "Let's get one thing straight right from the get-go. . . . We would rather be last in reporting returns than to be wrong. . . . If we say somebody has carried a state, you can pretty much take it to the bank." Yet all the networks initially called the election for Gore, then called the election for Bush, and finally decided it was too close to call for anybody. They botched it twice in the same night.

When the Supreme Court issued its decision in *Bush v. Gore*, ending the Florida recount controversy, the networks showed again that they would rather be fast than right. Under pressure to digest the decision on the steps of the Court, correspondents frantically flipped through the sixty-five-page opinion—and then they issued conflicting conclusions. Rather declared, "What [the ruling] does not do is in effect deliver the presidency to George Bush."[54] Wrong again. The networks felt they could not wait a half hour for their legal consultants to read the opinion, because viewers would switch to other networks that already would be proclaiming the result, even if erroneously.

Press Conferences

Press conferences also show the symbiotic nature of the relationship between reporters and politicians. Theodore Roosevelt, who was the first president to cultivate close ties to correspondents, started the **presidential press conference**.[55] He held occasional sessions while being shaved. Franklin Roosevelt, who was detested by newspaper publishers, realized that the press conference could help him reach the public. He held frequent sessions and provided a steady stream of news, which editors felt obligated to publish. This news publicized his policies and his efforts to implement them at the same time editors were writing editorials against them.

John Kennedy saw that the press conference could help him reach the public more directly if he allowed the networks to televise it live.[56] Then editors could not filter his remarks.

Of course, if a president wants to answer reporters, he can do so in private. If he wants to communicate with the public, he can do so in a formal speech, without risking an embarrassing question. But he might opt for a televised conference if he performs well in front of the cameras or, like the youthful Kennedy, feels a need to demonstrate his competence to the watchful public.[57] With his intellect and wit, Kennedy excelled at the televised conference.

As a result, presidents and their aides transformed the conference into a carefully orchestrated media show. Now an administration schedules a conference when it wants to convey a message. It might even limit questions to that topic. Aides identify potential questions, and the president rehearses appropriate answers. (Former press secretaries admit that they predicted at least 90 percent of the questions asked and often the exact reporters who asked them.[58]) During the conference, the president calls on the reporters he wants. Although he cannot ignore those from the major media, he can call disproportionately on those he knows will lob soft questions.

Beaming the conference to the nation results in less news than having a casual exchange around the president's desk, which used to reveal his thinking on programs and decisions. Appearing in millions of homes, the president cannot be as open and cannot allow himself to make a gaffe in front of the huge audience.

Televising the conference does not even provide much accountability, because one is scheduled when the administration wants, and nearly every aspect is scripted or predicted in advance. Televising the conference only offers an illusion of accountability.

The transformation of the conference frustrates reporters and prompts them to act as prosecutors. As one press secretary observed, they play a game of "I gotcha."[59] After Clinton's first conference, one reporter criticized him because "he didn't say a single thing he didn't mean to."[60] That is, the press could not trick him into saying something imprudent.

Still, reporters value the conference. Editors consider the president's remarks news, so the conference helps reporters do their job. It also gives them a chance to bask in the limelight. According to a former press secretary, it gives them "fame, power in the eyes of their peers, recognition by their families, ego gratification, and lecture fees from the Storm Door and Sash Associations of the world."[61] (Business and professional associations pay well-known journalists handsome fees to speak at their annual meetings.)

Media Events

Media events also show the symbiotic nature of the relationship between reporters and politicians. Staged for television, these events usually pair a photo opportunity and a speech to convey a particular impression of a politician's position on an issue.

The "photo op" frames the politician against a backdrop of things that symbolize the points the politician is trying to make. Photo ops for economic issues often use factories, whether bustling to represent a success or abandoned to represent a failure. Photo ops for President Bush's education proposals showed him in classrooms. The strategy is the same as that for advertisements of merchandise: Combine the product (the politician) with the symbols in the hope that the potential buyers (voters) will link the two.[62]

Photo ops can be misleading. To persuade people that President Bush's tax cuts, which were designed primarily to benefit wealthy taxpayers, would help working Americans, the Speaker of the House (Dennis Hastert, R-Ill.), asked well-heeled lobbyists who favored the tax cuts to dress as construction workers and appear in photo ops featuring "a sea of hard hats" and signs proclaiming, "Tax Relief for Everyone." The lobbyists were urged to participate: "WE DO NEED BODIES—they must be DRESSED DOWN, appear to be REAL WORKER types, etc."[63]

The speech at a media event is not a classical oration or even a cogent address with a beginning, middle, and end. It is an informal talk that emphasizes a few key words or phrases or sentences—almost slogans, because television editors allot time only for a short **sound bite.** And the amount of time is less and less. In 1968, the average sound bite of a presidential contender on the evening news was about forty-two

President Richard Nixon, who moved awkwardly—his gestures were out of synch with his words—was not effective on television. He reminded some people of a marionette; one man made this doll for the president.

Henry Groskinsky, New York City

Democratic leaders Representative Dick Gephardt (Mo.) and Senator Tom Daschle (N.D.) use a photo op to criticize President Bush's tax cut. They said it would enable wealthy people to buy a Lexus but the average laborer just a muffler.

P. F. Bentley/PFPix/Timepix

seconds, but in 1988, it was under ten seconds and since then under eight seconds.[64]

Speechwriters plan accordingly. "A lot of writers figure out how they are going to get the part they want onto television," a former presidential aide explained. "They think of a news lead and write around it. And if the television lights don't go on as the speaker is approaching that news lead, he skips a few paragraphs and waits until they are lit to read the key part."[65] This approach does not produce coherent speeches, but the people watching on television will not know, and the few watching in person do not matter because they are just props. But such writing does not provide either group of people with enough explanation or much inspiration.

Perhaps more than any other source of news, media events illustrate the reliance of politicians on television and of television on politicians. The head of CBS News said, "I'd like just once to have the courage to go on the air and say that such and such a candidate went to six cities today to stage six media events, none of which had anything to do with governing America."[66] Yet television fosters these events, and despite occasional swipes by correspondents, networks continue to show them.

Adversarial Relationship

Although the relationship between the media and politicians is symbiotic in some ways, it is adversarial in others. Since George Washington's administration, when conflicts developed between Federalists and Jeffersonians, the media have attacked politicians, and politicians have attacked the media. In John Adams's administration, Federalists passed the Sedition Act of 1798, which prohibited much criticism of the government.

Federalists used the act to imprison Jeffersonian editors. Not long after, President Andrew Jackson proposed a law to allow the government to shut down "incendiary" newspapers. Even now, a former press secretary commented, "There are very few politicians who do not cherish privately the notion that there should be some regulation of the news."[67]

The conflict stems from a fundamental difference in perspectives. Politicians want the media to help them accomplish their goals, so they hope the media will pass along their messages to the public exactly as they deliver them. But journalists see themselves as servants not of the government but of the public. They question officials until the public knows enough about a matter to hold the officials accountable. According to correspondent Sam Donaldson, "My job is not to say here's the church social with the apple pie, isn't it beautiful?"[68] But some go beyond skepticism to cynicism. In the eyes of a Clinton aide, they walk in the door "assuming that something is wrong and asking, 'What are you hiding?' "[69]

In contemporary society, information is power. The media and the government, especially the president, with the huge bureaucracy at his disposal, are the two primary sources of information. To the extent that the administration controls the flow of information, it can achieve its policy goals. To the extent that the media disseminate contradictory information, they can ensure that the administration's policy goals will be subject to public debate.

Inevitably, politicians fall short of their goals, and many blame the media for their failures. They confuse the message and the messenger, like Czar Peter the Great, who, when notified that the Russian army had lost a battle in 1700, promptly ordered the messenger strangled.

When President Kennedy became upset by the *New York Times* coverage of Vietnam, he asked the paper to transfer the correspondent out of Vietnam. (The paper refused.) When President Nixon became angry with major newspapers and networks, he had Vice President Spiro Agnew lash out at them. He also ordered the Department of Justice to investigate some for possible antitrust violations and the Internal Revenue Service to audit some for possible income tax violations.

However, it would be incorrect to think that the relationship between the media and politicians is usually adversarial. Normally, it is symbiotic. Although journalists like to think of themselves and try to portray themselves as adversaries who stand up to politicians, most rely on politicians most of the time.[70]

Yet the relationship has become more adversarial since the Vietnam War, and the Watergate scandal fueled cynicism about government's performance and officials' honesty. After Watergate, Congress became more willing to launch investigations of administration officials, and reporters became more aggressive in reporting possible scandals.[71] Many reporters, according to the editor of the *Des Moines Register*, "began to feel that no journalism is worth doing unless it unseats the mighty."[72] New reporters especially began to feel this way. Senator Alan Simpson (R–Wyo.) asked the daughter of old friends what she planned to do after graduating from journalism school. "I'm going to be one of the hunters," she replied. When he asked, "What are you going to hunt?" she answered, "People like you!"[73] With this attitude, "young reporters, without a sense of history, context, or proportion, saw scandal where none existed or at least treated any mistake, no matter how minor, as worthy of being called a 'gate.'"[74] During the Clinton years alone, reporters talked about "Filegate," "Travelgate," "Korea-gate," "Troopergate," "Paulagate," and "Monicagate," as well as "Whitewatergate"—questions about a failed real estate development in which the Clintons lost money years before reaching the White House. Yet none of these rivaled Watergate or the Iran–Contra affair in scope or significance. (At least reporters ought to be able to think of more creative names.)

In response, politicians have restricted access for reporters, out of fear that they will say something that will be used against them. Then reporters have complained that politicians are not accessible and that they cannot get the information to do their job.

At the same time, politicians have become more sophisticated in their efforts to "spin" the media—to portray themselves and their programs in the most favorable light, regardless of the facts, and to shade the truth where necessary. Then reporters have become more cynical. "They don't explicitly argue or analyze what they dislike in a political program but instead sound sneering and supercilious about the whole idea of politics."[75] This prompts politicians to increase their efforts to spin the media, which, in turn, prompts reporters to escalate their comments that politicians are insincere or dishonest. And so the cycle continues.

After Vice President Al Gore announced his candidacy for president from his family's farm in Carthage, Tennessee, ABC correspondent Diane Sawyer, while smiling and oozing charm, conducted an interview replete with disrespect. She began, "Are you really a country boy?" He replied, "I grew up in two places. I grew up in Washington, D.C. [as the son of a senator from Tennessee], and I grew up here. My summers were here. Christmas was here." Sawyer taunted Gore, "You mucked pigpens?" Gore answered, "I cleaned out the pigpens . . . and raised cattle and planted and plowed and harvested and took in hay." Sawyer, not satisfied, challenged Gore in an attempt to show that he was a hypocrite: "I have a test for you. Ready for a pop quiz? . . . How many plants of tobacco can you have per acre? . . . What is brucellosis? . . . What are cattle prices roughly now? . . . When a fence separates two farms, how can you tell which farm owns the fence?" By announcing from his family's farm, Gore was trying to convey his rural roots; by interviewing him in this manner, Sawyer was trying to question his sincerity.[76]

In this poisoned relationship, "the most embarrassing, humiliating thing" for a journalist, according to one, is not to have accused someone falsely but to have been perceived by one's peers as getting taken.[77] During the 1992 presidential campaign, George H. Bush aides complimented a *New York Times* reporter for a fair article. "He looked at us like we had the plague. . . . The next thing we heard, a bunch of other reporters were grousing about [him] and accusing him of being a shill for Bush, of being 'in the tank.' By paying him a compliment we had compromised him."[78]

The increasingly adversarial relationship is also due to other factors mentioned earlier. There are so many media, with so much space to fill, that they have a voracious appetite for news and a strong incentive to compete against each other for something "new." As a result, they often magnify trivial things. And because the fringe media play a more prominent role, and because their stories eventually appear in the mainstream media, the media pay more attention to politicians' personal shortcomings with sex, drugs, and alcohol and raise more questions about politicians' "character" than they ever used to.[79] In 1977, one of every two hundred stories on network newscasts was about a purported scandal; in 1997 (*before* the Monica Lewinsky affair was revealed), one of every seven stories was![80]

Yet the apparent toughness usually is "a toughness of demeanor," rather than a toughness of substantive journalism.[81] Reporters exhibit tough attitudes rather than conduct thorough investigations and careful analyses. In fact, few engage in investigative journalism. An examination of 224 incidents of criminal or unethical behavior by Reagan administration appointees found that only 13 percent were uncovered by reporters. Most were discovered through investigations by executive agencies or congressional committees, which then released the information to the press. Only incidents reflecting personal peccadilloes of government officials, such as sexual offenses, were exposed first by reporters.[82]

Few reporters engaged in investigative journalism of the Clinton administration, either. For the Whitewater scandal, reporters got most of their tips from a Republican Party operation run by officials from Republican presidential campaigns.[83] For the sexual matters, reporters got most of their tips from prosecutors for the independent counsel, lawyers for Paula Jones, or a book agent for Linda Tripp. "The big difference between this and Watergate," Bob Woodward said, "is that in Watergate Carl [Bernstein] and I went out and talked to people whom the prosecutors were ignoring or didn't know about. . . . And we were able to look these people in the eye and decide if they were credible and get the nuances of what they were saying. . . . Here, the reporting is all about lawyers telling reporters what to believe and write."[84]

Relationship between the Media and Recent Administrations

Franklin Roosevelt created the model that most contemporary presidents use to communicate with the public. Newspaper publishers, who were conservative businessmen, had no use for Roosevelt and his policies. In fact, a correspondent recalled, "The publishers didn't just disagree with the New Deal. They hated it. The reporters, who liked it, had to write as though they hated it too."[85] Roosevelt saw that he would not receive favorable coverage and knew that he would have to reach the public another way. He used press conferences to provide a steady stream of news about his policies and his efforts to implement them. Editors felt obligated to print this news. This tactic enabled him to overcome the views of the publishers. Roosevelt also used radio talks, called **fireside chats,** to advocate his policies and reassure his listeners in the throes of the Depression. He had a fine voice and a superb ability to speak informally—he talked about his family, even his dog. He drew such an audience that he was offered as much airtime as he wanted (though he was shrewd enough to realize that too much would result in overexposure). This tactic enabled him to avoid the filters of editors and reporters and to take his case directly to the people.

In addition, Roosevelt was the first to seek systematic feedback from the people. He used public opinion polls to gauge people's views on his policies. Thus, for him communication was a two-way process—to the people and from the people.

Reagan Administration

Ronald Reagan refined the model. As a young man, Reagan idolized FDR, even developing an imitation with an appropriate accent and a cigarette holder.[86] As president, Reagan duplicated Roosevelt's success in using the media. Although Reagan was fuzzy on the facts about government programs and the details about his proposals, and sometimes he made bizarre assertions (once he said trees cause most air pollution), he had an uncanny ability to convey his broad themes. Reporters dubbed him the "Great Communicator."

As Roosevelt used radio, Reagan used television. By the time he reached the White House, Reagan had mastered the art of speaking and performing in front of live audiences on stage and in front of the cameras in film. He had also mastered the demands of radio and television.[87] Not only tall and handsome, he knew exactly how to use an inflection or a gesture, or just a tilt of his head. As a result, his speeches and casual comments were highly effective.

His aides knew how to make his appearances especially effective. The administration approached its relationship with the media as "political jujitsu."[88] A jujitsu fighter tries to use the adversary's force to his or her own advantage through a clever maneuver. The administration knew the media would cover the president extensively to fill their news columns and newscasts. An aide explained the strategy: "The media, while they won't admit it, are not in the news business; they're in entertainment. We tried to create the most entertaining, visually attractive scene to fill that box, so that the networks would have to use it."[89]

Aides sent advance agents days or weeks ahead of the president to prepare the "stage" for media events—the specific location, backdrops, lighting, and sound equipment. A trip to Korea was designed to show "the commander in chief on the front line against communism." The advance man went to the demilitarized zone separating North and South Korea and negotiated with the army and the Secret Service for the most photogenic setting. He demanded that the president be allowed to use the most exposed bunker, which meant that the army had to erect telephone poles and string thirty thousand yards of camouflage netting to hide Reagan from North Korean sharpshooters. The advance man also demanded that the army build camera platforms on a hill that remained exposed but offered the most dramatic angle to film Reagan surrounded by sandbags. Although the Secret Service wanted sandbags up to Reagan's neck, the advance man insisted that they be no more than four inches above his navel so viewers would get a clear picture of the president wearing his flak jacket and demonstrating "American strength and resolve."[90]

The Reagan administration also developed the technique of highlighting a single theme with a single message for every week and every day to emphasize whatever proposal the president was pushing then. The administration offered the media information and appearances that reinforced that proposal. Aides strictly controlled the president. They determined "the line of the day" and instructed him what to say. He refused to answer reporters' questions about other matters, except when emerging crises made this practice impossible. When reporters asked questions inside a building, aides frequently demanded that the television lights be shut off so the answers could not be televised; outside they often ordered the helicopter's engines revved up so the answers could not be heard. They did not want other remarks to overshadow the message of the day. The strategy was to set the agenda and to prevent the media from setting it.[91]

By alternately using and avoiding the media, President Reagan's administration managed the news more than any administration before or since. The administration of George W. Bush now is making a similar effort.

Clinton Administration

In his use of the media, Clinton emulated Roosevelt and Reagan. Like Roosevelt, he tried to leapfrog journalists to reach citizens directly.[92] Like Reagan, he tried to focus on one issue at a time to shape public opinion on that issue.

Clinton was knowledgeable about policies, perhaps the most knowledgeable president ever, and he was articulate when speaking. Unlike Roosevelt and Reagan, however, Clinton was not enthralling. He lacked discipline and, as a result, talked too long and gave too many details for most listeners. He strayed from his message of the day or the week and thus blurred this message. Consequently, many people said they did not know what he stood for or wanted to do. Yet Clinton was empathetic; he conveyed the feeling that he cared for others. So

President Reagan, staged to reflect "American strength and resolve" in Korea.

Corbis-Bettmann

many people said they thought he understood the problems of people like them.

Clinton was very effective one-on-one because of his knowledge and his charm. One network correspondent who was not a supporter said, "He is the most charming man I have ever met."[93]

But Clinton inspired visceral hatred from some opponents even before he set foot in the White House. Perhaps it was because he represented the excesses of the baby boom generation, such as sexual affairs and drug use, or because his wife, Hillary, reflected the nontraditional gender roles of that generation. Or perhaps it was because his election cast doubt on conservatives' expectations that Republicans had a lock on the White House and would continue the "Reagan revolution." For whichever reason, some conservative commentators, interest groups, and congressional investigators made a concerted effort at the outset of his administration to undermine his presidency. They magnified minor miscues into major scandals and fed accusations and rumors, some completely bogus, to the media.[94] The media allowed themselves to be used as conduits because, with the atomization of the media, they were competing with other organizations and trying to fill their news columns and newscasts. They aired charges before verifying them because other organizations, including fringe media, had done so or would do so if given a chance. Also, as one reporter later acknowledged, "[T]here's no denying that we give more coverage to stories when someone is shouting."[95]

So Clinton faced a hostile press from the start.[96] According to a joke at the time, he went on a fishing trip with reporters. After their boat left the shore, Clinton realized he had left his tackle on the dock. He stepped out of the boat, walked to the shore, picked up his tackle, and returned to the boat while staying on the surface of the water. The next day's headline read, "Clinton Can't Swim."[97]

As the investigations into the Whitewater land deal, the revelations about the president's personal life, and the concerns about his party's fund-raising prompted ethical questions, they dominated the news and hindered his efforts to convey his messages and accomplish his goals. The Clintons became bitter toward the media, while the reporters became cynical toward the administration. They thought Clinton did not tell the truth or at least did not leave an accurate impression. They considered him "a master of lawyerly evasion."[98] So they looked for manipulation, hypocrisy, or falsity behind every action or statement by the president.

George W. Bush Administration

Early in his administration, President George W. Bush shunned the role of "communicator in chief." Unlike most presidents, who used public occasions to celebrate a national accomplishment or mourn a national tragedy, Bush avoided the spotlight. Even when twenty-four military personnel whose surveillance plane was forced down in China came home to a hero's welcome, Bush spent the weekend in Texas. When aides scheduled public appearances, he bristled. As governor of Texas, he had worked behind the scenes and evidently expected to do the same as president.[99]

His reluctance to make public appearances reflected his discomfort in giving formal speeches or even informal remarks. He usually looked awkward and frequently sounded inarticulate. Reporters observed that he was "perhaps the least confident public performer of the modern presidency."[100] An aide to the previous president commented, "In the Clinton administration, we worried the president would open his zipper, and in the Bush administration, they worry the president will open his mouth."[101]

The terrorist attacks thrust Bush into the public role he had avoided. Initially he stumbled. On the day of the attacks, he failed to return to the White House to reassure the public from the Oval Office.[102] Later he called our task a "crusade," unintentionally linking the war against terrorism to the Crusades by European Christians against Eastern Muslims in the Middle Ages. Then, sounding like a frontier sheriff in the Wild West, he declared Osama bin Laden was "wanted, dead or alive." But gradually Bush grew into his new role, appearing more comfortable on the national stage. At times his informal remarks touched people, and even his formal speeches sounded better. Converting "grief to anger to action,"[103] he rallied the public behind the war.

Bush's strength is to speak to moral clarity. The terrorist attacks, revealing a wide chasm between good and evil, allowed Bush to talk in these terms. But September 11 was "one of history's rare unnuanced days," a presidential adviser admitted.[104] On other issues where there is less moral clarity, such as the clash between Israelis and Palestinians, Bush is less effective. His black-and-white view of the world and his "poverty of language"[105] make it difficult for him to reflect any nuances in his comments and in his policies. For these issues he can seem crude and simple-minded, and he has sent confusing and contradictory messages to the public and to foreign countries affected by our policies.

Although his speechwriters are very good, Bush still stumbles when he speaks without a script. At times he forgets his train of thought, makes up words, and leaves listeners bewildered.[106] But his lack of polish does not seem to hurt him in the polls. He talks like many American men, in his tone and simple words—even the belligerence in his voice—and thus relates well to many American voters.

The climate created by the attacks and his popularity in the polls have muted potential criticism of the president in the press. And all along there has been no concerted effort from the left, as there was against President Clinton from the right, to undermine Bush's presidency.[107] Consequently, he has received relatively gentle treatment from reporters during his term in office.

Relationship between the Media and Congress

Members of Congress also use the media but have much less impact. Since 1970, nearly all have hired their own full-time press secretary who churns out press releases, distributes television tapes, and arranges interviews with reporters.[108] The Senate and House of Representatives have established recording studios for members, allowed television cameras into committee rooms, and supported creation of C-SPAN. Yet members still have trouble attracting the eye of the media. One president can be the subject of the media's focus, whereas 535 members of Congress cannot. Only a handful of powerful (or, occasionally, colorful) members receive much notice from the national media. Other members get attention from their home state or district media, but those from large urban areas with numerous representatives get little publicity or scrutiny even there.[109]

Congressional committees also try to use the media to influence public opinion. After Arizona and California voters supported initiatives on their state ballots in 1996 to allow sick people to use marijuana to control pain, the Senate Judiciary Committee held a hearing to discredit the initiatives and discourage people in other states from following their lead. The hearing, titled "A Prescription for Addiction? The Arizona and California Medical Drug Use Initiatives," included five opponents and just one proponent of marijuana use for sick people. The chair, Senator Orrin Hatch (R-Utah), opened the hearing by stating that the voters were fooled by millions of dollars spent on "stealth campaigns designed to conceal their real objective: the legalization of drugs." Hatch also asserted that marijuana has no medical value. One witness, representing the Federal Drug Enforcement Administration, charged that proponents of the initiatives "cynically used the suffering and illness of vulnerable people to further their own agenda." Witnesses predicted that allowing sick people to use marijuana would result in other people using the drug and then trying harder drugs as well. All the charges are debatable—for example, a federal judge concluded that medical evidence shows that smoking marijuana can ease the symptoms of some patients with AIDS, cancer, or glaucoma—but the committee was not trying to investigate the facts; it was trying to sway public opinion.[110]

Relationship between the Media and the Supreme Court

Unlike presidents and members of Congress, justices of the Supreme Court shun the media. They rarely talk to reporters, and they also forbid their law clerks from talking to them. They try to convey the impression that they are not engaged in politics and therefore should not answer reporters' questions or concern themselves with public opinion.

As a result, the media do not cover the Supreme Court nearly as much as the presidency or Congress. Few newspapers have a full-time Court reporter; no newsmagazines or television networks do. In one recent year, only 27 reporters had Court press credentials, while an estimated 1,700 reporters had White House press credentials.[111]

When the media do cover the Supreme Court, they focus on the rulings of the Court. They seldom run stories on the personalities of the justices, and they seldom investigate or peer behind the scenes of the Court. They often ignore even relevant concerns, such as the periodic questions about the justices' health. The correspondent for *USA Today* violated the norm when he discovered that only 29 of the 394 clerks who had been hired by the current justices were minorities (and that most of these were Asians). His investigation irritated other correspondents, some of whom refused to report the story for their media.[112]

Most reporters on this beat, called "Washington's most deferential press corps,"[113] reject the role of watchdog. Consequently, the justices are shielded from both the legitimate investigation and the excessive scrutiny that officials in the other branches are subjected to. It is probably not a coincidence, then, that the public holds the Court in higher esteem than either of the other branches of government.

Bias of the Media

Every night Walter Cronkite, former anchor for *CBS Evening News,* signed off, "And that's the way it is." His statement implied that the network reported the news exactly the way it happened, that the network held a huge mirror to the world and reflected an image of the world to the viewers—without any distortion. Yet the media do not hold a mirror. They hold a searchlight that seeks and illuminates some things instead of others.[114]

From all the events that occur in the world every day, the media can report only a handful as the news of the day. Even the fat *New York Times,* whose motto is "All the News That's Fit to Print," cannot include all the news. The media must decide what events are newsworthy. When the Wright brothers invited reporters to Kitty

Hawk, North Carolina, to observe the first plane flight in 1903, none considered it newsworthy enough to cover. After the historic flight, only seven American newspapers reported it, and only two reported it on the front page.[115]

After the media decide what events to report, they must decide where to report them—on the front page or top of the newscast, or in a less prominent position. Then they must decide how to report them. Except for magazines, most media attempt to be "objective"; that is, they try to present facts rather than their opinions. Where the facts are in dispute, they try to present the positions of both sides. They are reluctant to evaluate these positions, although sometimes they do explain or interpret them.

In making these decisions, it would be natural for journalists' attitudes to affect their coverage. As one acknowledged, a reporter writes "from what he hears and sees and how he filters it through the lens of his own experience. No reporter is a robot."[116]

Political Bias

Historically, the press was politically biased. The first papers, which were established by political parties, parroted the party line. Even the independent papers, which succeeded them, advocated one side or the other. The attitudes of publishers, editors, and reporters seeped—sometimes flooded—into their prose. But papers gradually abandoned their ardor for editorializing and adopted the practice of objectivity to retain as many of their readers as possible.

Yet the public thinks the press is still biased. Many people think the press is "out to get" the groups they identify with: Executives believe the press is out to get businesses, and laborers believe it is out to get unions. Liberals believe it is biased against liberals, and conservatives believe it is biased against conservatives. Republicans believe it is biased against Republicans, and Democrats believe it is biased against Democrats.[117]

Indeed, the public seems more critical today, when most media at least attempt to be objective, than in the past, when they did not even pretend to be. Then, citizens could subscribe to whichever local paper reflected their own biases (without ever recognizing that the paper reflected any biases). Now, as local newspapers, radio stations, and television stations have given way to national newspapers and networks, and as independently owned newspapers, radio stations, and television stations have given way to large chains and conglomerates, people have less opportunity to follow only those media that reflect their views. People who hold strong views inevitably are disappointed with more moderate coverage. So partisans on both sides simultaneously criticize the same media for being biased.

Bias for Established Institutions and Values

The media generally do reflect a bias for established institutions and values. This should not come as a surprise. Because the media are major businesses owned by large corporations, and because they need to retain their readers and viewers to make a profit, they consciously or unconsciously mirror the mainstream.

The media have a long history of bias against noncapitalist economic systems—democratic socialism as well as authoritarian communism. They play up the failures and play down the successes of these economic systems. They also exaggerate the health of our economic system in boom times, such as in the 1990s. As the stock market soared in that decade, they discounted the risks and entertained the possibility that there would no longer be periodic cycles of boom and bust in the "new economy."[118] (The real economy proved otherwise.) In foreign affairs, the media toe the government line. During the Cold War, this meant harsh attacks on the Soviet Union and leftist Latin American regimes.[119] During the Persian Gulf War, this meant jingoistic coverage and unquestioning acceptance of administration claims.[120] Even for the Vietnam War, which is cited as an example of journalistic rejection of governmental policies, the media offered blindly positive coverage for most years and then relatively restrained criticism near the end.[121]

This bias was apparent after the terrorist attacks. For understandable reasons, the networks, featuring patriotic logos and melodramatic music, made no effort to be neutral. But some media went further. Cable systems yanked *Politically Incorrect* after the host criticized the use of the word *cowardly* to refer to the terrorists, and two newspapers fired columnists after they criticized the president's delayed return to the Capitol on September 11.[122] CBS anchor Dan Rather, who prides himself on his independence, declared, "George Bush is the president. He makes the decisions and . . . wherever he wants me to line up, just tell me where." The patriotic fervor diminished media coverage and, therefore, public awareness of important matters. In contrast to the British Broadcasting Corporation (BBC), American media presented less information about Arab opinion, the lack of progress in resolving the Israeli-Palestinian conflict, and the cracks in the American-led coalition against terrorism.[123]

Correlated with the media's support for established institutions and values is their reliance on government officials for their news.[124] Heavy reliance on government officials means that the stories will bear their imprint. Reporters turn to officials for news because it is easy and because, ironically, they want to avoid charges of bias. Reporters believe their peers, their superiors, and the public all consider officials newsworthy. Ignoring them or downplaying them might be construed as showing bias against them.[125]

Bias for Particular Candidates and Policies

Most debate about media bias revolves around charges that the media exhibit a preference for particular candidates and policies over others. Conservative groups, in particular, claim that the media are biased toward liberal candidates and policies.

In studying media bias, social scientists have examined the characteristics and behavior of journalists. They have found that journalists are not very representative of the public. They are disproportionately college-educated white males from the upper middle class. Furthermore, they are disproportionately urban and secular, rather than rural and religious. They are disproportionately Democrats or independents leaning to the Democrats, rather than Republicans or independents leaning to the Republicans. Likewise, they identify themselves disproportionately as liberals rather than conservatives.[126]

Journalists who work for the most influential organizations—large newspapers, wire services, news magazines, and radio and television networks—are more likely to be Democrats and liberals than those who work for less prominent organizations—small newspapers and radio and television stations.[127]

Journalists in the most influential organizations are more likely than the public to support the liberal position on issues. At the same time, they support capitalism and do not think that our institutions "need overhaul."[128] Thus, they are not extremely liberal.

Examination of journalists' backgrounds and attitudes assumes that these color journalists' coverage. But several factors mitigate the effect of these traits. Most journalists chose their profession not because of a commitment to political ideology, but because of the opportunity to rub elbows with powerful people and be close to exciting events. "Each day brings new stories, new dramas in which journalists participate vicariously."[129] As a result, most journalists "care more about the politics of an issue than about the issue itself,"[130] so they are less likely to express their views about the issue.

In addition, mainstream organizations pressure journalists to muffle their views because of a conviction that it is professional to do so and a desire to avoid the headaches that could arise otherwise—debates among their staffers, complaints from their local affiliates, complaints from their audience, perhaps even complaints from the White House or Congress. Sometimes media executives or editors pressure reporters because they have contrary views.[131]

For these reasons, mainstream media do not exhibit nearly as much **political bias** as would be expected from journalists' backgrounds and attitudes. Although they do show a bias for established institutions and values, they do not show much bias for particular candidates in elections.

To measure bias, researchers use a technique called content analysis. They scrutinize newspaper and television stories to determine whether there was an unequal amount of coverage, unequal use of favorable or unfavorable statements, or unequal use of a positive or negative tone. They consider insinuating verbs ("he conceded" rather than "he said") and pejorative adjectives ("her weak response" rather than "her response"), and for television stories they evaluate the announcers' nonverbal communication—voice inflection, eye movement, and body language.

Studies of coverage of presidential campaigns found relatively little bias. The media typically gave the two major candidates equal attention, and they usually avoided any favorable or unfavorable statements in their news stories. They typically provided diverse views in editorials and columns, with some commentary slanting one way and other commentary slanting the opposite way. Thus, the authors of a major study examining forty-six newspapers concluded that American newspapers are "fairly neutral."[132] Some studies did find some bias against incumbents, front-runners, and emerging challengers.[133] For these candidates, the media apparently took their watchdog role seriously.

Overall, then, there is less bias than the public believes or the candidates feel. When candidates complain, they usually are objecting to bad news or trying to manipulate the media. The strategy is to put reporters on the defensive so they will go easier on the candidate or harder on the opponent in the future. In the 1996 election, Bob Dole learned that reporters were considering publishing a story that he had an extramarital affair in 1968. Although the story did not appear in the major media, Dole criticized them for being biased. Later his aide admitted the criticism was "a preemptive strike."[134]

Yet the way in which the media cover campaigns can have different implications for different candidates. The media report the facts and all the details that contribute to the facts: that one candidate is leading while the other is trailing, that one campaign is surging while the other is slipping. This coverage has positive implications for the former—swaying undecided voters, galvanizing campaign workers, and attracting financial contributions—and negative implications for the latter. Such coverage does not benefit one party over the other party in election after election, but it can benefit one party's candidate over the other party's candidate in a particular election.[135] People who support the losers consider such reporting biased. Journalists, however, consider it a reflection of reality. In 1992 and 1996, the media's coverage of the success of Clinton's campaigns and the failure of Bush's and Dole's campaigns mirrored the reality of these elections.[136]

The 2000 election was fraught with allegations of bias. Some observers pointed to the cracks about Bush's intelligence, though most observers saw more bias against Gore's candidacy.[137] Studies confirmed this pattern.[138] Reporters acknowledged that Bush was more accessible and chummy, even bestowing nicknames on them, while Gore was remote and reserved. "If this were high school," one reporter remarked, "the press would be the drama nerds and the history club freaks. Bush would be the popular boy who has lots of friends. And the popular boy is courting the geeks."[139] But reporters denied that their personal feelings toward Bush resulted in favorable coverage, noting that their political views did not necessarily match his.

Actually, the 2000 coverage can be explained by the habitual practices of political reporting. Reporters covered candidates as they rose and fell in the polls. For much of the campaign, coverage favored Bush while he was riding high. Then it favored Gore when he was surging from behind. "We all respond like Pavlov's dogs to polls," an experienced correspondent explained.[140]

Another habitual practice also has positive implications for some candidates and negative implications for others. The press pays more attention to minor things that are easy to report—and easy to ridicule—than to substantive issues that are difficult to explain.[141] Hence all the emphasis on Gore's exaggerations or "lies."[142] The vice president was rebuked for saying that he and wife Tipper were the models for the couple in *Love Story.* In fact, he was a model for the male character, though Tipper was not a model for the female character. He was the butt of late-night comedy for claiming credit as a senator for creating the Internet—comedians cracked that he said he "invented" it.[143] In fact, he was instrumental in securing the government funding that made it possible (as Newt Gingrich later acknowledged), though he did not invent it. These incidents exemplify a pattern throughout the campaign. The straight arrow—Gore was so straight that unlike most politicians he could not fake sincerity at campaign events he thought were silly or annoying—was portrayed as a serial liar. He was called "Pinocchio."

In contrast, there was little emphasis on Bush's misstatements about his proposals or about Gore's proposals.[144] For reporters to call attention to these misstatements would require more knowledge about substantive policies or more nerve to draw conclusions about such policies than most have. Although they are frequently willing to criticize or even ridicule candidates about minor matters, they are usually reluctant to challenge them on substantive issues. Thus, as a senior correspondent wrote after the election, "we do not write stories that begin: 'Governor George W. Bush today proposed a $1.6 trillion tax cut that will destroy the budget surplus unless prosperity continues at current record levels for the next ten years.'"[145]

Similarly, when covering the debates, the press pays more attention to style and tactics than to substantive issues—more attention to how they said it than to what they said.[146] Reporters act as though they are theater critics. Hence all the emphasis on Gore's mannerisms—the rolling eyes and loud sighs during Bush's answers. (Although the debate rules forbade the television networks from showing the opponent's reactions to a candidate's answers, the networks ignored these rules in their quest for more drama in their telecasts.)[147] In contrast, correspondents spoke of Bush's appeal to "ordinary people" and his ability to "remain cool" in the face of Gore's attacks. Although Bush seemed overmatched—at times he appeared lost when addressing substantive issues—correspondents declared that he "held his own."[148] Consequently, a study found that coverage of Gore was "decidedly more negative" than coverage of Bush.[149]

In the 2000 election, these tendencies rebounded to Bush's advantage—not because reporters favored the Republican candidate but because they followed their normal practices. In other elections, these tendencies might boost the Democratic candidate. These practices do not reflect bias by reporters as much as they reflect superficiality in reporting.

There are two exceptions to the generalization that overt political bias in elections is minimal. First, the media usually give short shrift to third-party candidates.[150] In 2000, Ralph Nader ran for president. Although he was well known and his views were partly shared by various blocs of voters, and although his Green Party offered an appealing alternative to the major parties, Nader received scant coverage. When he held a press conference announcing his candidacy, none of the networks and few of the newspapers even reported it. When he held enthusiastic rallies on college campuses and in large coliseums, including Madison Square Garden in New York City, the national media virtually ignored them. Only when the election between Gore and Bush tightened and it appeared that Nader might be a spoiler did the national media pay attention. Then they focused on his potential as a spoiler rather than on his views that had attracted the crowds.[151]

Second, newspapers traditionally print editorials and columns that express opinions. In editorials before elections, papers often endorse candidates. Most owners are Republican, and this is one time many seek to influence the content of their papers. Since the first survey in 1932, more papers have endorsed the Republican presidential candidate, except in the election between Democratic president Lyndon Johnson and Republican senator Barry Goldwater in 1964 and in the election between Clinton and Bush in 1992.[152]

The relative lack of bias in coverage of elections does not necessarily mean there is a lack of bias in coverage of other events. Because elections are highly visible and candidates are very sensitive about the coverage, the media might take more care to be neutral here than elsewhere. Researchers have not examined coverage of other events as much. Studies of coverage of social policies, such as abortion, school busing, and nuclear power, found a tilt toward the liberal positions.[153] Anecdotal reports also suggest some bias to the left on social issues.[154] Yet studies of coverage of foreign policies found a tilt toward the conservative positions.[155]

Examination of coverage of religion shows how difficult it is to assess bias. The religious right and its leaders get far more coverage than the religious left or the religious middle, which are nearly invisible in the mainstream media. Most coverage of religion in politics focuses on the agenda of Christian conservatives—abortion, homosexuality, and school issues—which helps them garner support and gain leverage. But the religious right sometimes is mocked.[156] So is the net result a bias in favor of the religious right or against it?

Because of the real or perceived bias in the mainstream media, conservatives established their own media in the 1980s and 1990s. This vocal complex includes newspapers, such as the *Wall Street Journal,* the *Washington Times,* and the *New York Post,* various magazines, numerous radio and television talk shows, plus a network of columnists, commentators, and think tanks. These journalists, seeing themselves as part of an ideological movement, as members of the same team, are unabashedly conservative, more biased toward the right than the mainstream media are toward the left.

This vocal complex also includes the Fox News Channel, which competes with CNN and MSNBC. Fox is the first network to *narrowcast*—intentionally appeal to a narrow segment of the entire audience—rather than broadcast. Fox appeals to conservatives disenchanted with the mainstream media. For instance, when reporting on the debate over President Bush's tax cut proposal, the network ran a line at the bottom of the screen urging, "Cut 'em already."[157] Yet the network retains a veneer of neutrality. It repeats: "Fair and balanced," "spin-free." The marketing strategy is to attract viewers by offering them conservative commentary but also the reassurance that this commentary is truth rather than opinion.[158]

The conservative media additionally include Christian radio networks, television organizations, and more than 1,300 radio and television stations.[159] These media address political issues as well as spiritual matters.

Although public questions about bias revolve around liberalism and conservatism, perhaps the questions should be pointed toward class differences. An examination of coverage of the debate over the North American Free Trade Agreement (NAFTA) in 1996, drafted to ease trade between American and Canadian and Mexican companies, showed more emphasis on the benefits of free trade than on the loss of jobs that would result from the treaty. Thus, the media reflected the views of business more than those of workers. Analysts now suggest that the most significant bias is not liberal or conservative but upper middle class over working class.[160] Such

bias usually favors the liberal positions on social issues and the conservative, or business, positions on economic issues. These views closely match not only the social class of most journalists but also their urban background and college education (see Table 3).

This chapter focuses on the news media, not the entertainment media. Popular television programs, movies, and records often promote ideas or trends that sometimes are characterized as liberal, such as diversity, multiculturalism, acceptance of racial minorities, acceptance of casual sex, and disparagement of traditional religion. (However, these media also glorify violence and possession and use of guns, which do not reflect liberal values.) Such entertainment might have as much or even more effect on individuals' views than the news does. But consideration of this aspect of the media is beyond the scope of this text.

Bias against All Candidates and Officials

Some critics charge that a general bias exists against all candidates and officials—a negative undercurrent in reporting about government, regardless of who or what is covered. President Nixon's first vice president, Spiro Agnew, called journalists "nattering nabobs of negativism." Critics think this bias increased after the Watergate scandal made reporters more cynical.

There seems to be considerable validity to this charge. Analyses of newspapers, magazines, and television networks show that the overwhelming majority of the stories about government are neutral.[161] However, the rest of the stories are more often negative than positive.[162]

Emphasizing the negative distorts what occurs. In the 1996 presidential campaign, 85 percent of the candidates' comments made a positive case for the candidates, but 85 percent of the media's coverage focused on

TABLE 3	Do the Media Reflect Class Bias?

Differences in opinion and income between the public and journalists suggest that the media may reflect a class bias.

President Clinton's economic plan in 1993 did not increase taxes on the wealthy enough.

Respondent	Percentage Who Agreed
Public	72
Washington, D.C., journalists	18

U.S. economic conditions in 1998 are "excellent" or "good."

Public	66
Washington, D.C., journalists	92

Household income of $50,000 or more.

Public	34
Washington, D.C., journalists	95

SOURCE: David Croteau, "Examining the 'Liberal Media' Claim," *Fairness and Accuracy in Reporting* (June 1998); U.S. Department of Commerce Bureau of the Census, cited in "Ticker," *Brill's Content* (October 1998): 148.

negative attacks by the candidates.[163] In 1997, the *Washington Post* reported that Senator Robert Byrd (D–W.V.) got the National Park Service to fund a project for his state, including the renovation of a train station—for his "personal pork barrel." "Why did the National Park Service spend $2.5 million turning a railroad station into a visitor center for a town with a population of eight? The compelling reason—Senator Robert C. Byrd . . . who glides past on Amtrak's Cardinal Limited from time to time, heading to and from his home in Sophia, a few miles south." But Byrd did not ride that train, and that train did not go to that town. Moreover, the Interior Department recommended the project; it was not "slipped" into other legislation "unwanted," as the article claimed. When the reporter was questioned, he replied with disgust, "Look, everyone knows that this is the way the world works in Washington. What's the big deal?" Indeed, this is the way things work in Washington sometimes, but apparently not this time. This article, which prompted editorials in newspapers across the country, reinforced readers' cynicism. When Byrd challenged the accuracy of the article, the paper made no effort to confirm the accuracy or correct the record.[164]

Emphasizing the negative conveys the impression that neither the candidates are worthy of the office they seek nor the officials of the office they hold. It ultimately conveys the impression that the political process itself is contemptible.[165]

Commercial Bias

Although the public dwells on charges of political bias, commercial bias is far more pervasive and significant in understanding media coverage of politics.

Reasons for Commercial Bias

Except for public radio and television, American media are private businesses run for a profit. They must attract readers and listeners and viewers. With an audience, they can sell advertising. The larger the audience, the higher the price they can charge. A change of 1 percent in the ratings of a television news program in New York City, for example, can mean a difference of $5 million in advertising for a station in a year.[166] The opportunity to make a profit from newscasts is so enormous that CBS's *60 Minutes* made more money in one decade than the entire Chrysler Corporation did during the same years.[167] NBC's news division generated 40 to 50 percent of NBC's overall profit in recent years, with its entertainment and sports divisions dividing the rest.[168] One financial analyst estimated that local stations' news programs also garner 40 to 50 percent of the stations' overall profit.[169] (For racial implications of the pressure to make a profit, see the box "Color and the Clicker.")

With chains and conglomerates taking over most media, the pressure to make a sizable profit has escalated. In the 1970s, big-city newspapers expected to make a 7 or 8 percent return; today chains and conglomerates expect these papers to make over a 20 percent return.[170] Corporate executives worry that financial analysts will rank them lower and mutual fund managers will unload their stock if their earnings fall below those available "from investments anywhere else in the financial universe, from a shirt factory in Thailand to the latest Internet start-up."[171]

The pressure to make a profit and the need to attract an audience shape the media's presentation of the news and lead to a **commercial bias.** Sometimes this means that the media deliberately print or broadcast what advertisers want. In 2001, CBS bowed to demands by Proctor & Gamble that it drop episodes of *Family Law* dealing with gun ownership, capital punishment, interfaith marriage, and abortion.[172] Other times the media censor themselves. Numerous magazines, in health articles, avoided references to smoking's dangers for fear of losing advertising from tobacco companies. A poll of reporters and executives found that a third admitted to avoiding stories that would embarrass an advertiser or harm the financial interests of their own organization.[173]

Usually, though, commercial bias means that the media must print or broadcast what the public wants, which means that the media must offer what the public

COLOR AND THE CLICKER

Television news features African Americans in "lights-and-sirens" stories about crimes and drugs and in other stories about "urban pathologies," such as single parenthood, that reinforce negative stereotypes.[1] However, television news shuns African Americans in other contexts—not just in the newscasts that focus on government officials but in the newsmagazines, such as *Dateline, 20/20, 60 Minutes,* and *48 Hours,* that air human dramas.[2] A network staff member lamented, "Can't we do a story about day-care centers and have a black day-care owner . . .? Why can't they be regular, normal people doing regular, normal things that aren't just associated with their ethnic backgrounds? It makes me sick."[3]

A producer working on a story about a mental disability was searching for a family who had a child with that disability. "I found a great, great upper-middle-class family in Miami, but they were black. I was told . . .: 'Find another family.' " Many network staff members have had similar experiences.

"It's a subtle thing," said one. "A story involving blacks takes longer to get approved. And if it is approved, chances are that it will sit on the shelf a long time before it gets on the air. No one ever says anything. The message gets through."

Sometimes it's not so subtle. Staffers were told by executives that a particular story was "not a good story for us" or that it would "not have broad appeal in the Midwest and in the South." Instead, they were told to feature "families with lots of blond-haired, blue-eyed children."[4]

One reporter observed, "They whisper it, like cancer: 'Is she white?'
'Yeah, she's white.'
'Are you sure?'
'Well, it says they are from Slovakian descent; I'm assuming.'
'Well, go out and check.' "

A producer on an evening newscast, working on a health series, found a story about a doctor who encouraged women to get mammograms. The doctor hauled her equipment to beauty parlors where she could test the women conveniently. But when the executive producer saw the piece, he exclaimed, "You didn't tell me that the doctor was black . . . that the people were black!" And he spiked the story.

This pattern is pervasive. A senior executive at a major network confessed, "It's our dirty little secret."

The reason? Research shows the demographic makeup of the audience for every program, and minute-by-minute ratings reveal which stories attract and keep an audience. Many middle-class whites do not want to watch stories about either lower-class people or racial minorities. When such stories come on, these viewers click to another channel. The networks, under pressure to boast the most viewers to generate the most profits for their corporate owners, cater to the tastes of middle-class whites—the largest segment of the audience.

What appears to be racial bias by the networks is actually commercial bias, just as we have seen that what appears to be political bias by the media is usually commercial bias. But the commercial bias here has racial implications, just as the commercial bias elsewhere has political implications. As a result, television news, which could forge understanding between the races by showing sympathetic people of all colors facing common challenges, makes little effort to do so. Instead, it accepts the subtle racism of some white viewers who will not watch the same story if it portrays black folks rather than white folks.

1. Jeff Cohen, "Racial Tension," *Brill's Content,* October 1999, 54.
2. The record of *60 Minutes* is not as bad as the others', perhaps because *60 Minutes* is the only one without prime-time competition. Robert Schmidt, "Airing Race," *Brill's Content,* October 2000, 145.
3. Av Westin, "The Color of Rating," *Brill's Content,* April 2001, 84. Quotations are from this article, unless otherwise noted.
4. Schmidt, "Airing Race," 114–115.

finds entertaining. This creates a "conflict between being an honest reporter and being a member of show business," a network correspondent confessed, "and that conflict is with me every day."[174] When Dan Rather was asked why he devoted time to the demolition of O. J. Simpson's house two years after his trial, Rather answered, "[F]ear . . . the fear that if we don't do it, somebody else will, and when they do it, they will get a few more readers, a few more listeners, a few more viewers than we do. The result is the 'Hollywoodization of the news.' "[175]

The dilemma is most marked for television. Many people who watch television news are not interested in politics; a majority, in fact, say it covers too much politics.[176] Some watch the news because they were watching another program before the news and left the television on, others because they were going to watch another program after the news and turned the television on early. Networks feel pressure "to hook them and keep them."[177]

Therefore, networks try to make the everyday world of news seem as exciting as the make-believe world they depict in their other programs. One network instructed its staff, "Every news story should, without any sacrifice of probity or responsibility, display the attributes of fiction, of drama. It should have structure and conflict, problem and denouement, rising action and falling action, a beginning, a middle and an end."[178] As one executive says, television news is **"infotainment."**[179]

So television anchors and newscasters, hired for their appearance and personality as much or more than their experience and ability, become show business stars. And show business stars become television anchors and newscasters. CNN hired comely detective Andrea Thompson from *NYPD Blue,* despite her lack of any experience (as ABC had previously hired noted authority Leonardo DiCaprio to interview President Clinton about the environment).

Consequences of Commercial Bias

The commercial bias of the media has important consequences. One is to sensationalize the news. The anthrax infections after the terrorist attacks deserved our full attention. But the media would not let up. Even after the initial flurry of reports, they ran one overwrought account following another. *Time* magazine featured families who bought gas masks. The *Washington Post* wrote that America is "on the verge" of "public hysteria."[180] In fact, few people other than journalists panicked. In polls, large majorities expressed concern but not fear. (Eight percent said they spoke to a doctor, and 4 percent said they bought antibiotics.[181]) However, the media realized that generating fear would expand their audience, as people would pay attention to see if they had to worry about anthrax infecting them.

The emphasis on sensationalism leads to an emphasis on scandals. Since Watergate, the media have played up—blown up—other, lesser scandals. In the Clinton era, the public was subjected to saturation coverage of the Whitewater scandal[182] and then extensive coverage of all the other "gates" mentioned earlier in the chapter. And we should not forget the "scandal"—the outrage *du jour*—over the president's $200 haircut on Air Force One. Perhaps there was something important in these incidents, though a succession of special prosecutors could find nothing more damning than that the president lied about having sexual relations with Monica Lewinsky.[183]

One journalist observed:

> When a scandal is breaking, talk show figures wring their hands about the "agony" of Watergate or Iran–Contra; but the truth is that journalists are happier at such moments than at any other time. The country's attention is turned toward Washington. People hang on disclosures of the latest "inside" news. Life is energizing and sweet for Washington journalists, even if the scandal of the moment is a big wheel-spinning exercise for the country as a whole.[184]

Another, related consequence of commercial bias is to emphasize human interest in the news. When a small boat fleeing Cuba sank, drowning eleven refugees including his mother, six-year-old Elian Gonzales survived. He was rescued by fishermen and taken to relatives in Miami, but his father wanted him returned to Cuba. The relatives and Cuban Americans in South Florida demanded that he remain there, and they provided made-for-television demonstrations for the journalists who had

The media frenzy after the anthrax infections prompted some families, such as this one in Chicago, to buy gas masks.

Steve Liss/Timepix

round-the-clock stakeouts at the house. The plight of this boy became the story of the summer. A *Wall Street Journal* columnist wrote that "the dolphins who surrounded him like a contingent of angels pushed him upward" so he would not drown.[185] Experts explained his presumed state of mind. Diane Sawyer, in an interview, insisted that he tell the national audience just whom he wanted to live with.

The emphasis on human interest includes an emphasis on sex. Although American newscasts do not go as far as the Bulgarian program *The Naked Truth,* which had young women disrobe as they read the news,[186] the media do dwell on sexual affairs of public officials. The escapades of President Clinton received extraordinary attention. When the allegations involving Monica Lewinsky arose, the media dropped important stories to focus on what the president did with the intern.[187] The *Los Angeles Times* assigned twenty-six reporters to examine Lewinsky's life, interviewing baby-sitters and kindergarten classmates.[188] *Time* magazine solicited personal information from college classmates. The networks interviewed one person who ate lunch with her three years earlier.

During the investigation by the special prosecutor, titillating details were leaked to the media and then announced to the public. There were breathless reports about phone sex, the president's cigar as a sex toy, and the intern's dress with a semen stain. There was tittering about the "distinguishing characteristics" of the president's genitals—and speculation about how this would be proven or disproven in court.

The emphasis on sensationalism and human interest include an emphasis on crime. Although the national media give crime extensive coverage, this emphasis is most apparent for the local media, where television news is, in Ralph Nader's words, "something that jerks your head up every ten seconds, whether that is shootings, robberies, sports showdowns, or dramatic weather forecasts."[189] Media consultants advise local stations how to attract the largest audience and make the most money for their corporate chain or conglomerate.[190] The saying "If it bleeds, it leads," expresses, tongue in cheek, the programming philosophy of many stations. Crime coverage fills about one-third of local newscasts.[191] A week before the presidential election of 2000, television stations in Columbus, Ohio, devoted more than twice as much time to various crimes than to the election, though the outcome was in doubt, with Ohio a key state and Columbus the state's capital.[192] (One station, however, was able to find time for an undercover investigation of a topless car wash.) A jaded reporter put it bluntly, "It doesn't matter what kind of swill you set in front of the public. As long as it's got enough sex and violence in it, they'll slurp it up."[193] (For an example of local news reporting, see the box "Investigating Mickey Mantle?")

The emphasis on sensationalism and human interest leads to another consequence of commercial bias—an emphasis on controversy rather than agreement. Stories about conflict provide drama. Reporters, one admits, are "fight promoters" rather than consensus builders.[194] Reporters frame disputes as struggles between opposite camps. Thus, some stories about survivors of the Holocaust include bizarre statements by deniers of the Holocaust, claiming that there was no plan to exterminate European Jews, or that Hitler was unaware of the effort, or that few Jews were ever killed. The stories present these statements as though they constitute an opposing opinion that deserves a public platform.[195] With their focus on controversy, the media allow themselves to be manipulated by people who are unscrupulous or ignorant. And with the justification that there are two sides to every story, the media promote public confusion in the process.

Once the media frame an issue as a struggle between two sides, they depict attack and counterattack, using dueling sound bites from politicians and interjecting metaphors from wars. They talk about politicians who are "targets," who are "under fire," who receive "shots across their bow." They talk about politicians who engage in "search-and-destroy missions" and who "hold back no ammunition." Occasionally, they refer to a "cease-fire," but eventually they return to a "war of attrition" with "do-or-die" battles. Ultimately, they lament the politicians who "crashed in flames."[196]

A researcher studying the coverage of the debate over health care reform in 1994 sat with reporters listening to Hillary Clinton present the administration's plan. For two hours she discussed the plan, including its substance and the arguments raised against it.

The reporters

found it completely uninteresting. They were talking to each other, passing notes around. But as soon as she made a brief attack on the Republicans, there was a physiological reaction, this surge of adrenaline, all around me. The pens moved. The reporters arched forward. They wrote everything down rapidly. As soon as this part was over, they clearly weren't paying attention any more.[197]

Not surprisingly, an experimental study later found that people who read fifteen newspaper articles on the health care debate knew no more about the proposals than people who read just one article.[198]

By focusing on conflict and by framing most issues as though they have two—and only two—sides, the media polarize the public. After the rampage at Columbine High School in Littleton, Colorado, the public was subjected to a moronic debate about whether the incident was caused by the availability of guns in our society *or* by the glorification of violence in the media. The coverage prodded people to choose sides, as though it had to be one or the other, and could not be the result of any other factor, too. In contrast, Japanese television talk shows about controversial issues typically have more than two guests, thus reducing the polarization while conveying the impression that the issues are complex and might have multiple answers.[199] American media prefer to focus on two opposing extremes. "The middle ground, the sensible center," one reporter admits, "is dismissed as too squishy, too dull, too likely to send the audience channel surfing."[200]

These practices make it harder for people to accept compromises as solutions to problems and, therefore, harder for politicians to forge compromises. In fact, the media belittle compromises. They portray politicians on one side as losing or "giving in" when they should have been fighting to win. Thus, the media reinforce some citizens' naive belief that politicians need not and should not compromise.

Another consequence of commercial bias is to use a **game orientation** in political reporting.[201] The underlying assumption is that politics is a game and politicians, whether candidates campaigning for election or officials performing in office, are the players. The corollary to the assumption is that the players are self-centered and self-interested. They are seeking victory for themselves and defeat for their opponents and are not concerned about the consequences of their proposals or of government's policies. With this orientation, reporters highlight politicians' strategies and tactics, and they present new developments according to how these developments help some politicians and hinder others. Reporters slight the substance and impact of politicians' proposals and policies.

The game orientation appeals to journalists because it generates human interest. It offers new story lines as new information comes to light, much like a board game where "chance" cards inject unexpected scenarios and alter the players' moves and the game's outcomes.

This orientation also appeals to journalists because it is easy and relatively free from charges of partisan or ideological bias. (Stories highlight which contestants are winning, not which ones should win or what consequences might result.) Analyzing policy lacks all of these advantages for journalists.

The game orientation attracts an audience, but it breeds more cynicism. It creates the impression that politics is just a game, not an essential activity for a democratic society; that politicians are just the players, not our representatives; that politicians act just in their self-interest, not in the public interest; and that politicians' goal is just to beat others, not to make good public policy.

The assumption that politics is a game and the corollary that the players are concerned solely with their own interests leads to the conclusion that their strategies and tactics are based mostly on manipulation and deception. Journalists, casting their wary eyes on politicians, look for manipulation and deception and interpret even sincere action in those ways.

For elections, the game orientation results in what is called horse race coverage, with "front-runners," "dark horses," and "also-rans." This coverage accounts for much of the total coverage of campaigns.[202]

Horse race coverage is not new and is not confined to television. An examination of presidential election coverage by metropolitan newspapers since 1888 shows that the race was a staple of journalism long before the advent of broadcast media.[203] Yet other research suggests that the proportion of coverage focusing on the race has been increasing in recent decades.[204]

Now horse race coverage dominates election reporting. In 2000, about two-thirds of the reporting by newspapers, television networks, and Web sites featured the horse race, and much of the remaining reporting featured the candidates' strategies. Although there were major differences in the candidates' stands, far less reporting examined the issues or their proposals.[205]

The quintessential reflection of horse race coverage, reporting of candidates' poll standings, has increased greatly. Not only have the media reported more results of polls taken by commercial organizations, but they have conducted more polls themselves.[206] Now coverage of polls takes more space than coverage of candidates' speeches, and it usually appears as the lead or next-to-lead story.[207]

Even after elections, the game orientation continues. When Clinton proposed a plan to overhaul the welfare system, all major newspapers focused on the political implications for his reelection; few even explained the plan, let alone its substantive implications. When he proposed more money for law enforcement, to put "more cops on the beat," the media pointed out how this would sound in campaign ads but ignored where the extra officers would be, how much they would cost, and whether they would have any effect on crime.[208]

Commercial bias of the media leads to additional consequences for television specifically. One is to emphasize events, or those parts of events, that have visual interest. The networks have people whose job is to evaluate all film for visual appeal. Producers seek the events that promise the most action, camera operators shoot the parts of the events with the most action, and editors select the portions of the film with the most action.[209] Television thus focuses on disasters, crimes, and protests far more than they actually occur, and it displays the interesting surface rather than the underlying substance of these events—for example, the protest rather than the cause of the anger.

Another consequence of commercial bias for television is to cover the news very briefly. A half-hour newscast has only twenty-one minutes without commercials. In that time, the networks broadcast only about one-third as many words as the *New York Times* prints on its front page alone. Although cable television has an abundance of time, it follows this format, too.

Television stories are short—about one minute each—because the networks think viewers' attention spans are short. Indeed, a survey found that a majority of eighteen- to thirty-four-year-olds who have remote controls typically watch more than one show at once.[210] Thus, networks do not allow leaders or experts to explain their thoughts about particular events or policies. Instead, networks take sound bites to illustrate what was said. Their correspondents usually do not have enough time to explain the events or policies or to provide background information about them.

A network correspondent was asked what went through his mind when he signed off each night. "Good night, dear viewer," he said. "I only hope you read the *New York Times* in the morning."[211]

When the chairman of the board of one network, in conversation with a former Reagan aide, asked what the networks could do to provide more responsible report-

"Hey, do you want to be on the news tonight or not? This is a sound bite, not the Gettysburg address. Just say what you have to say, Senator, and get the hell off."

ing, the aide answered, "Easy, . . . just eliminate ratings for news. You claim that news is not the same as entertainment. So why do you need ratings?" The chairman sighed, "Well, that's our big money-maker, the news."[212] A former network executive concluded, "Because television can make so much money doing its worst, it often can't afford to do its best."[213]

Overall, commercial bias of the media results in no coverage or superficial coverage of many important stories. This, more than any political bias, makes it difficult for citizens, particularly those who rely on television, to become well informed.

Impact of the Media on Politics

It is difficult to measure the impact of the media on politics. Because the many media provide varied though similar coverage and reach different though overlapping audiences, it is exceedingly difficult to isolate the impact of particular media on particular groups of people. Other factors also influence people's knowledge, attitudes, and behavior toward politics. But there is considerable agreement that the media have a substantial impact on the public agenda, political parties and elections, and public opinion.

Impact on the Public Agenda

The most important impact of the media is **setting the agenda**—influencing the process by which problems are considered important and solutions are proposed and debated.[214] The media publicize an issue, and people exposed to the media talk about the issue with their fellow citizens. Eventually, enough consider it important and pressure officials to resolve it.[215]

The media's impact is most noticeable for dramatic events that occur suddenly. It is less noticeable for issues that evolve gradually. Watergate required months of coverage before making it onto the public agenda, and AIDS required the death of actor Rock Hudson before making it.[216]

Even for issues that evolve gradually, however, cumulative coverage by the media can have an impact. After years of extensive coverage, people told pollsters that drug use was the "most important problem" facing the country, and then they told pollsters that crime was.

Studies comparing people's views with the media coverage of these problems and with the actual rates of these activities show that people's views fluctuated more according to the media coverage than to the actual rates. When the media coverage increased, people considered the problems more serious, even when the actual rates of crime or drug use remained steady or decreased.[217]

The impact usually is greatest for stories that appear on the front page of the newspaper or at the top of the newscast rather than those buried in the back or at the end.[218] Many people who do not follow the news fully check the beginning of the newspaper or newscast for the "important" stories. Without being aware of it, they are accepting the media's role in identifying these stories as the important ones. Moreover, the impact usually is greatest on people who are most interested in politics, because they are most likely to follow the news.[219]

The media's power to influence the agenda has important implications. The media play a key role in deciding which problems government addresses and which it ignores. They also play a key role in increasing or decreasing politicians' ability to govern and to get reelected.

By publicizing some issues, the media create a golden opportunity for politicians with the authority and ability to resolve these issues. At the same time, the media create a pitfall for those who lack the power to resolve these issues. Thus, the Iranian seizure of the American embassy and hostages became the prominent issue in the country in 1980. Every night CBS's Walter Cronkite signed off, "And that's the way it is, the _____ day of American hostages in captivity," as if anyone needed reminding.

President Carter's lack of success in persuading Iranian officials to release the hostages or in directing an American invasion to rescue them cost him dearly in his reelection bid that year.

Yet the role of the media in shaping the agenda should not be overstated. Individuals' interests prompt the media to cover some things in the first place. Individuals' experiences lead them to consider other things unimportant even when the media do cover them.[220]

Moreover, politicians play an important role in shaping the agenda. For much legislation, Congress initiates action and then the media publicize it.[221] For many issues, the president initiates action. President Clinton launched a campaign to reduce smoking by teenagers. The media ran many stories about this problem. They could have done so years before or after, of course, but they followed the president's lead. For elections, candidates usually establish the agenda of *policy* issues. By emphasizing issues, they think will resonate with the public and reflect favorably on themselves, candidates pressure the media to cover these rather than other issues. But the media usually establish the agenda of *nonpolicy* issues, involving the candidates' personality and behavior.[222] The media are able to set the agenda for nonpolicy issues because these are more likely to catch the public's fancy.

Impact on Political Parties and Elections

The media have had an important impact on political parties and elections. In particular, they have furthered the decline of parties, encouraged new types of candidates, and influenced campaigns.

Political Parties

Political parties have declined in power on the national level, as will be addressed in Chapter 7, in large part because of the influence of the media.

In the young republic, political parties created and controlled most newspapers. Naturally, the papers echoed the parties' views and the journalists bowed to the parties' leaders. (The editor of one Democratic Party paper made sure a pail of fresh milk was left on the White House doorstep for President Andrew Jackson every morning, even if the editor had to deliver it himself.[223]) Yet people received much of their political information, however biased, from these papers.

When independent newspapers arose as profit-making businesses, the party papers declined and then disappeared. Eventually, people came to receive most of their political information from independent newspapers, magazines, radio stations, and television stations. Thus, people are no longer dependent on parties for their political information; they can make up their own minds about how to vote or what to support rather than rely on parties to tell them.

In other ways as well, the media, especially television, have contributed to the decline of parties. In place of selection of the candidates by party bosses, television allows the candidates to appeal directly to the people. If the candidates win the primaries, parties have little choice but to nominate them. In place of management of the campaign by party bosses, television requires new expertise, so the candidates assemble their own campaign organization. Television advertising requires substantial amounts of money, so the candidates approach other donors. Thus, the media have supplanted parties as the principal link between people and their leaders.

Types of Candidates

Television has encouraged new types of candidates for national offices. No longer must candidates be experienced politicians who worked their way up over many years. Celebrities from other fields with name recognition can move into prominent positions without political experience. Jesse Ventura, who had been a professional wrestler, got elected governor of Minnesota. In recent years, Congress has had an actor (Fred Grandy, R-Iowa—"Gopher" on *Love Boat*), a rock singer (Sonny Bono, R-Calif.), a professional baseball pitcher (Jim Bunning, R-Ky.), a professional football quarterback (Jack Kemp, R-N.J.), a professional basketball player (Bill Bradley, D-N.J.), and two astronauts (John Glenn, D-Ohio, and Harrison Schmitt, R-N.M.). (After one term, however, Schmitt was defeated by an opponent whose slogan was "What on Earth has he ever done?") Tom Osborne, who as the former football coach at the University of Nebraska was the best-known person in the state, got elected to Congress from a district in which he did not even live.[224]

Alternatively, unknowns with talent can achieve rapid name recognition and move into prominent positions. Jimmy Carter, who had served one term as governor of Georgia, was relatively unknown elsewhere in the country when he ran for the Democratic nomination for president in 1976. People kept asking "Jimmy who?" But through effective use of television, he won enough primaries so the party had to nominate him, even though the leaders were uncomfortable with him.

At the same time that television has allowed newcomers to run, it also has imposed new requirements on candidates for national office. They must demonstrate an appealing appearance and performance on camera; they must be telegenic. President Franklin Roosevelt's body, disabled from polio and supported in a wheelchair, would not be impressive on television. President Harry Truman's style—"Give 'em hell"—would not be impressive on television, either. Although effective in whistlestop speeches, it would be too "hot," too intense, to come into people's homes every day. A "cool," low-key style is more effective.

President Reagan was the quintessential politician for the television age. He was tall and trim with a handsome face and a reassuring voice. As a former actor, he could project his personality and convictions and deliver his lines and jokes better than any other politician. It is not an exaggeration to conclude, as one political scientist did, "Without a chance to display his infectious smile, his grandfatherly demeanor, and his 'nice guy' qualities to millions of Americans, Ronald Reagan, burdened by his image as a superannuated, intellectually lightweight movie actor with right-wing friends and ultraconservative leanings, might never have reached the presidency."[225]

Television has not created the public desire for politicians with an appealing personality. "When candidates shook hands firmly, kissed babies, and handed out cigars, the thrust was not on issues."[226] Yet television has exacerbated this emphasis on their image.

The media have imposed other requirements on candidates for national office. In recent decades, the intense scrutiny and constant criticism screen out those who are unwilling to relinquish most of their personal privacy and individual dignity. Candidates, of course, have always expected to sacrifice some privacy and be subjected to some criticism, but now they are expected to endure even more. One columnist wonders whether public service will attract only those with the "most brazen, least sensitive personalities."[227]

Retired admiral Bobby Ray Inman, who had held positions in both Democratic and Republican administrations, was nominated to be secretary of defense by President Clinton. During the confirmation process, he came under attack by some senators and some newspa-

Franklin Roosevelt spent much of his life in a wheelchair, but journalists did not photograph him in it. A friend snapped this rare picture. Journalists were reluctant to photograph or write about officials' afflictions or behaviors until a new era of more personal coverage after Watergate.

pers. One editor told him, "Bobby, you just have to get a thicker skin. We have to write a bad story about you every day. That's our job." Although he was assured by members of both parties that he would be confirmed—the *New York Times* reported that his nomination was "unusually well received in Washington"—Inman withdrew his nomination, saying he did not want "the daily diet" of media criticism. Then, when he withdrew, the newspapers criticized him for being insecure.[228]

Campaigns

The media affect nomination and election campaigns through their news and commentary and candidates' advertisements. They help set the campaign agenda, as already explained. They also inform and persuade.

The media provide information about the candidates and the issues, and they also interpret this information.[229] The public learns about the candidates and the issues,[230] but in the process the public is influenced in making its choices.

Information about the candidates can have a major impact especially at the nomination stage. In presidential elections, a party without an incumbent president running for reelection might field a dozen candidates. The media cannot cover all adequately, so they narrow the field by considering some "serious" and giving them more coverage. Once the primaries begin, they label some "winners" and others "losers," and they give the "winners" more coverage.[231] In the Democratic race in 1992, even before a single primary, the press proclaimed Clinton the front-runner, and several magazines put his picture on their cover, although half of the public did not know who he was.[232]

By making these judgments, the media strongly influence the election process at this stage.[233] Because few people have formed opinions about the candidates this early, they are open to impressions from the media. Therefore, when the media declare some candidates winners, they help create a bandwagon effect.[234] When they declare others losers, they make it hard for these candidates to attract contributors and volunteers and eventually supporters in the next primaries.

The media also can persuade voters directly. This influence can be seen in several ways.

Televised debates do not sway most viewers because people tend to engage in **selective perception,** which is a tendency to screen out information that contradicts their beliefs. Consequently, most people conclude that their candidate performed better.[235] However, the debates do sway some viewers, usually those who have moderate education and some interest in politics but who are not decided or at least not strongly committed to one candidate. In 1960, the debates might have caused enough voters to cast their ballots for Kennedy that he won the election.[236]

Media commentary about the debates also might sway some viewers.[237] Yet this effect usually does not last long; after the media frenzy wears off, the candidate usually bounces back.[238]

Newspaper endorsements of candidates apparently sway some readers, especially those with a ninth-through twelfth-grade education. People with less education are less likely to read editorials, while those with more education have more sources of information and more defined ideologies to guide their decisions.[239] Even if endorsements sway only a small percentage of voters, they can determine the outcome of tight races.[240] Although endorsements have some effect on well-publicized races, such as those for president,[241] they probably have greater effect on less-publicized races, such as those for state legislator or local tax assessor, because voters have little other information to guide them.

Talk radio also influences listeners. People who tune in to talk radio are more likely to turn out to vote and even to participate in campaigns.[242]

For the 2000 election, the media appeared to have an impact after the votes were cast. By calling the election for Bush, after retracting their previous call for Gore, the networks established the presumption that Bush had won.[243] Although later they admitted the election was too close to call, by this time they had already declared Bush the president-elect and flashed their graphic labeling him the forty-third president of the United States. Then Gore was placed in the position of trying to take the election away from Bush through legal maneuvers. These dynamics generated public pressure on judges, legislators, and election officials to do what was necessary to make Bush's election official. As the wrangling continued, the media heightened this pressure by encouraging Gore to concede and by exaggerating the possibility that there would be a constitutional crisis if the election were not resolved quickly.[244]

Impact on Public Opinion

Social scientists long thought that the media influenced the things people thought about but not the opinions they held about these things. Some contemporary research, however, demonstrates that the media do have a substantial impact on public opinion on things besides elections. A comparison of the networks' newscasts with the public's policy preferences in a wide variety of foreign and domestic issues shows that the media influence opinion about issues.[245] Other research shows that the media influence opinion about particular presidents.[246] They affect opinion indirectly, by providing the news and transmitting the views of various opinion leaders, as well as directly, through editorials and commentaries intended to sway opinion.

THE CNN OF THE MIDDLE EAST

After the terrorist attacks, the initial reports from the Middle East showed some people rejoicing and many others voicing satisfaction that the United States got its comeuppance. This reaction raised questions about the news coverage and the American image in the Arab world.

Almost all media in Arab countries are state run. Although they mimic American news formats, they are not independent.[1] To preserve the regime, whether a monarchy, a dictatorship, or another government, they are censored. Along with bland entertainment, they offer staid and sycophantic coverage of their government and its officials. They feature the formal announcements of the ministries and the comings and goings of the officials.

Then there is Al-Jazeera, a television station based in the small country of Qatar, which wields little influence in regional politics compared with Egypt and Saudi Arabia, which have controlled media. Al-Jazeera is independent and lively. It broadcasts news twenty-four hours a day, reaching viewers with private satellite dishes in twenty Arab countries.

People starved for news about their country and other countries in the Middle East tune in. The station's popularity has prompted millions of people, many of whom can barely afford basic necessities, to buy satellite dishes. Some women have sold their jewelry to finance a dish for their family.[2]

Al-Jazeera began operating in 1996 after a coup in Qatar installed a young ruler who was educated in England and prepared to break from the country's conservative political traditions. Seeking a more liberal political system, with greater emphasis on voting and on educating girls, he announced the end of government censorship. He allowed the station to operate and even agreed to finance it until it becomes self-supporting. (Qatar, with the third largest reserve of natural gas in the world, is a wealthy country.) He promised the station its independence.[3] The station hired Arab journalists from the BBC's (British Broadcasting Corporation's) Arabic radio and television network. These staffers, trained in Western journalistic practices, tailored Al-Jazeera after CNN.

The station attracted a large audience with its coverage of the Palestinian *intifadeh*—the uprising against Israeli occupation—in 2000. Then the station scooped the media around the world by showing film clips of Osama bin Laden talking menacingly about the September 11 attacks and future terrorist attacks against the United States.

After these film clips, the Bush administration asked the Qatari emir to restrict the station, and it asked the station to stop broadcasting bin Laden's statements. (Both the emir and the station refused. The station noted that CNN aired an interview with Iraqi President Saddam Hussein during the Persian Gulf War in 1991.) The administration claimed that bin Laden might be sending signals through coded language to terrorists in the United States, although it is more likely the administration feared that bin Laden was inflaming public opinion in the Middle East.[4] During the bombing in Afghanistan, the Bush administration objected to the station broadcasting film clips of civilian casualties. Then a United States missile destroyed Al-

Relatives and neighbors in Pakistan watch Al-Jazeera's coverage of the war in Afghanistan.

Ruth Fremson/The New York Times

Jazeera's office in Kabul. (It is not clear whether the attack was intentional.[5])

Al-Jazeera, whose motto is "The opinion, and the other opinion," presents competing views on topics of interest to Arabs. The station breaks taboos as it addresses topics shunned by the state-run media. In addition to examining the Palestinian *intifadeh* and the Western aims in the Middle East, Al-Jazeera uncovers the corruption in some governments in the region. Talk shows pit fundamentalists against secularists and Iraqis against Kuwaitis, and they address topics such as polygamy among Muslims. The coverage reflects heresy according to some viewers, but the programs mirror the arguments that many Arabs have with their relatives and friends.

Whether Al-Jazeera is balanced or biased is the subject of debate among Western observers. At the outset of the war in Afghanistan, the station seemed skeptical of American aims. A poster of bin Laden hung in its headquarters, and film clips juxtaposed a serene bin Laden with a scowling George Bush. Reporters spoke about the United States' policy against "what it calls terror" and questioned the United States' policy of bombing.[6] But much that American observers complained about—airing competing views, sampling the opinions of ordinary people, showing the casualties among Afghan civilians—represented standard Western journalistic practices. In fact, some coverage, such as broadcasting film clips of bin Laden, was duplicated by Western television networks.

It does seem clear that the station supports the Palestinian side in the struggle with Israel. Although the station conducts interviews with Israeli officials, which other Arab media avoid, it highlights Israeli attacks on Palestinians more than Palestinian attacks on Israelis. It shows graphic images of Palestinian victims and reports personal details about their lives, thus stirring the emotions of Arab viewers. It refers to Palestinian suicide bombers as "martyrs," thus justify-ing their actions. In these ways it reflects the perspective of its audience, just as American media reflect the perspective of their audience. Arabs believe that American media are biased toward Israel's side, depicting Palestinian attacks more than Israeli attacks and referring to Israeli assassinations of Palestinian activists as "targeted killings."[7] A CBS executive acknowledges, "You could argue that Al-Jazeera is too pro-Mideast or pro-Arab, but our news organizations are all pro-Western."[8] A journalism professor who had been a correspondent in the Middle East observes that the American media, which emphasize objectivity, nevertheless report "from the American point of view."[9]

Already Al-Jazeera has had a major impact in the Middle East. By attracting so many viewers, it has set the standard for television news in the region, prodding state-run media to begin loosening up. Yet by criticizing authoritarian Arab rulers, it has infuriated these leaders who fear instability in their countries. Some governments have recalled their ambassador to Qatar to protest Al-Jazeera's coverage of their policies. Other governments have closed Al-Jazeera's bureaus in their countries or denied visas to Al-Jazeera's reporters seeking entry into their countries. To prevent its citizens from seeing a program about their country, the Algerian government turned off the electricity in its capital city. In addition to infuriating Arab leaders, the station has inflamed Arab masses, especially in the struggle between the Palestinians and the Israelis. This has pressured Arab governments to do more to help the Palestinians, which has worried Arab rulers who are trying to walk a line between appeasing their own citizens but not antagonizing the United States.

In the long run, Al-Jazeera might have a significant impact in encouraging the rights of Arab women and, most obviously, in promoting the right to a free press. In the process, it might help nour-ish a sense of freedom and a desire for democracy among Arab people. Ironically, then, while galvanizing Arab radicalism on particular issues, Al-Jazeera could be promoting Western values in other ways.

Yet the U.S. government has been slow to realize the influence and the potential of Al-Jazeera. American officials, while solicitous of the views of Arab leaders of friendly states, have ignored Arab opinion on the street. They have especially ignored the opinion of Arab youths, who due to a population bubble in most countries are numerous and approaching a future where they will find few jobs and face considerable frustration. Until 9/11, American officials refused to appear on Al-Jazeera programs. After 9/11, high-ranking officials agreed to appear, but they might not be the most effective speakers to reach Arab youths. Our officials have been slow to realize that our country was, is, and in the future will be embroiled in a propaganda war for the hearts and minds of Arab people. After the military battles conclude, the media war will continue.

1. A United Nations report ranks the media in these Arab countries as the least independent in the world. Nadia Abou El-Magd, "Fifty Years after Revolution, Arabs Ponder Nasser's Legacy," *Lincoln Journal-Star,* July 22, 2002. There is a large independent television station in Lebanon.
2. Mohammed El-Nawawy and Adel Iskandar, *Al-Jazeera: How the Free Arab News Network Scooped the World and Changed the Middle East* (Boulder, Colo.: Westview, 2002), 46.
3. Apparently sensitive to this unusual arrangement, the station practices self-censorship in covering its host country and government. Ibid., 199–200.
4. There are more efficient means to communicate than relying on a speech that is cut by journalists from thirty minutes to six minutes and then broadcast with a voiceover in English. For a discussion, see ibid., 177–179, 187.
5. The Bush administration claimed that it was a mistake, but the location of the office was well known, and the building was easily identified.
6. For development of this view, which might have been affected by the terrorist attacks shortly before publication of his article, see Fouad Ajami, "What the Muslim World Is Watching," *New York Times Magazine,* November 18, 2001, 48.
7. For development of this view, see El-Nawawy and Iskandar, *Al-Jazeera,* 175–196.
8. Ibid., 182.
9. Ibid.

Photographs can have an impact too. After courts ruled that Elian Gonzalez should be returned to his father in Cuba, his relatives in Miami refused to give him up. Federal agents, who had received threats, entered the house not knowing if they would be resisted. A photographer waiting in the house shot this image, which prompted some people to oppose federal efforts to obey the courts.

Al Diaz/AP

Many speculate that the media have contributed to the public's cynicism toward government in recent decades. The media have undermined the public's perception of the integrity of government and officials not just by reporting real shortcomings of programs and administrators, but by engaging in several practices already addressed in this chapter. The negative bias in coverage of all candidates and officials directly undermines them, while the game orientation more subtly undermines them. The emphasis on conflict leads to a focus on politicians' most extreme statements, which alienates the public and, at the same time, polarizes it. The practice of objectivity—reporting what he said versus what she said without evaluating the truth of either—passes along some false statements and some misleading ones and confuses the public.[247] Many people complain, "You can't believe any of them."

Some researchers have concluded that the result of these practices is to foster **media malaise** among the public.[248] This is a feeling of cynicism and distrust, perhaps even despair, toward government and officials. Indeed, according to a 1995 survey, the public is even more cynical than journalists themselves. Seventy-seven percent of the public gave government officials a low rating for honesty and ethics, while only 40 percent of the journalists did.[249] Most of the public believed that politicians could "never" be trusted to do the right thing. Yet the journalists saw the American political process as "a flawed but basically decent means of reconciling different points of view and solving collective problems."[250] They apparently report in a more cynical fashion than they actually feel because of the conventions of contemporary journalism. But the public, while deploring these practices, evidently sees them as reflections of reality. So cynical coverage by the press leads to even more cynical attitudes in the citizenry.[251]

The cynical attitudes have important implications for politics. They probably reduce satisfaction with candidates and officials and reduce turnout in elections. At the same time, they probably increase votes for "outsiders" who present themselves as "nonpoliticians."

Ironically, observes one writer, "The press, which in the long run cannot survive if people lose interest in politics, is acting as if its purpose was to guarantee that people are repelled by public life."[252]

Conclusion: Are the Media Responsive?

The media have to be responsive to the people to make a profit. They present the news they think the people want. Because they believe the majority desire entertainment, or at least diversion, rather than education, they structure the news toward this end. According to a number of studies, they correctly assess their consumers.[253] For the majority who want entertainment, national television and radio networks and local television and radio stations provide it. For the minority who want education, the better newspapers and magazines provide it. Public radio, with its morning and evening newscasts, and public television, with its nightly newscast, also provide quality coverage. In addition, now numerous Web sites on the Internet provide news on demand. The media offer something for everyone.

When officials or citizens get upset with the media, they pointedly ask, "Who elected you?" Journalists reply that the people—their readers or listeners or viewers—"elected them" by paying attention to their news columns or newscasts.

To say the media are responsive, however, is not to say they perform well. Giving the people what they want most is not necessarily serving the country best. "This business of giving people what they want is a dope pusher's argument," says a former president of NBC News. "News is something people don't know they're interested in until they hear about it. The job of a journalist is to take what's important and make it interesting."[254] But people get what they want. The media personalize and dramatize the news. The result is to simplify the news. Superficial coverage of complex events leaves the public unable to understand these events and, ultimately, unable to force the government to be responsive.

The media give us the big hype—"Hey, listen to this! Here's something new you can't miss!" They reflect a crisis *du jour* mentality in which everything is important but ultimately nothing is important. Almost any political development is important for a day or a week or occasionally a month. But almost no political development is important for long. The headlines and the stories clamoring for attention go by in such a blur that after a while they all become a jumble for many people. They leave no sense of what's actually a crisis, what's only a problem, what's merely an irritant, and what's truly trivial.[255]

Thus, most news coverage is episodic, presenting an event as a single, idiosyncratic occurrence, rather than thematic, presenting the event as an example of a larger pattern. For instance, a story might focus on one hungry person or group of persons rather than on malnutrition as a national problem. Episodic coverage is more common because it is more entertaining—dramatic, with human interest—than thematic coverage. But episodic

coverage makes it hard for people to see the connection between the problems in society and the actions of government. Then the people do not hold their leaders accountable for addressing or resolving the problems.[256]

Although the media give people what they want, people criticize the media. Almost three-fourths tell pollsters the media get in the way of society's efforts to solve its problems. Only one-fourth say the media help solve the problems.[257]

People have gotten so critical that they rank reporters the lowest in public esteem of any profession (lower even than lawyers).[258] People also express less support for freedom of the press. In 1999, a majority said the press has too much freedom. In fact, a majority went so far as to say the media should not be allowed to endorse or criticize political candidates, and a third went further to say the media should not be allowed to publish a story without government approval.[259] Thus, at the same time the media are competing to give people what they want, their practices are alienating people.

The media's desperation is aggravated by a declining interest in politics and a decreasing number of people who read newspapers or watch newscasts. Although the public is better educated now than in the 1960s, it is less likely to follow the news and less able to answer questions about the government.[260] People under thirty-five especially reflect these trends. To retain their shrinking audience, many newspapers and newscasts have revamped their formats to replace hard news with soft features. If this process continues, it will have disturbing implications. Citizens who are not aware of the news or who do not understand it cannot fulfill their role in a democracy.

These trends come at a time when the media, despite their shortcomings, provide more news than ever and—with journalists better educated and better able to understand and explain complex topics—better news than ever. Think how useful their reports about the terrorist attacks and the Afghanistan war were.

Today American media provide very fast and relatively accurate reports of events. They also probe wrongdoing in society. They have become powerful enough to serve as a check on government in many situations. This was

evident during two major crises of the past half century. During the war in Vietnam, the media stood up to two presidents when Congress and the courts were relatively passive. During the Watergate scandal, the media led Congress and the courts in standing up to a president. Even local media serve as a check on government. In recent years, a Newark newspaper exposed racial profiling by New Jersey state police, a Miami newspaper revealed voter fraud in a mayoral election, and a Houston television station prompted a regulatory agency to investigate the blowouts of Firestone tires on Ford Explorers. The media serve as a check on government in countless other situations. As a former government official noted, "Think how much chicanery dies on the drawing board when someone says, 'We'd better not do that; what if the press finds out?' "[261]

Evans Pursued the Admiral

You decided to meet with Admiral Boorda to confront him with your allegations and give him an opportunity to respond. But you did not want to give him much warning, so you did not tell his office why you wanted to meet other than that you were preparing a story about the admiral. Two hours before the meeting, Boorda's aide called for more information. Then, you revealed the purpose. Later, you explained, "If you go in too soon, the navy can counterattack, and the opposition gets the story."[262]

After Thomas revealed the purpose of the meeting, Boorda's aides checked with navy officials about the ribbons. A previous secretary of the navy had questioned why admirals wore so many ribbons. When the navy investigated the 257 admirals, it found that many wore ribbons, including the V, who technically should not have. Apparently the navy's practice of awarding ribbons deviated from its regulations. When Boorda was informed last year that he should not have worn the V, he took it off. "It was an honest mistake," he commented to an aide. He has not worn it since then.

After Boorda learned the purpose of the meeting, he went home for lunch. He typed a letter to his wife and another to the sailors. He said to the sailors:

What I am about to do is not very smart but it is right for me. You see, I have asked you to do the right thing, to care for and take care of each other and to stand up for what is good and correct. All of these things require honor, courage and commitment our . . . core values.

I am about to be accused of wearing combat devices on two ribbons I earned during sea tours in Viet Nam. It turns out I didn't really rate them. When I found out I was wrong I immediately took them off but it was really too late. I don't expect any reporters to believe I could make an honest mistake and you may or may not believe it yourselves. That is up to you and isn't all that important now anyway. I've made it not matter in the big scheme of things because I love our navy so much, and you who are the heart and soul of our navy, that I couldn't bear to bring dishonor to you. . . .

Finally, for those who want to tear our navy down, I guess I've given them plenty to write about for a while. But I will soon be forgotten. You, our great navy people, will live on. I am proud of you. I am proud to have led you if only for a short time. I wish I had done it better.

Then Boorda went out to his garden and shot himself in the chest. At his funeral, Boorda was hailed as "the sailors' sailor." In Washington, however, he was criticized by some for having "thin skin." Yet, as one columnist observed, "Thin skin is the only kind of skin human beings come with."[263]

Newsweek's efforts to pursue the story did not reflect political bias against the navy or the admiral or the changes he was implementing. (Other critics of Boorda did have political motives—opposition to new policies that challenged navy traditions.) Newsweek's efforts instead reflected commercial bias. The magazine was trying to attract more readers by running provocative articles by prominent writers.

Of course, Newsweek had not even run the article when Boorda decided to kill himself. A columnist for Newsweek pointed out, "It is possible [Boorda] could have moved the story in a different direction, or talked the magazine out of publishing anything on the matter at all."[264] Evidently Boorda, who had considerable experience with the press, did not think this was likely.

No doubt Newsweek's editors were as surprised as other people when Boorda killed himself. They were just trying to do their jobs. Yet their behavior reflects journalists' mind-set that public officials are not motivated by a desire to serve the public but to advance their career or enhance their power. Moreover, journalists see public officials as insincere. With this mind-set, journalists look for wrongdoing and seek to expose it. Essentially, journalists consider officials fair game for relentless attack.[265]

To learn more about the nature of the Admiral Boorda incident and its aftermath, go to this chapter's "You Are There" exercises on the text Web site.

Key Terms

symbiotic relationship	political bias
adversarial relationship	commercial bias
leaks	infotainment
scoop	game orientation
presidential press conference	setting the agenda
media events	selective perception
sound bite	media malaise
fireside chats	

Further Reading

Timothy Crouse, *The Boys on the Bus* (New York: Random House, 1972). An irreverent account of press coverage of the 1972 presidential campaign, focusing on the reporters rather than on the candidates.

Beth J. Harpaz, *The Girls in the Van: Covering Hillary* (New York: St. Martin's, 2001). An account of press coverage of Hillary Clinton's Senate campaign.

Marvin Kalb, *One Scandalous Story: Clinton, Lewinsky and Thirteen Days That Tarnished American Journalism* (New York: Free Press, 2001). As the scandal unfolded, the press abandoned its standards.

Howard Kurtz, *Spin Cycle: Inside the Clinton Propaganda Machine* (New York: Free Press, 1998). An examination of the Clinton administration's press operation.

John R. MacArthur, *Second Front: Censorship and Propaganda in the Gulf War* (New York: Hill & Wang, 1992). A searing critique of media coverage of the war.

Joe McGinniss, *The Selling of the President 1968* (New York: Simon & Schuster, 1969). An account of the often-comical efforts by Richard Nixon's advisers to transform him into a media candidate.

Electronic Resources

www.msnbc.com
For overall news.

www.nytimes.com
The New York Times, *for in-depth reports on international and national affairs.*

www.washingtonpost.com
For political news from the capital.

www.sfgate.com
The San Francisco Chronicle, *described as an "oasis of attitude" in the world of news.*

www.alternet.org
Alternative journalism, for news and opinion not found in most media outlets.

www.slate.com
A "Webzine" with columns and wit and perhaps the best media analysis on the Web.

www.ajr.org
A variety of stories about the media from the University of Maryland College of Journalism.

InfoTrac College Edition

Search for the following articles in the InfoTrac database:

Hanson, Chrisopher. "All the News That Fits the Myth," *Columbia Journalism Review* (January 2001).

Kunkel, Thomas, and Gene Roberts. "Leaving Readers Behind: The Age of Corporate Newspapering," *American Journalism Review* (May 2001).

O'Brien, Meredith, "A Growing Divide: War Coverage Has Pushed **Press** Values and the Public's Values Even Farther Apart," *The Quill* (January 2002).

Ruscio, John. "Risky Business," *Skeptical Inquirer* (March 2000).

For more articles, enter:

"mass media" in the Suject Guide;

"press" in the Subject Guide;

"elections" in the Subject Guide, and then go to subdivision "media coverage."

American Government Resources

Visit the Political Behavior section of the Wadsworth American Government Resources Web site (politicalscience.wadsworth.com/amgov/) for a variety of tools to help you explore news media further. Included are simulations, video clips, Microcase exercises, and a wealth of other activities.

CHAPTER 6

INTEREST GROUPS

Damian Dovarganes/AP/ Wide World Photos

Some interest groups are loosely organized and fleeting like this group of students who rallied in support of Clinton-Gore in the 1996 presidential election campaign.

Do You Make More Concessions, or Do You Fight?

You are Steven Goldstone, the CEO of RJR Nabisco. Your company owns RJ Reynolds, the nation's second largest tobacco company. It is June 1998, and you are faced with a crucial decision about how hard to fight some antitobacco proposals being considered by Congress.

You and the rest of the tobacco industry, historically one of the strongest and most powerful interests in Washington, are under siege. Families of those who have died from lung cancer are suing for damages, and in one recent case they won a huge settlement. This success is encouraging others to sue. In addition to possibly owing billions of dollars in damages, the federal and state governments are threatening stricter regulation of tobacco advertising, regulation of nicotine as a drug, and heavy fines if youth smoking does not decrease over the next ten years. In the past, you might have been able to stave off such threats, but today you are willing to accept higher taxes and government restrictions, if they are coupled with protection from unending lawsuits with the potential to bankrupt the industry.

But your political position has weakened. Public opinion has turned against you, and you have lost major allies in Congress. Recent polls show that more than 70 percent of Americans, many of them smokers, distrust tobacco companies and believe they are run by

greedy executives who make a profit from marketing cigarettes to children and teens. Indeed, one news article labeled the tobacco industry "the Libya of American commerce."[1] This view is supported by research that shows that Joe Camel, an RJ Reynolds creation, is as recognizable to six-year-olds as Mickey Mouse. Your industry's image has also been tarnished because you knew of the dangers of smoking long before warnings appeared on cigarettes. But the companies suppressed the evidence of health risks and publicly denied that there were any. Many Americans recall you and your fellow CEOs swearing before a congressional committee that cigarettes are not addictive. Recent disclosure of internal company documents confirms that your industry did indeed target teenagers with ads—and with some success. Three thousand teens and preteens begin smoking every day, a statistic the president has labeled "a national tragedy."

Republicans in Congress, once your staunch supporters, are also turning away. House Speaker Newt Gingrich recently told you and other CEOs that the party would not protect you against lawsuits. Gingrich, whose father and grandfather died of lung cancer, is fearful that protection for tobacco companies will lead to other industries descending on Washington seeking protection and that Clinton and the

The tobacco industry has been fighting desperately to avoid restrictions. Here a tobacco company lawyer argues in court.

Democrats will use the issue against the Republicans in the 1998 elections.

Your opponents have also gained strength. There is no doubt that smoking causes cancer and exacerbates heart and lung diseases. Smoking is the leading cause of preventable death in the United States, claiming more than four hundred thousand lives a year and $100 billion in medical costs. Public health organizations have spread the word about tobacco's dangers through their own advertising campaign.

Furthermore, you and the industry are feeling pressure to strike a deal. A jury recently ruled for the first time that a tobacco company was liable for the death of a lung cancer victim. The jurors awarded the victim's family

$750,000. More suits are already in litigation, and even more are likely to follow. President Clinton has granted the Food and Drug Administration authority to regulate tobacco as a drug. Four states have successfully settled lawsuits recouping billions of dollars in claims against the tobacco industry for the costs entailed in treating sick smokers. More state suits are pending.

A year ago you were a key figure in an agreement that was worked out between the industry and a number of state leaders. In it, industry leaders agreed to pay $370 billion over twenty-five years and restrict the marketing and advertising of cigarettes. In return, state leaders agreed to limit the liability that tobacco companies face in lawsuits. Though by no means a good deal for tobacco, the agreement will enable the industry to survive. By supporting it, the industry may avoid more severe restrictions or even an outright ban on tobacco. Your task now is to get Congress to accept the package.

While your position is weakened, you still have some bargaining power. The number of teens who begin smoking each day is likely to decrease only if the industry raises the price of cigarettes and restricts advertising, and you will not agree to these measures without legal protection. You are prepared to argue in court that the First Amendment allows you to advertise your product. There are 50 million Americans who smoke and can be mobilized to oppose any increase in the cost of

cigarettes. Cigarettes also provide tax revenue to the states and national government and seven hundred thousand jobs. Legislators from tobacco-growing states, such as Kentucky and North Carolina, are also supportive of your industry.

On the other side, many groups opposed to tobacco, including the Campaign for Tobacco Free Kids, the American Medical Association (AMA), and the American Cancer Society, endorsed the agreement as a way to immediately curb youth smoking. State leaders who negotiated it are lobbying Congress to accept it.

But some in Congress have their own ideas and have introduced bills that differ from the agreement. The bill with the most support would cost the industry $526 billion over twenty-five years, impose restrictions on tobacco aids, set goals for reducing teenage smoking, and regulate tobacco as a drug. It would not, however, include the protection against lawsuits that you think is necessary for the industry to survive.

What do you do? In addition to the concessions you have already made, you can make one more. You can abandon your demand for protection against lawsuits, a concession you believe will kill the industry. Or you can fight the bill by mobilizing what few friends you have on Capitol Hill and among the grassroots public. It will be an uphill fight with little chance of success. Which will you choose, and why?

In the United States, everything from fruits to nuts is organized. From apple growers to filbert producers, nearly every interest has an organization to represent it. These organizations touch every aspect of our lives; members of the American College of Obstetrics and Gynecology bring us into the world, and members of the National Funeral Directors Association usher us out.

Organizations that try to achieve at least some of their goals with government assistance are called **interest groups.** Fruit and nut growers want government subsidies and protection from imported products; doctors and funeral directors want to be free of government controls. The efforts of interest groups to influence government

are called **lobbying.** Lobbying may involve direct contact between a lobbyist, or consultant or lawyer, as they prefer to be called, and a government official; or it may involve indirect action, such as attempts to sway public opinion, which will in turn influence officials.

People organize and lobby because these are ways for them to enhance their influence. As one lobbyist remarked: "The modern government is huge, pervasive, intrusive into everybody's life. If you just let things take their course and don't get involved in the game, you get trampled on."[2]

The Founders feared the harmful effects of interest groups. Madison was intent on "curing the mischiefs of faction" through separation of powers, checks and balances, and federalism. Today, many people bemoan the "mischiefs of faction" or "special interests" because they seem to block government actions favoring the larger interests of society.[3] Sometimes it seems that everyone is represented in Washington but the people.

Do interest groups undermine the people's interests? Or do they make government more responsive by giving people greater representation in the political process? These are the difficult questions explored in this chapter.

Group Formation

Throughout most of its history, America has been a nation of joiners. As early as the 1830s, the Frenchman Alexis de Tocqueville, who traveled in America, noted the tendency of Americans to join groups: "In no country in the world has the principle of association been more successfully used or applied to a greater multitude of objects than in America."[4] Even now Americans are more likely than citizens in other countries to belong to groups.[5] The United States is especially fertile for the growth of groups. Compared to most other countries, it is racially, religiously, and ethnically diverse. These differences give rise to different interests and views on public issues and often lead to the formation of groups that express those views.[6]

Groups can also organize because of the freedom to speak, assemble, and petition government, guaranteed in the First Amendment to the Constitution. Without such freedom, only groups favored by the government—or groups whose members are willing to be punished for their actions—can exist.

The federal structure also encourages the proliferation of groups. It is not enough to have a national organization. Because state and local governments have significant authority, groups also must be organized at those levels to protect their interests.

Why Interest Groups Form

The formation of interest groups occurs in waves.[7] In some periods formation is rapid and extensive, whereas at other times very little activity takes place.

Social and economic stress often account for these surges.[8] The stress of the Revolutionary War period activated groups for and against independence. The slavery controversy in the decades before the Civil War energized groups on both sides of the issue. After the Civil War, rapid industrialization led to the formation of trade unions and business associations. Economic problems in agricultural areas spurred the development of farm groups.

© 1989 Ken Heinen

In 1773, a group of colonists organized to protest British taxes on tea by throwing tea into Boston Harbor. In 1989, groups organized to protest a congressional pay increase by sending teabags to their representatives in Washington.

The greatest surge in group formation occurred between 1900 and 1920. Stimulated by the shocks of industrialization, urbanization, immigration, and the government's response to them, groups such as the United States Chamber of Commerce, American Farm Bureau Federation, National Association for the Advancement of Colored People (NAACP), Socialist and Communist Parties, and countless others formed.[9]

The 1960s and 1970s witnessed another interest group explosion, directed primarily toward Washington. As the national government expanded in power and influence in the post–World War II period, it increasingly became the center of interest group efforts to satisfy demands for favorable public policy. Spurred by the success of civil rights and war protest movements in the 1960s, other groups representing racial minorities, women, consumers, the poor, the elderly, and the environment organized. Business lobbying surged in the late 1970s as a response to the success of consumer and environmental groups in prompting government to enact and enforce occupational safety and environmental standards.[10]

Technological changes also accelerate group formation. A national network of railroads and the telegraph contributed to the surge in the early 1900s. Computer-generated direct mail appeals to solicit funds and mobilize members to action as well as WATS lines (wide-area telephone service) increased the ability of groups to form and mobilize in the 1960s and 1970s. The number of groups increased by 60 percent between 1960 and 1980, and the number sending representatives to Washington doubled.[11] In the 1990s, the spread of personal computers and the growth of the

Internet facilitated communication between people with an endless variety of narrow interests. The Internet continues to be particularly essential for those who wish to organize citizens groups on a low budget.[12] It's also useful for groups outside the mainstream who can operate relatively anonymously. For example, members and sympathizers of militia groups spread throughout the country, often in remote locations and with few resources, can stay in touch and keep each other informed via the Web.

The government is also important to group formation. Government efforts to deal with problems often prompt the organization of groups opposed to such efforts.[13] In addition, government provides direct financial assistance to some groups, particularly nonprofit organizations. Groups as diverse as the American Council of Education, the National Governors Association, and the National Council of Senior Citizens obtain a large percentage of their funds through federal grants and contracts.[14]

Group organizers also play a role in group formation.[15] These entrepreneurs often come from established groups. They gain experience and then strike out on their own. Many civil rights activists of the 1950s and early 1960s founded organizations in the late 1960s. Some used their skills to organize groups against the war in Vietnam and later to organize groups for women's rights and environmental causes.[16] Thus, the formation of one group often opens the door to the formation of others.

Why People Join

Some people join a group because of the group's political goals or cause. But many join for economic and social reasons.[17] Some groups offer monetary benefits to members such as discounted prices for goods and services. The large nonfarm membership of the Farm Bureau often is attributed to the cut-rate insurance policies offered through the organization.[18] The American Association of Retired Persons (AARP) provides health, home, and auto insurance; a motor club; a travel service; investment counseling; discount drugs and medicines; and a magazine. These services attract members and generate millions of dollars for the organization. In an effort to cultivate new members and reach an increasingly diverse aged population as well as generate additional advertising revenue from its publications, the group markets two versions of its mainline magazine and just launched another aimed at those forty-five to fifty-five years of age.[19]

Because members pay dues, providing groups with resources to accomplish their goals and enhance their influence with government, most groups provide a mix of benefits in an effort to maximize their membership. The National Rifle Association (NRA) lobbies against gun regulation and control. Some people join for this reason. Others join to secure other NRA services: *The American Rifleman* (a monthly magazine), a hunter's information service, low-cost firearm insurance, membership in local gun clubs, and shooting competitions.[20] Still others join because they enjoy associating with fellow gun enthusiasts.

Some people join groups because they are coerced. For example, in many states lawyers must join the state bar association to practice law.

Who Joins?

Not all people are equally likely to join groups. Those with higher incomes and education are more likely to belong. They can afford membership dues, have free time necessary to take part, and have the social and intellectual skills that facilitate group participation. They also appear more attractive to many groups and therefore are more apt to be recruited. Whites more often belong to groups than blacks, but mostly because of their higher average income and education.[21]

Have Americans Stopped Joining?

Some observers have pointed to a decline in Americans' propensity to join organizations.[22] Church membership and church-related activities, for example, have declined over the past twenty years. Membership in labor unions, once the most common organizational affiliation among American workers, has been declining for nearly four decades. Membership in the PTA has decreased during the past generation. In general, fewer people are joining and volunteering for a variety of civic and fraternal organizations.

The declining impulse to join with others in common pursuits may even have influenced recreational activity. Although more Americans than ever bowl, league bowling is down by more than 40 percent. If the decline represented just a loss of revenue from the pizza and beer consumed by leagues, only bowling proprietors would care. However, the decline also means the loss of close personal relationships that foster discussion of public issues and trust among citizens, which are important to the success of government.

Some argue that the decline in membership in organized groups is not a serious problem, because informal social ties provide the same opportunity.[23] People may not join bowling leagues, but they visit with others when they attend their children's soccer games, for example. Yet being part of an organized group does provide networks that casual contact does not.

People today claim that they are busier than ever before and that, between their work life and their family life, they have little time for other pursuits. Women's lives, in particular, have changed over the past generation, with most women now in the paid workforce while still carrying the largest share of household and child-raising duties. Women used to be the backbone of most local civic, religious, political, and educational groups, but working women now have far less time to devote to such volunteer activity.

While formal membership in voluntary organizations is down, membership in mass organizations is increasing.[24] Many of these organizations are "checkbook organizations," in which members' only link to the organization is the occasional check they send to support it.[25] They pay dues but do not interact with each other. Although these organizations can be successful politically, the benefits of social interaction are lost. Members do not discuss and share information that helps in discerning one's real stake in public affairs and politics.

Some argue that television has replaced memberships as a preferred leisure activity. Even busy people usually find time to watch TV. And while TV can be educational, as well as entertaining, there is no discussion; the information flow is one-way.

Types of Interest Groups

Interest groups come in all sizes. Some have large memberships, such as the American Federation of Labor–Congress of Industrial Organizations (AFL-CIO) with 13 million members. Others have small memberships, such as the Mushroom Growers Association with fourteen. Some have no members at all.

Corporations have no members but act as interest groups when they lobby government.[26] Some groups lobby on behalf of specific interests and are funded by the government, private foundations, other groups, or fees but have no members. The Children's Defense Fund (CDF) is

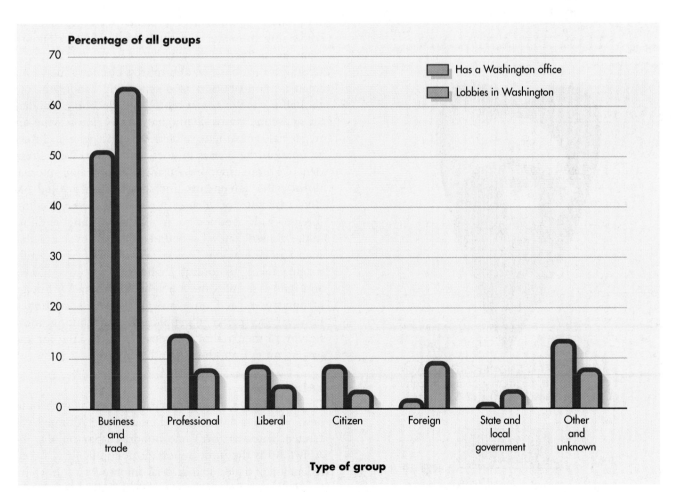

F I G U R E 1 ■ Business Interests Dominate the Contemporary Interest Group System

NOTE: Groups with a Washington office number 2,810, and 6,601 groups lobby there. "Liberal" groups are those representing women, minorities, the poor, labor, and the elderly. "Citizen" includes public interest groups such as Common Cause.

SOURCE: K. L. Schlozman and J. T. Tierney, *Organized Interests and American Democracy* (New York: Harper & Row, 1986), 67.

an example. Founded in 1973, it is funded entirely from private funds and lobbies on behalf of children.[27]

Some interest groups are formally organized, with appointed or elected leaders, regular meetings, and dues-paying members. Some are large corporations whose leaders are the corporate officers hired by boards of directors. Others have no leaders and few prescribed rules.

"Checkbook groups" have members, who send money but have no say in group decisions. Many **political action committees (PACs)** operate this way. They raise money through direct mail and channel it to political candidates. How the money is spent is determined solely by the organization's leaders.

Thus, interest groups can be distinguished according to their membership and organizational structure. They also can be distinguished by their goals. Some groups pursue economic goals, primarily of benefit to their members. Others pursue political goals or causes that have consequences for all or, at least, consequences that are not limited to those who hold membership in the group.

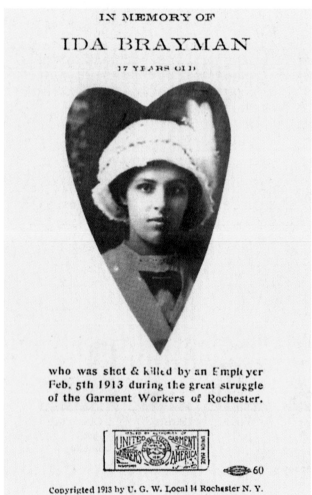

IN MEMORY OF

IDA BRAYMAN

17 YEARS OLD

who was shot & killed by an Employer Feb. 5th 1913 during the great struggle of the Garment Workers of Rochester.

Copyrighted 1913 by U. G. W. Local 14 Rochester N. Y.

Gotham Book Mart, New York

This postcard commemorates the death of a seventeen-year-old woman striking for recognition of her union, an eight-hour day, and extra pay for overtime and holidays.

Private Interest Groups

Private interest groups seek economic benefits for their members or clients. Examples include business, labor, and agriculture.

Business

Business organizations are the most numerous and among the most powerful interest groups in Washington (see Figure 1). Scholars have argued that politics is essentially a confrontation between business and government.[28] Business seeks to maximize profit, whereas government hopes to protect society from the harshness of profit-seeking businesses.

Today, however, there is little confrontation between the two. While the Republican Party has traditionally favored business, in recent years Democrats have also been supportive.[29] In spite of who occupies the White House or which party controls Congress, business has generally done well. This reflects in part the disincentives in a capitalist economy for politicians, liberals or conservatives, to antagonize business, which is so important to the nation's economic success.[30] If the economy falters, politicians get blamed. Rather than do something to undermine business confidence, politicians are inclined to do what business wants. Democratic support for business also reflects business's increasing financial contribution to Democratic candidates (although Republicans get more), the election of moderate and conservative Democrats, like Clinton, who are in general sympathetic to business, and a general climate of opinion that favors business over labor. With President Clinton's support, business won major international trade agreements, including "most favored nation" trading privileges for China, which allow foreign-made products to be sold free of import duties in the United States. Labor and other groups charge that such agreements cost American jobs as firms transfer manufacturing to countries where labor costs are lower and ignore serious human rights violations by foreign manufacturers and governments. Business continues, however, to prefer Republicans, contributing more heavily to their political campaigns and asking for and getting more from them than Democrats.

Labor

Organized labor is the principal competitor with business, but runs a distant second in influence. Although the United States has over one hundred labor unions, the AFL-CIO is the most important politically. It is a confederation of trade and industrial unions with a staff of five hundred and some of the most skillful lobbyists in Washington. Through its Committee on Political Education (COPE), it provides substantial sums of money as well as a pool of campaign workers to candidates for public

There is no lobby in Washington as large, as powerful, or as well-financed as the pharmaceutical industry. Battle-tested over the years involving a number of health care issues going back to the creation of the Medicare program in the 1960s, the industry spent $177 million lobbying government in 1999–2000 and another $20 million in campaign contributions. Lobbying expenditures outdistanced its nearest rivals, the insurance and telecommunications industries, by $50 million.

Walking down the fabled K Street corridor, home to Washington's most famous lobbying-law firms, you can count 134 firms on the industry's payroll. Bristol-Myers Squibb, manufacturer of a popular cholesterol-lowering drug and one for the treatment of diabetes, boasts fifteen firms with fifty-seven lobbyists, including Haley Barbour, former chair of Republican National Committee, and the well-known Democratic lobbyist Tommy Boggs. Over half of the industry's 625 registered lobbyists are either former members of Congress or former congressional staff members and government employees.

Why should the nation's manufacturers of pills require so much fire power in Washington? The answer: profits. At issue is drug patents that give manufacturers monopoly control for an extended period of time. Exclusive rights to make and market a drug means billions of dollars for the manufacturer. Opening the market to gener-

ics, non-name-brand equivalents, sold at a fraction of the cost, cuts profits. William Nixon, chief executive of the Generic Pharmaceutical Association, which battles the big drug companies, says they will do "everything to maintain their monopoly."[1]

Of course, there is a legitimate argument that no drug company will invest in development of new drugs if it does not have the exclusive right to sell them over an extended period of time. But, on the other hand, granting that monopoly also means that the industry can charge users who need the drug very high prices.

Take, for example, Claritin. If you suffer from hay fever or other allergies, you probably have taken it. Manufactured by Schering-Plough, the company generated $9.8 billion in revenue last year and spent $7.9 million lobbying Congress to, among other things, extend its patent on the drug. Income from sales last year totaled $2.3 billion, paid by consumers and their insurance companies.

However, after several years of pressuring Congress to extend its patent and spending millions in the process, Schering-Plough announced that the medication would soon be available over the counter. If approved by the Food and Drug Administration, the drug would be available without a prescription and at a fraction of the cost. Why the shift?

First, the company was having little success in getting Congress to extend

its patent. Insurance companies tired of paying higher costs for the drug, and competing companies wanting to tap into the lucrative allergy drug market were pressuring in the opposite direction. There was also concern that continuing double-digit increases in the cost of drugs and the perception that drug companies are only concerned with profits might lead to government controls. Concessions by the industry to assist the government in manufacturing drugs to deal with acts of terrorism, such as the anthrax scare, are motivated, some suggest, by a desire to improve its image and win additional favors from government. The industry says it just wants to help.

Of course, another factor, as it turned out, was that Schering-Plough was about to launch a new prescription drug, Clarinex, to fill the market void left by Claritin. The new drug, presumably, will be sold at premium prices, while the old one will sell for much less.

When each of us purchases a prescription drug, we are only interested in whether it makes us feel better. For the industry, this is only one of several concerns.

1. Leslie Wayne and Melody Petersen, "A Muscular Lobby Rolls Up Its Sleeves," *New York Times*, November 4, 2001, BU1 and BU13; Charles Babcock, "An All-Campaign That's Nothing to Sneeze At, *Washington Post National Weekly Edition*, November 8, 1999, 30.

office, typically Democrats. In the 2000 general election, the union spent nearly $40 million on campaign literature, phone banks to get out the vote, television issue aids, and voter registration.[31] In spite of misgivings regarding Al Gore based on his support for trade agreements that cost American jobs, labor made an all-out effort to elect him president. In Michigan, which Gore carried, auto workers took advantage of their union-negotiated Election Day holiday to get people to the polls.[32] Once in office, George W. Bush did reverse several Clinton Admin-

istration policies favorable to unions, including requiring them to inform workers that they have a right not to pay the portion of their dues used for political activities.[33] The administration hopes to reduce campaign funds used against Republican candidates.

The political influence of labor unions has waned considerably since the 1960s. One reason is that union membership, even though it has increased in numbers in recent years, continues to decline as a percentage of the workforce.[34] Only 14 percent of the nonagricultural

FEEDING FRENZY

Efforts of special interests to secure benefits from government do not stop because of a national tragedy. The efforts are simply refocused to take advantage of the situation. In the wake of 9/11, scores of Washington lobbyists, trade associations, interest groups, and members of Congress pleading for special interests rushed to repackage their demands in patriotic wrapping. While not new to Washington politics, post-9/11 may represent a new low in trying to exploit a national disaster for personal and private gain. PBS television producer Bill Moyers put it this way: "It didn't take long for wartime opportunists—the mercenaries of Washington, the lobbyists, lawyers, and political fundraisers—to crawl out of their offices on K Street to grab what they can for their clients."[1]

It began with the nation's airline industry. By September 22, the government gave the airlines a sweet deal: $5 billion in cash, plus another $10 billion in loan guarantees. The airlines also won protection from lawsuits arising from the attacks, which would have cost them billions more. Former Secretary of Labor Robert Reich has pointed out that the bailout exceeds the combined value of all America's major airlines: United, American, Delta, Northwest, US Airways, America West, and Continental.[2] Of course, American taxpayers received no ownership in the airlines for their sizeable investment. In the wink of an eye and with virtually no debate, Congress approved the measure for an industry in which several carriers were near bankruptcy before 9/11.

Following on the heels of the airline bailout, the insurance industry pressed the Bush administration to shift liability

for future terrorist attacks to the federal government. It also sought to have claims confined to the federal court in Manhattan rather than reviewed in state courts where judges would more likely approve punitive damages potentially in the billions. If the White House refused, the industry warned it would cease to cover future terrorist attacks and bring the country's economy to a standstill.

The request was not a hard sell to the administration. Insurance companies spent $1.6 million to elect George Bush in 2000. The industry also had friends in Congress after donating $20 million in soft money to both Republicans and Democrats. By October 12, the White House outlined a plan where tax payers would cover all but $12 billion of the first $100 billion in future claims. In November, the House approved the "Terrorism Risk Protection Act." However, the plan stalled in the Democrat-controlled Senate.

Others picked up the strategy of the airlines and insurance industry. Steel lobbied for direct subsidies as well as restrictions on imports of less costly foreign steel. The Democratic senator from West Virginia, Jay Rockefeller, made the case. "Without steel, we cannot guarantee our national security."[3] Carl Levin, the Democratic senator from Michigan, went a bit further. "Our weapons are made of steel." Before a group of cheering steelworkers, he shouted "We go to war with what you make."[4] "Absolute baloney" was the response of a researcher at a Washington think tank. "One or two steel mills could provide all the steel needed for defense."[5] Of course, Rockefeller's and Levin's views may have been tainted by the $2.7 million the steel producers contributed to Democratic candidates in 2000. The

president eventually approved restrictions on steel imports at a tremendous cost to U.S. taxpayers and opening the U.S. to retaliation by our European allies for our violation of free trade agreements.

The $167 billion farm subsidy labeled the Agricultural Act of 2001 became the Farm Security Act of 2001 following 9/11. On September 24, Capitol Hill was deluged with letters from growers of twenty federally subsidized commodities with the message that "food production is vital to the national interest."[6] Like steel, the growers pumped $58 million into the 2000 elections. The measure passed the House in October 291 to 120 and was later signed into law by the president.

Manufacturers of traffic signs, barricades, and other equipment wanted their share, too. In an effort to bolster federal highway safety spending, a spokesman argued that increased spending for traffic-routing devices would help motorists flee cities faster and more safely during terrorist attacks. The American Bus Association, representing a thousand private companies providing intercity bus service, had been lobbying for $400 million to improve bus security and safety. After 9/11, the association maintained that it would help companies retain drivers who have come to fear potential terrorist attacks.

A capital gains tax cut was marketed as a national security initiative by the National Tax Payers Union. According to the association, a reduction in capital gains taxes would "revitalize the sagging economy and bring new revenues to Washington—aiding our war against terrorism."[7] Having succeeded in winning $135 million to shore up public beaches, the American Shore and Beach

Preservation Association sought additional funds arguing that "America needs to make a major commitment to its energy and water infrastructure, both for security and economic reasons."[8] Lobbyists also sought a $10 million subsidy for bison producers because, as they put it, the fear of terrorism drove patrons from the fancy restaurants that serve bison steaks and burgers.

Flight schools, operators of skydiving companies, manufacturers of small aircraft, and owners of small airports seeking compensation for business lost since the attacks also bellied up to the trough. Ethanol producers proposed blending its product with gasoline to check the nation's dependence on foreign oil. Travel agents sought $4 billion arguing that without travel agencies, the nation's travel industry cannot survive. Date growers in California petitioned the White House and Pentagon to buy dates and include them in food packages being dropped into Afghanistan. They argued that dates would be a real treat for the Afghans during Ramadan (a Muslim holy period).[9]

Of course, none of these groups were asking for anything different from what they sought before 9/11. But 9/11 offered an opportunity to provide a stronger argument for their causes. One lobbyist expressed what many were thinking, "What happened was a tragedy certainly, but there are opportunities. We're in business. This is not a charity."[10] A member of Congress captured the view of many lawmakers and lobbyists by saying, "It's an open grab bag, so let's grab."[11]

Perhaps the biggest grab was the economic stimulus package put forth by House Republicans. The measure

"Pardon me, but could you tell us where the public trough is?"

would allow companies to write off expenses they hadn't yet incurred, take advantage of loopholes to avoid paying any taxes at all, and receive rebates on taxes they paid going back to 1986. The estimated stimulus effect was zero, but the lobbyist pushing it claimed it was his patriotic duty to bolster the bottom line of the nation's wealthiest corporations. Largely written by corporate lobbyists, the measure failed to win approval.

"Lobbyists are in the business of asking for things," says a researcher at the conservative Heritage Foundation. "And they adjust their message to whatever they think will sell. Right now its national security, economic stimulus, and disaster relief, and so they link what they want to one of those—better yet all three."[12]

1. Bill Hogan, "Star-Spangled Lobbyists," *Mother Jones,* March/April 2002, 59–63.
2. Alan Guebert, "Lugar's Proposal Calls Groups' Bluff," *Lincoln Journal-Star,* October 21, 2001.
3. Hogan, "Star-Spangled Lobbyists."
4. David E. Sanger and Joseph Kahn, "Bush's Plan to Raise Steel Tariffs Would Exempt Most Poor Nation," *New York Times,* March 4, 2002, A1 and A14.
5. Hogan, "Star-Spangled Lobbyists."
6. Ibid.
7. Ibid.
8. Ibid.
9. David E. Rosenbaum, "Since Sept, 11. Lobbyists Use New Pitches for Old Pleas," *New York Times,* December 3, 2001, B1.
10. Ibid.
11. Hogan, "Star-Spangled Lobbyists."
12. Ibid.

workforce belongs to a union (see Figure 2). Another reason for the decline in membership is the loss to foreign countries of manufacturing jobs, in which unions have traditionally been strong, and an increase in service jobs, in which unions have been weak or nonexistent. Another reason is business's efforts to check unionization. Many punish employees who promote it. National Labor Relations Board data show that 125,000 employees lost their jobs between 1992 and 1997 for supporting a union.[35] While illegal, such acts are rarely prosecuted and, if they are, take three to five years before a decision is reached and an employee reinstated. Moreover, penalties are minimal. Court decisions have also made it increasingly difficult, if not impossible, for workers to join a union. Where employers refrain from such blatantly illegal practices—namely the public sector (teachers and government workers)—union membership has increased. The antiunion message of business communicated through the largely antiunion media has also succeeded in convincing Americans that unions are something working men and women do not need.[36]

Labor's political influence has also declined as states in the South and Southwest, where the population is traditionally hostile to unions, have gained population and representation in Congress, while states in the North, with populations more sympathetic to unions, have lost representation, a trend that is likely to continue. Global competition and government's unwillingness to protect American workers has also hurt unions. Fearful of losing their jobs or putting an employer at a disadvantage in a competitive market, members are reluctant to strike. Without the threat of strikes, there is little reason to heed labor's demands or for employees to consider joining unions.

To expand their membership, unions have turned to the low-wage service sector. Labor won a major victory in 1999 when seventy-five thousand nursing home employees voted to be represented by the Service Employees International Union, making it the third largest union in the nation.[37] Unions are also expanding into the ranks of high-tech and professional workers. Efforts are under way to organize computer specialists where they are highly concentrated as in Silicon Valley.[38] Doctors employed by HMOs as well as those in private practice are organizing.[39] Graduate teaching assistants at the nation's major universities are organizing for purposes of

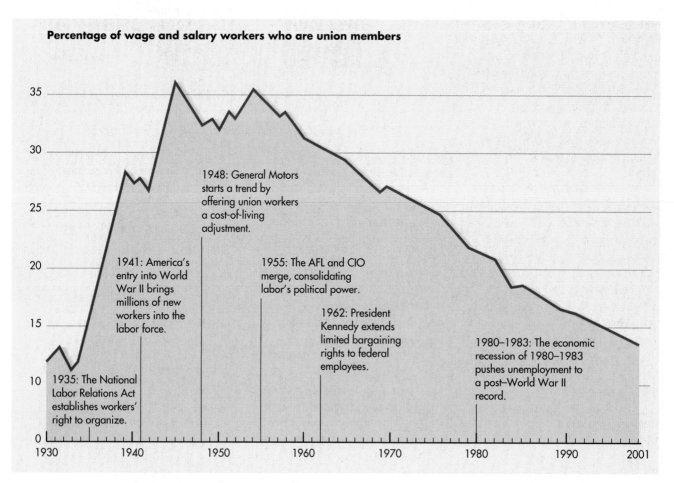

Percentage of wage and salary workers who are union members

1948: General Motors starts a trend by offering union workers a cost-of-living adjustment.

1941: America's entry into World War II brings millions of new workers into the labor force.

1955: The AFL and CIO merge, consolidating labor's political power.

1962: President Kennedy extends limited bargaining rights to federal employees.

1980–1983: The economic recession of 1980–1983 pushes unemployment to a post–World War II record.

1935: The National Labor Relations Act establishes workers' right to organize.

FIGURE 2 ■ Union Membership Has Decreased

SOURCES: Christoph Blumrich, *Newsweek*, September 5, 1983, 51; *Statistical Abstract of the United States, 1990*; *Lincoln Journal*, March 1993.

collective bargaining over wages and working conditions.[40] Even some undergraduates are organizing. Undergraduate resident hall advisors at the University of Massachusetts recently voted to affiliate with the United Auto Workers. The issue for this first unionized undergraduate group is job security. A residence hall assistant was fired for missing a staff meeting.[41] In spite of these efforts, union membership continues to decline as a percentage of the workforce.

Agriculture

Agricultural interests are represented by a number of general and specialized groups. Most groups support government subsidies to help farmers, others oppose such help.

The American Farm Bureau Federation, the largest of the general agriculture interest groups, began when the federal government established the agricultural extension service with agents in rural locations to help farmers. To encourage cooperation with agents, the government offered grants to states that organized county farm bureaus. By 1919, a national organization was formed.

Despite its roots, the Farm Bureau today is a conservative organization dominated by wealthy farmers with large land holdings. Although it generally opposes "big" government, it favors big government subsidies to farmers and corporate farmers, subsidies from which many of its members benefit.

The National Farmers' Union, which is considerably smaller than the Farm Bureau, represents small farming interests. It strongly supports government subsidies to farmers. The American Agriculture Movement (AAM), which began as a protest movement by farmers who were badly hurt by falling prices in the mid-1970s, also speaks out primarily on issues that benefit small farmers and ranchers.[42]

Along with the general interest groups, hundreds of commodity organizations promote specific products and operate much like business trade associations. Examples include cattle, cotton, milk, tobacco, and wool producers. Large agribusiness firms such as Cargill also have powerful lobbies in Washington.

At the start of the twenty-first century, American agriculture is dominated by agribusiness and large corporate farms. The small farmer plays a relatively insignificant role, although politicians often invoke the small farmer in pushing government subsidies for large corporate enterprises. Current farm subsidies provide a guaranteed income to producers of selected crops, and the lion's share of the subsidies in most states go to 10 percent of farmers.[43]

Public Interest Groups

Public interest groups lobby for political and social causes. If they succeed, benefits are shared more widely than by just the members of the group. For example, the National Taxpayers Union lobbies for reduced taxes not only for its members but for everyone who pays taxes. Amnesty International lobbies for the rights of political prisoners around the world even though none of its members are prisoners. Although nearly all groups think of themselves as pursuing the public interest, the label applies only to those working for other than personal or corporate interests. However, "public interest" does not mean that a majority of the public necessarily favors the goals of these groups.

Public interest groups increased dramatically in number and size during the late 1960s and early 1970s.[44] Now they number more than 2,500, with 40 million members.[45] Several factors account for this surge. Americans became increasingly distrustful of government, which appeared to favor special interests over more general interests. The need for a balance between the two led many to join public interest groups. Many middle-class Americans also had the financial means to support public interest groups. The new technology mentioned earlier also made it possible to reach and mobilize large numbers of them.

While many of the public interest groups that were established during the 1960s and 1970s were "shoestring" operations staffed by idealistic social reformers with few professional skills, the public interest organizations of today have larger budgets and memberships and a cadre of professionals—attorneys, management consultants, direct mail fund-raisers, and communications directors—handling day-to-day operations and seeking to influence government with a variety of strategies and tactics.[46]

Multiple-Issue Groups

Some public interest groups are multiple-issue groups, involved with a broad range of issues. Others have a narrower focus and are often referred to as single-issue groups. This section provides some examples of multiple-issue groups.

Women's Groups Groups advocating women's equality range from large, mass-based organizations with a broad agenda, such as the National Organization for Women (NOW), to much smaller groups with very specific interests such as electing women to public office.

NOW is the largest women's group with 250,000 total members and chapters in all fifty states.[47] It is well organized with field representatives and organizers, researchers, lobbyists, and specialists in various policy areas such as reproductive freedom and economic rights.

NOW is funded largely from membership dues but also actively solicits funds by mail. It also receives income from subscriptions and selling such things as T-shirts and posters. Private foundations interested in promoting women's rights also provide significant funding.

Although NOW began as a protest movement, today it lobbies at the national, state, and local levels. It provides leadership training and education for local and state groups and joins in coalitions with women's rights groups on different issues.

In recent years, the women's movement has divided between groups pushing an ideological agenda, such as NOW, which continues to see abortion as a major concern, and more pragmatic groups, such as the National Women's Political Caucus, which sees its task as electing women to public office regardless of their stands on the issues.

EMILY—short for "Early Money Is Like Yeast" (it makes the dough rise)—is an organization that recruits, trains, and endorses prochoice Democratic women candidates for the House and Senate and for state governor and then works to fund and elect them to public office. The organization holds seminars for candidates, campaign managers, and press secretaries. It has helped elect five women to the Senate and thirty-four to the House. In 2002, sixty-eight thousand EMILY's List members contributed $9.3 million to prochoice Democratic women running for House, Senate, and state governor and another $10 million mobilizing women voters in key battleground states.[48]

GenderPAC, which stands for Gender Public Advocacy Coalition, is not, strictly speaking, a women's group. It works to protect everyone's right to be free of gender stereotypes. Founded by Riki Wilchins, who started life as a boy and became a transsexual woman in the 1970s, refuses to identify with either gender and notes that "there are many people who do not fit or want to fit into binary genders."[49] Six years ago, the organization was a newsletter scribbled in Wilchins's New York apartment. With contributions from firms such as American Airlines and Verizon, GenderPAC has a Washington office and $250,000 budget. Its Congressional Gala drew two hundred people to hear an address by Colorado congresswomen Diana DeGette.[50]

While only 1,600 strong, the Independent Women's Forum is a conservative answer to NOW.[51] The group opposes government programs to achieve sexual equality, including extension of civil rights laws to cover discrimination against women's athletic programs in colleges and universities (see Chapter 15). Federal law requires institutions that receive federal funds to provide equality in athletic scholarships and opportunities for men and women. While a laudable goal, the group maintains that the provision forces institutions to cut men's programs. The group also opposes programs directed

The first wave of women's organizations campaigned for women's right to vote. Here, some of twenty thousand marchers parade for women's rights in New York City in 1917.

toward raising the performance of girls in public schools, arguing that it is boys who consistently underperform and suffer low self-esteem. The board of directors includes many who hold high-level government-appointed jobs in the Bush administration.

Religious Groups Religious groups often lobby on political issues. The National Council of Churches, representing liberal Protestant denominations, has spoken out on civil rights, human rights, and other social issues. Catholic groups have been active in both antiabortion and antinuclear movements. Jewish groups have been involved in lobbying for liberal issues, such as the rights of workers and minorities.

Jewish groups have been particularly active in lobbying for Israel. Since its beginning in 1951, the pro-Israel lobby has lost on only three key decisions, all involving the sale of U.S. arms to Egypt and Saudi Arabia. The success of Jewish groups in lobbying for Israel reflects their commitment, organization, and political skill, and an opposition Arab lobby that is weak by comparison.[52]

Conservative Christian groups have had an especially big impact on American politics in recent years. Identified by a "born again" experience, a desire to win converts, and a literal interpretation of the Bible, members of the Christian right, spurred by what they see as a decline in traditional values, became active in politics in the 1970s.[53] Growth in conservative denominations, while membership in mainline churches declined, raised the visibility and prestige of the Christian right and organizations like the National Association of Evangelicals and Christian Coalition.[54]

Opposed to abortion, divorce, homosexuality, and women's rights, conservative Christians were the major force behind the effort of television evangelist Pat Robertson to win the Republican presidential nomination in 1988. Following his defeat, Robertson converted a mailing list of 2 million names into the Christian Coalition. Unlike conservative Christian groups in the 1980s, primarily concerned with spreading their message via television and radio, the Coalition sought and won control of the Republican Party in many areas, enabling them to veto the nomination of candidates they deemed inappropriate.[55] By 1992, the organization gained dominance or leverage in twenty state party organizations.[56]

The Christian Coalition recruits members and communicates its message through schools, newspapers, magazines, radio and television stations, and thousands of politically mobilized churches. It prides itself as a counterweight to what it describes as the "liberal establishment" controlled by "secular humanists who exert every effort to debase and eliminate Bible-based Christianity from society."[57] To achieve its goals, the Coalition raises money for political candidates, registers

voters, operates phone banks to get out the vote, and grades legislators.[58] Since 1994, it has distributed in churches on the Sunday before election day voter guides rating Republican and Democratic candidates on key issues. In 1998, many pastors refused to allow the guides, claiming they were biased in favor of Republicans and fearful that such participation could be interpreted as political activity and jeopardize the church's tax-exempt status (no churches lost their tax exemption, nor did the IRS threaten action).[59] Robertson and the Coalition were outspoken critics of President Clinton during the impeachment process, calling on him to resign and requesting Christians to send money to make sure that he did.[60]

The Christian Coalition is not as singularly motivated by moral issues as it once was.[61] Support for George Bush in 2000 over several other candidates more closely aligned with the moral agenda of the Christian right reflects this. The shift represents an effort to broaden its appeal. At the same time, it may weaken the organizations as members oppose merging the family values agenda with the traditional economic concerns of the Republican Party.[62]

Robertson's credibility suffered when, on his television show, he agreed with his fellow Christian conservative leader Reverend Jerry Falwell that 9/11 was "God's punishment on America for tolerating feminists, gays and lesbians, libertarians and certain federal judges."[63]

It was the Christian right that delivered the Republican presidential nomination to George Bush in 2000 by mobilizing its followers in opposition to John McCain. Bush then appointed Christian conservative John Ashcroft as attorney general as a reward for their support.

Yet, the number of Christian conservatives is shrinking. With each new generation, social attitudes are becoming more liberal on abortion and gay rights. This fact caused one right-wing activist to declare that conservatives have already lost the "cultural war."[64] Perhaps mindful that time is working against him, Falwell recently told supporters in a fund-raising letter that he is organizing a campaign to take advantage of President Bush's popularity from the war to push the conservative family-oriented social agenda. He wrote, "Now is the time for President Bush to get his conservative family agenda through Congress because public support for him will never be stronger."[65] He added, "The Democrats and liberal media attacks will soon start taking their toll again."

The Interfaith Alliance began in 1994 to counter the message and political activity of the Christian Coalition and other conservative religious groups. Composed of mainstream and minority religious and secular groups, it has chapters in thirty-eight states and represents hundreds of churches, faith, and civic organizations. The group holds rallies and public forums dealing with family values, poverty, and discrimination. It opposes prayer in schools but takes no position on abortion. Like the Christian Coalition, it produces voter guides and campaign literature. The organization issues action alerts and often testifies before Congress.[66]

Racial and Ethnic Groups Groups promoting the civil rights of racial and ethnic groups have been an important part of twentieth-century history. Groups representing the interests of African Americans, such as the NAACP, Congress for Racial Equality (CORE), Urban League, and others pressed for equal rights for black Americans and eventually won major changes in American law and practice. Chapter 15 discusses these groups and their role in the civil rights movement.

Chapter 15 also discusses the civil rights struggles of Hispanics and American Indians. Though the roots of Hispanic American political groups date to the late nineteenth century, the longest existing organization, the League of United Latin American Citizens (LULAC), was founded in 1927 to combat discrimination against Mexican Americans. Another prominent group, the Mexican American Legal Defense and Educational Fund (MALDEF), focuses on court challenges to discriminatory practices—for example, the creation of election districts unfavorable to Hispanic voters.

Groups supporting the rights of Native Americans and Asians have also proliferated with the success of black civil rights movement. Among the targets of American Indian rights groups are school mascots that use American Indian tribal names or portray Indians in an offensive manner.

Gays and Lesbians Gay rights organizations have a shorter history than most other major political groups. The first groups formed after World War II in an era when gays were labeled as deviates on the rare occasions when they came to public attention. For example, in 1954, after a raid of a bar where gay men congregated, a Miami newspaper headline read "Perverts Seized in Bar Raids." Early gay and lesbian groups focused largely on sharing information about how to survive and how to fight police repression.[67]

In the mid-1960s, a few gays followed the example of the civil rights movement and organized small public demonstrations. Other gays argued that such demonstrations undermined the safety and well-being of the homosexual subculture, which then existed underground in many large cities. Nonetheless, during the 1960s, the gay rights movement became more radical and visible. Like Vietnam War protesters, women's rights advocates, and civil rights activists, many gays embarked on active protests to challenge the status quo. News of a violent confrontation between gays and the police after a 1969 police raid of a gay bar in New York City helped

fuel this new "gay liberation" movement. Street protests became common in large cities. Gays formed clubs on college campuses. The issue of civil rights for gays was discussed in the 1972 presidential campaign, and in 1973 the American Psychiatric Association removed homosexuality from its lists of mental disorders.

While gays are still barred from the military and often lose their jobs and are evicted if their sexual orientation becomes known, society has grown more tolerant of gays in the past twenty years. Gays and lesbians in the federal workforce and a dozen states are protected from job discrimination. Vermont approved civil unions for gay and lesbian couples. Eight out of ten Americans think discrimination in jobs and housing against gays and lesbians is wrong. Forty percent approve civil unions.[68] The AIDS epidemic, which began in 1981, opened a new chapter in the fight for gay rights. Media attention to the issue and its impact on the gay community raised the issue of discrimination against gays. Entertainers and celebrities who acknowledged their homosexuality, and in some instances, suffered from AIDS, raised public consciousness even more.

The election of Bill Clinton in 1992 also represented a turning point. While Clinton's public position on gay issues was mixed, he ended the federal policy treating gays as security risks and invited gay activists to the White House for the first time. The implicit message was that gays are part of the American community, have legitimate concerns, and are accepted as full participants in political life. With Clinton's election, the radical and confrontational style of gay groups such as Queer Nation have taken a backseat to more mainstream gay rights groups such as the Human Rights Campaign (HRC) with a membership of four hundred thousand. While HRC channels most of its campaign contributions to Democrats, it also supports Republicans. The hope is to elect supporters of gay rights in both parties. The strategy is paying off. Republicans in Congress have joined with Democrats in supporting a number of gay rights measures.[69]

The pragmatic approach of the HRC is rejected by old-guard activists on the left and emerging conservatives on the right.[70] Those on the left believe the gay-rights movement should be part of a larger campaign for "social justice" fighting for welfare benefits, abortion rights, affirmative action, and environmental causes. They see the Democratic Party as the principal vehicle for achieving this. Those on the right are drawn to the Republican Party, limit their agenda exclusively to gay-rights issues, and hope to win the party over to the point where sexual orientation is not an issue. HRC sees gay rights succeeding only with support from both parties.

All sides are united in wanting to be free of discrimination and enjoy the rights of other Americans, including access to spousal health and death benefits provided by employers. This desire for economic equality is the justification for legitimizing same-sex marriage, although the economic issues could be resolved without taking this step. At the moment, same-sex marriage is the most controversial and emotional gay issue.

Elderly While the population of the nation as a whole has tripled since 1900, the number of elderly has increased eightfold. Today, persons over sixty-five constitute nearly 13 percent of the population. Several groups, sometimes called the "gray lobby," represent their interests.

Founded in 1958 to provide insurance to the elderly, the American Association of Retired Persons, (now simply called AARP), with 35 million members, is the nation's largest and one of its most powerful interest groups in Washington. Recruited by direct mail and word of mouth, the AARP attracts eight thousand new members a day. For $12.50, anyone over fifty can join and use the numerous benefits provided by the organization.

With 1,800 employees and eighteen lobbyists, the AARP has become a potent political force. The AARP's lobbying efforts are directed primarily at preserving and expanding government benefits to the elderly. The organization generated $580 million in revenue in 2001; $56 million went for lobbying. The Reagan administration quickly dropped the idea of cutting cost-of-living increases in Social Security to reduce the nation's deficit when the AARP and others protested. Reagan's budget director lamented, "These are people who have plenty of time on their hands, who are well organized, who vote regularly, and they are a massive political force."[71] Although programs for the elderly (primarily Social Security and Medicare) represent one-third of the federal budget, politicians are reluctant to touch them. Those

who have suggested doing so have earned themselves the AARP label "granny-basher." Mindful of their political influence, Clinton got the AARP to support his effort to reform health care by including long-term nursing home care.

Influence is exercised primarily by a flood of correspondence to members of Congress from AARP members. There is no congressional district where the AARP is not at least fifty thousand strong.[72]

To counterbalance the power of the gray lobby, a number of groups such as Americans for Generational Equity and the Children's Defense Fund represent the interests of young people, but they are small by comparison. Increasingly, young adults have interests in common that raise the prospects of organizing them along the lines of the AARP. For example, college students have an interest in reducing tuition costs and expenses associated with a university education. Student groups often join university officials to lobby state legislatures for more funding and demonstrate on campus against higher tuition rates. Organizing can also check the economic exploitation of young people or at least raise their level of consciousness, reducing the likelihood of being taken advantage of. Consider the interest rates charged by credit card companies that routinely distribute cards to college students with an invitation to use them for whatever they wish.

Environmental Groups Environmental groups are another example of multiple-issue groups. Earth Day 1970 marked the beginning of the environmental movement in the United States. Spurred by an oil spill in California, what was to be a "teach-in" on college campuses mushroomed into a day of national environmental awareness with an estimated 20 million Americans taking part. A

Seniors demonstrate against Medicare cuts.

minority movement in the 1970s, the environmental lobby today is large and active, and its values are supported by most Americans.[73]

Some environmental groups, such as the National Audubon Society, Sierra Club, and the Natural Resources Defense Council, have permanent offices in Washington with highly skilled professionals who carry out a full range of lobbying activities. All experienced substantial growth in membership and finances during the 1980s, when the Reagan administration threatened to undo the environmental gains of the 1970s.[74]

The so-called Greens are environmental groups that shun conventional lobbying approaches and are more confrontational. Groups such as Greenpeace, Earth First!, and the Sea Shepherds seek a "green cultural revolution." Local citizen groups have also organized in support of local environmental concerns such as the location of toxic or nuclear waste dumps. Citizens, skeptical of government and corporate claims that such facilities are safe, want them located elsewhere.[75]

The election of George Bush saw the reversal of many Clinton-era environmental regulations such as the prohibition of road building in national forests, the use of snowmobiles in national parks, and restrictions on companies mining for gold and other minerals on public lands.[76] Many of the changes have been justified on national security grounds and environmentalists have been unwilling to challenge them for fear of appearing unpatriotic. In spite of the administration's national security argument to open up the Wildlife Refuge in Alaska to oil exploration, environmentalists found their voice in opposition and the measure was defeated in the Senate. With Republican success in the 2002 elections, it is expected that the administration will try again to open the refuge to exploration. Environmentalists also were able to get the administration to reverse itself and accept lower levels of arsenic in drinking water than those proposed by the Clinton administration.

Single-Issue Groups

Single-issue groups pursue public interest goals but are distinguished by their intense concern for a single issue and their reluctance to compromise. For example, members of the NRA passionately oppose control of firearms. Although a majority of Americans have supported gun control for years, the NRA has successfully lobbied Congress to prevent most gun control legislation. The group has members in every congressional district and is well organized to mobilize them. It spent a great deal of money in a losing battle to defeat the Brady Act, which requires a five-day waiting period to purchase a gun. It also failed to prevent a ban on sales of assault weapons.

More recently, the gun lobby is working hard to fend off potential lawsuits filed by cities and states against gun

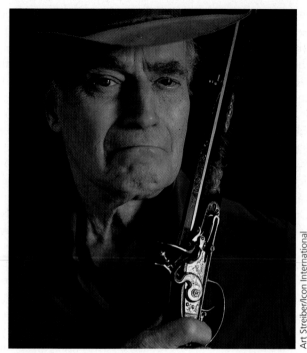

Charlton Heston strikes a tough-guy pose as president of the NRA.

Art Streiber/Icon International

manufacturers seeking compensation for police and health care expenses incurred as a result of gun violence. Local and state governments, spurred on by the success of state governments in suing tobacco companies, hope to win a similar kind of settlement.[77]

Although the NRA remains a major political force, antigun sentiment is growing as more and more Americans respond to increasing gun violence that touches cities, suburbs, and small towns. The result is an increase in the political influence of antigun groups such as Handgun Control and politicians more willing to take on the NRA. Demonstrations such as the Mother's Day march in Washington in 2000, in which nearly 1 million mothers gathered to hear speeches from celebrities and those victimized by gun violence, reflect the growing level of intensity among the population at large for what the marchers called sensible gun laws.

Demonstrations and expressions of antigun sentiment have energized the NRA and progun activists. Following a drop in membership, the organization now claims 3.6 million members. Fearful that the 2000 election of Democratic candidate Al Gore would mean gun control, the group waged an all-out effort to defeat him, pumping $15 million into the election campaign, making a major effort to register its members to vote, and training members in grassroots organizing. After Bush secured the Republican nomination in the spring, a high-ranking official boasted at an NRA gathering, "if [Bush] wins the election, we will have a president where we work out of their office."[78] While this was perhaps an exaggeration, the Bush Justice Department, led by Attorney General John Ashcroft, filed two briefs before the Supreme Court in cases involving gun regulation, arguing that the Second Amendment protects the right of individuals to keep and bear arms rather than a right that is tied to the nation's need to maintain an armed militia.[79] The administration's position reverses what had been the government's policy for sixty years and incorporates the view of Ashcroft expressed in a letter to an NRA gathering shortly after he was appointed. The NRA, which featured a picture of Ashcroft on its magazine a year ago and called him "a breath of fresh air to freedom-loving gun owners" lauded the decision.[80] The Violence Policy Center, a gun control group, chided the decision, adding that the Justice Department "has shown a willingness to throw red meat at the gun lobby and put its political agenda above its institutional obligations."[81]

The abortion controversy has generated a number of single-issue groups. The National Right to Life Committee seeks a constitutional amendment banning all abortions. The committee works to elect candidates who favor such an amendment and defeat those who do not. After the 1989 and 1992 Supreme Court decisions allowing more state regulation of abortion, prolife groups turned their attention to state legislators. They pushed for laws requiring informed consent, waiting periods, and parental consent for minors. More recently, it has lobbied Congress to outlaw human cloning for use in research.

Operation Rescue is a confrontational antiabortion group whose strategy has been to deny access to abortion clinics to women seeking abortions, as well as to disrupt abortion clinic operations and harass physicians who do abortions. Many "rescuers" have been jailed for their activities. The organization's direct action approach was dealt a blow when Congress passed the Freedom of Access to Clinic Entrances Act in 1994. The law made it a federal crime to hinder abortions by using threats, force, or obstruction. Although peaceful demonstrations that do not block clinic entrances are still legal, the law has discouraged some protesters as demonstrations at clinics have declined.

Under the 1994 law, prolife groups lost a multimillion-dollar lawsuit brought by Planned Parenthood involving Web postings of the names, addresses, and license plate numbers of doctors who perform abortions.[82] Prochoice advocates argued that the action, dubbed the "Nuremberg Files," was designed to threaten and intimidate doctors and likely to lead to violence, while the other side stated they were simply exercising their right to free speech. Initially overturned as a violation of speech protected by the First Amendment, upon review, the Appeals Court found the postings "to intimidate physicians from providing

Lynn Johnson/Aurora

The right-to-life movement is considered a single-issue group.

reproductive health services."[83] The case is likely to reach the Supreme Court, where justices will have to clarify the line between political expression and political violence.

Prolife forces lost in their efforts to prevent the Food and Drug Administration from approving RU-486, the so-called abortion pill. The movement divided on the issue of federal funding of stem-cell research, with several groups siding with President Bush's decision to permit it in a limited way and several others opposing his decision.[84]

Members of the National Abortion Rights Action League and Planned Parenthood are fervently committed to protecting women's right to abortion. Planned Parenthood is the oldest, largest, and best-financed advocate of reproductive freedom for women.

Since 1988, the organization has mounted a major effort to win policymakers to the prochoice point of view. Although often identified with abortion rights, they are also advocates for access to birth control, sex education in schools, and good reproductive health care for women. Using the theme that Americans want abortion to be safe and legal, Planned Parenthood uses newspaper ads, congressional testimony, a Web site, mailings, and local educational efforts to get out the message. They also sometimes use mass marches and rallies. Three months before the 1989 Supreme Court decision allowing state regulation of abortion (for more on this issue, see Chapter 14), three hundred thousand prochoice activists staged a march in Washington. Calling the event the "March for Women's Lives," the goal was to recast the issue in terms of freedom and choice rather than abortion. The three-day event received substantial publicity and demonstrated

Prochoice advocates form a human corridor to protect patients and workers entering a clinic in Buffalo, New York.

Lynn Johnson/Aurora

Tactics of Interest Groups

Interest groups engage in a variety of tactics to secure their goals. Some try to influence policymakers directly, whereas others seek to mold public opinion and influence policymakers indirectly. Some do both. Some interest groups form broad coalitions to maximize their influence. Others that have little chance of succeeding using conventional techniques turn to protest activity. Both coalition formation and protest activity can involve direct and indirect techniques.

Direct Lobbying Techniques

Direct lobbying techniques involve personal encounters between lobbyists and public officials. Some lobbyists are volunteers; others are permanent, salaried employees of the groups they represent; and others are contract lobbyists, "hired guns" who represent any individual or group willing to pay for the service. Contract lobbyists include the numerous Washington lawyers affiliated with the city's most prestigious law firms. Many have worked for government, so they can boast of contacts in government and access to policymakers to plead their clients' cases. Most firms recruit from the ranks of both Republicans and Democrats to assure access regardless of which party controls government. Some lobbying is done by corporate CEOs and board members.

Making Personal Contacts

Making personal contacts, in an office or in a more informal setting, is the most effective lobbying technique. Compared to other forms of lobbying, direct personal contact is relatively inexpensive, and it minimizes problems of misinterpretation by allowing questions to be answered on the spot.

Lobbyists know that whereas contacting every legislator is unnecessary, contacting key legislators, those who sit on the committees having jurisdiction over matters of interest to the lobbyists, and staff serving those committees is critical.[88] Conventional wisdom also suggests that only those legislators who support a group's position or who are known to be undecided should be contacted directly.[89] Putting undue pressure on known opponents may jeopardize prospects for working together in the future on other issues.

To a large extent, lobbying is building relationships based on friendship. As a former chair of the House Budget Committee put it, "The most effective lobbyists here are the ones you don't think of as lobbyists." Referring to one prominent Washington lobbyist, he said, "I don't think of him as a lobbyist. He's almost a constituent, or a friend." Barbara Boxer, then a Democratic representative from California, referring to the same gentleman, described him as "a lovely, wonderful guy. In the whole time I've known him, he's never

to members of Congress that the movement could mobilize a large number of supporters.[85]

Single-issue groups have proliferated in recent years. Some view this trend with alarm, because when groups clash over a highly emotional issue and are unwilling to compromise, it is difficult to resolve the issue.[86] The issue commands excessive time and energy of policymakers at the expense of broader issues that may be more important.

On the other hand, single-issue groups have always been part of politics.[87] These groups may even be beneficial because they represent interests that may not be well represented in Congress. Fears about single-issue groups may result from the groups' own exaggerated claims of influence, their heavy media coverage, and, in the case of some antiabortion and environmental groups, their confrontational tactics.

asked me to vote for anything." At a gathering, she joked that he's almost "a member of the family."[90]

Direct personal contact was the principal strategy of the airline industry in seeking government aid following 9/11. Senator Peter Fitzgerald, Republican from Illinois and the only senator to vote against the $15 billion aid package, said, "The airline industry made a full-court press to convince Congress that giving them billions in taxpayer cash was the only way to save the republic."[91] Twenty-seven in-house lobbyists and several hired lobbyists from forty-two Washington firms, including former White House aides, cabinet secretaries, retired members of Congress, and former Republican National Party chair Haley Barbour, went to work. Additionally, the CEOs and board members of several airlines pitched in. One lobbyist remarked, "It was the most high-level surgical strike that I have ever seen."[92]

Rather than pursue the usual path of congressional lawmaking, committee hearings, and floor debate—which would have delayed action, allowing opposition to form, and undercut the effort—the airlines targeted a few congressional and administration leaders. "Their tactic was to bring all their top people to meet with top people in government and to say the sky is falling."[93] The result, as Representative George Miller, Democrat from California, put it, was that "[t]he big dog got the bone."[94]

Providing Expertise

Although all groups provide information to public officials, some are known for providing information based on accurate and reliable research. Ralph Nader's organization, Public Citizen, which says that it lobbies for the average citizen, has such a reputation. In recent years, Public Citizen has lobbied against the erosion of government regulations dealing with clean air and water, safe drugs, food, and the workplace. It has also worked to limit corporate gifts, such as fancy vacations, to members of Congress and to enact campaign finance reform (see Chapter 9).

Lobbyists often have a great deal of knowledge and expertise that are useful in drafting legislation. A legislator may ask a lobbyist to draft a bill, or both may work together in drafting legislation. Sometimes interest groups themselves draft legislation and ask a sympathetic legislator to introduce it. General Electric drafted a tax reform measure that saved it millions in taxes. In an effort to tap the flow of federal money following 9/11, drug and biotechnology companies supplied Congress with the precise legislative language required to provide them with what they wanted.[95] Biotechnology firms want the government to pay any claims for injuries caused by vaccines they make to protect people from biological terrorism. Drug companies want the Food and Drug Administration to waive the usual review procedures when they are called on to supply drugs in an emergency.

Testifying at Hearings

Testifying at congressional hearings is designed to establish a group's credentials as a "player" in a policy area as well as to convince its own constituents that it is doing its job. Testifying has its own rules and norms. A member of a prominent Washington law firm with responsibility at his firm for prepping witnesses to testify identified the Boy Scout motto "Be Prepared" as the most important principle to follow in getting ready for a hearing. Beyond that, he offers a few other tips:

- Keep it short. No one has an hour to listen to you.

- Don't read your statement. Good salespeople know the product and can talk to you about it.

- Don't be arrogant. Some witnesses are short with members because they believe committee members don't understand their business. Most members of Congress don't care about your business; they are going to make a decision based on what they hear.

- Don't guess. If you don't know the answer to a question, say so and promise to supply the answer later.

- Don't be hokey, but illustrate whenever possible. It is easier to focus on a wrecked fender in a hearing room than to visualize a set of statistics.[96]

Another advantage of testifying is that it provides free publicity. Staging sometimes occurs. A lobbyist might ask a sympathetic legislator to raise certain questions that the lobbyist is prepared to answer or to indicate in advance

"Mr. Speaker, will the gentleman from Small Firearms yield the floor to the gentleman from Big Tobacco?"

what questions will be asked. Sometimes celebrities are invited to testify. In a not unprecedented but certainly rare move, Hillary Rodham Clinton, when she was the First Lady and the principal player in developing the president's health care reform, testified before several congressional committees. This White House effort prompted a former Reagan aid to quip that the Clinton White House "does PR the way [former chair of the Joint Chiefs] Colin Powell does war: maximum use of force."[97]

Giving Money

Lobbyists try to ensure access to legislators, and giving money is one way to guarantee this. A longtime financial backer of Ronald Reagan once said that having a dialogue with a politician is fine, "but with a little money they hear you better."[98] One Democrat commented in a similar vein, "Who do members of Congress see? They'll certainly see the one who gives the money. It's hard to say no to someone who gives you $5,000."[99]

The primary way groups channel money to legislators is through campaign contributions. Groups, including businesses and unions, may set up PACs to give money to campaigns of political candidates.

The number of PACs has grown dramatically since the mid-1970s, as has the amount of money they have contributed. (PACs are discussed more fully in Chapter 9.)

Lobbying the Bureaucracy

For lobbyists, the battle is not over when a bill is passed. Lobbyists also must influence bureaucrats who implement policy. Regulations outlawing sex discrimination in educational institutions were drafted largely in the Department of Education with only broad guidelines from Congress. Although the legislation was passed in 1972, both women's rights groups and interests opposing them continue to lobby over the interpretation of the regulations, particularly with regard to parity between men's and women's athletics.

In influencing bureaucrats, interest groups use most of the tactics described (see also "The Ten Commandments of Lobbying"). Ken Lay, former CEO of Enron, used the direct approach when he telephoned Curtis Hébert, appointed by President George Bush to chair the Federal Energy Commission, to let him know that Enron would continue to support him in his new job if he changed his views on electricity deregulation.[100] Lay also had access to those responsible for drafting the Bush administration's recommendation for the nation's energy policy. The final report included much of what Lay advocated, including finding ways to give the federal government, where Enron has substantial clout, more power over electricity transmission.[101]

Interest groups also try to influence who gets appointed to bureaucratic positions. The auto industry opposed a number of Clinton's nominees to head the Na-

tional Highway Traffic Safety Administration. While consumer groups want someone interested in promoting automobile safety, the industry is looking for someone more sympathetic to its interests and concerns. Senator Don Nickles (R-Okla.) held up the nomination of Clinton's nominee to head the Food and Drug Administration, until he was convinced she would not solicit a manufacturer for RU-486.[102] Nickles opposes abortion and was looking out for the interests of antiabortion groups. Public Citizen and the Natural Resources Defense Council opposed John Graham, Bush's choice to head the White House Office of Information and Regulatory Affairs, out of concern that he would water down Clinton-era health and environmental safeguards. Graham, a Harvard professor, promised to enforce current laws, even if he disagrees with them, and was confirmed.[103] Drug companies effectively vetoed Dr. Alastair Wood, a drug safety expert and early favorite of the Bush administration to head the Food and Drug Administration, because of his call for the agency to more aggressively monitor medicines currently on the market.[104] By influencing the appointments to an agency, an industry or group can improve their prospects for favorable treatment by the agency.

Lobbying the Courts

Like bureaucrats, judges also make policy. Some interest groups try to achieve their goals by getting involved in cases and persuading the courts to rule in their favor. Most groups do not litigate, but some use it as their primary tactic, particularly those that lack influence with Congress and the executive branch.

Litigation has been a favorite strategy of civil rights organizations. In 1999, five civil rights groups representing black, Hispanic, and Asian students sued the University of California.[105] At issue was an admissions policy giving students who took advanced placement courses an advantage. Such courses are rarely offered in poor, predominantly minority high schools; thus, the groups argued, minority students were being disadvantaged not on the basis of merit but wealth. Several civil liberties organizations are pursuing court action challenging President Bush's actions directed at noncitizens, including trying terrorists in military tribunals.[106] The American Civil Liberties Union maintains that the President is making law in authorizing tribunals and that lawmaking is a power granted by the Constitution to Congress. Thus, the group argues the president's actions are violations of the constitutionally established separation of powers. Environmental groups and public interest lobbies have also turned to the courts. The Natural Resources Defense Council along with Greenpeace, Physicians for Social Responsibility, and the Alaska Public Interest Research Group filed suit against Bush's missile defense plan asserting that it violates federal environmental laws.[107] In addition to filing civil suits, groups can represent defendants in criminal cases or file amicus curiae (friend of the court) briefs, written arguments asking the court to decide a case a particular way.[108]

Some groups use the courts to try to make their opponents negotiate with them. Environmental groups frequently challenge developers who threaten the environment in order to force them to bear the costs of defending themselves and to delay the project. The next time, developers may be more willing to make concessions beforehand to avoid lengthy and costly litigation.

Groups also try to influence the courts indirectly by lobbying the Senate to support or oppose judicial nominees.

Indirect Lobbying Techniques

Traditionally, lobbyists mostly employed direct lobbying techniques—providing information, advice, and occasionally pressure. More recently, interest groups are going public—that is, mobilizing their activists and molding and activating public opinion. A study of 175 lobbying groups found that most were doing more of all kinds of lobbying activity, but the largest increases were in going public.[109] Talking with the media increased the most, and mobilizing the grassroots to send letters and telegrams and make telephone calls was second. (See the box "Lobbying Goes High-Tech.")

Mobilizing the Grass Roots

The constituency of an interest group—a group's members, those whom the group serves, friends and allies of the group, or simply those who can be mobilized whether or not they have a connection to the group—can help in promoting a group's position as well as voting for a candidate sympathetic to the group. The National Rifle Association is effective in mobilizing its members. The NRA, like many mass membership organizations, can generate thousands of letters or calls to members of Congress in a short period of time. Calls from irate NRA members led one senator to remark, "I'd rather be a deer in hunting season than run afoul of the NRA crowd."[110]

Conservative Christian minister Jerry Falwell activated his "gospel grapevine" to flood the White House and Congress in opposition to President Clinton's plan to lift the ban on homosexuals in the military. Warning of a new radical homosexual rights agenda, he urged viewers of his *Old Time Gospel Hour* to call and register their opinions.

Senator John McCain (R-Ariz.), a sponsor of antitobacco legislation, was swamped with letters from members of the National Smokers Alliance, an organization funded by the tobacco companies.[111] Senator Tom Harkin (D-Iowa) was surprised to receive hundreds of letters opposing his antitobacco position, strangely enough from only one small region in his state. The mystery was solved when Harkin learned that all the letters came from employees of a Kraft food plant, owned by RJ Reynolds.[112]

Appeals to write or phone policymakers often exaggerate the severity of the concern and the strength of the opposition. To move members, it often takes the threat of a monstrous adversary or a catastrophic defeat.

To be effective, letters and phone calls must appear spontaneous and sincere. Groups often provide sample letters to aid constituents, but these are not as convincing as those written in a constituent's own words. Campaigns producing postcards with preprinted messages are seldom effective. While members of Congress often enlist organizations to mobilize constituents in support of legislation, many members are turned off by the flood of mail and calls they receive. As one lobbyist put it, "Members of Congress hate it when you call in the dogs."[113]

Grassroots lobbying was the hallmark of the successful effort to defeat President Clinton's health care reform proposal in 1994. Cigarette companies, drug manufacturers, health insurance agents, physicians, and hospital administrators mobilized their employees, clients, and friends to contact their representatives urging them to kill the measure.[114] Pressure or support of this kind can provide members of Congress in both parties with a reason to buck the president. As one lobbyist put it, "If done well, a member of Congress summoned to the Oval Office can turn to the president and say 'I can't go with you on this, Mr. President, because I promised the people in my district.'"[115]

The nature of grassroots lobbying has changed dramatically in the past decade. Almost all groups, particularly those with resources, use it as part of their overall lobbying strategy. With e-mail, faxes, and electronic media, it is quite easy to inform your supporters of threats and what to do about them. Dozens of public relations firms are willing to mobilize a group's constituency, if there is one, or manufacture the appearance of a constituency, if there is not. Washington firms in the business of producing citizen movements on demand advertise specialties such as "development of third-party allies," "grassroots mobilization and recruitment," and "grasstops lobbying."[116] (*Grasstops lobbying* involves identifying the person or persons that a member of Congress cannot say no to—a chief donor, campaign manager, political counselor or adviser—and persuading them to persuade the member of Congress to go along with the group.) In many respects, grassroots lobbying resembles a presidential election campaign, involving a number of specialists: a pollster to assess citizen opinion, a media consultant to produce and test market television ads, a communica-

tions adviser to enlist journalists to write stories and editorials, think tanks to provide supporting research, a recruiter to enlist local and community leaders, a Washington lobbyist to push the idea with members of Congress, and a legal expert to draft legislation. The grassroots industry spent upward of $800 million in 1998–1999 putting a "public look" on private interests.[117]

The strategy of massaging constituents and marshaling public opinion has become the method of choice for business lobbies and corporations. Relying on influential lobbyists with connections to party leaders and influential congressional committee chairs no longer works. Power is too dispersed. Today, you "send in the armies, ships, tanks, aircraft, infantry, Democrats and Republicans, grassroots specialists, and people with special relationships to members."[118]

Does grassroots lobbying enhance democracy or undermine it? Those in the business say their efforts mobilize real people with genuine and sincere interests in particular causes, whether they are members, employees, or simply isolated individuals identified by polling and research. Senator Carl Levin (D-Mich.) has a different view. "When public relations firms are paid to generate calls, it creates a distorted picture of public opinion. When a member gets 50 phone calls, what he doesn't know is that 950 other people were contacted and said no way."[119]

Groups also work hard to get their members and supporters to the polls on election day. Electing a sym-

Lobbying Goes High-Tech

The so-called information superhighway has changed the way lobbyists, public officials, and the public communicate. As personal contact with members of Congress or their staffs becomes increasingly difficult, more lobbyists are turning to electronic mail to communicate with members of Congress. Although e-mail is not a substitute for a personal visit, only veteran lobbyists with strong personal relationships developed over the years are likely to be consistently able to gain personal access. For those new to the profession or those who lack personal relationships, e-mail may be the only alternative. Moreover, it is quick and cheap.

The information superhighway is aiding lobbyists in other ways, too. Web pages allow lobbyists (and the public) opportunities to find out easily the status of bills, schedules of hearings, and other relevant information (some of these sites are listed in the note). One site, incongress.com, is described as a "one-stop shop of all the information that's floating around town." For a fee, lobbyists and interest groups can post issue-related information on the site. The information can be read by anyone who has access to the Internet.

Grassroots lobbying is also easier with the Internet. Interest groups have sites that not only provide information about an issue but also invite browsers to send e-mail messages to public officials. Some sites provide the message; others suggest talking points to include

in a message. By using this technique, the group avoids the time and expense of recruiting citizens to write letters or following up to ensure that letters have been written. Moreover, because the letters come from constituents, members of Congress and their staff will pay at least some attention to them. Of course, these mass e-mail campaigns, with each message the same, will soon be no more persuasive than mass postcard campaigns.

NOTE: The Web sites mentioned in the text are good places to start. Another useful site is http://congress.org/main.html, which will help you locate and send an e-mail to your member of Congress.
SOURCE: Ed Henry, "It's the '90s: Old Dogs, New Tricks," *Roll Call Monthly,* November 1997, 1.

pathetic member to Congress, not to mention a president, is more effective in the long run than relying on a continuing effort to mobilize constituents. Many groups worked hard to get their supporters to the polls in 2000 because of the anticipated closeness of the 2000 elections.[120] Labor unions in closely contested states made an effort to reach all of their current and retired members by phone or with a mailing. The AFL-CIO had a Web site capable of producing fliers comparing Gore and Bush on the major issues. The flier with a personal message from the local union official could be printed and mailed within a day. At get-out-the-vote rallies, NRA president Charlton Heston called "the 2000 election the most important since the Civil War."[121] If Gore won, he continued, his Supreme Court will "hammer your gun rights into oblivion."[122] As one journalist concluded, in an election where there are no great crises or burning issues, how do you get people to vote? The answer, "Scare the hell out of them."[123]

Molding Public and Elite Opinion

Groups use public relations techniques to shape public opinion as well as the opinions of policymakers. Ads in newspapers and magazines and on radio and television supply information, foster an image, promote a particular policy, or some combination of these. Tobacco companies spent a record $40 million to defeat antitobacco legislation in 1998. Lockheed Martin, a defense contractor, tried to persuade Congress to purchase the company's F-22 fighter jet with an ad appearing in several publications widely read by members. The ad featured a postcard on a black background. On the card, which is dated June 18, 2007, a wife and mother writes home telling her husband and son not to worry because "those F-22s upstairs" are "ruling the sky." Across the bottom of the ad is the caption "One day in the future, someone you love may be depending on the F-22." According to the company, the ad was an attempt to give a human dimension to an issue that often is shrouded in Pentagon jargon and mind-numbing statistics. But Senator Dale Bumpers (D-Ark.) accused the firm of pandering to the emotions of lawmakers.[124]

On occasion, groups will fabricate information. ExxonMobil is alleged to have distorted the debate on global warming by generating bogus reports and funding scientists who supported the corporation's point of view but who were not experts in the field of climatology and whose research was not reviewed by scholars in the field.[125] Conclusions by the Environmental Protection Agency in June 2002 that global warming is a significant problem discredits the corporate view that it is not. Of course, by themselves ads are unlikely to move policymakers to action or shift public opinion dramatically in the short run. They are most effective in combination with other tactics, in particular grassroots mobilization.

Groups may stage events such as rallies or pickets to attract media coverage to their cause. For example, during the Apartheid era in South Africa (when blacks and whites were strictly segregated), those opposing segregation won considerable attention picketing and protesting outside the South African embassy in Washington, D.C. They were especially effective because they enlisted members of Congress, community leaders, and other celebrities in their protests. Arrests of members of Congress and other celebrities for trespassing kept the issue in the limelight month after month.

Framing the terms of the debate is crucial in winning public support. Those arguing in favor of tort reform (limiting damages courts will award to those injured in auto accidents, air disasters, unsuccessful surgeries, or other mishaps) focus on the few outrageously huge settlements for seemingly innocuous injuries. Those arguing against such changes focus on the poor widows left penniless after being permanently incapacitated by the rapacious behavior of a wealthy corporation.[126]

A tactic increasingly used by interest groups to influence public opinion is rating members of Congress. Groups may choose a number of votes crucial to their concerns such as abortion, conservation, or consumer affairs. Or they may select many votes reflecting a more general liberal or conservative outlook. They then publicize the votes to their members with the ultimate objective of trying to defeat candidates who vote against their positions. The impact of these ratings is probably minimal unless they are used in a concerted effort to target certain members for defeat.

Coalition Building

Coalitions, networks of groups with similar concerns, help individual groups press their demands. Coalitions can be large and focused on many issues or small and very specific. Kingsford charcoal, 7-11 stores, amusement parks, and lawn and garden centers joined the Daylight Saving Time Coalition to lobby Congress to extend daylight saving time. All wanted additional daylight hours to snack, grill, play, or till the soil, which would mean more money in their pockets.

Huge coalitions formed around the health care reform issue in 1995. The AFL-CIO, American Airlines, Chrysler Corporation, the American College of Physicians, and the League of Women Voters supported health care reform, and the American Conservative Union, United Seniors Union, Citizens for a Sound Economy, and National Taxpayers joined a coalition of Citizens Against Health Rationing.[127] Similarly, shortly after the 2000 election, the National Coalition on Ergonomics, a coalition of corporations and business groups, pressured Congress and the White House to rescind regulations issued by the Clinton administration requiring employers to modify workplace conditions that result in injuries from repetitive motions.[128] Despite strong opposition from the AFL-CIO, business interests carried the day.

Coalitions demonstrate broad support for an issue and also take advantage of the different strengths of groups. One group may be adept at grassroots lobbying, another at public relations. One may have lots of money, another lots of members. Quite obviously, coalitions are likely to be part of a lobbying strategy when the goal is securing something that is sought by a wide array of interests rather than something that benefits a single group.[129]

The growth of coalitions in recent years reflects a number of changes in the policy process.[130] Issues have become increasingly complex. Legislation often affects a variety of interests, which makes it easier to form coalitions among groups representing those interests. In addition, changes in technology make it easier for groups to communicate with each other and with constituents. And the number of interest groups is larger than it used to be, especially the number of public interest groups. Many such groups have limited resources, and coalitions help them stretch their lobbying efforts. Some "black hat" business groups, with image problems, seek to associate themselves with "white hat" organizations ranging from labor unions to consumer groups.[131] The decentralization of Congress and the weakness of political parties have also led to coalition building to win needed majorities at the various stages of the policy process.

Coalitions vary in their duration—some are short term, whereas others are permanent. Coalitions involved with the health care issue remained only until the Clinton plan was dead. Coalitions supporting and opposing NAFTA ceased to exist when Congress approved the measure.

On the other hand, the Leadership Conference on Civil Rights is a permanent coalition of 185 civil rights, ethnic, religious, and other groups (Elks, Actors Equity, YMCA, and the National Funeral Directors and Morticians Association). Unlike short-term coalitions, permanent ones need to be sensitive to how today's actions will affect future cooperation. Some issues may be avoided even though a majority of coalition members want to deal with them. When a coalition is unified, however, it can be formidable.

In elections, coordination among PACs in channeling money to political candidates is a form of coalition. Business PACs, for example, take their lead from the Business Industry Political Action Committee (BI-PAC). Information is shared on candidates' issue positions, likelihood of winning, and need for funding.

Protest and Civil Disobedience

Groups that lack access or hold unpopular positions can protest. In the fall of 1999, for example, representatives from more than five hundred groups joined forces in

protesting the World Trade Organization (WTO) at its meeting in Seattle.[132] The WTO represents 135 countries with authority to force countries to change their labor, environmental, and human rights laws that restrict trade among countries. In addition to high-profile labor unions and environmental groups, the demonstration drew less well-known organizations such as the Ruckus Society, a group that provides training in nonviolent protest, and the Raging Grannies, a human rights organization. The protesters charged the organization with responding more to the profit needs of international corporations than those of the environment, working men and women, the poor, and native people. The Sierra Club and Steelworkers held a Seattle tea party with the slogan "No Globalization without Representation." Following their Boston forebears, they tossed steel imported from China, hormone-treated beef, and other goods they view as tainted by WTO decisions into the sea.[133] Taking a page from Vietnam War protests, the groups held a number of activities including teach-ins, concerts, and mock trials of corporations. Hundreds of protesters formed a human chain around Seattle's exhibition center, the site of the meeting, demanding the WTO cancel the debt owed by the world's poorest nations. The protest ended in violence as several hundred were arrested and jailed.

Peaceful but illegal protest activity, in which those involved allow themselves to be arrested and punished, is called **civil disobedience.** Greenpeace, the environmental and peace group, practices civil disobedience. It

© Pierre Gleizes/Greenpeace

Greenpeace attempts to influence public opinion with dramatic events. Here, Greenpeace protests dumping of nuclear waste at sea, while dumpers prepare to drop a barrel of waste on the Greenpeace protesters.

started in 1971 when a group of environmentalists and peace activists sent two boats to Amchitka Island near Alaska to protest a U.S. underground nuclear weapon test. The boats were named *Greenpeace*, linking the environment and peace. Although the boats failed to reach the island, the publicity generated by the affair led Washington to cancel the test.

Over the years, Greenpeace has staged a number of protests. To protest dumping of toxic wastes and sewage in the ocean, thirteen Greenpeace activists lowered themselves from a New York bridge and hung there for eight hours, preventing any sewage barges from carrying wastes out to sea. All were arrested. To protect endangered whales, members placed themselves in the path of a harpoon, narrowly missing being struck. Others parachuted over coal-powered power plants to protest acid rain. Their goal was to generate publicity and dramatic photographs that would activate the general population.

Greenpeace and several other protest organizations have moved away from the confrontational, "in your face" style of politics in recent years,[134] although four Greenpeace protesters chained themselves to a Canadian cargo ship in 1999, maintaining that it was loaded with paper made from rainforest trees,[135] and fifteen activists from seven countries delayed a U.S. missile defense test by rafting into an area beneath the rocket's flight path.[136] Felony charges were eventually dropped when all fifteen pleaded guilty to a misdemeanor charge of trespass.

Once organizations such as Greenpeace succeed in getting a hearing—that is, find someone in government who is willing to listen—they shift to an inside strategy, working with those in power rather than against them. Protest groups often drop the "yelling and screaming" for more conventional lobbying techniques once they have access to policymakers. It has also become increasingly difficult to draw media coverage to another story of a group of protesters willing to risk life and limb in the interest of preserving or preventing something, and it is publicity that makes such activities politically effective. The first time, these stories are front-page news. The second time, they are buried inside, if they get covered at all.

Protest can generate awareness of an issue, but to be successful, it must influence mass or elite opinion. Often it is the first step in a long struggle that takes years to resolve. Sometimes the result is hostility toward the group using it. Antiwar protest by college students in the 1960s and 1970s angered not only government officials, who targeted the leaders for harassment, but also many citizens. In the early years of the women's movement, the media labeled many female protesters "bra burners" even though it is not clear that any woman ever burned a bra.

Extended protests are difficult because they demand more skill by the leaders and sacrifices from the participants. Continued participation, essential to success, robs participants of a normal life. It can mean jail, physical

In 1920, a horse-drawn cart loaded with dynamite exploded on Wall Street and killed forty people. No one was ever charged with the murders, but they were thought to be the work of anarchists. Though anarchists were anticapitalist and anti–big business, reportedly most of the victims were clerks and secretaries, not Wall Street bankers.

Culver Pictures

harm, or even death and requires discipline to refrain from violence, even when violence is used against you.

The civil rights movement provides the best example of the successful use of extended protest and civil disobedience in twentieth-century America. By peacefully demonstrating against legalized segregation in the South, black and some white protesters drew the nation's attention to the discrepancy between the American values of equality and democracy and the southern laws that separated blacks from whites in every aspect of life. Protesters used tactics such as sit-ins, marches, and boycotts. Confrontations with authorities often won protesters national attention and public support, which eventually led to change. (See the box "Organizing Protest: The Montgomery Bus Boycott.")

All tactics can be effective, but some lend themselves better to some groups than others. Business groups with great financial resources can pay for skillful lobbyists and donate to political candidates. Labor unions have many members and can help candidates canvass and get out the vote. Public interest groups rely on activating public opinion and, where members are intensely committed to a cause, protest.

Violence

Sometimes groups become so frustrated and extreme that they move from routine ways of lobbying and nonviolent

The 1955 Montgomery, Alabama, bus boycott was the first successful civil rights protest, and it brought its twenty-six-year-old leader, Dr. Martin Luther King, Jr., to national prominence. Montgomery, like most southern cities, required blacks to sit in the back of public buses while whites sat in the front. The dividing line between the two was a "no man's land" where blacks could sit if there were no whites. If whites needed the seats, blacks had to give them up and move to the back.

One afternoon, Rosa Parks, a seamstress at a local department store and a leader in the local chapter of the National Association for the Advancement of Colored People (NAACP), boarded the bus to go home. The bus was filled, and when a white man boarded, the driver called on the four blacks behind the whites to move to the back. Three got up and moved, but Mrs. Parks, tired from a long day and of the injustice of always having to move for white people, said she did not have to move because she was in "no man's land." Under a law that gave him the authority to enforce segregation, the bus driver arrested her.

That evening a group of black women professors at the black state college in Montgomery, led by Jo Ann Robinson, drafted a letter of protest. They called on blacks to stay off the buses on Monday to protest the arrest. They worked through the night making thirty-five' thousand copies of their letter to distribute to Montgomery's black residents. Fearful for their jobs and concerned that the state would cut funds to the black college if it became known they had used state facilities to produce the letter, they worked quickly and quietly.

The following day black leaders met and agreed to the boycott. More leaflets were drafted calling on blacks to stay off the buses on Monday. On Sunday, black ministers encouraged their members to support the boycott, and on Monday, 90 percent of the blacks walked to work, rode in black-owned taxis, or shared rides in private cars. The boycott inspired confidence and pride in the black community and signaled a subtle change in the opinions of blacks toward race relations. This was obvious when, as nervous white police looked on, hundreds of blacks jammed the courthouse to see that Rosa Parks was safely released after her formal conviction. And it was obvious later that evening at a mass rally when Martin Luther King cried out, "There comes a time when people get tired of being trampled over by the iron feet of oppression. There comes a time when people get tired of being pushed out of the glittering sunlight of life's July, and left standing amidst the piercing chill of an Alpine November." After noting that the glory of American democracy is the right to protest, King appealed to the strong religious faith of the crowd, "If we are wrong, God Almighty is wrong. . . . If we are wrong, Jesus of Nazareth was merely a utopian dreamer. . . . If we are wrong, justice is a lie." These words and this speech established King as a charismatic leader for the civil rights movement.

Each day of the boycott was a trial for blacks and their leaders. Thousands

but illegal protest to violence and destruction. Examples include violence by the Ku Klux Klan in the late nineteenth and twentieth centuries against African Americans and sometimes their supporters; assaults by strike breakers employed by company owners against union organizers in the early twentieth century; violence by "prolife" anti-abortion forces, including burning abortion clinics and murdering abortion providers; and right-wing militia adherents who in 1995 blew up the Oklahoma City federal building, killing 168 people.

There is no evidence that these tactics work well in bringing permanent social change, though they are sometimes effective in intimidating opponents and delaying such change.

Success of Interest Groups

Although no interest group gets everything it wants from government, some are more successful than others. Politics is not a game of chance, where luck determines winners and losers. Knowing what to do and how to do it—strategy and tactics—are important, as are resources, competition, and goals.

Resources

Although large size does not guarantee success, large groups have advantages. They can get the attention of public officials by claiming to speak for more people or by threatening to mobilize members against them. Part of the airlines' success in securing a government bailout was the thousands of employees spread throughout the nation that were threatened with layoffs.

The geographical distribution of group members is also important. Because organized labor is concentrated in the Northeast, it has less influence in other parts of the country, particularly in lobbying Congress. The Chamber of Commerce, on the other hand, has members and influence throughout the country.

A group with well-educated members has an advantage because highly educated people are more likely than others to communicate with public officials and contribute to lobbying efforts.

Rosa Parks being fingerprinted after her arrest.

had to find a way to get to work and leaders struggled to keep a massive carpool going. However, each evening's rally built up morale for the next day's boycott. Later the rallies became prayer services, as the black community prayed for strength to keep on walking, for courage to remain nonviolent, and for guidance to those who oppressed them.

The city bus line was losing money. City leaders urged more whites to ride the bus to make up lost revenue, but few did. Recognizing that the boycott could not go on forever, black leaders agreed to end it if the rules regarding the seating of blacks in "no man's land" were relaxed. Thinking they were on the verge of breaking the boycott, the city leaders refused. Police began to harass carpoolers and issue bogus tickets for trumped-up violations. Then the city leaders issued an ultimatum: Settle or face arrest. A white grand jury indicted more than one hundred boycott leaders for the alleged crime of organizing the protest. In the spirit of nonviolence, the black leaders, including King, surrendered.

The decision to arrest the leaders proved to be the turning point of the boycott. The editor of the local white paper said it was "the dumbest act that has ever been done in Montgomery."[1] With the mass arrests, the boycott finally received national attention. Reporters from all over the world streamed into Montgomery to cover the story. The publicity brought public and financial support. The arrests caused the boycott to become a national event and its leader, Martin Luther King, a national figure. A year later, the U.S. Supreme Court declared Alabama's local and state laws requiring segregation in buses unconstitutional, and when the city complied with the Court's order, the boycott ended.

Rosa Parks became a hero of the civil rights movement. She has been honored many times since then, and millions saw her appearance at the 1988 Democratic National Convention.

1. Taylor Branch, *Parting the Waters: America in the King Years* (New York: Simon & Schuster, 1988), 83.
SOURCE: Taylor Branch, *Parting the Waters: America in the King Years* (New York: Simon & Schuster, 1988), Chapters 4 and 5; and Juan Williams, *Eyes on the Prize* (New York: Viking, 1987).

Group cohesion and intensity are also advantages. Public officials are unlikely to respond to a group if it cannot agree on what it wants or if it does not appear to feel very strongly about its position. In recent years, the NAACP has suffered from deep splits within its leadership. Some of this is over tactics. Should the organization be more confrontational and aggressive? Or should it work cooperatively within the system to secure its goals? Some is over allies. Should the NAACP work with groups like Louis Farrakhan's Nation of Islam or restrict itself to more moderate and mainstream civil rights organizations? Unresolved conflicts such as these undermine a group's claim and diminish the likelihood of success.

A large **market share,** the number of members in a group compared to its potential membership, is another advantage. For years, the AMA enrolled a large percentage (70 percent or more) of the nation's doctors as members. As its membership (as a percentage of the total number of doctors) declined, so did its influence.

The more money a group has, the more successful it will be. Not only does money buy skilled lobbyists and access to elected officials, it is also necessary for indirect lobbying efforts.

Knowledge is a major resource, too. If leaders of a group are experts in a policy area, they are more apt to get the attention of public officials. Knowledge of how things get done in Washington is also helpful, which is why many groups employ former members of Congress and the executive branch as lobbyists.

When Bob Dole resigned from the Senate in 1995 to run for president, he indicated that if he lost the presidency, he would have no place to go but back to his hometown of Russell, Kansas. If he had done that, he would have been quite unusual. Few members of Congress return to their roots once their political careers are over. Most move into high-paying positions with the dozens of law firms in Washington that lobby government. Indeed, Dole went to work for one that includes former senator and treasury secretary Lloyd Bentsen and former Senate majority leader George Mitchell. The firm refers to Dole and the others as our "rock stars." Dole's job is to "make rain," which means recruiting clients who will bring in millions of dollars for his firm's

168 other lawyers and lobbyists. Dole's motto is "a client a day."[137]

Finally, public image is important. A negative public image often troubles new, change-oriented groups, such as the animal rights movement. Many of the country's traditional interest groups, big business and organized labor, also suffer from a poor image, being viewed as too powerful and self-serving. A recent poll revealed 37 percent of Americans trust union leaders to tell the truth, and 43 percent trust business leaders (this poll was taken before the stream of revelations about corporate misdeeds in spring 2002).[138]

Few groups are blessed with all resources, but the more resources a group has, the better its chances of getting what it wants from government.

Competition and Goals

Success also depends on group competition and goals. Many groups are successful because they face weak opponents. Supporters of gun control have public opinion on their side, but their main lobbying group, the National Council to Control Handguns, has a membership and budget that are only a fraction of the NRA's. Used car dealers successfully lobbied against "the lemon law," which would have required them to tell customers of any defects in cars. Few lobbyists represented the other side. These mismatches between groups occur frequently on highly technical issues where one side has more expertise, the public has little interest, or both. Some groups—namely corporations—have no opponents at all in lobbying for government contracts, regulatory waivers, and government subsidies.[139] Such benefits cost taxpayers billions, but they are never mobilized to challenge them. The accountancy profession's well-organized lobbying against federal rules changes to tighten regulation over the profession had few opponents until Enron's financial dishonesty and auditor Arthur Andersen's complicity in it were revealed.

When a group competes with other groups of nearly equal resources, the outcome is often a compromise or a stalemate. The Clean Air Act was not rewritten for years because the auto industry, which wanted a weaker law, and the environmental lobby, which wanted a tougher one, were about equal in strength. The increased clout of the environmental forces finally led to a strengthening of the law in 1990.

Groups that work to preserve the status quo are generally more successful than groups promoting change; it is usually easier to prevent government action than to bring it about. Separation of powers among the Congress, executive branch, and the courts; checks and balances between and among the branches; and division of authority between the states and national government provide interest groups with numerous points in the political process to exercise influence. Groups wishing to change policy have to persuade officials throughout the political process to go along; groups opposed to change only have to persuade officials at one point in the process. Groups promoting change must win over the House, Senate, White House, bureaucracy, and courts; groups against change need convince only one of them.

Groups are more likely to be successful in securing very narrow and specific benefits than they are in promoting broad policy changes. For example, corporations are concerned with broad policy issues, but they are more likely to be successful in obtaining exemptions from major policy initiatives than they are in winning or losing on the policy itself. The tax code is riddled with exemptions for corporations; the beneficiaries are rarely identified by name. The 1986 changes in the tax code contained an exemption for Phillips Petroleum, identified in the bill as a "corporation incorporated on June 13, 1917, which has its principal place of business in Bartlesville, Oklahoma."[140] Phillips was not concerned about the basic tax changes because it was not affected by them. Such exemptions are unlikely to receive media attention or become controversial. In this way, politicians are able to satisfy a major interest group without risking a hostile public reaction.

Conclusion: Do Interest Groups Help Make Government Responsive?

Interest groups provide representation that helps make government more responsive. Although elected officials are representatives, they cannot adequately represent all interests in a diverse society. Interest groups pick up some of the slack by representing the views and opinions of their members and constituents and communicating these to political decision makers. This does not mean that all members agree with everything group leaders say or do or that group leaders are accountable to their members. Group leaders often develop perspectives somewhat different from those of their members. In most instances, however, groups do represent and speak for at least some of the interests of their members. In voluntary organizations particularly, leaders are likely to reflect the interests of their members. If they do not, members can simply exercise their option to leave. Even "checkbook" members can withhold their support if they disagree with group leaders.

Interest groups do not represent, however, all interests or all interests equally. In 1960, E. E. Schattschneider described the pressure system as small in terms of members and biased toward business and the wealthy. At

WHO CAN TAKE OUR GOVERNMENT BACK FROM THE SPECIAL INTEREST GROUPS? THE AMERICAN VOTER, THAT'S WHO-

that time no more than 1,500 groups were included, and more than 50 percent represented either corporations or trade and business associations.[141] Few groups represented consumers, taxpayers, the environment, women, and minorities.

The pressure system has changed since Schattschneider wrote, but its bias remains. The number of interest groups exploded in the 1960s and 1970s, with many of the new groups representing consumers, environmentalists, minorities, and other nonbusiness interests, but these were more than offset by an increase in the number of corporations in the pressure system. For those who would argue that America is a pluralist society where all groups are represented and the product of the struggle is balanced and fair, Schattschneider's observation from the 1960s remains valid today: "The flaw in the pluralist heaven is that the angelic chorus sings with an upper class accent."[142]

Business interests still dominate, as noted earlier. Indeed, business has a greater presence in Washington today than it did in the 1960s. Nearly two-thirds of the groups in Washington at last count represented either

corporations or trade associations. Groups representing minorities, women, the poor, and elderly are less than 10 percent of all groups with an office in Washington and only 5 percent of all groups that lobby.

This bias in the pressure system is a big advantage for business and wealthy interests, and it is increasing. Over the past three decades, business groups have gained in numbers and influence relative to other groups. Labor unions and the Democratic Party, strong supporters of legislation to improve the welfare of the working class, often in opposition to business and wealthy interests, have declined in the case of labor and shifted their focus, in the case of the Democratic Party. As one political analyst put it, "The nature of representative government in the United States has changed, so that more and more of the weight of influence in Washington comes from interest groups, not voters."[143] And interest groups are predominantly looking out for the interests of business. This is not to say that working- and middle-class Americans, or at least some of them, do not benefit from policies favoring the interests of business. But a system in which business interests must compete on a more equal basis with the interests of labor and other groups is likely to be more sensitive to the needs of average men and women.

How can we preserve the constitutional rights of interest groups to form and petition government and still keep government responsive to the needs of its citizens? Recognizing and correcting imbalances in group strength is not simple or easy. Reformers have waged a decades-long battle to limit financial contributions of interest groups to candidates (a topic we will discuss in greater detail in Chapter 9). But a balance of power in interests will more likely occur by mobilization of groups opposed to the status quo. We certainly would not expect that groups currently enjoying an advantage will easily give it up.

EPILOGUE

The Tobacco Industry Fights Back

With the survival of the industry at stake, not to mention high-paying jobs, Steven Goldstone and the other tobacco CEOs decided to fight by changing public opinion. Although Congress will ultimately decide the issue of liability from lawsuits, the public can push Congress one way or the other, particularly in an election year.

The tobacco industry decided to try to change the terms of the debate. The industry launched a massive advertising campaign portraying government efforts to regulate tobacco as just another attempt by "big government" to spend the "hard earned dollars of the American taxpayer" on a venture that will create another "government bu-

reaucracy" and still not solve the problem. The industry cast itself as a victim targeted by government. Goldstone commented, "I am very confident that the American people are more willing to listen than the people in Washington are."[144]

The industry's Republican allies were also more comfortable when the debate turned to taxes rather than teen smoking. Indeed, some, including Speaker Gingrich, who had backed away from tobacco in the fear that Clinton would use the issue against the Republicans, joined with the industry in its efforts to portray tobacco legislation as a back-door attempt to raise taxes and expand government regulation. Another central idea of the campaign was to convince Americans that a violent black market in cigarettes might develop if the legislation passed.[145] The campaign, costing $40 million, included a national radio, television, and newspaper ad campaign, along with one directed at members of Congress and opinion elites; an 800 number for citizens to call for more information, company spokespersons available to make the industry's case to the media and community and civics groups; a direct mail campaign enlisting potential allies such as tobacco employees, shareholders, distributors, and retailers; and a Web site.

Lawmakers' offices were suddenly deluged with calls and postcards from people opposing the bill. Even though the legislation's proponents responded with an ad campaign of their own, the newly created public opposition[146] provided some in Congress with a way to vote against what was initially a popular bill. As a result, the tobacco legislation, which seemed assured of passage in May 1998, died in June. Republicans wishing to avoid the appearance of knuckling under to an industry that contributes heavily to their party vowed to pass a leaner, less costly bill directed at curbing teen smoking.[147]

"If you still want to belong to an organization dedicated to killing Americans, there's always the tobacco lobby."

The tobacco industry ultimately settled with the states, agreeing to pay $246 million over twenty-five years to offset the cost of state expenditures for tobacco-related illnesses. The money was to be used to prevent smoking, which was responsible for one in five deaths in America. Then Governor of Wisconsin and current Secretary of Health and Human Services Tommy Thompson declared states could finally "do the things we all want to do, and that's the cessation of smoking, especially with our young."[148] However, only a few states are using their windfall to fight smoking.[149] Less than 5 percent of the $33 billion paid out to date has gone to prevent smoking. With declining state revenues, many have channeled settlement monies to other things. New York used a portion of its settlement to purchase new carts and sprinklers for public golf courses. Alabama used some of its settlement to build factories for Honda, Mercedes-Benz, and Lockheed Martin. It gave some of the money to public schools to fight satanic cults. Believe it or not, North Carolina, the nation's largest tobacco-producing state, gave three-quarters of their $59 million settlement to tobacco producers. The money paid for tobacco-curing equipment for farmers, a new tobacco auction hall, a video to greet visitors to a state-funded tobacco museum, and plumbing for a new tobacco-processing plant. In Virginia, $2 million went to a cigarette company that later sued the state to overturn the settlement. Other states have invested their settlement in tobacco company stocks. Texas channeled $3.6 million to investments in major cigarette manufacturers.[150]

In the meantime, the Supreme Court ruled that the federal Food and Drug Administration lacked authority to regulate tobacco as a drug, and the Congress and president are yet to take any action. In June 2002, a California judge fined RJ Reynolds $20 million, ruling that the company violated terms of its agreement by running ads in magazines aimed at teenagers. The company said it will appeal.

To learn more about Steven Goldstone and the tobacco industry, go to this chapter's "You Are There" exercises on the text Web site.

Key Terms

interest groups

lobbying

political action committees (PACs)

private interest groups

public interest groups

single-issue groups

coalitions

civil disobedience

market share

Further Reading

Jeffrey M. Berry, *The Interest Group Society*, 2d ed. (Boston: Little, Brown, 1989). A general survey of interest groups in American politics. It covers political action committees, lobbyists and lobbying, the internal dynamics of groups, and the problems that interest groups present to society.

Jeffrey Birnbaum, *The Lobbyists: How Influence Peddlers Get Their Way in Washington* (New York: Times Books, 1993). A study of lobbyists' activities surrounding major issues considered by Congress in the 1989–1990 session.

Osha Gray Davidson, *The NRA and the Battle for Gun Control* (Ames: University of Iowa Press, 1998). A useful account of how the battles over gun control are fought in Congress.

Michael Pertschuk, *Giant Killers* (New York: Norton, 1986). How low-budget lobbies can sometimes defeat the big guys by superior organization, tactics, and luck.

E. E. Schattschneider, *The Semi-sovereign People* (New York: Holt, 1975). A classical statement on how interest group politics benefit business and corporate interests by limiting the involvement of citizens in the political process.

Ernest Wittenberg and Elisabeth Wittenberg, *How to Win in Washington: Very Practical Advice about Lobbying, the Grassroots and the Media* (Cambridge, Mass.: Blackwell, 1989). A "how-to" book for average citizens.

Electronic Resources

Most of the organizations discussed in the chapter have their own home pages. Here is a sampling:

www.aflcio.org/home.html
The home page of the largest union in America, the AFL-CIO. It contains official union documents and press releases, news on issues important to the labor movement, a link to information on high corporate executive salaries in the United States, and links to other labor-related groups.

www.nam.org/
The National Association of Manufacturers' Web page. It contains material similar to that on the AFL-CIO page but from a business perspective.

www.fb.com/
The Farm Bureau's Web page. It contains similar information from the perspective of the more prosperous and conservative sector of agriculture, along with updates on the weather and a menu where you can register your favorite summertime activities.

www.nwf.org
The home page of the National Wildlife Federation, a major environmental group focuses on education about wild life and outdoor places.

www.thirdwavefoundation.org/
The Third Wave Foundation is the only national activist philanthropic organization for young women. The organization supports and involves young women in a broad range of movements from campaigning for a living wage, environmental protection, and reproductive rights.

www.aarp.org/
The AARP's excellent Web site. It allows you to learn about the AARP's position and congressional testimony on issues affecting the elderly, review the myriad of benefits offered by the organization, and much more.

www.apsanet.org/
The American Political Science Association's home page. Use it to find out about the organization to which your professor might belong.

www.house.gov/commerce-TobaccoDocs/ documents.html
This site allows you to read internal tobacco industry documents released by Congress.

Info Trac College Edition

Search for the following articles in the InfoTrac database:

Blakeslee, Nate. "A Naked Emperor Disrobed: Or, How Enron Did Texas," *The Nation* (March 4, 2002).

Dinan, John. "State Government Influence in the National Policy Process: Lessons from the 104th Congress," *Publius* (Spring 1997).

Golden, Marissa Martino. "Interest Groups in the Rule-Making Process: Who Participates? Whose Voices Get Heard?" *Journal of Public Administration Research and Theory* (April 1998).

Smith, Jonathan C. "Foreign Policy for Sale? Interest Group Influence on President Clinton's Cuba Policy, August 1994," *Presidential Studies Quarterly* (Winter 1998).

For more articles, enter

"pressure groups" in the Subject Guide;

"lobbying" in the Subject Guide;

"lobbyists" in the Subject Guide.

American Government Resources

Visit the Political Behavior section of the Wadsworth American Government Resources Web site (politicalscience.wadsworth.com/amgov/) for a variety of tools to help you explore interest groups further. Included are simulations, video clips, Microcase exercises, and a wealth of other activities.

Senator Jim Jeffords.

Should You Switch Parties?[1]

ou are Jim Jeffords, Republican senator from Vermont. Elected to the U.S. Senate in 1988, you were reelected in 1994 and again in 2000. Now it is spring 2001, and you are considering whether to leave the Republican Party. It's a decision that is important not only to you but to the U.S. Senate, too. If you switch, control of the Senate—that is, its majority party—will move from the Republicans to the Democrats.

You've been in politics most of your adult life. It's difficult to recall when you first thought of yourself as a Republican, but you mark the start of your political career in 1963 when at the age of twenty-nine you were chosen Republican Party chair in Shrewsbury, your hometown. Soon thereafter, you were elected to the Vermont state senate. You then served as state attorney general for four years and were elected to your first of eight terms in the U.S. House in 1974.

Ideologically you are a moderate, with one of the more liberal voting records among your Republican Senate colleagues. Throughout your career both in the House and Senate, you often found yourself voting with the opposition Democrats. As a member of the House, you voted against President Reagan's tax cut and, as a member of the Senate, against the confirmation of the senior Bush's conservative nominee to the Supreme Court, Clarence Thomas. Unlike most other

Republicans, you supported the Brady bill requiring a waiting period for the purchase of a handgun and opposed development of the Strategic Defense Initiative, a Reagan-era experimental proposal with the goal of shielding the United States from incoming missiles (resurrected more recently in the current Bush administration). You were the only Republican to cosponsor the Clinton health care reform proposal, and you were one of five Republicans to vote to acquit President Clinton on both articles of impeachment, preferring to censure him instead. Earlier this year, you opposed President Bush's $1.6 trillion tax cut, arguing that it was too costly and tilted toward the rich.

More than most other senators, you vote with the opposition party when a majority of Republicans line up against a majority of Democrats. You have voted with Republicans more since they gained control of the Senate in 1995, but you continue to be among the lowest in support of your party. While your defections from the party's positions have angered Senate Republicans and more recently President Bush, they seem quite consistent with the temperament and predispositions of your very independent state.

Your moderate voting record, particularly during your career in the House and your first term in the Senate, were not an issue. American political parties, if they are anything, are pragmatic, willing to abide members who take positions at odds with the party's majority, particularly if they reflect the wishes of a member's constituency. However, in recent years parties have become more distinct in their policy positions. The Republican Party, in particular, has moved noticeably to the right as religious conservatives have gained prominence. Moderates have become an endangered species in the party. There were nine when you joined the Senate in 1989. Today, there are five, including you. Your brand of Republicanism, conservative on fiscal issues but liberal on social issues, no longer seems welcome in the party.

Indeed, the party has shown its disdain. In 1990, you lost the job of Senate Conference chair, the number three leadership position in the party, with responsibility of presiding at party caucuses (meetings of Senate Republicans) where positions and strategy are debated and developed. Following your support of a Democratic campaign finance reform bill, conservative Texas Republican Senator Phil Gramm tore your photograph off the wall in the party's Senate campaign committee office, fuming "They're [a reference to you and Senator David Durenberger (R-Minn)] not Republicans anymore."[2] More recently, conservatives wanted to strip you of your chairmanship of the Health, Education, Labor and Pensions Committee in the Senate, but Majority Leader Trent Lott from Mississippi held them at bay, making an appeal to party unity. While you and Lott often disagree on the issues, you remain friends, singing together in a quartet known as the Singing Senators. Lott who introduces the quartet at social functions, identifies you as the senator "on my left, my far left."[3]

Winning the presidency with less than a majority of the popular vote and the smallest margin in modern history, Bush initially struck a conciliatory tone, pledging to work with the Democrats in a Senate evenly divided between the parties. His claim to end the partisan

bickering and work toward bipartisan solutions gives you reason to believe that perhaps the party needs moderates like you. News shows speculated on the potential new influence of moderates in the party to accomplish Bush's bipartisan agenda.

However, your optimism fades quickly. In spite of the rhetoric, the new Bush administration and Republican leaders in the House and Senate continue with an aggressively conservative agenda and the slights continue. In January, you were rebuffed in an attempt to secure a seat on the Environmental and Public Work Committee, an assignment important to Vermont. Acid rain from midwestern utilities continues to plague the state. Your response, "I think Republicans would rather not see the environmental side strengthened on the committee. And I am an environmentalist."[4] You have been a supporter of the environment and were one of ten Republicans endorsed by the Sierra Club in the 2000 election. Along with being denied a seat on Environment and Public Works, you were snubbed by the White House when Judd Gregg, a conservative senator from New Hampshire, was made the point man on an education bill being considered by the Education Committee that you chair. The White House also failed to invite you to a teacher-of-the-year event in the Rose Garden where a Vermont social studies teacher was honored. Normally, senators from the state of the honoree are invited to these sorts of White House functions.

You have reached a point where you no longer feel comfortable with or a part of the Republican Party. What do you do? You can switch to the Democrat party. Senate Democrats have been wooing you for some time. They have told you, should you switch, you may chair Environmental and Public Works, the seat denied you by Republicans. That would be possible because with your switch, the Democrats would become a majority and get to name the committee chairs.

In fact, if the Senate were not equally divided between the parties, your switch would not be much of a concern. Senators have switched parties before. New Hampshire senator Bob Smith jumped from independent to Republican in 2000, reversing a switch the year before from Republican to independent. Nothing much changed. This time a shift of one will put the Democrats in control. Tom Daschle (D-S.D.) will be majority leader with the power to set the Senate's agenda. Only issues approved by Daschle and the Democrats will come up for a vote. Democrats will chair committees where the Senate does its work. Edward Kennedy (D-Mass.) will replace you on Health, Education, Labor and Pensions. Patrick Leahy (D-Vt.) will chair the Judiciary committee in place of Orrin Hatch (R-Utah). Carl Levin (D-Mich.) will replace John Warner (R-Va.) on Armed Services. In short, liberals and moderates will replace conservatives. Democrats will also enjoy a majority on all committees, whereas now they are a minority.

Needless to say, such a shift will make it more difficult for President Bush to pursue his agenda. Democrats will be able to block the President or seek concessions in exchange for their support. Former Republican senator Warren Rudman of New Hampshire said that Washington "will become a city of compromise. There will be no laying down of agendas, take it or leave it."[5] One thing for sure, Bush's nominees to the federal courts are likely to move more slowly and be scrutinized more closely.

You also wonder about your supporters in Vermont. Party workers helped you and no doubt at least some voters voted for you because you are a Republican. Would you be treating them fairly by jumping ship now, so soon after the election?

Rather than join the Democrats, you could declare yourself an independent. Though less of a change than switching parties, your move would have the same effect on Senate organization.

You would no longer vote with the Republicans in choosing Senate officers, so the Democrats would be in charge. This might be more attractive to you. It is less of a repudiation of the party to which you have given a great deal and represents a change that you can accommodate more easily psychologically. Your Vermont constituency might be less concerned. But, from the perspective of your Republican colleagues, it is likely to have the same effect as switching parties.

A third option is to stay where you are. Even though the number of moderates in the party is small, should you leave, the number will be even smaller and the likelihood will be increased that the party will move further to the right. To leave would simply bring about more quickly a party committed to policies that you find objectionable. Moreover, if and when the president does seek accommodation with the Democrats, you might be able to play an important role.

As word of your possible defection spreads, you hear from every quarter, including the White House. You meet with Vice President Cheney and then President Bush. The president tells you "you can get more done for your state and the people who supported you if you remain in the party."[6] A half dozen GOP colleagues corral you in a room off the Senate floor and ask, "Jim, do you really believe you can further your dreams and aspirations by doing this?"[7] They tell you that the White House has pledged more money for education, something you feel very strongly about and that you may chair the Health, Education, Labor and Pensions committee for as long as you want it. They speak of lost jobs for hundreds of Republican staffers in Congress if you switch and the loss of coveted committee chairs that your Republican colleagues had worked long and hard to secure.

It's now up to you. What do you decide? Become a Democrat? Stay a Republican? Or compromise and become an independent?

George Washington warned against the "baneful" effects of parties and described them as the people's worst enemies. More recently, a respected political scientist, E. E. Schattschneider, argued that "political parties created democracy and that democracy was impossible without them."[8] The public echoes these contradictory views. Many believe that parties create conflict where none exists, yet most identify with one of the two major parties.[9]

These same feelings exist among candidates for office. They often bypass political parties by establishing their own personal campaign organizations and raising their own funds. If elected, they sometimes do not follow the party line. At the same time, candidates for national and state offices are nominated in the name of political parties, they rely on parties for assistance, and they have little chance of winning unless they are Democrats or Republicans.

This chapter examines American political parties to see why they are important and why many observers believe that if they become less important and effective, government will be less accountable to the people.

What Are Political Parties?

Political parties are a major link between people and government. They provide a way for the public to have a say in who serves in government and what policies government chooses. Political parties are organizations that seek to control government by recruiting, nominating, and electing members to public office. They consist of three interrelated components: the **party in the electorate,** those who identify with the party; the **party in government,** those who are appointed or elected to office as members of the party; and the formal **party organization,** the party "professionals" who run the party at the national, state, and local levels (see Figure 1).[10]

In linking the public and government policymakers, parties serve several purposes. They help select public officials by recruiting and screening candidates and then providing campaign resources. They help empower citizens by activating and interesting them in politics. Individually, citizens have little power, but collectively, through political parties, they can influence government.

Many voters feel an attachment to a political party, an affiliation they acquire early in life that aids them in deciding among competing candidates. Some voters simply vote their party identification, with little or no knowledge of candidates or issues. But a party vote is, in part, an issue vote. Political parties do have relatively consistent positions on issues, which are clear to most voters, and these differences have become sharper in recent decades. Since the 1930s, the Democratic Party has favored an expanded role for the national government in dealing with the country's economic problems, while the Republican Party has favored minimizing this role, preferring to leave economic issues to the marketplace—that is, the unregulated forces of supply and demand to resolve. Since the 1960s, the parties have also differed on issues related to lifestyle and morality. Here, Republicans favor government action to uphold certain standards of behavior, while Democrats prefer to leave such issues for individuals to decide for themselves. The difference is illustrated on abortion,

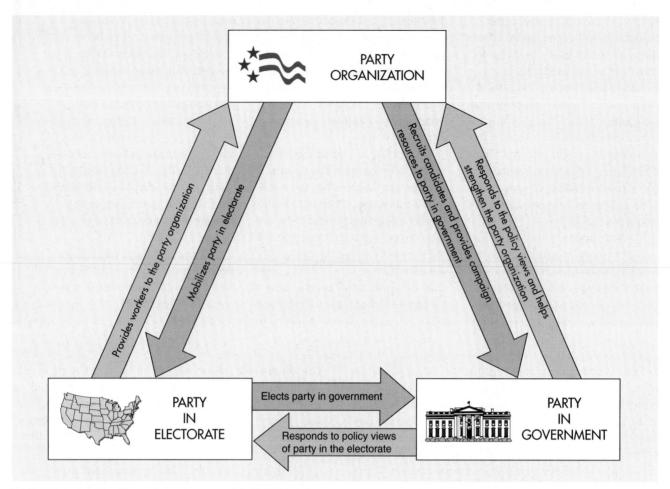

FIGURE 1 ■ The Three Components of Political Parties

where the Republican Party would make it illegal and the Democrat Party would support a woman's right to chose.

Most voters recognize these differences. Knowing a candidate belongs to a party is a clue to the candidate's general preference regarding the role of the national government in areas such as health care, energy, the environment, abortion, and gay rights. Voters therefore do not need to study each candidate's position on such issues in great detail, a difficult and time-consuming task. The party label provides a general understanding of where the candidate stands. This is one reason why Schattschneider believed democracy was impossible without political parties. When citizens select a party, they have a clearer understanding of what their selection means in terms of the policy direction of the nation. Without the party label, citizens have no idea of how their vote for an individual candidate will translate into public policy.

The party in government plays an important role in organizing and operating government; it formulates policy options and ultimately decides which to support or oppose. When political parties represent individuals from widely different backgrounds and interests, parties aid society by aggregating and mediating conflicts and contributing to political and social stability.

It is not fashionable to make the case for political parties these days or point to the contributions they make to popular democracy. Most Americans see political parties as part of the "mess in Washington." Many believe they are responsible for the government's inability to solve the nation's problems and that partisan differences are meaningless squabbles designed to secure political advantage. Many feel that political parties create differences where none exist rather than represent real and legitimate differences in how to solve the nation's problems. But without political parties, politics would be more fragmented, the media and interest groups would be more powerful, and the interests of average men and women would suffer.

Development and Change in the Party System

Most Americans think of the Democratic and Republican Parties as more or less permanent fixtures, and, indeed they have been around a long time. The Democratic Party evolved from the Jacksonian Democrats in

1832, and the Republican Party was founded in 1854. Nevertheless, the current party system is only one of five distinct party systems that have existed in American history (see Figure 2).

In tracing the development of these systems, two things need to be kept in mind. First, parties developed after the nation's founding, grew to be very powerful in the late nineteenth century, and have declined somewhat in influence since then.

Second, there have been periods of stability in the party system when one party has dominated American politics and won most elections. There have also been periods of transition and instability when neither party has dominated, and control of government has been divided between the parties or has shifted back and forth. In transition periods, issues have emerged that have been difficult to resolve, and voters have established new party loyalties based on them. The transition from one stable party system to another is called a **realignment.**

Preparty Politics: The Founders' Views of Political Parties

Most of the Founders viewed political parties as dangerous to stable government. This antiparty feeling was rooted in three basic beliefs. First, the Founders thought parties created and exploited conflicts that undermined consensus on public policy. Second, they thought parties were instruments by which a small and narrow interest could impose its will on society. Third, they believed that parties stifled independent thought and behavior.[11]

James Madison feared political parties as much as interest groups because he felt both pursued selfish interests at the expense of the common good. He referred to both as "factions" in *Federalist* 10. John Adams dreaded what he considered the greatest political evil, the formation of rival political parties.

Therefore, it is not surprising that the Constitution does not mention political parties. Nevertheless,

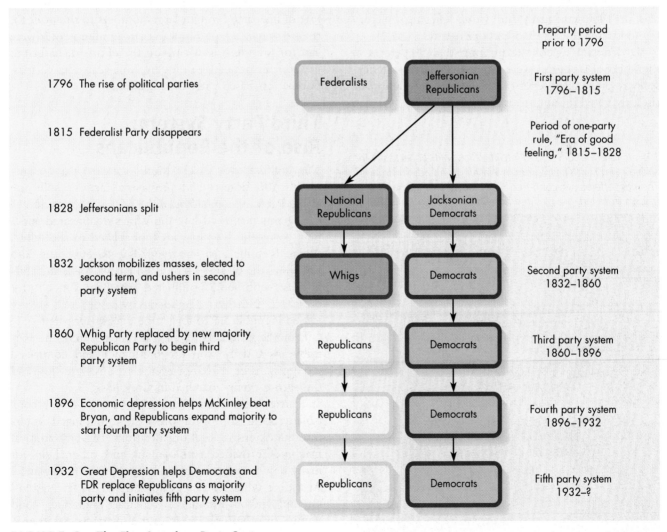

FIGURE 2 ■ **The Five American Party Systems**

it created a system in which parties, or something like them, were inevitable. When the Founders established popular elections as the mechanism for selecting political leaders, an agency for organizing and mobilizing supporters of political candidates was needed. Indeed, despite their initial antiparty feelings, Jefferson and Madison were instrumental in founding the first political party.

First Party System: Development of Parties

With George Washington's unanimous election to the presidency in 1788, it appeared the nation could be governed by consensus. But differences of opinion soon arose. Alexander Hamilton, Washington's secretary of the treasury, supported a strong national government. His following, the Federalists, were opposed by Thomas Jefferson, secretary of state, who feared a strong central government. The conflict led Jefferson to challenge Federalist John Adams for the presidency in 1796. Jefferson lost, but he then recruited able leaders in each state, founded newspapers, established political clubs, and in 1800 ran again and won. Jefferson's victory demonstrated the utility of political parties.

By Jefferson's second term, more than 90 percent of members of Congress were either Federalists or Jeffersonians (later called Jeffersonian Republicans) and consistently voted in support of their party.[12]

The factions that developed into the first political parties were already vying with each other in Washington's administration. Thomas Jefferson (second from left) and Alexander Hamilton (fourth from left) are pictured here with Washington (right).

The Granger Collection, New York

Second Party System: Rise of the Democrats

After a brief period of one-party rule ("the era of good feelings"), the Jeffersonian Republicans split into factions. One of these developed into the Democratic Party, led by Andrew Jackson, who won the presidency in 1828.

Jacksonian Democrats extolled the common person and encouraged popular participation in government. During Jackson's administration, the vote was expanded to all adult white males. Presidential electors were selected in popular elections rather than by state legislatures, and the party convention became the instrument for nominating presidential candidates. No longer did members of the party in Congress select the party's presidential nominee. Instead, conventions opened up decisions to local as well as national party elites.

Many political leaders deplored Jackson's efforts to mobilize the masses. John Quincy Adams called Jackson a "barbarian." An Adams supporter referred to Jackson's victory as "the howl of raving Democracy."[13]

Jackson's popular appeal and the organizational effort of his party brought large numbers to the polls for the first time. By 1828, more than a million votes were cast for president. Building on the efforts of Jefferson, Jackson introduced a uniquely American idea, a mass population-based party organization.

Third Party System: Rise of the Republicans

The conflict over slavery brought a new party alignment. Abolitionists and proslavery factions split the Whig Party, which had been the primary opposition to the Democrats. By 1860, the Whigs disappeared and a new party, the Republicans (not related to the Jeffersonian Republicans), emerged. The Republicans (also known as the GOP—Grand Old Party), reflecting abolitionist sentiment, nominated Abraham Lincoln for president. Northern Democrats who opposed slavery joined Republicans to form a new majority party.

For years after the Civil War (1861–1865), the Republicans usually won the presidency and controlled Congress. After 1876, however, elections were close and the parties evenly matched in Congress.

Parties were strong during this period. They controlled nominations for office and mobilized voters through extensive local organizations. Big-city political machines provided employment and other help for many new immigrants in exchange for their allegiance. At a time when there was no national welfare system, unemployment insurance, medical assistance, food stamps, or other safety nets, parties were crucial in providing assistance for poor families. Local businesses were

In 1828, opponents of Andrew Jackson called him a jackass (left). Political cartoonists and journalists began to use the donkey to symbolize Jackson and the Democratic Party. In the 1870s, Thomas Nast popularized the donkey as a symbol of the party in his cartoons and originated the elephant as a symbol of the Republican Party. His 1874 cartoon (right) showed the Democratic donkey dressed as a lion frightening the other animals of the jungle, including the Republican elephant.

tied to the machine through payoffs to get city contracts. Corruption—vote buying and political payoffs—linked poor immigrants, big business, and party leaders in strong party machines.

Fourth Party System: Republican Dominance

The election of 1896 ushered in another party alignment. Democrat William Jennings Bryan appealed to southerners and farmers of the plains. He played to their hostility toward the Northeast, with its large corporations and growing ethnic working class. His was a religious appeal too, pitting fundamentalists against Catholics. But his appeal was too narrow, and the Democrats were soundly defeated.

During this period a third party, the Progressives, gained strength, chiefly among middle-class Americans concerned with the corruption of big-city machines. The movement championed a number of reforms designed to wrench political control from political parties and the lower-class immigrant groups they served. These included voter registration and the secret ballot, which reduced election fraud; the direct primary, which allowed voters rather than party bosses to nominate candidates for public office; and a merit system, which eliminated political patronage in the awarding of government jobs and contracts. The Progressives never captured the presidency, but their ideas did win favor with a larger audience and were enacted into law. In addition

to checking corruption, the reforms weakened political parties, undermining their capacity to mobilize voters and their ability to use government to meet the needs of the citizens who support them.

Fifth Party System: Democratic Dominance

In the 1920s, the Republicans began to lose support in the cities. The party ignored the plight of poor immigrants and in Congress pushed through quotas limiting immigration from southern and eastern Europe. After the Depression hit in 1929, these immigrants, along with many women voting for the first time, joined traditional Democrats in the South to elect Franklin Roosevelt in 1932. This election reflected another party alignment.

The **New Deal coalition,** composed of city dwellers, blue-collar workers, Catholic and Jewish immigrants, blacks, and southerners, elected Roosevelt to an unprecedented four terms. The coalition was an odd alliance of northern liberals and southern conservatives. It stuck together in the 1930s and 1940s because of Roosevelt's personality and skill and because northerners did not seriously challenge southern racial policies.

But the coalition came unglued after Roosevelt's death. Even though the Democrats dominated Congress most of the time until 1994, they had much less success in winning the presidency. Democrats won the White House only three times after 1964, suggesting that the fifth party system may have ended.

The Republicans, by nominating a popular war hero, General Dwight D. Eisenhower, won the presidency in 1952 and 1956. Although the Democrats regained the White House in 1960, the civil rights movement and the Vietnam War divided them sharply, and they lost again in 1968 and 1972.[14] They won in 1976 by nominating a southerner—Jimmy Carter—and because the Republicans suffered from the Watergate scandal. Then Bill Clinton, another moderate southern governor, was elected in 1992 and 1996 by partially reconstructing the New Deal coalition.

The Post–Fifth Party System: Disengagement and Competition

The fifth party system has clearly changed, but what has replaced it? It is difficult to characterize the current party system in a single phrase, but we can explore several dimensions of it. This post–fifth party era is characterized by a southern realignment, modest realignments nationally, some indicators of dealignment (disengagement from partisanship), and intense party competitiveness.

Southern Realignment

Previous realigning periods were characterized by compelling issues that fracture the unity of the major parties.[15] Before 1860, slavery was such an issue. It divided the Democrats and destroyed the Whigs. In 1932, economic issues led many Republicans away from their party to the Democrats. In the post–fifth party system in the South, race is the issue that has produced a major realignment.

For nearly one hundred years, the South was solidly Democratic. This allegiance stemmed from white opposition to Abraham Lincoln and his Republican party. The Republicans were the party fighting against slavery and to preserve the Union in the American Civil War. They then implemented post–Civil War Reconstruction policies designed to improve the conditions and give some political voice to former slaves.

After the North lost interest in Reconstruction and the well-being of former slaves, African Americans in the South were deprived of their rights to vote (See Chapter 8 for a discussion of this topic). Thus, in the late nineteenth and most of the twentieth century, most African Americans in the South could not vote. (Those who could voted Republican, the party of Lincoln.) The white South controlled the elections and voted solidly Democratic until the 1950s when the Republicans first made some inroads.

At the time he signed the 1964 civil rights bill, President Johnson confided that he believed the event would deliver the South to the Republicans for the next fifty years. As predicted, in 1964 for the first time in more than a century, the Republicans carried several southern states in the presidential election.

Since 1968, Republicans have carried the South in all presidential elections, except for Carter's election in 1976. Even then, a majority of white southerners voted for Ford. Clinton carried his home state, Arkansas, and that of his running mate, Tennessee. He also picked up Louisiana and Georgia, but the Republicans recaptured these states in 2000.

White southerners increasingly vote for Republicans in congressional races, too. Since 1994, they have cast the majority of their votes for Republicans. The shift has led a few conservative Democratic members of Congress to change their party in an effort to take advantage of the changing loyalties of white southerners. Many governors, U.S. house members, and senators from the eleven southern states are Republican.

The change in party identification among white southerners is the main reason that polls have shown a decline in Democratic loyalties nationwide. The shift of white southerners to the Republican Party not only makes the South more Republican but also makes the Republicans more conservative. The change also makes the party system more ideological. The southern Democrats who changed tend to be conservatives and are more ideologically compatible with policies of the Republican Party.

The race issue, which spurred this realignment in the 1960s, continues to play a role. Where white southerners in the 1950s and 1960s claimed "betrayal" by the national Democratic Party for its policies urging equality for blacks, they now say they object to its policies accepting affirmative action for minorities. Black southerners, except for a few elderly ones who retain parental memories of Reconstruction, have largely moved to the Democratic Party. The polarization between the races reflects the national composition of each party. The Republican Party is largely white and the Democratic Party includes almost all the black population.

Modest Realignment

Realignment is not so clear outside the South. Although some issues have arisen that have brought about modest shifts in party allegiance, there has been no major issue that has realigned party coalitions dramatically.[16] These shifts that did occur largely took place in the 1970s and 1980s, particularly in response to Ronald Reagan.

The dominant Democratic coalition became less cohesive than in the heyday of the fifth party system. Blue-collar ethnics and Catholics found the Democrats much less attractive.[17] As New Deal policies succeeded, blue-collar workers became much less concerned with economic security and turned their attention to other issues. Many were upset with the party's promotion of civil rights. Divisions in the party over the Vietnam War pushed many who were in favor of the war, particularly blue-collar union members, to the Republicans. Some objected to the Democratic Party's positions on social issues such as opposition to capital punishment, prayer in schools, and support for abortion and the rights of criminal defendants.

In the 1980s, economic concerns returned. Blue-collar workers found their standard of living eroding and felt left behind.[18] This did not move all of them back to their Democratic roots, however. Many resented what they believed to be the Democrats' favoritism toward minorities and policies that seemed to free citizens from personal responsibility for their actions (for example, crime policies that some saw as "coddling criminals"). The big-city machines that once mobilized workers to vote Democratic are gone, and the labor unions, which did the same, were dramatically weakened. Ronald Reagan strongly appealed to blue collar workers and was successful in winning a large minority of them.

But the Republican coalition that won the presidential elections in 1980 to 1988 was not a stable one and did not reflect a permanent realignment. As one strategist put it later, "The Reagan coalition is not enough to win anymore."[19] The Clinton victories of 1992 and 1996 brought back many blue-collar workers and Catholics who had defected from the Democrats in the 1970s and 1980s. Other modest changes also led to these Democratic victories.

Although large majorities of small-business people, managers, and corporate executives remain in the Republican party, the Democrats made inroads into some other historically Republican groups. Northern white Protestants and white-collar workers are somewhat less Republican than they used to be. Many of them are employed by government and more sympathetic to government's role in solving social problems. The Democrats also increasingly appeal to better-educated voters, who support Democratic initiatives such as health care reform, commitment to the environment, and abortion rights.[20] In the closing decades of the twentieth century, the relationship between income and party allegiance weakened considerably and in some instances reversed. Many well-educated professionals (lawyers, doctors, scientists, and academics) have found a new home in the Democratic Party. In 2000, Al Gore did quite well in the nation's most affluent communities, winning better than 70 percent of the vote in some, while George Bush ran well in traditional bastions of Democratic strength such as the hills of West Virginia, Kentucky and Tennessee.[21]

Andy Levin

The Republican Party has tried to pull blue-collar workers away from their traditional home in the Democratic Party. Former President Ronald Reagan was especially effective in luring these voters.

The Democratic Party remains strong among African Americans, the growing Hispanic community, and white union members. The increasing numbers of Hispanic voters and working and single mothers are also providing more Democratic voters.

Religious belief was a factor in the New Deal coalition as Catholic and Jewish voters, many of them immigrants or children of immigrants, tended to be Democrats. Protestants tended to be Republicans. In the post–fifth party system, as cultural and social issues have gained strength relative to economic ones, new religious alignments are coming into play. Jews are still overwhelmingly Democratic, and a majority of Catholics are, too. Now the partisan division seems to be between those who are very religious and those who are not so religious. In fact, church attendance is more highly correlated with partisanship than either income or education. Among weekly church goers, Bush won 80 percent of the vote in 2000. For those who never attend, Gore won 60 percent.[22]

Other demographic shifts in the population add further instability to the coalitions. Immigration is changing the ethnic composition of the electorate. Both parties are trying to hold their bases of support and reach out to new groups. Hispanics are now 7 percent of the electorate, double that in California and Texas. Though most Hispanics vote Democrat, Republicans are also attempting to woo their vote. Asian voters have received less attention, but they also are a growing part of the electorate. Traditionally Republican, in 2000, they voted heavily Democratic.

The percentage of working women has also increased significantly. Working women have been voting Democratic by large margins, and in 2000, they preferred Gore to Bush by 19 percent.

Though Americans are still a "churchgoing" people compared to those in most other modernized nations, these numbers are declining. The proportions of voters who are nonreligious (or who may be religious but who profess other than Christian or Jewish faiths) rose from 5 to 16 percent since 1972, and nonchurchgoers are now one-third of the electorate.

Both Republicans and Democrats are trying to reach these growing groups. Right now, the demographic shifts favor the Democrats, and Republican strategists see a need to appeal to the growing number of Hispanics, secular (nonreligious) voters, working women, and socially tolerant, well-educated professionals.[23] These shifts, suggests one Republican strategist, require the party to "change the language of its message from a 'masculine' emphasis on 'order' and 'strength' to a more 'feminine' focus on fairness, compassion, and equality of opportunity.[24] Much like the Democrats under Clinton, Republicans feel some pressure to move or appear to move to the center.

Bush's centrist rhetoric in 2000 was an attempt to appeal to these voters.

The Republican problem is illustrated by the fact that if whites, blacks, and Hispanics vote in 2004 as they did in 2000, Bush would lose both the popular and electoral college vote. That is because of the increasing weight of California and Texas and other southwestern states in that college.[25]

Dealignment?

Some argue that the changes we have been describing have not led to a full-fledged realignment because citizens are disengaged from politics. *Dealignment* is the term used to describe that. **Dealignment** is a situation in which voters do not have strong party allegiances. Citizens who think parties are not important are unlikely to vote for the opposition when the party in power fails to deal with the nation's problems. Nor are independents likely to be drawn to a political party in search of answers to national problems. Perhaps neither party has offered a program sufficient to realign the electorate on a long-term basis in their favor.

Is there evidence for dealignment? One evidence is **ticket splitting,** voting for a member of one party for one office but a member of another party for a different one. Voters who split their ticket indicate that personalities, issues, or something else other than partisanship is driving their vote. Ticket splitting reached an all-time

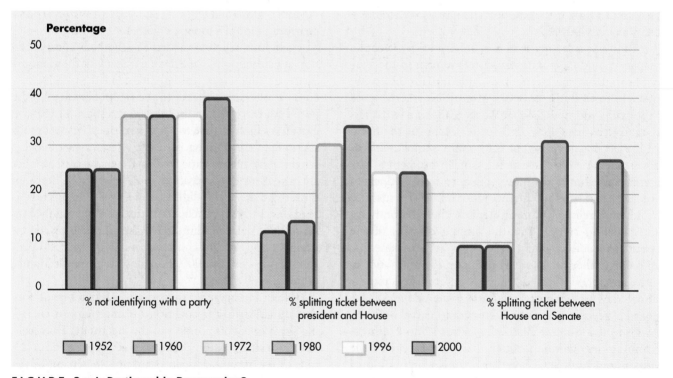

FIGURE 3 ■ Is Partisanship Reemerging?

SOURCE: CPS National Election Studies.

high in 1992, owing in part to the strong showing of third party presidential candidate Ross Perot. In 1996, ticket splitting fell off a bit but was still twice as common as it was in the 1950s (see Figure 3).[26] At the national level, the Republicans have occupied the White House and the Democrats have controlled Congress most of the time since 1968, indicating that voters, as a whole, are divided between Democratic and Republican allegiances.

Another indicator of dealignment is the number of independent voters, those who choose not to identify with either party. From 30 to 40 percent of citizens fit that category. Many voters who became eligible to vote for the first time during the 1980s and 1990s have not been attracted to either party, and some older voters lack firm attachments to their party.[27]

Many say that there is nothing that they like or dislike about parties. For example, the number who have something positive to say about one party and something negative to say about the other has declined; these trends suggest that parties are not as important to citizens as they were in the 1950s and 1960s. Nonetheless, the growth of independent voters leveled off in the 1980s.

Voter turnout has decreased over the past decades too (see Chapter 8 for a further discussion of this point). This is another indication that voters are not as interested in partisan politics as they were in the past.

Parties have lost the organizational bases that tied them to voters of the past. Party machines no longer dole out assistance to hungry families, find workers jobs, and expect in return a vote. (See the box "A Day in the Life of a Machine Politician".) They have also lost control over the nomination process with the widespread introduction of the primary. In general, Americans' ties with organizations of all sorts have weakened, and political parties are no exception.

Ticket splitting, failure to identify with a party, and declining voting turnout are signs of dealignment, loosening of traditional party ties.[28] Citizen indifference to political parties makes it difficult for parties to link citizens to government and to enhance citizens' influence over government actions.[29]

Competitiveness

At the same time, some indications point to increased partisan intensity and activity. The southern realignment has produced a party system in which the Republican Party is more conservative and the Democratic Party more liberal, leading to greater policy differences between the parties. An electorate not committed to either a liberal or conservative approach has produced an intense competition between the parties to spread their message and win the American people to their particular point of view.

Partisan intensity is reflected in the voting of Republicans and Democrats in elections and in voting in Congress. In the 2000 presidential election, 91 percent of those who identify with the Republican Party voted for Bush, and 86 percent of those identifying with the Democratic Party voted for Gore, a partisan pull stronger than in the three previous presidential elections. Partisan voting in Congress moved steadily upward during the 1980s, leveling off in the 1990s at 80 percent or better, which means that on issues where majorities in each party are opposed, party members vote together on average 80 percent or more (see Figure 5 later in the chapter).

Partisan intensity is also reflected in swings back and forth in party success in winning the presidency and in vote totals that are extremely close. Since 1977, the presidency has been held for twelve years by Democrats and fourteen years by Republicans, and the presidential vote in 2000 was the third closest in modern history. Moreover, although most congressional seats are not competitive, the division between the parties in Congress following the 2000 election is about as equal as it can be. Republicans enjoyed a modest seven-seat advantage in the House, and the Senate was split 50–50.

Are We Moving Toward a New Party System?

Although the South experienced a realignment and the rest of the nation some modest rearrangements of partisan support, the nation is yet to experience a 1930s-style realignment. That sort of alignment yielded a majority party with support allowing it to dominate American politics for an extended period of time. Instead, the post–fifth party system is a competitive one, reflecting realignment in the South, modest rearrangements of party support in the North, some indicators of dealignment, but other indicators of increased partisan intensity. This era also is characterized by sharpened differences between the parties.

Both parties seek to win new groups of voters. Republicans feel the need to improve their support from ethnic minorities, particularly Hispanics. Democrats also struggle with their dependence on corporate America for campaign funds and their traditional desire to represent the interests of working-class and middle-income Americans. Republicans are even more tied to big business, but that fits their overall ideology of limited government and little regulation. But reliance on big business as the source of campaign funds can, on some issues, make Democrats a "me, too" party and limit their interest in offering clear alternatives on issues such as government regulation and tax policies.

BIPARTISANSHIP FOR A WHILE

George W. Bush, sensing an electorate growing tired of partisan bickering, in his 2000 election campaign urged an end to the bitter partisan conflicts that characterized the Clinton years. He promised a fresh approach, seeking cooperation and building consensus with Democrats in Congress.

Bush worked cooperatively with the Democrats when he was governor of Texas. But Texas is not Washington. The Democratic Party in Texas is generally conservative, and, as in all states, the day-to-day workings of the legislature and state government are not covered by a national media driven to feature the conflicts that divide the parties.

Thus, in spite of Bush's rhetoric and his experience in Texas, few believed it possible that a bipartisan spirit would take hold in Washington. The parties have major disagreements about policy, disagreements that reflect differences of opinion in the public, ranging from health care to the Middle East. Moreover, Democrats were unlikely to forget the treatment of Bill Clinton by Republicans in Congress during his presidency. Many conservative Republicans hated Clinton in a way that went beyond partisanship. In addition to his policies, many objected to his personal life. Investigations of his financial dealings before becoming president dogged his presidency, and then the Lewinsky scandal and impeachment drove division even deeper. Talk radio, with the occasional Republican member of Congress as a guest, filled the airways with Bill and Hillary's real and alleged wrongdoings.

The 2000 election was also more partisan than usual with the Supreme Court stepping in to decide the Florida vote. Many Democrats, including some in Congress, believed Gore had won the election, and if not for Republican-appointed justices on the Supreme Court, Gore would be sitting in the White House instead of Bush.

Stung by the outcome, Democrats looked forward to the 2002 congressional races. Midterm elections typically turn on energizing the **party's base.** These voters respond to ideological appeals closer to the end of spectrum rather than centrist appeals designed for **swing voters** (those who swing back and forth between the parties). Providing alternatives to the Bush policies would be important in mobilizing the party's base.

In spite of Bush's efforts to establish personal relations with congressional leaders of both parties early on, the tone quickly turned sour. Bush's appointments were directed toward pleasing his conservative base rather than reflecting his moderate tone in the campaign and the closeness of the election. And the Republican leadership in Congress seemed to give up on the idea, if they ever had it, of moving toward the center, now that the party controlled both the presidency and the House.

Conflict between the parties was the order of the day. On the domestic front, the parties divided over a number of presidential initiatives. Bush hoped to privatize Social Security by allowing workers to put a portion of their contribution in the stock market. Democrats were skeptical that this was a workable solution that would provide real security for the millions who depend on Social Security. They argued that such a solution was easy to endorse when the market had gone up for eight straight years, but market volatility would lead to bad consequences if the market turned down and people saw their Social Security savings shrink.

The president proposed channeling funds to faith-based private organizations as an alternative to government programs to help individuals with their personal problems. Democrats were concerned that such organizations would discriminate on the basis of religion and break down the separation of church and state by providing public funds to religious groups (for more on church and state, see Chapter 14). The president also pushed a tax cut as part of an economic stimulus package. The Democrats thought that it gave too much tax relief to the wealthy and not enough to the working and middle classes. In foreign policy, Democrats criticized the president for going it alone, ignoring the nation's allies, and not paying sufficient attention to the Middle East. It was politics as usual.

Then came the 9/11 attacks. Suddenly "United We Stand" became the theme. In a moment, the usual political

Characteristics of the Party System

The American party system is characterized by some intriguing and even unique qualities.

Two Parties

First, the American party system is a **two-party system.** Only two parties win seats in Congress, and only two parties compete effectively for the presidency. The development and persistence of two parties is rare among the nations of the world.

In Western Europe, **multiparty systems** are the rule. Italy has nine national parties and several regional parties; Germany has five. Great Britain, although predominantly a two-party system, has several significant minor parties. Multiparty systems are also found in Canada, which has three parties, and Israel, which has more than twenty.

calculations were swept aside. The Senate voted 98–0 authorizing the president to use "all necessary and appropriate force" against those involved in the attack. The House followed 420–1. Singing the "Battle Hymn of the Republican," Democrats and Republicans joined hands in the Capitol. Commentators discussed the end to bipartisanship and division in American society, a new era of the nation working together. In spite of Bush's tainted election and an evenly divided Congress, bipartisanship arrived. Of course, the congressional response was bolstered by a public who overwhelmingly supported the president.

But politics is politics, and real differences about policy do not disappear because we are fighting terrorism. The president saw an opportunity to push his domestic agenda in the guise of fighting terrorism (see "You Are There" in Chapter 4), and while Democrats fearful of being labeled unpatriotic held back for a while, partisanship gradually reasserted itself. Standing outside the Capitol on September 25, House Democrats admonished the president that wartime deference would not extend beyond proposals to combat terrorism. The terrorist-induced infusion of bipartisanship lasted exactly forty-three days, by one count, from September 11 to October 24.

On October 24, Republicans and Democrats snapped at each other over an economic stimulus package as if the World Trade Center and Pentagon had never been attacked. Reverting to traditional party principles, the Democrats favored a stimulus targeted directly at the increasing number of Americans out of work, while the Republicans argued for corporate tax cuts to stimulate economic growth that would encourage business to hire new workers.

Some elements of bipartisanship did linger. The old adage about "politics stops at the water's edge" continues to be true. Democrats were hesitant to criticize the administration for the conduct of the war on terrorism even when it seemed to go badly. Likewise, most Democrats were reluctant to criticize the president's plans to attack Iraq. Nonetheless, by 2002, partisan discussions were in full bloom over a variety of domestic and foreign policy issues.

The short run of bipartisanship should not be a surprise. Disagreements are inevitable in a democratic society, and it is through political parties that they are resolved. In a time of extreme bipartisanship, when individuals are afraid or unwilling to challenge the dominant orthodoxy, individual rights can be trampled and bad decisions made. Bipartisanship plays well in campaign speeches, but it is partisanship that serves the interests of a diverse nation.

SOURCES: Helen Dewar, "United They Stand," *Washington Post National Weekly Edition*, November 26–December 2, 2001, 14; Karen Foerstel, "Congress and the President: A Recalibration of Power," *CQ Weekly*, September 29, 2001, 2248–2251; David S. Broder, "Fighting over the Economy," *Washington Post National Weekly Edition*, November 5–11, 2001, 4.

Why two parties? The most common explanation is the nature of American elections.[30] Officeholders are elected from **single-member districts** where the **winner takes all.** This means only one individual is elected from a district or state—the individual who receives the most votes. This contrasts with **proportional representation (PR),** in which officeholders are elected from multimember districts and the number of seats awarded to each party within each district is equal to the percentage of the vote the party receives in the district. Thus, in PR systems, representation in the national legislature is roughly proportional to the popular vote each party receives nationwide.

In single-member district, winner-take-all elections, only the major parties have much chance of winning legislative seats. With little chance of winning office, minor parties tend to die or merge with one of the major parties. However, where seats are awarded in proportion to the vote, even a modest showing in an election—15 percent or less—may win a seat or two in the national assembly. In PR systems, even parties representing only a small proportion of the electorate have voices in the legislature to speak in support of their policy positions and bases for mounting future campaigns.

While the nature of elections influences the number of parties, the number of parties also influences the conduct of elections. Where there are only two parties, they have strong incentives to conduct elections in a way that undermines the development and growth of other parties. For example, although the court eventually struck them down, Democrats and Republicans long supported laws that made it difficult for other parties to get their candidates placed on election ballots, requiring them to secure tens of thousands of signatures in order to qualify. Where there are more than two parties, it is to their advantage to conduct elections favorable to multiple parties.[31]

Fragmentation

The federal system, with its fragmentation of power among local, state, and national governments, leads to fragmentation within parties. State and local parties have their own resources and power bases separate from those of the national party, and the interests of state and local parties are often at odds with the national party.

Power is also fragmented within each level. At the national level, power is shared among the three branches of government. Control of the party is also shared. For the party of the president, control is shared between him and the members of his party in Congress. For the op-

position, it is shared between the party's members in the House and Senate. The national party organization may also seek a role, especially for the party that lacks control of the White House. Each of these agents has their own interests and stake in manipulating and using the party for their own ends. This is reflected in the difficult time that presidents often have in winning support for their policies among their party members in Congress.

For example, Democrats in Congress often broke with President Clinton on major issues. On the Clinton-negotiated North American Free Trade Agreement (NAFTA), two of the top three Democratic leaders in the House led in opposing him on the measure, and two of the top three Democratic leaders in the Senate joined the opposition in voting against him. (The measure passed anyway because many Republicans supported the agreement.) Three Democratic committee chairs and seventeen subcommittee chairs in both the House and Senate joined with Republicans in defeating a Democratic-sponsored crime bill. To their dismay, these leaders later learned that the party's failure to pass legislation dealing with crime and other issues contributed to voters' disgust with the party and the Republican takeover of Congress in the 1994 elections.

Thus, on some issues, members take an independent stance. To be reelected, members of Congress only need to satisfy a plurality of the voters in their district or state, not the president or the party. When Clinton considered a gas tax increase to reduce the deficit, Senator Herbert Kohl (D-Wisc.) told him the increase could be no more than 4.3 cents per gallon. Clinton had to accept Kohl's figure because the bill's outcome was in doubt and the president needed Kohl's vote. Kohl won election in his own right and was only obligated to the people of Wisconsin, not the president or the party. Such independence leads to fragmentation.

Nonetheless, party members do not act completely as free agents. In fact, the pull of party is strong and members normally support the legislative program of a president of their party. In Clinton's final year, Senate Democrats supported his position on 89 percent of the votes coming to the Senate; House Democrats 73 percent. In George Bush's first

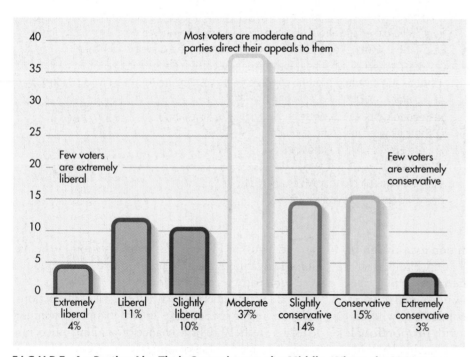

FIGURE 4 ■ Parties Aim Their Campaigns to the Middle, Where the Voters Are

SOURCE: Data from 2000 General Social Survey, National Opinion Research Center. The labels reflect how individuals identify themselves.

year, Senate Republicans supported his position 94 percent of the time; House Republicans, 86 percent.[32]

Moderation

Major American political parties tend toward moderation at least with respect to their appeals to voters in elections. The reason for this is that voters themselves are moderate (see Figure 4). To attract the most voters, parties direct their campaigns toward the middle. Historically, American political parties have been more interested in winning public office than in maintaining ideological purity and have been willing to sacrifice principles in order to win. While parties avoid the extremes in their campaign appeals, both the Democratic and Republican Parties have their elements—left of center in the Democratic Party and right of center in the Republican Party—that pull the parties toward the extremes. These tendencies are stronger in the Republican Party (though what is considered extreme is different to different people). Elected officeholders also tend to be more extreme than their rank-and-file supporters in the electorate, creating a tension between the personal predilections of officeholders and the preferences of voters.[33]

The desire to win directs the major parties to nominate moderate candidates at least for the presidency or for ideological candidates, when they are nominated, to obscure their issue positions or move to the middle. Ronald Reagan, when running for reelection, embraced a conciliatory stance toward the Soviet Union in contrast to his earlier "evil empire" posture. Bill Clinton became a "new kind" of Democrat. The implication was that, unlike those in the past who catered to minorities and special interests, he would deal with the problems of middle America. George W. Bush beat a hasty retreat from his conservative rhetoric in the South Carolina primary once the Republican nomination was secure. He avoided discussing issues such as abortion that would identify him with the right and focused on more centrist issues such as education, health care, and Social Security.[34] Once elected, Bush moved to the right again to satisfy his ideologically conservative base, by, among other things, appointing conservative John Ashcroft attorney general, backing tax cuts for the rich, and moving to undo as much regulation as he could.

Minor Parties in American Politics

What Do Minor Parties Stand for?

Sometimes called "third parties," minor parties are as varied as the causes they represent. Some are one-issue parties, like the American Know-Nothing Party (1856), which ran on a platform opposing immigrants and

Ralph Nader.

David La Spina/Birdboxarchives.com

Catholics, and the Prohibition Party (1869 to the present), which campaigns to ban the sale of alcoholic beverages.

Other parties advocate radical change. Economic protest parties, such as the Populist Party of 1892, occasionally appear when economic conditions are bad and disappear when the economy improves. Since the 1920s, the Communist Party USA has espoused the adoption of a communist system for the nation.

Some parties are simply candidates who failed to receive their party's nomination and decided to go it alone. In 1968, Alabama governor George Wallace split from the Democratic Party to run for president as the candidate of the conservative American Independent Party. Failing to get the Republican nomination, John Anderson launched a third-party campaign in 1980. Though both Wallace and Anderson had significant public support, neither won a large number of votes nor had any influence on the election outcome.

Ross Perot's third-party candidacy in 1992 had no association with either party. He simply decided to run. His willingness to use his personal fortune to fund his campaign, including buying large blocks of expensive television time, made him a highly visible alternative to the major-party candidates. Perot would have floundered quickly and with little notice if not for his capacity to buy hours of national TV time. Although he polled 19 percent of the vote, quite extraordinary for a minor party, his candidacy did not influence the election outcome. Diminished party loyalties among the electorate offer opportunities for other wealthy individuals to follow Perot's footsteps.

Ralph Nader, the consumer advocate, ran in 2000 for a second time as the nominee of the Green Party, an offshoot of the antinuclear and environmental movements. He campaigned on checking the influence of big business in government and received 3 percent of

Greens	Democrats	Republicans
Taxes		
Introduce a simple progressive income tax covering all income regardless of source; eliminate payroll taxes funding Social Security from progressive income tax; tax 100 percent of all income above ten times the minimum wage.	Provide tax cuts for middle-class families; eliminate the marriage penalty.	Reduce five income tax brackets to four with lower thresholds; double child-care credit; cap the top income tax rate; end inheritance tax; eliminate the marriage penalty.
Abortion		
Woman's right to choose abortion in all circumstances; coverage of abortion under publicly funded insurance programs.	Woman's right to choose abortion in all circumstances.	Constitutional amendment to support the right to life of the unborn; no public monies for abortion.
Social Security		
Basic income grants for all, funded by progressive income tax, which guarantees an adequate income sufficient for modest standard of living	Strengthen and save Social Security; supplement it with federal tax credits matching voluntary saving for retirement; rejects investing portion of Social Security in stock market.	Allow individuals to invest part of their Social Security contributions in the stock market.
Education		
Free public education from preschool through graduate school at public institutions; teacher pay scales comparable to other professions; no tax dollars for funding private schools.	Strengthen public schools; salary raises for teachers; increase number of teachers; accountability for student performance; opposes use of tax dollars (vouchers) for students to attend private schools.	Federal tax dollars (vouchers) to fund students to attend private schools; increases state and local control of education; establish English as common language in public schools.
Gay Rights		
Outlaw discrimination in housing, employment, benefits, and child custody; legalize same-sex marriage.	End workplace discrimination and full inclusion in the life of the nation.	Inclusion of homosexuals in armed forces incompatible with military service; silent on legal protection or standing in the law.
Environment		
Federal investments, purchases, mandates, and incentives to preserve and protect the environment.	Seek environmental protections in trade agreements; provide incentives to promote clean environment; Kyoto Protocol to limit CO emissions implicated in global warming.	Use market-based incentives to protect environment; balance private property rights and economic development with environmental protections; opposes Kyoto Protocol.
Missile Defense		
Eliminate nuclear, biological, and chemical weapons of mass destruction.	No missile defense.	Develop and deploy missile defense; change Anti–Ballistic Missile Treaty with Russia checking proliferation of nuclear weapons to allow missile defense.

the vote, well below the average of minor parties historically, but large enough to deny Al Gore the presidency.[35] Gore supporters harshly criticized Nader for drawing votes away and costing Democrats the White House. In the campaign, Nader argued that both Bush and Gore were pawns of corporate America, equally likely to do its bidding. On one level, the charge seems absurd. On important domestic issues, the Bush presidency has significantly differed in orientation from the national Democrats and presumably a Gore presidency. Still, Clinton's embrace of several traditional Republican policies such as welfare reform and free-trade, and the willingness of congressional Democrats to go along with deregulation of accounting firms, energy policy,

and other corporate activities, alienated many who found Nader an attractive alternative. They hoped to send a message against what one Nader supporter termed "money-polluted politics, battery-operated candidates, and policies that provide government welfare to corporations."[36]

Barriers to Minor Party Success

Minor parties face many obstacles in trying to establish themselves. Some are structural barriers. State laws, for example, present obstacles to minor-party and independent candidates seeking to get on the ballot. Federal laws make it difficult to secure public funding for third-party presidential campaigns.

There are also psychological barriers. Even though partisanship has weakened, minor-party and independent candidates confront the long-standing loyalty that most Americans have toward the major parties. Even when third-party or independent candidates are preferred to the major-party candidates, many voters are reluctant to cast a vote for them, believing that there is little chance they can win. Nearly one-third of those who expressed a first preference for Perot in 1992 voted for one of the major-party candidates. Many did so because they felt Perot could not win.

Often the major parties will encourage voters as a campaign tactic not to "waste their vote" by voting for a candidate who cannot win, as Gore did against Nader in 2000. Not only may voters waste their votes, but it may take away votes from their second choice and thus lead to the election of their least preferred candidate, as was probably true for many Nader supporters in 2000. Likewise, contributors are reluctant to donate money to a candidate who is unlikely to win.

For these reasons, third-party and independent candidates are rarely taken seriously by the media and thus receive less coverage than the major-party candidates. Limited media coverage adds to the perception that such parties are less legitimate and less worthy of voter and financial support.[37]

Practical barriers to third-party and independent candidates also exist. It is difficult for third parties to recruit qualified and experienced candidates. Most elected politicians are Republicans or Democrats and recognize that they are most likely to succeed in winning national office if they run as a major-party candidate.

The good ideas of third parties are usually co-opted by the major parties. Major parties are quick to back ideas that have voter appeal. Once a major party adopts an idea, the need for a third-party alternative is eliminated. Perot's strong stand on the need to eliminate the budget deficit in the 1992 campaign was at least partially responsible for the major parties' renewed efforts to deal with it.

Finally, third parties and independent candidates have done well only in elections when the nation has faced significant social and economic problems, and the parties failed to deal with them. Low support for third-party candidates in 2000 no doubt reflected a strong economy and a nation at peace.

Because third-party and independent candidates cannot win the presidency, their movements rarely extend beyond the defeat of their candidate. Perot was able to overcome this by spending his own money. His "United We Stand America" movement from the 1992 campaign became the Reform Party in 1996. But without Perot's financial support, Pat Buchanan, the party's nominee in 2000, received less than 1 percent of the popular vote. This dismal showing suggests that the party will go the way of most third parties.

In spite of the difficulties third parties face, many Americans say they want to see an alternative to the major parties. That support seems more rhetorical than real, however. Over one-half have indicated that the nation

needs a third party, although as we have seen, few actually vote for a minor-party candidate. Verbal support for a third party is fueled by the perception that the Democrats and Republicans in Congress are unable to work together to solve the nation's problems, and that an independent or another party is likely to do a better job.

Party in the Electorate

Earlier, the chapter identified three distinct but interrelated aspects of political parties: the party in the electorate, the party in government, and the party organization (Figure 1). The party in the electorate—those individuals who identify with a political party—are a party's grassroots supporters. **Party identification** is a psychological link that individuals feel toward a party; no formal or organization membership is implied. In contrast, European parties do have members; members pay dues and sign a pledge that they accept the basic principles of the party. The percentage of voters who are members ranges from 1 or 2 percent in some countries to over 40 percent in others.

Party Identification

A majority of Americans identify with a political party (see Table 1). In 2000, 35 percent said they were Democrats, 25 percent, Republicans; and 40 percent, independent.

Chapter 4 discussed how political socialization leads to party identification early in childhood. While this is true, party identification can change and often does as a person's life situation changes, such as moving to a new job or community, or in response to changes in issue positions that conflict with one's party. As noted earlier, the national Democratic Party's increased support for civil rights and other liberal policies caused many white southerners to leave the party.

Characteristics of Democrats and Republicans

Each party is more ideologically homogenous than it used to be. In fact, the Republican Party represents an

uneasy coalition of traditional conservatives, motivated primarily by a desire to minimize government intervention in the economy, and new conservatives, motivated primarily by a desire to institutionalize their religious and moral values. Called the *religious right,* the new conservatives want to increase government intervention in such areas as abortion, prayers in school, and pornography. In many states, the religious right controls the Republican Party. Since the 1992 Republican National Convention, the right has avoided open confrontations with moderate Republicans, and national party leaders have stressed issues such as lower taxes and smaller government, on which both agree. Winning elections may depend on keeping more divisive issues such as abortion in the background. The two Republican factions were united in their hate for communism and their support for Reagan. But the disintegration of the Soviet Union and the communist bloc and the departure of Reagan leave them with less in common.[38]

The Democrats are also divided. Some want to return to their liberal roots by appealing to working men and women and denouncing Republican support for big business and wealthy taxpayers. Others want the party to appeal to moderates who want lower taxes, less government, and more local control. Clinton directed his appeal toward the middle, angering many liberal Democrats in Congress. Clinton, who opened his second inaugural address with "The era of big government is over," thought it political suicide for him and the party to continue pushing a liberal agenda. As one of his aides put it, "We can't define ourselves as the party of government."[39] The party needs both its liberal base and the moderate middle to control the House and Senate.

Although people from all walks of life are found in each party, there are differences in the social compo-

TABLE 1	Party Identification, 2000	
Identifies self as:		**Percent**
Democrat		35
Independent		40
Republican		25

SOURCE: National Election Study, 2000.

sition of the parties. Republicans are somewhat younger than Democrats and those calling themselves independent (see Table 2). Republicans are somewhat better educated than Democrats, but independents have the highest percentage of college graduates. Women and blacks are better represented among the ranks of Democrats. Although the activities of religious fundamentalists are much more influential in the Republican Party, an equal percentage of Democrats and Republicans claim to be fundamentalists. Religious fundamentalists are an even larger proportion of independents.

Republicans have more supporters among high-income people and Democrats among low-income. Independents fall in between the two. Self-identified conservatives clearly dominate in the Republican Party, and self-identified liberals are more likely to be Democrats, though most Democrats are not liberals. Here also, independents fall between the two party groups.

TABLE 2	Characteristics of Republicans, Democrats, and Independents		
Total	Republican 25%	Independent 35%	Democrat 40%
Age 18–25	6	8	13
26–50	53	47	54
51–65	25	25	19
Over 65	17	19	13
Less than high school education	7	13	9
High school graduate	22	30	33
Some college education	32	30	30
College graduate	39	28	29
Men	49	37	45
Women	51	63	56
White	91	66	79
Hispanic/Latino	3	6	6
Black	2	23	8
Native American	1	1	1
Asian	2	2	2
Protestant	66	55	52
Catholic	34	39	43
Jewish	1	6	3
Born Again Christian	39	30	32
Professional and business	39	34	33
Other white collar	42	43	43
Blue collar	24	23	20
Under $25,000	39	48	52
$25,000–$50,000	31	35	31
$50,000–$75,000	16	10	11
$75,000–$125,000	10	6	5
Over $125,000	5	2	1
Conservative	61	20	28
Moderate	28	44	45
Liberal	12	36	27

SOURCE: National Election Study, 2000; General Survey Study, 2000.

Party in Government

Nationally, the party in government is the party's elected members of Congress and, for the party that occupies the White House, the president. The party in government links the party in the electorate to their government. The job of the party in government is to enact policies that party voters favor. This seems like a simple idea, but political scientists have waged great debates over how close the link between the party in government and the party in the electorate should be.

Proponents of **responsible party government** believe that political parties should take clear and contrasting positions on political issues and require their elected members to support the party's positions. "Responsible" party government is responsible in that

- voters have a choice among parties advocating different positions,
- elected members of the party support and vote for their party's position, and
- the party with a majority in the legislature enacts its position into law.

Given these conditions, voting for one party rather than another has definite policy consequences. It increases the prospects for popular control of government because a voter knows exactly what a vote for one party means for public policy. For example, in a responsible party system, if the Republican Party's position is prolife and the Democratic Party's position is prochoice, a vote for a Republican candidate will mean a prolife position. Should the Republicans win a majority, a prolife position would be enacted into law.

Great Britain is an example of responsible party government. Political parties are heavily involved in developing, articulating, and implementing public policy. If elected party members defect too often from the party's position, party leaders can deny them the right to stand for reelection as the party's candidates.

American political parties are not as responsible in this way. They do not always offer clear and contrasting policy positions. When they do, party leaders have only limited authority to force their elected members to accept the party's position.

Although the United States is not a responsible party government, it has some elements of party responsibility. Parties have important organizational and leadership functions in Congress. The majority in each chamber controls the agenda—that is, decides what issues will be debated and voted on. The majority also controls what happens in committees where the work of Congress is done. The party also links presidents with the members of their party in Congress. Members of the president's party in Congress support his policies substantially more often than members of the opposition. In 2001, the Republicans in the Senate supported George Bush 94 percent of the time, while Senate Democrats supported the president only 66 percent of the time; the Republican in the House supported him 86 percent and House Democrats, a scant 31 percent.[40]

Party influence on voting in Congress has increased dramatically during the 1980s.[41] This reflects in part the realignment of the South. In the days before blacks were allowed to vote and before the Republicans offered real challenges in most southern districts, the vast majority of southern members of Congress were white conservative Democrats who voted with the Republicans almost as often as with their own party.[42] As white conservatives have moved into the Republican Party, districts with conservative white majorities are much more likely to elect Republicans rather than conservative Democrats. Districts with large numbers of black voters are more likely than before to elect African Americans or moderate or liberal white Democrats. Thus, voting patterns of representatives from the South now divide along party lines as they do in the North.[43]

Republican control of both houses of Congress is also responsible for increased party unity. A number of conservative Republicans, committed to a very conservative agenda, were elected in 1994. Eager to retain control of Congress, moderate incumbent Republicans supported the program to show voters that the party could enact legislation and govern effectively.[44] Moderate Democrats, on the other hand, did not support the GOP's agenda, so division between the parties reached record highs. Partisanship fell off a little in both the House and Senate after 1995 but is still much higher than in the 1970s and 1980s. Roll call votes on which majorities of the parties opposed each other ranged from 43 to 56 percent in the House and 49 to 63 percent in the Senate. On these votes, better than 86 percent of the Republicans voted with each other in opposition to the Democrats, and 80 percent of the Democrats voted with each other in opposition to the Republicans (Figure 5).[45] Party voting in Congress rivals the British Parliament.

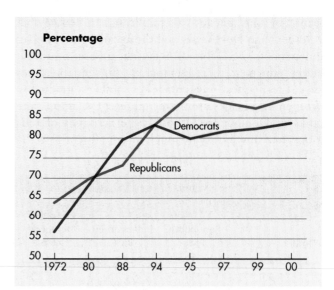

FIGURE 5 ■ Party Unity Increased in the 1980s and Has Remained High

Party unity is likely to remain high. Each party has a distinct vision of where it wishes the country to be, and each party finds electoral strength in ideologically opposed constituencies. For Republicans, it is constituencies that are right of center. For Democrats, it is those that are left. Both parties believe they can win support for their positions, are unwilling to give them up, or both.

To achieve higher levels of party unity would require major changes in government. Party leaders would have to be given more power to maintain party discipline in Congress, and the party of the president and congressional majority would have to be the same. This could be accomplished on a continuing basis only through a constitutional change providing for a parliamentary system similar to Britain's, in which Congress would elect the president. Such a change is unlikely, to say the least.

Party Organization

The party organization is the third component of the political party. The major levels of party organization—national, state, and local—coincide with political units responsible for administering elections. Within the local parties there are further subdivisions. The smallest unit is usually the precinct. Several precincts comprise a ward or district; several wards comprise a city or county. Each lower-level organization feeds into the next higher level.

Although party organization seems hierarchical (organized from the top down), it is not. Party organization is a layered structure with each layer linked to, but independent of, the others. Higher levels cannot dictate to or impose penalties on lower levels to ensure compliance.

Party organization is only loosely connected with the party in government. This contrasts with the British system, in which the party leaders in Parliament try to maintain a tight grip on the party organization.

National Party Organizations

The **national party chair** heads each national party organization, called the *national committee* (discussed later). The president appoints the chair of his party; this task falls to the national committee of the opposition party. The national party chair is a low profile position, and the person who serves is generally not very visible to the public. Haley Barbour, chair of the Republican National Committee from 1993 to 1998, was an exception. He was a frequent guest on TV talk shows and, before 1994, was the party's leading spokesperson and constant critic of Bill Clinton. Barbour was also responsible for GOP-TV, the Republican National Committee's television network. This network, available via satellite, cable systems, the Internet, and TV stations nationwide, provides information on party activities, issues, and personalities. Barbour was also an effective fund-raiser, wiping out the party's debt and raising million with the aid of state parties in 1996.[46] Following his resignation in 1998, Barbour was implicated in a campaign-funding scandal when information surfaced that he sought and accepted illegal contributions from foreign interests to fund a tax-exempt think tank used to develop Republican positions on issues.

Barbour's counterpart at the time was Donald Fowler, who shared the position with Senator Chris Dodd of Connecticut. Much less visible, Fowler was also implicated in campaign-funding scandals in 1996 and resigned his position in 1998.

Former governor of Montana, Marc Racicot was picked to chair the Republican Party by George Bush after his election in 2000. Racicot received some negative publicity when he agreed to serve as chair but refused to give up his lobbying business. While not unprecedented, past Democratic and Republican Party chairs have done the same thing, it is a conflict of interest.[47] Racicot's clients include the energy, agriculture, and recording industries, all with business currently before Congress and the White House.

While the **national committees** are the primary governing institutions of the Democratic and Republican Parties, they seldom meet, and it is the national chair and the permanent staff who are the de facto national party organization. The national committees do choose the site of their party's national convention and establish the formula for determining how many delegates each state receives.

National committee members are selected from each state using a variety of methods established by each state party. While states are represented equally on the Republican National Committee (RNC), the Democratic National Committee (DNC) awards states additional seats based on population and support for Democratic candidates in elections. The DNC also includes the party's leaders in Congress, the leaders of several state and local Democratic organizations, and representatives from elements of the party that are often underrepresented on the committee, including blacks, Hispanics, and youth.

Both major parties also have **House and Senate campaign committees,** which have grown in influence owing to their ability to raise and distribute campaign funds to their party's candidates for Congress.[48] The National Republican Senatorial Committee raised $33 million in 2000–2001; the National Republican Congressional Committee, $55 million. The Democratic Senatorial and Congressional Campaign Committees raised $19 million and $21 million, respectively. Most of the money was used to fund House and Senate candidates in the 2002 elections. New campaign finance laws that took effect following the 2002 election might slow down money flowing to the parties, but it will not end it (see Chapter 9).

Described as hollow shells in the 1950s and 1960s, the national party organizations are stronger today than they have been since the early twentieth century. Behind their success is a steady flow of cash from corporations, interest groups, and unions. The Republican Party has led the way in fund-raising, but Democrats are not far behind. Both parties actively recruit candidates to run for office, train them in various campaign technologies, and provide funds to mount an effective campaign. The RNC sponsors Nuts and Bolts seminars that are held throughout the country to provide training in fund-raising, developing a campaign strategy, using media, speech writing, polling, and getting out the vote. The party also has an array of how-to manuals for candidates and state and local party organizers. This past year the party launched "Winning Women," a program designed to overcome lack of support for the party among women.[49] Both parties have facilities to produce their own radio and television ads.

The Web has become a new tool in the arsenal of political parties.[50] Here, too, the Republicans are ahead of the Democrats. The GOP hopes to put everything it does online. One reason is that more Republican than Democratic voters are online. Another is the desire to bypass the mainstream media, which it considers unfair, in getting the party's message out.

The box "Party Political Clicks" gives a sample of Web sites sponsored by the national parties and candidates in the 2000 election; some remain active. Citizens were also able to link to each party's 2000 presidential nominating convention via the Web. Each site was linked to the candidates' main themes, including Spanish-language versions, ways for citizens to volunteer, and well-produced position statements on issues. The most prominent feature at each site was a little box that popped up on the screen asking for donations. Democrats could even participate and register their opinions on the party convention platform. Each party also set up sites critical of the other party's presidential candidate.

In a no-holds-barred fight to win control of Congress, both parties constantly upgraded their congressional sites with better messages, better artwork, and more sophisticated technology. The new technology allows the parties to communicate with their activists. Overnight they can send millions of e-mails on a particular issue and do so at minimal cost. Fund-raising is also possible and is more effective than traditional mail solicitations.

The increasing capacity of the national party organizations to offer candidates assistance in their campaigns may be responsible for the rising level of party voting in Congress. Members of Congress no doubt do feel beholden to the national party and perhaps a commitment to support party positions. At the same time, members are less beholden to state and local parties. Thus, national party organizations are growing in influence at the expense of state and local parties.[51] Today, the close link between the national party organizations and the parties in Congress moves us closer to the responsible party government model. However, the new campaign finance laws may give a boost to state and local party activities by restricting national party fund-raising (see Chapter 9).

State and Local Party Organizations

Each state and local party has a chair and committee to direct the activities of their party activists. In some communities, parties may be so weak and unimportant that there is little party organization. Because of this, someone who wants to become active in the party organization only has to show up at party meetings and be willing to work.

Big-City Party Organizations

Today's big-city political organizations vary in their strength and activity. But the **political machine** that flourished in some of the nation's largest cities in the late nineteenth and early twentieth centuries was strong and powerful. At the head of the machine was a boss, who often served as mayor and directed operations in such a way as to maintain control over the city and the organization. (See the box "A Day in the Life of a Machine Politician.")

The machine relied on the votes of the poor and working class, many of whom had only recently immigrated from Europe. Most accounts of machine politics are negative, dwelling on graft and corruption. However, the machine provided a number of valuable services. In a period when there were no welfare agencies, the machine provided jobs, food, and fuel for the thousands of immigrants who had no place else to turn. In return, party leaders expected individuals to vote for machine candidates.

Business also benefited from machines. The machine provided (for a fee) permits for business expansion, licenses, new roads, utilities, and police and fire protection.

The key to the machine's success was **patronage**—that is, giving jobs to party loyalists when the party controlled local government. An army of city employees, whose jobs depended on the political success of the machine, would dutifully bring family and friends to the polls on election day. One of the last of the big-city bosses, Mayor Richard J. Daley, head of the Chicago machine during the 1960s and 1970s, controlled thirty-five thousand public jobs and, indirectly through public contracts, ten thousand private ones.[52]

Reformers disturbed by corruption and by lower-class control of city politics eventually passed laws mak-

Party Political Clicks

whitehouse.gov	The White House
dpc.senate.gov	Senate Democrats
dccc.org	House Democratic campaign
rnc.org	Republican National Committee
gopnet.com	Republican National Committee
lott.senate.gov	Republican Senate leadership
senate.gov/~rpc	Senate Republican National Committee
nrcc.org	Republican House campaign
hillsource.house.gov	Republican House caucus
gop.gov	Republican House caucus
townhall.com	Republican discussions and groups
epn.org	Democratic discussions and groups

A Day in the Life of a Machine Politician

George Washington Plunkitt was a ward leader in the infamous Tammany Hall machine, the Democratic Party organization that governed New York City for seven decades in the late nineteenth and early twentieth centuries. Although Plunkitt was on the city payroll, he did not have a free ride. The demands of his job were exhausting. Yet by providing needed services to his constituents, he had many opportunities to build support for the party. Now government provides many of these services, thus making parties less vital. Entries from Plunkitt's diary illustrate the pervasive role of the party:

2:00 A.M. Aroused from sleep by a bartender who asked me to go to the police station and bail out a saloon keeper who had been arrested for violating the excise law. Furnished bail and returned to bed at three o'clock.

6:00 A.M. Awakened by fire engines. Hastened to the scene of the fire . . . found several tenants who had been burned out, took them to a hotel, supplied them with clothes, fed them, and arranged temporary quarters for them.

8:30 A.M. Went to the police court to secure the discharge of six "drunks," my constituents, by a timely word to the judge. Paid the fines of two.

9:00 A.M. Appeared in the municipal district court to direct one of my district captains to act as counsel for a widow about to be dispossessed. . . . Paid the rent of a poor family and gave them a dollar for food.

11:00 A.M. At home again. "Fixed" the troubles of four men waiting for me: one discharged by the Metropolitan Railway for neglect of duty; another wanted a job on the road; the third on the subway; and the fourth was looking for work with a gas company.

3:00 P.M. Attended the funeral of an Italian. Hurried back for the funeral of a Hebrew constituent. Went conspicuously to the front both in the Catholic church and the synagogue.

7:00 P.M. Went to district headquarters to preside over a meeting of election district captains, submitted lists of all the voters in their districts and told who were in need, who were in trouble, who might be won over [to Tammany] and how.

8:00 P.M. Went to a church fair. Took chances on everything,

bought ice cream for the young girls and the children, kissed the little ones, flattered their mothers, and took the fathers out for something down at the corner.

9:00 P.M. At the clubhouse again. Spent $10 for a church excursion. Bought tickets for a baseball game. Listened to the complaints of a dozen pushcart peddlers who said they were being persecuted by the police. Promised to go to police headquarters in the morning and see about it.

10:30 P.M. Attended a Hebrew wedding reception and dance. Had previously sent a handsome wedding present to the bride.

12:00 A.M. In bed.

SOURCE: Alistair Cooke, *Alistair Cooke's America* (New York: Knopf, 1973), 290–291; adapted from William L. Riordon, *Plunkitt of Tammany Hall* (New York: Dutton, 1963), 91–93.

George Washington Plunkitt holds forth in his unofficial office, a bootblack stand at the New York County Court House.

ing it difficult for machines to operate. Merit examinations for city jobs, nonpartisan elections, secret ballots, and voter registration undercut the means that machines had to secure voter loyalty. Political machines were dealt another blow when the federal government assumed responsibility for welfare needs in the 1930s; individuals no longer had to rely on the machine. And with a more educated population and greater employment opportunities, patronage jobs were no longer as desirable.

The Nominating Process

The major function of political parties is to nominate and elect candidates to office. Often several candidates of one party will seek the same office. Parties have devised three ways—caucuses, conventions, and primaries—to choose among the contenders.

Caucuses

A **caucus** is a meeting. In the early nineteenth century, party candidates were nominated by a small number of party leaders and officeholders in a caucus. Many criticized the system because so few people actually participated.

Conventions

By 1830, the increased number of voters and the desire of parties to win their continued support led to new procedures to broaden the nomination process. Caucuses of local residents selected delegates to attend county, state, and national conventions. These conventions then nominated candidates for public office.

Party conventions usually were controlled by party leaders who decided what happened and who was nominated. The leaders often made decisions behind the scenes in "smoke-filled rooms."

Primaries

In the early 1900s, progressive reformers argued that nominating conventions ignored the rank-and-file voter. Because they believed that party leaders in their "smoke-filled rooms" were corrupt and not to be trusted, reformers established the **direct primary** to increase citizen participation and check the influence of party bosses in nominations. The primary allows the voters in an election to choose the party's candidates. Today all states use primary elections, sometimes in conjunction with caucuses and conventions, to nominate candidates. (See also the box "Why Not Return to the 'Smoke-Filled Rooms'?")

Why Not Return to the "Smoke-Filled Rooms"?

Why not return the nomination process to the smoke-filled rooms of party conventions? The primary system has many flaws. Turnout in primaries is poor and unrepresentative. At the local and state levels, often there is little, if any, competition for a nomination or, in some cases, no candidates for a particular party at all. Presidential primaries place great weight on how much and how fast candidates can raise money.

But would conventions do better? At the presidential level, smoke-filled rooms produced Franklin Roosevelt and helped nominate John Kennedy. Perhaps the greatest argument for smoke-filled rooms is Harry Truman. Although a product of machine politics, Truman was honest and incorruptible. Tapped to be FDR's vice president in 1944 by party bosses who suspected Roosevelt would not live out his term, Truman became an excellent president.

In fairness, of course, smoked-filled rooms also produced Warren Harding, one of the most corrupt of the American presidents, and many other undistinguished nominees. At the state and local levels, where the parties are competitive, it is likely that conventions would produce strong candidates. This would give voters a real choice in the general election. However, in locales dominated by one party, the convention system would not necessarily produce stronger candidates than a primary. However, party leaders would almost always nominate a candidate so that the general election will be contested, something that frequently does not happen in a primary system.

Primaries are widely accepted today. They seem more democratic then conventions because more people are involved in making decisions. Party conventions are more exclusive and elitist. In the old days, they were also secretive.

However, while fewer are involved in conventions, numbers alone do not guarantee democracy. Democracy also requires that those involved are representative of the public. Primary electorates are not. Primary voters have higher incomes and greater formal education than the voters in general elections. Democracy also requires that voters be given a choice, but primaries undermine competition. And democracy at least implies openness; today, conventions could not operate in secret. Media coverage would change the nature of the deals made in the old-style conventions.

Although it is unlikely that we will abolish primaries and return to conventions, in recent years, in some states, party leaders have asserted more control through preprimary endorsements. Parties endorse candidates for nomination. The endorsed candidates are listed first on the primary ballot or are simply publicized as the "official" party candidate. Although on occasion the preferred candidate is defeated, the voters usually go along with the party's choice. Such arrangements give primary voters a choice while at the same time promoting party strength and ultimately responsiveness to voters.

In the days before polling and primaries, delegates to the party's presidential nominating conventions actually decided the party's nominee for president. Here, delegates to the 1924 Democratic convention are shown during a two-week convention that required 103 ballots to nominate John Davis for president. He lost to Calvin Coolidge in the election and quickly faded into obscurity.

Primaries vary from state to state according to who is eligible to vote in them. A **closed primary** limits participation to those who are registered with a party or declare a preference for a party. Thus, only Democrats can vote in the Democratic Party's primary. An **open primary** imposes no such limits; regardless of party registration, one may vote in either party's primary.

Party leaders and others favoring strong parties oppose open primaries. They argue that only voters who are party supporters should be permitted to vote in the party's primary. They fear that independents and opposition partisans will vote for candidates who are less sympathetic to the party's position on issues or who are less likely to win.

A minority of states use runoff primaries, which pit the two highest vote getters in the primary against each other for the party's nomination. Over the years, the inability of the Republican Party to compete effectively for office in the South meant that the winner of the Democratic Party's primary was virtually assured of winning the general election. Due to the large number of Democratic candidates, sometimes the winner of the primary did not have a majority of the vote. In those cases, some southern states used a runoff election between the two highest vote getters in the primary.

Although primaries have increased citizen participation in nominations, turnout in primaries is quite low and unrepresentative. Turnout in presidential primaries averages at best 10 percent. While it is higher for primaries held early in the year, such as New Hampshire's, which is always first, turnoff falls in those that come later. In 2000, turnout was again high in New Hampshire and the states immediately following, but it dropped dramatically when opponents to Bush and Gore withdrew from the race. Voters in primaries are also unrepresentative of the public at large. Primary voters tend to have higher incomes and education and to be older, more interested in politics, and, as one might expect, more partisan.[53]

In addition to attracting a small and unrepresentative group of voters to the ballot box, primaries have other flaws. In some ways, the primary process is less responsive to voters than party conventions, where candidates were once selected by a small group of party leaders meeting in smoke-filled hotel rooms.

Primaries do not necessarily provide voters with much choice. Many primaries are uncontested. Often the presence of an incumbent deters challengers, or at least strong challengers. In either case, incumbents are almost always renominated.

Primaries also may make the general election less competitive. The minority party (that is, the party less likely to win the general election) often has no strong candidate who can mount an effective campaign in the general election. In preprimary days, party leaders generally made sure there were some candidates running in the general election regardless of election prospects.

Another problem with primaries is that the electorate may nominate a candidate known by his or her party peers to be incompetent, difficult to work with, or lacking in character and integrity. Although the convention system does not guarantee that such candidates will be avoided, party leaders are more likely to know the real strengths and weaknesses of potential candidates than are voters, who must rely on the media for information. Indeed, voters have so little information about primary candidates that success often turns on name recognition.

Primaries hurt the most, however, by freeing candidates from supporting the party's program. Candidates can bypass leaders and appeal to voters directly. It is nearly impossible for party leaders to withhold nominations from candidates who are party members in name only or who often vote with the other party. Thus, party bonds are weakened, and members feel free to vote and act however they wish.

This outcome might seem desirable. But when candidates vote completely independent of their party, it is more difficult for voters to cast an informed vote. When parties offer a clear choice, voters know what they are voting for and can reward or punish the parties for what they do or plan to do in office. Thus, party voting can make government more responsive to voters.

Conclusion: Do Political Parties Make Government More Responsive?

Although the Founders initially opposed the idea of political parties, some later turned to parties when they began to have serious differences of opinion about public policies. They recognized that their ideas could prevail if they aligned with others who agreed with them and together elected a majority in government. Then, as now, parties were a vehicle to organize a stable majority. For Jefferson and Madison, the important issue was the scope and power of national government. Jefferson's views prevailed, but only with the aid of the party he created.

While organizing a political party was a way for Jefferson, one of America's most influential leaders, to influence government policy, parties are also a way for average Americans to influence government policy. Making government more accountable to voters is the major contribution of political parties to democratic government. Political parties provide an easily identifiable majority, at least in two-party systems, that voters can blame when things go wrong and reward when things go right, and in the process turn public policy in the direction they prefer.

While American political parties may not perform exactly as described here, Americans have an interest in maintaining strong and viable political parties. Without them, voters would be confronted with a hopelessly confusing array of candidates and have no idea of how a vote for any one of them will influence government policy. Without parties, the media, campaign consultants, lobbying groups, big donors, and self-financed wealthy candidates would play an even larger role in politics than they do now.

There is no doubt that parties are weaker than they were a century ago. They have, however, experienced a resurgence in the past three decades in several important ways. With respect to the party in the electorate, movement of voters toward independence and erosion of party attachments appears to have reached an end. The proportion of voters claiming partisan allegiance has grown slightly after steady declines since the 1960s. Split-ticket voting, after reaching an all-time high in 1992, decreased dramatically in 1996 (see Figure 3).

The party in government is also stronger. Party cohesion in Congress has increased. With the demise of the southern Democratic conservatives, the Democratic Party is much more homogeneous. Many members of both parties are more dependent on the national party committees for campaign support than they were a decade ago. Both these trends have contributed to the increase in party voting and support for the president by his own party.[54]

Finally, national party organizations have become much more powerful. Their activities are fueled by their ability to raise and spend essentially unlimited amounts of money. New campaign finance laws might check the flow, but it is unlikely to alter the situation significantly (for more on this topic, see Chapter 9).

While parties still compete for influence with interest groups, pollsters, campaign consultants, and the media, it is often funds raised by the national parties that buy the polling, campaign consultation, and media time. Both presidential and congressional candidates need the national party organizations because of their revenue-raising ability.

Each component of American political parties—party in the electorate, party in government, and party organization—has shown significant signs of revitalization. Parties have made no gain, however, where it might make a major difference—namely, control over the nomination process. Political parties have little influence over who can run for party office. In spite of name recognition, endorsements, and a cache of money to throw at the 1996 nomination, the Republican Party could not prevent Steve Forbes, a multimillionaire magazine publisher, and Pat Buchanan, a television personality—neither of whom had ever been elected to anything—and a host of others from entering the race and challenging the party's choice, Bob Dole. These candidates were taken seriously. They got airtime, coverage by national newspapers and magazines, and entrée into presidential debates. They attacked Dole, undermining his chance of winning the presidency, and there was nothing he or the party could do about it. George W. Bush faced a similar although less serious challenge in his quest for the Republican Party nomination in 2000. Today, anyone can claim to belong to a party and run for the party's nom-ination for president or any other office. In the past, the party organization could discourage candidates with little chance of winning an election, by withholding its support, or threatening sanctions if necessary if they choose not to obey.

Today, many indications point to a resurgence in party strength. Yet, split-ticket voting and the divided government it produces make it unclear how one's vote will affect what government does. Citizens elect a president of one party and a majority in Congress of another and wonder why there is gridlock in Washington. Voters see parties as instruments of delay and deadlock, not realizing that it is often lack of party discipline, and not the reverse, that causes the deadlock. Citizens have a greater prospect of influencing the direction of government if they elect those who are loyal and committed to a party. This factor is what led E. E. Schattschneider to reflect on the inevitability and necessity of parties in American democracy.

EPILOGUE

Jeffords Switches

f ollowing the lengthy meeting with his Senate colleagues, Jeffords was drained. He shared, "That's the worst emotional experience I've been through."[55] The last piece of advice they gave him was wait a few days before you make a decision, but he had scheduled a news conference the next day in Vermont. On the flight home that evening, he decided. He would declare himself an independent and vote with the Democrats, in effect giving them control of the Senate. That morning he told the press and a crowd outside the state capital, "I became a Republican not because I was born into the party but because of the kind of fundamental principles Republicans stood for—moderation, tolerance, fiscal responsibility."[56] As conservatives now dominate the party, Jeffords went on to say "It has become a struggle for our leaders to deal with me and for me to deal with them."[57] Jeffords pointed out that he disagreed with President Bush and the party on abortion rights, the shape of the judiciary, missile defense, energy, and the environment.

Reaction from fellow Vermonters dashed any thought that Jeffords's reelection in six years might some how be threatened. His announcement was met with cheers. In all likelihood, his switch will enhance his standing. The state elected Independent Bernie Sanders, a self-proclaimed "Democratic socialist," to his sixth term in the House with nearly 70 percent of the vote.

With Jeffords's defection and several other moderates in the party feeling out of step with the president's conservative agenda, some began to question Bush's strategy of governing from the right. The question: Should the president take Jeffords's switch as a signal and moderate his positions or continue to press the case for conservatives? Senator Olympia Snowe, a moderate Republican senator from Maine, admonished the party to treat the loss of Jeffords as a wake-up call to the party to welcome the voices of moderate Republicans. Senator John McCain from Arizona, Bush's challenger for the Republican nomination a year ago, was somewhat sharper in his criticism. "Tolerance of dissent is the hallmark of a mature party and it is well past time for the Republican party to grow up."[58]

Senator Trent Lott (R-Miss), majority leader at least for a few more days, countered that Republicans will not back down from their basic beliefs and are "unified and committed"[59] to pushing Bush's priorities.

In the months that followed, some of Bush's agenda did suffer a setback. Senate Democrats refused to support his economic stimulus package and to open up the Alaska Wildlife Refuge to oil exploration. These measures, of course, may have been difficult to pass even with the Republicans in control. Senate Democrats began scrutinizing Bush's conservative court nominations carefully too, though thus far, they have not held up as many as the Republican-controlled Senate did to Clinton.

The attacks on September 11, 2001, soon overshadowed Jeffords's switch as the nation's attention shifted to fighting terrorism. Republicans and Democrats joined to support Bush in dealing with the threat. Jeffords's switch was also rendered less important as the Republicans won control of the Senate in 2002. He lost the committee chairmanship given to him by the Democrats when he became an independent and they became the majority. In this respect, Jeffords may have miscalculated, but his shift still affords him more comfort in terms of taking positions he believes in rather than being forced to endorse party positions he finds objectionable.

 To learn more about the activities of political parties, go to this chapter's "You Are There" exercises on the text Web site.

Key Terms

party in the electorate

party in government

party organization

realignment

New Deal coalition

dealignment

ticket splitting

party's base

swing voters

two-party system

multiparty systems

single-member districts

winner-take-all

proportional representation

party identification

responsible party government

national party chair

national committees

House and Senate campaign committees

political machine

patronage

caucus

direct primary

closed primary

open primary

Further Reading

David Brooks, ed., *Backward and Upward: The New Conservative Writing* (New York: Vintage, 1996). This is a collection of combative, often funny essays from the political right. The authors lampoon various liberal beliefs, showing that conservatism is as much about personality as ideology.

James Carville, *We're Right, They're Wrong: A Handbook for Spirited Progressives* (New York: Random House, 1996). In this book, President Clinton's chief campaign adviser and one of Washington's most prominent Democratic strategists responds to the Republicans' platform during the 1994 and 1996 elections. Carville includes such features as the Republicans' "Biggest Lies" and "Most Expensive Boondoggles."

Congressional Quarterly, *National Party Conventions: 1831–1996* (Washington, D.C.: Congressional Quarterly Press, 1997). All you ever wanted to know about each party's national nominating conventions, including lists of keynote speakers, platforms, delegate selection rules, nominees, and more.

David J. Gillespie, *Politics at the Periphery: Third Parties in Two-Party America* (Columbia: University of South Carolina Press, 1993). This work provides both a historical review of the roles played by third parties in American politics and a look at the impact of recent third parties on election outcomes.

Stanley B. Greenberg, *Middle Class Dreams: The Politics and Power of the New American Majority* (New York: Times Books, 1995). President Clinton's adviser looks at the radical shape of American politics today and contends that both political parties have betrayed the middle class.

Edwin O'Connor, *The Last Hurrah* (New York: Bantam, 1957). A warm, intimate novel set in Boston in the 1950s that contrasts the old-style party election campaigns with new media-oriented ones.

William L. Riordon, *Plunkitt of Tammany Hall* (New York: Dutton, 1963). A series of witty talks by a ward boss of New York City's Democratic Party machine. A slice of Americana, this book discusses "honest graft" and other aspects of "practical politics" and in the process demonstrates why political machines flourished.

Mike Royko, *Boss: Richard J. Daley of Chicago* (New York: New American Library, 1971). An intriguing account of how the Chicago political machine operated under the late mayor Richard J. Daley.

Larry Sabato, *The Party's Just Begun* (Glenview, Ill.: Scott, Foresman, 1988). An overview of the American party system: why we need it, what it does, and how we can make it work better.

Ruy Teixeira and Joel Rogers, *Why the White Working Class Still Matters* (New York: Basic Books, 2000). An analysis of the need to capture the white working class in order to put together a new party coalition and what each party can do to succeed at it.

Electronic Resources

www.rnc.org/

The home page of the Republican National Committee. It provides many links to government institutions, important Republican officeholders, the national committee headquarters, and issue positions. See GOP-TV at www.rnc.org/webcast/webcast.html.

www.Democrats.org/index/html
The home page of the Democratic National Committee. It provides similar links from a Democratic perspective, as well as links to information about Democratic Party history and past Democratic conventions.

www.reformparty.org/
The home page of the Reform Party.

www.politicalindex.com/sect8.htm
This site gives you a flavor of many of the minor parties involved in U.S. politics. Check out the links to the U.S. Taxpayers Party, the Communists, the Libertarians, and many others.

www.greenparty.org
The site provides information on the Green Party, USA.

 InfoTrac College Edition

Search for the following articles in the InfoTrac database:

Lane, Charles. "Daddy's Boy: The Roots of Pat Buchanan's Authoritarianism," *New Republic* (January 22, 1996).

Lipset, Seymour Martin, and Gary Marks. "Social Democracy Lives On," *New Statesman (1996)* (June 26, 2000).

Lord, Lewis. "The Full Strom: Strom Thurmond and the History of Southern Politics," *U.S. News & World Report* (September 17, 2001).

Schecter, Cliff. "Extremely Motivated: The Republican Party's March to the Right," *Fordham Urban Law Journal* (April 2002).

For more articles, enter

"Republican Party" in the Subject Guide;

"Democratic Party" in the Subject Guide;

"third parties" in the Subject Guide.

 American Government Resources

Visit the Political Behavior section of the Wadsworth American Government Resources Web site (politicalscience.wadsworth.com/amgov/) for a variety of tools to help you explore political parties further. Included are simulations, video clips, Microcase exercises, and a wealth of other activities.

CHAPTER 8

ELECTIONS

Election official inspects Florida ballot for dimpled chads.

Najah Feanny/SABA

How Do You Recount?

ou are Al Gore. It is November 2000, and you have just won the popular election for president of the United States. Your vote margin is about a half million, close but larger than that of John F. Kennedy in 1960 and Richard Nixon in 1968. However, unlike Kennedy and Nixon, you might lose the election despite winning the popular vote. The outcome hinges on whether you or your opponent, George W. Bush, won the popular and hence the electoral college vote in Florida. And that outcome, in turn, depends on the decision of whether several hundred disputed votes belong to you or your opponent. The decision facing you is what kind of a recount should you ask for in deciding the razor-thin margin in Florida.

This should have been a Democratic election year, and a lot of your supporters as well as detractors think you made the race close by your mistakes. The economy is booming and the country is at peace, both normally good omens for the party in power. But you could not decide whether to run on Clinton's legacy or to separate yourself from him. Always a dilemma for a vice president running for the presidency, the issue was compounded for you by Clinton's policy successes but personal failures. Republicans rarely fail to mention that they want to bring a higher standard of morality and

integrity to the White House. You want to distance yourself from Clinton's moral and character flaws but associate yourself with the eight years of economic growth and prosperity during the Clinton–Gore administration. This dilemma is compounded by your own failings as a campaigner. Though in person you have a sense of humor and good conversational style, on the platform you are wooden and tend to lecture people. You appear phony, and people don't know who you really are.

Then there's your opponent, George W. Bush. A popular governor of Texas, Bush was thrust into the national limelight because of the Bush name and connections (just as you got a head start in your own congressional career because of the legacy of your father, the famous Tennessee senator Albert Gore). Though Bush lacks your understanding of public issues and often puts his foot in his mouth with malapropisms and misstatements, he is everything you are not when talking to large groups of people. He is relaxed and at ease, seemingly at peace with himself. Though a conservative with significant ties to big business, he has run a centrist campaign, emphasizing the "compassionate" in his self-described compassionate conservatism. His campaign has been a success in retaining the allegiance of the powerful Republican conservative wing while also appealing to moderates and independents.

So the race was close. As predicted, you have carried much of the Northeast, industrial Midwest, and the West Coast, especially the large urban centers of those regions, while Bush has run up huge margins in the South and Southwest, and he also won the mountain states and rural Midwest. Now it all comes down to Florida.

Florida was a state that a few months ago Bush was heavily favored to win. His brother is a popular governor there, and the Republicans are numerous and well organized. But you have made a race of it, appealing to the large Jewish and black communities in the state alongside traditional Democratic voters who have migrated there from the Northeast.

Election day exit polls of Florida voters show you winning by a small margin. And early in the evening the networks declare you the Florida winner. But then, actual precinct returns in some areas contradict the exit polls, and the networks pull back their call and declare Bush the Florida victor. In yet another reversal, in the early morning hours, the networks decide Florida is too close to call, and the election hangs in the balance (for a further description and explanation of the media performance on election night 2000, see Chapter 5). Bush has a tiny lead of just several hundred ballots.

Confusion reigns in the days afterward. The press and election observers report several problems, some of them serious. Most of the problems work to your disadvantage.[1] First you hear reports of losing thousands of votes because of the strange "butterfly" ballot configuration in Palm Beach County, a heavily Democratic liberal county. The odd format, designed by the supervisor of elections in the county, made it difficult for some voters to determine which punch hole corresponded to which presidential candidate. (It was labeled the butterfly ballot because candidate names appeared on

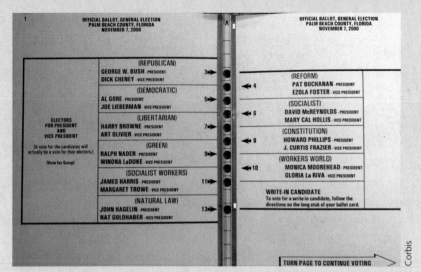

Butterfly ballot.

both sides of a row of vertical punch holes rather than only on one side, the standard, less confusing format; see the photo.) Even though the problem was recognized early on election day by some distraught voters leaving the polling places, there was no way that local election officials felt they could fix the problem then.

The punch hole registering a vote for Patrick Buchanan was to the right of Gore's name on the ballot, leading some voters to punch it rather than the next hole below. Probably as a result of that ballot, over three thousand votes were cast in the county for Buchanan, the right-wing candidate who got only a few hundred votes in neighboring counties. This is particularly ironic because the areas of Palm Beach County casting the most votes for Buchanan were those inhabited by mostly elderly Jewish voters, the least likely group to support Buchanan, who is thought to be anti-Semitic. As one elderly Jewish woman exclaimed after mistakenly voting for Buchanan, "I would rather have had a colonoscopy than vote for that son of a bitch Buchanan."[2]

And thousands of other votes in that county were invalidated because the presidential ballot was punched twice. More than 5,300 voters voted for Buchanan, apparently then discovered their error, and also voted for Gore; these "overvotes" were invalid, too.

Nearly three thousand voted for Gore and the socialist candidate whose punch hole was underneath Gore, apparently thinking they voted for Joseph Lieberman, Gore's vice presidential running mate, whose name was under Gore's. (Bush lost about 1,600 votes from those who voted for him and Buchanan.) While some spoiled ballots are normal in every election, you know that this erratic pattern in one county is a result of the badly designed ballot. The votes you lost there are far more than Bush's slim lead. But there is nothing you feel you can do about these. The ballot was designed by a Democratic supervisor of elections who made the candidates' names larger so elderly voters could read them easier. But the larger type actually made the format harder to understand. Nevertheless, a sample ballot had been printed in the local newspapers before the election, as is required in many states. Clearly there was no intention to deceive any voters.

But that is only the beginning of the troubles you are hearing about. In the Jacksonville area, African Americans turned out in huge numbers as a result of a voter turnout campaign urging them to vote for Gore and a black Democratic congresswoman, Corrine Brown. Democratic workers used voters to "Vote for Gore and Brown." Unfortunately, nine thousand voted for Gore and another Browne, a minor-party presidential candidate, leading to nine thousand ballots being invalidated. Of the twenty precincts in Florida with the highest rates of spoiled ballots, nineteen were in the Jacksonville area.[3]

Aside from this fiasco, newspaper accounts report thousands of presidential ballots that are not counted at all. Some Florida counties use punch card ballots where voters punch holes in the card opposite their candidate's name. But thousands of punch card ballots cannot be read by the machine and are reported as no vote. Statewide there are sixty-four thousand of these "undervotes." Some of these undervotes are from voters who in fact did not cast a vote in the presidential election, but most are those where the punches were incomplete. The term *chad* quickly becomes part of yours and the public's vocabulary. Machine counts of punch cards do not count partially punched holes; that is, the holes where the tiny piece of paper, called a *chad,* is still hanging by one or more corners or is simply indented (the so-called dimpled chads or pregnant chads).

Florida law mandated a recount because of the closeness of the election. The recount was done the same way the ballots were originally counted, so that in the punch card counties, the punch cards were run through the counting machine again. That recount registered several hundred more votes for you statewide but still left you behind.

Finally, there is a problem of overseas ballots. Americans overseas have a right to vote. They must ask for a ballot before the election and mail it by the day of the election, but the ballot does not need to be received by local officials until ten days after the election. (This time allows for mail delays.) Most overseas voters in Florida are members of the armed services, because Florida is home to large naval bases. There are strict rules about how these ballots are to be certified to

avoid vote fraud: The ballots have to have legible overseas postmarks showing the ballot was cast on or before election day; the voters had to have registered in advance, request a ballot, and sign their envelope; and the voting must be witnessed. But hundreds of these ballots are coming in without postmarks or with U.S. postmarks, from voters who were not registered, or that lacked a witness. You suspect that the Bush campaign, knowing that military personnel tend to be conservative voters, got servicemen and women from Florida who had not voted before the election to vote after the election when the outcome appeared uncertain. Hundreds of military votes could be decisive if courts eventually ordered recounts. You believe you should challenge these apparently illegal ballots, yet you know that has some risks. You don't want to be seen as being against voting by American troops.

Now you must decide your strategy. You are confident that thousands of Gore votes have not been properly counted. You believe a hand recount will be important so that humans can see the chads and thereby determine the intention of the voters. The punch card machines have a significant error rate. Sometimes voters push the stylus on the perforated square or oblong, but the square—the chad—does not completely detach, either because the voter did not push hard enough or because the buildup of punched chads from previous voters made it more difficult to punch through. If the chad does not completely detach, the machines do not count it as a vote. Yet it should be possible in a hand recount for officials to determine the voter's intention if a ballot has a hanging chad. (On the other hand, perhaps it would be less clear if the circle was only dimpled, suggesting that the voter might have started to vote for that candidate but then changed his or her mind.) Hand recounts, though subject to human fallibility, are considered more accurate than machine counts for

punch card ballots. Hand recounts would be undertaken with representatives of each party in attendance, so there would be little likelihood of fraud. Thus these recounts, you believe, would best illuminate what voters intended.

Although Florida has no law specifying how chads should be counted, some states do. Texas, for instance, has a law, signed by Governor Bush, that instructs officials to count hanging and indented chads when recounting the ballots.

As a candidate, you have a right to ask that every county be recounted. This strategy would seem principled. It would put you on record as wanting every vote counted. But a statewide recount would require a massive effort, and Republican counties might turn up more Republican votes. Alternatively, you have a right to ask that particular counties be recounted. You could ask that the counties with strong Democratic majorities where there have been reports of problems, as in Palm Beach County, be recounted. You feel you could get the necessary extra votes just from those counties. (Bush, of course, could then demand recounts of Republican counties, but most reports of problems have occurred in Democratic counties. Bush probably could not gain as many votes in Republican counties as you could gain in Democratic counties.) However, this strategy would not seem as principled as asking for a statewide recount. Even though it is allowed by state law, a partial recount would seem self-serving to many voters.

Then there is the issue of the overseas ballots. How aggressively should you challenge them? If you do so aggressively, perhaps this will look like you are upholding a double standard, wanting the benefit of the doubt for yourself in the "undervote" punch card ballots, but not wanting to give the benefit of the doubt to the returned overseas ballots.

What kind of a recount do you ask for and why?

Americans have fought and died in wars to preserve the rights of citizens to choose their leaders through democratic elections. Some have even died here at home, trying to exercise these rights. Despite this, most Americans take these important rights for granted; about half do not bother to vote even in presidential elections, and fewer still participate in other ways.

Moreover, the process by which we choose our leaders, especially the president, has been sharply criticized in recent years. Critics charge that election campaigns are meaningless and offer little information to the voters, that candidates pander to the most ill-informed and mean-spirited citizens, and that public relations and campaign spending, not positions on issues or strength of character, determine the winners. Then in 2000, it also became apparent that some voters' votes were not counted even when they went to the polls, largely due to defects in the election process itself.

In this chapter, we analyze why voting is important to a democracy and why, despite its importance, so few do it. We then examine political campaigns and elections to see how they affect the kinds of leaders and policies we have. We will see that the lack of participation by many reinforces the government's responsiveness to those who do participate, especially those who are well organized.

The American Electorate

During the more than two centuries since the Constitution was written, two important developments have altered the right to vote, termed **suffrage.** First, suffrage gradually has been extended to include almost all citizens aged eighteen or over. Second, deciding who may vote now lies largely in the hands of the federal government. The electorate has been widened mostly through constitutional amendments, congressional acts, and Supreme Court decisions.

Early Limits on Voting Rights

Although the Declaration of Independence states that "all men are created equal," at the time of the Constitution and shortly thereafter, the central political right of voting was denied to most Americans. States decided who would be granted suffrage. In some only an estimated 10 percent of the white males could vote, whereas in others 80 percent could.[4]

Controversial property qualifications for voting existed in many states. Some argued that only those with an economic stake in society should have a say in political life. But critics of the property requirement repeated a story of Tom Paine's:

> You require that a man shall have $60 worth of property, or he shall not vote. Very well . . . here is a man who today owns a jackass, and the jackass is worth $60. Today the man is a voter and he goes to the polls and deposits his vote. Tomorrow the jackass dies. The next day the man comes to vote without his jackass and he cannot vote at all. Now tell me, which was the voter, the man or the jackass?[5]

Because the Constitution gave states the power to regulate suffrage, the elimination of property requirements was a gradual process. By the 1820s, most were gone, although some lingered to midcentury.

In some states, religious tests also were applied. A voter had to be a member of the "established" church or could not be a member of certain religions (such as Roman Catholic or Jewish). However, religious tests disappeared even more quickly than property qualifications.

By the time of the Civil War, state action had expanded the rights of white men. However, neither slaves, Indians, nor southern free blacks could vote, although northern blacks could in a few states.[6] Women's voting rights were confined to local elections in a few states.[7]

Blacks and the Right to Vote

The Civil War began the long, slow, and often violent process of expanding the rights of blacks to full citizenship. Between 1865 and 1870, three amendments were passed to give political rights to former slaves and other blacks. One, the Fifteenth Amendment, prohibited the denial of voting rights on the basis of race and thus gave the right to vote to black men.

For a short time following the ratification of this amendment, a northern military presence in the South and close monitoring of southern politics enabled blacks to vote and hold office in the South, where 90 percent of all blacks lived. During this **Reconstruction** period, two southern blacks were elected to the Senate and fourteen were elected to the House between 1869 and 1876.

Although blacks did not dominate politics or even receive a proportional share of offices, whites saw blacks' political activities as a threat to their own dominance. White southerners began to prevent blacks from voting through intimidation that ranged from mob violence and lynchings to economic sanctions against blacks who attempted to vote.

Northerners tolerated these methods, both violent and nonviolent. The northern public and political leaders had lost interest in the fate of blacks or had simply grown tired of the struggle. In 1876, a compromise ended Reconstruction. In the wake of the disputed 1876 presidential election, southern Democrats agreed to support Republican Rutherford B. Hayes for president in return for an end to the northern military presence in the South and a hands-off policy toward activities there.

By the end of the nineteenth century, blacks were effectively disfranchised in all of the South. The last black southern member of Congress served to 1901. Another would not be elected until 1972.

The loss of black voting rights was legitimized in southern constitutions and laws. **Literacy tests** were often required, supposedly to make sure voters could read and write and thus evaluate political information. Most blacks, who had been denied education, were illiterate. Many whites also were illiterate, but fewer were barred from voting. Local election registrars exercised nearly complete discretion in deciding who had to take the test and how to administer and evaluate it. Educated blacks often were asked for legal interpretations of obscure constitutional provisions, which few could provide.

Some laws had exemptions that whites were allowed to take advantage of. An "understanding clause" exempted those who could not read and write but who could explain sections of the federal or state constitution to the satisfaction of the examiner, and a "good moral character clause" exempted those with such character. Again, local election registrars exercised discretion in deciding who understood the Constitution and who had good character. Finally, the **grandfather clause** exempted those whose grandfathers had the right to vote before 1867—that is, before blacks could legally vote in the South.

The **poll tax** also deprived blacks of voting rights. The tax, though only a couple of dollars, was often a sizable proportion of working people's monthly income. In some states, individuals had to pay not only for the present election but for every past election in which they were eligible to vote but did not.

In the **white primary,** blacks were barred from voting in primary elections, where party nominees were chosen. Because the Democrats always won the general elections, the real contests were in the Democratic primaries. The states justified excluding blacks on the grounds that political parties were private, rather than governmental, organizations and thus could discriminate just as private clubs or individuals could.

Less formal means also were used to exclude blacks from voting. Registrars often closed their offices when blacks tried to register, or whites threatened blacks with the loss of jobs or housing if they tried to vote. Polling places were sometimes located far from black neighborhoods or were moved at the last minute without notifying potential voters. If these means failed, whites threatened or practiced violence. In one election in Mobile, whites wheeled a cannon to a polling place and aimed it at about one thousand blacks lined up to vote.

The treatment of blacks by the southern establishment was summarized on the floor of the Senate by South Carolina Senator Benjamin ("Pitchfork Ben") Tillman, who served from 1895 to 1918. As he put it, "We took the government away. We stuffed ballot boxes. We shot them. We are not ashamed of it."

Over time, the Supreme Court and Congress outlawed the "legal" barriers to black voting in the South. The Court invalidated the grandfather clause in 1915 and the white primary in 1944. Through the Twenty-fourth Amendment, Congress abolished the poll tax for federal elections in 1964, and the Court invalidated the tax for state elections in 1966.[8] But threats of physical violence and economic reprisals still kept most southern blacks from voting. Although many blacks in the urban areas of the rim South (such as Florida, North Carolina, Tennessee, and Texas) could and did vote, those in the rural South and most in the Deep South could not; in 1960, black registration ranged from 5 to 40 percent in southern states.[9] (See also the "American Diversity" box.)

Library of Congress

Four of the men shown in this 1870 poster with Frederick Douglass (center) served in Congress: Hiram Revels in the Senate and Benjamin Turner, Josiah T. Walls, and Joseph Rainey in the House. Also pictured are writer William Wells Brown and Bishop Richard Allen, founder of the African Methodist Episcopal Church.

The Voting Rights Act and Redistricting

Despite our shameful history of depriving African Americans of the right to vote, today black voting rates approach those of whites. In the Deep South, much of this dramatic change was brought about by the passage of the **Voting Rights Act (VRA)** in 1965, which made it illegal to interfere with anyone's right to vote. The act suspended the use of literacy tests, and, most important, it sent federal voter registrars into counties where less than 50 percent of the voting age population (black and white) was registered. The premise of this requirement was that if so few had registered, there must be serious barriers to registration. All of Alabama, Mississippi, South Carolina, and Louisiana, substantial parts of North Carolina, and scattered counties in five northern states were included in the area covered by registrars.

Any changes in election procedures had to be approved by the Department of Justice or the U.S. District Court for the District of Columbia. States or counties had to show a clean record of not discriminating for ten years before they could escape this supervision. Those who sought to deter blacks from voting through intimidation now had to face the force of the federal government.

Though black registration had been increasing in the rim South due to voter registration and education projects, the impact of the VRA in the Deep South was dramatic.[10] Within a year after federal registrars were sent, hundreds of thousands of southern blacks were registered, radically changing the nature of southern politics. In the most extreme case, Mississippi registration of blacks zoomed from 7 to 41 percent. In Alabama, the black electorate doubled in four years.

Due to these increases, not only have dozens of blacks been elected, but white politicians must now court black voters to get elected. Even the late George Wallace, the segregationist Alabama governor who had opposed the civil rights movement in the 1960s, eagerly sought black votes in the 1970s and 1980s.

The VRA was renewed and expanded in 1970, 1975, and 1982. It now covers more states and other minorities, such as Hispanics, Asians, Native Americans, and Eskimos, and thus serves as a basic protection for minority voting rights. For example, states must provide bilingual ballots in counties in which 5 percent or more of the population does not speak English.

The VRA dramatically changed the face of the electorate in the South and then later in other parts of the nation. Given the success of the VRA and faced with an expanded black electorate, some white officials in areas of large black populations used new means to diminish the political clout of African Americans. Their technique was *gerrymandering*. (See the box "Racial Gerrymandering.") Through devices that political scientists call **"cracking, stacking, and packing,"** districts were drawn to minimize black representation depending on the size and configuration of the black and white populations. *Cracking* divides significant, concentrated black populations into

Before the Voting Rights Act in 1965, few African Americans held major public office. Only a handful were members of Congress, and few were state legislators, mayors of major cities, or other important political officers. Following the Voting Rights Act, southern blacks began to have the political clout to elect members of their own race to office for the first time. Progress, slow to be sure, has occurred; in 1968, there were only twenty-three African American legislators in southern legislatures, but by 1997, there were more than ten times as many. Virginia, the heart of the Confederacy, elected the nation's first black governor, Douglas Wilder. And six-

teen black members of Congress represent southern constituencies.

The number of northern black officeholders also has increased, reflecting heightened black political activity there too. Richard Hatcher, who became mayor of Gary, Indiana, in 1968, was the first black mayor of a major U.S. city. By 2000, 450 African Americans served as black mayors in northern and southern cities, nearly 60 percent in cities without black majorities. Nationally, the number of black officeholders has increased from an estimated 1,200 in 1969 to more than 9,000 in 2000. Although this is far from proportional representation, it is a dramatic increase.

Hispanics, too, have improved their representation in political office. From a total of little more than 3,000 Hispanic public officials in 1985, their numbers by 2000 had grown to about 5,200, including 233 state-elected legislators and executives.

In sum, though progress is slow, African Americans and Hispanics, like other ethnic groups, are achieving political power through elections.

SOURCE: *Statistical Abstract of the United States 2001* (Washington, D.C.: Government Printing Office, 2001), Tables 399 and 400; Web page, Joint Center for Political and Social Research, Directory of Black Elected Officials.

Blacks line up to vote in Peachtree, Alabama, after enactment of the Voting Rights Act of 1965.

two or more districts so that neither will be majority black; *stacking* combines a large black population with an even greater white population; and *packing* puts a huge black population into one district rather than two, where blacks might approach a majority in each.

Initially, the Supreme Court was reluctant to find these practices illegal without specific proof that their intent was to discriminate against black voters.[11] But in 1982, congressional revision of the VRA required states with large minority populations to draw boundaries in ways to increase the probabilities that minorities will win seats. The focus of the voting rights legislation, then, turned from protecting the right of suffrage to trying to ensure that voting rights result in the election of African American and other minority officeholders. With this new statute as an indication of congressional intent, the Court then did strike down districting in North Carolina as inappropriately diluting black voting power.[12]

After the 1990 census, eleven new **majority-minority districts** were created for blacks and six for Hispanics. All but one were actually won by blacks and Hispanics in the 1992 election. Partly as a result of this redistricting, blacks were elected to Congress for the first time since Reconstruction in Alabama, Florida, North Carolina, South Carolina, and Virginia. Hispanics were elected for the first time ever in Illinois and New Jersey. In all, thirty-nine blacks and nineteen Hispanics were elected to Congress, a dramatic increase from the twenty-five blacks and ten Hispanics serving before the 1992 election.[13]

However, after this post-1990 redistricting, which used extensive gerrymandering to create the majority-minority districts, some white voters challenged their legality. In a series of cases, the Supreme Court then ruled that racial gerrymandering, the drawing of district lines specifically to concentrate racial minorities to try to ensure the election of minority representatives, is as constitutionally suspect as the drawing of district lines to diffuse minority electoral strength.[14] To the surprise of many, despite the consequent redrawing of several majority-minority districts after the 1994 election, the African American incumbents were still able to win re-election in 1996 and after.

Women and the Right to Vote

When property ownership defined the right to vote, women property owners could vote in some places. When property requirements were removed, suffrage came to be seen as a male right only. Women's right to vote was reintroduced in the 1820s in Tennessee school board elections.[15] From that time on, women had the vote in some places, usually only at the local level or for particular kinds of elections.

The national movement for women's suffrage did not gain momentum until after the Civil War. Before and during that war, many women helped lead the campaign to abolish slavery and establish full political rights for blacks. When black men got the vote after the Civil War, some women saw the paradox in their working to enfranchise these men when they themselves lacked the right to vote. Led by Susan B. Anthony, Elizabeth Cady Stanton, and others, they lobbied Congress and the state legislatures for voting rights for women.

The first suffrage bill was introduced in Congress in 1868 and each year thereafter until 1893. Most members were strong in their condemnation of women as potential voters. One senator claimed that if women could hold political views different from their husbands, it would make "every home a hell on earth."

Racial Gerrymandering

This North Carolina district (the Twelfth), shown on the maps, was drawn after the 1990 census to create a black majority district. North Carolina, which is about 20 percent African American, had not elected a black representative to Congress since 1898. The state's seats, now twelve, went to whites because the black population was (and remains) relatively scattered. Responding to pressure from the Justice Department, the state legislature created two black majority districts after the 1990 census. Voters elected two African Americans from these districts in 1992.

Upset that the legislature created two black majority districts and at the same time protected white Democratic incumbents, the state Republican Party and white citizens sued, challenging the plan. One district, the Twelfth, snaked through parts of ten counties and seven of the former congressional districts as it followed Interstate 85.

The district was 160 miles long and in places no wider than the highway corridor and in other places not quite this wide—the northbound and southbound lanes were in different districts. One legislator famously remarked that "if you drove down the interstate with both car doors open, you'd kill most of the people in the district."

The bizarre shape was the result of the legislature's efforts to create the majority-minority district while also pro-

tecting white incumbents in other districts. Although its shape left the district, and the process, vulnerable to ridicule, in some ways at least these new districts were more homogeneous than the old districts had been. For example, the Twelfth was an urban district, drawing from the black populations of Charlotte, Winston-Salem, Greensboro, and Durham. Still, as one reporter noted, "In most electoral contests, candidates try to focus on finding out what the voters want. But in the 12th, the candidates face a challenge just *finding out who the voters are.*"[1]

Some white citizens challenged the districting plan. The case reached the Supreme Court, which overturned the North Carolina plan. The majority called the district "so irregular" and "so bizarre" that it can be understood "only as an effort to segregate the races for purposes of voting, without regard for traditional districting principles and without sufficiently compelling justification." North Carolina tried redrawing its districts twice more before the Court was satisfied. The last

---

When Wyoming applied to join the union in 1889, it already had granted women the right to vote. Congress initially tried to bar Wyoming for that reason but then relented when the Wyoming territorial legislature declared, "We will remain out of the Union one hundred years rather than come in without the women." Still, by 1910 women had complete suffrage rights in only four states.

Powerful interests opposed suffrage for women. Liquor interests feared that women voters would press for prohibition because many women had been active in the temperance (antiliquor) movement. Other businesses feared that suffrage would lead to reforms to improve working conditions for women and children. Southern whites feared that it would lead to voting by black women and then by black men. Political bosses feared that women would favor political reform. The Catholic Church opposed it as contrary to the proper role of women. According to some people, suffrage was a revolt against nature. Pregnant women might lose their babies, nursing mothers their milk, and women might grow beards or be raped at the polls (then frequently located in saloons or barber shops).[16] Others argued less

hysterically that women should be protected from the unsavory practices of politics and should confine themselves to their traditional duties.

About 1910, however, the women's suffrage movement was reenergized, in part by ideas and tactics borrowed from the British women's suffrage movement. A new generation of leaders, including Alice Paul and Carrie Chapman Catt, began to lobby more vigorously, reach out to the working class, and engage in protest marches and picketing, new features of American politics. In 1917, when the National Women's party organized around-the-clock picketing of the White House, their arrest and forced feeding during jail hunger strikes embarrassed the administration and won the movement some support. These incidents, plus contributions by women to the war effort during World War I, led to adoption of the Nineteenth Amendment guaranteeing women the vote in 1920. Although only 37 percent of eligible women voted in the 1920 presidential election, as the habit of voting spread, women's rates of voting equaled those of men. (See also the box "Women in Office.")

version did not have majority-minority districts though the black incumbents who had been elected continued to be reelected by the new white majorities.

The practice of drawing strangely shaped districts to fulfill political objectives, called *gerrymandering,* is hardly new in American politics. The name originated in 1812 when the Massachusetts legislature carved out a district that historian John Fiske said had a "dragonlike contour." When painter Gilbert Stuart saw the misshapen district, he drew in a head, wings, and claws and exclaimed, "That will do for a salamander!" Editor Benjamin Russell replied, "Better say Gerrymander," after Elbridge Gerry, then governor of Massachusetts.[2] Since then, gerrymandering has been widely used by politicians to benefit their own political parties.

Supporters of racial gerrymandering believe it is the best way to increase minority representation. It provides a favorable setting for members of a minority racial group to elect members of their own race. But others argue that low numbers of racial and ethnic minorities in Congress cannot appropriately be changed by the use of deliberate gerrymanders. Some also object to the creation of majority-minority districts because they see the dangers of thereby creating other districts with fewer minorities. These other districts will be more white than before, with representatives who are less sensitive to the interests of minorities.

One possible reform that meets the objectives of both groups is **cumulative voting.** Under that system, members of Congress would be elected not from single-member districts but from at-large districts in which several members of Congress would be elected at the same time. Voters would each have a number of votes equal to the number of seats in the district. They could apportion their votes among the candidates in any way that they preferred.

Members of any group, including racial, ethnic, religious, political, or economic groups, could target their votes on the candidates most likely to represent the group's interests. This election procedure could produce greater racial and ethnic diversity in representative bodies such as Congress without creating new districts on the basis of race or ethnicity.

This procedure is not totally new to the United States; it was used for many years in Illinois to elect members of their state's House of Representatives. Still, acceptance of cumulative voting for congressional districts seems remote.

1. Charles Mahtesian, "Blacks' Political Hopes Boosted by Newly Redrawn Districts," *Congressional Quarterly Weekly Report,* April 25, 1992, 1087.
2. *Guide to Congress,* 2d ed. (Washington, D.C.: Congressional Quarterly, 1976), 563; *Congressional Quarterly: The Race to Capitol Hill,* February 29, 1992, 103–105. OTHER SOURCES: Bruce E. Cain, "Voting Rights and Democratic Theory toward a Color-Blind Society?" *Brookings Review,* Winter 1992, 46–50; Carol M. Swain, "The Voting Rights Act: Some Unintended Consequences," *Brookings Review,* Winter 1992, 51; Douglas Amy, *Real Choices/New Voices: The Case for Proportional Representation Elections in the United States* (New York: Columbia University Press, 1993); John Gruhl and Susan Welch, "Representation and Race Conscious Districting," paper presented at the American Political Science Association meetings, 2002.

Women's contributions to the war effort during World War I helped lead to the ratification of the women's suffrage amendment in 1920. Here Broadway chorus women train as Home Guards during the war.

Brown Brothers

WOMEN IN OFFICE

Even before women were given the right to vote nationally, they held political office. Women officeholders in colonial America were rare but not unknown. In 1715, for example, the Pennsylvania Assembly appointed a woman as tax collector.[1]

Elizabeth Cady Stanton, probably the first woman candidate for Congress, received twenty-four votes when she ran in 1866.[2] It was not until 1916 that the first woman member of Congress, Jeannette Rankin (R-Mont.), was actually elected. In 1872, Victoria Claflin Woodhull ran for president on the Equal Rights Party ticket teamed with abolitionist Frederick Douglass for vice president.

More than one hundred thousand women now hold elective office, but many of these offices are minor. Inroads by women into major national offices have been slow. Geraldine Ferraro's 1984 vice presidential candidacy was historic but not victorious. In recent years, women have only gradually increased their membership in Congress. But in the 1992 elections, women candidates won striking increases in national legislative office. Women have continued to gain seats and after 2000 numbered thirteen in the Senate and sixty in the House. About 80 percent of the female senators and two-thirds of House members are Democrats.[3]

Real progress also has been made in state and local governments. Women hold 27 percent of all statewide elective offices, although only five women are governors (but seventeen women are lieutenant governors). In 1969, only 4 percent of the state legislators were women; today 23 percent are. However, this progress slowed in the late 1990s. In eight states, women hold at least 30 percent of state legislative seats, although in Alabama they hold less than 10 percent, and the Arkansas state senate has no women members.[4]

More than 20 percent of the city council seats in medium and large cities are now occupied by women, and 15 percent are mayors of cities of America's one hundred largest cities. Women are twice as likely to be found on school boards, however, where they make up 40 percent of the members.

Does it make a difference in terms of policy to have women officeholders rather than men? Studies of the behavior of women members of Congress and other legislative bodies indicate that they are, on the whole, more liberal than men.[5] Women tend to give issues relating to women, children, and the family higher priority than male legislators do.[6] Women are also less likely to be involved in corrupt activities.

More and more women are getting graduate and professional education and working outside the home. These

"Nothing against Rudy, I just feel that a woman would be instinctively better on dairy issues."

changes, coupled with increased public support for women taking an active role in politics, suggest that the trend toward more women in public office will continue.

1. Joseph J. Kelley, *Pennsylvania: The Colonial Years* (Garden City, N.Y.: Doubleday, 1980), 143.
2. Elisabeth Griffin, *In Her Own Right* (New York: Oxford University Press, 1983).
3. Data are from Center for the American Woman and Politics, National Information Bank on Women in Public Office, Rutgers University, www.rci.rutgers.edu/_cawp /pdf/elective.pdf.
5. Susan Welch, "Are Women More Liberal Than Men in the U.S. Congress?" *Legislative Studies Quarterly* 10, February 1985, 125–134.
6. Sue Thomas and Susan Welch, "The Impact of Gender on the Priorities and Activities of State Legislators," *Western Political Quarterly*, 1991.

Young People and the Right to Vote

Federal constitutional and legislative changes extended the franchise to young adults. Before 1971, almost all states required a voting age of nineteen or more. The service of eighteen-year-olds in the Vietnam War brought protests that if these men were old enough to die for their country, they were old enough to vote. Yielding to these arguments and to the general recognition that young people were better educated than in the past, Congress adopted and the states ratified the Twenty-sixth Amendment giving eighteen-year-olds the right to vote.

Felons and the Right to Vote

An exception to the general liberalization of the right to vote are the policies in thirteen states that bar all convicted felons from voting. In Florida, an estimated 525,000 people, most of them poor and black, were barred from voting in 2000.[17] In total, more than 1 million people are prevented from voting by felony convictions, including one in seven black men (in Alabama, one of three black men are barred).[18] Some states return the right to vote after a certain period of time, others, like Florida, bar them permanently. In some states, these laws stem from Reconstruction-era laws targeted to reduce voting power of blacks. Analyses of the impacts of these laws suggest they have had a significant effect in putting conservative Republicans in office in states with large black populations.[19]

In Florida, the secretary of state contracted with a private firm the job of purging felons from the registration lists. The firm also blocked several thousand people, mostly black, who were not convicted felons but rather had been convicted of misdemeanors. These people were also barred from voting.

Some might argue that we should not worry about the voting rights of felons. Loss of voting rights might be seen as part of their punishment. However, most felons barred from voting have served their time and returned to society. Many times they were convicted as a young person and have been a law-abiding citizen for years or even decades. Moreover, this particular punishment does not really seem to fit the crime.

In sum, only convicted felons, the mentally incapable, noncitizens, and those not meeting minimal residence requirements are unable to vote now. Voting has come to be an essential right of citizenship, except for felons, rather than a privilege just for those qualified by birth or property.

Voter Turnout

Paradoxically, as the *right* to vote has expanded, the proportion of eligible citizens *actually* voting has contracted.

Political Activism in the Nineteenth Century

In 1896, an estimated 750,000 people—5 percent of all voters—took train excursions to visit presidential candidate William McKinley at his Ohio home during the campaign.[20] This amazing figure is but one indication of the high level of intense political interest and activity in the late nineteenth century.

In those days, politics was an active, not a spectator, sport. People voted at high rates, as much as 80 percent in the 1840 presidential election,[21] and they were very partisan. They thought independents were corrupt and ready to sell their votes to the highest bidder. In colonial America, voters usually voted by voice. By the mid-nineteenth century, most states used paper ballots. Elaborate and well-organized parties printed and distributed the ballots. Voters, after being coached by party leaders, simply dropped their party's ballot into

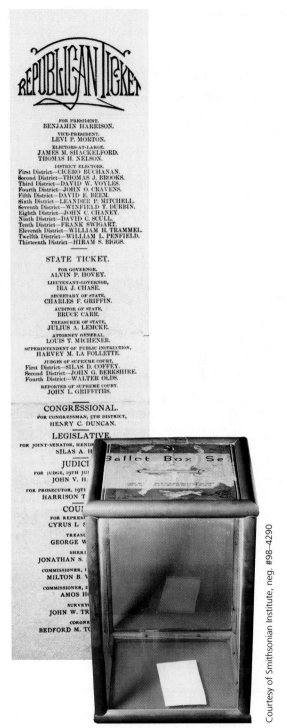

Until the turn of the twentieth century, there was no pretense of secrecy in voting. Each party's ballot was a different color. Voters chose their party's ballot, like this Republican ballot used in the 1888 Indiana elections. They then put that ballot in a clear glass-sided ballot box. Party ballots could make sure that "bought" voters stayed bought. The widespread vote buying in the 1888 election and the growing strength of party reform movements led to the secret ballot being adopted by thirty-eight states between the 1888 and 1892 elections and the remainder of states shortly thereafter. However, the 2000 election revealed that ballot format can still be both crucial and controversial.

the box. Split-ticket voting and secrecy in making one's choice were impossible.

Progressive Reforms

The **Progressive reforms** of the late nineteenth and early twentieth centuries brought radical changes to election politics. Progressive reformers, largely professional and upper middle class, sought to eliminate corruption from politics and voting. But they also meant to eliminate the influence of the lower classes, many of them recent immigrants. These two goals went hand in hand, because the lower classes were seen as the cause of corruption in politics.

The Progressive movement was responsible for several reforms: primary elections, voter registration laws, secret ballots, nonpartisan ballots (without party labels), and the denial of voting rights for aliens, which removed a major constituency of the urban party machines. The movement also introduced the merit system for public employment to reduce favoritism and payoffs in hiring.

The reforms, adopted by some states at the end of the nineteenth century and by others much later, were largely effective in cleaning up politics. But the reformers also achieved, to a very large extent, their goal of eliminating the lower classes from politics. Taking away most of the reason for the existence of the political parties—choosing candidates and printing and distributing ballots—caused the party organization to decline, which in turn produced a decline in political interest and activity on the part of the electorate. Without strong parties to mobilize voters, only the most interested and motivated participated. The new restrictions on voting meant that voters had to invest more time, energy, and thought in voting. They had to think about the election months in advance and travel to city hall to register.

As a consequence, politics began to be a spectator activity. Voter turnout declined sharply after the turn of the century.

Turnout figures from the nineteenth century are not entirely reliable and not exactly comparable with today's. In the days before voter registration, many aliens could vote, and some people voted twice. In some instances, more people voted in a state election than lived there! Nevertheless, it is generally agreed that turnout was very high in the nineteenth century and that it has diminished substantially; it dropped from more than 77 percent from 1840 to 1896 to 54 percent in the 1920–1932 era, when the Progressive reforms were largely in place. During the New Deal era, when the Democratic Party mobilized new groups of voters, turnout rose again, but it has never achieved anything close to the levels of the nineteenth century.

Recent Turnout

Between 1964 and 2000, turnout in presidential elections slowly declined, from 62 percent to 52 percent. That is, only half of all citizens voted in recent elections. This means that only one-fourth of the potential voters actually vote for the winning candidate.[22]

The turnout for off-year congressional elections is even lower. It has not exceeded 45 percent since World War II, and in 1998 it was 42 percent.[23] Only in Minnesota did more than half of the voters turn out. Turnout in primary elections is far lower still, sometimes as low as 10 percent.

Although nations count their turnouts differently, it is clear that Americans vote in much lower proportions than citizens of other Western democracies. Only Switzerland, which relatively recently gave women the right to vote, approximates our low turnout levels.

Within the United States, turnout varies greatly among the states (see Figure 1). In the 2000 presidential election, for example, 70 percent of Minnesota's citizens voted, but only 43 percent of Hawaii's did.[24] Turnout tends to be lower in the South and higher in the northern Plains and Mountain states.[25]

These differences suggest that not only are there certain kinds of people who are unwilling to vote, but there are also certain kinds of laws and political traditions that depress voting turnout.

Who Does Not Vote?

Before we can explain why some people do not vote, we need to see who the nonvoters are. The most important

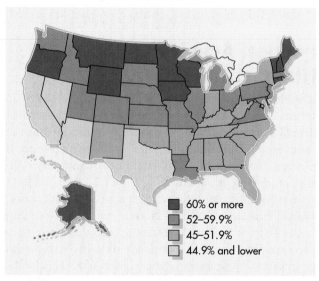

FIGURE 1 ■ State Electorates Differ in Voting Turnout Rates
These data report the official turnout for the 2000 presidential election. The average turnout was 52 percent.
SOURCE: *Statistical Abstract of the United States 2001,* Table 404.

60% or more
52–59.9%
45–51.9%
44.9% and lower

thing to remember is that voting is related to education, income, and occupation—that is, to socioeconomic class. For example, if you are a college graduate, the chances are about 70 percent that you will vote; if you have less than a high school education, the chances are less than half that.[26] Differences between higher- and lower-income people are also quite large and growing. Although voting among all groups of Americans has declined in the past forty years, the proportion of college-educated persons who participated fell by less than 10 percent, while that of high school–educated persons dropped by nearly 20 percent. Education apparently is linked to voting because those with more years of education are more interested in, and knowledgeable about, politics.

Though many people take it for granted that those in the working class vote at lower rates than those in the middle and upper classes, in the United States these differences are far wider than in other nations[27] and far greater than in nineteenth-century America. So there appears to be something unique about the contemporary American political system that inhibits voting participation of all citizens, but particularly those whose income and educational level are below the average.

Voting is also much more common among older than younger people. Since 1971, the minimum voting age has been eighteen. But in 1972, the first presidential election when all eighteen- to twenty-year-olds were eligible, less than half of young voters turned out, and even that small turnout has declined precipitously since. As Figure 2 indicates, only 31 percent of eighteen- to twenty-year-olds voted in 1996, compared with more than 55 percent in each age category over thirty-five and more than 60 percent among those fifty and older.

Why the low vote? One might expect that young people are more alienated from politics than their elders, but this does not seem to be true. Young voters are more trusting and less cynical. Others attribute low voting turnout to the high degree of mobility of young adults; they change their residences frequently and perhaps do not have time or do not take time to figure out how and where to register. Many young people are preoccupied with major life changes—going to college, leaving home, beginning their first full-time job, getting married, starting a family. If registered at all, the registration place may be in their home towns, far away from where they live. Those in their forties and older have established their careers and families, and they have more time and money to devote to voting and other political activities. Then, too, young people do not have the habit of voting.

Young people's initial tendency to vote is positively influenced by their parents' education and political engagement and by their own high school experiences and going on to college. Later in life, getting married, establishing a stable residence, and becoming active in

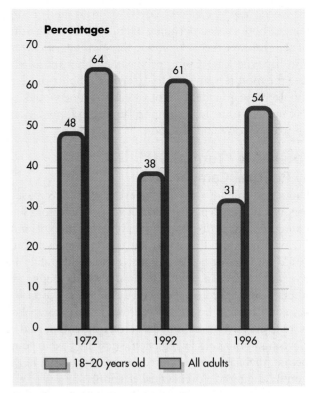

FIGURE 2 ■ Young People Vote Less

In 1996, Rock the Vote, a group organized to increase turnout among young adults, used a Web site to help those aged eighteen to twenty-four register to vote. The group also set up registration tables at rock concerts and surfing championships. Despite these efforts, voting by young adults decreased from 1992.

SOURCE: *Current Population Reports,* "Voting and Registration in the Election" (various editions), U.S. Census, Series P20.

the community are important to continuing their voting habits.[28]

Groups promoting voter turnout have recently focused on young people. MTV cosponsors a "Rock the Vote" promotion to encourage registration and voting as well as election reform.[29] Vote Smart, a nonpartisan group providing information about candidates and elections, also targets young people through special internship programs.[30]

Why Turnout Is Low

There are a number of other possible reasons more Americans, especially low-income and young Americans, do not vote.

Satisfaction among Nonvoters

One reason sometimes given for low rates of voter turnout is that nonvoters are satisfied; failing to vote is a passive form of consent to what government is doing.[31] This argument falls flat on two counts. First, voter turnout has decreased in an era when public trust in government has decreased, not increased. Levels of trust and voting turnout both started declining after 1964. Second, voter turnout is lower precisely among those groups of citizens who have the least reason to be content, not those who have the most reason to be so. If staying at home on election day were an indication of satisfaction, one would expect turnout to be lower among the well-off, not among the working class and the poor.

Voters Are "Turned Off" by Political Campaigns

About one-third of a group of nonvoters in the 1990 election, when asked why they did not vote, gave reasons suggesting they were disgusted with politics.[32] In explaining the low turnout in the 1988 campaign, one analyst commented, "The media consultants, media and politicians gave this nation an awful election, and the public responded with appropriately awful turnouts."[33] The analyst was condemning the lack of real issues in the campaign, the negative advertising, and the constant attention paid by television to the polls telling people how they were going to vote (there are now hundreds of campaign polls in the months leading to a presidential election).

These analyses surely contain some grains of truth, but how many? After all, people who are most likely to pay attention to the media, watch the ads, hear about the polls, and follow the campaigns are the most likely to vote, not the least. It is possible that the increasingly media-oriented campaigns have decreased overall turnout during the past generation (and we will have more to say about these campaigns later in the chapter). In fact, turnout is inversely related to media spending; the more the candidates spend, the lower the turnout. Moreover, voters who watch negative political ads are less likely to vote or to feel their vote counts.[34] But negative advertising does not affect turnout much, if at all,[35] and negative advertising and other media attention cannot explain the class bias in nonvoting.

In addition to the *quality* of the campaigns, some people think turnout has declined because our elections are so frequent, campaigns last so long, and so many offices are contested that the public becomes bored, confused, or cynical.[36] At the presidential level, the sheer quantity of coverage, much of it focused repetitively on "who's winning," may simply bore people. Moreover, the continual public opinion polling and the widely publicized results may lead some to believe they don't need to vote. To the extent that people feel their votes do not count, the close election in 2000 may change some minds.

At the local level, voters elect so many officeholders, all the way down to weed and mosquito control commissioners, that many have no idea for whom or what

In this chapter, there are eight photos, each marked with a blue band along the top, that illustrate American campaign tactics throughout the years. In this photo from the 1828 campaign, Andrew Jackson's opponents accused him of executing soldiers he commanded (as symbolized by the coffins). Jackson won anyway.

Courtesy of Smithsonian Institute

they are voting. This proliferation of elective offices, thought by some to promote democracy and popular control, may promote only voter confusion and alienation. The problem is compounded because elections for different offices are held at different times. For example, most states have decided to hold elections for governor in nonpresidential election years. This decision probably reduces presidential election turnout by 7 percent and may reduce by one-third the number of those who vote for governor in those states.[37]

Primary elections are another problem. One estimate is that holding primary campaigns diminishes the general election turnout by 5 percent.[38]

By contrast, in Britain the time between calling an election (by the current government) and the actual election is only a month. On May 9, 2001, Prime Minister Tony Blair called the election, and on June 7, 2001, it was held. All campaigning was done during that time. There are no primaries. Moreover, as in most other parliamentary democracies, British citizens vote only for their representative in parliament and (at one other time) for the local representative. Voters are not faced with choices for a myriad of offices they barely recognize.

Lack of Social Rootedness

Turnout is low partially because of what one analyst has called lack of "social rootedness."[39] Middle age, marriage, and residential stability lead to rootedness in one's community. Americans move around, marry late, and get divorced more than those in other nations. Mobility alone may reduce voting by as much as 9 percent. However, American turnout is still low even taking into account these factors.

Barriers to Registration

Most other democracies have nonpersonal systems of voter registration. That is, the state or parties are responsible for registering voters. Voter registrars go door to door to register voters, or voters are registered automatically when they pay taxes or receive public services. Consequently, almost everyone is registered to vote.

The United States puts the responsibility for registration on the individual, which has been a major impediment to voting. Only about 70 percent of U.S. citizens are registered.[40] About one-quarter of nonvoters surveyed in 1990 indicated they did not vote because it was too difficult. As one commentator put it, "The United States is the only major democracy where government assumes no responsibility for helping citizens cope with voter registration procedures."[41] Difficult registration procedures have a special impact on low-income Americans, who were 17 percent less likely to vote in states with difficult registration procedures than in other states.[42]

Some states make it more convenient to register by having registration periods lasting up to election day (most states require registration at least twenty-five days before the election), registration in precincts or neighborhoods instead of one county office, registration by mail, registration offices open in the evenings and Saturday, and a policy of not purging voters who fail to vote from the registration lists. (See the box "Same-Day Voter Registration" for another possible alternative.)

In other jurisdictions, voter registrars not only do not provide these options but actually try to hinder groups working to increase registration. They may refuse to allow volunteers to register voters outside the registration office.[43] Several states have attempted to intimidate minority voters from registering and voting. In fact, the states with the highest barriers to voting tend to be states with the largest minority populations.[44] In 1990, the North Carolina Republican state committee sent over one hundred thousand postcards, mainly to black voters, warning them they can't vote if they've moved within thirty days even though the law specifically gave them the right to vote in their old residence.[45]

Some states regularly purge the registration rolls of voters who fail to vote. They are fearful that people have moved, reregistered, and will vote twice. Sometimes less high-minded motives are at work, and this tactic is used to disenfranchise lower income and minority voters. This practice means that sometimes voters who think they are registered find they are not when they arrive at the polling places. In Florida, in the 2000 election, among other voting day problems, hundreds of black voters were turned away from the polls, finding they had been purged from the rolls.

One estimate is that voting turnout would be 9 percent higher if all states' procedures were similar to those of states that try to facilitate voter registration.[46]

To increase registration, Congress passed a law allowing people to register at public offices such as welfare offices and drivers' license bureaus (for this reason it is called the **motor voter law**).[47] Similar plans had increased registration in the twenty-nine states that had these policies before the federal government did.[48] The law led to the greatest expansion of voter registration in American history; 5 million new voters registered.[49] However, in the 1996 election, fewer voted than in 1992, indicating that the law did not have the desired effect of increasing turnout.[50]

A related proposal suggests that change-of-address cards filed with the post office be accompanied by cards that go to the voting registration offices in the voter's former residence and new residence. Registration in the new residence would be automatic. The proposal also would reduce election fraud by removing from voting rosters names of residents who move.[51]

Same-Day Voter Registration

Voting turnout in the United States is second from lowest among the nations of the industrialized world. There are a number of possible remedies to this problem. One popular proposal is to allow voters to register when they go to the polling place on election day. This would reduce the costs of voting by reducing the time spent in finding and going to the registration office and the foresight necessary to remember to do so weeks or months in advance of the election. Moreover, by allowing same-day registration, states would put less premium on permanence of residence. Since Americans are a mobile population, this would increase the number of citizens eligible to vote.

States that make registration difficult (closing registration long before the election, not allowing absentee registration, not having regular office hours at the registrar's office, and so forth) have voter turnout about 9 percent less than states that make registration easier.[1] Since same-day registration is another way of making registration easier, we would expect it to improve turnout.

Three states (Maine, Minnesota, and Wisconsin) adopted same-day registration beginning in the 1970s, and that experience allows us to compare turnout between them and the other states. Since those three states have adopted same-day registration, their turnout in presidential elections has increased over 3 percent. The turnout rates in the other states, on average, have decreased almost 2 percent during that same time.[2] In other words, with everything else staying the same, same-day registration appears to improve voting turnout by about 5 percent. Other indicators of turnout change also suggest that same-day registration does lead to increased turnout.

Does the increase in turnout outweigh possible negative effects of this change? Opponents of the reform believe that it might lead to increased voter fraud; it might be easier for voters to vote multiple times, for example, if they do not have to register before the election.

However, the existing system does not protect very well against voter fraud for someone determined to vote more than once, either. With the expansion of sophisticated computer tools, we might expect that the means to combat voter fraud are increasingly at hand, same-day voting or not.

Ultimately, though, we have to decide whether the expansion of the electorate by 5 percent, or, in another estimate, 8 million voters, is worth the additional risks that slightly more multiple voting might take place. And, whether or not we adopt same-day voting, we need to consider other means of increasing voter turnout, too.

1. Steven Rosenstone and Ray Wolfinger, "The Effect of Registration Laws on Voter Turnout," *American Political Science Review* 72, March 1978, 22–45; G. Mitchell and C. Wlezien, "Voter Registration Laws and Turnout, 1972–1982," paper presented at the annual meeting of the Midwest Political Science Association, 1989.
2. Mark J. Fenster, "The Impact of Allowing Day of Registration Voting on Turnout in U.S. Elections from 1960 to 1992," *American Politics Quarterly* 22, January 1994, 74–87.

Failures of Parties to Mobilize Voters

Traditionally, political parties mobilized voters to turn out. Parties have become less effective in this role. They are spending more time raising funds than mobilizing voters.[52] The lack of effectiveness on the part of political parties in mobilizing millions of nonvoters, most of them working class or poor, is another reason for low voter turnout. Because of their low income, a majority of these nonvoters are Democrats. If mobilized, they would probably vote for Democrats, but not to the degree many Republicans fear. In many elections, the preferences of nonvoters have simply reflected the preferences of voters.[53]

Republicans are most fearful of this potential electorate. But even some Democrats are wary. The party has embraced social and economic policies that attracted many middle-class and some business groups. The goals of these groups sometimes conflict with those of the working class and poor, and the party's leaders do not want to threaten these constituencies. They must be responsive to their funding sources as well as their potential voters. The party has thus muted its appeals to the working class. This further reduces the incentives of working-class people to

vote and in turn decreases the incentive of Democrats to appeal to working-class voters.[54] However, increasing voter turnout has now become a partisan issue, with most Democrats backing attempts to increase turnout (as they did with the motor voter plan) and most Republicans opposing them. States with the highest turnout tend to have active and liberal Democratic Parties, giving voters a choice and thus a motive to vote.

Voting as a Rational Calculation of Costs and Benefits

Nonvoting also may be the result of a rational calculation of the costs and benefits of voting. Economist Anthony Downs argues that people vote when they believe the perceived benefits of voting are greater than the costs.[55] If a voter sees a difference between the parties or candidates and favors one party's position over the other, that voter has a reason to vote and can expect some benefit from doing so. For that reason, people who are highly partisan vote more than those less attached to a party, and people with a strong sense of political efficacy, the belief they can influence government, vote more than others.

Voters who see no difference between the candidates or parties, however, may believe that voting is not worth the effort it takes and that it is more rational to abstain. In fact, 40 percent of nonvoters in 1990 gave only the excuse that they were "too busy," suggesting a large degree of apathy.[56] Nevertheless, some people will vote even if they think there is no difference between the candidates because they have a sense of civic duty, a belief that their responsibilities as citizens include voting. Most voters feel gratified that they have done their duties as citizens. In fact, more voters give this as an explanation for voting than any other reason, including the opportunity to influence policy.[57]

Downs assumes that the costs of voting are minimal, but, in reality, for many people the time, expense, and possible embarrassment of trying to register are greater than the perceived benefits of voting. This is especially true for lower-income people who perceive that neither party is attentive to their interests. Moreover, it is possible that the frequency, length, and media orientation of campaigns lower the perceived benefits of voting for people of all incomes by trivializing the election and emphasizing the negative.

Some analysts believe that voter turnout in the United States will not increase substantially until one of the political parties works to mobilize the traditional nonvoters through policies that appeal to them. For example, Roosevelt's New Deal mobilized thousands of new voters. If voters believe they have a reason to vote, then their calculation of the benefits of voting increases relative to the costs.

Other Campaign Participation

We have seen that only about half of all Americans vote in presidential elections, and even fewer vote in off-year

From this 1840 Whig campaign gimmick came the phrase "keep the ball rolling."

Courtesy of Smithsonian Institute

congressional races. Still fewer participate actively in political campaigns. For example, in a recent year, about one-quarter of the population said that they worked for a party or candidate. About an equal proportion claimed that they contributed money to a party or candidate. Smaller proportions attended political meetings or actually belonged to a political club.

Unlike voting, rates of participation in campaigns have not declined over the past twenty years. This suggests that people are about as political as they always have been but that something about elections themselves has decreased voter turnout. Indeed, more people give money to candidates and parties than they used to, probably because, unlike twenty years ago, candidates and parties now use mass mailing techniques to solicit funds from supporters.[58] Hundreds of thousands of potential donors can be reached in a very short time.

Just as there is a strong class basis to voting, there is also a strong class basis to participation in campaign activities.[59] Those with more education and income are more likely to participate. Those with some college education actually increased their participation over the past twenty years, whereas those with less than a high school education decreased theirs. Thus, the class bias in participation, as in voting alone, has increased over time.[60]

Gender, race, age, and regional differences in participation also appear. Even taking education into account, men usually participate slightly more than women, whites somewhat more than blacks, older people more than younger people, and southerners more than northerners. But these differences change over time. Young people participated more than their elders, and blacks more than whites, during the late 1960s and early 1970s.[61] The civil rights and anti–Vietnam War movements drew many young and black people into political activity.

Presidential Nominating Campaigns

Many Americans believe in the Horatio Alger myth, that with hard work anyone can achieve great success. This myth has its parallel in politics, where it is sometimes said that any child can grow up to be president. In fact, only a few run for that office, and even fewer are elected.

Who Runs for President and Why?

In deciding whether to run for president, individuals consider such things as the costs and risks of running and the probabilities of winning.[62] Most people have little chance of being president: They are unknown to the

In the nineteenth century, politics involved most people, and political parades and festivities were common. Here a torchlight parade honors Grover Cleveland in Buffalo in the late 1880s.

Corbis-Bettmann

public; they do not have the financial resources or contacts to raise the money needed for a national campaign; they have jobs they could not leave to run a serious campaign; their friends would probably ridicule them for even thinking of such a thing.

But a few people are in a different position. Take, for instance, a hypothetical U.S. senator from Texas or a governor of California. By their vote-gathering ability in a large state, they have demonstrated some possibility that they could win. Their decision to run might hinge on such considerations as whether they think they could raise the money necessary to run a campaign, whether they are willing to sacrifice a good part of their private life and their privacy for a few years, whether they have an embarrassing skeleton in the closet that would be discovered and lead to humiliation, and whether they would lose the office they currently hold if they run and lose.

These calculations are real. Most candidates for president are, in fact, senators or governors.[63] In recent decades governors (George W. Bush, Bill Clinton, Ronald Reagan, Jimmy Carter) have been more successful than senators (George McGovern, Robert Dole). Vice presidents also frequently run, but until George H. Bush's victory, they had not been successful in this century.

Why do candidates run? An obvious reason is to gain the power and prestige of the presidency. But they may have other goals as well, such as to gain support for a particular policy or set of ideas. Ronald Reagan, for example, clearly wanted to be president in part to spread his conservative ideology. Jesse Jackson wanted to be president in part to help those at the bottom of the social ladder. (See the "American Diversity" box for views

on electing an African American president one day.) Eugene McCarthy ran in 1968 to challenge Lyndon Johnson's Vietnam policy.

Sometimes candidates run to gain name recognition and publicity for the next election. Most successful candidates in recent years have run before. George H. Bush lost the nomination in 1980 before being elected in 1988; Ronald Reagan lost in 1976 before his victory in 1980; Richard Nixon lost in 1960 before winning in 1968.

Sometimes candidates run for the presidency to be considered for the vice presidency, probably viewing it as an eventual stepping stone to the presidency. But only occasionally, such as when Reagan chose Bush in 1980 or Kennedy chose Johnson in 1960, do presidential candidates choose one of their defeated opponents to run as a vice presidential candidate.

How a Candidate Wins the Nomination

The nominating process is crucial in deciding who eventually gets elected. Boss Tweed once said, "I don't care who does the electing, so long as I get to do the nominating."[64] American presidential candidates are nominated through a process that includes the general public, the financial supporters of each party, and other party leaders.

Over time, voters and fund-raisers have gained more power at the expense of party leaders. Presidential candidates try to win a majority of delegates at their party's national nominating convention in the summer preceding the November election. Delegates to those

CAN AN AFRICAN AMERICAN BE ELECTED PRESIDENT?

W ill the American presidency continue to be held only by white, non-Jewish males? Can an African American or a woman ever be elected?

These questions sound familiar. In 1960, some doubted that a Catholic could ever be elected president. At that time, only 71 percent of all voters said they would vote for a Catholic for president.[1] The only previous major-party Catholic candidate, Alfred Smith, had been soundly defeated by Herbert Hoover in 1928. But then John F. Kennedy was elected. Since then, two Catholics, Geraldine Ferraro and Sargent Shriver, have run as vice presidential nominees without much attention paid to their religion. And the candidacy of Joseph Lieberman, an orthodox Jew, for vice president on the 2000 Democratic ticket was widely applauded.

But race has been a more pronounced cleavage in American society than religion. Racism persists, and race influences all kinds of political debates, from welfare reform to the all-volunteer military. The party realignment that has occurred in the South is shaped by racial

as well as class issues. A majority of white southerners, resentful of the Democratic Party's support of the civil rights struggle, has turned to the Republican Party.

Race was important in the 1988 campaign. It surfaced when the Republicans succeeded in tying Michael Dukakis to Willie Horton, an African American convict who raped a woman while on furlough from prison. It also came up when Jesse Jackson's prominence in the Democratic Party was highlighted and made to seem somehow illegitimate and frightening. A campaign letter from the California Republican Party asked, "Why is it so urgent you decide now? Here are two [reasons]." Below were two photos, one of Bush and Reagan, the other of Jackson and Dukakis. "If [Dukakis] is elected to the White House," it continued, "Jesse Jackson is sure to be swept into power on his coattails."[2]

This is not to say that all of those who voted against Jackson in the primaries or against the Democrats in the general election were racists. Jackson had no experience holding office and is identified with the most liberal wing of the Democratic Party.

Race seemed less important in 1996 when Colin Powell, an African American former chair of the Joint Chiefs of Staff (the nation's highest military post) and currently secretary of state, was considered a strong presidential candidate. Many from both parties were quite disappointed when he chose not to run.

As the figure shows, 7 to 8 percent of the public say they would not vote for a black or a woman who was their party's nominee, and a slightly lower proportion say they would not vote for a Jew. Although 7 to 8 percent is enough to make a difference in a close race, many more people today say they would vote for a black, Jew, or woman than said they would vote for a Catholic in 1960. John Kennedy's victory suggests that 7 or 8 percent is not an insurmountable barrier.

1. Barry Sussman, "A Black or Woman Does Better Today Than a Catholic in '60," *Washington Post National Weekly Edition*, November 21, 1983, 42.
2. "Though This Be Meanness, yet There Is a Method in It," *Washington Post National Weekly Edition*, October 10–16, 1988, 26.

Declining Numbers Oppose Blacks, Women, and Jews for President

SOURCE: Gallup Polls. The question asked was "If your party nominated a generally well-qualified man for president and he happened to be a black [Jew], would you vote for him?" or "If your party nominated a woman for president, would you vote for her if she were qualified for the job?" No questions were asked about African Americans until 1958. The "1961" data for blacks are from 1963. The 1994 and 1996 data are from the NORC's General Social Surveys.

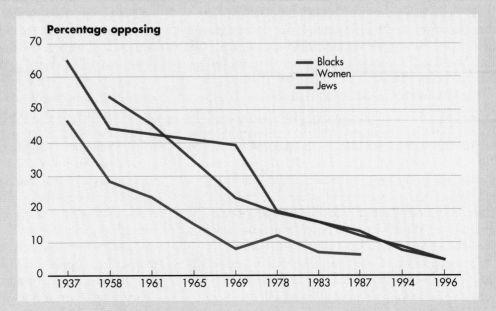

Percentage opposing

Blacks
Women
Jews

conventions are elected in state caucuses, conventions, and primaries. Candidates must campaign to win the support of those who attend caucuses and conventions and of primary voters.

Normally, candidates formally announce their candidacies in the year preceding the presidential election year. Then their aim is to persist and survive the long primary and caucus season that begins in February of election year and continues until only one candidate is left. Candidates use a number of methods to try to maximize their chances of survival. They carefully choose the primaries they will enter and to which they will devote their resources. Candidates must enter enough primaries so they are seen as national, not regional, candidates, but they cannot possibly devote time and resources to every primary or caucus. Especially important are the early events—the Iowa caucus and the New Hampshire primary—and the larger state primaries.

Candidates try hard to raise substantial amounts of money early. A large war chest can mark a candidate as unbeatable. George W. Bush started strong in the 2000 primaries because he had raised millions more than all his opponents combined. Candidates also try to survive by establishing themselves as *the* candidate for a particular policy or other constituency. In 2000, Gary Bauer and Steve Forbes each tried to combat their better known opponents by trying to win the loyalties of the new Christian Right within the Republican Party. They were unsuccessful in enlisting enough of these voters to offset Bush's head start.

To compete successfully, candidates also need considerable media coverage. They must convince reporters that they are serious candidates with a real chance of winning. Journalists and candidates establish expectations for how well each candidate should do based on the results of polls, the quality of a candidate's campaign organization, the amount of money and time spent in the campaign, and the political complexion of the state. If a candidate performs below expectations, even though garnering the most votes, it may be interpreted by the press as a weakness and hurt the campaign. On the other hand, a strong showing when expectations are low can mean a boost to a candidate's campaign.

Consequently, candidates try to lower media expectations. It is not enough to win a primary; you have to win by at least as much as the media claims you should, or you will be seen as a loser. In the Republican race in 1988, Pat Robertson's organizers tried to counter media predictions for the Iowa caucuses by urging supporters to tell pollsters that they were not going to attend the caucuses. Because pollsters do not count people who do not plan to vote, this tactic could result in an artificially low prediction—and then a surprisingly high vote.[65]

Sometimes even losers are portrayed as winners if they do better than expected. For example, in 1968 in the New Hampshire primary, antiwar candidate Senator Eugene McCarthy won 40 percent of the vote against President Johnson, who had become increasingly unpopular because of the Vietnam War. Although McCarthy did not win, he did much better than expected, and the press interpreted the vote as a repudiation of Johnson's leadership.

In sum, then, the primary season is a game among the media, the candidates, and the voters, with the candidates trying to raise voter enthusiasm and lower media expectations simultaneously. One commentator has called the political reporters, consultants, and pollsters "the expectorate," the group who decide whether the candidate has done well enough.[66]

The common wisdom about presidential primaries is that the key ingredient is "momentum." That is, a candidate needs to win early, or at least do better than expected, to gain momentum, and then keep winning to maintain momentum. The "expectorate" needs to pronounce him a winner. A classic illustration is that of Jimmy Carter in 1976. Then an unknown governor from Georgia, he won the Iowa caucuses, which attracted tremendous media attention and in turn led to further primary wins and eventually the nomination.

Bill Clinton finished second in the New Hampshire primary in 1992 but captured the momentum anyway. Coming far from behind, he pronounced himself "the comeback kid," a designation that became the story of the primary. Said one journalist, "Clinton's New Hampshire abracadabra remains . . . the furriest, plumpest rabbit any politician has ever pulled out of the battered New Hampshire hat."[67] In the modern era of primary elections, Clinton is the only president not to have won the New Hampshire primary.

Early in the primary season, candidates try to find the position, slogan, or idea that will appeal to the most voters. In 1984, Ronald Reagan presented himself as the candidate embodying traditional America. As one of his staff aides wrote in a campaign memo, "Paint RR as the personification of all that is right with, or heroized by, America."[68] George W. Bush capitalized on the sentiment that Bill Clinton's standard of personal morality was low, portraying himself as someone who would put morality back in the White House.

Candidates must avoid making a big mistake or, worse yet, being caught covering up a mistake or untruth. Edmund Muskie's front-running candidacy ground to a halt in 1972 when he cried at a public appearance while denouncing a newspaper attack on his wife. Gary Hart's 1988 candidacy collapsed when the media discovered that his marriage did not prevent him from having affairs with other women. He compounded the damage by lying. The Muskie incident was taken by the media and public to indicate that he could not handle the stress of a campaign or, by inference, the presidency. The Hart incident raised questions about his

Soliciting votes by giving speeches and making appearances was once considered beneath the dignity of the presidential office. William Jennings Bryan was the first presidential candidate to break this tradition. In 1896, he traveled more than eighteen thousand miles and made more than six hundred speeches in an effort to win voters. Although Bryan lost the election to William McKinley, his approach to campaigning became the standard. This photo illustrates how the term stump speech, used to refer to candidates' boiler-plate campaign speeches, may have developed.

character and honesty. (In contrast, during the primary campaign, Clinton admitted his marriage was not perfect but did not flaunt ongoing affairs; the Lewinsky scandal occurred after he was in the White House and was already a popular president.)

Incumbent presidents seeking renomination do not have the same problems as their challengers. No incumbent who sought renomination was denied it in the twentieth century.

In addition to these general strategies, candidates must deal specifically with the particular demands of caucuses, conventions, and primaries.

Presidential Caucuses and Conventions

Some states employ caucuses and conventions to select delegates to attend presidential nominating conventions. In 1992, one or both parties in sixteen states selected delegates in caucuses.

The Iowa caucuses, except for their timing and newsworthiness, are similar to those in other states. Normally, the campaign in Iowa starts months before the caucuses are actually held. In 1988, presidential candidates spent a total of 999 days campaigning in Iowa. Campaigning is, in large part, personal. In 1988, Democratic presidential

candidate Bruce Babbitt reported that one caucus participant, a tropical fish hobbyist, said he would deliver his vote to Babbitt if he could tell him the "pH and sediment density of the Congo River at its mouth." Babbitt assigned a staffer to look into the question.[69]

In early February, the caucuses are held in private homes, schools, and churches, and all who consider themselves party members can attend. They debate and vote on the candidates. The candidates receiving the most votes win delegates to later county and state conventions. The number of delegates is proportional to the vote that the candidate received at the caucuses (assuming the candidate got at least 15 percent).

Iowa, as the first state to hold its caucuses, normally gets the most attention. Thousands of representatives of the media cover these caucuses, which have gained importance beyond what one would normally expect for a small state. Although only a handful of delegates to the national convention are at stake, a win with the nation's political pros watching can establish a candidate as a serious contender and attract further media attention and financial donations important to continuing the campaign.

Presidential Primaries

Delegates to presidential nominating conventions are also selected in direct primaries, sometimes called **presidential preference primaries.** In these elections, governed by state laws and national party rules, voters indicate a preference for a presidential candidate, delegates committed to a candidate, or both. Some states have preference primaries, but delegates are actually selected in conventions. These primaries are often called "beauty contests" because they are meaningless in terms of winning delegates, though they can be important in showing popular support. Like other primaries, presidential primaries can be open or closed.

Until 1968, presidential preference primaries usually played an insignificant role in presidential nominations. Only a handful of states employed primaries to select delegates. The conventional wisdom was that primary victories could not guarantee nomination but a loss would spell sure defeat.

The insignificance of most primaries was illustrated in 1968 by Vice President Hubert Humphrey's ability to win the party's nomination without winning a single primary. Humphrey was able to win the nomination because a majority of the delegates to the convention in 1968 were selected through party caucuses and conventions, where party leaders supportive of Humphrey had considerable influence.

Humphrey's nomination severely divided the Democratic Party. Many constituencies within the party, particularly those opposed to the Vietnam War, were hostile to Humphrey and believed that the nomination was

Wendell Willkie, Republican presidential candidate in 1940, rides into Elmwood, Indiana. In the days before television, motorcades allowed large numbers of people to see the candidates and were a way for the candidates to generate enthusiasm among the voters.

controlled by party elites out of step with the preferences of rank-and-file Democrats.

Delegate Selection Reform

The response of the Democratic Party to these complaints was to change delegate selection procedures to make delegates more representative of Democratic voters. One change established quotas for blacks, women, and young people to reflect the groups' percentages in each state's population. These reforms significantly increased minority and female representation in the 1972 convention and, quite unexpectedly, made the primary the preferred method of nomination. Criteria of openness and representativeness could be more easily satisfied through primary selection. In recent years, more than 70 percent of the Democratic delegates were chosen in primaries.

The Democrats have replaced quotas for minorities with guidelines urging minority involvement in party affairs. However, the quota remains that half the delegates must be women.

The Democratic Party reforms diminished the participation of party and elected officials. Critics felt that this weakened the party and increased the probability of nominating a candidate who could not work with party leaders. To fix this problem and help ensure that the party's nominee would be someone who could work with other elected officials within the party, since 1984, 15 to 20 percent of the delegates have been "superdelegates" appointed from among members of Congress and other party and public officials.

The Republican Party has not felt as much pressure to reform its delegate selection procedures. Republicans have tried to eliminate discrimination and increase participation in the selection process.

Reforming the Nomination Process

Each election year political observers discuss changing the presidential nomination process. They correctly complain that primaries tend to weaken political parties and have very low, unrepresentative turnouts. Moreover, the current system gives disproportionate influence to two small states, Iowa and New Hampshire, that come first in the process. Voters in most other states do not get to see most candidates; they have already been weeded out by the time the April, May, and June primaries occur. Moreover, some charge that the media has too much influence in the current system. The press exaggerates the victories of the winners and makes the losers seem weaker than they actually are.

There are two advantages of giving disproportionate influence to small states that select their delegates early.

The train "whistlestop" campaign was a staple of many presidential races. Here President Harry Truman gives a speech from the back of a train in 1948.

Only in these first small states do candidates come in contact with voters on a very personal basis. In large states, the primaries are strictly media events. For example, a survey showed that in the 1996 campaign, one of every five New Hampshire voters had met a presidential candidate. In large states, most voters go through their entire lives without ever meeting a presidential candidate.[70] Moreover, when small states came first, the candidates could test their popularity without spending millions of dollars. Those who were successful could then attract funds for the larger, more expensive races. This system gave little-known candidates a better chance than most alternative arrangements would have.

But by 1996, large states such as California, New York, Texas, Florida, and Illinois moved their primaries earlier into the primary season to increase their influence on the nominating process. And, on **Super Tuesday,** most southern states hold their primaries simultaneously. Now candidates can no longer bank on doing well in the early small-state primary elections and then having some momentum to help in raising large sums of money. The demands for fund-raising have grown, because candidates must have money in hand long before the first primary to book and run the massive television campaigns needed to reach primary voters in these large states and in the South. As a result, little-known candidates have a tougher battle now than in previous election years.

Some observers are glad that we no longer have the "smoke-filled rooms" where party bosses chose nominees. Nevertheless, the primary system has weakened political parties, and the small primary electorate is unrepresentative of the general public. Indeed, these voters might be less representative of the public than the party bosses who met in smoke-filled rooms. And they know less about the nominees than did the party bosses. But the days when party leaders could anoint the nominees are probably gone forever.

The National Conventions

Once selected, delegates attend their party's national nominating convention in the summer before the November election. Changes in party rules have reduced the convention's role from an arena where powerful party leaders came together and determined the party's nominee to a body that ratifies a choice based on the outcome of the primaries and caucuses.

In the "old" days, often many ballots were necessary before a winner emerged. In 1924, it took the Democrats 103 ballots to nominate John W. Davis. Now nominees are selected on the first ballot. In most election years, some experts predict a close nomination race, which would force the decision to be made at the convention. But in fact, the recent national party conventions served the purposes they have served for nearly fifty years: to endorse the nominee and his choice for vice president, to construct a party platform, to whip up enthusiasm for the ticket among party loyalists, and to present the party favorably to the national viewing audience. Thus, even without the nomination job, national conventions give meaning to the notion of a national party.

Before 1972, delegates were predominantly white and male. After 1972, the percentage of delegates who were black, women, and under thirty increased substantially. In 1992, 52 percent of the Democratic and 45 percent of the Republican delegates were women; 17 percent of the Democratic and 4 percent of the Republican delegates were black. The latter figures are fairly close to the percentage of blacks among each party's supporters.

Convention delegates are still unrepresentative in terms of education and income. Compared to the population, delegates to national party conventions are well educated and well-off financially.

Delegates also tend to be more ideologically extreme than each party's rank and file. Democratic delegates are generally more liberal and Republican delegates more conservative than their party's supporters (see Figure 3).

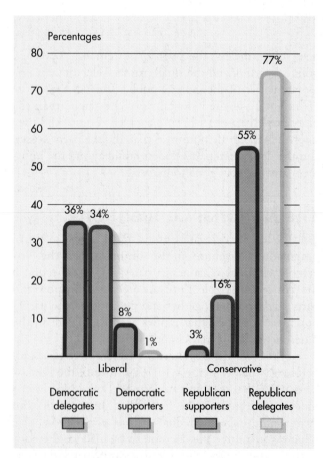

FIGURE 3 ■ National Convention Delegates Are More Ideologically Extreme Than Rank-and-File Members

SOURCES: Data are from delegate and public surveys reported in *Washington Post National Weekly Edition,* August 26–September 1, 1996, A4, and August 12–18, 1996.

The Activities of the Convention

National party conventions are full of color and at least a semblance of excitement. They are a montage of balloons, placards, and demonstrations. Candidates and their lieutenants scurry in search of uncommitted delegates. Behind-the-scenes negotiators try to work out differences among factions of the party. Journalists are everywhere covering everything from the trivial to the momentous. The keynote address reviews the party's glorious past and speaks to a promising future. Each candidate is placed in nomination by a party notable who reviews the candidate's background and experience. The roll call of the states ratifies the party's choice, and on the last night delegates cheer the acceptance speeches of the presidential and vice presidential nominees. Those who contested the nomination often join the nominees on the platform at the end in a display of party unity.

Aside from these very visible aspects, each convention has three important committees. The *credentials committee* reviews any challenges that may arise to the right of specific delegates to participate. The *rules committee* formulates convention and party rules, such as those governing delegate selection. The *platform committee* drafts the party's platform. The contents of the platform can generate conflict. For example, in 1968 the Democrats fought bitterly over a platform provision calling for an end to the Vietnam War. The failure of the party's nominee, Humphrey, to support the provision led many antiwar Democrats to sit out the election. After supporting the Equal Rights Amendment for years, the Republicans split over it and did not endorse it in their 1980s platforms. The abortion issue has spurred quarrels at more recent Republican conventions.

Apart from being important symbols of the direction the party wants to take, do platforms mean anything? Surprisingly, amid the platitudes, more than half of the platforms contained pledges regarding proposed future actions, and most of those pledges were fulfilled.[71] Platforms do provide observant voters with information about what the party will do if elected.

The Media and the Convention

Before 1932, nominees did not attend the convention. Acceptance of the nomination took place sometime afterward in a special ceremony. Franklin Roosevelt broke with tradition in 1932 and presented his acceptance speech to the convention and to a nationwide radio audience; he did not want to lose an opportunity to deliver his message to the American people. The Republicans did not follow his example until 1944. Since then, both parties' conventions have closed with the acceptance speeches of the presidential and vice presidential nominees.

With the beginning of radio coverage in 1924 and television coverage in 1940, the conventions have become media events. The parties try to put on a show they hope will attract voters to their candidates. Polls usually show the party's candidate doing better during and after the party's convention, called the "convention bounce," though the effect does not last long.

Major addresses, such as the acceptance speech, are planned for peak viewing hours. Potentially disruptive credentials and platform proceedings often are scheduled for the early morning hours. Conventions have become tightly organized and highly orchestrated affairs in which little is left to chance. The stakes are too high.

Control, however, has its limits. If there are deep cleavages in the party, it may be impossible to prevent them from surfacing at the convention during prime time. The 1968 Democratic Convention was filled with conflict—conflict inside the convention between the supporters of Hubert Humphrey and opponents of the Johnson policies on the Vietnam War and conflict outside the convention on the streets of Chicago between antiwar demonstrators and the Chicago police. Television covered both events, associating the division in the convention with the turmoil outside, and dimmed Humphrey's chances of winning the election.

In the 1950s, at the dawn of the television age, Democratic Party leaders instruct their delegates how to behave on camera.

Courtesy of Smithsonian Institute

In recent years, with the nomination settled well in advance of the convention and few vociferous floor fights over platforms, the conventions have been less dramatic and suspenseful. Consequently, the major networks are no longer showing them "gavel to gavel," leaving that coverage to specialty cable networks such as CNN and C-SPAN. Party leaders' control over the conventions backfired in terms of attracting and retaining a mass audience throughout.

Selecting a Vice Presidential Nominee

Selection of a vice presidential candidate normally is done by the party's presidential nominee and then merely ratified at the convention, although in 1956, Democratic nominee Adlai Stevenson broke with tradition and left the decision to the convention.

Presidential candidates usually select a vice presidential nominee who can balance the ticket. What exactly does "balance" mean? A careful analysis of vice presidential choices of both parties since 1940 revealed that presidential candidates tend to balance the ticket in terms of age, choosing a running mate from a different age cohort.[72] Those with little Washington experience usually balance the ticket by choosing a Washington insider as a running mate (as in 1992 outsider Clinton did in choosing Gore and as in 2000 outsider George W. Bush did in choosing Richard Cheney). However, Washington insiders tend to choose other insiders, as when Robert Dole chose insider Jack Kemp in 1996 and insider Al Gore chose insider Joseph Lieberman in 2000. Although common wisdom also suggests that presidential candidates balance the ticket in terms of region (John F. Kennedy from Massachusetts chose Texan Lyndon Johnson in 1960) or ideology (the more liberal Michael Dukakis picked the more conservative Lloyd Bentsen in 1988), this happens only occasionally.[73] In 2000, both presidential candidates picked running mates whose ideologies were similar to their own.

Gender traditionally has not been part of a ticket balancing effort, but since Walter Mondale's historic choice of Geraldine Ferraro in 1984, women are sometimes among those given consideration.

The most important factor, however, is choosing a vice presidential running mate from a large state—the larger, the better.[74] Presidential candidates believe that choosing a vice presidential candidate from a large state will help win that state in the November election. In fact, this is not true; the added advantage of a vice presidential candidate in their home state is less than 1 percent, and the bigger the state, the less the advantage.[75]

Bush Sr.'s 1988 selection of Indiana senator Dan Quayle illustrated the search for age balance and the tendencies for insiders to choose other insiders. Quayle was also from a different part of the country than Bush. Quayle, a conservative senator from Indiana, was

As a vice presidential candidate, Geraldine Ferraro drew large crowds and especially ignited the enthusiasm of many women.

youthful and charming but had little experience and was considered a lightweight. Though most of Bush's advisers seemed to think Quayle was a reasonably safe choice,[76] the media found that Quayle, though a hawk on the Vietnam issue, had spent his Vietnam years safely as a member of the Indiana National Guard. Debate raged over whether his family influence (his wealthy parents owned Indiana's largest newspapers) got him out of active service and into the guard. During the campaign, Bush's advisers would not let Quayle appear on network news shows or get close to metropolitan areas with major media markets.

Most observers believe Clinton's choice of Senator Albert Gore Jr. was more astute. Though Gore did not, at first glance, fit the traditional image of a candidate chosen to balance the presidential candidate's characteristics (he was about the same age, of the same Baptist religion, from the same region, and of the same moderate Democratic ideology) or to bring with him a state with a large number of electoral college votes (Tennessee), he in fact did balance some of Clinton's weaknesses. Gore was a war veteran, while Clinton avoided service in Vietnam, and Gore's credentials as a family man had never been challenged. Gore had foreign policy expertise while Clinton did not. Perhaps more important, Gore's own moderate political philosophy strengthened

Clinton's image as a moderate, Gore's youth strengthened Clinton's credibility as a candidate for change, and Gore's reputation as an environmentalist played well to many voters.

Do vice presidential choices affect the election outcome? In most cases probably not. As a cynical observer commented, "Pick anyone . . . if Quayle can't sink a ticket, nobody can."[77]

Independent and Third-Party Nominees

Independent and third-party candidates are part of every presidential campaign. Most of these candidates are invisible to all but the most avid political devotee. But in recent elections, strong independent candidates have emerged with some frequency, such as George Wallace in 1968, John Anderson in 1980, Ross Perot in 1992 and 1996, and Ralph Nader in 2000. The Perot candidacies were visible both because he had money to finance his campaign and because voters in recent years identify less strongly with parties and express more dissatisfaction with politics as usual. A strong independent candidate could influence the outcome of the election. Though many people thought Perot might have such an effect, his support was not strong enough. Nader did have an effect, however. His nearly one hundred thousand vote totals in Florida far exceeded the razor-slim Bush final margin, to take just one example. Though Pat Buchanan took some conservative votes away from Bush, too, his totals were far less than those of Nader's.

It is not easy for independent candidates to get on the ballot. State laws control access to the ballot, and Democratic and Republican legislators and governors make those laws. Thus, the candidates of the Democratic and Republican Parties are automatically placed on the ballot in all fifty states, but independent candidates must demonstrate significant support to get on the ballot through petitions signed by voters.

The General Election Campaign

We take it for granted that the election campaign is what determines who wins. But consider this: Only twice since 1952 has the candidate who was ahead in the polls in July, before the national conventions, lost the election. Those years were 1988 when Dukakis led and 2000 when Al Gore led (and since Gore won the popular vote, perhaps his case is only a partial exception to the rule).[78] This suggests that although campaigns can make a difference, a lot of other factors determine who is elected.

Campaign Organization

Staffing the campaign organization is crucial, not only to get talented people but also to get those with considerable national campaign experience and a variety of perspectives. In 1984 and 1988, the Republicans had the advantage in national campaign experience, but in the 1990s, the advantage shifted to the Democrats. In 2000, Al Gore's team had more national experience than that of George W. Bush.

The candidate's own personal organization is only one part of the overall campaign organization. The national party organization and state parties also have some responsibilities, especially in registering potential party voters, getting them to the polls, and trying to make sure that the presidential candidate's local appearances will help the party's congressional and state candidates.

Images and Issues

Largely through the media, candidates try to create a favorable image and portray the opponent in an unfavorable way. The George H. Bush campaign was remarkably successful at creating a negative image for Dukakis in 1988; Dukakis was unsuccessful in either creating a positive image for himself or reinforcing Bush's negative image.

In 1992, the Bush campaign struggled to create both a positive image for the president and a negative image for Clinton. But Bush could not find a focus for redefining himself, and his efforts to define a negative image for Clinton had limited success. The Clinton team had learned from the Dukakis debacle. They answered every attack Bush made, but at the same time they stayed focused on their own campaign message.

In 2000, Bush used his warm personality to establish a positive image despite the concerns many voters had about his abilities. Voters were comfortable with Gore's abilities but had reservations about his personality. Moreover, after eight years of Clintonian evasions and lies about personal issues, Gore's exaggerations may have seemed too much like those of Clinton.

Issues also can be the basis for an appeal to voters. As they did in 1996 and 2000, Democrats traditionally have used the "pocketbook" issues, arguing that economic times are better when Democrats are in the White House.

Issue appeals are usually general, and often candidates do not offer a clear-cut choice even on the most important controversies of the time. For example, the 1968 presidential election offered voters little choice on Vietnam policy, because the positions of candidates Nixon and Humphrey appeared very similar.[79] Voters who wanted to end the war by withdrawing and others who wanted to escalate the war had no real choice of candidates.

Ideally, the major campaign themes and strategies have been put into place by the end of the summer, but these themes and strategies are revised and updated on a daily, sometimes hourly, basis as the campaign progresses. Decisions are made not just by the candidate and the campaign manager but by a staff of key advisers who include media experts and pollsters. Sophisticated polling techniques are used to produce daily reports on shifts in public opinion across the nation and in particular regions. Thus, media ads can be added and deleted as polls reflect their impact. Campaign trips are modified or scratched as the candidate's organization sees new opportunities. And media events can be planned to complement the paid advertising the candidate runs.

The Electoral College

All planning for the campaign has to take into account the peculiar American institution of the **Electoral College.** In the United States we do not have a direct election of the president, although this came as a shock to many of those who voted for Gore or Bush but saw the popular vote become meaningless in the postelection wrangling over who won Florida.

Voters choose electors of the Electoral College. These electors are party notables who gather in each state capitol in December after the presidential election to cast their votes for president and vice president. Each state has as many electors as its total representation in Congress (House plus Senate) (see Figure 4). The smallest states (and the District of Columbia) have three, whereas the largest state—California—has fifty-five.

With the exception of Maine and Nebraska, which divide some of their Electoral College votes according to who wins in each congressional district, all of each state's electoral votes go to the candidate winning the most votes in that state. If one candidate wins a majority of the electors voting across the United States, that candidate wins. If no candidate wins a majority, the election is decided in the House of Representatives, where each state has one vote and a majority is necessary to win. This has not happened since 1824, when John Quincy Adams was chosen. If voting in the Electoral College for the vice president does not yield a majority, the Senate chooses the vice president, with each senator having one vote.

The Founders assumed that the Electoral College would have considerable power, with each elector exercising independent judgment and choosing from among a large number of candidates. They did not foresee the development of political parties or the development of a political climate where the popular vote is seen as the source of legitimacy for a candidate. As state parties developed, the electors became part of the party process, pledged to party candidates. Thus, electors usually rubber-stamp the choice of voters in each state rather than exercise their own judgment.

The Electoral College is based on states, so it encourages campaigns designed to win "states." In this sense, it reinforces the federal system and, because of the winner-take-all feature of the Electoral College, candidates concentrate their efforts in the larger states.

Campaign Strategies

Developing a strategy is an important element of a presidential campaign. But every strategy is surrounded by uncertainty, and even political pros cannot always predict the impact of a particular strategy.

Candidates seek to do three things: mobilize those who are already loyal to them and their party, persuade independent voters that they are the best candidate, and try to convert the opposition. Most candidates empha-size mobilizing their own voters. Democrats have to work harder at this than Republicans because Democratic voters often do not vote and are more likely to vote for the other party than are Republicans.

Both parties must try to persuade independent voters because independents are the swing voters; their votes determine the outcome. In 1964, when Johnson trounced Republican Goldwater, 80 percent of Republicans voted for Goldwater. In 2000, 86 percent of the Democrats voted for Gore, in the most partisan election in recent history. In these and other cases, it was the independent voters who determined the outcomes.

The crucial strategic question is where to allocate resources of time and money: where to campaign, where to buy media time and how much to buy, and where to spend money helping local organizations.

Candidates must always remember that they have to win a majority of the Electoral College vote. The most

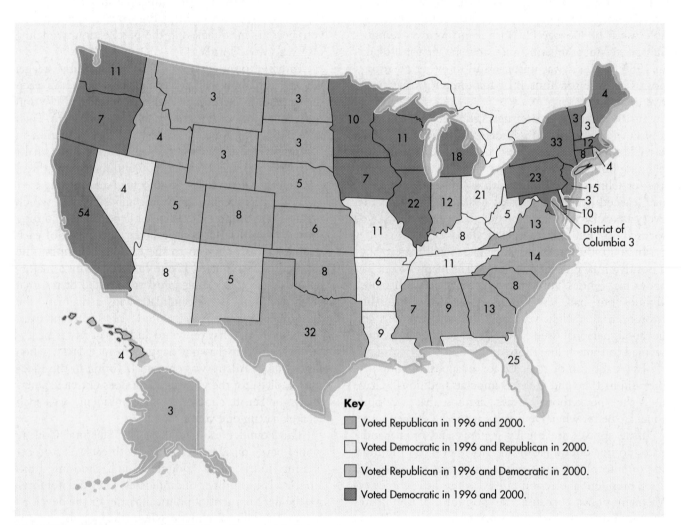

FIGURE 4 ■ Party Strength Displays Geographic Patterns
The numbers inside the states indicate the electoral votes, out of a total of 538.

SOURCES: Richard Scammon and Alice McGilliaray, *American Votes 19* (Washington, D.C.: Congressional Quarterly, 1991), 9–13; *Congressional Quarterly Reports,* November 7, 1992, 3549.

Though Al Gore won the popular vote, he lost the election. The discrepancy between the popular vote and the Electoral College vote highlights that what counts is the popular vote in each state, because that vote determines which candidate will receive the state's electoral votes. At the time the Constitution was written, the Founders neither wanted nor envisioned popular election of the president; selection of the president was placed in the hands of state elites. The Founders were less concerned with individual suffrage (states determined who could vote) than with the states' rights and with achieving a balance of power among the states.

A discrepancy between the Electoral College and the popular vote outcome occurred three times in the nineteenth century (1824, 1876, and 1888). However, after more than a century of presidential elections whose outcome was known once the popular vote was tallied, and since the principle of "one person one vote" has become enshrined in law and political culture, the American public has become used to thinking of elections as an expression of the will of the people.

When the 2000 election yielded an Electoral College winner who had not won the popular vote, there were immediate calls for the elimination or reform of the Electoral College system. One reform would be to abolish the Electoral College altogether and leave the choice of president to the popular vote because direct election is a more understandable system. However, supporters of a popular vote system disagree over whether we should have a run-off election if no candidate wins a majority.

Even though one might think support for such a reform would be overwhelming given the democratic values of our society, it is not. Small states wish to preserve what they see as an advantage. Because the number of Electoral College votes equals the number of congressional districts plus two, the smallest states are overrepresented relative to their populations, just as they are in the United States Senate.

On the other hand, many political and legal experts believe the Electoral College system gives greater weight to a vote cast in a large state; a one-vote margin in Pennsylvania, for example, yields twenty-two votes for the winning candidate compared to only three votes in North Dakota. So it is more important to get that extra vote in Pennsylvania. Therefore, candidates focus their campaigns in, and appeals to, the large states.

An even more undemocratic feature of the Electoral College is that not all states require their electors to cast their votes for the candidates who won the state vote. The **faithless elector** is one who casts his or her vote for a personal choice, even someone who was not on the ballot. Even though the intent of the Founders was to allow electors to cast their votes any way desired, today, most believe that in our more democratic era electors should be bound by the wishes of the voters in their states. However, no faithless elector has ever made a difference in the outcome of an election. But in the 2000 election, as few as three faithless electors could have made a difference.

Yet another undemocratic feature of the current system is the contingency for the vote to be thrown into the House of Representatives. There is no expectation that each state's House delegation will vote as its state's voters did; rather, states will follow the majority party in their House delegation.

populous states, with the largest number of electoral votes, are vital. Prime targets are those large states that could go to either party, such as Illinois, Texas, California, Ohio, New York, and of course Florida.

Candidates also have to expand their existing bases of support. Most of the Rocky Mountain states have been solidly Republican in their presidential loyalties. Republicans must build on this base and their strength in the South by carrying some of the large eastern or midwestern industrial states to win.

Democrats have a strategic problem given the western Republican bloc. Between the end of Reconstruction and 1948, the South was solidly Democratic, but there have been no solidly Democratic states in presidential elections since then (although Washington, D.C., has been solidly Democratic). Since 1976, the Democrats have consistently lost the South. During the 1980s, some strategists believed the Democrats should try to win back the South by choosing more conservative candidates. Others argued for a strategy to win without the South, aiming for the industrial states of the East and Midwest along with California and a few other states of the West. This strategy was used successfully by the Republicans between the 1870s and the 1920s, when they were able to capture the White House regularly without ever winning a southern state. This was Clinton's winning strategy (see Figure 4), although he did win three southern states in each election.

The Media Campaign

The media campaign consists of paid advertising, personal appearances on talk shows, debates, and coverage on news broadcasts and in print media. Candidates have the most control over paid advertising and the least over news coverage; but even there, campaigns spend hundreds of hours devising strategies to show their candidates to best advantage.

Campaigns are expensive because they rely so heavily on the media to get the candidate's message to the voters. As one observer argued, "Today's presidential campaign is essentially a mass media campaign. It is not that the mass media entirely determine what happens. . . . But it is no exaggeration to say that, for the large majority of voters, the campaign has little reality apart from the media version."[80]

Impact of the Media

The media, through news coverage, personal appearances by candidates, and paid advertisements, help shape voters' opinions and choices in three ways. They inform, they help set the campaign agenda, and they help persuade voters.[81] In Chapter 5, we discuss these effects.

Use of the Media

Media Events

Candidates try to use the media to their advantage by staging media events that allow them to be photographed doing and saying noncontroversial things in front of enthusiastic crowds and patriotic symbols. Candidates spend most of their time going from media market to media market, hoping to get both national and local coverage.[82] Candidates and their advisers try to design settings that will encourage television reporters to focus their stories on the candidate and put his or her policies in the best light.[83] In 1988, George H. Bush almost literally wrapped himself in the flag, frequently "pledging allegiance," until negative media reaction led his advisers to decide that they were overdoing it.

Advertising

Paid advertisements allow candidates to focus on points most favorable to their case or to portray their opponents in the most negative light. Most political ads are quite short, thirty or sixty seconds in length.

Television ads were first used in the 1952 campaign. One, linking the Democratic Truman administration to the unpopular Korean War, showed two soldiers in combat talking about the futility of war. Then one of the soldiers is hit and dies. The other one exposes himself to the enemy and is also killed. The announcer's voice says, "Vote Republican."[84] Today's ads are less melodramatic but still appeal to emotions. One classic example ad was the 1984 Reagan ad, depicting his policies as putting the country on the road to greatness again ("It's morning in America").[85]

Many ads are issue focused. Both Bush and Gore in 2000 sought to appeal to voters with ads on their stands on education and health care, for example.

Negative ads are prominent in some elections. However, negative ads are used more often by candidates who are behind. Strong frontrunners tend to stay positive.[86] Still some campaign advisers believe negative ads are very effective. Said one, "People won't pay any attention [to positive ads]. Better to knock your opponent's head off."[87] And polls show that negative ads can sometimes have a dramatic short-term effect on a candidate's standing.

Democratic consultants are more likely to find negative advertising distasteful than Republican consultants. However, we do not know how this translates into partisan differences in use.[88]

Negative campaign is as American as apple pie. When Thomas Jefferson faced John Adams in 1796, a Federalist editorial called Jefferson "mean spirited, low-lived . . . the son of a half-breed Indian squaw" and prophesized that if he were elected, "Murder, robbery, rape, adultery and incest will be openly taught and practiced."[89] When Andrew Jackson ran for president in 1832, his mother was called a prostitute, his father a mulatto (someone of mixed races, black and white), his wife a profligate woman, and himself a bigamist.[90] A British observer of American elections in 1888 described them as a "tempest of invective and calumny . . . imagine all the accusations brought against all the candidates for the 670 seats in the English Parliament concentrated on one man, and read . . . daily for three months."[91]

But why does negative advertising sometimes work when most people say they do not like it? People may say they like to hear about issues, but their actions belie their words. Politics is just not that important to most people, and indeed many are woefully ignorant about specific issues. If one out of seven Americans cannot find the United States on a world map, how interested are they going to be in a discussion of foreign policy?[92] Most people have a pretty good general picture of where the parties stand on a whole variety of general issues, but they are not particularly attuned to listening to debates on specifics, and the candidates realize this.

Negative ads have both virtues and drawbacks. On the positive side, such ads provide some helpful information about issues.[93] During a campaign, a candidate might produce ten or fifteen thirty-second ads, each providing new information, including information on issues. This material, though biased, is a valuable supplement to media news coverage, which focuses heavily on personalities, conflicts, and the "horse race" aspect of campaigns.

Negative ads tend to reinforce previous inclinations. Thus, negative ads are more believable than positive ones at least to Republicans and independents, who are more cynical about politics and government to begin with.

Still, there is little evidence, for example, that negative ads increase voter cynicism or depress turnout significantly.

Checks do exist on negative campaigns.[94] One check is the press, which could point out errors of fact. In recent campaigns, many in the press have tried to do this, but often end up simply giving more attention to the negative messages.[95] The voters, who might become outraged, are another check. The third check is the candidate under attack, who in most cases will hit back. Both candidates were aggressive in countering negative ads in 2000.

Televised Debates

Candidates also use televised debates as part of their media campaigns. In 1960, Kennedy challenged Nixon to debate during their presidential campaign. Nixon did not want to debate because as vice president he was already known and ahead in the polls. He remembered his first election to the House of Representatives when he challenged the incumbent to debate and, on the basis of his performance, won the election. Afterward he said the incumbent was a "damn fool" to debate. Nevertheless, Nixon did agree to debate, and when the two contenders squared off, presidential debates were televised to millions of homes across the country for the first time.

Nixon dutifully answered reporters' questions and rebutted Kennedy's assertions. But Kennedy came to project an image. He sought to demonstrate his vigor, to compensate for his youth and inexperience. He also sought to contrast his attractive appearance and personality with Nixon's. So he quickly answered reporters' specific questions and then directly addressed viewers about his general goals.

Kennedy's strategy worked. He appealed to people and convinced them that his youth and inexperience would not pose problems. While Kennedy remained calm, Nixon became very nervous. He smiled at inappropriate moments, his eyes darted back and forth, he had a five-o'clock shadow that gave him a somewhat sinister look, and beads of sweat rolled down his face.

According to public opinion polls, people who saw the debates thought that Kennedy performed better in three of the four. (The only debate in which they thought Nixon performed better was the one in which the candidates were not in the same studio side by side. They were in separate cities, and with this arrangement Nixon was less nervous.) Yet people who heard the debates on radio did not think Kennedy performed as well. They were not influenced by the visual contrast between the candidates. Clearly, television made the difference.

No more presidential debates were held for sixteen years. The candidates who were ahead did not want to risk their lead. But in 1976, President Ford decided to debate Carter, and in 1980, President Carter decided to debate Reagan. Both incumbents were in trouble, and they thought they needed to debate to win. Although President Reagan was far ahead in 1984, he decided to debate Mondale because he did not want to seem afraid. By agreeing to debate, he solidified the precedent begun anew in 1976. In 2000, the low expectation by the media for Bush's performance, coupled with his congenial,

Families all across the country gathered in front of their TV to watch the first televised presidential debates in 1960, featuring Senator John F. Kennedy (D-Mass.) and Vice President Richard Nixon (R-Calif.).

personal style, helped him win the debates in the view of many, even though the debates revealed his limited grasp of issues and misstatements. Gore's mannerisms seemed stiff and even phony to many, particularly in the first debate.

Because candidates have different strengths, each campaign wants the other to agree to a debate format that builds on its candidate's strengths. The "debate about debates" is a typical campaign issue that frequently overshadows other, more important issues. It has become as predictable a part of campaigns as the debates themselves.

E-campaigning

The contemporary candidacy would not be complete without an Internet address. These sites provide information on policies, report recent speeches, link to other relevant pages, offer opportunities to send messages to the candidates, and encourage Web browsers to volunteer. Some sites offer opportunities to register to vote. Candidates also use e-mail to communicate with supporters.

Sometimes, just as in business, e-campaigning provides more headaches. The campaign manager for Steve Forbes (Republican candidate in 2000), for example, sent out a message informing dozens of donors that they had "maxed out" on their federal campaign donations limits, so they could not send more money.[96] After dozens of messages back from confused recipients, he confessed to a computer glitch.

Some candidates find that opponents or pranksters have purchased rival Internet addresses to parody their candidacies. So, www.gwbush.com and www.Hillaryno. com parodied the Bush Web site (georgewbush.com) and the Hillary Clinton Web site (www.hillary2000.org), respectively.

Campaign Funding

Success in raising money is one of the keys to a successful political campaign. Although some of the money for presidential campaigns comes from public funds, much is raised privately. In Chapter 9 we will discuss campaign funding and its impact on politics.

The Permanent Campaign

The **permanent campaign** is a term coined by political scientists to describe the current state of American electoral politics. During each election cycle, the time between the completion of one election and the beginning of the next gets shorter and shorter. By summer 2001, only a few months after Bush's election, candidates were already busy visiting New Hampshire and other early primary states, assembling field operations,

hiring consultants and fund-raisers, and commissioning polls. No longer does the election campaign start in the election year; now it is nearly a four-year process.

Several factors are responsible for this change, some political and some technological. The political process has changed a great deal during the past twenty years. Primaries have become the chief means by which candidates get nominated, and parties have shrunk in importance in the nominating process. The necessity to win primaries in different regions of the nation means that potential candidates must start early to become known to key political figures, and ultimately to the voting public, in these states. In the "old days," candidates only had to woo party leaders, a process, which, though not easy, was much less public and much less expensive than campaigning for primary victories.

Technology has also contributed to the permanent campaign. Certainly, in comparison to the turn of the twentieth century, transportation and communication technology have revolutionized campaigns. Then, of course, travel was by rail, ship, or horse, and candidates could not simply dart about the country spending the morning in New York and the afternoon in Seattle. Telephone communication was primitive, and there were no radios or televisions. The idea of potential candidates spending four years publicly campaigning for office under these conditions would have been ludicrous.

But even in comparison with only thirty years ago, the media and information technology have revolutionized campaigning and thus have contributed to the permanent campaign. Modern computer and telephone technology enable the media and private organizations to take the pulse of the public through opinion polls almost continually. As polls have become more common, they have become a source of fascination by the media (and as pollsters have discovered that the media appetite for polls is nearly insatiable, polls have proliferated). Whereas in the 1950s polls were rarely done and poll results were rarely discussed in media coverage of elections, by the 1980s hundreds of stories about each election campaign focused on poll results. Indeed, much of the media coverage of the campaign focuses on exactly that (see Chapter 5 for more on this topic). Thus, candidates must pay attention to how well they do in the polls, which means they must begin campaigning early to earn name recognition by the public.

And, more generally, the fact that campaigns have become media events means that candidates must begin early to establish themselves as worthy of media attention. Until candidates have organizations, fund-raisers, and pollsters, the media does not take them seriously. Nor would it be very rational to do otherwise, because a modern campaign cannot succeed without these things.

All of these factors, then—the decline of the party organizations and the increased importance of primaries, the growth of polling, and the overwhelming role the media now play in campaigns—have contributed to the perpetual motion that modern elections have become. These trends seem irreversible. Only the rolling back of the primary system would seem to make much difference, and that change is highly unlikely.

Congressional Campaigns

Because reelection is an important objective for almost all members of Congress and *the* most important objective for many, members work at being reelected throughout their terms.[97] Most are successful, though senators are not as secure as members of the House.

Incumbents: Unsafe at Any Margin?

Most members are reelected even if they have not done that much for their home districts.[98] Indeed, one Republican member remarked, "Let's face it, you have to be a bozo to lose this job."[99] Still, incumbents believe the best way to ensure victory is to be so good at serving the home district, so successful in getting money for their districts, and so well known to the voters that no serious rival will want to run. Incumbents hope potential rivals will bide their time and wait for a better year or run for some other office.[100]

Given the advantages of office that incumbents have, in name recognition and in favors they can do their constituents (for more on this point, see Chapter 10), you may wonder why they worry about losing. But worry they do. One political scientist proclaimed that members feel "unsafe at any margin."[101] No matter how big their last victory, they worry that their next campaign will bring defeat. And despite the high reelection rate of incumbents, some do lose. This fear prompts members to spend even more of their energies preparing for the next campaign.

For the most part, this fear is misplaced. Turnover in Congress comes primarily from those who decide not to run. Even in the anti-incumbent elections of 1994, only 10 percent of House incumbents lost (all of them Democrats). In 2000, only 2 percent did. Senators are usually somewhat more vulnerable. House members really do have to offend their constituencies to lose. Most senators also are reelected, but the probabilities of defeat are higher than for the House. In the late 1970s and early 1980s, it was not uncommon for a third of the senators running to be defeated. Those proportions have decreased, but in 2000, 21 percent of senators running lost. Even so, the electoral benefit of incumbency still exists for the great majority of candidates who choose to run for reelection.[102]

Challengers

Another reason for the uneasiness of incumbents is that as their media and public relations sophistication has grown, so has that of challengers. Still, without the advantages of the free frank and other opportunities to become well known to constituents, challengers have a difficult time. The best advice to someone who wants to be a member of Congress is to find an open seat.

To beat an incumbent, challengers need money. The more they spend, the more likely they are to win. In recent House campaigns, a challenger needed to spend at least $250,000 to have even a one in four chance of winning—and the cost continues to rise.[103] Spending is important for challengers because they must make themselves known in a positive way, and they must suggest that something is wrong with the incumbent. Usually, challengers will charge incumbents with ignoring the district, being absent from committee hearings or floor votes, being too liberal or too conservative, or voting incorrectly on a key issue. Sometimes, of course, the incumbent has been involved in a scandal, which offers a ready target for the challenger.[104]

Sometimes challengers will try unusual tactics to make themselves known. Tom Harkin (D-Iowa) worked in a series of blue-collar jobs when running for the House to show people in his district that he understood their problems. Meanwhile, he got a lot of free publicity.

Senate challengers have a better chance than House challengers (Figure 5). One reason is that Senate seats are bigger prizes and so attract stronger candidates. Then, too, in a statewide constituency there is a larger pool of challengers to draw on. Because they are often former governors or members of the House with a statewide reputation, Senate challengers are better known than House challengers.[105] One analysis of this showed that about 80 percent of voters recognized the name of the person running against their incumbent senator; less than 60 percent recognized the challenger to their House incumbent.[106]

Another reason Senate challengers have greater success is that most incumbents have not had personal contact with as high a proportion of voters as a representative due to the much greater number of people they represent. Also there is a wider range of views and demands to satisfy in their larger and more heterogeneous constituencies.[107] Evidence indicates that senators from the largest states have about a six- or seven-point electoral disadvantage compared to senators from the smallest states. Senators from the smallest states do about as well in retaining their seats as House members from their states.[108]

PATRIOTISM AND PARTISANSHIP

When the nation is at war or is threatened by an external enemy, there is almost always a "rally 'round the flag" effect. For the moment, anyway, citizens put aside partisan differences to provide a common front to a threatening enemy. The Persian Gulf War in 1991 led President George H. Bush's public opinion ratings to skyrocket as the public supported the war. No president has had a bigger and more prolonged rally, however, than George W. Bush after the events of 9/11. In this case, America was attacked on its own soil, and millions of American witnessed through television the horrifying events that caused the death of almost three thousand people. Within a few days, Bush's public support rose to more than 90 percent, and it stayed near there for months. The president, whose very legitimacy was questioned by many because of the way he won the 2000 election and his reputation of having a shaky grasp on issues, suddenly became the articulate spokesperson for a united America.

Immediately after 9/11, the administration's policies seemed to win the approval of the vast majority of Americans, stunned by the suddenness and violence of the attacks on the World Trade Towers and the Pentagon. The tremendous popularity of the president made it difficult to ask questions about tactics let alone challenge fundamental policies. Even routine legislative matters, such as subsidies for airlines or crops, became entangled with 9/11 patriotic fervor (as we saw in Chapter 6) as supporters of this or that

policy announced that it was vital to America's security. In turn, the Democrats vowed their support for the war.

It is not surprising, then, that the events of 9/11 affected the 2002 congressional campaigns. Candidates of both parties attempted to wrap themselves in the flag and identify with the war on terrorism. Republicans were effusive in their praise of President Bush. Some Republicans encouraged the view that questions about the success of the war or the way we were fighting it were dangerous to our fighting troops, if not downright treasonous. The president implied that congressional Democrats were not interested in the security of America when they did not pass a resolution quickly enough giving him a free hand to invade Iraq.

Though most Democrats seemed afraid to challenge the president on his handling of the war, some Republican candidates tried to tar their opponents with actions taken before the war. Senator Tom Harkin's (D-Iowa) unsuccessful opponent, House Republican Greg Ganske, pointed out that Harkin had opposed a constitutional amendment to ban flag burning. Said Ganske, "America has a renewed sense of patriotism and a renewed appreciation for our American flag. Not everyone agrees."[1] An Iowa Republican leader accused Harkin of "trying to make America's war on terrorism a partisan issue."[2]

Norm Coleman, the challenger to liberal senator Paul Wellstone (D-Minn.), took him to task for having voted against increased military spending be-

fore 9/11 and again when Wellstone opposed invading Iraq. After Wellstone was killed in a plane crash a few days before the election, Coleman won. The Republican opponent of Senator Tim Johnson (D-S.D.) accused Johnson of voting consistently against the B-2 bomber and national missile defense system (again, before 9/11). The attack backfired, and Johnson won when his supporters ran an ad showing his son, an army sergeant, fighting in Afghanistan. Saxby Chambliss, the Republican opponent of Senator Max Cleland (D-Ga.) accused Cleland of breaking his oath to defend America by voting in favor of a chemical weapons treaty. This accusation offended even some Republicans who knew that Senator Cleland, a Vietnam veteran, had lost both legs and an arm in that war. Nonetheless, with George W. Bush's support, Chambliss won.

By the middle of 2002, Democrats began to speak more freely that the war on terrorism was not going well. Then as the economy sunk and unemployment rose, the president spent more and more time talking about the threat from Iraq and plans to remove its leader, Saddam Hussein. We do know that the patriotic rally-around-the-flag effect can, over time, turn to public hostility against wars that America does not win, as Presidents Johnson and Truman learned to their sorrow.

1. Helen Dewar, "War on Terror Colors the Battle for Congress," *Washington Post,* July 5, 2002, A1.
2. Ibid.

Campaigns

In the nineteenth century, political parties organized congressional and presidential campaigns, and the candidates had relatively little to do. Today, however, congressional as well as presidential campaigns are candidate centered.

Congressional candidates usually hire the staff, raise the money, and organize their own campaigns. They may recruit campaign workers from local political parties; interest groups they belong to; unions; church, civic, or other voluntary organizations; or they may simply turn to friends and acquaintances.[109]

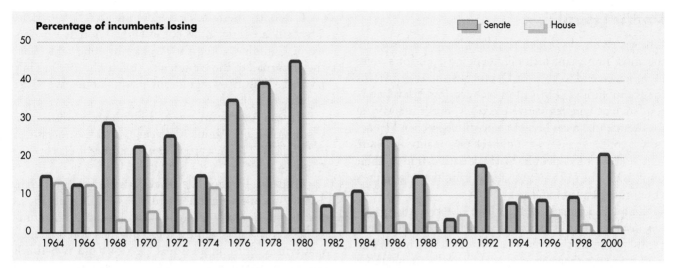

FIGURE 5 ■ House Incumbents Have Had Secure Jobs in Recent Years
In the 1980s and 1990s, more House incumbents lost in the reapportionment years (1982 and 1992); in the 1970s, most lost in 1974, the Watergate year. In the 1960s, reapportionment occurred before both the 1964 and 1966 election. Senate results do not reflect this cycle because, of course, there is no redistricting of Senate constituencies. Each Senator represents the whole state.
SOURCE: *Statistical Abstract of the United States 2001,* Table 389.

Political parties do have a significant role, however. National and local parties also recruit potential candidates. Presidents make personal appeals to fellow party members who they think can run strong races, and national campaign committees also recruit aggressively. Said one Democratic congressional campaign chair, "I'm not looking for liberals or conservatives. That's not my bag. I'm looking for winners."[110] Parties redouble their efforts when, as in recent elections, control of Congress is at stake.[111] Besides, if candidates are not closely linked to parties then, once elected, they are not as indebted to their party nor as obligated to reflect party views.[112] Recognizing this, national parties have increasingly provided services to congressional candidates—helping them manage their campaigns, develop issues, advertise, raise money, and conduct opinion polls. National party organizations give substantial sums of money to congressional candidates.[113]

Congressional Media Campaigns

To wage a serious campaign, the challenger or a contender for an open seat must wage a media campaign. Candidates hire media consultants and specialists in polling, advertising, and fund-raising. The old-style politician who might have been effective in small groups but who cannot appear poised and articulate on television has given way to one who can project an attractive television image. Candidates are elected on the basis of their media skills, which may not be the same skills as those needed to be a good lawmaker.

Campaign Money

The old adage says, "Half the money spent on campaigns is wasted. The trouble is, we don't know which

half." This bromide helps explain why congressional campaigns are expensive. There is a kind of "campaign arms race" as each candidate tries to do what the other candidate does and a little more, escalating costs year by year. In the next chapter, we review some of the escalating costs of running a winning House or Senate campaign.

Voting Choices

For fifty years, political scientists have argued about how voters make their choices. Are parties most important? Issues? Personalities? Political scientist Stanley Kelley has argued that voters go through a simple process in deciding how to vote. They add up the things they like about each candidate and party and they vote for the candidate with the highest number of "likes." If there is a tie, they vote on the basis of their party identification, if they have one. If they do not, they abstain. On the basis of this simple idea, Kelley explains more than 85 percent of the variation in voting choice.[114]

In making these calculations, then, voters consider three things:

■ The party of the candidate, which has a great effect on how the voter views everything else about him or her

■ The candidate's personality, style, and appearance

■ The issue stands of the candidates and parties

Despite considerable disagreement as to exactly how each of these is weighted in the voter's mind, political scientists can offer some general conclusions.

Party Loyalties

One's party loyalty, called *party identification,* is probably the most important factor influencing a person's vote: Democrats tend to vote for Democrats and Republicans for Republicans. This is most true for lower-level contests such as state legislative elections, but it is also true for presidential races because party preference influences how a voter perceives a candidate's personality and issue stance. For some people, party identification is their only source of information about candidates, and they vote on the basis of it alone.

Though political scientists have observed that partisan loyalties are not as strong as in the early twentieth century, it is still a powerful predictor of the vote. While it is true that there are more independents and more people who vote contrary to their partisan loyalties than there used to be, the best predictor of the vote is the person's party identification. In 2000, for example, among those who went to the polls, 86 percent of all Democrats voted for Clinton, and 91 percent of all Republicans voted for Bush. These proportions were similar in the 1998 off-year election.[115] Both were higher than they have been in decades.

How do people get to be Republicans and Democrats? Socioeconomic class is a very important predictor of the vote: The lower the income, the more likely to vote Democrat. But this general rule is cross-cut with distinctive ethnic and religious patterns (we use *ethnic* here to refer to differences of national origin and race).

For example, Jews are much more likely to vote Democratic than other whites of similar income. On the whole, they have a higher-than-average income, yet in both 1996 and 2000, over three-fourths of Jewish voters voted Democratic. As a group, they were exceeded in their Democratic allegiance only by blacks.[116]

Catholics used to be predominantly Democratic. They still are, but not as consistently. Though a majority of Catholics voted for Reagan in 1980 and 1984, they returned to the Democratic fold in the 1990s. They favored Clinton by significant margins but gave Gore only a small plurality.

African Americans are probably the most distinctive group politically. About 90 percent voted Democratic in 2000; this is a higher proportion than the black vote for Clinton.

Hispanics—who, like blacks, also have lower-than average incomes—are not as universally Democratic as blacks and have voted Republican in significant numbers. Nevertheless, almost three-quarters voted Democratic in recent congressional elections and two-thirds for recent Democratic presidential candidates. Among Hispanics, Cuban Americans are much more likely to be Republican than either Mexican Americans or Puerto Ricans. Many Cubans are refugees or descendants of refugees from Castro's Cuba and are intensely anticommunist.

The Bush administration has made a concerted effort to woo Hispanic voters. Bush has given his weekly radio address in Spanish, created a high-profile friendly relationship with the president of Mexico, and, before 9/11, suggested that Mexican illegal immigrants be given legal residence. Given the growth of the Hispanic population, especially in the Southwest, winning allegiance of significant numbers of Hispanics is crucial to Republican competitiveness in states like California and Texas.

The voting behavior of Asian Americans has been much less thoroughly studied than that of other groups (because until recently they were quite a small group). In 1992 and 1996, their voting patterns resembled those of whites, with a small plurality in favor of the Republican candidates, but in 1998 and 2000, a strong majority of Asian Americans voted Democratic.

"Not voting this year?"

White Protestants generally give a majority of their vote to the Republicans and have done so for decades. Evangelical Protestants (such as Southern Baptist and Assembly of God) are much more likely to vote for Republicans than are mainline Protestants (such as Episcopalians or Presbyterians). However, as for other groups, income differences are important in determining the vote of Protestants.

Ethnicity and religion are important in determining the vote because they are shorthand terms for many other factors influencing political behavior—class, historical treatment within the society, and basic culture and values. Jews are predominantly Democratic, for example, because as a persecuted minority throughout much of their history, they have learned to identify with the underdog, even when their own economic circumstances move them into the middle or upper class. Catholics were sometimes discriminated against, too; this discrimination plus their working-class status propelled them to the party of Roosevelt. As Catholics have moved into the middle class and as tolerance toward Catholics has grown, Catholics, like Protestants, have tended to vote their income.

Candidate Evaluations

Candidates' personalities and styles have had more impact as party influence has declined and as television has become voters' major source of information about elections. Reagan's popularity in 1984 is an example of the influence of a candidate and his personality. The perceived competence and integrity of candidates are other facets of candidate evaluation. Voters are less likely to support candidates who do not seem capable of handling the job, regardless of their issue positions. Jimmy Carter suffered in 1980 because of voter evaluations of his competence and leadership.

Clinton's popularity puzzled many observers. Many voters did not like his evasions and his public humiliation of his wife, but they voted for him anyway. During the impeachment debates, many journalists expressed amazement that Clinton's popularity remained high. The public, more than journalists, seemed to be able to separate his public and private roles. The public continued to support him because they felt he was doing a good job as president, not because they admired him personally.

Gore's personality was a negative in the 2000 campaign. He seemed tense and wooden. His personality would change from week to week. He often seemed to pander, as when he argued that Elian Gonzalez should stay in the United States, contracting the stance that the administration had taken. The press also charged him with shading the truth, and late-night jokesters made fun of his claim to have invented the Internet. (Yet, in

George W. Bush worked hard to win the votes of Hispanics for the Republican Party. Republicans believe they need Hispanic voters to be competitive in national elections.

fact, he was instrumental in securing federal funding for the precursor to the Internet.) Bush's evasions of the truth were the subject of much less comment, perhaps because the press took him so lightly and believed that maybe he really could not remember which policies he had supported as governor.

Issues

Issues are a third factor influencing the vote. Although Americans are probably more likely to vote on issues now than they were in the 1950s, issues only influence some voters some of the time. In 1984 and 1988, for example, voters' issue positions overall were closer to the positions of Mondale and Dukakis than to winners Reagan or Bush. In 2000, voters saw themselves as much closer to Gore than Bush on the issues.[117]

Although other factors also influence voters, many do cast issue votes. To cast an issue vote, voters have to be informed about issues and have opinions. In recent elections, more than 80 percent of the public could take a position on issues such as government spending, military spending, women's rights, and relations with Russia.[118] Knowledge about these issues may have been vague, but individuals were able to understand the issues enough to define their own general positions.

Also, for voters to cast issue votes, candidates must have detectable policy differences. A substantial minority of voters are able to detect some differences among presidential candidates. In recent elections, the percentages able to identify correctly general differences between the major party candidates varied between 26 and 55 percent.[119]

In every election since 1972, more than 70 percent of those who could correctly identify the positions of the candidates as well as their own position on an important issue cast a vote consistent with their own position.[120] We call this *issue voting*. Issues with the highest proportion of issue voting were those that typically divided Republicans and Democrats, such as government spending, military spending, and government aid to the unemployed and minorities. However, because only one-third to two-thirds of the electorate was able to define both their own and the candidates' positions on each issue, the proportion of the total electorate that can be said to cast an "issue vote" is usually less than 40 percent, and for some issues it is much less.[121] Abortion is an issue on which voters cast issue-related votes. In 1996, for example, about 60 percent of the voters cast issue-related votes on abortion. Of those voters (who had a position and also knew where the candidates stood), 15 percent of those who opposed abortion under any conditions voted for Clinton compared with 81 percent of those who believed that abortion should be a matter of personal choice.[122]

Some scholars have suggested that issue voting is really more of an evaluation of the current incumbents. If voters like the way incumbents, or the incumbent's party, have handled the job in general or in certain areas—the economy or foreign policy, for example—they will vote accordingly, even without much knowledge about the specifics of the issues.

Voting on the basis of past performance is called **retrospective voting.** There is good evidence that many people do this, especially according to economic conditions.[123] Voters support incumbents if national income is growing in the months preceding the election. Since World War II, the incumbent party has won a presidential election only once when the growth rate was less than 3 percent (Eisenhower in 1956) and lost only twice when it was more than 3 percent (Ford in 1976 and Gore in 2000). Unemployment and inflation seem to have less consistent effects on voting, and economic conditions two or three years before the election have little impact on voting.[124]

Table 1 shows the relationship of the presidential vote to beliefs about whether federal policies have made the nation better or worse off. Those who believe the nation is better off are considerably more likely to vote for the incumbent presidential party than others. The same general pattern holds true if the question focuses on individual economic success rather than national.

President Bush was defeated in 1992 when the economy stagnated; on the other hand, Clinton's reelection in 1996 was surely assisted by the booming economy. In fact, political scientists believe that economic growth in the months before the election is one of the best predictors of election results. For that reason, many were perplexed by

TABLE 1	Voting is Strongly Related to Views of the Economy		
Voters who believe that the policies of the federal government have made the nation's economy:	Percentage Who Voted for the Incumbent Party Nominee		
	1984	1992	1996
Better	84	79	82
Same	52	49	52
Worse	23	29	32

SOURCE: Paul Abramson, John Aldrich, and David Rohde, *Change and Continuity in the 1996 Election* (Washington, D.C.: Congressional Quarterly Press, 1998).

the close 2000 election and sought to explain it in terms of Gore's poor campaign. Other pundits, though, thought perhaps that the economy had been so good for so long that people took good times for granted.[125]

Parties, Candidates, and Issues

All three factors—parties, candidates, and issues—clearly matter. Party loyalties are especially important because they help shape our views about issues and candidates. However, if issues and candidates did not matter, the Democrats would have won every presidential election since the New Deal. Republican victories suggest that they often have had more attractive candidates (as in 1952, 1956, 1980, and 1984) or issue positions (in 1972 and in some respects in 1980). However, the Democrats' partisan advantage shrank throughout the 1980s. Though there are still more Democrats than Republicans, the margin is modest, and the number of independents is large.

Party loyalties have been even more important in congressional voting. The Democrats controlled the House continuously between 1954 and 1994 and controlled the Senate most of those years. However, the Democratic lock on the House was broken in the 1994 election, which found the Republicans winning control in a sweeping victory. Clearly, issues overcame traditional partisan habits in that election. Exactly which issues, however, were less than clear.

Voting for Congress

Party loyalty, candidate evaluations, and issues are important factors in congressional elections just as in presidential ones.[126] Party loyalty is even more important for congressional than for presidential elections because congressional elections are less visible, so more people base their vote on party identification. Incumbency is also more important than in presidential races. The result is that increasingly, since about 1960, voters have split their tickets in voting for presidential and congressional candidates. Democrats especially are likely to

"This year i'm not getting involved in any complicated issues. I'm just voting my straight ethnic prejudices."

desert their party when casting a vote for president. For example, one out of five Reagan voters in 1984 voted for a Democratic member of the House, leaving Reagan with only a 41 percent Republican House despite his commanding personal victory.

Normally, the party of a winning presidential candidate gains seats during a presidential election year and loses a number of seats in the midterm election. This maintains a sort of equilibrium in party control of Congress.[127] In most recent elections, these losses have been modest. In 1998, the Democrats actually gained five seats in the House and lost no seats in the Senate. The same pattern was true in 2002 when George Bush's incumbent Republican Party gained two Senate and six House seats. To some extent, midterm election results are a referendum on how well citizens think the president is doing. In 1998, Clinton was given credit for the economic good times the country was experiencing, and in 2002 voters rewarded the Republicans for Bush's strong antiterrorist stance. The percentage of the total vote for congressional candidates that went to Democrats in 1996 and in 1998 was within a percentage point of the vote Clinton won in 1996. (In 2000, though George Bush won the presidency, the Democrats gained five Senate seats while losing two in the House.)

Conclusion: Do Elections Make Government Responsive?

Although election campaigns are far less successful in mobilizing voters and ensuring a high turnout today than they were in the past century, in a democracy, we

expect elections to allow us to control government. Through them we can "throw the rascals out" and bring in new faces with better ideas, or so we think. But other than to change the party that controls government, do elections make a difference?

In the popular press, we hear a lot about "mandates." A president with a **mandate** is one who is clearly directed by the voters to take some particular course of action—reduce taxes or begin arms-control talks, for example. George H. Bush had a substantial majority in his 1988 victory. But did he have a mandate? If so, what for? The campaign hardly talked about the budget deficit even though the election-day polls showed that this was the issue of concern to the largest group of voters. They, in turn, gave an overwhelming majority of *their* votes to Michael Dukakis. On other issues, such as protecting the environment, Bush portrayed himself as a liberal. On many issues, ranging from abortion to day care to defense policy, the two candidates clearly differed. But did Bush's victory mean that he was to limit abortions, leave it to the states to fund day care, or continue the Reagan defense policy? Did he have a mandate on any of these issues?

Like most things in politics, the answer is not simple. Sometimes elections have an effect on policy, but often their effects are not clear-cut. In close elections, few would argue that there is a mandate. In 2000, voters favored the Democratic policy positions and did so in a time of peace and prosperity. A plurality gave their votes to Gore. Yet, Bush is president and acts as though his narrow electoral college victory is a mandate in support of his foreign policies and conservative domestic policies.

It is primarily political parties that translate the mix of various issues into government action because voters' issue positions influence their party loyalties and their evaluations of candidates. Over time, a rough agreement usually develops between public attitudes and policies.[128] A vote for the candidate of one's own party is usually a reflection of agreement on at least some important issues. Once in office, the party in government helps sort out the issues for which there is a broad public mandate from those for which there is not.

Elections that appear to be mandates can become "mandates for disaster." More than one observer has pointed out that every twentieth-century president who won election by 60 percent or more of the popular vote soon encountered serious political trouble. After his landslide in 1920, Warren Harding had his Teapot Dome scandal involving government corruption. Emboldened by his 1936 triumph, Franklin Roosevelt tried to pack the Supreme Court and was resoundingly defeated on that issue. Lyndon Johnson won by a landslide in 1964 and was soon mired in Vietnam. Richard Nixon smashed George McGovern in 1972 but then had to resign because of Watergate. Ronald Reagan's resounding victory in 1984 (a shade less than 60 percent) was followed by the blunders of the Iran-Contra affair. Of these presidents, only Roosevelt was able to recover fully from his political misfortune. Reagan regained his personal popularity but seemed to have little influence on policy after Iran-Contra. One recent observer has argued that these disasters come because "the euphoria induced by overwhelming support at the polls evidently loosens the president's grip on reality."[129]

Elections can point out new directions for government and allow citizens to make it responsive to their needs, but the fact that many individuals do not vote means that the new directions may not reflect either the needs or wishes of the public. If election turnout falls too far, the legitimacy of elections may be threatened. People may come to believe that election results do not reflect the wishes of the majority. For this reason, this slow and steady decline of turnout should concern all of us. If elections promote government responsiveness to those who participate in them, higher turnouts help increase responsiveness.

EPILOGUE

Gore Asks for a Limited Recount

In the end, you pursued a conservative strategy that likely cost you the election. You asked only for a recount in four strongly Democratic counties. You felt that these counties would give you enough more votes to win the election. Even though this was your right under Florida law, it made you appear to be manipulating the process for your own ends rather than seeking an accurate recount. The Bush campaign took advantage of this impression, hammering away in the media.

Later, after the Bush campaign sued to stop the recount, you did challenge Bush to have a recount in every county, but you did not emphasize it or file suit to accomplish it.[130] When finally the Florida Supreme Court mandated a recount in every county, so much time had elapsed that the U.S. Supreme Court threw up its hands and gave the election to Bush (see Chapter 13 for the description of the U.S. Supreme Court's controversial actions).

Although your strategy failed, the alternative strategy might have failed as well. The Bush campaign was determined to stop any recount. It did not propose, and would not have agreed to, a statewide recount. Republican aides claimed that hand recounts would be inaccurate and partisan

but in fact expected that they would turn up more Gore votes.

At the same time, you decided not to challenge the overseas votes, even the hundreds that were patently illegal under Florida laws. Indeed, 680 were flawed, including nearly 200 with United States postmarks, indicating that they had been mailed from within the country rather than from overseas; 344 with late, illegible, or missing postmarks; and even 38 reflecting double voting by 19 voters.[131] Clearly, the local election judges would have thrown these out had your Democratic Party representatives challenged them. But you did not, apparently not wanting to appear against voting rights of overseas armed forces personnel, even fraudulent ones. As a consequence of the illegal military ballots alone, you lost Florida by 537 votes when your election day margin was 202 votes.[132]

The Bush postelection campaign was, in hindsight, more skillful and more aggressive. At one point the Bush campaign even organized a demonstration to intimidate election officials in Miami-Dade to stop conducting a recount they were in the middle of. Demonstrators barged into the building, yelling and pounding on doors. Photos from that event showed that many of the "demon-

strators" were staffers in conservative congressional Republican offices who had been sent to Florida to do this, though at the time the election officials recounting the ballot did not know that. The demonstration succeeded in getting the officials to halt the recount.

The Bush campaign was also more aggressive in persuading election officials how to treat overseas ballots. Republican representatives urged election officials in Democratic majority counties to follow the law in handling overseas ballots, so illegal ballots would not be counted; in Republican counties, they urged election officials to disregard the law, so illegal ballots would be counted. (There is nothing illegal or even immoral about Republican supporters doing this, but the election officials should not have caved, and the Democratic representatives should have argued that the laws be followed.) Meanwhile, Democratic representatives, fearing a public backlash, did not try to counter Republican efforts. As a result, "Under intense pressure from the Republicans, Florida officials accepted hundreds of overseas absentee ballots that failed to comply with state laws."[133]

In addition, the Bush campaign had strong political allies in Florida. Not only was Bush's brother the governor, but the secretary of state, who oversees the election system, was cochair of Bush's Florida campaign. Making little effort to appear nonpartisan, at every opportunity she ruled in favor of the Bush campaign and forced the Gore campaign to go to court to obtain recounts and redress.

Time also worked in favor of the Bush campaign, as it held a narrow lead throughout these weeks and because it knew that the deadline for certifying Florida's electors would put pressure on the courts to stop the recount. Thus, the Bush campaign used delaying tactics to slow and stop the recounts, hoping that either the courts or, in the end, the Republican-dominated Florida legislature and executive branch would protect his narrow lead.

The outcome of this election will be argued as long as people are interested in politics. It is likely true that a bare majority of Florida voters in fact favored Gore.[134] Systematic analyses have proven that the Buchanan vote was inflated by at least 2,500 votes intended for Gore in Palm Beach County.[135] As one commentator noted, "No election analyst will say with a straight face that the butterfly design didn't cost Al Gore the presidency."[136]

Of course, the overseas ballot contributed, too, by an unknown amount. That is, we know how many ballots were illegal, but we don't know for sure their distribution between Bush and Gore.

Nearly two-thirds of the 2,400 overseas ballots counted after November 7 were for Bush.

If the Supreme Court had allowed the recount to go forward in just the four counties Gore asked for, it is unlikely Gore would have won. If the recount had gone forward in all counties, there is a good likelihood that Gore would have won. In fact, two independent scholars argue that the probability is about 99 percent that Gore would have won if the invalid overseas ballots were handled properly and a statewide recount was allowed under any reasonable standard for counting chads, whether it was a uniform state standard or standards each county set.[137]

The confusion surrounding the 2000 election outcome highlights an important but often ignored aspect of our electoral process: State law and local policies determine the mechanics of presidential elections. In this election, these mechanics also were important in determining the winner.

The Constitution gives the power to regulate elections to the states as part of the federal system. In some localities, votes are done on automatic voting machines, in other cases paper ballots are used. Other jurisdictions use electronic devices that scan shading on small round circles the voters have marked, like the mark sense sheets on college exams. And still others use the punch cards

that were the focus of the controversies in Florida. Even in a single state, like Florida, some localities use paper ballots, others machines, and still others punch cards.

In Florida, the embarrassment of 2000 did lead to election reform. Punch card machines, the ones that produced chads, were outlawed. Optical scan ballots and touch screen machines replaced them. The law also mandated the secretary of state to define a statewide standard for dealing with disputed ballots and further mandated a hand count of overvotes and undervotes in any election in which the margin was within one-fourth of 1 percent.[138] Had those reforms been in place in 2000, Gore would be the president.

But Americans have a surprising tolerance for election irregularities and even fraud, presumably because elections are run not by the federal government but by the states or, in many states, the counties. Indeed, part of American election folklore is that voter fraud in Illinois produced a Kennedy victory in Illinois and thus in the United States. Part of that folklore may be true—there is certainly evidence of fraud in Illinois's voting in 1960—but part is not, because Nixon wouldn't have won the national election anyway. Nonetheless, this is one of those cherished election war stories.

With so many local officials involved, Americans grudgingly accept

Republican protesters, some of them staffers in the Republican congressional offices, invade the Miami government center to protest the 2000 election recount.

"Oh, sure, it's stolen, but now we have to get on with our lives."

inevitable mistakes and even snicker over remarks such as that of Louisiana governor Huey Long, who commented, "When I die, I want to be buried in Louisiana so I can stay active in politics."[139]

But few elections are so close that irregularities make a difference. No doubt there were many communities in America where in 2000 voting machines did not work right or some part of the process confused many voters. Yet in most elections the margins are large enough that confusion or corruption on the part of a few does not change the outcome. But the election of 2000 brought into stark relief the problems that shoddy election procedures can create. Former president and Nobel Peace Prize winner Jimmy Carter, who through his Carter Center, now works for peace and social justice around the world, is often invited by governments or challengers to governments in Asia and Africa to monitor elections and

attest to their fairness in countries. He remarked, "I was really taken aback and embarrassed by what happened in Florida. If we were invited to go into a foreign country to monitor the election, and they had similar standards and procedures, we would refuse to participate at all."[140]

Perhaps we are coming to another era where election reform will be on the agenda. Over the past few decades, as a society we have become more concerned about fairness and equality. We have seen it with civil rights laws that require equal treatment of all individuals. We have seen it with regulations involving treatment of alleged criminals. There is an outcry when police stray from these procedures. Now that we have had an election where fair procedures were either nonexistent or not followed, the public appears to want more competence and professionalism among election officials just as it has demanded it from various other officials in recent decades.

Months after the election, half of the electorate thought that the outcome was unfair or downright crooked. But most Americans, even those who think that, are willing to move on. The exceptions include strong Florida Democrats and many African Americans who believe they were systematically disenfranchised by the way the election was run in Florida. One of ten votes in largely African American precincts in Florida were thrown out as invalid, compared to one of thirty-seven in white precincts.[141]

Certainly the events of 9/11 took the election of 2000 off the front page. Yet, it is likely that the way the Florida election was handled will continue to reverberate through American politics.

The crowning indignity of the Florida election confusion was the joking comment of Cuba's Fidel Castro that he'd be glad to come over and straighten the system out.

 To learn more about Gore's post-election strategy and the controversy surrounding the Florida election results, go to this chapter's "You Are There" exercises on the text Web site.

Key Terms

suffrage

Reconstruction

literacy tests

grandfather clause

poll tax

white primary

Voting Rights Act (VRA)

cracking, stacking, and packing

majority-minority districts

cumulative voting

Progressive reforms

motor voter law

presidential preference primaries

Super Tuesday

Electoral College

faithless elector

permanent campaign

retrospective voting

mandate

Further Reading

Stephen Ansolabehere and Shanto Iyengar, *Going Negative* (New York: Free Press, 1996). Two political scientists report the results of their research on the impact of negative television ads on voters and voting.

Taylor Branch, *Parting the Waters: America in the King Years* (New York: Simon & Schuster, 1988). An excellent, readable account that illustrates the impact of political protest in changing America's race laws and to a considerable extent its attitudes about race.

Robert Darcy, Susan Welch, and Janet Clark, *Women, Elections, and Representation* (Lincoln: University of Nebraska Press, 1994). An examination of the potential barriers faced by women candidates.

Kathleen Hall Jamieson, *Packaging the Presidency* (New York: Oxford University Press, 1984). The history and impact of presidential campaign advertising.

David Kaplan, *The Accidental President: How 413 Lawyers, 9 Supreme Court Justices, and 5,963,110 Floridians (Give or Take a Few) Landed George W. Bush in the White House* (New York: Morrow, 2001). A humorous look behind the scenes of the Bush and Gore organizations fighting for the election after election day.

Zachary Karabell, *The Last Campaign* (New York: Knopf, 2000). The story of the Truman-Dewey 1948 campaign that some campaign experts believe was the best in the second half of the twentieth century.

Frances Fox Piven and Richard Cloward, *Why Americans Don't Vote* (New York: Pantheon, 1988). The authors attribute nonvoting to restrictive registration laws and the disinterest of parties in mobilizing the working class.

Theodore H. White, *The Making of the President,* 4 vols. (New York: Atheneum, 1961, 1965, 1969, 1973). Journalistic accounts of presidential elections from 1960 to 1972. White was the first journalist to travel with the candidates and give an inside view of campaign strategy.

Electronic Resources

allpolitics.com
Chat online with presidential candidates and keep up with the political news of the day.

democrats.org/party/ and www.rnc.org
Links to the Democratic National Committee and the Republican National Committee. Each of these pages contains information about the campaign organizations of the two national parties.

washingtonpost.com/wp-dyn/politics/
Go to a map of the United States, and click on a state to get information about the politics and elected officials of that state.

odwin.ucsd.edu/idata/icpsr.html
This site, sponsored by the University of California at San Diego, provides access to information from national election studies done by political scientists since 1952. You can find out what voters thought on a broad variety of issues asked in each national election (presidential and most congressional) study.

politics.com
Check who donates to which campaign, and keep current with the campaign stories of the day, the results of the latest polls, and links to other sites.

www.vote-smart.org/ce/
Project Vote Smart provides nonpartisan information about campaigns and issues on this site.

InfoTrac College Edition

Search for the following articles in the InfoTrac database:

> Conniff, Ruth. "It's Not Easy Being Green," *The Progressive* (August 2000).
>
> Cook, Jr., Charles E. "Election Season Heats Up," *Washington Quarterly* (Summer 2000).
>
> Pitney Jr., John J. "Chad All Over," *Reason* (August 2001).
>
> Walsh, Kenneth T. "In the Homestretch, Hitting His Stride," *U.S. News & World Report* (November 6, 2000).

For more articles, enter

> "Democratic Party" in the Subject Guide;
>
> "Republican Party" in the Subject Guide;
>
> "third parties" in the Subject Guide.

American Government Resources

Visit the Political Behavior section of the Wadsworth American Government Resources Web site (politicalscience.wadsworth.com/amgov/) for a variety of tools to help you explore elections further. Included are simulations, video clips, Microcase exercises, and a wealth of other activities.

CHAPTER 9

MONEY AND POLITICS

Patrick J. Kennedy (D-Mass.) and House Minority Leader Richard A. Gephardt (D-Mo.) work the phones to raise funds for Democrats running for the House.

Should You Vote to Regulate?

t is 2000, and you are Charles Schumer, a Democratic senator from New York. You are weighing a proposed rule to restrict potentially corrupt practices in the financial industry. Elected to public office immediately after graduating from Harvard Law School, you have served in the New York state assembly, the U.S. House of Representatives, and, now, the U.S. Senate.[1] Though a relatively junior senator, you are highly visible. As a member of the House, you were known both for your legislative activism and success and for your nose for publicity. Bob Dole once joked that "the most dangerous place in Washington was in between Schumer and a television camera."[2] In 1998, you won a Senate seat, beating a popular incumbent in the most expensive Senate race ever waged up till then.

Given your New York constituency, it is not surprising that you have a liberal voting record, strongly supporting gun control and abortion rights, for example. On the other hand, one of your special interests is the financial services industry—that is, banks, savings and loans, brokerage houses, and related financial institutions—and there you have established a less liberal record, voting frequently to lighten government regulation.

In both the House and Senate, you served as a member of the Banking, Housing, and Urban Affairs Committee. Though most members do not consider seats on the banking committee desirable or prestigious, in a time of change and deregulation in the financial services industry, the committee has been considering much significant legislation. Moreover, it has oversight powers over the Security Exchange Commission (SEC), the federal agency that regulates the stock exchange. Of course, New York City is the heart of the nation's and the world's financial system, so legislation and regulations affecting the financial industry are of keen interest to many of your most influential constituents. Moreover, membership on the Banking Committee offers access to interest groups with significant wealth, an important factor given the cost of running statewide races in New York.

During the past decade, Congress has been busy deregulating the financial services industry, giving banks, savings and loans, insurance companies, and investment bankers more flexibility to do business with each other and to compete for business normally handled by other sectors of the financial industry. This allowed banks to sell stocks, real estate, and insurance and savings and loan firms to offer checking accounts, for example. Deregulation has also meant that some federal laws have been repealed, lightening federal oversight and weakening protection for consumers and investors.

With the New York financial world part of your constituency, you, too, have supported legislation to deregulate much of the financial services industry. Last year, you worked closely with conservative Republicans and other Senate leaders to win approval to allow banks more flexibility in dealing with investment securities.

Now Arthur Levitt, chair of the SEC, the government agency that regulates stock trading, proposes to tighten regulations involving auditing firms. In recent years, auditing firms are increasingly providing consulting services for companies that they are auditing. The consulting business often yields more revenue than the auditing contracts. Levitt believed that there was an increasing chance that auditors' reports were being corrupted. Indeed, in a speech in 1998, he complained of "accounting hocus-pocus" by corporations and their auditors.[3]

The reason is the obvious potential for conflict of interest. Auditors with firms that have lucrative consulting contracts with corporations they are auditing may feel they can't come down hard on suspicious accounting practices. As consulting becomes more and important to the top accounting firms, their independence is more and more compromised.

Because of these conflicts, Levitt wants the SEC to pass a rule requiring firms to choose between being auditors of corporations and being consultants for them. In the complex world of corporate finance, accounting principles govern how profits are calculated. Auditors, hired by the company boards of directors, but with ostensible independence from the company, are charged with investigating adherence to these accounting principles and then certifying that they have been met. Certifying that the company's books are accurate assures investors and potential investors that finances of the corporation are as portrayed. And, favorable reports reassure investors and allow the corporation's stock to continue increasing in value, whereas unfavorable reports worry investors and prompt them

to unload their stock in the corporation, causing its value to decline.

As the economy boomed in the 1990s, pressure increased on corporations to boost their earnings and thus benefit from the high-flying stock market. A rosy earnings picture was among the factors that drove stocks to record highs. One way to increase earnings is to increase revenue and cut costs; the other way is to cook the books. And indeed, the demand to show stockholders large profits have put pressures on auditors to falsely certify that the healthy financial pictures that corporations painted were accurate. By the end of the 1990s, the SEC regulators begin to find that accountants were not holding corporations to the appropriate standards for calculating profits and losses; indeed, in some cases they were participating in outright fraud. In many cases, these were auditing firms that made millions from their consulting contracts with companies they were auditing. (By the late 1990s, big accounting firms were making more from consulting than by their auditing business.)

Levitt argued that lax oversight could have catastrophic consequences if a business overstated its earnings and investors invested their money on the basis of this false information. When the truth was uncovered, stock prices would plummet, and investors would lose some or all of their investment in the business. Moreover, if one large corporation's unethical accounting practices were uncovered, other companies could suffer as mistrust would dampen investors' willingness to invest in stocks. In a nutshell, poor accounting practices, as dry and boring as they might seem, could threaten our capitalist system.

The rules that Levitt proposes are not legislation; they do not need to be passed by Congress. However, rule making by agencies such as the SEC relies on support from the various constituencies the agency serves. In particular, the members of the Banking, Housing, and Urban Affairs Committee have considerable clout with the SEC. As a government agency, the Security and

Exchange Commission is subject to congressional oversight, and the banking committees in each house do much of that oversight. The committees have the power to reward the agency through favorable budget recommendations or to make the lives of the officials of the SEC miserable by holding hearings, demanding information, failing to endorse the president's recommendations for high-level appointments to the agency, proposing unfavorable legislation affecting the agency (such as reducing its jurisdiction), and cutting their budget, among other ways. And committee members have an influence on the larger membership of Congress when it comes to budgets affecting the SEC.

The SEC would like to have your support for this proposed rule because you are an influential Democrat on the Banking Committee. What is your response? Do you support this regulation or not?

Your first instinct is to oppose these rules. You have generally supported deregulation of the financial industry, and the rules Levitt are proposing are more regulation, not less. Moreover, the accounting lobby has mobilized to oppose the rules. This is a lobby with significant clout; in fact, five years ago they succeeded in getting legislation through Congress that would shield companies and their auditors from suits by stockholders. This legislation was opposed by the SEC and vetoed by President Clinton, but his veto was overridden and the bill became law. Now the accountants' lobby has hired high-powered lawyers and is working to persuade individual members to, in turn, lobby the SEC against the bill. They are even helping draft letters that members of Congress can send to the SEC.

These lobbyists have access to you and other influential members of Congress because you have worked together over the years on legislation of interest to the accounting profession. Moreover, over the past few years, they have made significant contributions to your campaign and those of many others. For example, you have received nearly $330,000 from the accounting lobby since 1995, more than any other member of Congress. The chair of the Banking, Housing, and Urban Affairs Committee, Phil Gramm (R-Tex.), has received $200,000, and many members have received more than $100,000. Of course, you and your colleagues have also received campaign donations from many corporations that are also opposing this bill. One such aggressive corporation, Enron, a high-flying Texas energy company, has donated more than $70,000 to you and much more to other members.

On the other hand, among your constituents, there are certainly more investors than there are accountants and corporation executives. Yet, though approximately 100 million Americans, including millions of New Yorkers, own stocks, they are not well organized as a lobby. So constituency pressure to support the rules is weak. As Levitt said, "[Investors are] potentially the most powerful lobbying force in the country, and . . . the least well-organized." Investors don't stand a chance of winning in a face-off with most business interest groups that are well organized.[4]

You, too, have heard warning signals that some firms might be operating unethically in terms of their earnings reports. Just last year, one of the nation's largest accounting firms, Ernst & Young, agreed to pay over $300 million to shareholders who blamed the accounting firm for misleading profit statements by a large corporation it had audited. Ernst & Young claimed it was the victim of fraud by the company but paid anyway.[5] Obviously, you have no interest in seeing scandal overtake the accounting industry or corporate America more generally; this would hurt the country and it would certainly hurt New York's economy. Levitt's rule might help prevent such scandal.

Whatever you decide on this proposed rule, your position will be immediately known to the accounting lobby and to the large corporations who do not want the rule to be adopted. Your position is not so likely to be known by those unorganized groups in favor of the rule, and certainly it is not likely to be known by most of your constituents. Most will never know, unless corrupt auditing practices cause a corporation's stock to tank and the investors—including your constituents—to lose their money. Then they might blame you. But, of course, this scenario might never occur. Public interest in this rule is weak. Short of some scandal, it will remain weak. This fight is mostly an "inside the beltway battle"[6] between the head of the SEC and the big accounting firms. What do you do and why?

Former speaker of the House of Representatives Tip O'Neill once said, "There are four parts to any campaign. The candidate, the issues . . . , the campaign organization, and the money. Without money you can forget the other three."[7] Conventional wisdom holds that "money is the mother's milk of politics." But we are not sure whether that milk is tainted or pure. On the one hand, without money, candidates or people with new political ideas could never become known in our massive and complex society. Television spreads names and ideas almost instantaneously, so having money to buy television time means your ideas will be heard. In that sense, money contributes to open political debate.

On the other hand, money can be a corrupting influence on politics. At the least, it can buy access to those making decisions. At the worst, it can buy decisions. Money allows some points of view to be trumpeted while others are forced to whisper. Some candidates or groups can afford to spend hundreds of thousands of dollars for each prime-time minute of national television or for prestigious Washington law firms to lobby; others can afford only Web pages and letters. Money increases inequities in political life.

Money, then, leads to a dilemma in politics. In our largely capitalist society, we expect substantial differences in wealth and income. In most cases, we see nothing wrong when those of great wealth are able to buy goods and services that others cannot afford. But in politics, many people feel uneasy when high-income individuals or well-bankrolled groups are able to buy political favors. We feel so uneasy that we have outlawed certain kinds of buying of political favors, such as politicians paying voters for their votes or interest groups paying politicians and bureaucrats for their support.

But we are uneasy about other ways of limiting the influence of money. Many people feel that individuals or groups should be allowed to contribute as much money to candidates as they want and that candidates should be permitted to buy as much media time to get their point of view across as they want and can afford. This view holds that contributing money and buying media time are forms of constitutionally guaranteed freedom of speech. The opposite view says that these practices distort the democratic process.

These issues are growing more important as the cost of political campaigns increases. In 2000, candidates at all levels spent $4 billion. Only a fraction came from public funds. So it is not surprising that political candidates scramble for money. Limiting the amounts individual groups give tracking those amounts are the subject of campaign finance laws. Journalists and other analysts also try to determine what the donors received in return for their gifts.

In this chapter, we first focus on the development of laws that regulate how money can influence politics, then we turn to the role and impact of money in elections, and finally we briefly examine conflict of interest on the part of decision makers in Congress and the executive branch.

Money and Politics in Earlier America

Concern about the illegitimate influence of money on politics is nearly as old as the Republic. In 1699, after asking how campaign money could be regulated, Virginia House of Burgesses (their legislature) voted to prohibit bribing voters.[8] In his campaign for the Virginia House of Burgesses in 1757, George Washington was accused of vote buying. He had given out twenty-eight gallons of rum, fifty gallons of rum punch, thirty-four gallons of wine, forty-six gallons of beer, and two gallons of cider.[9] Because there were only 391 voters in his district, he had provided more than a quart and a half of beverages per voter![10]

Obviously, Washington survived these charges, and his constituents probably survived the effects of the rum and cider. But most discussions of the impact of money on politics were more sober. In his well-known analysis of controlling factions, James Madison, in *Federalist* 10, recognized that "the most common and durable source of factions has been the various and unequal distribution of property." Madison went on to say that although ideally no one should be allowed to make decisions affecting his or her own self-interest, almost any subject of legislation—taxes, tariffs, debts—involves self-interest. For those making laws, "every shilling with which they overburden the inferior number is a shilling saved to their own pockets."[11]

Madison hoped that the design of the new nation, with the power of the government divided among the branches of government and between the nation and the states, would mean that no one interest or faction would overwhelm the others. The interest of one person or group would check the interest of another.

This view of counterbalancing interests is an optimistic one and has not always worked. Over the decades, Americans have found it necessary to make additional rules to restrict the ways that those with money can try to influence policymakers.

Money in Nineteenth-Century American Politics

The influence of money on politics has shaped several epochs of American history. For example, from the earliest westward expansion of the nation, charges of graft and corruption surrounded the government's sale and giveaway of land. Indeed, the West was developed by giving land to speculators and railroads, sometimes after bribes. When Congress was debating whether to give federal land to the railroads, the lobbyists "camped in brigades around the Capitol building."[12]

The impact of money on political life was probably at its peak in the late nineteenth century. The United States grew from a small agrarian society to a large in-

This Puck cartoon mocks President Ulysses S. Grant's involvement in various corrupt activities. Grant (dressed in the flag suit) is shown supporting various political bosses and profiteers.

dustrialized one. This industrialization produced great wealth in such fields as oil exploration and refining, the steel industry, and the railroad companies that were spanning the nation. This was the era of "robber barons," when the owners of giant corporations (called *trusts*) openly bought political favors.

Business contributions to campaigns and to politicians were routine. One railroad president justified bribery of political officials by noting, "If you have to pay money to have the right thing done, it is only just and fair to do so."[13] Mark Hanna, a Republican fundraiser in the presidential election of 1896, assessed banks at a fixed percentage of their capital and also collected substantial sums from most insurance companies and large corporations.[14] However, Cornelius Vanderbilt, one of the wealthiest men of his time, refused to contribute to election campaigns, believing that it was cheaper to buy legislators after they were elected!

Not only did lobbyists bribe politicians, but politicians bribed reporters. In the 1872 presidential campaign, the Republican Party gave money to about three hundred reporters in return for favorable coverage.[15] (See the box "Honest Graft" for more on money's role in nineteenth-century politics.)

Early Reforms

Around the turn of the century, the Progressive reformers and their allies in the press, called the **Muckrakers,** began to attack this overt corruption. They wanted to break the financial link between business and politicians. In 1907, a law prohibited corporations and banks from making contributions to political campaigns, and a few years later, Congress mandated public reporting of campaign expenditures and set limits on campaign donations. Prohibitions against corporate giving to political campaigns were broadened over time to forbid utilities and labor unions from giving as well.

The **Teapot Dome scandal** of 1921 stimulated further attempts to limit the influence of money on electoral politics. The secretary of the interior in the Harding administration received almost $400,000 from two corporations that then were allowed to lease oil reserves in California and Wyoming (one of them was called the "Teapot Dome"). This led to the Federal Corrupt Practices Act (1925), which required the reporting of campaign contributions and expenditures.

Because none of these laws was enforced, each had only a momentary effect. Nevertheless, the reforms did seem to make open graft and bribery less acceptable and less common. Instead of outright bribes, political interests now sought to influence politicians through campaign contributions.

Labor unions, for example, set up **political action committees (PACs)** funded from dues. These committees then raised "voluntary" money from members to support candidates for elections. Then many businesses did the same.

Regulating Money in Modern Campaigns

Waging a campaign in state or national politics is expensive. And, because most funding for such campaigns is private, candidates for office must continually look for sources to fund their campaigns. At least some of those who give money see donations as an opportunity for access and influence. Since the early 1970s, Americans have been at least intermittently concerned about the influence of campaign money on modern politics.

Reforms of the 1970s

Prompted by the increasing use of television in campaigns and the rising cost of buying television time, Congress passed a law regulating spending on advertising in 1971. The law limited the amount that candidates could donate to their own campaigns and required candidates to disclose the names and addresses of donors of more than $100.

In the course of the Watergate investigations, it became clear that corporations were not abiding by these restrictions. Several corporations secretly funded President Nixon's reelection campaign. For example, Nixon's Justice Department negotiated a settlement favorable to the ITT Corporation in a pending legal dispute soon after an ITT subsidiary gave the Republican National Committee $400,000.[16] Altogether, twenty-one individuals and fourteen corporations were indicted for

At the turn of the century, rich New Yorkers, wearing vine leaves on their heads, enjoy their wealth.

The influence of money on local politics reached a high point in the late nineteenth century. Urban machines used money to cement a complex network of businesses, voters, and political party organizations. Business payoffs to government and party officials for licenses and contracts, and party payoffs to voters for their support, were the norm. Graft was tolerated and even expected.

As we saw in Chapter 7, George Washington Plunkitt was a famous leader of the New York City machine, Tammany Hall. Plunkitt, born in 1842, began life as a butcher's helper and ended up a millionaire through deals made in his role as a party leader and public official. He held a number of state and local public offices; at one point, he held four at the same time. He drew a salary for three of them simultaneously.

Plunkitt's view of graft illustrates the casual attitude about the influence of money on politics common among many of his time:

There's all the difference in the world between [honest graft and dishonest graft]. There's an honest graft, and I'm an example of how it works. I might sum up the whole thing by sayin': "I seen my opportunities and I took 'em."

Just let me explain. . . . My party's in power in the city, and it's goin' to undertake a lot of public improvements.

Well, I'm tipped off, say, that they're going to lay out a new park at a certain place. I see my opportunity and take it. I go to that place and I buy up all the land I can in the neighborhood. Then the board of this or that makes its plan public, and there is a rush to get my land, which nobody cared particular for before. Ain't it perfectly honest to charge a good price and make a profit on my investment and foresight? Of course, it is. Well, that's honest graft.

Tammany was beat in 1901 because the people were deceived into believin' that it worked dishonest graft. . . . [They supposed] Tammany men were robbin' the city treasury or levyin' blackmail on disorderly houses, or workin' in with the gamblers and lawbreakers. . . . Why should the Tammany leaders go into such dirty business when there is so much honest graft lyin' around?

. . . I don't own a dishonest dollar. If my worst enemy was given the job of writin' my epitaph . . . he couldn't do more than write: George W. Plunkitt. He Seen His Opportunities, and He Took 'Em.

Source: William L. Riordon, *Plunkitt of Tammany Hall* (New York: Dutton, 1963).

illegal campaign contributions, mostly but not entirely to the Nixon reelection campaign.

In response to these scandals, Congress again attempted to regulate campaign financing. The objectives of the 1974 law were to limit spending, to make the campaign finance system more open, and to force candidates to be less reliant on a few big donors. Thus, the 1974 law called for public financing of presidential campaigns, limits on contributions of individuals and committees to campaigns for federal office, limits on overall expenditures by candidates' organizations in presidential and congressional campaigns, limits on overall expenditures by national party committees, limits on expenditures by PACs, limits on individual donations to PACs and to individual candidates, and prohibitions on cash contributions of more than $100. The act also established a bipartisan Federal Election Commission to enforce the law. The 1974 act also imposed limits on so-called **independent spending,** spending by groups not under the control of candidates. These limits were ruled unconstitutional and no longer obtain.

Because of the importance of money in campaigns, both elected officials and those who want something from the officials found ways to get around the campaign finance laws. Indeed, by the 1990s, the 1974 campaign finance law no longer had any practical effect.

Failures of the Campaign Finance Laws

Very quickly after 1974, the law's regulations began to be eroded. The Supreme Court judged some spending limits were unconstitutional, and other parts of the law were easy to get around. These loopholes set the stage for a new round of campaign finance reform in 2002.

Spending Limits

In 1976, the Supreme Court knocked a hole in the law when it ruled that some portions of the act were unconstitutional.[17] The Court struck down spending limits except for presidential elections that were publicly funded. Because spending often goes to buy advertising, the Court argued that spending restrictions violated individuals' First Amendment rights of free speech. Spending in a campaign enables candidates to get their message out. Giving money is a form of expression protected by the Constitution.

Spending limits still do obtain in presidential races, where candidates have the option of accepting public money. Presidential candidates who accept public financing, as most do, may not spend more than a fixed amount (in 2000, $57 million was spent on seventeen candidates) to get the nomination (the money comes from a voluntary checkoff of $3 on individuals' tax returns; the spending limit increases each year to take inflation into account). Candidates who do not accept public funding can spend as much as they can raise. In 2000, George W. Bush did not accept federal funds but raised over $91 million in private funds for the primary campaign (Gore did accept $15 million and raised $33 million in additional private funds).[18] Once candidates receive their parties' nominations, public funding pays them each about $62 million for the general election campaign (also adjusted each election for inflation), and they can accept several million more from their party's national committee. At this point, fund-raising is supposed to be officially over for the candidates.

Disclosure

Though the court knocked down some spending limits, it did uphold the provisions of the act that mandate disclosure of contributions. Through this part of the law, journalists and the public can see who is giving how much to whom.

Contribution Limits

The 1974 law aimed to limit individual and group contributions to campaigns. The Court did uphold these limits. But these parts of the law were negated in other ways. One way of negating these limits was through independent spending. The independent spending loophole was created by a little-noticed portion of the law reaffirming the right of unions and corporations to establish PACs using voluntary contributions. Now that there were limitations on the amount of money individuals could give to campaigns, PACs became the vehicle by which individuals could channel more money to their favorite candidates. Individuals could give a limited amount directly to candidates and then give $5,000 to each of several PACs, which in turn could give it to candidates.[19]

PACs quickly sprang up. Business and trade PACs multiplied especially quickly, from around one hundred in 1974 to over four thousand in the late 1980s and slightly fewer today. Business-related PACs comprise the largest number, around 1,500. Next are "unconnected" PACs, those set up to promote various kinds of issues, ranging from free trade to protecting the environment, and then various PACs related to trade or occupations, such as hospitals, attorneys, or accountants. Finally, about three hundred are labor-related PACs. Labor had dominated the PAC game before 1974; now, it finds itself substantially outnumbered.

Individuals and PACs avoided most rules and limitations by "independent spending." In 1985, the Supreme Court ruled that PACs could spend unlimited amounts working on behalf of issues or candidates, publicly funded or not, as long as they do not give funds directly to parties or candidates.[20] The Court assumed this spending would be meaningfully independent. However, "independent spending" often is done by organized groups with indirect links to the candidate.

By the 1990s, interest groups and political parties themselves spent as much as they wanted as long as they are not actually campaigning for a candidate. Instead, they engaged in "issues advocacy" usually advocacy that was targeted to promoting one candidate or party. In 1996, for instance, the AFL-CIO spent as much as $35 million on an advertising campaign urging support for many of President Clinton's priorities. The union targeted its television ads at congressional districts with Republican incumbents.[21] Because contributions to groups engaged in "issues advocacy" are not limited by law, large donors could provide a great deal of indirect support to candidates for office without violating laws limiting campaign contributions.

The Court's rule to judge whether an ad is a campaign ad is whether it uses terms such as "vote for" or "vote against." However, this is a meaningless criterion because only a small proportion (4 percent) of ads sponsored by the candidates themselves use these phrases.[22] So this criterion had no teeth in discriminating between campaign ads and other ads sponsored by PACs or parties.

Soft Money

Soft money provides the largest loophole in the campaign funding regulation. *Soft money* is the term for donations given to political parties, ostensibly for uses other than campaigning. Soft money was exempted from limitations of the 1974 act because it was not to be used for campaigns. Instead, it is supposed to be used for such

"Some of it is soft and some of it is hard, but the main thing is that all of it is money."

© The New Yorker Collection 2000; J. B. Handelsman from cartoonbank.com. All rights reserved.

"party-building" activities as national party conventions, voter registration drives, direct mailings, polling, issue ads, and advertisements for nonfederal party candidates. Donors who want to give more than their legal federal maximum can give soft money to national party committees. Some of those funds are channeled to state parties, which spend under even less stringent state regulations.

In reality, most soft money is spent for national television advertisements for the parties' candidates. Even though the parties claim they are running issue ads that contribute to party building, only 15 percent of the ads mention the party, while 99 percent mention a candidate.[23] As a spokesperson for the National Rifle Association commented, "It is foolish to believe there is any practical difference between issue advocacy and advocacy of a political candidate. What separates [them] is a line in the sand drawn on a windy day."[24]

In 2000, the Democrats' ads prominently featured Gore, and the Republicans' Bush. As Robert Dole, the Republicans' 1996 presidential candidate, explained about an ad that spent fifty-six seconds dealing with his life and four seconds on the issues, "It never says that I'm running for President. I hope that it's fairly obvious since I'm the only one in the picture."[25]

The soft money loophole allows people with money to spend as much as they want. By 2000, the growth of soft money signaled to everyone not in solitary confinement that the campaign finance regulations dealing with contributions to candidates and parties were simply irrelevant. George W. Bush held a fund-raiser for the Republicans where the take exceeded $21 million in large donations from individuals and corporations; a few weeks later, President Clinton and Vice President Gore held one raising over $26 million from the same sorts of

Selling Access to the White House

Following the 1996 elections, the Lincoln Bedroom in the White House became a staple of editorial writers and late-night comedians. To raise soft money for the Democratic National Committee and thus for his campaign, President Bill Clinton had invited big donors to the White House to have coffee with him and, in some cases, to stay overnight. Vice President Al Gore made phone calls from the White House soliciting funds. These and other revelations about fund-raising practices prompted new calls for campaign finance reform and for an independent investigation of Democratic fund-raising practices.

But as any student of campaign finance knows, these examples are only variants of practices that are endemic. Soft money is an ever-growing loophole that has made campaign finance laws irrelevant. And selling access appears to be routine in both hard- and soft-money fund-raising.

Republicans were the first to formally reward large soft-money donations when, in 1975, they established the Republican Eagles. In exchange for a gift of $10,000 or more, members were invited to presidential functions at

the White House. Donors of $25,000 or more could meet the Reagans and "wander through the entire second floor of the White House."[1] By 1988, the Republicans, reflecting increased costs of campaigns, had created "Team 100," with a gift of $100,000—the minimum for entrance. Eight members were made ambassadors when Bush was elected to office. A study showed that companies of Team 100 givers enjoyed "a clear pattern of favorable government treatment," including action on criminal charges and awarding of federal grants.[2] The Democrats responded with their own $100,000 group during the 1988 campaign but, of course, had no federal largesse to dispense, having lost the election.

Given the clear Republican success in fund-raising (Republicans have outspent Democrats in every modern presidential election, including 2000), and with the Democrats' failure to raise money from smaller givers in 1992 (a direct-mail campaign raised $9 million from middle- and working-class donors but cost $8 million), President Clinton believed Democrats must radically improve their fund-raising capacity to win the 1996 election. He

apparently agreed with his experts that enticements such as personal access to the White House and to him were necessary.

One journalist-expert on campaign finance arranged recent campaign finance activities into five categories. Though partly tongue-in-cheek, these categories illustrate just how confusing and probably noncommonsensical campaign finance laws are.[3]

"Tacky but Legal." Sleepovers at the White House, as long as no solicitations for contributions took place, are legal. However, the degradation of a national shrine into a national joke was an unhappy side effect of these activities.

"Offensive and Questionable." White House coffees with President Clinton meeting donors are ethically offensive and legally questionable, even if the idea is not new. They seem particularly offensive if the donors had specific policy interests for which they are lobbying the government. And they are legally questionable because campaign donations that result in "any benefit" for the giver from the recipient are illegal.

"Possibly Illegal but No Big Deal." President Clinton and Vice President

donors. For the 2000 elections, each party had raised and spent nearly $250,000,000 in soft money, nearly double what each spent in 1996 and four times the official hard-money limit.

Another unappetizing aspect of soft money is the way it is raised. The Democratic National Committee offered the incentive of dinner with President Clinton and Vice President Gore or visits to the White House. Though criticisms of Clinton's exploitation of the presidential office for fund-raising were a staple of the 2000 Republican campaign, once in office, the Republicans offered their big donors a chance to "dine with diplomats and embassy officials and discuss international affairs at one of Washington's famous embassies."[26] Later, the Republicans, capitalizing on a national tragedy, gave, in exchange for a donation, photos of George W. Bush calling Vice President Cheney on September 11, 2001.

(See the box "Selling Access to the White House.) Naturally the Democrats called it "a strategy to use the war for political gain."[27]

Secret Spending

The fig leaf that spending by PACs is independent is hypocritical, but, again, until 2000, contributions to PACs were on the public record so the press and other watchful observers could at least trace the flow of money from donors to candidates. But in 2000, new loopholes were found that returned the situation to the pre-1974 days in which money can be given secretly.

Discovering a loophole in the law, some groups (called "527 groups" after the section number in the relevant tax code) accepted contributions and spent without reporting donors and spending. For example, a group called "Republicans for Clean Air" spent $2.5 million on

Gore made phone calls from the White House soliciting donors. Conceivably, this is illegal, because there is to be no fund-raising on federal property. For example, members of Congress cannot solicit funds from their offices. (At least one drives around the Capitol in his car using his cell phone.) However, the Justice Department in the 1970s declared the president's part of the White House "private," and this may stretch to cover the vice president, too (though the vice president lives elsewhere). As the noted late-night political analyst (!) Jay Leno has joked, "Where do you expect the president to make fund-raising phone calls from—the local 7-11?"

"Seriously Troubling." There is nothing *illegal* about the president or vice president dialing for dollars. However, many people believe that it is clearly inappropriate for them to do this. Yet members of Congress routinely do this, too.

"Over the Line." One of the most troubling aspects of the Democratic fund-raising activities in 1996 was the number of donors with unsavory backgrounds who bought access. One was a convicted felon, another an arms dealer. Individuals with specific policy

interests were admitted to the White House repeatedly. One such individual, who paid $300,000 to the Democratic National Committee and was promoting a plan to build an oil pipeline in Central Asia, later told congressional investigators, "Sure I bought my way in. What of it?"[4] He then proceeded to reveal that, though he was invited to six functions at the White House, he did not get a private meeting with Clinton or support for his pipeline. But would he donate again? Yes, because other oil company executives were there, and "Now they know [I was] also there so they can't bluff me."

George W. Bush and the Republicans sharply criticized Clinton's use of the White House for fund-raising. Said Bush, "Will we use the White House . . . as a fundraising mechanism—in other words, you give money and you get to sleep in the Lincoln Bedroom? The answer is no."[5] But the Bush administration just as blatantly exploited his office for partisan fund-raising, as the president invited big donors to dine with diplomats at an embassy and meet with cabinet officials.[6]

Even if all that is being bought and sold is access, access is worth some-

thing. If access did not influence policy, most people would not be trying to buy it. Even if no favors were exchanged for money and nothing illegal transpired, most Americans probably believe that these activities are unethical and unbecoming a president. Indeed, the most troubling activities are the ones that are apparently legal. If the public believes such activities should be cleaned up, voters must elect members of Congress who agree. Otherwise, campaign finance activities will continue to provide material for cartoonists and comedians, embarrassment for public officials, and ultimately loss of public trust in both business and politics.

1. Quoted in Jane Mayer, "Inside the Money Machine," *New Yorker,* February 3, 1997, 34.
2. Ibid., 35.
3. The following paragraphs are drawn from Elizabeth Drew, "Washington's Scandal Scale," *Washington Post National Weekly Edition,* March 31, 1997, 21–22. The categories are hers.
4. Clarence Page, "The Real Scandal in Campaign Finance Probe Is What's Still Legal," *Lincoln Journal-Star,* September 27, 1997.
5. Mike Allen, "Does an Embassy Trump the Lincoln Bedroom?" *Washington Post National Weekly Edition,* May 7–13, 2001, 14.
6. Ibid.

television ads attacking John McCain right before the New York primary in 2000. Later it turned out the "Republicans" were two Texans, both large donors to the Bush campaign. In a Senate race that same year, a group called "Citizens for Better Medicare" ran ads against one candidate who was running on a platform to lower prescription drug costs. Voters did not know that "Citizens" was largely a creation of the pharmaceutical industry. Of course, PACs have always been free to give themselves names suggesting they represent broad, public interests when they may represent a quite narrow interest, but with 527 groups it is much more difficult to determine who the backers of the group really are.

Gifts from Children

In an attempt to give more than the campaign limits, sometimes individuals will give money in the names of their spouse and children, thus enabling a bigger gift than they alone would be entitled to. Gifts by children as young as nine have been accepted, although donors are supposed to be in control of funds they give.[28]

With all of these loopholes in the law, by 2002, we came full circle back to the pre-1974 conditions that led to the campaign finance reforms. As one observer indicated even earlier, "The fat cats have returned."[29]

Reforms in 2002

By the early 1990s, calls for reforms became deafening to all but the legislators who were dependent on donations to finance their campaigns and the powerful interest groups who supported them. Elected officials do not want to tie their own hands by limiting their abilities to raise funds from friendly interest groups. After all, when one party starts spending money in a close race, the impulse is for the other party to match or exceed it, a kind of campaign finance arms race. In a close contest, both

sides want to do everything possible to win, and a few extra hundreds of thousands of dollars might indeed make the difference. And most powerful interest groups with money to spend wanted to retain the ability to spend it and acquire the influence their donations bought.

Democrats tended to offer more rhetorical support for campaign finance, though Democratic incumbents were wary of giving up large contributions on which they had become dependent. President Clinton tried, but not very hard, to get a campaign finance reform bill, but Republicans, who controlled one or both houses through most of his terms, easily beat back those efforts. Republicans, with access to the most campaign donations, did not want to relinquish this electoral advantage. Other Republicans were opposed in principle to government regulation of campaign spending.

Efforts for campaign finance reform were led by a pair of Senate mavericks, John McCain, an Arizona Republican senator, and Russ Feingold, a Wisconsin Democrat. Success of their efforts came in the wake of revelations of corporate scandals.

In the 2000 presidential campaign, McCain, the Republican challenger to the front-runner George W. Bush in the 2000 presidential primaries, made campaign finance reform a major issue. His candidacy died. Al Gore supported campaign finance reform but did not make it one of his central issues. With the election of Bush, an opponent of campaign reform, change was seemingly postponed for several more years. But in 2002, when the Enron collapse made it all too obvious that Enron money had bought at least a decade of lax regulation, Congress passed, and the president signed, a new campaign finance law. The Democrats voted overwhelmingly in favor of the bill, the Republicans against, but enough Republicans crossed party lines to pass the bill.

Taking effect after the 2002 elections, the **Bipartisan Campaign Finance Reform Act** (also called the **McCain-Feingold Act** after its sponsors) bans soft-money contributions to national political parties. This is the largest prospective change in campaign finance laws. However, soft-money contributions to PACs are still legal. As of this writing, it also appears that such contributions to state and local parties will also be legal.

Because inflation since 1974 had eroded the real value of the contribution limits established then, the new law raises several of these limits: Individuals can now give $2,000 per candidate per election instead of only $1,000. Upward adjustments were also made in donations to national party committees ($25,000) and to state or local committees ($10,000). The overall aggregate donations permitted rose from $25,000 per year to $95,000 over a two-year election cycle (the odd-numbered year before each federal election and the election year itself). Limits on PAC contributions to candidates and parties were not changed.

TOO MUCH CAMPAIGN FINANCE REFORM WILL DISRUPT OUR SACRED TRADITION OF CHECKS AND BALANCES.

HOW MUCH REFORM IS THE RIGHT AMOUNT?

IT DEPENDS. HOW MUCH CAN YOU AFFORD?

Russ Feingold (D-Wisc.) and John McCain (R-Ariz.) on top of the Russell office building.

Most observers believe that the reforms will weaken political parties at the expense of political action committees. With tighter regulations on party fund-raising, PACs will be the conduit for soft-money funds. As long as PACs spend independently of parties and candidates, they are free to raise and spend as much as they like.

Even the sponsors of the act do not believe that it will dramatically decrease the amount or influence of campaign donations. After all, John McCain himself says, "Money is like water: it finds cracks in the wall."[30] The hopes of reformers is that the law will slow the growth of money in politics as the big donors and their recipients figure out ways to evade the new regulations, and perhaps give reformers more time to develop support for further regulations.

But those opposed to reform immediately began planning how to evade these new rules. It is safe to predict that loopholes will eventually erase the intended effect of the law. The Federal Election Commission, charged with overseeing the campaign finance laws, immediately adopted rules to weaken the impact of the reforms. The law forbids federal officeholders from soliciting soft-money donations, so the commissioners interpreted "solicited" very narrowly to include only a direct ask rather than a suggestion or an invitation to contribute. The commission broadened the ability of members of congress to ask for money for state parties, and it widened the definition of what state parties could use the money for. The commissioners, an equal number of Democrats and Republicans, adopted these rules despite advice from their legal counsel that the rules "have the potential for great mischief."[31] Several of the appointees were appointed precisely because they did not favor tough finance rule.

Many PACs are single-interest groups, but many are unofficially affiliated with parties or wings of parties. Already, party leaders are planning how to organize more of these sorts of PACs to serve as a channel for partisan funds. For example, the Democrats have such a PAC called DaschleDemocrats.org, a group that claims to be independent from the senator whose name it bears. Tom DeLay, the majority leader of the House, has several committees that support a full political operation, including staff, consultants, speechwriters, candidate recruiters, and other support for Republican candidates.[32]

One type of further reform might avoid the pitfalls of the attempts to limit soft money. A large part of the cost of campaigns is buying media ads. Television stations have free use of the public airwaves. In what Bob Dole called "a giant corporate welfare program," in 1996, Congress gave away even more airwave space to facilitate the transition to digital technology.[33] Political ads on television cost over $1 billion in the 2000 election, a number that increases each election.[34] Nearly 10 percent of TV profit is earned through political ads, which are stations' third largest advertising category, bigger than, for example, fast-food or movie ads.[35] A New York television sales manager, contemplating the media ads from the Hillary Clinton–Rudy Giuliani Senate race, exulted, "It's like Santa Claus came."[36]

In light of the fact that the public provides the airwaves free to broadcasters who in turn profit from campaign spending, a panel of broadcasters and reformers are asking stations to donate five minutes of free airtime each day for thirty days before the elections for political discussions among national, state, and local candidates for office. Five minutes a day sounds rather minimal, but currently the major networks broadcast each evening less than one-half minute of candidate dialogue, and local stations offer less.[37] Although twenty of the nation's 1,300 commercial television stations agreed to meet this standard in the 2000 election, the proposal was opposed by the National Association of Broadcasters, in fear of lost revenue. We can expect this proposal to continue to be on the reform agenda because it is unlikely we can stem the flow of money into campaigns without curbing the costs of the campaigns themselves.

Sources of Campaign Funds

There are three sources of campaign funds: individuals, party organizations, and corporations and unions.

Individuals

Donations from individuals are an important source of campaign funds. Large donations come from business executives, entertainers, and lawyers.

Party Organizations

Individuals' giving to PACs and candidates is limited, but they can give unlimited amounts of soft money to parties. Party organizations, in turn, can give legally to candidates' campaigns and can support advertising for candidates across the nation. In the 2000 campaigns, the Republicans raised and disbursed $466 million and the Democrats $275 million in "hard" money.[38] This is in addition to the soft-money activities of the parties that we have already described (Figure 1).

Corporations and Unions

Corporations and unions are not entitled to give directly to campaigns, according to the 1974 law. However, as with individuals, they can give unlimited amounts of soft money to political parties and can create and support PACs. Under the 1974 law, there were few limits on the ability of these organizations to contribute, and influence, campaigns. The 2002 law promises little different.

PACs

The funding activity of PACs differs greatly. Although there are nearly 4,000 PACs, about one-third do not contribute to any candidates, while about 400 give over $100,000 in total. Less than 10 percent of the PACs account for three-fourths of all PAC donations. Thus, the number of key PACs is relatively small. Table 1 lists the biggest spending PACs, most of which are occupational groups, unions, and some special interest organizations.

PACs differ in the targets of their donations, but some patterns are clear. PACs show a distinct preference for Republicans in the presidential races and for incumbents—Republicans or Democrats—in congressional races (Figure 2). PACs usually want to give to the candidate they believe will win so they will have access to a policymaker. Enron's PAC donations are illustrative of spending patterns. Substantially more Republicans were supported than Democrats, but Democrats on key committees, such as Charles Schumer, were supported.

If they guess wrong, PACs often give to the winner *after* the election, a practice called "catching the late train." After the surprise Republican victories in the 1994 congressional elections, PACs raced to help winning Republicans pay their campaign debts. As one noted, "We gave to Democrats because they were in control, and we're likely to do the same for Republicans. [T]hose who affect our company and our customers are in another party."[39]

Although the majority of PACs are business related and are ideologically much more sympathetic to the Republicans, before 1994 PACs gave predominantly to the Democrats because they were the majority party. When the Republicans gained control of both houses of Congress, they began receiving the majority of PAC donations. However, in 2000, when the Republicans controlled the House and Democrats the Senate, 53 percent of PAC donations to House candidates went to the Republicans, and 52 percent of PAC donations to Senate candidates went to the Democrats, nicely reflecting the political reality of party control.[40]

What other criteria aside from incumbency guide PAC donations?[41] Most PACs give money to members in districts where the PACs have a substantial interest, such as a large number of union members for a union PAC or a large factory for a corporate PAC. Enron focused much of its support for Democrats on Texas Democrats, where Enron's headquarters resided. And Enron's substantial support for Bush was partly due to his powerful position in Texas (as governor) before he became president.

PACs also target contributions to members of key congressional committees. For example, PACs organized by defense contractors give disproportionately to members who serve on the Armed Services Committees, which have a big role in deciding what weapons to purchase. Unions and shipping companies involved in the maritime industry give large sums to those on the House Merchant Marine and Fisheries Committee and its Senate counterpart, Commerce, Science, and Transportation.[42] Members of congressional committees that specialize in tax law (Ways and Means, and Finance) and business regulations (Commerce) receive generous contributions from business PACs.[43]

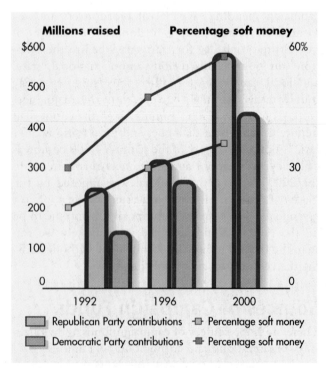

FIGURE 1 ■ Republicans Raise More Money; Democrats Rely More on Soft Money

SOURCE: FEC data on contributions to political parties, reported in Harold Stanley and Richard Niemi, *Vital Statistics in American Politics, 2001–2002* (Washington DC: CQ Press, 2001), Table 5.1.

Rank	PAC	Overall Spending
Overall Spending Leaders		
1	NRA Political Victory Fund	$16,821,436
2	EMILY's List	14,746,248
3	Democrat Republican Independent Voter Education Committee	9,000,564
4	American Federation of State, County and Municipal Employees—PEOPLE, Qualified	8,557,040
5	International Brotherhood of Electrical Workers Committee on Political Education	6,236,036
6	NEA Fund for Children and Public Education (FKA NEAPAC)	6,108,964
7	Association of Trial Lawyers of America Political Action Committee	6,082,160
8	Elect Life	4,882,154
9	New Republican Majority Fund	4,692,690
10	American Medical Association Political Action Committee	4,496,150
Leaders in Contributions to Congressional and Presidential Candidates		
1	Realtors Political Action Committee	$3,423,441
2	Association of Trial Lawyers of America Political Action Committee	2,656,000
3	American Federation of State, County and Municipal Employees—PEOPLE, Qualified	2,590,074
4	Dealers Election Action Committee of the National Automobile Dealers Association (NADA)	2,498,700
5	Democrat Republican Independent Voter Education Committee	2,494,450
6	International Brotherhood of Electrical Workers Committee on Political Education	2,455,325
7	Machinists Non-Partisan Political League	2,181,113
8	UAW-V-CAP (UAW Voluntary Community Action Program)	2,155,050
9	American Medical Association Political Action Committee	1,942,623
10	Service Employees International Union Political Campaign Committee	1,887,649

NRA—National Rifle Association; EMILY's List—promotes prochoice Democratic women candidates; NEA—National Education Association; Elect Life—promotes antiabortion policies; UAW—United Auto Workers.

SOURCE: Federal Election Commission, reported in Harold Stanley and Richard Niemi, *Vital Statistics in American Politics, 2001–2002* (Washington, D.C.: CQ Press, 2001), Table 2.15.

Women's PACs, including EMILY's List, one of the biggest-spending PACs, are unusual in focusing most of their money on nonincumbents. Their goal is to get more women elected, which often means supporting nonincumbents with strong chances of winning.

Special Interests as Victims?

PAC, corporation, and union contributions to campaigns are products of mutual need. Special interests need access to and votes of members of Congress and the president, and elected officials need (or think they need) large sums of money to win elections. Thus, donations are useful to officials and to the donors. The question is whether they are useful to the public.

Although special interests try to buy access and sometimes votes, members of Congress are not simply victims of greedy PACs and corporations. Indeed, as one observer remarked, "There may be no question that the money flowing into campaign coffers is a crime. But there is a question whether the crime is bribery of public officials or extortion of private interests."[44]

Members themselves are aggressive in soliciting for donations. They fear defeat in the next election and think that raising a lot of money can protect them. Senators, for example, must raise more than $18,000 each week during all six years of their term to fund an average-cost winning reelection campaign. A senator from a high-cost state needs to raise $60,000 a week. On the other hand, many incumbents raise millions even when they face little-known opponents. Phil Gramm (R-Tex.) continued to solicit funds from lobbyists even after he had raised more than $6 million and his opponent had only $20,000.

Until the 1960s, most fund-raising by members of Congress was done in their home districts. Members did not want their constituents to think they were influenced by Washington lobbyists. Today, the majority of PAC funds are raised in Washington.[45] Members of Congress continually hold fund-raisers to which dozens of lobbyists for PACs are invited. Well-known lobbyists get hundreds of invitations to congressional fund-raisers every year.[46] Indeed, the number of these events is so large that a private company sells a special monthly newsletter listing all of them.

Pressure on corporations and unions is unrelenting. Some members keep lists of PACs that have given to them on their desks as an implicit indication that it is those groups that will have access. Others play one PAC off against another. Tom DeLay (R-Tex.), the majority

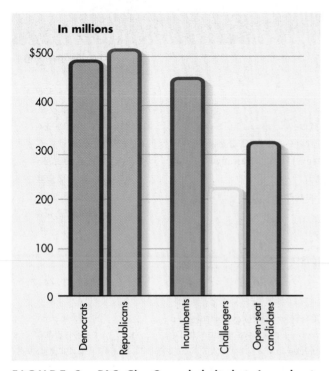

FIGURE 2 ■ PACs Give Overwhelmingly to Incumbents

SOURCE: 1999–2000 election cycle, *Statistical Abstract of the United States 2001*, Table 411. Donations include those to House and Senate candidates.

whip in the House, is called "The Hammer" as a testament to his strong-arming potential donors. He offers lobbyists and corporate interests an open quid pro quo: They give, and they get to help develop Republican strategy and interests and shape legislation that Republican leaders will support.[47]

In recent years, some corporations, including General Motors, Ameritech, and Monsanto, have said that they do not intend to give more political contributions. Companies such as this should favor campaign finance regulation, which could provide a defense to fund-raising pressure. Effective legislation would put a lid on spending and eliminate the "arms race" aspect of campaign funding in which candidates make ever bigger demands on potential donors. Regulations forcing television stations to donate time to candidates should have the same effect.[48]

Whatever the problems with the current system, we should be careful not to contrast it with an idealized version of the past. After all, over one hundred years ago Mark Twain observed, "It could probably be shown by facts and figures that there is no distinctly native American criminal class except Congress." Big interests always have had influence and access in Washington. The ways in which they exercise that influence are different now. In some ways, this influence is more open because the campaign finance reforms have made public the organizations working for special interests and the money they spend doing it. Thirty years ago we would not have known how much each member of Congress received from each lobbying group; today we do.

The Impact of Campaign Money

We have discussed several aspects of money in elections: how much there is, who contributes it, and how they do so. Now we turn to the question of what difference campaign money makes. An obvious question is whether money influences the outcomes of elections. But we also will focus on three other kinds of potential effects of money and the way it is raised: the recruitment of good candidates, the policy decisions of elected leaders, and the cynicism of the public.

Does the Campaign Finance System Deter Good Candidates?

When John Glenn, an unsuccessful Democratic candidate in 1984, was asked whether running for president had been worth it despite his defeat, Glenn replied, "My family was humiliated. I got myself whipped. I gained 16 pounds. And I'm more than $2.5 million in debt. Except for that, it was wonderful."[49] In 1998, nearing the end of his career, Glenn remarked in a similar vein: "I'd rather wrestle a gorilla than ask anyone for another 50 cents."[50]

Other presidential candidates have lamented the difficulties and humiliations of having to raise money; Jack Kemp, Richard Cheney, and Dan Quayle, all potential 1996 presidential candidates, bowed out early in 1995 indicating that the magnitude of necessary fund-raising was one reason. In 2000, George W. Bush's huge campaign war chest deterred several potential candidates from entering the race. Others, such as Elizabeth Dole, dropped out after losing early primaries partly because of the impossibility of matching Bush's funding levels. Bush had raised and spent more money before the first primary than Bob Dole did in his entire 1996 election campaign.[51]

The necessity of raising a lot of money deters congressional candidates, too. As one leading congressional scholar noted, "Raising money is, by consensus, the most unpleasant part of a campaign. Many candidates find it demeaning to ask people for money and are uncomfortable with the implications of accepting it."[52] As one senator commented, "I never imagined how much of my personal time would be spent on fund raising. . . . I do not think a candidate for the U.S. Senate should have to sit in a motel room in Goldendale, Washington, at 6 in the morning and spend three hours on the phone talking to political action committees."[53] And, once elected, many new members of Congress are surprised and chagrined to find that they

must begin raising funds for their next campaign almost before they are sworn into office.

Does Money Win Elections?

Money helps win elections. It's not the only factor, of course. Many candidates have tried to "buy" elections with their own money and failed. But money certainly aids in getting the candidate's message out.

Looking first at presidential elections, the evidence is mixed as to the impact of money on winning presidential primaries. Primaries are the crucial elections that lead to each party's nomination. Some candidates are never considered serious contenders because they do not have sufficient money to mount a large campaign. In that sense, money is crucial.

In primaries, candidates of each party run against others of their party to achieve the nomination. Most primary candidates start out with little name recognition. Moreover, candidates cannot count on party loyalty to win votes. In primaries, voters choose among candidates of their own party; that is Republican voters have to choose among Republicans rather than between a Republican and a Democrat. For both those reasons, money is crucial to increase candidate visibility.

Primary candidates who appear to be doing well generally attract money.[54] "Doing well" includes favorable media coverage that suggests the candidate is gaining popularity and momentum. Actual success in early primaries also stimulates giving. Money, in turn, allows further purchases of media ads to become known in the next primaries.

Other things being equal, spending does influence voting in primaries. Money appears to be a necessary condition for primary victory, although not sufficient by itself. One analysis suggests that every 1 percent increase in spending buys 1/3 percent more votes.[55] Money is most important in multicandidate races, as is often typical early in the primary season where candidates are seeking to distinguish themselves from other also little-known contenders.[56] Money is less important in two-candidate primary contests, often the situation late in the primary season where one candidate has emerged as a front-runner already.

By the time presidential candidates are nominated, they already have spent a great deal. The name recognition achieved during the primaries and at the national conventions carries into the general election campaign. Presidential candidates receive extensive free media coverage in news stories. The amount that they spend after the convention is less likely to be as crucial. This is just as well for the health of the two-party system, because if money determined elections, the Republicans would have won every presidential election since World War II. However, of the presidential elections lost by the Democrats during that time, probably only the election of 1968 between Richard Nixon and Hubert Humphrey was close enough that it might have turned out differently had the Democrats been able to spend more.[57] When the elections are close, as in 1968, the Republicans definitely have the advantage by having more money.[58] However, the Democrats are catching up; in the past two presidential elections, they have been aggressive in raising soft money.

In congressional races, incumbents usually start with a huge advantage. Some estimate that their advantage is about 5 percent of the vote just by being incumbents.[59] Their name is recognized by many, if not most, of their constituents. And as incumbents, they are able to raise money early to finance their campaign. In many cases, the incumbents' huge war chests deter potentially strong challengers from even entering the race.[60] Challengers know they must raise considerable money to fund media ads even to be competitive. Thus, the ability of challengers to raise and spend money is crucial to any chance of success in the election.

But incumbent fund-raising and spending are also important. Fund-raising is important early in the campaign to deter potential opponents. And campaign spending is important, especially so for relatively new members of Congress. That is because those who have served only a few terms are less well known than more senior incumbents and thus are considered vulnerable.[61] Of course, incumbents tend to spend the most when they have the toughest opponent. In general, as challengers spend more, so do incumbents.[62]

Most of the time, the person who spends the most to win a congressional seat wins. In 1998, for example, the biggest spender in a particular election won 94 percent of Senate and 95 percent of House races.[63] Most of these winners were incumbents, and the link between spending and victory is also a link between incumbency and victory. The average incumbent is able to raise significantly more money than challengers. In 1998, for example, on average House incumbents raised $733,000, their challengers less than $200,000. In the 2000 Senate races, more than one-third of the challengers spent less than $1 million, while only two of the incumbents did so. Most Senate incumbents spent at least $3 million, a figure matched by only seven challengers.[64]

Sometimes the biggest spender loses, but the relative rarity of this occurrence only highlights the general link between spending and victory. In 2000 Senate races, only five of thirty-three winners were outspent by their opponents. In probably the most publicized Senate race, in an open-seat contest in New York, Hillary Clinton won by a large margin over Congressman Rick Lazio, despite being outspent by more than $10 million in one of the most expensive races ever (in total, the candidates spent nearly $70 million). But Clinton was well known before she ran her first TV ad, so she did not have to spend money just to become visible. Three Senate incumbents were beaten by challengers who outspent them, but three other incumbents lost despite having outspent their opponents.

Does Money Buy Favorable Policies?

As we have seen, donors are not a random cross section of the public. Money usually buys access, and that access is by the wealthiest segment of the population, whose views on public issues, especially economic issues, are more conservative than the larger population.

In recent years, corporate interests have pushed hard to deregulate and to lower taxes and have used substantial gifts to help gain access to rule makers. The accounting industry, for example, in the early 1990s helped fund more than three hundred congressional races, including both Democrats and Republicans, and spent $2 million for lobbyists. This clout led to Congress passing a law erasing liability for accountants and lawyers aiding and abetting securities fraud. Though President Clinton vetoed the law, his veto was overridden.[65] The law provided a disincentive for auditors to uphold strict accounting standards and removed a tool by which stockholders could hold companies accountable. Enron money bought considerable access (See the box "Buying Energy and Influence.")

If money buys access, does it also buy votes? Both anecdotal and systematic evidence suggest that money does buy votes, although only under some conditions.

Money is not likely to buy votes on issues that are highly publicized, because legislators' constituents usually have strong views on these issues and legislators feel pressured to follow them.[66] For the same reason, money is less likely to buy roll-call votes on the floor

"It says here that you gave a lot of money to both parties and neither expected nor received anything in return. Very nice, but we'll have to put you in the crazy section."

of each house than votes in committees. The former are public and recorded; the latter are not as visible to the public. Compared to their activity on the floor, in committees, legislators with PAC support are more active in speaking and negotiating on behalf of the PAC's positions and offering amendments that reflect these positions.[67]

Money is also not likely to buy votes on moral issues, because legislators themselves often have firm views on these issues. These sorts of issues (abortion and school prayer, for example) also tend to be publicized.

But most matters that come to a vote are neither highly publicized nor moral issues. Most are relatively technical matters that constituents and legislators do not care as strongly about as do PACs. For these, members are susceptible. The deregulation of the accounting and energy industry was done when the public had no interest. "You can't buy a Congressman for $50,000. But you can buy his vote," a member admitted. "It's done on a regular basis."[68]

One survey of members found that about one-fifth admit that political contributions have affected their votes on occasion, and another one-third are not sure.[69] Analysis of voting has revealed that contributions from the AFL-CIO affected voting on the minimum wage legislation, and contributions from the trucking interests led senators to vote against deregulation of trucking. Those senators facing reelection the year in which the vote was taken were most susceptible.[70] Voting is also related to donations in such disparate areas as minimum wage legislation, gun control, and billboard regulation.[71]

One classic example concerns used-car legislation. Auto dealers spent $675,000 in the 1980 congressional elections. This investment seemed to pay off in 1982 when Congress voted against a rule requiring dealers to inform prospective buyers of any known defects in used cars. The senators who opposed the measure received twice as much money from the auto dealers' PAC as those who voted for it. In the House, those who opposed the measure received on average five times as much money as those who voted for it. Almost 85 percent of the representatives opposing the legislation had received PAC money.[72]

The relationship between PAC money and votes still existed even when the party and ideology of the members were taken into account. For conservatives, who might have voted against requiring auto dealers to list defects anyway, PAC contributions made only a marginal difference in their voting; but for liberals, PAC money substantially raised the probability that they would vote with the used-car dealers.[73] "'Of course it was money,' one House member said. . . . 'Why else would they vote for used-car dealers?'"[74]

The relationship between PAC contributions and voting should not be exaggerated, however.[75] Even on these low-visibility votes, a member's party and ideology are important. The constituency interests of members are also key factors explaining votes. For example, members with many union workers in their districts are going to vote for those interests regardless of how much or little they get in PAC contributions.[76] Members without these constituents, though, may be more swayed by PAC contributions.

Money not only can help buy votes; it can buy influence with the executive branch, too. Presidential candidates tend to have widely publicized views, and their actions as president are subject to intense scrutiny and publicity. Once in office, presidents need donors less than donors need them, thus making the leverage of a campaign donation uncertain. Contributors sometimes find, as did one contributor to the campaign of Teddy Roosevelt, "We bought the son of a bitch but he did not stay bought."[77]

However, on actions not widely visible to the public, donors can help shape policy. In 1999, for example, the Clinton administration imposed a 100 percent tariff on several specialty goods imported from Europe (a 100 percent tariff, a tax, raises the cost of the goods to the importer, and hence the customer, by 100 percent). A number of U.S. businesses dependent on these imports were forced to take big losses and go out of business or stop selling the product.

The reason for this tariff was that a major contributor to both the Democratic and Republican campaigns, American Financial Group, owned the Chiquita banana firm. The European Union had placed barriers to the import of those bananas, thus potentially causing the owners a multimillion-dollar loss. In response to the pressure of the banana company owners, the United States retaliated, despite the fact that the banana company (in Latin America) employed no U.S. workers and that many U.S. small businesses were hurt by the retaliation of the U.S. government. But the contributor was a business partner of one of the Democrats' chief fund-raisers and had given the vast majority of his $5 million contributions to the Republicans. Many recipients of this largesse were among those pressuring the administration to take action on behalf of the banana company.[78]

Analyses of large donors to, and fund-raisers for, the 1992 Bush campaign reveal that many were given special favors or benefits from the federal government. The Department of Labor reduced a proposed fine by nearly 90 percent against a large sugar farmer who gave $200,000 to the campaign.[79] The president proposed incentives for using corn-based ethanol in auto fuels, a proposal that would cost consumers three-tenths of a cent per gallon of gas purchased and yield a profit of $30 to $75 million. Archer-Daniels-Midland, a producer of such fuels, gave the Republican campaign more than $1 million.

President Clinton created a furor when, on his last day in office, he pardoned the fugitive ex-husband of a major campaign donor, Denise Rich. Rich had contributed generously to the Democratic Party and later to the Clinton presidential library.[80]

While it is impossible to prove a cause-and-effect relationship in these cases, clearly large donors who expect favorable treatment have plenty of precedents to lead them to that conclusion. Thus, the leader of a watchdog group said, "The point is, we're not just electing politicians. . . . We're also electing their patrons and their priorities."[81]

The influence of big money in presidential campaigns probably makes both parties more conservative.

Buying Energy and Influence

"No company in America did more to help George W. Bush get elected president than Enron." So reports the *Wall Street Journal*.[1] Enron's CEO Kenneth Lay was "the biggest sugar daddy in [George W.] Bush's political career."[2] During Enron's heyday, its funds helped elect friendly lawmakers, mostly Republican but also many Democrats; gain access at the highest levels; and buy loosened regulation and favorable tax policies. It made billions and benefited greatly from government deregulation of the energy industry. In the end, when Enron crashed, though, its substantial influence was not enough to get government to bail it out.

This seeming contradiction illustrates well the point that money is most influential when the public is not paying attention. Most congressional legislation does not get featured on the evening news or in local papers. It is subject mostly to "inside the beltway" battles. It is often dry, seemingly affecting only a few. On those issues, the influence of well-organized and powerful lobbies can greatly profit corporations or other groups.

But on well-publicized issues, those that CNN, the nightly news, and the local papers are featuring, it is more difficult for money to have the dominant influence. Thus, a Bush aide spoke of the Enron affair as a "tribute to American capitalism" because the government let it fail.[3] This point of view, of course, ignores what went on before and after Enron failed, including the enrichment

of a few at the expense of workers and investors and the loss of public and investor confidence in the truthfulness of corporate financial statements.

What did Enron give, and what did it get in return? While undoubtedly much more of the story will be revealed in future investigations, and the full story of such a complex corporation is unlikely to ever be known, we do know some of the story.

One estimate was that Enron gave, from 1989 to 2001, nearly $6 million to parties and candidates, three-fourths going to Republicans.[4] Enron's gifts include gifts from its executives and other employees, corporate soft-money gifts, and gifts from Enron's PAC, funded by contributions by individual Enron employees. The fund-raising for the PAC was done by high-level executives who kept track of who gave and who did not. In 1999, the CEO, Kenneth Lay, himself sent letters asking for contributions for the Bush campaign. One employee recalls a "menacing reference" to her husband's job and felt compelled to give even though she hadn't even decided whether she favored Bush.[5] In response to that one solicitation, more than one hundred employees gave nearly $114,000. In 2000, the Enron PAC again sent a memo to employees urging "voluntary" contributions ranging from $500 for a lower-level manager to $5,000 for a senior executive. As one former employee stated, "The higher you go, the more pressure there is to give."[6]

I-DID-NOT-HAVE-RELATIONS WITH *THAT* COMPANY!

ENRON

© 2001 Stahler/Cincinnati Post

Separate from corporate gifts, Lay and his wife donated more than $600,000 to the campaigns of George W. Bush, beginning when he first ran for governor and including $325,000 in 2000.[7] Lay also was a major fund-raiser for Bush, raising millions of dollars for the Bush campaigns. Their connection was close. During the Republican primaries in 2000, Bush used Enron's planes to fly staff and even his parents. Indeed, an Enron jet flew George H. Bush to his son's inauguration in January 2001, and a $100,000 donation from Lay helped fund the inaugural expenses.

But Enron also bought access to top Democrats. When Clinton beat George H. Bush in 1992, Lay began contributing to the Democrats. Enron gave nearly as much in soft money to Democrats as to Republicans in the 2000 election. The Enron PAC gave $10,000 to the New Democrat Network, led by Joseph Lieberman (D-Conn.), who now chairs the Senate Government Affairs Committee, one of those investigating Enron.[8] Overall, one

Environmental Defense Fund once
out a mass fund-raising mailing
ising new members a copy of the
*50 Simple Things You Can Do to
the Earth.* The book's number one
estion: stop junk mail. Ironically,
onmental groups, like others, fill
oxes with junk mail, which even-
y amounts to 3 percent of the vol-
in our landfills.

'ACs and political parties soliciting
bers and funds send out hundreds
illions of letters annually. For exam-
he American Association of Retired
le is reported to send 50 million a
just prospecting for new members.[1]
Most people look forward to receiv-
nail more than other daily activities
as watching television, eating, and
uing hobbies.[2] Mail solicitations for
ey by PACs and other political
ps provide an interesting diversion.
y read the letters, are convinced by
rguments, and write checks.
Getting a good response from mail
tations appears to be both an art
a science. Here are some of the
of the trade used by successful
.

he *mailing list* is one key to suc-
Letters are not sent out randomly.
ng lists of potential contributors are
d among like-minded groups, so
are likely to receive such mailings if
have already contributed to a candi-
or cause or even if you buy goods
mail-order catalogs. One estimate
t average Americans in profes-
l occupations spend eight months
eir lives simply opening and sorting
cal and business junk mail.
he *envelope* should be personal-
with real stamps, not metered
Often the words *URGENT* or *RE-
REQUIRED* stimulate a better re-

sponse. One PAC sent out a mailing
with the "FEDERAL TAX REDUCTION
INFORMATION ENCLOSED" prominently displayed on the envelope (the
letter dealt with the activities of a PAC
working to reduce taxes).

The *letter* often is written on
expensive-looking paper. The text is
written in short paragraphs at the sixth-
to eighth-grade level to capture the
reader's attention. On the other hand,
the letter is often fairly long. Four pages
are typical, but many are longer.

The *opening paragraph* is usually
an attention grabber such as "I need
your advice" or "This is the most urgent letter I have ever written."[3] On a
different note, Molly Ivins, the syndicated columnist who sent a letter on
behalf of the American Civil Liberties
Union, began, "I am writing you on
the cheerful topic of croaking."[4] She
goes on to urge recipients to "sign up
now saying you've put the ACLU in
your will, and they get the money after
you're gone. And think of the hell the
ACLU can raise with your money."

The *language* is usually emotional,
overblown, and, Molly Ivins to the contrary, very negative. One 1995 Democratic fund-raising letter called Newt
Gingrich a terrorist (the authors later
apologized). The National Rifle Association's labeling of government agents as
"jackbooted thugs" caused former
president George Bush to resign his
membership. One NCPAC letter from
Jesse Helms warned, "Your tax dollars
are being used to pay for grade school
courses that teach our children that
cannibalism, wife swapping, and the
murder of infants and the elderly are
acceptable." Campaigning against
PACs, an independent action PAC
(IAPAC) warned that "money doesn't

just talk, it leads many elected officials
around on a leash." And Ivins, reflecting on the gift to the ACLU in her will
that she hopes others will emulate,
notes that "every time the press . . .
takes on some pinhead in Congress or
the biggest employer in town and kicks
his ass from hell to breakfast, you know
I'll be there. Now that's immortality."

Mailers use a personal approach,
and their letters are sprinkled with
yous. A mailing from the National Taxpayers Union offered instructions as to
how "you can save America from
Washington." Well-heeled PACs sometimes use computers to intersperse
your name throughout the letter.

Enclosures are common. Solicitors
often promise you something for your
membership or send along a small gift,
such as a signed picture, stickers, or a
pin. "While trying to appeal to you
with flattery for your intelligence and
compassion, direct mail packages are
designed on the assumption you are a
self-indulgent idiot," commented one
observer of the direct mail scene.

A *donor card* is crucial. Cards are
enclosed to make it easy for recipients
to give. This card can be pretty emotional, too. For example, one conservative PAC offered recipients two choices
on the donor card. If they contributed
to the PAC, they could stick a stars and
stripes flag on the card. If they refused
to contribute, they should stick on the
white flag of surrender!

1. Jill Smolowe, "Read This!!!!!!!!" *Time,*
November 26, 1990, 63.
2. Larry Sabato, "Mailing for Dollars,"
Psychology Today 18, October 1984, 38–43.
This box draws heavily on the Sabato article.
3. Ibid. The remainder of the quotations are
from this article, unless otherwise noted.
4. Quotes from the Ivins letter are from a letter
dated May 2002 sent by the ACLU Office of
Planned Giving.

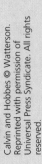

The biggest contributors to the Republicans in the last few presidential elections have been some of the most conservative people within that party. The big-money contributors to the Democrats are, on the whole, less liberal than the mainstream of the party.

Some Democratic House leaders were surprised when members said they could not vote against a capital gains tax cut (which would benefit the wealthy) be-cause it would anger their busine[...] elected by voters. I get financed l[...] don't care about this, contributor[...]

Large contributions to preside[...] lead to appointments to public of[...] sadorships. The "spoils system," a[...] with us since at least the time of [...] cannot be blamed on modern PA[...]

estimate is that Enron has provided funds for nearly half of all members of the House and three-fourth of the Senators.[9]

Enron also spent lavishly to influence public opinion. It provided handsome consulting fees (up to $50,000 a year) for high-level journalists, think tank leaders, and others to spend a couple of days a year at Enron talking about political issues and Enron.

What favors did Enron get from politicians? Enron profited from Democrats. In 1992, the Democratic-majority Congress approved an energy bill that set the stage for Enron's growth, and later Clinton took an interest in a large Enron project in India. In 1997, Lay met with Clinton, Gore, and other administration officials to discuss the U.S. position at the Kyoto Global Warming conference.[10]

But Enron profited even more consistently from its Republican ties. For example, when Bush was governor, he signed an energy deregulation bill that opened lucrative markets for Enron. He established a panel that acted in secret to grant exemptions allowing power plants to exceed legal pollution limits, and Enron got several of these exemptions.[11] When Bush arrived in D.C., he rolled back efforts to crack down on American corporations using offshore banks (banks set up in the Caribbean, for example, to help U.S. firms—and others such as drug dealers—evade American tax and criminal laws), a move of great benefit to Enron with re-portedly eight hundred off-shore accounts. As a consequence of this and other creativity, Enron avoided taxes in four of its last five years.[12]

Bush also established an energy policy task force headed by Vice President Dick Cheney. The task force, meeting in secret and whose membership and agenda have not been released, reportedly included Kenneth Lay and other lobbyists for the utility and energy industries, the past and present chair of the Republican Party, along with the secretary of energy and other administration officials. The past Republican chair, Haley Barbour, at the same time was lobbying utilities for large campaign contributions, which were given around the same time that the task force was working.[13] It is not surprising that the task force recommended a weakening of a major clean air rule opposed by the utilities and energy industries. It also endorsed increasing coal and nuclear power. The General Accounting Office is suing, on behalf of the public, to obtain information about the membership and proceedings of the task force.

Other benefit of Enron's access was that Kenneth Lay was allowed to "interview" candidates for positions on the Federal Energy Regulatory Commission, the agency that was Enron's regulator.[14] This seems to be a first for letting those to be regulated be involved so directly with the choice of the regulator.

Enron's investm[...] cials over a dozen y[...] end save the firm f[...] But as one observer[...] lowed the Enron lea[...] to town. . . . Everyo[...] get anything. . . . Bu[...] over the last five yea[...] get was no oversigh[...]

1. "Enron Lessons: Big P[...] Firms a Hearing, Doesn't [...] Street Journal, January 1[...]
2. Howard Fineman and [...] "Light's Out: Enron's Faile[...] Newsweek, January 21, 2[...]
3. Paul Krugman, "A Syst[...] York Times, January 18, 2[...]
4. Richard Stevenson and [...] Safeguards Failed as Enro[...] Times, January 20, 2002, [...]
5. Joe Stephens, "Hard M[...] and the 'Matrix,' " Washin[...] Weekly Edition, February 1[...]
6. "In Houston, the Lines [...] Business, and Society Are [...] New York Times, January 2[...]
7. Dan Morgan, "Enron's C[...] Democrats, Too," Washing[...] Weekly Edition, January 21[...]
8. Ibid.
9. Ibid.
10. These examples are fro[...]
11. "Big Political Giving Wi[...] Doesn't Assure Aid," Wall S[...] January 15, 2002, 1; Bob P[...] Friendship Is Study of Mutu[...] Journal-Star, February 4, 20[...]
12. Molly Ivins, "Enron Mes[...] Skin-Deep," Centre Daily Ti[...] Pa.), January 30, 2002. A6.
13. Michael Weisskopf and [...] "Getting the Ear of Dick Ch[...] February 11, 2002, 15.
14. Jonathan Alter, "Which [...] Next?" Newsweek, February[...]
15. Ibid.

Campaign Money and Public Cynicism

We have seen repeatedly that public confidence and trust in government have diminished greatly over time. Some of the reasons for this declining trust have nothing to do with money. But public trust was certainly affected by the Watergate scandal, and it is likely that revelations about big-money lobbying activity reinforce public cynicism and distrust.

American elections are funded, for the most part, by private money. It is therefore not surprising that candidates turn to people who have money to help with that funding. It is also not surprising that the current system alienates voters and probably reduces voting turnouts. Even if we believe that no votes are actually bought, the appearance of conflicts of interest that permeates the existing system and clearly disturbs the public should give pause to those interested in the health of our political system.

Walter Lippman, a famous American journalist, once said that American communities govern themselves "by fits and starts of unsuspecting complacency and violent suspicion." We think nothing is wrong, and then we think everything is wrong. So it is with our views of campaign money. For several years after the 1974 reforms, we thought things were going along pretty well. More recently, many have become convinced that the nation is in terrible jeopardy because of the influence of money. This fear is compounded because money has helped bring about regulatory lapses, which in turn have been partly responsible for failures to check the dishonesty of many corporations, which in its turn has led to eroding confidence in corporate America. So, instead of only leading Americans to grow cynical about government, the campaign finance system has also indirectly helped lead to the loss of confidence in business, too.

Although Congress did pass a campaign finance reform, it is not clear that the practical effect will be great. Both parties rely on the largesse of private givers, corporations, and unions, and it is unlikely that the disasters of 2002 in the corporate world will be enough to change the system. Elected officials appear to be more afraid of being without campaign donations than they are that the campaign finance system will further erode confidence in the system.

And while most of the opposition to campaign finance reform comes from Republicans, the commitment of many Democrats is also questionable. Ideologically, Democrats are more sympathetic to limiting the influence of big money, but practically, Democratic incumbents are heavily dependent on their PAC "fixes." When a Republican president was in office, Democratic members of Congress could vote their ideological inclinations for campaign finance reform, resting assured that the president would veto any serious reforms. When Clinton took office and indicated his support for reform, Democrats found innumerable ways to avoid passing a serious bill. In 2002, after Enron, most Democrats supported reform, but some party officials are working with the Federal Election Commission to

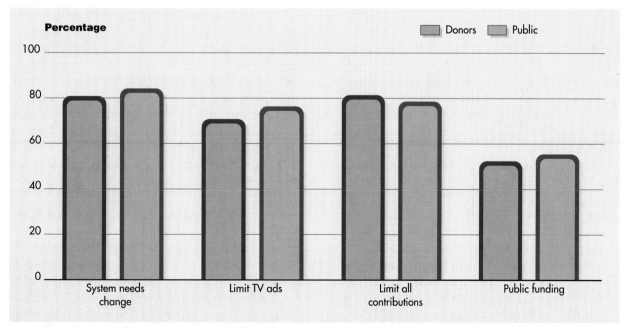

FIGURE 3 ■ The Public and Donors Agree That the Campaign Finance System Needs to Be Fixed

SOURCE: *Washington Post* national survey, reported in Ruth Marcus and Charles Babcock, "Feeding the Election Machine," *Washington Post National Weekly Edition,* February 17, 1997, 10.

water down those reforms. Thus, as we begin the twenty-first century, it is not clear that either party has much incentive to support campaign finance reform. What does seem to be true is that the public is repelled by the existing system.

As Figure 3 shows, support for change is overwhelming in the general public. The 2002 bill did not go as far in reform as most voters seem to want. However, it is unlikely that any reform is going to be able to limit the impact of private money as long as our election system relies on private support rather than public financing or limitation of spending. Campaign finance reform continues to wait for its champions who can rally sustained public interest and support around a realistic new finance system.

Conflicts of Interest

In addition to money's influence on political campaigns and policymaking, it also leads to **conflicts of interest.** This term refers to officials making decisions that directly affect their own personal livelihoods or interests. The campaign contribution system we have just described is certainly a huge conflict of interest. Presidents and members of Congress make decisions about policies affecting those who give them campaign money. But conflicts of interest are not confined to decisions involving sources of campaign money. As James Madison noted, almost every decision involves potential conflicts of interest. Decisions made by presidents, bureaucrats, and members of Congress can affect their personal financial interests (including stocks, bonds, or other investments).

Despite periodic attempts to limit conflicts of interest, violations of ethics codes still occur in Congress and in the executive branch. In 1981, six House members and one senator were convicted in an FBI undercover operation known as Abscam. Five were even videotaped accepting cash. Incidents of blatant bribery such as this are rare, but conflicts of interests are more common. They are harder to deal with, however, because the issues are less clear-cut.

It is difficult to untangle the effects of personal financial interests, constituency interests, and party loyalties. For example, people on the Agriculture Committee with agribusiness interests, as most have, often represent districts with large agricultural interests. If those members vote in favor of agricultural interests, they are voting both for their own interests and for their constituents' interests. And they are likely to think that they are advancing the national interest at the same time. It appears that the impact of these personal interests on voting is fairly small once constituency interests are taken into account.[83]

In the executive branch, decision makers operate under much less direct public and media scrutiny. Yet they, too, may be acting on matters that affect their personal economic position. Since the Carter administration, all high-level administrative officials have been required to file public financial disclosure statements to allow the public to see when they are making decisions that benefit their own financial interests. But the rules do not require officials to step aside on matters that would affect them financially.

It is also a conflict of interest to use one's government position to line up a job following a public service career. The Ethics in Government Act of 1978 tries to regulate this. The act bars former public servants from lobbying their former agencies for a year and on matters in which they "personally and substantially" participated as public officials, for life. Current employees also are prohibited from participating in decisions affecting interests with which they are negotiating about future employment. But the act is not very stringently enforced.

Because many companies that regularly deal with government think experience in government is an asset, especially experience in the agency that regulates the company's activities, many officials take well-paying jobs in the industry they came to know while in government. Critics call this the "revolving door," referring to the movement of people from government service to the private sector and, sometimes, back again.

Using a government job to line up lucrative private employment also can involve **influence peddling,** or using one's access to powerful people to make money. Former high-government officials can and do use their access to former colleagues to win jobs representing clients in business or labor. A well-publicized case of influence peddling was that of Michael Deaver, the deputy chief of staff and one of President Reagan's closest advisers during his first term. Deaver left government, immediately set up a public relations and lobbying firm, and began soliciting clients largely on the basis of his close relationship with the president.[84]

Conflicts of interest and influence peddling are bipartisan phenomena. Such accusations swirled around the Clinton White House, although no high official was convicted of illegal acts in office. But President Clinton and Hillary Clinton were accused of conflicts of interest in the long-running investigation of the "Whitewater affair," but they were never found guilty of anything from that investigation. A number of Clinton administration members, including a cabinet secretary, Mike Espy, left office under ethical clouds relating to conflicts of interest and interest peddling. Some of the allegations of improper behavior (such as Whitewater) took place before the accused persons assumed their current roles in the federal government.

George W. Bush came to Washington saying that the ethical standards of his administration would be higher than those of the Clinton White House. While it certainly is true there has been nothing like the Monica Lewinsky scandal in the Bush White House, if anything, influence peddling seems to be at a higher level than before. In some cases, corporate interests have been part of secret policymaking process within the White House in ways not seen before.

Conflicts of interest can never be completely eradicated from government, but presidents can make their expectations clear. Presidents George W. Bush, Bill Clinton, and George H. Bush have shown more concern about ethical issues than their predecessors, though conflicts of interest of administration officials have been regularly reported during all three administrations. Ironically, when such conflicts are made public instead of being ignored, public perceptions of lower ethical standards in government than elsewhere in society may be reinforced. However, the recent revelations of dishonesty and greed in the corporate world illustrate clearly that people in government are as, or perhaps more, ethical than those in business, labor, or other parts of the private sector. (See the box "Are There Democratic and Republican Kinds of Corruption?")

Conclusion: Does the Influence of Money Make Government Less Responsive?

The influence of money in American politics is a perennial source of concern to those who want to live up to the democratic ideals of political equality and popular sovereignty. Our democratic values tell us that government should represent all, the poor as well as the rich, and that everyone should have an equal chance to influence government. We know that in the real world things do not work this way. We tolerate much inequality in access because that seems to be the way the world works in the private as well as in the public sphere, because everyone is not equally interested in influencing government, and because for

Are There Democratic and Republican Kinds of Corruption?

Some observers have pointed out that while both Democrats and Republicans have ethical lapses, the kinds of ethics problems they have are quite different. Corrupt Democrats steal. They accept bribes and improper campaign donations, divert public funds to their own pockets, and, in general, engage in personal financial aggrandizement. This style of corruption is reminiscent of the "honest graft" of the big-city political machines (see the box on Boss Plunkitt and "honest graft" earlier in the chapter). While some Republicans also steal—for example, former vice president Spiro Agnew, who pleaded no contest to charges of kickbacks, bribery, and extortion, and former representative Joseph McDade (R-Pa.), who was convicted of bribery and racketeering—most of these sorts of scandals involved Democrats. Examples

include Daniel Rostenkowski (D-Ill.), former chair of the House Ways and Means Committee, convicted of corrupt acts involving mail fraud; and Robert Torricelli (D-N.J.), censured by his Senate colleagues for accepting gifts from lobbyists.

Republican ethical failings tend to be related to the use of government for improper means. President Nixon's Watergate scandal involved trying to use the powers of government to punish his personal enemies and then lying about it. He also ordered Cambodia to be bombed and tried to keep it a secret. President Reagan tried to subvert the constitutional powers of Congress by secretly selling arms to Iran and supplying weapons to rebels in Nicaragua, both expressly against the law. While Democratic presidents have also been guilty of misuse of government power

(for example, President Johnson lying about alleged attacks by the North Vietnamese on an American ship to justify getting the United States more deeply involved in the Vietnam War, and President Kennedy ordering the FBI to wiretap Reverend Martin Luther King), subverting government seems more a Republican style of corruption.

Why do these differences exist? They could be coincidental, of course. But one Democrat argued that these differences were tied to the class basis of the parties: "The lower classes steal, the upper classes defraud." A prominent Republican had a different view: "Most Republicans are contemptuous of government; few Democrats are." Whatever the reason, these examples suggest that partisanship extends to more than presidential preferences.

most people the effort of changing this pattern would be greater than the benefits gained.

Nevertheless, our reaction to the influence of money seems to be cyclical. We tolerate it; then when stories of inside deals, influence peddling, and buying access and even votes become too frequent, we act to do something about it. We then slip back into apathy until the next cycle comes along.[85]

In recent history, the low point of the use of money to buy access was probably during the Watergate scandals associated with the 1972 election. We then reacted strongly to those scandals by passing new laws and cleaning up our campaign finance system. But as the years went by, we found ways to get around the laws until they became nearly meaningless with the important exception that we know how much money is being given to candidates. Now it appears we are in another era of growing concern over ethical standards in government, and the 2002 campaign finance reforms are one indication of that.

We should not think of our times as the low point in government morality. In political campaigns, big money is certainly less influential than it was a century ago. Campaign funding disclosure legislation means that the public can at least know who is buying influence.

Some commentators believe the standards of public conduct decreased during the 1980s and have remained low. But although conflicts of interest and influence peddling in government may shock some, they reflect the ethical standards of the larger society. Making money in any way possible seems to be the hallmark of modern times, the age of "pin-striped outlaws." In the 1980s, numerous Wall Street bankers bought and sold illegal insider tips, savings and loan officers looted their institutions of millions of dollars, military contractors cheated government, and many other executives made millions in shady deals that were just this side of legality. One businessman lamented, "We are all embarrassed by events that make the *Wall Street Journal* read more like the *Police Gazette*."[86]

In the 1990s and on into the new century, many business leaders have also seemed intent on making their fast buck, regardless of the ethics or legality of their actions. Corporate leaders falsifying corporate income and plundering corporate funds for personal gain while shareholders lose their investments have been common occurrences in the new century. A prominent CEO remarked, "In my lifetime, American business has never been under such scrutiny, and to be blunt, much of it deserved. You pick up the paper, and you want to cry."[87]

We should also not exaggerate the amount of money involved in politics. Corporations spend much more to attract consumers than politicians spend to attract voters. We reported that the cost of all political campaigns in 2000 was $4 billion. This is an extremely large sum, until we compare it to the $4.7 billion a year that Americans spend on laundry detergent, or the $1 billion a month that car companies spend selling their wares.[88] It is not the amount of money in politics as much as its possible effects that concern us.

But the effects of money are hard to pin down. It is difficult to measure exactly the influence of money on political outcomes. Money sometimes influences votes and policies. Campaign contributions have some impact on voting in Congress. Money seems to have moved both parties toward more conservative policies. But at some times, especially when the public is paying attention, money appears to have little impact.

We do not know exactly how presidential candidates might be influenced by huge campaign donations or whether bureaucrats are using promises of future jobs as trade-offs for current favors. We think that good candidates are hindered or deterred from running by a shortage of money or even just by the knowledge that they need to raise big money, but it is difficult to measure exactly how many. Even though money is very tangible, its influence sometimes is quite intangible.

To the extent that money has an impact, it limits the responsiveness of government to the average citizen. It causes some policymakers to be more responsive to the big interests than to the average person. This does not mean, though, that those with the most money always win. Organization and a sense of the public interest can sometimes defeat even big money.

In designing laws to regulate the use of money in political life, perhaps the best that reformers can reasonably hope for is a system in which public officials who want to be honest will not feel under pressure to be influenced by money. Certainly, there will always be a few "bad apples," and no political system can protect us completely from them. It should be enough to design rules and structures that ensure that people of average honesty who serve in public office are rewarded for putting the public interest, rather than their private interests, first. Our current laws, especially our congressional campaign finance laws, do not always do that. The penalties we suffer are less in politicians stealing from the public till (relatively little of this occurs, certainly in comparison with the stealing that has been revealed in corporate America). They are more in the loss of public trust, an increasing alienation from government, and anger at politicians who seem to be putting their interests before the public interest. Perhaps, then, even a largely symbolic effort by our legislators to limit the influence of money on the political process is important, because it sends the signal that they are aware of and accountable to, public concerns.

Schumer Discourages Tighter Accounting Regulations

enator Schumer joined many of his colleagues on the Senate and House banking committees in urging the SEC not to impose this tighter regulation on the accounting industry. Collectively, the members of Congress who wrote to the SEC arguing against this new regulation had received more than $3,500,000 in campaign donations from the accounting industry. Eleven of the fourteen senators writing the SEC against the proposed regulation were on the Banking, Housing, and Urban Affairs Committee. And, most of the House members who wrote were on the parallel House committees that oversee the SEC.

Schumer's comments were more moderate than some, but he challenged the assumption that consulting conflicts with audit responsibilities. Later, the SEC briefed members of the committee about the conflicts in several cases it was currently investigating. Few minds were changed, and Phil Gramm, the chair of the banking committee, charged that the rule was "too draconian." The rule was never adopted, though a watered-down version requiring auditing firms to disclose their consulting relationships was put in place. Levitt left the SEC at the end of President Clinton's term. He was replaced by a Bush appointee with close ties to the accounting profession (he had been the attorney representing the auditing industry in early lobbying for decreasing the liability of accounting firms when companies were charged with securities fraud).

Perhaps we would have heard little more about the SEC's failure to approve this rule, at least not so soon, if it had not been for the failure of Enron. Enron was a $100 billion–a–year Texas-based energy trading company, number 7 on the Fortune 500 and one of America's most admired and visible companies. After an announcement that its earnings had been vastly overstated, possibly by more than $1 billion, its stock plummeted to almost nothing and it declared bankruptcy. Enron's auditor, Arthur Andersen, had overlooked Enron's inflated earnings and illicit ways of hiding debt. Before the announcement that Enron was bankrupt instead of making excellent profits, Arthur Anderson attested that Enron's internal accounting system "was adequate to provide reasonable assurance as to the reliability of financial statements" and that the financial reports of Enron "present fairly, in all material respects, the financial condition of the company."[89]

Enron executives who had advance knowledge of the announcement that earnings were inflated sold out before the announcement and made millions (Kenneth Lay, the CEO, had made $103 million in the year before the bankruptcy; seven others made more than $5 million; and the top one hundred made $300 million). Lower-level Enron employees, many of whose pension plans were invested heavily in Enron, collectively lost millions, many of them their life savings. Enron had forbidden its employees to sell their Enron stock invested in company pension plans, telling them all was well, until the stock had plummeted to 26 cents per share. Ordinary investors, also without insider knowledge of the financial shenanigans, also found their stocks worthless.

Individuals had invested in Enron because they believed it was a profitable company. They believed it was a profitable company because one of the nation's largest accounting firms, Arthur Andersen, attested it was profitable. It did so despite Enron's obvious violations of basic accounting principles and despite the fact that the directors of the corporation were asked to waive ethics rules at least twice so officers of the company could become partners in one of Enron's many phony companies and subsidiaries.

Arthur Andersen did $27 million of consulting business with Enron in addition to its $25 million auditing contract. Would Andersen have been less likely to go along with these shady practices if Schumer and his Senate colleagues had supported the rule that Arthur Levitt proposed forbidding auditing firms to do consulting business? It may be that it would have. However, much else of the regulatory system had been corrupted. Corporate boards of directors turned their head away from shady practices; some because they were too busy, others because they didn't want to sacrifice their lucrative positions on the board. Securities regulatory agencies were underfunded and overworked, as well as partially declawed by a Congress eager to deregulate. Securities analysts evaluating Enron and other companies and making recommendations to the public to buy Enron stock made money on those stock transactions.

Capitalism depends on a set of institutions, some private and some governmental. These institutions include accounting rules, independent auditors and boards of directors, securities regulation, and prohibitions against insider trading. As one economist pointed out:

> None of the checks and balances that were supposed to prevent insider abuses worked; the supposedly independent players were

compromised. *Arthur Andersen was told of these concerns, but . . . gave Enron a free pass . . . and the regulators were nowhere to be seen, partly because politicians with personal ties to Enron . . . took care to exempt Enron from regulation.*[90]

Some serious analysts argue that the Enron debacle was more damaging to America than 9/11. Why? Because our entire financial system, the stock market, and the health of American business rests on the assumption that investors have accurate information about the profitability of companies as they make their decisions to buy or sell. When they don't, when companies lie about their profits, and when both private accounting firms and government regulators look the other way, the capitalist system itself is threatened.[91] As one columnist declared luridly, "Enron is a cancer on capitalism . . . the disease may be in the nodes of the marketplace, poisoning the rest of the financial system."[92]

After the Enron shenanigans were revealed, other companies, too, revealed that their earnings were not as reported. In fact, from 1997 to 2002, nearly one thousand companies had restated their earnings, indicating their original estimates were incorrect.[93] The SEC is investigating fraud and other criminal activity at numerous well-known companies such as Xerox and others less well known such as Qwest, WorldCom, Global Crossing, Tyco, Adelphia, Waste Management, MicroStrategy, and Halliburton, all of which found their names in the headlines as examples of firms that had grossly exaggerated their profits.[94] The press has been particularly interested in Halliburton, whose CEO was Dick Cheney, now vice president; SEC charged that it falsely inflated its income statements by as much as $100 million a year, again certified as appropriate by Arthur Andersen.[95]

These and other examples created at least a short-term crisis of confidence in the integrity of the markets, as the stock market slowly declined during the months after these revelations. After all, said one analyst, "Might not Arthur Andersen have offered a few of its other clients the same tips for scamming the IRS, the SEC, and the average investor just trying to make sense of quarterly earnings reports written in corporate Sanskrit?"[96]

After Schumer learned of the extent of the Enron fiasco and its effect on its former employees, the senator, like many others who had accepted campaign donations from the now pariah firms, decided to donate his contributions from Arthur Anderson and from Enron to a fund for former Enron employees.

Under strong pressure from the media and public, in the summer of 2002, Congress did pass a new corporate accountability law (known as the Sarbanes-Oxley Act, after its sponsors) that mandates new, higher penalties for those who violate laws on corporate accounting and related practices. Though initially opposing finance reform, the president signed the law in the face of public pressure to do something about the mounting corporate scandals. The law created a new board within SEC to oversee audits of companies, set up new accounting rules, and make sure that accounting firms are not also providing consulting services.

The passage of this law led accounting firms to divest themselves of their consulting businesses. However, only a few months after the bill was passed and after public attention had moved on to the president's plan to invade Iraq, the accounting and corporate lobbies went to work to try to undermine

Former Enron employees revised the company's block E logo to reflect the company's unscrupulous practices.

Pat Sullivan/AP

the new law. Oxley himself, chair of the House Financial Services Committee, and with close ties to the accounting industry, led efforts to undermine by fighting against the appointment of a strong chair of this new committee.[97] After all, laws mean little unless they are effectively implemented.

Accounting regulation, like many other kinds of regulation, is generally of little interest to the public. But when Enron and other companies crashed, taking the life savings of thousands with them, suddenly the public became temporarily very interested. But now that the public's attention has waned, Schumer and others are free to work again on behalf of those with whom they have strong financial ties. Whether new regulations are implemented or ignored will depend on whether the public's attention can be refocused on the issue.

To learn more about the troubles of the accounting industry and efforts to reform it, go to this chapter's "You Are There" exercises on the text Web site.

Key Terms

Muckrakers

Teapot Dome scandal

political action committees (PACs)

independent spending

soft money

Bipartisan Campaign Finance Reform Act (McCain-Feingold Act)

conflicts of interest

influence peddling

Further Reading

Bruce Ackerman and Ian Ayres, *Voting with Dollars* (New Haven, Conn.: Yale University Press, 2002). The authors propose a novel way of financing political campaigns through "Patriot Dollars," anonymously given donations from the public at large.

Jeffrey Birnbaum, *The Money Men* (New York: Times Books, 2000). The real scandal in Washington isn't what's illegal; it's what's legal. This book follows the money in a very readable way.

Larry Sabato and Glenn Simpson, *Dirty Little Secrets: The Persistence of Corruption in American Politics* (New York: Times Books, 1996). A look at corruption in politics.

Bradley Smith, *Unfree Speech: The Folly of Campaign Finance Reform* (Princeton, N.J.: Princeton University Press, 2001). Smith, once nominated to the FEC, argues that restricting campaign donations is unconstitutional and ineffective besides.

Frank Sorauf, *Inside Campaign Finance: Myths and Realities* (New Haven, Conn.: Yale University Press, 1992). An overview that challenges conventional wisdom.

Electronic Resources

www.commoncause.org

The home page of Common Cause, the public interest group whose major focus is reforming the campaign finance system. Linked to the page are the group's reports tracking relevant legislation, periodic reports on campaign spending, coverage of the Enron and accounting scandals, and reports on financial ties of those voting against major regulatory legislation such as the tobacco bill.

www.pbs.org/wgbh/pages/frontline/president/

The home page for the PBS special "So You Want to Buy a President." Contains much useful data on how much is contributed and who the contributors are.

www.fec.gov/index.html

The Federal Election Commission does not have much regulatory power, but it does publish useful reports of campaign spending. This page describes election rules and links to FEC reports on campaign spending and on voter turnout.

www.politics.com

Links to news stories and polls, and allows you to see who in your neighborhood (or any other, by ZIP code) gave to which campaigns.

www.enron.com/corp

Enron's site, now featuring bankruptcy news and advice for laid-off workers.

InfoTrac College Edition

Search for the following articles in the InfoTrac database:

Faucheux, Ron. "New Campaign Law: Whose Ox?" *Campaigns & Elections* (July 2002).

O'Beirne, Kate. "Cash Bar: How Trial Lawyers Bankroll the Democratic Party," *National Review* (August 20, 2001).

Schaumberg, Ron, and Timothy Kelley. "Got Money?" *New York Times Upfront* (March 27, 2000).

Tumulty, Karen, and Michael Weisskopf. "What $6 Million Can Buy: Connection between George W. Bush and Enron," *Time* (January 28, 2002).

For more articles, enter

"campaign finance reform" in the Subject Guide;

"campaign funds" in the Subject Guide, and then go to subdivision "analysis";

"campaign funds" in the Subject Guide, and then go to subdivision "finance."

American Government Resources

Visit the Political Behavior section of the Wadsworth American Government Resources Web site (politicalscience. wadsworth.com/amgov/) for a variety of tools to help you explore money and politics further. Included are simulations, video clips, Microcase exercises, and a wealth of other activities.

CHAPTER 10

CONGRESS

The Senate convenes to decide whether to remove President Clinton from office after he was impeached by the House of Representatives.

George Tolbert/Senate Photo Office

Should the President Be Removed from Office?

You are Olympia Snowe, a first-term senator from Maine, and you are sitting in judgment of the forty-second president of the United States. It is February 1999, and the trial of William Jefferson Clinton on two articles of impeachment is under way in the Senate. In the year since Clinton was accused of misconduct in office for having an affair with a young White House intern and later of lying under oath about that relationship, Washington has been in political turmoil, the press in a feeding frenzy, and the public transfixed by the barrage of accusations flying between Congress and the White House and by one lurid media story after another.

The controversy reached its penultimate stage in December 1998, when the Republican-controlled House of Representatives voted to impeach (indict) the president on two charges of failing to execute his oath of office by obstructing justice through (1) perjuring himself in testimony about his affair with Monica Lewinsky and (2) by encouraging witnesses in a federal civil rights suit to conceal evidence or give misleading testimony. Now it is the Senate's job to sit as a jury, with the chief justice of the Supreme Court presiding, and decide whether the president should be found guilty of either or both of these charges and removed from office.

The vote in the House, where only a simple majority is needed to impeach, had been along party lines. Things are shaping up this way in the Senate, too, and the pressure is on you, a junior Republican senator, to stick with the party leadership. The president cannot be removed from office unless two-thirds of the Senate votes to convict him of at least one of the articles of impeachment. The Republicans hold fifty-five seats in the Senate, so to remove Clinton from office, which the Republican leadership wants to do, it would take the vote of every Republican senator and twelve Democrats as well.

It has been decades since such a period of fierce partisanship has gripped the Congress. After their resounding victory at the polls in 1994, the conservative wing of the Republican Party, led by House Speaker Newt Gingrich, has been in heated battle with the Clinton administration and its legislative agenda. They have authorized a series of investigations of actions taken by Clinton, some before he became president, so many investigations that some observers are calling it the criminalization of politics. The obstruction of justice Clinton is now charged with stemmed from testimony given in a civil sexual harassment suit brought against him for alleged actions taken while governor of Arkansas. Vocal opponents of the Clinton administration were involved in the lodging of the suit and in paying the defendant's legal costs. While acting independently, these political enemies of the president have found allies among conservative Republicans who control the House leadership.

It was this faction of your party that had led the impeachment fight in the House. Even though you won your Senate seat in the same election that brought the Gingrich revolution to power, you are not an ally of the conservative movement. You were the only moderate Republican elected to the Senate in 1994, and you have since been labeled a centrist—someone who prefers negotiating compromise, middle-ground solutions.

Orphaned at age nine and raised in the blue-collar household of relatives, you have spent all of your working life in public service.[1] One of only seven women ever to have served in both the House and Senate, you began your political career as a staff aide to Republican William S. Cohen, the former Maine congressman who is now serving as Clinton's secretary of defense. In 1973, after your husband was killed in a car accident, you were elected to his seat in the Maine House of Representatives, and a few years later you won a seat in the Maine Senate. In 1978, when Cohen ran for the Senate, you won his House seat, entering Congress at age thirty-one. Although a moderate like Cohen, you served as a deputy to the conservative House whip Trent Lott.

Now both you and Lott are in the Senate. Lott is majority leader, one of Clinton's most vociferous critics, and you know he will vote for conviction and removal. You are still seen as Lott's ally, but your voting records are quite different. While Lott is a hero to conservative forces, you muster only about a 40 percent rating from the American Conservative Union. You share the Republican commitment to lower taxes and smaller government but oppose the party's anti–abortion rights position, and you are a leading advocate of government funding for women and children's health issues.

You have voted with the Clinton administration more often than most of your Republican colleagues. But some of your differences with the party are over tactics; you think the Republican agenda has prevailed, and the parties should be talking to one another now, not drawing lines in the sand. You say every time your party turns an issue debate into an ideological or partisan battle, it loses the public relations war.[2] However, in matters of floor strategy when bills come to a vote, you stick with your party. On core issues like tax cuts, too, you vote with the party even when you have preferred smaller cuts or a compromise between Republican and Democratic bills.

But now you are not facing a legislative decision, something that can be undone or modified down the line if later seen as mistaken. The vote in the impeachment trial will lead to the president's exoneration or removal from office. It cannot be undone, and its impact on the office of the president will reverberate through history.

The public seems to have made up its mind; Clinton's approval ratings have never been higher. And those of Congress have seldom been lower. However irresponsibly they may believe the president to have acted in having an affair with a White House intern and lying to conceal it, the great majority of the public clearly does not believe his actions are equivalent to the high crimes or treason necessary to impeach a president. Furthermore, it seems clear it will be impossible to get enough Democratic votes to win conviction. In some sense, despite the great tension and high drama surrounding the proceedings, the trial could be regarded as over before it begins because the votes to convict just do not appear to be there. This means you could do what your party wants you to do, and what your ally Trent Lott wants you to do, without causing a president to be removed from office. Who outside your own state will ever remember, or care, how you voted? You could walk the party line, and down the road it might add to your clout within the Republican caucus.

But there is more to think about than what the national party leadership wants you to do. You will be standing for reelection in 2000, and you should give some thought to how your vote in

Senators Barbara Mikulski (D-Md., foreground) and Olympia Snowe lead Chief Justice Rehnquist to Senate chambers for trial of President Clinton.

this trial will play at home. You won your first term with 60 percent of the vote, but could your decision in this trial turn the 2000 race into a close election? Senate seats are not nearly as safe as House seats. But is it likely that Maine voters would punish you for going against the Republican leadership when they tend to be moderates like yourself and to like "against-the-grain politicians."[3] Maine has two Republican senators and an Independent governor, but Clinton carried the state in 1996. Maybe it is more likely that voters would punish you for voting *with* the party leadership. After all, when the House impeached Clinton, his approval ratings jumped to 73 percent while those of the Republican Party fell to 31 percent.[4]

Last but certainly not least, there is what you think is right. You believe Clinton's behavior was wrong and that it should not go unpunished. But you are afraid the Republican leadership may be handling the whole impeachment process in a way that makes it appear more like an ideological battle than a legal process. It would set a terrible precedent to have impeachment seen as just one more political weapon. Yet if Clinton was wrong—and you think he *was* wrong—can you vote "not guilty" on the articles of impeachment if removal from office is the only option for sanctioning him?

How do you vote?

Scott J. Ferrell/Congressional Quarterly

The Founders clearly intended Congress to be the dominant branch of government. They laid out its role and powers in Article I, and their discussion takes up almost half the document. Through its formal powers, Madison believed, Congress would dominate the presidency because it alone had "access to the pockets of the people." But Congress has not always been first in the hearts of the people, nor has it always been the most respected or trusted branch of government. Americans continue to love the Congress described in Article I—the Congress the Founders created—but they are not so thrilled about the actual behavior of its current members. On the other hand, most people like their own representatives and senators, at least well enough to return them to office at impressively high rates.

In this chapter, we look at current members of Congress, their backgrounds, and what they do that makes them so popular back home that they usually get reelected. Then we look at Congress itself, how it is organized, how it carries out its constitutional responsibilities, and why, as an institution, it is so often a focus of public criticism. To understand Congress, one must also understand the process by which members are elected, a topic covered in Chapter 8.

Members and Constituencies

Alexis de Tocqueville was not impressed with the status of members of Congress, noting that they were "almost all obscure individuals, village lawyers, men in trades, or even persons belonging to the lower class." His view was shared by another European visitor, Charles Dickens, who was shocked in 1842 to find Congress full of tobacco spitters who committed "cowardly attacks upon opponents" and seemed to be guilty of "aiding and abetting every bad inclination in the popular mind."[5] However one views their behavior, members of Congress were not then, and are not now, a cross section of the American public. But the Congress of today is slowly beginning to look more like the people it represents, and it is more responsive to the public at large than the Congresses of the eighteenth and nineteenth centuries ever were or thought they should be.

Members

The Constitution places few formal restrictions on membership in Congress. One must be twenty-five years old to serve in the House and thirty in the Senate. One has to be a citizen for seven years to be elected to the House and nine to the Senate. Members must reside in the states from which they were elected, but House members need not reside in their own districts. As a practical matter, however, it is highly unlikely that voters will elect a person to represent their district who is not from the district or who does not maintain a residence there.

Tenure

Every member of the House stands for election every two years, while each senator serves a six-year term, with one-third of the membership standing for election every two years. Although the Articles of Confederation set a limit on the number of terms a representative could serve, the Constitution places no cap on how many times an individual can be reelected. In the late eighteenth and early nineteenth centuries, leaving one's home to serve in Congress was considered by most a great sacrifice. Perhaps the Founders thought that no one would want to serve more than a few terms. In fact, during Congress's first forty years, 41 percent of House members, on average, dropped out every two years.

The first members of Congress made $6 a day, which paid for boardinghouse accommodations, firewood, candles, and their meals, and a mileage allowance for travel to and from the capital.[6] Washington was a muddy swamp, with debris-filled streets, farm animals running loose, and transportation so poor almost no one got home during a session.

But in the twentieth century, as Washington became a power center and a much more livable city, and later as seats went uncontested in the one-party South, more legislators became career politicians, spending thirty and even forty years in Congress. These long-serving members began to dominate committee work and to control the legislative agenda. Although they by no means comprised a majority of Congress, they were probably in the minds of many Americans who began to see government as increasingly unresponsive to the public.

During the height of public anger with government in the 1990s, there was a nationwide move to limit the number of terms both state and national legislators could serve. By 1995, over 70 percent of the public said they favored term limits.[7] Though Congress narrowly defeated term-limit legislation, in twenty-three of twenty-four states that allow ballot initiatives, voters adopted term limits for their members of Congress and state legislators.

But in 1995, in a 5–4 vote, the Supreme Court held term limits for members of Congress unconstitutional. The majority argued that permitting individual states to have diverse qualifications for Congress would "result in a patchwork of state qualifications, undermining the uniformity and national character that the framers envisioned and sought to ensure."[8] By adding to the qualifications spelled out in the Constitution (age and citizenship), the states were in effect "amending" the Constitution. The Constitution can be amended only through the processes of adoption and ratification specified in the Constitution, not by state or congressional laws.

Some supporters of term limits cling to the mid-nineteenth-century image of "citizen lawmakers," who set aside their personal business for a few years to attend to the public's business and then return home. Most supporters believe that by not having to worry constantly about getting reelected, legislators would be free to consider the "public interest," not "special interests," and would have no desire to build personal empires. Others also see term limits as a way to weaken the power of government by having a more rapid turnover in the membership of Congress and state legislatures.

By the late 1990s, the enthusiasm for term limits had waned, and measures to weaken or repeal term limits were pending in ten states. Opponents of the limits said they had "drained statehouses of veteran leadership and institutional memory."[9] Some thought term limits gave lobbyists and special interests more power, because they knew more about the functioning of state governments than some novice legislators did. In 2001, Idaho became the first state to repeal term limits.

Social Characteristics

For the first century of the republic, the possibility of having citizen-legislators who were a cross section of the general public was just a romantic notion. Only certain landed, business, or professional white men could even think about running for Congress. It was not until 1920 (with ratification of the Nineteenth Amendment giving women the right to vote) that a majority of Americans could vote or realistically stand for office. Today, though adults of all social classes can meet the minimum requirements needed to stand for office, the nomination and selection process limits the range of people who choose to run. Members tend to rank well above average in education; nearly all have college degrees, and a majority have graduate or professional degrees. (In addition to the 160 law degrees in the House, there are 20 Ph.D.s and 16 M.D.s.) Although blue-collar workers constitute nearly one-third of the working population, there are only six members of the 108th Congress who list their occupation as blue-collar.

The single most common occupation of congressional members has been the law. Over the past decade, almost 40 percent of the members of the House and over 50 percent of the Senate were lawyers. But this pattern is beginning to change as legislative careers have become more demanding. Today it is difficult for lawyers to maintain their practices and also serve as legislators. Ethics laws requiring financial disclosure and information about client relations have also discouraged practicing attorneys from running. While the Senate is still dominated by lawyers, their numbers in the House are falling, and the numbers of people in agriculture, real estate, and education are increasing. In the 107th Congress, for the first time in the modern era, businessmen and bankers outnumbered lawyers.[10]

Members are also quite well-off financially. A number are multimillionaires, and it is increasingly common for congressional candidates to use their personal finances to fund their campaigns. Senators Corzine (D-N.J.) and Fitzgerald (R-Ill.) are just two who have loaned their campaign treasuries millions of dollars in their election bids.

Members of Congress always have been predominantly of white European descent and male. It is somewhat less so today, as Table 1 shows. Nonetheless, white, non–Hispanic males, who make up about 37 percent of the total population, comprised about 72 percent of the House and 83 percent of the Senate in 2003.

Another dent in the citizen-legislator ideal has been the presence of "dynasty" families (for example, the Adamses, Harrisons, Lodges, and Kennedys). By one estimate, over the years sixteen dynasty families have produced thirty senators and fifty-six House members. In the 106th Congress, fifteen members of Congress held seats that had previously been filled by members of their families;[11] in the 107th, seventy-seven members were relatives of elected officials at some level of government; and in the 108th, there are three pairs of siblings.[12]

But it does not appear that Congress is going to be dominated by career politicians anytime soon. One

TABLE 1	Members of 108th Congress Are Not Representative of the Public (2003–2005)		
	Population (%)	House* (%)	Senate* (%)
Lawyer	0.3	37	60
Blue-collar	30	1.3	0
Race and ethnicity			
Black	12.5	8.5	0
Hispanic	13	5.3	0
Asian	4	.7	2
American Indian	0.7	0.5	1
Women	51	13.5	14
Catholic	27[†]	28.5	25
Jewish	2[†]	6	11
Muslim	1–2[†]	0	10
Median age	35	54	60

*Does not include nonvoting members from Puerto Rico, Guam, Samoa, the Virgin Islands, or the District of Columbia.
[†]Estimates. Census does not collect data on religion.
SOURCES: *Congressional Quarterly Weekly Report,* January 25, 2003, 192–193; *Statistical Abstract of the United States 2001.*

hundred fifty-four members in the 107th Congress listed public service or politics as their only occupation, but for a growing percentage of the membership, the race for a House or Senate seat was a first campaign. Despite the public tendency to think of Washington as full of professional politicians, most U.S. Representatives are relative greenhorns. Seventy-three percent of all House members, and only 64 percent of all senators serving in 2001–2002, had held prior elective office at the state or local level. Almost two-thirds of all House members were elected in 1992 or later.[13]

Remuneration

Members of Congress receive an annual salary, plus money for office and staff. The Twenty-seventh Amendment prohibits pay raises passed by Congress from going into effect until a new Congress convenes, but in 1999, Congress passed a bill indexing their salaries to inflation. This qualifies them for automatic annual cost-of-living pay increases and spares them the negative publicity of voting on pay increases every few years, although they can vote to refuse the increase. In the first four years of indexing, salaries jumped from $136,700 to $155,000, an increase of close to $5,000 per year. Leadership salaries are just slightly higher, except for the Speaker of the House, who earns $192,000.

Many of the members' constituents probably wish that their salaries had kept pace with inflation, too. But seen in the context of professional salaries in the private sector, the cost of living in Washington, D.C., and the need for almost all members to maintain a residence in their home districts as well as in the capital, the salaries are not high. However, members do have generous benefits. In exchange for modest monthly premiums, they receive first-class health care or, if they choose, free care at one of two military hospitals. Taxpayers spend about $2 million a year to keep a doctor and staff on site at the Capitol.

All members of Congress are required to pay Social Security taxes, but they are also participants in a generous federal pension program that is adjusted each year for inflation. The longest-serving members—those retiring with several decades of service—receive about 75 percent of their salaries. This amounted to slightly less than $100,000 per year for those retiring in 2000.[14] But for the average member, who serves many fewer years, pensions range from $47,000 to $51,000 a year.

Party Identification

The party composition of Congress corresponds rather well with the party identification of the public. During most years since World War II, Democrats have held majorities in both houses of Congress, just as a greater percentage of the public have identified as Democrats than as Republicans (see endpapers).

Members are more likely to share the issue position of constituents when the issue is important to constituents and when their opinions are strongly held.[15] However, evidence indicates that members are more responsive to the opinions of independent voters than to those from their own parties.[16] This is probably because members believe they can count on the support of their partisans but need to appeal to voters not strongly committed to either party.

In general, however, if districts are filled with farmers, the members must represent farmers, whether or not they know anything about farming. Representatives of districts with large universities must be sensitive to the reactions of students and professors even if they personally think academics have pointed heads.

Constituencies

The district a member of Congress represents is called a **constituency.** The term is used to refer to both the area within the electoral boundaries and its residents. There are two senators from each state. Each senator's constituency is the entire state and all its residents. Because every House district must have (in accordance with the one-person, one-vote rule) roughly the same number of residents, the number of districts in each state depends on total population. But six states have populations so small they are allotted a single seat in the House of Representatives; therefore, the states themselves constitute the House as well as the Senate district. In all other states, the geographic size of a constituency is determined by distribution of the population. In states with large urban populations, several districts may exist within a single city. The logistics of campaigning are thus very different for a representative from Manhattan, whose district can be measured in a few square miles, and one from Wyoming, who must cover the entire state.

Initially, the House of Representatives had fifty-nine members, but as the nation grew and more states joined the Union, the size of the House increased too. Since 1910, it has had 435 members except in the 1950s, when seats were temporarily added for Alaska and Hawaii. Every ten years, in a process called **reapportionment,** the 435 seats are distributed among the states based on population changes. Since the first Congress, the number of constituents each House member represents has grown from 30,000 to roughly 650,000.

Within a constant 435-seat House, states with fast-growing populations gain seats, while those with slow-growing or declining populations lose seats. Since World War II, population movement in the United States has been toward the South, West, and Southwest and away from the Midwest and Northeast. This has been reflected in the allocation of House seats. From 1950 through 2000, California gained twenty-three seats and

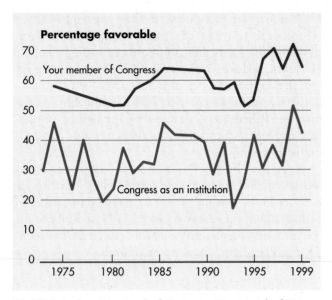

Percentage favorable

F I G U R E   1 ■ Approval of Congress/Approval of Own Representative

Sources: Roger H. Davidson and Walter J. Olesak, *Congress and Its Members,* 7th ed. (Washington D.C.: CQ Press, 2000), 414; Gallup Poll, June 2002 (www.gallup.com).

New York lost fourteen, for example. Illinois, Wisconsin, Pennsylvania, and Ohio also continued to lose House seats after the 2000 census, while Arizona, California, Colorado, Florida, Georgia, Nevada, and Texas continued to gain.

States that gain or lose seats and states whose population shifts within the state must redraw their district boundaries, a process called **redistricting.** This is always a hot political issue. The precise boundaries of a district can influence the election prospects of candidates and parties. In fact, districts often are formed with weird shapes to benefit the party in control of the state legislature. The term *gerrymander* is used to describe a district where boundaries are set to maximize the political advantage of a party or a racial group (see also Chapter 8). Majority parties in state legislatures continue to secure political advantage by drawing districts of bizarre shapes, while still complying with the Supreme Court ruling that all congressional districts be approximately equal in population.

Before 1960, states were often reluctant to redistrict their state legislative and congressional boundaries to conform to population changes within the state for fear it would endanger incumbents and threaten rural areas whose populations were declining. After decades without reapportioning, some legislative districts in urban areas had as much as nineteen times the population of rural districts.

When state legislatures, frequently dominated by rural representatives, still refused to reapportion themselves, the Supreme Court in *Baker v. Carr* (1962) issued the first in a series of rulings forcing states to reapportion their legislative districts.[17] In 1964, the Court required congressional districts to be approximately equal in population, thus mandating the principle of "one person, one vote."[18] As a result, most states had to redraw district lines, some more than once, during the 1960s. These decisions fueled heated controversy, including a proposed constitutional amendment to overturn them. But after a while the principle of one person, one vote came to be widely accepted.

Because of the important role state legislatures play in the redistricting process, the 2000 state legislative elections were crucial for both parties. In the early 1980s, Democratic-controlled state legislatures were able to help Democratic candidates in states such as California by drawing lines that concentrated Republican strength in a few areas and created districts with small Democratic majorities.[19] After the 1990 state legislative elections, which gave Republicans more clout, many states drew boundaries favoring Republicans, a factor in the Republicans' victories in 1994.

The 2000 election left sixteen state legislatures under Democratic control, eighteen in Republican hands, and fifteen states with divided control. The split was so close in Illinois that the decision on whether the Republican- or the Democratic-drawn redistricting map would go into effect was decided by drawing a name of out of a hat to determine whether a Democrat or a Republican would be added to the committee to break the deadlock. A Democrat won and his party's map was approved.

The redistricting process has been very important to underrepresented minorities. As we saw in Chapter 8, before the 1992 election, redistricting produced eleven new districts with black majorities and six with Hispanic majorities; all but one were won by blacks and Hispanics. However, the Supreme Court has since ruled that while race may be taken into consideration, it cannot be the primary basis for creating districts.[20]

Racial redistricting also can affect the partisan composition of Congress because more minorities are Democrats than Republicans. In some southern states, black voters were redistricted from solid Democratic districts to create new majority black districts. This left their old districts with Republican majorities and helped Republicans got their first victories in eighteen congressional districts in the 1994 elections.[21]

Another significant factor for increasing minority representation in Congress is getting an accurate count in the decennial census. The Census Bureau estimated an undercount of 3.3 million in the 2000 census, and most of those not counted are believed to be urban or inner-city minorities.[22] Census response rates fell from 78 percent in 1970, the first year the forms were sent by mail, to 65 percent in 1990. There was a small bump up to 67 percent in 2000, in spite of the fact that some members of Congress encouraged citizens who felt it an invasion of their privacy *not* to respond to the long census form. Because Congress has refused to authorize the use of sampling to estimate the size and racial breakdown of the uncounted portion of the population, it is possible that states with the most minorities might not gain as many seats in the reapportionment as population trends suggest they should.

The Representative on the Job

Because reelection is an important objective for almost all members of Congress and *the* most important objective for many, much of the work members do throughout their terms is targeted at getting reelected. As shown in Chapter 8, most incumbents are successful, though Senate seats are not as secure as those in the House. Going into the 2002 midterm election, for example, 343 of the 435 House seats were considered safe.[23] Nevertheless, few members take anything for granted, and they use the many advantages of incumbency to keep them in office.

In this section, we describe how members go about their day-to-day business and how this work and some of the perks of office give incumbents an edge over challenges in their bids for reelection. (For an example of a representative's workday, see the "A Day in the Life" box.)

The Advantages of Incumbency

Before they even take the oath of office, newly elected representatives are given an introduction to the advantages of incumbency. At meetings arranged by the Democratic and Republican leadership and by the House Administrative Committee, new members learn about free mailing privileges, computers and software to help them target letters to specialized groups of constituents, facilities to make videotapes and audiotapes to send to hometown media, and other "perks" designed to keep members in touch with their constituencies and not coincidentally to help win reelection.

Incumbents win because they are better known than nonincumbents and voters evaluate them more positively. Almost all voters can recognize the name of their representatives and senators; they have seen them on television or received mail from them, and they can give a general rating of their performances.[24] Although most voters can correctly identify their representatives and senators as liberal or conservative, only a small minority know how they voted on any issue.[25] Therefore, incumbents have the advantage of name recognition without the disadvantage of having voters know how they actually cast their votes on most pieces of legislation.

Incumbents' high level of public recognition is not so surprising given that members of Congress spend most of their time and energy looking for and using opportunities to make themselves known to their constituents. Members visit their home districts or states an average of thirty-five times a year—at taxpayers' expense.[26] To accommodate these trips, the House usually operates on a three-day week, Tuesday through Thursday, allowing legislators four-day weekends in their districts. The Senate operates on a five-day week but takes off every fourth week to make longer home district visits possible.

Franking Privilege

The **franking privilege** is a great asset of incumbency because it allows members to write their constituents without using postage. Its main advantage is helping each member increase name recognition (and newly elected members can begin using the frank immediately, even before their swearing in). The frank cannot be used to send personal correspondence to constituents or to ask them for their vote or a campaign contribution, and the House has a committee that is supposed to screen all mailings. But members can send out newsletters that inform constituents of their work for the district or to survey constituents' issue positions. Much of the time, however, the frank is used to send constituents material they have requested, such as government forms or publications.

The frank is literally a facsimile of the member's signature, and it works like metered mail, with the frank appearing where the stamp would be. It is not free; the Post Office records all franked mail and sends Congress a bill at the end of each year. That means the cost of the frank goes up with each postal increase. During the 1970s and 1980s, costs soared and Congress often spent more than it appropriated for mailings, sometimes for political advantage. This led to restrictions on its use, and over the next decade, spending on mailings fell over $80 million. But even with the ban on mass mailings just before elections, use of the frank still increases by as much as 50 percent in election years and sometimes much more. In a tight House race in 2002, George Gekas (R–Pa.) increased his franked mail by 2,524 percent over his average in the previous four years.[27]

Through the 1990s, Congress apportioned the franking budget among its members according to size of their constituency, and it required public disclosure of how these allotments were spent. Evidence that public disclosure accounts for a good part of the decline in use of the franking privilege was found when spending

There is no such thing as a "typical" day for a member of Congress. But this is one of those ordinary workdays for Representative Timothy V. Johnson, who represents Illinois's Fifteenth District. His newly redistricted constituency will be 350 miles long and will include twenty-two counties. Much of the district is occupied by thousand-plus acre farms, but it also includes the University of Illinois and Illinois State University.

Johnson shares a Washington apartment with staff and flies home at the weekend. Those days are spent traveling the district, making rounds of coffee shops and visiting schools, and, in the summer months, visiting fairs and local celebrations. He also works with his press secretary to prepare a weekly radio spot to update constituents and makes many calls to local TV and radio stations.

Face time with constituents: Representative Timothy Johnson talks to customers of the Edgar, Illinois, County Farm Credit Services agency at an annual gathering in a nearby state park.

Photo by Matt Bisbee. Used with permission.

6:00 A.M.–8:00 A.M. Johnson begins every day with a workout, either on the stationary bike or swimming at the House gym. While he bikes, he reads *Roll Call* and the major daily newspapers.

8:00 Johnson walks a few short blocks to speak at a breakfast fundraiser for Speaker of the House Dennis Hastert. Johnson is not fund-raising himself, but it is an occasion to make contacts with representatives of business and labor interest groups as well as to pay tribute to a powerful member of his state delegation.

9:30 Johnson returns to the House office building for a meeting of the Agriculture Committee. Today it is re-

---

more than quadrupled during a brief period of suspension of the disclosure requirement, and it immediately declined when disclosure was reinstated. However, heading into the 2000 election with a large budget surplus and control of Congress at stake, the House removed the spending cap and allowed members to use whatever portion of their office budgets they chose on the frank.[28] One political consultant estimates that the frank is worth at least $350,000 in campaign funds.[29]

The franking privilege becomes even more useful when combined with sophisticated software that allows members to target very specific constituency groups with "personalized" letters. Members can maintain incredibly specialized lists, not just of Republicans and Democrats but of those living near federal prisons, small-business owners, veterans, teachers, and government employees, for example. No group is too specialized or ostensibly apolitical to be targeted. Senator Charles Grassley (R–Iowa) even sent a letter to a thousand Iowans who had had intestinal surgery in honor of Ostomy Awareness Month.[30]

Media Advantage

In addition to "old-fashioned" mail, members use increasingly sophisticated production equipment and technology to make television and radio shows to send home. For example, one evening, on any of three local television news shows, residents of Boise, Idaho, might have seen their Republican congressional representative, Larry Craig, state in an interview that he was strongly opposed to a pay increase for Congress and would not take it if it were passed. The viewers were not told that the "interviewer" was one of Craig's congressional staffers and that the camera crew was that of the Republican Congressional Campaign Committee, which also paid for the taping.[31]

Members also like to tape themselves at committee meetings asking questions or being referred to as "Mr. (or Madam) Chairman" (because many members are chairs of at least a subcommittee). The tape then is edited to a thirty-second sound bite to be sent to local television stations. Often stations run these productions as news and do not tell their viewers that they are essen-

viewing provisions in the Homeland Security Act of 2002 that recommend transferring Agriculture Department agencies into the proposed new cabinet department. Before this meeting ends, Johnson departs for another, leaving behind a staff member who specializes in agricultural affairs.

11:00 A.M.–12:30 P.M. Johnson walks over to Rayburn House Office Building for a meeting of the Transportation and Infrastructure Committee, which is looking at how provisions of the Homeland Security Bill will affect the agencies under its jurisdiction. A noon appointment makes it impossible to take his usual midday exercise break; he leaves the meeting in session while a staff member specializing in transportation stays behind to take notes.

12:00–1:00 Johnson arrives at the Cannon Building for the annual meeting of the Alliance for Disability Sport and Recreations, which is holding a lunch honoring Olympic medallist Jean Driscoll. Driscoll works in physical rehabilitation at the University of Illinois. This is a chance to honor a constituent

and to promote the University's work in wheelchair athletics.

1:00–2:00 By one o'clock, Johnson is back in the Capitol, heading toward the Family Room where he will attend, as he does every week, a private prayer and Bible study meeting with a dozen or more other House members.

2:00–2:15 Johnson heads back to his office in the House Office Building for a meeting with a board member of the National Institute for Deafness and Other Hearing Disorders. Johnson is interested in funding possibilities for research going on his district.

With a little time to spare between this and his next meeting, he walks the hallways with his cell phone making calls to constituents, using the computer printout of names and phone numbers that he carries with him everywhere. On the average weekday day, he spends four hours making upward of two hundred calls to constituents. To help with casework, the congressman has a staff of sixteen, but Johnson's calls are not about specific problems, just a way of "checking in," he says.

3:00–4:00 Johnson goes to the House floor for a members-only briefing on the war on terrorism by high-level officials from the State Department and Pentagon. A briefing of the full House in chambers is an unusual event, and this one is very high-security.

Because so much of members' time is taken up in committee meetings, the House does much of its business in these late afternoon and early evening hours Tuesday through Thursday. Except for a 2.5-hour break to accommodate the briefing, the House has been in session most of the day. Eighteen public bills and four resolutions were introduced. There were two yea and nay votes, both on technical issues concerning executive branch agencies. The House recessed just after 8 P.M.

This is a short day for the congressman.

SOURCE: This summary is based on the *Congressional Record* for July 11, 2002, and interviews with Congressman Johnson and his press secretary, Matt Bisbee, who provided copies of the congressman's daily schedules.

tially campaign features prepared by the members. But television is not alone in portraying members' self-publicity as "hard news." Congressional staffers write press releases about accomplishments of the member and fax them to local newspapers, which often print them as written. Local media, whether print or television, are often short of news with local content and eagerly take whatever members give them.

Fund-Raising

Media access enhances another advantage of incumbency—the opportunity to raise funds from the hundreds of PACs that populate Washington. Eager to gain access to members of Congress, PACs make fund-raising much easier for incumbents than challengers, as we pointed out in Chapter 9.

Working for Constituents

Arguably the main advantage of incumbency is the opportunity that being in office gives representatives to perform services and do favors for their constituents.

This is one of the best ways members of Congress have to make themselves known in their districts and to create a kind of patron–client relationship. You will not read about this in the Constitution where the duties of Congress are defined. But in practice, electoral politics have meant that members must spend a great deal of their time serving the specific interests of their districts, which are not necessarily synonymous with the interests of the nation as a whole. However, all members take this aspect of their representational responsibilities very seriously.

This work of answering questions and doing personal favors for constituents who write or call for help is called **constituency service** or **casework.** Members and their staffs function as red-tape cutters for everyone from elderly citizens having difficulties with Social Security to small-town mayors trying to get federal grants for new sewer systems. They provide information to students working on term papers and citizens puzzled about which federal agency to ask for assistance. Typically, responsibility for mediating with federal agencies is divided among the staffers doing casework, allowing them to specialize and resolve constituents' problems—passports, immigration, Social Security payments, and the like—more efficiently. Members send calendars, U.S. flags that have flown over the Capitol, and brochures and publications of the federal government.

Requests for service often come by post or e-mail. House members receive an average of two hundred letters per day from their constituents and senators well over five hundred. Some offices get five to ten thousand requests per year for assistance.[32] Congress also receives thousands of e-mails each day, but since it is not always apparent from an e-mail address that it has been sent by a constituent, members are more likely to respond to posted mail that comes with a ZIP code attached.[33] More than half of all congressional staffers in Washington work on the flood of mail that pours in. In addition, every senator and representative has one or more offices in their state or home district to deal personally with constituents and their casework. More than 30 percent of senators' staffs and 44 percent of all representatives' staffs are located in the home state or district.[34]

Citizens turn to their congressional representatives because they see them as allies in their struggles with bureaucracy.[35] Members of Congress, who are in large part responsible for the establishment of the huge Washington bureaucracy, are able to score with voters by helping them cope with the bureaucracy they have created.[36] Individual members may have limited power in trying to get important legislation passed, but in dealing with a constituent's problems, their power is much greater because of their clout with bureaucrats. A phone call or letter to a federal agency will bring attention to the constituent's problem.

Of course, not all casework is directed toward winning reelection. Some members say they enjoy their casework more than their policy roles, perhaps because the results of casework are often more immediate and tangible. Casework does allow members to build nonpartisan and seemingly nonpolitical ties with their constituents, an advantage in this antipolitical era.

Pork Barrel

Incumbents can gain the attention of or curry favor with constituents by obtaining funds for special projects, new programs, buildings, or other public works in their districts or states. Such benefits are sometimes defined as "federal spending with a ZIP code attached"[37] but are best known as **pork barrel** projects. A pork feature of virtually every annual budget is money for yet another bomber, fighter plane, weapon, or military construction project the Pentagon has not requested. Universities are also perennial winners in the pork sweepstakes; in 2001,

representatives whose districts include a college or university obtained almost $1.7 billion in funding for campus projects.[38] Pork spending is popular with constituents because it brings jobs, benefits, and business to the district.

Citizens against Government Waste (CAGW), which publishes an annual "Pig Book" and gives an "oinker of the month" award, estimated that about $20 billion was spent on pork in the 2002 election year. This was 32 percent more than the previous year when Congress had a budget surplus to work with. But even after tax cuts, the recession, and the cost of the war on terrorism had sent the federal budget into deficit, Congress still approved well over eight thousand pork barrel projects. This is a good illustration of how important spending is to incumbents in an election year. Funding was approved for tattoo removal in California, a sheep institute in Montana, statue refurbishing and orange research in Alabama, and $2 million was allocated for the Oregon Groundfish Outreach Program.[39]

Because members consider pork barrel projects crucial to reelection chances, there is little support in Congress for eliminating projects most know to be unwise or wasteful. David Stockman, former president Reagan's director of the Office of Management and Budget, observed, "There's no such thing as a fiscal conservative when it comes to his district."[40] Liberals and conservatives, Democrats and Republicans, protect these kinds of projects. Former Senator Alfonse D'Amato (R-N.Y.), who identified himself as a fiscal conservative, was called "Senator Pothole" for his ability to win highway and transportation projects for New York. And the biggest pork producers of all are—not surprisingly—the most senior and powerful members of budget and appropriations committees.

Working with Colleagues

To be successful, representatives and senators must not only serve their constituents and get reelected, they must also know how to work with their colleagues and how to maneuver within the intricate system of parliamentary rules, customs, and traditions that govern the House and Senate.

Informal Norms

First among the many lessons every new member must learn are the customary ways of interacting with colleagues both on and off the floor of Congress.[41] These **informal norms** help keep the institution running smoothly by attempting to minimize friction and allowing competition to occur within an atmosphere of civility. As in other American institutions, the norms of Congress are changing.

Institutional Loyalty

Throughout much of the twentieth century, the most important norm was **institutional loyalty,** the expectation that members would respect their fellow members and the Congress itself, especially their own chamber. Personal criticism of one's colleagues was to be avoided, and mutual respect was fostered by such conventions as referring to colleagues by title, such as "the distinguished senator from New York," rather than by name. This norm has seriously eroded in the last two decades, leading some to call for a return to "civility."

Reciprocity

Reciprocity, or "logrolling," is summarized in the statement "You support my bill, and I'll support yours." Sam Ervin, the late Democratic senator from tobacco-growing North Carolina, is reported to have told an audience from North Dakota, "I got to know Milt Young [then a senator from North Dakota] very well. And I told Milt, 'Milt, I would just like you to tell me how to vote about wheat and sugar beets and things like that, if you just help me out on tobacco.'"[42]

Specialization

Tied to reciprocity is the norm of **specialization.** Given the scope of Congress's legislative authority, members cannot be knowledgeable in all areas, so they specialize in subject areas related to their committee work. The Senate's smaller membership cannot support such an extensive division of labor. In any case, the Senate traditionally has been more individualistic than the House and less willing to give way to specialists. And some senators see themselves as potential presidential candidates who need to be well versed on a variety of issues.

Specialization and reciprocity increase the influence of individual members but also facilitate the smooth running of the institution. By specializing, a member can become an expert. Reciprocity helps each member get the votes needed to pass legislation favored in his or her district. This is another informal norm that is increasingly threatened. Open meetings, media scrutiny, and a decentralized Congress have made it more difficult for members to "go along" on bills unpopular in their constituency.

Special Interest Caucuses

An increasingly common venue for cooperation among members, especially in the House, is the **special interest caucus.** Caucuses are organized by members who share partisan, ideological, issue, regional, or identity interests to pool their strength in promoting shared interests and gaining passage of related legislation. Caucus size ranges from a handful to more than a hundred. There are more than one hundred caucuses in the

House, and almost every member belongs to at least one. In some cases, they are the source of a member's closest political allies. With the exception of its Centrist Coalition, caucuses are not that important in the much smaller Senate, which has only six. There, personal friendships might count for more than committee or caucus membership, and strong relationships of trust sometimes develop across party lines. A notable example is the close friendship between the very liberal Edward Kennedy (D-Mass.) and the very conservative Orrin Hatch (R-Utah).

Prior to the 1995 Gingrich reforms that reduced spending on caucuses, the most important caucuses had their own office space and budgets. Today they are run out of members' offices and are supported by their office staff and budgets, just as the smallest of the caucuses have always had to operate. Among the most significant of the caucuses are those designed to pool the strength of women and minorities. (See the "American Diversity" boxes.)

"Going Public"

We have seen that members must serve their constituents and learn how to work with their colleagues. But sometimes achieving one's legislative objectives requires reaching beyond either group and appealing directly to the larger public.

Twenty years ago the workday routine in both House and Senate for resolving most issues involved bargaining with other members, lobbyists, and White House aides. Working privately, one-on-one in small groups, or in committees, members and staff discussed and debated issues, exchanged information, and planned strategies. Even though many issues still are resolved through these private channels, much has changed in the way Congress operates.

Today leaders and individual members believe it is as important to "go public" to further their goals as it is to engage in private negotiation.[43] *Going public* means taking an issue debate to the public through the media as Congress does when it televises floor debates and important hearings.

C-SPAN

In the past, television networks only broadcast important congressional proceedings such as the McCarthy hearings, those for the Watergate scandal, and hearings for the Iran-Contra affair. In 1979, after considerable controversy and anxiety, the House began routinely to televise its proceedings. Fearful of being overshadowed by the House, in 1986 the Senate followed suit. But today exposure comes daily on C-SPAN (the Cable Satellite Public Affairs Network), which is seen by more than 20 million viewers each week. Regular

WOMEN IN CONGRESS

Women make up 51 percent of the nation's population but only 14 percent of the Senate and slightly less than 14 percent of the House. These paltry proportions are an increase from the 1980s when the percentage of women in the House was stuck at around 5 percent. Today twenty-nine states have at least one woman in their delegation, and California has twenty (one-third of all women in Congress). Five states (Alaska, Iowa, Delaware, Vermont, and New Hampshire) have never elected a woman to Congress.

The first woman in Congress was Representative Jeannette Rankin (R-Mont.), who was elected in 1916 even before women got the right to vote. It was not until 1932 that the first woman served in the Senate. Hattie Caraway (D-Ark.) won the seat after the death of her husband, the former occupant. Margaret Chase Smith, a Republican from Maine who spent a distinguished career in the Senate from 1949 to 1973, entered Congress by succeeding to the House seat of her deceased husband before winning election to the Senate on her own. It was not until 1978, with the election of Nancy Kassebaum (R-Kan.) that a "non-widow" was elected to the Senate.

In 1992, which many called "The Year of the Woman," the proportion of women in the House began to increase because women targeted the extraordinarily large numbers of open seats available. Women fare about as well as men when they run for open seats.[1] Indeed, of the sixty-five open seats in the 1992 election, twenty-two were won by women. However, six of these new incumbents were swept out of office in the 1994 Republican landslide.

Although gains have been small since 1992, and the 2002 election brought losses at the state level, overall more women are being elected to state legislatures and other offices that traditionally have been stepping stones to Congress. The 2002 reapportionment offered opportunities for challengers by creating twelve new seats, but only one was won by a woman.

Women's problems are not over when they are elected, however, because the male leadership of both houses has often been condescending. In 1977, to pool their strength, women in the House founded the Women's Caucus, which they reorganized four years later as the Caucus for Women's Issues, inviting men to join. But more than a decade later they still had trouble

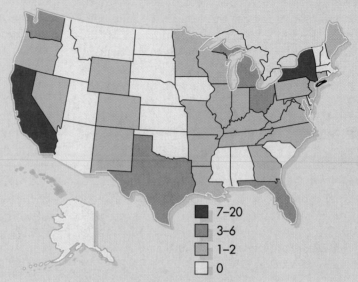

Number of women in 108th Congress, 2003–2005.
SOURCE: *CQ Daily Monitor,* November 7, 2002, 46–48.

7–20
3–6
1–2
0

---

viewers watch twelve hours of programming per week and—of greater importance to the legislators they are watching—nine out of ten C-SPAN viewers voted in the 2000 election.[44]

Two of the three C-SPAN advertisement-free channels are available with almost all basic cable service. Local television listings provide times for daily coverage of House and Senate floor proceedings as well as for committee hearings and other official business. In addition, C-SPAN covers members of Congress on the campaign trail, attending fund-raisers, giving stump speeches, and just chatting with con-

stituents. Besides its unbroken coverage of events, what sets C-SPAN apart from commercial network coverage of Congress is that there is no intermediary between the viewer and the events and people they are watching. C-SPAN does not use reporters, so televised events are free of commentary and on-the-spot analysis.

Other Media

During the 1980s, use of the media by congressional leadership increased tremendously. Newt Gingrich's (R-Ga.) rise to power was attributed in part to his un-getting a foothold in the House's power centers. Said one woman who tried for a seat on the prestigious Appropriations Committee three times, "Each time I've been nicely told that the women's slot is already filled in that committee." And in 1993, Nancy Johnson (R-Conn.), one of the Republicans' leading health care experts, was told by her subcommittee chair at a public hearing that she must have learned about a particular health issue through "pillowtalk" with her physician husband.[2]

But in the 1990s, women began to make a substantive difference. In 1993–1994, Congress passed a record sixty-six bills of special importance to women. That nearly equaled the number of such bills passed in the entire previous decade.[3]

The Caucus for Women's Issues lost some of its steam during the Gingrich years when funding for all caucus work was eliminated, but in 1998 it regrouped and, working across party, racial, and ethnic lines, recruited all but two House women to membership. (More than a quarter of all women House members are black, Asian, or Hispanic.) With a Republican and a Democrat serving as cochairs, the caucus is regarded as one of the most bipartisan in Congress. Its legislative agenda includes supportive measures for woman-owned businesses, pay equity, and women in the military.

By the 107th Congress, women were gaining more assignments to the most powerful committees such as Budget and Appropriations, and more women were chairing subcommittees in both the House and the Senate. Because of the term-limit rule for chairs passed during the Gingrich years, a few women were well positioned to assume chairs after the 2000 election, yet none were appointed. Marge Roukema (R-N.J.), the longest-serving Republican woman in the House, announced her retirement from the House when she was denied the chair of the Banking Committee. But in the 108th Congress, two women won chairs of standing committees in the Senate.

In addition to the standing committees and their subcommittees in each chamber, each party has its own committees for planning policy and strategy. Women fare somewhat better here, holding a number of secondary leadership positions on conference committees and as assistant and deputy whips. In 2001, when the Democratic Caucus elected Nancy Pelosi (D-Calif.) as minority whip, second in command to House minority leader Dick Gephardt, she became the highest-ranking woman in congressional history. With her election as minority leader the following year, Pelosi became the first woman ever to head a congressional party caucus.

There is still a way to go. Of the 11,637 Americans elected to Congress between 1789 and 2000, 185 (1.6 percent) were women.[4] If all 185 could be seated in the same congressional session, it would still leave women well below representational parity.

1. Philip Paolino, "Group-Salient Issues and Group Representation: Support for Women Candidates in the 1992 Senate Elections," *American Journal of Political Science* 39, May 1995, 294–313; Barbara Burrell, "Did We Get More Than One 'Year of the Woman'?" Paper presented at the 1995 Annual Meeting of the Midwest Political Science Association, Chicago.
2. Kevin Merida, "A Woman's Place on the Hill," *Washington Post National Weekly Edition*, April 11–17, 1994, 15.
3. Leslie Laurence, "Congress Makes Up for Neglect," *Lincoln Journal-Star*, December 5, 1994, 8.
4. For a list of all women ever elected to Congress, see www.loc/gov/thomas.
OTHER SOURCES: *2001 Congressional Staff Directory;* Sue Kirchoff, "Dollars and Sensitivities: Finessing the Gender Gap," *Congressional Quarterly Weekly Review,* April 24, 1999, 951–953; "Congress of Relative Newcomers Poses Challenge to Bush, Leadership," *Congressional Quarterly Weekly Review,* January 20, 2001, 178–182; *CQ's Politics in America 2002: The 107th Congress* (Washington, D.C.: Congressional Quarterly, 2002).

derstanding of the potential of electronic media and other technology and his strategic use of television. His stated goal was to shape the entire nation through the news media, and he used language that appealed to the public. As one reporter noted, he was "absolutist, aggressive, hyperbolic, informed, topical, unpredictable, and studied in his use of supercharged symbolic language."[45] Even before becoming a party leader, Gingrich illustrated strategic use of the media on the House floor, denouncing Democrats regularly. Because the camera was stationary, on TV it looked as if he were speaking to an interested audience of members. In reality, he was talking to an empty chamber. Today, the camera pans the chamber.

The congressional leadership goes public, too. Leaders of both parties regularly call producers of television talk shows to suggest guests. They meet with the press and often have prepared statements. Before important congressional votes on key issues, the leadership plans letters to the editors of important newspapers and floor speeches designed for maximum television coverage. For example, when the Republican leadership refused to allow the Democrats to bring their bill providing prescription drug benefits to a vote

House Minority Leader Richard Gephardt goes public, leading a walkout of Democratic members from a House session where the Republican leadership refused to consider their version of a prescription drug benefit bill.

before the 2000 election, the Democratic leadership organized a walkout of party members, while the vote on the Republicans' version of the bill was taking place. Striding down the Capitol steps to a battery of cameras, Minority Leader Gephardt excoriated, just in time for the evening newscasts, both the Republicans' bill and their parliamentary tactics.

The more media-oriented among the rank-and-file members are also experts in providing short and interesting comments for the nightly network news, writing articles for major newspapers, and appearing on talk shows and as commentators on news programs.

Voting as Representation

We have seen that members of Congress represent their constituents through service and by obtaining special benefits for their districts or states. A third major kind of representation is voting on policy. In the eyes of most people, members are sent to Washington to make laws. By casting hundreds of votes each year, members try to represent the interests of their constituencies as they see them and in the process win support for reelection. Increasingly, constituents are becoming more active in communicating with their legislators. Members are flooded with faxes, e-mails, poll results, and mailgrams, often stimulated as a result of radio or television talk shows. These individuals, however, do not represent the entire constituency. Talk show callers and listeners, for example, are more likely than other voters to be conservative, Republican, and male.[46]

Constituents are often uninformed, divided, or apathetic. Because most votes in Congress are on subjects the electorate knows little about, members cannot, and often do not want to, rely on a simple polling of constituents to tell them how to vote. The opinions of constituents do matter, but other influences are also important: the party, the president, the members' ideology, staffers, and caucus membership. Members often take cues from these sources on how to vote.

Party and Constituency

Paradoxically, given the heated rhetoric, by the end of the Clinton administration the number of partisan votes in Congress had reached its lowest level in several years.[47] Partisan votes are those on bills on which the Republican and Democratic leadership have taken a position and the majority of one party opposes a majority of the other. In 2000, 49 percent of all roll call votes in the Senate and 43 percent of those in the House were partisan.[48] On most of those votes 80 to 90 percent of party members followed their party leadership.

However, on other votes, although tempers ran high, with heated exchanges in committee and conference negotiations, those differences often did not translate into party unity voting. It is in part a consequence of both parties trying to position themselves nearer the center where a large part of the electorate is clustered.

When Newt Gingrich was House Speaker, voting along an ideological party line was expected of Republicans. With new leadership, there has been an attempt to move away from hard-line policy positions in order to keep moderate Republicans from crossing over and voting with Democrats. But there have also been much more negotiating and compromising in committees on the final version of legislation. Once a bill reaches the floor, a middle position may already have been reached, and the vote on it may not reflect the intensity of the partisan haggling of the earlier stages of the process.

Two events increased partisan voting in the Senate in 2001. First was the 50-50 party split after the 2000 election. Second was James Jeffords's decision to leave the Republican Party to become an Independent (Chapter 6 "You Are There"). Having lost their control of the chamber, the Republican leadership had greater motive for taking positions on bills to keep their members in line. Also in these circumstances, moderates found it harder not to stick with the leadership when it declared a position.

In the House, where the Republicans were working with a ten-vote majority in 2001 and where the leadership had a less confrontational approach, partisan voting declined slightly.[49] The atmosphere of national unity after 9/11 also had an impact on partisan voting as members were trying to present a united front in responding to the emergency situation.

Party affiliation continues to be central. All members of Congress are elected on a partisan ballot, and Congress organizes itself on a partisan basis. Members tend to have policy views similar to others in their party, at least more similar than to those in the opposite party. Many members receive significant campaign support from their party organization, and party leaders try hard to influence their members to vote the "right" way by dispensing "perks" or exerting pressure. Party votes reflect constituency needs, too, because Democratic and Republican constituencies have different policy preferences.

Members must be responsive to their own constituents as well as to party members in general. Members must consider what benefits their districts as a whole as well as the needs of subgroups within the district, such as party voters, socioeconomic groups, and personal supporters.[50] Sometimes the interests of these groups may be in conflict. The representatives' personal constituency may be more liberal or conservative than the district as a whole. When members vote against what seems to be the sense of the majority of voters in the district, it may be that they are responding to their staunchest supporters. Of course, in those rare instances where most of the representative's constituents feel strongly about a core issue, the member cannot buck an overwhelming majority and expect to win reelection.

When neither the member nor the member's constituents have strong feelings on an issue, it is certainly in the member's interest to go along with party leaders. Although their efforts to collar votes are usually low-key, party leaders sometimes do turn on the heat. In a successful vote to override a Reagan veto, Democratic Senate leaders adopted a "baby-sitting" strategy to make sure that wavering Democrats did not get near anyone who might persuade them to uphold the president's veto. These Democrats were accompanied at all times by two other Democrats with the "right" views.

Ideology

On the whole, the member's ideology is usually not far from that of his or her party or constituency.[51]

In general, Democrats vote for more liberal measures than do Republicans. Historically, this was not true of southern Democrats, who often deserted the Democratic leadership and voted with Republicans because they shared their more conservative outlook. Thus, for about thirty of the years when the Democrats "controlled" Congress, they did not have a working majority on many issues.

Today, southern conservatives usually run as Republicans and have captured much of the formerly solid Democratic South. Southern Democrats are still more conservative than the Democratic Party in the North, but many districts are increasingly urban and contain voters who are more liberal than those of thirty years ago. Black voters are a substantial bloc in many southern districts and counterbalance the more conservative white vote.

Members within both parties still hold a sufficiently wide range of views for there to be issue-based or ideological alliances within each party. Among House Republicans, for example, there are a group of about fifty moderates, the New Republicans, and a forty-member Conservative Action Team. Among the Democrats, the House's moderate-leaning New Democrat Coalition, with seventy-two members, comprises almost a third of the party caucus. The Blue Dog Coalition, a group of thirty-two socially conservative Democrats, have helped defeat bills on gun control and increased funding for the National Endowment for the Arts.[52]

The President

The president is also a factor in congressional voting, due in part to his role as party leader.[53] The president appeals to fellow partisans to support a program and tries to persuade those in the other party to go along as well. Presidents can win support by granting or withholding favors, such as support for a bill a member is sponsoring or for a pet project in his or her district.

Interest Groups

Interest group lobbyists are most effective when their interests overlap constituency interests or when the issue is technical or little publicized. They are also more likely to be effective when a bill is still in committee than when it is being debated on the floor of the House or the Senate.

Staffers

Staff can be a very important influence on a member's vote. Staff members are likely to have done the research and briefed the member on an issue. They probably have the greatest influence on technical, low-profile issues or those the member does not care or know much about.

Other Members

Members are influenced by other members of their party or their state's delegation and by colleagues whose judgment or expertise they respect, or whose ideology or background they share. In fact, on most routine bills, cues from trusted fellow members are among the most important influences on members' votes. House members in particular are influenced by colleagues who share membership in a special interest caucus.

How Congress Is Organized

An institution with 535 voting members that must make thousands of policy decisions every year without benefit of a unified leadership is an institution not likely to work quickly or efficiently. Like all organizations, legislatures need some structure to be able to accomplish their purposes. Congress does have both a leadership system and a committee structure but each is organized along party lines. Alongside this partisan organization exist many other groups—caucuses, coalitions, work and study groups, and task forces—whose membership cuts across party lines or reflects the division of interests within party caucuses. Some of this micro-organizing is a means of bypassing the committee system that dominates Congress's legislative and oversight functions.

How Congressional Organization Evolved

The Constitution calls for the members of the House of Representatives to select a **Speaker of the House** to act as its presiding officer and for the vice president of the United States to serve as president (or presiding officer) of the Senate. But the Constitution does not say anything about the powers of these officials, nor does it require any further internal organization. So little is said about the Speaker in the Constitution that it is not even required that he be a member of the House.

The first House, meeting in New York in 1789, had slow and cumbersome procedures. For its first several sessions, Congress's legislative work was accomplished by appointing ad hoc committees. By the Third Congress, there were about 350, and the system had become too unwieldy. Soon permanent committees were created, each with continuing responsibilities in one area, such as taxes or trade.[54]

As parties developed, the selection of the Speaker became a partisan matter, and the Speaker became as much a party leader as a legislative manager. The seventh Speaker, Henry Clay (Ky.), who served ten of the years between 1811 and 1825, transformed the speakership from a ceremonial office to one of real leadership. To maintain party loyalty and discipline, he used his powers to appoint committee members and chairs. Under Clay's leadership the House was the dominant branch, but its influence declined when it, like the rest of government, could not cope with the divisiveness of the slavery issue. By 1856, it took 133 ballots to elect a Speaker. In many instances, there were physical fights on the House floor and duels outside.[55]

The Senate, a smaller body than the House, was less tangled in procedures, less rule bound, and more effective in its operation. Its influence rose as visitors packed the Senate gallery to hear the great debates over slavery waged by Daniel Webster (Mass.), John C. Calhoun (S.C.), and Henry Clay (who had moved from the House). During this era, senators were elected by state legislatures, not directly by the people. Thus, they had strong local party ties and often used their influence to get presidential appointments for home state party members. But the Senate, too, became ineffective as the nation moved toward civil war. Senators carried arms to protect themselves as debates over slavery turned to violence.

After the Civil War, with the presidency weakened by the impeachment of Andrew Johnson, strong party leadership reemerged in the House, and a period of congressional government began. Speaker Thomas Reed (Me.), nicknamed "The Czar" by his colleagues, assumed the authority to name members and chairs of committees and to chair the Rules Committee, which decided which bills were to come to the floor for debate. A major consequence of the Speaker's extensive powers was increased party discipline. Members who voted against their party might be punished by a loss of committee assignments or chairmanships.

At the same time, both the House and the Senate became more professional. The emergence of national problems and an aggressive Congress made a congressional career more prestigious. Prior to the Civil War, membership turnover was high; members of the House served an average of only one term, senators only four years. After the war, the strengthening of parties and the growth of the one-party South, when Democrats controlled virtually all elective offices, made reelection easier, thus offering the possibility of a congressional career.

This desire for permanent careers in the House produced an interest in reform. Members wanted a chance at choice committee seats and did not want to be controlled by the Speaker. Resistance against the dictatorial practices of Reed and his successor Joseph Cannon (R-Ill.) grew. Cannon, more conservative than many of his fellow Republicans, used his powers

Vitriolic exchanges are not just a phenomenon of the contemporary Congress. Shown here is a fight in the House in 1798. After Representative Matthew Lyon (R-Vt.) spit on Representative Roger Griswold (Fed-Conn.) and the House refused to expel Lyon, Griswold attacked Lyon with a cane. Lyon defended himself with fire tongs as other members of Congress looked on (with some amusement, it seems).

Library of Congress

to block legislation he disliked, to punish those who opposed him, and even to refuse to recognize members who wished to speak. In 1910, there was a revolt against "Cannonism," a synonym for the arbitrary use of the Speaker's powers.

The membership voted to remove the Speaker from the Rules Committee and to strip him of his authority to appoint committees and their chairs. The revolt weakened party influence. Party discipline could no longer be maintained by the Speaker punishing members through loss of committee assignments. And it gave committees and their chairs a great deal of independence from leadership influence.

The Senate also was undergoing a major reform. As part of the Progressive movement, pressure began to build for the direct popular election of senators. The election of senators by state legislatures had made many senators pawns of special interests—the big monopolistic corporations (called "trusts") and railroads. In a day when millionaires were not as common as now, the Senate was referred to as the "Millionaires Club."

Not surprisingly, the Senate first refused to consider a constitutional amendment providing for its direct election, although in some states popular balloting on senatorial candidates took place anyway. Finally, under the threat of a call for a constitutional convention, which many members of Congress feared might lead to other changes in the Constitution, a direct election amendment was passed in the House and Senate in 1912 and ratified by the states a year later.

These reforms of the early twentieth century dispersed power in both the House and Senate and weakened leadership. House members no longer feared the kind of retribution levied by Speaker Cannon on members who deviated from party positions. In the Senate, popular elections made senators responsive to the diverse interests of the electorate rather than to party leaders.

Contemporary Leadership Positions

The modern leadership of Congress cannot be understood from reading the Constitution. Not only is the Speaker now a party leader, but none of the secondary leadership positions in the House and none of the current top posts in the Senate are provided for in Article I. This is because they are party leadership positions, and the Founders did not plan for or take into account party organizations. Nor were there party organizations in Congress when it first met.

The leaders in each party are selected by their full memberships meeting in caucus. The full House must vote on the Speaker, of course, but it is a straight party line vote, so the real selection is made in the majority party's caucus. The Speaker is typically someone who has served in the House a long time and is usually a skilled parliamentarian and an ideological moderate. The institutional task of the Speaker is to act as presiding officer and to see that legislation moves through the House. He is also second in line to the presidency after the vice president. The Speaker's partisan task is to secure the passage of measures preferred by his (thus far all have been men) party. By tradition, the Speaker does not cast a vote on most bills before the House, participating only on "symbolic or party-defining issues."[56]

Nancy Pelosi (D-Calif.), House minority leader and the first woman in American history to lead a congressional party caucus.

Trying to win partisan support is often difficult. The Speaker has some rewards and punishments to dispense for loyalty and disloyalty, but they are small compared to the power wielded by Reed and Cannon. The Speaker, however, does influence committee assignments, which committees will be given jurisdiction over complex bills, what bills will come to the House floor, and how his party's congressional campaign funds are allocated. He also decides who will be recognized to speak on the floor of the House and whether motions are relevant. He has the authority to appoint members to the conference and select committees, and he controls some material benefits, such as the assignment of extra office space. He also has the power to name the chair of the Rules Committee and all of his party's members on the committee. Despite these formal powers, the Speaker must be persuasive to be effective.

The few strong Speakers of the nineteenth and early twentieth centuries—Clay, Reed, Cannon—have already been mentioned. In modern times the only Speaker to attempt the level of control of Reed and Cannon was Newt Gingrich (R-Ga.). Gingrich was not an ideological moderate; he had been the intellectual and tactical leader of conservative House Republicans. Although a sixteen-year veteran of the House, his only formal prior leadership service had been as a whip; he had never had the chance to chair a committee, or even a subcommittee, because the Republicans were in the minority during his pre-Speaker years. Like other Speakers who were too controlling, Gingrich met with rebellion in his own party and had to fight back a challenge to his leadership in his third year. Gingrich's demands for party discipline in support of a national legislative program (Contract with America) left many

members with too little flexibility to respond to their constituencies and risked their chances for reelection. This is one reason that an ideological moderate with a conciliatory manner is often sought for the Speaker's position.

The current House Speaker, Dennis Hastert (R-Ill.), is more in the mold of a traditional Speaker. He is from the mainstream of the party and a mediator and persuader rather than an agenda-driven leader who uses a heavy hand to enforce party discipline. When he took over as Speaker, Hastert had only a five-vote margin to work with, the smallest majority any Speaker had had in fifty years. His approach to the Speakership is to "do things in regular order" and "not to throw his weight around." His low-key approach has its disadvantages with the public. Few people know anything about him, and those who do give him lower approval ratings than they give House Republicans.[57] But a Speaker does not need public approval to be successful; he needs to have good working relationships with his colleagues so that he can see his party's bills through to passage.

The party leadership in the House includes a **majority leader,** a **minority leader,** and majority and minority **whips.** The majority leader is second in command to the Speaker, and the minority leader is, as the name suggests, the leader of the minority party. Whips originated in the British House of Commons, where they were named after the "whipper in," the rider who keeps the hounds together in a fox hunt. This aptly describes the whips' role in Congress. Party whips try to maintain contact with party members, see which way they are leaning on votes, and attempt to gain their support. The current majority whip has twelve deputies and twenty-two assistant whips who keep tabs on their assigned state delegations. The minority whip currently has four deputies.

The party apparatus in the House also includes committees that assign party members to standing committees, discuss policy issues, plan legislative strategies, and allocate funds to party members running for reelection.

The Senate has no leader comparable to the Speaker of the House. The vice president of the United States is formally the presiding officer but in reality attends infrequently and has relatively little power. He is allowed to cast the tie-breaking vote in the rare instances in which the Senate is split evenly, but this rarely happens. Vice President Gore cast three tie-breaking votes during the Clinton administration, but Cheney has yet to cast a vote despite the even split in the Senate in 2001. The Senate has an elected president pro tempore, by tradition the senior member of the majority party. It is an honorific post with few duties except to preside over the Senate in the absence of the vice president. In practice, during the conduct of routine day-to-day business, presiding duties are divided among junior senators. This releases the senior member from boring work while giving the Senate's newest members a chance to learn rules and procedures.

The position of Senate majority leader was not created until 1911 and has often been held by men of no particular distinction in their parties. The office has none of the speakership's potential for control of chamber proceedings. A congressional watcher once said the majority leader "is often more a coat-check attendant than a maitre'd or chef."[58] The instances of powerful majority leaders are few, the most notable being Lyndon Johnson. He assumed office at a time when the Democrats had a slim hold on the Senate, giving him an opportunity to exercise his extraordinary powers of personal persuasion to keep party members in line on key votes. Johnson's reputation was made through a combination of personality and mastery of the legislative process (he had been an aide to the House Speaker and served in the House before election to the Senate). There is nothing inherent in the office to give a majority leader the power Johnson had, and no one has had it since.

The Senate majority leader is a spokesperson for his party's legislative agenda and is supposed to help line up members' votes on key issues. But procedurally the Senate is a free-for-all compared to the House, with "every man and woman for him- or herself."[59] Unlike the Speaker, the majority leader cannot control the terms under which a bill is considered on the floor, since rules are assigned by unanimous consent in the Senate, and he has little power to stop a filibuster if a member wants to block legislation. This means a majority leader needs to do much more than keep his own party in line to keep legislation moving through the Senate.

The leader can influence the general atmosphere of deliberation in the Senate by adopting an approach to working with the minority party that is either conciliatory or partisan. When Robert Dole left the Senate to run for president in 1996, Republicans selected Trent Lott (R–Miss.) to replace him as majority leader. In contrast to Dole, who worked very much in the conciliatory, clubby style common to the Senate, Lott chose a rather aggressively partisan approach closer to the leadership style of Newt Gingrich, who was then House Speaker. But Lott's partisanship was less strident because Gingrich's style would never be accepted in the more equalitarian atmosphere of the Senate.

In 2001, when James Jeffords (R–Vt.) left the Republican Party to become an Independent, the Democrats became a majority of one in the Senate and the leadership changed hands. Majority leader Lott had to trade places with Tom Daschle (D–S.D,), who had been Senate minority leader. Daschle had a less aggressively partisan or confrontational style in his dealings with the press and public, but he was no less partisan behind the scenes than his predecessor and was very good at keeping party members in line. But Daschle's leadership was complicated by his presidential ambitions. When Congressional leaders are seeking higher office they may

Senate majority leader Lyndon Johnson, persuading. LBJ "used physical persuasion in addition to intellectual and moral appeals. He was hard on other people's coat lapels. If one were shorter than Lyndon he was inclined to move up close and lean over the subject of his persuasive efforts." Here that subject is Senator Theodore Green (D-R.I.). "If a Senator were taller than [Johnson], he would come at him from below, somewhat like a badger." Senator Edmund Muskie (D-Me.), who was taller, "emerged from a meeting with Johnson with the observation that he had not known until this meeting why people had the hair in their nostrils trimmed." Quotes are from Eugene McCarthy, Up 'til Now *(New York: Harcourt Brace, 1987).*

have difficulty convincing the members of their caucuses that actions they are being asked to take are in the interests of the party rather than in support of the leaders' own political agenda. When the Republicans regained control of the Senate in the 2002 elections, Daschle and Lott again traded leadership positions.

Daschle gave up his presidential aspirations to concentrate on organizing the Democratic opposition. But Lott immediately undermined his position with Republican colleagues and the White House by making comments that appeared to endorse segregation. Having damaged his party's credibility with minority voters and having lost the confidence of Senate colleagues and the White House, Lott was forced to resign as majority leader even before the new Congress met. He was replaced as majority leader by Bill Frist (R–Tenn.), a heart surgeon with a much less combative style than Lott's and a close ally of George W. Bush.

The Senate minority leader's job is similar to that of the majority leader in that its effectiveness depends on a limited package of incentives and procedural ploys to enforce party discipline. Both parties also elect assistant floor leaders and whips to assist in this task; the Republicans have nine whips and the Democrats three. These are important, if not essential, positions for working one's way into the top leadership.

Committees

Most of the work of Congress is done in committees. Observers of American politics take this for granted; yet the power of legislative committees is rather rare among Western democracies. In Britain, for example, committees cannot offer amendments that change the substance of a bill.

Standing Committees

Today there are nineteen **standing committees** in the House and sixteen in the Senate. Each deals with a different subject matter, such as finance or education or agriculture. Each has a number of subcommittees, totaling seventy-five in the House and sixty-eight in the Senate.[60] Nearly all legislation introduced in Congress is referred to a standing committee and then to a subcommittee. Subcommittees hold public hearings to give interested parties a chance to speak for or against a bill. They also hold **markup** sessions to provide an opportunity for the committee to rewrite the bill. Following markup, the bill is sent to the full committee, which also may hold hearings. If approved there, it goes to the full House or Senate.

Standing committees vary in size from nine to seventy-five members in the House and from twelve to twenty-eight in the Senate. The number of seats on any committee can change from one session to another as party caucuses try to satisfy as many of their members' preferences as possible. Trying to accommodate members' requests for committee assignments that will be most beneficial to their constituencies has led to ever-larger committees. Party ratios—that is, the number of Democrats relative to Republicans on each committee—are determined by the majority party in the House, and negotiated by the leadership of both parties in the Senate. The ratios are generally set in rough proportion to party membership in the particular house, but the majority party gives itself a disproportionate number of seats on several key committees to ensure control.

When the Senate was evenly divided at 50-50 in the early months after the 2000 election, the negotiations were particularly hard fought, with Republicans arguing that Vice President Cheney's role as presiding officer and his ability to cast a tie-breaking vote gave them a de facto majority and entitled them to chair all committees. With Jeffords's party switch, the chairs were turned over to Democrats, and the ratio of seats on all committees were renegotiated, only to be reappointed again when the Republicans gained a two-vote majority.

Committee Membership

New members and those members seeking committee changes express their preferences to their party's selection committee. As a general rule, preferences will be granted, although there is some self-selection by seniority. Historically, junior members did not ask for the most prestigious posts, but this tradition is breaking down as freshmen are bolder in their requests and even receive instruction in how to get the assignments they want. And if there are freshmen members whose reelection races are likely to be tough or whom the party leadership believes have the potential to be future leaders, those members will likely be given helpful committee assignments.

The committees dealing with appropriations, taxes, and finance are always sought after because having a say in the allocation of money or tax policy gives members power and enhances their ability to help their districts. Most members want committee assignments that let them tell constituents that they are working on problems of the district. Members from agricultural districts, for example, strive to get on the agriculture committees.

The practice of filling committees with representatives whose districts have an especially strong economic interest in its work makes committees rather parochial in their outlook. It also encourages costly and wasteful legislation; if committee members' constituents benefit from programs under their jurisdiction, committee members have no incentive to eliminate them or pare them back. This is one of the biggest weaknesses in the system for making committee assignments.[61]

Committees are also often filled with members who have financial interests in the businesses they make policies for. Most members who sit on the banking committees own bank stock, many on agriculture committees own agribusiness stock, and those on the armed services committees hold stock in defense industries.[62] Phil Gramm, the ranking Republican on the Senate Banking Committee and instrumental in deregulating the banking industry in the 1990s, gave up his Senate seat in 2003 to become an investment banker.

Media coverage is another criterion important in deciding committee preference. The work of some committees is more likely to be covered by television. In one five-year period, the Senate Foreign Relations Committee had 522 network television cameras covering it, whereas the Indian Affairs Committee had 0.[63] Getting on the right committee is important to those who want to become nationally known. When a journalist once asked Senator Joseph Biden (D-Del.) why he was so newsworthy, Biden replied, "It's the committees, of course." Biden had served on the three committees with the greatest media exposure.

Committee Chairs

The chair is usually the leader and most influential member of a committee. Chairs have the authority to call meetings, set agendas, and control committee staff and funds. In addition, chairs are usually very knowledgeable about matters that come before their committees, and this, too, is a source of influence. Some chairs have used their power to rule their committees with an iron hand.

Usually, the member of the majority party with the longest service on a committee becomes its chair by the so-called **seniority rule.** The rule was adopted to protect committee members from powerful Speakers of the House who often used their authority to award committee chairs to friends and allies. Under the ironclad seniority rule, chairs might have been senile, alcoholic, or personally disliked by every member of the committee. ...the party had ...House, they became chairs.

Many members believed the custom of seniority led to chairs who were dictatorial and out of step with the rest of their party. In response to those complaints, in the early 1970s both parties agreed that the seniority rule no longer had to be followed. Since then, a Committee on Committees in the Republican Party and a Steering and Policy Committee in the Democratic Party have recommended chairs in addition to assigning committee seats. All members of each party caucus vote on these recommendations by secret ballot, although in some cases the result is a foregone conclusion.

In 1975, in the first application of the new rule, the Democratic membership stripped three senior Democrats of their chairs. They did so to others in later years. The Republicans also ignored the seniority principle in

their choice of chairs in 1995.[64] In the House, Speaker Gingrich elevated less senior members who were more conservative over other Republicans on the all-important Budget, Appropriations, and Banking Committees.

Still, the seniority principle is observed most of the time because Congress assumes that members with long service on the committee will have the most expertise in its subject matter. That is usually true. Applying the seniority rule also eliminates potentially damaging intraparty fights over who will chair important committees. Some argue the seniority system is also the best protection for women and minorities as they gain seniority in the institution. However in 2001, when Marge Roukema (R–N.J.) was in line to chair the Banking Committee, that supposition was put to the test and failed. The Republican leadership divided Banking's jurisdiction, and the chairs of the two reorganized committees went to men.

Choosing chairs by means other than strict seniority has ended the days of the autocratic chair. And the reform has brought about an interesting change in the behavior of senior members. Before 1975, committee chairs were less supportive of their party than other party members in roll-call votes.[65] Since 1975, committee chairs have been much more likely than other members to vote with their party. The same pattern holds true of those who are second, third, and fourth in seniority on each committee. Thus, removing seniority as a sole criterion for choosing committee chairs has meant that senior party members are much less likely to deviate from their party's position. In that sense, the reforms have strengthened party influence in Congress.

Facing vacancies in the chairs of several important committees in 2001, Hastert indicated that, unlike Gingrich, he would look to the committees to submit nominations should the Republicans retain control of the House. His approach did not sit well with many House Republicans because they believed it fostered a spirit of competitiveness among those who wanted to chair committees. One of Hastert's colleagues said, "His weakness may be that he doesn't understand how much influence he has."[66]

This illustrates the dilemma of the autocratic versus the conciliator approach to leadership. Gingrich created a great deal of tension and a splintering within the party because he tried for too much control. Now some claim Hastert is fostering division by *not* using the full powers of his office to control the assignment of committee chairs. An effective Speaker needs to find a balance between control and conciliation.

Subcommittees

Each standing committee is divided into subcommittees with jurisdiction over part of the committee's area of responsibility. The House International Relations

Committee, for example, has six subcommittees—one each for the geographic areas of Africa, East Asia and the Pacific, the Western Hemisphere, the Middle East and South Asia, and Europe, and the sixth for international operations (trade) and human rights.

Committee chairs traditionally dominated not only their committee but its subcommittees as well. Chairs chose the chairs of the subcommittees and controlled the subcommittees' jurisdiction, budget, and staff. Chairs thus could manipulate the subcommittees' action on proposed legislation as they saw fit.

The rule changes made by House Democrats in 1973 and 1974 reduced the control of the standing committee chairs by allowing each subcommittee to operate semi-independently of the parent committee. Similar changes took place in the Senate. These reforms, sometimes called the subcommittee bill of rights, allowed more members, especially newer members, to share in important decisions. In this way, they made Congress more democratic.

But by diffusing power, they also made it less efficient because the very number of subcommittees contributed to government gridlock. Complex legislation might be sent to several subcommittees, each with its own interests and jurisdiction. For example, seven different House committees managed the 1990 clean air bill. When the House had to meet in conference with the Senate to work out a unified version, the House ended up sending 140 members.[67]

Under the Republican majority in the House, standing committee chairs reasserted control over their subcommittees. In 1999, when the House had eighty-four subcommittees and the Senate sixty-nine, new rules were adopted to streamline the legislative process and reduce the number of subcommittees. All but a few House committees were limited to five subcommittees (excluding oversight) and House members to no more than four subcommittee assignments. No restrictions were placed on subcommittee numbers in the Senate, but no senator is supposed to sit on more than five.[68] These reforms have not ended the problem of overlapping jurisdictions. When President Bush proposed establishing a cabinet-level department of Homeland Security, for example, twelve House committees were involved in marking up the bill.

One of the most significant rule changes under the Republican majority was term limits for committee chairs, with most limited to three terms. This meant that thirteen mostly younger men whom Gingrich had nominated to chair standing committees had to relinquish their seats after the 2000 elections. Two powerful chairs, John Kasich (R-Ohio) of Budget and Bill Archer (R-Tex.) of Ways and Means, decided to retire from the House when their terms were up, some say because of their impending loss of power. Opponents argue that term limits punish experience and weaken oversight as chairs are forced out just when they have become familiar with the operations of the agencies they oversee.[69] An attempt to repeal term limits for chairs was defeated in 2001, but Senate Republicans did adopt a modification. Committee chairs who lost their positions when Jeffords switched parties will not have the remainder of their terms counted against the six-year limit. And each member is now allowed to serve six years as ranking member in addition to three terms as chair.

The typical senator sits on four standing committees and five subcommittees, while a House member averages two or three standing and several subcommittee assignments. These multiple assignments mean that members have impossible schedules, and at times committees cannot obtain quorums because members are tied up in other committee work. This leaves it to the committee chair, a few colleagues, and staff to do much of the work and make many of the decisions.

Other Committees

There are a few other types of congressional committees. Select or special committees are typically investigative committees organized on a temporary basis to study a specific problem or to hold hearings and issue a report on special problems that arise, such as Watergate or intelligence agency failures prior to 9/11. These committees are disbanded when their work is completed. The exceptions are the House and the Senate Select Committees on Intelligence, and the Senate Select Committee on Ethics, which are in effect permanent committees. In 2003, the House added a Select Committee on Homeland Security. Joint committees include members from both houses with the chair rotating between a House and Senate member. There are four permanent joint committees, two of which study budgetary and tax policy. The other two administer institutions _____ _____ ___ Congress, such as the Library of Congress.

Conference committees also are composed of members from both chambers. They are appointed whenever the Senate and the House pass different versions of the same bill. Members from the committees that managed the bill in their respective chambers work out a single version for the full membership to vote on. Conference committees are dissolved after the compromise version is agreed on. (See the section "Conference Committees.")

Task Forces

The traffic jams and turf wars surrounding much committee work has led members of Congress with strong interests in particular areas to look for ways to bypass the committee structure. This is a major reason for the use of a task force, or ad hoc committee, to study major issues and draft legislation.[70] Task forces have existed in the House for decades, used by Democratic and Republican leadership alike, usually to get around foot-dragging committees. Currently the House has a dozen task forces, about half working on issues as important as Medicare, AIDS, and drug policy.

Task forces achieved their greatest visibility when Gingrich was Speaker, when they became a vehicle for his "adhocracy" approach of aggressively pursuing a legislative agenda and moving it through the legislative process as fast as possible. To do that, the Speaker sometimes bypassed committees, hand-picking members for a task force to draft bills such as a Republican version of Medicare reform. Democrats used the same strategy to bypass Ways and Means to write a welfare reform bill. But the most significant contribution of the task force has been writing bills that offer an alternative to what the relevant standing committees are likely to produce, and doing it more quickly.

A good example can be found in the attempt to pass legislation regulating tobacco. When the agreement between tobacco companies and the states reached Congress, the leadership, President Clinton, and key legislators such as Senator John McCain (R-Ariz.) worked outside the committee system to draft an acceptable bill. The tobacco bill did not pass, in large part because the tobacco industry "went public" with an advertising campaign against the bill, so it is doubtful that a committee-drafted bill would have fared better.

The use of a task force does have some advantages. It can overcome the paralysis that results from the divided partisan control of Congress and the presidency. Direct negotiations between the White House and congressional leaders can sometimes break long-standing deadlocks. On the other hand, task forces bypass mechanisms for accountability to the public and to most rank-and-file members. Bills are written without formal hearings or the opportunity to point out potential pitfalls and problems of the legislation. Rank-and-file members often are faced with voting on a huge package of legislation about which they know only what they read in the newspaper.

The general impact of task forces under Gingrich was to weaken the power of standing committees and their chairs. However, with Hastert as Speaker, committee chairs receive much more deference, and task forces have declined in importance.

Evaluating Committee Government

The division of labor provided by committees and subcommittees enables Congress to consider a vast number of bills each year. If every member had to review every measure in detail, it would be impossible to deal with the current workload. Instead, most bills are killed in committee, leaving many fewer for each member to evaluate before a floor vote. Committees also help members develop specializations. Members who remain on the same committee for some time gain expertise and are less dependent on professional staff and executive agencies for information.

But committee government also has disadvantages. By splitting off into subcommittees and developing expertise in a few areas, a House member runs the danger of being more responsive to narrow interests and constituencies and less responsive to national objectives when making national policy.

Over time, members of congressional subcommittees develop close relationships with lobbyists for the interest groups and staff in executive branch agencies affected by their work. Over the years, these three groups—legislators, lobbyists, and bureaucrats—get to know each other, often come to like and respect one another, and seek to accommodate each other's interests. These personal relationships can result in favorable treatment of special interest groups.

The division of authority and specialization of individual members mean that Congress as a whole often cannot get things done because both energy and power are fragmented. Most members of the majority party in the Senate and about half of those in the House chair committees or subcommittees. With their own bases of power, they are somewhat independent from party leaders. Thus, the opposition party in Congress often has difficulty mounting a coherent alternative to the president. The fragmentation of power also means it is relatively easy for the president's own party to block his initiatives.

However, without powerful committees, if the majority leaders are not strong, bargaining over legislation can become a free-for-all, with dozens of legislators striking individual deals for their favorite programs. Without strong committee chairs, individual members of Congress, often with no expertise or interest beyond a special interest, can hold a piece of legislation hostage in exchange for a tax loophole or bit of pork.

Many people believe that Congress is still ripe for reform. However, its burst of legislative energy early in 1995 suggests that when Congress fails to get things done, committee structure is only part of the reason. A cohesive House majority with strong leadership can pass legislation even with a complex committee structure. Conversely, if the public is divided and there is little strong leadership or incentive for members to carry out a legislative agenda, congressional structure only reinforces other impediments to action. As one member remarked, "How is a committee overhaul going to make me more courageous to do things I don't want to do now?"[71]

MINORITY POWER IN CONGRESS

In 1970, the thirteen African Americans then serving in the House of Representatives organized the Black Caucus, determined to gain some clout. Today, with all black Democrats in the House and some of their white colleagues holding membership, the Black Caucus encompasses one-fifth of the House Democratic Caucus. Paradoxically, in 2002, at a time when the caucus was at its all-time high in number of members, it wielded the least influence it had for two decades. The reason is that all of its members are Democrats, and they lost control of the House in 1995. The last year the Democrats were the majority party, black members chaired 26 percent of all House committees and many subcommittees, too. Black Caucus members have held their strength within the party organization, with two serving as chief deputy whips for the Democrats. (The House is currently the only venue for a leadership position because the only black member of the Senate lost her seat in 1998.) But a secondary party leadership position does not compare to the influence of a committee chair.

To be influential when Democrats are not in control of the House, Black Caucus members have had to find new allies while continuing to speak for their constituencies. This is a difficult task because there are deep policy divisions between the Black Caucus and the Republican leadership. One obvious reason why the caucus has little influence with the Republican majority is because it has no Republican members; another is that the black constituents of Republican House members tend to vote Democratic. More than 90 percent of black voters cast their votes for Al Gore in 2000, the largest, most solid bloc of voters for any party.

The only black Republican in Congress, J. C. Watts (who refused to join the Black Caucus), was chair of the Republican Conference, a member of its national campaign committee, and a spokesman for Republican policy. But in 2002, he announced that he would not stand for reelection, citing family reasons. Some believed he was unhappy with his party's failure to assign him a committee chairmanship. In fact, the Republican House leadership had few black allies among ranking committee

members or in the electorate in general, despite the fact that the party has been actively courting African Americans.

Members of the Hispanic Caucus are probably better positioned than the Black Caucus to form alliances with Republican leaders and chairs. This caucus, formed in 1976, had only eighteen members in 2000, but they are not nearly as unified on issues as are members of the Black Caucus. This is because Hispanic Caucus membership draws on a diverse group of Mexican, Puerto Rican, and Cuban Americans, whose constituencies split their votes among Republicans and Democrats. Also, like the Democrats, Republicans are aggressively pursuing the votes of Hispanics, who are now the largest minority in the United States. With population trends showing that the main base of their electoral support—white men—is eroding, Republicans have little choice but to increase minority representation within the party if they are to hold their majority.

Asian and Pacific Americans also have a caucus but publish no membership figures. The five Asians in the House and Senate (this excludes one

Staff

The term *Congress* encompasses not only elected representatives but also a staff of 17,700 people. This does not include the 7,000 that Congress employs in support positions—security, maintenance, and so forth. The cost of running Congress is substantial at nearly $3 billion per year, and almost $4 billion if the costs of all affiliated agencies are included.[72] As large as current numbers may seem, staff size has been falling since the early nineties, when Democrats made a 10 percent reduction. Much larger hits were sustained in 1995 when Republicans assumed control.

Still, Congress hires far more staff members than any other legislative body. The Canadian legislature, which is second in staff size, has only about 3,300 people.[73]

Types of Staff

Of the 17,700 aides, 2,500 are employed as committee staff, a number equal to the entire congressional staff in 1947. Another 11,700 serve as personal aides to members and are divided among the members' Washington and home district offices. Many are engaged in full-time constituency service; others are legislative aides, and one or two in each office do media work. Each House member receives a staff budget of about $600,000 and on average hires about twenty aides. Senators, who have no limit on staff size, are allotted from $1 to $2 million depending on state population. They employ anywhere from thirty to forty aides and in addition receive roughly $400,000 to hire three legislative assistants.[74]

The remainder of the 17,700 serve as administrative personnel in congressional support agencies or work

nonvoting delegate) are a diverse group of Chinese, Japanese, and Pacific Islander descent, but all are Democrats. Like Hispanics, Asians are substantially underrepresented in the House and hold no top leadership positions.

Currently only seven states and Puerto Rico have Hispanic representation in the House (there are no Hispanic senators), and only three states and two territories have Asian representation, compared to twenty states and the District of Columbia who send black representatives to the House. With the population gains registered in the 2000 census, and given their concentration in a small number of states, Hispanic representation should increase dramatically, but Hispanics do not vote in proportion to their numbers. (They are 13 percent of the population but only 7.5 percent of registered voters.) Yet, Hispanics did make the best showing of any underrepresented group in the 2002 elections, winning four more seats in the House. This will not automatically translate into greater power in the House, however. Because African Americans have a stronger show of voters, across the board and in a greater number of

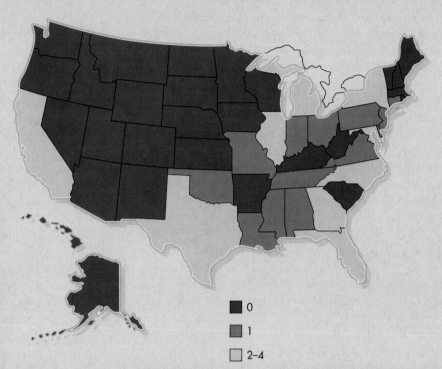

■ 0
■ 1
□ 2–4

Number of African American members of 108th Congress, 2003–2005.

states, they have a say in far more state delegations than do Hispanics and Asians. While black Americans went overwhelmingly Democratic in the 2000 election, Hispanics divided their votes 62 to 35 percent between Gore and Bush.

Unless this changes, the Black Caucus, with its greater political unity, will probably remain the special interest caucus best able to target its clout.

SOURCE: *CQ Daily Monitor,* November 7, 2002, 46–48.

for the Senate and House leaders, who have much larger staffs than rank-and-file members. One of the reasons for staff size is the heavy demand for constituency service. Another reason is that members of Congress try to develop their own expertise and sources of information so they will not have to rely on the executive branch. To this end, staff in support agencies carry out various research functions. The General Accounting Office checks on the efficiency and effectiveness of executive agencies, the Congressional Research Service conducts studies of public issues and does specific research at the request of members, the Office of Technology Assessment provides long-range analyses of the effects of new and existing technology, and the Congressional Budget Office provides the expertise and support for Congress's budgeting job.

Staffers do most of the background work on the complex foreign and domestic issues that cross the members' desks every day. To research difficult problems, they can call on the seven hundred full-time congressional research staff (CRS) in the Library of Congress. To illustrate how important their work is, we can consider the early days of the Gulf War in 1991 when Congress was scrambling to keep up with the president's fast-moving policy. CRS was called on to research everything from Iraq's economic strengths and weaknesses, weapons programs, and culture, to the historical applications of the War Powers Resolution. All this information was pulled together in a briefing paper that "outlined the issues, analyzed the options, described legislation already on the books, listed applicable congressional hearing reports, and presented a chronology of events." Such reports are available to all members online and are periodically updated.[75]

Impact of Staff

The size and competence of staff have both positive and negative effects. By giving testimony at hearings and markup sessions, legislative and research staff can have great influence on the technical content of bills. The two top CRS social security experts have a combined fifty-five years of experience working on the issue and have contacts with experts in the academic world, in all the relevant federal agencies, and with the interest groups that lobby on behalf of Social Security recipients.[76] No member of Congress on his or her own would have the time to develop this kind of expertise, yet without it, competent legislation could not be written, and Congress would not have the background it needs to challenge facts and figures presented in communications from the executive branch.

On the negative side, some scholars have argued that although large numbers of congressional aides may be necessary, they create paperwork and have a tendency to produce ever more research, committee work, and hearings. More information is collected than is possible for members to digest. Some argue that members have become office managers rather than legislators who have time to think about policy. Congressional staffers have been accused of reducing the amount of discussion members have with one another over policy issues. As former senator David Boren (D-Okla.) complained, "Very often, I will call a senator on an issue, and he won't know anything about it. He'll ask me to get someone on my staff to call someone on his staff. It shuts off personal contact between senators."[77] This means the compromises and adjustments necessary to make policy are sometimes made by technicians rather than elected representatives.

Through their service, staffers gain a great deal of experience and the opportunity to create a network of contacts that can help them should they decide to run for Congress. Almost one hundred members of the 107th Congress were former congressional staffers.

What Congress Does

The importance of Congress is reflected in the major, explicit constitutional powers the Founders gave it: to lay and collect taxes, coin money, declare war and raise and support a military, and regulate commerce with foreign governments and among the states. Essentially, most of the named powers the Constitution gives to the national government were given to Congress. (See the "After 9/11" box for a discussion of plans to keep Congress functioning after a terrorist attack.) These and other powers specifically mentioned in the Constitution are called the *enumerated powers* of Congress.

Congress also has *implied* powers; that is, it can make all the laws "necessary and proper" to carry out its enumerated powers. Although the Founders did not necessarily foresee it, this tremendous grant of power covers almost every conceivable area of human activity.

Lawmaking

In each congressional session in the past decade, between six thousand and nine thousand bills and resolutions have been introduced. From 5 to 9 percent of these measures have passed, but most die in committee. Of the measures passed, many are trivial, such as resolutions congratulating the winners of the Super Bowl or World Series or bills naming local courthouses. A number of the bills passed each year are private; they resolve an issue an individual or private party has with the government, such as citizenship status or a monetary claim. Our concern is with public bills, those that, when passed, become laws affecting the general public.

Turning a bill into a law is like running an obstacle course. Because of the need to win a majority at each stage, the end result is almost always a compromise. The formal steps by which a bill becomes a law (see Figure 2) are important but do not reveal the bargaining and trade-offs at every step in the process. Those opposing a bill have an advantage because it is easier to defeat a bill than pass it.

Introduction

Bills may be introduced in either the House or the Senate, except for tax measures (which according to the Constitution must be initiated in the House) and appropriations bills (which by tradition are introduced in the House). This reflects the Founders' perceptions that on fiscal issues Congress would be more responsive to the people than the president and that the House would be more responsive than the Senate.

Although the president initiates about half of all legislation passed, only members of Congress can introduce bills. Interest groups or the president must find a congressional sponsor for a proposed bill.[78]

Referral and Committee Action

After a bill's introduction, it is referred to a standing committee by the Speaker of the House or the presiding officer in the Senate. The content of the bill largely determines where it will go, although the Speaker has some discretion, particularly over complex bills that cover more than one subject area. Many such bills are referred to more than one committee simultaneously.

Once the bill reaches a committee, it is assigned to a subcommittee. Bills receiving subcommittee approval go to full committee, and after approval there go to the full House. Bills that get out of committee usually become law. One of the main functions of committees is to screen

	HOUSE	SENATE	PRESIDENT
Bill Introduction ↓	Given a number	Given a number	
	Referred to committee	Referred to committee	
In Committee ↓	Referred to subcommittee	Referred to subcommittee	
	Hearings held	Hearings held	
	Markup	Markup	
	Recommend passage or kill the bill	Recommend passage or kill the bill	
	Rules committee action (setting terms of debate)		
On the Floor ↓	Debate and amendment, if allowed under rule (usually one day)	Debate and amendment (days or weeks)	
	Vote on passage	Vote on passage	
In Conference ↓	Conference Committee reconciles different versions		
	Conference report adapted	Conference report adapted	
To President	Vote on veto override (if necessary)	Vote on veto override (if necessary)	Signs or vetoes

F I G U R E 2 ■ How a Bill Becomes a Law

These formal steps do not include the informal negotiations, discussions, and compromises that take place throughout the process. Neither do they include the efforts interest groups make to influence the decisions or the comments legislators receive from their constituents.

bills with little chance of passage. (If a committee kills a bill, there are procedures that members can use to try to get the bill to the floor, but these are used infrequently.)

The markup stage in both committee and subcommittee is legally open to the public yet barely visible to it. Consequently, lobbyists fill most of the hearing rooms. For critical meetings, lobbyists will hire messengers to stand in line for them, sometimes all night, and then pack the hearing room. Members who receive financial or other support from groups affected by the legislation often face intense and direct pressure to vote a particular way in committee. Sometimes lobbyists mob members as they leave the hearing room.

Scheduling and the Rules Committee

Once a House committee approves a bill, it is placed on one of four "calendars," depending on the subject matter of the bill. The Senate has just two calendars separat-

ing private and public bills from treaties and nominations. Bills from each calendar are generally considered in the order that they are reported from committee. In the House, the **Rules Committee** sets the terms of the debate over the bill by issuing a rule on it. The rule either limits or does not limit debate and determines whether amendments will be permitted. A rule forbidding amendments means that members have to vote yes or no on the bill; there is no chance to change it. If the committee refuses to issue a rule, the bill dies.

The Rules Committee is not as independent or powerful as it once was. In earlier years, the committee was controlled by a coalition of conservative Democrats and Republicans who used the committee to block liberal legislative proposals including, for decades, meaningful civil rights proposals. But the committee now functions as an arm of the majority leadership.[79] The Speaker uses his majority to fashion rules to control and expedite floor action.

CONTINUITY IN GOVERNMENT

The hijacked plane that crashed into the Pennsylvania countryside on September 11, 2001, was believed headed for Washington, D.C., to slam into either the White House or the Capitol building. The White House is protected against such attacks in ways the Capitol is not. Safeguards include antiaircraft artillery on the White House roof and bunkers nearby for speedy evacuation. In addition, since the Cold War, there has been a drill for loading the president and designated key officials onto planes and keeping them aloft during an attack. And if all this fails, the Constitution provides a line of succession to the presidency and vice presidency (see Chapter 11).

There has never been a comparable emergency security plan for Congress as a whole, even though the Capitol building, with its large cupola and fewer fortifications, is more vulnerable than the White House. No one wants the seat of a popularly elected government to look like an armed camp. Historically, the main arrangement for the physical safety of members of Congress during an enemy attack has been their evacuation from Washington to a bunker in the hills of West Virginia.

What would have happened if the plane had hit the Capitol and killed or maimed dozens or even a few hundred members of Congress? While Congress

was beginning to grapple with that possibility, it was faced with a variation on the dilemma when anthrax spores sent through the mail contaminated its offices. Speaker Dennis Hastert (R-Ill.) decided to shut down the House, the first closure in its history. Senate majority leader Tom Daschle (D-S.D.) kept the Senate in operation, but members had to evacuate much of their meeting space while the areas were checked for anthrax exposure and decontaminated where necessary.

Of at least equal importance to protecting the lives of members of Congress is having a comprehensive plan for the continuity of government should its members be killed or disabled. During the early weeks after the 9/11 attacks, the White House began assembling a shadow government at a secret location outside Washington. These one hundred or so officials, including Vice President Dick Cheney, were to provide continuity in government in the event that high-level executive branch officials were killed in a subsequent attack on Washington.[1] The fact that no similar provisions were made for the legislative branch, even though it is legally the heart of representative government, led to calls for Congress to make its own continuity plans.

In a time of national emergency, possibly even chaos, continuity in leadership is essential. Who would make decisions on measures necessary to respond to and recover from a terrorist attack? In the first nine months after the 9/11 attacks, Congress passed fourteen new laws and nineteen resolutions, and it had seventy-three other bills and resolutions under consideration. The resolutions may not have been necessary, but much of the legislation dealt with the emergency situation by providing funds for disaster relief, ordering new security measures in mass transport and public facilities, authorizing the manufacture and stockpiling of antidotes in the event of a bioterrorism attack, and appropriating money for recruiting and training special personnel and the acquisition of new weapons systems. Then, too, the normal daily business of government was conducted. And having a visible government carrying on day-to-day business and taking necessary defense measures would be essential for maintaining public order and social stability in times of national disaster. To plan for such emergencies, both the House and the Senate have established Continuity Committees.

One of the first contingencies planners had to deal with is that the Constitution does not adequately provide for the replacement of dead or stricken members of Congress. Governors can appoint temporary successors to Senate seats, but there is no legal mechanism other than by special election for replac-

Debate in the House

Debate on a bill is controlled by the bill managers, senior members of the committee that sent the bill to the full chamber. The opposition, too, has its managers who schedule opposition speeches. "Debates" are not a series of fiery speeches of point and counterpoint. They are often boring, given to sparse audiences, some of whom are reading, conversing, or walking around. After the time allotted for debate is over, usually no more than a day, the bill is reported for final action.

The Senate

Because the Senate is a smaller body, it can operate with fewer rules and formal procedures. (Table 2 summarizes House and Senate differences.) It does not have a rules committee. A lot of work is accomplished through the use of privately negotiated unanimous consent agreements, which allow the Senate to dispense with standard rules and define terms for debate and amending a specific bill. As the Senate's workload has increased and its sense of collegiality decreased, it has become more difficult to get opponents to accept

When anthrax contaminated House offices, Gary Ackerman (D-N.Y.) set up an office outside.

Susana Raab photography

House or Senate members. The Senate had foreseen the dangers of such loopholes during the Cold War and passed a constitutional amendment with provisions for temporary appointments to the House. The House chose not to act on the proposal.

Areas of legal ambiguity about how and where a dislocated Congress would conduct its business also need to be clarified. The Constitution stipulates that neither chamber of Congress can meet away from its usual place of business unless it is approved by the other chamber. This may be a minor technicality in time of emergency, but the reality is that Congress has had no fixed backup office and assembly space. Congress is now searching for a permanent backup facility, considering sites as far as one thousand miles from Washington.

Another legal uncertainty is whether a regrouped Congress could conduct official business if it did not meet the constitutional standard for a quorum. A legal quorum has come to be defined as half of the living membership, but if more than half of Congress were incapacitated but not dead, would any action Congress took be legal?[2]

In addition to filling in the legal loopholes, Congress has been dealing with some of the practical problems as well, such as how the two chambers would stay in communication should

an evacuation of the Capitol or city occur. Evacuation drills and simulation exercises were also planned to prepare for quick and orderly departure. All senators were given Blackberry e-mail machines and have had their whip pagers (the devices that call them to the floor when a vote is pending) connected to a police notification system. Key congressional staff have been designated for evacuation, too, and have been provided with "fly-away" kits with all the materials and equipment needed to conduct legislative business. In addition, provisions have been made to include members of the press in the evacuation and perhaps even a mobile recording studio. The secretary of the Senate said, "The press has got to be there because the American people need to know that their government is functioning."[3]

1. A comprehensive source for reviewing congressional proceedings on these issues is the "Continuity of Congress" site created by the American Enterprise Institute. It includes the texts of, and hearings on, proposed constitutional amendments and new legislation, as well as links to dozens of newspaper and journal articles on the subject. See www.aeipoliticalcorner.org/continuity.htm.
2. This issue is discussed by Norman Ornstein in "Preparing for the Unthinkable: Bush's 'Shadow Government' Plan Is a Start—But Only a Start," *Wall Street Journal,* March 11, 2002; and "What If Congress Were Obliterated? Good Question," *Roll Call,* October 4, 2002.
3. This quote and other material in the paragraph are drawn from Mark Preston, "Senate Plans Disaster Drill," *Roll Call,* May 16, 2002.

ing House members who have died. Special elections take from three to six months to organize even in the best of times (candidates have to declare and campaign for office). And in the case of incapacitation rather than death, there are no mechanisms for replacing either

a unanimous consent agreement. A few senators can and do delay or kill important bills.

Without a unanimous consent agreement, there is no rule limiting debate, and there are no restrictions on adding amendments. Opponents can add all sorts of irrelevant amendments to pending legislation. One senator held up an antibusing bill for eight months with 604 amendments.

The other major mechanism for delay in the Senate is the **filibuster.** This is a continuous speech made by one or more members to prevent the Senate from tak-

ing action on a bill. Before 1917, only unanimous consent could prevent an individual from talking. Today a **cloture** vote of three-fifths of the members closes or ends debate on an issue thirty hours after cloture is invoked. Then the measure must be brought to a vote.

Both liberals and conservatives use filibusters (as they do nongermane amendments). The filibuster developed in the 1820s when the Senate was divided between slave and free states. Unlimited debate maintained the deadlock.[80] For over a century, the filibuster was used primarily to defeat civil rights legislation. It took a cloture

TABLE 2   Important Differences between the House and Senate

House	Senate
Constitutional Differences	
Must initiate revenue bills	Confirmation power over many major presidential appointments
Initiates impeachment and votes on impeachment bills	Tries impeached officials
Apportioned by population	Ratification power over treaties
	Two members from each state
Differences in Operation	
More centralized; procedures more formal:	Less centralized; procedures less formal:
Speaker's assignment of bills to committee hard to challenge	Assignment of bills to committee appealable
Rules Committee fairly powerful in controlling time and rules of debate	No rules committee; limits on debate come through unanimous consent or cloture of filibuster
Nongermane amendments forbidden	Nongermane amendments permitted
Scheduling controlled by majority party	Schedule and rules negotiated between majority and minority leaders
More impersonal, less clubby	More personal
Power less evenly distributed	Power more evenly distributed
Members highly specialized	Members are generalists
Emphasizes tax and revenue policies	Has more foreign policy responsibilities
Changes in the Institution	
Power of key committees and the leadership increasing	Senate workload and partisanship increasing; informality breaking down
House procedures more efficient with less debate and fewer amendments	Members are becoming more specialized; debate and deliberation are less frequent
More organizing and bill writing outside committees	

vote to end seventy-three days of debate and get the 1964 Civil Rights Act to the floor for a vote.

During Clinton's first year in office, Republicans used the filibuster quite frequently to block proposals from the Democratic Senate majority. In fact, in 1991–1992 alone, the filibuster was used thirty-five times, compared with only sixteen times during the entire nineteenth century. After Republicans took control of the Senate in 1995, the new majority leader, Trent Lott (R–Miss.), found himself frustrated by Democratic filibusters. "We are completely balled up and it's not my fault. I want us all to sober up here now and get on with the business of the Senate," he complained.[81]

Filibusters prevent domination and precipitous action by the majority. But by requiring sixty votes to end debate, they impede the majority's right to legislate and contribute to gridlock.[82]

Conference Committee

The Constitution requires that the House and Senate pass an identical bill before it becomes law. Thus, the House and Senate versions of the bill must be reconciled. Sometimes the house that passed the bill last will simply send it to the other house for minor modifications. But if the differences between the two versions are not minor, a **conference committee** is set up to try to resolve them. The presiding officers of each house, in consultation with the chairs of the standing committees

that considered the bill, choose the members of the committee. Both parties are represented, but there is neither a set number of conferees nor a rule requiring an equal number of seats for each chamber.

If the leadership of both parties is really committed to passing a version of a bill, they may negotiate the compromise themselves and essentially impose it on the committee. They may even negotiate the final version with the president to avoid a veto.

But on many bills, conference committees have tremendous latitude in how they resolve the differences between House and Senate versions. One White House aide has described them as "a no man's land," because there are no formal rules governing how they operate.[83] Sometimes a bill is substantially rewritten, and occasionally a bill is killed. It is even possible to add provisions to a bill that were not in the version passed by either chamber. The power of conference committees to alter bills after their passage is why they are sometimes called "The Third House" of Congress.[84]

Once the conference committee reaches an agreement, the bill goes back to each house, where its approval requires majority votes. It cannot be amended at that point, so Congress must either "take it or leave it." In the Senate, however, any individual member can challenge a provision added in conference that was not related to the original bill. In practice, both House and Senate accept most conference reports, because members of both parties in each chamber have participated in working out the compromise version.

Conference committees clearly can be very influential in determining the final provisions in major legislation, yet the work they do happens almost completely out of public view. Knowing how to win a seat on a conference committee—that is, to participate in rewriting an important piece of legislation—is an essential skill for any legislator.

As should be clear from this overview of the complex legislation process, to be a successful member of Congress—to get bills passed or to keep them from being passed, to influence other members, or to rise to a position of leadership—a legislator must know how to use to his or her advantage the inner workings of the legislative process. The conference committee is an important part of that process, as is the tactical use of a full range of parliamentary rules and procedures within the congressional system.

Presidential Action and Congressional Response

The president may sign a bill, in which case it becomes law. The president may veto it, in which case it returns to Congress with the president's objections. The president also may do nothing, and the bill will become law after ten days unless Congress adjourns.

Most presidents have not used the veto lightly, but when they do, Congress does not usually override them. A two-thirds vote in each house is required to override a presidential veto. Congress voted to override only nine of former President Reagan's seventy-eight vetoes, only one of President George H. Bush's forty-six, and only two of Clinton's thirty-four.

Overseeing the Federal Bureaucracy

As part of the checks-and-balances principle, it is Congress's responsibility to make sure the bureaucracy is carrying out the intent of Congress in administering federal programs. This monitoring function is called **oversight** and has become more important as Congress continues to delegate authority to the executive branch. For a variety of reasons, Congress is not especially well equipped, motivated, or organized to carry out its oversight function. Nevertheless, it does have several tools for this purpose.

One tool is the General Accounting Office, created in 1921, which functions as Congress's watchdog in oversight and is mostly concerned with making sure that money is used properly.

Another, but not very effective, method of oversight is committee hearings. Members can quiz representatives from agencies on the operation of their agencies, but often the hearings go into great detail about some particular problem of minor importance and neglect broader policy questions. Scheduling conflicts and the pressure of other business often mean that a member's attention is not focused on committee hearings. Nevertheless, officials in agencies view hearings as a possible source of embarrassment for their agency and spend a great deal of time preparing for them. This is never more true than when Congress decides, often for political reasons, to seek maximum media coverage for hearings.

This points to one of the problems with the use of these proceedings to carry out the oversight function: Hearings are often held after oversight has failed. This was painfully clear after the corporate collapses of 2002—Enron, Global Crossing, and WorldCom, for example—when four Senate and three House committees held hearings in succession, all vying for media time. If Congress had been monitoring federal agencies such as the Securities and Exchange Commission to see whether they were carrying out their regulatory mandates, some of the enormous costs to employees and investors might have been prevented. Indeed, in this case, Congress not only did not exercise oversight but contributed to weakening the SEC's regulatory powers (see "You Are There" in Chapter 9 for an example). Prominent members of oversight committees, such as Joseph Lieberman (D-Conn.) and Christopher Dodd (D.-Conn.), who represent a state where some of the failed businesses were headquartered and who had received large campaign contributions from them, actively worked to prevent new regulations from being adopted. Occurring after the failures, the hearings were more aftersight than oversight but served as a way for Congress both to consider remedial measures and to make it seem like it was doing something about the problem.

The incentive of committee members to place constituent protection—these businesses bring a lot of jobs to their home districts—and big campaign donor interests above rule enforcement is one weakness of oversight. But the fragmentation of oversight responsibility is also a problem for its effective implementation. There were at least seven Senate committees and six House committees with some oversight responsibility for the accounting and financial practices that led to so many industry bankruptcies in 2002. And many more committees were responsible for oversight of the defense and intelligence agencies whose failures were so widely publicized after 9/11 (see Chapter 12).

Congress can also exercise its oversight function through informal means.[85] One way of doing this is to request reports on topics of interest to members or committees. In a given year, the executive branch might prepare five thousand reports for Congress.[86] Moreover, the chair and staff of the committee or subcommittee relevant to the agency's mission are consulted regularly by the agency. But one can question whether any serious oversight is exercised informally. There are few electoral or other incentives for members to become involved in the drudgery of wading through thousands of pages of reports or for doing a really thorough job in any area of oversight, at least until a crisis arises or public confidence in the economy or government institutions is threatened.

The primary means for congressional oversight is its control over the federal budget. Congress can cut or add to agencies' budgets and thereby punish or reward them for their performance. It strengthened its control when it shifted in the 1970s from permanent to short-term authorization for many agencies.[87] Members with authority over an agency's budget can use that power to get benefits for their constituents, and by going along with the members' wishes, agencies may stand a better chance of having their budget requests approved. There is an incentive in this relationship for congressional committees to exercise oversight.

Budget Making

An increasingly large part of the job of Congress is to pass a budget. The Constitution gives Congress the authority to control the federal purse by collecting taxes and spending money, but in the 1920s, Congress delegated the authority to prepare the annual budget to the president (the Office of Management and Budget, or OMB). In years when the president's party does not control Congress, the congressional majority produces its own budget, with priorities distinctly different from the president's.

Congress is aided in its budget setting by the Congressional Budget Office (CBO), which provides expertise to Congress on matters related to the budget and economy. Before the establishment of the CBO, members of Congress felt they were junior partners in budget making because they had to depend on information provided by the president, his budget advisers, and the Office of Management and Budget. Because the CBO is responsible to both parties in Congress, it provides a less politically biased set of forecasts about the budget than does the administration or the leadership of either party.

The topic of budget making may sound dull, but without money, government cannot function. Real priorities are reflected not in rhetoric but in the budget.

Congressional budgeting has two basic characteristics. First, the process is usually incremental; that is, budgets of one year are usually slightly more than budgets of the past year. Normally, Congress does not radically reallocate money from one year to the next; members assume agencies should get about what they received the previous year. This simplifies the work of all concerned. Agencies do not have to defend, or members scrutinize, all aspects of the budget.

A second feature is that Congress tends to spend slightly more on federal agencies in election years.[88] This tendency increases in times of unemployment and moderates in times of inflation. Members are also more likely to vote for increasing federal payments to individuals (such as veterans' benefits or Social Security cost-of-living increments) in the years they are up for reelection.[89]

There are exceptions to this general rule, such as times of war or domestic crisis. The first budget submitted after 9/11, for example, requested a huge increase in defense spending. There are also instances of ideological budgeting. Reagan's domestic budget cuts and increased military spending in 1981 were clearly an exception to incrementalism. The Contract with America approach to cutting programs wholesale is another exception.

The budget for any fiscal year is not approved in a single piece of legislation. Since the 1970s, the budget has been reviewed and passed as thirteen separate bills, each of which focuses on a different area of expenditure, such as defense. All budget legislation goes through a process similar to but more complicated than other bills. To grasp the complexity, we have to understand the distinction between budget authorizations and budget appropriations. **Authorizations** are acts that enable agencies and departments to operate, either by creating them or by authorizing their continuance. They also establish the guidelines under which the agencies operate. Although authorization bills might specify funding levels, they do not actually provide the funding. **Appropriations** are acts that give federal agencies the authority to spend the money allocated to them. Both authorizing and appropriations bills must pass each house, and differences must be resolved in conference.

Typically, authorizations precede appropriations, although in practice it is not always so clear. These budgetary procedures are not defined in the Constitution but are determined by House and Senate rules, which can be, and often have been, changed. The standing committees that oversee the work of the agency or program being funded usually work out the authorizations. The House Interior and Insular Affairs Committee and the Senate Energy and National Resources Committee, for example, review the authorization of the Park Service in the Department of the Interior; the agricultural committees write authorizations for the Department of Agriculture. Close ties often exist between the agency being reviewed and the authorizing committee, which can cause proposed funding levels to be set without consideration of the overall demand on federal revenues. But the real power to limit spending rests with the Appropriations Committees.

The House and Senate each have an Appropriations Committee, and each of these has thirteen subcommittees corresponding to the thirteen functional areas into which budget allocations are divided. The Appropriations Committee assigns a spending limit for each area, and the relevant subcommittee then decides how to apportion it among the agencies in its jurisdiction. In reviewing an agency's proposed budget, the subcommittee is not bound to fund it at the level requested in the president's budget proposal or the authorization bill. Nor do the subcommittee's funding proposals have to be accepted by the whole committee. Although appropriations subcommittees may develop close ties with the

agencies they review, the committee as a whole does not, and thus it may not be as generous as its subcommittees. In the bills it sends to the floor for a vote, the Appropriations Committee can increase or cut the previous year's funding levels, or it can eliminate an agency altogether.

Both the House and Senate also have Budget Committees, but these are not as powerful as the Appropriations Committees. The Budget Committees have existed only since 1974 and were created to work with the CBO on big-picture issues such as economic forecasting and fiscal planning, including deficit management and controlling overall spending. Each year the House Budget Committee has to prepare a budget proposal that sets out spending goals in the context of projected federal revenues. The House and Senate committees cannot enforce their guidelines, however.

During the budgetary process, committees hold hearings, but these have become a sideshow to the main event. The real decisions are made in private negotiations, and budgets produced after months of direct negotiations among congressional leaders, their staffs, administration aides, individual members, and the president. The rest of Congress is often left with a "take it or leave it" budget package laid out in the thirteen separate appropriations bills.

Congress and the Public

As we have noted, one of the most frustrating things about Congress for the average citizen is the "messiness" of the legislative process. Not only is the process of crafting laws incredibly complex, but it provides so many places along the way where individual legislators and interest groups, often for seemingly (or truly) selfish motives, can exact concessions from the people who want to pass the bill. Add to that the partisan bickering, with

Democrats picking a proposal apart simply because a Republican introduced it or vice versa, and casual observers are ready to throw up their hands in exasperation.

It seems that the more media exposure Congress gets, the less supportive the public is of its work. Now, as never before, every step—or misstep—that members of Congress take is carried to every part of the nation. Or, as the *New York Times* commented, "Modern Washington is wired for quadrophonic sound and widescreen video, flashed by fax, computer, 800 number, overnight poll, FedEx, grassroots mail, air shuttle and CNN to every citizen in every village on the continent and Hawaii too. Its every twitch is blared to the world, thanks to C-SPAN, open meetings laws, financial-disclosure reports, and campaign spending rules, and its every misstep is logged in a database for the use of some future office seeker."[90]

Some media attention is good, because we prize open government in a democracy. But too much is not so good, because in a heterogeneous society we rely on compromise to achieve our public goals, and, under the harsh glare of media, there are fewer opportunities to compromise and deliberate without fear of losing votes back home.

Of the three branches of government, the public has been least supportive of Congress, where the processes of democracy are exposed for all to see. For some years, the public gave its highest level of support to the Supreme Court, the institution that is most isolated from the public. Historically little of the disagreement, negotiation, and compromise of the Court has taken place in public view. This has changed somewhat at the beginning of the twenty-first century with a deeply divided Court and its highly publicized split ruling that decided the 2000 presidential election (see Chapter 13). The Court lost ground to the president and Congress in approval ratings after 9/11 when the nation was rallying around its leaders in the war on terrorism. But whereas President Bush's public approval ratings stayed high for months, those of Congress quickly plunged (see Figure 3).

Too often, for the public's taste, congressional debates are rancorous rather than measured and more focused on how prospective legislation will affect private interests rather than the public interest. None of this is surprising, of course, in a complex society where people and groups do have quite different interests and views of the world. Members themselves contribute to the poor image of Congress by belittling the institution and promising voters a change when they campaign for office. They denigrate Congress to get themselves elected.[91]

That being said, however, public attitudes about Congress are themselves conflicted. One famous political scientist once observed that Americans hate their Congress but love their own member of Congress.[92] Two-thirds of the public approve of their own representative, compared to just over half who approve of Congress as a whole and about the same percentage who approve of congressional leaders (see Figure 1, page 284).[93]

The public thinks that most members of Congress care more about power than about the best interests of the nation, care more about special interests than the people, and lose touch with the people quickly after being elected. In early 2002, members of Congress placed sixteenth on a list of seventeen professions ranked by trust, one notch below business leaders. Only 42 percent said they trusted members of Congress to tell the truth.[94]

The public is not mistaken in its impression of a cozy relationship between Congress and special interest lobbies. The U.S. Association of Former Members of Congress estimates that as many as 15 percent of ex-members become lobbyists after the one-year cooling-off period mandated by a 1989 ethics law. In 1999, 142 former members were registered lobbyists; others worked as "consultants" and were not required to register.[95] Even during the cooling-off period, a former member can work as a lobbyist, as long as it is not on Capitol Hill. Within six months of resigning as Speaker-elect of the House, Robert Livingston had signed up thirty-one clients for about $350,000 worth of business, more than double his annual salary as a representative.

After one year, ex-House members have easy access to their former colleagues because they retain rights to use the dining room and gym and have floor privileges for life—although they are prohibited from lobbying on the floor. (The Senate has no such restrictions.)

Despite all this, the idea of Congress as enshrined in the Constitution is esteemed by the public. It is the people *in* Congress and the way Congress works that the public dislikes. But most of the public is poorly informed about the work of Congress. They are much more likely to know about ethics violations and sexual improprieties of members of Congress than they are about the legislation passed in any session. Thus, the public evaluation of Congress as accomplishing "not

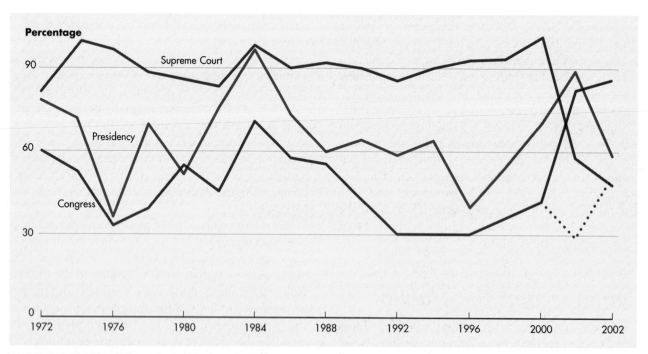

FIGURE 3 ■ Confidence in Political Institutions

A higher percentage of the public consistently said it had more confidence in the Supreme Court than in the presidency and Congress until the Supreme Court's decision to settle the 2000 election in what appeared to be a partisan way reduced confidence in the Court. Then, after the terrorist attacks of September 11, 2001, confidence in both the presidency and Congress soared.

SOURCE: Gallup Poll, June 2002 (www.gallup.com).

By Paul Szep for the *Boston Globe*

much" or "nothing at all" stems in part from the public's lack of awareness of what Congress has actually done. This pattern persists even with C-SPAN coverage and even though most local papers each week print a congressional scorecard with the voting records of local legislators.

Conclusion: Is Congress Responsive?

Congress is certainly responsive to individual constituents, but is it responsive to the policy demands of the national constituency?

The pressures of elections and of constituency service seem to undermine Congress's ability to focus on public policy. Pressure to be in the home district meeting constituents competes with legislators' desires to do a good job at lawmaking and to work more efficiently. The public wants Congress to be responsive to their individual needs and group interests, but then it looks down on the institution for its pork barrel politics and big spending.

Pressure to raise money for reelection campaigns incurs obligations to interest groups that may not be consistent with either the members' or constituents' views. Indeed, part of the problem congressional leadership from both parties has in articulating a clear vision is that so many of them have become dependent on the contributions of PACs for their campaign funding. This puts them in the position of having to support some interests that are not consistent with voters' views or interests.

The procedures and organization of Congress also give individuals and small groups opportunities to block or redirect action. This is particularly true in the Senate, where procedures allow a minority of senators to engage in unlimited debate, unless sixty members vote to stop it. The fragmented committee and subcommittee structure in both houses offers many venues in which action can be killed. Political parties have been strengthened in recent years but are not strong enough to protect against the pressure of lobbyists or outraged constituents. All of these factors mean that Congress continues to be more responsive to individual than to national needs. It is difficult to get consistently good legislation when special interests, partisan concerns, and pork-hungry legislators dominate the lawmaking process.

Perhaps surprisingly, Congress can legislate better than people commonly think, both despite and *because* of its frustrating procedures. The legislative process sometimes works well *because* individual legislators (especially senators) can derail bills, *because* interest groups can make their voices heard effectively, and *because* parties nitpick at each others' proposals. Our whole system of government is based on checks and balances. Laws are effective only if people accept them. That means that representatives have to try to build a consensus for their legislation. If legislators build a consensus from competing views, all sides have an incentive to make the outcome work.

Consensus takes time to develop. But occasionally Congress does pass bills with lopsided margins of approval from both parties. We learn more from the media about conflict than compromise, however. Yet by resolving conflicts and developing a consensus, Congress can legislate effectively. It might be said that some of the faults people find with Congress are in fact its greatest strengths, because those "shortcomings" allow Congress to accomplish its objective: passing legislation that has widespread support in an increasingly fragmented society.

Snowe Votes against Removal

rue to her reputation as a middle-grounder, Senator Snowe and other moderate Republicans, including fellow Maine senator Susan Collins, tried to devise an exit strategy from the trial by drafting a "finding of fact."[96] This resolution contained a list of the offenses they believed Clinton had committed but took no position on whether they warranted removal from office. Snowe said they wanted to avoid the certainty of legal terms like *guilty* and *conviction*.[97] The drafters proposed bringing the resolution to a vote in the Senate before the vote on the formal charges. This would give those who did not believe Clinton guilty of impeachable offenses the option to censure him for misconduct while voting not guilty on the articles of impeachment. A group of moderate Democrats devised their own censure resolution that they hoped to put to a vote after the vote on articles of impeachment.

These compromises were labeled "impeachment plus" and "conviction lite" and were brushed aside.[98] The Republican leadership was set on Clinton's guilt and wanted a straight vote for or against conviction. The Democratic leadership, knowing the Republicans did not have the votes to convict, resisted any alternative to exoneration.

Quite possibly, either resolution drafted by moderates could have served as an alternative to impeachment proceedings had their supporters been able to bring them to the floor before the impeachment momentum was underway.

But once the politics were in motion and lines firmly drawn, partisans on either side began lining up their votes. The process passed out of reach of those compromisers who feared the institutional damage to both congress and the presidency that a partisan struggle could bring.

With a vote on the articles unavoidable, the senators stood at their desks as the chief justice polled them in alphabetical order: "Senators, how say you? Is the respondent, William Jefferson Clinton, guilty or not guilty?" When he reached the S's, Senator Snowe answered, "Not guilty," twice. Snowe was joined by her junior colleague from Maine and three other moderate Republicans from the Northeast, including James Jeffords, who two years later left the Republican Party. Five other Republicans joined them in voting not guilty on the perjury charges in Article I. All forty-five Democrats also voted to acquit the president on both articles.

In explaining her vote, Snowe said that there was insufficient evidence to support some charges, and where there was convincing evidence, the charges did not meet the constitutional standard of high crimes and misdemeanors necessary to remove a president from office. At the same time, she was unsparing in her criticism of Clinton's behavior.[99] She wanted to censure the president for inappropriate behavior, but she did not want to make it more than it was

nor to help set a precedent for removing a president for what would appear to be partisan reasons.

As one Democratic senator said, "the Founders made it extremely hard to remove a popularly elected president." A Republican colleague agreed, saying that while everyone is entitled to an opinion of the president, impeachment is hard and "was meant to be hard."[100]

Snowe got some satisfaction in her calls for a limited form of censure. The judge hearing evidence in the sexual harassment case, although dismissing the suit for lack of cause, fined Clinton for misleading the jury in his testimony. Ultimately Clinton agreed to a temporary suspension of his right to practice law in Arkansas. But by the end of the year, Snowe was so tired of the ideological warfare in Congress that she joined with a Democratic colleague and other moderates in reestablishing the Centrist Coalition. "Everything up here is very divided. There's no instrument for breaking down those walls of separateness. It is degrading to the Senate. I hear it at home. It has not gone unnoticed by the public."[101]

Snowe went on to easy victory in her 2000 reelection campaign, unopposed in the Republican primary and winning 69 percent of the vote in the general election. And she did no permanent damage to her position in the party. In 2001, she became the first Republican woman ever to win a full-term seat on the Senate's powerful Finance Committee.

 To learn more about Senator Snowe's decision and the Clinton impeachment process, go to this chapter's "You Are There" exercises on the text Web site.

Key Terms

constituency

reapportionment

redistricting

gerrymander

franking privilege

constituency service

casework

pork barrel

informal norms

institutional loyalty

reciprocity

specialization

special interest caucus

going public

Speaker of the House

majority leader

minority leader

whips

standing committees

markup

seniority rule

Rules Committee

filibuster

cloture

Conference Committee

oversight

authorizations

appropriations

Further Reading

Michael Barone et al., *The Almanac of American Politics* (Washington, D.C.: National Journal, since 1980). Offers background on each member, his or her district, and voting record. Revised every two years since 1980. A volume similar in format and publication schedule is *Congressional Quarterly's Politics in America,* compiled by CQ staff. The most recent edition is for the 107th Congress (Washington, D.C.: CQ Press, 2001).

Robert A. Caro, *Master of the Senate* (New York: Knopf, 2002). When you have some time on your hands, check out this monumental study of a master legislator at work. This is the second in a projected three-volume study that tracks the House and Senate career of former president Lyndon B. Johnson, arguably the most powerful Senate majority leader in U.S. history.

Timothy Cook, *Making Laws and Making News* (Washington, D.C.: Brookings Institution, 1989). A revealing account of how media coverage affects the legislative process in the U.S. House.

Roger H. Davidson and Walter J. Oleszek, *Congress and Its Members,* 7th ed. (Washington, D.C.: CQ Press, 2000). Now a classic general reference work on Congress, revised every few years.

Marjorie Margolies-Mezvinsky, *A Woman's Place: The Freshmen Women Who Changed the Face of Congress* (New York: Crown, 1994). Representative Margolies-Mezvinsky reflects on the changes brought about in Congress by the largest group of women representatives ever.

Timothy Phelps and Helen Winternitz, *Capitol Games: Clarence Thomas, Anita Hill and the Story of a Supreme Court Nomination* (New York: Hyperion, 1992). A close look at the Senate hearings on Clarence Thomas's nomination to the Supreme Court.

Pat Schroeder, *24 Years of House Work and the Place Is Still a Mess: My Life in Politics* (Kansas City, Mo.: McMeel, 1998). One of the most outspoken women in Congress from 1973 to 1995, Schroeder tells how a woman succeeded in this male-dominated institution.

Steven Waldman, *The Bill: How the Adventures of Clinton's National Service Bill Reveal What Is Corrupt, Comic, Cynical—and Noble—about Washington* (New York: Viking, 1995). How a bill became a law in the 1990s, with a focus on Clinton's national service and student loan proposals.

 ## Electronic Resources

thomas.loc.gov/

Links to texts of bills, the Congressional Record (reporting entire floor debates), and committee hearings and reports. It is also a good site for congressional history and information about individual members. Want to know how many Asian Americans are in Congress and who they are? How much members of Congress make? Who the leadership is? This page links to all kinds of statistics about Congress, along with links to the home pages and e-mail addresses of members.

www.c-span.org/

The Web site of the two cable stations that cover congressional proceedings. It is a treasure trove of information on congressional history as well as current affairs. It also has an archive of frequently asked questions about Congress and resources for students of American government.

www.washingtonpost.com/

This is the Web site of the Washington Post, *whose news coverage of Congress is unrivaled.*

www.cq.com/

The Web site of Congressional Quarterly, *publisher of the most authoritative weekly review of congressional affairs.*

 ## InfoTrac College Edition

Search for the following articles in the InfoTrac database:

Adler, David Gray. "Virtues of the War Clause," *Presidential Studies Quarterly* (December 2000).

Crowley, Michael. "On the Hill: Switch Hit (Jim Jeffords)," *New Republic* (December 31, 2001).

Devins, Neal. "Congress as Culprit: How Lawmakers Spurred on the Court's Anti-Congress Crusade," *Duke Law Journal* (October 2001).

Loomis, Burdett. "The Senate and Executive Branch Appointments," *Brookings Review* (Spring 2001).

For more articles, enter:

"United States Congress" in the Subject Guide;

"United States Congress House" in the Subject Guide;

"United States Congress Senate" in the Subject Guide.

 ## American Government Resources

Visit the Government Institutions section of the Wadsworth American Government Resources Web site (politicalscience.wadsworth.com/amgov/) for a variety of tools to help you explore Congress further. Included are simulations, video clips, Microcase exercises, and a wealth of other activities.

THE PRESIDENCY

Eric Gay/AP

Should the President Get a New Cabinet Department?

ou are California congresswoman Jane Harman, the most senior Democrat on the House Intelligence Committee's Subcommittee on Terrorism and Homeland Security. Over the past few years, your committee work has made you one of the House's leading experts on counterterrorism.[1] It is July 2002, and you must decide whether to support President Bush's proposal to create a new cabinet department for homeland security.

This bill would authorize the most massive reorganization ever attempted in the executive branch. The president described the new agency as having "clear and efficient organizational structure" divided into four responsibilities: Border and Transportation Security; Emergency Preparedness and Response; Chemical, Biological, Radiological and Nuclear Countermeasures; and Information Analysis and Infrastructure Protection. But the proposed $38 billion agency seems to have an organizational structure that is anything but "clear and efficient." It involves reshuffling departments within twenty-two different agencies and reassigning as many as 170,000 employees. The responsibilities of the new department would extend to border security, coastal patrols, immigration, biological and nuclear weaponry, public health, airport security, disaster management, police work and firefighting, domestic surveillance, and other intelligence gathering and

analysis, to name just a few. The department would assume responsibility for the United States Coast Guard, the United States Customs Service, the Immigration and Naturalization Service (including the Border Patrol), the Animal and Plant Health Inspection Service, the Federal Emergency Management Agency, and programs scattered other places in the federal bureaucracy, from the Department of Justice to the Department of Health and Human Services. Such a large segment of the executive branch would be affected by this legislation that yours is only one of twelve committees marking up the bill.

You have as much expertise as any member of Congress to evaluate this proposal. You were a special counsel to the Department of Defense in the Carter administration. Since coming to Congress in 1993, you have served on the Intelligence and Armed Services committees and developed a reputation as a hawk on both budget deficits and defense spending. After serving three terms, you decided to run for governor of California, but, entering the race late in the campaign, you lost the primary. You had plenty to keep you busy: engaging in activism on women's health issues and reproductive rights, practicing law and running a business that made you a multimillionaire, not to mention raising four children.

In 2000, you were reelected to the House and regained your seat on

Jane Harman (D-Calif.) and the organizational chart of the Office of Homeland Security.

Richard Drew/AP

the Intelligence Committee. You are also a member of the powerful Energy and Commerce Committee, where you deal with telecommunications, the Internet, trade, and some environmental issues, including hazardous materials. You were cochairing an investigation into terrorism and homeland security needs when 9/11 happened and were subsequently asked to submit a report on intelligence lapses prior to the attacks.

At one level, the president's proposed plan makes sense to you. The existing agencies to fight terrorism are uncoordinated and do not communicate very well. To remedy this, the president did create, by an executive order shortly after September 11, the Office of Homeland Security. As director, Bush named his old friend Tom Ridge, the governor of Pennsylvania and a former House member. But this office has little authority and, moreover, is not very accountable to the Congress or the public. The White House even resisted congressional calls for the director to testify on the work of the new office.

If Homeland Security became a cabinet department, its head would be a cabinet secretary subject to Senate approval. He would be obligated to appear before congressional committees, give testimony on the department's work, and justify its budgets. Such status would help Congress better fulfill its oversight responsibilities, as well as be able to mandate further reorganizations if necessary.

The current organization seems neither effective nor efficient. You wonder how one man with a small office in the White House and a staff of fewer than twenty can coordinate the counterterrorism work that is currently divided among forty-six different agencies overseen by more than eighty congressional committees and subcommittees. The organizational chart for the agency was so complicated and impenetrable, it looked like a parody of bureaucratic organization (see photo). Ridge had no authority to cross all these jurisdictional lines, and even if he tried, the bureaucratic turf issues would surely defeat him. To remedy this problem, you had sponsored a bill to strengthen the office.

But is the proposed new cabinet department the best solution? You do not want to be—or to be seen as—a partisan grandstander on the issue of homeland security. Yet there are serious nonpartisan issues to consider. Three questions have come to the fore: Is the proposed agency the most effective means for achieving homeland security? Is the authority the president asks for consistent with the constitutional separation of powers? And will the new agency erode civil liberties?

In the many hearings held since 9/11 on government failures that may have contributed to the disaster, the major theme has been the bureaucratic morass and turf wars that diminish the effectiveness of intelligence and other security agencies. Your reaction: "'Turf' is the dirtiest four-letter word in Washington. To win any turf war, the Office of Homeland Security needs sufficient authority."[2]

But it is not clear that the new organization would resolve turf problems. In fact, there already are serious turf problems. For example, neither the FBI nor the Central Intelligence Agency would be part of the proposed new department. These omissions seem less a result of some organizational rationale than of the power of the agencies

to resist being suborned in a new cabinet department. Intelligence gathering should be at the core of what a homeland security organization would do, and you are not sure how the new agency can be successful with the FBI and CIA on the outside.

Moreover, in the president's bill you are confronted by a different turf battle—that between the executive and legislative branches. The president has been asking for extraordinary powers for executive agencies ever since the 9/11 attacks. In the immediate weeks after 9/11, the general mood in the Congress was to give the president what he thinks necessary to fight terrorism. But as time passes, many members in both parties are concerned about eroding the constitutional separation of powers. The bill calls for Congress to give the White House discretionary power over up to 5 percent of the money appropriated to any account within the new cabinet department, even for the purpose of liquidating some function Congress had authorized. He is also asking for a suspension of civil service and bargaining rights guaranteed executive agency employees so that he or the department head would have the authority to hire, fire, and transfer employees.

Defending the country against terrorist attacks is essential, but is it necessary for Congress to surrender some of its constitutional powers to do so? And what is your responsibility to one of your party's most loyal constituencies: organized labor. Should you open the door to narrowing job security and bargaining rights of executive branch employees?

You and others are also concerned about the loss of civil liberties in the war on terrorism, and this huge agency could further accelerate that loss. One prominent civil liberties lobbyist said of the bill, "If you like the idea of a government agency that is 100 percent secret and 0 percent accountable, you'll love the new homeland security department." As someone whose legal specialization was constitutional rights, this is a serious concern. While you did not oppose Bush's earlier proposal to try suspected terrorists by military tribunals, you did introduce legislation to guarantee some of the defendant's most basic civil liberties.

The president is pushing for a quick decision; he submitted the bill mid-June, demanding action before the August recess. How can Congress carry out its proper function of checking executive power, overseeing the bureaucracy, and guarding the purse strings if it does not take the time to give thorough consideration to the bill?

The president prepared the bill in secret, with no consultation with Congress or other leaders. This is unprecedented for legislation with such far-reaching consequences, and it is not at all clear that the effects have been carefully thought through. Dick Armey (R-Tex.), whom the Speaker chose to lead the bipartisan committee that will take the bill through the House, says, "I don't see this as a task of daunting challenge."[3] But in the Senate, Fred Thompson (R-Tenn.) thinks differently: "We don't do anything for years, and then try to do the biggest reorganization of government in fifty years real fast."[4]

You want to rely mainly on your expertise in deciding how to vote on this bill. But there are other considerations. Yours is a district of moderates, and Bush's approval ratings have been astronomical; it is not a great time to oppose his initiatives, especially on counterterrorism, and especially when many in Congress pushed him to create a cabinet department in the first place. You have never won your district by a big margin, and your seat is considered far from safe in 2002. But if you are vulnerable in the next election, it will almost certainly not be on defense issues. The aerospace industry is very important to your district's economy, and you earned your reputation as a defense hawk supporting their interests.

You realize this is an extraordinary situation that calls for some balance between protection of civil liberties and ensuring domestic security. But the war on terrorism is ill defined and may go on for decades; civil liberties given up in the heat of emotion over 9/11 may be very difficult to reclaim.

Moreover, you wonder about the efficacy of this plan. Moving boxes around on an organizational chart does not necessarily bring about change. The same lack of communication between agencies could continue in a new structure. And there is no guarantee that old turf battles will not carry over into the new department, defeating the purpose of the reorganization.

Do you approve the new cabinet position and expanded powers for the executive branch, and do it quickly, before the recess? Or should you side with those who want to delay the vote until Congress can study the organizational plan and delegation of authority more thoroughly?

Pharaohs, consuls, kings, queens, emperors, czars, prime ministers, and councils of varied size served as executives in other governments before 1789. But no national government had a president, an elected executive with authority equal to and independent of a national legislature, until George Washington was elected president of the United States.

The Founders viewed their creation as a chief executive officer, someone who would serve as both a check on bills passed by Congress and the administrator of those enacted into law. He would also be head of state, chief diplomat, and commander of the armed forces. At its inception, the presidency was a not very powerful office in a fledgling country that had few international ties and virtually no standing army. The office's first occupants were drawn from among the Founders; a few of them, Washington and Thomas Jefferson especially, served with some reluctance. Nevertheless, they were willing to lend their reputations and abilities to the cause of stabilizing the new government, and as a result, they had the opportunity to influence the direction of its development.

Throughout the nineteenth century, except for the Civil War period, real power at the national level resided in Congress, so much so that Woodrow Wilson characterized the federal arrangement in the 1880s as "congressional government."[5] Thus, between Andrew Jackson and Franklin Roosevelt, many who sought the presidency were "ordinary people, with very ordinary reputations."[6] There were powerful exceptions, such as Abraham Lincoln, Theodore Roosevelt, and Woodrow Wilson, and a few men of exceptional achievement before their presidencies, such as Ulysses Grant and Herbert Hoover, who failed badly in the White House.

Today the president of the United States is among the most powerful people in the world. By the 1970s, the scope of that power led one historian to write about an "imperial" presidency.[7] Yet most presidents since World War II have suffered reelection defeats and at times have seemed almost powerless to shape events affecting the national interest. The immensely popular war hero Dwight Eisenhower was unable to buck Cold War sentiment and prevent the buildup of the military-industrial complex. John Kennedy (1961–1963), who enjoyed an extraordinary success rate in a conservative Congress, was stymied in getting civil rights legislation accepted. Lyndon Johnson's (1963–1968) domestic goals and chances for reelection were derailed by a war that took Richard Nixon (1969–1974) six years to end. And Nixon had to resign from office because of his Watergate cover-up. Ronald Reagan (1981–1988), one of our most popular recent presidents, was so frustrated when Congress thwarted his foreign policy initiatives that he condoned illegal activities, producing the Iran-Contra scandal and a tarnished personal reputation. Gerald Ford (1974–1976), Jimmy Carter (1977–1980), and George H. Bush (1989–1992) failed to get re-elected. At century's end, Bill Clinton (1993–2000) discovered that instead of an imperial presidency, the country had something closer to an "impossible" or "imperiled" presidency.[8] Although he won reelection handily, most of his domestic agenda, other than economic growth and deficit reduction, was sidetracked by one congressional investigation after another.

Little wonder that one survey of the time found that 52 percent of Americans would rather spend one week in jail than serve one term as president and that many Americans, instead of believing the president was too powerful, believed he was too weak to battle Congress and interest groups.[9] When George W. Bush entered office at the beginning of the twenty-first century, he brought with him a retinue of Washington professionals and set out to restore the presidency to its former preeminence.

In this chapter, we will consider the paradox of presidential power and presidential weakness. After describing the growth of the modern presidency, we look at the constitutional provisions—the qualifications for the office and its responsibilities. We explain why a bureaucracy grew up around the presidency at the same time the president was becoming a more personal and accessible representative of the American people. Inevitably, the growth of the modern presidency has affected the balance of power between the executive and legislative branches, and that is another topic of this chapter.

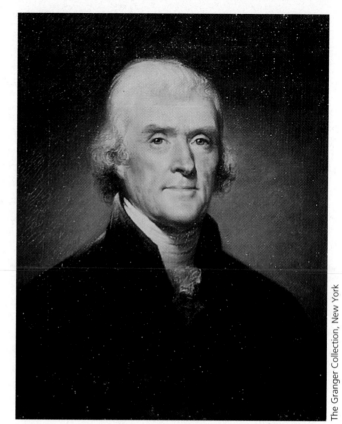

Although political scientists rank Jefferson as a great president, he did not consider the office, or his performance in it, very important. His instructions for an epitaph listed what he thought were his three main accomplishments in life: authoring the Declaration of Independence and a Virginia law guaranteeing religious freedom and founding the University of Virginia. He did not include his two terms as president.

The Growth of the Presidency

Someone once said that Americans were lucky because we always got presidential leadership when we needed it: during the birth of the nation, the Civil War, and foreign crises. This implies that our needs change, that we need more government and executive leadership during crises and less at other times. Presidential power was traditionally supposed to return to its "normal" low profile after we resolved special problems.

This expectation may have been realistic before the United States became a unified country that accepted Washington as the center of governmental power. But once the country stretched from Mexico to Canada and from the Atlantic to the Pacific, once it had a standing army, international trade aspirations, and the ambition to dominate the hemisphere, governmental power gravitated to Washington. The image of Thomas Jefferson sitting at his desk in isolation week after week conducting the presidency by personal correspondence was a quaint memory even twenty years later when Andrew Jackson was dubbed the "people's president."[10] Jackson was the

first to act assertively to fulfill the popular mandate he saw in his election—the first to veto a bill because *he* did not like it. Thirty years later, Lincoln assumed extraordinary powers during the Civil War, suspending civil liberties, overturning state laws, and boldly interpreting the Constitution to say the Union was indivisible.

Teddy Roosevelt, who has been called the "preacher militant," used the presidency in an unprecedented way to challenge corporate power and to argue for labor reform and better living conditions for average Americans. He also saw an imperial role for the United States in world politics, especially through military expansion, and led the country toward those "entangling alliances" that George Washington had warned against. Eight years after Roosevelt left office, Wilson became the first twentieth-century president to lead us into a major foreign involvement, World War I, and was the first president ever to travel to Europe while in office.

As we have already seen in Chapter 3, the Great Depression and World War II led to a large expansion in the role of the national government and tremendous growth in presidential power. Franklin Roosevelt was elected president in 1932 because people thought he would help them. His policies, which he called the New Deal, put the national government and the presidency in direct contact with many citizens for the first time. People saw presidential leadership as a way to deal with national needs. It was Roosevelt, not Congress, who provided the vision and legislative program to cope with the economic emergencies of the Great Depression. In his first inaugural address, he told Americans that he would ask Congress for "broad executive power" to fight the crisis, equivalent, he said, to what he might be granted if an enemy had invaded the country. The enactment of New Deal programs led to an expansion of the executive branch because new agencies had to be created and new civil servants hired. This increased the president's power by making him more important as a manager and policymaker. And after the United States entered World War II, Roosevelt assumed additional powers as a hands-on commander in chief.

Radio and television contributed significantly to the expansion of presidential power. As an integral part of national life by the 1930s, broadcasting made the news seem more immediate and compelling. Along with the wire services, it gave people a way to follow presidents and a way for presidents to "sell" their policies and provide leadership. Because it is easier to follow one person than many (as in Congress), the media helped make the presidency the focal point of national politics. With his radio broadcasts during the Great Depression, Roosevelt became a kind of national cheerleader, a one-man band of optimism, persuading the public that solutions were at hand.

Congress is not structured to provide this kind of national leadership. Its 535 members are divided into two houses and hundreds of committees and subcommittees and come from both major political parties. It is difficult for either the majority or minority leadership to develop and articulate national policy goals or to keep its members faithful to them.

Even after the fifteen years of crisis receded, Roosevelt's successors had little opportunity to shrink the presidency. With the United States emerging from World War II as the preeminent world power, and with the onset of the Cold War, Congress was willing to cede even more leadership to the president to counter Soviet rivalry. Responsibilities as chief diplomat and commander in chief of the world's largest military establishment have made the president a principal actor in world politics, a platform not afforded to any other government official or institution.

Of his postwar administration, Harry Truman said, "Being president is like riding a tiger. You have to stay on or get swallowed." And thus we have today's presidency, with everyone looking to see whether the man is riding the tiger or the tiger is swallowing the man.

Terms of Office

Qualifications

There are formal, constitutional qualifications to be president: One must be a "natural born citizen," at least thirty-five years old, and have resided in the United States for at least fourteen years before taking office.

Informally, it also helps to be a white male with roots in small-town America; a Protestant of English, German, or Scandinavian background; a resident of a state with a large population; and a good family man. In recent years, however, this profile has broadened considerably as society has become more tolerant of diversity. Nevertheless, although eroding, gender and racial barriers remain.

Rewards

In return for services rendered, the Constitution authorized Congress to award the president "a Compensation," which could be neither increased nor decreased during a president's term of office. Our first seventeen

America does not have a monarchy, but it does have political dynasties. Both major party candidates in 2000 were sons of important American political leaders. George W. Bush, shown with his father, former president, vice president, CIA director, and Republican House member George Bush, is also the grandson of a U.S. senator.

George Bush Presidential Library

presidents received an annual salary of $25,000. Grant got the first raise in 1873, a doubling to $50,000; by the time Nixon took office, the salary was $200,000, where it stayed through the end of the Clinton years. A majority of the public was not eager to see it go higher, even as executive salaries skyrocketed in the 1990s, and by century's end, the president's salary ranked 785 among those of the 800 highest-paid CEOs.[11] Supporters of a pay increase argued that the president's low salary was holding down the base pay for all other top-level officials and interfering with government recruitment. Congress agreed, and in 2001 the president's salary was bumped to $400,000; he continues to receive $50,000 for expenses and $100,000 for travel.

In addition, there are *substantial* fringe benefits. These include living quarters in one of the world's most famous mansions, a rural retreat in Maryland (Camp David), the best health care money can buy, and fleets of cars and aircraft. After leaving office, the president is entitled to a generous pension, as well as a security detail and money for an office and staff. In 2001, Americans spent $2.5 million on their five surviving ex-presidents, with more than one-quarter going to the ailing Ronald Reagan.[12]

Tenure

Presidents serve four-year terms. The Twenty-second Amendment limits them to serving two terms (or ten years if they complete the term of an incumbent who dies or resigns). Four presidents died in office from illness (Harrison, Taylor, Harding, and Franklin Roosevelt), and four were assassinated (Garfield, McKinley, Lincoln, and Kennedy).

Presidents can be removed from office for "Treason, Bribery, or other high Crimes and Misdemeanors" (Article II). The Founders established the impeachment option as part of the system of checks and balances, a final weapon against executive abuse of power. It was adapted from British law, where it had served, according to Jefferson (who was not present at the writing of the Constitution), as "an engine more of passion than of justice."[13] (Britain last used impeachment in 1788, just as the United States was writing it into its Constitution.) James Madison, who *was* present at the drafting, objected to the inclusion of the phrase "and other high crimes and misdemeanors" in the impeachment article precisely because he thought it was so vague it could be used for political purposes. Through a compromise, it was retained.[14]

As retained then, impeachment was intended to be a legal procedure for removing a president who had committed crimes, not as a means for removing a president for political or partisan reasons. The charges brought against a president in an impeachment proceeding would be "political," only in the sense, Alexander Hamilton wrote in *Federalist* 65, that they are "injuries done immediately to society itself."

The procedure is cumbersome and meant to be; the Founders did not intend for the president, as head of state and the only nationally elected official in government, to be removed from office easily. Like the other major powers, the impeachment process is divided. The House has the power of **impeachment**—that is, the authority to bring formal charges against the president (similar to an indictment in criminal proceedings)—but the Senate has the power of removal. The Founders recognized that impeachment could become the partisan tool Jefferson feared because the process itself would "agitate the passions of the whole community." If trying the charges were left to the popularly elected House, Hamilton wrote in *Federalist* 65, "There will always be the greatest danger that the decision will be regulated more by the comparative strength of parties, than by the real demonstrations of innocence or guilt." What body, Hamilton asked, other than the (then-unelected) Senate would be likely to feel *confidence enough in its own situation,* to preserve, unawed and uninfluenced, the necessary impartiality between an *individual* accused, and the *representatives of the people, his accuser?*" (italics in original).

The House holds hearings to determine whether there is sufficient evidence to impeach, and if a majority votes yes, the president is impeached, and the process moves to the Senate, where a trial is held with the chief justice presiding. Conviction requires a two-thirds vote of members present in the Senate and results in removal from the presidency and, if the Senate so votes, loss of the right to hold other federal office. Under a 1958 law, conviction also results in the loss of all benefits, including pension, office and staff allowance, and Secret Service protection. The Senate can assign no additional punishment. Where applicable, however, a president removed from office can be subject to criminal charges and prosecuted through the court system.

Only three presidents have been targets of full impeachment proceedings. Andrew Johnson, who came to office on Lincoln's assassination, was a southerner who was unpopular in his own party; he was impeached by the House in a dispute over enforcement of Reconstruction policies in the post–Civil War South. The Senate failed to convict by a single vote. A century later the House Judiciary Committee voted to impeach Richard Nixon on obstruction of justice and other charges stemming from the Watergate scandal, but by resigning, Nixon prevented a vote by the full House and almost certain conviction in the Senate. Once out of office he avoided possible indictment on criminal charges through a full pardon granted by his successor, Gerald Ford.

In 1998, Bill Clinton became the third target of the process when the House voted to open an unrestricted

inquiry into possible grounds for his impeachment. After a $47 million investigation by Independent Counsel Kenneth Starr, the House held hearings and voted two articles of impeachment against the president. (See Chapter 10's "You Are There.") All eleven charges of perjury and obstruction of justice stemmed from Clinton's testimony in the Paula Jones civil suit and from statements about his relationship with a White House intern. After a nationally televised trial, the Senate failed to convict, with neither article receiving even a majority of the vote.[15] Still, Clinton stands as the only *elected* president ever to be impeached. He was also cited for contempt and fined by a federal judge for giving misleading testimony to a grand jury. At the end of his term, Clinton made a deal with the independent counsel that any remaining charges would be dropped in exchange for his acceptance of a temporary suspension of his license to practice law in Arkansas.

Succession

The original wording of the Constitution provided only that presidential powers "shall devolve on the Vice President" should the president die, resign, be removed, or become incapacitated. At the time the Constitution was written, it was assumed that the vice presidency would be occupied by the man who had been the runner-up in the presidential election. It was left to Congress to make provisions for a situation in which both the presidency and the vice presidency had been vacated. When Lincoln was assassinated, there were no provisions for replacing the vice president when the office was left vacant. Had Andrew Johnson been convicted in his impeachment trial, the presidency would

have gone to the president pro tempore of the Senate who, according to rules in effect at the time, was the next in line of succession.

Not until 1947, two years after the death of Franklin Roosevelt had put the virtually unknown Harry Truman in the White House, did Congress pass the Presidential Succession Act. It establishes the order of succession of federal officeholders should both the president and the vice president be unable to serve. The list begins with the Speaker of the House, followed by the president pro tempore of the Senate, and then proceeds through the secretaries of the cabinet departments in the order in which the departments were created.

The Succession Act has never been used because we have always had a vice president when something happened to the president. The Twenty-fifth Amendment was ratified in 1967 to ensure, as much as possible, that this will always be the case. In the event that the vice presidency falls vacant, the amendment directs the president to name a new vice president acceptable to majorities in the House and Senate. The amendment has been used twice. Nixon chose Gerald Ford to replace Spiro Agnew, who resigned after pleading no contest to charges of taking bribes when he was a public official in Maryland. After Nixon resigned and Ford became president, Ford named Nelson Rockefeller, the former governor of New York, as his vice president.

The Twenty-fifth Amendment also charges the vice president and a majority of the cabinet—or some other body named by Congress—to determine, in instances where there is doubt, whether the president is mentally or physically incapable of carrying out his duties. This provision was meant to provide for situations in which it is unclear who is or should be acting as president, such as when James Garfield was shot in July 1881. He did not die until mid-September, and during this period he was completely unable to fulfill his duties. In 1919, Woodrow Wilson had a nervous collapse in the summer and a stroke in the fall and was partially incapacitated for seven months. No one was sure about his condition, however, because his wife restricted access to him.

Under the amendment's provisions, the vice president becomes "acting president" if the president is found mentally or physically unfit to fulfill his duties. As the title suggests, the conferral of power is temporary; the president can resume office by giving Congress written notice of his recovery. Reagan followed the spirit of this section in 1985. Before undergoing cancer surgery, he sent his vice president, George H. Bush, a letter authorizing him to act as president while Reagan was unconscious. George W. Bush took the same precaution in 2002 when he was briefly under anesthesia during a medical checkup.

If the vice president and other officials who determined the president unfit do not concur in his judgment that he has recovered, they can challenge his return to office by notifying Congress in writing. Then it falls to Congress to decide whether the president is capable of resuming his duties.

The issue of succession arose again after the terrorist attacks of 2001. Faced with the possibility of an attack on Washington that might take the lives of, or incapacitate, everyone in the immediate line of succession, the Bush administration, just hours after the attack, activated an emergency plan established during the Eisenhower administration to provide for continuity of government in case of a nuclear attack. As we described in Chapter 10, a shadow government of from seventy-five to one hundred senior executive branch officials (serving in a rotation system) were removed to a secret, fortified location outside the capital where they lived and worked underground twenty-four hours a day. They were given responsibility for carrying on essential work if elected leaders were disabled. Bush also issued executive orders defining a line of succession in each cabinet department. As an added precaution, in the immediate months after the 9/11 attacks, Vice President Dick Cheney spent much of his time at undisclosed locations that the press referred to collectively as "the Bunker."

Duties and Powers of Office

The foundation of presidential power lies in the formal duties assigned by the Constitution. Additional authority stems from powers the federal courts have ruled are implied by the president's constitutional mandate, dele-

gated authority from Congress, and informal powers acquired through the exercise of office.

Chief Executive

The enumeration of the president's formal duties begins with the simple statement that "Executive power shall be invested in a President." The Founders expected Congress to make policy and the president to administer it. The Constitution has few provisions that describe the president's administrative duties, but it does invest the president with the authority to demand written reports from his "principal officers." It also directs the president to nominate the most important officers of the executive branch.

The president was given power neither to create executive branch departments and agencies nor to fund them—this authority resides with Congress—so his means for controlling the bureaucracy over which he presides lies in his formal powers of appointment, his implied power to remove those he appoints, and his delegated authority to propose reorganizations and to make budget recommendations.

Appointing Officials

The total number of appointments sent by the president to the Senate is in the tens of thousands, but almost all of these receive approval without review, including the military commissions and promotions the president makes as commander in chief. The president nominates about three thousand people to civilian positions in the

State Department and other federal agencies, two-thirds of whom do not require confirmation. Only about six hundred of the most important policymaking jobs—heads of regulatory agencies, boards and commissions, cabinet secretaries and ambassadors, and federal judges, for example—receive careful review by the Senate.[16] In many cases, televised hearings are held prior to a confirmation vote in the Senate.

In practice, the president's freedom to name people to some positions is limited by the custom of **senatorial courtesy.** This gives senators from the president's party a virtual veto over appointments to positions, including judicial appointments, in their states. As the leader of his party, the president has a political (not governmental) obligation to help senators from his party get reelected. So he usually defers to their political needs and wishes when making federal appointments in their home states, even though doing so limits to some extent his freedom to choose.

Presidents have more latitude in nominating people to positions with national jurisdictions, such as cabinet posts and seats on regulatory boards and independent agencies. It has become customary to give preference in some appointments to people with politically useful backgrounds, such as naming a westerner secretary of the interior, a person with union ties to be labor secretary, or a close associate of the president to be attorney general. But these considerations were never confining and, as traditions, are weakening.

It has also been customary for the Senate, no matter which party controls it, to approve the president's nominations to policymaking positions on the grounds that, having won the election, he is entitled to surround himself with people who can help put his policies in place. In the contentiousness of recent years, this practice also seems to be weakening. A Democrat-controlled Congress challenged several high-profile appointments made by Reagan and George H. Bush, and under Republican control, Congress tabled or defeated many of Clinton's nominations. George W. Bush's nomination of former senator John Ashcroft to be attorney general inspired a nationwide campaign against confirmation. But most unusual among attempts to stop Bush nominees was a filibuster led by Senator John McCain, Bush's rival in the 2000 Republican presidential primaries, to block all of Bush's nominees until he approved McCain's choice of a reform-minded candidate for the Federal Elections Commission. Until he was able to work out a compromise with McCain, Bush was forced to seek Democratic support to win cloture votes and to make provisional appointments when Congress was in recess.

Removing Officials

Although the power to remove appointees is not in the Constitution, presidents have it. Their power to name people they trust implies a power to remove those they find wanting, but because the power is not explicit, Congress has not always recognized it. The battle over removal powers was fought and largely won by Grover Cleveland, who on entering office in 1885 insisted on replacing many policymaking officials with his own appointees. Although the Senate challenged Cleveland, he persevered. His persistence is credited with helping revitalize a presidency still weakened by Andrew Johnson's impeachment.

In 1935, the Supreme Court refined this removal power by saying that presidents can remove appointees from purely administrative jobs but not from those with quasi-legislative and judicial responsibilities. Although this ruling protects many appointees, distinguishing quasi-legislative and judicial positions from those with no policymaking authority can be subjective.[17]

There is no ambiguity, however, about a president's removal authority over people he has appointed to policymaking positions with fixed-terms, such as regulatory boards, the Federal Reserve Board, and the federal courts. Presidents cannot remove these people. To grant the president the power to remove federal judges would interfere with the system of checks and balances between the executive and judicial functions of government.

Of course, presidents can appoint and remove their political aides and advisers at will; none of these appointments require Senate approval. Presidents also have wide latitude in replacing cabinet heads and some agency directors—even though these positions do require Senate confirmation—because they are seen as agents of presidential policy. This does not keep the Senate from trying at times to badger a president into firing one of his appointees, as it did repeatedly with Clinton's attorney general, Janet Reno. A president may give in for political reasons, but the Senate cannot compel him to do so.

Reorganizing Executive Branch Agencies

When the president enters office, a huge bureaucracy is already in place. Each new president has to be able to reorganize offices and agencies to fit his administrative and working style and to be consistent with the issue priorities he has set.[18] This can mean redrawing agency boundaries to promote coordination when actions overlap or duplicate each other. It may involve merging or abolishing offices or creating new ones.

Under a law existing from the Truman to the early Reagan administrations, presidents had the authority to submit such reorganization plans to Congress and, absent a veto by either chamber, the plans went into effect. But since the Supreme Court struck down the legislative veto in 1984, approval has been harder to win. Now every reorganization proposal is likely to get a thorough review in each house, and most are altered, sometimes severely.[19]

Thus, as we saw, when George W. Bush wanted to create a new cabinet-level Department of Homeland Security, reorganizing the jurisdictions of dozens of executive branch agencies, it required congressional approval. And because it required reassigning tens of thousands of federal employees, transferring funds, and authorizing new spending authority, this reorganization set up a classic turf battle, both within the bureaucracy and between the White House and Congress.

Within the White House Office itself, the president has a fairly free hand to reshuffle staff and offices (see the later discussion of the White House Office). Clinton created the National Economic Council to coordinate departments and agencies that shape economic policy and to show that economic issues were a high priority for him. He also established an office within the National Security Council to oversee counterterrorism efforts. And Bush created an office of Homeland Security within the White House, where it will remain even though Congress approved a cabinet department of the same name in 2002.

Budget Making

The Founders gave Congress, and particularly the House of Representatives, the power of the purse. For many years the president had a negligible role in managing executive branch budgets. Agency funding requests went to the House unreviewed and unchanged by the White House. But by the end of World War I, a general awareness had developed that a larger government required better management. In the Budget and Accounting Act of 1921, Congress delegated important priority-setting and managerial responsibilities that have given presidents so inclined the opportunity to dominate budgetary politics.

The 1921 act requires the president to give Congress estimates of how much money will be needed to run the government during the next fiscal year. The president's annual budget message contains recommendations for how much money Congress should appropriate for every program funded by the national government. Formulating the message requires the White House to examine all agency budget requests and to decide which to support or reject. This exercise allows the president and his staff to initiate the annual budget debate on their own terms.

In addition, the act created the Bureau of the Budget (BOB). Originally a part of the Treasury Department, BOB was meant to be the president's primary tool in developing budget policy. It was made a part of the newly created Executive Office of the President in 1939. Nixon changed BOB's name to the Office of Management and Budget (OMB) to stress its function of helping the president manage the executive branch.

The process of writing and passing the annual budget resolution is one of the greatest sources of friction in presidential-congressional relations, especially when the president and Congress have different priorities. Without funding, little is possible. Having the OMB within the Executive Office of the President gives the president an edge in dealing with Congress on budget issues because its hundreds of experts work only for the president. Congress's nonpartisan budget office, the Congressional Budget Office (CBO), prepares budget reports that are regarded as substantially more reliable than those of the OMB, but the policy initiative lies with the OMB and the White House because they prepare the first budget draft. The annual budget is huge and hard to read and understand. Because the president presents it to Congress and the public, he has the opportunity to shape the debate over spending priorities. Presidents who are little interested in the details of domestic policy, such as Reagan and both Bushes, do not get maximum political leverage out of the budgetary powers Congress has delegated them. But a president whose strength lies in the mastery of detail may be able to use those powers, as Clinton did, to dominate budgetary politics and the debate over deficit reduction.

The OMB not only proposes allocations for each department, agency, and program of the federal government, but it also monitors how and when executive branch agencies spend appropriated funds, their operating procedures, and the policies they develop. This gives the president another advantage over Congress, one that Reagan used to great advantage. By appointing agency and department heads who oppose policies he opposes but that Congress has funded, the president can issue directives that effectively bring policy implementation to a halt.

Other Executive Powers

In addition to the formal administrative powers granted under Article II and those delegated by Congress, federal courts have affirmed additional powers that presidents have claimed are necessary to the administration of the executive branch.

Executive Privilege Since the 1970s, the courts have upheld the presidential claim to **executive privilege,** the right of a president to refuse to make public some internal documents and private conversations. The rulings have argued that executive privilege is a power inherent in the president's duty as chief executive because without it, a president would not be able to get full and frank advice from his aides. Although ruling that the power is limited rather than absolute in scope, the courts have not defined its limits. In the landmark ruling ordering President Nixon to turn over tapes of Oval Office conversations to the Watergate special prosecutor (see Chapter 2's "You Are There"), the Supreme Court did establish that executive privilege cannot be invoked to withhold evidence material to an investigation of criminal wrongdoing.

In the 1970s, the federal courts requested that Congress specify the limits of the privilege, but it declined, leaving it to the courts to resolve each invocation of privilege that the president and Congress cannot resolve. President Clinton interpreted this power very broadly. He claimed that senior aides could not be required to answer certain questions put to them by a grand jury convened by the special prosecutor investigating possible obstruction of justice charges against the president. His reason was that their answers would make public the content of privileged conversations with the president. Clinton asked the federal courts to extend the cover of executive privilege to his conversations about political strategy with his aides and to those between his aides and the First Lady, who served as his political adviser and whom the courts had already recognized as serving in a quasi-official role. In 1998, the lower federal courts again confirmed the right to executive privilege and its application to conversations between the president, aides, and the First Lady. But it ruled against the president on the circumstances under which he invoked the privilege (withholding information from a grand jury hearing evidence about possible criminal wrongdoing), saying the aides' testimony might be relevant to the investigation. The administration did not appeal the ruling.

In 2002, President Bush took this power a step further when Congress, in its investigation of Enron's financial collapse, subpoenaed records of Vice President Cheney's meetings with executives from energy industries. The White House, claiming that executive privilege extended to the vice president, refused to turn over most of the documents, even after ordered to do so by a federal court.

Executive Orders Because the Constitution charges the president with ensuring that "the laws be faithfully executed," the courts have ruled that the president has inherent power to take actions and issue orders to fulfill that duty. This gives the president the authority to issue directives or proclamations, called **executive orders,** that have the force of law and are therefore a form of legislative power residing in the executive branch. In arguing for these powers, presidents have claimed that Article II of the Constitution grants them inherent power to take whatever actions they judge to be in the nation's best interests as long as those actions are not prohibited by the Constitution or by law. The

rationale is that Congress often lacks the expertise and ability to act quickly when technological or other developments require fast action and flexibility.[20] Recent examples of this use are the numerous Bush directives responding to problems created by the 9/11 attacks.[21]

The recording and numbering of executive orders did not begin until 1907, and although an effort was made to identify and retroactively number orders issued back to the Lincoln administration, it is uncertain how many have been issued over the years. Since 1946, Congress has required all executive orders, except those dealing with classified national security issues, to be published in the *Federal Register.*[22] Many of these orders have had a significant impact. Truman, for example, used an executive order to integrate the armed forces, Kennedy to end racial discrimination in public housing, and Lyndon Johnson to require affirmative action hiring by firms with federal contracts.

Presidents more commonly use executive orders to deal with organizational problems and internal procedures, such as Bush's post-9/11 orders establishing a line of succession in cabinet departments. Executive orders are also used to implement the provisions of treaties and legislative statutes that are ambiguously stated (perhaps deliberately) by Congress. In fact, presidents have used executive orders to make policies opposed by congressional majorities. Reagan and Bush used this power to ban abortion counseling in federally financed clinics and financial aid to United Nations–sponsored family planning programs. Clinton canceled these orders in his first week in office, but when George W. Bush succeeded him, he returned to the policies of Reagan's and his father's administrations.

Another significant use of executive orders is to manage the controversial system for classifying government documents and withholding information from the public. Clinton used his powers to declassify a huge number of documents, and again Bush used his powers to do the opposite, making public access to presidential papers and many other government documents much more difficult (see this chapter's "After 9/11" box). Thus, through the exercise of this inherent power of office, the presidency has acquired significant legislative authority. But as these examples illustrate, they are much more easily overridden than congressional acts.

The legality of executive orders can be, and occasionally are, challenged in federal court. Early in his presidency, George W. Bush ordered the posting of signs in union shops informing workers that they were not required to allow union dues to be withheld from their paychecks. A federal court ruled this was a misuse of an executive order.

A RETURN OF THE IMPERIAL PRESIDENCY?

Often in wartime or crises situations, a president demands greater latitude in exercising his powers of office in order to respond quickly to the problems the country is facing. Sometimes this demand corresponds to a president's own wishes to strengthen the office.

After the terrorist attacks of 9/11, George W. Bush assumed extraordinary powers both for himself and the executive agencies he presides over, especially the Department of Justice and the newly created Office of Homeland Security. He had no reluctance in exercising this power because he came into office with the goal of strengthening the presidency. He said the inherent powers of the office had eroded to "an unsettling degree over the past thirty years" and that he would use his administration to reclaim those powers. "I have an obligation to make sure that the presidency remains robust and that the legislative branch doesn't end up running the executive branch."[1]

His press secretary said Bush was especially unhappy about the president not having enough control over budgetary matters and use of the military. But Bush was clearly worried about personal privacy as well, as any president might after seeing the extraordinary invasion of the Clintons' personal lives during the previous administration. He told a group of schoolchildren at the end of his first year in office that the biggest sacrifice he had made in running for the presidency was privacy.[2]

Bush was especially unhappy with the rule established by FDR in 1934 that presidential papers belonged to the public rather than to the individual president. He stopped his daily habit of e-mailing his daughters and other relatives and friends because he did not want the messages to become part of the presidential record to which the public might someday have access. He did not believe that scholars or the public, or even congressional oversight committees, should have access to his personal communications or his discussions with White House staff or advisers. Although every president does have considerable right to privacy in communications with his advisers while he is in office, Bush believed it was not sufficient. Thus, shortly after taking office, he began exploring how he could use the inherent powers of office, such as executive privilege and executive orders, to bolster the presidency against congressional and public scrutiny.

After the attacks of 9/11, Bush was given an additional reason to make claims for less scrutiny of White House activities: national security. He referred to the period following the attacks as "wartime" and demanded he be granted the right to exercise the powers of a president leading a country at war. In the past, this has given presidents a platform from which to demand that Congress rubber-stamp any action taken in the name of national security. In this and earlier chapters, we have given examples of the uses and abuses of such powers: suspension of habeas corpus, limits on free speech rights, and internment of American citizens without indictments or trials and confiscation of their property. Woodrow Wilson got Congress to pass a law during World War I that permitted the arrest of any-

At a visit to an elementary school, the president first learns about the attack on the World Trade Center towers.

one who spoke publicly against the war or conscription. It was used to imprison third-party presidential candidate Eugene Debs for three years.

Bush asked for, and Congress granted, authority to fight the war against terrorism as he saw fit, including committing troops to a prolonged period of combat in Afghanistan without an act of war; permitting the indefinite detention of material witnesses to, or those suspected of, acts of terrorism; and establishing military tribunals that denied defendants due process or lawyer–client privilege (see Chapter 14). He also was successful in getting Congress to accept the kind of covert operations by intelligence agencies that had been outlawed in the 1970s because of their abuse and lack of success. He es-

Head of State

As chief executive, the president is the presiding officer or head of government. But in our form of republic, the head of government is also the head of state; this arrangement is not common among Western democracies. A **head of state** is the official representative of a country, the person whose office symbolizes the collective unity and identity of the nation. When our president stands in public behind the Great Seal of the

tablished a Homeland Security office within the White House and made its director answerable only to him. When he finally bowed to congressional will to establish it as a cabinet department, he demanded concessions of budgetary and other powers for himself and the cabinet secretary and threatened to veto any bill that did not grant these powers.

Because the security threat the country faces is very real, most in Congress went along with most of the president's demands. In the political climate created by a direct attack on the country and significant loss of lives, Congress was reluctant to exert its oversight or checking powers against these executive actions. As the Democratic chair of a powerful Senate committee said in voting for a presidential request he did not support, he did not "wish to create dissent where we need unity."[3]

Bush used this opportunity of bipartisan acquiescence to help restore other presidential initiatives he thought had been thwarted by Congress. He got money appropriated for an antimissile defense shield program that had many opponents in both parties before 9/11 and even more after the attacks suggested defense priorities lay elsewhere. Bush went on to extend the "national security" rationale to a number of situations where its application is very questionable. A month after the attacks, he issued an executive order making public access to the papers of past presidents much more difficult to obtain (an order immediately challenged in court, but not by Congress). Although he justified the order citing national security concerns, Bush was predisposed to taking this ac-

tion well before 9/11 ever happened. He also gave the attorney general broad discretion in limiting public access to any information or documents that might have national security implications.

Two months after 9/11, Bush invoked executive privilege to deny Congress access to documents on federal prosecutors' decision-making process, even in cases dating back decades. A memo to the Justice Department explaining his denial said simply, "I believe congressional access to these documents would be contrary to the national interests." He also used executive privilege to protect his vice president against congressional oversight committees investigating his possible collusion with energy industry officials in writing energy legislation.[4] And he often refused to let his advisers testify before congressional committees, especially on foreign policy or defense matters, by saying they have no obligation to do so. While it is true that his personal staff and advisers do not have legal obligations to give testimony to Congress, it has often been the case that advisers have been willing to do so, both to help Congress understand White House policy and to gain support for it. Clinton's national security adviser frequently and voluntarily went before congressional committees to answer questions. His actions led members of both parties to accuse Bush of creating a monarchy or imperial presidency "to keep Congress from overseeing the executive branch and guarding against corruption."[5] When the Senate and House Intelligence Committees undertook an investigation of intelligence failures, most of the records on what the

relevant agencies knew prior to 9/11 were declassified. But Bush refused to declassify records that would reveal how much he had been told in briefings prior to the attacks.

Bush is one of a number of presidents who believed strongly in presidential prerogatives and the right to set policy and to function relatively freely of congressional oversight. The insistence on unchecked executive authority destroyed the presidencies of Lyndon Johnson and Richard Nixon, and FDR's reputation took a beating over such abuses as the internment of Japanese Americans and his attempt to pack the Supreme Court. When presidents use war or other national crises to justify expansion of their powers—whatever the hardships on individuals or the impact on society in the short run—the results are usually undone when the crisis eases, and the separation of powers reasserts itself. In the process of trying to make a lasting imprint on the office, presidents can do serious harm to their own legacies while the office itself gets reshaped by its next occupant.

1.Quoted by Bill Straub in "A Debate Concerning the Use or Abuse of Presidential Powers," *Champaign-Urbana News-Gazette,* May 15, 2002, B5.
2.Carl M. Cannon, "For the Record," *National Journal,* January 12, 2002, 96.
3.Jeffrey Toobin, "Can Democrats Still Play the Game?" *New York Times,* October 28, 2001, WK 13.
4.Jill Barshay, "A Closer Look at GAO vs. Cheney: Politics and Separation of Powers," *Congressional Quarterly Weekly Review,* February 2, 2002, 289–291.
5."Bush Invokes Executive Privilege," *Champaign-Urbana News-Gazette,* December 12, 2001, A5.

United States of America, he is not just a politician who was elected to govern but a nonpartisan representative of all the people, entrusted with the symbols, emblems, and traditions of the country. The unifying, nonpolitical nature of the role that the head of state is meant to serve

is the reason why some countries separate this office (sometimes filled by a king or queen) from that of head of government. The latter is usually filled by the leader of a political party, who is by definition partisan. But the American president has to wear two hats, and members of Congress, the press, or the public who may attack him freely in his partisan role as head of government usually show more deference when the president is acting in his capacity as head of state.

These duties include serving as official representative of the United States at a variety of state and ceremonial occasions both at home and abroad. It could be opening the baseball season; lighting the White House Christmas tree; attending the swearing in, coronation, or funeral of a foreign head of state; or serving as official greeter when a foreign head of state visits this country. The head of state is also empowered to take actions that symbolize national sentiment, such as issuing proclamations to commemorate events, or making gestures that express a humane national spirit, as in the granting of reprieves and pardons to people convicted of federal crimes. The president's role as unifier of the nation was acted out by Clinton in leading the national mourning for victims of the bombing of the federal building in Oklahoma City, and by Bush participating in a memorial service at Washington's National Cathedral for the victims of 9/11.

In exercising the power of pardon, the president usually consults Justice Department lawyers and the relevant U.S. attorneys, but he is not required to do so. On his own authority, he can erase guilt and restore the civil rights of anyone convicted of a federal crime, except an impeached president. One of Lincoln's last acts, signed the day he was assassinated, was to pardon a Union army deserter. Blanket pardons have been issued to Confederate Army veterans and Vietnam draft dodgers, but most presidents have used the power to clear the names of minor offenders who have served their sentences. Using it to absolve government officials or persons convicted of crimes with political overtones can evoke strong public reactions, as George H. Bush found out when he pardoned Reagan's secretary of defense and five other officials charged with or convicted of crimes related to the Iran-Contra scandal.

Many presidents have come under fire for pardoning a few individuals for what appear to primarily political reasons. Clinton's last-minute pardon of a fugitive commodities trader whose ex-wife was a large donor to the Democratic Party, and whose pardon was also being sought by Israeli prime minister Barak, drew strong negative media and public reaction. But many presidents have slipped questionable pardons onto their lists. In addition to his pardon of former Reagan officials, the first George Bush pardoned the famous head of an oil company who had pleaded guilty to making illegal campaign contributions and who had just made a large donation to the Republican Party. Under pressure from his son Jeb, who was running for governor of Florida, Bush also pardoned a jailed Cuban convicted of terrorism. Reagan pardoned Yankees owner George Steinbrenner, who

had pleaded guilty to conspiring to violate federal election laws in his over-the-limit campaign donations to Republicans.[23] Despite these and similarly controversial pardons by other past presidents, the overwhelming majority of pardon requests are vetted by government lawyers and refused.

As head of state, the president is required by the Constitution to report to Congress "from time to time" about the "State of the Union." He notes the successes of the past year, addresses problems, and outlines his policy agenda for the coming year. Part of the report inevitably deals with the mood of the country and identifies goals for maintaining or increasing national unity.

Today these addresses are televised and delivered in the House of Representatives before a joint session of Congress at the start of each congressional session. The president is received as head of state, rather than as partisan head of government. Even when presidents are mired in political controversy at the time of the speech—Nixon during the Watergate investigation or Clinton in 1998, delivering the State of the Union address just weeks after the revelation of allegations of personal wrongdoing—congressional leaders usually caution the membership to show due respect to a person who is speaking in his constitutional role as head of state.

Chief Diplomat

As head of state, the president is given ceremonial powers "to receive Ambassadors and other public Ministers." Ambassadors are those appointed by other nations to represent their country's interests in the United States. An ambassador must present his or her credentials to the president and have them accepted before taking up office. What appears to be a ceremonial duty has real potential for foreign policymaking. Recognition is not automatic. The power to accept or reject foreign ambassadors, by extension, gives the president the power to decide which governments the United States will recognize and which will be shut out. We did not recognize the Soviet government until sixteen years after the Bolshevik Revolution of 1917 or that of the communist government of mainland China until over twenty-five years after it took power.

As chief diplomat, the president also appoints ambassadors and consuls to represent us abroad, subject to Senate approval. But he frequently conducts diplomacy directly with other heads of state or government, such as at summit conferences where leaders gather to discuss economic, trade, environmental, or arms issues. The president can negotiate treaties and trade deals, although the former must be ratified by the Senate and the latter approved by both chambers.

Some of these powers are implied in Article II and were acknowledged by the Supreme Court in a 1936

As the nation's foreign policy leader, President Franklin Roosevelt edited his own speech to Congress about the Japanese attack on Pearl Harbor. He added the word that made memorable his phrase "a date which will live in infamy."

decision.[24] Congress had authorized Franklin Roosevelt to ban arms sales to warring Bolivia and Paraguay, but a military aircraft manufacturer claimed that Congress lacked the constitutional authority to delegate such power. The Court ruled against the corporation, saying that the United States, like every nation, has implied powers to promote its interests in the world. The Court said there is logic behind presidential power in foreign policy. A nation's government must be able to speak with one voice because having more than one voice can lead to confusion about what is official policy and therefore about what actions might be taken.

Commander in Chief

Using the military to achieve national goals is one way presidents conduct foreign policy. The Founders made the president "commander-in-chief." By this they meant that the president would be the "first general" and "first admiral," as Hamilton wrote in *Federalist* 69.

But the Founders did not want to give the president the sole power to make war. In the words of Connecticut delegate (and later representative and senator) Roger Sherman, they believed "the Executive should be able to repel and not to commence war." The Founders feared

that presidents, like the British kings from whom they had recently freed themselves, would be too eager to go to war.[25] So they gave Congress the power to declare war. James Madison expressed the view of several of the Founders when he argued that "the executive is the branch of power most interested in war and most prone to it. [The Constitution] has, accordingly, with studied care, vested the question of war in the legislature."[26] Thus, the Founders created a system of checks and balances in military affairs; the president commands the troops, but Congress has the power to declare war and to decide whether to authorize funds to pay for it. Thomas Jefferson thought this arrangement would be an "effectual check to the dog of war, by transferring the power of letting him loose from the executive to the legislative body, from those who are to spend to those who are to pay."[27]

Of forty-two presidents (Grover Cleveland served two nonconsecutive terms), all but twelve have had military experience. Nine achieved the rank of general, and six were propelled to the presidency by virtue of military fame (Washington, Jackson, W. H. Harrison, Taylor, Grant, and Eisenhower). Both Theodore and Franklin Roosevelt served as secretary of the navy, and FDR played an active role in directing the naval war against Japan. On the other hand, Lincoln led the Union through the Civil War with only brief military experience in the Illinois state militia.

It is likely that few future presidents will have the kind of military experience their predecessors had, given the absence of the draft and the rise of a professional military. Clinton, an opponent of the Vietnam War, evaded the draft in his youth, while George W. Bush avoided conscription by joining the Texas Air National Guard. John McCain, Bob Kerrey, John Kerry, and Al Gore are among the few recent presidential contenders to have served in the regular armed forces, although Gore was a noncombatant. McCain's background as a Naval Academy graduate, combat veteran, and prisoner of war makes him an exception among recent contenders for the White House.

No sitting president has ever led troops into battle, but modern weaponry has led to more presidential involvement, especially in setting limits on the scope of battle. The decisions to wage limited wars in Korea and Vietnam, for example, were based on presidential beliefs that victories over North Korea and North Vietnam were not worth risking a nuclear holocaust. Under our Constitution, decisions on goals and containing the costs and consequences of war are for elected civilian leaders to make, not the professional military.

The development of high-tech weaponry has also given presidents more military leadership opportunities. Johnson and Nixon used sophisticated communications equipment to select targets in Vietnam. In the Persian Gulf War, Bush used modern transportation facilities to

President Lincoln, as commander in chief, consults his generals at the Antietam battlefield during the Civil War. Lincoln wanted a more active role in Civil War battles, but his generals worried about his safety and made sure he was gone when there was fighting. Limited by an inability to maintain close communications with field commanders, he could not direct ongoing battles.

send large numbers of troops to the Gulf quickly with the latest "smart" weapons. His White House sent so many orders to General Norman Schwarzkopf in the Gulf (from how to stop a blockade-running Iraqi tanker to ending the ground war before Iraq's army was destroyed) that the general complained when the flow of instructions slowed.[28]

Despite congressional oversight of military policy, presidential power is wide-ranging and increasingly controversial as troops frequently are used without a declaration of war or even congressional approval. But presidents have historically assumed and exercised the most power during wars endangering our national survival. During the Civil War, Lincoln suspended the use of writs of habeas corpus, seized control of some eastern railroads, and blockaded southern ports. He took these actions as commander in chief and without congressional authorization. The survival of the Union was at stake, and Lincoln believed he had to take extraordinary measures. Because most people in the North agreed with him, he was able to do what he thought necessary.

Acting under his self-defined authority as commander in chief, Franklin Roosevelt put one hundred thousand Americans of Japanese descent into camps during World War II. He had the government seize and operate more than sixty industries important to the war effort and vulnerable to union strikes. In addition, he created special agencies to control the consumption and price of gasoline, meat, shoes, and other goods.

Wars that do not threaten our national survival tend not to generate high levels of support for executive actions. When Truman had his secretary of commerce seize most of the nation's steel mills during the Korean War to keep them operating in the face of a possible labor strike, one of the steel companies took him to court to stop him. In 1952, the Supreme Court sided with the company by ruling that Truman had not exhausted other, legal remedies to the problem.[29] But Truman, a World War I infantry officer, surrendered none of his power as commander in chief. When General Douglas MacArthur, commander of U.S. and United Nations Forces in Korea, refused to carry out his orders to keep the war contained in Korea, Truman ordered him home, effectively ending his military career.

The extent of the war-making power exercised by Presidents Johnson and Nixon during the undeclared war in Vietnam inspired the 1970s characterization of the presidency as "imperial" and led Congress to take action to limit the power of the president to take unilateral military action. But after the attacks on the United States in 2001, Congress gave George W. Bush extraordinary latitude in carrying out the military response in Afghanistan. (See "The Return of the Imperial Presidency" box.)

Presidential Staff and Advisers

For the first 150 years of the presidency, staff size was small. George Washington paid a nephew out of his own pocket to be his only full-time aide. Congress did not appropriate funds for a presidential clerk until 1857. Lincoln's staff "exploded" to four people, but he often opened and answered the daily mail himself.

Cleveland answered the White House telephone, and Wilson typed many of his own speeches.[30] Today, as presiding officer of the executive branch, the president heads a bureaucracy of fifteen cabinet departments, including the new Homeland Security department, and 2 million civil servants, whose work is described in Chapter 12. To carry out the day-to-day duties of his office, the president has a large staff of policy specialists and liaisons to Congress and federal agencies.

The Executive Office of the President

The bureaucracy that surrounds the modern president had its origins in the administration of Franklin Roosevelt. Because his small staff was overwhelmed by the workload of administering New Deal agencies and programs, FDR called in a team of public administration experts to help restructure his office. In 1937, they recommended the creation of the Executive Office of the President (EOP), but FDR had to wait until 1939 before issuing the executive order that established the EOP. Angry at FDR, Congress withheld approval for two years.[31]

The size of the EOP grew rapidly in the Nixon administration and continued to grow until 1993. Bush's EOP employed more than 1,700 people, over four hundred times the size of Lincoln's staff. Clinton cut this number by 25 percent in his first year in office to show his commitment to downsizing government and deficit reduction. Since FDR's administration, the EOP has been reorganized many times to reflect changing national problems and the issue priorities of individual presidents. The EOP is not a single office but a group of offices, councils, and boards devoted to specific functional or issue areas such as national security, trade, the budget, and drug abuse (see Figure 1). Their offices are divided among the White House and the two Executive Office Buildings, except for the Office of Management and Budget (OMB), which has its own building. Many EOP staffers are career civil servants, but the president appoints those who fill the top policymaking positions, and these are the most influential people in the EOP.

Given the centrality of budget issues, the head of the OMB is an influential adviser in almost every administration. The influence of other EOP heads varies with the president's issue priorities, but those who count as the president's closest advisers are usually concentrated in the White House Office. This office, headed by the president's chief of staff, has grown from sixty-four when Truman took office to more than eight hundred today. To put staff growth in perspective, Nancy Reagan's staff was larger than Roosevelt's at the height of the New Deal.[32]

The EOP is essentially the president's bureaucracy, sitting atop the executive branch and monitoring the work done in cabinet departments and agencies to see that the president's policies are carried out. Although the president also appoints cabinet secretaries and directors

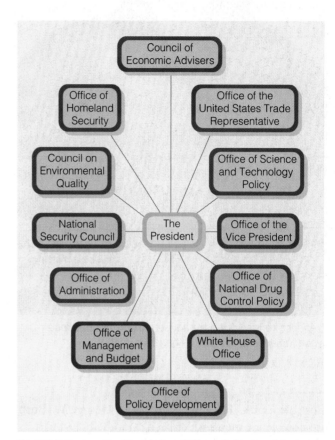

FIGURE 1 ■ The Executive Office of the President in 2002

SOURCE: Adapted from *United States Government Manual, 2001–2002* (Washington, D.C.: U.S. Government Printing Office, 2001).

of independent agencies, some of them head huge bureaucracies with vested interests that may be at odds with the president's agenda. Not surprisingly then, some scholars see the growth in influence of EOP officials as having come at the expense of cabinet secretaries.[33]

The White House Office

Presidents seek advice from different people depending on the issue, but they tend to consult some more than others. Andrew Jackson was the first to call the advisers he consulted frequently his "kitchen cabinet."

Jimmy Carter and Bill Clinton are notable among recent presidents for their degree of reliance on longtime associates. Unlike Kennedy, Nixon, Johnson, and George H. Bush, neither Carter nor Clinton had experience in Washington, and they filled their top staff positions with old friends and political operatives from Georgia and Arkansas. George H. Bush was a consummate Washington insider but relied heavily on his fellow Texan and longtime friend James Baker to serve on the White House staff, in the cabinet, and as his campaign manager. Of recent presidents, only Ronald Reagan, who did not have close personal friends in politics, did not fill his top staff positions with longtime friends and

President Kennedy's closest adviser was his brother Robert, whom he appointed attorney general.

Timepix

close associates. The appointments of George W. Bush are notable for their insider backgrounds; three-quarters had previous Washington experience, and 43 percent had served in his father's administration.

Among their most trusted advisers, presidents often count friends who do not hold official positions but whom they have come to trust for candid, unguarded conversation. The lawyer and former civil rights activist Vernon Jordan, for example, became well known as Clinton's "first friend." Richard Nixon had businessman Bebe Rebozo as a confidante, and Lyndon Johnson had lawyer and lobbyist Abe Fortas, whom he eventually appointed to the Supreme Court. Many presidents have counted their wives among their closest advisers. (See the box "Who Elected Her?") Among George W. Bush's closest advisers, Karl Rove and Karen Hughes worked for him in Texas, while his chief of staff, Andrew Card, and national security adviser, Condoleeza Rice, his closest foreign policy adviser, served in his father's administration.[34] Bush is said to be so close to Karen Hughes that she can finish his sentences.

Members of the White House staff have greater influence than most advisers because the president appoints all of them, works daily with them, and tends to trust them more than others. They are often people who helped him get elected or worked for him when he held other offices.

Presidents have used different styles in running the White House Office. Roosevelt and Kennedy cared little for rigid lines of responsibility. They gave staffers different jobs over time and fostered a competitive spirit: Who could serve the president best? Lyndon Johnson's style was the archetype of aggressive, hands-on management. Known for his commitment to using all resources at his disposal to find government solutions to virtually every problem, Johnson was often accused of overworking and bullying his staff. In an incident that captures this approach, Johnson once turned to an aide who was desperately trying to keep him from engaging in an unscheduled event and asked in a "low threatening tone, 'Are we gonna join the Can't Do It Club right here?'"[35]

In contrast, Eisenhower's administration has been characterized as "the hidden hand presidency," because his management style masked his involvement in decision making.[36] He did not want to risk his popularity by being out front on issues and often appeared diffident around his advisers and cabinet officers. A skilled administrator and conciliator from his years as a staff officer and as supreme commander of the allied forces in World War II, Eisenhower delegated authority yet closely monitored all decisions.

Like Eisenhower, Nixon valued formal lines of authority. Nixon's chief of staff, H. R. Haldeman, saw his job this way: "Every president needs a son of a bitch, and I'm Nixon's. I'm his buffer and his bastard. I get done what he wants done and I take the heat instead of him."[37] Part of Nixon's approach was to be reclusive and keep his cards close to his vest. He demanded at least two days a week when he would see no one so he could work in seclusion; even his closest staff often did not know what he was working on.[38]

The Watergate scandal led Presidents Ford and Carter to avoid the appearance of strong staff chiefs. Reagan prided himself on delegating authority to the best people and letting them do their work without interference.[39] Serious problems developed, however, because no one had authority to make final decisions on more important matters, and Reagan was too removed from daily affairs to do so. This detached management style had its costs, most noticeably the Iran-Contra scandal.[40] To compensate for his detachment, Reagan appointed a series of strong staff chiefs whose coordination of White House operations helped restore his image.

George H. Bush had greater hands-on involvement in policy, but he spent more time on foreign policy and delegated domestic issues to his staff. Clinton's appointment of many staffers with little Washington experience and diverse policy positions showed his determination to immerse himself in policy details and to be the final arbiter of many competing views. He directed his first staff chief to channel all paperwork to him. He did not want his appointees to experience the frustration of a Bush cabinet member who had to mail his views to Bush because Bush's first staff chief, John Sununu, sat on them.

However, running the White House this way made it difficult for Clinton to keep his and the nation's focus on important issues. He got so bogged down in details that his wife complained that he had become the "mechanic-in-chief."[41] In addition, the young, unruly staff and Clinton's penchant for sitting up all night with them talking issues and policy were taken by some as symptomatic of a chaotic and disorganized management style.[42] Under Clinton's second and third staff chiefs, lines of authority and communication were tightened. But his White House operation still reflected his love of policy details and an inability to maintain a schedule and stick to a few clear policy themes in communicating with the public and the media.

George W. Bush employs a near-opposite approach to staff management. With experience as an enforcer of political loyalties on his father's White House staff, and as the only president to hold an MBA, Bush set out to run his staff along corporate lines. He believes in delegating work along crisp lines of authority, keeping to a tight schedule, and demanding complete team loyalty with no public dissent from administration policy.[43]

Office of the First Lady

A small number of special presidential assistants on the White House Office staff are assigned to work full-time for the First Lady.[44] The First Lady's role is ill defined: There is no mention of a presidential spouse in the Constitution, and she has no official position, no title, and no salary. Yet she is definitely expected to serve, especially as what Martha Washington called "the hostess of the nation."[45]

The visibility of the First Lady increased enormously after the arrival of photography in the mid-nineteenth century; mass circulation newspapers and magazines provided new means for satisfying public curiosity about the president's private life. There was heightened interest in seeing presidents' wives in public, and early in the twentieth century, First Ladies began accompanying their husbands at official functions.

A quantum leap in the conception of the First Lady's role occurred during the administration of Franklin Roosevelt. Eleanor Roosevelt held press conferences (for women journalists shut out of the president's briefings), wrote a syndicated newspaper column read by millions, and made regular radio broadcasts. She discussed policy with her husband, bombarded him with memos, and brought supporters of the causes she advocated into the White House. She served on countless committees and traveled around the world promoting racial equality, women's and social justice issues, and the war effort.

Mrs. Roosevelt's stature was attained under the exceptional circumstances of her husband's long tenure in the White House during a prolonged period of national crisis (the Great Depression and World War II). Furthermore, after his incapacitation from polio years earlier, FDR had become dependent on Eleanor to keep his political career afloat by serving as his stand-in and surrogate campaigner. In combination with their strained marriage, this meant that Mrs. Roosevelt entered the White House as much FDR's political partner as his wife.

But the evolution of the role of First Lady is not just simple incremental growth of duties and staff over time. The personality and orientation of the woman who fills the position, and the relationship she has with her husband, also affect the nature of the position. Eleanor Roosevelt's successor, Bess Truman, saw herself more as Harry Truman's wife than as First Lady. Uninterested in Washington politics or social life, she carried out as few functions as her title allowed and spent as much time as possible away from the capital.

With the era of television campaigns, the wives of presidential candidates began to figure much more prominently in campaign strategy. Even those not interested in electoral politics were used to great effect in getting votes. For example, Dwight Eisenhower considered his wife a better campaigner than he was, and Jacqueline Kennedy attained a level of popularity and celebrity that surpassed her husband's. First Ladies have been fixtures on the campaign trail ever since.

It has become the custom for First Ladies to identify causes, usually nonpartisan, on which they will focus special effort. Jacqueline Kennedy devoted herself to historic preservation; Lady Bird Johnson to environmental issues; Betty Ford to the creative arts and welfare of the elderly; Nancy Reagan to drug prevention; Barbara and Laura Bush to literacy; Hillary Rodham Clinton to child welfare.

In addition, all First Ladies have the domestic staff of the White House residential quarters to oversee, as well as an intense schedule of state social functions. These traditional duties, combined with charity and issue-oriented work and the heavy demand for public appearances, have given the First Lady a formal, if not an institutionalized, role, complete with office, staff, and budget—but still no salary. For decades, funding her office presented legal problems since, officially, the First Lady is a private citizen and government funds could not be used to pay her staff. It was not until 1978 that Congress made formal budgetary provisions for the office.[46]

Nixon made a concerted attempt to modernize the office, located in the East Wing of the White House, and to integrate the activities of the First Lady's staff with those of the president's in the West Wing. Hillary Rodham Clinton, in a show of intent to be a close policy adviser, moved into the West Wing with sixteen personal aides, including schedulers, publicity handlers, and a chief of staff, whose duties she described as equivalent to those of the president's chief of staff. Laura Bush, who has said she is very satisfied with a traditional role, moved back into the East Wing, but staff size is unlikely to decrease given the many demands on all contemporary First Ladies.

Does this sound familiar: A president's wife is accused of being a radical, more activist than her husband, and in danger of leading him in policy directions his opponents, and perhaps even his own party, do not support? Voters, pundits, and political columnists ask, "Who elected her?" The name of Hillary Rodham Clinton or Eleanor Roosevelt may come to mind. Yet the controversy over the First Lady and how her proximity to the president and the special confidence she shares with him might affect policy decisions has been with us since the administration of John Adams.

The president's wife has always had to walk a fine line, presiding over state social functions and being supportive of her husband without looking as though she is politically out in front of him. Martha Washington and Louisa Adams (wife of John Quincy Adams) were just two First Ladies who felt they were in a prison, hemmed in by the limits of acceptable behavior.[1] Barbara Bush's chief of staff described the position as "filled with banana peels and land mines."[2]

The first and second presidential wives—they did not yet have a formal title—Martha Washington and Abigail Adams, were preoccupied with the problems of keeping their families afloat economically while their husbands led public lives. Abigail Adams managed the family farm in Massachusetts, and Martha Washington ran the plantation at Mount Vernon. Although not always happy with it, neither rejected the role of manager of the domestic sphere and hostess for state social occasions. But whereas Martha Washington was basically unschooled and not much interested in public affairs, Abigail Adams was an accomplished writer with strong political opinions and not afraid to express them (for example, that women would "foment a Rebellion" if they were made subject to laws without representation). Her views on women's rights and other issues, coupled with the fact that her long and happy marriage to John Adams made her his principal adviser, led both supporters and opponents of the president to believe she might have "undue" in-

fluence on policy decisions. When Adams's opponents referred to his wife as "Mrs. President," they meant something more than her marital status.

Abigail's daughter-in-law, Louisa Adams, and Dolley Madison are other nineteenth-century First Ladies who played crucial roles in their husbands' political careers. Dolley Madison was so highly regarded among Washington's influential that in 1844 Congress reserved a seat for her whenever she chose to attend sessions.[3]

Influential First Ladies of the early twentieth century include Edith Wilson, who served what she called a "stewardship" (but what others called "bedside government") during a seven-month period when her husband was disabled by a stroke.[4] She decoded classified diplomatic and military messages, encoded presidential responses, controlled access to her husband, and kept information about his condition from the public. Much of the work organizing and financing Warren Harding's presidential campaign was done by Florence Harding, which explains her widely repeated query: "I got you the presidency; now what are you going to do with it?"

Although many First Ladies since have been political advisers to their husbands, no one did it quite so publicly, or from such an independent platform, as Eleanor Roosevelt. Her tenure as First Lady was unique in that she had a pol-

icy agenda that sometimes was at odds with the president's; she had her own coterie of supporters and direct access to the public through her news conferences, broadcasts, and newspaper column. In later years, she served as a delegate to the United Nations and was a member of John Kennedy's Committee on the Status of Women. Her efforts for human rights and international cooperation earned her the title "First Lady of the World." More than any other First Lady, she can be said to have developed a reputation independent from her husband's legacy as president. Although some thought her too powerful, Mrs. Roosevelt always deferred to her husband in joint appearances, saying it was the job of a wife to offer no personal opinions, limit her appearances, and "lean back in an open car so voters [can] always see *him*."[5]

Mrs. Roosevelt's term may have been a type unto itself, but most First Ladies were not traditional wives who limited themselves to the domestic sphere. In modern times, Bess Truman, Mamie Eisenhower, Pat Nixon, and Barbara Bush come closest to the image of traditional wife. But these were hardly women without influence on their husbands. Despite her lack of interest in electoral politics, Bess Truman was called "The Boss" by Harry, who said he frequently consulted her on the content of his speeches and in making impor-

A shy woman who once said, "I hate politics," Eleanor Roosevelt became the most influential First Lady ever.

UPI/Corbis-Bettmann

tant decisions. Mamie ("Ike runs the country; I turn the pork chops") Eisenhower cut as traditional a figure as possible in the 1950s, but that did not keep her husband from listening to her opinion when she gave it or from wearing an "I Like Mamie" button when campaigning. In most long and close marriages, it is natural for husbands and wives to become confidantes and to rely on one another's judgment. Presidential husbands and wives who have led relatively separate lives, such as John and Jacqueline Kennedy—she, like Bess Truman, having little interest in electoral politics—are not that common among first couples. But Mrs. Kennedy did have an interest in the social and symbolic aspects of her role, and in that capacity she was extremely important to an administration that was in large part about style.

A number of strong-willed women followed Jacqueline Kennedy into the White House. Lady Bird (Claudia) Johnson helped finance her husband's congressional campaigns and in his presidential race had her own campaign train to tour the South while her husband worked on in Washington. She is said to have greeted him in the evenings with the query, "Well, what did you do for women today?" Betty Ford was an outspoken supporter of the Equal Rights Amendment and abortion rights in defiance of her party's position, and she argued for a salary for her successors as First Lady. Her popularity often surpassed her husband's. Rosalynn Carter sat in on cabinet meetings, had weekly policy lunches with her husband, met with foreign heads of state to discuss policy, chaired the Commission on Mental Health Reform, and was at times derisively referred to as "copresident." Nancy Reagan's stepfather helped shape her husband's political philosophy, and she often controlled access to the Oval Office and weighed in on the hiring and firing of key advisers. The term *copresident* was revived for Hillary Clinton, a lawyer and lobbyist for child welfare causes, who was one of her husband's closest advisers and strate-

gists throughout his career in elective office, while also serving as the family's principal wage earner.

Although some political commentators and at least part of the public appear leery of activist First Ladies, it does not seem to bother many of their husbands. FDR often disagreed with Eleanor's policy positions, but he depended on her to fill a public role he was physically unable to sustain, and the political circle that developed around her never appeared to threaten him. Reagan depended heavily on Nancy's advice. Carter called Rosalynn a "full partner" and his costrategist in the presidential campaign.[6] And Clinton clearly saw his wife's activist role as a natural continuation of the political partnership they had had throughout their marriage. "It doesn't bother me for people to get excited and say she could be president. I always say she could be president, too."[7] An exception perhaps was Gerald Ford, who told his wife that her outspokenness cost him millions of votes in the 1976 election.[8]

Although Rosalynn Carter had more public hands-on involvement in policy, Hillary Clinton prompted greater opposition to the activist conception of the office than anyone since Eleanor Roosevelt. In response to public criticism, she retreated into a more traditional role before the 1996 reelection campaign. But in 2000, Mrs. Clinton—now Senator Clinton (D-N.Y.)—became the first presidential wife to run for elective office, moving out of the White House and taking up separate residence in the state of New York.

In some ways, the concern over the influence and accountability of presidential spouses is moot. The First Lady is not subject to congressional approval, but neither are the members of the White House staff nor the president's close advisers outside government. But as Hillary Clinton discovered, First Ladies are not immune from investigation of criminal wrongdoing, and when they serve by official appointment, as she did on the health care task force, they are subject to the same rules as other public officials.

How is issue advocacy of a presidential spouse different from that of any lobbyist? In cases in which wives have played active roles in getting their husbands nominated and elected, how realistic is it that they will expect that their advice will no longer be needed after the election? And how realistic is it to expect that their advice will no longer be offered when important decisions are being made? Yet some seem to worry that the special nature of a marital relationship provides opportunities to influence—the kind Betty Ford called "pillow talk"—unavailable to others. We frequently refer to lobbyists as "getting into bed" with politicians, but wives do not have to pay to get there, and if they are successful in changing their husband's views, it is not likely that money will have had anything to do with it.

Will the president's wife continue to be the "First Lady" in the twenty-first century? There probably will not be many more in the mold of Bess Truman or Mamie Eisenhower. Laura Bush is closer to their example, and to that of her mother-in-law, than to Hillary Clinton's, but she had a career as a schoolteacher and librarian. It is increasingly likely that professional couples like the Clintons and Robert and Elizabeth Dole will be occupying the White House in this century. And inevitably there will be a First Gentleman. Will his influence be as feared as that of a presidential wife?

1. Edith P. Mayo, ed., *The Smithsonian Book of First Ladies* (Washington, D.C.: Smithsonian Institution, 1996), 11, 43.
2. Henry Louis Gates Jr., "Hating Hillary," *New Yorker,* February 26 and March 4, 1996, 121.
3. Mayo, *Smithsonian Book of First Ladies,* 31.
4. Phyllis Lee Levin, *Edith and Woodrow* (New York: Scribner's, 2001).
5. Carl Sferrazza Anthony, "The First Ladies: They've Come a Long Way, Martha," *Smithsonian,* October 1992, 150.
6. Gil Troy, *Affairs of State: The Rise and Rejection of the First Couple since World War II* (New York: Free Press, 1997), 236–272.
7. Mayo, *Smithsonian Book of First Ladies,* 277.
8. Troy, *Affairs of State,* 222.
OTHER SOURCES:Carol Chandler Waldrop, *Presidents' Wives: The Lives of 44 American Women of Strength* (Jefferson, N.C.: McFarland, 1989); *The Presidency A to Z: A Ready Reference Encyclopedia* (Washington, D.C.: Congressional Quarterly, 1992), 179–182; Lewis L. Gould, ed., *American First Ladies* (New York: Garland, 1996).

Office of the Vice President

The Office of the Vice President was made part of the EOP in 1972. Not long afterward, the vice president got his own white mansion (the former home of the chief of naval operations), when the government decided maintaining an official residence was much less expensive than paying for the necessary security arrangements on the homes of each new vice president.[47] In 2002, the vice president's salary was $192, 600, but it is subject to the same automatic cost-of-living allowance granted to Congress and other executive branch officials, excluding the president. The vice president also has his own office budget and staff (housed in the old Executive Office Building adjacent to the White House), and an official airplane (*Air Force Two*). As president of the Senate, he is also provided with an office next to the Senate chamber.

That vice presidents have succeeded to office unexpectedly nine times (eight presidential deaths and one resignation) may be responsible for the growing importance of the office.[48] Most recent vice presidents have been seasoned public servants with considerable experience and personal records of achievement. That they were willing to take the job suggests that it has become more than "standby equipment," as Nelson Rockefeller called it.

The only formal duties the vice president has are to preside over the Senate, cast tie-breaking votes, and succeed to the presidency should it be vacated. Historically, presidents gave their vice presidents little information and few opportunities to prepare for succession. Harry Truman did not even know about the atom bomb until after Franklin Roosevelt's death, but within months he had to decide whether to use it against Japan.

Woodrow Wilson's vice president, Thomas R. Marshall, said that holding the job was like being "a man in a cataleptic fit. He cannot speak, he cannot move. He suffers no pain. He is perfectly conscious of all that goes on. But he has no part in it." Franklin Roosevelt's first vice president, John Nance Garner, was less elegant in observing that his job was not worth a "pitcher of warm piss."

Until recent times, presidents had difficulty delegating important jobs to their vice presidents. One reason is that vice presidential candidates have often been chosen to balance a ticket geographically and ideologically, not because of closeness to the presidential candidate. (Before the Twelfth Amendment, when the vice presidency was filled by the runner-up in votes to the president, the vice president was actually an electoral opponent of the president.) And once in office, some vice presidents have used the position to build an independent political base from which to run for the presidency. This has not always made them the most loyal supporters of the president's agenda.

President Bush and Vice President Cheney in synch.

Until recently, vice presidents were asked to deal mainly with partisan or ceremonial matters. There is no legal basis for institutionalizing an expansion of the office because, beyond the few duties specified in the Constitution, the work vice presidents assume, and the advising or policymaking authority they acquire, are at the president's discretion. Therefore, much depends on the personal relationship of the two people filling the positions, how needy the president is for assistance, or how generous he is about sharing power.

Jimmy Carter was the first president to delegate to his vice president responsibilities for day-to-day White House operations.[49] Carter had no national experience before his election and considered Walter Mondale, a former U.S. senator, a major asset. He gave Mondale a White House office, scheduled weekly lunches with him, included him in all White House advisory groups and all important meetings, and asked him to lobby Congress and read the paperwork that crossed Carter's desk. Ronald Reagan, Bill Clinton, and both George Bushes added to this new tradition. Indicative of their added responsibilities, Mondale, Gore, and Cheney were all assigned some of the scarce office space in the West Wing of the White House.

Prior to the Bush–Cheney administration, the closest working relationship between a president and vice president was undoubtedly that between Bill Clinton and Al Gore. Gore became so influential in the Clinton White House that he was referred to as a "shadow president" and his staff as a "shadow cabinet." Divisions did not surface until Gore was running his own presidential campaign and trying to establish an identity apart from Clinton's.

Reuters/Timepix

The relationship of Bush and Cheney surpasses that of Clinton and Gore. Cheney was already well known to Bush from service in his father's administration, and he had far more administrative, and Washington, experience than the new president. In fact, Cheney's influence and visibility were so great in the early months of the administration that he had to be pushed to the background so that Bush would have the chance to establish his own identity as president. Even then many continued to believe that the far more experienced and policy-savvy Cheney was running a large part of the White House operation; this would not be surprising given Bush's preference for delegating work. He ran Bush's transition team, chose many staff members, and heads the most important policymaking groups in the White House. Cheney has unprecedented access to the Oval Office, meeting the president every morning and sometimes several times more during the day. Outperforming the president carries political liabilities for the vice president. Midway through Bush's term, some of his supporters advocated dropping Cheney from the 2004 ticket in favor of Condoleeza Rice.

The heightened visibility of the office apparently has raised it in the estimation of its occupants: Speaking to a group of high school students, Cheney said, "Who knows, a few of you may even dream of becoming vice president. It's not that bad a job. Although it takes a while getting used to being a character on *Saturday Night Live*."[50]

The President and the People

Our earliest presidents had little contact with the general public and even communicated with Congress in writing. George Washington and Thomas Jefferson averaged only three speeches a year to the public, while John Adams averaged one. Adams, in fact, spent eight months of his presidency living in Quincy, Massachusetts, avoiding Congress and the need to make a decision over involvement in a war between England and France.[51]

Abraham Lincoln thought it prudent to avoid giving speeches. He told people gathered at Gettysburg the night before his famous address, "I have no speech to make. In my position it is somewhat important that I should not say foolish things. It very often happens that the only way to help it is to say nothing at all."[52] It has been many years since we have had such a diffident public speaker in the White House.

Until the advent of radio and television, presidents had to speak to the nation indirectly through newspapers. The development of new transportation and communication technologies has given presidents more opportunities to utilize the presidency as a "bully pulpit," as Teddy Roosevelt called it. Franklin Roosevelt's fireside chats were the first presidential effort to use the media to speak directly and regularly to the nation. They helped make him, and his office, the most important link between people and government. In a personalized style, he began, "My friends." People felt Roosevelt was talking to each of them in their own homes, and they gathered around their radios whenever he was on. Whereas President Herbert Hoover had received an average of forty letters a day, Roosevelt, after beginning his chats, received four thousand letters a day.[53] He even received some addressed not to "The President" but simply to "My Friend, Washington, D.C."

There has been no turning back. Now when a president is not heard from frequently, the media begin to speculate about what is wrong. But how often a president wants to address the public—or how often his staff wants him to do so—depends on his communications skills. Reagan, often called the "great communicator" although he always read from notes, spoke in public on average two hundred times a year. Bill Clinton, considered one of the best extemporaneous speakers ever to occupy the presidency, spoke in public an amazing 550 times a year.[54]

The Personal Presidency

Political scientist Theodore Lowi believes that we have had a **personal presidency** since the New Deal era.[55] He argues that, consciously or unconsciously, the American people have had a "new social contract" with the president since the 1930s. In return for getting more power and support from us than we give to other government officials, the president is supposed to make sure we get what we want from government. The personal presidency ties government directly to the people and gives us someone to rally around during times of crisis. To the extent that it serves as a focal point for national unity, the personal presidency also contributes to our ability to achieve national goals.

Polls have consistently shown that Americans consider "leadership" very important in evaluating presidents.[56] Somewhat paradoxically in light of their fear of "big government," most people want a president who can get government to "do" things. Franklin Roosevelt was the first president to use survey data to identify public needs and to use the media to tell people that he would give them what they wanted. Making himself the major link between public opinion and government often enabled him to overcome the inertia and divisions associated with a system of fragmented powers.

However, Roosevelt's actions also revealed a cost of the personal presidency: Presidents with great power often seek more. Roosevelt won reelection in 1936 by a landslide, confirming popular support for his New Deal. This led him to seek more power by trying to expand the size of an unfriendly Supreme Court so he could appoint judges who supported him. He also tried to get local and state parties to nominate congressional candidates he favored by using federal funds as an inducement. The defeat of pro-Roosevelt congressional candidates in 1938 ruined both his plans. People did not want the Court politicized, and state and local parties wanted to pick their own nominees.

Nixon and Reagan also tried to override constitutional limitations on their power after their landslide reelections in 1972 and 1984, as evidenced in the Watergate and Iran-Contra scandals. The use of popular mandates to amass power in the Oval Office illustrates the relationship between the growth of the modern presidency and the rise of the personal presidency.

Practitioners of the personal presidency have sought more power because they promised more than they could deliver. To win approval for their programs, they needed more power to compete successfully with other parts of government and maintain their public support. Thus, they were caught in a cycle of making great promises, seeking more power to honor them, and making even greater promises to get more power. Inevitably, they promised more than they could deliver. George H. Bush promised to send astronauts to Mars, protect the environment, be the "education president," and do many other things while cutting the budget deficit without raising taxes. After the Reagan and Bush administrations had doubled the national debt, promising *less* from government became the tactic of the personal presidency. So while Clinton also began by making

promises and saying he wanted "to do it all as quick as we can," he started his second term by announcing that "the day of big government is over."[57]

Yet Clinton had his own angle on the personal presidency, an approach that is said to "have changed the very nature of what the public expects of its Presidents." While deemphasizing big government, Clinton dwelt on "little initiatives," such as his proposal to adopt uniforms in public schools. These are what one of his top advisers called "kitchen table issues," problems that families deal with on a daily basis and may discuss around the kitchen table.[58] Not only was Clinton extremely adept at speaking directly to people in a conversational style, but he projected an intimate knowledge of domestic, school, and community problems that were of great concern in everyday life.

Lowi might have been right in calling the personal presidency the "victim" of democracy, but irresponsible leadership is not an inevitable consequence of the age of mass media. The separation of powers and the vote should check the short-term excesses of presidents. However, every president since the 1960s has needed and sought media exposure and in turn has had to submit to intense scrutiny by media that delve into every detail of his personal life, as well as his performance of official duties. Few people can withstand such prolonged exposure without losing public esteem. The continuous congressional and special prosecutor investigations of Bill Clinton resulted in the media being saturated with the most graphically presented private and intimate details of a president's life ever revealed. "It is entirely possible," one reporter observed, "that the Clinton era will be remembered by historians primarily as the moment when the distance between the President and the public evaporated forever."[59] (For attitudes toward the presidency by its occupants, see the box "Match the Quote to the President.")

Persuading the Public

The relationship of the president to the people starts well before inauguration day. Changes in electoral laws have established a relationship with the public quite different from the one that the Founders saw for their head of state. The president is no longer just an elder statesman chosen by the Electoral College or a politician selected by party professionals to run for the presidency; he is a politician with a national constituency who convinced the rank-and-file voters in his party to choose him in the primaries and at least a plurality of the general population to vote for him in the general election. The modern president comes into office with extensive experience in persuading the public.

As presidential scholar Richard Neustadt pointed out long ago, presidents need more than their formal

When President Franklin D. Roosevelt died, most Americans felt a personal loss. Here Chief Petty Officer Graham Jackson plays "Nearer My God to Thee" as the president's body is carried to the train that returned him to Washington.

Edward Clark/*Life* magazine © Time Inc.

1. "I don't even remember that I ever was President."

2. "No man who ever held the office would congratulate another on attaining it."

3. "War and politics are so different."

4. His mother said of him, "I hardly can believe that this is the same son I threatened with death and destruction if he didn't do his homework and clean his room."

5. His law partner said of him, "His ambition is a little engine that knows no rest."

6. He wanted to put a sign on the Oval Office that said, "Don't shoot; he's doing his damnedest."

7. Called having both home and office in the White House "an evil combination."

8. "This country is for white men and, by God, as long as I am President, it will be a government for white men."

9. "The Presidency is hell; there is no other word to describe it."

10. "I can use it [the presidency] for any damned thing I want to."

11. "Unpredictability is the greatest weapon a president can have."

12. "You are only fit to be president when you are not obsessed with it."

13. "Above all try something."

14. "No man ever lived a really worthy life unless he possessed power."

15. "[The presidency] is the greatest sacrifice I ever made; I felt like I was facing my executioner."

SOURCES: 4, *CQ Daily Monitor*, June 6, 2002 (www.CQ.com); 12, *NewsHour with Jim Lehrer*, March 2000; 7, Louis Achincloss, *Woodrow Wilson* (New York: Penguin, 2000), 55; all others from the PBS series *The American President* (www.pbs.org).

A. Warren G. Harding
B. William J. Clinton
C. Ulysses S. Grant
D. John Quincy Adams
E. Woodrow Wilson
F. Abraham Lincoln
G. George Washington
H. Richard Nixon
I. Andrew Jackson
J. Franklin Delano Roosevelt
K. Andrew Johnson
L. William Howard Taft
M. Theodore Roosevelt
N. Benjamin Harrison
O. George W. Bush

Answers

1, L; 2, D; 3, C; 4, O; 5, F; 6, E; 7, N; 8, K; 9, A; 10, I; 11, H; 12, B; 13, J; 14, M; 15, G.

---

powers to achieve their goals. They need the **power to persuade.**[60] In addition to the public, presidents must be able to win over interest group leaders; newspaper and magazine publishers, reporters, and columnists; judges who hear challenges to their policies; and a majority in Congress. These policymakers and opinion elite, who Neustadt called Washingtonians, are, in short, the people the president needs to get his policies enacted. Because the Washingtonians also need him to get what they want, a president can bargain and persuade.

The effective president is "one who seizes the center of the Washington bazaar and actively barters to build winning coalitions."[61] Presidents "remember" their friends by putting their pet projects in the budget, by campaigning for them, and by naming the people they want to public office.

In pursuit of his policy agenda, a president can use his powers to persuade the public as a means to bring pressure on reluctant Washingtonians, or when the public is disinterested or slow to accept, he can try to persuade Washingtonians to shape public opinion. In doing so, he has much more to rely on than his rhetorical skills. A president's powers give him considerable favors and penalties to dispense. As the chief maker of foreign policy, he can seek support from Irish, Cuban, and Jewish Americans by supporting their objectives in Northern Ireland, Cuba, and the Middle East. As de facto leader of his party, he can use the symbolic resources of the presidency in campaigning for candidates he supports. And as chief budget maker, he has many favors to give and withhold, including support for hundreds of pork barrel projects.

The strategy of making a direct presidential appeal to the people to gain cooperation from Washingtonians is called *going public*.[62] The strategy includes giving primetime television and radio addresses, holding press conferences, making speeches at events around the country, and using satellite technology to give interviews to local television stations, conventions, and other audiences.

Why have some presidents found going public attractive? One reason is that the weakness of party identification forces presidential candidates to appeal as widely as they can for support. They continue doing so after taking office because they have seen its value. In addition, national parties have been unable to represent the larger number of interests produced by government's larger role in society. This has helped disperse power among alliances that interest groups form with congressional committees, subcommittees, and executive agencies that write and administer the laws they lobby for and against. It is difficult for presidents to know, bargain with, and persuade all these Washingtonians. It is often easier to go public.

Although the public did not always agree with President Reagan's policies or views, he was popular in part because of his image as a rugged individualist.

Ronald Reagan Library

tify public reactions, presidential staff regularly gather data just as they did on the campaign trail. A White House aide described the Reagan administration as "a P.R. outfit that became President and took over the country."[65]

Going public leads presidents to use "sound bites" to simplify their positions to build public support while working behind the scenes to build congressional and interest group support. This approach worked for Reagan, who publicly described his 1982 budget package as "a line drawn in the dirt" to stress his resolve. He traveled around the country to generate public support, and his staff used focus groups to identify popular reactions to his proposals. These analyses told his advisers where he could hold firm and where he should compromise. And he made the necessary changes in his package to build congressional support for it.

Clinton used Reagan's sound bite and compromise strategy to gain congressional passage of the North American Free Trade Agreement and a ban on assault weapons. But Clinton's health care reform plan was too complex and difficult to understand, making it an easy target for interest groups to oppose by playing on fears of "socialized medicine." His effort to build support for his position failed, and Congress defeated his bill.

Going public may sometimes lead presidents to emphasize public relations over results and to blame the media rather than themselves for low poll scores. For example, Nixon claimed the media had hounded him from office, Reagan said they exaggerated the importance of the Iran-Contra scandal, and Clinton complained they did not give him credit for his first-year accomplishments. "I have fought more damn battles than any president has in twenty years with the possible exception of Reagan's first budget and not gotten one damn bit of credit from the knee-jerk liberal press," Clinton said. "I am sick and tired of it, and you can put that in the damn article."[66]

George H. Bush's use of the going public strategy in garnering support for the Persian Gulf War was very skillful. He decided to use military force soon after Iraq invaded Kuwait in August 1990. Until January, when Congress approved this option, Bush made many speeches comparing Iraq's Saddam Hussein to Hitler, condemning his use of chemical and biological weapons on his own people, and warning that Iraq would soon have nuclear weapons. Bush's efforts won more public support for using force, which in turn made congressional support more likely. George W. Bush needed no strategy to win popular support for responding to al Qaeda's terrorist network because military action followed a direct attack on the United States. But in trying to rally the public behind his goal of expanding the war to Iraq, he used a tactic similar to his father's, referring to Saddam Hussein as part of an "axis of evil."

As outsiders, or presidential candidates without national political experience, Carter, Reagan, and Clinton used the strategy of going public because they lacked ties with the Washingtonians they needed to govern.[63] In a 1981 television address to stimulate support for major tax cuts, Reagan asked viewers "to put aside any feelings of frustration about our political institutions [and] contact your senators and congressmen."[64] The public's reaction was swift and overwhelming. Many Democrats decided to support the president, and the cuts passed.

Going public has a number of important effects. It makes the workings of the presidency resemble an election campaign because presidents fly around the country to get their views in the media. Seeking coverage and support, they use the same simple, dramatic style to sell their positions that they used as candidates. To iden-

Public Opinion and Effectiveness in Office

Americans pay more attention to the president than to other public officials, and we typically link government's success to the effectiveness of his leadership. Although many factors affect public opinion about presidential effectiveness, a positive image of a president's leadership skills helps protect his ratings after serious policy failures.

Many people are predisposed to support the president and to look at his overall record rather than the short term.[67] Failure on specific issues does not always produce low scores on general performance. For example, majorities of respondents simultaneously disapproved of Reagan's handling of environmental and foreign policy issues, which the public thinks are important, *and* registered approval of his overall performance.

Crises called *rally events* affect presidential popularity.[68] President Clinton's approval ratings increased after the bombing of the federal building in Oklahoma City, and George W. Bush's rose by forty points after 9/11. Public support increases significantly at such times because people do not want to hurt the president, the symbol of national unity. However, the higher levels of support produced by rally events are rarely sustained.[69] The rise in support among those who were critical of a president before the event tends to be short-lived.

Support for George H. Bush's policies toward Iraq after its invasion of Kuwait also demonstrates public readiness to rally around the president. In November 1990, the public was divided over Bush's decision to send more troops to the Persian Gulf, with 47 percent approving and 46 percent disapproving. By January 1991, after fighting began, almost 90 percent approved of the way he was handling the situation. As Figure 2

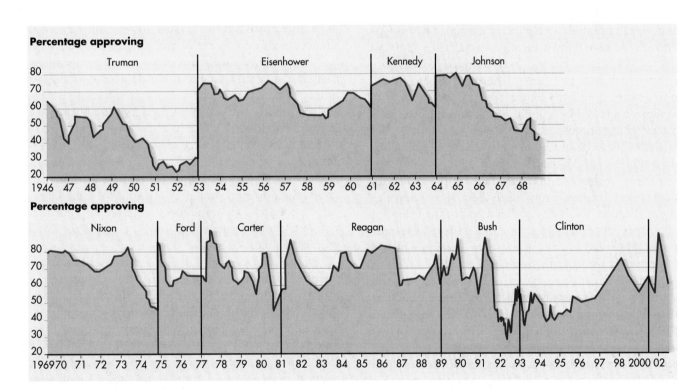

FIGURE 2 ■ Presidential Popularity Usually Declines over Time

Eisenhower and, to some extent, Reagan are exceptions to the post–World War II tendency for presidential popularity to fall during their tenures. Although Reagan's popularity plunged twenty points at the end of 1986 because of the Iran-Contra scandal, it partly rebounded by the end of his term. Most commentators thought this reflected popular fondness for Reagan as a person and Reagan's early successes rather than policy achievements late in his term. George H. Bush began his term with high ratings typical of new presidents; after falling in 1990, his ratings rebounded to record heights during the Persian Gulf War, then began falling dramatically in 1991. Despite Clinton's modest showing at the polls (49 percent) in 1996 and continuing scandals, his approval ratings soared to 67 percent in 1998 and were still high when he left office. George W. Bush's ratings were in the mid-50s before 9/11, soared to 90 percent, but declined to near his pre-9/11 level by early 2003.

SOURCES: William Schneider, "Reagan Now Viewed as an Irrelevant President," *National Journal*, November 28, 1987, 3051. See also George Gallup Jr., and Alec Gallup, "The Former President," *The Polling Report,* January 30, 1989, 1 and 5. Figure data: Gallup Polls, reported in *Public Opinion* (January/February 1989) and updated at www.gallup.com. The question asked is "Do you approve or disapprove of the way [name of president] is handling his job as president?"

shows, this increasing support helped raise Bush's general approval ratings from 54 percent in October 1990 to 89 percent in February 1991. The unexpectedly swift defeat of Iraq with surprisingly few American casualties kept Bush's poll scores high for some time.[70] However, the effect of the Gulf War faded as Americans began focusing on domestic concerns, especially economic problems. Bush's approval rating fell to 33 percent by mid-1992, leading to his defeat by Clinton in November.[71] George W. Bush's approval ratings fell from 92 to 58 percent over a nine-month period after 9/11, also in the wake of bad economic news.

Clinton's up and down scores during his first term reflected public anxiety about his leadership skills. In 1995 polls, 56 percent of Americans described Clinton as a weak president, and 80 percent expected the Republican Congress would have more influence than Clinton on the nation's direction.[72] But Clinton was far more adept at going public than the Republican leadership, and by the end of his first term, his approval rating was at 53 percent and Congress was in legislative retreat.

Winning consistently good ratings when public anger and frustration with government are widespread is difficult. Although short-term crises or rally events can help a president's ratings, long-term conditions will continue to influence them. Clinton's 67 percent approval rating during the impeachment investigation may have been sparked by a public backlash against the salaciousness of congressional and media commentary, but it is more likely that he got a positive bounce from public confidence in the overall state of the economy.

The more important issue is whether a president with high approval ratings can translate them into policy successes. Reagan had only qualified success in using his popularity to get Congress to enact his legislative proposals. He relied heavily on his own appointment and budgetary powers and the issuing of executive orders to accomplish much of his agenda. The problem with this approach is that it is easily reversible by a successor. Clinton, with higher sustained approval ratings than either Reagan or Bush late in their terms, and a substantial legislative agenda, was not able to translate his popular support into victories in Congress. George W. Bush used his high approval ratings to win concessions of power rather than to push legislation. He won his first two major goals—education reform and tax cuts—in his first year and had a limited legislative agenda beyond that.

The President and Congress

One thing the Founders did not anticipate is that the president would one day be dealing with Congress as the popularly elected leader of a national political party. The president is the nominal head of his party and chief advocate for its policy agenda. This adds another dimension to the relationship between the executive and legislative branches: The president is never just the head of state or chief executive; he is also an electoral adversary of members of the House and Senate who do not belong to his party. He can use his reputation and the weight of his office not only to challenge their legislative priorities but also to try to unseat them.

Party Leadership

To improve the electoral chances of their party, presidents try to help recruit good candidates for House and Senate races. In addition, presidents help raise money by being the headliner at fund-raising events and by staying on good terms with major contributors. They also send their aides around the country to help fellow Democrats or Republicans with their campaigns and sometimes even go themselves. Seeing presidents in person—seeing a little history in the making—is exciting, and they almost always draw a crowd and good media coverage. But the president usually tries to camouflage his role as party leader when trying to persuade people to support him or to vote for his party's candidates, because people are more likely to listen to a president when they see him as head of state.

Candidates for any office are usually eager for a presidential visit, although in 1992 some Republican candidates avoided being photographed with Bush when he visited their districts, and in 1994 and 1998 some Democratic congressional candidates preferred to campaign without Clinton's support, as did Al Gore in the 2000 presidential race.

Presidential partisanship has a purpose: The more members of a president's party who sit in Congress, the more support he gets for his policies. However, a president's support, when he chooses to give it, is no guarantee of electoral success for congressional candidates, especially in off-year elections (see Table 1). Since 1932, the president's party has lost an average of twenty-six House and four Senate seats in off-year elections. Indeed, the 1998 election was the first off-year election since 1934 that the president's party increased its seats, a feat also achieved by Bush in 2002.

In presidential election years, the average gains for the winning presidential candidate's party in Congress are close to their losses in off-year elections, twenty-one in the House and three in the Senate. The 1988 and 1992 elections were unusual. The Republicans lost House and Senate seats when Bush was elected, and the Democrats lost House seats when Clinton was elected.

TABLE 1	Congressional Candidates Fall Off the President's Coattails in Off-Year Elections		
		Seats Gained or Lost by President's Party in	
Year	President	House	Senate
1934	Roosevelt (D)	+9	+10
1938	Roosevelt (D)	−71	−6
1942	Roosevelt (D)	−45	−9
1946	Truman (D)	−55	−12
1950	Truman (D)	−29	−6
1954	Eisenhower (R)	−18	−1
1958	Eisenhower (R)	−47	−13
1962	Kennedy (D)	−4	+4
1966	Johnson (D)	−47	−3
1970	Nixon (R)	−12	+2
1974	Ford (R)	−48	−3
1978	Carter (D)	−11	−3
1982	Reagan (R)	−26	0
1986	Reagan (R)	−6	−8
1990	Bush (R)	−8	−1
1994	Clinton (D)	−52	−9
1998	Clinton (D)	+5	0
2002	Bush (R)	+6	+2
Average, all off-year elections		−27	−4
Average, all presidential elections years		+21	+3

D = Democrat; R = Republican.
SOURCE: *Congressional Quarterly Weekly Review,* various issues.

The pattern of presidential party gains in presidential elections and losses in off-year elections seems to be weakening due to the increasing numbers of safe seats and the influence of campaign contributions. These factors help make candidates safe even when their presidential candidate loses or is unpopular at midterm.

Divided Government

Presidents are normally active in support of House and Senate candidates not just because they are policy leaders but also because one of the major factors influencing the working relationship between the president and Congress is whether the president's party controls the House and Senate. For all but two years since 1981, one party has controlled the White House and the other one or both houses of Congress. This is called **divided government.** The Founders made divided government possible by giving each branch its own powers and distinctive constituency and providing for different methods of election. This contrasts with parliamentary systems, in which voters elect members of the legislative

branch, who in turn choose the head of government (see the box "Presidents and Prime Ministers").

In the first half of the twentieth century, divided government did not occur very often. From 1900 to 1950, only four of twenty-six presidential and midterm elections resulted in divided government.[73] From 1952 to 2000, however, sixteen of twenty-five elections produced divided government (seventeen if one does not count the brief months after the 2000 election when Republicans controlled the White House and both houses of Congress). Even with Reagan's overwhelming victory in 1980, the Republicans captured only the Senate. Their dominance lasted until 1986, when the Democrats regained majority control. George H. Bush had to work with a Democratic Congress, and Clinton had a Republican-controlled Congress after 1994.

Some believe that divided government is partially responsible for the failure to solve many of the country's important problems. The term *gridlock* has often been used to suggest this policy stalemate. The president presents a program, and Congress does not accept it. Or Congress passes a bill, and the president vetoes it. The result can be a lot of squabbling but few results. The impeachment proceedings in 1998 were a period of especially bitter rivalry between the White House and Congress, and it brought legislative action to a halt. But in times of national emergency, a divided Congress is not necessarily a barrier to action; witness the significant amount of legislation passed by Congress in the first months after 9/11. And united government does not always eliminate gridlock. During 1946 to 1990, as many major laws passed during periods of divided government as in periods of united government. Adoption of policies that address major problems is usually the result of strong presidential leadership, national crisis, policy failure, or a change in public opinion rather than united government.[74] Failure to adopt policies may mean there is no national consensus on the issue, or it may signify that the electoral needs of Congress and the president differ, as Bush discovered in 2003.

Legislative Leadership

Because he is the head of a political party with an issue agenda, and because the public has come to expect policy leadership from the White House, a president usually takes office with legislative goals. This can mean a few key proposals such as for tax cuts, tax reforms, or downsizing government, or it can mean a comprehensive package of proposed legislation, such as Teddy Roosevelt's Square Deal, Wilson's New Freedom, Franklin Roosevelt's New Deal, and Johnson's Great Society. People often evaluate presidential leadership in terms of the content and impact of these programs.

Many Americans are frustrated by our system's fragmentation and by "gridlock," the inability of our elected officials to agree about how to solve our nation's problems. These differences can be exacerbated when different parties control the White House and Congress, as has been the case most years since World War II. Divided government makes it more likely that the president and congressional leaders will advocate different policies and priorities. It also makes it easier for elected officials to play the "blame game" and avoid taking responsibility for failed policies and inaction. We even have problems when the White House and Congress are controlled by the same party. The president and members of Congress often have different interests because they are elected by different constituencies at different times. And they can use the system's checks and balances to thwart each other's efforts.

In contrast, British heads of government, called *prime ministers*, seem to be better party leaders and more accountable to the public. Like most democratic nations, Britain has a **parliamentary government**—that is, a system in which the executive is chosen by the legislature. The British government is marked by a unity of authority. The prime minister, or PM, is an elected member of the House of Commons, the lower house of Britain's national legislature called *Parliament*. (Parliament's other house, the House of Lords, is unelected and has more limited power.) The PM is elected like other members of the Commons—by the voters of a constituency—and then is chosen by his or her party as its leader. The PM is always the leader of the majority or plurality party in the Commons and usually decides when elections to the Commons will occur. However, elections must take place within five years of the last election. As members of the Commons, the PM and the cabinet ministers appointed by the PM must argue for their policies and respond to criticism from minority party members in debate.

Rank-and-file members of the Commons have very little independent power and often do not live in the constituencies that elect them. National party organizations have a great deal of influence over who is selected to run for election to the Commons. Members who do not vote the party line sometimes lose their party's support for re-election. This helps explain why 97 percent of the bills sponsored by the PM and cabinet from 1945 to 1987 were enacted.[1]

Although this is an attractive picture in some respects, the Founders designed our system to represent the diverse interests of a large, heterogeneous population. While more effective leadership in government is appealing, greater centralization can mean less opportunity to accommodate diverse local interests.

Many Americans would not like a national party organization to decide who would stand for election in their congressional districts. Some would also be angry if representatives advocated positions contrary to local majority opinion on an important issue because they had to follow party discipline. America is a much more diverse and decentralized society than Britain, making party cohesion more difficult.

Considering whether parliamentary forms would improve the workings of our government requires us to weigh a difficult trade-off. Do we want to pay the costs of frequent gridlock and inefficiency to keep a system that is more responsive to diverse local and other interests?

1. Richard Rose, *Politics in England: Change and Persistence,* 5th ed. (London: Macmillan, 1989), 113.

All presidents have advisers who serve as congressional liaisons; they lobby for the president's agenda and facilitate exchange of information with members of Congress on pending legislation. How active the president's personal role is depends on his involvement in policy detail, knowledge of congressional operations, and powers of persuasion. In all, twenty-four presidents have served in Congress and presumably understood how that institution works. But not all were knowledgeable or effective members of Congress. For example, Truman, Kennedy, and George H. Bush had short and undistinguished congressional careers, while Nixon used his short time in the House and Senate to build a national reputation rather than to sponsor legislation. In contrast, Gerald Ford and Lyndon Johnson rose to leadership positions in their long years of congressional service. As a former Senate majority leader of legendary persuasiveness, Johnson is the classic example of president as inside dopester and congressional coalition builder. He knew how to approach members and was a masterful lobbyist. In working for a foreign aid bill, he invited key members to the White House for one-on-one talks described by an aide as "endless talking, ceaseless importuning, torrential laying on of the facts for several days."[75]

Johnson was essentially a persuader and a deal maker, but sometimes White House staffers are more heavy-handed in seeking support. A Reagan aide described how the White House changed one senator's vote: "We just beat his brains out. We stood him in front of an open grave and told him he could jump in if he wanted to [oppose Reagan]."[76] Such tactics can succeed but can also make a president look bad. In 1990, George H. Bush was criticized for the way White House staff lobbied Congress for a budget plan. His chief of staff, John Sununu, called Trent Lott (R-Miss.), who was soon to become majority leader of the Senate, "insignificant" on television after Lott refused to support the plan. And Sununu alienated others with petty reprisals.

Presidents also use the prestige of their office as an instrument of persuasion. In 1975, Ford persuaded eighteen House members to change their votes to support one of his vetoes. He took them on his jet, *Air Force One,* and "lectured" them.[77] Because many members rarely, if ever, talk to a president, most consider these conversations memorable events and listen.

Reagan's leadership style in dealing with Congress involved going public to pressure it for support. In contrast, Clinton tried to generate congressional support for his policies by personally lobbying individual members and by trying to get backing in those parts of the country and from those interest groups most affected by the policies. One way he and his aides did this was to give interviews to journalists whose work reached those he wanted to influence. Clinton then tried to use popular support to build congressional backing by lobbying members both directly and indirectly, through intermediaries such as business and union leaders. During his administration, the final versions of many pieces of legislation were worked out in direct negotiations between conference committee leaders and White House staff or with Clinton himself. Clinton was often criticized for having so much hands-on involvement with Congress because such a strategy invests the prestige of the office in too many issues while also risking the political capital of the president himself.

George W. Bush avoids this involvement, taking positions on far fewer issues and keeping his distance from Congress. This fits with his idea of a more imperial presidency but has frustrated many in Congress who criticize him for being too distant and uninvolved in legislative matters.[78] Bush relies to a great extent on Cheney to handle relationships with congressional leaders. Cheney served in the House and also worked as a legislative liaison when he was a White House staffer. Bush reportedly told one senator repeatedly, "When you're talking to Dick Cheney, you're talking to me."[79] Cheney goes to Capitol Hill at least once a week to meet the Republican caucus, and unlike many vice presidents who used their Senate office only for ceremonial purposes, Cheney has a working office there. For lobbying purposes, he also keeps an office in the House of Representatives; he is the only vice president in history to have an office in that chamber.

Presidents cannot always get the support they need, however. Members of Congress have their own constituencies and careers. And presidential persuasion does not always involve bargaining. Presidents also remind fellow Republicans or Democrats of the need to stick together to promote their party platform and achieve party goals. Bipartisan appeals can sometimes be effective, too, especially in foreign affairs.

Veto Power

No president has to rely solely on his persuasive powers to affect legislation. The Constitution has given the chief executive veto power over bills passed by Congress. The veto power is not listed among the president's formal powers in Article II but rather is included in Article I as a check on Congress's power to legislate.

When the president receives a bill passed by Congress, he has three options: He can sign it into law; he can veto it and send it back to Congress along with his objections; or he can take no action, in which case the bill becomes a law after ten congressional working days. An unsigned bill returned by the president can be passed into law if two-thirds of both houses vote to override the veto. But if Congress adjourns within ten working days after sending legislation to the White House, and the president chooses to pocket the bill—that is, not to act on it—the legislation dies. This option, called a *pocket veto,* is a means by which the president can kill a bill without facing an override attempt in Congress.

Given the presence of White House supporters in Congress and the president's ability to go public, mobilizing two-thirds majorities in both houses to override a veto is usually very hard. As a result, presidents can try to influence the content of bills by threatening to veto them if they do not conform to presidential wishes.

Only eight presidents never vetoed a bill. Franklin Roosevelt holds the record for most vetoes with 635 vetoes in fourteen years, only 9 of which were overridden. But Grover Cleveland used his veto 584 times in just eight years. Clinton did not use the veto until his third year in office and cast 37 in all. The seventeen cast during his first full term was the lowest number for a full term since Woodrow Wilson's administration. Presidents who use the veto too often may appear isolated or uncooperative or seem to be exercising negative leadership. But the fact that presidents are rarely overridden reminds us of their power when they decide they really want something.

In 1997, after decades of lobbying by presidents, Congress gave the president the *line item veto* for appropriations bills. This change allowed a president to strike down parts of bills. It increased presidential power relative to Congress, because the president could eliminate only those parts of bills he did not like, keeping those he did. After Clinton exercised a line item veto eighty-two times, the Supreme Court struck it down as a violation of separation of powers. The ruling pointed to the constitutional provision that bills be accepted or rejected in their entirety by a president, implying that if Congress wants to change this requirement, it will have to be done by constitutional amendment rather than by legislation.

Congressional Support

A president's reputation for effectiveness is based in part on how successful he is in getting congressional support. Franklin Roosevelt's ranking as one of our greatest presidents can be attributed in part to his legislative effectiveness. He was able to persuade Congress to enact much of his legislative program within the first one hundred days of his administration. Those were extraordinary times, and few presidents since have been able to match his success in Congress.

Reagan's effectiveness with Congress was greatest in his first year in office when he got Congress to approve a major tax cut and increase military spending. Economic problems produced in part by these changes and a growing public awareness that he was uninformed about White House activities led to a drop in his effectiveness with Congress during the remainder of his administration. As Figure 3 shows, Reagan's congressional support fell after 1981 and was low compared to other presidents.

Congressional support for George H. Bush was weak throughout his term. Figure 3 shows that his first-year success with Congress was the lowest of any elected president since 1953, when scores were first computed. Bush had fewer congressional Republicans to work with than any GOP president in this century, but he even had low support among congressional Republicans. He lacked a well-articulated legislative program. He also failed to capture the public's attention with clear themes, what he once called the "vision thing." This prevented Bush from securing more congressional support, even after the Persian Gulf War when his popularity was very high.

Clinton tried to emulate Reagan's successful first-year strategy of asking Congress to vote on a few high-priority bills. This strategy lets presidents define their positions in relatively simple terms and seek congressional support when they are in their postelection honeymoon periods and before other influences on Congress have time to make mobilizing majorities more difficult. Enjoying early successes with Congress can help presidents build their professional reputations.

With both houses of Congress controlled by Democratic majorities, Clinton did not have to deal with a divided government. Despite substantial disagreements among congressional Democrats, Clinton succeeded in getting majority support for most of his early economic proposals. In fact, Clinton had the highest first-year success score with Congress (86 percent) since Eisenhower's in 1953 and Johnson's in 1964. Surprisingly, Clinton's congressional approval record during his first two years exceeded that of every president since Johnson.

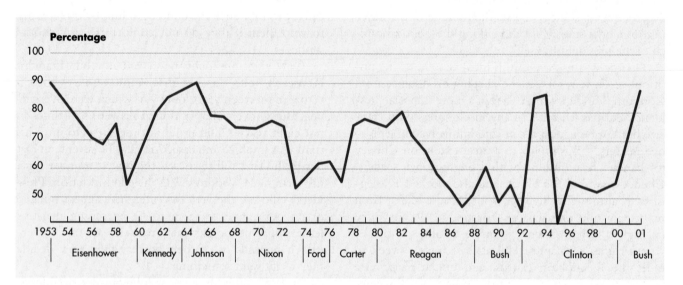

FIGURE 3 ■ Presidential Success on Congressional Votes Often Declines over Time
Presidents usually have the most success with Congress early in their first terms. This figure shows the percentage of votes that presidents have won when they took a position. Clinton's 86.4 percent score ranks the highest of any president in his first year since Johnson's 88 percent in 1964 and Eisenhower's 89 percent in 1953, while his 1995 and 1999 scores of 36.2 percent and 37.8 percent are the two lowest in CQ's nearly fifty years of record keeping. George H. Bush had the smallest first-year success of any of these presidents, while George W. Bush hit 87 percent in his first year and 88 percent in his second.
SOURCES: *Congressional Quarterly Weekly Report,* January 12, 2002, 112; and December 14, 2002, 3237.

Clinton's early legislative record was impressive, but it did not give him a reputation for effectiveness. It was overshadowed by the scandals that followed him into his second term and by his failure to articulate larger goals so the American people knew where he wanted to lead them. In 1995 and 1998, he had the lowest success rates in Congress of any president in the second half of the century (see Figure 3).

George W. Bush's first-year success rate of 87 percent was nearly identical to that of Clinton's first year, an impressive performance given the very partisan post-election atmosphere. He achieved this by taking positions on only half as many bills as Clinton had. In addition, Bush usually took a public stand only after Congress had drafted a bill in a form likely to pass.[80] With this strategy of doing and risking far less than his predecessor, Bush equaled Clinton's success rate in a divided Congress.

Foreign Policy and Military Leadership

Over the years, the president has become more powerful than Congress in foreign policy, assuming powers that were not explicitly given to either the legislative or the executive branch. One reason for this dominance is that in foreign policy, more than in domestic, the president has more information than others do. He can often stifle debate by citing classified or secret information from the CIA, Defense Department, State Department, and other agencies and saying, "If you knew what I knew, you would agree with me." The president can also share certain information with Congress (and the public) while withholding other material, putting members of Congress at a distinct disadvantage. In 1984, the Reagan administration mined harbors in Nicaragua after telling the Senate Intelligence Committee it was not doing so. When the facts became known, the chair of that committee, Barry Goldwater (R-Ariz.), wrote a blistering public letter to the head of the CIA saying, not so formally, "I am pissed off."[81]

The White House also has a large role in shaping the agenda of debate. Alternatives acceptable to the administration are advanced through public statements, background briefings of the press and Congress, and "national" newspapers such as the *New York Times* or the *Washington Post*. Many reasonable alternatives may never be suggested or receive support. Thus, media outlets did little to initiate discussions of our goals in the Persian Gulf, choosing instead to cover troop commitments largely as a logistical challenge and human interest story. Media acceptance of Pentagon restrictions on news gathering also helped Bush generate support for his policies by producing news of successful, but not unsuccessful, attacks and by concealing information describing casualties on both sides.

Although different presidential advisers sometimes advocate conflicting views publicly, it is much easier for a president than for Congress to have a coherent policy. Thus, another advantage the president has over Congress is that he can act decisively, whereas Congress must reach agreement and vote in order to act, and this takes time. George H. Bush ordered American troops to Somalia in December 1992, but the House Foreign Affairs Committee did not meet until May 1993 to authorize this action—the day after the United Nations had assumed responsibility in Somalia, and most of our troops had come home.

Because the president is one and Congress is many, the president is usually more effective in appealing for public support. There is almost always a "rally 'round the flag" effect on both Congress and the public when the president takes a strong stance in foreign policy, especially if troops are involved. In these cases, Congress may hesitate to oppose the president because it fears doing so may be seen by other nations as a sign of United States weakness.

Vietnam is a good example of presidential dominance in foreign policy. Presidential policy prevailed even with demonstrations, mass arrests, opposing editorials, negative opinion polls, and congressional criticism. The Vietnam War raised major questions about presidential authority in foreign and military policy. Although Congress never declared war in Vietnam, it routinely appropriated money for it. Nonetheless, many members of Congress believed that Johnson and Nixon exceeded their authority in pursuing the war. This painful experience led Congress to try to supervise use of military force more closely.

In 1973, Congress passed the **War Powers Act** to limit the president's ability to commit troops to combat. It says the president can use troops abroad under three conditions: when Congress has declared war, when Congress has given him specific authority to do so, or when an attack on the United States or its military creates a national crisis. If a president commits troops under the third condition, he is supposed to consult with Congress beforehand, if possible, and notify it within forty-eight hours afterward. Unless Congress approves the use of troops, the president must withdraw them within sixty days, or ninety days if he needs more time to protect them. Congress can pass a concurrent resolution (not subject to presidential veto) at any time ordering the president to end the use of military force.

Congress passed the War Powers Act over Nixon's veto. He believed it violated his constitutional authority to protect the nation from military threats. Although presidents have not questioned Congress's constitutional

Signaling the growing importance of Asia in United States foreign policy, Clinton became the first president since Jimmy Carter to visit India, the world's second most populous country and an emerging nuclear power.

authority to declare war, all have fought congressional involvement in the use of troops. As a result, enforcement of the act has proved difficult. For example, President Carter did not inform, let alone consult, Congress before using U.S. troops in an attempt to free the Iranian hostages in 1980. Congress did not protest. Neither did it protest after Bush sent troops to invade Panama in 1989. Bush did not even refer to the War Powers Act in the two-page letter he sent to Congress justifying the invasion sixty hours after it began.

On the whole, then, the War Powers Act has not stopped presidents from sending American troops abroad. This was certainly true in the Persian Gulf. President Bush sent 250,000 troops to the Gulf between August and November 1990 on his own authority. He also delayed announcing his decision to double this number until after the November elections, even though he had made the decision in October. This kept the decision that changed our mission

from defense (Operation Desert Shield) to offense (Operation Desert Storm) from coming to Congress until Bush had mobilized United States and world opinion and gained United Nations support. By the time Congress authorized using force in January 1991, the question of whether to do so was, practically speaking, already decided.

Congress has special need to be vigilant in election years because a president's public opinion scores, especially before national elections, can influence the use of military force abroad.[82] Presidents may be tempted to use rally events to increase their popularity and congressional support for their policies. A White House aide, acknowledging low presidential popularity in October 1983, said Reagan needed "a major victory somewhere to show that we can manage foreign policy." The United States invaded Grenada soon after. When Bush's scores were falling in 1990, his staff chief told associates that a short successful war against Iraq would guarantee Bush's reelection (he was wrong).[83] In late 1998 and early 1999, when Clinton was the subject of impeachment hearings, he was accused of bombing Iraq and advocating NATO's bombing of Kosovo to detract attention from his political problems. But when NATO did bomb Kosovo in March 1999, Clinton's approval ratings fell five points in one week.[84]

Historically, a president's use of military force tends to raise his congressional support for about a month.[85] This led one observer to note that, based on U.S. experiences in Vietnam and Grenada, presidents who start military actions abroad must win them in a hurry if they want to stay popular.[86]

As this discussion suggests, despite the advantages presidents have in foreign policy, Congress has often refused to give its backing to presidential initiatives. Though some scholars have argued that the presidency is really "two presidencies"—that presidents have substantially more success in winning support from Congress on foreign policy votes than on domestic policy—the evidence does not provide much support for that idea.[87]

A president needs to be able to act decisively in international affairs. But we want to make sure the president does not make any prolonged or costly commitments against the public's wishes. Congress has historically served as the most important check on the president, but its power to influence military policy is limited in emergency or crisis situations. An uneasy balance exists between presidential powers adequate to do the job and controls necessary to prevent abuse.

After the end of the Vietnam War, Congress sought to reassert its authority in foreign policy in a number of ways, including closer monitoring of intelligence agencies, limiting the president's authority to enter into trade or other agreements with foreign countries, refusing to approve arms control and other treaties negotiated by presidents, and requiring congressional approval of major arms sales.

The end of the Cold War temporarily threatened presidential foreign policy dominance. Without the threat of a challenging external enemy of superpower status, Congress was less willing to give the president the benefit of the doubt in major foreign policy initiatives, certainly not those involving a commitment of military forces. Clinton, the first post–Cold War president, was not able to count on congressional support even when he had committed troops, as in Bosnia and Haiti. In 2000, the Senate tried, and narrowly failed, to use the War Powers Resolution to force Clinton to withdraw U.S. troops from the NATO contingent in Kosovo. And many of his trade and economic initiatives met with similar resistance.

Prior to 9/11, Bush tried to recover some of the power lost to Congress. He withdrew from prior treaty agreements, such as on antimissile defense and global warming, with little consultation with Congress. The war on terrorism has strengthened presidential power further. The shock of the first attack on U.S. soil since Pearl Harbor and the uncertainty of how to deal with a new kind of warfare resulted in Congress giving the president a virtual free hand in planning the initial response. In a strengthened position after the attacks, Bush was successful in winning greater latitude in covert operations for intelligence agencies and regaining the "fast track" trade authority that allows the president to negotiate trade deals that Congress can reject but cannot change.

Limits on Presidential Power

As government grew during the first seventy-five years of the twentieth century, so did the office of the president. Some of these new powers came at the expense of Congress, but in large part they were delegated (budget making), voluntarily ceded to the president (foreign policymaking during the Cold War and now in the war against terrorism), or assumed by default through congressional inaction. What the executive branch gained was not the simple sum of what the legislative branch lost, as if the president and Congress were contestants in a zero-sum game. Much of the power FDR assumed in dealing with the Great Depression and World War II had not been exercised by any branch of the national government before. Crises arose, presidential incumbents responded, and in the process they assumed powers of government not yet established at the federal level. Indeed, several extraordinary extensions of presidential authority occurred in wartime or at a time of national crisis, including Lincoln's suspension of habeas corpus in the Civil War and, most recently, George W. Bush's authorization of military tribunals to try suspected terrorists in the absence of an act of war or a uniformed enemy.

Today a person elected to the presidency is the recipient of the respect bestowed on the office itself: People stand when the president enters a room; "Hail to the Chief" is played when he appears on a dais or at ceremonial events; men and women in uniform salute him; he is surrounded by bodyguards and aides; the public and media scrutinize every detail of his personal life and public performance. He is almost universally regarded as the most powerful person in the world. Yet some presidents have become so frustrated by limitations on their power that they try to overcome those limitations by exceeding their constitutional authority. The most famous example of illegal presidential action in the face of perceived frustration is Nixon's attempt to gather intelligence on his political opponents by invading personal privacy with phone taps, break-ins, and unauthorized reviews of income tax returns and then obstructing justice by trying to cover up evidence of these acts.

Even the most persuasive presidents like FDR, Reagan, and Johnson do not get everything they want. There are many formal checks on their constitutional powers as well as many limitations inherent in the office or the men who have served there. Formal checks include the independence of the federal judiciary; the budgetary, confirmation, oversight, and removal powers of Congress; term limitations; and the power of the electorate to throw an incumbent out of office. When formal checks do not work, or do not work quickly enough, there is also the power of a free press. The abuses of office during the Nixon administration are instances where Congress and the public did not initially serve as a check on the president; illegalities might never have been revealed had it not been for investigative reporting by the *Washington Post*. Only after evidence was uncovered by the press did the Democratic-controlled Congress deal seriously with accusations of wrongdoing.

Many idiosyncratic and situational factors also can impose restrictions on executive power, including the president's competence, personality, and attitude toward the exercise of power; the opportunity to exercise power presented by international or domestic crises, including warfare; the president's popularity and his reputation in Congress and with other Washingtonians; and the mood of Congress to use its powers fully to check the president.

In the last twenty-five years of the twentieth century, the power of the presidency appeared to wane. The decline began in reaction to the sometimes arrogant or imperial exercise of power during the Johnson and Nixon administrations, especially with respect to the conduct of the Vietnam War and abuses of the electoral process during Nixon's reelection campaign. Reagan's personal popularity and conception of the office of presidency—emphasizing the head of state and symbolic roles of the office over governance—restored some of the prestige or grandeur of the presidency, but the illegalities of the Iran-Contra affair and ethics scandals involving his appointees eroded public confidence again.

The end of the Cold War also restricted the president's freedom to act unilaterally in international affairs and reduced his role as a rally figure to mobilize public opinion against foreign enemies. In domestic affairs, decades of budget deficits, the return of many respon-sibilities to the states, and a tendency toward downsizing national government limited how much the personal presidency could credibly promise or deliver to the American public. As the presidency grew with the expanding role of national government, so it began to shrink under the weight of scandals beginning with Watergate and followed by the illegalities of the Iran-Contra dealings. With the Clinton presidency, the personal presidency seemed to be imploding. Six years of ethics investigations, a record number of special prosecutors, sensational headlines, and constant scrutiny of the First Family's personal lives all contributed to the diminution of the office. However, neither Congress nor the media would have had the inclination to concentrate on such matters had the country not been in a period of prolonged prosperity and free of foreign policy crises.

Some historians and analysts claimed that Clinton's impeachment would be similar in impact to Andrew Johnson's, which weakened the presidency for the next half-century.[88] This argument is based in large part on precedents set by federal court decisions issued during the investigation. These rulings limited a president's ability to use executive privilege to deny Congress access to records of conversations he has with his advisers and to exercise attorney–client privilege to protect such records in cases in which the advice is provided by government lawyers. The court also allowed Secret Service agents to testify before grand juries about the president's activities, including his personal conduct. But perhaps most important was the court's ruling that a sitting president can be sued for private conduct that occurred before he took office. In the latter decision, judges reasoned it was unlikely that the need to defend himself in a civil suit would divert a president's time and energy from carrying out his duties. This was clearly not the case in the sexual harassment suit brought against Clinton, and critics of the decision wondered whether the filing of civil suits would become one more maneuver to hamstring the presidency. However, other observers saw Clinton's personal conduct as having done far more damage to his professional reputation and legacy than to the office of president.[89]

While Clinton maintained throughout the impeachment process the highest sustained public approval ratings attained by any second-term president, Congress's public approval ratings took a serious dip. The president's ability to carry out his legislative agenda was severely damaged, but congressional influence also suffered when leaders were cut out of the normal routine of consultation with the White House on foreign and domestic policy. Furthermore, the public backlash against Congress during the impeachment process and against the continuous investigation of the Clintons' lives before and during their White House years contributed to Congress's decision in 1999 not to renew the independent counsel law, one of its own mandated checks on the abuses of executive power.

But the normal ebb and flow in the balance of power resulted in a strengthening of the presidency in George W. Bush's first two years in office. Determined to restore power drained from the office during the Clinton years, Bush used executive privilege to shield the office from congressional and public scrutiny and his inherent legislative authority to repeal policies of the Clinton administration. He also distanced the presidency from the political fray. It is impossible to say for certain whether he could have achieved as much of what he wanted as he did without the political climate created by the events of September 11. But it is likely that Bush's early successes resulted from a convergence of his will to reassert the powers of the presidency and the opportunity handed to him by a national emergency to do so.

What Makes an Effective President?

Every president develops a track record of his effectiveness as a leader. Richard Neustadt calls it the president's professional reputation.[90] A president with an effective reputation has a record of getting what he wants, helping his allies, and penalizing the opposition. This reputation contributes to his continuing ability to persuade the public, Congress, and other Washingtonians. Few modern presidents were more adept at getting what they wanted from Congress than Lyndon Johnson, yet Johnson often is not ranked among the great presidents. A president's professional reputation is of great importance to him while he is in office and is a commentary on his political and administrative skills. But having the ability to get what he wants is not the same as being able to do what is best for the country, and therefore presidents seen as highly effective in office are not always judged by history to have been great presidents.

It is not always immediately clear how deep an impact a president's tenure has had on the direction of the country, and over time assessments of presidential performance do change. Truman exemplifies a president who was very unpopular during his tenure and in the immediate years afterward but who left a legacy of directness, personal integrity, and decisiveness on key decisions during an extremely difficult time (the national trauma of FDR's death while we were engaged in a world war).

Neustadt has called the presidency a "choice-making machine," and presidents who can act decisively are of-

ten well regarded. Truman epitomized the decisive style and has probably benefited from the contrast with the more waffling approaches of recent presidents who are often seen as driven by polls and focus groups. The "Buck Stops Here" sign that Truman kept on his desk illustrated both his sense of accountability and his nononsense rhetoric. In historical perspective, his leadership skills have looked more impressive than they did while he was in office, and this view has helped move him to the ranks of near-great presidents.

Scholarly assessment of Eisenhower's administration has also changed significantly. Early on after he left office, he was judged an average president, a good and honest man with strong administrative skills, but one who took few chances and lacked an overall vision for the country. In retrospect, analysts see as level-headed and prescient both his leadership during an extremely volatile period in the nuclear arms race and his warnings about the dangers the military-industrial complex would present to the economy and our sense of national purpose.

How can presidential performance be measured? In characterizing the role of the president, the nineteenth-century historian Henry Adams wrote that he "resembles the commander of a ship at sea. He must have a helm to grasp, a course to steer, a port to seek."[91] That is, the incumbent must have a goal, a destination where he is leading the nation; he must have programs and a course of action to enable the nation to get there; and he must be a leader who is willing and able to use the instruments of office to achieve his goals.

Franklin Roosevelt fit the definition of a great president as a leader "of thought at times when certain ideas in the life of the nation had to be clarified."[92] This reminds us that an opportunity factor is involved in rising to the highest ranks of performance. FDR's examples of our best presidents—"Washington embod[ying] the idea of the federal union, Jefferson and Jackson the idea of democracy, Lincoln union and freedom"—are men who served at critical times in the country's development.[93] These are presidents whom almost all scholars rank among our greatest, and they are associated with ideas and policies that took root and affected the course of our country.

Any concept of presidential effectiveness inevitably involves the "vision thing." A president will likely be seen as effective only if he has a clear idea of where he wants to take the country. This is why Reagan is regarded by much of the public as a more effective president than George H. Bush, even though scholars of the presidency give Reagan and Bush comparable rankings. To rank with the "greats," however, vision must be coupled with the political and administrative skills necessary to achieve it. In the scholarly consensus, Bush was willing and able to grab the helm but was steering to no port in particular; Reagan had a fixed destination but no firm hand on the helm and insufficient knowledge or interest to steer the ship. Like Bush, Reagan had a mediocre legislative record and an abysmal fiscal record, but in the public eye, Reagan had a clear vision of what he wanted for the country. In contrast, Clinton had all the political and communication skills to steer the ship but kept changing his destination. He was unsuccessful in projecting to the public a clear and consistent vision of where the country should be headed. In a recent survey, Reagan, Bush, and Clinton were all ranked as average presidents. (See the box "Rating the Presidents.")

It is far too early to evaluate the second Bush presidency, but in his early years, Bush gave a clearer idea of what he wanted to do with the office of president than he did about where he wanted to lead the country. He was also limited by weak speaking skills, which made it difficult for him to publicly articulate his ideas and positions.

Rating the Presidents

As children, we learned that George Washington, Abraham Lincoln, and Franklin Roosevelt were great presidents, but few of us think about most of the other presidents. How do they rate? Presidential ratings surveys have been taken periodically since the historian Arthur Schlesinger Sr. first polled fifty-five leading historians in 1948. While presidents have moved up and down the rankings over the years, almost all polls agree on Washington, Lincoln, and Franklin Roosevelt as the Greats and Jefferson, Jackson, Theodore Roosevelt, Wilson, and Truman as the Near Greats. The placement of Madison in the top ten in the ranking shown here differs sharply from a 1996 *New York Times* poll of thirty-two presidential scholars; they rated Madison average.[1] Some presidents—Taylor, Harding, and Ford—spent such short periods in office that they are hard to rank. In a survey of viewers and historians conducted by C-SPAN in 2000, the historians bumped John Kennedy and Lyndon Johnson into the top ten, while dropping Madison back into the middle of the pack. Former presidents sometimes get a bounce in the poll ratings: Truman, Eisenhower, Carter, and Reagan, for example, received much higher favorable ratings in retirement than they had at the end of their terms. But higher approval does not necessarily lead to a higher ranking, as one can see in Clinton's case. Both George H. Bush and Clinton remain dead in the middle. You can review the survey results at http://americanpresidents.org/.

1. Arthur M. Schlesinger Jr., "The Ultimate Approval Rating," *New York Times Magazine,* December 18, 1996, 46–51.

Ranking U.S. Presidents

The Greats

U.S. President in Order of Overall Ranking	Leadership Qualities	Accomplishments and Crisis Management	Political Skill	Appointments	Character and Integrity
1 Lincoln	2	1	2	3	1
2 F. Roosevelt	1	2	1	2	15
3 Washington	3	3	7	1	2
4 Jefferson	6	5	5	4	7
5 T. Roosevelt	4	4	4	5	12
6 Wilson	7	7	13	6	8
7 Truman	9	6	8	9	9
8 Jackson	5	9	6	19	18
9 Eisenhower	10	10	14	16	10
10 Madison	14	14	15	11	6

The Failures (Listed Chronologically)

Pierce, Buchanan, A. Johnson, Grant, Harding, Hoover, Nixon

SOURCE: *Champaign-Urbana News-Gazette,* February 8, 1997, D-2.

Conclusion: Is the Presidency Responsive?

The presidency has become the most consistently visible office in government as well as one of the most personalized and responsive. Americans expect leadership from the president even in these days of "less" government. The presidency is responsive in that whoever holds that office has an almost direct relationship with the public. Using the media, a skillful president can tell us what he wants and attempt to shape our opinion. Through public opinion polls and the ballot box, we tell the president what we think. In this relationship, there is a danger of overresponsiveness. To remain popular, a president may seek short-term solutions to the nation's problems and neglect long-term interests. And short-term responsiveness that caters to public opinion can siphon off the attention and resources a president should be devoting to the real needs of the nation.

But most recent presidents gradually come to understand the limits of presidential power, sometimes the hard way. Indeed, the moral of the personal presidency suggests that presidents who become popular by making exaggerated promises have trouble keeping them, and their popularity, in a system of fragmented power. The Clinton years illustrated another danger in exercising the personal presidency in the age of tabloid media: the risk of diminishing the office when scrutiny of the occupant's private life overtakes evaluation of his public role.

One of the most interesting aspects of this unusual office is its resilience and elasticity. It can be stretched and shrunk from one administration to another, or even within a single administration. Each occupant is likely to make something quite different of it than his predecessor, either by the attitude and skills he brings to it or because the times force him to do so.

EPILOGUE

Harman Votes with the President

Harman voted for the president's proposal to establish a new cabinet office, even though just six weeks earlier she had been touting her own legislation as providing the strategy and the organizational plan the president had failed to produce.

As the Homeland Security Act of 2002 moved through the House, members of both parties looked skeptically at the provisions calling for Congress to cede some of its budgetary authority to the executive branch. The House Appropriations Committee was reluctant to grant the president independent authority over any part of the new department's budget. The committee chair said what he was asking for was "overly broad and unprecedented" and "would constitute a major erosion of the separation of powers abrogating the central role of the Congress—the direction and oversight of public expenditures." The ranking Democrat was harsher in claiming that if Congress granted the president this authority, the Department of Homeland Security "would become a $30 billion slush fund for the executive branch."[94] But the provisions ceding some budgetary authority to the executive branch and to waive workers' rights remained in the House bill over the objections of many Democrats.

From the beginning of the legislative process, Bush had courted Harman, knowing that, because she was the ranking minority member on the Terrorism and Homeland Security Subcommittee and a sponsor of competing legislation, her support was crucial. She was one of only three Democrats the president invited to the White House for consultation and photo-ops after requesting the new office. Bush knew Harman's support was winnable; she was a centrist, a defense hawk, and up for re-election in what would probably be a close contest. And Harman did abandon her own bill after negotiations between House leaders and White House staff produced some minor alterations in the president's legislation. Harman called the final version "ambitious and bold" and said it would help win both the war on terrorism and the war on turf.[95]

In the Democratic-controlled Senate, there was a less generous view of the president's plan. Senate leader Daschle called the bill a "power grab of unprecedented magnitude."

Appropriations Committee Chairman Robert Byrd (D-W.V.), a forty-year veteran and outspoken defender of congressional prerogatives, said he would not vote for passage without careful, and maybe even lengthy, review. He refused to join a "stampede." "With the level of endorsement the Congress has given to this idea, you would think that the proposal had been engraved in the stone tablets that were handed down to Moses at Mount Sinai. But in reality, the idea was developed by four presidential staffers in the basement of the White House. For all we know, it could have been drafted on the back of a cocktail napkin."[96] Byrd was worried that the powers the president was asking for "could upend the system of checks and balances." Some of his Republican colleagues agreed that everything was going too fast for such a major restructuring, but one said "the train is moving forward, so we have to get on it."[97]

Harman and other House Democrats who supported the Bush bill did have allies in the Senate, especially Joseph Lieberman. But Harman and Lieberman represent constituencies where defense industry, corporate, and professional interests are far more important than those of unionized workers. With the midterm election looming, Senate Democrats were unwilling to vote on the House version of the bill because they did not want to give the president the power to waive bargaining rights and civil service protections for workers. And the White House was unwilling to negotiate a compromise version because the lack of action on the bill allowed Republicans to accuse Democrats of blocking the creation of an office the president claimed was vital to national security. So the Homeland Security Act was put aside until after the November elections determined whether the composition of the new Congress would strengthen the president's hand or that of Senate Democrats.

When the Repulicans gained a Senate majority, the bill passed with only nine dissenting votes in a form that gave Bush almost all he asked for.

 To learn more about the Homeland Security Act of 2002 and the struggle to pass it, go to this chapter's "You Are There" exercises on the text Web site.

Key Terms

impeachment	personal presidency
senatorial courtesy	power to persuade
executive privilege	divided government
executive orders	parliamentary government
head of state	War Powers Act

Further Reading

Anonymous [Joe Klein], *Primary Colors: A Novel of Politics* (New York: Random House, 1996). Inspired by the first Clinton presidential campaign, this is one of the most insightful and readable books on modern presidential politics, and certainly the funniest.

Michael R. Beschloss, ed., *Reaching for Glory: The Secret Johnson White House Tapes, 1964–65* (New York: Simon & Schuster, 2001). The second in a series of books based on White House conversations secretly taped by President Johnson. This volume contains Johnson's private thoughts on the Vietnam War and reveals that even as he committed more men and resources to the war, he believed we could not win.

Doris Kearns Goodwin, *No Ordinary Time* (New York: Simon & Schuster, 1994). An engaging study of life in the White House and the leadership of Franklin Roosevelt during World War II.

Philip B. Kunhardt Jr., Philip B. Kunhardt III, and Peter W. Kunhardt, *The American President* (New York: Riverhead, 1999). This is a companion volume for the PBS series on the presidency. It describes all presidencies through Clinton's, grouping them by shared char-acteristics rather than chronologically. It also offers a marvelous pictorial history of the office and presidential families.

Kati Marton, *Hidden Power: The Impact of Presidential Marriages on Our Recent History* (New York: Pantheon, 2001). Portraits of eleven presidential marriages with a focus on how influence wielded within these relationships affected policy.

Richard E. Neustadt, *Presidential Power and the Modern Presidents* (New York: Free Press, 1990). The most cited book on the presidency, it argues that presidential power is based on the ability to persuade.

Gary Wills, *James Madison* (New York: Penguin, 2001) A biography of one of the best-known Founders but one of our least-known presidents. This book is one in a series of presidential biographies being published by Penguin in small book format (about two hundred pages). Each is, or will be, written by a well-known American writer.

Electronic Resources

whitehouse.gov/
The White House home page has links to the Office of the Vice President, the First Lady, Homeland Security, and all EOP offices. You can tour the White House, read presidential speeches, and email the president. The link to the First Lady's home page allows viewers to send email, look at the work of the office, and link to biographies of each of America's First Ladies.

www.historyplace.com/
Contains sound bites from speeches made by all presidents since Franklin Roosevelt.

americanpresidents.org/
C-SPAN's Peabody Award–winning Web site for historical coverage of the American presidency.

www.access.gpo.gov/usbudget/
*A Citizen's Guide to the Federal Budget, Fiscal Year 2003.
Reading the president's annual budget message is one way to find
out the basic goals of any administration.*

InfoTrac College Edition

**Search for the following articles in the InfoTrac
database:**

Edwards III, George C., and B. Dan Wood. "Who Influences Whom? The President, Congress, and the Media," *American Political Science Review* (June 1999).

Greenstein, Fred I. "The Contemporary Presidency: The Changing Leadership of George W. Bush: A Pre- and Post-9/11 Comparison," *Presidential Studies Quarterly* (June 2002).

Reed, Bruce. "Monkey Do: Similarities between Presidencies and Management Decisions of President George W. Bush and Former President Bill Clinton," *Washington Monthly* (June 2001).

Rose, Melody. "Losing Control: The Intraparty Consequences of Divided Government," *Presidential Studies Quarterly* (December 2001).

For more articles, enter

"George W. Bush" in the Subject Guide;

"Bill Clinton" in the Subject Guide;

"Presidential Studies Quarterly" for journal name in PowerTrac.

American Government Resources

Visit the Government Institutions section of the Wadsworth American Government Resources Web site (politicalscience.wadsworth.com/amgov/) for a variety of tools to help you explore the presidency further. Included are simulations, video clips, Microcase exercises, and a wealth of other activities.

CHAPTER 12

THE BUREAUCRACY

FBI whistleblower Coleen Rowley faces media at her congressional hearing.

Can the FBI Hold Its Ground?

You are Robert S. Mueller III; it is summer 2002, and you are in your first year as director of the Federal Bureau of Investigation (FBI). You took office on September 4, 2001, and exactly one week later nineteen terrorists hijacked four planes and plowed three of them into the Pentagon and the World Trade Center. After a series of bungled operations, and with the eyes of the public focused on fighting terrorism, you must make a decision about the FBI's future. Should you fight to keep the agency in the Justice Department, where it has been since its creation and where career agents prefer to stay? Or should you support the call of many in Congress to move the FBI into the president's proposed Homeland Security department, despite the opposition of career professionals?

The FBI has a long history, some of it inglorious. For decades after its 1924 founding to enforce federal criminal laws, the FBI was headed by J. Edgar Hoover, who made it into a respected agency, even an icon of popular culture. However, it was also feared. During his fifty years as director, Hoover turned the FBI into his own personal fiefdom, grossly abusing his powers by keeping personal files on presidents and members of Congress, then using the information to get what he wanted for the agency and to protect his own position. Hoover was followed by a series of political appointees, many

with substantial backgrounds in criminal law but until the 1990s, none from inside the agency. Then President Clinton appointed an FBI insider, Louis Freeh. Having one of their own head the agency lifted morale, yet Freeh was unable to break the old culture or redefine the FBI's mission.

You are a lawyer who spent much of your career as a U.S. district attorney and as a political appointee in the Justice Department, which oversees the FBI. You have had some experience in counterterrorism work by virtue of your involvement in the prosecution of terrorists involved in blowing up a passenger plane several years ago (Pan Am 103). But you have been much more involved with the usual kind of cases the FBI handles: violations of federal drug and civil rights laws, public corruption, white-collar and organized crime.

You had been appointed to replace Freeh because the agency was increasingly seen as adrift and in urgent need of reform. It had weathered one foul-up after another. In a standoff with a right-wing separatist at Ruby Ridge, Idaho, an FBI sniper killed the rebel's wife. Freeh and senior agents narrowly escaped formal censure from the Justice Department for their handling of that case. Next came the debacle at Waco, Texas, where dozens of women and children, members of a religious cult, were killed in a fire while your agency had their compound surrounded. This time the FBI had not taken the lives, but the agents at the site were widely regarded as having provoked the situation that led to the deaths. Then, just as the agency was starting to make a recovery with its swift resolution of the bombing of the federal building in Oklahoma City, agents investigating espionage at a government weapons lab in Las Alamos, New Mexico, ham-handedly fingered a Chinese American scientist as a spy, accusing him of leaking classified information on weapons of mass destruction to the Chinese. When all but one of fifty-nine charges had to be dismissed for lack of evidence, the FBI ended up with egg on its face for what appeared to be a case of racial profiling.

In a grave lapse, the agency discovered that one of its own veteran agents, Robert Hanssen, had been spying for the Soviet Union for years. A man living way beyond his means and whose brother-in-law suspected him of spying continued to pass muster at the FBI. No one knows how many agents lost their lives because of information sold by Hanssen. That story played day after day in newspapers and evening newscasts, and there were other well-publicized failures.[1] By the time you were named director, six separate reviews of the agency were in progress.[2]

Then came 9/11, an incredible initiation into your new job. Local law enforcement officials and the public received no warning of the attacks from your agency or the CIA. During the first days afterward, the country was in shock, preoccupied with rescue efforts, finding survivors, mourning victims, and worrying about when another attack might occur. But gradually the questions began: Where were American intelligence agencies, and why had they not picked up any signs that such an attack was coming? What was being done to prevent new attacks?

As the questions proliferated, intelligence agencies started pointing fingers at one another. There was talk of interagency competition and turf wars, outdated computer equipment, ineffec-

tive means of information-sharing, inadequate surveillance of visa violators, lack of on-the-ground intelligence gathering in countries harboring terrorist organizations, too few agents with language skills, not enough data analysts, and more. You admit to Congress that the agency is woefully short of intelligence analysts and that you had to borrow twenty-six from the CIA for the antiterrorist investigation. No wonder everyone is beginning to see the FBI as just another part of the bureaucratic forest, at best, or a group of incompetents, at worst.

Then details of specific failures in fighting terrorism before September 11 emerge. A flight school administrator in Arizona called the local FBI to report a suspicious student who wanted to learn to take off but not to land. The agent passed that information to Washington, but there was no follow-up. Messages were intercepted warning that "D-Day was here," but because of the backlog of information and shortage of trained personnel, the message was not translated until September 12.

In May, one of the most egregious FBI lapses was revealed in a scathing eight-page memo sent to you by Coleen Rowley, a Minneapolis-based agent and counsel involved in the case of Zacarias Moussaoui, an Algerian, now under indictment as the so-called twentieth hijacker. He had been arrested just weeks before the attacks and held on suspicion of terrorist activities. In her attempt to get a search warrant to go through Moussaoui's personal belongings and the contents of his computer, Rowley had been thwarted by a midlevel manager.[3] She criticized you for doing what FBI directors usually do when they get bad news—you protected the agency. You said that the search of Moussaoui's

China now says it will withdraw its opposition to the missile-defense shield if the F.B.I. builds it.

home probably would have made no difference. Rowley was outraged, charging that you could not possibly know that for certain.

The memo went to Congress, and Rowley testified before the Senate Judiciary Committee. Even though Rowley's critics said she could have gotten a warrant on her own by going through the criminal courts, you cannot ignore her memo. Rowley is a twenty-one-year veteran with a law degree and an unblemished record in the agency. So you go public to commend her for her actions. You say henceforth when agents request search warrants in terrorism cases you will review them personally. You promise big changes at the FBI, in part because Congress is promising even bigger changes. You want to get out in front of Congress and present your own plan for reorganization before reforms from outside the agency are your only option.[4]

The question now facing you is what kind of internal reform to propose. You must keep in mind that you are a political appointee and to some extent must follow the bidding of your superiors. But you also want to protect the agency and try to ensure that its legacy is not swallowed up in the larger bureaucracy of Homeland Security.

Because terrorists are committing crimes within the United States as well as acts of aggression from outside, the

FBI has to play a central role in homeland security. But the turf battles between the FBI and other agencies, especially the CIA, are notorious. Historically, the FBI was charged with domestic law enforcement; the international work was left to the CIA. Each agency protected its role from intrusion by the other. A wall of separation developed between them, contributing to pre–September 11 intelligence lapses.

You understand that better coordination of counterterrorist work is essential; that case has been well and tragically made. But does the bureau have to lose its identity by being moved to a new cabinet department where all the focus will be on counterterrorism? What will happen to the other missions of the FBI? Your predecessor, who some agents thought was obsessed with terrorism, tried to reshuffle agency priorities and asked for more counterterrorism agents, equipment, and a

bigger budget. You sent that proposal to the Justice Department, and the day before 9/11 Attorney General Ashcroft turned it down.

But now everyone wants the FBI on board in fighting terrorism, and becoming part of the new cabinet department would put the agency at the heart of the fight. But many agents are resisting giving up the agency's historical role in law enforcement. How can you reorganize the FBI while salvaging the historic mission and iconic status of the agency?

Much of what the agency does has little to do with terrorism. More than eleven thousand special agents have spent years developing expertise in areas of law enforcement basic to the FBI's historic mission, fields such as violations of federal drug and civil rights laws, public corruption, and white-collar and organized crime. These crimes will still need to be fought even

as the war on terrorism proceeds. Of course, most of the FBI's career agents and other employees would prefer that the agency remain as it is. Not only would this approach allow them to apply the skills it took years to acquire, but it would leave the agency with the clout in Congress and visibility with the public it took decades to build.

What do you do? Do you accept the argument that much of the bureau's traditional mission is passé and go along with its reassignment from Justice to the proposed department of Homeland Security? Not only will this anger many of your career agents, but it may even write off the bureau's involvement in some areas of law enforcement. Or do you defend the agency's turf against all reorganization plans, promising instead to fix specific problems and improve the agency's responsiveness in the antiterrorism fight?

When George Wallace ran as a third-party candidate for president in 1968, he campaigned against "pointy-headed bureaucrats" in Washington making decisions that regulated good people's lives. Bureaucrats, according to Wallace, were out of touch with everyday citizens and their concerns. Wallace did not invent bureaucracy bashing, but he helped make it popular among candidates for federal office.

President Reagan never tired of talking about his dissatisfaction with big government and liked to say he preferred flying over Washington because being in the air made government look smaller. Presidential candidates Patrick Buchanan and Ross Perot ran for office by disparaging the people who run the government they wanted to lead. And not long after taking office, George W. Bush discounted a report on global warming "put out by the bureaucracy," implying that, given its source, it need not be taken seriously.

When these men refer to "Washington," they mean big government using too much money to do things that are not needed. Does government do unneeded things? And if so, why? These critics would argue that bureaucrats are not like ordinary citizens. Instead, the argument goes, they are busybodies committed to expanding government's size, spending taxpayers' money, and designing regulations to make life more difficult for individuals and business.

To some people the federal bureaucracy has become the symbol of big government and the embodiment of

everything they dislike about it. It is seen as equivalent to a fourth branch of government—powerful, uncontrollable, and with a life of its own. But, in fact, the federal bureaucracy has no independent legislative authority, only that delegated by Congress, and it has no budgetary powers. The bureaucracy's official role is to implement and enforce policies made by elected officials—that is, by Congress and the president. In doing this, bureaucrats do, in some instances, make new law. But departments and agencies exist at the pleasure of Congress, which can eliminate them or trim their budgets if it does not approve of their behavior. If an agency within the bureaucracy consistently supersedes its authority, it is because Congress is willfully letting it do so or because it is not fulfilling its oversight duties.

And, as we shall see, government bureaucrats are a lot like everyone else. They are ordinary citizens with attitudes that mirror those of their fellow citizens.

Bureaucratic decision making is involved in so much of our lives because government has come to serve many different purposes and interests. The federal government employs butchers, truck drivers, engineers, and three-quarters of all the math Ph.D.s working in the United States. In all, it employs 2.6 million civilians who work in one hundred agencies at more than eight hundred different occupations. (The armed forces, exclusive of the reserves, put another 1.4 million on the federal payroll.) Federal bureaucrats do crop research and soil analysis, run hospitals and utilities, fight drug trafficking, check manufacturers' claims about their products, inspect mines, develop high-tech weapons systems, send out Social Security checks, authorize Medicare payments, administer student loan programs, and regulate air traffic, to mention only a few responsibilities.

In this chapter, we look at the evolution of the federal bureaucracy, its growth in size, function, and lawmaking powers. We describe the people who staff the bureaucracy, how they are recruited, what rules govern their work, and how Congress and the president set guidelines for the executive branch and oversee its work. Finally, we describe ways in which the public can join in the work of monitoring the bureaucracy and have a say in the rules it makes.

The Nature of Bureaucracies

Many people automatically associate the word *bureaucracy* with the federal government. They may visualize rows of cubicles with nameless clerical workers doing monotonous work very inefficiently. Trying to cash in on this stereotype, a Virginia company once sold a "Bureaucrat" doll, as "a product of no redeeming social value. Place the Bureaucrat on a stack of papers on your desk, and he will just sit on them."[5] The problem with this joke is that the parodied traits are not necessarily common to government bureaucrats, nor are they unique to them. All organizations except the very smallest have bureaucracies: Your college or university has

one, as did your local school district; corporations, most religious denominations, and large philanthropic foundations have them, too, not to mention the Olympics, your favorite sports league, and the unions that represent the players in that league.

All these bureaucracies, public and private, share some common features. For example, all have hierarchies of authority; that is, everyone in a bureaucracy has a place in a pyramidal network of jobs, with fewer near the top and more near the bottom. Almost everyone in a bureaucracy has a boss, and, except for those in the bottom tier, most have some subordinates. People advance up the hierarchy based on performance or seniority, so those with more authority tend to be those with more experience and expertise.

Because of the hierarchical structure, bureaucratic behavior is not always consistent with democratic principles. Most bureaucrats are not elected, and, as in any hierarchical organization, higher-level authorities can restrict the opportunity of someone lower in the pyramid to express an opinion or share expertise in the decision-making process. In their relative lack of openness, bureaucracies have the potential to restrict consumer and client access to information about their products and services and how they operate, and to limit citizens' access to information about their own government. In effect, organizational tendencies, if unrestrained in a government bureaucracy, could transform "citizens" into "subordinates."[6] But our constitutional system provides checks on the power of federal bureaucrats and ways for the public to participate in decision making that few know about or take advantage of.

Bureaucracies are not only structurally similar in different types of organizations, but they do the same types of work. Employees in both private and public bureaucracies perform a lot of routine tasks. Auditing expense vouchers, managing employee travel, and creating personnel systems, for example, are as routine in business firms as in public agencies. And both also have workers who are productive, honest, and efficient and others who are not. Executives in the Defense Department bought $600 toilet seats and spent more than $75 apiece for metal screws sold elsewhere for 57 cents. In the 1970s and 1980s their private counterparts at Chrysler, Lockheed, Penn Central, and hundreds of banks and savings and loans ran their businesses into the ground, then looked to the government for bailouts or buyouts. During the 1990s, corporations paid out hundreds of millions of dollars in stock options and bonuses to executives who, in return, lied about company earnings and cost investors billions of dollars.

To some extent, the distinction between private and public bureaucracies has become blurred, but differences remain, and here we look at several.[7]

"I'm sorry, dear, but you knew I was a bureaucrat when you married me."

Goals

Businesses are supposed to make a profit; if they do not, they fail. Public agencies are supposed to promote the "public interest"; if they do not, they fail to serve the people who pay their salaries. Although people disagree over what the public interest is, it is not the same thing as making a profit, just as a government is not a business. This is why we have different words for these two kinds of organization that exist for completely different reasons.

The goals of a public bureaucracy are defined by elected officials, who collectively determine what is in the public interest. They are sometimes accused of setting goals as if they were in a private bureaucracy—that is, making policies that will sell at the polls rather than those that serve the public good. But in general, the goals set by these officials are supposed to accomplish tasks and provide services that private bureaucracies cannot. In some cases, such as providing for national security during wartime, they must do so irrespective of cost.

Some part of the public's varying perception of how well the bureaucracy does its job stems from a lack of agreement on the work it is given to do. One person's lazy, red-tape-ridden, uncaring bureaucracy is another's responsive agency. But even when unhappy with the delivery service, Americans still expect government to provide a vast array of services, costing billions of dollars annually, from highways that accommodate high-speed cars to Social Security payments that arrive on time, from clean tap water to safe neighborhoods, from protection from foreign enemies to a cure for cancer.

Performance Standards

A major problem with the difference in goals between public and private bureaucracies is that it creates the need for a standard other than profit for evaluating performance. One obvious method is to determine whether a public agency is accomplishing its goals in the most efficient and cost-effective way possible. That sounds logical, but any method of assigning dollar value to bureaucratic output must of necessity be partly subjective. It is usually easier to place a value on a commodity than on a government service. We can estimate what price to place on a chair or a house by computing the cost of constructing it. But placing a dollar value on such public goals as education or consumer safety is much harder. How many children have to die from swallowing pills and medications before government requires pharmaceutical manufacturers to use childproof caps on bottles? Or how many lives saved makes it worthwhile for government to require auto manufacturers to install air bags? These are questions bureaucrats must answer on a daily basis. They are required to cal-

culate how much a human life is worth and how productive an individual will be during his or her lifetime. Then they have to estimate the costs of putting the policies in place to protect lives, as well as to monitor and enforce them.

Private bureaucracies ask the same questions before their leaders decide whether it is profitable to install safer fuel tanks in cars or to remove a low-risk flaw from a child's toy. Although the federal bureaucrat, too, is always weighing costs against benefits, many believe the government should not use costs as the primary standard when lives are at risk.

Another way to evaluate performance is to measure waste that stems from inefficiency and corruption. This is not that difficult to do once exposed. It is not hard to calculate how much more an agency paid out for equipment and supplies because it failed to get competitive bids when it hired more employees than necessary to do a job, contracted consultants to do imaginary work, or erred in calculating welfare payments or farm subsidies. But other kinds of government "waste" are hard to measure.

Some people judge a program wasteful, no matter how well run, because they are opposed to its goals. Perhaps the program is providing services the taxpayer thinks inappropriate for government or maybe it serves relatively few people at a large cost. These were the criteria many Americans used to evaluate welfare programs. Accusations of waste and fraud were common, but, as a percentage of overall expenditures, there was little client fraud in the welfare program. Most criticism stemmed from opposition to the program itself and services provided at large cost to a small clientele without appropriate results.

When a government commission called it wasteful to keep open hundreds of very small post offices that served rural communities, they were not alleging fraud or mismanagement. To the Commission, the post offices cost too much for the small number of people served. To the residents of these communities their post offices were a good return on their tax dollars and more efficient than having to drive miles to a station in a larger town.

Citizens have rarely applied, at least not prior to our more environmentally conscious era, this standard of waste to corporate behavior. If a business or industry makes a profit, most people think it is a job well done, without asking whether the product or service offered is in itself wasteful. Marketing a hundred different kinds of breakfast cereal in packaging twice the size of the contents may not be an efficient use of resources, but if they sell, consumers are inclined to say, "Why not?" We may not like chocolate-covered fruit loops, but we do not consider their manufacturer wasteful for making them as long as the product is profitable.

Historically, private corporations have been able to waste more than a government agency of comparable size without the public ever taking notice. In 2001, when senior managers in the federal bureaucracy got bonuses averaging $11,000, it prompted public scrutiny of their agencies' performances.[8] When CEOs of corporations that lost money got multimillion-dollar bonuses, much of the public simply said, "Whatever the market will allow."

We see government expenditures as *our* money, and we feel entitled to complain, especially since payment of that money (taxes) is not voluntary. Only recently has such a large percentage of the public invested in stock that they have begun paying attention to how private bureaucracies manage *investors'* money. Yet, private investments often are made through public bureaucracies, such as a university's or a school district's pension fund, and when losses occur because of corruption or poor performance by the corporate bureaucracy, it may still be the public bureaucracy that takes much of the heat.

Openness

The openness of public bureaucracy is another feature distinguishing it from a private bureaucracy. Private firms operate with much more secrecy than do public agencies, even when private actions have a significant impact on the public. For example, tobacco companies' lack of openness, while long assumed to be their right, cost the lives of many people. The courts ordered tobacco companies to open their files only after much scientific evidence on the dangers of tobacco had accumulated.

In contrast, the greater visibility, or openness, of public agencies helps make them more responsive. Only by having knowledge of both the process and the content of public decisions can interested groups and individuals express their preferences effectively. No one articulated this better than James Madison when he wrote, "A popular Government without popular information or the means of acquiring it, is but a Prologue to a Farce or a Tragedy or perhaps both. Knowledge will forever govern ignorance, and a people who mean to be their own Governors, must arm themselves with the power knowledge gives."[9]

To this end, in 1813, Congress established a system for making government documents accessible to the public by placing them in local libraries around the country. But as government grew and agencies and paper proliferated, it became harder for the public to keep track of what government was doing. In 1934, Congress passed the Federal Register Act requiring that all government rules, regulations, and laws be published in the **Federal Register** and that all rules in

their final version appear in the *Code of Federal Regulations.* (Today both are available online.)

Congress went further in 1946 by passing the **Administrative Procedure Act (APA),** which provides for public participation in the rule-making process. All federal agencies must disclose their rule-making procedures and publish all regulations at least thirty days in advance of their effective date to allow time for public comment. Today citizens often can post comments on proposed rules at an agency's Web site, but it is common for public hearings to be held on controversial rules or those with wide impact. Environmental rules frequently provoke citizen reactions, with comments sometimes numbering in the tens of thousands.

Congress increased public access to the bureaucracy in another way by passing the Freedom of Information Act in 1966. **FOIA** (pronounced "foy-ya"), as amended in 1974, lets any member of the public apply to an agency for access to unclassified documents in its archives. The government also puts out a handbook telling how to take advantage of this right, and every government Web site is required to have a link to its FOIA office.[10] The FOIA cannot be used to gain access to internal records such as personnel files, for example, or sensitive documents on a living person. But FOIA can be used to get your FBI file, should you have one, or the file of a person no longer living. Requests must be made according to a formal procedure, and they must

---

The Under Secretary of Energy
Washington, D.C. 20585

December, 1992

MEMORANDUM FOR SECRETARIAL OFFICERS

SUBJECT:　　　NE/NE-60 Concurrence

Recently, memoranda have been prepared for my signature or directed to departmental offices from other departmental offices which contain statements regarding whether the direction contained in the memorandum is applicable to Naval Reactors (NE-60). Several memoranda have been incorrect in their assumption regarding the effects on NE-60, resulting in unnecessary further correspondence to correct the misunderstanding.

Applicability to NE-60 of a contemplated action is not always obvious. In many cases, the impact is either indirect or the direct impact is not appreciated due to lack of understanding of the scope of NE-60 responsibility. To avoid misunderstandings in the future, you are requested to consult NE regarding applicability statements <u>before</u> they are made and before memoranda are presented to me, the Secretary, or Deputy Secretary for signature.

I appreciate your attention to this matter.

Hugo Pomrehn
Hugo Pomrehn

Sometimes real examples of bureaucratic thinking are stranger than ones we might imagine. This example was reprinted in Washington Monthly. *Is it any wonder ordinary people think bureaucrats have their own language?*

cite specific documents. Agencies are not obligated to give "information," only to provide copies of the documents requested, if they have them and if they are not in an exempt category.

Most FOIA requests still come from businesses, interest groups, lawyers, scholars, and the media. But members of the general public are increasingly taking advantage of it. Government agencies received 2 million FOIA requests in 2001 and employed over five thousand administrators to process them. Groups that are directly affected by an agency's decisions have a strong incentive to use the act. Thus, in one year, 85 percent of the requests for information submitted to the Food and Drug Administration came from companies that it regulates. That information enabled the companies to evaluate their strategies for influencing agency decisions that affect them.

Efforts to make government agencies more open often run up against a desire to limit the distribution of critical or embarrassing information. It is the rare public or private bureaucracy that wants to reveal its failures. Thus, an evaluation of FOIA found that agencies used many tactics to discourage people from seeking information, such as delaying responses to requests, charging high fees for copies of records (the State Department once charged $10 a page for copying records), and requiring detailed descriptions of documents requested.[11] The FBI once refused to expedite the release of information to a prisoner on death row who was afraid he would be executed before the information was available. The FBI's judgment that his situation did not show "exceptional need or urgency" was overruled by a federal court.[12]

As the chief executive, a president's views on the openness of agencies have also been important. The president's policy on FOIA implementation is communicated to federal agencies by the attorney general at the beginning of each administration. Republican presidents have been more reluctant to release information than Democratic ones. Under Reagan and Bush Sr., federal agencies adopted a narrow reading of the act, making it more difficult to get information.[13] George W. Bush adopted a policy of rolling back FOIA access, justifying it on national security grounds. (See the "After 9/11" box.) In contrast, Carter banned classification of documents unless they were clearly related to national security. Clinton issued an executive order that directed that most documents twenty-five years old or older be declassified and put a ten-year limit on how long documents can remain classified unless a review determines that they should remain so.[14]

There is also disagreement over which public documents are subject to FOIA requests and which are exempt. The federal government, like private businesses, stores an increasing amount of information electronically. Retrieving the growing mass of information stored on

Stefano Paltera/Gamma

Federal employees are often on the front line of danger. A mail carrier protects herself after other postal workers were infected by anthrax spores sent through the U.S. mail in 2001.

computer can be easier than finding information on paper. However, FOIA neither defined when electronic information was in the public domain nor required agencies to save and release it. The aides of Reagan, George H. Bush, and Clinton used email extensively. Bush took his aides' email tapes with him when he left office and argued that they were not public property. A federal appeals court ruled that these tapes are public records and must be preserved, and they applied the same ruling to Clinton administration requests for exemption. Because of these rulings, George W. Bush's administration has been very cautious about exchange of views by email.

Despite the limitations of FOIA, it has enabled individuals and groups to gain important and useful information. Citizens have used it to gather injury and fatality information on defective cars, to assess dangerous infant formulas, to reveal a link between aspirin and a disease known as Reye's syndrome, to learn that J. Edgar Hoover authorized the FBI to carry on a four-year investigation of women's rights groups, and to force the IRS to release a forty-thousand-page manual on its auditing procedures.[15] Scholars have used FOIA to retrieve thousands of documents on Cold War diplomacy, to get records of medical experiments on the effect of radioactivity conducted on unwitting subjects, and to retrieve the FBI files of anthropologists kept under surveillance during the Cold War and McCarthy era.

Public access to records that document experiments on human subjects and surveillance of private citizens is an essential check on abuse of power by federal bureaucrats. Yet some categories of information and types of deliberation among decision makers require privacy. It is not always easy to strike the right

A few months after the destruction of the World Trade Center, federal officials contacted the head of the Documents Library at the University of Illinois and told her to destroy a CD with information on the nation's largest water supplies. The library had received the CD under the federal depository library program, established in 1813 "[t]o guarantee public access to government information by making it available free of charge." Illinois is one of 1,350 libraries designated as depositories, and faced with the possibility of losing that designation, the documents librarian destroyed the CD.[1]

The water supply CD was one of more than 6,600 scientific and technical documents the government began removing from public release at the beginning of 2002, some from libraries and many from government Web sites. The EPA, for example, deleted a database on chemicals used at industrial sites.[2] The government also asked scientists' professional associations to restrict what they publish.[3]

In the public eye, the tightening of access to public documents could be justified in the face of a palpable threat to national security. It was widely believed that one of the reasons terrorists were able to carry out part of their plans on September 11 was that they knew how to take advantage of the openness of American society. No one wants to make it easier for terrorists to plan new attacks by having access to detailed site information on nuclear waste dumps, nuclear power plants, or other utilities and public facilities or information on how to construct nuclear, biological and chemical weapons.

But information of interest to potential terrorists is not all that has been removed from public view. By executive orders from President Bush and directives from Attorney General John Ashcroft, new rules on access to all government documents and reports have been put in place, most of them having nothing to do with the war against terrorists.

In a dramatic departure from Reno Justice Department policy in the Clinton era that "encouraged agency compliance" with FOIA, Ashcroft sent a memo to all federal agencies one month after the 9/11 attacks that changed the standard for release of government documents to the public.[4] The memo assured FOIA administrators that when they "decide to withhold records, in whole or in part," the Justice Department "will defend your decisions unless they lack a sound legal basis or present an unwarranted risk of adverse impact on the

This comment was all that remained of an email after the Bush administration censored it before release to a congressional committee.

New York Times, March 31, 2002.

ability of other agencies to protect important records."[5] The Clinton administration standard for FOIA access to government records had been to exempt a document from a FOIA request only if there was a "foreseeable harm" in its release. Under the Bush standard, any FOIA request denied by an agency for any "sound legal basis" can expect Justice Department backing.

The Bush–Ashcroft guidelines also place special emphasis on protecting the privacy of federal bureaucrats and gov-

balance between the need for privacy and openness to the public, interest groups, and the media.

Another significant law mandating openness in government is the aptly named *Sunshine Act.* Adopted in 1977, it requires most government meetings to be conducted in public and for there to be public notice of them. Regulatory agencies, for example, must give advance notice of the date, time, place, and agenda of their meetings and follow certain rules to prevent unwarranted secrecy. State governments have adopted their own sunshine laws, and today it is difficult for any public body—city council or planning commission or any

of their subgroups—to meet in secret to conduct official business. Results of meetings conducted in closed, unannounced sessions are open to citizen challenge.

Growth of the Federal Bureaucracy

The Founders did not discuss the federal "bureaucracy," but they did recognize the need for an administration to carry out laws and programs. They envisioned adminis-

ernment officials as a reason for exempting documents from FOIA requests. Bush also signaled his position on privacy by amending, on executive order, public access to presidential papers and by refusing to turn over White House papers to congressional oversight committees.

By executive order, Bush also reversed the Clinton policy that made it more difficult for department and agency heads to classify records as "secret." When Clinton came to office, there were about a half-million federal employees with the authority to stamp documents secret; over the previous quarter-century, an estimated 1.5 billion pages of classified material had accumulated.[6] Clinton's order that all documents more than twenty-five years old be declassified by the year 2000 resulted in the release of 800 million pages of material, four times as much as in the previous fifteen years.[7] With his order, Bush reauthorized department and agency heads to stamp documents secret on their own authority.

The narrow definition of rights of public access and the penchant for secrecy have left the administration open to criticism from across the political spectrum. The head of the independent Judicial Watch interest group said the administration's attitude has been "arrogant throughout—that the government is not to be questioned."[8] And when a

civil rights lawyer was refused permission to see a court order that gave approval to the government's jailing hundreds of foreigners after 9/11, she complained, "They say, 'There's a secrecy order barring us from telling you this. But the language of the secrecy order is secret, so you'll just have to take our word for it.' "[9]

Some critics charge that the justification of "national security" for all the secrecy is just an excuse. Limiting access to information was administration policy before the terrorist attacks. Bush came into office saying publicly that he wanted to strengthen the office of president and reduce both congressional and public oversight of the executive branch. (See Chapter 11's "After 9/11" box.) Vice President Cheney and Secretary of Defense Donald Rumsfeld are long-standing opponents of FOIA. Both encouraged President Ford to veto the 1974 bill strengthening FOIA rights when they were part of his administration. (Congress passed the bill over Ford's veto.) Thus, the administration's well-known commitment to strengthening the executive branch has led critics to suspect that the war on terrorism is being used to pursue long-held policy goals that have nothing to do with national security.[10]

The libertarian think tank, Cato Institute, has accused the administration of being "a law unto itself,"[11] while one

of Bush's strongest supporters, Representative Dan Burton (R-Ind.) has said even though he understands that every president wants to protect himself from oversight, "a veil of secrecy has descended around the administration."[12]

1. Greg Kline, "Information at Risk," *Champaign-Urbana News-Gazette,* January 20, 2002, 1.
2. A list of excised material appears at www.ombwatch.org.
3. William S. Broad, "U.S. Is Tightening Rules on Keeping Scientific Secrets," *New York Times,* February 17, 2002. 1, 13.
4. The quote is from the Clinton administration's last annual report (2000) on compliance with FOIA, "Description of Department of Justice Efforts to Encourage Agency Compliance with the ACT," 1. It is available at the Federation of American Scientists' (FAS) Web site (www.fas.org) or at www.usdoj.gov by linking to the department's FOIA page.
5. Memo from Attorney General John Ashcroft, October 12, 2001. The text of this memo and all major Bush administration statements and documents on its FOIA and access to government information policies are posted at the FAS Web site (www.fas.org). The FAS maintains a site on government secrecy that users can link to from the main page.
6. Evan Thomas, "Uncle Sam's Classification Compulsion," *Washington Post National Weekly Edition,* March 17, 1997, 22.
7. Ellen Nakashima, "Frustration on the Left—and the Right," *Washington Post National Weekly Edition,* March 11–17, 2002, 29.
8. Ibid.
9. Laura Parker, Kevin Johnson, and Toni Locy, "Secure Often Means Secret," *USA Today,* May 16, 2002, 1A.
10. Linda Greenhouse, "A Penchant for Secrecy," *New York Times,* May 5, 2002, WK1.
11. Ibid.
12. Interview by Bill Moyers, "Behind the Freedom of Information Act," on *Now with Bill Moyers,* PBS, April 5, 2002.

trators with only a little power, charged with "executive details" and "mere execution" of the law. But the growing size and complexity of modern society and increasing demands that government do more have dramatically changed the nature of the federal bureaucracy.

George Washington's first cabinet included only three departments and the offices of attorney general and postmaster general, all combined employing just a few hundred people. More people worked at Mount Vernon, Washington's plantation, than in his executive branch in the 1790s.[16] The Department of State had just nine employees. By 1800, the bureaucracy was still

small, with only three thousand civil servants. Only the Treasury Department had much to do, collecting import and excise taxes and purchasing military supplies for an army of a few thousand. From then until 1990, the bureaucracy grew continuously, though at an uneven rate.

Periods of Growth

The Civil War years (1861–1865) and the fifty years following the war were the first period of growth. Early in the twentieth century, reformers highlighted unsafe food and drugs and dangerous working conditions for millions of workers. Congress passed laws regulating food and drugs, and new agencies were created to apply the regulations. This era of industrialization, westward expansion, and population growth saw increasing demands for government to provide benefits to business, labor, and farmers. So Congress established the Departments of Commerce, Labor, and Agriculture. Worries about abuses by big business also led to the creation of new bureaucracies, such as the Interstate Commerce Commission, and expanded powers for others, such as antitrust law enforcement in the Justice Department.

A second surge of bureaucratic growth took place during the Great Depression in the 1930s. President Roosevelt changed Washington from a sleepy southern city to an activist capital of a powerful nation. Roosevelt and Congress created a plethora of new agencies to combat the Depression, from the Social Security Administration and Civilian Conservation Corps to the National Labor Relations Board and Federal Deposit Insurance Corporation. In Washington alone, the federal workforce rose from 63,000 in 1933 to 287,000 a decade later.[17] A substantial part of that growth was due to U.S. entry into World War II and the creation of new agencies to mobilize the public and the economy for the war effort.

A third era of bureaucratic growth came during the 1960s and 1970s as a response to public demands that government do more to fight poverty, protect the environment, promote civil rights, and ensure consumer and worker safety. During this time, Congress created several new cabinet departments (Housing and Urban Development, Transportation, Energy, and Education) and agencies (Environmental Protection Agency [EPA], Occupational Safety and Health Administration [OSHA], and the Equal Employment Opportunity Commission [EEOC]).

Why the Bureaucracy Has Grown

As we have seen, over time, government responded to public wishes by creating federal agencies to assist and promote emerging economic interests of business, agriculture, and labor and, more recently, to provide health and economic benefits to workers, consumers, retirees, and other groups.[18] One scholar explained the bureaucracy's growth by pointing to Americans' discovery that "government can protect and assist as well as punish and repress."[19] Thus, at the same time we criticize government's growth, we demand educational services, irrigation projects, roads, airports, job training, effective policing, consumer protection, and many other bene-

fits. Each of us might be willing to cut benefits for someone else, but most of us want to keep the benefits we have.

When new bureaucracies are created, the intent is to hold them to their original size, but most grow over time. After World War II, the Department of Defense did not return to its prewar size or scope because the Cold War gave us a new reason to support a massive military establishment. It also created additional demands for health care and other services for veterans. After the Cold War, when thoughts turned to downsizing the Defense Department, supporters of military spending found new justifications for expansion, including the threat of global terrorism.

Bureaucracy usually grows during a national crisis, and the war on terrorism that began in late 2001 was no exception. The PATRIOT Act (Providing Appropriate Tools Required to Intercept and Obstruct Terrorism), which was rushed through Congress with virtually no opposition (and thus little thoughtful consideration) shortly after the attacks, greatly increases the surveillance powers of the federal bureaucracy. Implementation of government's extraordinary new power to wiretap, search email, and gain access to library borrowing records and to many business records, paper and electronic, will require more personnel and increase spending, although the problems of size and money are dwarfed by that of privacy loss.

Bureaucrats cannot produce growth on their own. Every agency exists because it is valuable to enough people with enough influence to sustain it. Every agency needs congressional and presidential approval of its programs, appropriations, staffing, and procedures. But there are periods when Congress may be preoccupied with urgent issues or when it is in a losing battle for control of the bureaucracy with an imperial president, as was the case during the Roosevelt, Johnson, and Nixon administrations. One explanation why Congress passed the Administrative Procedure Act in 1946 is that it had been overwhelmed by the growth in size and power of the executive branch during the Depression and World War II and needed to redefine the oversight role of the legislative branch.[20]

Sometimes, ironically, government grows because the president and Congress want it to be more accountable. This often results in hiring more managers, greater inefficiency, and, ironically, more difficulty in holding agencies accountable.[21]

It is also ironic that support for the growth of the bureaucracy often comes from those who are antigovernment and critical of the bureaucracy. For example, many of the supporters of the PATRIOT act, which increases government power, are those who deplore "big government."

WOMEN AND MINORITIES IN THE CIVIL SERVICE

Americans expect their public bureaucracies to be open and responsive. Andrew Jackson recognized this when he opened the civil service to frontiersmen of "common" origins. He hoped to make the bureaucracy more responsive and more representative by putting his frontier supporters in office. In the twentieth century, the expectation that public agencies should be open to all qualified applicants gave some groups, such as the Irish, Jews, and African Americans, more job opportunities than in the more restricted private corporate world.

In the past decade, significant progress has been made in making the federal bureaucracy more reflective of American diversity. Thirty-one percent of Americans identified as minorities in the 2000 census, and today 30 percent of federal workers are minorities.[1] African Americans are particularly well represented, being a substantially larger portion of the federal workforce (almost 18 percent) than of the general population.[2] Both Asian Americans and

American Indians have a slightly larger share of federal jobs than population share. Hispanics, on the other hand, are underrepresented in the federal workforce despite an aggressive Hispanic recruitment program.[3] Women are slightly underrepresented, too, filling 44 percent of federal positions compared with 46 percent of private sector jobs.

The relatively good news about the overall profile of the bureaucracy fades as we move up the pay scale (see the table). Women and minority men have not yet broken completely through the "glass ceiling" that has kept them out of top management positions. Even after passage of civil rights and equal opportunity legislation, barriers did not fall because often those who enforced the new regulations were white men opposed to the policies. Indeed, the Justice Department backed white males who sued the government for reverse discrimination.

There is progress, however. Women now fill about 24 percent of all positions at senior pay grade, tripling their proportion of 1985. Collectively, minorities hold about 14 percent of all senior positions.[4]

Federal court rulings and out-of-court settlements in discrimination cases account for some of the improvement in upward mobility. African Americans won a suit against the Education Department charging management abuse of a system designed to promote those who took on extra work. The additional responsibilities were usually given to whites, putting them on a faster promotion track.[5] Women agents charged the FBI with a similar tactic to restrict their promotion. They were prohibited or discouraged from joining SWAT teams, even

Ted Thai/*Time* magazine

Federal employment has historically opened opportunity for African Americans. Shown here are two Bureau of Engraving and Printing employees checking the quality of $20 bills (the woman at right is holding $8,000 in printing mistakes).

though service on them was crucial to advancement. When they threatened to sue, the FBI changed its promotion procedures.[6]

1. Office of Personnel Management, *The Fact Book, 2001 Edition,* Table 11 (www.opm.gov).
2. The comparison of public and private sector employment is from "Diversity Trickles Up in Government," *Champaign-Urbana News-Gazette,* July 17, 2001, A3.
3. "Hispanics Sought for Federal Work Force," *Champaign-Urbana News-Gazette,* February 3, 2002, A6; "Diversity Trickles Up."
4. *The Fact Book,* Table 46.
5. "Diversity Trickles Up."
6. Katherine C. Naff, "Through the Glass Ceiling: Prospects for the Advancement of Women in the Federal Civil Service," *Public Administration Review,* November/December 1994, 513.

Percentage of Senior Federal Civil Service Who Are Women and Minorities

	1985	1990	2000
Women	8	12	24
African Americans	4	5	7
Hispanics	1	2	3
Asians and Pacific Islanders	1	1	2

Data are for those at senior pay levels. Overall, about 1 percent of all federal employees are in this grade.
SOURCE: Office of Personnel Management, *The Fact Book: Federal Civilian Workforce Statistics,* 2001 (www.opm.gov).

In its early years Washington was described as "a miserable little swamp." When this photo was taken in 1882, the government was still comparatively small.

The growth of the bureaucracy should be seen in the perspective of the overall growth of our economy and population. For example, the number of federal bureaucrats for every one thousand people in the United States decreased from sixteen in 1953 to ten in 1999.[22] Civilian personnel costs will take about 15 percent of total federal spending in 2003.

The major growth in public employment has been at the state and local levels. Over 37 percent of all government workers were federal employees in 1953; in 1999, fewer than 14 percent were.[23] And only a small fraction (12 percent) of these federal civil servants work in the Washington, D.C., metropolitan area. Check the U.S. government listing in your telephone book and see how many offices are located in or near your hometown. All the people who work in these local offices are bureaucrats in one sense or another. But they are your neighbors, pretty ordinary people you meet on the street every day. (See the "American Diversity" box on the roles of women and minorities in the federal bureaucracy.)

Controlling Growth

Once they are established, the consolidation or elimination of departments is rare. It is more common for departments to become so large they must subdivide (Labor and Commerce; Health, Education and Welfare) or for agencies to become so big or their work so important they are made into cabinet departments (Veterans Affairs, Homeland Security) where they become even larger.

Yet almost every president since Lyndon Johnson has tried to streamline or downsize the bureaucracy. Nixon tried to merge seven departments into four but could not gain approval, and despite many attempts to ax the Department of Education, it is stronger than it ever has been. Jimmy Carter was a committed deregulator and a micromanager who oversaw the elimination of thousands of rules and some regulators. He unsuccessfully tried to introduce a budgeting process that would have required every agency to justify its budget every year on the basis of its success in achieving agency goals.

For all Reagan's talk against big government, it grew by over two hundred thousand employees during his administration. Although many agencies lost personnel (the biggest loser was the Department of Housing and Urban Development), others such as the Defense, Justice, and Treasury Departments gained. In addition, he created a new cabinet office, the Department of Veterans Affairs, from what had been an independent agency. He had entered office with a plan to wage a "war on waste," but he left office with the country another trillion dollars in debt and the Defense Department buying $600 toilet seats.

The Clinton administration's initiative on "reinventing government" also attempted to reduce the size of the bureaucracy with limited success, although it did decrease by 1.5 percent during his administration. It shrunk by almost 3 percent for the decade as a whole.

There is a general assumption that size and performance are linked. So presidents often think they can establish more efficient management plans and then cut employees. George H. Bush, for example, came into office with a plan for "total quality management," and George W. Bush, the only president to hold an MBA, adopted a system for grading the performance of every agency. The OMB, which performs much of the executive branch's internal oversight, evaluated each department or agency on five management categories: personnel, competitive bidding, financial management, e-government (using technology to improve efficiency), and whether program achievements justify a budget (similar to Carter's zero-based budgeting).[24] Those who fall short or whose work is duplicating that in another department are to have their budgets slashed. The money is to be redirected to programs that work. Almost all agencies and departments received poor or failing marks in some categories, and OMB even gave itself a failing grade. It is too early to evaluate how this approach to reforming the bureaucracy will work, but some agencies did receive budget cuts. However, in 2003, the Department of Defense, which got poor marks in all five categories, received its largest one-year budget increase since the Reagan era.

Career civil servants are skeptical about the attempt of every administration to take on the bureaucracy and cut it down to size. Despite good intentions, they see nothing new or bold in any of the reforms. In the view of a former OMB official, it is mostly "three yards and a cloud of dust."[25] (See the box "What Do Bureaucrats Want Anyway?")

What Do Bureaucrats Want, Anyway?

Overall, bureaucrats are not much different from any of the rest of us. They are no more likely to favor raising taxes or government spending; they have about the same confidence in government and other institutions—such as organized religion, business, labor, and the press—as other citizens; and they are about as likely to favor busing and gun control.

When civil servants do differ from other citizens, they seem more open to diversity. For example, they are more likely to say they would vote for a black or woman as president and less likely to accept traditional gender roles. And they are somewhat *less* likely than other Americans to approve government intrusions into people's private lives. They also are less likely to approve censoring people who hold unpopular views or laws banning pornography or interracial marriage. On only one issue are they more liable to favor "big government." They are somewhat more likely to favor wiretapping.

According to a Brookings Institution survey, federal bureaucrats, like many other Americans, are critical of their own institutions. "Having endured a decade of downsizing, two decades of bureaucratic bashing, three decades of constant reform, four decades of increasing workloads, and five decades of pay and hiring freezes," the attitudes of many federal bureaucrats do not add up to a "healthy public service."[1]

They do not have a particularly high opinion of the political appointees who wander into their agencies for short periods to fill leadership positions and quickly disappear, often without ever learning very much about what the agency is all about. What most bureaucrats seem to want is for Congress and the president to stop using them as guinea pigs for their management experiments and instead to provide the tools and training they need to do their jobs right. Sixty percent of federal employees said that Congress "generally acts in ways that worsen the management of their organizations, while 41 percent said the same about the president." Overall, the report concludes that the attitude of federal employees is not "Show me the money," but "Let me do my job."[2]

At lower levels of the civil service, employees are especially apt to complain about their lack of access to training, and at most levels there is dissatisfaction over the lack of equipment, especially state-of-the-art computers, necessary to do their work properly

and efficiently. Other major concerns are the impact of past reforms that have left many programs without sufficient personnel to carry out their work, and the increasing number of positions within the bureaucracy that have been removed from civil service and made appointive. Some believe this has made the work of the bureaucracy too politicized. In addition, many of those at lower levels believe there is too much bureaucracy—that is, too many layers of administration between top and bottom, impeding communications and making their jobs more difficult.

Bureaucrats are very hard on themselves, both their performance and their agencies, citing too many people in positions they are unqualified for, especially senior people and political appointees. They want "to eliminate the 'yes' men (and women) and give responsibility back to the employees."[3]

1. Paul C. Light, "What Federal Employees Want from Reform: Reform Watch Brief #5" (Washington, D.C.: Brookings Institution, 2002), 1.
2. Ibid., 10.
3. Ibid., 7.
OTHER SOURCE: Gregory B. Lewis, "In Search of the Machiavellian Milquetoasts: Comparing Attitudes of Bureaucrats and Ordinary People," *Public Administration Review,* May/June 1990, 220–227.

Types of Offices within the Federal Bureaucracy

The Constitution says little about the organization of the executive branch other than indicating a need for the president to have a cabinet. As government's role expanded, it became clear that a single type of organization would not be appropriate for every task assigned to the bureaucracy. Cabinet departments, for example, are headed by people who serve at the president's pleasure and are there to help carry out his policies. But other agencies must implement law without reference to an individual president's preferences. These agencies require protection from political interference, as do those established to carry out highly technical work. In this section, we review the major types of agencies in the executive branch.

Departments

Departments are those organizations within the executive branch that form the president's cabinet. Their heads, called secretaries (or attorney general, for the head of the Justice Department), are appointed by the president with the consent of the Senate, and they are directly responsible to the president. There are fifteen departments; the newest is Homeland Security, which was created in 2002 (see Figure 1). These departments constitute the lion's share of the federal bureaucracy,

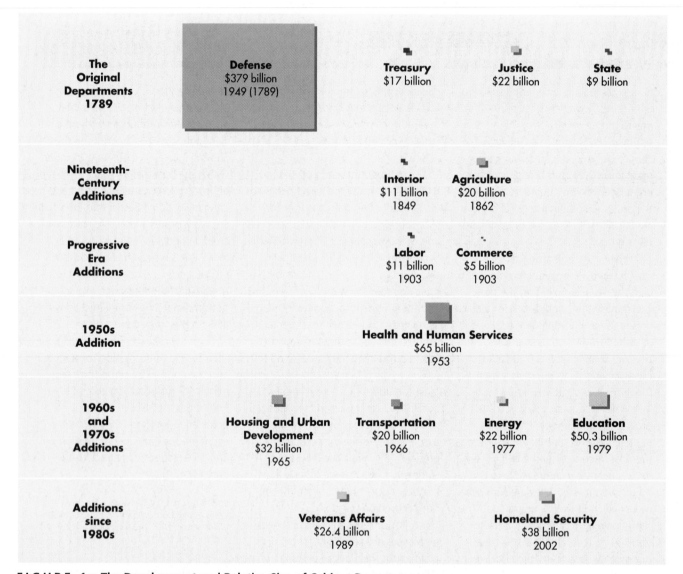

FIGURE 1 ■ The Development and Relative Size of Cabinet Departments

NOTE: The dollar figure in each box is the 2003 budget estimate for that department's discretionary budget; founding dates are below. The modern Defense Department (1949) replaced the Departments of War (1789) and Navy (1798); the Justice Department (1870) replaced the Attorney General (1789); the Commerce and Labor Departments were first established in 1903 as a joint enterprise; and the Health and Human Services Department and the Education Department (1979) replaced the Department of Health, Education, and Welfare (1953).

SOURCE: *Manual of the United States Government, 2001–2002* (Washington, D.C.: Government Printing Office, 2001), United States Budget for Fiscal Year 2003, Table S-7.

employing over 60 percent of all nonmilitary personnel. The largest employer is the Defense Department with 38 percent of all civilian workers.

Cabinet departments exist to carry out the president's policy in specific functional areas: national security, federal law enforcement, fiscal policy, health and welfare, foreign relations, and so forth. They are staffed by career civil servants, but all top policymaking positions in each division of a department are held by presidential appointees. The fourteen departments had 327 such positions, and Homeland Security will add another 23.[26] The increase in number of top positions that are appointive is a trend that the permanent staff believe makes their work more difficult (see the section on professional standards).

Independent Agencies

Independent agencies differ from departments in that they are usually smaller and their heads do not sit in the cabinet. Agency heads are, however, appointed by and responsible to the president. And occasionally a president does extend cabinet status to the head of an independent agency, most notably the director of the Environmental Protection Agency (EPA). Some of these agencies, such as the EPA, the CIA, the Social Security Administration, the Peace Corps, and the National Aeronautics and Space Administration (NASA), are well known to the public. Others, such as the Office of Government Ethics, are known to few.

Some independent agencies deal with highly specialized areas of policy such as space exploration or law enforcement, and therefore their heads usually need to have an appropriate professional background, not just a political profile acceptable to the president. However, if the agency deals with policy that has widespread impact, as the EPA and CIA do, political credentials are likely to be the president's first consideration in naming a director.

Independent Regulatory Boards and Commissions

Examples of independent regulatory boards include the Federal Communications Commission (FCC), which regulates the electronic media; the Securities and Exchange Commission (SEC), which makes and enforces rules regarding stocks, bonds, and securities; and the Federal Reserve System (the Fed), which sets prime interest rates and controls the amount of money in circulation. These and other regulatory agencies are designated "independent" because the work they do is supposed to be removed from politics insofar as possible. Congress created the first such commission, the Interstate Commerce Commission, in 1887 to decide such things as interstate freight rates, railroad ticket prices, routes, and conditions of service.

Each of these and other boards and commissions regulates a specific area of business or the economy. Five to ten presidential appointees head every independent regulatory board and commission. By law, each board and commission must be balanced with members of both major political parties. Appointees serve staggered terms and cannot be removed by presidents who dislike their decisions. Because of the technical knowledge needed for decision making, appointments are supposed to be based on expertise rather than partisan considerations. Of course, it is almost impossible for politics, in the sense of an individual's values, not to have some impact on decision making. Presidents who want less government regulation appoint commissioners who share that value. Commissioners, in turn, can then make it difficult for the professionals in the agency to carry out their regulatory mission. However, the goal of having these independent commissions is to make politics secondary to professional expertise.

Government Corporations

Government corporations are businesses run by government to provide services the public needs but that no private company will provide because they are not profitable—or were not profitable at the time government began providing the service. The first government corporation, the Tennessee Valley Authority (TVA), was created when no utility company was willing to invest in the infrastructure necessary to bring electricity to what was then a very poor, undeveloped region of the country. The TVA still supplies electricity to its part of the country.

The Postal Service, which was originally a cabinet department, was converted to a business operation in 1971. Formerly a government monopoly, it now has competition for some of the services it provides. In the 1960s, when railroads were no longer willing to provide passenger service, the government created the National Railroad Passenger Corporation (Amtrak). And because no private insurance company would ever bear the risk of insuring private bank deposits, the government established a corporation to protect your savings account (Federal Deposit Insurance Corporation). Similarly, the government is about to become the main purveyor of terrorism insurance, because after 9/11, private firms are no longer willing to assume the risk.

Government corporations charge for their services or products, just like private firms, but their primary objective is to provide a needed service, not to make a profit. Of course the government is quite happy if they do, or if they at least break even. When a government corporation does become profitable, its assets may be sold to private businesses and the corporation closed. This is, for example, what happened with CONRAIL, the government corporation that took over rail freight and turned it back into a profitable enterprise. Some people argue the government should privatize the unprofitable rail passenger and postal systems, too, but the services provided are so important to the national economy that, without certainty that private businesses would continue providing them indefinitely, government would have difficulty justifying the sale of their assets.

Currently there are seven government corporations and fifty independent agencies, boards, and commissions. Although unfamiliar to most Americans, these agencies affect almost every aspect of our daily lives—the air we breathe; the water we drink; the interest on a bank loan; the fee at an ATM; the terms under which we buy or sell stock; labeling on food and manufactured goods and conditions in the plants where they were made; phone and mail service; the construction of every car, train, plane, or bus we ride on; and the shuttles that astronauts take to outer space.

What Bureaucracies Do

We have described forms of bureaucratic organization and specific things that bureaucrats do. In this section, we look in greater detail at the source of the bureaucracy's authority and the categories of responsibility assigned to it.

After elected officials make a law, someone must carry it out. That is the primary job of the bureaucracy. Bureaucrats convert laws passed by Congress and signed by the president into rules and actions that have an actual impact on people and things. We call this process **policy implementation.** The general process of policy implementation has two major components: administering policies and making them.

Administering Policy

Public bureaucracy's oldest job is to administer the law. To "administer" is to execute, enforce, and apply the rules that have been made either by Congress or the bureaucracy itself. Thus, if policymakers decide to go to war, they must empower agencies to acquire weapons, recruit and train soldiers, and devise a winning strategy. Policymaking without administration is usually tantamount to having no policy at all.

Administration includes thousands of different kinds of activities. It involves writing checks to farmers who receive payments for growing—or not growing—crops, providing direct services to the public, evaluating how well programs are working, prosecuting those who try to defraud the government, and maintaining buildings and offices. For forest rangers, administration involves helping backpackers in the Grand Canyon or putting

out a forest fire in northern Minnesota. For postal employees, it includes delivering the mail or repairing an automatic sorting machine.

Making Policy

Responsibility for administering policy inevitably conferred lawmaking powers on the bureaucracy. This can be illustrated with the example of the Americans with Disabilities Act (ADA). The ADA directs employers to make a "reasonable accommodation" for a competent worker with a disability that "substantially limits" a major life activity such as seeing or walking, except when this causes "undue hardship."[27] Although the act went into effect in 1992, the Equal Employment Opportunity Commission (EEOC), which has responsibility for its implementation, is still clarifying what specific provisions in the act mean. What is the difference between a "reasonable accommodation" and an "undue hardship"? When voters want local governments to spend less, is the $2 million Des Plaines, Illinois, spent for sidewalks and curb cuts an "undue hardship" or not?[28] Will the EEOC let colleges and universities make only some classrooms and offices accessible to students and staff in wheelchairs? Or must every classroom and faculty office be accessible to people with disabilities, at a cost of millions of dollars for large universities?

Answering such questions and formulating rules to implement them is de facto policymaking. Implementation requires disseminating the rules and negotiating interpretations with those who have to put them in place and enforce them. State and local counterparts of the EEOC and their clients must be informed of the rules, assisted in their attempts to use the rules, and monitored in their progress. Bills must be paid, disputes resolved, and information collected as to how successful the program is. If affected parties reject the EEOC's interpretation or how officials implement it, the rules can be challenged in federal court. This is where almost all disputed provisions of the ADA are being decided. Bureaucrats very often do not have the last word in determining how a policy is implemented.

Passage of thousands of complex bills like the ADA over time explains how the policymaking functions of public bureaucracies have grown. Industrialization, population growth, urbanization, and profound changes in science, transportation, and communications have put problems of a more complex nature on government's agenda. The large number and technical nature of these problems, as well as policy differences among its members, have often limited Congress's ability to draft specific policy responses.

Congress often responds to this situation by enacting a general statement of goals and identifying actions that would help achieve them. Congress then has an agency with the relevant expertise draft specific rules that will achieve these goals. Thus, Congress gives agencies **delegated legislative authority**—the authority to draft, as well as execute, specific policies. Just as the ADA left rule making to the EEOC, the Tax Reform Act of 1986 required thousands of rules to be written by the Internal Revenue Service (IRS) and the Treasury Department.

Agency-made policy is just as binding as acts of Congress because agencies make it on Congress's behalf. In strictly numerical terms, agencies make much more policy than Congress. On average, for example, executive agencies issue about seven thousand new rules and regulations a year compared to Congress's annual production of about seven hundred new laws.

Many political scientists believe Congress abdicates its authority and acts in an irresponsible manner by refusing, because of political pressures and its heavy workload, to develop specific guidelines for agencies.[29] Thus, agencies sometimes are left to implement policies without much guidance from Congress beyond the bill itself. This congressional inaction has contributed to partisan conflicts, especially over regulatory policy. Republican presidents have appointed agency heads who drag their feet or outright refuse to execute regulations passed by a Democrat-controlled congress.

Sometimes, however, agency complaints about the ambiguities or lack of specificity in legislation are just excuses not to implement disliked policies. When this happens, Congress has to adopt more detailed directives to agencies. But this does not prevent the political appointees who head executive branch agencies from resisting congressional directives they dislike on the grounds they are too complex and unrealistic to follow.

In effect, the competition between the White House and Congress was extended to the bureaucracy when Congress delegated legislative authority to agencies. This competition can intensify or subside, depending on whether there is divided or undivided government. However, the competition continues even in the undivided government of George W. Bush. Sometimes agencies are in the difficult position of having to satisfy competing demands. To figure out what Congress, the president, and others want, agency officials read congressional debates and testimony and talk to members of Congress, committee staffers, White House aides, lobbyists, and others. While agencies also try to determine what the public wants, they are more likely to respond to well-organized and well-funded interests that closely monitor their actions. As a result, agency-made policy is often less responsive to the general public than to particular interests.

Wanted: Young Bureaucrats

The attractiveness of government service ebbs and flows over time, reflecting the ethos of the era, the number of job opportunities and national needs. The Great Depression and World War II era presented the challenge of true national crises. Many in the generation of the 1960s and 1970s were called to public service by the civil rights movement and the War on Poverty. Each generation sees somewhat differently the importance of public service and the potential for government to make positive changes in society.

During the 1980s and 1990s, there were no national crises to draw people together in a common enterprise that could be expressed through government service. Those having grown up in this era seem less inclined to believe that government can make a positive difference. Indeed, young people heard a generation of politicians railing against government. In the 1990s, given the alternative lure of the booming economy and the dot-coms, young people saw government service as less attractive than the private sector. Public service took a back seat to "make as much as you can as quickly as you can." And even those who chose public service had choices outside government, as the growth of nonprofit philanthropic organizations provided alternatives.

Consequently, it is not surprising that from 1990 to 2000, the average age of government employees rose from forty-two to over forty-six. The average length of service rose form thirteen to seventeen years.[1] As the century turned, about 20 percent of the federal workforce was under thirty-four compared with 38 percent for the civilian labor force as a whole, a rather dramatic difference.

As the 1960s generation approaches retirement, the need to recruit young people into the federal civil service has gained urgency. Diminished private sector job opportunities have now increased applications for federal job openings. And after 9/11, when trust in government figures shot up, the numbers of Americans who said they would recommend a government career to their children rose from 30 to 39 percent. But is still appears to be a job choice of last resort for many people.[2]

1. Office of Personnel Management, *The Fact Book*, 2001 Edition, 10 (www.opm.gov/).
2. Paul C. Light, "What Federal Employees Want from Reform: Reform Watch Brief #5" (Washington, D.C.: Brookings Institution, March 2002), at www.brookings.edu.

Regulation

A special kind of policymaking called **regulation** produces rules, standards, or guidelines conferring benefits and imposing restrictions on business conduct and economic activity. Regulations have the force of law and are made by agencies whose directors and board members are appointed by the president and whose operating procedures are generally governed by the Administrative Procedure Act. Regulatory agencies include not only independent regulatory boards and commissions but also some independent agencies, such as the Environmental Protection Agency, and some agencies within cabinet departments, such as the Food and Drug Administration in Health and Human Services and OSHA within the Labor Department.

Regulatory actions include two steps: making rules and adjudicating their enforcement. Rule making is the establishment of standards that apply to a class of individuals or businesses. Adjudication occurs when agen-

Your Hamburger: 41,000 Regulations

The hamburger, staple of the quick, inexpensive meal, is the subject of 41,000 federal and state regulations, many of them stemming from 200 laws and 111,000 precedent-setting court cases. These rules, cited in a three-volume study by Colorado State University, touch on everything involved in meat production, including cattle-grazing practices, conditions in slaughterhouses, and methods used to process meat for sale to supermarkets, restaurants, and fast-food outlets. If government does not regulate pesticide use on crops, there is a significant risk of serious illness to consumers who eat the crops. If the government does not inspect to make sure livestock are free of tuberculosis, the incidence of TB bacteria in meat will be higher. If regulators do not tighten inspection procedures at slaughterhouses, the recent series of outbreaks of potentially deadly food poisoning from *E. coli* bacteria in ground beef could continue.

When examined closely, most of the regulations have a plausible rationale. But regulation is not free. The cost of regulating hamburger is about 8 to 11 cents per pound. Is this a high cost? It depends on the probability of contracting a serious disease and the value you as a consumer place on having some confidence in the quality of products you buy.

Then, of course, there are some regulations that are mystifying even to those not especially opposed to government regulation. What is the danger in eating a pickle sliced too thin? Only Uncle Sam knows!

SOURCES: *U.S. News & World Report,* February 11, 1980, 64 (copyright 1980, U.S. News & World Report, Inc.); Carole Sugarman, "A Beef with the Cattlemen," *Lincoln Journal-Star,* September 15, 1997, 32.

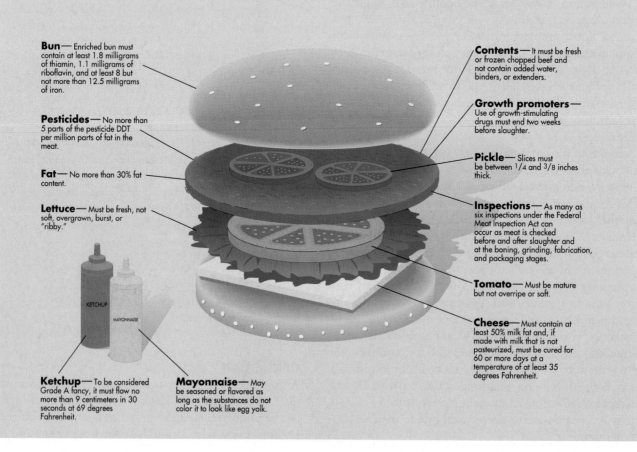

Bun— Enriched bun must contain at least 1.8 milligrams of thiamin, 1.1 milligrams of riboflavin, and at least 8 but not more than 12.5 milligrams of iron.

Pesticides— No more than 5 parts of the pesticide DDT per million parts of fat in the meat.

Fat— No more than 30% fat content.

Lettuce— Must be fresh, not soft, overgrown, burst, or "ribby."

Ketchup— To be considered Grade A fancy, it must flow no more than 9 centimeters in 30 seconds at 69 degrees Fahrenheit.

Mayonnaise— May be seasoned or flavored as long as the substances do not color it to look like egg yolk.

Contents— It must be fresh or frozen chopped beef and not contain added water, binders, or extenders.

Growth promoters— Use of growth-stimulating drugs must end two weeks before slaughter.

Pickle— Slices must be between 1/4 and 3/8 inches thick.

Inspections— As many as six inspections under the Federal Meat Inspection Act can occur as meat is checked before and after slaughter and at the boning, grinding, fabrication, and packaging stages.

Tomato— Must be mature but not overripe or soft.

Cheese— Must contain at least 50% milk fat and, if made with milk that is not pasteurized, must be cured for 60 or more days at a temperature of at least 35 degrees Fahrenheit.

cies try individuals or firms charged with violating standards. To do this, they use procedures that are very similar to those of courts.

Most regulations derive from laws passed by Congress that direct agencies to take actions to accomplish the goals established in the legislation. Environmental legislation, for example, requires regulatory agencies to set standards for clean air, safe disposal of toxic wastes, or safe workplaces that businesses must meet. Businesses are often allowed some flexibility in the methods used to meet the standard. But failure to comply can result in fines or other legal penalties.

Consumer protection legislation directs federal regulators to set quality or safety standards for certain types of products, such as cars, toys, food, and medical equipment. This is why there are seat belts, air bags, and shatterproof windows in cars and why materials used to make children's toys or clothing cannot be flammable or toxic.

Another form of regulation is licensing the right to own or use public properties. For example, the Federal Communications Commission licenses the publicly owned airwaves to people who own and operate radio and television stations. Regulations may also require businesses to provide information through labeling, such as the cancer warnings on cigarette packages and lists of ingredients noting fat, sugar, salt, and vitamin content on packaged food. The box "Your Hamburger: 41,000 Regulations" illustrates how far-ranging regulatory authority is and gives examples of some of the nitpicking rules opponents of regulation prefer to focus on rather than those guarding worker and consumer safety.

Data Collection and Analysis

In the course of policymaking and administration, the bureaucracy performs other functions. It collects data, such as in the decennial census, and it makes information available to the public. Much of what we know about ourselves as a people comes from the government's collection of data on births and deaths, occupations and income, housing and health, crime, and many other things. A cursory glance at the annual *Statistical Abstract* shows that the government reports to us everything from the incidence of abortions to the exports of zinc and in between informs us how much celery we eat and how many VCRs we own.

Bureaucracy also keeps us informed about what government is doing, and the Internet is a valuable tool to assist in this function. Every federal agency has a Web site with information about its policies and programs, and electronic mail for feedback from the public. If we want to know the rules governing camping in national parks, we can call the National Park Service or go to its Web site. If we want to know the fate of a bill in Congress or how our representatives voted on it, we can find it posted on the Internet.

The bureaucracy engages in research, too. A prime example is the Department of Agriculture, which for nearly 140 years has conducted research on how to grow bigger and better crops, raise healthier animals, and transport and market products more effectively. Government researchers, such as those at the National Institute of Health and the National Centers for Disease Control, do much of country's medical research, especially on mental health and epidemiology. Many vaccines and prescription drugs are also developed in government labs.

In addition, providing continuity is an important offshoot of the bureaucracy's activities. Presidents and members of Congress come and go, and political appointees in the bureaucracy stay an average of two years. Many barely learn their jobs by the time they leave. Career civil servants have a much deeper knowledge of their agencies' work, which can make them more productive. (See the box "Wanted: Young Bureaucrats" for more on civil service recruitment.)

Politics and Professional Standards

As the part of government that implements policies made by elected officials, the bureaucracy cannot escape politics and is subject to constant lobbying. That does not mean that civil servants have the green light to implement policy in a partisan manner. Today's civil servants are governed by laws that place professional competence above political loyalties. Most Americans want fair, apolitical competence applied so that the quantity and quality of any government service they receive is not dependent on whether they belong to the same party as the president or their member of Congress. And most of us would prefer to have a civil engineer rather than a political crony in charge of the dam being built near our town. The chances that the engineer will get the job over the crony have improved significantly since patronage was outlawed in the federal bureaucracy.

Patronage

For decades, American public bureaucracies were staffed by the **patronage** system, which allowed elected officials to fill administrative jobs on the basis of political loyalty rather than merit. By providing their supporters with jobs, elected officials could strengthen their political base, and for many in the public it was simply a means of government agencies providing employment to citizens. It operated in rough accordance with the

Andrew Jackson made the bureaucracy more representative of the nation's population. He also opened the doors to the White House. The guests at a White House party open to the public consumed or carried away much of a 1,400-pound cheese.

principle "To the victor belong the spoils," as the newly elected filled jobs with their own supporters. At the federal level, Andrew Jackson's presidential election in 1828 was a watershed in using the patronage system. Jackson believed that any white male citizen of average intelligence and goodwill could do a government job well. So he reversed the existing practice of naming mostly well-off people from the East Coast by appointing less well-off supporters from frontier areas.

The most obvious problem with staffing the bureaucracy with political supporters rather than through competitive recruitment is that jobs will go to people who are not competent to perform their duties. This became a major problem as government work became more technical and specialized. Furthermore, patronage could, and did frequently, lead to corruption, in particular to deal making between candidates and voters or individuals who controlled blocks of voters. Voters supported candidates who promised them jobs or other favors. Such corruption increasingly sullied city councils, state legislatures, and Congress during the 1800s.

Neutral Competence

Although patronage was affecting government performance, the influence wielded by the political machines that had grown powerful through its use kept Congress from acting until an unsuccessful job seeker assassinated President James Garfield in 1881. The Pendleton Act of 1883 established a **Civil Service Commission** to fill designated positions within the bureaucracy with people who had proved their competence in competitive examinations. Jobs under the commission's jurisdiction were part of the **merit system.** The new law also pro-

tected people holding merit positions from pressure to support or oppose particular candidates and from dismissal for political reasons.

The merit system established **neutral competence** as the professional standard for those in the civil service. It requires that those filling merit positions are chosen for their expertise in executing policy and that they carry out their work in a nonpartisan or neutral manner. This standard assumes that there is no Republican or Democratic way to build a sewer, collect customs, or fight a war. In effect, it says partisan politics has no place in bureaucracy. It also implies that bureaucrats should not profit personally from the decisions they make.

Woodrow Wilson, a major advocate of neutral competence, believed that bureaucrats could learn to execute policy both expertly and responsively.[30] He saw government jobs as either political or administrative in nature and that by knowing which was which, we could create a bureaucracy that elected officials could control. Most current observers are less sanguine about the possibility of completely separating politics from administration.[31]

The Pendleton Act authorized the president to extend merit system coverage to additional federal jobs by executive order. In 1884, the merit system covered about 10 percent of the jobs in the federal bureaucracy. Today that figure is over 75 percent, down from a high of 90 percent as changes in civil service law exempted positions covered by other merit systems, such as the State Department's Foreign Service and the Executive Senior Service, and created more political appointments.

Merit is not all that counts in the merit system however. The system favors veterans by adding a five-point bonus to their test scores (disabled veterans get ten points). And positioning counts as well; people already in the system are favored because they know about job openings first and may have skills identical to those in the job listing. Sometimes, job descriptions are written to fit particular individuals.

Another consequence of removing patronage from federal hiring was passage of a law to limit the partisan political activities of federal workers. The **Hatch Act** of 1939 prohibited federal employees from active participation in partisan campaigns, even at state and local levels. Political activities were restricted to voting, attending rallies, and having private conversations. But federal employees cannot participate in party-sponsored voter registration drives, endorse party candidates, or work for or against them in any way. These prohibitions also apply to state and local government workers supported by federal funds.

The Hatch Act has been the subject of considerable controversy. Supporters argue that it protects the neutral competence of civil servants from partisan influences. Critics of the act say it makes civil servants second-class

A disappointed office seeker assassinated President Garfield. This act alerted federal officials to the level of public anger over the use of patronage to staff the bureaucracy and led to adoption of the Civil Service Act.

citizens by denying them the First Amendment guarantees of freedom of speech and association. In 1993, Congress changed the law to allow most federal employees to hold office within a political party, to participate in political campaigns, and to raise funds for political action committees when they are off-duty. However, all employees of law enforcement and national security agencies remain under the earlier, more stringent prohibitions.[32]

The neutral competence standard prohibits bureaucrats from gaining materially from their decisions. Civil servants are supposed to make decisions based on their professional judgment and not to advance the cause of something in which they have a financial stake. For example, bureaucrats who are stockholders in chemical companies are not supposed to be making policy about chemical waste. Even if it were possible for policymakers to put aside self-interests, their stakes in firms they are regulating would in themselves produce an appearance of conflict of interest. This in turn would allow critics of a decision to charge a lack of neutral competence. When this happens often, it lowers public confidence in government.

Responding to concerns about conflicts of interest, Congress passed the Ethics in Government Act in 1978. The act sought to prevent former public officials with inside information from using it and their contacts to give their new employers an unfair competitive advantage. The act barred former public servants from lobbying their agencies for one year and prohibited for life lobbying on matters in which they "personally and substantially" participated as public officials. In 1989, news that ex-Reagan officials had used their government service for substantial financial gain led to the passage of

a law designed to strengthen the 1978 act. These new rules had little more impact than the old ones.

President Clinton issued an executive order requiring many of his political appointees to sign a pledge that they would not lobby the agencies in which they worked for five years and would never lobby for foreign political parties and governments. In 2002, four of Clinton's former cabinet members and other high-level political appointees, including his trade representative and the heads of the FCC and SEC, each held multiple seats on corporate boards. It is not unthinkable that they were hired for their government contacts, although the positions do not violate any ethics rule. George W. Bush appointed more corporate executives to head government agencies than any other president. Some are now regulating industries in which they held stock or were recently on the payroll.

Sometimes the range within which bureaucrats can exercise neutral competence is severely restricted by their superiors. Agencies and department heads are political appointees, and many are specifically charged with carrying out the programs of the president who appointed them. In addition, some of the policy that bureaucrats are implementing was made by presidential directive or executive order. EPA bureaucrats gearing up to implement Clinton's executive orders on clean water and clean air in December 2000 were required to write very different rules several months later when Bush rescinded Clinton's orders and substituted radically different policies. When an agency appears to be partisan in the way it implements, or fails to implement, congressional acts, it may be because of presidential directives or orders issued by the short-term political appointee temporarily heading the agency.

There is no greater health concern in the world today than AIDS (acquired immune deficiency syndrome), a disease unknown to the medical community until the early 1980s. AIDS involves a virus that weakens the body's immunity, making it vulnerable to deadly infections. Other diseases claim more lives than AIDS, but many of these are curable if victims can be reached with appropriate medical care. There is no cure for AIDS, and most countries still have inadequate programs of testing, blood screening, and public education. Therefore, many people live with the disease without knowing they have it, passing their infection along to others. This might have been the case in the United States if government had not undertaken a program of public education in the 1980s.

AIDS was believed introduced in the United States by a widely traveled French tourist who happened to be homosexual. The disease spread swiftly among male homosexuals, taking thousands of lives before the federal government began to formulate a policy to curb the epidemic. From the victims' standpoint, the government came too late to the problem, but compared to the way the disease has been handled in many countries, our federal health bureaucracy did far better than most. Many thousands, perhaps even millions, of lives were saved through the introduction of preventive measures.

The government's first AIDS prevention program was the work of a federal bureaucrat, a man who put professional responsibilities above political preference. In 1986, President Ronald Reagan asked the government's top medical officer, Surgeon General C. Everett Koop, to report to him on the AIDS crisis. By that time there were more than thirty-five thousand cases reported in the United States, and twenty thousand had already died. An estimated 1.5 million people had been exposed to the virus, and it was projected there would be 270,000 full-blown cases by 1991.[1] At the time, intravenous drug users and homosexual men were at the greatest risk.[2] However, AIDS was beginning to spread among non-drug-using heterosexual men and women through contact with prostitutes and bisexuals and from blood transfusions received before the spring of 1985, when blood banks began testing for the HIV virus.

As AIDS began to spread to the general population, there was increasing public anxiety. Americans knew little about the illness or how it was contracted. Many people thought they could be infected through social contact, or just by being in proximity to an infected person. Some parents tried to bar children with AIDS from the schools their children attended; some people were afraid of even indirect physical contact with an HIV-infected person and began to worry about contamination of swimming pools and other public facilities.

The government needed a policy to address both the illness and the fear of it. Certain preventive and diagnostic steps, such as mandatory blood testing, were already required of military recruits and Foreign Service officers. But should the public, or at least individuals at high risk, be made subject to the same mandatory measures? Or would voluntary preventive measures work better? The government also had to decide to what extent it should be involved, and how much left to the private sector, in trying to find a treatment for the disease and a vaccine to prevent it.

The atmosphere surrounding AIDS policy was very politicized.[3] Social conservatives saw AIDS as a moral issue, and believed it was necessary to change teen behavior by teaching sexual abstinence in the schools. Extremists even said AIDS was a punishment for homosexuality and drug use. They pressured Surgeon General Koop to recommend mandatory testing for convicted prostitutes and intravenous drug

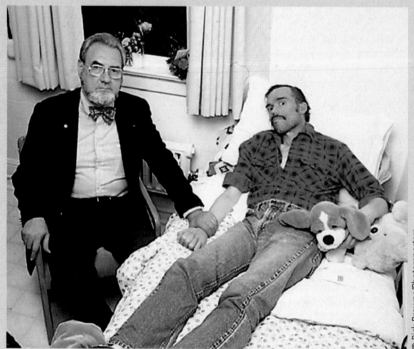

Former Surgeon General Koop visits an AIDS patient.

© Rick Browne/Photoreporters

users, venereal disease patients, immigrants, and couples seeking marriage licenses. Some wanted government to quarantine those infected to keep them from infecting others (as is done in Cuba). At least one member of Reagan's cabinet recommended a policy of mandatory notification of the spouses and past sexual partners of those who tested positive.

Public health experts rejected almost all of the politically driven recommendations as unworkable or as likely to backfire, driving people at risk to go underground to avoid being tested. They opposed mandatory notification as a violation of doctor–patient confidentiality and thought few would identify their sexual partners. They worried about increased social and employment discrimination against those infected but without full-blown AIDS as well as those just thought to be at risk. Health professionals also believed, given human nature, that teaching abstinence was unrealistic and therefore very risky; they recommended educating young people about "safe sex" and contraception.

Reagan was more comfortable with conservative views on AIDS. He had appointed Koop surgeon general not so much for his medical reputation but because he was a born-again Christian with conservative views on abortion and birth control. In preparing his report, Koop would have moved in the direction of the man who appointed him had he relied only on his political instincts or preferences. But Koop was also a doctor who respected the views of health care professionals and took his responsibility to respond to a health crisis more seriously than the political demand to remedy what some regarded as a cultural or social crisis.

Koop's 1986 report to the president emphasized prevention through public education and voluntary over mandatory measures, which he could

have argued was a more truly conservative response than the Orwellian testing, quarantine, and abstinence program advocated by others among the president's political appointees. The thirty-six-page report concluded that a lack of sex education would impede the effort to contain the spread of AIDS while we still had no vaccine or cure, and it recommended expanding sex education to include new material on the dangers of AIDS for schoolchildren. In a radio broadcast, Koop called on the nation's networks to lift their self-imposed ban on condom advertising. He argued that "anyone who is sexually active should use a condom from start to finish. AIDS kills and sexually active people have to be told this." The most visible aspect of the government's new program was a brochure mailed to 107 million households in 1988 describing how AIDS is contracted and how to avoid it. That same year, a presidential commission and a National Academy of Sciences panel on AIDS made recommendations that echoed those in the Koop report.

Koop put his professional foot forward, exercised neutral competence, and in essence bit the political hand that fed him. Political appointees in the bureaucracy are supposed to serve the public interest just as civil servants do, but they must also be responsive to their superiors, in this case the president. But as Koop said, "I'm not afforded the luxury of bringing ideology or morals into my job, especially with the sort of threat we have with AIDS."[4]

Koop's public education campaign changed the direction of public thinking and helped people see the necessity of confronting the disease head-on as a public health crisis instead of treating it as a marginalized problem best left to patients and their doctors. The campaign helped calm fears driven by ignorance of how the disease was contracted and spread. Later Koop ac-

knowledged weaknesses in his approach, especially that health workers had been "singularly unsuccessful in penetrating the drug-addicted culture" with educational messages.[5]

By 2002, AIDS had killed almost 468,000 people in the United States, but that number would almost certainly have been far higher without the public education campaign and other preventive measures, including blood screening. Greater public awareness also helped win support for federal funding for AIDS research that was instrumental in developing a treatment program that allows many AIDS patients to live relatively normal, active lives for indefinite periods.

Partly in response to having an effective treatment program, complacency has set in in some parts of the at-risk population, and infection rates are increasing again, especially among poor minorities. And the government has still not resolved the problems of holding down drug costs or delivering a treatment program to all who need it. But it would be hard to fault the government for any lack of public awareness about how to avoid contracting the disease or its lethal nature. In some countries where no steps were taken until infection rates extended to as much as 20 to 30 percent of their populations, AIDS-related deaths are predicted to reach into the tens of millions over the next several decades.

1. "AIDS: Who Should Be Tested?" Newsweek, May 11, 1987, 64–65.
2. Stephen Jay Gould, "The Exponential Spread of AIDS Underscores the Tragedy of Our Delay in Fighting One of Nature's Plagues," New York Times Magazine, April 19, 1987, 33.
3. "AIDS Becomes a Political Issue," Time, March 23, 1987, 24.
4. Koop's 1987 remark is quoted in Julie Kosterlitz, "Health Focus," National Journal, January 28, 1989, 259.
5. Lawrence K. Altman, "Who's Stricken and How: AIDS Pattern Is Shifting," New York Times, February 5, 1989, 1 and 16. See also Sandra Panem, The AIDS Bureaucracy (Cambridge, Mass.: Harvard University Press, 1988).

Overseeing the Bureaucracy

The principal overseers of the bureaucracy are of course the president, who heads it and appoints its top policy-makers; the Senate, which holds confirmation powers; and the Congress as a whole, which has authority to create, monitor, and fund agencies. Congress also has given the public a significant, if vastly underutilized, role, through legislation mandating openness in government.

President

Means of Control

The development of the bureaucracy led to demands for **executive leadership**—that is, some central leader to set the direction of the agency and monitor its responsiveness. The president, constitutionally the "chief executive," has several tools to control the bureaucracy. One is budgeting. Presidents can try to cut agency appropriations to limit agencies' range of actions, or they can tie conditions to appropriations to make them take specific actions. Using this strategy effectively can be difficult, but presidents may directly affect the work of regulatory agencies through their appointment powers and the use of executive orders.

The presidents can try to control agencies by appointing people who share his views. This is expected in the case of cabinet departments. Reagan and Bush filled health-care-related positions in the Department of Health and Human Services with people who were pro-life, while Clinton filled them with people who were prochoice. In appointments to regulatory agencies, Republican presidents tend to appoint probusiness people and Democratic presidents, proconsumer and prolabor individuals. Reagan chose heads for regulatory agencies such as OSHA, the Consumer Products Safety Commission, and the EPA who agreed with his goal of reducing government regulation. Clinton named a life-long environmental activist to head the EPA. Despite being screened for issue positions, presidential appointees may end up representing agency policies rather than the president's interests. Most appointees have less expertise and experience in agency operations than career civil servants, and some come to rely on career officials for information about agency history, procedures, and policy questions. But much depends on the president's leadership and insistence on his policy agenda.

Administrative reform is a third means a president can use to increase his control over the bureaucracy. Generally, the more sweeping a president's recommendation for change, the more he must anticipate congressional and interest group resistance. For example, Reagan wanted to abolish the Departments of Education and Energy and merge the Commerce and Labor Departments, but Congress would not support him. The most audacious attempt at bureaucratic control by a modern president has been George W. Bush's reorganization of the executive branch to create a new cabinet-level Department of Homeland Security. The plan had great scope, affecting twenty-two agencies and 177,000 employees, but what made it bold was Bush's request for exemption from worker protection laws and the authority to transfer funds and personnel from agency to agency without congressional approval. In other words, he asked Congress to cede substantial budgetary and oversight powers to the White House. (See Chapter 11's "You Are There.")

In addition, the White House can try to influence independent agencies and commissions by lobbying and mobilizing public opinion. Attempts by presidents to influence Federal Reserve Board decisions on interest rates, for example, are legion.

Strengthening Presidential Control

Despite these powers, there are many limits on the president's ability to control the bureaucracy. Given its size and complexity, the president cannot possibly control every important decision. Moreover, presidents have found it increasingly difficult to lead an executive branch containing large numbers of merit system employees deliberately insulated from presidential control. This is one reason Bush asked for exemptions from the system for many Homeland Security department positions.

Presidential control problems escalated in the 1930s with the establishment of many new programs and agencies. In 1935, Franklin Roosevelt appointed the Brownlow Committee, named after its chair and composed of public administration specialists, to draft a statement on principles of executive leadership. Its 1937 report was very influential. At its suggestion, the Bureau of the Budget (BOB), which had been created in 1921, was put into the new Executive Office of the President to help the president manage the bureaucracy.

Perhaps the most significant development for monitoring the bureaucracy was the establishment of the Office of Management and Budget (which absorbed BOB) in the Executive Office of the President. OMB has specific responsibility for overseeing agency performance, and it reports its findings to the public as well as the president by posting them at its Web site.

Congress also increased the president's appointive powers with a reclassification of civil service positions. The Civil Service Reform Act of 1978 replaced the Civil Service Commission with two agencies. One agency promotes executive leadership by working with the president in writing and administering civil service regulations. The other is intended to protect civil servants from violations of these regulations. It also created the Senior Executive Service (SES), positions outside the regular civil service. Today just over three-quarters of positions in the federal bureaucracy are within the civil service; all others are in exempt categories. In addition, the act gave managers more opportunity to fire incompetent subordinates and authorized bonuses and a new pay scale for managers to encourage better performance.

Despite this legislation, executive leadership is still thwarted by the difficulty of removing poor performers from the civil service. Although job security is not meant to shield public servants who do poor work, it does make firing incompetent workers difficult and time-consuming. The organization of public employees into unions contributes to this, although unions also protect workers from being dismissed without grounds. The government's rate of discharging people for inefficiency, 0.01 percent a year, did not increase after the 1978 reforms, though no doubt others left after being threatened with firing or demotion. As one public employee said, "We're all like headless nails down here—once you get us in you can't get us out."[33]

Agencies that have strong allies in Congress, in powerful interest groups, or in the public provide another limit to presidential leadership. Presidents have more success controlling agencies that lack strong congressional allies and domestic clientele groups, such as the Treasury and State Departments, than agencies *with* such allies, such as the Social Security Administration and the Agriculture and Health and Human Services Departments.

Congress

Congress has the power to create, reorganize, or eliminate agencies and the ultimate instrument of control—the power of the purse strings. Much of the bureaucracy's power is delegated authority from Congress, and much of its work is implementing laws passed by Congress. While the president has the edge in leadership through his appointment powers, Congress has greater scope for oversight and control. This is not just because of its budgetary powers but because Congress has dozens of committees (supported by a staff of thousands) to which executive agencies must report.

Just as an agency's outside allies can work to thwart presidential control, they can also limit congressional oversight. Agencies frequently work closely with certain congressional committees and interest groups for mutual support and outcomes favorable to all. (These relationships are sometimes called *iron triangles*.) Agencies may adjust their actions to suit the preferences of the congressional committees that authorize their programs and appropriate their funds. For example, decisions by members of independent regulatory commissions are sensitive to the views of members of their congressional oversight committees. When the membership of the committees becomes more liberal or more conservative, so, too, do the decisions regulators make.[34]

Iron triangles make oversight look less like monitoring the bureaucracy and more like collusion. Constituent service, on the other hand, provides a motive for members of Congress to try to shape bureaucratic decision making. Members often try to influence agencies to take some action on behalf of constituents or that is in the interest of their districts. In fact, congressional staff who do casework often have their duties assigned according to the agencies they are responsible for contacting about constituent complaints. This can lead to inefficiencies when bureaucrats are pressured to act not on neutral competence but solely on the needs of members to satisfy constituent demands. It is this kind of pressure that kept military bases open years beyond their usefulness simply because they were good for the economy of a member's district. This pressure from Congress makes it difficult for bureaucrats to act with neutral competence.

Courts

Federal courts act as another check on the bureaucracy. Judicial decisions shape agency actions by directing agencies to follow legally correct procedures. Of course, the courts cannot intercede in an agency's decision making unless some aggrieved person or corporation files a suit against the agency. Nevertheless, in almost any controversial agency action, there will be aggrieved parties, and possibly some with sufficient resources to bring a court action.

The courts interpret lawmakers' intentions by deciding what congressional majorities and the president had in mind when they made a law. This can be difficult. Sometimes, in their haste, lawmakers may have neglected to specify crucial elements of a law or, as a Supreme Court justice put it, they may have to "agree to disagree."[35] Lawmakers may also have written a certain amount of vagueness into a law so agencies would be able to adapt it to unknown future conditions. How the courts read a law may add to or reduce the ability of Congress and the president to influence its implementation. In the current Supreme Court, the conservative majority has increasingly used its authority to interpret the intent of congressional acts in ways that expand the Court's own powers. We discuss these issues in Chapter 13.

Regulators as well as other agency policymakers appear to be quite sensitive to federal court decisions. For example, when the courts overturn the National Labor Relations Board's decisions in a prolabor direction, NLRB decisions soon become more prolabor. Similarly, decisions drift the other way when courts overturn agency decisions in a probusiness direction.[36]

Interest Groups and Individuals

As we have indicated, the public has numerous opportunities to oversee and to influence bureaucratic decision making. Most of these rights stem from laws designed to ensure openness in government.

Openness laws also extend to media access and thus provide another important check on bureaucratic abuses. But the media can also make the bureaucracy's work more difficult. Reporters like to cover conflict and bad news and are usually on the lookout for stories about internal policy disputes. They even may fan the flames to make a better story.

Interest groups and their lobbyists are also part of the public. Lobbyists tend to take much greater advantage of their rights of access than does the general public, and they provide much of the "public" comment on proposed rules received by agencies. Interest groups want to make sure bureaucracies adopt rules and enforcement practices they favor. An environmental group cannot rest on its laurels just because Congress has passed a law placing new safeguards on toxic waste disposal. Their job is not over until they make sure the Environmental Protection Agency writes strict rules to enforce the law. Thus, the group must lobby the regulators as well as Congress. Sometimes interest groups pressure an agency so effectively that the agency is said to be "captured."[37] This term is used most frequently for regulatory agencies thought to be controlled by the groups they are supposed to be regulating.

If an agency seems to be sabotaging the intent of Congress, interest groups can work with friendly congressional committees to put pressure on the agency to mend its ways. And interest groups can also try to rally public opinion to their side to pressure Congress or the president to do something about the agency. Environmental groups are especially skilled at this.

During the corporate accounting scandals of 2001–2002, the Securities and Exchange Commission was headed by a lawyer who had just moved from defending Wall Street firms into a position of having to regulate them. Shortly after he took office, he announced that under his direction the SEC would be "a kinder place for accountants," a statement he undoubtedly wished he had not made after the Enron scandal broke. Then Congress began asking whether he had the

neutral competence necessary to toughen regulations. Public outrage over the scandal was so great that the SEC head had to reverse his position and call for much tighter regulation of insider trading, accounting practices, and law firms that consult on corporate finance. Then, he quietly worked to weaken new rules until public pressure forced his resignation.

We know interest groups can influence the bureaucracy, but can individual citizens, too? It can be argued with some truth that it is difficult for an individual to influence public agencies when acting alone, but that does not mean there are no opportunities to do so. Perhaps one person posting a comment on a Web site will not change agency policy, but if all residents opposed to a decision on cleaning up a hazardous waste in their neighborhood file comments, it can make a difference. Rules have been reversed or amended.

An individual who used FOIA to retrieve documents that exposed agency corruption or abuse can also make a difference by going public with the story. But few individuals take advantage of their FOIA rights, and it is not made easy for those who try. There is a lot of paperwork involved, some costs, and often a long wait. The main problem is that most people do not use the tools that Congress has given them to oversee and to influence the bureaucracy.

Individual bureaucrats, called **whistleblowers,** can sometimes make a big difference by opening their agencies to public view. Their purpose is usually to expose mismanagement and abuse of power in order to make their agencies more responsive and productive. One of the most famous whistleblowers was Ernest Fitzgerald. In 1968, as an Air Force cost accountant, he exposed bad management by revealing problems with the Lockheed C-5A transport plane. The plane vibrated so much in flight that its wings actually fell off if they were not replaced after only two hundred hours of flying time. Saying it wanted "to save expenses"—his $32,000 salary—the Air Force reacted by firing Fitzgerald. He sued to get his job back and won, but all he got was his title, office, and pay. The Air Force gave him nothing to do, and he had to wait for a court order in 1982 before the Air Force gave him responsibilities equal to his qualifications. The wings were repaired, and the C-5A operated successfully for many years.[38] But two decades later, the Air Force was still trying to neutralize what one Pentagon veteran called "the most hated man in the Air Force" by juggling his assignments.[39]

Partly in response to experiences like Fitzgerald's, Congress provided for an agency to protect whistleblowers in the 1978 Civil Service Reform Act. In that act and later amendments, bureaucrats who blow the whistle on mismanagement, sexual or political harassment, or other abuses of power in their agencies are protected from arbitrary firing. Private citizens can be

"It's not mailmen per se. I'm just very antigovernment these days."

whistleblowers, too, by suing companies with government contracts that defraud the government.[40]

Despite the legal protections, it is the rare person who will set aside cordial relations with colleagues and ambition for promotion in order to challenge the status quo. Most people, whether working in the private or the public sector, find it difficult to expose the dirty laundry of the agency employing them. And even if the law does protect their jobs, their careers may be effectively ruined. More than one-third of federal whistleblowers report suffering some form of reprisal or threat of reprisal.[41] A lawyer specializing in whistleblower cases says that, still today, any bureaucrats "committed to bringing out the truth need to steel themselves, as well as their families, for difficult times."[42]

In a case foreshadowing agency failures uncovered after 9/11, a Justice Department employee complained in 1997 of "a cesspool of official misconduct" that included "sexual favoritism in hiring, breaches of security and visa fraud in their department's overseas criminal training program."[43] As a reward, he was sent to work in a warehouse where he was given no responsibilities. He settled for a small payment and left the agency. After 9/11, he was given a public service award for his whistleblowing.

Rarely does an agency publicly thank an employee for blowing the whistle, as FBI director Mueller did when Coleen Rowley went public with that agency's mishandling of 9/11-related investigations. But Mueller's actions were not so much an indication of changing attitudes toward whistleblowers as a measure of the trouble the agency was in with Congress. And it is by no means clear that Rowley's career with the FBI will be unaffected.

Conclusion: Is the Bureaucracy Responsive?

At this writing, Congress is overseeing the biggest reorganization of the federal bureaucracy in a half century. The changes were prompted by failures in performance that helped make possible the terrorist attacks of September 2001. Particular targets of the reform are intelligence and law enforcement agencies and customs and immigration services. A reporter noted the bureaucratic morass in the INS was encapsulated in the title of the official put in charge of the reorganization: the "assistant deputy executive associate commissioner for immigration services."[44]

Is the federal bureaucracy an impenetrable forest or an uncontrollable fourth branch of government as some portray it? The turf wars, miscommunications, and fragmented authority that surfaced after 9/11 certainly indicate that at least part of the federal bureaucracy is an impenetrable forest. It is not surprising that most of the agencies who failed so badly are among the least open to citizens or the media or, for that matter, even to congressional oversight.

But the bureaucracy as a whole is not an errant fourth branch of government. With the exception of supersecret agencies like the National Security Agency, where Congress has forfeited much of its oversight responsibility in the interests of national security, most of the bureaucracy is subject to presidential and congressional control. Indeed, one of the by-products of the Bush administration's current attempts to increase presidential control of executive branch agencies at the expense of Congress is that it has reawakened Congress to its oversight lapses.

Our fragmented political system has created an environment of uncertainty and competition for public agencies. Bureaucrats have many bosses: a president, his appointees, Congress, and its many committees and subcommittees. In addition, numerous interest groups try to influence them. The often-contradictory demands for responsiveness and neutral competence contribute to an uncertainty of expectations, too. As a result, agencies try to protect themselves by cultivating the support of congressional committees and interest groups. Even presidents have trouble influencing agencies because of these alliances. Although some presidents, such as Franklin Roosevelt and Lyndon Johnson, have occasionally rearranged the status quo, their successes in articulating a vision of national priorities are more the exception than the rule.

Then there is the issue of a vaguely defined, but frequently articulated, public suspicion that any bureaucracy is destined to be intransigent and inefficient. We have tried to show that some of that attitude stems from lack of consensus on what the work of government should be. If you do not like the work Congress and the president have assigned the bureaucracy, there is not much chance you will view it as responsive to your needs. If the dissatisfaction is more over how the bureaucracy does its work, there is hope that at least some areas of performance will meet with your approval. The public does have tools to influence how bureaucrats do their work, but they have many more ways to lobby Congress and the president to change the work they give the bureaucracy to do.

Despite people's negative feelings about the bureaucracy, the mail is delivered, bridges get inspected, and passports are issued. As Charles Goodsell points out, "Unmistakably, bureaucracy works most of the time."[45] It usually does what it is supposed to do.

While this is true for much of the bureaucracy, the investigation into INS, FBI, and CIA actions prior to September 11 made clear that these agencies had experienced catastrophic failures. While Americans' opinion of how the government was doing its job and its overall trust in government increased substantially after the attacks, there was also a more serious concern for poorly functioning government agencies. The head of one government watchdog group summarized the feeling this way: "Before September 11 there was a bit of a blasé attitude of 'O.K., the government screwed up again.' Now people see the consequences on their lives, and see the necessity of government functioning well."[46]

EPILOGUE

Mueller Keeps the FBI Out of the Homeland Security Department

In May 2002, less than a month before the president sent his plan for a new cabinet department for Homeland Security to the Hill, Mueller submitted a reorganization plan for congressional approval. By way of understatement, he said that "it was already clear that there was a need for change at the Bureau" before 9/11 and that afterward, there was no longer any doubt that "we needed to fundamentally change the way we do business."[47]

Mueller successfully prevented the FBI from being incorporated into the new Homeland Security department. He therefore was able to ensure that the agency continued to have the same department overseers and the same organizational ties and relationships with congressional committees as before.

In return for this concession, he gave those who wanted fundamental reorganization some of what they wanted. He proposed a complete restructuring of agency priorities, moving to the top of the list prevention of terrorist attacks, foreign espionage, and cyber-based attacks and high-technology crimes.[48] The more traditional mandates of the FBI, such as fighting public corruption and white-collar crime and protecting civil rights, were moved down the list. He surrendered a large part of the Bureau's involvement in fighting drug trafficking to other law enforcement agencies.

The FBI will also join a Joint Terrorism Task Force, but, under

Robert Mueller describes his proposed FBI reorganization.

Win McNamee-Reuters/Timepix

Mueller's plan, instead of becoming one of a few dozen agencies in a new cabinet office, the FBI would be a partner with the Department of Homeland Security in the task force. Mueller also stressed the need for better CIA–FBI cooperation. He improved his own relationship with CIA director George Tenet, and they began giving *joint* daily briefings to the president on terrorist threats.

In remarks to Congress, Mueller skillfully defended the continuance of the FBI as an independent agency within the Justice Department. He told Congress that moving the FBI into Homeland Security would "detract from the focus of both the new department and the FBI itself."

Bush's homeland security bill accepted this reasoning and left both the FBI and the CIA outside the new department. Mueller gave up some of the agency's turf, proposed a reorganization that will require massive retraining of current agents and recruitment of employees with new skills, but maintained the agency's identity and its historical place in the federal bureaucracy.

The fact that the administration accepted this reasoning illustrates the difficulty of significant bureaucratic reorganization even when an organization has failed. The Bush administration undoubtedly felt that to try to move the FBI against its wishes would spark a turf war that could endanger the entire plan. The FBI would call in its congressional allies, who would then join other forces opposing the bill.

To learn more about the FBI and homeland security, go to this chapter's "You Are There" exercises on the text Web site.

Key Terms

Federal Register
Administrative Procedure Act (APA)
FOIA
independent agencies
policy implementation
delegated legislative authority

regulation
patronage
Civil Service Commission
merit system
neutral competence
Hatch Act
whistleblowers

Further Reading

C. Fred Alford, *Whistleblowers: Broken Lives and Organizational Power* (Ithaca, N.Y.: Cornell University Press, 2001). A political science professor chronicles the impact on the lives and careers of individuals who reported corruption and mismanagement in government agencies.

David Burnham, *A Law unto Itself: Power, Politics and the IRS* (New York: Random House, 1990). An analysis of the enforcement of the federal tax code, a code so complex it seems to invite bureaucratic inefficiency and abuses.

Jonathan Kwitny, *Acceptable Risks* (New York: Poseidon, 1992). A fast-paced and well-written story of two men who prodded and fought the Food and Drug Administration to make potentially helpful medicines available to AIDS patients. A good illustration of both agency rigidity and, ultimately, responsiveness.

Paul C. Light, *The New Public Service* (Washington, D.C.: Brookings Institution, 1999). If you are interested in a career in a public bureaucracy, this is a useful handbook written by one of the leading scholars of the U.S. Civil Service.

George Orwell, *Nineteen Eighty-four* (New York: Harcourt, Brace, 1949). One of the most popular novels of the twentieth century gives you a look at an uberbureaucracy and its intrusion into private life. It will put any complaints you might have about the federal bureaucracy into perspective.

Mark Riebling, *Wedge: The Secret War between the FBI and the CIA* (New York: Knopf, 1994). Describes the different jurisdictions assigned to these agencies by Congress and how this division led to destructive turf wars.

Eileen Welsome, *The Plutonium Files* (New York: Dial, 1999). This is an account of secret government medical experiments that involved injection of radioactive plutonium into human subjects. The documents on which it is based were retrieved through a FOIA request.

Electronic Resources

www.gao.gov/
Site of the General Accounting Office, a congressional office that monitors performance of executive branch agencies.

www.opm.gov/
Review tables that reveal the composition of the federal workforce, demographics, occupation, pay, and many other stats.

www.fedstats.gov/
Federal agencies collect statistics about the American population, the economy, housing, employment, and many other areas of life. This Web site provides a guide to finding and using those statistics, whether they involve the mean household income of American families or last year's export trade data. Link to the most recent edition of the Statistical Abstract of the United States.

www.ombwatch.org
This is a site set up by interest groups and private individuals to monitor the performance of executive branch agencies. You can review agency evaluations, changes in FOIA, and other laws and rules governing openness in government. Maintains a list of information removed from government Web sites after 9/11.

www.usajobs.opm.gov/
At this site, you can see what jobs are open in the federal government and make an online application.

InfoTrac College Edition

Search for the following articles in the InfoTrac database:

Agranoff, Robert, and Michael McGuire. "American Federalism and the Search for Models of Management," *Public Administration Review* (November–December 2001).

Kirlin, John J. "The Big Questions of Public Administration in a Democracy," *Public Administration Review* (September–October 1996).

Leazes Jr., Francis J. "Public Accountability: Is It a Private Responsibility?" *Administration & Society* (September 1997).

Wise, Charles R. "Election Administration in Crisis: An Early Look at Lessons from Bush versus Gore," *Public Administration Review* (March 2001).

For more articles, enter

"Public Administration" in the Subject Guide, and then go to subdivision "Analysis";

"Public Administration" in the Subject Guide, and then go to subdivision "Evaluation";

"Public Administration Review" for journal name in PowerTrac.

American Government Resources

Visit the Government Institutions section of the Wadsworth American Government Resources Web site (politicalscience.wadsworth.com/amgov/) for a variety of tools to help you explore the bureaucracy further. Included are simulations, video clips, Microcase exercises, and a wealth of other activities.

THE JUDICIARY

Justice Sandra Day O'Connor

Do You Plunge into the Political Thicket?

ou are Justice Sandra Day O'Connor of the United States Supreme Court, and it is a month after the presidential election of 2000. The election is still undecided, and its outcome hinges on the results of the vote in Florida. Whichever candidate prevails in Florida will gain the state's twenty-five electoral votes and become the country's forty-third president.

The morning after the election it appeared that Governor George W. Bush had an 1,800-vote lead.[1] Because this was less than half of 1 percent of the votes cast, state law required a retabulation of the totals from the voting machines. The retabulation narrowed the gap to less than three hundred votes. Then Vice President Al Gore, claiming that the machines had failed to count some votes, sought a manual recount in four Democratic counties. Secretary of State Katherine Harris, who was the cochair of the Bush campaign in Florida, tried to prevent a manual recount.[2] In the meantime, a manual recount that had concluded in one disputed county would, if accepted, shrink the lead to just 150 votes. It appeared that a manual recount in the remaining counties might give the lead to Gore.

The Florida Supreme Court ruled that manual recounts from the disputed counties must be accepted and, hearing a related case three weeks later, ruled that manual recounts from the entire state must be undertaken.[3] The court set a general

standard for the recounts: The counties should ascertain "the intent of the voter." The court did not specify how counties should count hanging chads or dimpled chads. In these two decisions, the Florida justices interpreted the state's law, which was an incomplete and contradictory patchwork,[4] in ways that benefited Gore's campaign. Some legal scholars consider their interpretations questionable[5] (though others consider them plausible[6]). In several other cases, however, the court ruled in ways that hindered Gore's campaign.[7] Thus, although the Florida justices were mostly Democratic appointees,[8] they were not clearly partisan[9]—that is, favoring one party over the other. Even so, Republican commentators are accusing them of being partisan, and you have heard this charge.

Governor Bush appealed to the United States Supreme Court to stop the manual recounts ordered by the Florida Supreme Court. You have to decide whether to plunge into what one previous justice called the "political thicket" of state election law.[10]

You are a staunch Republican and an ideological conservative. You grew up on a ranch in Arizona with a father who opposed President Franklin Roosevelt's New Deal policies. You graduated in the top 10 percent of your class at Stanford Law School but did not get hired by a law firm because you were a woman, so you became a prosecutor instead.

Bush and Gore supporters argue the case outside the Supreme Court.

After returning to Arizona, you became an assistant attorney general, then a state legislator—eventually, the first woman elected majority leader of any state legislature—and then a state judge. In 1981, you were appointed to the United States Supreme Court—the first woman elevated to the high Court—by President Ronald Reagan.

On the conservative Rehnquist Court, you sit near the middle. There is a bloc of three arch conservatives, two moderate conservatives, three moderates, and one liberal.[11] Justice Kennedy and you are the two moderate conservatives. When you two join the other conservatives, you form a majority. When you two join the other justices, you form a majority in the opposite direction. Therefore, you are usually in the majority. Last term you wrote only one dissenting opinion.[12] As a swing justice on the Supreme Court, you may be the most powerful woman in America.

Unlike the three arch conservatives, you are cautious, reluctant to sweep away precedents, even precedents you might not have voted for had you been on the Court at the time. For instance, in 1992 you voted to reaffirm the precedent of *Roe v. Wade,* which established the right to abortion, despite demands to overturn it.[13] You expressed concern for the legitimacy of the Court if it abandoned its precedents:

The country's loss of confidence in the judiciary would be underscored by an equally certain and equally reasonable condemnation for . . . overruling unnecessarily and under pressure. . . . Unlike the political branches, a Court thus weakened could not seek to regain its position with a new mandate from the voters. . . . Like the character of an individual, the legitimacy of the Court must be earned over time.

In response to Bush's appeal, you have several choices. You could avoid this tangled thicket. The Supreme Court is not required to take the case; it has discretion. Sometimes it refuses to take a case if it thinks other branches or other levels of government should resolve the dispute.[14] Usually, in fact, it refuses to take cases that involve election outcomes.[15] It prefers elected officials, who have been chosen by the voters and are accountable to the voters when they run for reelection, to resolve these disputes rather than unelected judges..

This practice reflects "judicial restraint"—a tendency to avoid political disputes and to defer governmental policymaking to other branches. For the past half-century, conservatives have preached judicial restraint and attacked judges who they claim have practiced "judicial activism" instead. Republican candidates for president have promised to nominate as judges only individuals who have professed or demonstrated judicial restraint. The Rehnquist Court has echoed these views. At the same time, however, the Rehnquist Court has frequently practiced judicial activism by invalidating federal laws.[16]

If the Court does take the case, it could allow or disallow the Florida Supreme Court's order for a statewide recount. The argument for allowing the order is based on federalism. The states have primary responsibility for conducting elections, even federal elections, and a state's supreme court has primary authority to interpret the state's law. Normally, federal officials take a hands-off approach unless the state discriminates against some group of voters, as southern states did when they denied African Americans the right to vote.

The Rehnquist Court has emphasized the role of federalism in our system and has returned more power to state governments. As a former official in all three branches of Arizona's government, you have been especially sensitive to state concerns. You have, in fact, been *the* leader of the Rehnquist Court's movement. Your views on federalism might incline you to avoid the case or to allow the order. Either way, the result would be the same.

The argument for disallowing the order is based on the equal protection clause of the Fourteenth Amendment.[17] This clause, which was passed during Reconstruction, was designed to prevent southern governments from denying constitutional rights to former slaves. But the language in the clause is general, so the clause has been used to protect various groups of people, such as other minorities, poor people, illegitimate children, and women. The Rehnquist Court has also used it to protect white men, claiming reverse discrimination, in affirmative action cases.[18]

Bush maintains that the order would deny equal protection—that is, it would foster discrimination—because it does not set specific standards for counting hanging chads and dimpled chads. For example, Broward County officials decided that dimpled chads would be counted, but Palm Beach County officials decided that dimpled chads would be counted only if there was additional evidence of the voter's intent (such as dimpled chads for other offices on the ballot, too). Therefore, a small percentage of voters would not have their ballots counted the same as other voters in other counties because the standards in their county would be somewhat different than the standards in other counties. They could be Bush voters or Gore voters. There would be no intentional discrimination, and there would be no systematic pattern favoring one candidate or the other. There would be no identifiable group singled out for discriminatory treatment as there normally is in equal protection cases. Nevertheless, the absence of statewide standards for a statewide recount is troubling.

Yet courts have never insisted that manual recounts, which periodically have occurred, must use specific standards throughout the state.[19] Thirty states do not list specific standards in their laws for manual recounts.[20] Moreover, the Rehnquist Court has shown limited concern for voting rights[21] and has downplayed equal protection. The Court has even allowed states to use capital punishment when it reflects a pattern of racial discrimination.[22] You

have joined the majority of the Court in these decisions.[23]

Thus, the Court's pronouncements and its precedents suggest that it will not get embroiled in this controversy. Your past behavior suggests the same. Do you follow these pronouncements and precedents in this case?

Some media commentators have expressed alarm that the election is still unresolved. The American people themselves, while arguing for one side or the other, have remained calm. There have been no signs of unrest, no stockpiling of consumer goods, and no instability in financial markets. There have been no problems in our relations with other countries, though foreign leaders do not know which man they will have to deal with as president in January. But the situation is unsettled, and nobody knows what might happen if it drags on. Do you worry about the possibility that this high-stakes civics lesson might turn into political chaos?

Your decision could determine the outcome of the election. You realize that a manual recount might result in a Gore victory, yet you fervently hope for

a Bush victory. Of course, you know that a judge is not supposed to decide cases according to the persons or parties involved.

Your decision could affect future appointments to the Court as well. A President Bush would nominate very different justices than a President Gore. During the campaign, Bush pointed to two of the most conservative justices—Scalia and Thomas—as role models of the individuals he would appoint. Gore criticized these justices.

You have to be careful. The country is sharply divided, even polarized, over this election and its aftermath. If you make a mistake, you could exacerbate the split. At the same time, you could hurt the Court's legitimacy. Unlike the presidency and Congress, which derive their legitimacy primarily from the elections of their officials, the Court must derive its legitimacy primarily from the decisions of its justices. By *appearing* independent and wise, as well as by *acting* independent and wise, the justices nurture a sense of legitimacy among the people.

With these considerations in mind, what do you decide?

The public expresses more support for the Supreme Court than for the president or Congress.[24] The public dislikes the disagreements and debates and the negotiations and compromises among governmental officials, and it deplores the efforts of interest groups to influence governmental policies. These messy features of democratic government, which are visible in the executive and legislative branches, are not visible in the judicial branch. Many people conclude that they do not occur.

Indeed, many people assume that courts are nonpolitical and that judges are objective. People say we have "a government of laws, not of men." But this view is a myth. At any time in our history, "It is individuals who make, enforce, and interpret the law."[25] When judges interpret the law, they are political actors and courts are political institutions.

Thus, public support for the Supreme Court and the lower courts rests partly on false assumptions about the absence of politics in this branch. There is plenty of politics, as will be seen in each of the topics covered in this chapter—the history, structure, jurisdiction, composition, operation, and impact of the courts.

Development of the Courts' Role in Government

The Founders expected the judiciary to be the weakest branch of government. In the *Federalist Papers*, Alexander Hamilton wrote that Congress would have power to pass the laws and appropriate the money; the president would have power to execute the laws; but the courts would have "merely judgment"—that is, only power to resolve disputes in cases brought to them. In doing so, they would exercise "neither force nor will." They would not have any means to enforce decisions, and they would not use their own values to decide cases. Rather, they would simply apply the Constitution and laws as written. Consequently, the judiciary would be the "least dangerous" branch.[26]

This prediction was accurate for the early years of the Republic. The federal courts seemed inconsequential. The Supreme Court was held in such low esteem that some distinguished men refused to accept appointment; others accepted appointment but refused to attend sessions. The first chief justice thought the Court was "inauspicious,"[27] without enough "weight and dignity" to play an important role.[28] So he resigned to be governor of New York. The second chief justice resigned to be envoy to France.

When the capital was moved to Washington in 1801, new homes were built for Congress and the president but not for the Supreme Court. Planners considered the Court too insignificant for more than a small room in the Capitol. But the Court could not even keep this room. For decades it would be shunted from one location to another, from the marshal's office to the clerk's office, from the clerk's home to the Capitol's cellar—a dark and damp chamber in which visitors joked that Lady Justice would not need to wear a blindfold because she could not see anyway—and from one committee room to another.[29] It would not get its own building until 1935.

However, the status of the Court began to change after the appointment of the fourth chief justice—John Marshall. Under his leadership, the Court began to develop "weight and dignity" and to play an important role in government.

The development of the courts' role in government can be shown by dividing the courts' history into three eras: from the founding to the Civil War, from the Civil War to the Great Depression, and from the Great Depression to the present.

Founding to the Civil War

The first primary issue facing the courts, in the era from the country's founding to the Civil War, was the relationship between nation and state. In addressing this issue, the Supreme Court established judicial review and national supremacy.

Judicial Review

Judicial review is the authority to declare laws or actions of government officials unconstitutional. The Constitution does not mention judicial review. At the Constitutional Convention, the idea was proposed, but it was strongly opposed by some delegates who feared that it would give too much power to judges, who were unelected, and that it would weaken state governments. Proponents did not press for its inclusion, because they worried that doing so might jeopardize the Constitution's ratification. Regardless, they expected that federal courts would use judicial review eventually. In the *Federalist Papers,* Hamilton said the courts would have authority to void laws contrary to the Constitution,[30] and at the time some state courts did have such authority, although they did not exercise it vigorously.

The Supreme Court articulated the power of judicial review in the case of **Marbury v. Madison** in 1803.[31] The case had its origins in 1800, when the Federalist president John Adams was defeated in his bid for reelection by Thomas Jefferson and Federalist members of Congress were defeated by Jeffersonians. With both the presidency and Congress lost, the Federalists tried to ensure continued control of the judiciary. The lame duck president and Congress added more judgeships, most of which were unnecessary. (Forty-two were for justices of the peace for the District of Columbia, which was sparsely populated.) They hoped to fill these judgeships with loyal Federalists before the new president and Congress took over. In addition, Adams named his secretary of state, John Marshall, to be chief justice. At the time, though, Marshall was still secretary of state and responsible for delivering the commissions to the new appointees.

But he ran out of time and failed to deliver four commissions for District of Columbia justices of the peace. He assumed that his successor would deliver them. But Jefferson, angry at the Federalists' efforts to pack the judiciary, told his secretary of state, James Madison, not to deliver the commissions.[32] Without the signed commissions, the appointees could not prove that they had in fact been appointed.[33]

William Marbury and the three other appointees petitioned the Supreme Court for a writ of mandamus (Latin for "we command"), a writ that orders government

This portrait of William Marbury reflects the importance of Marbury v. Madison. *It is the only portrait of a litigant owned by the Supreme Court Historical Society.*

Supreme Court Historical Society

officials to do something they have a duty to do. In this case it would order Madison to deliver the commissions.

As chief justice, Marshall was in a position to rule on his administration's efforts to appoint these judges. Today this would be considered a conflict of interest, and he would be expected to disqualify himself. But at the time, people were not as troubled by such conflicts.

Marshall could issue the writ, but Jefferson would tell Madison to disobey it, and the Court would be powerless to enforce it. Or Marshall could decline to issue the writ, and the Court would appear powerless to issue it. Either way, the Court would reflect weakness rather than project strength.

Marshall shrewdly found a way out of the dilemma. He interpreted a provision of a congressional statute in a questionable way and then a provision of the Constitution in a questionable way as well. Marbury had petitioned the Court for a writ of mandamus under the authority of a provision of the Judiciary Act of 1789 that permitted the Court to issue such a writ. Marshall maintained that this provision broadened the Court's original jurisdiction and thus violated the Constitution. (The Constitution allows the Court to hear cases on appeal, and it gives the Court original jurisdiction—that is, the authority to hear cases that have not been heard by any other court before—in cases involving a state or foreign ambassador. Marbury's involved neither.) Yet it was quite clear that the provision did not broaden the Court's original jurisdiction—so clear, in fact, that Marshall did not even quote the language he was declaring unconstitutional. Furthermore, even if the provision did broaden the Court's original jurisdiction, it is not certain that the provision would violate the Constitution. (The Constitution does not say the Court shall have original jurisdiction *only* in cases involving a state or foreign ambassador.) Many members of Congress who had drafted and voted for the Judiciary Act had been delegates to the Constitutional Convention, and it is unlikely that they would have initiated a law that contradicted the Constitution.[34] But these interpretations allowed Marshall a way out of the dilemma.

Marshall concluded that the Court could not order the administration to give the commission because the provision of the act was unconstitutional. Thus, Marshall exercised judicial review. He wrote, in a statement that would be repeated by courts for years to come, "It is emphatically the province and duty of the judicial department to say what the law is."

Marshall justified judicial review this way: The Constitution is the supreme law of the land. If other laws contradict it, they are unconstitutional. So far, few of his contemporaries would quarrel with his reasoning. Marshall continued: Judges decide cases, and to decide cases they have to apply the Constitution. To apply it, they have to say what it means. They can be trusted to say what it

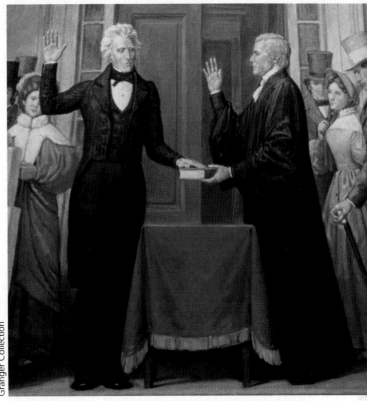

Chief Justice John Marshall (right) swears in President Andrew Jackson in 1829. Although Marshall's party, the Federalists, had dissolved, Marshall remained as chief justice, serving for thirty-four years.

means because they take an oath to uphold it. Here many would quarrel with his reasoning. Other officials have to follow the Constitution and take an oath to uphold it, and they could interpret it as appropriately as judges could.

But Marshall was persuasive enough to convince many. A sly fox, he sacrificed the commissions—he could not have gotten them anyway—and established the power of judicial review instead. In doing so, with one hand he gave the Jeffersonians what they wanted, while with the other he gave the Federalists something much greater. And all along he claimed he did what the Constitution required him to do.

Jefferson saw through this. He said the Constitution, in Marshall's hands, was "a thing of putty,"[35] adding that Marshall's arguments were "twistifications." But the decision did not require Jefferson to do anything, so he could not do anything but protest. Most of Jefferson's followers were satisfied with the result. They were not upset that the Court had invalidated a Federalist law or had articulated judicial review to do so.

Of course, they were shortsighted because this decision laid the cornerstone for a strong judiciary. Thus, the case that began as a "trivial squabble over a few petty political plums"[36] became perhaps the most important case the Court has ever decided. (See also the box "The Quintessential American?")

Thomas Jefferson is well known among Americans, with his face on nickels and a beautiful monument in Washington. His adversary, John Marshall, is relatively unknown despite the chief justice's historic accomplishments in strengthening the Supreme Court and the national government.

Though distant cousins and Virginia natives, these two great Americans detested each other, perhaps because they were so different from one another. Jefferson was an aristocrat, broadly educated, with an interest in science and a flair for inventing things, and also with an interest in architecture and real talent for practicing it, as evidenced by Monticello, his home. He owned slaves, yet he lived beyond his means and usually was over his head in debt. Marshall, the oldest of fifteen children from a frontier family, was a self-made man. He worked hard to establish himself as a lawyer. He also tried to increase his wealth as a land speculator. By combining law and business, Marshall reflected the American fascination with these two professions.

During the Revolutionary War, Marshall served with General George Washington through the long winter at Valley Forge. He witnessed American farmers selling their food to British troops rather than to American troops who desperately needed it, because the American army paid with worthless money. The American government under the Continental Congress was too weak to tax, so it lacked the resources to back up the money it printed. This experience would contribute to Marshall's belief in a strong government.

After the war, Marshall gained extensive political experience. He served in the Virginia legislature, the Virginia convention for ratification of the Constitution, and the United States House of Representatives, and he served as a United States minister to France. He led a delegation to France in 1797 to negotiate a treaty between the two countries. But when the French foreign minister demanded money in exchange for an agreement, Marshall rebuffed him and returned home a hero. Outraged Americans threatened war, but Jefferson, who admired French society and fancied French finery, upbraided Marshall for antagonizing French officials.

President John Adams appointed Marshall secretary of state and, at the end of his administration, chief justice of the Supreme Court. By the time Marshall reached the Court, his political experience certainly had sharpened his political acumen to the point where he could lead his brethren and write persuasive opinions for the Court over the opposition of other officials and opposing parties.

Throughout his career, Marshall dressed slovenly and got along well with people from all classes. He seemed as comfortable in rowdy taverns as in genteel homes. (They say that as a candidate for Congress, he provided the best whiskey on election day.) Even as chief justice, he often shopped for his sick wife. At market one day, a young dandy who did not recognize him said, "Here, my man. Just take this turkey to my house," and tossed a coin. Marshall took the coin and delivered the turkey.[1]

The aristocratic Jefferson envisioned an agrarian country and championed the poor farmers who seemed at the mercy of the commercial interests of the northern cities. He spoke against efforts to strengthen the national government, which, he believed, would be controlled by these powerful interests. The self-made Marshall, however, envisioned a commercial empire and advocated a strong government that could provide a stable economy in which business could flourish. Over the years Americans would talk like Jefferson— "That government is best which governs least" would become a perennial quotation—but they would act like Marshall, and the country would develop as Marshall envisioned far more than as Jefferson did.

In other ways Marshall was more advanced for his times, though less successful in furthering his views. He favored equality for women and opposed efforts to drive Indian tribes off their lands. When Georgia tried to force the Cherokees from the state, the Supreme Court held the laws unconstitutional.[2] But Georgia ignored the ruling, and former Indian fighter President Andrew Jackson reportedly said, "John Marshall has made his decision. Now let him enforce it."

1. Robert Wernick, "Chief Justice Marshall Takes the Law in Hand," *Smithsonian*, November 1998, 159.
2. *Worcester v. Georgia*, 31 U.S. 515 (1832).
SOURCE: Robert Wernick, "Chief Justice Marshall Takes the Law in Hand," *Smithsonian*, November 1998, 157–173.

National Supremacy

After *Marbury*, the Court did not declare any other congressional laws unconstitutional during Marshall's tenure, although it did declare numerous state laws unconstitutional.[37] These decisions entrenched the practice of judicial review and at the same time underlined the supremacy of the national government over the state governments.

The Court also furthered the supremacy of the national government by broadly construing the power of Congress. In *McCulloch v. Maryland*, explained in Chapter 3, the Court interpreted the "necessary and proper clause" to allow Congress to legislate in many matters not mentioned in the Constitution. Then the Court narrowly construed the power of the states to regulate commerce.[38]

When President Andrew Jackson named Roger Taney to replace Marshall, proponents of a strong national government worried that Taney would undo what Marshall had done. But, although Taney did not further expand national power, he upheld national supremacy and thus solidified most of Marshall's doctrine.

Yet in one case Taney severely undermined the Court's reputation. In the *Dred Scott* case,[39] the Court jumped into the thick of the slavery conflict and declared the Missouri Compromise of 1820, which controlled slavery in the territories, unconstitutional. This was only the second time the Court had declared a congressional law unconstitutional, and it could not have come in a more controversial area or at a less opportune time. The slavery issue had polarized the nation, and the ruling polarized it further. Southerners had been disenchanted with the Court because of its emphasis on a strong national government. Now northerners became disenchanted, too. The Court's prestige dropped so precipitously that it could play only a weak role for two decades. President Abraham Lincoln refused to enforce one of its rulings,[40] and Congress withdrew part of its jurisdiction.[41] As a result, the Court shied away from important issues.

The Taney Court naively thought it could resolve the clash over slavery and thereby resolve the conflict between nation and state. But no court could achieve this. It would take the Civil War to do so.[42]

Civil War to the Depression

With the controversy between nation and state muted, the next primary issue facing the courts was the relationship between government and business in cases involving regulation of business.

After the war, industrialization proceeded at a breakneck pace, bringing not only benefits but many problems. Some corporations abused their power over their employees, their competitors, and their customers. Although legislatures passed laws to regulate these abuses, the corporations challenged the laws in court. The Supreme Court, dominated by justices who had been lawyers for corporations, reflected the views of corporations—the laissez-faire attitudes of the late nineteenth and early twentieth centuries—and struck down the regulations on them.

Beginning in the 1870s, intensifying in the 1890s, and continuing in the 1900s, the Court invalidated laws that regulated child labor,[43] maximum hours of work,[44] and minimum wages for work.[45] It also discouraged employees from joining unions and unions from striking employers,[46] and it limited antitrust laws.[47] In just one decade, the Court invalidated forty-one state laws regulating railroads.[48]

In 1935 and 1936, the Court struck down twelve congressional laws,[49] nearly nullifying President Franklin Roosevelt's New Deal program to help the country recover from the Great Depression.

The Court's action precipitated another major crisis. Roosevelt was reelected resoundingly in 1936. Heady from his victory and frustrated by his lack of opportunities

National Archives 102-LH-1056

Although many children worked long days in unhealthy conditions, the Supreme Court declared initial laws prohibiting child labor unconstitutional. Addie Laird was a spinner in a Vermont cotton mill in 1910.

to appoint new justices in his first term, he retaliated against the Court by proposing what was soon labeled a **court-packing plan.** The plan would have authorized the president to nominate and the Senate to confirm a new justice for every justice over seventy who did not retire, up to a total of fifteen. At the time, there were six justices over seventy, so Roosevelt could have appointed six new justices and assured himself a friendly Court. The plan was the dominant political issue for five months. It was debated in Congress, in newspapers, and on the radio. Public opinion was divided. Even some of Roosevelt's supporters criticized him for tampering with the Court.

Before Congress could vote on the plan, two justices who often sided with four conservative justices against New Deal legislation switched positions to side with three liberal justices for similar legislation. Chief Justice Charles Evans Hughes and Justice Owen Roberts apparently thought the Court would suffer if it continued to oppose the popular president and his popular programs. Indeed, it is likely that the plan would have passed if the Court had not changed. Their "conversion" tipped the scales from votes of six to three against New Deal legislation to five to four for similar legislation. As a result, the plan became unnecessary, and Congress scuttled it. Hughes's and Roberts's switch was dubbed "the switch in time that saved nine."

Thus, the Court resolved this issue in favor of government over business. Since then it has permitted most efforts to regulate business.

Depression to the Present

With the controversy between government and business subdued, the next primary issue facing the courts was the relationship between government and the individual in cases involving civil liberties and rights. Often this issue featured a conflict between the majority, whose views were reflected in government policy, and a minority who challenged the policy.

Despite people's perceptions today, the courts paid little attention to civil liberties and rights historically. The courts allowed their governments to ignore these rights usually. But the courts' lax attitude began to change when President Dwight Eisenhower, fulfilling a campaign pledge to a presidential rival, Earl Warren, appointed him chief justice. From 1953 through the 1960s, Warren led the Court more effectively than any chief justice since Marshall. The **Warren Court** completely overhauled doctrine involving racial segregation, criminal defendants' rights, and reapportionment. It also significantly altered doctrine involving

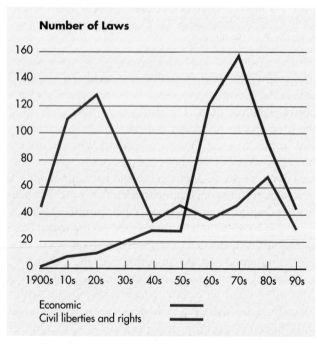

FIGURE 1 ■ Laws Regulating Economic Activity and Restricting Civil Liberties and Rights Declared Unconstitutional by the Supreme Court since 1900
The Supreme Court was nearly as activist in striking down laws in the 1910s, 1920s, and 1930s as it was in the 1950s, 1960s, and 1970s. But in the former years it was activist in economic cases (usually ones involving governmental regulation of business), while in the latter years it was activist in civil liberties and rights cases.

Sources: Congressional Research Service, *The Constitution of the United States: Analysis and Interpretation and 1998 Supplement* (Washington, D.C.: U.S. Government Printing Office, 1996 and 1999); Kenneth Jost, *The Supreme Court Yearbook, 1998–1999* (Washington, D.C.: CQ Press, 2000); Lawrence Baum, *The Supreme Court, 7th ed.* (Washington, D.C.: CQ Press, 2001), 208.

libel, obscenity, and religion. In the process it held many laws unconstitutional. It was more activist in civil liberties and rights cases than the Court had ever been (see Figure 1).

The Warren Court sympathized with unpopular individuals and powerless groups—alleged subversives, criminal defendants, racial minorities, and religious minorities—when they challenged governmental policies. Thus, the most elite institution in our government used its power to benefit many nonelites in our society. In its sympathies, the Warren Court sharply differed from previous Courts, which historically favored the haves over the have-nots and efforts to preserve the status quo over struggles to change it.

The Warren Court's decisions brought about a backlash in the late 1960s. President Richard Nixon vowed to change the direction of the Court, and in 1969 he appointed Warren Burger to be chief justice after Earl Warren retired. Then Nixon and his former vice president, President Gerald Ford, appointed four more justices when vacancies occurred. They sought to slow, halt, or even reverse the Warren Court's actions. They expected the **Burger Court** to make a "constitutional counterrevolution."

But the Burger Court did not. Although it eroded some of the Warren Court's doctrine, particularly in the area of criminal defendants' rights, it left most of the doctrine intact. Furthermore, it advanced doctrine in two areas where the Warren Court was silent: sexual discrimination and abortion. Although it was not as committed to civil liberties and rights as the Warren Court, the Burger Court was more committed to them than any earlier Court.

Presidents Ronald Reagan and George H. Bush also wanted to reverse the Court's liberal doctrine. When Burger retired, Reagan elevated William Rehnquist, the most conservative associate justice, to be chief justice in 1986. Then Reagan appointed three more conservatives, and Bush appointed two more conservatives. By this time, Republican presidents had named ten straight justices.

The election of President Clinton led to the appointment of the first Democratic justices since 1967. Although these two moderates slowed any further swing to the right, the conservatives control the **Rehnquist Court.** But conflicts among the conservatives have splintered the bloc. Some are bold, anxious to sweep away liberal precedents and substitute conservative principles. Others are cautious, willing to uphold liberal precedents they would not have agreed to set in the first place, and inclined to decide cases on narrow bases rather than on broad principles. In some terms, the former group has dominated, but in other terms, the latter group has dominated.[50] Overall, the Rehnquist Court, though markedly more

Chief Justice Earl Warren, flanked by Justices Hugo Black (left) and William Douglas.

Dennis Brack/Black Star

In sum, throughout its history the Court's role in government has been that of a policymaker—in relationships between nation and state, government and business, and government and the individual. In the first and second eras, the Court was a solidly conservative policymaker, protecting private property rights and limiting government regulation of business; in the third era, the Court was a generally liberal policymaker, permitting government regulation of business and supporting civil liberties and rights for the individual.

It now appears that the third era is over. Although the Rehnquist Court has not overturned most of the previous Courts' doctrine, it has deemphasized individual rights,[51] refusing to expand them and even cutting back on them in some areas.

The Next Era

If the third era is over, what controversy will the fourth era address? We probably will not know for many years, until we can look back with more perspective than we have now, but it is interesting to speculate.

Might the fourth era focus on information technology, including computers, the software they use, and the data they store? And might it resolve disputes about which people have access to this technology, when people have access to it, and how people can use it—in short, in what ways and to what extent the government and the private sector can impose restrictions on the new technology? These questions would be similar to ones the Court answered about freedom of speech, freedom of the press, libel, and obscenity in the third era. Or perhaps the emphasis will be on privacy from all the intrusions of this new technology. The Court has barely addressed invasion of privacy in the third era. (Chapter 14 explains the Court's doctrine in this area.)

Or might the fourth era focus on biotechnology? Advances in genetics herald a revolution promising the opportunity for people to live longer and for parents to choose various characteristics of their children, such as gender and eye color, and alter other characteristics, such as intelligence, personality, and athletic ability. Research even offers the possibility of cloning. Initial legal issues might involve restrictions on experiments and techniques. Once the techniques are developed, the legal issues might involve access to these procedures.

Information technology and biotechnology will experience exponential growth in the first half of the twenty-first century. Technological change, according to one scientist, "will appear to explode into infinity, at least from the limited and linear perspective of contemporary humans." This change will be "so rapid and so profound that it represents a rupture in the fabric of

conservative than the Burger Court, has not overturned most of the previous Courts' doctrine.

Yet the Rehnquist Court has altered some of the previous Courts' doctrine. The conservative justices have continued to erode criminal defendants' rights. They have also made it harder for racial minorities to use affirmative action and for religious minorities to follow the tenets of their religion. In two less obvious areas, the Rehnquist Court has altered doctrine in more fundamental ways. It has tightened access to the courts for individuals and groups trying to challenge government policies. And it has limited efforts by the federal government to impose new regulations on the states. The latter development is the most notable change by the Rehnquist Court. In these ways the Republican justices have mirrored the views of the Republican presidents and members of Congress in the 1980s and 1990s.

TABLE 1	Modern Supreme Courts
For convenience, scholars and journalists refer to the Supreme Court by the name of its chief justice, although the Court's doctrine is determined by all of its justices.	
Warren Court	1953–1969
Burger Court	1969–1986
Rehnquist Court	1986–present

Chief Justice William Rehnquist

Lynn Johnson/Aurora & Quanta

human history."[52] If this prediction is at all accurate, litigants and judges will be wrenched from their current preoccupations and forced to address new issues barely imagined now.

Courts

Most countries with a federal system have one national court over a system of regional courts. In contrast, the United States has a complete system of national courts side by side with complete systems of state courts, for a total of fifty-one separate systems. This setup makes litigation far more complicated than in other countries.

Structure of the Courts

The Constitution mentions only one court—a supreme court—although it allows Congress to set up additional, lower courts, which it did in the Judiciary Act of 1789. The act was a compromise between Federalists, who wanted a full system of lower courts with extensive jurisdiction—authority to hear and decide cases—in order to strengthen the national government, and Jeffersonians, who wanted only a partial sys-

tem of lower courts with limited jurisdiction in order to avoid strengthening the national government. The compromise established a full system of lower courts with limited jurisdiction. These courts were authorized to hear disputes involving citizens of more than one state but not disputes relating to the U.S. Constitution and laws. The state courts were permitted to hear all these cases.

In 1875, Congress granted the federal courts extensive jurisdiction. Sixteen years later Congress created another level of courts, between the Supreme Court and the original lower courts, to complete the basic structure of the federal judiciary.

The **district courts** are trial courts. There are ninety-four, based on population but with at least one in each state. They have multiple judges, although a single judge or jury decides each case.

The **courts of appeals** are intermediate appellate courts. They hear cases that have been decided by the district courts but are appealed by the losers. There are twelve, based on regions—"circuits"—of the country. They have numerous judges, although a panel of three judges decides each case.[53]

The Supreme Court is the ultimate appellate court. It hears cases that have been decided by the courts of appeals, district courts, or state supreme courts. (Although it can hear some cases—those involving a state or diplomat—that have not proceeded through the lower courts first, in practice it hears nearly all of its cases on appeal.) The group of nine justices decides its cases.

The district courts conduct trials. The courts of appeals and Supreme Court do not; they do not have juries or witnesses to testify and present evidence—just lawyers for the opposing litigants. Rather than determine guilt or innocence, these courts evaluate arguments about legal questions arising in the cases.

The state judiciaries have a structure similar to the federal judiciary. In most states, though, there are two tiers of trial courts. Normally, the lower tier is for criminal cases involving minor crimes, and the upper tier is for criminal cases involving major crimes and for civil cases. In about three-fourths of the states, there are intermediate appellate courts, and in all of the states there is a supreme court (although in a few it is called another name).

Jurisdiction of the Courts

Jurisdiction is the authority to hear and decide cases. The federal courts can exercise jurisdiction over cases in which the subject involves either the U.S. Constitution, statutes, or treaties; maritime law; or cases in which the litigants include the U.S. government, more than one state government, one state government and a citizen of another state, citizens of more than one state,[54] or a foreign government or citizen. The state courts exercise jurisdiction over the remaining cases. These include most criminal cases because the states have authority over most criminal matters and pass most criminal laws. Consequently, the state courts hear far more cases than the federal courts.

Despite this dividing line, some cases begin in the state courts and end in the federal courts. These involve state law and federal law, frequently a state statute and a federal constitutional right. For these cases there are two paths from the state judiciary to the federal judiciary. One is for the litigant who lost at the state supreme court to appeal to the U.S. Supreme Court.

The other path, available only in a criminal case, is for the defendant who has exhausted possible appeals in the state courts to appeal to the local federal district court through a writ of **habeas corpus.** Latin for "Have ye the body!" this writ demands that the state figuratively produce the defendant and justify his or her incarceration. If the district court decides that the state courts did not grant the defendant's constitutional rights, it will reverse the conviction. After the district court's decision, the losing side can try to appeal to the courts of appeals and Supreme Court (see Figure 2).

Judges

Selection of Judges

Benjamin Franklin proposed that judges be selected by lawyers because lawyers would pick "the ablest of the profession in order to get rid of him, and share his practice among themselves."[55] The Founders rejected this unique idea in favor of a plan whereby the president nominates judges and the Senate confirms them. There are no other requirements in the Constitution, although there is an unwritten requirement that judges be lawyers and an expectation that they be members of the president's political party. Most have been active party members who have served in office or contributed to candidates. In the twentieth century, presidents nominated members of their party from 82 percent of the time (William Howard Taft) to 99 percent of the time (Woodrow Wilson).[56] Thus, the process of selecting federal judges is highly political.

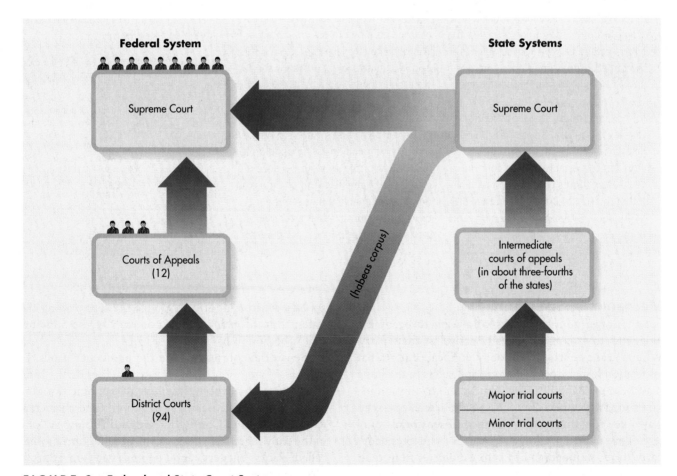

FIGURE 2 ■ Federal and State Court Systems
The arrows indicate the primary avenues of appeal, and the heads indicate the usual number of judges who hear cases in the federal system.

AFTER 9/11

SURVEILLANCE COURT

Behind closed doors in a windowless room in the Justice Department's basement, a highly secretive court meets for a few days each month. The court hears requests from the FBI for electronic surveillance of possible spies and terrorists (and sometimes for physical searches of their homes and computers).

The Foreign Intelligence Surveillance Court operates like no other court in the United States. It consists of district court judges from various judicial circuits who are chosen by the Chief Justice of the Supreme Court. The eleven members sit in panels of three judges, and they serve for seven years. Lawyers for the government, acting on behalf of the FBI, seek approval for electronic surveillance, much like law enforcement officers seek search warrants for routine searches in criminal cases. Lawyers for the defense— the targets of the surveillance—do not appear in court to protect the secrecy of the surveillance. In fact, they are not informed, and normally not aware, that a case involving the defendants is being heard at all.

Congress established the court in 1978 after abuses by the Nixon administration, which itself authorized the FBI to engage in wiretapping, bugging, and other forms of electronic surveillance.

The administration spied on American citizens active in the antiwar and civil rights movements, claiming that these protestors were threats to "national security." Despite these abuses, Congress thought the government should be allowed to engage in surveillance in genuine national security cases involving foreign agents or American citizens spying for foreign countries. Thus, Congress established the court to approve or disapprove such surveillance and thereby check future administrations.

Because of the need for strict secrecy, the court's decisions are shielded from virtually any scrutiny. Apparently, the court has turned down the government's requests only once while approving them some thirteen thousand times. Yet some FBI agents say they must have a strong case before seeking approval and occasionally have been denied the opportunity to seek approval by the Justice Department.[1]

After 9/11, Congress expanded the law to allow surveillance for the purpose of law enforcement—that is, to gain evidence for criminal trials—in addition to allowing it for the previous purpose of intelligence gathering. This change was designed to enable the government to prosecute terrorists easier after identifying them. Thus, Congress envisioned

this court, which some legal observers already viewed with a wary eye, playing a greater role as the country anticipates further terrorism.

However, this court, worried about possible abuses by the government, ordered the administration not to seek approval for surveillance simply to strengthen its prosecution of weak cases. The judges were furious that FBI agents had misled them about the purpose of the requested surveillance in many past cases, claiming that the purpose was intelligence gathering when in fact it was law enforcement.[2] Although the judges on this court seem aware of the possible abuses, the Foreign Intelligence Surveillance Court of Review, which hears appeals from this court, overruled the judge when the Bush administration appealed this ruling,.

1. "Court Will Wield Greater Power in Terrorist Hunt," *Champaign-Urbana News-Gazette,* November 5, 2001.
2. The standards for approval in the surveillance court, governed by the Foreign Intelligence Surveillance Act, are lower than the standards for a regular search warrant in the regular federal and state courts, under the Fourth Amendment. John Podesta and Peter Swire, "Speaking Out about Wiretaps," *Washington Post National Weekly Edition,* September 9–15, 2002, 27; Seymour M. Hersh, "The Twentieth Man," *New Yorker,* September 30, 2002, 56–76.

Mechanics of Selection

For the lower courts, lawyers who want to become a judge try to become politically active in their party. When vacancies arise, they lobby political officials, bar association leaders, or interest group leaders in the hope that these people will recommend them to the administration. They especially focus on their senators, who play a key role through the practice of senatorial courtesy. This tradition allows senators of the president's party to recommend and to veto candidates from their state. This practice applies not only to district courts, which lie within individual states, but sometimes to courts of appeals, which span several states. For courts of

appeals, senators informally divide the seats among the states. (But this practice does not apply to the Supreme Court because it has too few seats.)

Senatorial courtesy can tie the president's hands. In deference to southern senators, President John Kennedy, who advocated civil rights, appointed southern judges who advocated segregation. One characterized the Supreme Court's desegregation ruling as "one of the truly regrettable decisions of all time," and another called blacks "niggers" and "chimpanzees" in court.[57] However, senatorial courtesy is not as ironclad now as it was then. There is more give and take between the senators and the president.

For the Supreme Court, lawyers who want to become a justice try to become politically active in their party and also prominent in the legal profession. They write articles or give speeches designed to attract officials' attention. When vacancies arise, political officials, bar association leaders, and interest group leaders urge consideration of certain candidates. The administration also conducts a search for acceptable candidates. Sometimes even sitting justices make a recommendation. Chief Justice Burger recommended Harry Blackmun, a childhood pal and the best man at his wedding, and Justice Rehnquist recommended Sandra Day O'Connor, a law school classmate whom he had dated occasionally.

Once the president has chosen a candidate, he submits the nomination to the Senate, where it goes to the Judiciary Committee for hearings. Senators question the nominee about his or her judicial philosophy, and interest groups voice their concerns. If a majority of the committee consents, the nomination goes to the whole Senate. If a majority of the Senate consents, the nomination is confirmed.

The Judiciary Committee is the battleground for controversial nominations. The committee is controlled by the party that has a majority in the Senate, so the committee reflects the views of that party. If the committee confirms the nominee, normally the whole Senate will confirm the nominee. If the committee rejects the nomination, normally the nomination dies and the president submits another one.

The mechanics of selection for all federal courts are similar, but the process of selection for the Supreme Court is more politicized at every stage because the Court is more powerful and visible. Its seats are fought over more intensely.

Criteria Used in Selection

The Founders expected judges to be selected by merit; they did not foresee the policymaking role of the courts or the development of political parties and senatorial courtesy, which have thrust political criteria into the process of selection.

Criteria Used by Presidents Although presidents want judges who have merit, they select them primarily on the basis of politics. They look for members of their party, usually those who have some political experience, either in office or with the party behind the scenes, and often those who have certain ideological views. President Theodore Roosevelt sought judges who opposed monopolies and supported the rights of labor unions, and President Franklin Roosevelt sought judges who supported his New Deal policies. President Richard Nixon vowed to appoint judges who would change the direction of the Warren Court. But Presidents Ronald Reagan and George H. Bush made the most concerted efforts ever to appoint judges on the basis of ideological views. They sought judges who held conservative views and were willing to roll back the rulings of previous courts in a wide range of areas. They had candidates fill out lengthy questionnaires and then submit to day-long interviews probing their positions. They expected candidates, for example, to oppose the right to abortion, the Supreme Court's ruling establishing the right, and the Supreme Court's reasoning in the case.[58]

Sometimes presidents, under pressure from groups, look for judges who would provide more diversity on the courts. In the past, presidents chose Catholics and Jews to balance the Protestants who dominated the bench. In 1967, President Lyndon Johnson chose the first black justice, Thurgood Marshall; in 1981, President Reagan chose the first woman justice, Sandra Day O'Connor. Presidents have bowed to the pressure from various groups to solidify their support from these groups. Reagan, who was not a staunch advocate of women's rights, nonetheless made a campaign pledge to appoint a woman to the Supreme Court to shore up his support among female voters. (Then, after fulfilling this pledge, he felt no need to appoint many women to the lower federal courts.) Now Hispanics expect a seat on the Supreme Court. Both parties, who see support from this growing group as critical to future electoral success, would welcome the opportunity to appoint the first Hispanic to the High Court.

Presidents Carter and Clinton made the most concerted efforts to appoint women and minorities to the federal courts. Before Carter took office, only eight women had ever served on the federal bench.[59] Sixteen percent of Carter's appointees were women, and 21 percent were racial minorities.[60] Twenty-six percent of Clinton's appointees were women, and 17 percent were African Americans.[61]

Demands for diversity can limit presidents' choices, but presidents can acquiesce to these demands and still find candidates from their party with the desired political experience and ideological views. When Thurgood Marshall retired in 1991, President Bush felt obligated to nominate another black for this seat, but he wanted to nominate a conservative. He chose Clarence Thomas, a black conservative court of appeals judge. Whereas Marshall had been an ardent champion of civil rights, Thomas had opposed affirmative action and drawn the ire of most black leaders.

Individual justices do not always reflect their group's views. Justice O'Connor has voted against the feminist groups' position in some cases, while Justice Thomas has voted against the civil rights groups' position in many cases. Sometimes groups have to satisfy themselves with the symbolic benefits of having a "member" on the Court. (See also the box "Do Women Judges Make a Difference?")

DO WOMEN JUDGES MAKE A DIFFERENCE?

Some argue that there should be more women judges because women are entitled to their "fair share" of all governmental offices, including judgeships. Others argue that there should be more so women as well as men will feel that courts represent them. Still others argue that there should be more because women, compared to men, have different views and would make different decisions.

A study of Justice Sandra Day O'Connor, the first woman on the Supreme Court, shows that although she generally votes as a conservative, she usually votes as a liberal in sex discrimination cases. Moreover, her presence on the Court apparently sensitized her male colleagues to gender issues. Most of them voted against sex discrimination more frequently after she joined the Court.[1]

Some studies find similar results for women justices on state supreme courts. Even women justices from opposite political parties support a broad array of women's rights in cases ranging from sex discrimination to child support and property settlement.[2] But studies that compare voting patterns on issues less directly related to gender have less clear findings. Women judges appear more liberal than men in cases involving employment discrimination and racial discrimination. Perhaps the treatment they have experienced as women has made them more sympathetic to the discrimination others have faced. On the other hand, women judges do not appear more liberal or conservative than men in cases involving obscenity or criminal rights.[3]

Studies that compare sentencing of criminal defendants in state courts find small differences between men and women judges.[4] However, women judges do tend to sentence convicted defendants somewhat more harshly, especially black men who are repeat offenders. Apparently women judges consider these defendants more dangerous or more prone to commit new crimes after prison. Possibly women judges are influenced by the fact that these defendants are less often married and employed than other defendants.[5]

Women judges in Harris County, Texas, which includes Houston, have applied the death penalty with "greater ferocity" than their male predecessors. This county, a majority of whose judges are female, has given the death penalty to more defendants than all other *states* but one.[6]

But the studies comparing men and women judges find more similarities than differences. This should not be surprising, because the two sexes were subject to the same training in law school and the same socialization in the legal profession, and they became judges in the same ways as others in their jurisdiction.

Perhaps the most significant difference women judges have made has been to protect the credibility of women lawyers and witnesses. In court, occasionally men judges have made disparaging remarks about women lawyers, suggesting that they should not be in the profession—for example, calling them "lawyerettes." More frequently, men judges or lawyers have

made paternalistic or personal remarks to women lawyers or witnesses, referring to them by their first name or by such terms as "young lady," "sweetie," or "honey." Or the men, in the midst of the proceedings, have commented about their perfume, clothing, or appearance. "How does an attorney establish her authority when the judge has just described her to the entire courtroom as 'a pretty little thing'?"[7] Even if the men consider their remarks harmless compliments rather than intentional tactics, their effect is to undermine the credibility of women lawyers and witnesses in the eyes of jurors. Women judges have attempted to squelch such remarks.

1. Karen O'Connor and Jeffrey A. Segal, "Justice Sandra Day O'Connor and the Supreme Court's Reaction to Its First Female Member," in *Women, Politics and the Constitution* (New York: Haworth, 1990), ed. Naomi B. Lynn, 95–104.
2. David W. Allen and Diane E. Wall, "Role Orientations and Women State Supreme Court Justices," *Judicature* 77, November/December 1993, 156–165.
3. Sue Davis, Susan Haire, and Donald R. Songer, "Voting Behavior and Gender on the U.S. Courts of Appeals," *Judicature* 77, November/December 1993, 129–133; Thomas G. Walker and Deborah J. Barrow, "The Diversification of the Federal Bench," *Journal of Politics* 47, 1985, 596–617.
4. John Gruhl, Cassia Spohn, and Susan Welch, "Women as Policymakers: The Case of Trial Judges," *American Journal of Political Science* 25, May 1981, 308–322.
5. Darrell Steffensmeier and Chris Hebert, "Women and Men Policymakers: Does the Judge's Gender Affect the Sentencing of Criminal Defendants?" *Social Forces* 77, March 1999, 1163–1196.
6. Jeffrey Toobin, "Women in Black," *New Yorker,* October 30, 2000, 48.
7. William Eich, "Gender Bias in the Courtroom: Some Participants Are More Equal Than Others," *Judicature* 69, April/May 1986, 339–343.

Criteria Used by Senators Senators usually have been willing to confirm nominations to the lower courts but occasionally have been reluctant to confirm nominations to the Supreme Court. Because the high court is more important and appointments to it are more visible, these nominations are more likely to become embroiled in controversy. Since the late 1960s, senators have rejected six nominations to the Court—two by President Johnson, two by President Nixon, and two by President Reagan.[62]

Senators have decided whether to confirm a nomination primarily on the basis of the qualifications and ideology of the nominee.[63] If the qualifications were good, they usually have approved, regardless of the ideology. But if the qualifications were questionable, they often have considered how closely the nominee's ideology matches theirs. However, they have been reluctant to admit this because doing so would reveal the politics involved, and most of the public thinks politics should not be involved.

When Nixon chose court of appeals judge G. Harold Carswell, law scholars familiar with his record were dismayed. At Senate hearings they testified that he was undistinguished and opposed to civil rights. Nixon's floor manager for the nomination, Senator Roman Hruska (R–Neb.), blurted out in exasperation, "Even if he is mediocre there are a lot of mediocre judges and people and lawyers. They are entitled to a little representation, aren't they, and a little chance? We can't have all Brandeises, Cardozos, and Frankfurters, and stuff like that there."[64] This was the kiss of death. Once Carswell's supporters acknowledged his mediocrity, senators who objected to his views on civil rights could vote against him freely, and his nomination was doomed.

When presidents have nominated justices with unquestioned qualifications, they rarely have faced a problem. One exception was Reagan's nomination of Robert Bork in 1987. A former law school professor and, briefly, appellate court judge, Bork was clearly qualified. But he had addressed Supreme Court doctrine in his writings and speeches, and the debate focused on his ideology. He had rejected a right to privacy, which is the basis of Court decisions allowing birth control and abortion, and he had criticized Court decisions and congressional laws advancing racial equality and sexual equality. Although Bork had legal reasons for these positions—he had not advocated that whites should discriminate against blacks, for example, only that the Court should not have forbidden them from doing so—he seemed oblivious to the practical consequences of his positions. Senator Ted Kennedy (D–Mass.) gave an inflammatory speech:

> Robert Bork's America is a land in which women would be forced into back-alley abortions, blacks would sit at segregated lunch counters, rogue police could break down citizens' doors in midnight raids, school children could not be taught about evolution, writers and artists could be censored at the whim of the government, and the doors of the federal courts would be shut on the fingers of millions of citizens.

Bork's positions struck many Americans as extreme, and his nomination was voted down. Conservative activists were bitterly disappointed. At the high-water mark of the conservative movement, this defeat signaled that moderate Americans did not want to reverse judicial doctrine they considered settled. (One political cartoon, which appeared when daylight savings time ended in the fall, depicted Bork admonishing people, "Now, remember to turn your clocks back thirty years.") In the 1990s, conservative activists still cited the battle over Bork's nomination as the justification for their efforts and their tactics in blocking even moderate nominees of President Clinton to the courts and his cabinet.[65]

This battle prompted some observers to ask whether anyone with a record could be nominated again. Indeed, when George H. Bush had his first vacancy, he chose a man who had left no trail of controversial writings and speeches. David Souter, though a former New Hampshire attorney general and then state supreme court justice, was called the "Stealth candidate" (after the bomber designed to elude radar). Souter was a private person, living alone in a house at the end of a dirt road and not answering his neighbors' phone calls some nights. He had expressed few positions and made few decisions reflecting his views on constitutional doctrine. Then in his confirmation hearings he refused to reveal his views. Although it was assumed that he was another conservative, he offered a small target and won confirmation easily.

When Bush had his second vacancy, he chose a better-known conservative: Clarence Thomas, the head of the Equal Employment Opportunity Commission in the Reagan administration and then a judge on a federal court of appeals. Bush knew that the nomination would be controversial but saw that it would split the Democratic coalition: some Democrats would be sympathetic because of Thomas's race, while others would be critical because of his views. Even blacks were divided. Most black leaders were opposed, but many black citizens were pleased that another black man was nominated. (The allegations and the law of sexual harassment, which also arose here, are explained in Chapter 15.) Ultimately, the nomination was confirmed by four votes.

The Bush administration instructed Souter and Thomas not to reveal their views during their hearings on the grounds that they would have to decide these issues on the bench, so they would need to preserve their impartiality.[66] Yet their general views would not necessarily determine their votes in specific cases. Nevertheless, this rationale has become the standard excuse for refusing to answer the senators' questions.

When Clinton had his first vacancy, he was wary because the Republicans had vowed to avenge Bork's defeat and because the Senate had forced him to withdraw several nominations to other positions. The president chose Ruth Bader Ginsburg, a court of appeals judge for thirteen years. The nomination satisfied Republicans because Ginsburg had often voted with Republicans on the bench, yet it also pleased some Democratic constituencies. Women's groups, of course, expected more seats, and Jews, who had not had a representative on the Court since 1969, also wanted a seat.

Ginsburg refused to discuss doctrine at her hearings, but her record showed a commitment to abortion rights and sexual equality. Although she had tied for first in her graduating class from Columbia Law School in 1959, she was turned down for a clerkship by Justice Felix Frankfurter and for a job by New York City law firms. The firms, just beginning to hire Jews, were not ready to hire mothers with young children. She taught law and then served as an attorney for the American Civil Liberties Union (ACLU). In the 1970s, she argued six sex discrimination cases before the Supreme Court and won five.

When Clinton had his second vacancy, he was still wary of a confirmation fight and so chose another moderate: Stephen Breyer, a court of appeals judge.

Nominations to the Court, which were contentious during the nineteenth century but not during the first half of the twentieth century, have become contentious again partly because of the Court's activism—both liberals and conservatives have seen what the Court can do—and partly because of the struggle for control of the divided government since the late 1960s. In most years, Republicans have dominated the presidency while Democrats have dominated Congress (though in the 1990s, the situation was just the reverse), so both have fought over the judiciary to tip the balance. Republicans, especially, have been frustrated by their inability to push their civil liberties and rights policies through Congress, so they have hoped that their appointees to the Court would do what their members in Congress have not been able to do.

Even nominations to the lower courts have become contentious in recent decades. The Senate has confirmed fewer nominations to the lower courts in the fourth year of a president's term, especially when the Senate has been controlled by the other party.[67] Senators in the other party hope their candidate will capture the White House in the next election. They delay confirmation so there will be numerous vacancies for the new president and, through senatorial courtesy, for themselves to fill as well.

Efforts to delay confirmation became more pronounced in the 1990s. Republicans, who controlled the Senate, dragged their feet even at the beginning of President Clinton's second term, following a pace that kept about one hundred seats vacant.[68] After Chief Justice Rehnquist complained about the Senate's inaction, the Republican leaders responded that the Judiciary Committee needed to make sure the nominees were not "liberal activists." In reality, Clinton, who was unwilling to risk a confirmation fight over any judicial nominee, nominated moderates almost exclusively, disappointing liberals by not trying to balance the conservatives still on the bench from the Reagan and Bush years.[69]

The Republicans' tactics served several goals. Their efforts to delay confirmation and their complaints about

liberal activists were like brushback pitches in baseball: they warned the president, as he stepped up to the plate to select his candidates, not to choose the ones he might prefer. Furthermore, their complaints fired up their supporters, who sent in more money to conservative organizations, and appealed to some independents. One Republican strategist advised party officials that complaints about liberal activists enabled them to "both channel populist anger at the notion of elitist judges with a general sense of resentment that the federal government is controlling people's lives too much."[70]

The result of these tactics, according to a political scientist who studies the nomination and confirmation process, was a polarization and a delay "unprecedented in its scope."[71]

When the Democrats controlled the Senate in 2001 and 2002, they delayed confirmation of the president's nominees just as Republican senators did before.

Results of Selection

Judges are drawn primarily from the lower federal and state courts, the federal government, or large law firms. These established legal circles are dominated by white men, so, not surprisingly, most judges have been white men. Although recent presidents have appointed more minorities and women, the composition of the bench changes slowly because of life tenure for the judges.

Most judges have been wealthy. A third of George H. Bush's appointees to the lower courts were millionaires. Seven justices on the Supreme Court are millionaires.[72]

Despite some efforts to provide diversity, no effort has been made to represent various groups according to their proportion of the population. Throughout history, judges have come from a narrow, elite slice of society. Most have been born into families of Western European stock (especially English, Welsh, Scotch, and Irish), profess the Protestant religion (especially Episcopalian, Presbyterian, Congregational, and Unitarian), and are upper middle or upper class. Moreover, they have been born into families with traditions of political or even judicial service, families with prestige and connections as well as expectations for achievement.[73]

With the power to nominate judges, presidents have a tremendous opportunity to shape the courts and their decisions (see Table 2). Bush and Reagan together appointed about 65 percent of the lower court judges and five Supreme Court justices (in addition to elevating Rehnquist from associate to chief justice).

Tenure of Judges

Once appointed, judges can serve for "good behavior." This means for life, unless they commit "high crimes and misdemeanors." These are not defined in the Constitution but are considered serious crimes or, possibly, political abuses. Congress can impeach and remove

	Percentage of Liberal* Votes by Appointees of					
Issue	Nixon (R)	Ford (R)	Carter (D)	Reagan (R)	Bush (R)	Clinton (D)
Criminal justice	30	32	38	23	29	34
Civil rights and civil liberties	37	39	52	33	33	39
Labor and economic regulation	48	55	62	49	51	62

*Liberal votes were defined as ones in favor of criminal defendants' or prisoners' rights in criminal justice cases; individuals' rights, involving freedom of expression or religion and equality between the races or sexes, in civil rights and liberties cases; and workers' or economic underdogs' interests, rather than businesses' or economic upperdogs' interests, in labor and economic regulation cases. Cases from 1992 to 1996 are included.
Source: Ronald Stidham, Robert A. Carp, and Donald R. Songer, "The Voting Behavior of President Clinton's Judicial Appointees," *Judicature* 80 (July/August 1996): 16–20.

judges as it can presidents, but it has impeached only thirteen and removed only six. The standard of guilt—"high crimes and misdemeanors"—is vague, the punishment drastic, and the process time-consuming, so Congress has been reluctant to impeach judges.

As an alternative, in 1980 Congress established other procedures to discipline lower federal court judges. Councils made up of district and appellate court judges can ask judges to resign or can prevent them from hearing cases, but they cannot actually remove them. The procedures have been used infrequently, although their existence has prompted some judges to resign before being disciplined.

Qualifications of Judges

Given the use of political criteria in selecting judges, are judges well qualified?

Political scientists who study the judiciary consider federal judges generally well qualified. This is especially true of Supreme Court justices, apparently because presidents think they will be held responsible for the justices they nominate and do not want to be embarrassed by them. Also, because presidents have so few vacancies to fill, they can confine themselves to persons of their party and political views, and even to persons of a particular region, religion, race, and sex, and still locate good candidates. This is less true of lower court judges. Presidents and senators jointly appoint them, so both can avoid full responsibility for them. These judges are also less visible, so a lack of merit is not as noticeable.

Presidents do appoint some losers. President Truman put a longtime supporter on a court of appeals who was "drunk half the time "and "no damn good." When asked why he appointed the man, Truman candidly replied, "I . . . felt I owed him a favor; that's why, and I thought as a judge he couldn't do too much harm, and he didn't . . . he wasn't the worst court appointment I ever made. By no means the worst."[74]

Sometimes presidents appoint qualified persons who later become incompetent. After serving for many years they incur the illnesses and infirmities of old age, and perhaps one-tenth become unable to perform their job well.[75] Yet they hang on because they are allowed to serve for "good behavior." The situation has prompted proposals for a constitutional amendment setting a mandatory retirement age of seventy. This change would have a substantial impact because fully one-third of all Supreme Court justices, for example, have served past seventy-five. But constitutional amendments are difficult to pass, and mandatory retirement ages are out of favor now. Further, some of the best judges have done some of their finest work after seventy.

Independence of Judges

Given the use of political criteria in selecting judges, can judges be independent on the bench? Can they decide cases as they think the law requires? Or do they feel pressure to decide cases as presidents or senators want them to?

Because judges are not dependent on presidents for renomination or senators for reconfirmation, they can be independent to a great extent. In the Watergate tapes case, three Nixon appointees joined the decision against President Nixon. In a case involving a law authorizing a special prosecutor to investigate and prosecute misconduct by governmental officials, Chief Justice Rehnquist wrote the majority opinion, and another Reagan appointee joined the decision upholding the law against a challenge by President Reagan (whose aides had been prosecuted under the law).[76]

After surveying Warren and Burger Court decisions involving desegregation, obscenity, abortion, and criminal defendants' rights, one scholar observed, "Few American politicians even today would care to run on a platform of desegregation, pornography, abortion, and the 'coddling' of criminals."[77]

Presidents have scoffed at the notion that their appointees become their pawns. A study concluded that one-fourth of the justices deviated from their president's expectations.[78] Theodore Roosevelt placed Oliver Wendell Holmes on the Court because he thought Holmes shared his views on trusts. But in an early antitrust case, Holmes voted against Roosevelt's position, which prompted Roosevelt to declare, "I could carve out of a banana a judge with more backbone than that!"[79] Holmes had plenty of backbone; he just did not agree with Roosevelt's position in this case. Likewise, President Eisenhower placed Earl Warren on the Court, in part because he thought Warren was a moderate. But Warren turned out to be a liberal. Later Eisenhower said his appointment of Warren was "the biggest damn fool thing I ever did."[80] President Truman concluded that "packing the Supreme Court simply can't be done . . . I've tried it and it won't work. . . . Whenever you put a man on the Supreme Court he ceases to be your friend."[81]

Truman exaggerated, although some presidents have had trouble "packing" the courts. They have not been able to foresee the issues their appointees would have to rule on or predict the ways their appointees would change on the bench. Nevertheless, presidents who have made a serious effort to find candidates with similar views usually have not been disappointed.

Access to the Courts

In this litigation-prone society, many individuals and groups want courts to resolve their disputes. Whether these individuals and groups get their "day in court" depends on their case, their wealth, and the level of court involved.

Courts hear two kinds of cases. **Criminal cases** are those in which governments prosecute persons for violating laws. **Civil cases** are those in which persons sue others for denying their rights and causing them harm. Criminal defendants, of course, must appear in court. Potential civil litigants, however, often cannot get to court.

Wealth Discrimination in Access

Although the courts are supposed to be open to all, most individuals do not have enough money to hire an attorney and pay the costs necessary to pursue a case. Only corporations, wealthy individuals, or seriously injured victims suing corporations or wealthy individuals do. (Seriously injured victims with a strong case can obtain an attorney by agreeing to pay him or her a sizable portion of what they win in their suit.) In addition, a small number of poor individuals supported by legal aid programs can pursue a case.

The primary expense is paying an attorney. In 1996, new lawyers in law firms charged an average of $95 per hour, while established partners charged an average of $183 per hour.[82] Other expenses include various fees for filing the case, summoning jurors, paying witnesses, and also lost income from the individual's job due to numerous meetings with the attorney and hearings in court.

Even if individuals have enough money to initiate a suit, the disparity continues in court. Those with more money can develop a full case, whereas others must proceed with a skeletal case that is far less likely to persuade judges or jurors. Our legal system, according to one judge, "is divided into two separate and unequal systems of justice: one for the rich, in which the courts take limitless time to examine, ponder, consider, and deliberate over hundreds of thousands of bits of evidence and days of testimony, and hear elaborate, endless appeals and write countless learned opinions" and one for the non-rich, in which the courts provide "turnstile justice."[83] (During the week that one judge spent conducting the preliminary hearing to determine whether there was sufficient evidence to require O. J. Simpson to stand trial for murdering his ex-wife and her friend, other judges in Los Angeles disposed of 474 preliminary hearings for less wealthy defendants.) Consequently, many individuals are discouraged from pursuing a case in the first place.

Interest Group Help in Access

Interest groups, with more resources than most individuals, help some individuals gain access. The groups sponsor and finance these individuals' cases. Of course, the groups do not act purely out of altruism. They choose selected cases they hope will advance their goals. An attorney for the ACLU, which takes cases as a way to prod judges to protect constitutional rights, admitted that the criminal defendants the ACLU represents "sometimes are pretty scurvy little creatures, but what they are doesn't matter a whole hell of a lot. It's the principle that we're going to be able to use these people for that's important."

Some liberal groups—especially civil liberties organizations such as the ACLU, civil rights organizations such as the National Association for the Advancement of Colored People (NAACP), environmental groups such as the Sierra Club, and consumer and safety groups such as Ralph Nader's organizations—use litigation as a primary tactic. Other groups use it as an occasional tactic. In the 1980s and 1990s, some conservative groups began to use litigation as aggressively as these liberal groups. The Rutherford Institute, for example, arose to help persons who claimed their religious rights were infringed, representing children who were forbidden from reading the Bible on the school bus or praying in the school cafeteria. The institute also funded Paula Jones's suit against President Clinton.

Interest groups have become ubiquitous in the judicial process. About half of all Supreme Court cases in-

Both sides in Paula Jones's suit against President Clinton used the media to influence public opinion. They expected the jurors to reflect the public's views. Jones's team, financed by conservative interest groups, had her made over (from left to right) to appear more appealing.

volve a liberal or conservative interest group,[84] and many lower court cases do as well. Even so, interest groups can help only a handful of the individuals who lack the resources to finance their cases.

Restrictions on Access

Even if litigants have enough wealth or interest group help, they must overcome various restrictions on access imposed by the courts. According to the Constitution, litigants can get access only for a "case" or "controversy." Courts interpret this to mean a real dispute—one in which the litigants themselves have lost rights and suffered harm. This major restriction is called **standing to sue.**

This principle is illustrated by a series of cases challenging Connecticut's birth control law. Passed in 1879, the law prohibited giving advice about or using birth control devices. Actually, the law was not enforced much; women with a private doctor could get advice and a prescription. But the law effectively prevented opening birth control clinics that would help poor women without a private doctor or young women who did not want to go to their family doctor.

In the 1940s, a doctor challenged the law, arguing that it prevented him from advising patients whose health might be endangered by childbearing. The courts said he did not have standing because he could not point to any injury he had suffered.[85] In the 1960s, a doctor and two patients, who had experienced dangerous pregnancies in the past, challenged the law, claiming that it forced them to choose between stopping sexual activity or risking dangerous pregnancies. Again the courts said they did not have standing because they could not point to any injury they had suffered, or would suffer, because the law was rarely enforced.[86] Finally, the head of Connecticut's Planned Parenthood League and the head of

Yale's obstetrics and gynecology department opened a birth control clinic. Within days they were arrested. Although they could not get access in a civil suit, they could in the criminal case. In the process of defending themselves, they claimed the law was unconstitutional, and the Supreme Court agreed.[87]

Although this doctrine is technical, its implications are highly political. Without access, of course, individuals and groups have no chance to get courts to rule in their favor. And whether they get access depends, to a considerable extent, on the ideology of the judge presiding.

According to one study, Reagan's appointees to the district courts denied access to underdogs (individuals, groups representing individuals, or unions) in 78 percent of the cases in which they sued but denied access to upperdogs (governments or corporations) in only 41 percent of the cases in which they sued. These rulings contrast with those of Carter's and Nixon's appointees, who were both less strict in denying access and more evenhanded in treating underdogs and upperdogs.[88]

Proceeding through the Courts

Cases normally start in a district court. Individuals who lose have a right to have their case decided by one higher court to determine whether there was a miscarriage of justice. They normally appeal to a court of appeals. Individuals who lose at this level have no further right to have their case decided by another court, but they can appeal to the Supreme Court. However, the Court can exercise almost unlimited discretion in choosing cases to review. No matter how important or urgent an issue seems, the Court does not have to hear it.

Litigants who appeal to the Supreme Court normally file a petition for a **writ of certiorari** (Latin for "made more certain"). The Court grants the writ—that is, the Court agrees to hear the case—if four of the nine justices vote to do so. The rationale for this "rule of four" is that a substantial number, but not necessarily a majority, of the justices should think the case is important enough to review. Generally, the Court agrees to review a case when the justices think an issue has not been resolved satisfactorily or consistently by the lower courts.

From almost seven thousand petitions each year, the Court selects less than one hundred to hear, thus exercising considerable discretion. The oft-spoken threat "We're going to appeal all the way to the Supreme Court" is usually just bluster. Likewise, the notion that the Court is "the court of last resort" is misleading. Most cases never get beyond the district courts or courts of appeals.

That the Supreme Court grants so few writs means the Court has tremendous power to control its docket and therefore to determine which policies to review. It also means the lower courts have considerable power because they serve as the court of last resort for most cases.

Deciding Cases

In deciding cases, judges need to interpret statutes and the Constitution and determine whether to follow precedents. In the process they make law.

Interpreting Statutes

In deciding cases, judges start with statutes—laws passed by legislatures. If statutes are ambiguous, judges need to interpret them in order to apply them to their cases.

Sometimes statutes are ambiguous because of the nature of legislation. To be broad enough to cover many situations, their words and phrases must be so general that they might not be clear. Other times statutes are ambiguous because of the nature of the legislative process. To satisfy public demand for action on problems, legislators are urged to move quickly, even if they are not prepared. They are encouraged to act symbolically, even if they cannot alleviate the problems this way. They are pressed to compromise, even if they must include fuzzy provisions in statutes to avoid upsetting fragile agreements negotiated among themselves. Thus, a member of Congress, tongue in cheek, told one justice that they purposely use "unintelligible language" in statutes so the courts will "tell us what we mean."[89]

When statutes are ambiguous, judges try to ascertain the legislators' intent in passing them. They scrutinize the legislators' remarks and debates. But they often find that different members said different things, even contradictory things, and most members said nothing about the provisions in question. This gives judges considerable leeway in construing statutes.

Congress passed the Americans with Disabilities Act to protect people from discrimination in employment and public accommodations (businesses open to the public, such as stores, restaurants, hotels, and health care facilities). The act applies to people who have a "physical impairment" that "substantially limits" any of their "major life activities." The statute does not define these terms. Thus, the courts have had to, and in the process they have determined the scope of the act.

When a dentist refused to fill a cavity in a woman with HIV, she sued, claiming discrimination under this act. The Supreme Court agreed by a 5–4 vote.[90] The majority concluded that HIV was a physical impairment, although the woman was in the early stages and was not prevented from performing any activity yet. And the majority concluded that HIV could limit the major life activity of reproduction, because the disease could infect her fetus if she got pregnant. (Of course, HIV would also affect other major life activities eventually.) The dissenters denied that reproduction is a major life activity, and they denied that HIV in its early stages limits reproduction. They interpreted the statute to ap-ply to repetitive activities that are essential for daily existence rather than important activities that rarely, if ever, occur in a person's life.

When twin sisters who were severely near-sighted were denied the opportunity to become global airline pilots, they sued. This time the Court ruled the opposite by a 7–2 vote.[91] Because their condition could be corrected with glasses, they were not limited in any major life activity. Although they could not get jobs as global pilots, they could get jobs as regional pilots. The majority observed that 100 million Americans have impaired vision that requires glasses (and 28 million have impaired hearing, and 50 million have high blood pressure), and they concluded that Congress could not have intended the act to apply to so many people.[92]

When a woman developed carpal tunnel syndrome on the assembly line at a manufacturing plant, she sued, claiming that the company did not make the reasonable accommodation—in this situation, give her a job that did not require repetitive manual labor—that it was required to under the act. She said her condition limited her major life activities of performing manual tasks at work and at home, including lifting, sweeping, and gardening; playing with her children; and driving long distances. The Court unanimously ruled that these are not major life activities.[93] For the act to apply, the activities must be of central importance to most people's daily lives.

Thus, although the Court interpreted the act broadly when it covered persons with HIV, it interpreted the act narrowly when it refused to cover workers with less serious ailments. In these cases, the Court protected employers from having to make individual arrangements for many employees. From these cases it should be evident that judges can make law when they interpret statutes.

Interpreting the Constitution

After interpreting statutes, judges determine whether they are constitutional. Or, if the cases involve actions of government officials rather than statutes, judges determine whether the actions are constitutional. For either, they need to interpret the Constitution.

Compared to constitutions of other countries, our Constitution is short and therefore necessarily ambiguous. It speaks in broad principles rather than in narrow details. The Fifth Amendment states that persons shall not be "deprived of life, liberty, or property without due process of law." The Fourteenth Amendment states that persons shall not be denied "the equal protection of the laws." What is "due process of law"? "Equal protection of the laws"? Generally, the former means that people should be treated fairly and the latter means that they should be treated equally. But what is fairly? Equally?

These are broad principles that need to be interpreted in specific cases.

Sometimes the Constitution uses relative terms. The Fourth Amendment provides that persons shall be "secure . . . against unreasonable searches and seizures." What are "unreasonable searches and seizures"? Other times the Constitution uses absolute terms. These appear more clear-cut but are deceptive. The First Amendment provides that there shall be "no law . . . abridging the freedom of speech." Does "no law" mean literally no law? Then what about the proverbial example of the person who falsely shouts, "Fire!" in a crowded theater? Whether relative or absolute, the language needs to be interpreted in specific cases.

Occasionally, politicians assert that judges ought to be "strict constructionists"; that is, they ought to interpret the Constitution "strictly." This is nonsense. Judges cannot possibly interpret ambiguous language strictly.

When the language does not give sufficient guidance, some judges believe they should follow the intentions of the framers.[94] Yet these intentions are difficult to ascertain. James Madison's notes from the Constitutional Convention and the *Federalist Papers* are considered the most authoritative sources, but relying on them is fraught with problems. Because Madison edited his notes many years after the convention, his experiences in government or lapses of memory might have colored his version of the intentions of the delegates. Because Madison, Hamilton, and Jay published the *Federalist Papers* to persuade New York to ratify the Constitution, their motive might have affected their account of the intentions of the delegates. Furthermore, there were fifty-five delegates to the Constitutional Convention and many more to the state ratifying conventions, and the sources do not indicate what most thought about any of the provisions. Undoubtedly, all did not think the same.

Other judges believe they need not follow the intentions of the framers. They maintain that the Constitution was designed to be flexible and adaptable to changes in society.[95] These judges try to distill the general meaning of the provisions of the Constitution and apply this meaning to contemporary situations facing them. The Fourteenth Amendment's equal protection clause does not refer to schools, and its framers did not intend it to apply to schools. However, they did intend it to grant blacks greater equality than before, and therefore the Court applied this meaning to segregated schools. Then the Court applied it to other segregated facilities, then to other racial minorities, and then to women. In short, the Court extracted the general meaning of equality and extended it to prohibit discrimination in many situations. In this way the Court put into practice Chief Justice John Marshall's statement that the Constitution is "intended to endure for ages to come."[96]

When judges interpret the Constitution, they exercise discretion. As former Chief Justice Hughes candidly acknowledged, "We are under a constitution, but the Constitution is what the Supreme Court says it is."[97]

Restraint and Activism

All judges exercise discretion, but not all engage in policymaking to the same extent. Some, classified as restrained, are less willing to declare laws or actions of government officials unconstitutional, whereas others, classified as activist, are more willing to do so.

Restrained judges believe that the judiciary is the least democratic branch because (federal) judges are appointed for life rather than elected and reelected. Consequently, they should defer to the other branches, whose officials are elected. That is, they should accept the laws or actions of the other branches rather than substitute their own views instead. They should be wary of "government by judiciary." "Courts are not the only agency of government that must be presumed to have the capacity to govern," Justice Harlan Stone said. "For the removal of unwise laws from the statute books appeal lies not to the courts, but to the ballot and the processes of democratic government."[98] Restrained judges also believe that the judiciary is the least capable branch because judges are generalists who lack the expertise and resources that bureaucrats and legislators use to make policy.

Restrained judges further maintain that the power to declare laws unconstitutional is more effective if it is used sparingly. Justice Louis Brandeis concluded that "the most important thing we do is not doing."[99] That is, the most important thing judges do is declare laws constitutional and thereby build up political capital for the occasional times that they declare laws unconstitutional.

Ultimately, restrained judges contend that showing appropriate deference and following proper procedures are more important than reaching desired results. When a friend encouraged Justice Oliver Wendell Holmes one morning, "Well, Mr. Justice, I hope you do justice today," Holmes replied that "my job is not to do justice, but to follow the law."

Activist judges are less concerned with showing appropriate deference and following proper procedures. They seem more outraged at injustice. Chief Justice Earl Warren said the courts' responsibility was "to see if justice truly [had] been done." He asked lawyers who emphasized technical procedures during oral arguments, "Yes, yes, yes, but is it right? Is it good?"[100]

Activist judges do not believe that the judiciary is the least democratic branch. Warren, who served as governor of California, saw that the legislators, though elected, were often the captives of special interests. As a

Two clerks meet with Justice Stevens.

result of these attitudes, activist judges have a more flexible, pragmatic view of separation of powers. District court judge Frank Johnson, who issued sweeping orders for Alabama's prisons and mental hospitals, replied to critics, "I didn't ask for any of these cases. In an ideal society, all of these . . . decisions should be made by those to whom we have entrusted these responsibilities. But when governmental institutions fail to make these . . . decisions in a manner which comports with the Constitution, the federal courts have a duty to remedy the violation."[101]

Activist judges do not believe that the power to declare laws unconstitutional is more effective if it is used sparingly. Rather, they claim that the power is enhanced if it is used frequently—essentially, they urge their colleagues to "use it or lose it"—because the public gets accustomed to it.

Thus, judicial restraint and judicial activism are belief systems and role concepts that people think judges should adopt and follow when they decide cases. In response to the liberal activism of the Warren Court, many people insist judges should adhere to judicial restraint as a way to limit further liberal activism. Justice Harry Blackmun, appointed by President Richard Nixon, reflected this view in a capital punishment case:

I yield to no one in the depth of my distaste, antipathy, and, indeed, abhorrence, for the death penalty, with all its aspects of physical distress and fear and of moral judgment exercised by finite minds. That distaste is buttressed by a belief that capital punishment serves no useful purpose that can be demonstrated. For me, it violates childhood's training and life's experiences, and is not compatible with

the philosophical convictions I have been able to develop. It is antagonistic to any sense of "reverence for life." Were I a legislator, I would vote against the death penalty.

But as a judge, he voted for it.[102]

Although these are useful concepts, we should not make too much of them. It usually is more important to know whether a judge is conservative or liberal than whether the judge purports to be restrained or activist. Political science research shows that justices' ideology accounts for most of their votes. That is, conservative justices vote for the conservative position and liberal justices vote for the liberal position in most of their cases. Sometimes justices claim to be restrained, but usually their decision—allowing a particular policy to continue—produces the conservative or liberal outcome they prefer.[103] Thus, some political scientists conclude that "judicial restraint" is little more than "a cloak for the justices' policy preferences."[104] That is, it enables them to proclaim their "restraint" while actually voting on the basis of their ideology—without ever admitting this to the public. We should be skeptical when we hear judges or politicians using these terms, whether touting their "restraint" to pacify the public or deriding opponents' "activism" to inflame the public.

Conservatives and liberals have practiced restraint or activism according to the political climate at a given time. In the late nineteenth and early twentieth centuries, the Court was conservative and activist; it struck down regulations on business. After the switch in the late 1930s, the Court was liberal and restrained; it upheld regulations on business. But in the 1950s and 1960s, the Court was liberal and activist as it struck down restrictions on individual rights. Then conservatives demanded that the Court be restrained.

The Rehnquist Court has shifted between restraint and activism, with the conservative justices accepting some liberal laws and rejecting others. Although they have proclaimed their restraint, they have struck down laws implementing gun registration, affirmative action, legislative districts that help racial minorities elect their candidates, and governmental policies that help religious minorities practice their religion.

Following Precedents

In interpreting statutes and the Constitution, judges are expected to follow precedents established by their court or higher courts in previous cases. This is the rule of **stare decisis** (Latin for "stand by what has been decided").

When in 1962 the Supreme Court held unconstitutional a New York law that required public school students to recite a nondenominational prayer every day, the ruling became a precedent.[105] Then in 1963 the Court held unconstitutional a Baltimore school board policy that required students to recite Bible verses.[106] The Court followed the precedent it had set the year before. Then in 1980 the Court held unconstitutional a Tennessee law that forced public schools to post the Ten Commandments in all classrooms.[107] Although this law differed from the previous ones in that it did not require recitation, the majority concluded that it reflected the same goal—to use the public schools to promote the Christian religion—so it violated the same principle, separation of church and state. Then in 1992 the Court ruled that clergy cannot offer prayers at graduation ceremonies for public schools.[108] Although this situation, too, differed from the previous ones in that it did not occur every day at school, the majority reasoned that it, too, reflected the same goal and violated the same principle. Finally, in 2000 the Court ruled that schools cannot use, or allow clergy or students to use, the public address system to offer prayers before high school football games.[109] Thus, for almost four decades the Court followed the precedent it originally set when it initially addressed this issue.

The primary advantage of stare decisis is that it provides stability in the law. If different judges were to decide similar cases in different ways, the law would be unpredictable, even chaotic. "Stare decisis," Justice Brandeis said, "is usually the wise policy; because in most matters it is more important that the applicable rule of law be settled than that it be settled right."[110] A related advantage of this practice is that it promotes equality in the law. If different judges were to decide similar cases in different ways, the courts would appear discriminatory.

The primary disadvantage of stare decisis is that it can lead to excessive stability—inflexibility—in the law when society's attitudes are changing. At these times

precedents of past generations can bind present and future generations. Justice Holmes declared, "It is revolting to have no better reason for a rule of law than that it was laid down in the time of Henry IV. It is still more revolting if the grounds upon which it was laid down have vanished long since, and the rule simply persists from blind imitation of the past."[111]

Even when judges agree to follow precedents, sometimes they have discretion to decide which ones to follow. There might not be any that are controlling but several that are relevant, and these might point in contrary directions. This situation often arises when courts face technological changes in society. In 1996 the justices weighed government regulation of indecent programming on cable television. They had precedents that governed broadcast television, telephones, and bookstores. But, as Justice Breyer observed, none of these really paralleled cable television, which looks like broadcast television but uses telephone lines rather than airwaves to transmit its signals. Thus, he was uncertain which precedents to use. Apparently, the others were uncertain also, as the nine justices split three ways and wrote six opinions while upholding one section and striking down two other sections of the law.[112]

Making Law

Many judges deny that they make law. They say that it is already there, that they merely "find" it or, occasionally, "interpret" it with their education and experience. They imply that they use a mechanical process. Justice Roberts wrote for the majority that struck down a New Deal act in 1936:

> It is sometimes said that the Court assumes a power to overrule . . . the people's representatives. This is a misconception. The Constitution is the supreme law of the land. . . . All legislation must conform to the principles it lays down. When an act of Congress is appropriately challenged in the courts as not conforming to the constitutional mandate, the judicial branch of government has only one duty—to lay . . . the Constitution . . . beside the statute . . . and to decide whether the latter squares with the former.[113]

In other words, the Constitution itself dictates the decision.

However, by now it should be apparent that judges do not use a mechanical process, that they do exercise discretion. They *do* make law—when they interpret statutes, when they interpret the Constitution, and when they determine which precedents to follow or disregard.[114]

In doing so, they reflect their own political preferences. As Justice Benjamin Cardozo said, "We may try to see things as objectively as we please. Nonetheless, we can never see them with any eyes except our own."[115] That is, judges, too, are human beings with their own perceptions and attitudes and even prejudices. They do not, and cannot, shed these the moment they put on their robes.

But to say that judges make law is not to say that they make law as legislators do. Judges make law less directly. They make it in the process of resolving disputes brought to them. They usually make it by telling governments what they cannot do, rather than what they must do and how they must do it. And judges make law less freely. They start not with clean slates but with established principles embodied in statutes, the Constitution, and precedents. They are expected to follow these principles. If they deviate from them, they are expected to explain their reasons, and they are subjected to criticism within the legal profession.

Deciding Cases at the Supreme Court

The Supreme Court's term runs from October through June. Early in the term the justices decide which cases to hear, and by the end of the term they decide how to resolve these cases.

After the Supreme Court agrees to hear a case, litigants submit written arguments. These "briefs" identify the issues and marshal the evidence—statutes, constitutional provisions, precedents—for their side. (The word *briefs* is a misnomer, as some are over one hundred pages long.) Often interest groups and governments submit briefs to support one side. These "friend-of-the-court" briefs[116] present additional evidence or perspectives not included in the litigants' briefs. Major cases can prompt many briefs. An abortion case in 1989 prompted a record seventy-eight briefs.[117]

Several weeks after receiving the briefs, the Court holds oral arguments. For these the justices gather in the robing room behind the courtroom. They put on their black robes and, as the curtains part, file into the courtroom and take their places at the raised half-hexagon bench. The chief justice sits in the center, and the associate justices extend out in order of seniority. The crier gavels the courtroom to attention and announces:

The Honorable, the Chief Justice and Associate Justices of the Supreme Court of the United States! Oyez, oyez, oyez! [Give ear, give ear, give ear;!] All persons having business before the Honorable, the Supreme Court of the United States are admonished to draw near and give attention, for the Court is now sitting. God save the United States and this Honorable Court.

The chief justice calls the case. The lawyers present their arguments, although the justices interrupt with questions whenever they want. When Thurgood Marshall, as counsel for the NAACP before becoming a jus-

tice, argued one school desegregation case, he was interrupted 127 times. The justices ask about the facts of the case: "What happened when the defendant . . . ?" They ask about relevant precedents that appear to support or rebut the lawyers' arguments: "Can you distinguish this case from . . . ?" They ask about hypothetical scenarios: "What if the police officer . . . ?" With these questions the justices want to know what is at stake, how a ruling would relate to existing doctrine, and how a ruling might govern future situations. They are experienced at pinning lawyers down. Chief Justice Rehnquist, who is affable toward his colleagues, is tough on the lawyers appearing before him. When asked whether the lawyers were nervous, he replied, "I assume they're all nervous—they should be."[118] Occasionally, a lawyer becomes unnerved and faints on the spot.

The chief justice allots half an hour per side. When time expires, a red light flashes on the lectern, and the chief justice halts any lawyer who continues. Rehnquist, who values efficiency and punctuality, cuts lawyers off in midsentence when their time expires.

The oral arguments identify and clarify the major points of the case for any justices who did not read the briefs, and they assess the potential impact of the possible rulings. The oral arguments also serve as a symbol: They give litigants a chance to be heard in open court, which encourages litigants to feel that the eventual ruling is legitimate. However, the oral arguments rarely sway the justices, except occasionally when the lawyer for one side is especially ineffective.

The Court holds Friday conferences to make a tentative decision and assign the opinion. The decision affirms or reverses the lower court decision; it indicates who wins and who loses. The opinion explains why. It expresses principles of law and establishes precedents for the future. It tells judges on lower courts how to resolve similar cases.

A portrait of Chief Justice Marshall presides over the conference. To ensure secrecy, no one is present but the justices. They begin with handshakes. (During his tenure, Chief Justice Marshall suggested that they begin with a drink whenever the weather was rainy. But even when it was sunny, Marshall sometimes announced, "Our jurisdiction extends over so large a territory that the doctrine of chances makes it certain that it must be raining somewhere."[119] Perhaps this accounts for his extraordinary success in persuading his colleagues to adopt his views.) Then the justices get down to business. The chief justice initiates the discussion of the case. He asserts what he thinks the issues are and how they ought to be decided, and he casts a vote. The associate justices follow in order of seniority. Although the conference traditionally featured give and take among the justices, under Rehnquist discussion has been perfunctory as the conference has become a series of quick votes.[120]

The job of a justice is unlike that of other political officials. Even after three decades of experience, Justice William Brennan often ate at his desk so he could finish his work.

The Court reaches a tentative decision based on these votes. If the chief justice is in the majority, he assigns himself or another justice to write the opinion of the Court. If not, the most senior associate justice in the majority assigns one to write it. This custom reveals the chief justice's power. Although his vote counts the same as each associate justice's vote, his authority to assign the opinion can determine what the opinion says. If he assigns it to some colleagues, he knows it will lay down broad principles and use strong language; if to others, he knows it will hew closely to specific facts of the case and use guarded language.

Before Marshall became chief justice, each justice wrote his own opinion. But Marshall realized that one opinion from the Court would hold more weight. He often convinced the other justices to forsake their opinion for his. As a result, he authored almost half of the Court's 1,100-some opinions in his thirty-four years. Recent chief justices have assigned most opinions— from 82 to 86 percent—but have authored just slightly more than their share—from 12 to 14 percent.[121] Some Court watchers believe Rehnquist downplayed his conservative views after he became chief justice (but before the Court veered to the right) to stay in the majority and retain control of the opinion.[122]

After the conference, the Court produces the opinion. This is the most time-consuming stage in the process. After Justice Brandeis died, researchers found in his files the thirty-seventh draft of an opinion he had written but still had not been satisfied with.

Because the justices are free to change their vote anytime until the decision is announced, the justice assigned the opinion tries to write it to command support of the justices in the original majority and possibly even some in the original minority. The writer circulates the draft among the others, who suggest revisions. The writer circulates more drafts. These go back and forth, as the justices attempt to persuade or cajole, nudge or push their colleagues toward their position.

These inner workings underscore the politicking among the justices. Justice William Brennan, a liberal activist on the Warren and Burger Courts, was a gregarious and charming Irish American who was well liked by his colleagues. After drafting an opinion, he sent his clerks to other justices' clerks to learn whether the other justices had any objections. Then he tried to redraft it to satisfy them. If they still had qualms, he went to their offices and tried to persuade them. If necessary, he compromised. "He [didn't] want to be 100% principled and lose by one vote," a law professor observed.[123] Brennan was so adept at persuasion that some scholars consider him "the best coalition builder ever to sit on the Supreme Court."[124] In fact, some say the Warren and Burger Courts should have been called the Brennan Court.

Justice Antonin Scalia, a conservative activist on the Rehnquist Court, is a brilliant and gregarious Italian American who, when appointed by President Reagan, was expected to dominate his colleagues and become the leader of the Court. Yet he has not fulfilled this expectation. He has been brash and imprudent, appearing to take more pleasure in insulting his colleagues than in persuading them.[125] In a case in which Justice O'Connor, also conservative but more cautious, did not want to go as far in limiting abortion rights as he did, Scalia wrote that her arguments "cannot be taken seriously."[126] In another case in which Chief Justice Rehnquist, who usually votes with Scalia, voted opposite him, Scalia wrote that his arguments were "implausible" and suggested that any lawyer who advised his client as Rehnquist urged should be "disbarred."[127] As a result, Scalia has not been as effective in forging a consensus among conservatives as Brennan was among liberals.

As a result of the maneuvering and politicking, opinions often are compromises among justices in the majority. As Justice Harlan Stone explained to a law professor who criticized one of his opinions:

> I should have preferred to have written your opinion than the one which will actually appear in the books. Had I done so, I should have been in a minority of two or three, instead of a majority of six. Someone else would have written the opinion [of the Court]. . . . I proceed upon the theory . . . that the large objectives should be kept constantly in mind and reached by whatever road is open, provided only that untenable distinctions are not taken, and that I am not in the process, committed incidentally to the doctrine of which I disapprove or which would hinder the Court's coming out ultimately in the right place.[128]

If the opinion does not command the support of some of the justices in the original majority, they write a concurring opinion. This indicates that they agree

"My dissenting opinion will be brief. You're all full of crap."

with the decision but not the reasons for it. Meanwhile, the justices in the minority write a dissenting opinion. This indicates that they do not agree even with the decision. Both concurring and dissenting opinions weaken the force of the majority opinion. They question the validity of it, and they suggest that at a different time with different justices there might be a different ruling. Chief Justice Hughes used to say that a dissenting opinion is "an appeal to the brooding spirit of the law, to the intelligence of a future day."

Unlike the high courts of many other countries, which do not report any dissents, the United States Supreme Court routinely does and the American people normally accept the existence of such disagreements about the law.[129] But too many dissents indicate a fractious Court. One-third of the Rehnquist Court's cases were decided by a 5–4 vote in 2001, possibly the highest proportion ever.[130]

Finally, the Court's print shop in its basement prints the opinions. Then the Court announces its decisions and distributes the opinions in public session.

The Power of the Courts

Alexis de Tocqueville observed that unlike in other countries, "Scarcely any political question arises in the United States that is not resolved, sooner or later, into a judicial question."[131] Because Americans are more inclined than other people to bring suits, courts have many opportunities to try to wield power. The courts have been able to capitalize on these opportunities because they interpret the Constitution and enjoy relative, though not absolute, independence from the political pressures on the other branches.

The use of judicial review and the use of political checks against the courts reveal the extent of the power of the courts.

Use of Judicial Review

Judicial review—the authority to declare laws or actions of government officials unconstitutional—is the tool that courts use to wield power. When courts declare a law or action unconstitutional, they not only void that particular law or action, but they also might put the issue on the public agenda, and they might speed up or slow down the pace of change in government policies.

When the Supreme Court declared a Texas abortion law unconstitutional in *Roe v. Wade* in 1973, the Court put abortion on the public agenda.[132] The issue had not been a national controversy before the decision.

The Court used judicial review as a catalyst to speed up change in the desegregation cases in the 1950s. At the time, President Eisenhower was not inclined to act, and Congress was not able to act because the houses were dominated by southerners who, as committee chairs, blocked civil rights legislation. The Court broke the logjam.

The Court used judicial review as a brake to slow down change in the business regulation cases in the first third of the twentieth century. The Court delayed some policies for several decades.

Judicial review, an American contribution to government, was for years unique to this country. It is now used in numerous other countries but not as extensively or as effectively as in the United States.

The Supreme Court alone has struck down more than one hundred provisions of federal laws and more than one thousand provisions of state and local laws. The Court has struck down more of the latter because state and local legislatures enact more laws; these legislatures reflect parochial, rather than national, interests, so they enact more laws that the national Court considers in conflict with the national Constitution; and these legislatures are less risky to confront than Congress.

The number of laws struck down, however, is not the true measure of the importance of judicial review. Instead, the ever-present threat of review has undoubtedly prevented legislatures from enacting many laws they feared would be struck down.

By using judicial review to play a strong role in government, the Court has contradicted the Founders' expectation that the judiciary would always be the weakest branch. Usually it has been the weakest branch, but occasionally it has been stronger. Arguably, these times include some years during the early nineteenth century, when the Court established national supremacy; the late nineteenth century and early twentieth century, when the Court thwarted efforts to regulate business; and the 1950s and early 1960s, when the Court extended civil liberties and rights.

Nevertheless, the extent to which the Court has played a strong role in government should not be exaggerated. The Court has not exercised judicial review over a wide range of issues; in each of the three eras of its history, it has exercised review over one dominant issue and paid relatively little attention to other issues. Moreover, the one dominant issue always has involved domestic policy. Traditionally the Court has been reluctant to intervene in foreign policy.[133] Even when the war in Vietnam was the most contentious issue in the country, with many people questioning its constitutionality and numerous men challenging the draft, the Court refused to review the issue.

When the Court has tackled an issue, it has been cautious. Of the provisions of congressional laws held unconstitutional, more than half were voided more than four years after they had been passed, and more than one-fourth were voided more than twelve years after they had been passed.[134] These laws were voided after many members of Congress who had initiated and voted for them had left Congress. The Court confronted Congress when it was safer to do so.

Use of Political Checks against the Courts

Although the courts enjoy relative independence from the political pressures on the other branches, they certainly do not enjoy absolute independence. Because they are part of the political process, they are subject to political checks, which limit the extent to which they can wield judicial review.

Checks by the Executive

Presidents can impose the most effective check. If they dislike judges' rulings, they can appoint new judges when vacancies occur. A sizable proportion of these appointees remain on the bench even two decades after presidents leave the White House.[135] Nevertheless, it can be difficult to get judges to reverse precedents or to make decisions beyond the existing political consensus, as Presidents Reagan and Bush discovered.

Presidents and state and local executives, such as governors and mayors and even school officials and police officers, can refuse to enforce courts' rulings. School officials have disobeyed decisions requiring desegregation and invalidating class prayers. Police officers have ignored decisions invalidating some kinds of searches and interrogations.

Yet executives who refuse to enforce courts' rulings risk losing public support, unless the public also opposes the rulings. Even President Nixon complied when the Court ordered him to turn over the incriminating Watergate tapes.

Checks by the Legislature

Congress and the state legislatures can overturn courts' rulings by adopting constitutional amendments. They have done so four times (Eleventh, Fourteenth, Sixteenth, and Twenty-sixth Amendments).[136] They can also overturn courts' rulings by passing new statutes. When courts base decisions on their interpretations of statutes, or when they make decisions in the absence of statutes, legislatures can pass new statutes to negate the decisions. The Supreme Court ruled in 1986 that the Air Force did not have to allow an ordained rabbi to wear his yarmulke with his uniform.[137] The next year Congress passed a statute permitting military personnel to wear some religious apparel while in uniform. From 1967 through 1990, Congress passed statutes to negate 121 Supreme Court rulings.[138]

Legislatures can refuse to implement courts' rulings, especially when money is needed to implement them. The legislators simply do not appropriate the money.

Although these checks are the most common, Congress has invoked others, although only rarely: It can alter the structure of the lower federal courts, it can limit the appellate jurisdiction of the Supreme Court, and it can impeach and remove judges.

As a result of occasional checks or threatened checks, the courts have developed a strong sense of self-restraint to ensure self-preservation. This, more than the checks themselves, limits their use of judicial review.

Conclusion: Are the Courts Responsive?

Courts tend to reflect the views of the public. A study comparing 110 Supreme Court rulings from 1936 through 1986 with public opinion polls on the same issues found that the rulings mirrored the polls in 62 percent of the cases.[139] Thus, the justices either responded to the public or, having been appointed by officials elected by the public, simply reflected the views of the public.

Research shows that citizens know little about the cases (and less about the judges; more adults can identify the character names of the Three Stooges than a single justice on the Supreme Court[140]), but they do remember controversial decisions, and they do recognize broad trends. A study of public opinion toward the Supreme Court from 1966 to 1984 found that the public became more negative when the Court upheld more criminal rights and struck down more congressional statutes.[141] This opinion pressured presidents and members of Congress to appoint justices with different views. Thus, these officials responded to the public, and ultimately they got the Court to respond to the public.

Although the courts are directly or indirectly responsive to the public, the Founders did not intend for them to be very responsive. The Founders gave judges life tenure so courts would be relatively independent of officials and the public.

Indeed, the courts are more independent of political pressures than the other branches are. This enables them, in the words of appellate court judge Learned Hand, to stand as a bulwark against the "pressure of public panic." They provide a "sober second thought."[142]

The courts can even protect the rights of various minorities—racial minorities, religious minorities, political dissidents, and criminal defendants—against the demands and the wrath of the majority. Chapters 14 and 15 will show how courts extended civil liberties and rights to unpopular individuals and groups who lacked clout with the executive and legislative branches and support from the public. Yet protecting the rights of these individuals and groups historically has been the exception rather than the rule. It was typical of the Warren Court era and to some extent the Burger Court era, but it was not typical of most years before and has not been typical of most years since.

The courts are part of the political process and are sensitive to others in the process, especially to the president, Congress, and public. Although they enjoy relative independence, they do not have absolute independence from political pressure. Thus, they have "learned to be a political institution and to behave accordingly." They have "seldom lagged far behind or forged far ahead" of public opinion.[143]

EPILOGUE

O'Connor Plunges into the Political Thicket

In the disputed presidential election of 2000, a majority of the Supreme Court, including Justice O'Connor, intervened aggressively and decisively when prudence counseled restraint. The Court decided the case of *Bush v. Gore.*

First the Court temporarily set aside the Florida Supreme Court's order for a manual recount throughout the state.[144] Although this decision did not resolve the dispute, the majority tipped its hand when Justice Scalia justified the ruling: "The counting of votes that are of questionable legality does . . . threaten irreparable harm to . . . [Bush] by casting a cloud upon what he claims to be the legitimacy of his election." Three days later the Court permanently set aside the Florida Supreme Court's order.[145] This decision essentially gave the election to George W. Bush.

In a contentious case, it is desirable for the justices to be unanimous or nearly unanimous, as they were in the Watergate tapes case that also arose from a controversy involving the presidency (covered in Chapter 2). Unanimity helps dispel fears that their decision is partisan. But in the 2000 election case, the justices were sharply split, 5–4. The majority included the five most conservative justices, including O'Connor, while the minority included the four moderate-to-liberal justices. The majority were all Republicans, while the minority included two Republicans and two Democrats.[146]

The majority ruled that manual recounts throughout the state denied equal protection to some voters, because there was no uniform standard specifying how hanging chads and dimpled chads would be counted.[147] Some counties were using more forgiving standards than other counties. A small number of unknown voters in other counties that were using more strict standards were not having their ballots counted. According to the majority, these voters were being discriminated against because of where they were living. Of course, any discrimination was not intentional, and it was not partisan; these voters included both Bush supporters and Gore supporters.

The Court could have allowed Florida to set statewide standards and proceed with the recounts, but there was limited time, and the majority refused to give the state the opportunity to try specific standards.[148]

By intervening, the majority was activist rather than restrained. Moreover, the majority rejected the federalism principle that allows state supreme courts to interpret state laws.[149] The justices seemed contemptuous of the Florida Supreme Court. Justice Scalia called that court's reasoning "peculiar" and "absurd."

Much public reaction to the Court's decision was strictly partisan. Bush supporters liked it because it meant their candidate would become president. Gore supporters disliked it for the same reason. Legal scholars, however, had more interest in and concern for how the Court's decision reflected established legal doctrine and affected the Court's legitimacy.

Most legal scholars were stunned when the Court intervened in the first place.[150] They assumed the Court would avoid this tangled thicket because it was a political dispute, it could be resolved through the political process, and the public was sharply divided. Also, the Court normally did avoid such election controversies. But the legal scholars underestimated the intense feelings aroused on the right by this election. Around the country, political and social conservatives wanted to repudiate Gore to rebuke Clinton, who had survived their impeachment effort. Former law clerks for the conservative justices, who formed a powerful network in conservative law firms and interest groups, encouraged Bush's legal team to take the case to the Supreme Court. The clerks knew these justices had strong feelings about this election and predicted they would hear the case.[151]

Most legal scholars also criticized the Court's rationale for its ruling. One said it was "embarrassingly weak."[152] Even conservative scholars were baffled; one called it "weird."[153] The majority's use of the equal protection clause here was novel. "It was not consistent," a constitutional scholar observed, "with anything they have done in the past twenty-five years."[154] It departed from precedents in several ways.[155] States' recount procedures had not been held in violation of the federal Constitution before.[156] Counties' election procedures had not been required to be standardized by the federal courts before.

In our decentralized governmental system, states often deviate from other states, and counties often deviate from other counties in the same state. Even for a policy with critical consequences as capital punishment, courts allow variations among states and among counties. A defendant convicted of murder in one part of Florida might be executed, while a defendant convicted of murder in another part of Florida might be imprisoned.[157]

Although the majority focused on the absence of statewide standards for evaluating chads, it ignored the greater problem of the absence of statewide standards for voting machines. In Florida, wealthier counties used newer machines with near-

Steve Benson/*Arizona Republic*. Reprinted by permission of United Media.

perfect counting rates, while poorer counties used older machines with lower counting rates.[158] These variations produced a bias toward the candidates favored by the voters in wealthier counties.

Even the majority seemed uncertain about its use of the equal protection clause. The majority said its use was "limited to the present circumstances." That is, it would not serve as a precedent for future cases. Thus, the majority rejected the role of precedents both in making its ruling and in following this ruling in subsequent cases involving electoral procedures. This made the majority look as if it were concerned with the outcome of this particular case rather than with the establishment of a valid principle that would govern other cases too. "Like a great spot-relief pitcher in baseball," a law professor remarked, "this equal protection argument was trotted out to do its singular job of striking out Vice President Gore and was immediately sent to the showers, never again to reappear in the game."[159]

But legal scholars were most taken aback by the willingness of the majority justices to forsake their judicial philosophies. Most people understand that the justices, like other politicians, have their own ideologies. People assume that the justices

hold these ideologies sincerely and will follow them consistently. By doing so, the justices may be political but nevertheless demonstrate an integrity that comes from deciding particular cases according to their established principles rather than their preferred outcomes. Thus, we would expect justices who have a strong view about, say, freedom of speech, to follow that view regardless of their distaste for the individual and the expression involved in a given case. Otherwise, it would appear as though they are deciding cases according to the individual and the expression involved rather than the principles they hold. In *Bush v. Gore,* the majority justices abandoned long-held principles about judicial restraint, federalism, and equal protection.[160] Their ruling was "wildly out of character."[161] Nearly six hundred law professors signed an open letter calling the majority justices hypocritical and devious.

As a result, the ruling appeared partisan.[162] A former law school dean, a conservative, called it "an unmistakably partisan decision without any foundation in law."[163] Legal scholars questioned whether the majority justices could have passed "the shoe-on-the-other-foot test." Would they have ruled the same way if Gore had been ahead and Bush had been seeking a recount? A senior law professor who had voted for Bush said, "I don't want to believe it. I don't want to have to tell my students to believe it. It goes against everything I've been saying and teaching for decades. But there is no escaping the conclusion that if Bush had been the one seeking the recount, at least some of the majority justices would have voted the other way."[164]

The entire pattern of decision making, from taking the case to disregarding established precedents to abandoning their own principles, suggests that the majority justices were reacting viscerally to what was occurring.[165] One dissenting justice reportedly said the mind-set of some majority justices was "If the Florida Supreme Court is going to act like a bunch of Democratic political hacks, well, by God, we will act like a bunch of Republican political hacks."[166]

The charges of partisanship were fueled by reports that Justice O'Connor, who was seventy, was hoping for a Bush victory so she could retire and a Republican president could appoint her successor. At an election night party, she exclaimed, when the networks projected Gore as the winner in Florida, "This is terrible!" After she left the room in disgust, her husband explained that they wanted to retire to Arizona and now would have to wait another four years.[167] Reports also indicate that Justices Kennedy and Scalia want to be chief justice when Rehnquist retires.[168] As Republicans, they would have a chance only if the president is a Republican. In addition, Justice Scalia's two sons were working as lawyers for the Republicans' law firm in the case, and Justice Thomas's wife was already screening applicants for jobs in a Bush administration.

Despite the appearance of partisanship, we do not know whether the justices were influenced, either consciously or subconsciously, by such concerns. They might have been influenced as much or more by a fear of potential chaos. When several Russian judges visited the Supreme Court after the decision, one Russian judge criticized the United States for letting judges choose the president. Justice Kennedy replied, "Sometimes you have to be responsible and step up to the plate."[169]

Some legal scholars defended the decision (though not its rationale), saying that it prevented a crisis by bringing the election to a prompt and decisive conclusion. Thus, it enabled a smooth transition to the next administration.[170]

What would have happened if the Court had not intervened? Bush might have won the recount. But if Gore had won the recount, the Republican secretary of state and the Republican governor, Bush's brother, probably would have refused to certify Gore's slate of electors. Then the Republican legislature probably would have submitted another slate of electors pledged to Bush. Thus, two slates of electors probably would have been sent to Congress—one pledged to Gore and one pledged to Bush. According to the Constitution, Congress would select one. The House of Representatives had a Republican majority, while the Senate, after the election, was divided, 50–50. As the current vice president, Gore might be in the position to cast the tie-breaking vote in the Senate, which could stalemate the two houses. Then the selection would revert to the governor, Bush's brother. But there would be tremendous pressure to avoid this unseemly prospect, and politicians would engage in politics—negotiating and brokering some agreement.

This scenario would be messy, as politics often is. It might polarize people further, as politics sometimes does. But it might also continue the civics lesson already in progress—about how a stable democracy deals with its electoral problems.[171] Should it be frightening to realize that an electoral deadlock might be settled by elected officials accountable to the voters?

But the best that can be said of the Court's decision is that the majority disregarded the law as a way to avoid chaos and maintain order.[172] The worst that can be said is that the majority disregarded the law because of their partisan feelings.

Either way, the Court deprived the new president of the public confidence that he was fairly elected. And perhaps the Court deprived itself of the public legitimacy that it had carefully nurtured. Half of the respondents to a survey said they believed the justices were "influenced by their personal political views." A year later, after 9/11 and the increase in Bush's popularity, almost half of the respondents still said they believed Bush either "won on a technicality" or "stole the election."[173] But the decision was not as disastrous for the Court's legitimacy as some others in its history. Unlike the Dred Scott decision, *Bush v. Gore* was not linked to any controversy, such as slavery, that already was at a flashpoint. Unlike the business regulation cases in the 1930s, *Bush v. Gore* was not linked to any series of decisions that previously had eroded public support. It was a one-of-a-kind case. Thus, large majorities say they support the Court and would obey its decisions even if they disagreed with them.[174] (Republicans increased their support 20 percent, but Democrats decreased their support 28 percent, while independents decreased their support 3 percent.[175]) However, future vacancies on the Court could reopen the wound, especially if the president nominates judicial conservatives.

Meanwhile, Justice O'Connor decides other cases in her office, where a hand-stitched pillow offers a motto: "Maybe in error but never in doubt."[176]

To learn more about the Supreme Court's decision in *Bush v. Gore*, go to this chapter's "You Are There" exercises on the text Web site.

Key Terms

judicial review	habeas corpus
Marbury v. Madison	criminal cases
court-packing plan	civil cases
Warren Court	standing to sue
Burger Court	writ of certiorari
Rehnquist Court	restrained judges
district courts	activist judges
courts of appeals	stare decisis
jurisdiction	*Bush v. Gore*

Further Reading

Vincent Bugliosi, *No Island of Sanity:* Paula Jones v. Bill Clinton (New York: Ballantine, 1998). A readable examination of this Supreme Court case.

Robert Chrisman and Robert L. Allen, eds., *Court of Appeal: The Black Community Speaks Out on the Racial and Sexual Politics of* Thomas vs. Hill (New York: Ballantine, 1992). Passionate and provocative essays by black writers reflecting on the nomination and confirmation of Justice Thomas.

Richard D. Kahlenberg, *Broken Contract* (Boston: Faber & Faber, 1992). A memoir by a student at Harvard Law School that tells you a lot about law schools, the legal profession, and the nature of American law.

David M. O'Brien, *Storm Center,* 5th ed. (New York: Norton, 2000). A lively account of the Supreme Court and its very human justices.

LeRoy Phillips and Mark Curriden, *Contempt of Court* (New York: Faber & Faber, 1999). The story of the Supreme Court's only criminal trial—of the Chattanooga sheriff for allowing a lynch mob to murder a defendant whose appeal was pending before the Supreme Court in 1906.

Bob Woodward and Scott Armstrong, *The Brethren* (New York: Simon & Schuster, 1979). A behind-the-scenes look at the politicking among Supreme Court justices for major cases during the 1970s.

Electronic Resources

supremecourtus.gov
The Supreme Court's official site, with decisions and opinions posted the day they are announced. A similar site, operated by Cornell University, is supct.law.cornell.edu/supct/index.php.

oyez.nwu.edu/
This site, developed by Northwestern University, has biographies of all the Supreme Court justices, current and previous. You can hear the marshal cry, "Oyez, oyez," listen to oral arguments in important cases, take a virtual tour of the Court, and search for Court decisions by subject, date, or citation.

www.courttv.com/library/supreme/
Current legal news, recent court cases, and links to historical criminal cases from Court TV.

www.law.umkc.edu/faculty/projects/ftrials/manson/manson.html
Information on over thirty famous American and international trials by a law professor at the University of Missouri.

InfoTrac College Edition

Search for the following articles in the InfoTrac database:

Balkin, Jack M. "The Use That the Future Makes of the Past: John Marshall's Greatness and Its Lessons for Today's Supreme Court Justices," *William and Mary Law Review* (March 2002).

Lazarus, Simon. "The Most Dangerous Branch? The Supreme Court Has Been Signaling That It Will Treat Congress Roughly in the Coming Decade—But Nobody Seems to Be Paying Attention," *Atlantic Monthly* (June 2002).

Mauro, Tony. "The Education of Clarence Thomas," *American Lawyer* (August 2001).

Schroeder, Christopher H. "Causes of the Recent Turn in Constitutional Interpretation," *Duke Law Journal* (October 2001).

For more articles, enter

"United States Supreme Court" in the Subject Guide;

"United States Constitution" in the Subject Guide;

"federal courts" in the Subject Guide.

American Government Resources

Visit the Government Institutions section of the Wadsworth American Government Resources Web site (politicalscience.wadsworth.com/amgov/) for a variety of tools to help you explore the judiciary further. Included are simulations, video clips, Microcase exercises, and a wealth of other activities.

James Dale (foreground) as a Boy Scout.

Jonathan Barth/Gamma

Can the Boy Scouts Discriminate against Homosexuals?

ou are Justice John Paul Stevens of the United States Supreme Court, which is deciding whether the Boy Scouts of America can expel an assistant scoutmaster who is openly gay.

James Dale grew up in Middletown, New Jersey, where he became a Cub Scout when he was eight. Later he became a Boy Scout, earning twenty-five merit badges and attaining the Eagle Scout rank. After he turned eighteen, he was too old to remain a Boy Scout, so he became an assistant scoutmaster of a local troop. The next year he left town to attend Rutgers University. In his sophomore year, he came out of the closet and joined a gay group on campus. Elected copresident of the group, he spoke at a conference on why gay teens had high rates of suicide. An article and a photograph from the conference appeared in the newspaper and were noticed by local scout officials, who promptly revoked his scout membership. There was no evidence that he had advocated his views to his troop and no complaints that he had acted improperly.

Dale hoped to become a scoutmaster after college, so he took his case to the Lambda Legal Defense Fund, which offers legal services to homosexuals. It sued the Boy Scouts, claiming that a New Jersey statute against discrimination, including discrimination based on sexual orientation, prohibits the organization from expelling or excluding homosexuals.

The Boy Scouts of America is divided over the issue of homosexuality, as the people of America are. One faction of liberal religious groups, whose churches sponsor 20 percent of all scout troops, opposes any ban on homosexuals. But another faction of conservative religious groups, including the Mormons, who furnish 21 percent of all Boy Scouts, favors a ban. This faction controls the organization from its headquarters in Texas.[1] It defended the ban in the courts.

After the New Jersey Supreme Court ruled unanimously for Dale, the Boy Scouts appealed to the U.S. Supreme Court in 2000.

The Boy Scouts maintains that Dale, as a gay rights advocate, cannot communicate the scouts' moral values to his troop or to the public. The Boy Scouts emphasizes helping others and becoming more self-reliant. Its values are found in the Scout Oath and the Scout Law. The Scout Oath says, "On my honor I will do my best to do my duty to God and my country and to obey the Scout Law; to help other people at all times; to keep myself physically strong, mentally awake, and morally straight." The Scout Law says, "A scout is trustworthy, loyal, helpful, friendly, courteous, kind, obedient, cheerful, thrifty, brave, clean, reverent." Neither the oath nor the law, nor the mission statement nor the membership policy, addresses sexual orientation.[2] At the time the Boy Scouts expelled Dale, it had no clear policy forbidding gays. However, the Boy Scouts argues that "morally straight" precludes gays, although that phrase was coined a century ago, before it carried any sexual connotations. In addition, the Boy Scouts argues rather offensively that "clean" precludes gays.

But it does not matter whether the Boy Scouts is "in the vanguard or the rear-guard of social thinking."[3] It, like other organizations, has a First Amendment right to **freedom of association.** Although association is not mentioned in the amendment, the Supreme Court has interpreted the right to speak, assemble, and petition the government for a redress of grievances, all of which are in the amendment, to encompass a right to associate with others to do these things. And the right to associate implies a right not to associate. Thus, groups can exclude others.

This right allows a minority to pursue interests, whether political, religious, economic, educational, or social, without prevention from the majority. In theory, this right preserves diversity.

The right is strongest when the organization forms for "expressive association"—that is, when it speaks, assembles, and petitions the government for a redress of grievances. The right is also strong when the organization forms for "intimate association"—that is, when it is relatively personal, selective, and small, such as a social club or a country club. Organizations formed for expressive association or intimate association usually can exclude others. The right is weakest when the organization forms for "commercial association"—that is, when it is designed to enhance business interests of its members and is relatively impersonal, unselective, and large.

The right is not absolute; it can be overridden if there is a "compelling interest," which is the legal phrase for a good reason. For example, Minnesota and California adopted laws prohibiting sex discrimination in various organizations. The Court ruled that the Jaycees (the Junior Chamber of Commerce), which was a business organization of young men, and the Rotary Club, which was a civic organization of men, could not discriminate against women in these states because the laws forbade such discrimination.[4] The right to freedom from discrimination overrode the right to freedom of association because the organizations were formed for commercial association rather than expressive or intimate association.[5]

Here the Boy Scouts insists that it practices expressive association because it tries to instill its values in its scouts. Dale counters that its recent opposition to homosexuality is not one of these values and, regardless, the state's law banning discrimination overrides the scouts' opposition. So this case pits two competing rights: freedom of association and freedom from discrimination.

In addition to precedents involving association and discrimination, a speech case is relevant. Organizers of the St. Patrick's Day parade in Boston refused to allow a group of gays, lesbians, and bisexuals (GLB) to participate and display their banner. The members of GLB said they wanted to express their pride in being Irish and openly gay, lesbian, and bisexual. Essentially, they wanted social acceptance, which their participation in the parade would advance. But parade organizers opposed social acceptance of gays, lesbians, and bisexuals. Because parade organizers were private individuals—the parade was not sponsored by the city—the Supreme Court ruled that they did not have to allow any views contrary to their views.[6] The Court emphasized that a parade is inherently expressive and that the organizers have the right to express what they want. Thus, this case was decided on the basis of freedom of speech rather than freedom of association, but it has a bearing on freedom of association.

To resolve this dispute between competing rights, you need to answer specific questions: Is the Boy Scouts of America an expressive organization?

If so, is its opposition to homosexuality one of the values it expresses or merely a discriminatory reaction to the newspaper coverage of Dale?

If its opposition to homosexuality is one of the values it expresses, would the inclusion of Dale, as an openly gay assistant scoutmaster, undermine that value?

Regardless, does the state have a compelling interest in preventing discrimination against homosexuals?

When you were appointed by President Ford in 1975, you were selected because of your merit. As a student at Northwestern University's law school, you had the highest grades in the school's history, and as a judge on a federal appellate court in Chicago, you were well respected. You were not appointed because of your ideological views. Initially a moderate, you gradually became more liberal as the Supreme Court became more conservative.

Whether liberal or conservative, you realize that judges in this case should not be swayed by their own views toward homosexuality, but of course it is difficult for judges to disregard their own views on hot-button issues.

How do you decide?

Americans value their "rights." Eighteenth-century Americans believed that people had "natural rights" by virtue of being human. Given by God, not by government, the rights could not be taken away by government. Contemporary Americans do not use this term, but they do think about rights much as their forebears did.

Yet Americans have a split personality about their rights. As Chapter 4 described, most people tell pollsters they believe in various constitutional rights in the abstract, but many do not accept these rights when applied to concrete situations. For example, most people say they believe in free speech, but many would not allow communists, socialists, or atheists to speak in public or teach in schools.

Surveys in recent years show that Americans remain divided over their support for civil liberties. Even before the terrorist attacks, many respondents were ready to ban expression that might upset other people. One-third said they would not allow a rally that might offend community members. Two-thirds said they would not allow persons to say things in public that might offend racial groups, and over one-half said they would not allow persons to say things in public that might offend religious groups. One-fifth said they would not allow newspapers to publish without government approval of the articles.[7]

After the terrorist attacks, people's opinions reflected their fears. More respondents were skeptical about the value of the First Amendment; half said the amendment "goes too far" in guaranteeing rights (49 percent in 2002 compared with 22 percent in 2000). Two-fifths said newspapers should not be allowed to "freely criticize" the government's military strategy and performance. The same proportion said professors should not be allowed to criticize the government's military policy. Half said the government should be able to monitor religious groups for security purposes even if doing so infringes on religious freedom. (However, two-fifths said, "It's more important to ensure people's constitutional rights, even if it means that some suspected terrorists are never found.")[8]

Conflicts over civil liberties and rights have dominated the courts since the Great Depression. This chapter, covering civil liberties, and the next, covering civil rights, describe how the courts have interpreted these rights and tried to resolve these conflicts. We will explain the most important rights and recount the struggles by individuals and groups to achieve them. We will see how judges act as referees between litigants, brokers among competing groups, and policymakers in the process of deciding these cases.

The Constitution and the Bill of Rights

Individual Rights in the Constitution

Although the term *civil liberties* usually refers to the rights in the Bill of Rights, a few rights are granted in the body of the Constitution. The Constitution bans religious qualifications for federal office and guarantees jury trials in federal criminal cases. It bans **bills of attainder,** which are legislative acts rather than judicial trials pronouncing specific persons guilty of crimes, and **ex post facto laws,** which are legislative acts making some behavior illegal that was not illegal when it was

done. The Constitution also prohibits suspension of the writ of habeas corpus, except during rebellion or invasion of the country. These rights are significant, but they by no means exhaust the rights people believed they had at the time the Constitution was written.

The Bill of Rights
Origin and Meaning

The Constitution originally did not include a bill of rights; the Founders did not think traditional liberties needed specific protections because federalism, separation of powers, and checks and balances would prevent the national government from becoming too powerful. But to win support for ratification, the Founders promised to adopt amendments to provide such rights. James Madison proposed twelve, Congress passed them, and in 1791 the states ratified ten, which came to be known as the Bill of Rights.[9] Of these, the first eight grant specific rights. (See the box "Civil Liberties in the Bill of Rights.") (The Ninth says the listing of these rights does not mean they are the only ones the people have, and the Tenth says the powers not granted to the federal government are reserved for the state governments.)

The Bill of Rights provides rights against the government. According to Justice Hugo Black, it is "a collection of Thou shalt nots" directed at the government.[10] Essentially, the Bill of Rights provides rights for minorities against the majority, because government policy concerning civil liberties tends to reflect the views of the majority.

As Chapter 2 explained, the Founders set up a government to protect property rights for the well-to-do minority against the presumably jealous majority. Separation of powers, checks and balances, and various specific provisions of the Constitution were intended to limit the ability of the masses to curtail the rights of the elites. However, as Americans became more egalitarian and as the masses got more opportunity to participate in politics, the importance of property rights has declined while the importance of other rights has increased. At the same time, the role of the Bill of Rights has increased to protect the have-nots of society—the unpopular, powerless minorities in conflict with the majority.

Responsibility for interpreting the Bill of Rights generally falls on the federal courts. Because their judges are appointed for life, they are more independent from majority pressure than elected officials are.

Application

For many years the Supreme Court applied the Bill of Rights only to the federal government—not to state governments (or local governments, which are under the authority of state governments). The Court ruled that the Bill of Rights restricted only what the federal government could do.[11]

The Founders thought that states, being closer to the people, would be less likely to violate their liberties. Also, they knew that many states had their own bills of rights, and they expected the rest to follow.

The Court applied the Bill of Rights this way because the Founders did not realize that states would come to violate people's liberties more frequently than the federal government. The state governments, representing smaller, more homogeneous populations, tended to reflect majority sentiment more closely than the federal government, and they often rode rough-shod over criminal defendants or racial, religious, or political minorities. When disputes arose, state courts tended to interpret their bills of rights narrowly.

However, starting in 1925[12] and continuing through 1972,[13] the Supreme Court gradually applied most provi-

sions of the Bill of Rights to the states, using the Fourteenth Amendment's due process clause as justification. This clause, adopted after the Civil War to protect blacks from southern governments, reads, "Nor shall any state deprive any person of life, liberty, or property, without due process of law." The clause refers to states and "liberty." It is ambiguous, but the Court interpreted it to mean that states also have to provide the liberties in the Bill of Rights.

The Court has applied all but two provisions of the First and the Fourth through the Eighth Amendments to the states: guarantee of a grand jury in criminal cases and guarantee of a jury trial in civil cases. In addition, the Court has established some rights not in the Bill of Rights, and it has applied these to the states, too: presumption of innocence in criminal cases, right to travel within the country, and right to privacy. Thus, most provisions in the Bill of Rights, and even some not in it, now restrict what both the federal and state governments can do.

To see how the Court has interpreted these provisions, we will look at three major areas—freedom of expression, rights of criminal defendants, and right to privacy.

Freedom of Expression

The **First Amendment** provides freedom of expression, which includes freedom of speech, assembly, and association;[14] freedom of the press; and freedom of religion.

The amendment states that "Congress shall make no law" abridging these liberties. The language is absolute, but few justices interpret it literally. They cite the example of the person who falsely shouts "Fire!" in a crowded theater and causes a stampede that injures someone. Surely, they say, the amendment does not protect this expression. So the Court needs to draw a line between expression the amendment protects and that which it does not.

Freedom of Speech

Freedom of speech, Justice Black asserted, "is the heart of our government."[15] By creating an open atmosphere, it promotes individual autonomy and self-fulfillment. By encouraging a wide variety of opinions, it furthers the advancement of knowledge and discovery of truth. The English philosopher John Stuart Mill observed that individuals decide what is correct by comparing different views. Unpopular opinions could be true or partially true. Even if completely false, they could prompt a reevaluation of accepted opinions. By permitting citizens to form opinions and express them to others, freedom of speech helps them participate in government. It especially helps them check inefficient or corrupt government. The American philosopher John Dewey remarked that "democracy begins in conversation."[16] By channeling conflict toward persuasion, freedom of speech promotes a stable society. Governments that deny freedom of speech become inflexible; they force conflict toward violence.[17]

Seditious Speech

The first controversies to test the scope of freedom of speech involved **seditious speech,** speech that encourages rebellion against the government.[18] The government historically prosecuted individuals for seditious speech during or shortly after war, when society was most sensitive about loyalty.

Numerous prosecutions came with World War I and the Russian Revolution, which brought the Communists to power in the Soviet Union in 1917. The Russian Revolution prompted a "Red Scare," in which people feared conspiracies to overthrow the U.S. government. Congress passed the Espionage Act of 1917, which prohibited interfering with military recruitment, inciting insubordination in military forces, and mailing material advocating rebellion; and the Sedition Act of 1918, which prohibited "disloyal, profane, scurrilous, or abusive language about the form of government, Constitution, soldiers and sailors, flag or uniform of the armed forces." Many states passed similar laws. In short, government prohibited a wide range of speech.

During the war, the federal government prosecuted almost two thousand and convicted almost nine hundred persons under these acts, and the states prosecuted and convicted many others. They prosecuted individuals for saying that war is contrary to the teachings of Jesus, that World War I should not have been declared until after a referendum was held, and that the draft was unconstitutional. Officials even prosecuted an individual for remarking to women knitting clothes for the troops, "No soldier ever sees those socks."[19]

These cases gave the Supreme Court numerous opportunities to rule on seditious speech. In six major cases, the Court upheld the federal and state laws and affirmed the convictions of all the defendants.[20] The defendants advocated socialism or communism, and some advocated the overthrow of the government to achieve it. Except for one—Eugene Debs, the Socialist Party's candidate for president—the defendants did not command a large audience. Even so, the Court concluded that these defendants' speech constituted a "clear and present danger" to the government. Justice Edward Sanford wrote, "A single revolutionary spark may kindle a fire that, smoldering for a time, may burst into a sweeping and destructive conflagration."[21] In reality, there was nothing clear or present about the danger; the defendants' speech had little effect.

More prosecutions came after World War II. In 1940, Congress passed the Smith Act, which was not as broad

Eugene Debs, the Socialist Party's candidate for president, criticized American involvement in World War I and the draft. He was convicted for violating the Espionage Act and sentenced to ten years in prison. When President Harding pardoned him early, Debs commented, "It is the government that should ask me for a pardon."

as the World War I acts because it did not forbid criticizing the government. But it did forbid advocating overthrow of the government by force and organizing or joining individuals who advocated overthrow.

The act was used against members of the American Communist Party after the war. The uneasy alliance between the United States and the Soviet Union had given way to the Cold War between the countries. Politicians, especially Senator Joseph McCarthy (R-Wisc.), exploited the tensions. McCarthy claimed that many government officials were communists. (He said he had a list of 205 "known communists" in the State Department alone.) He had little evidence (and provided no "list"). His tactics were called "witch-hunts" and, eventually, **McCarthyism.** Other Republicans also accused the Democratic administration of covering up communists. They goaded it into prosecuting members of the Communist Party so it would not appear "soft on communism."

In 1951, the Court upheld the Smith Act and affirmed the convictions of eleven top-echelon leaders of the Communist Party.[22] These leaders organized the party, and the party advocated overthrowing the government by force, but the leaders had not attempted overthrowing it. (If they had, they clearly would have been guilty of crimes.) Even so, the Court majority concluded that they constituted a clear and present danger, and Chief Justice Fred Vinson wrote that the government does not have to "wait until the putsch is about to be executed, the plans have been laid and the signal is awaited" before it can act

At congressional hearings, Senator Joseph McCarthy identified locations of alleged communists and "fellow travelers."

against the party. The minority argued that the Communist Party was not a danger. Justice William Douglas said that the party was "of little consequence. . . . Communism has been so thoroughly exposed in this country that it has been crippled as a political force. Free speech has destroyed it as an effective political party." Following the Court's decision, the government prosecuted and convicted almost one hundred other communists.

But the Cold War thawed slightly, the Senate voted to condemn McCarthy, and two new members, including Chief Justice Earl Warren, joined the Court. In a series of cases in the 1950s, the Court made it more difficult to convict Communists,[23] thereby incurring the wrath of the public, Congress, and President Eisenhower. In a private conversation, Warren asked Eisenhower what he thought the Court should do with the communists. Eisenhower replied, "I would kill the S.O.B.s."[24]

The government took other action against communists. The federal government ordered communists to register, and then some state governments banned them from public jobs such as teaching, or private jobs such as practicing law or serving as union officers. Legislative committees held hearings to expose and humiliate them. The Court heard numerous cases involving these actions and usually ruled against the government.

The Vietnam War did not prompt the same fears that World Wars I and II did. Congress did not pass comparable laws, perhaps because many "respectable" people opposed this war and also because the Court in the 1950s and 1960s increasingly allowed seditious speech.

The Court developed new doctrine for seditious speech in 1969. A Ku Klux Klan leader said at a rally in Ohio that the Klan might take "revengeance" on the president, Congress, and Supreme Court if they

continued "to suppress the white, Caucasian race." The leader was convicted under a statute similar to those upheld after World War I, but this time the statute was unanimously struck down by the Court.[25] The justices said people can advocate—enthusiastically, even heatedly—as long as they do not incite illegal action. This broad protection for seditious speech remains in effect today.

Thus, after many years and many cases, the Court concluded that the First Amendment protects seditious speech as much as other speech. Justice Douglas noted that "the threats were often loud but always puny."[26] Even the attorney general who prosecuted the major Communist cases later admitted that the cases were "squeezed oranges. I didn't think there was much to them."[27] Nevertheless, the Court had permitted a climate of fear to overwhelm the First Amendment for many years.

The collapse of the Soviet Union and the demise of the Cold War have made communism less of a threat, but this doctrine remains important. After the Oklahoma City bombing in 1995, government surveillance of right-wing militia groups increased, but prosecution of the members, under terrorism laws, was limited because most of the "evidence" was fiery rhetoric, which is protected speech (unless it urges immediate action to violate any laws).

After the terrorist attacks in 2001, there was some pressure to conform and to support the government's response. An organization identified forty college professors with "un-American" agendas, in an apparent effort to force the schools to discipline and restrain their professors. However, negative reaction prompted the organization to remove the names from its Web site.[28] Yet a tenured professor at the University of New Mexico who cracked, "Anyone who can blow up the Pentagon gets my vote," was reprimanded, and a lawsuit demanding his termination was filed.[29] And a tenured professor at the University of South Florida, who as a Palestinian activist gave speeches supporting the *intifadeh*—the Palestinian uprising against the Israeli occupation—was suspended and barred from campus. After Fox Network's Bill O'Reilly challenged the professor on the air, the school was criticized, and its president was fearful that its donations would dry up. Although the professor, who had campaigned for George W. Bush, praised America and condemned the September 11 attacks, the school's president panicked and ignored his academic freedom.[30]

Now we will turn to other speech—nonseditious speech—to see how the Court has interpreted the First Amendment in these situations.

Public Forum

People usually communicate with each other in private. But sometimes speakers want more listeners and use public places where people congregate. This means speakers will be heard by some listeners who do not like their message or their use of public places to disseminate it, and it also means speakers might disrupt the normal purposes of these places.

The Court holds that individuals have a right to use public places, such as streets, sidewalks, and parks, to express their views on public issues. These places constitute the **public forum** and serve as "the poor person's printing press."

When speakers seek to use other public facilities, the Court has to determine which ones are also part of the public forum. It decided that federal and state capitol grounds,[31] Supreme Court grounds,[32] and public school grounds[33] are part of the forum. It decided that blacks could protest library segregation at a public library[34] and promoters could show the rock musical *Hair* at a public theater[35] because these, too, are part of the forum.

On the other hand, the Court decided that civil rights activists could not demonstrate against jail segregation outside a jail because of the need for security[36] and that Dr. Benjamin Spock—the baby doctor—and other antiwar activists could not encourage opposition to the Vietnam War at an army base because of the need for discipline in the army.[37]

Normally, only publicly owned facilities are considered part of the public forum, but the proliferation of shopping centers and malls prompted speakers to use these privately owned facilities to reach crowds of shoppers. The Warren Court permitted them to do so, saying that shopping centers and malls are similar to downtown shopping districts where streets and sidewalks are part of the public forum.[38] But the Burger Court overruled the Warren Court; it allowed the shopping centers and malls to prohibit speech. Thus, the Burger Court emphasized property rights over First Amendment rights in this situation.[39]

Even in public forums people cannot speak whenever and however they want. The Court has divided speech into three kinds—pure speech, speech plus conduct, and symbolic speech—and established doctrine for each.

Pure Speech

Pure speech is speech without any conduct (besides the speech itself). Individuals can say what they want as long as they do not cause a breach of the peace or a riot, or hurl "fighting words" at specific persons, except at police officers, who are supposed to be trained and disciplined to take abuse.[40]

Before the Court's ruling in 1972, arrests for swearing were common. In the District of Columbia, for example, more than half of the fifteen thousand to twenty thousand arrests for "disorderly conduct" each year involved swearing, usually at police.[41]

Individuals can use offensive language in many situations.[42] During the Vietnam War, a man walked through the corridors of the Los Angeles County courthouse wearing a jacket with the words "Fuck the Draft" emblazoned on the back. Police arrested him. The Court reversed his conviction, and seventy-two-year-old Justice John Harlan remarked that "one man's vulgarity is another's lyric."[43]

The media, however, cannot broadcast some offensive language. A California radio station broadcast a monologue by comedian George Carlin. Titled "Filthy Words," it lampooned society's sensitivity to seven words that "you couldn't say on the public airwaves . . . the ones you definitely wouldn't say, ever." The seven words, according to the Federal Communications Commission report, included "a four-letter word for excrement" repeated seventy times in twelve minutes. In a close vote, the Court ruled that although the monologue was part of a serious program on contemporary attitudes toward language, it was not protected under the First Amendment because people, including children, tuning the radio could be subjected to the language in their home.[44]

Yet the Court struck down a Utah law restricting "indecent material" on cable television. The difference apparently is that people choose to subscribe and pay for cable television.[45]

Speech Plus Conduct

Speech plus conduct is speech combined with conduct that is intended to convey ideas—for example, a demonstration in which protesters chant slogans or carry signs with slogans (the speech) and march, picket, or sit in (the conduct).

Individuals can demonstrate, but they are subject to some restrictions. Places in the public forum are used for

other purposes besides demonstrating, and individuals cannot disrupt these activities. They cannot, Justice Arthur Goldberg remarked, hold "a street meeting in the middle of Times Square at the rush hour."[46] Thus, abortion protesters can demonstrate on public streets and public sidewalks by abortion clinics, and they can approach staffers and patients who come and go. But protesters cannot block access (and, to ensure this, judges can order them not to come within a certain distance—for example, fifteen feet—of driveways and doorways).[47]

To help enforce the restrictions, governments can require groups to obtain a permit, which can specify the place, time, and manner of the demonstration. However, officials cannot allow one group to demonstrate but forbid another, no matter how much they dislike the group or its message. They cannot forbid the group even if they say they fear violence, unless the group actually threatens violence. In short, officials may establish restrictions to avoid disruption, but they may not use these restrictions to censor speech.

Accordingly, lower federal courts required the Chicago suburb of Skokie to permit the American Nazi Party to demonstrate in front of the town hall in 1978.[48] About forty thousand of Skokie's population of seventy thousand were Jews. Of these, hundreds survived the German Nazi concentration camps during World War II, and thousands had relatives who died in the camps. The city, edgy about the announced demonstration, passed ordinances that prohibited wearing "military-style" uniforms and distributing material that "promotes and incites hatred against persons by reason of their race, national origin, or religion." These ordinances were thinly disguised attempts to bar the demonstration, and the courts threw them out. One quoted Justice Oliver Wendell Holmes's statement that "if there is any principle of the Constitution that more imperatively calls for attachment than any other it is the principle of free thought—not free thought for those who agree with us but freedom for the thought we hate."[49]

The Rehnquist Court, however, did uphold a Milwaukee suburb's ordinance that prohibited picketing at a residence.[50] The city passed the ordinance after antiabortionists had picketed, six times in one month, the home of a doctor who performed abortions. Although protesters can march through residential neighborhoods, the Court said, a city can prohibit them from focusing on a particular home. Thus, the Court emphasized the right to privacy at home over the right to demonstrate in this situation.

Symbolic Speech

Symbolic speech is the use of symbols, rather than words, to convey ideas.

During the Vietnam War, men burned their draft cards to protest the draft and the war. This was powerful expression, and Congress tried to stifle it by passing a law prohibiting destruction of draft cards. The Supreme Court was uncomfortable with symbolic speech and reluctant to protect it. Even Chief Justice Warren worried that this would mean that "an apparently limitless variety of conduct can be labeled 'speech.'" The Court upheld the law.[51]

One year later, however, the Court was willing to protect symbolic speech. A junior high and two senior high school students in Des Moines, Iowa, including Mary Beth Tinker, wore black armbands to protest the war. They were suspended, and they sued school officials. Public schools, Justice Abe Fortas said, "may not be enclaves of totalitarianism." They must allow students freedom of speech, providing students do not disrupt the schools.[52]

Young men burned their draft cards to protest the Vietnam War, but the Supreme Court refused to protect this symbolic speech. (Until the late 1960s, student protesters did not look like the image we associate with them today.)

Kubota/Magnum

In the 1960s and 1970s, many students wore long hair or beards in violation of school policy. Some claimed they did so to protest "establishment culture." Blacks and Indians claimed they wore Afros and braids to show racial pride. Federal courts of appeals split evenly as to whether this was symbolic speech. The Supreme Court refused to hear any of these cases, so there was no uniform law across the country.

Some individuals treated the American flag disrespectfully to protest the Vietnam War. A Massachusetts man wore a flag patch on the seat of his pants and was sentenced to six months in jail. A Washington student taped a peace symbol on a flag and then hung the flag, upside down, outside his apartment. The Court reversed both convictions.[53]

When a member of the Revolutionary Communist Youth Brigade burned an American flag outside the Republican National Convention in Dallas in 1984, the justices faced the issue of actual desecration of the flag. The Rehnquist Court surprisingly permitted this symbolic speech.[54] Two Reagan-appointed conservatives joined the three most liberal members of the Court to forge a bare majority. The foremost free speech advocate on the bench, Justice William Brennan, wrote that the First Amendment cannot be limited just because this form of expression offends some people. "We do not consecrate the flag by punishing its desecration, for in doing so we dilute the freedom that this cherished emblem represents." The ruling invalidated laws of forty-eight states and the federal government.

Chief Justice Rehnquist emotionally criticized the decision. He said the First Amendment should not apply because the flag is a unique national symbol. He recounted the history of the "Star-Spangled Banner" and the music of John Philip Sousa's "Stars and Stripes Forever," he quoted poems by Ralph Waldo Emerson and John Greenleaf Whittier that refer to the flag, and he discussed the role of the Pledge of Allegiance.

Civil liberties advocates praised the decision. One lawyer for the defendant said, "If free expression is to exist in this country, people must be as free to burn the flag as they are to wave it." Another said veterans should cheer the decision because it shows that the values in the Bill of Rights that they fought for are intact. Yet veterans groups were outraged.

After administration officials assessed public opinion by monitoring talk shows, President George H. Bush stood in front of the Iwo Jima Memorial and proposed a constitutional amendment to override the decision.[55] Members of Congress, always anxious to appear patriotic, lined up in support. But some, especially Democrats, later came out in opposition. They criticized the proposal for creating an unprecedented exception to the First Amendment. Instead of the proposed amendment, Congress passed a statute prohibiting flag desecration.

Mary Beth Tinker, here with her mother and brother, wore a black armband at school to protest the Vietnam War.

Apparently, a majority felt that this less permanent substitute would be an adequate shield against the public's wrath. Yet in 1990, the justices, dividing the same way, declared the statute unconstitutional for the same reasons they reversed the Dallas conviction.[56] President Bush, this time waving a model of the Iwo Jima Memorial, proposed another constitutional amendment, and Senate Republican leader Robert Dole (Kan.) warned Democrats that their opposition to the amendment "would make a good thirty-second spot" for the upcoming elections, but Congress rejected the amendment. Members sensed less pressure from the public. By the second year of debate on this issue, the initial emotional reaction of the public had ebbed. More voices had spoken out against dilution of the First Amendment. Then in 1995, after Republicans became the majority in Congress, they renewed efforts to adopt a constitutional amendment but fell three votes short in one house.

Freedom of the Press

Unlike most civil liberties cases, which pit a relatively powerless individual or group against the government, freedom of press cases usually feature a more powerful publisher or broadcaster against the government. Even so, these cases still involve rights against the government.

Prior Restraint

The core of freedom of the press is freedom from **prior restraint**—censorship. If the press violates laws prohibiting, for example, libelous or obscene material, it can be punished after publishing such materials. But freedom from prior restraint means the press at least has the opportunity to publish what it thinks is appropriate.

Freedom from prior restraint is not absolute. At the height of the Vietnam War, the secretary of defense in the Johnson administration, Robert McNamara, became disenchanted with the war and ordered a thorough study of our involvement. The study, called "The Pentagon Papers," laid bare the reasons the country was embroiled—reasons not as honorable as the ones officials had been giving the public—and it questioned the effectiveness of military policy. The study was so revealing that McNamara remarked to a friend, "They could hang people for what's in there."[57] He printed only fifteen copies and classified them "Top Secret" so few persons could see them. One of the thirty-six authors, Daniel Ellsberg, originally supported the war but later turned against it. Haunted by his failure to act sooner, he photocopied the papers and gave them to the *New York Times* and *Washington Post* in the hope that their publication would sway public opinion and force the government to end the war. The newspapers did publish excerpts.

Although the papers embarrassed the Kennedy and Johnson administrations, President Nixon, who was in office at the time, was continuing to fight the war, so the excerpts infuriated him. Meeting with his chief of staff and his national security adviser, he demanded:

> I have a project I want somebody to take. . . . This takes 18 hours a day. It takes devotion and loyalty and diligence such as you've never seen. . . . I really need a son of a bitch . . . who will work his butt off and do it dishonorably. . . . And I'll direct him myself. I know how to play this game and we're going to start playing it. . . . I want somebody just as tough as I am for a change. . . . We're up against an enemy, a conspiracy. They're using any means. We're going to use any means.[58]

The chief of the presses of the Washington Post hails the Supreme Court's decision allowing publication of the Pentagon Papers.

This tirade set in motion the developments that eventually would culminate in the Watergate scandal.

But immediately Nixon sought injunctions to restrain the newspapers from publishing more excerpts. However, the Supreme Court refused to grant them.[59] Most justices said they would grant injunctions if publishing the papers clearly jeopardized national security. But information in the papers was historical; it did not directly hinder the war effort.[60] Thus, the rule remained—no prior restraint—but exceptions were possible.

One exception occurred in 1979 when *The Progressive,* a monthly political magazine, planned to publish technical material about designing a hydrogen bomb. The article, "The H–Bomb Secret: How We Got It, Why We're Telling It," argued for open debate rather than secret classification. Although the article was not a "do-it-yourself guide," a federal district court judge concluded that it might help a medium-sized nation develop a bomb sooner. He prohibited the magazine from publishing the article.[61]

The Rehnquist Court did approve prior restraint in a situation far removed from national security. When journalism students at a St. Louis high school wrote articles for their newspaper about the impact of pregnancy and of parents' divorce on teenagers, the principal deleted the articles and three of the students sued. The Court, noting that students below the college level have fewer rights than adults, decided that officials can censor school publications.[62]

Principals typically have exercised their authority over articles covering school policies or social issues. A Colorado principal blocked an editorial criticizing his study hall policy while allowing another editorial praising it. A Texas principal banned an article about the class valedictorian who succeeded despite the death of her mother, the desertion of her father, and her own pregnancy. An editorial urging students to be more responsible about sex was censored by a Kentucky principal, who feared it could be interpreted as condoning sex, while a survey on AIDS was censored by a Maryland principal, who prohibited students from defining the term *safe sex.* A North Carolina high school newspaper was shut down and its adviser was fired because of three articles, including a satirical story about the "death" of the writer after eating a cheeseburger from the school cafeteria.

High school newspaper advisers say that principals have tightened their control in recent years. Over a third of the advisers report that principals have rejected articles or required changes in articles for their paper.[63]

Some principals have disciplined students who have used the Internet to criticize school officials or policies. But, like underground newspapers of the 1960s and 1970s, Web pages created off campus (rather than in computer class) cannot be censored by administrators.

Leanne Tippell and Leslie Smart, two of the St. Louis high school students who sued their school for suppressing their student newspaper story, meet with their attorney, Leslie Edwards (left).

Web pages cannot be used to make terroristic threats, however. A Georgia student was arrested for suggesting that the principal be shot, his daughter kidnapped, his car keyed, and its locks clogged with Superglue.

Despite these exceptions to freedom from prior restraint, the press in the United States is freer than that in Great Britain, where freedom from prior restraint began. Britain has no First Amendment and tolerates more secrecy. The government banned radio and television interviews with all members of the outlawed Irish Republican Army (IRA) and its political party, including its one representative in Parliament.[64] The French government banned the sale of a song—"Go for It, Saddam"— that criticized the West during the Persian Gulf War. The German government banned the sale of music by skinhead groups after neo-Nazi violence.

Restrictions on Gathering News

Although prior restraint is an obvious limitation on freedom of the press, restrictions on gathering news in the first place are less obvious but no less serious. They also keep news from the public.

The Burger Court was not vigilant in guarding the press from these restrictions. Most important, it denied reporters a right to keep the names of their sources confidential. In investigative reporting, reporters frequently rely on sources who demand anonymity in exchange for information. The sources might have sensitive positions in government or relations with criminals that would be jeopardized if their names were publicized. A Louisville reporter was allowed to watch persons make hashish from marijuana if he kept their names confidential. But after publication of the story, a grand jury demanded their names. When the reporter refused to reveal them, he was cited for contempt of court, and his conviction

was upheld by the Supreme Court.[65] The majority said reporters' need for confidentiality is not as great as the judicial system's need for information about crimes. So either reporters cannot guarantee a potential source anonymity, or they may have to choose between breaking their promise or being cited for contempt and jailed for an indefinite period of time.

Invasion of Privacy

The right to a free press can conflict with an individual's right to privacy when the press publishes personal information. The Supreme Court has permitted the press to publish factual information. For example, although a Georgia law prohibited the press from releasing names of crime victims to spare them embarrassment, an Atlanta television station announced the name of a high school girl who was raped by six classmates and left unconscious on a neighbor's lawn to die. The girl's father sued the station, but the Court said the press needs freedom to publish information that is a matter of public record so citizens can scrutinize the workings of the judicial system.[66]

In 1975, a man in a crowd of people watching President Gerald Ford noticed a woman pull out a gun. He grabbed the gun and prevented the assassination. Reporters wrote stories about this hero, including the fact that he was a homosexual. This caused the man embarrassment and some practical problems, and he sued. The courts sided with the press again. The man's good deed made him newsworthy, whether he wanted to be or not.[67] Persons who become newsworthy are permitted little privacy. Justice Brennan said this is a necessary evil "in a society which places a primary value on freedom of speech and of press."[68]

Libel and Obscenity

Despite broad protection for the press overall, courts grant much less protection for libelous and obscene material. Traditionally, they considered such material irrelevant to the exposition of ideas and search for truth envisioned by the framers of the First Amendment. Whatever benefit such material might have was outweighed by the need to protect persons' reputations and morals. Courts thus allowed states to adopt and implement libel and obscenity laws as they saw fit.

Libel

Libel consists of printed or broadcast statements that are false and that tarnish someone's reputation. Victims are entitled to sue for money to compensate them for the damage.

The Warren Court decided that traditional state libel laws infringed on freedom of the press too much and forced radical changes in these laws. Its landmark decision came in *New York Times v. Sullivan* in 1964.[69]

The *Times* ran an ad by black clergymen who criticized Montgomery, Alabama, officials for their handling of racial protests. The ad contained some trivial inaccuracies. It did not mention any officials by name, but the commissioner of police claimed it referred to him implicitly, and he sued. The local jury ordered the *Times* to pay him a half million dollars! The Court could see that the law was used to punish a detested northern newspaper for an ad that criticized the handling of controversial civil rights protests. And the Court could not ignore the size of the award or the fact that another jury had ordered the *Times* to pay another commissioner a half million dollars for the same ad. It was apparent that libel laws could be used to wreak vengeance on a critical press.

The Court ruled against the police commissioner and made it harder for public officials to win libel suits. It said officials must show not only that the statements about them were false but also that the statements were made with "reckless disregard for the truth." This provides the press some leeway to make mistakes and print false statements, as long as the press is not careless to the point of recklessness.

This protection for the press is necessary, according to Justice Brennan, because "the central meaning of the First Amendment" is that individuals should have the right to criticize officials' conduct. This statement prompted one legal scholar to herald the decision as "an occasion for dancing in the streets."[70]

In later cases, the Court extended this ruling to public figures—persons other than public officials who have public prominence or who thrust themselves into public controversies. It held several persons to be public figures: candidates for public office,[71] a retired general who spoke for right-wing causes,[72] a real estate developer,[73] and a university athletic director.[74] The Court justified making it harder for public figures to win libel suits by saying that they sometimes influence public policy as much as public officials do. They also are newsworthy enough to get coverage to rebut any false charges against them.

The Burger Court was less inclined to consider various persons public figures,[75] but it maintained the core of the Warren Court's doctrine, which shifted the emphasis from protection of personal reputation to protection of press freedom.

This shift in emphasis has aided the press tremendously at a time when its coverage of controversial events has angered much of the public. Increasingly, since the 1960s, individuals and groups have sued the press not primarily to win compensation for damage to personal reputations but to punish it. A lawyer for a conservative organization admitted that the organization sought "the dismantling" of CBS by suing the network for its depiction of the army general commanding the U.S. military in Vietnam.[76]

Although the press has an advantage in the law when public officials or figures bring suits, lawsuits are expensive to defend against. One case cost the *Washington Post* over a million dollars in defense expenses at the trial court level alone.[77] The expense puts pressure on the press to refrain from publishing controversial material. Large news organizations can withstand most of this pressure, but many small ones cannot. After twelve libel suits in as many years, the publisher of six weekly newspapers in suburban Philadelphia halted his papers' investigative reporting. "I found myself vigorously defending the First Amendment and watching my business go to hell," he said. "Now the communities our papers serve no longer learn about the misconduct of their officials."[78]

Another emerging problem is for foreign figures to sue American writers or publishers in foreign courts where protection against libel suits is much less. A British historian, called a "Holocaust denier," sued the American publisher of a book on Holocaust denial. Although the book was published in the United States, the suit was filed in Great Britain. The publisher was required to mount a lengthy defense, proving that the Holocaust occurred and showing that the historian's provocative statements could, indeed, be categorized as Holocaust denial.[79]

Obscenity

Obscenity also pits conservative groups against the media, albeit a small and specialized part of the media. Yet there are important differences. Whereas it is relatively clear what libel is and who the victim is, it is not at all clear what obscenity is and who, if anyone, the victim is. It is not even clear why the law needs to deal with it. Some say it is necessary because obscenity is immoral; others say it is necessary because obscenity leads to improper behavior (although this link is uncertain). The justices themselves have disagreed, perhaps more than in any other area, and their decisions reflect this. They have been neither clear nor consistent.

The Warren Court decided that state obscenity laws restricted publication of sexual material that should be allowed. While still maintaining that the First Amendment does not protect obscenity, the Court narrowed the definition of obscenity in a series of cases in the 1950s and 1960s.[80]

The Burger Court, however, thought the Warren Court went too far. When a man and his mother received an ad for a book entitled *Orgies Illustrated,* their suit prompted the justices to broaden the definition of obscenity somewhat.[81] Now the Court defines obscenity as sexual material that is patently offensive to the average person in the community and that lacks any serious literary, artistic, or scientific value. The Court generally permits state legislatures and local juries, in passing

The Internet enables people to get pornography in the privacy of their home, without having to go to a seedy adult bookstore or movie theater and without risking the embarrassment that might occur. Users can type in key words, such as *sex*, and easily find their way to, for example, "Bianca's Smut Shack." Perusing pornography is one of the most common, if not the most common, recreational uses of computers. (At one university, thirteen of the forty most visited sites had names like "rec.arts.erotica.")[1] Much of this pornography depicts sex with children or animals or other deviant practices such as bondage or sadomasochism.

Shocked by the amount and the nature of online pornography and worried about its availability to children, Congress passed a law prohibiting people from knowingly circulating "obscene" or "indecent" material online "in a manner available" to those under eighteen. Thus, the law banned sexual material that would be defined, under existing law, as "obscene" and additional material that would be considered "indecent." However, the latter was not clearly defined.

A coalition of forty-seven groups filed suit to have the law declared unconstitutional. These included the ACLU, the American Library Association, and the computer companies Microsoft and America Online. The U.S. Chamber of Commerce filed a supplementary brief arguing that the law threatened corporations' ability to compete globally in an age of new communications.

The new technology of the Internet has made the old laws under the First Amendment difficult to apply. A commentator observed that "it's one thing to support the free speech rights of bookstore owners, quite another to have an 'XXX' store open at the end of the block, and still another to have its contents available in your rumpus room."[2]

So what precedents should apply? Is the Internet like the print media, which have substantial freedom so long as they do not publish the narrow category of sexual material defined as obscenity? Or is the Internet more like the broadcast media, which have less freedom because they are pervasive and reach into people's homes? Or, because the goal is to protect children, is the law more analogous to child pornography laws that prohibit a broader range of material than regular obscenity laws?

A lower federal court recognized that the Internet is a different medium and is, in fact, the most participatory speech medium yet developed. As such, the judges concluded, it should be nurtured, not stifled. In 1997 the Supreme Court, in its initial effort to apply the First Amendment to cyberspace, agreed.[3] It did not want the Internet censored more than other media. Thus, the Internet would receive as much protection as books, magazines, and newspapers (and more than radio and television). As a result, the portion of the law banning "obscene" material was upheld, while the portion banning additional "indecent" material was struck down. This portion was too broad and too ambiguous. It might lead to prosecution of people for discussing homosexuality or prison rape. It could even lead to prosecution of parents for sending their child information about birth control. Or the stiff penalties, two years in prison and a $250,000 fine, might cause people to avoid subjects they should feel free to address. Then the law would have a chilling effect on speech, which the First Amendment is supposed to guard against.

Although the goal of protecting children was worthy, the justices said, the result would be to prevent adults from communicating with each other, because the nature of the Internet made it impossible to know who might receive the material. Adults might be prosecuted if children obtained the material even though the adults were unaware that the children were doing so.

Congress passed another law, this one prohibiting people from circulating virtual child pornography, which is computer-simulated images that depict children engaged in sex. Virtual and actual child pornography can be hard to tell apart, and Congress assumed that either type led to child abuse. But the Court invalidated the statute because virtual pornography does not involve real people, so no children were harmed in its production.[4]

1. Philip Elmer-DeWitt, "On a Screen Near You: Cyberporn," *Time*, July 3, 1995.
2. John Schwartz, "The New Cultural Battleground Comes with a Mouse," *Washington Post National Weekly Edition*, February 23, 1998, 22.
3. *Reno v. American Civil Liberties Union*, 138 L.Ed.2d 874 (1997).
4. *Ashcroft v. Free Speech Coalition* (2002).

statutes and deciding cases, to determine whether this definition applies to certain types of material.

But some local officials got carried away. A prosecutor in Charlottesville, Virginia, announced that he would prosecute persons who sold *Playboy* magazine. Jurors in Albany, Georgia, convicted a theater manager who showed the movie *Carnal Knowledge*. The movie, which featured explicit language and occasional nudity, was nominated for an Academy Award as the best film of the year. The Burger Court reversed the conviction, announcing that local communities have discretion but not "unbridled discretion."[82]

A prosecutor in Cincinnati put the director of an art gallery on trial for an exhibit of photographs by Robert Mapplethorpe. The homoerotic pictures, which the director called "tough, brutal, sometimes disgusting," included three showing penetration of a man's anus with various objects. Yet the prosecutor could not prove that the photographs lacked serious artistic value, because the photographer had received praise from art critics and the pictures were displayed in an art gallery, so the jury acquitted the director.

The Burger Court did not succeed in its efforts to reduce the availability of sexual material. Prosecutors report that they actually prosecute fewer cases, because the public is less concerned about obscenity than it used to be, so jurors are less likely to convict.[83]

The continuing flow and increasing violence of pornography prompted some radical feminists, in alliance with religious fundamentalists, to advocate new anti-pornography statutes. They maintain that pornography discriminates against women by degrading them and portraying them as willing targets for violent sex. In response, Indianapolis passed a statute that defined pornography as "the sexually explicit subordination of women"—material in which women were "sexual objects for domination . . . or use" or depicted in "positions of servility or submission or display." The statute allowed women who believed themselves victims of pornography to sue for a court order banning such material and for monetary damages. The proponents' aim was to encourage enough women to sue to drive the purveyors out of business.

A coalition of book and magazine publishers, distributors, and sellers challenged the law. They said it was so broad and vague it could apply to many nonpornographic books and magazines. The American Civil Liberties Union (ACLU) maintained that it could apply to books such as Ian Fleming's James Bond stories and movies such as *Last Tango in Paris.* Some feminist writers said it could apply to feminist literature.

The federal district court judge, a woman, ruled the statute unconstitutional. She said its breadth and vagueness would prohibit much sexual material now permitted by the Supreme Court and would severely restrict the First Amendment. The Supreme Court affirmed the decision.[84]

Despite the Court's refusal to broaden its definition of obscenity further, it does allow cities, through zoning ordinances, to scatter "adult" theaters and bookstores to avoid seedy districts that might attract criminals, or to concentrate them to avoid location in neighborhoods where they might offend residents or passersby.[85] The Court acknowledged that such ordinances help preserve the quality of urban life. (See also the box "Regulating Cyberporn.")

Freedom of Religion

Some people came to America for religious liberty, but once they got here, many did not want to allow others this liberty. Some communities here were as intolerant as the ones in the Old World from which people had fled.[86] But people came with so many different religious views that the diversity gradually led to tolerance, and by the time the Bill of Rights was adopted, widespread support existed for religious liberty. The First Amendment states, "Congress shall make no law respecting an establishment of religion, or prohibiting the free exercise thereof." The two clauses concerning religion—the establishment clause and the free exercise clause—were intended to work in tandem to provide freedom of religion and, by implication, freedom from others' religions.

The Founders recoiled from the Europeans' experience of continuous conflict and long wars fought over

Amish children head for the cornfields to avoid school officials in Iowa.

religious differences. Thus, Thomas Jefferson said, the clauses were designed to build "a wall of separation between church and state." Each would stay on its own side of the wall and not interfere or even interact with the other. **Separation of church and state** was a novel idea; according to one historian, it was the "most revolutionary" aspect of the Constitution.[87]

Today some deeply religious people scorn the idea of separation of church and state. They think this idea devalues the importance of religion. But the Founders did not propose separation because they considered religion less important than government. Rather, they saw it as a practical means to preserve the peace that had eluded European states. In addition, they saw it as a way to protect religion. Without the interference of government officials, whether to help or hinder, churches would be free to flourish. Perhaps for this reason, religion is stronger in the United States than in Europe, where churches sit mostly empty.

Despite the Founders' intention, as society became more complex and government became more pervasive, church and state came to interact, sometimes interfere, with each other. Inevitably, the high wall began to crumble, and courts had to devise new doctrine to keep church and state as separate as possible but still accommodate the needs of both.

Free Exercise of Religion

The **free exercise clause** allows individuals to practice their religion without government coercion. Government occasionally has restricted free exercise of religion directly. Early in the country's history, some states prohibited Catholics or Jews from voting or holding office, and as late as 1961 Maryland prohibited nonbelievers from holding office.[88] In the 1920s, Oregon prohibited students from attending parochial schools.[89] More recently, prisons in Illinois and Texas prohibited Black Muslims and Buddhists from receiving religious publications and using the prison chapel.[90] The Supreme Court invalidated each of these restrictions.

A suburb of Miami, Florida, tried to ban the Santeria religion in 1987. Santeria blends ancient African rites and Roman Catholic rituals, but its distinguishing feature is animal sacrifice. Adherents believe animal sacrifice is necessary to win the favor of the gods, and they practice it at initiations of new members and at births, marriages, and deaths. They kill chickens, ducks, doves, pigeons, sheep, goats, and turtles. When adherents, who had practiced their religion underground since refugees from Cuba brought it to Florida, announced plans to construct a church building, cultural center, museum, and school, the city passed ordinances against ritualistic animal sacrifice, essentially forbidding adherents from practicing their religion. The Court struck down the ordinances.[91] "Although the practice of animal sacrifice may seem abhorrent to some," Justice Anthony Kennedy wrote, "religious beliefs need not be acceptable, logical, consistent, or comprehensible to others in order to merit First Amendment protection."

Government also has restricted free exercise of religion indirectly. As society has become more complex, some laws inevitably have interfered with religion, even when not designed to. The laws usually have interfered with minority religions, which do not have many members in legislatures looking out for their interests.

At first the Court distinguished between belief and action: Individuals could believe what they wanted, but they could not act accordingly if such action was against the law. In 1878, male Mormons who believed their religion required polygamy could not marry more than one woman.[92] The Court rhetorically asked, "Suppose one believed that human sacrifices were a necessary part of religious worship?" Of course, belief without action gave little protection and scant satisfaction to the individuals involved.

In the 1960s, the Warren Court realized this and began to broaden protection by granting exemptions to laws. A Seventh-Day Adventist who worked in a textile mill in South Carolina quit when the mill shifted from a five- to six-day workweek that included Saturday—her Sabbath. Unable to find another job, she applied for unemployment benefits, but the state refused to provide them. To receive them she had to be "available" for work, and the state said she was not available because she would not accept jobs that required Saturday work. The Court ordered the state to grant an exemption to its law.[93] The Burger Court ruled that employers need to make a reasonable effort to accommodate employees' requests to fit work schedules around their Sabbath.[94]

Amish in Wisconsin withheld their children from high school, although the law required attendance until age sixteen. The parents sent their children to elementary and junior high school to learn basic reading, writing, and arithmetic, but they complained that high school would subject their children to worldly influences that would interfere with their semi-isolated agricultural life. The Warren Court ruled that the Amish could be exempt from the additional one to two years the law required beyond junior high school.[95]

Congress, too, has granted some exemptions. It excused the Amish from participating in the Social Security program, because the Amish support their own elderly. And in every draft law, it excused conscientious objectors from participating in war.

The Court has been most reluctant to exempt individuals from paying taxes. It did not excuse either the Amish[96] or Quakers, who as pacifists tried to withhold the portion of their income taxes that would go to the military.[97] The Court worried that many other persons would try to avoid paying taxes, too.

The Rehnquist Court refused to grant exemptions.[98] The Native American church uses peyote, a hallucinogen from a cactus, in worship ceremonies. Members believe the plant embodies their deity and eating it is an act of communion. Although peyote is a controlled substance, Congress has authorized its use on Indian reservations, and almost half the states have authorized its use off reservations by members of the church. But when two members in Oregon, a state that did not allow its use off reservations, were fired from their jobs and denied unemployment benefits for using the substance, the Court refused to grant them an exemption.[99] A five-justice majority rejected the doctrine and precedents of the Warren and Burger Courts. Justice Scalia, a Catholic, admitted that denying exemptions will put minority religions at a disadvantage but said that this is an "unavoidable consequence of democratic government." That is, denying minority rights is acceptable because of majority rule. This rationale, of course, could be used to emasculate not only the free exercise clause but other provisions of the Bill of Rights as well.

Although Congress overturned the narrow focus of the decision, involving Indians' use of peyote,[100] the broad implications of the decision remained. Some adherents of minority religions were not allowed to practice the tenets of those religions. Families of deceased Jews and Laotian immigrants who reject autopsies on religious grounds were overruled. Muslim prisoners whose religion forbids them from eating pork were refused other meat instead. Members of the Sikh religion, who wear turbans, had been exempted from the federal law requiring construction workers to wear hard hats, but the Occupational Safety and Health Administration (OSHA) rescinded the exemption in the wake of the ruling.[101]

Even mainstream churches worried about the implications of the ruling, and a coalition of religious groups lobbied Congress to overturn it. Congress passed and President Clinton signed an act that reversed the ruling and substituted the previous doctrine. But the Rehnquist Court invalidated the act in 1997 because it challenged their authority and altered their interpretation of the First Amendment without going through the process required to amend the Constitution.[102]

Establishment of Religion

Two competing traditions regarding the role of government have led to conflict over the **establishment clause.** Many early settlers in America wanted government to reinforce their religion, yet the framers of the Constitution were products of the Enlightenment, which emphasized the importance of reason and deemphasized the role of organized religion. The two individuals most responsible for the religious guarantees in the First Amendment, Jefferson and Madison,

Alfred Smith, fired for using peyote in religious ceremonies, challenged Oregon's law.

© Phil Schofield

feared the divisiveness of religion. They wanted separation of church and state, advocating not only freedom *of* religion for believers but freedom *from* religion for others.[103]

Early decisions by the Supreme Court usually reflected the first of these traditions. In 1892, Justice David Brewer smugly declared that "this is a Christian nation."[104] But as the country became more pluralistic, the Court moved toward the second of these traditions. Since the early 1960s, the Court generally has interpreted the establishment clause to forbid government not only from designating an official church, like the Church of England in England, which receives tax money and special privileges, but also from aiding one religion over another or even from aiding religion over nonreligion.

Courts have used the clause to resolve disputes about prayer in public schools. In 1962 and 1963, the Supreme Court issued its famous (or infamous) prayer rulings. New York had students recite a nondenominational prayer at the start of every day, and Pennsylvania and Baltimore had students recite the "Lord's Prayer" or Bible verses. The Court, with only one justice dissenting, ruled that these practices violated the establishment clause.[105] The prayers technically were voluntary; students could leave the room. But the Court doubted that the prayers really were voluntary. It noted that nonconforming students would face tremendous pressure from teachers and peers, and that leaving the room usually connotes punishment for bad behavior. Thus, the Court said the prayers fostered religion. According to Justice Black, "Government in this country should stay out of the business of writing and sanctioning official prayers and leave that purely religious function to the people themselves and to those the people choose to look to for religious guidance." Schools could teach about religion, but they could not promote it.

For similar reasons, the Court ruled that Kentucky could not require public schools to post the Ten Commandments in classrooms.[106]

Many people sharply criticized the rulings. A representative from Alabama lamented, "They put the Negroes in the schools, and now they've driven God out."[107] Actually, the justices had not driven God out because students could pray on their own anytime they felt the need.

A survey of teachers two years after the rulings found that prayers and Bible readings had decreased but by no means disappeared. Schools in the West, East, and, to a lesser extent, the Midwest generally complied with the rulings, but schools in the South overwhelmingly refused to.[108] For example, just 1 of 121 districts in Tennessee fully complied. A local official said, "I saw no reason to create controversy," and another asserted, "I am of the opinion that 99 percent of the people in the United States feel as I do about the Supreme Court's decision—that it was an outrage. . . . The remaining 1 percent do not belong in this free world."[109]

Despite the passage of time, periodic news reports indicate that many schools, especially in the rural South, still use prayers or Bible readings in violation of the Court's rulings. These practices are reinforced by social pressure. In 1993, a woman whose family had moved to Pontotoc, Mississippi, to be near relatives discovered that Christian prayers were being broadcast on the intercom and the Bible was being taught in a class. When she objected, rumors circulated that she was an outside agitator paid by the ACLU to force the town to change. One of her children said his teacher told the class that he did not believe in God, while another of her children said he kept "getting jumped" in the bathroom. Then the woman lost her job in a convenience store after customers threatened to boycott the store.[110]

News reports also indicate that schools in Kentucky and Ohio at least allowed volunteers to put the Ten Commandments inside or outside public schools in violation of the Court's ruling.[111]

Congress considered a constitutional amendment to overturn the rulings but did not pass one for several reasons. Some people support the rulings. Others support the Court and do not want to challenge its authority and thereby set a precedent for other groups on other matters.

The country's religious diversity has led to demands for some exotic exemptions. Inspired by the Bible's statement that Jesus' followers "shall take up serpents" and "if they drink any deadly thing, it shall not hurt them," members of the Holiness Church of God in Jesus' Name handle snakes and drink strychnine. Some become enraptured and entranced to the point of hysteria, and occasionally some die. In 1975, the Tennessee Supreme Court forbade such practices, saying that the state has "the right to guard against the unnecessary creation of widows and orphans." However, the practices continue in some places.

Some religious leaders doubt that groups would ever agree about specific prayers. America's religious diversity means that the prayers would offend some students or parents. Prayers that suit Christians might not suit Jews; those that suit Jews might not suit persons of other faiths. Recent immigrants from Asia and the Middle East, practicing Buddhism, Shintoism, Taoism, and Islam, have made the country even more pluralistic. Now, according to one researcher, America's religious diversity is greater than that of any country in recorded history.[112] Thus, asking students in this country to say a prayer would be like "asking the members of the United Nations to stand and sing the national anthem of one country."[113] Other religious leaders expect that officials anxious to avoid controversy would adopt the religious equivalent of canned peas—bland and watered-down prayers. They also expect that prayers would become rote exercises while students were daydreaming or checking out their classmates. In either event, the prayers would trivialize religious faith.

In lieu of an amendment, about half the states have passed laws providing for a "moment of silence" to begin each school day. Although the laws ostensibly are for meditation, some legislators admit they really are for prayer. Yet a majority of justices indicated that they would approve a moment of silence if students were not encouraged to pray.[114]

The Rehnquist Court reaffirmed them. It held that clergy cannot offer prayers at graduation ceremonies for public elementary, middle, and high schools.[115] The prayers in question were brief and nonsectarian, but the majority reasoned, "What to most believers may seem nothing more than a reasonable request that the nonbeliever respect their religious practices, in a school context may appear to the nonbeliever or dissenter to be an attempt to employ the machinery of the state to enforce a religious orthodoxy." Although attendance at the ceremony was voluntary, like participation in school prayers, the majority did not consider it truly voluntary. Justice Kennedy wrote, "Everyone knows that in our society and in our culture high school graduation is one of life's most significant occasions. . . . Graduation is a time for family and those closest to the student to celebrate success and express mutual wishes of gratitude and respect." The Court's decision was by a bare majority, but the opinion's wording was emphatic.

The Court's stance on student-led prayers at graduation, however, is ambiguous. In 1992, the Court refused to review a federal court of appeals ruling that allowed student-led prayers at graduation ceremonies.[116] A Texas school board permitted the senior class to decide whether to have a prayer and, if so, which student to give it. The appellate court held that this policy was not precluded by the Supreme Court's ruling, because the decision was not made by officials and the prayer was not given by a clergy member, so there would not be any official coercion. But in 1996, the Court also refused to review a federal court of appeals ruling from a different circuit that would prohibit student-led prayers at various school events.[117] The Court's reluctance to resolve this controversy means that the ruling of each court of appeals remains but applies only to schools in its circuit and that no appellate ruling governs schools in the rest of the country.

The first appellate court's holding encouraged opponents of the Supreme Court's school prayer rulings to use the same approach to circumvent these rulings as well. Several southern states passed laws allowing student-led prayers. Some school officials, who selected the students, let them give the prayers over the intercom. Federal courts in Alabama and Mississippi invalidated these laws, because school officials were involved and because all students were required or at least pressured to listen to the prayers.

The Rehnquist Court did invalidate the use of schools' public address systems by clergy or students to give prayers at high school football games.[118] Although student attendance is voluntary, the games are official school events.

The public demand is fueled by the symbolism of school prayer and a nostalgia for the less troubling times before the 1960s. As one writer perceived, the demand "doesn't have much to do with prayer anyway, but with a time, a place, an ethos that praying and pledging allegiance at the beginning of school each day represent."[119] Many people echo the feelings of a Pennsylvania school board member who said, "The country has certainly gone downhill since they took it out."[120] For these people, reinstitutionalization of school prayer would be a symbol that our society stands for appropriate values. For some religious leaders, however, calls for school prayer are "a cynical exploitation" of the public by politicians who imply that "two-minute pieties" will make up for the decline of values in society.[121]

Muslim students in Dearborn, Michigan, reflect our religious pluralism. The Detroit area has the second largest concentration of Arabs outside of the Middle East.

"Under God" under Fire

A federal appellate court caused a furor for ruling that the phrase "under God" in the Pledge of Allegiance was unconstitutional when recited in the public schools. In 2002, the Court of Appeals for the Ninth Circuit, which covers the western United States, held that the phrase constituted an establishment of religion and thus violated the First Amendment. Although the phrase is general, the court said it promotes religion as much as if it professed that we are a nation "under Jesus" or "under Vishnu" or "under Zeus" or "under no god." It promotes Christianity most clearly, leaving out not only atheists and agnostics but believers of other deities, such as Buddhists and many Native Americans.

A minister's son and a Republican appointee, the judge who wrote the opinion was ridiculed as a California wacko, but he followed the logic of the school prayer rulings. For the same reason that schools cannot endorse religion by making prayers a part of the school day, according to the court, they cannot do so by making this phrase a part of the school day. Classes can recite the pledge without this phrase, and individual students can recite this phrase on their own, as they can pray on their own if they do not disrupt class. Presumably, the pledge with this phrase would be tolerated for adults in legislatures and courts, just as prayers are tolerated in these bodies.

Yet the school prayer rulings do not require courts to hold the phrase "under God" unconstitutional. In an early school prayer case, Justice William Brennan wrote a concurring opinion suggesting that traditional and symbolic references to God, such as the phrase in the pledge, might be permissible because they are patriotic and, in his view, no longer have religious meaning.[1] But Brennan's thoughts were not part of the Court's

ruling and are not binding on the Court or lower courts.

Just as the school prayer rulings have not been accepted by many people, the pledge ruling was viewed as yet another assault on traditional values. The timing, less than a week before the Fourth of July and less than a year after the terrorist attacks, was not sensitive to the public mood. Why poke this beehive with a stick now?[2] The public uproar brought out the politicians' pandering. President Bush criticized the ruling, repeating the pledge and using the phrase at his appearances; members of the House marched to the steps of the Capitol to recite the pledge, including the phrase; and members of the Senate voted unanimously to condemn the ruling.

Despite the furor, the pledge originally did not include the phrase "under God." For the nation's first celebration of Columbus Day in 1892, Francis Bellamy wrote, "I pledge allegiance to my flag and the republic for which it stands, one nation indivisible, with liberty and justice for all."[3] For Bellamy, the key words were "indivisible," which referred to the Civil War and emphasized the Union over the states, and "liberty and justice for all," which emphasized a balance between freedom for individuals and equality between them.[4]

During the Cold War in the 1950s, Americans feared "godless communism." Some objected to communism as much because of the Soviet Union's official policy of atheism as they did because of its totalitarianism. A religious revival swept the United States, as preachers such as Billy Graham warned that Americans would perish in a nuclear holocaust unless they opened their arms to Jesus Christ. Congress replaced our traditional motto— "E Pluribus Unum" ("Out of Many, One")—with "In God We Trust," and it

added this new motto to our paper money. Fraternal organizations, especially the Catholic Knights of Columbus, and religious leaders campaigned to add "under God" to the Pledge of Allegiance. The Presbyterian pastor of President Eisenhower's church in Washington urged the addition in a sermon as the president sat in a pew. With little dissent, Congress passed and the president signed a bill to do so in 1954. The legislative history of the act stated that the intent was to "acknowledge the dependence of our people and our government upon . . . the Creator . . . [and] deny the atheistic and materialistic concept of communism." The president stated that "millions of our school children will daily proclaim in every city and town . . . the dedication of our nation and our people to the Almighty."[5] Thus, the phrase was adopted expressly to endorse religion.

Although Bellamy was no longer alive, his granddaughter said he would have opposed the change. " 'One nation indivisible,' " she observed, "conveyed the deep meaning that after the Civil War our nation could not be divided." The change "tampered with the original meaning of the pledge as well as spoiling its rhythmic cadence."[6]

Whether the phrase ultimately stays or goes, it would be refreshing if people got as worked up about what comes after the phrase as they do about the phrase itself.

1. *Abington School District v. Schempp,* 374 U.S. 203 (1963).
2. Hendrik Hertzberg, "Comment" Two Little Words," *New Yorker,* July 15, 2002, 28.
3. In 1924, Congress changed "my flag" to "the flag of the United States of America."
4. David Greenberg, "The Pledge of Allegiance: Why We're Not One Nation 'under God,'" *Slate,* http://slate.msn.com/?id=2067499 S, June 28, 2002. This article was the source for much of this box.
5. Ibid.
6. Arthur Schlesinger Jr., "When Patriotism Wasn't Religious," *New York Times,* July 7, 2002, WK9.

In the United States, Sikhs from India sometimes were mistaken for Muslims after the 9/11 terrorist attacks. One was killed in Arizona.

Robert Nickelsberg/Timepix

The public demand is also aggravated by occasional reports of school officials who mistakenly believe that court rulings require them to forbid all forms of religious expression. Thus, some confused administrators have prohibited a few students from wearing religious jewelry, reading the Bible while riding the bus, and praying before eating their lunch.[122]

In another case, the Supreme Court said that the University of Missouri at Kansas City had to make its meeting rooms available to students' religious organizations on an equal basis with other organizations, even if the religious organizations used the rooms for prayer or worship.[123] Otherwise, the university would be discriminating against religion. After this decision, Congress passed a law that requires public high schools as well to allow meetings of students' religious, philosophical, or political groups outside class hours. The Court accepted this law in 1990.[124] Justice O'Connor said high school students "are likely to understand that a school does not endorse or support student speech that it merely permits on a nondiscriminatory basis." Students have established Bible clubs in a quarter of the public schools, according to one estimate.[125] (As a result of this act, students have also established gay-straight clubs—organizations of gay and straight students who support the rights of gays, lesbians, and bisexuals—in more than seven hundred high schools.[126]) Yet students' desires for Bible clubs have not always been the driving force. Adults who are anxious to put prayers back into the schools have often taken the initiative. Organized networks encourage the clubs and provide advice, workshops, and handbooks for them.

The Rehnquist Court also said that the University of Virginia had to provide funding, from students' fees, to students' religious organizations on an equal basis with

other campus organizations, even if a religious organization sought the money to print a religious newspaper.[127] On the basis of this precedent, a federal court of appeals ruled that the University of South Alabama had to provide funding to a gay organization.

Despite its prayer rulings, the Court has been reluctant to invalidate traditional religious symbols. It has not questioned the motto "In God We Trust," on our coins since 1865 and paper money since 1955, or the phrase "One nation under God," in the Pledge of Allegiance since 1954.

The Burger Court upheld the display of a nativity scene on government property, at least if it is part of a broader display for the holiday season.[128] Pawtucket, Rhode Island, had a crèche, Santa Claus, sleigh with reindeer, Christmas tree, and talking wishing well. Although the nativity scene was an obvious symbol of Christianity, the Court said it was a traditional symbol of a holiday that has become secular as well as religious. Moreover, the presence of the secular decorations diluted any religious impact the nativity scene would have. A crèche by itself, however, would be impermissible.[129]

Courts have also used the establishment clause to resolve disputes about teaching evolution in schools. In 1968, the Supreme Court invalidated Arkansas's forty-year-old law forbidding schools from teaching evolution.[130] Arkansas and Louisiana then passed laws requiring schools that teach evolution to also teach "creationism"—the biblical version of creation.[131] In 1987, the Court invalidated these laws, because their purpose was to promote the fundamentalist Christian view.[132] Yet teaching evolution remains controversial. Many science teachers skip it to avoid confrontations with conservative parents or religious groups.[133]

Courts have also used the establishment clause to resolve disputes about aid to parochial schools. Historically, most parochial schools were Catholic schools. Protestants opposed aid to these schools because they feared growth of the Catholic Church. But changes in society, beginning with the desegregation of public schools, prompted more Protestants to form their own schools.[134] Now millions of students attend either Catholic or Protestant schools, and their parents pay tuition and other expenses. Schools have asked legislatures to provide money to defray part of the costs of their nonreligious activities. Courts have had to decide whether providing the money helps religion or whether denying it hinders religion. In addition, courts have had to determine whether providing the money leads to excessive entanglement of church and state because of the monitoring required to ensure that the money is not spent for religious purposes.

The Court has upheld some types of aid[135] but has rejected most types.[136] Yet the Court, reflecting shifting coalitions of justices, has not drawn a clear line separating permissible from impermissible forms of assistance.[137]

A Christian Bible club meets in a Minneapolis school.

The Rehnquist Court, reflecting its justices' greater tolerance for aid to parochial schools and perhaps the majority's Republican affiliations, narrowly upheld tuition aid, in the form of school vouchers, for some students to attend private schools.[138] Although this case involved a pilot program for failing schools in Cleveland, the ruling has been used by conservatives to push for similar programs throughout the country.[139]

Despite frequent tensions and periodic conflicts, the effort to separate church and state over the years has enabled the United States to manage, and even nourish, its religious pluralism. The effort has kept much religious debate and potential religious fights out of the political arena. But this practical arrangement is opposed primarily by religious conservatives, whether Protestant, Catholic, or Jewish, who most fear the changes in modern society. They believe that their religion is so important that it should be reinforced by the government.

Rights of Criminal Defendants

The Fourth, Fifth, Sixth, and Eighth Amendments provide numerous **due process** rights for criminal defendants. When the government prosecutes defendants, it must give them the process—that is, the procedures—they are due; it must be fair and "respect certain decencies of civilized conduct,"[140] even toward uncivilized people.

One defense attorney said many of his clients "had been monsters—nothing less—who had done monstrous things. Although occasionally not guilty of the crime charged, nearly all my clients have been guilty of something."[141] Then why do we give them rights? The reason is that we give all individuals rights. As Justice Douglas observed, "respecting the dignity even of the least worthy . . . citizen raises the stature of all of us."[142]

But why do we give all individuals rights? We do so because we have established the **presumption of innocence.** This presumption is "not . . . a naive belief that most or even many defendants are innocent, or a cavalier attitude toward crime. It reflects mistrust of the state. Requiring the state to prove guilt is a way of saying, 'We won't take your word for it.' "[143] Of course, when the crime rate is high or a crime is particularly heinous, many people fear the state less than the criminals. Then they want to give officials more authority and defendants fewer rights. But this is the way people eventually lose rights.

Search and Seizure

England fostered the notion that a family's home is its castle, but Parliament made exceptions for the American colonies. It authorized writs of assistance, which allowed customs officials to conduct general searches for goods imported by colonists without paying taxes to the crown. The English tradition combined with the colonists' resentment of the writs of assistance led to adoption of the Fourth Amendment, which forbids **unreasonable searches and seizures.**

One type of seizure is the arrest of a person. Police must have evidence to believe that a person committed a crime. Another type of seizure is the confiscation of illegal contraband. The general requirement is that police

What about the Second Amendment?

Individuals and interest groups opposed to gun control cite the **Second Amendment,** which provides "the right of the people to keep and bear arms." But these opponents seldom quote the rest of the amendment, which reads in its entirety, "A well regulated militia, being necessary to the security of a free state, the right of the people to keep and bear arms, shall not be infringed." The amendment was adopted at a time when there was no standing army to protect people from foreign invasions, Indian uprisings, or mob riots. The language links the right to bear arms with the security of the state. The language suggests that the right belongs to each state or, if to individuals, only to individuals when they are protecting their state—that is, when they are serving in the militia of their state. Today the militia is the National Guard in each state. Therefore, the amendment might be a useless anachronism.

Accordingly, the federal courts routinely uphold gun control laws when they are challenged as violations of the Second Amendment. The Supreme Court rarely reviews these decisions, even one in which an appellate court allowed a Chicago suburb to ban possession of handguns.[1]

Conservative Chief Justice Warren Burger criticized the National Rifle Association for misleading people by insisting that the Second Amendment right should prevent gun control legislation. He said the amendment "has been the subject of one of the greatest pieces of fraud—I repeat the word 'fraud'—on the American public."[2]

Yet the persistent views of the American public have prompted legal scholars to take a closer look at the adoption of the Second Amendment. Some have concluded that there might be a right for individuals, separate from the right for states and National

"You know, if she weren't part of a well-regulated militia I'd be a little nervous."

Guards, to own and use guns. Their rationale is that the original notion of a militia encompassed all individuals who had political rights, such as the right to vote in elections and serve on juries—that is, all white males who owned property. Today individuals who have political rights include all adult citizens (except felons in most states). Thus, the word *militia* in 1791 might mean all adult citizens today. However, this expanded view of the Second Amendment would provide a right only for individuals to own and use guns to defend their state or, possibly, their homes or themselves.[3] It would not provide a right to own and use guns for hunting or other recreational purposes because the language—"the security of a free state"—indicates that the justification for the right is just protection.

Even if this expanded view of the Second Amendment becomes more common—the Bush administration is the first to advocate an expanded view—it would not bar most gun control proposals. The amendment refers to a "well regulated militia," making

clear that arms can be regulated (as they were even in colonial times). As Justice Stevens observed, arms have "long been subject to pervasive governmental regulation because of the dangerous nature of the product and the public interest in having that danger controlled."[4]

So a huge gap remains between what many people think and what most judges and legal scholars have concluded.

1. *Quilici v. Morton Grove,* 695 F.2d 261 (7th Cir., 1982). A federal district court did make headlines in 1999 when it ruled unconstitutional a federal law that prohibits a person under a restraining order from owning a gun. This apparently was the first time a court struck down a law because it infringed on the Second Amendment.
2. Joan Biskupic, "A Second (Amendment) Look at Bearing Arms," *Washington Post National Weekly Edition,* May 15–21, 1995, 33.
3. In the original debate over the proposed amendment, the framers apparently never discussed the use of firearms for personal protection. Garry Wills, *A Necessary Evil: A History of American Distrust* (New York: Simon & Schuster, 1999).
4. *U.S. v. Thompson/Center Arms Co.,* 504 U.S. 505, 526 (1992).
SOURCE: Except where noted, Laurence H. Tribe, *American Constitutional Law,* 3d ed., vol. 1 (New York: Foundation Press, 2000), 894–903.

should get a search warrant from a judge by showing evidence that a particular thing is in a particular place.

However, the Supreme Court has made exceptions to this requirement that complicate the law. These exceptions account for the vast majority of searches. If persons consent to a search, police can conduct one without a warrant. If police see contraband in plain view, they can seize it; they do not need to close their eyes to it. If police have suspicion that a person is committing a crime but lack evidence to arrest him, they can "stop and frisk" the person—give him a pat-down search. If police have evidence to arrest someone, they can search her and the area within her control. If police face an emergency situation, they can search for weapons. If police want to search motor vehicles in some situations, they can do so because vehicles are mobile and could be gone by the time police get a warrant.

Customs and border patrol officials can search persons and things coming into the country to enforce customs and immigration laws. Airport guards can search passengers and luggage to prevent hijackings and terrorism. And prison guards can search prisoners to ensure security.

These are all general principles that need to be interpreted in specific cases. The law is so complex that it is difficult to determine the legality of many searches and seizures.

In defining reasonable and unreasonable searches and seizures, the Court has tried to walk a fine line between acknowledging officials' need for evidence and persons' need for privacy.

Exclusionary Rule

To enforce search and seizure law, the Court has established the **exclusionary rule,** which bars from court any evidence obtained in violation of the Fourth Amendment. The rule's goal is to deter police from illegal conduct.

Although the Court issued the rule for federal courts in 1914,[144] it did not impose the rule on state courts until 1961. Even so, the Warren Court's decision, in the case of *Mapp v. Ohio,*[145] was one of its most controversial. Until this time, police in many states had ignored search and seizure law.

The decision still has not been widely accepted. The Burger Court created an exception to it. In a pair of cases, the justices allowed evidence obtained illegally to be used in court because the police had acted in "good faith."[146]

Electronic Surveillance

The Fourth Amendment traditionally applied to searches involving a physical trespass and seizures producing a tangible object. Electronic surveillance, however, does not require a physical trespass or result in a tangible object.

This posed a problem for the Supreme Court when it heard its first wiretapping case in 1928. Federal prohi-

bition agents tapped the telephone of bootleggers by installing equipment on wires in the basement of the bootleggers' apartment building. The majority of the Court rigidly adhered to its traditional doctrine, saying this was not a search and seizure so the agents did not need a warrant.[147]

In a classic example of keeping the Constitution up-to-date, the Warren Court overruled this precedent in 1967.[148] Because electronic eavesdropping might threaten privacy as much as traditional searching, officials must get judicial authorization, similar to a warrant, to engage in such eavesdropping.

Yet judicial authorization is easy to get. In a recent four-year period, the FBI requested 2,686 wiretaps, and the courts granted all but one.[149]

Self-Incrimination

The Fifth Amendment provides that persons shall not be compelled to be witnesses against themselves—that is, to incriminate themselves. Because defendants are presumed innocent, the government must prove their guilt.

This right means that defendants on trial do not have to take the witness stand and answer questions, and neither prosecutor nor judge can call attention to their failure to do so. Neither can suggest that defendants must have something to hide and thereby imply that they must be guilty. (But if defendants do take the stand and testify, this constitutes a waiver of their right, so the prosecutor can cross-examine them and they must answer.)

This right also means that prosecutors cannot introduce into evidence any statements or confessions from defendants that were not voluntary. However, the meaning of "voluntary" has changed over time.

For years law enforcement officials used physical brutality—"the third degree"—to get confessions. After

1936, when the Supreme Court ruled that confessions obtained this way were invalid,[150] officials resorted to more subtle techniques. They held suspects incommunicado, so the suspects could not notify anyone about their arrest, and delayed bringing them to court, so the judge could not inform them of their rights.[151] Officials interrogated suspects for long periods of time without food or rest, in one case with alternating teams of interrogators for thirty-six hours.[152] They tricked suspects. In one case, police told a man they would jail his wife if he did not talk, although they knew she was not involved, and in another they told a woman they would take away her welfare benefits and even her children if she did not talk, although they did not have authority to do either.[153] The Court ruled that these techniques, designed to break the suspects' will, were psychological coercion, so the confessions were invalid.

The Warren Court still worried that many confessions were not truly voluntary, so it issued a landmark decision in 1966. Arizona police arrested a poor, mentally disturbed man, Ernesto Miranda, for kidnapping and raping a woman. After the woman identified him in a lineup, police interrogated him for two hours, prompting him to confess. He had not been told that he could remain silent or be represented by an attorney. In *Miranda v. Arizona,* the Court decided that his confession was not truly voluntary.[154] Chief Justice Warren, himself a former district attorney, noted the tremendous advantage police have in interrogation and said suspects needed more protection. The Court ruled that officials must advise suspects of their rights before interrogation. These came to be known as the **Miranda rights:**

- You have the right to remain silent.
- If you talk, anything you say can be used against you.
- You have the right to be represented by an attorney.
- If you cannot afford an attorney, one will be appointed for you.

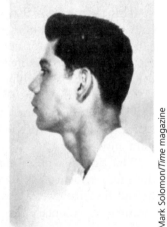

Ernesto Miranda.

The Burger and Rehnquist Courts have not required police and prosecutors to follow *Miranda* as strictly as the Warren Court did but, contrary to expectations, have not abandoned *Miranda*. In 2000, the Rehnquist Court reaffirmed *Miranda* by a 7–2 vote.[155]

Even with the warnings, most suspects talk anyway. Some do not understand the warnings. Others think police, who may rattle off the warnings fast or in a monotone, give them only because they are required to, not because they actually mean them. Also, all suspects in an interrogation are in a coercive atmosphere and face tactics designed to exploit their weaknesses. Detectives are trained to persuade suspects to talk despite the warnings. One said, "Before you ever get in there, the first thing an investigator usually thinks about is . . . how can I breeze through this *Miranda* thing so I don't set the guy off and tell him not to talk to me, song and dance it, sugarcoat it, whatever."[156]

Counsel

The Sixth Amendment provides the **right to counsel** in criminal cases. Initially, it permitted defendants to hire an attorney to help them prepare a defense, and later it permitted defendants to have the attorney represent them at trial. But it was no help to most defendants because they were too poor to hire an attorney.

Consequently, the Supreme Court required federal courts to furnish an attorney to all indigent defendants as long ago as 1938.[157] But most criminal cases are state cases, and although the Court required state courts to furnish an attorney in some cases, it was reluctant to impose a broad requirement on these courts.[158]

In 1963, the Warren Court accepted the appeal of Clarence Earl Gideon. Charged with breaking into a pool hall and stealing beer, wine, and change from a vending machine, Gideon asked the judge for a lawyer. The judge refused to appoint one, leaving Gideon to defend himself. The prosecutor did not have a strong case, but Gideon was not able to point out its weaknesses. He was convicted and sentenced to five years. On appeal, the Warren Court unanimously declared that Gideon was entitled to be represented by counsel.[159] Justice Black explained that "lawyers in criminal courts are necessities, not luxuries." The Court finally established a broad rule: State courts must provide an attorney to indigent defendants in felony cases.

Gideon proved the Court's point. Given a lawyer and retried, he was not reconvicted. The lawyer did the effective job defending him that he had not been able to do himself.

In 1972, the Burger Court expanded the rule: State courts must provide an attorney to indigent defendants in misdemeanor cases too, except those that result in no incarceration,[160] because even misdemeanor cases are

Clarence Earl Gideon, convinced he was denied a fair trial because he was not given an attorney, read law books in prison so he could petition the Supreme Court for a writ of certiorari. Although he had spent much of his life in prison, he was optimistic. "I believe that each era finds an improvement in law each year brings something new for the benefit of mankind [sic]. Maybe this will be one of those small steps forward."

Both courtesy of the National Archives

too complex for defendants to defend themselves. In 2002, the Rehnquist Court expanded the rule further: State courts must provide an attorney to indigent defendants even in cases that result in no incarceration, if the defendants receive probation or a suspended sentence, which could eventually result in incarceration if the defendants fail to follow the terms of such sentence.[161]

In addition to an attorney for the trial, the Supreme Court decided that courts must provide an attorney for one appeal.[162]

Receiving counsel does not necessarily mean receiving effective counsel, however. Some assigned attorneys are inexperienced, some are incompetent, and most are overworked and have little time to prepare the best possible defense.

Some places make little effort to provide effective counsel, even in murder cases where capital punishment looms. In Illinois, at least thirty-three convicts on death row had been represented at trial by attorneys who later were disbarred or suspended.[163] In Louisiana, a defendant was represented by an attorney who was living with the prosecutor in the case. In Florida, a defendant was represented by an attorney who was a deputy sheriff at the time. In Georgia, a black defendant was represented by a white attorney who had been the Imperial Wizard of the local Ku Klux Klan for fifty years.[164] In another case from Georgia, the attorney was so unversed in criminal law that when he was asked to name criminal rulings he was familiar with, he could think of only one (*Miranda*).[165] In three murder cases in one recent year in Texas, defense attorneys slept through the trials. When one of these defendants appealed his conviction on the ground that he did not receive his constitutional right to counsel, the appellate court announced that "the Constitution doesn't say the lawyer has to be awake."[166] (Stung by criticism, the appellate court sat en banc and overruled itself. The Supreme Court refused to hear the case, thus allowing the final appellate court ruling to stand.) At least these attorneys were present. In Alabama, a defendant was represented by an attorney who failed to appear when his case was argued before the state supreme court. The defendant lost and was executed.[167]

In recent years, the issue of counsel for those subject to the death penalty has received some attention, partly

CHAPTER 14 ■ *Civil Liberties*   **445**

CIVIL LIBERTIES AT RISK?

In response to the terrorist attacks, the Bush administration has adopted tactics intended to disrupt terrorist cells and thereby delay or prevent further attacks. The tactics are directed primarily at Muslim men from the Middle East or South Asia (including Afghanistan and Pakistan) who are not American citizens. These measures raise questions about the continuing viability of some civil liberties.

Detentions

The administration rounded up almost one thousand men and detained them in undisclosed locations for an indefinite time. Apparently they were put in solitary confinement and subjected to harsh conditions, including rough treatment by prison guards, and allowed limited access to their lawyers.[1] They were held in secret; little information was released to indicate who was detained, what they were charged with, and who was representing them.

The men were singled out because of anonymous tips or miscellaneous information discovered by officials. One man had a book that had an ad for another book that had a photo of Osama bin Laden. Another man had materials for a correspondence course on becoming a private investigator. An Egyptian antiques dealer had made plane reservations at the same place and about the same time as one of the hijackers. A Pakistani gas station attendant had renewed his driver's license at the same place and about the same time as another of the hijackers. The government cast its net widely on the chance that it might snare sleeper agents of al Qaeda.

Normally the government can detain persons only if they are actually suspected of particular crimes. Within forty-eight hours, the government must charge them or release them. If the government charges them, it must bring them to court so the judge can approve their detention and advise them of their rights. However, there are some exceptions to these requirements. Persons who are material witnesses to particular crimes and who might be unavailable to testify at the trials can be held for a "reasonable" (not an indefinite) time. Persons who are immigration violators can be held until they are deported.[2] The administration stretched these laws to the legal limit—and perhaps beyond. It is not clear whether the men detained as material witnesses were real witnesses to particular crimes or whether they were held for a reasonable, rather than an indefinite, time.

Enemy combatants can be captured and held as prisoners of war for the duration of the conflict. One American citizen, fingered during interrogation of an al Qaeda official, was suspected of volunteering to detonate a bomb within the United States. He was apprehended and held in a military brig. Although an American citizen, he was detained without bail, without counsel, and without charges being filed. The administration claimed that it alone could determine whether this detainee was an enemy combatant and thus subject to indefinite detention. Some legal scholars, however, insist that courts have authority to review such executive decisions.

Many detainees have been released, and many others have been charged with immigration violations—for example, overstaying their visa. Those charged with immigration violations have been deported and not allowed to return, including some who were legal residents and married to American citizens. By fall 2002, however, only four detainees had been charged with terrorism crimes. Yet it is difficult to evaluate the validity or success of the detention policy because it is shrouded in secrecy. Even the lawyers for the detainees are afraid to talk out of fear that the prosecutors will make conditions harder for their clients.

Interviews

The administration sought to interview about five thousand young, Middle Eastern men—all those from eighteen to thirty-three who had entered the United States since 2000 from countries with links to terrorism. The purpose was to get information about sleeper agents of al Qaeda or future attacks.

According to the administration's policy, the interviews were voluntary, but for young foreign men whose nationality put them under a cloud of suspicion, the interviews seemed mandatory. Moreover, the interviews seemed risky, forcing many men to contact a lawyer.

The interviews were wide ranging, with FBI agents or law enforcement officials asking the men about not only their travel history but their religious beliefs, political views, and even their future marriage plans. Also, the Justice Department instructed the interviewers, "You should remember to ask the catch-all question whether the individual is aware of any criminal activity whatsoever, whether related to terrorism or not." Lying to a federal officer can result in deportation of a person on a visa, so a no answer could have serious consequences for a person who was aware of, say, underage drinking or any other minor offense.

Normally, under the Fourth Amendment, law enforcement officers can ask people questions but cannot force them to answer or even to stop and listen. Officers can force only suspects to stop, and then officers must give them their *Miranda* rights to silence and counsel. Because the interviews were voluntary, they did not violate the Fourth Amendment. But, again, the administration stretched the law to its legal limit.

It is uncertain whether any information obtained was worth the ill will generated among Middle Eastern residents in the United States. For this reason, when the government asked local police departments to help conduct the interviews, some departments refused. They said the policy resembled racial profiling, which they were trying to avoid.

Military Tribunals

President Bush, in his capacity as commander in chief, established military tribunals to try some terrorists. Neither civilian courts nor military courts-martial, the tribunals deviate in significant ways from each.

Defendants will not be allowed to hear the evidence against them if this evidence is classified (though their attorneys will). The "jury" will consist of three to seven military officers, and it will reach its decision by a two-thirds vote (though it will need seven officers and a unanimous vote to impose the death penalty). Any appeals will go only to another military tribunal, whose members will be picked by the president. The tribunals might be held outside the United States to prevent a federal court from hearing an appeal and assuming jurisdiction. The procedures and the records will be kept secret indefinitely. (In theory, it is possible that tribunals have already been held by the time you read this.)

These procedures deviate less from civilian courts and military courts-martial than the administration's original procedures did. Those procedures were roundly criticized as a shortcut to a certain conviction, causing the administration to revise them.[3]

The administration claims that the tribunals are necessary to preserve classified information, but it seems to worry more that the juries of civilian courts might not convict—although they did convict in two cases in the 1990s—and that the openness of civilian courts might permit the terrorists to publicize their cause. Attorney General John Ashcroft recoiled from the prospect of "Osama TV."

Presumably the tribunals would be ruled legal, if federal courts would ever hear a challenge to their legality. The Supreme Court upheld the last tribunal, of eight German saboteurs who landed on our coast during World War II.

But the reason for that tribunal is not reassuring. The government used a military tribunal rather than a civilian court because it was embarrassed that the FBI had ignored clear evidence of the sabotage earlier. The secrecy promised by military tribunals was tempting

to the government then, and it might be tempting now.

These policies—and others not addressed here, such as interrogating and profiling (covered in Chapters 2 and 15)—demonstrate that the Bush administration essentially is developing a parallel judicial system, with fewer protections and rights, for some Arabs and Muslims in the United States. The president of the Arab-American Institute observed, "Military tribunals, secret evidence, no numbers on how many people the government is detaining. We're looking like a Third World country."[4]

The system is not bereft of protections and rights, and it offers a plausible rationale for each of these policies. And, of course, the terrorist threat is real and substantial. Perhaps this in itself justifies the deviations from our established procedures. But each of these policies stretches the law to its legal limit. Moreover, one critic noted, each reflects "some combination of overreaching, arbitrariness, and unwisdom."[5] The nature of the war on terrorism could exacerbate these problems. The United States is fighting a vague enemy and has a broad objective—stopping terrorism—that together predict a long war. What will become of these tactics, and other heretofore unannounced tactics, as time drags on? Will this administration, or its successor, stop before jeopardizing civil liberties of everyone? Can some people in our society be deprived of civil liberties without everyone's rights being put at risk? Or will these policies, now that they are in place, continue to expand?

At least the climate in the country is different than in previous wars. There is nothing comparable to the prosecution of thousands of dissenters in World War I. There is nothing comparable to the internment of over a hundred thousand Japanese Americans in World War II. There is nothing comparable to the government harassment of the antiwar movement in the Vietnam War. And this

time Congress and the courts are showing a willingness to check the president and attorney general.[6] Even liberals who are the first to identify any assaults on civil liberties and rights acknowledge the difference. "Perhaps because the stakes were so high," a magazine editor wrote, "Americans approached this new war with a sense of sad necessity, rather than with relish. There has been relatively little blind anger, and a genuine desire—from almost everyone except John Ashcroft [the attorney general]—to make sure that the rights and dignity of fellow citizens who happen to be Muslim are protected."[7]

The legal precedents and the political culture that developed in the twentieth century, especially in the second half of the twentieth century, have made the abuses of past wars less likely today. But this has come about only because citizens have been sensitive to potential abuses and willing to speak up against them.

1. Steve Fainaru, "Lives on Hold," *Washington Post National Weekly Edition,* April 22–28, 2002, 29.
2. In addition, a congressional law passed after the attacks allows the government to detain suspected terrorists seven days rather than forty-eight hours or, if national security is at stake, six months. Reportedly the Bush administration has relied on the existing laws rather than upon this new law.
3. Even so, military officials are upset by comparisons of the tribunals with courts-martial, which have a tradition of fairness and openness. For an examination of the differences, see William Glaberson, "Arguing Tribunals v. Courts-Martial," *New York Times,* December 2, 2001, B6.
4. George Lardner Jr., "Are Civil Liberties in Jeopardy?" *Washington Post National Weekly Edition,* November 26–December 2, 2001, 29.
5. Hendrik Hertzberg, "Comment: The Wrong Man," *New Yorker,* December 10, 2001, 46.
6. Jeffrey Rosen, "A Lesson on Liberties," *Washington Post National Weekly Edition,* September 23–29, 2002, 21.
7. Roger Cohn, "Editor's Note," *Mother Jones,* January/February 2002, 4. In one area—guns—Ashcroft bent over backward to protect "rights." He refused to allow the FBI to check its records to determine whether any of the detainees had purchased weapons. During the Clinton administration, the FBI preserved these records for 90 days, the maximum allowed by congressional law. Ashcroft, however, ordered the records destroyed within twenty-four hours of being received. This order forced the FBI to discard evidence of weapons purchases by terrorist suspects. Jeffrey Toobin, "Ashcroft's Ascent," *New Yorker,* April 15, 2002, 61.

because new investigations and technologies have shown definitively that dozens of people on death row were not guilty of the crime for which they were convicted and sentenced. Nonetheless, in most cases, including death penalty cases, there is little effort to provide effective counsel because no powerful constituency urges adequate representation. Criminal defendants have no political power in our system, and the public has little sympathy for their rights. Government responds to the public by increasing the funding for prosecutors while ignoring the representation of defendants.[168]

Jury Trial

The Sixth Amendment also provides the **right to a jury trial** in "serious" criminal cases. The Supreme Court has defined "serious" cases as those that could result in more than six months' incarceration.[169]

The right was adopted to prevent oppression by a "corrupt or overzealous prosecutor" or a "biased . . . or eccentric judge."[170] It also has served to limit governmental use of unpopular laws or enforcement practices. Regardless of the extent of evidence against a defendant, a jury can refuse to convict if it feels the government has overstepped its bounds.

The jury is to be "impartial," so persons who have made up their minds before trial should be dismissed. It also is to be "a fair cross section" of the community, so no group should be systematically excluded.[171] But the jury need not be a perfect cross section and, in fact, need not have a single member of a particular group.[172] Most courts use voter registration lists to obtain names of potential jurors. These lists are not truly representative because poor people do not register at the same rate as others, but courts have decided that the lists are sufficiently representative. And Congress passed and President Clinton signed the "motor voter bill," which requires drivers' license and welfare offices to offer voter registration forms. Presumably, more poor people will register and be eligible to serve on juries.

Cruel and Unusual Punishment

The Eighth Amendment forbids **cruel and unusual punishment** but does not define it. The Supreme Court had defined it as torture or any punishment grossly disproportionate to the offense, but the Court had seldom used the provision until applying it to capital punishment in the 1970s.

Because the death penalty was used at the time the amendment was adopted and had been used ever since, it was assumed to be constitutional.[173] But the Burger Court, albeit with Chief Justice Burger and the other three Nixon appointees in dissent, held that capital punishment as it was then being administered was cruel and unusual.[174] The Court said the laws and procedures allowed too much discretion for those who administered the punishment and too much arbitrariness and discrimination for those who received it. It was imposed so seldom, according to Justice Potter Stewart, that it was "cruel and unusual in the same way that being struck by lightning is cruel and unusual." Yet when imposed, it was given to blacks disproportionately to their convictions for murder.

The decision invalidated the laws of forty states and commuted the death sentences of 629 inmates. But because the Court did not hold capital punishment cruel and unusual in principle, about three-fourths of the states adopted new laws that permitted less discretion in an effort to be less arbitrary and discriminatory.

These changes satisfied a majority of the Court, which ruled that capital punishment is not cruel and unusual for murder if administered fairly.[175] But the death penalty cannot be imposed automatically for everyone convicted of murder, for the judge or jury must consider any mitigating factors that would call for a lesser punishment.[176] Also, capital punishment cannot be imposed for rape, because it is disproportionate to that offense.[177]

The new laws apparently have reduced but not eliminated discrimination. Although past studies showed discrimination against black defendants, recent studies show discrimination against black or white defendants who murder whites. People who affect the decision to impose the death penalty—prosecutors, defense attorneys, judges, and jurors—appear to value white lives more. Despite evidence that in Georgia those who kill whites are more than four times as likely to be given the death penalty as those who kill blacks, the Rehnquist Court, by a 5–4 vote, upheld capital punishment in the state.[178]

The new laws have not addressed an equally serious problem: the inadequate representation provided for poor defendants who face the death penalty.

In recent decades, the primary criticism against capital punishment was that it discriminated against racial minorities and the poor. Although the punishment is irrevocable, most people dismissed any suggestions that innocent defendants might be put to death. They assumed that criminal justice systems used careful procedures and made no mistakes in these cases at least. However, since capital punishment was reinstated in the 1970s (with stricter procedures), one hundred inmates awaiting execution have been released because new evidence, sometimes DNA tests, revealed their innocence. This amounts to one exoneration for every seven or eight executions, which is a disturbing frequency for this ultimate punishment.[179] Some were the victims of sloppy or biased police or overzealous prosecutors; some were the victims of mistaken witnesses; others were the victims of emotional or prejudiced jurors. Many were the victims of inadequate representation.

Due to the patterns of racial discrimination and inadequate representation, the American Bar Association called for a moratorium on the use of capital punishment in 1997. After Illinois released its thirteenth innocent inmate from death row, most after investigations by Northwestern University journalism students, its governor announced a moratorium in 2000.

Reflecting the public's recent unease about capital punishment, the Rehnquist Court, long a staunch supporter of the death penalty, ruled in 2002 that states cannot execute the mentally retarded.[180] The six-justice majority observed that there was a new "national consensus" against such executions.

Rights in Theory and in Practice

Overall, the Supreme Court has interpreted the Bill of Rights to provide an impressive list of rights for criminal defendants (although one of the greatest changes from the Warren Court to the Burger and Rehnquist Courts has been a decline in support for criminal defendants). Yet not all rights are available for all defendants in all places. Some trial court judges, prosecutors, and police do not comply with Supreme Court rulings. If defendants appeal to a high enough court, they probably will get their rights, but most defendants do not have the knowledge, the resources, or the perseverance to do this.

When rights are available, most defendants do not take advantage of them. About 90 percent of all criminal defendants plead guilty, and many of them do so as part of a **plea bargain.** This is an agreement between the prosecutor, the defense attorney, and the defendant, with the explicit or implicit approval of the judge, to reduce the charge or the sentence in exchange for a plea of guilty. A plea bargain is a compromise. For officials it saves the time, trouble, and uncertainty of a trial. For defendants it eliminates the fear of a harsher sentence. However, it also reduces due process rights. A plea of guilty waives defendants' rights to a trial by a jury of their peers, in which defendants can present their own witnesses and cross-examine the government's witnesses, and in which they cannot be forced to incriminate themselves. A plea of guilty also waives the right to counsel to some extent because most attorneys appointed to represent defendants are overworked and inclined to pressure defendants to plead guilty so they do not have to prepare a defense. Despite these disadvantages for due process rights, the Court allows plea bargaining because of its practical advantages.[181]

Right to Privacy

Neither the Constitution nor the Bill of Rights mentions "privacy." Nevertheless, the right to privacy, Justice Douglas noted, is "older than the Bill of Rights,"[182] and the framers undoubtedly assumed that people would have such a right. In fact, the framers did include amendments that reflect a concern for privacy: The First Amendment protects privacy of association; the Third, privacy of homes from quartering soldiers; the Fourth, privacy of persons and places where they live from searches and seizures; and the Fifth, privacy of knowledge or thoughts from compulsory self-incrimination. The Supreme Court would use these to establish an explicit **right to privacy.**

So far, the Court's right-to-privacy doctrine reflects a right to autonomy—what Justice Louis Brandeis called "the right to be left alone"—more than a right to keep things confidential. As noted earlier in the chapter, the Court has been reluctant to punish the press for invasion of privacy.[183]

Birth Control

The Warren Court explicitly established a right to privacy in 1965 when it struck down a Connecticut law that prohibited distributing or using contraceptives.[184] To enforce the law, the state would have had to police people's bedrooms, and the Court said the very idea of policing married couples' bedrooms was absurd. Then the Court struck down Massachusetts and New York laws that prohibited distributing contraceptives to unmarried persons.[185] "If the right of privacy means anything," Justice Brennan said, "it is the right of the individual, married or single, to be free from unwarranted governmental intrusion into matters so fundamentally affecting a person as the decision whether to bear or beget a child."[186]

Abortion

When twenty-one-year-old Norma McCorvey became pregnant in 1969, she was divorced and already had a five-year-old daughter, and she sought an abortion. But Texas, where she lived, prohibited abortions unless the mother's life was in danger. She discovered, "No legitimate doctor in Dallas would touch me. I found one doctor who offered to abort me for $500. Only he didn't have a license, and I was scared to turn my body over to him. So there I was—pregnant, unmarried, unemployed, alone, and stuck."[187]

Poor and unaware of states that permitted abortions, McCorvey put her baby up for adoption. But the state law rankled her. When she met two women attorneys who recently graduated from law school and who also disliked the law, they offered to take her case to challenge the law. She adopted the name Jane Roe to conceal her identity.

In *Roe v. Wade* in 1973, the Burger Court extended the right to privacy from birth control to abortion.[188] The majority concluded that doctors, theologians, and philosophers cannot agree when life begins. Therefore, judges should not assert that life begins at conception, which would make a fetus a person and abortion murder. Because of the uncertainty as to when life begins, the majority decided that a woman's right to privacy of her body is paramount.

The Court ruled that women can have an abortion during the first six months of pregnancy. States can prohibit an abortion during the last three months. Thus, the right is broad though not absolute.

The justices, as revealed in memos discovered years later, acknowledged that their division of the nine-month term was "legislative," but they saw this as a way to balance the rights of the mother in the early stages of pregnancy with the rights of the fetus in the later stage.[189]

Although *Roe* was not even the lead story on the news when it was decided, it has had an enormous impact on American politics. The Court's ruling invalidated the abortion laws of forty-nine states[190] and increased the abortions performed in the country (see Figure 1). It put abortion on the public agenda, and it

galvanized conservative groups who saw it as a symbol of loosening societal restraints at a time of rampaging social problems. Disparate groups, such as Roman Catholics and evangelical Protestants (and some Orthodox Jews), rural residents and urban ethnics, who rarely saw eye to eye, coalesced around this issue and exercised leverage within the Republican Party.

The right-to-life movement pressured presidents and senators to appoint justices and lower court judges who opposed the ruling. The movement also lobbied members of Congress and state legislatures to overturn or circumvent the ruling. Although Congress refused to pass constitutional amendments banning abortions or allowing states to regulate them, Congress and state legislatures did pass statutes limiting abortions in various ways.

The Burger Court invalidated most of these statutes,[191] but it upheld a major limitation. The Medicaid program, financed jointly by the federal and state governments, had paid for abortions for poor women. As a result, the program had paid for a third of the abortions in the country each year.[192] But Congress eliminated federal funding (except when pregnancy threatens their life or is the result of rape or incest), and most state legislatures eliminated state funding. Consequently, poor women need to pay the entire cost. The Court upheld these laws, ruling that governments have no obligation to finance abortions, even if this means that some women cannot take advantage of their right to have them.[193]

For some women, these laws delay abortions, making them more risky, while the women search for the money. For an estimated 20 percent of the women, these laws deny abortions, because the women cannot obtain the money.[194]

Many people, including many prochoice advocates, support these bans because they dislike welfare spending. Yet, according to an analysis of the states that do provide funding for poor women, the states save money. For every $1 they spend on abortions, they save $4 in welfare (and medical) expenses in what would have been the first two years of the child's life.[195] They save much more over a longer period. Ironically, then, public distaste for welfare spending leads to more welfare spending in this area.

Presidents Reagan and Bush sought justices who opposed *Roe,* and after they filled their fifth vacancy on the Court, prolife advocates expected the Court to overturn it. Yet the Rehnquist Court, while narrowing *Roe,* has not overturned it.[196] In 1992, a bare majority of five justices reaffirmed the right to abortion.[197] At the same time, the majority signaled a willingness to allow more restrictions on the right—as long as the restrictions do not place an "undue burden" on women seeking abortions.

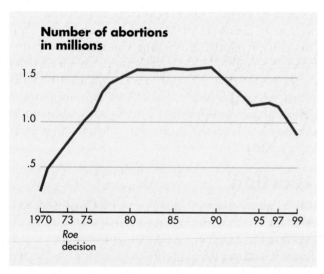

Number of abortions in millions

FIGURE 1 ■ The Number of Abortions Has Declined
The number of abortions in the United States was already increasing before the Supreme Court's Roe decision because some states had liberalized their laws. After the Roe decision, the number increased sharply but leveled off in the 1980s and declined in the 1990s.

Sources: 1970–1972: Susan Hansen, "State Implementation of Supreme Court Decisions: Abortion Rates since *Roe v. Wade,*" *Journal of Politics* 42 (May 1980): 372–395; 1973–1981: Stanley K. Henshaw and Ellen Blaine, *Abortion Services in the United States, Each State, and Metropolitan Area, 1981–1982* (New York: Alan Guttmacher Institute, 1985), 64; 1982–1983: Stanley K. Henshaw, "Characteristics of U.S. Women Having Abortions, 1982–1983," *Family Planning Perspectives* 19 (1987): 6–7; 1984–1985: Stanley K. Henshaw, Jacqueline Darroch Forrest, and Jennifer Van Vort, "Abortion Services in the United States, 1984 and 1985," *Family Planning Perspectives* 19 (1987): 64; 1986–1988: *Abortion Fact Book* (New York: Alan Guttmacher Institute, 1992); "Number of Abortions at Lowest Level since '79," *Lincoln Journal-Star* (June 16, 1994); 1993–1994: Tara Meyer, "Abortion Rate Lowest since 1976 in U.S.," *Lincoln Journal-Star,* (January 4, 1997); "U.S. Abortions Continue Decline," *Lincoln Journal-Star* (January 7, 2000).

Therefore, the majority upheld Pennsylvania's twenty-four-hour waiting period between the time a woman indicates her desire to have an abortion and the time a doctor can perform one. Although a twenty-four-hour waiting period is not a burden for many women, it can be for poor women who live in rural areas and must travel to cities to obtain abortions. One woman in Mississippi hitch-hiked and planned to sleep on outdoor furniture in the K Mart parking lot across the street (until the clinic offered to pay for her motel room).[198]

A waiting period can also affect teenagers. Prolife groups in some cities note the license numbers of cars driven to clinics by teenagers. After looking up the name and address of the family, they inform the parents in the hope that the parents will persuade or pressure the daughter to change her mind during the waiting period. (See the box "Teen Pregnancies and Abortions.")

The majority struck down Pennsylvania's requirement that a married woman notify her husband before having an abortion. This was an undue burden because a

Teen Pregnancies and Abortions

Of American teenagers from fifteen to nineteen, about 10 percent become pregnant, and about 35 percent of these have an abortion. This teen pregnancy rate is higher than that of every other developed country except Russia. The high rate apparently is not because American teens are having more sex but because they are using fewer contraceptives. In European countries, contraceptives are readily available and widely encouraged.

However, the American teenage pregnancy rate has been falling. After peaking in 1990, it has dropped 17 percent since. The primary reason is not abstinence. Delayed onset of sexual activity accounts for a quarter of this decline, whereas increasing use of contraceptives (though still less than in other countries) accounts for three-quarters of the drop.

The teen pregnancy rates of African Americans and Latinos, which are similar, are more than twice that of whites who are not Hispanic. The teen pregnancy rates also vary from region to region and state to state. The rates are highest in the South and Southwest and lowest in the North Central region and Northeast. The conservatism of the South evidently does not prevent teen pregnancies. On the other hand, Massachusetts, one of the most liberal states, has a rate well below average. Perhaps its liberalism fosters greater use of contraceptives.

The states with the highest teen pregnancy rates are

1. Nevada,
2. California,
3. Arizona,
4. Florida, and
5. Texas.

The states with the lowest teen pregnancy rates are

50. North Dakota,
49. Minnesota,
48. Maine,
47. New Hampshire, and
46. Iowa.

The American teen abortion rate is also higher than that of most other developed countries. However, the abortion *rate,* which is the number of abortions per one thousand teens, and the abortion *ratio,* which is the percentage of those teens who get pregnant who have an abortion, have been falling. Since 1986, the abortion ratio has dropped from 46 percent to 35 percent. That is, 46 percent of teens who got pregnant in 1986 had abortions; a decade later just 35 percent did. More gave birth, perhaps because abortions became more restricted, due to state laws requiring parental notification and consent, or less available, due to fewer providers, or perhaps because single

parenthood became less stigmatized. But the decline has occurred only among whites who are not Hispanic.

African Americans have the highest abortion ratio, at 41 percent, while Latinos have the lowest, at 28 percent. Whites who are not Hispanic are in between, at 34 percent.

The teen abortion rates are highest in the most urban states, where abortions are more available. The states with the highest teen abortion rates are

1. New York,
2. Nevada,
3. New Jersey,
4. Maryland, and
5. California.

The states with the lowest teen abortion rates are

50. Utah,
49. North Dakota,
48. South Dakota,
47. West Virginia, and
46. Idaho, Iowa (tied).

For all racial and ethnic groups, older teens (eighteen to nineteen) had more pregnancies and abortions than younger teens (fifteen to seventeen), because the older teens are more sexually active.

SOURCE: Based on statistics for 1996, the most recent year for which data are available, from the Alan Guttmacher Institute, 2000.

woman who fears physical abuse from her husband would be deterred from seeking an abortion. Justice O'Connor said a state "may not give to a man the kind of dominion over his wife that parents exercise over their children."

But the Court upheld some states' requirement that unmarried minors notify their parents before having an abortion and other states' requirement that unmarried minors obtain their parents' consent before having an abortion.[199] For either requirement, if a daughter does not want to tell her parents, she can seek permission from a judge. She must convince the judge that an abortion would be in her best interest or that she is mature enough to make the decision herself. If she is not mature enough, she must become a mother. These laws, Justice Marshall wrote in dissent, force "a young woman in an already dire situation to choose between two fundamentally unacceptable alternatives: notifying a possibly dictatorial or even abusive parent or justifying her profoundly personal decision in an intimidating judicial proceeding to a black-robed stranger."

Prolife groups advocated these laws with the expectation that they would result in fewer abortions. They believed that many teenagers would go to their parents rather than face the forbidding atmosphere of a court hearing and that their parents would persuade or pressure them not to have the abortion. Some evidence indicates that the laws have had this effect.[200]

When teenagers do go to court, they routinely get waivers in some states but not in others. The Nebraska Supreme Court ruled that a fifteen-year-old was too immature to decide to have an abortion, because although she could discuss the consequences of keeping the baby or giving it up for adoption, discuss her philosophy of abortion, and explain the procedures involved, she was unable to explain the risks involved (even though the risks are less than giving birth).[201]

After the Rehnquist Court reaffirmed the right to abortion, prolife groups tried to have one abortion procedure, called "intact dilation and extraction" in medicine but referred to as "partial-birth abortion" in politics, prohibited. In this procedure, a doctor delivers the fetus except for the head, punctures the skull and drains the contents, and then removes the fetus from the woman. The procedure is used occasionally for late-term abortions when other methods might be more dangerous. Because the procedure is gruesome, prolife groups used it to try to sway people who were undecided in the abortion debate. Numerous states passed laws banning the procedure, but the Supreme Court struck down Nebraska's law in 2000.[202] The five-justice majority said the law was too broad—the language might ban other methods as well—and this procedure might be the safest one sometimes.

In recent years, prolife groups have quietly pressed state legislatures to enact extrastringent building codes for abortion clinics. These codes specify such things as the heights of ceilings, widths of hallways and doorways, dimensions of counseling rooms and recovery rooms, rates of air circulation, and the types and angles of jets in drinking fountains. (All states have construction codes for their buildings, but some new laws apply only to abortion clinics.) Some codes require equipment or levels of staffing, such as a registered nurse rather than a licensed practical nurse, beyond what is normally used in these clinics. Although the stated goal is health and safety, the real purpose is to drive up the clinics' expenses so they have to increase their patients' fees to the point where many women can no longer afford to get an abortion.[203] When South Carolina's law, which mandates twenty-seven pages of requirements just for abortion clinics, was challenged, a lower court upheld the law and the Supreme Court refused to hear the case, thus allowing the law to stand.

Despite the dissatisfaction of activists on both sides—prolife groups were disappointed that the conservative Supreme Court upheld the right to abortion, while prochoice groups were critical that it upheld some restrictions on abortion—it is worth noting that the nonelected, nonmajoritarian Supreme Court has come closer to forging a policy reflective of public opinion than most politicians have. Polls show that the public is ambivalent. A majority believes abortion is murder, but a two-thirds majority opposes banning it. This two-thirds majority favors letting women choose. (Over half of those who believe abortion is murder nonetheless favor letting women choose.)[204] Thus, many people support the right to abortion but are uncomfortable with it and presumably willing to permit restrictions on it. The Court's doctrine essentially articulates this position.

But the Court's rulings are not necessarily the final word in this controversy, as they have not been the final word in some other controversies. Frustrated by the Court's refusal to overturn *Roe*, activists in the prolife movement (not most of the prolife supporters) adopted more militant tactics. First they targeted abortion clinics. Organizations such as Operation Rescue engaged in civil disobedience, blockading clinics and harassing workers and patients as they came and went. Some activists sprayed chemicals inside clinics, ruining carpets and fabrics and leaving a stench that made the clinics unusable. Such incidents occurred fifty times in one year alone.[205]

Protesters in Charleston, South Carolina, distributed fliers in the city's poorest neighborhood encouraging residents to rob an abortion clinic: "The killers accept only cash! They kill about 60 babies each week. That is $16,500 of CASH taken to the bank each week. That means that an average of $5,500 is waiting there each day of business in cash before closing hours."[206]

Norma McCorvey, a carnival barker, was used as a tool by prochoice lawyers and then became a symbol fought over by both prochoice and prolife forces.

Young lawyers Sarah Weddington and Linda Coffee were planning to challenge antiabortion laws when they met the pregnant McCorvey, who said she had been gang-raped. She wanted an abortion, and although the lawyers knew how she could get an illegal one, they did not tell her. So she agreed to be the plaintiff in a test case. After signing a one-page affidavit and authorizing the suit, she was not involved or even informed of its progress. When the Supreme Court issued its ruling, she learned about it from newspapers.

She lived in anonymity, partly to protect her privacy and partly to conceal her lie: Her pregnancy had been the result of romance rather than rape. In 1989, feeling proud of her involvement in the landmark case, she decided to go public. As a result, she received hate mail, found baby clothes scattered across her lawn, and was shot at through the window of her home.

Prochoice groups considered her a useful symbol and gave her a job at an abortion clinic in Dallas. But otherwise they ignored her. Yet she had a difficult life and craved more attention. She had been born to an alcoholic parent, sexually abused as a teenager, married at sixteen but deserted soon after, and hooked on drugs. She was "so spiritually needy that she ran through religions as if channel surfing." She said, with dismay, that she could not remember any prochoice representatives calling and asking, "Good morning,

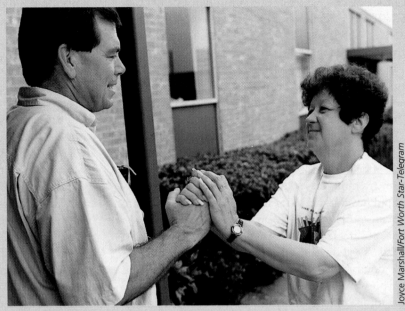

Operation Rescue's Flip Benham moved Norma McCorvey—"Jane Roe"—to his side.

Norma, are you having any trouble in your life?" Indeed, when prochoice groups hosted a twentieth anniversary party for *Roe v. Wade,* they did not bother to invite her.

She felt uncomfortable with the upper-middle-class women who predominated in the movement. "I am a rough woman," she said. "I don't have a degree from Vassar."

When Operation Rescue, a prolife group, moved its headquarters into the same building that housed the abortion clinic where she worked, she called its workers "a pack of whores." But their charismatic leader, Flip Benham, wooed McCorvey, and eventually she warmed to him. "He doesn't make me feel bad about myself," she said.

In 1995, after watching a second-trimester abortion, she quit her job at the abortion clinic and became a volun-

teer for Operation Rescue. She dramatically announced that she was "prolife" (though at the same time said that she favored the right to first-trimester abortions). One activist gleefully remarked, "The poster child has jumped off the poster." So the woman whose case was used to further the prochoice cause is now being used to advance the prolife cause.

McCorvey says she wants to be "a regular person," but she has become too valuable as a public symbol in the abortion debate for that. Both sides, with their eyes on the ambivalent views of the people in the ideological center of the spectrum, want her to help them move these people.

SOURCES: David Van Biema, "An Icon in Search Mode," *Time,* August 21, 1995, 36; Ellen Goodman, "Poster Child for Ambivalence," *Lincoln Journal-Star,* August 17, 1995.

Then activists targeted doctors, nurses, and other workers of the clinics. Operation Rescue ran a training camp in Florida that instructed members how to use public records to locate personal information about employees, how to tail them to their homes, and how to organize demonstrations at their homes. Activists put up "Wanted" posters, with a doctor's picture, name, address, and phone number, and then encouraged people to harass the doctor, his or her spouse, and even their children. (One thirteen-year-old was confronted in a restaurant and told that he was going to burn in hell.)[207] Letters containing powder and threats of death by anthrax were sent to over one hundred doctors and clinics, both before and after anthrax infected people in

2001. (The letters to the doctors and clinics were hoaxes.)[208] Some extremists even came out in favor of killing the doctors. One minister wrote a book—*A Time to Kill*—and marketed a bumper sticker—"EXECUTE ABORTIONISTS-MURDERERS."[209]

In this climate, three doctors, two clinic receptionists, and one clinic volunteer were killed, and seven other doctors, employees, and volunteers were wounded.[210] Numerous clinics were fire-bombed.

The tactics have had their intended effect on doctors.[211] They have made the practice of providing abortions seem dangerous and undesirable. Fewer medical schools offer abortion classes, fewer hospitals provide abortion training, fewer doctors study abortion procedures, and fewer gynecologists and obstetricians, despite most being prochoice, perform abortion operations.[212]

One prolife leader proclaimed, "We've found the weak link is the doctor." Another observed, "When you get the doctors out, you can have all the laws on the books you want and it doesn't mean a thing."[213]

Abortions remain available in most metropolitan centers but not in most rural areas. Eighty-six percent of U.S. counties, with 32 percent of the American women from fifteen to forty-four, have no doctor who performs abortions. Some states have only one, others have only two, cities where women can obtain abortions.[214]

Despite the debate over this issue today, abortion is not likely to fuel such contentious arguments in the future. Expanded use of contraceptives, especially the "morning after pill," undoubtedly will occur. (The morning after pill is considered a contraceptive by the medical profession because it prevents conception/implantation, but it is considered an abortion drug by the Catholic Church because the sperm and egg have already united.) Other pharmaceutical remedies, which actually induce abortions, probably will be accepted because they will seem more like contraceptives than abortions to most people exposed to the pictures of aborted fetuses and the descriptions of grisly procedures. Even when they act like abortions, they will seem akin to contraceptives. Thus, these pills, though feared and opposed by the prolife movement, eventually will defuse the debate over early-term abortions. The debate over middle-term abortions, which are less common, may continue along with secondary arguments over government funding, parental consent, and other issues. The ban on late-term abortions, except when necessary to save the life of the woman, probably will remain.[215]

Homosexuality

The Court has not extended the right to privacy to protect homosexual acts. Thirteen states have laws prohibiting sodomy—oral and anal sex.[216] Although these laws are primarily symbolic and rarely enforced, they can be invoked against either homosexuals or heterosexuals.[217] For example, when police delivered a summons to residents of a house and discovered them violating the law of Georgia, police arrested them. Although prosecutors did not file charges, one of the men sued to have the courts declare the law unconstitutional. In 1986, the Supreme Court, by a one-vote margin, refused to do so.[218]

Justice Louis Powell believed the law was unconstitutional, but after voting against it in conference, he switched before the decision was announced in court because the man had not been prosecuted. After public reaction to the *Roe* ruling, Powell was leery of potential reaction to another controversial ruling, especially when the law might never be enforced. When he retired, however, he admitted he made a mistake.[219]

Although the Court has not extended the right to privacy to homosexual acts, it has struck down laws directed against homosexual individuals. Colorado voters adopted a constitutional amendment prohibiting laws that bar discrimination against homosexuals, but in 1996 the Court invalidated the amendment.[220] The majority said it was based on animus toward homosexuals. They were singled out and denied the opportunity, enjoyed by everyone else, to seek protection from discrimination. The ruling put the brakes on the movement to adopt similar provisions in other states.

Although some state and local legislatures have passed laws barring discrimination in employment, housing, credit, insurance, and public accommodations, Congress, by one vote, rejected a bill in 1996 barring discrimination in employment. At the same time, it passed the Defense of Marriage Act, which forbids federal recognition of same-sex marriages and thus denies federal benefits, such as Social Security, for same-sex

ALL WE WANT IS A MARRIAGE, A MORTGAGE AND MANY YEARS TOGETHER

HELP! IT'S AN ASSAULT ON FAMILY VALUES!!

GAYS

POLS

WASSERMAN © '00 BOSTON GLOBE DIST. BY L.A. TIMES SYNDICATE

couples. The act also allows states to disregard same-sex marriages performed in other states.[221] About thirty states have passed laws to do so.[222] (Under the full faith and credit clause of the Constitution, states normally must recognize the public records and judicial proceedings of other states.) The act was prompted by speculation that some states might approve same-sex marriages, thus allowing homosexual couples to get married in one of these states and then return to their home state as married couples.

Courts in Alaska and Hawaii did rule in favor of same-sex marriages, but their decisions were negated by voters in initiatives to restrict marriages to unions between men and women. However, the Vermont Supreme Court ruled that the state must either legalize same-sex marriages or equalize the benefits received by same-sex couples and traditional married couples. The legislature decided to equalize the benefits, such as family leave, bereavement leave, health insurance, pension benefits, and inheritance rights. To implement this policy, the legislature established "civil unions," with procedures for couples to become official partners (similar to marriage) and procedures for them to dissolve their relationship (similar to divorce). These civil unions provide most of what regular marriages would provide, except the unions do not apply to federal benefits, and, for couples who move from Vermont, the unions do not apply in other states.[223] Also, of course, the unions do not provide the same symbolism that the marriages would. Thus, homosexuals see them as a long stride but not the final step.

Private employers, especially large corporations, have been willing to grant health care packages to same-sex couples as a way of attracting and retaining good workers. Some cities and states also offer these benefits.

Congress also blocked President Clinton's pledge to issue an executive order barring discrimination against homosexuals in the military.[224] Since World War II, the military has rejected recruits who admit to being homosexual and discharged troops who are found to be homosexual. According to the military, having homosexuals in the trenches or on ships undermines the discipline and morale essential for combat.[225] However, when more troops were needed during the Korean, Vietnam, and Persian Gulf Wars, the military did not find this to be such a problem, as it relaxed its policy.[226] And most other democracies do not find this to be such a problem either. Western European countries, Canada, Japan, and Israel, which has a battle-tested military, tolerate homosexuals in their services.[227]

But strident opposition from military officials and members of Congress forced President Clinton to ac-

Steven E. Frischling/Corbis/Sygma

Two women exchange rings in a civil union ceremony in Vermont.

cept a compromise, a policy called "don't ask—don't tell." The military (including the Reserves and National Guard) is not allowed to ask questions about sexual orientation on enlistment or security questionnaires but is allowed to discharge members for statements admitting homosexuality or conduct reflecting homosexuality (or bisexuality). Such conduct is defined broadly to encompass not only sexual actions but also holding hands, dancing, or trying to marry someone of the same sex. The restrictions apply off-base as well as on. They do not encompass reading gay publications, associating with gay people, frequenting gay bars or churches, or marching in gay rights parades.

The policy has not helped much. Many commanders have seemed confused, and some have been unwilling to accept the policy; they continue to ask and pursue. And the debate about the policy called attention to homosexuality, so "everyone from private to general openly speculated about who in their unit might be gay, and as a result there are some people who've had a bull's eye on their back."[228] In fact, more homosexuals have been discharged since the policy went into effect. Female homosexuals have been discharged at a disproportionate rate, perhaps because women in general have not been fully accepted in the services.[229]

Right to Die

The Court has broadened the right to privacy to provide a limited right to die. When Nancy Cruzan's car skidded off an icy road and flipped into a ditch in 1983, doctors were able to save her life but not her brain. She never regained consciousness. She lived in a vegetative state, similar to a coma, and was fed through a tube. Twenty-five at the time of the accident, she was expected to live another thirty years. When her parents asked doctors to remove the tube, the hospital objected and the state of Missouri, despite paying $130,000 a year to support her, also objected. This issue, complicated enough in itself, became entangled in other controversial issues. Prolife groups said denying life support was analogous to abortion; disability groups said that her condition was merely a disability and that withholding food and water from her would lead to withholding treatment from other people with disabilities.[230]

In this case, the Rehnquist Court established a limited right to die.[231] The justices ruled that individuals can refuse medical treatment, including food and water, even if this means they will die. But states can require individuals to make their decision while competent and alert. (Presumably, individuals can also prepare a "living will" or designate another person as a proxy to make the decision in the event that they are unable to.)

Several months after the Court's decision, Cruzan's parents returned to a Missouri court with evidence that their daughter would prefer death to being kept alive by medical machines. Three of Cruzan's former coworkers testified that they recalled conversations in which she said she never would want to live "like a vegetable." Her parents asked for permission to remove her feeding tube, and the court agreed. She died twelve days later.

Although the legal doctrine seems clear, practical problems persist. Many people do not indicate their decision. Approximately ten thousand people in irreversible comas now did not indicate their decision beforehand.[232] Some people who do indicate their decision beforehand waver when they face death. Some doctors, who are in the habit of prolonging life even when their patients have little chance of recovering or of enjoying life, resist their decision. The doctors try to persuade the patients or their families not to "pull the plug."[233]

The Rehnquist Court has resisted patients' pleas to extend the limited right to die to encompass a broader right to obtain assistance in committing suicide.[234] Thus, the Court has drawn a distinction between stopping treatment and assisting suicide; individuals have a right to demand the former but not the latter. The justices seemed tentative, as is typical with an issue new to the courts. Chief Justice Rehnquist emphasized, "Our holding permits this debate to continue, as it should in a democratic society." Under the Court's doctrine, states can prohibit assisted suicide, as the majority have done, or they can allow it, as Oregon has done. Yet the prolife Bush administration has challenged Oregon's law in court, claiming that states cannot allow assisted suicide.

A majority of the public favors a right to assisted suicide,[235] but conservative religious groups oppose one. They insist that people should not take a life. Some ethicists worry that patients will be pressured to give up their life because of the costs, to their family or health care provider, of continuing it. Thus, they fear that a right will become a duty.

Meanwhile, the practice, even where officially illegal, is widely condoned, much as abortion was before *Roe.* Almost a fifth of doctors who treat cancer patients in Michigan admitted in a survey that they have assisted suicide, and over half of two thousand doctors who treat AIDS patients in San Francisco also admitted that they have done so.[236]

Conclusion: Are the Courts Responsive in Interpreting Civil Liberties?

The Supreme Court has interpreted the Constitution to provide many important civil liberties. The Warren Court in the 1950s and 1960s expanded civil liberties more than any other Court in history. It applied many provisions of the Bill of Rights to the states. It substantially broadened rights in the areas of speech, libel, obscenity, and religion. It enormously broadened rights of criminal defendants in the areas of search and seizure, self-incrimination, counsel, and jury trial. And it established a right to privacy.

Observers predicted the Burger Court would lead a constitutional counterrevolution. However, it did not. The Burger Court in the 1970s and 1980s narrowed rights in some areas, especially for criminal defendants. But the Court accepted the core of the Warren Court's doctrine and, in fact, even extended the right to privacy.

Nor has the Rehnquist Court produced a constitutional counterrevolution. It, too, has narrowed rights in some areas, but it also has accepted most of the Warren Court's doctrine.

The decisions of these Courts show the extent to which the Supreme Court is responsive to the people in civil liberties cases. The majority of the people support civil liberties in general but not necessarily in specific situations. Elites support civil liberties more than the masses. As the Court has expanded civil liberties, it has not been very responsive to the majority. But it has been more responsive to elites, and it has been very responsive to minorities.

When the Supreme Court has upheld civil liberties, it has fulfilled what many legal scholars consider "the quintessential role" of the highest court in a democracy—"to vindicate the constitutional rights of minorities, of dissidents, of the unrepresented, of the disenfranchised, of the unpopular." The other branches of government, whose officials are elected every two, four, or six years, are sensitive to the needs of "the majority, the politically powerful, the economically influential, and the socially popular."[237]

Because the Court was not intended to be very responsive to the majority, it was given substantial independence. Therefore, it does not have to mirror public opinion, although it cannot ignore this opinion, either. It must stay within the broad limits of this opinion, or it will be pulled back. Thus, the Warren Court went too far too fast for too many people. It produced a backlash that led to the Burger and Rehnquist Courts, which have been more responsive to majority opinion. At the same time, they have been less vigilant in protecting civil liberties.

EPILOGUE

The Court Allows the Boy Scouts to Discriminate against Homosexuals

By a 5–4 vote, the Supreme Court ruled that the Boy Scouts can expel and exclude homosexuals.[238] For the majority, Chief Justice Rehnquist held that the Boy Scouts is an expressive organization. He accepted its assertion that opposition to homosexuality is one of the values it expresses. He assumed that the inclusion of Dale, as an openly gay assistant scoutmaster, would undermine that value, even though there was no evidence that Dale had discussed or promoted his orientation to his troop or even evidence that families with boys in the troop had been aware of his orientation.

The majority relied on the precedent involving the St. Patrick's Day parade, which allowed parade organizers to bar gays, lesbians, and bisexuals from participating and displaying their banner, rather than the precedents forbidding the Jaycees and the Rotary Club, to bar women from joining.

Thus, the majority concluded that the Boy Scouts' right to freedom of association is more important than homosexuals' right to freedom from discrimination and more important than states' interest in limiting such discrimination. That is, the majority concluded that

there was no compelling interest in limiting antigay discrimination.

The dissenters, including Justice Stevens, agreed that the Boy Scouts, like other organizations engaged in expressive activity, can hold whatever views they want and can bar persons with contrary views. But the dissenters questioned whether the Boy Scouts actually opposes homosexuality as one of the values it expresses. Justice Stevens concluded that the commands to be "morally straight" and "clean" do not say "the slightest thing about homosexuality." He concluded that opposition to homosexuality did not become policy until after Dale was kicked out, and then only because the organization worried about the reaction of the families of Boy Scouts if it became known that gays were tolerated. The result of the Court's decision, Stevens observed, was to transform "the right to associate into a free pass out of antidiscrimination law." It creates "a constitutional shield for a policy that is . . . the product of a habitual way of thinking about strangers."

Instead, the dissenters argued, the scouts could tolerate homosexuals but forbid them, as well as heterosexuals, from discussing their sexuality during scout activities. Al-

At the time of the Supreme Court case, James Dale was the advertising director of an AIDS magazine.

ready scout rules urge scoutmasters to avoid addressing sex, religion, and politics. They are to leave these to families. Thus, the organization could discipline homosexual leaders for violating these rules just as it can discipline other leaders for fostering their religious or political views.

With competing rights—freedom of association and freedom from discrimination—at stake, there is no inherently conservative or liberal position. Both provide individual rights and group rights. But with homosexuality involved, the dispute becomes a struggle between conservatism and liberalism, between the status quo and change. In this climate, the Rehnquist Court, as a conservative court, sided with the conservative position on homosexuality and with the established institution of the Boy Scouts.

 To learn more about the controversy over homosexuals and the Boy Scouts, go to this chapter's "You Are There" exercises on the text Web site.

Key Terms

freedom of association

bills of attainder

ex post facto laws

First Amendment

freedom of speech

seditious speech

McCarthyism

public forum

pure speech

speech plus conduct

symbolic speech

prior restraint

libel

obscenity

separation of church and
  state

free exercise clause

establishment clause

due process

presumption of innocence

unreasonable searches and
  seizures

Second Amendment

exclusionary rule

Miranda rights

right to counsel

right to a jury trial

cruel and unusual
  punishment

plea bargain

right to privacy

Further Reading

Dan T. Carter, *Scottsboro: A Tragedy of the American South* (Baton Rouge: Louisiana State University Press, 1979). An examination of the infamous Scottsboro, Alabama, rape case that prompted the Supreme Court to begin to provide counsel to poor defendants.

Fred W. Friendly, *Minnesota Rag* (New York: Random House, 1981). A lively chronicle of the Court's first important freedom of the press case—*Near v. Minnesota* in 1927.

David J. Garrow, *Liberty and Sexuality: The Right to Privacy and the Making of* Roe v. Wade (New York: Macmillan, 1994). An exhaustive account of the hard road to *Roe*.

Franz Kafka, *The Trial* (numerous editions, 1937). One of the great novels of the twentieth century, which shows, perhaps more dramatically than anything else written, what life without due process rights would be like.

James Kirby, *Fumble: Bear Bryant, Wally Butts, and the Great College Football Scandal* (New York: Dell, 1986). Law for football fans—the story of the libel suit against a national magazine for writing that the coach of Alabama and athletic director of Georgia fixed a football game

between the two schools. The author, a lawyer, was hired by the Southeastern Conference to determine what really happened in the dispute.

Anthony Lewis, *Gideon's Trumpet* (New York: Vintage, 1964). A wonderful account of Clarence Earl Gideon's suit and the Court's landmark decision.

Patricia G. Miller, *The Worst of Times* (New York: Harper-Collins, 1992). Recollections of women who had abortions before *Roe* made them legal and interviews with abortionists, doctors, and police who witnessed the effects.

Helen Prejean, *Dead Men Walking* (New York: Vintage, 1993). An account, from the front lines, of capital punishment in the United States.

Electronic Resources

w3.trib.com/FACT/

A home page for the First Amendment, sponsored by the Casper, Wyoming, Star-Tribune, and winner of a national award for best online newspaper services. Links to First Amendment issues and to Supreme Court decisions.

www.perkinscoie.com

A site maintained by a law firm, featuring the latest cases involving Internet legal issues.

www.aclu.org/index.html

The home page of the American Civil Liberties Union, the foremost group dedicated to protecting civil liberties through legal and political action. Links to information and position papers on many issues covered in this chapter.

www.loc.gov/exhibits/religion

The role of religion in the founding of the country, by the Library of Congress.

www.naral.org and **www.prolifeinfo.org**

The first site is the home page of the National Abortion Rights Action League, a prochoice group, and the second site is a link to prolife groups.

InfoTrac College Edition

Search for the following articles in the InfoTrac database:

Lewis, Penney. "Rights Discourse and Assisted Suicide," *American Journal of Law & Medicine* (Spring 2001).

Loconte, Joe. "Lead Us Not into Temptation: A Christian Case against School Prayer," *Policy Review* (Winter 1995).

O'Neil, Robert M. "Rights in Conflict: The First Amendment's Third Century," *Law and Contemporary Problems* (Spring 2002).

Radelet, Michael L., and Ronald L. Akers. "Deterrence and the Death Penalty: The Views of the Experts," *Journal of Criminal Law and Criminology* (Fall 1996).

For more articles, enter

"Prayer in public schools" in the Subject Guide;

"Assisted suicide" in the Subject Guide;

"Capital punishment" in the Subject Guide;

"Gay liberation movement" in the Subject Guide.

 American Government Resources

Visit the Government Foundations section of the Wadsworth American Government Resources Web site (politicalscience.wadsworth.com/amgov/) for a variety of tools to help you explore civil liberties further. Included are simulations, video clips, Microcase exercises, and a wealth of other activities.

CHAPTER 15

CIVIL RIGHTS

The civil rights movement led to the integration of some communities, such as this suburb in New Jersey.

Justine Parsons

Friend or Foe?

Y ou are Justice William Douglas of the Supreme Court facing a decision in the case of **Korematsu v. United States.** Fred Korematsu, a Japanese American, was born and raised in California. He was working as a welder when Japan bombed Pearl Harbor and forced the United States into World War II. As an American citizen, he tried to enlist in the army but was rejected because of ulcers. A few months later, President Franklin Roosevelt, under pressure from West Coast politicians and newspapers, issued an executive order, which Congress ratified, that allowed the secretary of war to exclude persons of Japanese ancestry from the three West Coast states and part of Arizona to prevent espionage and sabotage. Under the order, persons of Japanese ancestry were required to report to assembly centers—often fairgrounds, racetracks, or stockyards, from which the animals had been removed just days before. Then, allowed to take only what possessions they could carry, they were relocated to camps in deserts and swamps farther inland, presumably for the duration of the war. Enclosed by barbed wire and patrolled by armed guards, these camps resembled prisoner-of-war camps.

Korematsu did not leave with the others. He had fallen in love with an Italian American woman, and they planned to marry. He had un-

dergone plastic surgery to appear Spanish Hawaiian instead of Japanese. But the surgery was not successful, and while walking down the street in his hometown, he was identified and arrested for violating the order. At trial he was convicted, and on appeal his conviction was upheld. On further appeal, his case has reached the Supreme Court.

The government claims the order is justified. Although officials do not expect an invasion of the West Coast, they do fear espionage and sabotage. Before the war, some Japanese Americans supported Japan's efforts to expand its territory in Asia. Some contributed money, tinfoil, and scrap metal, while a few formed an espionage ring. Intelligence officials crushed the ring but now fear renewed attempts. Already Japanese submarines have attacked American merchant ships off our coast, sinking two and damaging another. Officials speculate that Japanese Americans were signaling Japanese ships. (The *Los Angeles Times* even reported that Japanese American farmers were guiding Japanese pilots to their targets: "Caps on Japanese Tomato Plants Point to Air Base."[1])

Officials question Japanese Americans' loyalty. Most, born here, are U.S. citizens, but they have been granted citizenship by Japan also because of their ancestry. And they have formed semiclosed communities and adhered to Old World cultural patterns. The army general in charge of evacuation expressed the prevalent attitude toward them: "There isn't such a thing as a loyal Japanese."[2]

Many groups characterized the Japanese as rats. Some West Coast restaurants have placed signs in their windows: "This Restaurant Poisons Both Rats and Japs." Some West Coast drivers have put stickers picturing a rat with a Japanese face on their cars. A patriotic parade in New York City included a float the crowd reportedly "loved"—an eagle leading a squadron of American bombers toward a herd of yellow rats trying to escape.[3]

Korematsu claims the order discriminates against him on the basis of his race and thereby violates his Fifth Amendment right to due process of the law. As evidence, he notes that the order does not apply to persons of German or Italian ancestry. (Although the order was general, the military commander was told not to remove the many persons of Italian descent on the West Coast. The mayor of San Francisco was Italian, and baseball star Joe DiMaggio, whose parents were aliens, was a national idol.) Anyway, President Roosevelt said he was not worried about the Italians. "They are a lot of opera singers."[4]

Korematsu also notes that there has been widespread discrimination against Asians on the West Coast. For decades there has been talk of the "yellow peril." In 1913 Congress refused to allow more Japanese to become citizens and in 1924 refused to allow more to immigrate. The discrimination has resulted in segregated neighborhoods and schools and, in at least one city—Bakersfield—even the omission of their names from the telephone directory.

The hostility has fueled efforts to drive Japanese Americans off their productive farmland. Many Japanese, brought over as cheap laborers, worked hard enough to become successful owners. At the outbreak of the war, according to some estimates, they grew about half the fruits and vegetables in California, and an acre of their land was worth more than seven times the average value of an

Courtesy of Franklin D. Roosevelt Library, NLR-PHOCO-A-7420 (394)

A Japanese American family with the belongings it was allowed to take to the relocation camp.

acre of farmland on the coast. Competitors covet their land.

You are torn. You were appointed by President Roosevelt, yet you are strongly committed to individual rights. What do you decide?

Civil rights refer to equality of rights for persons regardless of their race, sex, or ethnic background. The Declaration of Independence proclaimed that "all men are created equal." The author, Thomas Jefferson, knew that all men were not created equal in many respects, but he sought to emphasize that they should be considered equal in rights and equal before the law. This represented a break with Great Britain where rigid classes with unequal rights existed; nobles had more rights than commoners. The Declaration's promise did not include nonwhites or women, however. Thus, although colonial Americans advocated equality, they envisioned it only for white men. Others gradually gained more equality, but the Declaration's promise remains unfulfilled for some.

Race Discrimination

African Americans, Hispanics, and Native Americans all have endured and continue to face much discrimination.

Discrimination against African Americans

Slavery

The first blacks came to America in 1619, just twelve years after the first whites. The blacks, like many whites, initially came as indentured servants. In exchange for passage across the ocean, they were bound to an employer, usually for four to seven years, and then freed. But later in the seventeenth century, the colonies passed laws requiring blacks and their children to be slaves for life.

Once slavery was established, the slave trade flourished, especially in the South. But slavery was also common in the North. There were large plantations in Connecticut, Massachusetts, and Rhode Island, which shipped agricultural products to the West Indies in exchange for molasses used to make rum. (Newport, Rhode Island, had more than thirty distilleries.) There were also slaves in the cities. In the middle 1700s, New York City had more than any city in the colonies except

Charleston. After the middle 1700s, most northern slaves were freed. By the time of the Constitutional Convention, there were sharp differences between northerners and southerners in their attitudes toward slavery.

As a result of compromises between northern and southern states, the Constitution accepted slavery. It allowed the importation of slaves until 1808, when Congress could bar further importation, and it required the return of escaped slaves to their owners.

Shortly after ratification of the Constitution, northern states officially abolished slavery. In 1808, Congress barred the importation of slaves but did not halt the practice of slavery in the South. Slavery became increasingly controversial, and abolitionists called for its end. Southerners began to question the Declaration of Independence and to repudiate its notion of natural rights. They attributed this idea to Jefferson's "radicalism."[5]

The Supreme Court tried to quell the antislavery sentiment in the **Dred Scott case** in 1857.[6] Dred Scott, a slave who lived in Missouri, was taken by his owner to the free state of Illinois and the free territory of Wisconsin and, after five years, was returned to Missouri. The owner died and passed title to his wife, who moved but left Scott in the care of people in Missouri. They opposed slavery and arranged to have Scott sue his owner for his freedom. They argued that Scott's time in a free state and a free territory made him a free man even though he was brought back to a slave state. The owner, who also opposed slavery, had the authority to free Scott, so the purpose of the suit was not to win his freedom. Rather, she and others sought a major court decision to keep slavery out of the territories.

In this infamous case, Chief Justice Roger Taney stated that no blacks, whether slave or free, were citizens and that they were "so far inferior that they had no rights which the white man was bound to respect." Taney could have stopped here—if Scott was not a citizen, he could not sue in federal court—but Taney continued. He declared that Congress had no power to control slavery in the territories. This meant that slavery could extend into the territories Congress already had declared free. It also raised the possibility that states could not control slavery within their borders.[7]

By this time, slavery had become the hottest controversy in American politics, and this decision fanned the flames. It provoked vehement opposition in the North and prompted further polarization, which eventually led to the Civil War.[8] Meanwhile, Scott got his freedom from his owner.

The North's victory in the Civil War gave force to President Lincoln's Emancipation Proclamation ending slavery.[9] But blacks would find short-lived solace.

Reconstruction

After the war, Congress passed and the states ratified three constitutional amendments. The Thirteenth prohibited slavery. (Mississippi became the last state to ratify the amendment—in 1995—but of course the ratification was only of symbolic value by then.) The Fourteenth granted citizenship to blacks, thus overruling the Dred Scott decision, and also granted "equal protection of the laws" and "due process of law." The **equal protection clause** eventually would become the primary guarantee that government would treat people equally. The Fifteenth provided the right to vote for black men.

These amendments not only provided specific rights for blacks but also transformed the relationship between the federal and state governments. Each amendment included a stipulation that "Congress shall have power to enforce" the provisions of the amendment. This stipulation granted the federal government new power—whatever power was necessary to guarantee these rights. This new power stands in marked contrast with the original understanding of the Founders that the federal government would have limited power. The Civil War and these amendments together thus constituted a constitutional revolution, as explained in Chapter 2.[10] This transformation was intentional; Congress did not trust southern states to enforce constitutional provisions they had just fought a war against.

Congress also passed a series of Civil Rights Acts to reverse the "Black Codes" that southern states had enacted to deny the newly freed slaves legal rights. These Civil Rights Acts allowed blacks to buy, own, and sell property; to make contracts; to sue; and to be witnesses and jurors in court. They also allowed blacks to use public transportation, such as railroads and steamboats, and to patronize hotels and theaters.[11]

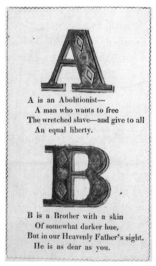

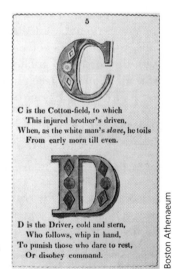

A is an Abolitionist—
A man who wants to free
The wretched slave—and give to all
An equal liberty.

B is a Brother with a skin
Of somewhat darker hue,
But in our Heavenly Father's sight,
He is as dear as you.

C is the Cotton-field, to which
This injured brother's driven,
When, as the white man's *slave*, he toils
From early morn till even.

D is the Driver, cold and stern,
Who follows, whip in hand,
To punish those who dare to rest,
Or disobey command.

Slavery became a polarizing issue years before the Civil War. The Anti-Slavery Alphabet, *a children's book, was first published in 1847.*

Boston Athenaeum

BLACK MASTERS

Although most slave owners were white, some were black. William Ellison of South Carolina was one. Born a slave, he bought his freedom and then his family's by building and repairing cotton gins. Over time he earned enough to buy slaves and operate a plantation. With sixty slaves, Ellison ranked in the top 1 percent of all slaveholders, black or white.

Ellison was unusual, but he was not unique. In Charleston, South Carolina, alone, more than one hundred African Americans owned slaves in 1860. Most, however, owned fewer than four.

Although part of the slave-owning class, black slaveholders were not much more acceptable to whites. Ellison's family was granted a pew on the main floor of the local Episcopal church, but they had to be on guard at all times. Failure to maintain the norms of black–white relations—acting deferentially—could mean instant punishment. And as the Civil War approached, whites trying to preserve the established order increasingly viewed free blacks, even slaveholders, as a threat. Harsher legislation regulated their lives. For example, they had to have a white "guardian" to vouch for their character, and they had to carry special papers to show their free status. Without these papers, they could be sold back into slavery.

Some black slaveholders showed little sign that they shared the concerns of black slaves. Indeed, Ellison freed none of his slaves.

SOURCE: Michael Johnson and James L. Roark, *Black Masters* (New York: Norton, 1984).

Even so, most freed blacks faced bleak conditions. Congress rejected proposals to break up plantations and give former slaves "forty acres and a mule" or to provide aid to establish schools. Without land or education, they had to work for their former masters as hired hands or sharecroppers. Their status was not much better than it had been. Landowners designed a system to keep the former slaves dependent. They allowed sharecroppers to sell half their crop and keep the proceeds, but they paid so little, regardless of how hard the farmers worked, that the families had to borrow to tide them over the winter. The next year they had to work for the landowner to pay off their debt. The following year the cycle continued. And, lacking education, most sharecroppers did not keep records of how much they owed and how much the landowner owed them, and many were cheated.

During the period of Reconstruction, the Union army enforced the new amendments and acts. While the army occupied the South, military commanders established procedures to register voters, including the newly freed slaves; hold elections; and ratify the Fourteenth Amendment. The commanders also started schools for children of the newly freed slaves. But in state after state, the South resisted, and eventually the North capitulated. After a decade, the two regions struck a deal to end what was left of Reconstruction. The 1876 presidential election between Republican Rutherford Hayes and Democrat Samuel Tilden was disputed in some states. To resolve the dispute, Republicans, most of whom were northerners, and Democrats, many of whom were southerners, agreed to a compromise: Hayes would be named president, and the remaining Union troops would be removed from the South.

In hindsight, it should not be a surprise that Reconstruction did not accomplish more. It was not easy to integrate 4 million former slaves into a southern society that was bitter in its defeat and weak in its economy. Northern citizens who expected progress to come smoothly were naive. When it did not come quickly, they became disillusioned. At the same time, there was a desire for healing between the two regions and lingering feelings for continuity with the past.

However understandable, public attitudes during Reconstruction thus began a recurring cycle that continues to this day: The public gets upset about the treatment of African Americans and supports some efforts to improve conditions. But the public is naive, and when the efforts do not immediately produce the expected results, the public becomes disillusioned and dissatisfied with the costs. The public's lack of patience then forces officials to put the race problem on the back burner for some future generation to handle.[12]

Segregation

In both the South and the North, blacks came to be segregated from whites.

Segregation in the South The reconciliation between Republicans and Democrats—northerners and southerners—was effected at the expense of blacks. Removing the troops enabled the South to govern itself again, and this enabled the South to reduce blacks to near-slave status.

Before the Civil War, slavery itself had kept blacks down, and segregation would have been inconvenient when blacks and whites needed to live and work near each other. There was no residential segregation—not in rural areas, where former slaves' shacks were intermixed with plantation houses, and not in urban areas, where few blocks were solidly black. But after slavery, southerners established segregation as another way to keep blacks down. Initially, they did so haphazardly—one law here, another there. By the early 1900s, however, there was a pervasive pattern of **Jim Crow laws**.[13]

Jim Crow laws segregated just about everything. Some segregated blocks within neighborhoods, others neighborhoods within cities. Laws in some small towns excluded blacks altogether. Some did so explicitly; others simply established curfews that required blacks to be off the streets by 10 P.M. Laws also segregated schools, which blacks had been allowed to attend during Reconstruction, and even textbooks (black schools' texts had to be stored separately from white schools' books). Many laws segregated public accommodations, such as hotels, restaurants, bars, and transportation. At first the laws required the races to sit in separate sections of streetcars; eventually, they required them to sit in separate cars; finally, they also forced them to sit in separate sections of waiting rooms. Other laws segregated parks, sporting events, and circuses. Laws segregated black and white checkers players in Birmingham and established districts for black and white prostitutes in New Orleans. They segregated drinking fountains, restrooms, ticket windows, entrances, and exits. They segregated the races in prisons, hospitals, and homes for the blind. They even segregated the races in death—in morgues, funeral homes, and cemeteries.

The harm from segregation was not primarily that blacks were denied access to better facilities or locations, though they were, but that they were degraded. The system of Jim Crow laws was "an officially organized degradation ceremony, repeated day after day." Segregation told blacks that they were inferior and that they did not belong in the community where they lived.[14]

Blacks were forced to defer to whites in all informal settings as well, and failure to do so could mean punishment or even death. Blacks were "humiliated by a thousand daily reminders of their subordination."[15]

Meanwhile, northern leaders, who had championed the cause of the slaves before and during the Civil War, abandoned blacks a decade after the war; Congress did not pass new laws, presidents did not enforce existing laws, and the Supreme Court gutted the constitutional amendments and Civil Rights Acts.

The Supreme Court struck down the Civil Rights Act allowing blacks to use public accommodations, including transportation, hotels, and theaters.[16] Where the Fourteenth Amendment said that "no state" shall deny equal protection, the Court interpreted this to mean that "no government" shall, but private individuals—

owners of transportation, hotels, and theaters—could. The Court's interpretation might seem plausible, but it was clearly contrary to Congress's intent.[17]

Then the Court upheld segregation itself. Louisiana passed "an Act to promote the comfort of passengers," which mandated separate accommodations in trains. New Orleans black leaders sponsored a case to test the act's constitutionality. Homer Adolph Plessy bought a ticket and sat in the white car. When the conductor ordered him to move to the black car, Plessy refused. He maintained that the act was unconstitutional under the Fourteenth Amendment. In *Plessy v. Ferguson* in 1896, the Court disagreed, claiming that the act was not a denial of equal protection because it provided equal accommodations.[18] Thus, the Court established the **separate-but-equal doctrine,** which allowed separate facilities if they were equal. Of course, government required separate facilities only because it thought the races were not equal, but the Court brazenly commented that the act did not stamp "the colored race with a badge of inferiority" unless "the colored race chooses to put that construction on it." Only Justice John Harlan, a former Kentucky slaveholder, dissented: "Our Constitution is color-blind, and neither knows nor tolerates classes among citizens."

Three years later, the Court accepted segregation in schools.[19] A Georgia school board turned a black high school into a black elementary school. Although the board did not establish a new high school for blacks or allow them to attend the ones for whites, the Court did not object. This set a pattern in which separate but equal meant separation but not equality.

Segregation in the North Although Jim Crow laws were not as pervasive in the North as in the South, northerners imitated southerners to the point where one writer proclaimed, "The North has surrendered!"[20]

Job opportunities were better in the North. Southern blacks were sharecropping—by 1930, 80 percent of those who farmed were still working somebody else's land[21]—and northern factories were offering jobs. Between 1915 and 1940, more than a million southern blacks headed north in the "Great Migration." But they were forced to live in black ghettos because they could not afford better housing and because they could not escape discrimination in the North, either.

Denial of the Right to Vote

With the adoption of the Fifteenth Amendment, many African Americans voted and elected fellow African Americans to office during Reconstruction, but southern states began to disfranchise them in the 1890s (as explained in Chapter 8). Thus, they were unable to elect black representatives or even pressure white officials to oppose segregation.

Violence

To solidify their control, whites engaged in violence against blacks. In the 1880s and 1890s, whites lynched about one hundred blacks a year. In the 1900s, vigilante "justice" continued (Table 1). For example, a mob in Livermore, Kentucky, dragged a black man accused of murdering a white man into a theater. The ringleaders charged admission and hanged the man. Then they permitted the audience to shoot at the swinging body— those in the balcony could fire once; those in the better seats could empty their revolvers.[22]

Lynchings often began with a false report of a white woman being sexually assaulted by a black man. Then a mob would gather and force the hapless man to endure a humiliating and excruciating ordeal. Usually they tortured him before killing him. The mob routinely castrated him, often before lynching him, and frequently hacked off his fingers and ears as well.[23]

Lynchings were not the result of a few troublemakers but were a social institution in the southern society. The ritualized spectacles were used to cling to the antebellum order that had been upset by the Civil War. Lynchings also were related to the increase in white women who worked outside the home at the turn of the century. As women experienced greater independence, insecure men evidently feared that the women would leave them for black men. Hence the ritual of castration.[24]

In 1919, twenty-five race riots erupted in six months. White mobs took over cities in the North and South, burning black neighborhoods and terrorizing black residents for days on end.[25]

In 1921, ten thousand whites burned down thirty-five blocks of Tulsa's black neighborhood. The incident that precipitated the riot was typical—a report of an assault by a black man on a white woman. The report was false, fabricated by the woman (and later retracted), but

TABLE 1 Why Whites Lynched Blacks in 1907	
Whites gave the following reasons for lynching blacks, who may or may not have committed these acts.	
Reason	**Number**
Murder	5
Attempted murder	5
Manslaughter	10
Rape	9
Attempted rape	11
Burglary	3
Harboring a fugitive	1
Theft of 75¢	1
Having a debt of $3	2
Being a victor over white man in fight	1
Insulting white man	1
Talking to white girls on telephone	1
Being wife or son of rapist	2
Being father of boy who "jostled" white women	1
Expressing sympathy for victim of mob	3
	56

SOURCE: Adapted from Ray Stannard Baker, *Following the Color Line* (New York: Harper & Row, 1964), 176–177.

residents were inflamed by a racist newspaper and encouraged by the city's officials. Up to three hundred people were shot, burned alive, or tied to cars and dragged to death. Survivors reported corpses stacked like firewood on street corners and piled high in dump trucks.[26]

Sometimes the violence was intended to drive black families off their land. In addition to lynchings and burnings, bands of white farmers known as Whitecaps nailed notes, with a drawing of a coffin and a warning to leave or die, on the doors of black farmers. Then the cities or counties put the land up for auction or simply

Tulsa's black neighborhood after whites burned it down in 1921.

gave it to white families who owned adjacent land.[27] This process affected not only the black families at the time but their descendents for many generations. The black families lost wealth that is accumulating value for the white owners today, many of whom may be unaware of how the land changed hands.

The Ku Klux Klan, which began during Reconstruction and started up again in 1915, played a major role in inflaming prejudice and terrorizing blacks. It was strong enough to dominate many southern towns and even the state governments of Oklahoma and Texas. It also made inroads into some northern states such as Indiana.

Federal officials said such violence was a state problem—presidents refused to speak out, and Congress refused to pass legislation making lynching a federal offense—yet state officials did nothing.

For at least the first third of the twentieth century, white supremacy reigned—in the southern states, the border states, and many of the northern states. It also pervaded the nation's capital, where President Woodrow Wilson instituted segregation in the federal government.[28] (See also the box "Passing the 'Paper Bag Test.'")

Lynching occurred not only in the South but also in northern cities such as Marion, Indiana, in 1930. The girls on the left hold pieces of the victims' clothing, torn off as "souvenirs."

Overcoming Discrimination against African Americans

African Americans fought white supremacy primarily in three arenas: the courts, the streets, and Congress. In general, they fought in the courts first and Congress last, although as they gained momentum they increasingly fought in all three arenas at once.

The Movement in the Courts

The first strategy was to convince the Supreme Court to overturn the separate-but-equal doctrine of *Plessy v. Ferguson*.

The NAACP In response to white violence, a group of blacks and whites founded the **NAACP,** the National Association for the Advancement of Colored People, in 1909. In its first two decades, it was led by W. E. B. DuBois, a black sociologist. In time it became the major organization fighting for blacks' civil rights.

Frustrated by presidential and congressional inaction and its own lack of power to force action, the NAACP decided to converge on the federal courts, which were less subject to pressures from the majority. The association assembled a cadre of lawyers, mainly from Howard University Law School, a black university in Washington, D.C., to bring lawsuits attacking segregation and the denial of the right to vote. In 1915, they persuaded the Supreme Court to strike down the grandfather clause (which exempted persons whose ancestors could vote from the literacy test);[29] two years later, they convinced the Court to invalidate laws prescribing residential seg-regation.[30] But the Court continued to allow most devices to disfranchise blacks and most efforts to segregate.

In 1938, the NAACP chose a thirty-year-old attorney, Thurgood Marshall, to head its litigation arm.[31] Marshall, whose mother had to pawn her engagement and wedding rings so he could go to an out-of-state law school because his in-state school—the University of Maryland—did not admit blacks, would become a tireless and courageous advocate for equal rights. (In 1946, after defending four blacks charged with attempted murder during a riot in rural Tennessee, he would narrowly escape a lynch mob.)[32] In the next two decades, presidents appointed more liberals to the Supreme Court. These two developments led to the NAACP's success in the courts.

Desegregation of Schools Seventeen states and the District of Columbia segregated their schools (and four other states allowed it by local option). The states gave white students better facilities and paid white teachers more. Overall, they spent from two to ten times more on white schools than on black ones.[33] Few of these states had graduate schools for blacks: As late as 1950, they had fifteen engineering schools, fourteen medical schools, and five dental schools for whites and none for blacks; they had sixteen law schools for whites and five for blacks.

The NAACP's tactics were first to show that "separate but equal" really resulted in unequal schools and then to attack "separate but equal" head-on, arguing that it led to unequal status.

The NAACP began by challenging segregation in graduate schools. Missouri provided no black law school

Passing the "Paper Bag Test"

Whites' preoccupation with skin color affected blacks even in their relationships with other blacks. In the early twentieth century, African Americans who wanted to join certain African American clubs and churches had to pass the "paper bag test." They had to put their hand into a paper bag to see whether their hand was lighter than the brown bag. If so, they were eligible for membership. A social club in Nashville had a similar test. Aspiring members had to demonstrate that their blue veins showed through their pale skin on the inside of their wrists.

This concern for lighter skin stemmed from the slavery era, when light-skinned blacks often brought higher prices and got better jobs as household workers than as field hands. After emancipation, lighter skin continued to be a social and economic advantage. Many blacks with darker skin used bleach, lye, or other products to lighten their color.

Although black colleges did not restrict admission to African Americans with lighter skin, in the 1930s most of their students did have lighter skin. They were the children of doctors, dentists, lawyers, and morticians, who themselves had lighter skin and were more successful in their community. They were predominant among African Americans who could afford to send their children to college in those years. At college, their children took up whites' pastimes such as cotillions and tennis, in an attempt to distinguish themselves from poor blacks and to gain acceptance from whites. (But ac-

Sorority sisters at Fisk University, a historically black college, in 1936.

ceptance was not granted.) As late as the 1960s, when the slogan "Black is beautiful" became popular, the homecoming queen at Howard University usually had light complexion.

This concern for lighter skin persists. Fashion models on *Ebony*'s covers usually have pale skin, and the sales of bleaching products still are very heavy.

SOURCE: "For Black College Students in the 1930s, Respectability and Prestige Depended on Passing the Brown Bag Test," *Journal of Blacks in Higher Education*, Winter 1998/1999, 119–120.

but offered to reimburse blacks who went to out-of-state law schools. In 1938, the Supreme Court said the state had to provide a black law school.[34] Texas established a black law school clearly inferior to the white law school at the University of Texas in size of faculty, student body, library, and opportunities for students to specialize. In 1950, the Court said the black school had to be substantially equal to the white school.[35] Oklahoma allowed a black student to attend the white graduate school at the University of Oklahoma but designated a separate section of the classroom, library, and cafeteria for the student. The Court said this, too, was inadequate, because it deprived the student of the exchange of views with fellow students necessary for education.[36] The Court did not invalidate the separate-but-equal doctrine in these decisions, but it made segregation almost impossible to implement in graduate schools.

The NAACP continued by challenging segregation in grade schools and high schools. Marshall filed suits in two southern states, one border state, one northern state, and the District of Columbia. The suit in the northern state was brought against Topeka, Kansas, where Linda Brown could not attend the school just four blocks from her home because it was a white school. Instead, she had to go to a school twenty-one blocks away.[37]

When the cases reached the Supreme Court, President Eisenhower pressured his appointee, Chief Justice Earl Warren, to rule in favor of segregation. Eisenhower invited Warren and the attorney for the states to the White House for dinner. When the conversation turned to the segregationists, Eisenhower said, "These are not bad people. All they are concerned about is to see that their sweet little girls are not required to sit in schools alongside some big overgrown Negroes."[38] However, Warren not only voted against segregation but persuaded the other justices, some of whom had supported segregation, to vote against it too.

In the landmark case of ***Brown v. Board of Education*** in 1954, the Court ruled unanimously that school segregation violated the Fourteenth Amendment's equal protection clause.[39] In the opinion, Warren asserted that separate but equal not only resulted in unequal schools but was inherently unequal because it made black children feel inferior. In overruling the *Plessy* doctrine, the

Court showed how revolutionary the equal protection clause was—or could be interpreted to be. The Court required the segregated states to change their way of life to a degree unprecedented in American history. After overturning laws requiring segregation in schools, the Court overruled laws mandating segregation in such places as public parks, golf courses, swimming pools, auditoriums, courtrooms, and jails.[40]

In *Brown,* the Court ordered schools to desegregate "with all deliberate speed."[41] This was a compromise between those who wanted schools to do so immediately and those who wanted schools to do so gradually.[42] The ambiguity of the phrase, however, allowed them to take years to desegregate. The ruling prompted much deliberation but little speed.

The South engaged in massive resistance. The Court needed help from the other branches of government to implement its ruling but failed to get any cooperation for some time. President Eisenhower was reluctant to tell the states to change. In fact, he joined their representatives in Congress in criticizing the decision. With his position and popularity, the president could have speeded implementation by speaking out in support of the decision, yet he did not do so for more than three years. When nine black students tried to attend a white high school under a desegregation plan in Little Rock, Arkansas, the governor's and state legislature's inflammatory rhetoric against desegregation encouraged local citizens to take the law into their own hands. Finally, Eisenhower acted; he sent federal troops and federalized the state's national guard to quell the riot.

A few years later, President Kennedy used federal marshals and paratroopers to quell violence after the governor of Mississippi blocked the door to keep James Meredith from registering at the University of Mississippi. Kennedy again sent troops when the governor of Alabama, George Wallace, proclaiming "segregation now, segregation tomorrow, segregation forever," blocked the door to keep blacks from enrolling at the University of Alabama.

After outright defiance, some states attempted to circumvent the ruling by shutting down their public schools and providing tuition grants for students to use at private schools, which at the time could segregate. They also provided other forms of aid, such as textbooks and public recreation facilities, for private schools. These efforts hindered desegregation and hurt black education because the black communities seldom had the resources to establish their own schools.

The states also tried less blatant schemes, such as "freedom of choice" plans that allowed students to choose the school they wanted to attend. Of course, virtually no whites chose a black school, and due to strong pressure, few blacks chose a white school. The idea was to achieve desegregation on paper, or token desegregation in practice, in order to avoid real desegregation. But the Court rebuffed these schemes and even forbade discrimination by private schools.[43]

The Court's firm support gave blacks hope. Thurgood Marshall said, "Chief Justice Warren became the image [of the Court] that allowed the poor Negro sharecropper to say, 'Kick me around Mr. Sheriff, kick me around

When nine black students attempted to enroll at a white high school in Little Rock, Arkansas, in 1957, they were confronted by a white crowd. "Lynch her! Lynch her!" someone yelled. "Nigger! Nigger!" the girl behind her called. Six years later, the girl phoned to apologize, and forty years later the two met for the first time in front of the high school.

Busing led to rioting in some cities, such as Boston. Here protesters assault a black man in 1976.

Mr. County Judge, kick me around Supreme Court of my state, but there's one person I can rely on.' "[44]

Nevertheless, progress was excruciatingly slow. If a school district was segregated, a group like the NAACP had to run the risks and spend the time and money to bring a suit in a federal district court. Judges in these courts reflected the views of the state or local political establishment they came from, so the suit might not be successful. If it was, the school board had to prepare a desegregation plan. Members of the school board reflected the views of the community and the pressures from the segregationists, so the plan might not be adequate. If it was, segregationists would challenge it in a federal district court. If the court upheld the plan, segregationists would appeal to a federal court of appeals. Judges in these courts came from the South, and they sat in Richmond and New Orleans. However, they were not as tied to the state or local political establishment, and they usually decided against the segregationists. But then segregationists could appeal to the Supreme Court. Segregationists knew they would lose sooner or later. But the process took several years, so they were able to delay the inevitable.

Thus, segregationists tried to resist, then to evade, and finally to delay. In this they succeeded. In 1964, a decade after *Brown*, 98 percent of all black children in the South still attended all-black schools.[45]

By this time, the mood in Congress had changed. Congress passed the Civil Rights Act of 1964, which, among other things, cut off federal aid to school districts that continued to segregate. The following year it passed the first major program providing federal aid to education. This was the carrot at the end of the stick: School districts began to comply to get the federal money.

Finally, by 1970, only 14 percent of all black children in the South still attended all-black schools. Of course, some went to mostly black schools. Even so, the change was dramatic. Since then, though, many white students have left the public schools for private schools, causing creeping resegregation of the public schools.

Busing *Brown* and related rulings addressed **de jure segregation**—segregation enforced by law. This segregation can be attacked by striking down the law. *Brown* did not address **de facto segregation**—segregation based on residential patterns—typical of northern cities and large southern cities, where most blacks live in black neighborhoods and most whites live in white neighborhoods. Students attend their neighborhood schools, which are mostly black or mostly white. This segregation is much more intractable because it does not stem primarily from a law, so it cannot be eliminated by striking down a law.

Civil rights groups proposed busing some black children to schools in white neighborhoods and some white children to schools in black neighborhoods. They hoped to improve black children's education, their self-confidence and aspirations, and, eventually, their college and career opportunities. They also hoped to improve black and white children's ability to get along together.

The Burger Court authorized busing within school districts—ordinarily cities—including southern cities where there was a history of de jure segregation and northern cities where there was a pattern of de facto segregation but evidence that school officials had located schools or assigned students in ways that perpetuated this segregation.[46]

But even extensive busing within cities could not desegregate most large cities, where blacks and other minorities together became more numerous than whites. After World War II, affluent whites began to leave central cities for their suburbs, and after the courts upheld busing, more did so. Then the birthrates of whites fell and the immigration rates of whites from foreign countries also fell, relative to those of nonwhites. Due to these factors, there were not enough whites to desegregate the schools in most large cities. Consequently, civil rights groups proposed busing some white children from the suburbs to the cities and some black children from the cities to the suburbs. This approach would provide enough of both races to achieve balance in both places.

The Burger Court rejected this proposal by a 5–4 vote in 1974.[47] It said busing is not appropriate between school districts unless there is evidence of intentional segregation in both the city and its suburbs. Otherwise, such extensive busing would require too long a ride for students and too much coordination by administrators. Although there was intentional segregation by many cities and their suburbs,[48] the evidence is not as clear as that of the segregation by southern states at the time of *Brown,* so it is difficult to demonstrate a pattern by the cities and their multiple suburbs to the extent expected by the judges. Consequently, the Court's ruling made busing between cities and suburbs very rare.

Thurgood Marshall, by then on the Court, dissented and predicted that the ruling would allow "our great metropolitan areas to be divided up each into two cities—one white, the other black." Indeed, the ruling did contribute to this result.

During these years, relatively few students were bused for desegregation—4 percent in one typical year. These students were far fewer than those bused, at public expense, to segregated public and private schools.[49]

Nevertheless, busing ran up against a wall of public opinion. White parents criticized the courts sharply. Their reaction stemmed from some mixture of prejudice against blacks, bias against poor persons, fear of the crime in inner-city schools, worry about the quality of inner-city schools, and desire for the convenience of neighborhood schools. They also resented the courts for telling local governments what to do. In addition, some black parents opposed busing because it disrupted their children's lives and exposed them to the hostility of white students in their new schools. Black parents also resented the implication that their children could learn only if sitting next to white children. But other black parents favored busing because of the opportunity for their children to go to better schools.

Due to the opposition of white parents, busing prompted an increase in white flight, so there were fewer white students to balance enrollments and fewer middle-class students to provide stability in the cities' schools. It also furthered the deterioration of minority communities, because it diminished the neighborhood schools that had helped define these communities and hold them together.[50]

Busing could not accomplish all that civil rights groups and federal judges expected—or at least hoped—it could. Busing could not compensate for massive residential segregation. It could not overcome students' poverty or their parents' lack of involvement in their education. Thus, studies of the performance of minority children bused to white schools showed disappointing, mixed results.

In 1991, the Rehnquist Court decided that school districts have no obligation to reduce de facto segregation and, in fact, limited obligation to reduce the vestiges of de jure segregation.[51] This ruling relieved the pressure on school districts, and by the mid-1990s, most had stopped mandatory busing. When some tried other programs to balance enrollments, the Court looked askance at these programs.[52] The rulings in the 1990s reflected none of "the moral urgency of *Brown."*[53] Instead, the justices decided that desegregation is less important than minimizing judicial involvement in education and judicial authority over local governments. In these ways, the majority of the justices mirrored the views of the Republican presidents who had appointed them.

The Movement in the Streets
After the NAACP's early successes in the courts, other blacks, and some whites, took the fight to the streets. Their bold efforts gave birth to the modern civil rights movement.

The movement began in Montgomery, Alabama, in 1955, when Rosa Parks refused to move to the back of the bus. Her refusal and arrest prompted blacks to

Martin Luther King, under arrest in 1958.

boycott city buses. For their leader they chose a young Baptist minister, Dr. Martin Luther King Jr. The boycott catapulted the movement and King to national attention (as explained in Chapter 6).

King was the first charismatic leader of the movement. He formed the Southern Christian Leadership Conference (SCLC) of black clergy and adopted the tactics of Mahatma Gandhi, who had led the movement to free India from the British. The tactics included direct action, such as demonstrations and marches, and civil disobedience—intentional and public disobedience of laws considered unjust. The tactics were based on nonviolence, even when confronted with violence. This strategy was designed to draw support from whites by contrasting the morality of the movement's position with the immorality of discrimination and violence against blacks.

For a long time some whites, focusing on civil rights leaders such as King and even fearing foreign communists, deluded themselves into thinking that "outside agitators" were responsible for the turmoil in their communities.[54] But the movement grew from the grass roots, and it eventually shattered this delusion.

The movement spread, especially among black students. In 1960, four black students of North Carolina A&T College sat at the lunch counter in Woolworth's and asked for a cup of coffee. The waitress refused to serve them, but they stayed and were arrested. On following days, as whites waved the Confederate flag and jeered, more students sat at the lunch counter. Within a year, such sit-ins occurred in more than one hundred cities.

When blacks asserted their rights, whites often reacted with violence. In 1963, King led demonstrators in Birmingham, Alabama, for desegregation of public facilities. Public Safety Commissioner Eugene "Bull" Connor had police unleash their dogs to attack the marchers. In 1964, King led demonstrators in Selma, Alabama, for voting rights. State troopers clubbed some marchers, while vigilantes beat and shot others.

In the summer of 1964, black and white college students mounted a voter registration drive in Mississippi. By the end of the summer, one thousand had been arrested, eighty beaten, thirty-five shot, and six killed.[55] These included one southern black and two northern whites who were murdered by Klansmen, allegedly with aid from a sheriff and deputy sheriff, in Neshoba County.

Perpetrators of the violence usually were not caught. When they were, they usually were not punished. Law enforcement was frequently in the hands of bigots, and juries generally were all white. The Supreme Court had struck down discrimination in choosing juries,[56] but discrimination continued through informal means.

During these years, most whites told pollsters they disliked the civil rights movement's speed and tactics: "They're pushing too fast and too hard." At the same time, most said they favored integration more than ever. And they seemed repelled by the violence. The brutality against blacks generated more support for them.

Although the movement's tactics worked well against southern de jure segregation, they did not work as well against northern de facto segregation or against both re-

Students sit in at a lunch counter in Jackson, Mississippi.

Fred Blackwell/*Jackson Daily News*. Used by permission of the *Clarion Ledger*.

When three civil rights workers were murdered in Neshoba County, Mississippi, no one was ever indicted by the state. After an investigation, eighteen persons, including the sheriff (right) and deputy sheriff (left), here in court, were indicted by the federal government for the lesser charge of conspiracy. (There was no applicable federal law for murder.) Ultimately, seven persons, including the deputy, were convicted by the federal court.

AP/Wide World Photos

gions' job discrimination. By the mid-1960s, a decade after the *Brown* decision, progress had stalled and dissatisfaction was growing. Young blacks from the inner city, who had not been involved in the movement, questioned two of its principles: interracialism and nonviolence. As James Farmer, head of the Congress of Racial Equality (CORE), later explained, these blacks began to say, "What is this we-shall-overcome, black-and-white together stuff? I don't know of any white folks except the guy who runs that store on 125th Street in Harlem and garnishes wages and repossesses things you buy. I'd like to go upside his head. [Or] the rent collector, who bangs on the door demanding rent that we ain't got. I'd like to go upside his head."[57] These blacks criticized King and his tactics. In place of the integration advocated by King, some leaders began to call for "black power." This phrase meant different things to different people. To some it meant political power through the ballot box; to others, economic power through boycotts of segregated businesses or ownership of their own businesses. At least it implied black pride and self-reliance. And in place of the nonviolence practiced by King, some leaders began to urge violence in retaliation for the violence of whites. The movement splintered further.

The Movement in Congress

As the civil rights movement expanded, it pressured presidents and members of Congress to act. Presidents Kennedy and Johnson supported civil rights but felt hamstrung by southerners in Congress who, through the seniority system, had risen to chair key committees and dominate both houses. As a result, the presidents considered civil rights leaders unreasonable and the movement a nuisance that alienated the southerners on whom the presidents had to rely. But once the movement demonstrated its strength, it was able to prod officials to act. After two hundred thousand blacks and whites marched in Washington in 1963, President Kennedy introduced civil rights legislation, and President Johnson, with his consummate legislative skills, forged a coalition of northern Democrats and northern Republicans to overcome southern Democrats and pass the Civil Rights Act of 1964. After one thousand blacks and whites had been arrested and many had been attacked in Selma, the public outcry led Johnson to introduce and Congress to pass the Voting Rights Act of 1965. Three years later, Johnson introduced and Congress passed the Civil Rights Act of 1968. Within a span of four years, Congress passed legislation prohibiting discrimination in public accommodations, employment, housing, and voting.

Although President Johnson believed he was doing the right thing, he realized the political ramifications. Upon signing the first of these acts, he commented that he was handing the South to the Republican Party "for the next fifty years."[58] He was perceptive. In the next election, he became the first Democrat since the Civil War to lose the white vote in the southern states. In less than a decade, the South, which had been solidly Democratic since the Civil War, would go from the most Democratic region of the country to the least.[59]

Desegregation of Public Accommodations The **Civil Rights Act of 1964** prohibits discrimination on the basis of race, color, religion, or national origin in public accommodations. This time, unlike after the Civil War, the Court unanimously upheld the act.[60]

The act does not cover private clubs, such as country clubs, social clubs, or fraternities and sororities, on the principle that the government should not tell people with whom they must associate in private. (The Court has made private schools an exception to this principle to help enforce *Brown*.)

Desegregation of Employment The Civil Rights Act of 1964 also prohibits employment discrimination on the basis of race, color, religion, national origin, or sex and (as amended) physical disability, age, or Vietnam-era veteran status. The act covers employers with fifteen or more employees and unions.[61]

In addition to practicing blatant discrimination, some employers practiced more subtle discrimination. They required applicants to meet standards unnecessary for their jobs, a practice that hindered blacks more than whites. A high school degree for a manual job was a common example. The Court held that standards must relate to the jobs.[62] However, standards that hindered blacks more than whites were not necessarily unlawful. Washington, D.C., required applicants for police officer to pass an exam. Although a higher percentage of blacks failed to pass, the Court said the exam related to the job.[63]

The Court has allowed employers to reduce their workforce by laying off workers with less seniority, even if these workers are disproportionately black.[64] The principle of "last hired, first fired" thwarts desegregation of employment when an employer hires more blacks to compensate for past discrimination but then lays off the newer workers when the economy slows.

Desegregation of Housing Although the Supreme Court had struck down laws that prescribed segregation in residential areas, whites maintained segregation by making **restrictive covenants**—agreements among neighbors not to sell their houses to blacks. In 1948, the Court ruled that courts could not enforce these covenants because doing so would involve the government in discrimination.[65]

Realtors also played a role in segregation by practicing **steering**—showing blacks houses in black neighborhoods and whites houses in white neighborhoods. Unscrupulous realtors practiced **blockbusting.** After a black family bought a house in a white neighborhood, realtors would warn white families that more blacks would move in. Because of prejudice and fear that their houses' values would decline, whites would panic and sell to the realtors at low prices. Then the realtors would resell to blacks at higher prices. In this way, neighborhoods that might have been desegregated were instead resegregated—from all white to all black.

Banks and savings and loans also played a role. They were reluctant to lend money to blacks who wanted to buy a house in a white neighborhood. Some engaged in **redlining**—refusing to lend money to those who wanted to buy a house in a racially changing neighborhood. The lenders worried that if the buyer could not keep up with the payments, the lender would be left with a house whose value had declined.

The government also played an important role. The Veterans Administration and the Federal Housing Authority, which guaranteed loans to some buyers, were reluctant to authorize loans to blacks who sought to buy a house in a white neighborhood. And the federal government, which funded low-income housing, allowed local governments to locate such housing in ghettos. In these ways, the governments helped perpetuate segregation.[66]

But the **Civil Rights Act of 1968** bans discrimination in the sale or rental of housing on the basis of race, color, religion, national origin, and (as amended) on the basis of sex, having children, or having a disability. The act covers about 80 percent of the available housing and prohibits steering, blockbusting, and redlining.

Restoration of the Right to Vote After years of skirmishing with the states, the Supreme Court and Congress barred measures designed to keep blacks from voting. The Voting Rights Act of 1965 permitted large numbers of blacks to vote for the first time (as explained in Chapter 8).

Continuing Discrimination against African Americans

African Americans have overcome much discrimination but still face continuing discrimination. Overt laws and blatant practices have been struck down, but subtle manifestations of old attitudes and habits persist—and in ways far more numerous and with effects far more serious than this one chapter can convey.[67] Moreover, African Americans must cope with the legacy of generations of slavery, segregation, and discrimination and, for many of them, the effects of generations of poverty. And they must cope with the attitudes of whites. Although few people say they want to return to the days of legal segregation, about half reject the dream of an integrated society.[68] (See the box "How Much Is White Skin Worth?" for a hypothetical but telling response to coping with discrimination.)

Discrimination in Education

For blacks who can afford it, a great deal of desegregation has occurred in education. Affluent parents who can pay for private schools or live in expensive neighborhoods with good public schools can send their children to integrated schools. However, for most blacks in big cities, medium cities, or areas where private schools predominate, much less desegregation has occurred.

Although de jure segregation of schools has been eliminated, de facto segregation remains. In fact, this segregation is getting worse. After progress in the mid-1960s and 1970s, the trend toward desegregation reversed itself in the 1980s and got worse in the 1990s. "For the first time since the *Brown v. Board* decision," according to one study, "we are going backwards."[69]

The reversal is due to white flight to the suburbs, leaving fewer white children, and higher nonwhite

How Much Is White Skin Worth?

"You will be visited tonight by an official you have never met. He begins by telling you he is extremely embarrassed. The organization he represents has made a mistake, something that hardly ever happens.

According to their records, he goes on, you were to have been born black—to another set of parents, far from where you were raised.

However, the rules being what they are, this error must be rectified, and as soon as possible. So at midnight tonight, you will become black. And this will mean not simply a darker skin, but the bodily and facial features associated with African ancestry. However, inside, you will be the person you always were. Your knowledge and ideas will remain intact. But outwardly you will not be recognizable to anyone you now know.

Your visitor emphasizes that being born to the wrong parents was in no way your fault.

Consequently, his organization is prepared to offer you some reasonable recompense. Would you, he asks, care to name a sum of money you might consider appropriate? He adds that his group is by no means poor. It can be quite generous when the circumstances warrant, as they seem to in your case. He finishes by saying that their records show you are scheduled to live another fifty years—as a black man or woman in America.

How much financial recompense would you request?

A professor who puts this parable to white college students finds that most feel $1 million per year—$50 million total—would be appropriate. This much would protect them from, and reimburse them for, the danger and discrimination they would face if they were perceived as black. In acknowledging that white skin is worth this much, the students also are admitting that treatment of the races, even today, is not nearly equal.

SOURCE: Andrew Hacker, *Two Nations: Black and White, Separate, Hostile, Unequal* (New York: Scribner's, 1992), 31–32.

birthrates and immigration rates, producing more non-white children. In our forty-seven largest cities, only one of four students in public schools is white.[70] To a lesser extent, the reversal is due to the Burger and Rehnquist Courts' limited acceptance of busing or alternatives to balance enrollments and to the Reagan and Bush administrations' lax enforcement of desegregation

orders. School districts got the message that school desegregation was no longer an important national goal.[71]

As a result of these trends, there is more segregation today in northern cities, where the segregation has been mostly de facto, than in southern cities, where the segregation was mostly de jure.[72] Yet both regions are experiencing increasing segregation.

The persistence of de facto segregation and the waning of commitment to integration have led national, state, and local officials to adopt the attitude "We still agree with the goal of school desegregation, but it's too hard, and we're tired of it, and we give up."[73]

Reforms proposed for urban schools rarely include desegregation. Officials speak of a ghetto school that is more "efficient" or one that gets more "input" from ghetto parents or offers more "choices" for ghetto children. But the existence of segregated education as "a permanent American reality" appears to be accepted.[74]

A writer who visited many central city classrooms and talked with students, teachers, and administrators observed that Martin Luther King was treated as

> an icon, but his vision of a nation in which black and white kids went to school together seemed to be effaced almost entirely. Dutiful references to "The Dream" were often seen in school brochures and on wall posters in February, when "Black History" was celebrated in the public schools, but the content of the dream was treated as a closed box that could not be opened without ruining the celebration.[75]

Indeed, many cities have a school named after King—a segregated school in a segregated neighborhood—"like a terrible joke on history," a fourteen-year-old, wise beyond her years, remarked.[76]

Many minorities have gotten so frustrated that they themselves have questioned the goal of school desegregation. Instead, they have voiced greater concern about improving the quality and safety of their schools and neighborhoods.[77]

Unequal Funding In areas where schools are segregated, the quality varies enormously—from "the golden to the godawful," in the words of a Missouri judge.[78] And, of course, minorities are more likely to be in the "godawful."

Schools are financed largely by property taxes paid by homeowners and businesses. Wealthy cities get more in property taxes than poor ones. In modern America, this means suburban school districts get more to spend per pupil than central city school districts. Moreover, although many suburbs tax their residents at a lower rate than cities do, suburbs still bring in more revenue because their property is valued at a higher level. Thus, these suburbs ask their residents to sacrifice less but still provide their children with an education that costs more.[79] It is common, therefore, for a suburb to spend $3,000 to 4,000 more per pupil than the central city near it.[80]

Spending-per-pupil figures do not take into account that the needs of poor children, after years of neglect and with scores of problems at home and in the neighborhood, are greater than the needs of other children. Schools for poor children would require *more* funding to provide their students an equal education.

So, many inner-city schools are bleak institutions, reflecting disrepair and filth. An East St. Louis, Illinois, school had, a visitor discovered, a boys' bathroom in which "[f]our of the six toilets do not work. The toilet stalls, which are eaten away by red and brown corrosion, have no doors. The toilets have no seats. One has a rotted wooden stump. There are no paper towels and no soap. Near the door is a loop of wire with an empty toilet-paper roll." Yet the visitor was told, "This is the best school we have in East St. Louis." At another school in the city, sewage repeatedly backed up into the bathrooms and kitchen and flooded the gym and parking lot.[81]

Numerous inner-city schools are overcrowded. Classes routinely are held in former coatrooms and closets. At one school, two classes are held in converted coal bins, while another is held in the current bathroom. Some cities in New Jersey literally ran out of classrooms and tried to rent space in vacant schools in the suburbs. But the cities were turned down because the suburbs did not want the mostly nonwhite children entering their communities.[82]

Many inner-city schools do not have texts for all their students, texts that are at the appropriate grade levels, or

A Philadelphia teacher tries to teach English in the hallway of an overcrowded school in an underfunded system.

texts that are up-to-date. Some schools cannot afford to hire science, art, music, or physical education teachers. Almost all cannot afford to offer competitive salaries to hire good teachers in the subjects the schools do offer. A New York City principal said he is forced to take the "tenth-best" teachers. "I thank God they're still breathing."[83]

Despite the pervasive pattern of unequal funding, cash alone would not solve all the problems. Cultural and economic factors in inner cities also restrict the quality of education available. But cash would help. According to one calculation, if New York City schools had been funded at the same level as the highest-spending suburban schools on Long Island, a typical fourth grade class of thirty-six children would have had $200,000 more invested in their education in one year. The difference would have been enough to divide the class in half, hire two excellent teachers, and provide the classrooms with computers, new texts, reference books, learning games, carpets, air conditioning, and new counselors to help the children cope with problems in their environment outside school.[84]

Some states have equalized funding, but moves to do so in other states have encountered fierce opposition. After the New Jersey Supreme Court in 1990 ordered the state to reduce disparities between districts, the Democratic governor and legislature increased some taxes and cut some spending in other areas. The governor also redirected a portion of state aid from suburban schools to inner-city schools to comply with the order. Suburbanites were furious; the next year they elected veto-proof majorities of Republicans to both houses of the state legislature in an attempt to block the program, and in the next election they ousted the governor.

An alternative to equalized funding would be for states to provide supplementary funding for schools in inner cities. But peoples' priorities run in other directions. In 1999, the Pennsylvania legislature approved $160 million of public financing for new stadiums for the Eagles and Phillies and another $160 million of public financing for new stadiums for the Steelers and Pirates, while the schools in Philadelphia and Pittsburgh languished.[85]

Second-Generation Discrimination Even where desegregation of schools has been achieved, segregation within schools exists. This "second-generation discrimination" isolates many minority students by placing them in separate programs or classes from white students. Black children are more likely to be put in "special education" classes for slow learners and less likely to be put in programs for gifted students. They are more likely to be put in classes for the educable mentally retarded (EMR).[86]

These facts by themselves are not necessarily evidence of second-generation discrimination, because the long legacy of discrimination and the dismal living conditions of many blacks make it harder for them to succeed in school. However, in school districts where more minorities are school board members or are administrators or teachers, less disparate treatment occurs.[87] The presence of minorities in authoritative positions apparently sensitizes white administrators or teachers to this discrimination.

Black children are also more likely to be disciplined. After the shootings at Columbine High and other schools, administrators are quick to sanction unruly students. If suspended, the students fall behind in their studies and may quit school. Poor students are disproportionately disciplined, and African Americans are disproportionately lower class. But there are racial reasons as well. Cultural misunderstandings between white teachers and black students—for example, misinterpretation of body language that signals respect or disrespect—and "racial paranoia" explain the more frequent discipline meted out to black students. One education professor observed, "We see this a lot with black boys who are cute until about the fourth grade, and then teachers start to fear them."[88]

Discrimination in Public Accommodations

Black newlyweds no longer have to spend their wedding nights in a funeral parlor, as Martin Luther and Coretta Scott King did. Most businesses comply with the Civil Rights Act of 1964 prohibiting discrimination in public accommodations.[89]

However, Jim Crow still lives in some places. For example, numerous blue-collar bars and lounges in New Orleans operate as though the act is not on the books. One serves blacks through a side window, while it allows whites to drink inside. Others keep separate rooms for blacks and whites. Others use separate entrances—blacks through a back or side door, whites through the front door. "I can go to the front door, now," a black patron says. "But no one is going to let me in. All I'll do is get my feelings hurt. If you want service, you go around to the back room—that's for blacks."[90] Although illegal, these practices persist if no one files a complaint or brings a lawsuit.

Periodic examples of other incidents are reported. A restaurant in Maryland refused to serve a group of black men, who turned out to be Secret Service agents. A car-rental franchise in North Carolina refused to rent cars to blacks. A gas station in North Carolina refused to sell gas to blacks. When a thirty-one-year-old black man, traveling through the state, pulled into the station, the white attendant said, "Boy, you can't get gas here." The man figured the pumps were broken. "No," the attendant said. "Boy, you can't get any gas." At that point a black police officer pulled up, asked what was going on, and then directed the motorist to another station.[91]

Some businesses try to circumvent the act. For instance, some restaurants give blacks poor service so they will not return. A suburban mall refused to allow city buses from Buffalo in its parking lot, although it allowed Canadian buses to bring their shoppers from across the border. Mall executives assured shopkeepers that "you'll never see an inner-city bus on the mall premises."[92]

Even some businesses that try to comply with the act have employees who treat blacks differently and embarrassingly. As one writer notes:

You stroll into a shop to look at the merchandise, and it soon becomes clear that the clerks are keeping a watchful eye on you. Too quickly, one of them comes over to inquire what it is you might want, and then remains conspicuously close as you continue your search. It also seems that they take an unusually long time verifying your credit card. Then you and a black friend enter a restaurant, and find yourselves greeted warily, with what is obviously a more anxious reception than that given to white guests. Yes, you will be served, and your table will not necessarily be next to the kitchen. Still, you sense that they would rather you had chosen some other eating place.[93]

Because the Civil Rights Act does not apply to private clubs, many country clubs and golf clubs discriminate against blacks. One estimate is that three-fourths of these clubs have no black members, and many of the remainder have only one or a few token members.[94] Thus, the business, professional, and political elites who form the membership perpetuate inequality in their circles and also send a message that discrimination is acceptable for others in society.

Discrimination in Employment

Although the Civil Rights Act of 1964 and affirmative action (discussed later in the chapter) have prompted more employers to hire and promote African Americans, discrimination remains.

A 1991 study of Chicago and Washington, D.C., used pairs of white and black male college students who were matched in education, experience, age, speech, demeanor, and physical build. The men applied for nearly five hundred advertised jobs involving retail, service, clerical, or physical labor. The whites advanced farther in the hiring process 20 percent of the time, while the blacks did 7 percent of the time. (They were equal in the remainder.) The blacks found the most discrimination in white-collar jobs—one who had applied for a job as a hotel desk clerk was offered a job as a bellboy—and those requiring contact with customers.[95] These results not only reflect discrimination against blacks but also contradict the perception that there is widespread reverse discrimination against whites.

A 1992 investigation by the Equal Employment Opportunity Commission (EEOC) uncovered discriminatory practices by employment agencies that hire workers for many companies. The agencies devised code phrases the companies could use to screen out applicants of a particular race or sex or age as a way to violate the law without being caught. If, for example, a business did not want any blacks, it was instructed to specify, "No Z." If it simply preferred whites, it was instructed to say, "Talk to Mary." Through these phrases, one Los Angeles agency alone discriminated against 3,900 applicants.[96]

Many blacks who are hired are passed over when they believe they should be promoted.[97] But discrimination at this point is more subtle and difficult to prove. Black employees at Texaco filed suit but felt stymied until a white executive, who was being forced to retire early, disclosed secret tape recordings of a meeting at which top executives discussed the suit and admitted shredding and hiding incriminating documents subpoenaed by aggrieved employees.

On the job, some blacks are subjected to racial slurs in comments, notes, and graffiti. More common are negative stereotypes that question their competence and value. Often they endure an unfriendly or hostile environment.[98]

Upper-level executives realize that it is economically advantageous to have a diverse workforce, but some middle-level white managers and lower-level white workers interact poorly with the black employees.

Discrimination in Housing

The Civil Rights Act of 1968 prohibiting discrimination in housing has fostered some desegregation of housing, especially big apartment complexes, which are visible and therefore susceptible to pressure from civil rights groups and the government. And the act has resulted in large penalties on individuals found guilty of violations. Lawyers for fair-housing organizations say white jurors think discrimination has been eliminated—until they hear the testimony, which jars them into granting large awards.[99]

But the act is working at a snail's pace to change housing patterns. One reason is economic. Most blacks do not have enough money to buy homes in white neighborhoods. This problem is aggravated by local zoning laws designed to establish a certain type of community. Often these laws require large lots and large houses, which command high prices.

Another reason is continuing discrimination. Occasional violence and considerable social pressure discourage blacks who try to move into white neighborhoods. Actual discrimination by homeowners, realtors, lenders, and insurers also stymies them. A study of twenty metropolitan areas, using white and minority testers responding to house and apartment advertising, found that blacks who try to buy a house face discrimination 17 percent of the time, and those who try to rent an apartment do so 22 percent of the time. (These figures from 2002 are about 25 percent lower than the results from 1989, which was the last time the government had conducted this research.)[100] If callers sound black, landlords might claim the apartment "for rent" has been filled. Research shows that most Americans can identify most callers as black or white.[101]

Some realtors still practice steering. Many lenders apparently require extra proof that blacks will repay their home loans. A study by the Federal Reserve Board examined 5.3 million mortgage applications to 9,300 financial institutions in nineteen major cities in 1990. It found that applications from blacks were denied more than twice as often as those from whites with comparable income. As a result, applications from high-income

A Grand Rapids artist put up this billboard to prompt white motorists to think about how they would feel if discrimination were directed at them instead. By the next day the word NIGER [sic] had been scrawled on the billboard, and the mayor had gotten so many complaints that the artist had to take the billboard down.

blacks were rejected about as often as those from low-income whites.[102]

The Clinton administration proposed that the government phase out its public housing projects and give residents vouchers—government coupons—to use for any housing unit they locate on their own. The goal was to let them escape the dreary environment of the huge projects, but one consequence would be to desegregate more neighborhoods, as the minorities in the projects fanned out through the city or, possibly, adjacent suburbs. Congressional Republicans blocked the proposal. Although they support the concept of vouchers—allowing individuals to choose a service rather than having the government determine what particular service is best for them—and the use of vouchers to enable children to attend religious schools, many oppose the use of vouchers to enable minorities to move into white neighborhoods.[103]

For all of these reasons, residential segregation remains pervasive in metropolitan areas. However, it is declining slowly. The 2000 census shows that people in the fast-growing suburban areas in the West and South are more likely to live in integrated neighborhoods than a decade earlier. At the same time, however, people in the stagnant "rust belt" cities in the East and Midwest are as likely or more likely to live in segregated neighborhoods than a decade earlier, partly because of continued white flight from the central cities.[104] Even middle-class blacks who escape the ghetto often end up in black neighborhoods in the suburbs of these cities[105] (see Table 2).

Segregation does not continue because blacks "want to live by their own kind," as some whites insist. Surveys show that only about 15 percent want to live in segregated neighborhoods, while 85 percent would prefer mixed neighborhoods. (Many say the optimal level would be about half blacks and half whites.) Yet whites tend to move out, and new ones do not move in, when blacks reach 8 to 10 percent.[106] These very different views make integration an elusive goal, particularly because blacks make up 12 to 13 percent of the American population and a much larger percentage of some cities.

These patterns and attitudes are all the more troublesome because residential segregation, of course, leads to further school segregation.

To add potential injury to the insult for blacks, a study of the Environmental Protection Agency's enforcement of air, water, and hazardous waste pollution laws from 1985 to 1991 concluded that the government took longer to act in minority communities, imposed smaller fines against polluters in those communities, and required less stringent solutions in those communities.[107] Such "environmental discrimination" continues.[108]

Discrimination in Other Ways

African Americans face discrimination from police officers. The practice of **racial profiling,** which is based on the assumption that minorities, especially males, are more likely to commit crimes, especially ones involving drugs, targets minorities for stops and searches. So without any evidence, officers stop minority drivers and search them and their car.[109] Racial profiling sometimes is directed toward pedestrians and passengers in airports as well. Although police departments deny following this practice, statistics show clear evidence that dispro-

TABLE 2	Residential Segregation Varies by Region

■ Hispanics   ■ Blacks

Census Region	Least Integrated	Most Integrated	Least Segregated	Most Segregated
East				
Philadelphia				
New York				
Boston				
Midwest				
Chicago				
Detroit				
St. Louis				
South				
Atlanta				
Austin				
Baltimore				
Charlotte				
Nashville				
New Orleans				
Washington				
West				
Denver				
Las Vegas				
Los Angeles				
San Jose				
Seattle				
Average of all metropolitan areas				
All large cities				
All suburbs*				

*Excludes outlying areas.
SOURCE: U.S. Census Bureau, Washington Post National Weekly Edition, April 9—15, 2001,6.

portionate numbers of minorities are stopped and searched. Interstate 95 from Florida to New York is notorious. On I-95 through Maryland, while 18 percent of the speeders were black, 29 percent of those stopped and 71 percent of those searched were black. On the New Jersey Turnpike, while 15 percent of the speeders were black, 35 percent of those pulled over were black.[110] The practice of racial profiling contributes to the tensions between minorities and police.

Now African Americans speak of the moving violation "DWB"—Driving While Black. A Chicago journalist who was stopped at least every other time he traveled through the Midwest learned not to rent flashy Mustangs or wear his beret. Others avoid tinted windshields or expensive sunglasses—any flamboyance—to avoid the cops.[111]

Profiling might be justified if this tactic led to the apprehension of dangerous criminals, but apparently it does not. Although minorities, especially young men, evidently do commit a larger percentage of certain crimes,[112] the profiling does not lead the police to many criminals. When police stop motorists, they find no greater evidence of crimes by minorities than by whites.[113] Some states and many counties and cities have taken steps to reduce profiling, such as recording data on every stop to see whether the police, or individual officers, are prone to profile. Yet the cops on the beat, who feel that profiling is useful, are reluctant to change their habits. (See the "After 9/11" box.)

Other discrimination from police officers is less common but more serious. Sometimes officers arrest black citizens without legal cause, and occasionally they use excessive force against them. Numerous examples attest to improper beatings.[114] Sometimes officers lie while testifying against black suspects in court. As a result, even prominent African Americans say their "worst fear is to have to go before the criminal justice system."[115] It is little wonder, then, that black jurors hearing the O. J. Simpson trial and black citizens following it put less faith in the police testimony than white observers did.

Cautious parents feel obligated to teach their children how to avoid sending the wrong signals to police. Some parents urge their children not to wear street fashions and not to use cell phones, which from a distance might be mistaken as weapons. Some schools offer survival workshops for police encounters. Minority officers instruct the students what to do when they get stopped: Don't reach for an ID unless the officer asks for one; don't mumble or talk loudly; don't antagonize by asking for a badge number or threatening to file a complaint.[116]

Most blacks, even those in the upper and middle classes and those in professional occupations, face insults because of their race. Black women tell of being mistaken for hotel chambermaids. One family therapist, invited to speak at a conference, was stopped in the hall-

way by a white attendee who asked where the restrooms were. When the therapist appeared taken aback, the attendee said she thought the woman worked at the hotel. Although the therapist was wearing her official name tag and presenter's ribbon, the attendee did not look past her black face.[117] Black women also tell of waiting for friends in hotel lobbies and being mistaken for prostitutes by white men and police officers. A distinguished black political scientist tells of people who assume he is a butler, in his own home. Black doctors tell of dressing up when they go shopping to avoid being regarded as shoplifters. But even dressing up is no guarantee. A black lawyer, a senior partner in a large law firm, arrived at work early one morning, before the doors were unlocked. As he reached for his key, a young white lawyer, a junior associate in the firm, arrived at the same time, blocked his entrance, and asked, repeatedly and demandingly, "May I help you?" The white associate had taken the black partner for an intruder.[118] Although in these encounters the insults were unintentional, the stings hurt just the same.

The accumulation of these incidents—poor service, fearful movements, disrespectful comments—which more than eight in ten blacks say they occasionally experience, has created a "black middle-class rage" among many.[119]

Overall, discrimination against African Americans continues. Whites speak of "past discrimination"—sometimes referring to slavery, sometimes to official segregation—but this phrase is misleading. Of course, there is a lot less discrimination now due to the civil rights movement, Supreme Court decisions, and congressional acts. However, there is nothing "past" about much "past discrimination."[120] The effects linger, and, indeed, the discrimination itself persists.

Even when blacks point out the discrimination, some whites insist little discrimination is left. These whites apparently assume they know more than blacks do about what it is like to be black. Indeed, the perceptual gap between blacks and whites about the existence of discrimination is one of the real barriers to making progress on the issue of race. Whites who believe nothing is wrong do not favor actions to fix what they see as a nonexistent problem.

As African Americans have become frustrated with the slow pace of progress, some have been attracted to the black separatist movement. These blacks, seeing themselves as realistic, consider integration a naive ideal from the 1950s and 1960s—an impossibility even in the future. They want to direct their energy toward building up the black community.[121] (Supreme Court Justice Clarence Thomas seems to hold this view.) But most blacks, remaining hopeful, consider separatism premature and risky; they fear it will play into the hands of the most prejudiced whites trying to perpetuate discrimination.

PROFILING OF ARABS?

Soon after racial profiling of African Americans and Latinos became discredited, the terrorist attacks have prompted governments to engage in profiling of Arabs. Because the September 11 attackers were all young men from Arab countries with terrorist groups, governments have made a determined effort to prevent further attacks from similar people.

Despite its denials, the federal government has focused on young men from the Middle East. The Justice Department has sought to interview five thousand men between eighteen and thirty-three who have entered the country since 2000 from Middle Eastern countries with links to terrorist groups. Federal officials have contacted college administrators from over two hundred campuses for information on students from Middle Eastern countries—what they are studying, where they are living, how they are doing. And the officials have made unannounced visits to the students, asking their educational plans, political views, and so on. Federal officials keep tabs on an unknown number of Arab men, monitoring their movements, telephone calls, email messages, Internet use, and credit card charges around the clock.

Local officials have trained a wary eye on local Arabs. For example, New York City police culled their lists of outstanding warrants for petty crimes for names that sound Middle Eastern. Then they picked up and questioned nearly one hundred people, using the warrants as leverage to demand full cooperation.[1]

The Federal Aviation Administration (FAA) requires airports to use an automated system for deciding which checked bags to screen, because airports cannot screen most luggage. The criteria are confidential, though buying a one-way ticket is one factor. Using a stolen credit card to pay for a ticket is another. The FAA, however, insists that speaking Arabic, being Muslim, or wearing a veil or a beard are not other factors.

Soon after September 11, opinion polls showed that 58 percent of Americans approved more extensive airport screening of Arabs; 49 percent approved ID cards for Arabs, including those who are American citizens; and 32 percent approved "special surveillance" of Arabs.[2] Perhaps surprisingly, African Americans were more supportive of these measures than other Americans.[3]

The profiling disturbs some people. One law professor said it shows that "[w]e have decided to trade off the liberty of immigrants—particularly Arabs and Muslims—for the purported security of the majority."[4]Another observer asked, "How would you feel about the IRS' auditing Italian Americans' taxes in order to deter Mafia activity?"

Others believe profiling is legitimate because of the severity of the threat. Others justify it because the attacks did come only from young male Arabs (though they overlook the earlier Oklahoma City bombing done by a native-born American.)

In an effort to appear not to profile, airports are instructed to search passengers randomly. Is it silly, even counter-productive, to search a seventy-year-old grandmother head to toe? "Random searches," one columnist asserts, "are a ridiculous charade . . . that not only gives a false sense of security but, in fact, diminishes security because it wastes so much time and effort on people who are obviously no threat."[5]

The alternative, at least for airports and other transportation hubs, may be to employ far more sophisticated screening systems than we use now. In fact, such systems are in development. Basically they will use a computer network to link multiple databases. They will be able to scan every passenger's travel history, living arrangements, and other personal information gleaned from driver's licenses, credit cards, magazine subscriptions, and who knows what else.[6] Such systems will be so sophisticated that they can look at many factors without considering race or ethnicity. Will they be better for this reason? Or will they be worse because they will pose a threat to the privacy of everyone? That is the trade-off.

1. Matthew Purdy, "Bush's New Rules to Fight Terror Transform the Legal Landscape," *New York Times,* November 25, 2001, A1.
2. CNN/*USA Today*/Gallup poll, Ruben Navarrette Jr., "All of a Sudden, Profiling Is OK," *Lincoln Journal-Star,* October 5, 2001.
3. These results were found in polls by both Gallup and Zogby International. Clarence Page, "Look Who's Profiling Now," *Lincoln Journal-Star,* October 6, 2001.
4. David Cole, quoted in ibid., B4.
5. Charles Krauthammer, "The Case for Profiling," *Time,* March 18, 2002, 104.
6. Robert O'Harrow Jr., "Will Passenger Profiling Fly?" *Washington Post National Weekly Edition,* February 11–17, 2002, 29; Jeffery Rosen, "Silicon Valley's Spy Game," *New York Times Magazine,* April 14, 2002, 46.

Improving Conditions for African Americans?

Despite the continuing discrimination affecting some, African Americans have taken great strides toward achieving equal rights. These strides have led to much better living conditions for them and to a healthier racial climate in society.

Since the 1960s, blacks' lives have improved in most ways that can be measured.[122] Blacks have a longer life expectancy and a lower poverty rate than before. They have completed more years of education, with larger numbers attending college and graduate school. They have attained higher occupational levels—for example, tripling their proportion of the country's professionals[123]—and income levels. Many more have reached the middle class. About half of all blacks consider themselves middle class, and even more are classified as middle class or higher—fully 59 percent are "middle class" and another 11 percent are "affluent," according to one calculation.[124] A third have moved to the suburbs,[125] and nearly half own their own homes.[126]

During the same years that blacks' lives have improved, whites' racial attitudes have also improved. Although answers to pollsters' questions cannot be accepted as perfect reflections of people's views, especially on emotional matters such as racial attitudes, the answers can be considered general indicators of these views. Polls encompassing a wide variety of racial questions show that whites' views have changed significantly (even assuming that some whites gave more socially acceptable answers than they really felt).[127] Just as one example, in the mid-1980s, a Louisville sportswriter cracked that a Martian would sit in the White House before a black man would coach basketball at the University of Kentucky. But in 1998 the university hired a black man, Tubby Smith, who guided the team to a national championship in his first season.

Whites and blacks both report more social contact with members of the other race since the 1960s (see

TABLE 3	Blacks and Whites Have Had More Social Contact since the 1960s

The percentages of respondents who say that members of the other race do the following:

	Blacks	Whites
Live in their neighborhood		
1964	66	20
1976	70	38
1994	83	61
Are friends of theirs		
1964	62	18
1976	87	50
1989	82	66
Are "good friends" of theirs		
1975	21	9
1994	78	73
Have been dinner guests in their home		
1973	39	20
1994	53	34
Attend their church		
1978	37	34
1994	61	44

SOURCE: Stephan Thernstrom and Abigail Thernstrom, *America in Black and White* (New York: Simon & Schuster, 1997), 521.

Table 3), and both report more approval of interracial dating and marriage (see Table 4). The acceptance of interracial dating and marriage is especially significant, because these practices were the ultimate taboos in segregated society. Interracial couples represented the clearest breach and their potential offspring the greatest threat to continued segregation.

Some whites, of course, remain blatant racists (perhaps from 2 to 24 percent, according to various estimates by social scientists).[128] But blatant racist behavior occurs less frequently and is condemned more quickly than before.

Even so, blacks have pessimistic views of whites' attitudes. In 1989, one-fourth of blacks believed that at least a quarter of whites were in the Ku Klux Klan; one-fourth of blacks also believed that most whites shared the views of the KKK. In 1992, two-thirds of blacks believed that about half of whites were "basically prejudiced." (Whites also believed this about whites.)[129] One sociologist estimates that, despite the improvement in whites' attitudes, there are still two white racists for every African American. For socioeconomic reasons, blacks are more likely to come into contact with prejudiced whites, who live and work in closer proximity to blacks, than they are to come into contact with tolerant whites, who are more educated and prosperous.[130] Furthermore, some blacks have not experienced the overall improvements. It would be more surprising if they were not pessimistic.

When the push for civil rights opened doors, some blacks were not in a position to pass through. About a quarter of the black population lives in poverty—two and one half times the rate among the white population—and about a tenth, the poorest of the poor, exists in a state of economic and social "disintegration."[131] This "underclass" is trapped in a cycle of self-perpetuating problems from which it is extremely difficult to escape. These people are isolated from the rest of society and demoralized about their prospects for improvement.

The problems of the lower class and underclass were exacerbated by economic changes that began in the 1970s and hit the poor the hardest. Good-paying manufacturing jobs in the cities—the traditional path out of poverty for immigrant groups—disappeared. Chicago lost over three hundred thousand jobs, New York over five hundred thousand.[132] Many jobs were eliminated by automation, while many others were moved to foreign countries or to the suburbs. Although service jobs increased, most were outside the cities, required more education, or paid lower wages than the manufacturing jobs had.

As a result, many black men, especially, lost their jobs and lost their ability to support a family. This led not only to pressure on intact families but to a decrease in the number of "marriageable" black men and an increase in the number of households headed by black women.[133] The percentage of such households rose from about 20 percent in 1960 to 45 percent in 2000.[134] And 60 percent of

TABLE 4	Approval of Interracial Dating and Marriage Has Increased since the 1960s

The following percentages say it is all right for blacks and whites to date each other.

	Blacks	Whites
1963	NA	10
1987	72	43
1994	88	65
Ages 18–24	NA	85
Age 65 or over	NA	36

The following percentages say it is all right for blacks and whites to marry each other.

	Blacks	Whites
1958	NA	4
1968	48	17
1978	66	32
1983	76	38
1994	68	45

SOURCE: Stephan Thernstrom and Abigail Thernstrom, *America in Black and White* (New York: Simon & Schuster, 1997), 524–525.

black children live in such households. These families are among the poorest in the country (see Chapter 17).

Meanwhile, much of the black middle class fled the inner cities to the suburbs. Their migration left the ghettos with fewer healthy businesses, strong schools, or other institutions to provide stability and fewer role models to portray mainstream behavior.[135] By 1996, one Chicago ghetto with sixty-six thousand people had just one supermarket and one bank but forty-eight state-licensed lottery agents and ninety-nine state-licensed liquor stores and bars.[136] The combination of chronic unemployment in the inner cities and middle-class migration from the inner cities created an environment that offers ample opportunity and some incentive to use drugs, commit crimes, and engage in other types of antisocial behavior.

The development of crack, a cheap form of cocaine, in the mid-1980s aggravated these conditions. It led to more drug use and drug trafficking that overwhelmed whole neighborhoods. Crack ravaged the lives of users in ways that other drugs did not, and by producing steady demand by users and huge profits for dealers, it stimulated more violence.[137] The spread of AIDS, rampant among intravenous drug users, further aggravated these conditions.

Half of the victims of murder and more than half of those charged with murder are black, although the population is only 12 percent black.[138] Two-thirds of the defendants sent to state prisons for drug offenses are black. According to one study in Washington, D.C., one-fourth of black males born in the 1960s were charged with drug dealing between the ages of eighteen and twenty-four.[139] (Of course, part of this is due to harsher treatment of black drug offenders than of white ones.)

The plight of young black men is worse than that of any other group in society. A black man in Harlem had less chance of living past forty than a man in Bangladesh.[140] Moreover, by 1995, almost one of every three black men between the ages of twenty and twenty-nine was serving a criminal sentence in prison or was on probation or parole.[141] This situation, too, exacerbated the problem of "marriageable men" and female-headed black households.

After the riots in the 1960s, the Kerner Commission, appointed by President Johnson to examine the cause of the riots, concluded, "What white Americans have never fully understood—but what the Negro can never forget—is that white society is deeply implicated in the ghetto. White institutions created it, white institutions maintain it, and white society condones it." After the riots, however, governments did little to improve the conditions that precipitated the riots. Now the conditions in the ghettos are worse.

After the 1992 riots in Los Angeles that followed the trial of the police officers who beat Rodney King, there was more talk about improving conditions in the ghetto. But a columnist who had heard such talk before commented, "My guess is that when all is said and done, a great deal more will be said than done. The truth is we don't know any quick fixes for our urban ills and we lack the patience and resources for slow fixes."[142]

These problems are all the more difficult to resolve, because the cities have lost political power as they have lost population due to white flight and black migration. In 1992, for the first time, more voters (including many blacks) lived in the suburbs than in the cities. Suburban voters do not urge action on urban problems. Sometimes, in fact, they resist action if it means an increase in their taxes or a decrease in their services.

For the black lower class, and especially for the black underclass, it is apparent that civil rights are not enough. As one black leader said, "What good is a seat in the front of the bus if you don't have the money for the fare?"[143]

But most blacks do not fall in the lower class or underclass, and most do not dwell in the inner cities. It would be a serious mistake to hold the stereotypical view that the majority reside in the inner cities and that a majority of them live in dysfunctional families filled with crackheads and prone to violence.

Discrimination against Hispanics

Hispanics, also called Latinos, are people with Spanish-speaking backgrounds. The first Latinos came to America from Spain in the 1500s. They settled in the Southwest, and when the United States took this land from Mexico in 1848, they became U.S. citizens. Other Latinos came to America more recently (see Figure 1).

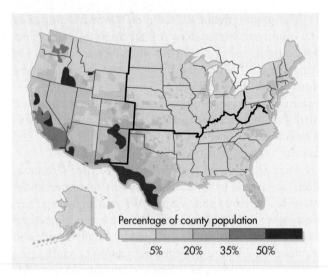

FIGURE 1 ■ Hispanics Are Concentrated in Southwest and West

Percentage of county population

5%   20%   35%   50%

SOURCE: *New York Times*, April 1, 2001, 184.

Latinos include groups with different cultural traditions. In fact, until rather recently, most Mexicans did not think of themselves as "Latinos" or "Hispanics" but rather in terms of their ancestral group, such as Mexican.[144] Many still do not identify with the larger group. About 61 percent trace their ancestry to Mexico and live mainly in the Southwest, though some live in large cities in the Midwest. About 15 percent are from Puerto Rico, which is a commonwealth—a self-governing territory—of the United States. As members of the commonwealth, they are U.S. citizens. Most live in New York, Boston, Chicago, and other cities in the North. Another 6 percent are from Cuba. Following the establishment of a communist government in Cuba in 1959, many fled to the United States and settled in south Florida. In recent years, Latinos from other Caribbean or Central American countries have immigrated to the United States to escape turmoil and oppression.

Despite the diversity of their origins, Latinos are heavily concentrated in six states. More than half live in California and Texas, where they make up one-third of the population, and many of the rest live in Florida, New Jersey, New York, and Illinois. But there are growing pockets elsewhere.

Latinos represent over 12 percent of the U.S. population. According to the 2000 census, they have overtaken blacks as the largest minority. Already the United States has the seventh largest Latino population in the world, and within the United States this group is the second fastest-growing minority (after Asians).

Latinos never endured slavery, but they have faced discrimination. Although numerous Latinos are Caucasian, many Puerto Ricans and Cubans have African ancestry, and many Mexicans have some Indian ancestry, so they have darker skin than non-Hispanic whites.

Like blacks, Hispanics have faced discrimination in education, employment, housing, and voting.[145]

Latinos also encounter discrimination due to continuing immigration. The illegal immigrants pouring in from Mexico exacerbate hostility and discrimination against Latinos, especially in the Southwest. U.S. Border Patrol and local law enforcement officials, who cannot tell the difference between Latinos who are citizens or legal residents and those who are not, often stop them for questioning not only at the border but inland as well. (Agents stopped the mayor of Pomona, California, more than one hundred miles from the border, and ordered him to produce papers to prove that he is a legal resident.) Even if officials are well intentioned, their conduct is considered harassment by law-abiding legal residents.

Latinos also encounter discrimination from police, as African Americans do. Police use racial profiling, suspecting them of crimes involving drugs as well as illegal immigration. In Illinois, Latinos constitute 8 percent of the population but 30 percent of those stopped by police.[146]

Discrimination in Education

For years Latino children in some areas were not allowed to attend schools at all. In other areas they were segregated into "Mexican" schools whose quality was not comparable with Anglo schools.[147]

In the 1940s, Mexican American organizations asked the courts to find that Mexican Americans were "white" so that they could not be segregated. The federal courts agreed. This strategy backfired, however, after the Supreme Court declared segregation by race illegal. Many school districts accomplished "integration" by combining blacks with Latinos, leaving non-Hispanic whites in separate schools.[148]

Even when admitted to schools, Latinos faced discrimination due to their language. Traditionally, teachers and administrators forbade students from speaking their native Spanish to each other in school. They reprimanded, spanked, or expelled those who did. Some even anglicized students' names in class and in school records so that "Jesus" became "Jesse" and "Miguel" became "Michael."[149]

Although de jure segregation has been struck down,[150] de facto segregation exists in northern and southwestern cities where Latinos are concentrated, due to residential segregation and white flight to the suburbs. Many Latinos attend schools with more than 90 percent minorities, and most attend schools with more than half minorities.[151]

Even where Latinos go to desegregated schools, they are often segregated within the schools. They face "second-generation discrimination," though not as much as blacks.[152]

Predominantly Latino schools, like predominantly black schools, are not as well funded as other schools. Because minority schools are frequently in poor communities, they do not receive as much revenue from property taxes. In San Antonio, Mexican American families were concentrated in the poorest districts, while wealthy families were concentrated in a section that was incorporated as a separate district, though it was surrounded on four sides by the rest of the city. Its property taxes financed its schools only. When Mexican American parents sued, the Burger Court ruled that the Fourteenth Amendment's equal protection clause does not require states to equalize funding between school districts.[153] Although some states proceeded to equalize funding, other states have not.

Latinos' primary problem in education, however, is the language barrier. Many are unable to speak English, causing them to fail in school and drop out of school at higher rates than other students, even African Americans. One-third of Latinos leave school at some point; one-fourth drop out in high school.[154]

Bilingual education was established to help such students. These classes use the students' native language to teach them English and also substantive subjects such as math. The goal is to transition from their native language to English within three years. In 1968, Congress encouraged bilingual education by providing funding, and in 1974, the Supreme Court, in a case brought by Chinese parents, held that schools must teach students in a language they can understand.[155] This can be their native language, or it can be English if they have been taught English. These federal actions prompted many states to establish bilingual education programs. More than 150 languages, from Chinese to Yapese, have been offered nationwide. Because almost three-fourths of the students who do not speak English are Hispanic, Spanish is the most common.[156]

Bilingual education programs have been controversial. Latino parents want their children to learn English and to learn it well. A survey of Latinos in forty cities found that more than 90 percent thought U.S. citizens and residents should learn English.[157] A survey of Cuban Americans in south Florida found that 98 percent thought it was important for their children to read and write "perfect English."[158] And their children apparently agree. More than four-fifths of immigrant children in south Florida and more than two-thirds of those in San Diego prefer English to their familial language.[159] Latino parents and children worry that bilingual programs will delay the mastery of English. Seventy-five percent of recent immigrants, including 56 percent of Mexican immigrants, oppose these programs.[160]

In fact, bilingual programs have not worked as well in practice as they have promised in theory. Although their results are difficult to measure because the programs vary, being staffed at different levels and for different lengths of time, they have been disappointing. Perhaps these results should not be surprising, given that the programs grew partly out of political as well as pedagogical needs. Latino groups in the Southwest saw them as a way to tap into federal antipoverty funds.[161]

Indeed, the debate revolves around politics as much as education. Some Latino groups see bilingual education as a way to preserve their native language and culture. They consider it to be a component of multiculturalism. So they want it not as a temporary bridge until students learn English but as a permanent fixture through high school. Many Anglo citizens, especially those who fear the influx of immigrants, also see bilingual education as a way to preserve Latinos' native language and culture. But these Anglos discount the need for multiculturalism. Instead, they want the students to be exposed only to English so that they will be more likely to assimilate into society. Some Latino leaders accuse these Anglo citizens of "cultural genocide."[162]

For both sides, then, bilingual education is a symbolic issue. It prompts concerns, even fears, about the relative dominance of Anglo culture and Hispanic culture and about the extent to which Anglo Americans will make room for Hispanic Americans in society.

The debate is complicated by economic and bureaucratic problems in bilingual programs. Because they require more teachers and smaller classes, the programs are expensive and impractical. Many schools cannot find enough teachers in the necessary languages. California, where half of all students in bilingual programs lived, fell twenty-one thousand teachers short in 1998.[163] Schools were unable to offer bilingual education to two-thirds of the students who were eligible.[164]

Stephanie Maze/Corbis

Cuban Americans are more likely to be middle class than are members of other Latino groups.

For all of these reasons, California citizens voted to abolish bilingual programs in 1998. Now non-English-speaking students receive intensive immersion in English for one year and then move into regular classes. Initial research indicates that Spanish-speaking students are improving rapidly in their ability to read English and to understand other subjects taught in English.[165]

Despite the disappointing results of bilingual programs and the common perceptions of many Americans, current immigrants throughout the country are learning English. Among Spanish speakers in the United States, over 90 percent speak English.[166] Although about half of those who arrived as teenagers or adults do not speak English proficiently, almost all of those who arrived as younger children or who are in the second generation do speak English proficiently.[167] Cuban Americans are learning it as fast or faster than any group in history.[168] Mexican Americans are learning it as they live longer in the United States. Although many of those who come for work and plan to return to Mexico do not speak English, most of those who plan to remain in the United States learn to speak more English, and almost all of their children learn to speak fluent English.[169]

It is true that some immigrant communities, especially Cubans in south Florida and Mexicans in parts of the Southwest, are so large that people can survive without learning English. But most feel pressure to learn English to function in the broader society and for their children to succeed in school.

Combating Discrimination against Hispanics

In the 1960s, Latino advocacy groups tried to imitate African American groups by using protests and other forms of direct action. The Chicano movement attempted to forge a powerful bloc from the diverse population of the Hispanic people. Cesar Chavez successfully led a coalition of labor, civil rights, and religious groups to obtain better working conditions for migrant farm workers in California. But few other visible national leaders or organizations emerged.

In 1977, when the first Hispanic member of Congress from California approached the Speaker of the House about the possibility of establishing an Hispanic caucus, as other groups had established various caucuses, the Speaker teased, "Where are you going to hold the meetings—in a telephone booth?"[170]

Latinos are more diverse and less cohesive than blacks. Most do not even consider themselves part of a large group of Hispanics.[171] They profess strong loyalty to people of their national origin and have little contact with Hispanics with other ancestry. Thus, most do not call themselves "Hispanics" or "Latinos," but "Mexican Americans," "Puerto Ricans," or "Cuban Americans."[172] Also, they have different legal statuses. Puerto

Latinos are gradually improving their status. This woman toils as a migrant farm worker, but her son graduated from college and now runs personnel management programs for farmers.

Ricans have American citizenship by birth, but many Latinos do not have it at all. And they lack a common defining experience in their background, such as slavery for blacks, to unite them.

But where they are highly concentrated, they are increasingly powerful at the local and state levels of government. Rather than portraying themselves as a victimized group, they are moving into the mainstream. Rather than focusing primarily on immigration issues, bilingual education, and affirmative action, they are addressing broader concerns, such as health care and school class-size reduction. Yet Latino politicians have not shaped a common agenda, perhaps because Latino people, of diverse origins, do not share a common agenda.[173]

They are potentially powerful at the national level as well. With their huge numbers, Latinos are a coveted bloc of voters. Yet many are not citizens, and many of those who are do not register and vote. Although the Latino and African American populations are nearly the same size, 6 million more blacks are registered to vote.[174] Nevertheless, the Latino voters are numerous enough to be courted. Although most, except Cuban Americans, are Democrats, the Republicans believe they need to attract more if their party hopes to win national elections in the future. The Bush administration has adopted a strategy to entice them. President Bush appointed a Cuban American as secretary of the Department of Housing and Urban Development and a Mexican American as counsel to the White House. He proposed granting legal status to the Mexican immigrants illegally living in the United States now, though this proposal died a quiet death after September 11 turned the focus to problems with illegal immigrants. And he sprinkles Spanish into his speeches before Hispanic or mixed audiences.

At the same time, Latino individuals are moving up society's ladder. More attend college and become managers and professionals. At least those who speak educated English appear to be following the pattern of Southern and Eastern European immigrants—arriving poor, facing discrimination, but eventually working their way up. At the same time, they are also assimilating through high rates of marriage to non-Latinos.

Discrimination against Native Americans

More than 2 million Native Americans live in the United States. Although some are Eskimos and Aleuts from Alaska, most are Indians, representing more than 550 tribes with different histories, customs, and languages. Most are proud of their tribal heritage and prefer to be known by their tribal name, such as Cheyenne or Sioux, than by the collective terms, Native Americans and Indians. About half live on reservations (see Figure 2).

Although Native Americans have faced some discrimination similar to that against blacks and Hispanics, they have endured much discrimination of a different nature.

Government Policy toward Native Americans

The government's policy toward Native Americans has varied over the years, ranging from forced separation at one extreme to forced assimilation at the other.

Separation Initially, the policy was separation. For many years people believed the continent was so vast that most of its interior would remain wilderness, populated

"I love the way you make those yams. You'll have to give me the recipe before your culture is obliterated from the face of the earth."

by Indians who would have ample room to live and hunt. The Constitution reflects this belief. It grants Congress authority to "regulate commerce with foreign nations, and among the several states, and with the Indian tribes." In early cases, Chief Justice John Marshall described the tribes as "dependent domestic nations."[175] They were within U.S. borders but outside its political process.

Early treaties reinforced separation by establishing boundaries between Indians and non-Indians. The government thought these boundaries were necessary for its growth, the Indians for their survival. The boundaries were intended to minimize conflict. White hunters or settlers who ventured across the boundaries could be punished as the Indians saw fit.

But as the country grew, it became increasingly difficult to contain settlers within the boundaries. Mounting pressure to push Native Americans farther west led to the Indian Removal Act of 1830, which authorized removal of tribes east of the Mississippi River and relocation on reservations west of the river. At the time, people considered the Great Plains to be the great American desert, unfit for habitation by whites but suitable for Indians. At first, removal was voluntary, but eventually it became mandatory for most and was supervised by the U.S. cavalry.

Assimilation and Citizenship As more settlers moved west, the vision of separate Indian country far enough beyond white civilization to prevent conflict faded. In the 1880s, the government switched its policy to assimilation. Prompted by Christian churches, officials sought to "civilize" the Indians—that is, to incorporate them into the larger society, whether they wanted to be incorporated or not. In place of their traditional means of subsistence,

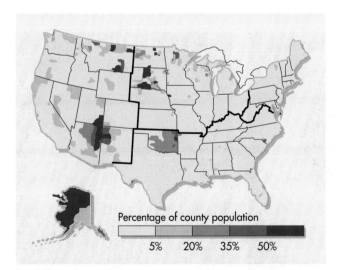

FIGURE 2 ■ Concentration of Native American Populations

SOURCE: *New York Times*, April 1, 2001, 184.

Percentage of county population

5%   20%   35%   50%

rendered useless once the tribes were removed from their homeland, the government subdivided reservation land into small tracts and allotted these tracts to tribe members in hopes that they would turn to farming as white and black settlers had. (In the process, the government reclaimed "surplus" land and sold it to white settlers. Ultimately, the Indians lost about two-thirds of their reservation land.)[176] Bureau of Indian Affairs agents, who supervised the reservations, tried to root out Native American ways and replace them with white dress and hairstyles, the English language, and the Christian religion. Government boarding schools separated Native American children from their families to instill these new practices.

Early in the history of the United States, Native Americans were not considered citizens but members of separate nations. Treaties made exceptions for those who married whites and for those who left their tribes and abandoned their tribal customs. But in 1890, after government policy switched to assimilation, Congress permitted some who remained with their tribes on reservations to become citizens by applying to the U.S. government. Citizenship was sometimes marked by a formal ceremony. In one, the Indian shot his last arrow and then took hold of the handles of a plow to demonstrate his assimilation.[177] After World War I, Congress granted citizenship to those who served in the military during the war, and finally, in 1924, Congress extended it to all those born in the United States.

Citizenship enabled Indians to vote and hold office, though some states effectively barred them from the polls for decades. Arizona denied them the right to vote until 1948, Utah until 1956.[178]

Tribal Restoration By the 1930s, the government recognized the negative consequences of coerced assimilation. Most Indians could speak English, but they were poorly educated in other respects. And with their traditional means of earning a living gone, most were poverty stricken. The policy led to destruction of Native American ways without much assimilation into white society. Consequently, in 1934, Congress implemented a new policy of tribal restoration that recognized Indians as distinct persons and tribes as autonomous entities encouraged to govern themselves once again. Traditional cultural and religious practices were accepted, and children, no longer forced to attend boarding schools, were taught some Indian languages.

The government even made an effort to settle claims for wrongful taking of tribal land. For several decades, the Indian Claims Commission authorized the payment of money—not the return of property—to tribes whose land was illegally taken by the government any time since 1776. But the commission faced an impossible task. Most tribes had a hazy conception of land ownership and did not keep written records. How would disputed land be valued—according to the earlier subsistence living of the Indians or the later market value to farmers, ranchers, and miners? And how would religious land be valued? (Native religions focus on particular parcels of land or prominent features of the landscape, rather than on buildings such as churches or figures such as Jesus.) Ultimately, the commission authorized as much money as it thought was politically feasible, but this amounted to less than $1,000 for every Native American.[179]

Reflecting the policy of tribal restoration and the efforts of other minorities in the 1960s and 1970s, Indian interest groups became active. Indian law firms pursued cases in court, seeking to protect not only tribal independence and traditional ways, but also land, mineral, and water resources. The diversity and the dispersion of the tribes—they are divided by culture and by geogra-

Tom Torlino, before and after his transformation at a boarding school in Carlisle, Pennsylvania. Native Americans were shorn of their hair and clothes and trained to adopt white ways.

Denver Public Library, Western History Collection, J. N. Choate (X-32984)

Denver Public Library, Western History Collection, J. N. Choate (X-32985)

phy, often located in the remotest and poorest parts of the country—make it difficult for them to present a united front. Nevertheless, they have been able to wrest some autonomy from the government. In particular, they have gotten more authority over the educational and social programs administered by the Bureau of Indian Affairs for the tribes.[180]

In recent years, Indians have fought for an end to digging up old gravesites and for a return of bones and artifacts unearthed from them. With little regard for Native American culture, "pothunters" have searched for artifacts to sell to collectors. Such looting raises the ire of archaeologists who say, "We'll never know what's been taken or how it relates to what remains in the ground. Everything has been scrambled." But digging for scientific purposes itself enrages some Indians, who say that archaeologists are "hardly any better than grave robbers themselves; only difference is they've got a state permit." Until recent years, in fact, many laws about exhumation of bones applied only to those of whites.[181]

In recent years, Indians also have fought for the return of some tribal land and for an accounting of the money owed them for the use of their individual land held in trust by the government. In the early nineteenth century, the government took tribal land and put it in trust for the Indians. But then the government divided the land, paying individual Indians a pittance and offering the parcels to white settlers. In this way the Indians lost most of their territory. The government held the remaining land in trust for the Indians, leasing it to ranchers, loggers, and miners who contracted with the government to use it. The government collected the rents and royalties for the Indians. But the BIA did not bother to keep accurate records or even to preserve its records. Now a class-action lawsuit, dubbed "the Indian Enron Case," seeks a reckoning of the accounts and a payment to the Indians who are owed money.[182]

Some tribes are enjoying renewed vitality with the income they receive from mineral rights or gambling casinos. After a Supreme Court ruling and a congressional law in the 1980s underscored tribal sovereignty on tribal land, tribes could establish gambling casinos on reservations, even if their state did not allow casinos.[183] Almost three hundred tribes have done so, although less than a dozen have found a bonanza.[184] With their new revenues, the successful tribes have begun to buy into the political process, as other groups have done. Threatened by gambling interests in Las Vegas and Atlantic City, which fear that tribal casinos will lure away potential customers, the tribes have formed their own lobby, the National Indian Gaming Association, and made their own contributions to politicians.

Overall, Native Americans enjoy renewed pride. From 1970 to 1990, according to birth and death records, the Indian population increased by 760,000.

Native Americans feel renewed cultural pride but also the lure of modern American technology.

Yet, according to people's self-identification for the census, this population rose by 1.4 million.[185] Evidently, many people, including those with only distant Indian ancestry, who did not wish to identify themselves as Indians in 1970 did so two decades later. Now more Indians share the views of one activist who says, "You have a federal government, state governments, and tribal governments—three sovereigns in one country. This is the civil rights movement of Native Americans."[186]

Nevertheless, Indians remain at the bottom of America's racial and ethnic ladder. They are the least educated and most unemployed group, the poorest and sickest group, with the highest rates of alcoholism and the lowest life expectancy, of any people in the country.

Sex Discrimination

Discrimination against Women

For many generations, people believed that natural differences between the sexes required them to occupy separate spheres of life. Men would dominate the public domain of work and government, while women would dominate the private domain of the home. Both domains were important, and men were considered superior in one while women were considered superior in the other. Unlike racial minorities, women were not held in disdain in every aspect of life.

Thomas Jefferson, the most egalitarian of the Founders, reflected this widespread view when he said, "Were our state a pure democracy there would still be excluded from our deliberations women, who, to prevent deprivation of morals and ambiguity of issues, should not mix promiscuously in gatherings of men."[187] That is, women are more moral than men, so they would be corrupted by politics, but also more irrational, so they would confuse the issues. For both reasons, they should not be involved in politics.

Women were denied the right to vote in most places, and married women were denied other rights. They did not have the right to manage property they owned before marriage, to manage wages they received from jobs, to enter into contracts, or to sue. Although some states eventually enacted laws granting women these rights, when disputes arose within families, male judges hesitated to tell other men how to treat their wives. Often, then, these rights did not exist in practice until well into the twentieth century.

Even women's citizenship was tied to their husbands'. If a foreign woman married an American man, she automatically became a United States citizen. But if an American woman married a foreign man, she automatically lost her United States citizenship. (Women's citizenship would not become independent of their husbands' until 1922, shortly after women gained the right to vote.)

Women were also barred from schools and jobs. Before the Civil War, they were not admitted to public high schools. Because they were being prepared for motherhood, education was considered unnecessary, even dangerous. According to the *Encyclopaedia Britannica* in 1800, women had smaller brains than men.[188] Education would fatigue them and possibly ruin their reproductive organs. Similarly, before the Civil War, women were not encouraged to hold jobs. Those who sought employment were shunted into jobs that were seen as extensions of the domestic domain, such as producing textiles, clothes, and shoes in sex-segregated factories.[189]

This traditional conception of gender roles created problems for women who did not fit the mold. After the Civil War, Myra Bradwell ran a private school, founded a weekly newspaper, and worked for civic organizations. She was active in the women's suffrage movement and instrumental in persuading the Illinois legislature to expand women's legal rights. But after studying law, she was denied a license to practice law solely because she was a woman. The U.S. Supreme Court upheld the Illinois policy in 1873.[190] Justice Joseph Bradley declared:

> [L]aw as well as nature itself, has always recognized a wide difference in the respective spheres and destinies of man and woman. Man is, or should be the woman's protector and defender. The natural and proper timidity and delicacy which belongs to the female sex evidently unfits it for many of the occupations of civil life. . . . The constitution of the family organization . . . indicates the domestic sphere as that which properly belongs to the domain and functions of womanhood. The harmony . . . of interests and views which belong, or should belong, to the family institution is repugnant to the idea of a woman adopting a distinct and independent career from that of her husband. . . . The paramount destiny and mission of woman are to fulfill the noble and benign offices of wife and mother. This is the law of the Creator. And the rules of civil society must be adapted to the general constitution of things, and cannot be based upon exceptional cases.

Sometimes it was difficult to distinguish between this separate-but-equal view and discriminatory treatment. In the 1860s and 1870s, the doctors who practiced scientific medicine formed the American Medical Association (AMA) to drive out other people who offered medical services. These people included not only hucksters and quacks but also women who served as midwives or abortionists. Although abortions had been widely available, the AMA, drawing upon popular fears about the women's suffrage movement, convinced male state legislators that abortions were "a threat to social order and to male authority." The woman who seeks an abortion, the AMA explained, "becomes unmindful of the course marked out for her by Providence, she overlooks the duties imposed on her by the marriage contract. She yields to the pleasure—but shrinks from the pains and responsibilities of maternity. . . . Let not the husband of such a wife flatter himself that he possesses her affection."[191]

Sometimes the discriminatory treatment was even more blatant. The Mississippi Supreme Court acknowledged a husband's right to beat his wife.[192] Using the "rule of thumb," it claimed, a husband could not beat his wife with a weapon thicker than his thumb.

The Women's Movement

Early feminists were determined to remedy these inequities. Many had gained political and organizational experience in the abolitionist movement. It was not considered "unladylike" for women to campaign for the end of slavery, because the movement was associated with religious groups. Yet women were barely tolerated by the male leaders of the movement and not allowed to participate fully in the major antislavery society. They formed their own antislavery society, but when they attended a convention of antislavery societies, they were not allowed to sit with the male delegates.

Angry at such treatment, the women held a meeting to discuss the "social, civil and religious rights of women." This first Women's Rights Convention in 1848 adopted a declaration of rights based on the Declaration of Independence. It said, "We hold these truths to be self-evident: that all men and women are created equal." The convention also passed a resolution in favor of women's suffrage.

Following the Civil War, women who had worked in the abolitionist movement expected that women, as well as blacks, would get legal rights and voting rights. When the Fourteenth and Fifteenth Amendments did not include women, they felt betrayed and disassociated themselves from the black movement. They formed their own organizations to campaign for women's suffrage. This movement, led by Susan B. Anthony and Elizabeth

Cady Stanton, succeeded in 1920, when the Nineteenth Amendment gave women the right to vote.

Then dissension developed within the women's movement. Many groups felt the passage of the Nineteenth Amendment was but a first step in the struggle for equal rights. They proposed the Equal Rights Amendment to remedy remaining inequities. Other groups felt the battle had been won. They opposed the Equal Rights Amendment, arguing that it would overturn labor laws recently enacted to protect women. Because of this dissension and the conservatism in the country, the movement became relatively dormant.[193]

The movement reemerged in the 1960s. As a result of the civil rights movement, many women recognized their own inferior status. Numerous writers sensitized more women to this. Betty Friedan published *The Feminine Mystique*, which grew out of a questionnaire she circulated at her fifteenth college reunion. The book addressed the malaise that afflicted college-educated women who had been socialized into the feminine role but who were finding it unsatisfying.[194] Friedan's manifesto became the best-selling nonfiction paperback in 1964. In 1966, Friedan and other upper-middle-class, professional women formed the National Organization for Women (NOW). They resolved "to bring women into full participation in the mainstream of American society now."

Other women, also middle class but veterans of the civil rights and antiwar movements, had developed a taste for political action and gained political experience. They formed other organizations. Where NOW fought primarily for women's political and economic rights, the other organizations fought more broadly for women's liberation in all spheres of life. Together these organizations pushed the issue of discrimination against women back onto the public agenda.

Nevertheless, they were not taken seriously for some years. In 1970, *Time* magazine reported, "No one knows how many shirts lay wrinkling in laundry baskets last week as thousands of women across the country turned out for the first big demonstration of the women's liberation movement. They took over [New York City's Fifth Avenue], providing not only protest but some of the best sidewalk ogling in years."[195]

Although the movement tried to broaden its base beyond upper-middle-class and college-educated women, it was unable to do so. The movement generated an image of privileged women who looked with disdain on other women. *Housewife* became a derisive term. Traditional women viewed the movement as be-

During World War II, women were urged into the labor force to replace men called to war. "Rosie the Riveter" became a symbol of women working in the war effort. Following the war, they were told that it was patriotic to go home and give their jobs to returning veterans. The 1955 magazine cover on the right depicts the stereotypical women's role in this postwar era before the beginning of the modern women's movement.

"Some kids at school called you a feminist, Mom, but I punched them out."

ing antimotherhood and antifamily and, as it became more radical in the 1970s, prolesbian. This image gave "women's liberation" a bad name, even while most women agreed with most goals of the movement.[196] This image persists. More Americans believe that extraterrestrials have visited Earth than think that "feminist" is a compliment.[197] (It is unclear whether this says more about Americans' attitudes toward gender equality or about our penchant for paranoid conspiracy theories.)

The Movement in Congress and the Courts

Congress initially did not take the modern women's movement seriously, either. When civil rights proponents sponsored a bill to forbid racial discrimination in employment, eighty-one-year-old Representative Howard Smith (D-Va.) proposed an amendment to add sex discrimination to the bill. A foe of equal rights for blacks, Smith thought his proposal so ludicrous and radical that it would help defeat the entire bill. Indeed, during debate on the amendment, members of Congress laughed so hard that they could barely hear each other speak.[198] But the joke was on them, because the amendment, and then the entire bill, passed.

Congress later adopted legislation to forbid sex discrimination in credit and education. Congress also passed the Equal Rights Amendment.

The **Equal Rights Amendment (ERA)** simply declared, "Equality of rights under the law shall not be denied or abridged by the United States or by any state on account of sex." Introduced in 1923 and every year thereafter, Congress passed the amendment in 1972.

It appeared the amendment would zip through the states. Both parties endorsed it, and the majority of the public supported it. But after about half the states ratified it, the amendment bogged down. Observers noted

that it would make women subject to the draft and, possibly, combat duty. Opponents charged that it would result in unisex restrooms and homosexual rights. Legal scholars denied that it would lead to these latter consequences, but after the judicial activism of the 1950s, 1960s, and 1970s, some people distrusted the courts to interpret the amendment.

The main problem, however, proved to be the symbolism of the amendment. For many women, the ERA represented an attack on the traditional values of motherhood, the family, and the home. Early feminists emphasized equality in employment so much that they gave some women the impression that they were against these values. Traditional women sensed implicit criticism for being housewives.[199] To underscore the symbolism, women in anti-ERA groups baked bread for state legislators about to vote on ratification. Because of the symbolism, even some women who favored equality opposed the amendment itself. Although many young women supported it, fewer of their mothers and grandmothers did; and although many working women supported it, fewer housewives did. Women's organizations had not created an effective grassroots campaign to sway traditional women. Ultimately, the disaffection of many women allowed male legislators to vote according to their traditional attitudes. They did not need to worry that a strong majority of their female constituents would object.[200]

In 1980, the Republican Party became the first party not to endorse the ERA since 1940, and President Reagan became the first president not to support the amendment since Truman.

When the deadline set by Congress expired in 1982, the ERA fell three states short of ratification by the necessary three-fourths—thirty-eight—of the states. Like the Nineteenth Amendment, it was not ratified primarily by southern states.

Courts traditionally upheld laws that limited women's participation in the public domain and occasionally even laws that diminished their standing in the private domain. As late as 1970, the Ohio Supreme Court held that a wife is a husband's servant with "no legally recognized feelings or rights."[201]

The Burger Court finally reversed this pattern of decisions. In 1971, for the first time, the Court struck down a law that discriminated against women,[202] heralding a long series of rulings that invalidated a variety of such laws. In these rulings, the Court used the congressional statutes and also broadened the Fourteenth Amendment's equal protection clause to apply to women as well as to racial minorities.

The change was especially apparent in a pair of cases involving the selection of jurors. For the pool of potential jurors, some states drew the names of men, but not women, from voter registration or other lists. These states allowed women to serve only if they voluntarily signed

Women brokers at Merrill-Lynch, angry about bias in pay and promotion, have hired planes to pull banners over golf tournaments, auto races, and car shows sponsored by the firm. More than nine hundred sex discrimination claims were filed against Merrill-Lynch.

up at the courthouse. Consequently, few women served. In 1961, the Court let Florida use these procedures because the "woman is still regarded as the center of home and family life."[203] In 1975, however, the Court forbade Louisiana from using similar procedures,[204] thus overturning a precedent only fourteen years old.

The Court's rulings rejected the traditional stereotypes that men are the breadwinners and women the childrearers in society. The Court invalidated Utah's law that required divorced fathers to support their daughters until age eighteen but their sons until twenty-one.[205] The state assumed that the daughters would get married and be supported by their husbands, whereas the sons would need to get educated for their careers. But the Court noted, "No longer is the female destined solely for the home."

Employment The Civil Rights Act of 1964 forbids discrimination on the basis of sex as well as race in hiring, promoting, and firing. It prohibits discrimination on the basis of sex, except where sex is a "bona fide occupational qualification" for the job. The EEOC, which enforces the act, interprets it broadly and accepts sex as a legitimate qualification for very few jobs. For example, employers can seek only men or only women to fill particular jobs such as restroom attendants, lingerie salesclerks, models, or actors. On the other hand, employers cannot seek only males for jobs men traditionally held, such as those that entail heavy physical labor, unpleasant working conditions, late-night hours, overtime, or travel.

Some employers are reluctant to comply. For matched pairs of men and women, résumés were sent to sixty-five Philadelphia restaurants in 1995. The men were more than twice as likely to get an interview and more than five times as likely to get the job at the higher-priced restaurants than the equally qualified women were.[206]

The **Equal Pay Act** of 1963 requires that women and men receive equal pay for equal work. The act makes exceptions for merit, productivity, and seniority.

As a result of the act, the gap between what women and men earn has slowly been shrinking. For workers with the same job and experience, women earn $0.89 for every $1.00 men earn.[207] The gap is mostly between married women and married men. Single women and single men between twenty-one and thirty-five receive nearly equal pay. When the women get married, however, their pay starts to lag, and when they have children, it lags further, apparently because they work fewer hours due to child care and household responsibilities.[208]

Overall, working women make less than working men primarily because they have different jobs than men, and these jobs pay much less. Traditionally, women were shunted into a small number of jobs. These "pink-collar" jobs include secretaries (98 percent are women), household workers (97 percent), child care workers (97 percent), nurses (93 percent), bank tellers (90 percent), librarians (83 percent), elementary school teachers (83 percent), and health technicians (81 percent). In contrast, few women are carpenters (1 percent), firefighters (2 percent), mechanics (4 percent), or truck drivers (5 percent).[209]

Although the Equal Pay Act mandates equal pay for equal work, it does not require equal pay for comparable work—usually called "comparable worth." According to a personnel study in Washington state, maintenance carpenters and secretaries performed comparable jobs, but the carpenters, mostly men, made about $600 a month more than the secretaries, mostly women. In general, "men's jobs" paid about 20 percent more than comparable "women's jobs." These findings prompted unions representing government employees in the state to file a suit and demand an increase in pay for jobs held mostly by women. The federal court of appeals, in an opinion by Judge Anthony Kennedy, now on the Supreme Court, rejected comparable worth. Nevertheless, some state and city governments implemented comparable worth plans for their employees after prodding by unions and women's groups. Most private companies, however, did not adopt comparable worth because it would require them to pay many of their women employees more.

Although formal barriers against women have been lifted, informal ones remain. Women face male stereotyping. Their superiors and colleagues often assume that women are not serious about careers, will quit to have babies, are too emotional, and are not tough enough. Women also feel excluded from informal networks of communication that transact business.[210] In addition to these barriers, some women also face sexual harassment. (See the box "Sexual Harassment at Work.")

Mothers with young children confront more obstacles. Their male employers and coworkers think women should be responsible for child rearing, but these men do little to accommodate the demands of child rearing. Most companies do not provide paid maternity leaves, flexible schedules, or on-site day care. The United States lags far behind many other countries, ninety-eight of which grant partly paid maternity leaves for at least three months.[211] Only California provides partly paid family leaves (55 percent of a worker's wages for up to six weeks).

Congress passed and President Clinton signed a bill requiring employers to grant unpaid maternity and paternity leaves. Companies must allow unpaid leaves for up to three months for workers with newborn or recently adopted children or with seriously ill family members. The act applies to companies that have fifty employees and to workers who work twenty-five hours a week for a year.[212] This covers about half of American workers.

Relatively few workers have taken advantage of family leaves where they are available. Most workers cannot afford to take unpaid leave. Moreover, managers often do not support such measures, and coworkers resent the additional burdens, so employees are reluctant to take advantage of them. At a time when many companies have laid off workers to cut costs, "If you look like you are not career-oriented, you can lose your job."[213]

Mothers and fathers with young children often face unreasonable time demands from employers accustomed to hiring married men with a wife at home to rear the children, maintain the house, and run the errands. Now employers are putting the same demands on married women. Nobody is left to do the jobs of the housewife. Although women often continue to perform most of them, both spouses frequently feel stretched thin and stressed out.

Not surprisingly, among men with children, those who have a wife at home rise up the career ladder faster

Men resisted the expansion of women's athletics. The Boston Marathon traditionally was for men only, and when the first woman tried to participate in 1967, a marathon official assaulted her.

than those who have a wife working outside the home. The latter men apparently put in less "face time" at work. Executives who reach the higher rungs "almost always" are men who have a wife at home.[214] An executive of a Fortune 500 company, in a conversation with business professors at a southwestern university in a recent year, admitted that his company still prefers to hire men married to a woman who remains at home.[215]

Thus, women have gained some acceptance in the workplace, but they, and their spouses, have not yet overcome the expectations that developed long before they were ever allowed in the workplace.

Credit The Equal Credit Opportunity Act of 1974 forbids discrimination on the basis of sex or marital status in credit transactions. Historically, banks, savings and loans, credit card companies, and retail stores discriminated against women. Typically, these businesses determine how much money people can borrow according to how much they earn. Yet the lenders refused loans to single women, regardless of income, because they assumed that the women would work only until they got married and became pregnant. Likewise, the lenders did not count a wife's income as part of a couple's total income, again because they assumed the wife would work temporarily. Only if women were professionals or in their forties would lenders count their income the same as men's. When businesses lent money to a married couple, they put the transactions in just the husband's name. Upon divorce or widowhood, women had no credit record and little chance to obtain credit.

The Equal Credit Opportunity Act requires lenders to lend to single women and to count the wife's income as part of a couple's total income. It restricts lenders from asking women whether they intend to bear children. The act also requires lenders to put accounts in the names of both spouses if they request.

Education The Education Amendments of 1972 (to the Civil Rights Act of 1964) forbid discrimination on the basis of sex in schools and colleges that receive federal aid. The amendments were prompted by discrimination against women by undergraduate and graduate colleges, especially in admissions and financial aid.

The language of the amendments, often referred to as **"Title IX,"** is so broad that the Department of Education, which administers them, has established rules that cover more aspects of education than their congressional supporters expected.[216] The department has used the amendments to prod institutions into employing and promoting more female teachers and administrators, opening vocational training classes to women and home economics classes to men, and offering equal athletic programs to women. If institutions do not comply, the government can cut off their federal aid.

The amendments have affected athletic programs especially. Before the amendments, schools provided fewer sports for females than for males, and they spent far fewer dollars—for scholarships, coaches, and facilities—on women's sports. Now the department interprets the amendments to require a school either to have approximately the same percentage of female athletes as female undergraduates, to continually expand opportunities for female athletes, or to fully accommodate the interests and abilities of female students. (The latter would occur if a school's female students were satisfied that it offered sufficient opportunities for them, given their interests and abilities, even if the opportunities were not equal to those for men.)

Very few colleges meet the first requirement. To comply, most are trying to meet the second requirement by expanding the number of women's sports. But they worry that they will have to fulfill the first requirement eventually. And they fear that they will have to cap the squad size of their football team, which has the most players and costs the most money, to do so. This would lessen the imbalance in the numbers of male and female athletes, and it would free more money for women's teams.

Thus, some colleges have resisted enforcement of Title IX, partly because it comes at a time when athletic departments are struggling to make ends met and partly because it threatens deeply ingrained cultural values that are reflected in men's athletics. Administrators and boosters fear that women's sports will take money from men's sports and thereby weaken the primacy of men's athletics.

When Brown University tried to eliminate women's volleyball and gymnastics (at the same time it dropped men's golf and water polo), members of the women's teams sued. More than sixty schools filed briefs supporting Brown's decisions and criticizing the department's interpretations of Title IX. Lower courts ruled against Brown, and in 1997, the Supreme Court refused to hear the case, which left the lower courts' rulings in-tact. The Supreme Court's refusal signaled that the department's interpretations would remain and the schools would have to comply.

Already Title IX has had a major impact. Colleges have increased their women's teams, from an average of six to an average of eight.[217] The number of schools that offer women's soccer, for example, has more than tripled.[218] On the other hand, to reduce the gender imbalance, many colleges have eliminated low-profile men's teams, especially wrestling, gymnastics, tennis, and track (see Figure 3). Now women make up 42 percent of all college athletes and receive 42 percent of the scholarship money (though their teams have lower coaches' salaries and operating expenses).[219]

Colleges with a successful football or basketball program have increased their women's teams the most because these sports generate revenue that funds women's sports. Colleges with no football program have also increased their women's teams. Colleges with football programs that do not generate a profit (and most do not) lag behind. They pour money into football but lack revenue from television or bowl contracts to fund women's sports.[220]

Title IX has also had a major impact on high schools, which have increased their girls' teams, and on American Olympic teams, which have benefited from the women's training in college.

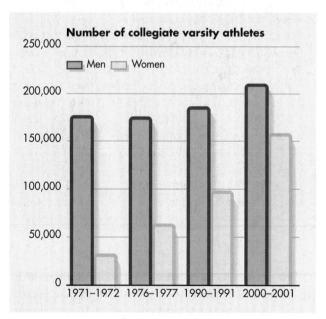

FIGURE 3 ■ **Men's and Women's Participation in Varsity Sports Has Increased since Title IX**
Both men's and women's participation in varsity sports has increased since passage of Title IX. Although many colleges have dropped some men's teams, more schools offer more sports than in the 1970s, so more men overall are participating despite the discontinued teams.

SOURCE: National Collegiate Athletic Association, reported in Welch Suggs, "Title IX at 30," *Chronicle of Higher Education*, June 21, 2002, 39.

Although the Supreme Court had ruled that sexual harassment was a form of job discrimination prohibited by the Civil Rights Act of 1964,[1] and Congress had passed a law allowing victims to collect monetary damages from employers for distress, illness, or loss of their job due to harassment, there was little public awareness of the law until Clarence Thomas's confirmation hearings for appointment to the Supreme Court in 1991.

The hearings propelled sexual harassment to the forefront of societal debate. For seven days the public was riveted to the televised hearings. Anita Hill's charges—that Thomas, as her supervisor at the Equal Employment Opportunity Commission, made lewd comments about her, about sex, about finding pubic hairs on Coke cans and watching animals have sex in films—led to many discussions around workplace office coolers.

After the hearings, more women recognized that behavior they had dismissed as merely annoying was actually harassment. The number of complaints filed with the EEOC doubled (though in recent years it has leveled off).

Courts recognize two types of sexual harassment. The most obvious is quid pro quo, in which a supervisor makes unwanted sexual advances and either promises good consequences (for example, a promotion) if the employee goes along or threatens bad consequences (for example, an undesir-able reassignment) if the employee refuses. Less obvious is creating a hostile environment that interferes with the employee's ability to do the job. To prove a hostile environment, the employee must demonstrate that the conduct was severe or persistent.

Paula Jones's suit against President Clinton was dismissed because the alleged sexual advance was considered neither severe enough nor, as a single incident, persistent enough to constitute a hostile environment. If it happened, the judge said, it was "boorish and offensive" but not technically harassment. Although many men seem to worry that innocuous comments will be classified as sexual harassment, Justice Antonin Scalia emphasized that the law did not create "a general civility code."[2]

Yet considerable confusion persists, because the law is relatively recent and different courts have issued varying interpretations. In addition, employers, who can be held responsible for sexual harassment by their employees (even if the employers are unaware of the harassment), can defend themselves by having policies to prevent such conduct.[3] Some have adopted "zero tolerance" policies to insulate them from employee lawsuits. These policies are stricter than the law, and they have led to the firing of a few men who would not have been convicted under the law. For example, an executive told a woman coworker about the plot of the Seinfeld show he had seen the night before. Seinfeld was telling his friends about a woman he met but whose name he could not remember except that it rhymed with a female body part. The coworker complained of sexual harassment, and Miller Brewing Company fired the executive, despite his nineteen years of service to the company. (When the executive sued the company, however, a mostly female jury awarded him millions of dollars for being wrongfully dismissed.)

Consultants who advise employers have observed that women in traditional female jobs, such as secretary, are more likely to be subjected to quid pro quo harassment from supervisors, whereas women in traditional male jobs, especially blue-collar jobs, are more likely to be subjected to hostile environment harassment from coworkers. Hundreds of women in the Mitsubishi auto plant in Normal, Illinois, experienced incidents ranging from finding plastic penises in tool buckets to being asked their sexual habits and preferences; being called "bitches," "sluts," and "whores," rather than their names; and being grabbed by their breasts, buttocks, and genitals. Some women had their work sabotaged to make their performance seem slow and shoddy.[4]

The dynamics of sexual harassment do not revolve around sex as much as they reflect abuse of power. A supervisor or coworker makes a woman feel

---

But supporters have a broader goal in mind as well. "If girls are socialized the way boys are to take part in sports," the editor of a women's sports magazine says, and "if boys and girls grow up with the idea that girls are strong and capable, it will change the way girls and women are viewed—by themselves and by society."[221]

Discrimination against Men

Although most sex discrimination has been directed at women, some has been directed at men. The traditional conception of gender roles has created problems for men who did not fit the standard mold either.

When the Burger Court rejected stereotypes that led to discrimination against women, it also rejected some that led to discrimination against men. It invalidated Mississippi's law that barred men from one of the state's university nursing schools.[222] It also invalidated Alabama's law that allowed just women to seek alimony upon divorce.[223] Thus, the Court rejected stereotypes that only women become nurses and only women are dependent on their spouses.

vulnerable and thus exercises psychological dominance over her.

Consultants have also observed that a very small percentage of men harass women, but these men do it a lot. One consultant has found that perhaps three to five men out of one hundred create problems, but these men might affect fifty women in the same workplace. The harassers typically feel bitter toward women or threatened by them. Some have long been bullies toward men as well as women.[5]

Surveys how that a third of female workers say they have been sexually harassed on the job.[6] After twenty-three women acknowledged in 1992 and 1993 that they had to fend off sexual advances by Senator Bob Packwood (R-Ore.), the *Washington Post* conducted a survey of women who worked as aides to members of Congress or staffers for congressional committees. It found the same results. A third of the women had been sexually harassed in the hallowed halls of Congress, and a third of these had been harassed by a member of Congress. (The others had been harassed by supervisors, coworkers, or lobbyists.)[7]

Yet few victims file formal complaints, let alone bring lawsuits, because they need their jobs. According to several studies, only 3 percent of women who have been harassed have filed formal complaints.[8] On Capitol Hill, 80 percent of the women surveyed said they would lose their job if they did, 80 percent said they would never find another job there if they did, and 70 percent said nothing would be done to the harasser anyway.[9]

Sexual harassment can be directed toward men as well.[10] About 15 percent of male workers say they have been sexually harassed by men or women on the job.[11]

Recently, a backlash has set in, apparently because of the legal confusion in the courts and zero tolerance policies of some employers. A majority—57 percent of men and 52 percent of women—say that "we have gone too far in making common interactions among employees into cases of sexual harassment."[12]

Defining sexual harassment too broadly jeopardizes free speech. One library employee filed a complaint against another because the other had posted an innocuous *New Yorker* cartoon in his cubicle.[13] One graduate teaching assistant filed a complaint against another because the other had placed a photograph of his wife, wearing a bikini, on his desk in their office at the University of Nebraska.

While companies and courts have been sensitive, sometimes overly sensitive, to sexual behavior, they have been callous toward the discrimination that sexual harassment law originally was intended to prevent. When women have coworkers who will not train them and will not work with them, coworkers who repeatedly subject them to verbal abuse or obscene gestures, the women face discrimination, but the courts usually rule against them because the coworkers' behavior was not sexual. Yet these women face more discrimination than women whose sensibilities are offended by a sexual remark or off-color joke. Some judges have interpreted the law to be puritanical toward sex but indifferent toward discrimination.[14]

1. *Mentor Savings Bank v. Vinson,* 91 L.Ed.2d 49 (1986).
2. *Oncale v. Sundowner Offshore Services,* 140 L.Ed.2d 201 (1998).
3. *Faragher v. Boca Raton,* 141 L.Ed.2d 662 (1998); *Burlington Industries v. Ellerth,* 141 L.Ed.2d 633 (1998).
4. Kirsten Downey Grimsley, Frank Swoboda, and Warren Brown, "Trouble on the Line," *Washington Post National Weekly Edition,* May 6–13, 1996, 6–7.
5. Kirsten Downey Grimsley, "Confronting Hard-Core Harassers," *Washington Post National Weekly Edition,* January 27, 1997, 6.
6. Richard Morin, "Think Twice before You Say Another Word," *Washington Post National Weekly Edition,* December 28, 1992–January 3, 1993, 37.
7. Richard Morin, "Jack and Jill Went up the Hill," *Washington Post National Weekly Edition,* March 1–7, 1993, 37.
8. Daniel Goleman, "Sexual Harassment: About Power, Not Sex," *New York Times,* October 22, 1991, B8.
9. Morin, "Jack and Jill Went up the Hill,"
10. *Oncale v. Sundowner Offshore Services.*
11. Janice Castro, "Sexual Harassment: A Guide," *Time,* January 20, 1992, 37.
12. John Cloud, "Sex and the Law," *Time,* March 23, 1998, 49.
13. Henry Louis Gates Jr., "Men Behaving Badly," *New Yorker,* August 18, 1997, 5.
14. For further analysis and a critique, see Jeffrey Toobin, "The Trouble with Sex," *New Yorker,* February 9, 1998, 48–55.

On the other hand, the Burger Court upheld some laws that were designed to protect women but that discriminate against men. It affirmed laws that prohibit statutory rape—intercourse with a minor, with consent—by males but not by females.[224] It also affirmed draft registration, required for males but not for females.[225] In 1980, President Carter asked Congress to reinstate draft registration, though not the draft itself, to show our "toughness" to the Soviet Union and other communist countries. He also urged Congress to include women in the program. Although Congress had admitted women to the military academies in 1975, it was not ready to include them here. The Court upheld the law, rationalizing that registration eventually could lead to the draft and the draft eventually could lead to combat. And it insisted that most women are not capable of combat. Thus, the Court accepted the stereotypes that only men initiate sex with underage partners and only men can fight in war.

In the absence of war, the most significant discrimination against men may occur in divorce cases, where the norm is to grant custody of children to mothers and require payment of support by fathers. Although courts

Although most single parents are women, an increasing number are men, such as this father of an eleven-year-old in Dallas.

Brent Humphreys

give fathers visitation rights, they permit mothers to move miles away, making visitation difficult and sporadic. And although governments have taken steps to enforce support payments, they have done little to enforce visitation rights. This practice reflects the stereotype that fathers are capable of financing their children's upbringing but not of bringing them up themselves. The Supreme Court has ignored this problem.

Overall, however, Congress and the courts have moved steadily toward legal equality for the sexes. Women, and men, have accomplished through congressional and judicial action much of what they would have accomplished with the ERA. It is an indication of the success of the movement that young women today take their equality for granted, that they focus on their personal lives rather than see the need for further reform.

Affirmative Action

Assume there is a track meet. A black runner and a white runner start together. But the officials force the black runner to carry heavy weights, and he falls behind. Eventually, the officials realize this is unfair, and they take the weights off. Of course the black runner is still behind. Would this be fair? Assume, instead, the officials not only take the weights off but allow him to catch up. Would this be more fair? Or would it be unfair to the white runner who was not responsible for the weights and who might have run faster than the black even without the weights?[226]

This scenario captures the dilemma of civil rights policy today. Although most race and sex discrimination has been repudiated by the courts and legislatures, the effects of past discrimination survive. Now the question is whether civil rights policy should ignore race and sex or take race and sex into account to compensate for the effects of past discrimination. That is, should the policy require nondiscrimination only or **affirmative action** as well?

Affirmative action applies to employers in hiring and promoting minorities and women, governments in reserving a portion of their contracts for businesses owned by minorities and women, and colleges and universities in admitting minorities and women.

The Civil Rights Act of 1964, which bars discrimination in employment, does not mention affirmative action, but it does authorize the bureaucracy to make rules to help end discrimination. In 1969, the Department of Labor called for affirmative action by companies doing business with the federal government. Later, the Equal Employment Opportunities Commission called for affirmative action by governments and the Office of Education by colleges as well. Presidents from Nixon through Carter supported it with executive orders, and the Supreme Court sanctioned it in a series of cases.[227] Many state and local governments also adopted it.

Affirmative action applies most extensively to employment. It requires positive steps to ensure that qualified minorities and women receive a fair share of jobs at all levels. Just what the positive steps and the fair share should be are the subject of much controversy.

If the number of minorities and women in a company or government agency, at any level, is less than the number in the local labor force, the company or agency must agree to recruit more or, in serious cases, draw up an affirmative action plan. The plan must include goals to hire or promote more minorities or women and a timetable to reach these goals. If the company or agency does not reach them, it must show that it made an effort to reach them. If the company or agency cannot satisfy the government, it can be denied future contracts or aid, but employers rarely are penalized.

Some government pressure evidently is necessary. White men dominate public and private institutions, and as the personnel director of a Fortune 500 company observed, "People tend to hire people like themselves."[228]

Although the requirements for affirmative action plans speak of "goals," some people say they really mean quotas. Critics charge that quotas would result in both lower standards and reverse discrimination.[229] But affirmative action usually does not require actual quotas. Admittedly, the terms blur; if employers are pressured to meet "goals," they might interpret them to be quotas. But only occasionally, and only after a finding of deliberate and systematic discrimination, does affirmative action entail actual quotas.

The Supreme Court has issued mixed rulings on the legality of quotas. In *University of California Regents v. Bakke* in 1978, the Court upheld the policy of the medical school at the University of California at Davis to consider race as a factor in admissions, but it struck down the policy to establish a quota of sixteen spaces for minorities out of one hundred spaces in the class. On the other hand, the Court upheld quotas for skilled workers, firefighters, and state police.[230] The primary factor in determining the legality of quotas is whether the employer or union discriminated in the past. The University of California at Davis had no history of discrimination, but the other employers did.

In reviewing an affirmative action plan, the Court also looks at two crucial elements: The plan must not prevent all white men from being hired and promoted, and it must be temporary (usually until the percentage of black employees approaches the percentage of black workers in the community).

Because of concern that affirmative action should not pose too great a burden on innocent individuals, the Court has struck down affirmative action in laying off workers—that is, struck down protection for minorities and women when employers pare their workforce for economic reasons. Instead, the Court has accepted the traditional practice, based on seniority, that the last hired is the first fired.[231]

The Rehnquist Court, however, has signaled a change of direction in affirmative action doctrine. Although the Court has not barred affirmative action programs, a slim majority has made it more difficult for governments to adopt some programs.[232] Governments must have clear evidence of specific discrimination, rather than cite the general pattern of historical discrimination, and they must show how particular programs would ameliorate the problems.

Affirmative action programs have helped minorities and women. Companies that do business with the federal government, and therefore are subject to affirmative action, have shown more improvement in hiring minorities and women than other companies. And state and local governments, also subject to affirmative action, have shown more improvement in hiring than private companies. Organizations subject to affirmative action have shown even more progress in promoting minorities and women previously kept in low-level positions.[233]

The state of Alabama, for example, made dramatic gains. After a court found that the state troopers had never employed any blacks, it ordered them to hire one new black for every new white until the force reached 25 percent black. The force became the most integrated force in the country. Faced with the threat of a similar order, other departments of the state government quickly hired more blacks at all levels.

Affirmative action has helped middle-class and some lower-class blacks get jobs in government and business.[234] It has noticeably increased the number of blacks in government agencies, police departments, fire departments, construction trades, and textile companies. Affirmative action has also helped women get jobs in government and business that traditionally went only to men.

But affirmative action has not pulled blacks out of the "underclass." Many, from families that have suffered long-term poverty, experience continual unemployment because they lack the education and the skills necessary to compete for available jobs.[235] And affirmative action, of course, cannot create new jobs or better jobs. Thus, it is not as helpful to minorities or women as a flourishing economy is.

In short, affirmative action should not be credited by proponents for more benefits or blamed by opponents for more harms than it actually causes. It has boosted some minorities and women, but it cannot help many others. It has displaced some white men, but it has not affected most.

Thirteen percent of white men think they lost a job or promotion because of their race, and 10 percent think they did because of their sex.[236] Many others claim they "heard about" another white man who did. Yet affirmative action is not as pervasive as many people assume.[237]

Similarly, some students think they lost a seat at a college they applied to because of their race. But 60 percent of colleges admit nearly all students who apply; only 20 percent are selective enough to use affirmative action much.[238] Students who apply to elite schools are more likely to lose a seat because other applicants' parents are alums of these schools. Typically, a fifth of Harvard's students have had preferential treatment because their parents attended the school. Harvard's "legacies" are more than twice as likely to be admitted as blacks or Latinos. A similar advantage exists at other selective schools, including public schools such as the Universities of California and Virginia.[239] Affirmative action may be more widespread in graduate schools, however.[240]

Many people subconsciously view affirmative action as they do handicapped parking. When looking for a parking space in a crowded lot, numerous drivers see the handicapped space and think, "If it weren't for that reserved space, I could park here." In reality, if the space wasn't reserved, only one other driver could park there.[241] So it is with affirmative action. Many white men think they would get a particular job or school seat if it weren't for affirmative action, but only one would. Meanwhile, the rest feel victimized by the policy.

For both sides in the controversy, affirmative action has become a symbol. For civil rights leaders, it represents fairness and real progress toward equality. For critics, it represents unfairness and an attack on individuality and meritocracy. It is important to debate these values, but it is also important to recognize that affirmative action is neither the key public policy for racial and sexual equality nor the biggest stumbling block for individual achievement as supporters and detractors seem to assume.

Public opposition to affirmative action has been festering for years. According to opinion polls, a majority of whites agree with the statement "We have gone too far in pushing equal rights in this country."[242] More specifically, 75 percent of Americans oppose giving a "preference" for blacks and other minorities in hiring, promoting, and admitting to college "to make up for past discrimination." Seventy-three percent oppose a "preference" for women. Although large majorities of whites and males think affirmative action programs have increased opportunities for minorities and women, only 34 percent of whites and 37 percent of males think this is "a price worth paying" if these programs result in less opportunity for white men.[243]

Despite the public opposition, the public debate over affirmative action had been muted until recently. In the late 1960s and 1970s, when affirmative action was introduced, government policy was initiated by executive orders, implemented by bureaucratic agencies, and sanctioned by judicial rulings. The legislative branch, controlled by Democrats sympathetic to civil rights, acquiesced, so Congress never staged a sharp debate on affirmative action as it has done for other controversial policies.

Republican candidates realized the volatility of this issue and reopened—some might say reignited—the debate. When the Republicans wrested control of Congress from the Democrats in 1994, affirmative action was no longer protected. Republicans in Congress called for a review of affirmative action programs, with an eye toward shrinking or dismantling them.

Voters in California and Washington and the governor of Florida mandated an end to the use of race in admissions to public universities. U.S. courts of appeals in two circuits ignored the *Bakke* precedent and ordered an end to the use of race in admissions to public universities. However, courts of appeals in two other circuits affirmed the *Bakke* precedent and upheld the use of race. The Rehnquist Court has agreed to revisit the issue.

The moves against affirmative action prompted concerns that minority enrollments would plunge. The Texas legislature passed a law guaranteeing admission to its state universities for all high school graduates in the top 10 percent of their class. The Florida governor guaranteed admission to the top 20 percent, and the University of California Board of Regents guaranteed admission to at least one of its campuses to the top 4 percent. This idea uses geography instead of race; it uses residential segregation, which has stymied the efforts to desegregate the schools from grade schools through high schools, as a way to diversify the universities. Minority students who do well in their segregated schools can still get admitted to the universities, even if their schools provided a less competitive education than predominantly white schools provide.[244]

Despite the attempt to eliminate affirmative action by governments (including public universities), the practice of affirmative action by businesses, especially large corporations, has increased. Although businesses initially resisted affirmative action, many now champion it, under the name of "diversity." They have found new pools of untapped talent in overlooked groups, and they have reached new markets in these groups. That is, hiring more minority and female workers has led to insights that enable the corporations to sell products to more minority and female consumers.[245]

Conclusion: Is Government Responsive in Granting Civil Rights?

Blacks and women have made tremendous progress in obtaining civil rights since the time when a federal official who fired competent blacks could insist, "A Negro's place is in the cornfield,"[246] or employers who refused to hire women could insist, "A woman's place is in the home." The black movement and the women's movement initiated the changes. They protested legal inequality and put the issue on the public agenda. As they grew and garnered support, they pressured the government. Finally, approximately one century after the first significant agitations for change, the government responded.

Within the government, the Supreme Court exercised decisive leadership. Historically, the Court was both activist and restrained toward blacks—whichever was necessary to deny their rights—while it was restrained toward women. Then in the 1950s and 1960s, the Warren Court was activist in striking down racial segregation. In the 1970s and 1980s, the Burger Court was activist in striking down sexual discrimination. As with the Warren Court's decisions against racial discrimination, the Burger Court's decisions against sexual discrimination may go down in history as its major achievement. But the Court's rulings themselves did not guarantee the rights. Because the Court lacks the means to enforce its decisions, the president and Congress had to help overcome the resistance.

Thus, the areas of racial and sexual discrimination show the power, and the limit of the power, of the courts. The Supreme Court exercised power because it articulated emerging views in society—that racial segregation by law and sexual discrimination by law are wrong. But the Court was unable to accomplish the changes alone. The Court has struggled, mostly in vain, to accomplish further changes in the area of racial discrimination. It has made little progress in overcoming residential segregation and the accompanying problems of school segregation and school inequality and in ameliorating the poverty that makes it difficult for many minorities to take advantage of their rights.

The changes in policy illustrate the responsiveness of government. In its subjugation of minorities until the 1950s and treatment of women until the 1970s, government was responding to the majority view. When minorities and women organized to protest their status, government began responding to them and to shifts in the majority view that their protest prompted.

In pressuring government to respond, African Americans have benefited from being numerous, visible, and—with their common legacy of slavery, segregation, and discrimination—relatively cohesive. Their concentration in large northern cities and some southern states has helped them exercise political power. Their long legacy, though, has fostered debilitating ghetto conditions and denied them resources to make quicker and greater progress.

Latinos have become more numerous. Their concentration in some western and southwestern states has enabled them to influence state and local governments.

Their diversity and lack of cohesiveness, however, have hindered their ability to influence the national government. The increasing size of their electoral bloc will give them more clout in coming years.

Native Americans are the smallest, most isolated, and least organized minority, so they have had the poorest success in pressuring government to respond.

As minority groups grow in size, they will be able to pressure governments more effectively. But as minority groups expand, they will increasingly come into conflict with each other, especially when economic conditions are stagnant. Competition for scarce resources will widen the cracks in the coalition. Already there are tensions. Some blacks resent the faster progress of Latinos and Asians. Blacks say they were here before most Latinos and Asians, they suffered more and struggled more, and so they should reap the rewards sooner. On the other hand, some Latino leaders resent the reluctance of black groups to help them with their civil rights problems.[247] Sometimes there are conflicts over issues. Occasionally, there have been riots. Blacks have rioted in Miami from frustration with the Cuban-dominated leadership. Latinos have rioted in Washington, D.C., out of anger with their lack of city services and jobs and with gerrymandering by the black power structure.

Nonminority women were never subjugated as much as minority men and women, so they have had less to overcome. Moreover, women are a majority, they vote as frequently as men, and they have well-organized and well-funded interest groups. Consequently, since the 1970s they have made the greatest strides toward equality.

EPILOGUE

Exclusion of Japanese Is Upheld

*I*n *Korematsu v. United States,* the Supreme Court, by a 6–3 vote, upheld the order excluding 120,000 Japanese Americans from the West Coast.[248] Although Justice Douglas voted against the order in conference, he switched to the majority just before the decision was announced.[249]

The majority held that the government could take precautions to prevent espionage and sabotage during wartime, and it noted that the president and Congress agreed that the order was necessary.

Thus, the majority was restrained, deferring to the combined force of the other branches. These justices did not question whether officials had a valid fear of espionage or sabotage by Japanese Americans. In contrast, the minority was activist, challenging the other branches. These justices disputed the suspicions of disloyalty and suggested that discrimination against Japanese Americans led to the order.

The minority raised the specter that the Court's ruling would set a dangerous precedent. "A military order, however unconstitutional, is not apt to last longer than the military emergency," Justice Robert Jackson wrote. "But once a judicial opinion rationalizes such an order . . . the Court for all time has validated the principle of racial discrimination . . . and of transplanting American citizens. The principle then lies about like a loaded weapon ready for the hand of any authority that can bring forward a plausible claim of an urgent need."

In December 1944—two and a half years after it began the evacuation and one day before it heard the Court's decision—the military ordered the release of "loyal" Japanese Americans.

Upon their release, they discovered that the government had failed to keep its promise to protect their property. Many of their possessions, stored in warehouses, had been vandalized or stolen. Some of their homes had been taken over by strangers, and some of their land had been seized for unpaid taxes. "They did me a great wrong," Korematsu said. But he returned to live in the same town where he was arrested. "I love this country and I belong here."[250]

Near the end of his career, Justice Douglas expressed regret that he and others in the majority had gone along with the government. The case "was ever on my conscience."[251] He did not live long enough to learn that the War Department had presented false information to the Court. The department had altered some reports and destroyed others demonstrating the loyalty of the Japanese Americans.[252] In fact, from

A Japanese relocation camp in Amache, Colorado.

Pearl Harbor until the end of the war, the government had no record of any incident of espionage or sabotage by a Japanese American citizen or alien in the United States.

With help from the lawyer who discovered the false information, Korematsu reopened his case through a rarely used procedure available only when the original trial was tainted with prosecutorial misconduct and fraud. In 1983, a federal judge reversed his conviction.[253]

In 1988, Congress passed a law offering a public apology for the internment and $20,000 compensation to each surviving internee.[254]

After the September 11 terrorist attacks, there was renewed talk about the Japanese relocation. Should legal immigrants from countries with links to terrorist groups be rounded up and put in internment camps? A majority of Americans rejected this proposal, but nearly a third said they might accept it.[255]

To learn more about *Korematsu v. United States* and the controversy surrounding it, go to this chapter's "You Are There" exercises on the text Web site.

Key Terms

Korematsu v. United States

Dred Scott case

equal protection clause

Jim Crow laws

Plessy v. Ferguson

separate-but-equal doctrine

NAACP

Brown v. Board of Education

de jure segregation

de facto segregation

Civil Rights Act of 1964

restrictive covenants

steering

blockbusting

redlining

Civil Rights Act of 1968

racial profiling

bilingual education

Equal Rights
    Amendment (ERA)

Equal Pay Act

Title IX

affirmative action

Further Reading

Edward Ball, *Slaves in the Family* (New York: Farrar, Straus & Giroux, 1998). A search by the descendant of a plantation owner for the descendants of his family's slaves.

Jennifer Baumgardner and Amy Richards, *ManifestA: Young Women, Feminism, and the Future* (New York: Farrar, Straus & Giroux, 2000). A primer on feminism for Generation X.

Taylor Branch, *Parting the Waters: America in the King Years, 1954–63* (New York: Simon & Schuster, 1988). A readable account of Martin Luther King Jr. and the first decade of the civil rights movement.

Seth Cagin and Philip Dray, *We Are Not Afraid: The Story of Goodman, Schwerner, and Chaney and the Civil Rights Campaign for Mississippi* (New York: Macmillan, 1988). An American crime in the steamy summer of 1964.

Ian Frazier, *On the Rez* (New York: Farrar, Straus & Giroux, 2000). A personal guide to life on Indian reservations.

David Halberstam, *The Children* (New York: Random House, 1998). The lives of eight students who attended college in Nashville and helped launch the civil rights movement. The book shows how a small group of courageous students helped transform the country.

Peter Irons, *Justice at War* (New York: Oxford University Press, 1983). The story of Korematsu and other cases involving the Japanese American relocation by the attorney who uncovered the government's false information.

Randall Kennedy, *Nigger: The Strange Career of a Troublesome Word* (New York: Pantheon, 2002). A history of the most explosive word in the English language by an African American law professor.

Gregory Howard Williams, *Life on the Color Line: The True Story of a White Boy Who Discovered He Was Black* (New York: Dutton, 1995). How the life of a ten-year-old boy changed the day he learned that his father was black.

 ## Electronic Resources

www.naacp.org/
The Web site of the NAACP, the largest and oldest civil rights organization. Links to discussions of policy issues and information about the organization and its mission.

www.census.gov/statab/www/
The Statistical Abstract of the United States *online. Information about the state of the American people, their incomes, family structures, occupations, and many other characteristics. Includes detailed information about individual ethnic and racial groups as well as men and women.*

www.americanwest.com/pages/indians.htm
A link to information about Native Americans and their cultures. Includes links to various tribal home pages.

oyez.nwu.edu/
Read important civil rights cases on-line from this Web page. Allows you to search for and access cases by name or topic. See also the civil rights page, wwwsecure.law.cornell.edu/topics/civil_rights.html.

www.yforum.com
Questions about blacks or whites, or Latinos or Asians that you have never understood? Post your questions and have people from those communities respond.

 ## InfoTrac College Edition

Search for the following articles in the InfoTrac database:

Kier, Elizabeth. "Homosexuals in the U.S. Military: Open Integration and Combat Effectiveness," *International Security* (Fall 1998).

Kim, Elaine H. " 'At Least You're Not Black': Asian Americans in U.S. Race Relations," *Social Justice* (Fall 1998).

Langham, Sylvia. "Sacred Cows? (The Success of the Feminist Movement and Gender Discrimination)," *Sociology Review* (February 2001).

Rubenfeld, Jed. "The Anti-Antidiscrimination Agenda (of the U.S. Supreme Court)," *Yale Law Journal* (March 2002).

For more articles, enter

"Race relations" in the Subject Guide;

"Feminism" in the Subject Guide;

 ## American Government Resources

Visit the Government Foundations section of the Wadsworth American Government Resources Web site (politicalscience.wadsworth.com/amgov/) for a variety of tools to help you explore civil rights further. Included are simulations, video clips, Microcase exercises, and a wealth of other activities.

CHAPTER 16

ECONOMIC POLICY

The Internet has spawned many new businesses, including online retailers—"e-tailers." Greater reliance on high technology spurred big productivity gains in the 1990s.

Can the Country Afford a Permanent Tax Cut?

You are Patty Murray, junior senator from Washington. It is June 2002, and the Senate is trying to clear the deck for its summer recess. One item on the agenda is a permanent repeal of the estate tax, sometimes called the "death" tax because it is levied against inherited wealth. When a person dies, if the estate is not passed on to a spouse and if its value is $1 million or more, it is subject to a federal tax. Most Americans are not aware that only 2 percent of all estates are large enough to be taxed and that half of all revenue generated by the tax comes from estates worth more than $5 million.[1]

Still, you are no fan of the estate tax. You have always thought there was something to the Republicans' argument that the estate tax has ruined some family farms and mom-and-pop businesses.[2] So you sponsored legislation to raise the exemption limit for farmers and small businesses and worked for partial or total repeal of the tax, just as you had promised in your campaigns. Two years ago, despite heavy opposition from your own party, you voted for a Republican bill that is now phasing out the tax over a ten-year period. But that law had a "sunset" provision—a time limit or expiration date—that will nullify the tax cut at the end of ten years if Congress does not reauthorize it. The bill you are looking at now, already passed by the Republican-

controlled House, would permanently abolish the estate tax. With control of both houses of Congress at stake in the upcoming midterm election, and President Bush's popularity riding high, the Republicans are hoping to make permanent all tax cuts passed with time limits. The House leadership knows that some of these taxes (income, estate, marriage penalty, pension deductions, and so on) have broader support than others, so they decided to have a separate vote on each instead of presenting them in one all-or-nothing bill. They see the estate tax as the least popular of all taxes, and they believe they can get it through the Senate despite Majority Leader Daschle saying he "will go all out to kill the legislation."[3] Republicans believe they cannot lose on this issue. If enough Democrats vote with them, Republicans will get the credit for abolishing an unpopular tax; if the bill is killed, they can blame Democrats for taxing the dead. You must decide whether to stick with your party as it heads into the election or to vote again for estate tax repeal.

You ran for the Senate as "the mom in sneakers." The daughter of a disabled veteran, you were a stay-at-home mom after college, only later returning to the labor force as a teacher. You served on the local school board and have made increased funding for education one of your major issues. You see the problems of women and children, and low- and middle-income families, especially rural families, as your special concern. In fact, you have started your own "Rural Initiative" to benefit Washington's rural residents.[4] Your state still has a number of family farms and orchards, as well as many small high-tech start-ups.

But Washington is also home to many multimillionaires, including Bill Gates and others made wealthy by the success of Microsoft. It the tax were repealed, these multimillionaires would be as free to transfer their wealth untaxed to the next generation as would the owners of family farms and businesses. However, Bill Gates's father, the president of the Gates Foundation, has repeatedly stated his support for retention of the estate tax. But for every Mr. Gates you have a constituent who says that estate taxes ruined the family farm or mom-and-pop business by forcing its sale to pay taxes.

One of the reasons the estate tax has so few active supporters is its depiction as a tax on the dead and a double billing on wealth that had been taxed during a person's lifetime. But the dead cannot be taxed, and spouses of the deceased are exempt form the tax. The loss is to heirs who in many cases did not contribute to earning the wealth. That is because most inherited wealth does not come from family farms and mom-and-pop businesses; it comes from stocks, bonds, and nonfarm real estate. At the time the phase-out bill passed two years ago, 96 percent of all farm estates were not worth enough to be subject to estate tax. And family-owned farms and businesses already have a higher exemption than other estates; if it were raised by just another half million or so, virtually no family-owned farm would ever pay an estate tax.

Most Democrats had opposed the ten year phase-out, just as they now oppose making it permanent. They believe eliminating the tax would benefit only the wealthiest Americans, widen the income gap, and substantially reduce federal revenues. Democrats had argued then that the best use of the surplus was to pay down nearly $6 trillion of national debt and bolster Social Security reserves so that when the economy slowed or took a downturn, as it always does after a boom period, the federal treasury would be prepared. There was nothing put away for an emergency. Congress had gambled on the tax cuts stimulating economic growth and generating new revenues.

But the phase-out passed in a presidential election year when the unified budget was in surplus and Congress was sprinkling benefits and tax breaks everywhere. Now conditions are very different: The economy is faltering, and the costs of the war against terrorism coupled with billions in lost revenue from all the tax cuts have sent the federal budget into deficit. Forty-five of the fifty state budgets are in deficit, and most states that have an inheritance tax get a percentage of the federal tax.

Revenue losses during the decade of estate tax phase-out are expected to be $135 billion, and five times that during the following decade if the cut is made permanent—all to benefit the wealthiest 2 percent of the country.[5] And this does not count further losses from the Bush income tax cuts, also weighted toward the highest income groups, which constitute the biggest tax reduction in two decades.[6]

A vote with the Republicans will help guarantee huge revenue losses at a time of budget deficits, thereby undermining your position as a fiscal moderate and supporter of balanced budgeting. And you would be putting more money in the pockets of the wealthiest Americans, few of whom support your party. You have criticized the Republicans for offering so many new benefits without "debate on how tax cuts fit in with our long-term budget goals . . . , reducing the national debt . . . and extending the long-term solvency of Social Security and Medicare."[7]

You are not up for reelection until 2004, so your vote on the permanent repeal will not be an issue this November. You probably could go against your party's leadership with little political fallout. You have shown you can win without much help from the national party: In your last race, you ran eight percentage points better than Clinton had in 1996, winning Microsoft's hometown of Seattle with 63 percent of the vote. But the Senate Democrats have treated you well. You got good committee assignments, and although still a junior member of the Senate with only a few years' prior legislative experience in your state's senate, you were given a role in the Senate's minority leadership. After your big 1998 win, you were named vice chair of the Democratic Senatorial Campaign committee, and now you are a deputy whip. You think that the confidence the party has shown in you might deserve, even require, loyalty on a partisan vote. And if Daschle decides to run for president in 2004, there will be openings in the Senate leadership. Going against the party on one of its bread-and-butter issues will not win you any support in the party caucus.

Nevertheless, you have stated your opposition to the tax countless times, and that is how you have voted every time the issue has come to the floor. Can you reverse your position now? Do you stick with your party and call it a vote for fiscal responsibility, or do you vote for permanent repeal and defend it as support for small farms and businesses?

How do you vote?

"I've noticed our tax system tends to favor bigger, meaner citizens."

Americans pride themselves on their free market economy. Yet when economic problems occur, they want government to do something. The degree to which government should be involved in the economy is a perennial source of conflict. Only a few people believe government should not be involved at all. Most agree, for example, on the following:

1. Government, not volunteer efforts, must pay for a military force. Thus, government must tax. We cannot individually decide whether to contribute to maintaining our nation's defense. If we did, some citizens would become "free riders."[8] Without paying, they would benefit from the voluntary contributions of others.

2. The market cannot determine which television or radio company should have the right to broadcast at a specific frequency. If broadcasting companies competed on the same frequency, none would be intelligible to listeners.

3. Market forces alone cannot regulate supply and cost of food and lifesaving medicine. Deaths from malnutrition and treatable illnesses would be much more frequent than they already are without government aid to the poor, disabled, and elderly.

Despite broad consensus on points such as these, there is much honest disagreement about how far government should go in regulating the economy and altering the distribution of wealth.

Types of Economic Systems

Capitalism

The role of government in the economy largely determines the kind of economic system a country has. An economy in which individuals and corporations own its capital goods or productive capacity—businesses, factories, and farms—is called a **capitalist economy,** or sometimes a free market, free enterprise economy.

In a pure capitalist economy, prices, profits, working conditions, and wages would be totally determined by private sector decisions rather than by the government. Manufacturers would sell goods at what the market could bear, pay workers as little as possible, and manufacture products as cheaply as possible, concerned with health and safety only to the extent dictated by individual morality and the necessity to maintain consumer loyalty.

The idea that a capitalist economy would promote prosperity was popularized in 1776 by the British economist Adam Smith in *The Wealth of Nations.*[9] In his view, as each person seeks to maximize his or her own economic well-being, the collective well-being is enhanced. Businesses become more efficient, sell more at lower cost, hire more workers, and hence promote the economic well-being of the workers as well as the owners.

Socialism and Communism

Socialism, in theory, is an economic system in which a country's productive capacity is under the collective ownership and control of the people. In real socialist systems, however, it has been the state that controls capital goods and production and has the power to set wages and determine the supply of, and demand for, goods.

There have been many well-known theorists of socialism, but none so famous as Karl Marx. He was even better known for his writings on communism; perhaps this is why *socialism* is often used interchangeably with *communism.* But in theory, communism is a more advanced form of economic organization than socialism. Collectively owned economic units would also become self-governing, and the need for formal government or "the state" would disappear. No country that called itself communist ever came close to achieving this utopian goal. In fact, in those countries labeled communist, the state grew large and became increasingly more invasive in the economy and private lives.

At the core of the debate between capitalists and socialists is intense disagreement about how much control government should have over the economy and the consumption and work habits of its citizens. Sometimes in American public debate, one candidate will accuse another of supporting "socialism"; in this context, socialism is often just a synonym for something a person does not like, especially bigger government.

Mixed Economies

In practice, there are no pure capitalist or socialist systems, and there never have been. In the United States, for example, government owns power-generating dams, some railroads, and 27 percent of all land, and it acts as an insurer of individual and corporate assets. It has loaned money to corporations to save them from bankruptcy and has bailed out large banks in danger of failing. In other modern societies, such as Britain, France, Sweden, Germany, and the former communist nations of Eastern Europe, government owns airlines, television networks, and telephone systems.

Just as all capitalist nations have socialist components, socialist nations have capitalist aspects. Even before the reforms of the late 1980s, which led to socialist governments being swept away across Eastern Europe, most of these nations found it useful to tolerate or even encourage some private enterprises, and some, such as Hungary, had quite large private economies.

Most countries, then, have a **mixed economy.** Some are more capitalist, others more socialist, but all have elements of both. Government plays a large role in the economies of most mixed systems. For example, government directly influences the behavior of business and industry through regulation and taxation. Even Adam Smith believed there was some role for government intervention in a capitalist system, such as to ensure conditions for fair competition in the marketplace.

Our own system is a mixture of private enterprise and government ownership combined with considerable government intervention through taxation and regulation (see Chapter 18). In nineteenth-century America, government involvement in the economy was much less than it is today. Initially, we moved toward a more active economic role for government because of abuses by big business in the late nineteenth century: Child labor was widely used, workers were paid a pittance, filthy and unsafe working conditions (as suggested by the term *sweatshop*) led to thousands of workers' deaths from industrial accidents, foods and drugs were often unsafe, and the markets for some products came to be dominated by a few large producers who controlled prices and wages. Public anger led to increased government regulation of wages, working conditions, content of foods and drugs, and more.

Government also intervenes in the economy by taxing and spending. Budget policies can make the rich richer and the poor poorer, or it can make the poor better off at the expense of the rich. Most Western democracies have fairly elaborate social welfare systems that redistribute some wealth from the rich to the poor in order to provide them with a minimal standard of living. In the United States, we do less of this than do most other industrialized nations.

Despite our mixed economy, we have a very individualistic, capitalistic ethic. The idea that individuals, not government, should provide services and that government should be small influences a wide range of public policies. The belief that individuals are poor because of their own failings limits our sense of responsibility to provide support for low-income families. The idea that private business is inherently self-regulating makes it difficult to enact higher standards for worker health and safety. The belief that private profit is not only the most important goal of business, but perhaps the only one, means that those fighting to protect the environment from abuse by both industry and consumers must either defeat or find compromise with powerful lobbies.

Economic Systems and Political Systems

Our Constitution specifies only a little about the nature of our economic system. It emphasizes private property rights and gives government taxation and regulatory powers. By contrast, the governments of most other mixed and socialist economies, whether democracies or dictatorships, have constitutions that link their political system to a form of economic organization and give government major responsibilities for achieving economic goals.

Economic distinctions between capitalism and socialism are not necessarily linked to gradations in democracy. Capitalist systems are not inevitably democratic. The most democratic systems in the world are mixed economies with strong elements of capitalism (such as Sweden, Britain, and Denmark), but many capitalist systems are undemocratic (the most blatant example being South Africa under white rule). Indeed, there is an inevitable tension between capitalism and democracy. The capitalist marketplace rewards and encourages inequities that, if unchecked, threaten democratic beliefs about individual equality.

For example, capitalist systems place no upper limits on the accumulation of wealth, even though wealth can be used to buy greater access to decision makers. The potential for greater exercise of influence by the wealthy weakens the concept of one person, one vote.

Socialist systems promote equality in wages, but in practice most socialist systems have tolerated significant disparity in overall standard of living. Socialist theory also advocates democratic control by workers, but in countries such as the former Soviet Union and China, the Communist Party has used its dictatorial powers to deny individual freedom. Today, in Eastern Europe and the independent republics formed from the old Soviet Union, many of the political parties working to establish democratic governments retain some elements of socialism in their economies.

Regulating the Economy

Economic cycles of boom and bust have been one of the constants of human history. Good times with rising living standards are followed by bad times when harvests are poor, people go hungry, unemployment is rife, and living standards decline. Until modern times, governments did little to regulate these cycles, although some tried to ease the consequences of the bad times by distributing grain to people who were starving or by providing temporary shelters for the homeless. In the United States, it was not until the 1930s that government tried, through economic policies, to prevent these cycles from occurring.

The idea that government intervention could ease the boom-and-bust cycle of the economy was revolutionary. Classical economists had argued that the market would adjust itself without government action. But in democratic societies, as government became larger and more powerful, people expected government at least to try to alleviate economic problems.

In Germany in 1923, inflation was so high that a basket of money barely sufficed to buy a few groceries. This hyperinflation was caused by the German government's printing ever more money to pay penalties they were assessed by the victors of World War I. The government finally ended the inflation by issuing new currency, one unit of which was equal to one trillion of the old. This made the lifetime savings of many people worthless.

Economic Problems

One of the familiar economic problems that modern government is expected to do something about is unemployment. Even in a "full employment" economy, several percent of the labor force will be out of work—people who quit their jobs to look for others, those just entering the workforce, those unable to work, and those who do not want to work for one reason or another. But most Western countries experience periods when there are many people unemployed because the economy does not create enough jobs.

A **depression** is a period of prolonged high unemployment. During the Great Depression (1929–1935), over one-quarter of the American working population were without jobs. A second recurring economic problem is **inflation**—a condition of increasing prices during which wages and salaries do not keep pace with the price of goods. As a dollar becomes worth less, there is little incentive to save and great incentive to borrow. In the late 1950s and early 1960s, inflation in the United States was quite low, as little as 2 or 3 percent a year, but the Vietnam War and the high cost of imported oil during the early 1970s stimulated a sharp rise. It was not until the 1990s that inflation returned to pre–Vietnam War levels.

Though some economists believe moderate inflation is not a bad thing,[10] many people feel threatened by it. It erodes the value of savings and gives people an incentive to consume rather than save. Bankers hate inflation because the dollar paid back to them in the future is going to be worth less than the dollar they lend today. Inflation drives interest rates up as banks charge higher and higher interest to compensate for the declining value of the dollar. Credit becomes more expensive, which makes it difficult for businesses and industries to expand. And, of course, inflation is bad because people think it is bad—they worry about it getting out of control.

A third economic problem is stagnant production—that is, the failure of the economy as a whole to produce increasing amounts of goods and services. Two or more consecutive quarters (a quarter is three months) of falling production are termed a **recession.** During the peak of the recession in 1981–1982, over 10 percent of the American workforce was unemployed, and many others had only part-time work or had simply quit looking for work. In 2001, the United States went into a milder recession with unemployment rising by "only" 2 percent. Some economists believe this downturn was a "double dip" recession, so called because just as a recovery seems to be under way, the economy experiences reversals that push it back into recession.

Productivity, one measure of the country's economic health, is the ratio of the total hours worked by everyone in the labor force to the dollar value of goods and services they produce (the gross domestic product, or GDP). When businesses and industries discover new ways to produce goods and services using less labor, or when a healthier, better-educated, more mobile and efficient labor force can produce more product in less time, productivity rises. To achieve improvement in the overall standard of living without increasing inflation, productivity must steadily rise. Productivity is also a measure of competitiveness; businesses must become increasingly more efficient to be competitive at home and abroad.

For decades the United States has had the highest productivity rates in the world. Although Japan and Germany began to close the gap in the 1980s, the American labor force, when measured by worker output per hour, is still the most efficient in the world. But productivity growth is slowing, in part because the sharp increases in the 1990s were spurred by the introduction of computers, Internet access, and businesses streamlining, including reduction of their labor forces. Since much of the gain from these efficiencies has been realized, productivity is not growing as quickly.

The sum of inflation and unemployment, known as the "misery index," is an economic indicator that is especially important for anyone holding or running for office. As the number of people looking for work and the prices people have to pay for basic goods and services rise, the misery index goes up; the higher the index, the more likely people will be thinking about the economy when they enter polling booths. Because depression, inflation, and recession all affect people's standard of living, most people expect government to take action to stimulate or slow the economy. But they do not agree on which are the most appropriate or effective responses.

The ultimate goal in any economy is to have low unemployment, low inflation, and increasing productivity while total economic output grows steadily. Achieving all of this simultaneously is rare, however. There has long been a consensus among economists that unemployment and inflation are inversely related and that if unemployment falls below about 6 percent, wages and prices will begin to rise. Historically, inflation had been at its lowest when unemployment was high and production sagging. Conversely, increasing employment often brought high levels of inflation. This often meant some trade-off among these three goals. At least that was the assumption before 1995, when the U.S. economy entered a period of economic growth with rising productivity, the lowest unemployment (3.9 percent) in a quarter century, and a low, stable inflation rate around 2 percent.

Government's Economic Tools

Government has two primary tools to help achieve its economic goals: fiscal policy and monetary policy.

Fiscal Policy

Government decisions on how much money it will spend and how much tax it will levy determine **fiscal policy.** Increased spending stimulates the economy and increases employment; lower government spending helps slow the economy and decreases inflation. How great an impact government has depends on how much it spends in relation to the size of the economy.

Tax policy can also help regulate economic cycles. Tax cuts can be used to leave more money in the hands

of the consumer, thus stimulating private spending and reducing unemployment. Increased taxes take more money out of the hands of the consumer, slow the economy, and thus reduce inflation.

Government's ability to regulate economic activity through spending and taxation is limited, however. Sometimes the economy responds to government changes too quickly, other times not quickly enough. International trends also affect our economy, as we shall see in the last section.

Who makes fiscal policy? In the United States, laws regarding taxation and spending require approval by Congress and the president. In making his recommendations to Congress about taxes, spending, and other economic matters, the president has the assistance, among others, of three key people: the secretary of the treasury; the head of the Office of Management and Budget (OMB), who is responsible for preparing the annual budget message; and the chair of the Council of Economic Advisers, a group of economists who are specialists in fiscal policy matters. Sometimes, of course, these three advisers to the president are at odds with each other or with the president's political aids, or uncertain their advice is sound. Indeed, Harry Truman once said he was in search of a one-armed economist so that the person could never make a recommendation and then say "on the other hand."[11] Economics, like political science, is an inexact science!

To improve communication and policy coordination among his economic advisers in the cabinet and the Executive Office of the President (EOP), President Clinton created the National Economic Council, a new office within the EOP's Office of Policy Development. Its members include the vice president and the heads of Labor, Commerce, Treasury, the OMB, and the Council of Economic Advisers. The council's chair briefs the president and helps translate the needs and demands of executive branch agencies into workable policies. Its primary responsibility in the Clinton administration was to monitor the implementation of economic policies to ensure they were consistent with the achievement of the administration's overall goals. The Bush administration has retained this office.

Congress has its own fiscal specialists on committees such as Appropriations and Budget and members also rely heavily on the director of the Congressional Budget Office.

Approaches to Fiscal Policy

That government can have a substantial impact on the economy through its fiscal policy has been accepted wisdom since the British economist John Maynard Keynes published *A General Theory of Employment, Interest and Money.*[12] In 1935, Keynes argued that government could stimulate the economy by increasing spending in a time of high unemployment. This would put more money into the economy, thus stimulating the demand for goods and services and, in turn, causing factories to produce more and hire more workers. Therefore, even if government had to borrow to increase spending, the deficit could be justified because eventually higher employment rates would increase tax revenue.

Keynesian economics ran counter to the conventional wisdom of the time. At the outset of the Great Depression in 1929, President Hoover believed that if the government went into debt, it would make the Depression worse, not better. His opponent in the 1932 election, Franklin Roosevelt, also ran on a pledge of a balanced federal budget. It was only after he was elected that Roosevelt adopted the Keynesian idea that the government could stimulate the economy by spending money, borrowing it if it had to, and in this way help the nation get out of the Depression.

Keynesian thinking dominated fiscal policy for several decades. Well into the 1960s, economists were optimistic that government could successfully regulate the economy to maintain high levels of employment and reasonable inflation. But by the 1970s, this confidence disappeared because of simultaneous high unemployment and high inflation. No government policies coped well with **stagflation,** the word coined to describe this combination of economic stagnation and inflation. Stagflation dealt a blow to Keynesian economics, which predicts that high unemployment and inflation cannot exist simultaneously (because, historically, higher levels of unemployment had driven prices down). The arrival of stagflation signaled a new era in the development of the American economy and led to increasing dissatisfaction with existing fiscal policy.

In 1981, the Reagan administration came to the White House with a new policy, **supply-side economics,** that promised to reduce inflation, lower taxes, and balance the budget simultaneously. The basic premise of this theory is that as government taxes less, more money is freed for private investment. Therefore, when the economy is sluggish, supply-siders advocate tax cuts to stimulate growth. They believe people will save some of the money they would have paid in taxes, thus making more money available to lend to businesses for expansion and modernization. Taxpayers would also be left with more money to spend on consumption; and to satisfy the increased demand, businesses would hire more workers. With increased employment, there would be more people paying taxes and fewer collecting unemployment compensation. So, according to supply-side economics, it is possible both to promote economic growth and to balance the budget by lowering the tax rate.

These ideas appealed to conservatives because they offered an economic rationale for smaller budgets and thus smaller government. They also have broad appeal to Republicans who, since the Great Depression, have drawn substantial electoral support from the wealthiest Americans. Whereas Keynesian economics has been used to endorse across-the-board tax cuts to stimulate consumer spending, the supply-side approach puts more emphasis on tax cuts for the highest income groups as a means of encouraging private investment.

Keynesians and supply-siders have fundamentally different views on government regulation of the economy. Keynesians believe that government intervention can be effective both in steering the economy and in cushioning the blow to consumers of a sluggish or overheated economy. Supply-siders believe that taxing and spending for these purposes are inappropriate and inefficient uses of governmental powers. They believe it is better to leave as many decisions on spending and investing, and as much money as possible, in the hands of consumers.

Supply-side economics, as implemented by Reagan's economic team and continued by the first Bush administration (despite Bush having labeled it "voodoo economics"), led to disillusionment with the policy. It created record-smashing budget deficits. Dramatically increased spending for the military combined with small cuts in spending for social programs and the loss of billions of dollars in tax revenues left the country with $2.5 trillion of new debt.

The fiscal policies of the Republican leadership that assumed control of Congress in 1995 had much in common with supply-side thinking, especially its emphasis on tax cuts for the wealthy and the belief that government attempts to redistribute wealth through tax and spending policies are a misuse of power. However, until

John Maynard Keynes's ideas revolutionized economics.

UPI/Corbis-Bettmann

the George W. Bush administration, post-Reagan Republican leaders had no patience with deficits and assumed an aggressive posture toward coupling tax and spending cuts.

Monetary Policy

Whereas fiscal policy affects the economy through spending and taxation decisions, **monetary policy** attempts to regulate the economy through control of short-term interest rates and the supply of money. Monetary policy is made by the Federal Reserve Board (Fed), composed of a board of governors, twelve Federal Reserve Banks located in major cities around the country, and the Federal Open Market Committee (FOMC).[13] The FOMC meets several times a year to determine monetary policy. Since 1978, its primary mandate from Congress has been to achieve price stability and full employment (remember that full employment is considered achieved when the unemployment rate falls somewhere between 5 and 6.5 percent).

The Federal Reserve Board is largely, but not completely, independent of the president. Fed members are appointed by the president, with the consent of the Senate, but their terms are fourteen years. The terms are staggered in such a way that, barring resignations, the maximum number any president could appoint in a four-year term is two. Another factor that helps maintain the independence of the Fed is that it does not depend on Congress for funding; its operating costs come out of the more than $20 billion in annual interest earned on its holdings of U.S. government securities. The chair, however, serves only a four-year term, although reappointment is possible and often happens. The relatively short-term appointment opens the door to influence by Congress and the president, especially when the Fed chair wants to be reappointed. The current chair, Alan Greenspan, is an adept Washingtonian now in his fourth term and known for his ability to cultivate members of Congress and the cabinet.[14]

The role of the Fed as governing body of the nation's central banking system is crucial. As Will Rogers once said, "There have been three great inventions since the beginning of time: fire, the wheel, and central banking!" The Fed is *the* bank for the federal government; it distributes our currency, supervises and regulates some national banks, and acts as clearinghouse for many of the checks written on those banks. But from the standpoint of the overall health of the economy, its most important work is using its monetary powers to maintain a balance between demand for and supply of currency.[15]

The Fed controls the supply of money in several ways. It can buy and sell hundreds of millions of dollars of treasury notes and bonds. When it buys, it pumps money into other banks; when it sells, it depletes the money reserves of the banks and thus takes money out of the economy. The Fed also changes the interest rates it charges banks to borrow its money. Low interest rates stimulate borrowing and put more money into the economy. As a last resort, the Fed can increase or decrease the amount of reserves (cash on hand) it requires banks to have. If the reserve requirement is increased, banks take money out of circulation to build up their reserves. If the reserve requirement is decreased, banks take money out of their reserves and lend it to customers, thus increasing the money supply.

When the Fed makes money scarce, interest rates go up, and businesses and industries find it harder to borrow money for plant expansion. As a result, production and inflation may slow. When the Fed allows more money into the economy, interest rates go down, making it easier for businesses to borrow for expansion.

Monetary policy is a dry subject, but its effects can be dramatic. In the nineteenth century when fiscal policy was not yet a major factor in the economy, "tight" money was often the main issue in elections. In 1982, when the Fed tightened the money supply, forcing interest rates, unemployment, and bankruptcies up, one man entered the offices of the Fed and tried to kill its chair.[16] Other groups drew up "wanted" posters for the board members. And still others, thrown out of work or off their farms, killed themselves.

Today, the chair of the Federal Reserve Board is one of the most powerful people in the country. The chair is required by law to give testimony to Congress twice a year on monetary policy, but Greenspan, perhaps the most visible head the Fed has ever had, averages a dozen appearances before congressional committees and fifteen public speeches each year. His comments on the state of the economy can cause the stock market to soar or plummet. The Fed's influence grew in the 1980s as huge budget deficits limited the options available to the president and Congress to stimulate or slow the economy through taxing and spending. With little flexibility left in fiscal policy, monetary policy was the principal means for fine-tuning the economy. Even in the late 1990s, Wall Street and business continued to look on monetary policy as the primary means for stimulating growth and productivity as well as for slowing the economy when it becomes overheated. This is the view favored by *monetarists,* who believe that if government has to intervene in the economy, it should do so through monetary, not fiscal, policy.

Monetary policy is made primarily to protect the value of currency and ultimately to protect investors. Fiscal policy is geared much more toward protecting the average consumer against unemployment and the effects of inflation (rather than toward *preventing* inflation). While many people are both investors and consumers, and while fiscal and monetary policy should be complementary and not at odds, at times they may seem to be at cross-purposes.

To see how this works, we can look at the fiscal policy of the Clinton administration and the monetary pol-

Many people credited Federal Reserve Board chair Alan Greenspan with a large share of the responsibility for the economic boom of the 1990s, but his reputation was dented by his easy acceptance of Bush tax cuts that led to deficit spending in 2002.

Michael O'Neill/Corbis

icy of the Fed under Greenspan's chairmanship. Clinton came into office with the goal of "growing" the economy and increasing the real wages of workers. Primarily a politician, his eye was on the earning and buying power of the average voter. As protector of the currency, Greenspan did not want to see Clinton achieve his goals through a too-rapid expansion of the money supply or by wage increases that were too quick or precipitous. Primarily a banker, his eye was on investors.

During Clinton's first two years in office, the growth rate soared, 5.5 million new jobs were created, and inflation stayed at or below 3 percent. But as the unemployment rate fell toward 6 percent and then below it, the Fed began imposing a series of interest rate hikes.

Greenspan also started jawboning (see the next section), trying to slow the economy and offset a rise in inflation. Although it is arguable whether the impact of monetary policy can be felt so quickly, by early 1995, the rate of growth did slow and unemployment rose for the first time in two years.

To a large extent, the concerns of the Fed and the Clinton administration should have overlapped. In an era of flat wages, workers did not want higher prices, and Clinton certainly would not have wanted to take the rap for high inflation and a devalued dollar. On the other hand (remember that expression?), most workers would rather have a job and higher prices than have no

job and stable prices, especially in an era of decreased spending for welfare. And while no politician may claim to favor it, the devalued dollar can lead to more exports, and more exports can mean more jobs.

In addition to the difference in the priorities of fiscal and monetary policymakers, accountability is also an issue. If greater power to regulate the economy *has* gravitated toward monetary policymakers, it has passed into the hands of men and women who are not directly accountable to voters and who most Americans cannot identify. This is especially significant because of the value we place on equality of economic opportunity. The Fed cannot determine which sectors of the economy will grow or who will reap the benefits of growth, just as it has no authority to make policy on how wealth is distributed across the population. To the extent government can influence this aspect of the economy, the responsibility falls to the elected officials who set fiscal policy.

Of all federal agencies, the Fed is the most independent as well as the most powerful. In part this stems from the fact that it never needs to go to Congress to justify a budget. But the Fed can do more with its money than pay its own operating costs. On its own authority, it can extend billions of dollars in credits and loans to businesses, other banks, and even to foreign countries. During the 1995 financial crisis in Mexico, the Clinton administration wanted to make a loan quickly to avoid the crisis spreading to other countries, but it found the Treasury without enough money and Congress unwilling to approve the loan. So Clinton went to the Fed, which used its own funds to loan Mexico $50 billion—something it can do *without* congressional approval. In this case, the initiative came from the White House, but it is part of the Fed's responsibilities to makes independent decisions on loans and credits. Because it can act independently, it can act quickly, and it can have a significant impact on the economy without the public ever being aware of its actions. After September 11, for example, the Fed, fearing a possible economic meltdown, freed up currency and extended billions of dollars in credits and loans to businesses.

Another aspect of the Fed's independence is its ability to escape openness rules that apply to other federal agencies. Although some consider the Fed under Greenspan far more open than it was in the past because of the frequency of his public appearances and pronouncements on Fed policy, Greenspan also uses his power to protect the agency from oversight. On his own authority, in reaction to a House Banking Committee demand to see transcripts of a Fed meeting, he ordered some Fed proceedings not to be taped, even though the committee was well within its oversight rights in requesting the minutes. In addition, Greenspan has ruled that the only transcripts of Fed meetings that will ever be available to archives, and hence to the public, will be versions edited by Fed staff.[17]

It is not likely that any other agency head could exercise this kind of power with respect to Congress.

Jawboning, or Persuasion

The government, and the president in particular, has an informal means for affecting the economy—trying to persuade businesses or individual consumers to behave in a certain way. *Jawboning,* or persuasion, can make a difference because psychological factors affect economic behavior. For example, economists recognize the importance of consumer confidence—that is, the degree of optimism individuals have about the economy. Confidence is rooted in the real performance of the economy, but sometimes there is a lag between the economy's performance and consumers' perception of its health. A president can try to persuade businesses to expand or consumers to spend, for example, by expressing his confidence in the country's economic direction. Lyndon Johnson was extremely skillful in persuading business and labor leaders to accept his economic policies, and Kennedy and Reagan were remarkably adept at persuading both business and the public. In contrast, Carter's calls for sacrifice to meet economic problems seemed to decrease consumer confidence, and George H. Bush's inability to convince the public that the country was coming out of recession in 1992 contributed to his defeat by Clinton.

Perhaps the most impressive feats of jawboning in recent years have come from Fed chairs. However, when the economy is in a prolonged period of expansion, as it was during the 1990s, and consumer confidence is very high, the Fed chair's persuasive powers are not as strong. At those times the economy seems to run on its own momentum. In 1999, when Greenspan tried to cool what he saw as a dangerously overheated economy by accusing investors in the stock market of "irrational exuberance" and threatening new interest rate hikes, his comments produced only a short-term flurry of activity, and the stock market continued to climb.[18]

Managing the Economy for Political Purposes

Partisan differences exist in the management of the economy. Conservatives and Republicans tolerate higher unemployment more easily than do liberals and Democrats, whereas liberals and Democrats are more tolerant of inflation.[19] The business and middle-class supporters of the Republican Party are more concerned about inflation, whereas the working class has more to fear from unemployment and other attempts to "cure" inflation. Thus, Republicans first try to bring down inflation, while Democrats first try to stimulate the economy.[20]

However, the shift in spending that occurs when control of Congress changes hands shows that both parties

adhere to the old adage "To the victor go the spoils." In the early 1990s when Democrats were in the majority, $34 million more per year on average was spent in Democratic than in Republican congressional districts. After Republicans assumed control in 1995, spending shifted from urban and poor rural areas to suburban and farm counties until by 2001, $612 million more was being spent in Republican than in Democratic congressional districts. While spending increased in all districts during these years, it rose by 52 percent in Republican districts compared to 34 percent in Democratic districts.[21]

There is also little difference between parties, either in Congress or the White House, in their willingness to adjust economic policy during election years.[22] Cuts in government spending and increases in taxes reduce real personal income, so budget cuts and tax increases are unlikely in election years. And congressional spending on pork barrel projects almost always increases in an election year.

The 2000 election year was especially lucrative for constituent interests for two reasons. Control of Congress was up for grabs, with the Republicans holding only a five-seat majority and twenty-one of its members retiring. Second, a much higher than expected budget surplus made it possible to fund a cornucopia of benefits. Among them were new subsidies for farmers, tax breaks for married couples, removal of caps on the earnings of Social Security recipients, and higher deductibles for individual retirement accounts. In all, Congress approved more than $700 billion in tax cuts and deductions in the year before the 2000 election.

The prediction before the 2002 election of multiyear budget deficits did not stop Congress from proposing additional tax cuts or making permanent existing tax breaks. Democrats and Republicans vied for the leading role in providing a prescription drug benefit to seniors, who not only vote in large numbers but are represented by one of the country's most powerful interest groups, the AARP. Congress also approved billions in pork barrel projects. (See the "After 9/11" box.)

"There, there it is again—the invisible hand of the marketplace giving us the finger."

President George W. Bush approved steep tariffs on imported steel and steel products to protect aging American mills from efficient foreign competition and to gain electoral support in critical states. Almost immediately, international trade agreements forced him to remove more than seven hundred products from the tariff list.

Making no adjustments in fiscal policy can also have an electoral impact, as the first President Bush found out in 1992. Believing that the economy was on the road to recovery and that he had already interfered too much, Bush took no action. He also apologized to voters throughout the campaign for raising taxes early in his term. Although he presented the outlines of a new fiscal plan two months before the election, when it was clear Clinton's lead in the polls was related to the state of the economy, by then it was too late. In November 1992, 43 percent of all voters said the economy and jobs were the issues that most affected their vote, and 53 percent of them voted for Clinton.[23]

Monetary policy is also subject to partisan influence from elected officials. During an election campaign when the economy is the central issue, there is enormous potential for politicization of the Fed despite its independence. In the summer before the 1992 election, following a jump in the unemployment rate, the Fed lowered its prime lending rate (in an attempt to increase borrowing and thus consumer and business spending). President Bush had publicly demanded such a reduction just several days earlier. His secretary of the treasury was accused of pressuring the Fed's chair to lower rates even further as a condition of his renomination for another term.[24] Although he denied placing any condition on Greenspan's renomination, Bush reportedly blamed the Fed chair for his 1992 reelection loss. The Fed chair does not have to listen to the president, even less a chair as powerful as Greenspan has been.

But Greenspan treated Bush's son, George W., better. Having advised Clinton throughout his administration of the need to hold down spending and end budget deficits, Greenspan was very receptive to the huge tax cuts passed in the second Bush administration, even though they clearly contributed to the budget deficits of 2002. The explanation, according to longtime Fed watchers, lay in Greenspan's politics: He is not so much an opponent of deficit spending as he is of spending for social programs—education, health, and welfare. Because higher amounts of social spending are more likely in a Democratic than Republican administration, Greenspan urged Clinton to avoid deficit spending, while later accepting Bush's increased spending on tax cuts and defense without comment. As the deficits grew larger and the economy continued to falter, and as Bush continued proposing additional tax cuts, Fed watchers and business reporters increasingly called attention to the differential treatment. Prior to the 2002 elections, when Bush was looking for tacit Fed endorsement of his fiscal policies, Greenspan began making fewer optimistic statements about economic recovery.

The economy has an impact on the vote, although it is not as simple as one might suspect. Those who have studied the impact of economic hard times on individual vote choices have reported that how people feel they are doing compared to a year or two before does have some mild influence on their presidential and congressional voting choice. If they feel things are improving, they are somewhat more likely to favor the incumbent; if they

BUDGETARY POLITICS: BUSINESS AS USUAL

Since the Great Depression, Americans have had an expectation that government will intervene when things are going badly, and certainly when there is a crisis. By late summer 2001, things were starting to go badly with the economy; it had been in mild recession for five months and then took another jolt from the terrorist attacks in September (an estimated $95 billion and eighty-three thousand jobs). By the end of the year, more than a million jobs had been lost, and another three-quarters of a million were expected to disappear before the economy improved. In addition, the military response to 9/11 was expected to cost between $60 to $80 billion during its first months. After four years of surpluses, the budget was heading toward a major deficit. New economic woes came in 2002 with a major stock market crash.

The government was in the position of having to respond to terrorism, recession, increased unemployment, revitalizing the airline industry and New York City's economy, beefing up regulation of the stock market and financial industries, and having to do it all with declining revenues. State revenues shrank, too, leaving states and localities in need of federal help. With demands like these, decisions about where to invest public resources tells a great deal about what policymakers value most.

Under the best of circumstances, few members of Congress, let alone average Americans, know any details about what is in an appropriation bill; even fewer look closely at what gets passed under the cover of a national security crisis. A lot of taxpayer money tends to get spent in a hurry, and in the first few months after 9/11, Congress approved billions of dollars in new appropriations. As cynical as it may sound, such times become "opportunities" for lobbyists and decision makers to get money appropriated for favored programs that may or may not be related to the situation. Many who were lobbying for programs, subsidies, or tax breaks restated their requests in a national security context or justified them as remedies for the economic effects of 9/11. The airline industry, for example, got a $15 billion bailout; it did take a serious hit from the attacks, but the major carriers were already in serious

trouble from bad management. And the bailout included nothing for the one hundred thousand airline workers who had been laid off. The head of a lobbying association said it was "a free-for all. . . . It's like squirrels running around finding acorns and putting them in the ground for winter."[1]

Elected officials are not above using these times to get approval for programs they favor, pork for home districts, or policies that play to their party's political base. A month after the 9/11 attacks, when a $20 billion antiterrorism package was attached to a Pentagon appropriations bill, the Senate added 103 amendments with $400 million in funding requests. Any pet project that was indirectly, or just vaguely, related to national security got tacked on to the bill. Senator Collins (R-Maine) asked for $4 million to support research at the University of Maine on hand-held computerized maps for soldiers. Senator Shelby (R-Ala.), a member of the Appropriations Committee, attached an amendment for $2 million to develop communications software in Huntsville, saying, "If they weren't good decisions, I don't believe they would pass." There

believe their financial situation is eroding, they are somewhat more likely to vote against the incumbent.

Voters are more concerned, however, with the state of the overall economy than with their own family's situation. But they do not seem to respond decisively to changes in unemployment or inflation levels. The 1994 election provided evidence for this. With the economy strong and unemployment low, voters were strongly anti–status quo, expressing deep pessimism over the country's future.[25] But in 1998, after four years of economic boom, the president's party gained seats in Congress for only the second time in this century.

Some observers believe the 1990s run of prosperity changed, if only temporarily, the economy's impact at the polls. Whereas in the past, a prolonged period of low unemployment, low inflation, and rising wages would have helped incumbents, it did not give Vice President

Al Gore much of a lift in his 2000 presidential campaign. He had to emphasize other issues such as "family values," income inequality, and health care to catch up to Bush in the polls. The reason, some argue, is that people were doing so well that they took continued growth and near full employment for granted. In addition, factors other than government policy, such as individual hard work, are given credit for the good times.

The stock market is also a factor. Half of all Americans now own stock, and many of those who profited most in the nineties boom did so from stock market investments. Business innovation is another factor: One economist argues that it would have made little difference whether a Republican or a Democrat occupied the White House during the nineties because almost all the economic growth was technology driven.[26] If voters adopt the view that most of the credit for economic

was even a request for money for Marine shirts made in Massachusetts. John McCain (R-Ariz.) said the defense bill was "going to have more Christmas tree goodies on it than the North Pole."[2] Although a conference committee reconciling House and Senate versions of the appropriations bill would remove some of these requests, there was virtually no debate or opposition to adding the amendments.

In an example of how each party played to its base, we can compare the economic stimulus bills of Republicans and Democrats. Only 2.3 percent of the Republicans' $100 billion stimulus package went to support for the newly unemployed, the rest for business subsidies.[3] The Democrats, who draw more votes from workers than from big business, emphasized short-term income support and medical care for the unemployed, although they also included many temporary tax breaks for business in their $90 billion stimulus bill. A compromise ended up allocating about 13 percent to income and health support for the unemployed and the remainder to business in the form of tax breaks.[4]

In his budget requests, the president played the same game as Congress. Other than military appropriations, most of his requests were for tax breaks for corporations rather than small business or workers. They were subsidies he had favored before the country was feeling the economic consequences of 9/11. And, although labeled as economic stimulus measures, the proposed breaks extended two years beyond the time when the economy was expected to have recovered from both 9/11 and the recession. Just one of Bush's requested tax breaks, deduction for depreciation of business equipment and facilities, was projected to cost more than seven times the $14.4 billion that had been approved for unemployment assistance.[5] Of $25 billion in retroactive corporate tax cuts approved by Congress, $800 million in subsidies went to GM alone. One economist pointed out that it was unlikely to lead to more investment at a time when GM already was sitting on $8 billion in cash reserves.[6]

The appropriations process is always an opportunity to reward constituents, political supporters, and campaign donors. In other words, even in a national crisis, the fattest squirrels get the biggest acorns. But in the end—in a kind of pork barrel irony—there were "fewer oinks on the campaign trail" than expected.[7] In the nearly evenly split Congress, with each party trying to deny the other an electoral advantage, members were unable to pass many of the appropriations bills that would have authorized money for all the special projects they had approved. So incumbents went back to their home states and districts for the midterm election bearing far fewer gifts than expected.

1. Leslie Wayne, "So Friend, It's Time for That Tax Cut," New York Times, November 18, 2001, BU1.
2. "Senators Put Pet Projects into Defense Bill," Champaign-Urbana News-Gazette, December 15, 2001, A5.
3. Sara Mosle, "Capitalize on Blue-Collar Heroism," New York Times Magazine, November 11, 2001, 124.
4. Paul Krugman, "Another Useful Crisis," New York Times, November 11, 2001, WK13.
5. Joel Friedman and Isaac Shapiro, "Multi-Year Business Tax Cuts Still Dwarf Aid to Unemployed Workers in New House Bill," report of the Center on Budget and Policy Priorities, March, 2002 (www.cbpp.org).
6. Paul Krugman, "An Alternate Reality," New York Times, November 25, 2001, WK11.
7. "Fewer 'Oinks' on the Campaign Trail," New York Times, October 27, 2002, 22.

good times lies outside the White House and Congress, then incumbents will gain little at the polls in times of prosperity. Gore did win the popular vote in 2000, but it was far closer than it would have been had economic conditions been the deciding factor in how people cast their ballots.

In leaner times, the economy is more likely to be a campaign issue. Incumbents can easily become scapegoats, deserved or not. Much depends on where voters place the economy in the constellation of issues that concern them and who they hold accountable. Private investment and the stock market got most of the credit for the boom of the 1990s and apparently absorbed all of the blame for the crash of 2002. Voters did not punish elected officials for being slow to regulate big campaign donors who had perpetrated corporate fraud. During the 2002 election, polls suggested that voters

were making a distinction between what they saw as the country's most pressing problem (terrorism) and the issue on which they would base their votes in congressional races (jobs and the economy). Yet incumbents were not punished; the Republicans gained six seats in the House and two in the Senate as voters accepted Bush's message on Iraq and terrorism rather than Democrats' emphasis on the weak economy.

The Budget in the Economy

The size of the annual budget tells us the federal government's share of the domestic economy and indicates the potential for fiscal policy to affect the nation's economy. The federal budget also reflects the country's political goals and values, because who is taxed, at what rates, and what government spends the money on reflect national priorities. Government spending is often discussed within the larger debate over fundamental political values, and disagreements on taxation have always been linked to the debate over the proper size and role of government in both a democracy and a free market economy.

The United States spends a smaller percentage of its GDP on government than other Western industrial countries. For the past forty years, federal government spending has hovered near 20 percent of GDP, while state and local government spending has been growing, now adding 10.4 percent to the cost of government. Thus, nearly 70 percent of our $11 trillion economy is accounted for by private spending.

Our Tax Burden

Many believe our tax rates are high, yet except for Japan's, our tax burden is the smallest in the industrial world (Figure 1). Reasons for this include our aversion to taxes and big government, our less than comprehensive social welfare system, and the low percentage of government ownership of economic enterprises.

In 2003, personal and corporate income taxes will account for 57 percent of all federal revenue, and Social Security taxes paid by workers and their employers for another 35 percent. The proportion of revenue coming from corporate income tax (10 percent) is dramatically below the level of the 1950s and 1960s, when it accounted for about 25 percent of all federal revenue. Social insurance payroll taxes, in contrast, are the fastest-growing source of federal revenue (see Figure 2).

The income tax burden for most Americans fell throughout the 1990s. Overall, in 2001 federal personal income, payroll and other taxes (such as taxes on alcohol, gasoline, and cigarettes) took an average of 16.3 percent of the income of the middle fifth of American taxpayers.[27] This is the lowest percentage since the CBO began publishing such data.[28] Of course, most households pay state and local in addition to federal taxes. In 2001, a household with median income of $64,600 paid about 7 percent of it in *income* taxes, the lowest amount since 1957.[29] Those in the top 1 percent of earnings paid about 36 percent, while those in the bottom half of earnings paid only 4 percent in income tax.

However, lower-income people pay a higher proportion of their income in payroll taxes than do upper-income people. Such taxes (for Social Security and Medicare) take, on average, about 9 percent of income, but only up to about $80,000 of earned income. Income beyond that is not subject to payroll tax, nor are interest and dividends. However, on retirement, the majority of workers get benefits well in excess of what they have had withheld in payroll taxes.

The wealthiest Americans account for the largest share of income tax revenue, but that is simply because they have most of the country's wealth. In fact, by the end of the 1990s, they were receiving a larger percentage of (before-tax) national income than at any time since 1936.[30] Even while paying a higher percentage of their income in taxes than less well-off Americans, the after-tax income of the wealthiest 1 percent still grew by 157 percent from the late 1970s to the late 1990s, while that of the middle fifth grew by only 10 percent[31]

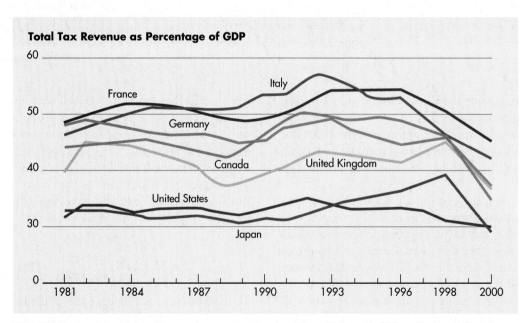

FIGURE 1 ■ Americans Have a Lower Tax Burden Than Citizens of Most Industrialized Nations

SOURCE: Organization for Economic Cooperation and Development (www.oecd.org).

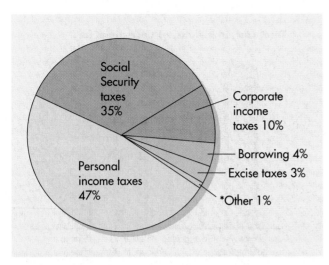

FIGURE 2 ■ Estimated Federal Revenue Sources, 2003† ($2 trillion)

*Customs duties; fines; penalties, Federal Reserve earnings.
†Does not include revenue from business activities such as park fees. This is subtracted from spending.
SOURCE: *Citizen's Guide to the Budget of the United States Government, Fiscal Year 2003* (Washington, D.C.: Government Printing Office, 2002), 3.

(see Table 1). The impact of the 2001 tax cuts will make that inequality even greater, since those cuts favored the highest income groups.

The distribution of the federal tax burden across the population differs from that in other industrial democracies, in part because the overall tax burden on the wealthiest Americans is much lower. Japan and Western European countries rely more heavily on taxing goods and services, which means that, relative to the United States, a larger share of the tax burden falls on consumption than on income. By placing greater emphasis on Social Security and personal income taxes, our tax policy allows the average worker to keep a smaller part of a paycheck than his or her counterpart in Europe or Japan. In 1998, a middle-income family paid about $3,575 in Social Security and Medicare taxes compared to $72 in Social Security tax in 1954 (Medicare did not exist at the time). That amounts to a 4,865 percent increase, a pace far from matched by wage increases over the same period. While the effective rate of payroll taxes for the average household is 7.65, it is only 1.66 for a

TABLE 1	Average After-Tax Income Gains, 1979–1997
The income gap between rich and poor has grown significantly in the past two decades.	
Income Group	**After-Tax Income Gain**
Top 1 percent	$414,200
Middle fifth	$3,400
Bottom fifth	−$100

SOURCE: Congressional Budget Office (analysis of data at www.cbpp.org).

family with an income of $2 million (the difference is due to the ceiling on the amount of income subject to the tax).[32] At the same time, the wealthiest Americans have a double advantage over their counterparts in that both their incomes and their consumption are taxed at substantially lower levels than in other developed countries. This helps explain why the United States now has the most unequal distribution of wealth of all the industrial democracies.

Tax Policies

President Franklin Roosevelt once stated that our tax code "might as well have been written in a foreign language," and the laws are dozens of times more complex now. (To get a good idea of just how complex our tax system is, go to the IRS Web site, click on "Forms and Publications," and scroll through the vast array of forms that must be filed when claiming deductions.) The complexity occurs because tax policy is used to achieve a variety of social goals. Congress wants to encourage families where both parents work to have adequate care for their children, so it allows credits for child care; it wants to encourage business growth, so it gives credits and deductions for investment. (A *deduction* is the amount taxpayers have spent for some item, such as mortgage interest or business equipment, that they are allowed by law to subtract from their income before figuring their tax liability.) Congress believes that voluntary giving to charitable organizations is good, so it creates deductions for that, too. Congress wants to help people buy homes and stimulate new housing construction, so deductions are allowed for interest on mortgage payments. Though each of these and hundreds of other exemptions and deductions may be desirable, together they create a tax code that is difficult to understand and favors wealthier Americans who are able to take advantage of more loopholes.

In 1986, Congress passed major income tax reform in an effort to make the tax structure fairer, simpler, and more efficient. The code's definition of fairness is spreading the tax burden among households according to their ability to pay. A tax structure based on the principle of wealthy and middle-income households paying higher percentages of their income in taxes than poorer households is called a **progressive tax.** A tax that requires the poor to pay proportionately more than those in middle- and upper-income brackets is a **regressive tax.**

The 1986 tax law tried to achieve greater fairness by reducing deductions and exemptions and by lowering the number of tax rates from fifteen to four (counting the zero rate for low-income households). These simplifications in turn were to make the system more efficient. Taxes should have been easier to calculate and the forms less time-consuming to complete.

One of the reasons they were not is that the reform did not go far enough in reducing deductions and loopholes. That so many exemptions and special provisions were retained is testimony to the power of a variety of interests. For example, middle-income homeowners, along with housing, construction, and real estate lobbies, ensured that mortgage interest on first and some second homes would remain deductible. Part of the cost of travel, meals, and entertaining for business purposes is still deductible, as is interest on business loans. In addition, loopholes in the tax code have made it possible for a majority of foreign corporations to pay little or no tax.[33] (The cost of some of the major deductions is shown in Figure 3.)

Current Tax Issues

Most Americans felt no tax relief from the 1980s tax cuts because of increases in Social Security taxes and hikes in state and local taxes to compensate for reduced federal funding for social services. And because the benefits of the Reagan tax cuts and the 1986 tax reform went lopsidedly to the wealthy, the income tax was somewhat more regressive after the 1986 reform than before it. Therefore, when faced with the problem of how to increase revenue to help balance the budget, the Clinton administration submitted legislation designed to make the income tax more progressive by forcing the wealthiest Americans to carry a larger share of the burden. In 1993, Congress increased the highest tax rate on ordinary income from 31 to 36 percent. When income exceeded $250,000, a 10 percent tax surcharge applied, making the effective rate 39.6 percent for those in the highest income group. The top corporate tax rate rose from 34 to 35 percent. The purpose of the Clinton bill was to raise more revenue by making the tax structure more progressive; it did little to make it simpler or more efficient.

Achieving a tax policy that is both fair and simple is difficult given our complex occupational and income structure, and perhaps impossible without a total overhaul of the system of deductions. One solution to some of these problems is to abolish our present tax code and replace it with a **flat tax**—that is, a single rate for all income groups.

One version of the flat tax advocated by former majority leader Dick Armey and many Republicans calls for a single rate of 17 percent for all Americans and the elimination of all deductions except for one large standard deduction (about $35,000 for a family of four; currently, every taxpayer receives a standard deduction and a personal exemption, for a total of $7,450 per individual each year).

Such a plan would greatly simplify the tax code, cut millions for administering the IRS from the federal budget, and reduce the present U.S. 1040 form to a

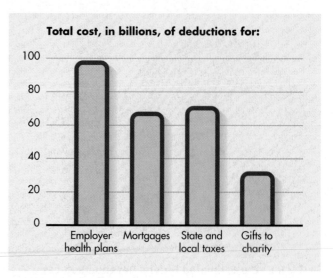

Total cost, in billions, of deductions for:

F I G U R E   3 ■ Tax Deductions Mostly Benefit Middle- and Higher-Income Families
Billions of dollars of tax revenue are lost through deductions, largely benefiting middle- and upper-class families.

SOURCE: "Estimates of Total Income Tax Expenditures," in *Analytic Perspectives on FY 2003 Budget of the United States* (Washington, D.C.: Government Printing Office, 2002), Table 6.1.

single-page or a postcard-sized form. Flat tax advocates believe that a progressive tax policy punishes people for earning more and creating wealth. They argue that fairness can be better achieved by requiring all Americans to pay the same proportion of their income to the government. Supporters also claim that with the large personal exemption, lower-income individuals would pay a smaller percentage of their income in taxes than under the present system and that there would be a de facto zero tax rate for an estimated 10 million of the poorest Americans.

Opponents of the bill argue that a flat tax promotes simplicity and efficiency over fairness. The tax code historically has defined fairness as requiring a multirate structure, so tax burdens would increase in proportion to one's ability to pay. Although most agree that this principle has been deeply compromised by a system of deductions favoring wealthier Americans, supporters of progressive taxation would rather reform and simplify the present code. Opponents also point out that it is unlikely that higher-income groups who want special exemptions and deductions would go away even if the flat tax plan were adopted; thus, the flat tax would soon become very regressive.

Others, such as House Energy and Commerce Committee chair Billy Tanzin (R-La.), would like to eliminate the personal income tax in favor of a 15 percent national sales tax. To reduce the regressivity of the tax, it would exempt basic necessities such as food and clothing, on which the lowest-income groups spend a high proportion of their earnings, but not large-ticket items such as homes, cars, and furniture. With a national sales tax, there would be no need to file a return because taxes would be paid as one spends. But Social Security and Medicare taxes would still be withheld from paychecks. Many people find the prospect of a simplified procedure for filing taxes very attractive, but critics argue that the rates proposed thus far are too low to recover the revenues that would be lost by eliminating the personal income tax.

For all the talk of simplifying the massive and complex tax code, tax laws grew 10 percent faster after the Republicans took control of Congress in 1995 than in the five previous years, adding another 6,400 pages to the code. In addition, while giving the agency 1,200 more laws to comply with (many resulting from the new deductions), Congress cut the number of IRS agents by 16,000.[34]

The trend has continued with the Bush tax cuts. In the absence of any consensus on reforming the tax code, Congress continues to pass laws reducing or eliminating specific taxes and targeting income groups. Bush's income tax legislation aimed to lower the 39 percent rate on the highest-income group to 33 percent, for example. Because the repeal of the estate tax and the 2001 income tax cuts are both phase-in programs, they will require taxpayers to deal with different numbers and rules each year until 2010. And if they are not renewed or made permanent, the rules will all revert to those valid in 2001.

In addition, Congress regularly approves "extenders" or special, limited-time tax breaks for business groups or other special categories of taxpayers. Each year it has to either suspend or renew them. All of this piecemeal legislating adds thousands of pages to the tax code.

Thus, the current tax code, with its 17,500 pages of explanation for filling out 650 different forms, will continue to grow. The rules are so Byzantine that a 2001 Treasury Department survey of IRS walk-in services found that taxpayers received insufficient or incorrect answers 73 percent of the time.[35] This is probably why more than half of all Americans hire professionals to prepare their tax reports.

Spending Policies

In 1999, for the first time in thirty years, the federal government proposed spending approximately the same amount it raised in revenues. Under an agreement reached with Congress in 1997, the president was committed to balancing the budget by 2002. But continued economic growth and low unemployment produced greater-than-anticipated federal revenues, leading to a surplus in 1998 and the passage of a balanced budget three years ahead of schedule. In 2001, the government actually proposed spending 9 percent *less* than it expected to receive in revenues.

Discretionary and Mandatory Spending

Legislation passed in 1990 to bring the budget deficit under control divided federal spending into two categories: discretionary, and direct or mandatory (Figure 4). **Discretionary spending** is set by annual appropriations bills passed by Congress, and as the label suggests, amounts are established at the discretion of members of Congress in any given year. Included in this category of spending are such items as government operating expenses and salaries for many federal employees. Spending on each item is limited by the dollar ceilings, or caps, that Congress authorizes for the year.

Mandatory spending, in contrast, is mandated by permanent laws. Even though some of these outlays are provided for by annual appropriation bills, Congress *must* spend the money because there are laws that order it to do so. Examples of mandatory spending are payments made for Medicare and Medicaid, various government subsidies such as farm price supports, and unemployment insurance. In 2003, discretionary spending is expected to account for about one-third of all budgetary outlays, and mandatory spending for two-thirds.

As its name implies, mandatory spending is harder than discretionary spending for Congress to control.

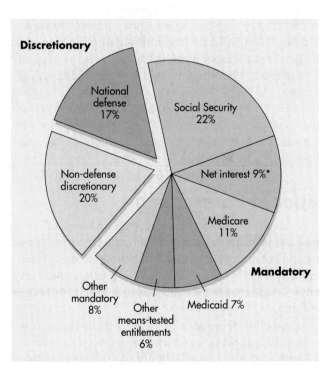

FIGURE 4 ■ **Estimated Federal Spending, 2003 ($2.1 trillion)**

*Does not include interest paid on government securities held by the Social Security Trust Fund.
SOURCE: *Citizen's Guide to the Budget of the United States Government, Fiscal Year 2003* (Washington, D.C.: U.S. Government Printing Office, 2002), 4.

Yet mandatory spending is not uncontrollable in every instance. In considering the president's budget, Congress cannot simply refuse to fund Medicaid, for example, nor can it decide to drastically lower its funding level. But it can amend the law that created Medicaid to change eligibility, or it can repeal the law and remove any need for appropriations. After 1990, Congress was barred by law from passing any bill that increased mandatory spending without offsetting spending cuts or increased revenue to support it. If a program had a net cost—that is, if new spending was not matched by a revenue increase—the funds were sequestered. This provision is called pay-as-you-go, or simply "pay-go." These rules helped provide the discipline that resulted in a balanced budget.

Most mandatory spending then, while not controllable through the budgetary process alone, can be altered by legislation. An expenditure such as interest on the national debt, however, is truly mandatory and can be reduced only by paying down the debt.

Clearly, any serious effort to reduce budget deficits required reductions in mandatory spending or substantial tax increases. That is why, when Republicans committed both to tax cuts and to balancing the budget assumed leadership of Congress in 1995, they immediately introduced legislation to alter the permanent laws that created, and ordered spending for, welfare, farm subsidies, and other programs.

Once the budget went into surplus, however, Congress immediately began modifying the rules that had constrained spending. It has been raising caps annually since 1999, and Bush asked for additional increases for 2003. More important, the rule that tied increases in mandatory spending to available revenues has been all but discarded.[36] This helps explain why surpluses lasted only four years and the budget was back in deficit by 2002.

Budget Forecasting

Deciding how large the budget should be and how much should go to each government activity is part of the political process. Because the amount the government can spend is supposed to be a function of the revenue it collects, revenue projection is crucial to budget making.

Predicting revenue is not a science, as much as we would like to think otherwise; it is rooted in political as well as economic considerations. To estimate accurately what revenues are likely to be and what outlays will be needed, budget writers have to estimate future rates of economic growth, inflation, unemployment, and productivity. With economic growth comes greater revenue from taxes. With economic slowdown, factories are idle, workers are laid off, tax revenues fall,

and more money is be needed for unemployment insurance, welfare support, crime control, and even mental health care.

Small errors in predictions make an astoundingly large difference. For example, underestimating unemployment by 1 percent can mean a multibillion-dollar error in budgeting because unemployment reduces revenue and increases expenditures.

Presidents usually rely on estimates of economic growth, inflation, and unemployment that are most favorable to their own economic program. President Reagan's projections were especially far off the mark. David Stockman, Reagan's first budget director, described how such estimates were made for his first budget. To justify a huge tax reduction and show a balanced budget, significant economic growth and low inflation had to be projected. The administration's initial figures included a 2 percent projected inflation rate, a figure far below the existing rate. The chair of the Council of Economic Advisers, Murray Weidenbaum, said, "Nobody is going to predict 2 percent inflation on my watch. We'll be the laughingstock of the world."[37] So Stockman and Weidenbaum bargained over what the forecasts would be; Weidenbaum selected an inflation figure he could live with, and Stockman raised the economic growth projections. Of course, both were horribly wrong, and that is why the real deficit was a hundred times bigger than projected.

In preparing its first multiyear budget forecast, the current Bush administration was able to come up with much more optimistic projections than the Congressional Budget Office by not factoring in the long-term costs of tax cuts and by using lower estimates of increases in mandatory spending for Medicare. While it predicted a return to a balanced budget in 2005, the CBO saw deficits running into 2006 and well beyond if the tax cuts were made permanent. The CBO, because it serves both parties and the political agenda of neither, is not compelled to accept the most or the least rosy estimates of economic performance, and thus its projections are usually more reliable than those of the White House.

In this case, Bush administration projections did not include the cost of tax cuts that it was asking Congress to make permanent. That omission alone could account for a difference of $4 to $5 trillion in long-term projections. And while the administration talked about $1 trillion in surpluses over the next decade, all of that surplus was from Social Security payments, money that is off-budget and supposedly reserved for future payment to retirees (or, as candidate Al Gore said repeatedly, in a lockbox). The administration's budget outside Social Security was actually showing a $1.5 trillion deficit.[38] After studying these projections one economist said, "No company, other than Enron, would think of counting its pension funds as surplus operating funds."[39]

But that is a sleight of hand used by many earlier administrations. No chief executive wants to predict a decade of red ink.

Deficits and Debt

Politically driven economic forecasting, tax cuts unmatched by spending cuts, dramatically increased health care costs for the poor and elderly, and huge outlays for unforeseen events such as the savings and loan bailout or war all contribute to deficits in the federal budget. A budget deficit occurs when federal spending exceeds federal revenues. The accumulation of money owed by the government from all budget deficits is the **national debt.** Between 1980 and 1995, our national debt quadrupled to more than $4.6 trillion and in 2002 stood at $6 trillion.

Despite the widespread conviction that moderate deficits are sometimes needed to stimulate the economy, most experts agree that the huge recurring deficits of the 1980s and the early 1990s impaired the country's long-term health. When government borrowing reaches a high level, it crowds out private borrowing and therefore private investment. And the intense competition for investment dollars drives up interest rates. Budget deficits, coupled with private debts, left too little money in the United States to finance this mass borrowing, and we had to borrow from foreign as well as domestic sources. The outflow of interest and other payments made by our government to foreign investors in the 1980s and 1990s also contributed to our trade deficit and made us increasingly vulnerable to the uncertainties of international markets.

The economy also suffered from government's reduced flexibility in fiscal policy when as much as $0.15 of every tax dollar was designated for interest payments. There was less money for spending to meet urgent needs in education, health care, research, and infrastructure improvements necessary to economic growth.

A continuing problem is the amount of the national debt owned by government agencies. The public (domestic and foreign institutions and individual investors) holds a little more than half the debt, and state, local, and federal government agencies a little less than half.

The Social Security Trust Fund, for example, is required by law to invest its surplus (money paid in each year by workers and employers in excess of what is needed to meet outlays to Social Security recipients) in government securities. Just as you, a private investor, might loan the government money by buying a Treasury bond, so does the Social Security Trust Fund. The interest paid on these securities stays in the Trust Fund along with the bonds. The government uses the cash received from the Trust Fund purchase of securities, just as it uses

the cash you spend to buy a bond, to offset the budget deficit. It means less money has to be borrowed from banks and other institutions. The question is whether the government will have the money to pay off the securities held by the Trust Fund when they mature, and if not, who will pay the benefits due retiring workers.

For some, the solution to recurring deficits is amending the Constitution to require a balanced budget. The most recent call for a constitutional convention had won support in thirty-two states by 1990, just two short of the minimum needed, before the time limitation on ratification expired. But changing the Constitution is usually regarded as a last-ditch alternative, and shepherding an amendment through to ratification can take years. Therefore, many in Congress look to legislative action as a quicker and surer route to deficit reduction.

Because the Treasury Department cannot borrow beyond limits set by Congress, one obvious option is for Congress to refuse to approve an increase in the debt ceiling and force the Treasury Department to stop borrowing money. Congress has done this a few times, but when the government runs out of operating funds, it must shut down, just as it did in 1996, when Congress failed to pass appropriations bills.

Hypothetically, the government could print more money or stop making interest payments when budget shortfalls occur. Defaulting would destroy the government's financial credibility at home and abroad with the banks and corporations who help finance the debt, and it would betray millions of private citizens who invest in government bonds individually or through their pension plans. If the Treasury Department simply printed more money, the market would be flooded with dollars, setting off an inflationary spiral.

Congress's 1985 attempt to legislate a balanced budget was a travesty. The balanced budget act, more commonly referred to by its cosponsors' names—Gramm-Rudman-Hollings (GRH), was supposed to trigger automatic cuts in most programs if annual goals for deficit reduction were not met. What really happened was even more playacting than usual. The deficit was artificially reduced by selling off public land and public enterprises, a one-shot infusion of money that does nothing to solve any long-range spending problems (it is like selling your house to pay off a vacation) and by gimmicks such as delaying military pay raises for a day. Spending items were put into an "off-budget category" and not counted in the estimate of the deficit.

More successful were the spending caps agreed to in 1990 by President George H. Bush and the Democratic majority in Congress. These caps were approved for three years, along with a requirement that tax cuts and increases for entitlement programs had to be offset by new revenue or offsetting spending cuts (the pay-as-you-go system). This was the first serious measure to bring

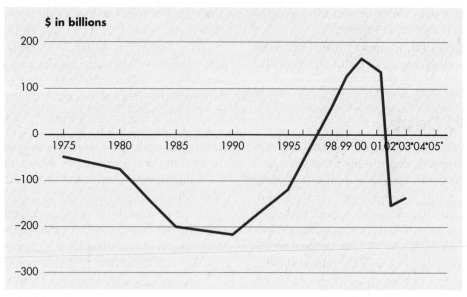

FIGURE 5 ■ The Deficit Returns

The country had four years of budget surpluses before the combination of recession, the 2001 tax cuts, and increases in military and other spending related to terrorist attacks sent the budget back into deficit in 2002. It is projected to stay there through 2005.

*All numbers from 2002 to 2005 are Congressional Budget Office estimates (August 2002) and do not include cost of a war with Iraq.

spending in line with revenue. In 1993, against the wishes of many Democrats, Clinton proposed a renewal of the spending caps. His offer was one part of a larger package designed to bring mandatory spending under control through sweeping reforms in the permanent laws governing spending for health care and welfare.

The size of the deficit fell each year of Clinton's first term (Figure 5), and midway through his second term, the budget went into surplus. Despite budget politicking, the deficit disappeared in large part due to increased revenues generated by economic growth and low unemployment.

Our $6 trillion national debt sounds staggering, but the picture is not all gloom and doom. In 1790, the fledgling U.S. government had run up a national debt of $75.4 million, mainly from the costs of the Revolutionary War. This figure was fifteen times greater than the new government's annual revenues, whereas in 2002 our national debt was "only" three times larger than the $2 trillion in revenues. It took almost fifty years to pay off that first debt, but by 1835, the United States was virtually debt-free.[40] During that period of steady debt reduction, the country continued to grow and prosper.

A small part of the publicly held debt was paid off during the budget surplus years at the end of the Clinton administration and in Bush's first year. Clinton's fiscal 2001 budget contained a plan for paying off all of the public debt by 2013, but with the return of deficit spending, we are again borrowing rather than repaying holders of the debt.

Economists disagree about how urgent it is to pay off the debt. Those who support reducing debt level point

to the amount of money tied up in annual interest payments. In the single year between 1998 and 1999 as the budget went into surplus, money spent on net interest payments on the debt dropped by $13 billion; if the budget had stayed in surplus in the decade from 1998 to 2009, as then projected, annual interest payments would have declined from $243 billion to $71 billion instead of being on the increase, as they are now. Even to Bill Gates, a savings of $172 billion is a lot of money.

Opponents of rushing to pay off debt fall into two general categories: those who believe cutting taxes is important for continued economic growth, and those who believe it is more important to invest in education, train future workers, and improve infrastructure necessary for industrial growth and increased productivity. But since virtually all of the surplus came from payroll taxes withheld for Social Security and Medicare benefits and was needed for future retirees, experts did not even agree whether the surpluses were real or just an accounting device.

Postwar Boom and Bust

The health of any economy depends on many factors, only some of which government can influence and none of which it can completely control. But the role of government has to change over time if it is to be responsive to public needs and to structural changes in the economy. As we entered the twenty-first century, the relationships between governments and economies were everywhere in flux.

In the United States after the Great Depression, the Keynesian-influenced activist role of the government was not seriously challenged until the Reagan years, and even then without great impact. But the collapse of one-party socialist systems in Eastern Europe and a relative decline in U.S. economic strength revived the debate over government's role in a free market economy. Before looking to the future, we look back briefly at the U.S. economy since World War II and government's contributions to current problems and successes.

The American Quarter Century

In the late 1940s, following World War II, we were the undisputed economic power of the world. Optimistic (and perhaps jingoistic) Americans talked of the "American century," in which America would dominate the world much as Britain had done in the nineteenth century and other powers had done in earlier eras. The economies of World War II allies (Britain, France, the Soviet Union) and enemies (Germany, Italy, and Japan) alike were shattered by the expense and human loss of the war, the dislocation of populations in some nations, and the destruction of factories, businesses, and public facilities such as highways and railroads in others. In these circumstances, our economy boomed, and we produced goods for the entire world.

The economic good times continued for twenty-five years, fueled in part by our growing population. Slowdowns in economic growth and increases in unemployment were temporary, inflation was not serious, and productivity marched steadily upward. Our standard of living zoomed as Americans bought cars, new homes, household appliances, and luxury items in quantities unheard of before. Most people could anticipate being better off in the future than in the present and felt sure that their children would be even better off. Economic improvement seemed inevitable, not for everyone, of course, but for most people.

The late 1960s brought the first obvious signs of trouble as inflation rose along with spending on the Vietnam War. Then in 1973 the bottom fell out of our economic machine. A group of oil-producing nations (called OPEC), which controls much of the world's

The American postwar economy lifted millions of families into middle-class status. At left is thirty-two-year old Florence Thompson and her three daughters in 1936 after drought and depression drove them from Oklahoma to look for a better future in California. The family was living in a migrant labor camp and surviving on vegetables dug up from fields and birds the children killed. Publication of the photo prompted the government to send twenty thousand pounds of food to the camp, but by then the Thompsons had moved on. At right is the same family forty-three years later in Modesto, where Mrs. Thompson's children eventually were able to buy her a home. But before her last illness and death in 1983, they had to solicit contributions to pay for her medical care.

Library of Congress

Photo by Bill Ganzel, from *Dust Bowl Descent*, University of Nebraska Press

known reserves, forced a large price increase in oil. Dependent on foreign oil, Americans found prices skyrocketing, not only for gas for their cars but for almost everything else. Petroleum products ran our factories and our farm machinery and were essential ingredients in the manufacture of goods ranging from plastics to pesticides, petrochemicals to Chapstick. The United States was not alone in its distress. All of the industrialized and much of the developing world also experienced rampant inflation. But the United States, used to being "on top of the world," may have been shaken more deeply.

The oil price shock was not the only blow to our economy. During the 1970s, the baby boom generation—those born in the late 1940s and early 1950s—entered the workforce in record numbers. As a consequence, unemployment increased because the economy was not growing fast enough to absorb millions of new workers. To add to our woes, other industrial nations of the world had long since recovered from the devastation of World War II and were giving us stiff competition in the international marketplace. Developing nations of Asia were also beginning to industrialize and, with low wage rates for their workers, were underselling us in international markets. Many of our heavy industries shriveled as U.S. and foreign manufacturers discovered they could buy steel and machinery cheaper in Japan, Korea, or Germany, and consumers at home and abroad decided they preferred energy-efficient, foreign-made cars to those produced by the American auto industry. These developments increased unemployment as workers in declining industries were laid off.[41]

Despite these woes and the fact that inflation made the dollar worth less in 1979 than in 1970, real income in the 1970s increased by over one-fourth, and the distribution of income between the rich and poor changed little.[42] The average person was better off but felt worse off because of the specter of rising inflation, which reached double-digit figures during some months of the late 1970s. Economists could not agree on any solution to inflation that would not increase unemployment. Pessimists, looking at the shattered U.S. economy, noted that the "American century" had lasted only twenty-five years.

The Reagan–Bush Years

During his eight years in the White House, Ronald Reagan succeeded in reviving public confidence in the economy. As promised, he reduced income taxes, increased military spending, and lowered inflation. Inflation rates after 1982 were the lowest since the early 1970s, due in part to a big drop in oil prices. However, most of the decrease in inflation was due to the Federal Reserve Board's policies of taking money out of the economy by raising prime interest rates and making it very expensive for businesses to borrow money. This tight money policy slowed growth, and with it inflation, but it also contributed to a severe recession in 1981 and 1982. High unemployment drove down wages as workers threatened with layoffs agreed to forgo pay increases and in some cases even to accept pay cuts and reduced fringe benefits.

With the Fed's tight money policy and the sharp drop in inflation, farmland plummeted in value, deflating even more than wages. Having borrowed amounts for expansion far in excess of the new value of their land, farmers were unable to sell the land at prices equal to their debt when banks called in their loans. Thousands of farmers lost their land and homes and were thrown into an uncertain job market.

In 1982, unemployment reached 11 percent—its highest level since the Great Depression—but then began to fall as an economic recovery took hold. Higher levels of consumer spending, stimulated by the tax cut, and record levels of government spending increased the demand for goods, which in turn fueled more production and employment. Moreover, in the latter part of the 1980s, the smaller number of children born during the "baby bust" era (the mid- to late 1960s) entered the workforce, leaving many parts of the country with labor shortages. By the time Reagan left office, the unemployment rate was around 5 percent.

Unfortunately, the boom in our economy was built in large part on a foundation of debt. Supply-side economics did not work; though production increased, new business did not generate enough tax revenue to make up for that lost from lower rates. Individuals borrowed heavily, too. Buying on credit became such a way of life for Americans that, in 1990, 90 percent of all bankruptcies were filed by individual consumers unable to pay their debts.[43]

During the Reagan years, we did not save or invest for the future. We consumed about as much as we earned. Indeed, if it were not for pension funds and the Social Security Trust Fund, collectively as consumers we would have spent all we earned. Most public borrowing paid for consumption rather than modernization of our nation's industries or improvement of our rapidly deteriorating infrastructure of roads, bridges, and water treatment plants. By the time the first President Bush took office, 42 percent of America's highway bridges were closed or restricted to light traffic; a bridge failed every two days.[44]

Bush rode into office on the Reagan administration's successes in reducing inflation and unemployment and building up the military. Due to the growing deficit, he did agree to new taxes but otherwise veered little from the Reagan economic path, despite his earlier rejection of supply-side policies. As Bush turned his attention to foreign policy and the end of the Cold War, economic conditions at home deteriorated. Inflation rose, and more than 1 million private sector jobs were lost in 1990–1991. Corporate profits fell by almost 6 percent, and economic growth slowed almost to a halt. The nation was declared to be in recession as unemployment rose to 7.5 percent. With the budget and trade deficits soaring, Bush could not turn to the supply-side cure of further tax reductions to stimulate the economy. Yet government continued to spend. By the time he left office, another trillion dollars had been added to the national debt.

Age of Diminished Expectations

When Clinton entered the White House, Americans were pessimistic about the country's economic future. They were living in an era of diminished expectations with declining real wages and living standards.[45] In real dollars (that is, dollars adjusted for inflation), the average family in 1995 earned only about as much as it did in 1975, even though by 1995 most families had two wage earners, rather than one.

From the post–World War II decades into the 1970s, family income grew over 3 percent a year.[46] Indeed, in 1966, a fifty-year-old man could look back over a ten-year period in the workforce and see that his income had risen over 30 percent. At the end of the 1980s, he could look back over the same number of years and find his income had risen only 10 percent.[47] In real terms, workers were earning less than their parents did at a comparable age, and growth in living standards had nearly stopped.

Opportunities knocked for most college-educated young adults, but getting a college education became increasingly difficult for students from poor families.[48] There were fewer well-paying jobs for blue-collar workers than there had been twenty years earlier because heavy industries that traditionally paid high wages to unionized workers fell on hard times. By 1995, of all men between the ages of twenty-five and thirty-four, 32 percent earned "less than the amount necessary to keep a family of four above the poverty line." Mothers had to work longer hours to maintain the old standard of living.[49] Wage concessions were made by workers worried about job security.[50]

The 1990s were a time of taking stock of what the 1980s' private and public spending binge had wrought. The president and Congress reined in spending, and businesses that had overexpanded in the 1980s began cutting back their labor forces, eliminating unnecessary jobs and computerizing clerical work.[51] With fewer employees turning out more goods and services, productivity began to increase sharply in 1992–1993.

"The poor are getting poorer, but with the rich getting richer it all averages out in the long run."

Recovery and Recession

During the last decade of the twentieth century, the United States had experienced a remarkable nine years of low unemployment, economic growth, and low inflation. It appeared that the country had completed a difficult transition from an economy based on manufacturing to one where jobs are generated primarily by high-tech and service industries, just as we earlier had made the difficult transition from agriculture to manufacturing. At century's end, Americans' confidence in the economy was at its highest point in fifty years.

But the recovery was a song in two keys. Employment was high, but income inequality increased dramatically and working people lost benefits. From the standpoint of a job hunter, the economy looked good; jobs were plentiful, and real income moved upward for almost all workers except farmers. Although for a few years in the late 1990s, unskilled workers were earning more than they had for two decades, they were losing benefits at an alarming rate.[52] The number of Americans without health insurance was and is increasing.[53] One in six children still lived in poverty in 1999. To the millions of uninsured Americans in low-paying jobs, a million immigrants, many of them poorly educated, were being added each year. (See the "American Diversity" box.)

By 2002, personal bankruptcies accounted for 97 percent of all bankruptcies, and Americans were spending 14 percentage of their income servicing their debts.[54] Nevertheless, in a departure from the usual call from government for Americans to spend

DOES IMMIGRATION BENEFIT THE ECONOMY?

Concerns about the number and national origins of immigrants have been with us almost since settlers began colonizing North America. But during the 1980s and early 1990s, as the arrival of millions of new Americans coincided with slow economic growth, serious unemployment, and huge budget deficits, another round of anti-immigration sentiment surfaced. It led to new state and federal laws restricting benefits and services available to both legal and illegal immigrants, calls for suspending immigration, and even for the elimination of the Immigration and Naturalization Service (INS). Concern over immigration policy continued to mount in the 1990s even as unemployment and inflation dropped to record lows, the deficit declined, and the economy grew. Is immigration benefiting the economy or hurting it? Experts disagree. (There are many noneconomic benefits and costs of immigration, but we focus here only on the economic issues.)

Without doubt, the population growth brought by immigration stimulates the economy by increasing the demand for goods and services. A certain portion of immigrants come with very high or even unique job skills, adding to economic growth and productivity. People who receive residency visas within the quota reserved for priority job skills are likely to be well educated, as are those who come on nonimmigrant student visas and stay on. (Immigrants are disproportionately represented among university professors.) Immigrants have also helped economic revitalization of a number of major cities, bringing new small businesses to the central city.

A 1997 study by the National Academy of Sciences (NAS) concluded that immigration produces a small net gain for the economy, while having a very small negative impact on the wages and job opportunities of native workers.[1] While the majority of immigrants need more services than native residents and have fewer resources to pay for them, the study concluded that, on average, adult immigrants pay more in taxes over a lifetime than they receive in benefits. Most of these revenues, however, go to the federal government, while states and localities pick up much of the cost for education, health care, and other social services.

But there is another side. Most illegal immigrants and the majority of immigrants who come in under one of the family preference programs have lower educational levels than native workers. By one estimate, during the 1980s immigration "contributed to an increase of 15 percent in the number of high school dropouts in the U.S. workforce—causing a 5 percent decline in wages for native workers who had dropped out of high school."[2] In California, where competition for low-wage laborers is fierce, businesses have turned to nonunionized immigrants, driving native workers out of unskilled positions and slashing the going wage rates.[3] In Pittsburgh, the asbestos workers union saw the going wage drop from $31 to $19 per hour and safety conditions deteriorate, under competition from nonunionized immigrants willing to work for as little as $11 or $12 an hour.[4]

Moreover, the calculation of economic benefits depends on whether the study includes both parents and children in immigrant households. The national net gain figures cited earlier hold true only if one looks at the cost incurred per adult worker. When the costs of benefits for children are factored in, each immigrant produces a net loss in revenue.[5]

One independent study concluded that over his or her lifetime, an immigrant never repaid in taxes an amount equivalent to benefits received, unless one counted in the tax contributions of grown children. And even then the immigrant would remain "a fiscal burden for twenty-two years."[6] In fact, the same NAS study that concluded immi-

less and save more, President Bush called for Americans to spend even more to stimulate the sluggish economy after 9/11.

The boom of the 1990s left many people very rich, but it widened the gap between the rich and everyone else, a gap likely to be further widened by the cutbacks in spending for human services and the tax reductions for the wealthy being phased in over the next decade. In 2000, families' net worth fell for the first time in fifty-five years.[55] Furthermore, except for the most highly educated, the *lifetime* earnings of men have been declining for thirty years, while lifetime earnings inequality between low- and high-skill workers has continued to increase over the same period.[56]

As real wages were stagnating and the average income of the poorest fifth was falling, the average corporate executive was paid $11.9 million per year, earning more in one day than the average American worker earned in a year.[57] This is one reason the 1990s has been labeled the "decade of greed." Yet the difference in total wealth is far greater than wages alone suggest, because those in the highest income brackets have had money to save, invest in the stock market, and buy homes, which made it possible for them to take advantage of the real

gration produced a small net gain for the country as a whole also estimated that states and localities lose $25,000 a year per immigrant. And, since most immigrants cluster in six states and several major cities, these costs are not evenly distributed. In California, which absorbs a very disproportionate share of both legal and illegal immigrants, the total cost of immigration per year for each nonimmigrant household was estimated to be $1,778 in 1994–1995.[7]

Because states have little control over the level of new arrivals each year and therefore over how to budget for them, governors of high-impact states like California and Florida have sued the federal government for reimbursement of the cost of providing education, health care, and social services. Public health facilities have been especially taxed by mounting illegal immigration. The number of people living in the country illegally rose from about 5 million in 1995 to 8 million in 2000. During those five years, 86 percent of counties surveyed reported an increase in uncompensated health care, and two-thirds of them attributed the rise in county hospital and rescue services cost to illegal immigration. In 2002, hospitals were writing off as much as $2 billion a year from the unpaid bills of illegal immigrants.[8]

On the surface, these problems do not seem radically different from the problems of economic integration this country has always faced. But there are some reasons to think that they could be. For example, older economies, as ours is, cannot grow at the same rate as young economies. Current levels of immigration have added additional pressure on schools and the health care and welfare systems, about whose adequacy Americans are deeply concerned. Six percent of immigrants receive some form of welfare on arrival in the country, double the rate for U.S. citizens.[9] Immigration also contributes to growing economic inequality in our society in that the economic benefits of immigration go disproportionately to the well-off (such as employers of low-paid unskilled labor), while the costs fall disproportionately on the poor (competition for low-wage labor and for social services).

We do need to consider factors other than the economic costs and benefits to the country in evaluating current immigration policy, principal among them that immigration is at the core of American identity. But in 2001, the economic arguments were dwarfed by security concerns stemming from violations of INS rules that allowed terrorists to plan attacks on the United States while living in the country, many of

them on overstayed visas. This has prompted a reorganization of the INS and much closer scrutiny of immigrants from countries with ties to terrorist organizations. But these changes are likely to have little impact on the economic pressures on states and localities in responding to the needs of legal immigrants, or of illegal immigrants, over 90 percent of whom come from Central and Latin America.[10]

1. Robert Pear, "Academy's Report Says Immigration Benefits the U.S.," New York Times, May 18, 1997, 1, 12.
2. Dick Kirschten, "American Dreamers," National Journal, July 5, 1997, 1367.
3. Roy Beck, "The Wages of Immigration," Washington Post National Weekly Edition, April 29–May 5, 1996, 24. Also see Beck's The Case against Immigration: The Moral, Economic, Social and Environmental Reasons for Reducing U.S. Immigration Back to Traditional Levels (New York: Norton, 1996).
4. Peter Passell, "Benefits Dwindle along with Wages for the Unskilled," New York Times, June 14, 1998, 23.
5. Pear, "Academy's Report," 12.
6. John Cassidy, "The Melting-Pot Myth," New Yorker, July 14, 1997, 42, citing a study by Berkeley economist Ronald Lee.
7. Kirschten, "American Dreamers," 1366.
8. Dana Canedy, "Hospitals Feel Strain of Illegal Immigrants," New York Times, August 26, 2002, 12. Data are from a 2002 survey conducted by the National Association of Counties.
9. William Booth, "Diversity and Division," Washington Post National Weekly Edition, March 2, 1998, 7.
10. New York Times, June 18, 2000, 18; "Fees Draining Money Hispanics Send Home," Champaign-Urbana News-Gazette, March 1, 2002, 2.

estate and stock booms of the 1990s in ways unavailable to those with little capital. The concentration of wealth and privilege (especially access to higher education in elite institutions) has become so pronounced that one observer refers to the formation of an "overclass."[58]

The United States is now the most economically stratified country in the modern industrial world. At the beginning of this century, 1 percent of the population controlled 40 percent of the country's wealth, twice the share it had twenty-five years ago. America's children are among the poorest in the industrialized world (ranking sixteenth out of eighteen).[59]

This overall picture has given rise to a grassroots movement to win wage support policies at local levels in lieu of Congress's refusal to raise the minimum wage. By 2002, the Living Wage movement had convinced eighty-three local governments to enact laws that set hourly wages for public employees, or those hired with public funds, at a level that allow full-time workers to meet the basic costs of living in the area.

Education is the key to getting ahead in this economy, but aid for lower-income students is also declining in the private sector. In the competition for students, many universities no longer consider need as the

The booming economy of the late 1990s gave the illusion that money grows on trees, but many people were left in the dirt. The stock market crash of 2002 brought the rest back to reality.

"The economy's never been better. Here's another potato!"

primary factor in awarding grants and scholarships. Three-quarters of all grants awarded by colleges and universities between 1989 and 1995 went to middle- and upper-income students, with the fastest rate of increase among students from upper-income homes.[60] This aggravates the trend in tuition costs: In the twenty years between 1980 and 2002, the percentage of household income required to send a child to a four-year state school rose from 13 to 25 for the poorest fifth of Americans. For the middle-income groups, the increase was from 3 to 6 percent of household income in 1980 to 5 to 11 percent in 2000. But for the wealthiest households the cost was 2 percent in 1980 and 2 percent in 2000.[61]

This is a good example of how much faster income has increased for wealthier than middle-income households and also an indication of how hard it will be to close the wealth gap. The gap in lifetime earnings between the high school– and college-educated workers continues to widen, while it becomes increasingly difficult for poorer households to send their children to college. And given the current direction of the economy, job opportunities will be declining for the less well educated; of the 23 millions jobs projected to be created over the coming decade, the majority are expected to be in management, teaching, the professions, and skilled trades.[62] If the middle class is declining, this is clearly a

danger sign because democratic stability rests in part on a large middle class. A society of haves and have-nots with relatively few in the middle is not likely to be very stable.[63]

The American Economy in the Twenty-First Century

At least one-third of world production is controlled by multinational corporations.[64] This international dispersion of economic activity—investment, research and development, production, and distribution—through the networking of companies across national borders is called **globalization.** By definition, globalization means that business is not as nation centered today as it was in the mid-twentieth century. Because business exists primarily to make a profit, loyalty to a particular place is less important than favorable economic conditions for production and distribution. Thus, corporations are continuously scouting for those locations where, for example, labor costs are cheapest and regulation least burdensome. To trade unions and environmental and consumer groups, it means that U.S. corporations are becoming less dependent on and less responsive to American workers and consumers. It also means that they may be moving beyond the reach of government regulation that was adopted to safeguard workers' and consumers' rights and to protect the public against environmental abuses or other negative consequences of business activity.

Japan, the European Union, China, Taiwan, Hong Kong, South Korea, Singapore, and several Latin American countries are now major rivals in world trade. We cannot dominate markets with our manufactured or agricultural products, and we cannot keep jobs within our borders when it is more profitable for businesses to operate elsewhere. The competition is good in that it forces us to become more efficient and brings greater prosperity to the citizens of other countries (who are potential consumers of goods and services we produce). But it has had an impact on the kinds of jobs available to Americans and the wages paid: 20 to 25 percent of the growth in wage inequality in the United States has been attributed to labor competition in a global market.[65]

As the U.S. economy's position in the global economy has changed, so has the government's ability to effect economic change. The days when the board chairman of General Motors could say "What is good for GM is good for the country and what is good for the country is good for GM" are over. The American economy is now a region of the global economy, and both business and labor must compete in an international market. We may still jealously guard our territorial boundaries, but today no border can contain financial and intellectual activities.

A revolution in technology—computers, telecommunications, and transportation—brought us to this new era. Money can be transferred to foreign banks instantaneously through computerized accounts, making competition for investment international. The most highly paid workers—scientists, systems planners and analysts, lawyers, and artists, for example—are very mobile; modern transportation makes it feasible to travel to employment opportunities anywhere in the world, and telecommunications makes it easy to transmit their ideas. They are part of an international labor pool.

Blue-collar workers, too, compete in an international market, not just against available labor in the United States. Manufacturers relocate where low overhead and wages ensure higher profits, and highly paid North Americans lose jobs to poorly paid Latin Americans and Asians.

Businesses do not make decisions on relocating to another city or country based on how their departure will affect the local economy. Workers do not worry (unless restricted by national security laws) about whether the company they sell their invention, new software, or design idea to is an American-based or a foreign company as long as they get the highest possible price for their services or product.

Some say that we need to stop thinking about how to maintain an "American" economy and prepare the American labor force to compete in the global economy.[66] In today's world, national competitiveness no

longer depends on the amount of money the nation's citizens save and invest in building more factories on American soil. It depends instead on the skills and insights workers can contribute to the global economy. Given our great university system and leadership in high technology, the United States has a greater potential than almost any other country to train workers for the economy of the twenty-first century. But doing this will mean upgrading the educational system so that it does an equally good job for people in all income groups. In the global economy of the twenty-first century, our economic well-being will depend on it.

The question is how to make available to all Americans the technology necessary to close what some call a "digital divide." This is a term for the gap in access to computers and Internet hookups that exists between the well-off and the poor, whites and minorities, the well educated and the less educated, and urban and rural residents. The gap between those with computer experience and those without can widen rapidly because those with training and access are able to keep pace with the almost daily changes in technology and software, while those without do not just stand still but lose ground rapidly.

The economic significance of the digital divide is that opportunities for both job seekers and consumers are increasingly tied to computer training and Internet access. In 1998, for example, the Internet created 1.2 million jobs in the United States, jobs considerably better paid on average than other jobs.[67] Government has granted tax deductions for computers purchased for use as educational and job tools. But the major government response to the digital divide has been to levy a surcharge on telephone service, the revenue from which has paid for wiring 98 percent of all public schools and 95 percent of all public libraries for Internet service.

In the twenty-first century, the American economy is moving faster than the ability of many of its citizens to keep pace in education and training, leaving them without the chance to participate in the new prosperity. If the gap in opportunity and income is not to get increasingly wider, all Americans will have to have access to the essential tools to participate in the new economy. As one senator told a group of schoolchildren, "Not everyone can be a Michael Jordan, but if you have technology, all of you can play this game."[68]

Even if an "American economy" no longer exists, there is little evidence to suggest that Americans have stopped thinking that there is an economy contiguous with the country's borders and that their government is responsible in some way for its performance. This creates a set of expectations that government officials may be increasingly less able to meet.

While our government cannot control developments in the global economy or dictate to corporations where they will do business or how many or what kind of jobs they will create, the government can take actions to encourage economic growth. For example, it can adopt fiscal policies that avoid another cycle of huge budget deficits, thus freeing more money for private borrowing and investment, and it can support programs for retraining workers who have lost their jobs and for upgrading their technology skills.

The federal government can also monitor trade practices to see that foreign markets are open to American products, encourage reform of the educational system, fund repair and upgrading of the country's infrastructure, and target new technologies and industries for government support. Government could also do nothing and allow the market to set the terms of competition and the distribution of wealth, but this option has not been chosen by any modern industrial country.

Conclusion: Is Our Economic Policy Responsive?

The prosperity we enjoy and the economic problems we face have never been totally the result of government policy. Private spending accounts for 70 percent of our economy, so economic policies of the private sector and the consumption and saving habits of Americans play an enormous role in the state of the economy at any time. But government can help protect us from recession and depression, create jobs, and guarantee minimum wages and safety conditions.

It should be evident now that our country passes through cycles of economic boom and bust and how we weather these periods depends to a great extent on fiscal and monetary policies. We expect fiscal policy to be more directly responsive to the public because it is made by elected officials. Monetary policy is made by individuals shielded to some extent from the short-term wishes of both the public and elected officials, except perhaps in crisis situations. The fact that fiscal policy is made in more open and democratic processes does not make it necessarily more responsible. Fiscal policy is, and has to be, more responsive to the voters, while monetary policymakers are freer to respond to macroeconomic conditions—*as they see them.*

Fiscal policymakers, while eager to give voters what they want, have not been especially good stewards of the American economy over the past several decades. During the 1970s and 1980s, economic policymakers, both government and private, were living for the short term. In the 1980s, corporate America improved its profit margin at the expense not only of investment but also of workers, many of whose real wages fell significantly. Government policymakers preferred politically popular tax cuts to either balancing the budget or investing in programs to improve our nation's infrastructure, promote research, or upgrade human capital through education and training. Moreover, government was content to let income inequalities grow and even exacerbated them by cutbacks in social programs.

The mid-1990s also saw a movement away from policy geared toward short-term electoral results and toward longer-term solutions to the problem of maintaining the country's economic vitality. Coming out of the transition to a high-tech, service economy, the United States began a period of economic growth and deficit reduction and entered the twenty-first century as the largest and most productive economy on earth. It also had the greatest income disparity of all the industrial democracies, fostered in part by public policy (a tax structure that placed the heaviest burdens on middle- and lower-income groups) and in part by private policies (market changes in the job and wage structure that favored the wealthiest Americans) that government was less and less willing to ameliorate.

Indeed, in the 1990s, in part due to pressure from corporate lobbies and the new Republican congressional majority, but with the support of many Democrats, government relaxed controls on large corporations, deregulating accounting standards and business behavior in fields such as telecommunication and energy. These policies allowed some corporate leaders to run free, accumulating private wealth at the expense of investors and consumers.

Congress and the White House have been divided over how government should respond to growing income disparity. The Clinton administration argued that a responsive government is one that uses fiscal policy both to foster economic growth and to regulate the distribution of income generated by that growth. George W. Bush and the Republican leadership in Congress argue that the country's economic difficulties stemmed precisely from this overresponsive, interventionist, Keynesian approach. In their view, the most responsive government is that which leaves an unfettered market to "grow" the economy and distribute its wealth. This is the essence of the long-standing debate in American political life over the proper relationship of government to the economy.

EPILOGUE

Murray Says No to a Permanent Tax Cut

despite her opposition to the estate tax, Senator Patty Murray voted against making its repeal permanent. The measure was stopped by a technicality in Senate rules that required sixty yea votes to bring the bill to the floor for a straight up or down vote. Only two Republicans defected, while nine Democrats crossed over to support the repeal, three of them up for reelection. On a straight up or down vote, if all had held their ground, the measure would have passed 54–44.

Why did Murray choose to stick with her party this time? Several things had changed since her earlier votes for repeal of the estate tax. When Clinton was in the White House, Murray knew he would veto it. She was able to vote for the Republicans' bill, pleasing some of

Our Hero

her constituents, knowing that Clinton's opposition would send the bill to a reconciliation process. In the Clinton administration, any bill that emerged with the possibility of getting a presidential signature was likely to target tax reductions for small business owners and family farmers and smaller estates. But in 2002, the White House was a strong advocate of estate tax repeal. If the Senate passed the House version of the bill, it would sail through to enactment with permanent tax cuts that went entirely to the wealthiest people in the country.

Second, the original bill had passed during a time of budget surpluses when it was easy to make the case that some of those dollars should go back to taxpayers. With money to spend and voters to woo during the presidential campaign, the timing was perfect. But in 2002, the budget was in deficit, the country was in a recession, and it was fighting a war on terrorism that had already cost billions and was threatening to spread to Iraq. When coupled with the double-digit increase in defense spending, disaster relief, and antirecession measures, the cumulative costs of all the new tax cuts

would explode. Government borrowing would skyrocket, and the amount of the budget devoted to interest payments escalate. This could send the budget into the downward spiral of the 1980s when military spending coupled with tax cuts doubled the national debt. Such a situation would make it impossible to fund programs for the rural working class and poor that Murray wanted.

Third, Democrats did not want to vote for tax cuts that overwhelming favor the wealthy at a time when we have the biggest inequality in income and wealth of any developed country. This would be a slap at their own voting base. Furthermore, during the Clinton administration, when balanced budgets and surpluses were achieved, the Democrats had cut into traditional Republican territory and were now regarded by the public as the better budget managers. Democrats were not eager to surrender this ground as they positioned themselves for the upcoming midterm and the next presidential election. They were happy to portray Bush as the spend-but-don't-tax president.

In voting against permanent repeal of the estate tax, Murray again stated her complete opposition to it as bad for family-owned businesses, workers, and new job creation. She promised there would be future votes on estate tax repeal, and in better economic times she would again vote yes. But between now and then, she says, "Congress and the Administration need to reach agreement on a basic budget framework that makes room for estate tax repeal." Otherwise, she says, they will just be "playing politics."[69] But of course Murray, too, was playing politics.

Murray was right about there being occasion for another vote. The Republicans immediately announced their intention to regroup and present the measure again, after the summer recess when the Senate rule that prevented it being considered in a straight up or down vote will have lapsed. The president's senior adviser Karl Rove said it should not be looked on as a defeat but as one battle in a "war."[70] Furthermore, the president told Congress he had another new package of tax cuts he wanted to send to the Hill.

 To learn more about the estate tax and contrasting views of its fairness, go to this chapter's "You Are There" exercises on the text Web site.

Key Terms

capitalist economy

socialism

mixed economy

depression

inflation

recession

productivity

fiscal policy

Keynesian economics

stagflation

supply-side economics

monetary policy

progressive tax

regressive tax

flat tax

discretionary spending

mandatory spending

national debt

globalization

Further Reading

Donald L. Bartlett and James B. Steele, *The Great American Tax Dodge: How Spiraling Fraud and Avoidance Are Killing Fairness, Destroying the Income Tax, and Costing You* (Boston: Little, Brown, 2001). Two Pulitzer Prize–winning reporters describe off-shore tax shelters and other tax evasion schemes, summarize flat tax and national sales tax proposals, and warn they could shift the tax burden to poorer Americans.

William Grieder, *Secrets of the Temple* (New York: Simon & Schuster, 1988). It is hard to imagine a book about the Federal Reserve Board being interesting, but this one is. Reveals the human face behind this most technical institution.

Friedrick von Hayek, *The Road to Serfdom,* 50th anniversary ed. (Chicago: University of Chicago Press, 1994). The seminal statement of anti-Keynesian economics written by an Austrian economist later championed by Milton Friedman and the University of Chicago school. Van Heyack argues too much government intervention in the economy is dangerous and could turn people into slaves.

Robert Heilbroner and Lester Thurow, *Economics Explained* (New York: Random House, 1982). A readable discussion of major economic concepts and issues.

Kevin Phillips, *Wealth and Democracy* (New York, Broadway Books, 2002). A former Republican political operative explains why he is fed up with the economic policies of both major parties for doing so little to stop influence buying by the wealthy and growing income inequality. The main focus is on the negative impact on democracy of a maldistribution of wealth.

Amartya Sen, *Development as Freedom* (New York: Knopf, 1999). A Nobel laureate in economics and one of the world's leading authorities on development explains the relationship between income and well-being and between economic development and democracy.

David Stockman, *The Triumph of Politics: Why the Reagan Revolution Failed* (New York: Harper & Row, 1986). Reagan's budget director tells all.

Steven R. Weisman, *The Great Tax Wars: Lincoln to Wilson, the Fierce Battles over Money and Power That Transformed the Nation* (New York: Simon & Schuster, 2002). A history of the long political battle to establish a permanent income tax. Among its many interesting facts: In 1939, only 7 percent of the labor force earned enough to pay income tax.

 Electronic Resources

interactive.wsj.com/14_regchoice.html
The Wall Street Journal *probably has the best coverage of economic news of any U.S. newspaper. However, if you want to see the Web edition, you must subscribe.*

www.whitehouse.gov/fsbr/esbr.html
An "Economic Briefing Room," with links to national economic statistics, GDP, income, unemployment, prices, and interest, in addition to international economic statistics

www.whitehouse.gov/omb
The Web site of the Office of Management and Budget links to A Citizen's Guide to the U.S. Budget. Revenue sources and government spending by category are explained with a minimum of jargon. The site also contains a glossary of budget terminology.

www.whitehouse.gov/cea
Even the Council of Economic Advisers has its own Web page, with numerous links to economic statistics, budgets of the United States, and other useful information.

www.federalreserve.gov
This is the Web site of the Federal Reserve System with links to the regional banks. The site offers a history of the Fed, a description of the work of its constituent parts, testimony and reports to Congress, consumer information, and publications free to the public.

www.irs.gov/
The Web site of the Internal Revenue Service offers a history of the agency and its work and provides help with personal income taxes. Users can download forms and publications and get information on the reform of the IRS passed by Congress in 1998.

www.cbpp.org
Web site of the Center for Budget and Policy Priorities where you can find reports on taxing and spending policy with a different perspective than that at government agencies.

 InfoTrac College Edition

Search for the following articles in the InfoTrac database:

Auerbach, Alan J. "Formation of Fiscal Policy: The Experience of the Past Twenty-Five Years," *Federal Reserve Bank of New York Economic Policy Review* (April 2000).

Fisher, Patrick. "Political Explanations for the Difficulties in Congressional Budgeting," *Social Science Journal* (January 1999).

Jones, George G., and Mark A. Luscombe. "Making Sense of the New Tax Legislation," *Journal of Accountancy* (September 2001).

Tager, Michael, and William Van Lear. "Fiscal and Monetary Policy Rules Revisited," *Social Science Journal* (January 2001).

For more articles, enter

"Monetary policy" in the Subject Guide, and then go to subdivision "United States";

"Fiscal policy" in the Subject Guide;

"Tax reform" in the Subject Guide.

 American Government Resources

Visit the Public Policy section of the Wadsworth American Government Resources Web site (politicalscience.wadsworth.com/amgov/) for a variety of tools to help you explore economic policy further. Included are simulations, video clips, Microcase exercises, and a wealth of other activities.

CHAPTER 17

SOCIAL WELFARE AND HEALTH POLICY

This 55,000-ton pile of raw sugar is part of the surplus that costs taxpayers $1.4 million a month to store. Sugar subsidy programs cost American consumers about $2 billion annually.

Brad Doherty, Brownsville, TX

Should the Government Subsidize Corporate Farming?

You are Tim Hutchinson, Republican from Arkansas nearing the end of your first term in the Senate. It is April 2002, and the Senate is facing a vote on a bill to provide price supports and other financial aid to farmers. The Republican majority in the House has already passed a version of the bill that you could have given wholehearted backing. But the Democrat-controlled Senate is bringing to the floor its own bill, one that sets a cap on the amount of support from the federal government any farmer or corporate farm can receive in a given year. It also would increase the amount of money available to help small farmers and promote conservation. Your decision is whether to vote *against* the bill because it is opposed by corporate farmers in your state or to vote *for* it so some legislation on farm support gets through Congress before the midterm election.

Like other senators standing for reelection in farm states, you have been pressing for additional relief for the country's struggling farmers. You represent one of the poorest states in the Union; per capita personal income is little more than half that of the wealthiest state. More than 40 percent of Arkansas is farmland, close to half its population is rural, and one-fifth of the state's employment is agriculture related. In the past year, Arkansas farmers received $740 million in subsidies from the federal government, but you say it was not enough.[1]

Because of your state's economic profile, you sought and won a seat on the Agriculture Committee. But farming is also a personal issue; before attending Bob Jones University and becoming a pastor and teacher at a Christian college, you lived and worked on your parents' farm. You see farmers as the bedrock of the country, economically and morally, and agriculture as "the first industry of America," essential to national security and economic well-being.[2]

Farm subsidies are a means by which government underwrites part of the cost of agriculture; they include direct payments to farmers or agribusinesses to reduce the economic risks of growing food and other crops. The original objective was to make it economically feasible for farmers to stay in business and guarantee the United States a domestic supply of cotton, sugar, and basic foodstuffs. More than 90 percent of subsidies are paid out in price supports; the government guarantees set prices—usually more than the market commands—for crops like corn, wheat, rice, cotton, and soybeans, to name the most heavily subsidized. If the market price falls below the guaranteed level, the government pays the difference, while also purchasing and storing tons of surplus crops each year. Some of that surplus goes to federal programs such as food stamps and subsidized school lunches.

The government also pays farmers to withhold land from production, either to promote conservation or to reduce the production of crops or farm products (cheese, butter, dried milk) that the government holds in surplus. Collectively, these farm-support programs have made agriculture the most subsidized industry in the United States.

The first farm subsidy legislation was adopted to protect family farms and marginal operations, and all of the rhetorical justification for continuing the program still focuses on family farms. But small farmers have been going out of business in droves since the 1970s. By 1997, there were only 2 million farms left in the United States, and about half of these were hobby farms, having less than $10,000 in gross sales.[3] In reality, most of the money goes to large farm operations and agribusiness corporations. The media has had some fun calling attention to well-off subsidy recipients like basketball star Scottie Pippen, the billionaire Ted Turner, founder of CNN and TNT, and one of the heirs to the Rockefeller fortune, but they are not exceptions. By the 1980s, when farm subsidies accounted for half of all farmers' income, most of the payments were going to the wealthiest farmers. Over the past five years, the average payment for the top 1 percent of subsidy recipients has been $558,698, while the average for the bottom 80 percent was $5,830.[4] Just 10 percent of farm owners receive two-thirds of all subsidies.[5]

In principle, conservative Republicans have opposed farm subsidies and most other government income support programs. So when more ideological Republicans like Newt Gingrich seized the party leadership, they succeeded in passing the 1996 Freedom to Farm bill to phase out crop supports over a seven-year period. Gingrich vowed to return market forces to agriculture and to wean the industry from "East German socialist farm programs."[6] Not only did you agree with that goal; you

cowrote the bill, which lifted government restrictions on acreage and crops and was supposed to greatly reduce subsidies, while promoting farm exports. But the effort failed when grain prices dropped abroad and U.S. crops were no longer competitive in the global marketplace. Producers asked for emergency payments, and a big bailout package passed in 2001. Now here you are a year later looking at a bill that calls for spending even more on price supports and adds new crops—peanuts and apples—to the program. In fact, if this bill passes, direct payments to farmers will have increased sevenfold since the Republicans gained control of the House.[7]

Opponents of the ten-year, $171 billion bill passed by the House have been unsparing in their criticism of the program's size and cost. Two members argued that "[i]t represents the most sweeping non-military expansion of the federal government since the Great Society [of the 1960s]," while a fellow Republican warned that "[w]e are in danger of systematically turning farmers into dependent serfs of the federal government."[8]

This might have been your view when you were writing the Freedom to Farm bill. You won your Senate seat running on a platform of balanced budgeting, tax relief, welfare, and education reform. Nevertheless, you want a farm subsidies bill passed. You justify your support, saying, "Unfortunately, a confluence of factors has crippled the ability of American farmers to compete internationally. High energy prices, closed markets, heavily subsided foreign competition, natural disasters, and burdensome federal environmental regulations have pushed many farmers to and over the brink of bankruptcy."[9]

You cannot afford to be against something so important to your state's economy and to some of your biggest campaign donors. Your problem is with the Senate version of the bill. The cap it places on how much an individual can receive in direct payments in any year would reduce the current support level from $460,000 to $275,000. The

House version you favor retains the higher limit. The Senate bill also would channel more money to food subsidies for the poor and about $55 billion to smaller farmers, especially through increases to the conservation programs that pay for not planting or grazing on land that is depleted or eroding. In short, the Senate bill would reduce benefits for large-scale farming and redirect some of that money to smaller farm operations.

Family farmers are an important part of your political base, but agribusiness is preeminent in Arkansas. In fact, your state has three of the country's top ten recipients of farm payments: Tyler foods, Riceland Foods, and Rice Mill all own multiple farms and collected millions in subsidies last year. Tyler Farms alone has received $24 million in various kinds of support over the past five years, but its CEO insists that "it's not like a welfare check."[10] Grain farms like Riceland's, along with cotton growers, are the most highly subsidized farmers in the United States.

If you vote for the Senate bill, you would send a message to small farmers that you are in favor of giving more aid to them and less to corporate operations. And if the bill does pass, it would go to a conference committee where you can be certain the compromise version will push the ceiling on payments closer to current levels. In this way, you could give something to both small and large farmers, and you would help push a farm support bill through to passage.

But do you want to cast a vote that will anger agribusiness, the source of some of your biggest campaign donations? Your reelection race in the fall is shaping up as an uphill battle; in fact, the White House is privately saying that your defeat is a strong possibility. It is not the best time to aggravate the most powerful economic interests in the state. But you have other constituents and campaign promises to consider. How will it look for a supporter of education reform to vote for a bill that proposes to spend three times the amount on farm subsidies that Congress voted to spend on Bush's new education program?[11] How will you defend your position as a budget balancer if, after supporting big tax cuts, you vote for a bill that adds to the post-9/11 double-digit spending increases? And some constituents may compare your support for increasing payments to wealthy farmers and ranchers to your

vote to reform welfare and lower income support for the poor. Though recipients of federal farm subsidies are quick to deny their program is welfare, income support payments to farmers dwarf welfare payments to poor non-farm families.

Should you vote against the Senate bill and protect the higher payment

caps for large farm interests, perhaps alienating small farmers and damaging your image as a fiscal conservative? Or should you risk antagonizing the agribusiness lobby and vote for a bill that will give more benefits to small farmers and the poor and that might also please conservationists? How should you vote?

In almost all areas of American politics, it is those who give the most to candidates, vote, belong to the most influential interest groups, and are politically active in other ways who have the most impact on government policies. It should come as no surprise then that these are the same people who benefit most from social welfare policies. All the same, it probably *will* come as a surprise because the term *social welfare* usually brings to mind images of welfare mothers, elderly people in nursing homes, and indigents receiving welfare and surplus food and living in shelters or public housing welfare, not images of the wealthy farmers, shareholders, and CEOs who benefit from billions of dollars in tax subsidies every year.[12]

Americans tend to see welfare as largesse for the other guy, and his or her own benefits—scholarships and guaranteed loans for students; price supports and credit assistance to farmers; preferred mortgage rates to veterans; retirement benefits and medical care for seniors; and billions in annual tax deductions for savings plans, home ownership, education, private health care, and charitable giving—as their tax dollars at work. Although federal social welfare programs aid almost all groups—rich, poor, and almost everyone in between—more social welfare spending is targeted at the well-off than at the poor.

In this chapter, we will discuss the political and legal bases for social welfare policies, briefly review how they have evolved, and then describe programs and tax policies adopted to serve the needs of specific groups of Americans.

The Political and Legal Bases of Social Welfare Policies

Imagine for a minute that you are a farmer in a chronically drought-stricken African country. If your cattle die or your crops fail, the chances of malnutrition and even starvation are fairly high. There is no crop insurance,

agricultural extension service, income support or food vouchers, public health service, and perhaps no schools to teach your children skills other than farming. Governments often do not have the reach, the resources, or sometimes even the will to provide a safety net. This is what pure capitalism without a social welfare program would be like. It is closer to what our system was like in the 1930s when American farmers fled the dust bowl states trying to find work to allow them to feed their children.

We use the term *social welfare policy* to refer broadly to direct or indirect government subsidies for individuals and families, who are often grouped by category such as the poor, the disabled, and the elderly. *Direct subsidies* are payments government makes to individuals by check, voucher, or credits. Social Security payments, price-support payments, cash assistance to the poor, and food vouchers are direct subsidies. *Indirect subsidies* are goods or services provided by the government to the public, or to a specified group, at below market value—for example, public education, health care, and public housing. If you are enrolled at a state college or university, chances are that your tuition and fees cover no more than half of real costs, probably a lot less—taxpayers pick up the difference.

Why does government do it—and should it be doing it? Whether it should be providing so many benefits is a philosophical question on which there will never be agreement. But there are many motivations for adopting such a wide variety of support programs. A political system like ours is predicated on equality of opportunity. The sick, the poor, the disabled, and the systemically discriminated against need assistance to put them on anything close to an equal footing. This support in turn helps foster economic growth because every country's development is dependent on a healthy, educated population. As government has grown and become involved in all segments of society, we have come to rely on its help to cushion life's blows for the least well-off. At the same time, we give even more support for the middle class and rich. Policymakers could not get elected if they were not responsive to the expectations of their constituents and most powerful supporters.

Few people in any industrialized country today think they should be left completely at the mercy of natural or market forces. They look to social welfare policies to take the worst risks out of living in a capitalist system, offering protection for the weak, ill, disabled, and unemployed, while also providing a very sturdy safety net for businesses.

Where does the authority come from to do all this? The Preamble to the Constitution says that promotion of the general welfare was one purpose for creation of the Union, but the phrase does not appear among the formal powers assigned Congress or the president. Congress's authority to enact social welfare programs stems from implied powers and its formal power to tax. Government's taxing authority allows it to accumulate the resources needed to provide social services as well as a means for taking income from some people and redistributing it to others. This is not unidirectional, however; sometimes government redistributes money from the rich to the poor and sometimes from the less well-off to the wealthy.

The Evolution of Social Welfare Policies

At the time the Constitution was written, no level of government was involved in providing aid to families and individuals. Local governments were responsible for the poor but gave little aid. Orphaned or destitute children were apprenticed to better-off families, where they worked as servants. Workhouses were established for the able-bodied poor, and some minimal aid was given to the old or sick.[13] Churches and other private charities helped the "deserving" poor and unfortunate. Those thought to be undeserving were treated harshly. These attitudes reflected the belief that individuals were mostly responsible for their own fate.

While government took little responsibility for the well-being of individuals, it was involved in the economic development of the country and the creation of jobs. In at least one case, the Homestead Act, this resulted in direct benefits to families and individuals: To encourage settlement of the western states, the government gave away 246 million acres of land, in 160-acre allotments, to 1.5 million homesteaders. If settlers stayed on the land for five years and developed it, they received title free and clear.

Government also encouraged development through its immigration policies, although it did little to help new residents after their arrival. The great waves of immigration at the end of the nineteenth and beginning of the twentieth century created a desperate need for health, housing, and education in the big cities, but what there was came primarily from private charities or settlement houses, such as Chicago's Hull-House, or from local political party organizations. Settlement houses taught literacy, work skills, and provided rudimentary health care. And ward heelers from the big cities' political machines recruited supporters by helping new arrivals find housing and jobs.

The idea that government should provide extensive common public services such as education, hospitals, and asylums developed in the nineteenth century. But the concept of paying individuals benefits is a twentieth-century idea. Gradually, the belief grew that government has a responsibility to help at least some of those

Hull-House helped new immigrants develop employable skills. This photo from the 1920s or 1930s shows a sewing class for women.

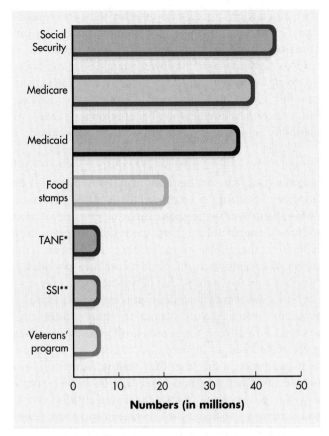

FIGURE 1 ■ Almost One-Third of All Americans Receive Direct Federal Aid

More than 80 million Americans receive direct federal aid. This does not include indirect subsidies or tax subsidies. The numbers in this figure add up to more than 80 million because some people benefit from more than one program, such as Social Security and Medicare, or TANF, Medicaid, and food stamps.

*TANF is Temporary Assistance for Needy Families, the replacement for the old AFDC "welfare" program.
**SSI is Supplemental Security Income, the aid program for the needy elderly and disabled.
SOURCE: *Budget of the United States, Fiscal Year 2003,* 68, 148, 150, 157, 363–373.

at the bottom of the ladder. These changed attitudes led to the enactment of state laws, beginning in 1911, to establish aid programs for poor children and their mothers. Fifteen years later, most states had such laws, freeing children from apprenticeships and poorhouses.

Most of our major national social welfare programs were first developed in the 1930s as part of the New Deal's response to the Great Depression. These programs provide support to farmers, poor families, and the elderly poor. No one need starve or go uneducated. Social welfare programs have expanded since the New Deal, and major additions such as Medicare were made during the 1960s War on Poverty.

Over the decades, the United States has amassed a large number of social welfare programs (see Figure 1), but that does not make us "a welfare state." Welfare

states have a coordinated set of income support programs to ensure access to basic necessities in a uniform way, not just for those in need but for the population as a whole. These are governments that accept the premise that jobs, health care, education, and the basic material necessities of life are entitlements or human rights, and some may even have that principle incorporated into their constitutions. In contrast, our social welfare programs are largely uncoordinated efforts designed to solve the particular problems of specific groups (for example, college students, the poor, farmers, the elderly) on a piecemeal basis. In the following sections, we look at some of these programs by category: income support programs, health care and other subsidized services, and tax subsidies.

Income Support Programs

Today the federal government has programs providing income support to retirees and their dependents, the disabled and their dependents, farmers, and poor families, in addition to pension plans for its civilian and military personnel.

Retirees and Their Dependents

The earliest and the most comprehensive of income support programs is the Old Age Survivors Disability and Health Insurance Program, adopted in 1935 to ensure that the elderly would not live in poverty after retirement. President Roosevelt and the other New Dealers who initiated the program would be astounded at its current magnitude. **Social Security** has evolved into a government-managed retirement fund for American workers from all income groups, a life insurance program for surviving dependents and spouses, and an income support program for people with disabilities. Participation is not voluntary, and over the decades the program has grown to cover 96 percent of all workers. Nearly one of every six individuals now receives a Social Security payment, and seven of ten can expect to be covered now or in the future. Social Security covers so many Americans that each of us is issued a Social Security identification number at birth.

Social Security is financed through a payroll tax on employees and employers. The employee's contribution, slightly over 7.7 percent of the first $80,400 of earnings, is withheld from wages; employers contribute an equal amount. Self-employed workers must pay both the workers' and employers' share (15.3 percent of their adjusted gross income) and send payments to the IRS with their annual income tax report. Social Security taxes are credited to a special off-budget trust fund and invested in government securities until needed to cover benefit payments. In other words, Social Security benefits are

One of the success stories of American public policy, Social Security gives most elderly the freedom to swim in society's mainstream. However, some changes are needed to maintain its benefits for the next generation.

not paid out of the general revenue funds that come from personal and corporate income or excise taxes.

Social Security taxes produce 35 percent of all federal revenues, and payments to beneficiaries account for 22 percent of federal spending. Lower-income workers are hardest hit by these taxes because all their earnings are subject to the tax. This is not the case for higher-income workers, whose income over $80,400 is not taxed for Social Security. But lower-income retirees receive more benefits relative to their earnings than wealthier participants. Still, given the purpose of the program, it is difficult to justify making payments to wealthy retirees beyond what they have paid in, and 60 percent of Social Security payments do go to those above the poverty line.[14] For this reason, and also to shore up the trust fund, middle- and upper-income beneficiaries are now required to pay taxes on 85 percent of their Social Security income at the same rate at which the rest of their income is taxed.

The size of the monthly stipend received by beneficiaries is determined by how many years they worked, how much they earned, and whether they are alone or have dependents. Currently a retiree can qualify for full benefits at age sixty-five and can request payments as early as age sixty-two at a lower stipend. For each year up to age seventy that retirement is postponed, the monthly stipend increases. Because Americans are living longer and therefore drawing benefits longer, the age of eligibility is gradually moving upward to sixty-seven.

Because it is an inclusive program—for people of all income groups—and because only those who have paid into the program, or their survivors, can collect benefits, Social Security is categorized as a social insurance rather than a welfare program. Since people do not have to show financial need to participate, millions can accept it without the public stigma of being on welfare. This aspect of the program increases its political popularity. Yet it is a mistake to think that beneficiaries are only getting back what they and their employers paid into the program through payroll deductions, plus accumulated interest. This is true for some short-lived people. But given today's longer life span, Social Security pays most of its recipients more than they paid in, something no private insurance program would do. In 1940, a sixty-five-year-old was expected to collect benefits for twelve and a half years and today for seventeen and a half years.

Social Security has grown from about 220,000 recipients in 1940 to 45 million in 2002. Ninety percent of Americans sixty-five years of age or older are currently receiving Social Security benefits. With their dependents, they account for about 70 percent of all benefits paid; beneficiaries' survivors account for another 15 percent. Disabled workers and their dependents account for the remaining 15 percent. The average benefit to a retired worker, a mere $13 per month in 1940, increased to $874 in 2001.[15]

In 1950, Social Security accounted for only 3 percent of all retirement income. It is now 34 percent of the income of elderly couples, and 51 percent for single

YOU WANT ME TO VOTE FOR YOU BUT YOU'RE ALL THE SAME. YOU GET IN AND NOTHING GETS DONE.

OK, YOU WANT ME TO LEVEL WITH YOU?

YES.

YOU WANT ME TO TELL YOU THE REAL PROBLEM? THE ONE EVERYONE IS SCARED TO DEATH TO SAY?

YES!

THE REAL PROBLEM IS THAT SOONER OR LATER WE'RE GOING TO HAVE TO CUT SOCIAL SECURITY AND MEDICARE. THERE'S NO WAY AROUND IT.

I'LL VOTE AGAINST ANYBODY WHO SAYS THAT.

IT'S MY OPPONENT'S POSITION.

I'M FOR BALANCING THE BUDGET~

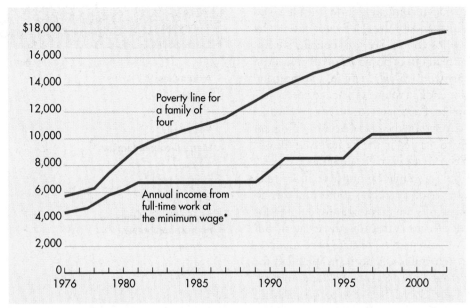

FIGURE 2 ■ Working at a Minimum Wage Job Is Not Enough to Support a Family
Although the minimum wage was increased in 1997, working full-time at minimum wage provides for less than a minimum standard of living.

*Assumes minimum wage of $5.15 per hour for forty hours per week, fifty weeks per year.
SOURCE: Poverty threshold from the U.S. Census Bureau.

women, who earn less over the life course and have fewer savings or other investments.[16] Without Social Security, almost half of our senior citizens would be poor, whereas today the poverty rate for those sixty-five and older is at a historic low of 10.2 percent.[17] To the extent that continued payments from the fund keep people above the poverty line, they are doing what Social Security was intended to do.

The program has stayed afloat because of ever-increasing numbers of people paying in at steadily rising rates. In 2001, there were 3.4 workers for each Social Security beneficiary.[18] These workers are supporting current retirees just as today's beneficiaries supported the generation before them.

Aid to the Poor

Federal income support programs for the poor began as part of the original Social Security legislation and later amendments to it. The original act established, along with the retirement program for seniors, a national program of unemployment insurance. This was during the Great Depression when nearly a quarter of the workforce was unemployed and state and local programs did not have the resources to meet demands. Except for Social Security itself, which is funded and managed entirely at the federal level, most income support programs have been run jointly by federal, state, and local governments. In most cases, state programs of assistance to the poor and unemployed predated federal programs;

federal money was sent to bolster these programs, sometimes with new guidelines set by Congress.

Eligibility

A major difference between beneficiaries of Social Security, a program for everyone, and programs that exclusively target the poor, is that qualification for participation requires a **means test.** Participants must periodically demonstrate eligibility by showing they are poor—they must have both limited income and few assets.

The definition of who is poor is revised each year by the Census Bureau, which makes adjustments to account for changes in inflation and the cost of living. It does not set a single income level but many, depending on age and household composition. In 2001, for example a single person under sixty-five years of age was considered poor if his or her income was below $9, 214; the comparable figure for a family of four was $17, 960 (see Figure 2). Not everyone agrees with the Census Bureau's estimates because they do not take into account many "in-kind" benefits poor people receive, such as food and housing subsidies and medical care. If we considered this income, it could reduce the poverty rate by about 4 percent. Others argue that the Census Bureau understates the amount of poverty by underestimating costs for food, housing, and fuel.[19]

The Elderly and Disabled

One of the first grant-in-aid programs established under Social Security authority, **Supplemental Security**

Income (SSI), provides income support for the blind and people with disabilities, and for the elderly not covered by Social Security or whose Social Security benefits are not large enough to lift them out of poverty. For 18 percent of seniors, Social Security is their *only* income, and for many these benefits are not enough to meet the basic cost of living. Other SSI recipients are workers or survivors of workers who were not covered by the Social Security program (something unlikely to happen in the future given the expansion of Social Security to virtually all jobs).

To qualify for SSI, a couple cannot have more than $3,000 in liquid assets (cash or stocks; homes and cars do not count). SSI recipients are automatically eligible for food stamps and health insurance (discussed later), but most remain in poverty, regardless of state of residence.

In 2001, about 6.5 million Americans qualified for SSI payments that ranged from $313 to $470 per month. About one-third were Social Security recipients, and the remainder were blind, people with disabilities, or dependents.

Poor Families

Aid to Families with Dependent Children (AFDC)

was another grant-in-aid program that grew out of Social Security legislation. The purpose was to strengthen maternal and child welfare services being provided by the states (see Figure 3). Coverage was soon extended to mothers as well as their dependent children and later for both fathers and mothers with dependent children. Because AFDC was a joint federal-state program and administered at the state level, eligibility and benefits varied from state to state.

TABLE 1	Poverty Is Much More Common in Female-Headed and Minority Families

	Percentage in Poverty
All families	**10**
White	6
Black	23
Hispanic	23
Married-couple families	**5**
White	4
Black	7
Hispanic	16
Female-headed families, no husband present	**30**
White	21
Black	41
Hispanic	44

Source: U.S. Census Bureau at www.census.gov.

Despite the success that AFDC had in providing food and shelter to dependent children, critics argued that it fostered dependency instead of encouraging independence and hard work. For example, though the number of AFDC recipients was fairly stable from the mid-1970s to the late 1980s, it zoomed up in the recession of the late 1980s and early 1990s. In contrast to the common stereotype, however, the increase in welfare recipients was not tied to the size of welfare stipends, which in real terms (taking inflation into account) began a steady decline in the 1970s.

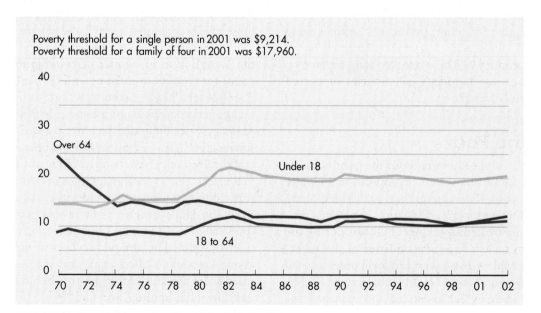

FIGURE 3 ■ Children Are Most Likely to Be Poor
The number of children living in poverty has declined in the past five years, but children are still more likely to be poor than any other age group.
Source: U.S. Bureau of the Census (www.census.gov/).

The largest growth in number of recipients came when economic times were hard; but when the economy improved, the rolls did not always fall back to their previous level. Part of the reason is that, even in years when the economy was growing, job growth was not in high-paying blue-collar jobs. Job prospects for people without college degrees have been deteriorating since the late 1970s and 1980s.

Welfare rolls also grew because of the increase in the number of births to unmarried women without job skills who were often still children themselves (see Table 1). The number of births to single women continues to be high, 68 percent of all African American, 26 percent of all white, and 42 percent of all Hispanic births. Over 80 percent of unwed mothers go on the welfare rolls for at least some time. But the number of unmarried teenage women giving birth began to decline in 1999.

It is extremely difficult for a single parent with no job skills to support children, especially without child care. Also, women who did choose low-paid work over welfare were often worse off because of child care costs and the loss of medical benefits. Nearly one-quarter of the women who went on AFDC stayed for ten years or more, and another 20 percent stayed for six to nine years. Though most AFDC recipients were white, long-term recipients were more likely to be black or Hispanic unmarried teenage mothers with no high school diploma (see Figure 4).

The majority of AFDC recipients collected benefits for a relatively short time.[20] They found a job, married someone who earned more than poverty wages, or both. However, AFDC became the main target for critics of cash assistance to the poor. Its cost was much lower than other income support programs, but to its critics it appeared to be rewarding the wrong kind of behavior while getting no results. They saw AFDC as discouraging work, encouraging out-of-wedlock births, and allowing fathers to take no responsibility for their children. While a consensus grew that the welfare system needed to be reformed, there were strong differences over how to do it.

In 1993, President Clinton took office promising to end welfare "as we know it." In the 1994 elections, the Republican "Contract with America" promised even more dramatic reform. After heated debate, in 1996 Congress passed, and the president signed, a welfare reform bill that abolished AFDC, and with it the concept of welfare as an entitlement to all those who met federal guidelines. Instead, in the new **Temporary Aid to Needy Families (TANF)** program, states were mandated to set up their own welfare systems under loose federal guidelines, to be funded by block grants from the federal government.

TANF is a results-oriented program that sets time limits on eligibility and requires participants to move "from welfare to work," the signature slogan of the reform bill. States receiving TANF funds were to have, at minimum, 30 percent of the people on their welfare rolls working at least thirty hours a week during the program's initial five years. "Work" included job training, community service, or continuing education. TANF recipients are required to hold jobs within two years of entering the program, and working families can receive assistance for a lifetime maximum of five years. States can exempt up to 20 percent of the people

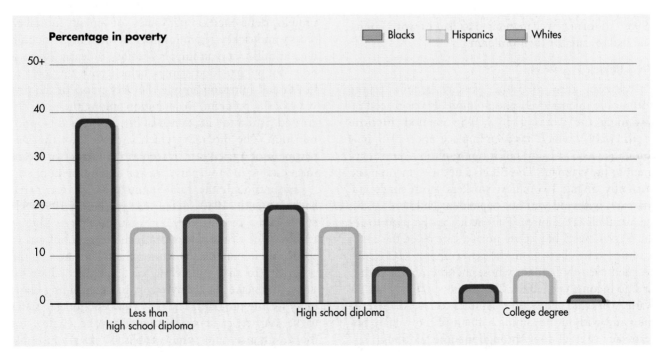

FIGURE 4 ■ Percentage of Families in Poverty by Education Level of Householder, 1999
SOURCE: *Statistical Abstract of the United States, 2001,* Table 686.

receiving assistance from this requirement (for example, people who are physically or mentally unable to hold a job, or a parent with young children and no child care).

Initially, those who feared the impact of TANF on children and those unable to find employment severely criticized the program. In response, some modifications were made to allow recipients to receive child care, transportation, and other noncash assistance beyond the two-year cutoff. These modifications were designed to help those who took low-paying jobs and who needed such additional assistance to keep their families intact.[21] However, states have the authority to enact more stringent limits.

Early evaluations of TANF were mixed.[22] On the positive side, by 1999, almost 7 million fewer people received welfare than in 1993, a 50 percent decline. Between 60 and 90 percent of those leaving found jobs. Although much of the decline reflected the economic boom of the late 1990s (employers needed workers and often hired the relatively unskilled and inexperienced), the overhaul of the welfare program was estimated to account for one-third of the reduction in the welfare rolls.[23] The new time limits and work requirements forced many states to reorient their efforts toward helping clients develop job and life skills and away from regulation and control.

The early years of implementing TANF were costly for those states that set ambitious goals.[24] Wisconsin, one of the first states to push for substantial welfare reform, found that efforts to create true self-sufficiency for former welfare recipients *increased* costs during the first years of transition, rather than cutting them. In reducing the number of welfare recipients by 65 percent over a decade, Wisconsin moved from spending $12 million on child care in 1987 to spending of $180 million in 1998.[25] If former welfare recipients had to work, someone had to care for their children.

The Working Poor

As criticism grew of paying welfare benefits to the chronically unemployed, more emphasis was placed on rewarding the working poor. The **earned income credit (EIC),** which has been in place since 1975, may sound like a tax subsidy, but it can result in a direct payment to the claimant. The EIC is a negative income tax, currently giving 19 million workers, both single and married, with and without dependent children, credits against their tax liability. The credit can be used to reduce taxes owed, but where no taxes are owed the credit is returned by check from the government. EIC can be accrued even by families whose income is so low they had no income tax liability. This approach to poverty rewards work and allows poor families to receive government aid without becoming a client of the welfare bureaucracy (it is all done through income tax filing).

The EIC has had bipartisan support (President Reagan noted it was the "best antipoverty, best profamily, best job-

Wasserman © 2000, *Los Angeles Times.* Reprinted by permission.

creation measure to come out of Congress"), and although at times attacked by conservative budget cutters, the program was expanded during the Clinton administration.

Food Stamps

Another major supplement to the income of the poor is **food stamps.** Food stamps are vouchers redeemable in grocery stores for food. They may be used only to purchase unprepared food and cannot be used for eating out or for liquor or tobacco. Their dollar value ranges from about $75 a month for one person to over $400 for a family of four.

The food stamp program grew from smaller origins, expanding most noticeably in the early 1970s in response to an investigation of hunger in America that revealed that tens of thousands of Americans suffered from malnourishment, resulting in retarded growth, anemia, protein deficiencies, high rates of infant mortality, scurvy and rickets (from insufficient vitamin C, vitamin D, and milk), and an impaired ability to learn. There is little doubt that food stamps helped raise the level of health and nutrition among the very poor. In the first years of the program, malnutrition among the poor decreased, as did the incidence of diseases caused by poor nutrition. The program, which is run out of the Department of Agriculture, is seen as a constructive means for reducing food surpluses as well as fighting hunger.

Even though the food stamp program was pared back during the 1980s, in the years just before 1996 welfare reforms, one of every ten Americans received food stamps. One of the objectives of the reform bill was to reduce these numbers by cutting fraud and abuse in the program. To that end, Congress established fines for states that make too many errors in determining eligibility for the program. The new rules encouraged states to be very strict about certifying anyone eligible for food assistance, and some established near-impossible standards. A Baltimore woman who applied for stamps after losing her job was required to produce eleven documents verifying her identity, residence, income, work history, and financial and family obligations. Most states now require recertification of eligibility every three or four months. In the two years following adoption of the certification procedures, participation in the program declined by 25 percent. One family lawyer called it a "bureaucratic disentitlement."[26]

Most legal immigrants were made ineligible for food stamp assistance by the 1996 reform, but the 2002 Farm Bill restored coverage to those who have been in the country at least five years. The program is currently providing benefits to about 21 million people at an annual cost of $20 billion, but it is believed to be reaching only about half of the people who could qualify.

Impact of Income Support

Overall, these programs in income support for the elderly, disabled, and dependent children have greatly reduced poverty in the United States. Due in part to the Great Society programs of the 1960s, the proportion of families in poverty dropped from 21 percent in 1959 to 10 percent in 1973, the lowest point ever achieved in the United States. It then increased rather steadily, reaching a high of 14 percent in 1993, before the booming economy of the 1990s sent the poverty rate downward again. In 2001, 11.3 percent of Americans were below the poverty level.[27]

Farmers

Income support programs for farmers are described in the "You Are There" earlier in this chapter. Direct federal aid has accounted for almost half of total farm income since the 1980s, and it has been as high as 70 percent in some farm states. Farming is the most heavily subsidized occupation in the Untied States.

Like Social Security, income support for farmers was motivated by the urgent needs and dire living conditions of one segment of the American population. Because food self-sufficiency is seen by many as essential to national security, and because many farmers were being driven off the land, providing federal aid took on a special urgency. But also like Social Security, farm aid has evolved into an income support program not for poor or marginal family farms but for all farming enterprises, including the largest and most profitable. In 2000, of 1.6 million receiving farm aid, about 57,500 got more than $100,000; at least 154 got more than $1 million. Seventeen million went to farms operated by government agencies, and millions more to university farms.[28] Almost 85 percent of the subsidies are received by fewer than one-quarter of the country's 2 million farmers. Sixty percent of farmers receive no subsidies at all.[29]

At least twenty Fortune 500 companies received checks from federal programs in 2000, as did eleven members of Congress. They included the Speaker of the House; the ranking Democrat on the House Agriculture committee, Marion Berry; and the chair of the Senate Finance Committee, Charles Grassley. Grassley, who claims to be primarily a farmer and not to live in Washington, D.C., "except Monday through Fridays," has received payments as large as $110,936—mailed to his Washington residence. The senator's claim to be living and farming in Iowa may stretch credulity, but his explanation that all but $20,000 of his payments went to meet equipment and operating expenses is believable.[30] The operating costs of large farms are staggering, and a good share of government aid is used to defray these expenses. The question is whether taxpayers' money should make the difference between agribusinesses and corporate farms staying in or going out of business.

Richard Lugar (R-Ind.), another Agriculture Committee member who receives subsidy payments for a corn and soybean farm and who says he could not grow these crops without subsidies, is still critical of the program. Subsidies, he says, "distort markets by encouraging overproduction to drive prices lower in a self-perpetuating cycle."[31]

The 1996 Freedom to Farm Act tried to phase out income supports for certain crops over a seven-year period, but instead payments quadrupled from $7.3 billion in 1995 to $32.2 billion in 2000. As American farmers lost their competitiveness in the global marketplace, Congress ramped up the subsidies. Agriculture and the "family farm" hold a special place in the American identity—they represent the country's breadbasket, its corn and Bible belt, conjuring up images of waving fields of grains, pioneers, and an "authentic" America that politicians love to be associated with.

In the 1930s, homelessness was largely caused by the Great Depression. Here is photographer Dorothea Lange's historic photo of a homeless Oklahoma family during that era.

But current programs are not well regarded by the small family farmers whom politicians like to claim they are saving. By 2001, 73 percent of rural Nebraskans polled believed that caps should be set on the amount of subsidies any individual can receive.[32] In Congress, the main division on this issue is more along regional than party lines. Senators from states where agriculture is dominated by family farms are in favor of the lower caps and shifting more of the money to small farmers. Senators from states with huge farms run by agribusinesses favor retaining the higher payment limit.

Veterans

Through the Department of Veterans' Affairs, the federal government provides income support to veterans with disabilities. To qualify for a disability pension, a veteran must be able to prove that the disability was acquired while on active duty. The level of support, whether full or partial, depends on the severity of the disability. Currently 2.3 million veterans receive disability pensions.

The government also funds a retirement program for career servicemen and -women. It would be hard to justify not having a pension system for military personnel, but the plan's eligibility standards have many critics. David Stockman, former president Reagan's budget director, called them a "scandal," partly because the typical beneficiary of the time started collecting at age forty-one. Because so many career service personnel retire at an early age, they go to work full-time while drawing full military pensions for the remainder of their lives. Thus, most military pensions are paid to individuals with above-average incomes who will also qualify for Social Security at age sixty-two.[33] At a cost of $29 billion annually, they are nearly twice the cost of TANF ($17 billion).

Health Care Programs

In the United States, government aid for health care is a social benefit for some people of all income groups, but not for all people. Nonetheless, health care is by far the most costly indirect government subsidy. Half of all federal, state, and local spending on means-tested programs is for medical care.[34]

The federal government has been involved in some aspects of health care for decades, but before 1965 there was no general federal support for individual health care. In 1965, after years of debate over government's responsibility, concern about the problems of millions of Americans who could not afford adequate health care prompted President Johnson to propose and Congress to pass two programs, Medicare (for the elderly) and Medicaid (for low-income people).

Health Care for Seniors

Medicare is a public health insurance program that funds many medical expenses for the elderly and disabled. It includes hospital insurance and additional, voluntary coverage that helps pay for physicians' services, outpatient hospital services, and some other costs.

Hospital insurance is paid for by Social Security taxes, while the elective portion is financed through general revenues and monthly premiums paid by participants. Everyone eligible for Social Security benefits is eligible for Medicare, and over 90 percent of Social Security recipients buy the optional insurance. In 2002, the program was covering 40 million people at a cost of $230 billion.

Although many factors affect our health, it is clear that Medicare has benefited the health of the elderly. Compared to the period before 1965, more people see doctors now, and the elderly have more but shorter hospital stays. There have been declines in death rates from diseases affecting the elderly, such as heart attacks and strokes, and a decrease in the number of days of restricted activity that older people experience.[35]

In spite of these substantial accomplishments, Medicare has not been a complete success. It is expensive, and many of those who need it have trouble paying their portion of the cost. Experts of both political parties continue to predict that the Medicare program will go broke in the next few years unless changes are made in the program or a national health care system is put in place. A similar cost problem afflicts the other major federal health care program, Medicaid.

Health Care for the Poor and Disabled

Medicaid is a federal-state program to help poor and disabled people pay their medical bills. States set their

Like most individuals in middle-class families, this young man gets good medical treatment for chronic illnesses, such as asthma. However, poverty-stricken Americans are much more likely to die from lack of treatment of such diseases.

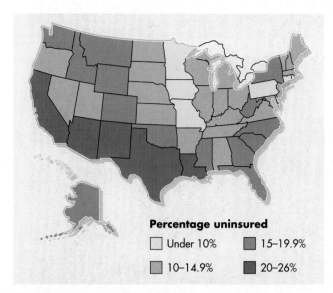

FIGURE 5 ■ Significant Numbers Are Uninsured
SOURCE: *Statistical Abstract of the United States, 2001,* Table 145.

Percentage uninsured

☐ Under 10%   ☐ 15–19.9%
☐ 10–14.9%   ☐ 20–26%

own Medicaid eligibility standards, within federal guidelines. In some states, almost all the poor are covered by Medicaid, but in others relatively few are.

Medicaid covers about 37 million people and costs $280 billion annually. It provides health care for one in every four children, pays for one in three births, and funds more than half of all the nursing home care in the country.[36] When a family's resources run dry paying for an aging relative's nursing home care, Medicaid takes over.

Even with Medicare, Medicaid, and private health insurance provided through the workplace, almost 40 million Americans remain without health insurance, two-thirds from wage-earning families whose income is above the poverty line. In five states, over 20 percent of the population remain uninsured (see Figure 5). To ensure greater coverage of children, in 1997 the government created the State Children's Health Insurance Program (S-CHIP). Working through existing state programs, it set a goal of insuring all children whose parents do not qualify for Medicaid and who cannot afford private insurance. Reaching all children who are eligible has been difficult because many families remain unaware of the program. And some states have done little to make them aware of their eligibility, instead diverting to other programs federal money allocated for S-CHIP.

The costs of providing health care to low-income families are now larger than those for seniors, and spending for all programs is rising rapidly as a percentage of GDP. In addition to Medicare and Medicaid, the government also funds, at an annual cost of $24 billion, a national system of hospitals to provide care to veterans of the armed services. In all, 40 percent of all health care is paid for by the government.

Other Aid for the Poor

In many states, poor families receiving TANF benefits can apply for child care assistance when they move off welfare and into jobs. Welfare reform authorized states to give assistance to any family earning up to 85 percent of the state's median income. More than 2 million children were receiving day care in federal- and state-funded child care centers in 2002.[37]

Government also funds an early-learning program for children from poor households. Head Start provides preschool education, with the objective of teaching children from poor families skills they will need to succeed in primary school. It also encourages parents to become involved in their children's education and to read to them at home. Head Start has been a widely supported program from its inception in the 1960s, but it is still underfunded in terms of the number of students who could benefit from it. With funding of only $650 million in 2002, it can accommodate only a small percentage of eligible children, even though studies show that preschoolers with Head Start experience do better in school than other poor children without preschooling. In 1995, the government began an experimental Early Head Start program to provide family services to pregnant women and their children from before birth until they become eligible for Head Start at age three.[38]

Because poorly nourished children do not learn as well as children with adequate diets, the government also funds school breakfast and lunch programs. After growing in the 1970s, the in-school meal programs, like food stamps, were cut back during the 1980s.

Other subsidized services for the poor include funding for job training and job placement centers, and about $30 million a year for housing and shelters.

Other Subsidized Services

Other subsidized services reach a broad swath of the American public. Virtually everyone who relies on a municipal bus system or intercity trains, for example, benefits from federally subsidized mass transit. Other federal aid mostly benefits middle- and high-income Americans.

Education

Education in the United States is primarily in the hands of local governmental units and funded largely through state and local taxes. But the federal government has become a major funder of higher education through grants and guaranteed loans to undergraduates and fellowships and low-interest loans to graduate students. The grand-daddy of all student support programs, and the most

Indiana University Photographic Services

It has been called the "greatest piece of legislation Congress ever passed," a "Marshall Plan for America," and "a magic carpet to the middle class." Virtually everyone has heard of the GI Bill of Rights, but few realize how broad its impact was on the country as a whole. When it was signed into law in 1944, just two weeks after D-Day, neither President Roosevelt nor Congress thought they were passing a transformative piece of legislation. They just wanted to provide the millions of veterans who would be returning from the war in Europe and Asia some help reintegrating into civilian life and the labor force.

Since the earliest days of the Republic, the national government has provided benefits to veterans for military service during wartime, but only after veterans organized to demand compensation for lost time and wages. Veterans of the Revolutionary and Civil Wars were promised a land bonus and eventually did receive a pension, but only after threatening revolt. Civil War veterans were extremely well connected in Congress, getting it to authorize pensions that by 1888 accounted for 20 percent of the federal budget.

Partly in reaction to this excess, World War I veterans received a tiny cash payment on mustering out but were promised a small annuity to be paid near retirement age. This was too long a wait for those who fell on hard times in the early years of the Great Depression. But in 1932, when they marched on Washington to demand early payment of their "bonuses," their

A federal law passed during World War II, the GI Bill of Rights, transformed American society by granting each veteran educational benefits and loans to buy housing and start businesses. Though skeptics believed that veterans would not use the bill, returning World War II vets flooded America's universities by the millions, changing the face of higher education. As at other schools, Indiana University's facilities were soon overtaxed, forcing relocation of student registration to its field house.

demonstration was violently suppressed by U.S. Army units under the command of General Douglas MacArthur.

The spectacle of the military assaulting veterans may have been on the mind of Congress when it approved benefits for the 12 million men and women returning from service in World War II. No one was looking for another march on Washington.

A comprehensive assistance package was opposed by all the powerful leaders in Congress and by President

Roosevelt. Some were opposed to providing cash assistance for fear it would encourage soldiers not to look for jobs, while others were against a bonus bill because it would single out for benefits only one group of people who contributed to the war effort. But some kind of bonus was supported by an overwhelming majority of the American public. In the end, the compromise bill—called the Bill of Rights for GI Joe and Jane—was written by a member of the American Legion. Its congressional sponsors were relatively unknown Re-

successful in terms of overall impact on the country, is the GI Bill of Rights (see the box).

Insurance

The government is one of the country's largest purveyors of insurance protection. In addition to the retire-

ment and unemployment insurance plans already discussed, the federal government insures farmer's crops, overseas business investments, everyone's savings accounts, and it provides disaster relief to supplement private insurance policies or coverage for damage private companies will not insure. For example, after 9/11 when private companies stopped offering policies to

publicans and conservative southern Democrats, some of whom supported the bill primarily as a way to prevent class warfare. Among the principal players was one woman, Edith Nourse Rogers, a liberal Republican from Massachusetts and the ranking minority member of the Veteran's Affair Committee, who had helped create the Women's Army Corps. She went on to become the first woman to chair a major House committee.

The Serviceman's Readjustment Act—or the GI Bill, as it was soon known—contained three major benefits: a living stipend and tuition vouchers for college, low-interest mortgages for purchase of a first home, and loans for starting new businesses. These measures set off a chain reaction that helped shape modern America. To understand how one bill could have such an impact, one has to keep in mind what the economic situation of the average GI was like when we entered World War II.

In 1940, the average soldier was twenty-six and had only one year of high school, and most came from families where college was financially impossible.[1] Had they not served in the war and received the GI benefit, most veterans could never have gone back to school. Many educators and college presidents opposed the voucher program, saying they would have to lower their standards and admit students with poor educational backgrounds. But veterans returned to school in record numbers, more than a million in 1946 alone, when they accounted for almost half of all college

enrollments in the United States. In 1950, almost a quarter of all college students were still veterans.[2] The GI Bill thus stimulated a tremendous growth in higher education, creating the need for many more faculty and new facilities, eventually giving rise to a new system of state colleges in many states.

In the first years after the war, however, most veterans chose private schools since at the time vouchers provided enough to cover tuition in the Ivy League. By 1946, the influx of veterans almost doubled Harvard's enrollment, and they "hogged the honor rolls,"[3] there and throughout the Ivy League. With college educations, many working-class families moved into the middle class, making it possible for them to afford to send their children to college and continue the families' upward mobility. With federally guaranteed mortgages, many vets were also able to leave rental housing in the cities for homes in the outlying areas. So many new homeowners entered the market that it prompted the building of housing developments like Levittown and began the suburbanization of America. This in turn fostered the building of highways and schools, and the whole infrastructure necessary to support new towns.

The bill did not work equally well for everyone, in part because African Americans did not have the same choices as whites in using their benefits. With housing segregation in most new suburban areas, including Levittown, the route out of the city to affordable housing was less possible. Al-

though black vets got the same educational benefits, they did not have the range of choices in schools, given segregation in some universities and the use of a quota system in others. But thousands did get to college, among them many of those who would become leaders of the modern civil rights movement.

What was so significant about this legislation was that its purpose was to provide financial help that made it possible for young men and women to become more productive citizens for the remainder of their lives. The GI bill provided education vouchers to 8 million veterans. It increased home ownership from one in three before the war to two in three afterward. According to a 1986 government study, "each dollar invested in the bill yielded 5 to 12 dollars in tax revenues."[4] The GI Bill was such a success that it was renewed in 1956 with scaled-back benefits for those who had served in Korea and later for Vietnam vets. Overall, the bill's single most important contribution may have been in its extraordinary expansion of higher education because it "signaled the shift to the knowledge society"; for this reason, its passage may in the future be seen "as one of the most important events of the 20th century."[5]

1. Doris Kearns Goodwin, "Remembering the GI Bill," *NewsHour with Jim Lehrer*, PBS, July 4, 2000.
2. Michael J. Bennet, *When Dreams Come True: The GI Bill and the Making of Modern America* (Washington, D.C.: Brassey's, 1996), 18.
3. Ibid., 19.
4. Spencer Michaels, "Remembering the GI Bill."
5. Peter Drucker, *Post-Capitalist Society* (New York: HarperBusiness, 1993), 3.

compensate for terrorist attacks, Congress passed legislation to establish a federal program.

Mortgages

The federal government is very big on home ownership and has several agencies that help veterans, farmers, and low-income families get mortgage loans at subsidized rates. The parent agency of these quasi-government corporations is the Federal Housing Finance Board, which supervises twelve Federal Home Loan Banks. In 2002, the loans issued and guaranteed by government-sponsored home loan agencies like Freddie Mac exceeded the $2.4 trillion debt held by the U.S. Treasury.[39]

The safety net has many holes for America's poorest, leaving hundreds of thousands homeless. Here a shelter provides a dinner in New York City.

Agriculture

The government has established separate loan agencies to help farmers buy homes, retain land, or expand operations. A former secretary of agriculture noted that some of the loans made by the Farmers Home Administration (FmHA) might more accurately be called grants. Once again, a program designed to help the average farm family hang on to their farms has acquired its own welfare queens. One southern California dentist spent thirteen years in default on a $3.5 million loan for his cattle ranch. Even after his account became delinquent, he was able to purchase an oceanfront house valued at $817,000 and an office building worth $1.7 million. Between 1988 and 1992, the FmHA wrote off $11.5 billion in bad loans and still carries about $5.2 billion in delinquent loans.[40]

Ranchers are subsidized by a Bureau of Land Management policy that allows them to graze their cattle on 270 million acres of public land at a cost per animal of $1.35 (private landowners charge an average of $9.26 per animal). Despite many attempts to revise these fees upward, ranchers believe they are entitled to use of these public lands, even though some land has been completely denuded and is eroding from overgrazing.

The federal government also offers ranchers and farmers billions of dollars in subsidized water. Most water project costs are never repaid. For example, the water brought to California by the $8.8 billion California Central Valley Irrigation Project has created wealth for huge corporate as well as family farms. But of the $36,000 per-acre cost of irrigation, only $527 per acre is returned to the government.

Because of federal subsidies, water is cheap, and farmers grow water-intensive crops even in naturally arid areas. The most water used by California farmers is for pasturing cows and sheep and by those growing crops that can be grown more economically elsewhere, such as alfalfa, cotton, and rice, which normally is grown only in very wet climates. These crops use far more water than the grapes, nuts, oranges, strawberries, and tomatoes we associate with California farming.[41]

Tax Subsidies

In addition to direct payments, such as farm subsidies and Social Security benefits, and indirect subsidies, such as for education and Medicare, a third type of federal subsidy is provided through tax breaks. The biggest government subsidies for the well-off take this form rather than the direct payment programs that characterize aid to the poor. A tax subsidy permits some people and corporations to pay much less in taxes than the assessed rate for their income level.

Corporations

The biggest winners in the aid to the well-off category are corporations. The ostensible reason for government extending so many tax incentives to business is to encourage economic and job growth that will benefit the population at large. While there is no doubt some tax breaks do lead to the creation of more jobs, many do not, or at least not within the United States.

The vast array of current tax breaks for business are seen by their critics as a form of welfare. **Corporate welfare** has been defined as "any action by local, state or federal government that gives a corporation or an entire industry a benefit not offered to others." The benefit can be in the form of services, low-interest loans, grants, concessions of land, or tax exemptions, deferrals, or lowered rates.[42] Mining and logging companies, for example, lease federal land at bargain-basement prices. The tax write-off for business for machinery and building depreciation costs the taxpayer more than SSI, and deductions for charitable contributions cost the Treasury 36 percent more than food stamps do (see Figure 6). The corporate tax exemption for income earned on exports is estimated to have resulted in $2.3 trillion in lost revenues since it was adopted thirty years ago.[43]

It would be easy to go on at length listing costs of various business tax breaks, but they only count as welfare if taxpayers get nothing back in return for the subsidies. In many instances, this seems to be the case. During the 1990s, when AT&T, Bechtel, Boeing, General Electric, and McDonnell Douglas were awarded 40 percent of all loans and grants made by the Export-Import Bank, employment by those firms dropped by 38 percent. During a period in the late 1980s and early 1990s when General Electric was buying up other companies, including RCA, it received several billion dollars in tax breaks, while reducing its workforce by 165,000.[44] And while Enron was receiving government subsidies for developing oilfields, it was bilking shareholders out of billions of dollars.

In addition to subsidies from the federal government, corporations also get huge tax breaks and grants from state and local governments. In the competition to attract new jobs, state governments try to outbid one another in offering financial aid to corporations. The town of Albert Lea, Minnesota, for example, gave $3.3 million in tax breaks to Seaboard Corporation to keep open its meat packing plant, and the state provided millions more. Seaboard lowered wages, brought in migrant labor, let its waste overwhelm the city's sewage treatment plant, and four years later relocated to another town that offered it more subsidies. Many of the migrant laborers who moved to Minnesota could not afford to live there and went on welfare, and the state spent hundreds of thousands of dollars retraining workers.[45]

In a study of state, local, and federal tax breaks offered to attract businesses to relocate, one study found that subsidies cost taxpayers from $44,000 to $29 million per job created.[46] Policymakers continue to find convincing the argument that tax breaks for corporations will produce new jobs despite the fact that most job growth in the United States has long come from small businesses. (They have their own government support agency—the Small Business Administration, which writes or sells off millions in loans.)

Another major cost of corporate welfare is cleanup of toxic emissions into the air and industrial waste deposited

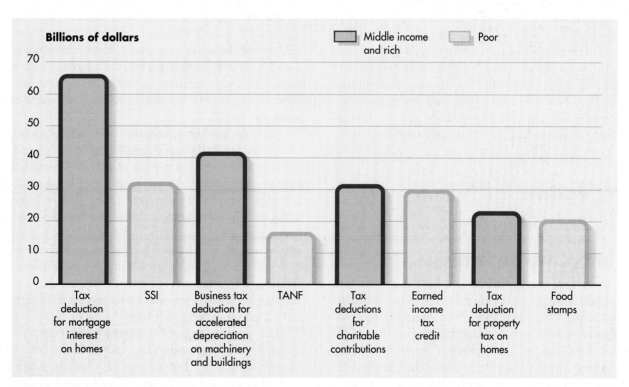

FIGURE 6 ■ A Comparison of the Cost of Federal Programs for the Poor and Selected Tax Breaks for the Middle Income and Rich

SOURCES: *Budget of the United States for Fiscal Year 2003*, 363–373; and *Analytical Perspectives*, Table 6-1.

in municipal sewage systems, waterways, and toxic waste dumps. Although corporations are required to bear more of the cleanup costs than they were before environmental protection laws were passed, taxpayers still bear most of the burden (see Chapter 18).[47]

With business tax subsidies currently costing between $125 and $150 billion annually, Congress is extending old breaks and passing new ones on the grounds they are necessary incentives during a period of economic sluggishness. As the share of federal taxes paid by corporations has declined from 25 to 10 percent since the 1960s, the burden for funding government spending falls more and more heavily on personal income and payroll taxes.

Families and Homeowners

Corporations may be the biggest winners of tax subsidies, but the government has not neglected mainstream America. It is "working families" that Congress most likes to cite as the beneficiaries of tax breaks and tax cuts, and, indeed, some are not trivial. In 2001, the tax deduction for mortgage interest, for example, cost the U.S. Treasury four times as much as payments to TANF recipients.

Families also receive tax credits for child care, adoption costs, school and college tuition, out-of-pocket health care costs, and tax deferrals for private savings plans.

Direct aid for the poor often produces outrage; even Medicare and Social Security and other largely middle-class programs are often subject to scathing criticism. But subsidized services and tax breaks for the well-off are subjected to public debate much less frequently, perhaps because benefits for the wealthy are less obvious and more diverse than benefits for the poor, and perhaps because the wealthy heavily influence political debate through corporate media control and campaign contributions.

The Future of Social Welfare Policies

Health Care Reforms

Our health care system suffers from both high costs and inadequate coverage for all Americans. The two immediate problems facing health care are access and rising costs.

One reason for higher costs is that the number of elderly is increasing, and the number of very elderly (those over eighty) is increasing even faster. The elderly have more health problems than others, so as their numbers increase, the demand for medical services rises. The growing reliance on high technology such as CAT scan-

ners, dialysis equipment, intensive care units, and other sophisticated medical tools cost millions of dollars. High technology has made possible organ transplants and other procedures unheard of a few years ago, but at a huge cost.

Hospitals all want the most sophisticated equipment, which drives up the overall costs and results in duplication and underutilization. Many Americans have become obsessed with state-of-the-art technology and do not want to drive a hundred miles to have access to it. If one hospital has a sophisticated machine, others nearby also want it, even if there are not enough patients in the city to use the extra machines. The resulting competition for patients encourages marketing to persuade doctors to use the equipment so that it can be paid for. The public—as patients, insurance buyers, and taxpayers—picks up the bill.

High-technology medicine also creates new demands for medical procedures. When better procedures become available, more people want them, so even if the new procedures are cheaper than the old, the total cost is higher. Surgery for cataracts, an eye disease affecting many elderly, is an example. Until two decades ago, surgery was painful and often ineffective. Now new techniques and materials allow plastic lenses to be inserted into the eye surgically, greatly improving vision. As a consequence, many more people receive the surgery, yielding a greatly increased total cost even though the individual procedures cost less.[48]

The pressure to perform many unnecessary procedures also drives up costs. One study estimated that one-quarter to one-third of all medical procedures are unneeded or are actually harmful.[49] For example, delivery of babies by caesarean (c-section) is the most common surgical procedure in the Untied States, and experts estimate that twice as many are done as are necessary. Doctors can charge more for caesareans than for a "normal" delivery, and a c-section can be done at the doctor's and patient's convenience. The incidence of caesareans done on women with private insurance is far higher than the incidence on women without insurance, suggesting that c-sections are done more frequently when doctors think they can get the additional fees for performing them.[50]

Given the aging population and the increasing expense of medical care, all people in the United States will never get all the medical care they want. Though we pretend otherwise, in reality we have a rationing system for medical care; it is rationing by ability to pay. If you can afford it, or if you have private or government insurance, then you can have the most expensive treatment, even if it will prolong your life only a few days or make you only marginally better off or not better off at all. If you do not have funds or insurance, then you may die at an early age even though you have a treatable condition.

Medical care is also not well rationed over the life cycle; we spend a very large proportion of health care resources on people in the last year of their lives. Thirty percent of all Medicare costs are incurred for last-year care, much of it for the last month of treatment. We are not accustomed, as are the British, French, Germans, Canadians, and Japanese, to thinking that maybe, if you are eighty-five years old, you shouldn't have triple-bypass surgery.[51]

Other nations also ration medical care, but they do it in a different way. In Canada, which has a government-funded national health care system, there is greater focus on preventive medicine. And expensive tests are reserved for those with a high probability of benefiting from them. People sometimes have to wait for elective surgery, imposing an inconvenience but ensuring that facilities will be used more efficiently. In several European countries, rationing is done by making decisions about who gets first priority for expensive procedures. For example, except in life-threatening circumstances, priority for an elective hip replacement would be given to a middle-aged working person over an elderly person (such choices would normally not be made if surgery were urgent).

The health care market has changed dramatically over the past decade because of the pressures of cost and access. The traditional "fee for service" method of health care now involves less than half of the privately insured public.[52] Employers shop around for the best "deal" for insurance for their employees, a process already leading to a managed competition plan for more than half of all Americans (compared to only 10 percent in 1988).

Health maintenance organizations (HMOs) were created as an alternative to the old fee-for-service practice. HMOs are groups of doctors who agree to provide full health care for a fixed monthly charge. This system provides direct incentives for doctors to keep costs low, avoid unnecessary hospitalization and procedures, and emphasize preventive medicine. Private insurers try to limit unnecessary operations and provide incentives for outpatient care rather than hospital stays. Critics claim that these incentives result in doctors undertreating patients by putting costs above the patients' best interests.

We spend more than twice the average per person on health care ($5,000) as other industrialized nations, but we help fewer. Our infant mortality rates are higher than in seventeen other nations, and our life expectancy is lower than Cuba's—and no better than China's. The quality of medical care received in the United States can be the best in the world for those who can pay for it, but overall it lags behind much of the industrial world and some of the less-developed world, too. A study done in 2000 showed that the United States spends more per person for health care than any other nation but ranks thirty-seventh in quality of care.[53] A more recent study by Dartmouth Medical School concluded that higher spending for more treatments does not produce significantly better results than lower spending and fewer treatments (Figure 7).[54]

Despite our large expenditures on health care, our public hospitals in big cities are overflowing with people suffering from diseases we thought we had conquered, such as tuberculosis. Analysts have concluded that neither income nor educational differences explain the poorer health of African Americans compared with people in the United States overall; instead, they conclude that racial discrimination plays a large part in explaining why blacks receive less and poorer-quality health care than others.[55] Rural hospitals are closing daily, unable to make ends meet, and great university teaching hospitals are going deeply into debt and fighting for survival.

"Kids, your mother and I have spent so much money on health insurance this year that instead of vacation we're all going to go in for elective surgery."

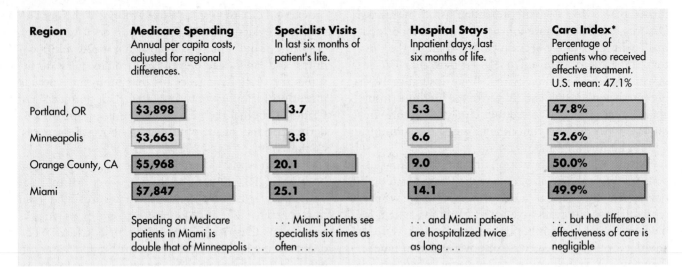

Region	Medicare Spending Annual per capita costs, adjusted for regional differences.	Specialist Visits In last six months of patient's life.	Hospital Stays Inpatient days, last six months of life.	Care Index* Percentage of patients who received effective treatment. U.S. mean: 47.1%
Portland, OR	$3,898	3.7	5.3	47.8%
Minneapolis	$3,663	3.8	6.6	52.6%
Orange County, CA	$5,968	20.1	9.0	50.0%
Miami	$7,847	25.1	14.1	49.9%
	Spending on Medicare patients in Miami is double that of Minneapolis . . .	. . . Miami patients see specialists six times as often . . .	. . . and Miami patients are hospitalized twice as long . . .	. . . but the difference in effectiveness of care is negligible

FIGURE 7 ■ More Spending, More Treatment, Similar Results
Medicare spending varies widely between regions, but evidence suggests the extra money has little or no beneficial effect for the overall population.

*Effective care index includes the following measures: vaccination for pneumococcal pneumonia; screening for breast and colon cancer; eye examinations for diabetics; HgA1c and blood lipid monitoring for diabetes; and, for heart attack victims, the prescription of aspirin therapy, beta blockers, ACE inhibitors, and reperfusion with thrombolytic agents or PTCA.
SOURCE: *New York Times*, July 21, 2002, 20.

The fact that government insurance programs cover many of those most likely to be sick—the elderly and the poor—while private health insurers cover those at least risk—the young, the well, and the well-off—means that it is very hard to hold down costs of publicly funded programs. To compensate, the federal government has tried to tighten access to Medicaid and limit the amount it pays on bills that doctors and hospitals submit to Medicare and Medicaid. But these are stopgap solutions that have led to doctors refusing to take patients covered by Medicare. Today Medicare and Medicaid costs continue to spiral upward at the same time that increasing numbers of Americans cannot afford private health care and are not eligible for either Medicare or Medicaid.

States are trying their own reforms. Maryland has attempted to standardize health insurance billing forms. Oregon decided it would not use Medicaid funds to pay for certain expensive procedures and will target more funds for preventive medicine, such as prenatal care. Hawaii requires employers to provide insurance benefits for all workers and regulates insurance costs (consequently, only 8 percent of Hawaiians do not have health insurance). Perhaps the biggest changes have come in how the states handle block grant money from the federal government to insure the poor. Increasingly, state governments have asked for waivers from the Department of Health and Human Services that allow them to spend this money as they see fit.

The public is unsure what it wants.[56] Over two-thirds believe the system needs significant change, and almost everyone believes it needs some reform, but there is little consensus on the kind of change. The public is divided on whether government or private insurers should cover costs and whether government should limit choice in exchange for cost savings.

Congress seems to have little stomach for major reform. Ever since it defeated the Clinton administration's bill to mandate employers to provide health insurance to all workers, Congress has approached each health care issue on a piecemeal basis. In recent years, the dominant issue has been holding down drug costs for seniors, but even on this issue, Congress could not agree on a plan when the House and Senate were controlled by different parties. Health care is approached much like all other social welfare issues, with changes and benefits targeted at specific groups. There is no commitment to an overall policy on health care and no consensus on who is responsible for providing it. In this sense, the United States remains at odds with all other developed countries.

Social Security

As a welfare program for everyone, Social Security continues to be politically popular among all groups because it has diminished many of the economic risks of growing old. It is a great public policy success story, but the program does have problems. Its popularity makes it difficult to change, but the program does come under attack periodically.

Two major problems face the Social Security system. One is the ratio of active workers to retirees. Social Security costs are increasing, largely because our population is getting older. The number of people aged sixty-five and older is expected to double from 35 million in 2002 to 70 million in 2030. Even though immigration keeps us from zero growth, there will be only 2.1 active workers for each Social Security beneficiary in 2030, compared to 3.4 today.[57]

The second problem is the integrity of the Social Security Trust Fund. Presidents and Congress continue to use its surpluses to offset online budget deficits. Because of 1980s reforms for funding Social Security—increasing payroll tax rates and the amount of income taxed, and expanding coverage to virtually all workers—the Trust Fund has accumulated a huge surplus. The surplus is deliberate, part of the planning for the drain on the fund that will occur as the baby boom generation (those born in the late 1940s and early 1950s) reaches retirement age. But during years when general revenue funds are insufficient to cover government spending, budget makers in the White House and Congress borrow from the Trust Fund to reduce deficits. This is part of the national debt held by government agencies. The question is, When the money is needed to pay benefits, will the government be able to repay what it has borrowed from the Trust Fund? Looking at this problem in combination with the aging of the population has led many young people to believe that Social Security will not be there when they retire. Some of their concern is undoubtedly fed by politicians constantly predicting that the Trust Fund and the Medicare program will go broke in the next few years unless changes are made.

Everyone agrees we need to put the program on a sounder financial basis for the future. We can raise the retirement age—something already being phased in—reduce the automatic annual cost-of-living increases recipients get (the 2003 increase was the lowest in four years), and tax a larger share of earnings. Taxing income up to an amount beyond the current $80,400 would tax people already well-off and generate more income for the system.

Another potential solution is to restructure the system. The most significant and persistent of these proposals is to privatize part of Social Security funding. The most comprehensive privatization plans advocate voluntary participation, allowing workers to join private pension plans or manage their own savings by investing them as they see fit, assuming as much or as little risk as they want. This plan has little support, because it runs the risk of millions of seniors not having enough retirement income if the stock market falters or if bad investment decisions were made. Most people have no special expertise in investment strategy; such a plan might provide a windfall for investment firms while leaving millions vulnerable.

The Bush administration has proposed a scaled-back, incremental privatization reform that would allow each individual to invest in stocks and bonds 3 percent of the first $10,000 earned and 2 percent of all other earnings. The remaining portion of the payroll tax obligation would be paid into the Social Security Trust Fund just as it is now. (The Trust Fund does not invest in anything but low-risk, low-interest government securities). But reductions in contributions in even these small percentages would put the Trust Fund in an even more tenuous financial position as the number of beneficiaries explodes over the next few decades. The Bush plan does call for a much speedier phase-in of sixty-seven as the age of eligibility and an increase in the amount of earnings subject to payroll tax, but still the estimates are that under this plan, beneficiaries would receive only about 80 percent of the stipend they are now guaranteed.[58] Since Social Security payments are already insufficient to meet the cost of living for more than 2 million seniors, the reform would probably force more beneficiaries into the SSI program. Because SSI is funded by General Revenues, not the Trust Fund, any large jump in the number of beneficiaries would increase budget deficits.

After the corruption scandals and the Wall Street crash of 2002, proposals for partial privatization were put on hold. The financial collapse of major corporations took with them billions of dollars of investments of state and private pension funds and diminished public confidence in the stock market. But some way will have to be found to keep benefits at least at existing levels because 53 percent of the workforce has no private pension coverage, and 35 percent of Americans have no retirement savings other than what they have paid into Social Security.[59]

Reforming Aid to the Poor

In 2001, Congress had to decide whether to reauthorize the 1996 welfare reform, which had been written with a five-year sunset provision. It passed the reauthorization with remarkably little debate considering how mixed the reports have been on the accomplishments of the 1996 reforms. In evaluating the reform, the point of reference was the number of people removed from the welfare rolls. Building on the initial success in moving people into the labor force, Congress, acting on Bush administration proposals, strengthened welfare-to-work requirements. Whereas the 1996 law mandated that a minimum of 30 percent of the people on state welfare rolls be job holders, the new rules require that at least 50 percent of those receiving welfare benefits find jobs immediately. Bush has asked that this number be increased to 70 percent by 2007 and that all jobholders be required to work a minimum of forty (up from thirty) hours per week. This will not be easy to achieve at a time of low job growth and increasing unemployment.

The Bush proposals also requested $300 million to encourage welfare recipients to marry, on the assumption that children do better in two-parent households and that child care would be more workable and less costly. It also would be easier for children to claim the benefits due to workers' dependents. It is a fact that there are fewer two-parent households in poverty. In most cases, both parents work, thus significantly increasing household income. Moreover, women earn on average 74 cents for every dollar earned by a man, so single-parent households headed by women are doubly disadvantaged.

One dark trend in the first five years of reform was that forcing women with dependent children into the labor force caused an increase in no-parent families. The reasons are unclear, but more mothers left their children with relatives. Possibly it is because of the burden of holding down jobs, often with irregular hours, combined with the demands of child care and a loss of benefits. Hardest hit have been African American children in inner cities, where the number living without a parent more than doubled after the welfare-to-work reforms.[60]

Another darker side to reform has been the reduction in state spending for welfare. Whereas in the early years spending in some states increased dramatically as they offered job training and other assistance to move people from welfare to work, after the decline in welfare rolls (by as much as two-thirds in midwestern states), spending has declined. That may seem logical since there are fewer clients, but most states still have 70 percent or more of welfare recipients who need training and other assistance if they are to find jobs. Although Congress set a requirement that states must spend at least as much as they were spending in 1996 to qualify for block grant money to cover income support, 2001 spending by most states was only 75 percent of the 1996 level.[61]

Part of the decrease in spending can be attributed to Congress giving states considerable flexibility in how they use a certain portion of block grant money, allowing them to create "rainy day funds." In this way, states can reserve for later use money they are entitled to receive for TANF, or they can divert it to other purposes.[62]

Despite the problems, TANF has worked for many. It has shown that at least in good economic times, welfare rolls can be reduced and more people employed. For people healthy and skilled enough to hold down jobs, and lucky enough to find them, welfare to work has been successful in ending dependency on cash assistance. But most have not been lifted out of poverty. Average incomes of the newly employed were $12,000 in Iowa and Ohio and $14,000 in Indiana and Michigan.[63] Other problems add to the job-seeking difficulties of welfare recipients. Lack of suitable skills for today's economy is a significant problem. Sizeable proportions of welfare recipients suffer from mental or physical disabilities, learning disabilities, and substance abuse problems. Any one of these conditions make finding and keeping a job difficult, and many unemployed have more than one of these problems.[64]

Although the cost to taxpayers is a frequently stated goal of reform and was one of the forces driving the 1996 welfare reform, it was probably not the primary objective. Income support for the poor pales in comparison to income support and indirect subsidies to millions of far better-off Americans. And no meaningful reform will cost less than the old AFDC program. It is likely that playing to the distaste people have for "welfare" and the idea that some recipients are getting

TABLE 2	Income Distribution Is Becoming More Lopsided		
Percentage of Households	Percentage of Income Earned		
	1980	1990	2000
Lowest fifth*	4.3	3.9	3.6
Next lowest	10.3	9.6	8.9
Middle fifth	16.9	15.9	14.9
Next highest	24.9	24.0	23.0
Highest fifth	43.7	46.6	49.2
Top 5%	15.8	18.6	21.0

*The fifth of households receiving the least income per houshold.
SOURCE: U.S. Bureau of the Census at www.census.gov/hhes/income/histinc/h02.html.

something for nothing was at least as important a motivation for reform as saving money.

Improving program performance and getting results for the individual are far more compelling reasons for trying to reform welfare than cost reduction. This would be better not only for the individual clients but for the economy and society as a whole. In America, we like to think everyone can have a chance to achieve to the best of his or her ability and that parents can have a reasonable hope that their children's lives will be better than their own. Moreover, democracies function better when there are no permanent classes of "haves" and "have-nots" (see Table 2). People who must worry about how to feed and house themselves are not going to be full participants in the political process. By helping sustain an underclass, we undermine the political system itself. But there will never be agreement between welfare reformers on what kinds of reforms are necessary because there is no basic agreement on why people are poor. Those who think that poverty is the fault of the poor because they are deficient in character or effort are far less likely to support government help for the poor than are those who believe that poverty is a product of the economic system, bad luck, and parentage (the wealth of your parents determines a lot about your own opportunities to get ahead).

Farm Subsidies

The commitment of Congress to continue business as usual in farm policy was made clear in its approval of large increases in subsidies in the 2002 farm bill. Even more impressive was that it was done during a period of recession, tax cuts, and budget deficits.

If farm subsidies are to be reformed, the pressure will probably come from abroad. Continued spending on price supports for agricultural commodities conflicts with the U.S. commitment to free trade and its obligations as a member of the World Trade Organization (see Chapter 19). The United States is a party to international trade agreements that, to ensure fair competition among the world's farm exporters, limit how much a government can pay in price supports. If the WTO rules against the United States in grievances filed by other member countries, payments to farmers would have to be cut if we want to be in compliance with international obligations.

Conclusion: Are Social Welfare Programs Responsive?

Looking at our vast array of social welfare benefits, it would be easy to conclude that government is not only responsive to the American public but hyperresponsive. Through income support programs, subsidized services, and tax breaks, social welfare provides something for everyone, while reflecting government's greater responsiveness to individuals and groups who wield political influence. The poor, although comprising more than 10 percent of the population, do not have the influence, organization, or access to win public support for programs benefiting them. In hard times, when support is most needed, programs for the poor often take the brunt of budget cuts. But not all Americans view politics only in terms of what they get, and most have learned that the growth of an underclass harms everyone.

Most taxpayers define themselves as middle income, and they support services for themselves and others like them. Benefits to the upper classes are tolerated to a large extent because they often take the form of technical or specially tailored tax breaks that most of the public has never heard of. When they do catch the public's attention, often because of abuse—such as offshore tax shelters or business deductions for stock options given to CEOs—they can trigger resentment and reform.

The making of social welfare policy also illustrates our government's lack of an overarching policy or philosophy about its responsibilities for ensuring basic human services. Instead, it responds in piecemeal fashion to crises or to pressure from the most influential interest groups and lobbyists and gives far too little attention to long-term planning. While Americans worry about the viability of the country's most comprehensive programs like Social Security and Medicare, Congress is too often preoccupied with responding to short-term demands.

Finally, it is clear that Congress has established a massive tangle of support programs to protect individuals and businesses from the risks of the same marketplace they like to eulogize. One of the central questions about social welfare policies today has to be whether government assumes too much risk for individuals and for business, and whether it assumes more risk for the powerful than for the weak.

Hutchinson Votes to Subsidize Big Farmers

utchinson voted against the Senate version of the farm bill. He said he preferred the House bill because it provided "the safety and certainty our farmers need. That safety and certainty was wiped out of the Senate bill by a misguided amendment that arbitrarily limits payments to farmers with high production costs." He added that the bill did "not reflect Arkansas priorities" and would be devastating for agriculture in his state.[65]

By the time the bill came to the floor, it was clear it would pass without Hutchinson's vote, so he knew farm subsidies would be approved without his having to go on record as supporting lower income support payments. The bill was sent to conference committee, where it took three months to work out a final report. Hutchinson, like most farm state senators who had voted against the Senate bill, voted yes on the conference report. It provides for $45 billion in new spending during the first five years, a 27 percent increase over existing programs. The ceiling on payments was lowered to a midway point ($360,000) between the House and Senate bills but "with enough exceptions to make it a symbolic compromise."[66]

Hutchinson said the final version provides the "safety net" farmers need until new markets open up abroad. He cited President Bush's description of farm and ranch families as embodying "some of the best

IT'S A HOOT.

ACTUALLY, WE'RE BOTH HIGHLY PAID CORPORATE EXECUTIVES. WE JUST LIKE TO DRESS UP THIS WAY WHEN WE PICK UP OUR FARM SUBSIDY CHECKS.

AKRON BEACON JOURNAL©02

Chip Bok/Creators Syndicate

values of our nation: hard work and risk taking."[67] He did not add that farms subsidies reduce, if not eliminate "risk taking" primarily for the wealthiest farm industries, not for the average family farmer. This is why some in rural America call it "farming the government, not farming the land."[68]

Hutchinson's vote, and that of many other subsidy supporters, is another example of why government continues to grow. We expect liberals to vote for agricultural price supports because they believe in government spending for social welfare. But government also grows as a result of corporate welfare, and much of its support comes from conservatives who decry big government while voting to expand it when it is bene-

ficial to their constituents. The farm support bill is also an example of how government welfare policies are most responsive to the lobbying influence of the well-off.

In the end, Hutchinson's decision to stand by Arkansas agribusiness did not help him at the polls. He had won his seat running as a social and fiscal conservative, loosely aligned with the Christian right. After divorcing his wife to marry a young member of his staff, Arkansas voters deserted him, and he went down to defeat in 2002. And for all the benefits extended to wealthy farmers, many farm families remain in need. The ink was barely dry on the $171 billion farm support bill when Congress approved an additional $6 billion in drought relief.

To learn more about this farm bill and the nature of agricultural subsidies, go to this chapter's "You Are There" exercises on the text Web site.

Key Terms

farm subsidies

Social Security

means test

Supplemental Security
Income (SSI)

Aid to Families with
Dependent Children
(AFDC)

Temporary Aid to Needy
Families (TANF)

earned income credit (EIC)

food stamps

Medicare

Medicaid

corporate welfare

health maintenance
organizations (HMOs)

Further Reading

Rebecca Blank and Ron Haskins, eds., *The New World of Welfare* (Washington, D.C.: Brookings Institution, 2002). A collection of essays edited by one of the drafters of the 1995 welfare reform legislation. Writers and policy-makers across the conservative-liberal spectrum evaluate the effectiveness of the reforms to date.

Walt Bogdanich, *The Great White Lie* (New York: Simon & Schuster, 1992). This description of the health crisis in America's hospitals probably should not be read if there is a hospital stay in your future!

Robert Coles, *The Youngest Parents: Teenage Pregnancy as It Shapes Lives* (New York: Norton, 1997). Based on several years of intensive interviews with a diverse group of teenage parents, this book illuminates their lives, largely by letting them speak for themselves.

Barbara Ehrenreich, *Nickel and Dimed: On (Not) Getting by in America* (New York: Metropolitan Books, 2001). A well-known writer and women's rights activist (a biologist by training) tells about her experience doing blue-collar work to find out what it would be like for a woman to try to support herself at minimum-wage jobs. She found that many who worked full-time, some holding several jobs, still could not afford both food and housing.

Frank Levy, *The New Dollars and Dreams: American Incomes and Economic Change* (New York: Russell Sage Foundation, 1998). Examines changes in the U.S. economy that have increased inequality in the distribution of income.

John E. Schwarz, *America's Hidden Success: A Reassessment of Twenty Years of Public Policy*, 2d ed. (New York: Norton, 1988). Argues that the Great Society programs of the 1960s and 1970s were largely successful in reducing poverty and achieving other goals.

William J. Williams, *The Truly Disadvantaged: The Inner-City, the Underclass and Public Policy* (Chicago: University of Chicago Press, 1987). Argues that the worsening plight of the black underclass is due to the changing structure of the national economy, which is increasing the number of poor-paying jobs, and to the success of the black middle class, who when they leave the ghetto leave an ever more concentrated underclass behind.

 ## Electronic Resources

www.aphsa.org/
This page of the American Public Human Services Association has information about and analysis of all welfare programs. It is a useful site for tracking the progress of welfare reform.

www.ncsl.org/
As part of its responsibility to state legislative bodies, the National Conference of State Legislatures provides assessments of changes in federal welfare law. In addition, this is a source of information on the welfare and Medicaid programs of individual states.

www.ssa.gov/
Like all other government agencies, the Social Security Administration has its own Web site, providing a broad array of information on its history and programs. Here employers can find out how to comply with laws governing Social Security taxation, and parents of disabled children can learn how to avoid losing SSI benefits.

www.hhs.gov/
This page links to the agencies of the Department of Health and Human Services, including the Food and Drug Administration, the Administration for Children and Families, and the Centers for Disease Control and Prevention.

www.ewg.org
A Web site maintained by the Environmental Working Group to make public farm subsidy disbursements. If you want to know who gets how much, this is the place to look.

 ## InfoTrac College Edition

Search for the following articles in the InfoTrac database:

James, Estelle. "Reforming Social Security in the US: An International Perspective," *Business Economics* (January 2001).

Jencks, Christopher. "Liberal Lessons from Welfare Reform: Why Welfare-to-Work Turned out Better Than We Expected," *American Prospect* (July 15, 2002).

Rank, Mark R., and Thomas A. Hirschl. "Welfare Use as a Life Course Event: Toward a New Understanding of the U.S. Safety Net," *Social Work* (July 2002).

Vladeck, Bruce C. "Can Its Benefits Be Sustained as Cost of Coverage Grows?" *Geriatrics* (May 2001).

For more articles, enter

"Social Security" in the Subject Guide;

"Welfare reform" in the Subject Guide;

"Medicare" in the Subject Guide.

 ## American Government Resources

Visit the Public Policy section of the Wadsworth American Government Resources Web site (politicalscience.wadsworth.com/amgov/) for a variety of tools to help you explore social welfare and health policy further. Included are simulations, video clips, Microcase exercises, and a wealth of other activities.

REGULATION AND ENVIRONMENTAL POLICY

Coal-burning plants are changing our environment, but the means to regulate them are a source of controversy.

Should Nevada Become the Country's Nuclear Waste Dump?

You are Kenny C. Guinn, Republican governor of Nevada. Since you were elected in 1998, you have been fighting attempts by the federal government to build a national nuclear waste storage facility in your state. Now, after the president and Congress have agreed to put the waste storage facility in Nevada, will you accept this decision, or will you continue to fight it in the courts and by going public?

The Department of Energy (DoE) is proposing to move seventy-seven thousand tons of nuclear waste to your state, waste that will remain radioactive for ten to twenty-four thousand years. Nevada's opposition to the plan dates back to 1987, when Congress first identified a former bomb-testing site at Yucca Mountain, an area of rocky hills and valleys and low rainfall, as the best place to store waste and spent fuel from the country's 103 nuclear power plants. The waste is currently stored at thirty-one temporary sites around the country, and Congress wants it all moved to a single, se-cure, and permanent repository.

You agree that nuclear waste should be in a safe and secure loca-tion, but it is a lot harder to accept Nevada as that location. When it comes to nuclear waste storage, everyone cries, "NIMBY" (not in my backyard). No one wants to be located next to a site that holds material that will be radioactive for millennia.

You are convinced that building a nuclear waste storage facility at Yucca Mountain presents dangers both for public health and the state's economy. Nevada is a small (2 mil-lion) but fast-growing state. Seventy-five percent of the population is in the Las Vegas metropolitan area, 90 miles away from the proposed waste site. With the storage of that much dangerous waste so close to Las Vegas, the risk of earthquake or accident, however small, could cre-ate a disaster. Even if there were no contamination, the scare would reduce the tourist trade on which the state relies so heavily.

You will be standing for reelec-tion this year, and the Yucca Moun-tain facility will be a major issue again. You never held elective office before getting elected governor. You moved to Nevada from your native California to work in the public schools, eventually becoming a superintendent. After retiring, you spent several years in business before doing a turn as interim president of the University of Nevada–Las Vegas when it was trying to come back from a basketball scandal. By donat-ing your salary to the school scholar-ship fund, you became a civic hero, and soon a local pundit was referring to you as "The Anointed One," the natural successor to the incumbent, term-limited governor.

You have promised Nevadans all along that you would do anything you can to prevent a permanent, or even a temporary, nuclear waste storage site from being built in the state. You even advocated banning the import of water necessary to construct the site, saying you would assess a fine of $1 million per gallon.[1]

The nuclear industry is eager to have the waste it produces moved away from the plants and stored at a distant site at taxpayer expense, and it has lobbied heavily to get approval for the Yucca Mountain facility. But until the past few years, Nevada had high-placed allies in Washington who kept the plan from gaining approval. During his two presidential campaigns, Bill Clinton told Nevadans he would veto any plan to designate Yucca Mountain as the storage site, and he did that. Presidential candidate Al Gore promised the same in 2000, and George W. Bush had said he, too, would oppose it until scientific study proved it safe.

Despite the state's overwhelming opposition, the proposal just would not die. In 2001, Congress gave the go-ahead to DoE to build the facility and now-president Bush approved it, saying that after $4.5 billion had been spent studying the site, current evidence indicated that Yucca Mountain was the best and safest site for the facility. You were livid, but the unusual legislation gave you, as governor, a chance to veto the plan. You did, and, in addition, the state filed four separate suits in federal court to overturn Washington's decision. But Bush asked Congress to approve it over your veto (it required only a majority vote in each chamber to override), and the House did so.

You did not give up. You set up the Nevada Protection Fund to raise money to hire lobbyists and prepare an ad campaign. The fund paid for a video on the safety risks and possible real estate impact in the forty-three states through which trains carrying radioactive waste would pass. They sent copies to 1,500 local chambers of commerce and 222 TV stations.[2] You hoped that if

other states declared they did not want trains full of radioactive waste passing through their cities, maybe members of Congress would reconsider the whole project.

You said in congressional testimony that the project is "the product of extremely bad science, extremely bad law, and extremely bad public policy."[3] As evidence, you argue that although the Nuclear Regulatory Commission has conducted extensive research on the casks the material will be stored in, they still do not know enough about the suitability of the terrain. You say it is like "making sure every deck chair on the *Titanic* can hold the heaviest passenger, without ever bothering to make sure the ship can float."[4]

You also argue that it is dangerous to transport thousands of tons of radioactive material across the country, especially in an era when the government is warning about the inevitability of more terrorist attacks. Shipments will pass through or near 106 cities and come within one-half mile of 123 million people.

You say that the Yucca Mountain repository will be too small. Built to hold seventy-seven thousand tons of waste and spent fuel, it will take only twenty-five years to fill what is intended to be the sole national repository. And by that time, the existing temporary sites near power plants would have produced fifty thousand additional tons of waste.[5]

The committee does not buy your arguments. The Senate also votes to override your veto and build at Yucca.

Now you have to decide what to do next. Yours is a tiny state with a part-time legislature and limited resources.[6] With the recession, there are many needs that the state is not meeting. Your congressional delegation consists of just two Democrats and two Republicans. It is not much to take on Washington, let alone the powerful lobbyists the nuclear industry has hired. The only serious allies your efforts have produced thus far are

those who would have opposed the facility in any case—environmental groups and Ralph Nader's consumer rights group, Public Citizen.

You are also being lobbied by a group representing Nevadans who believe that what the state wants is now beside the point because the facility is a done deal. They urge you to make the best of it and give you a long list of benefits you could negotiate for as the price for ending your opposition: fees for storage, more funding for highways, rights to draw more water from the Colorado, and the return to state ownership of federally held land in Nevada.[7]

On the other hand, you do have many reasons to continue the fight. Seventy percent of Nevadans say they oppose the Yucca Mountain project. The congressional delegation, the state legislature, the major city governments, the state medical and firefighters' associations, the PTA, the tourism commission, and the commission on nuclear projects all oppose building a national waste facility in Nevada.[8]

You do not like challenging a decision of a president from your own party, and you do not doubt the need for a solution to the waste problem. But you do not see why Nevada, which has no nuclear power plants, should be storing waste for the thirty-one states that do have them or why, after absorbing the fallout from years of nuclear testing, Nevada should have to be exposed to even more radioactivity. You want Congress to revisit the scientific evidence and understand your argument that it makes no sense to transport nuclear waste across the country to a site that may not be geologically stable.

Can the state afford to go on spending millions advertising and lobbying on what looks like a hopeless cause? Or is it time to stop fighting Washington and let the dispute play out in the courts? What do you do next?

Adam Smith believed the "invisible hand" of the marketplace works to increase production and make individual firms more efficient.[9] As each tries to maximize its profit, market forces push it toward increasing efficiency and productivity as the only means of staying competitive. In the process, in Smith's view, the greater good of society is served; jobs are created, economies grow, and the rising water lifts all boats. If the economy did work this way, and if everyone in business were honest and played by the unwritten rules, we would have little regulation. But unfortunately, the economy goes awry in ways that threaten the public good because market forces are not sufficient to protect us from the intended or unintended consequences of economic activity. So government regulates to limit or correct these effects: exploitation of labor, dangerous consumer products, unsafe foods and drugs, monopolies, insider trading, and pollution, to name a few.

But how much risk should government protect us from? How should the benefits of regulation be weighed against the costs of those regulations to business and industry? The public gives no clear-cut answer to these questions. Regulation that is seen as beneficial by one group is regarded by another as wasteful and unnecessary red tape. This is why there is continuing controversy over what should be regulated, how much regulation is needed, and the regulatory mechanisms that should be used.

In this chapter, we look at the evolution of government's regulatory authority, identify types of regulation and their objectives, and the standards used to measure their effectiveness. Then we look at how we cycle through periods of regulation and deregulation depending on the political climate in Washington. Finally, we look at one of the most strongly supported, yet controversial, areas of regulatory policy: environmental law.

Reasons for Regulation

Regulation is necessary for several reasons: (1) the damage to common property that would occur without regulation, (2) inefficient competition, (3) a lack of necessary coordination, and (4) unacceptable inequities.

Damage to Common Property

One reason for regulation has been called the **tragedy of the commons.**[10] The "commons" refers to the air we breathe and the water we drink, which belong to us all. The "tragedy" is that some individuals may seek to exploit them for their own uses to the detriment of

the common good. To maximize their profits, farmers pump as much irrigation water as they need from rivers or aquifers, even in water-short areas, and industries spew toxic chemicals into the air or bury them in the soil. They are acting in accord with the profit motive. Indeed, most individuals who exploit the commons gain economically and thus have considerable incentive to do so. But when many people exploit the commons, the community as a whole suffers.

Consider the case of Los Angeles and General Motors (GM). Los Angeles once had a low-pollution electric railway system. In the 1930s, GM bought the system and then destroyed it, because GM wanted to sell cars, trucks, and buses. The company replaced the electric system with noisy, polluting diesel buses, so uncomfortable and unreliable that Los Angelenos were given a great incentive to rely on private autos.

In 1949, after buying and destroying electric railway systems in more than one hundred cities, GM was fined a paltry $5,000 by the government for illegally conspiring to replace municipal services with its own. Meanwhile, the company made millions of dollars. Due in large part to reliance on cars, smog in Los Angeles became a major health hazard. Some studies claimed that children who grew up in Los Angeles lost up to 50 percent of their lung capacity from breathing in the polluted air.[11] Obviously, it is absurd to charge GM with creating the entire automobile culture of Los Angeles, but clearly its drive for private profits did not contribute to the common good.

When GM or any other entity, such as a chemical company that disposes of its toxic wastes in an unsafe way, imposes a cost on the public, it has created an **externality.** *Externalities* are costs or benefits that are not reflected in market prices. Environmental degradation is a negative externality because the social costs, the burdens imposed on society, are not reflected in the cost of the goods whose production caused the damage. When a coal-burning utility emits sulfur dioxide into the air, for example, the company is essentially disposing of a by-product at no cost by simply burning it off and releasing it into the air. This places an unfair burden on the public, both in terms of the health risks and the costs of environmental cleanup. It also leads to inefficiency in the marketplace because the utility is not made to bear the true cost of generating electricity. If companies are allowed to externalize costs in this way, they will produce more of a product than is "socially beneficial." But if they have to absorb or internalize the costs of emitting pollutants, instead of foisting them off on the public, they will have "an incentive to reduce production to acceptable levels or to develop alternative technologies."[12]

Houston, a center of the petrochemical industry, vies with Los Angeles as the smog capital of the United States.

To make the market more efficient and to get companies to stop producing goods and services whose real costs are not reflected in the prices charged for those goods and services—to get a petrochemical plant to stop releasing toxins into the air, for example—the government can set standards for how much of the pollutant can be emitted (and recover costs through penalties and fines from violators), or it can impose taxes on emissions or discharges and charge for pollution up front (more on this later in the chapter).

Inefficient Competition

In a capitalist system, government intervention is also justifiable when competition is inefficient. Adam Smith believed that in an open market, goods and labor would be used in a way that would maximize profit and limit cost. The competition among manufacturers trying to sell the same products to consumers would force them to make goods as cheaply as possible.

But sometimes competition does not work to drive down prices or increase efficiency. The large capital outlays required to build the infrastructure for public utilities—laying water pipes and gas lines, or building power grids—means that it is not cost-effective for every community to have more than one company. Thus, utilities (such as gas and electricity producers) have long been "controlled monopolies" regulated by state governments. A utility is allowed to be the only provider of a service in a given geographic area, but a state utility board regulates prices because people do not have a choice of sellers of electricity or gas. Smith himself agreed that this form of government intervention was appropriate.

However, the drive toward privatization of public services has led some states to deregulate electric util-

ities, to encourage the most efficient and cost effective use of power by transmitting it across the country to wherever it was most needed at any point in time. Consumers who, in the era of controlled monopolies, could count on the states to regulate prices and order local plants to maintain reserves strictly for local use found themselves without this protection, especially in California, where prices skyrocketed and there were frequent blackouts. California deregulated its utilities differently than other states. It kept the plants that distributed electricity to consumers and the authority to set consumer prices, but it sold all of its generating plants to private companies. It also sold the right to regulate the wholesale price of electricity that the generating plants still provided to the state-owned distribution plants. During a heat wave in the summer of 2000, prices spiked and stayed high even in times of low use. It turned out that the now privately owned generating plants that California had contracted with were producing enough electricity to cover demand even during high-use periods, but they were withholding electricity to drive up prices in a near-captive market. The state spent more than $9 billion purchasing electricity from other states to end the blackouts and dampen consumer rage. Essentially California had sold off public utilities to private companies that then held it ransom to exorbitant prices. Electric bills increased fivefold, and state-owned power distribution plants went into bankruptcy.[13]

In the end, California reinstated price controls and sued energy providers for price gouging. Its utilities have become a legendary example of how not to deregulate, leading other states to put their deregulation plans on hold. The deregulation of electricity illustrates that in some areas of economic activity privatization does not lead to greater efficiencies, more competition, or lower prices.

Lack of Necessary Coordination

Another reason for regulation is that sometimes the free market produces an unacceptable lack of coordination. An obvious example is regulation of airline flights. The free market is not well suited to determine which airline will have priority to schedule a departure at 2:00 P.M. on a certain runway at Kennedy International Airport in New York. Competition could lead to disaster. Thus, the Federal Aviation Administration (FAA) has been empowered to coordinate takeoffs, landings, and travel routes. Some of this authority has been privatized by allowing airlines to sell or trade their airport slots. But air traffic control remains a federal function.

Unacceptable Inequities

Another reason for regulation is to promote equity. *Equity* in this context does not refer to equality in outcome but to ensuring fair conditions for participation in the marketplace. Sometimes individuals or groups are severely disadvantaged by the private marketplace. For example, legislation setting minimum wages, banning child labor, protecting workers' rights to organize, and defining minimum standards for workplace health and safety is intended to redress the inequity in power between individual workers and employers. But government also protects employers from workers who organize for bargaining power. The conditions under which workers can unionize and the timing and conditions of strikes, or work stoppages, in certain sectors of the economy are also restricted by federal law.

Regulations forbidding race and gender discrimination are also designed to enhance equity. Consumer protection laws, such as those forbidding false advertising, and laws licensing pharmacists, physicians, lawyers, and public accountants are based on the assumption that consumers will often not have sufficient information to evaluate the competence of those selling the service or product. Government seeks to remedy an inequity in information between the buyer and the seller of a product or service.

The first major attempt to reduce inequities by regulating was **antitrust law,** which prohibits monopolies. A **monopoly** occurs when one or a few firms control the sale of a product or service in a particular market. Where a monopoly exists, the producer(s) can fix prices, setting them well above the cost of production, or they can sell below cost to drive small businesses out of the market. The Sherman Antitrust Act of 1890 and the Clayton Act of 1914 made uncontrolled monopolies and price rigging illegal.

Children working in a vegetable cannery. At the turn of the century, many young children worked twelve-hour days in unhealthy conditions. New Deal–era regulations outlawed most child labor, but abuse of child labor laws is increasing in some urban areas.

One firm may use antitrust laws to sue others, or the government itself may initiate antitrust actions. The enforcement of antitrust legislation has waxed and waned over the years.

Mergers can lead to monopolies as competitors combine forces to control a larger share of the market. Therefore, when large companies want to merge or acquire their competitors, they are required to submit their proposals for review to the Justice Department or the Federal Trade Commission so that government regulators can determine whether their combination would adversely affect competition and prices.

Our economy has experienced five major waves of business mergers: at the turn of the twentieth century and in the 1920s, the 1960s, the 1980s, and the 1990s. The number of merger proposals tripled during the nineties, with more than seventy thousand deals worth nearly $6 trillion during the Clinton years alone.[14] Some see this trend as a repeat of the corporate mergers that swept the American economy at the turn of the century, when General Motors was created from more than two dozen car companies, and U.S. Steel was formed by combining many small steel companies. In these situations, government regulators have to decide whether the mergers will make the economy more efficient and competitive or whether they will create monopolies and lead to price fixing.

I MISS DECEPTIVE LABELING...

LARD CAKES

Fat Nips

GREASY PIECES

SALTY SNAPS

Fried CHEMICAL TWISTS

SALTY FAT CHIPS

Sugar Fatty FLAKES

CHOLESTEROL CRISPS

OILY PUFFS

Reprinted with permission of Steve Kelley/*The Times-Picayune*, New Orleans

Ninety-five percent of the merger proposals made during the Clinton years went unchallenged by the Justice Department. A notable exception, on which it was joined by many state governments, was antitrust action against Microsoft, alleging it tried to corner the market in computer software. Although the case revealed that Microsoft made a 90 percent pretax profit on its Windows operating system, the government's case did not rest on the price-fixing standard. Instead, government lawyers established a new basis for challenging monopolies—constraint of innovation or technological change.[15]

Correcting inequities in the marketplace is one of the most controversial types of regulation. Conservatives often argue that this type of regulation is unnecessary because they believe the free market is self-regulating. They reason that unsafe or ineffective products will sooner or later end up unwanted: Pizza eaters can stop buying pizza with artificial cheese; unions can protect workers from unreasonable demands of corporations. But some opponents of regulation are against unions, too, believing they interfere with the free market for labor.

Defenders of equity-based regulations point out that the market works too slowly in providing vital information. People have been killed and injured before information about defective products became widely known. In the mid-1960s, many children were born with serious deformities because of the prescription drug thalidomide, which their mothers took during pregnancy. This incident caused Congress to set higher standards for drug safety and the Food and Drug Administration (FDA) to tighten its drug-testing rules. Before 1972, 20 million consumers were injured each year by unsafe products, and of those, thirty thousand were killed and more than one hundred thousand permanently disabled. This prompted Congress to establish the Consumer Product Safety Commission (CPSC), an independent regulatory agency mandated to establish safety standards for consumer products.

Some people believe education campaigns, not regulation, are the best way to protect people. But education campaigns are not cheap, especially over a long period of time, and not always effective, either. The government's campaign to educate the public about the health hazards of smoking has had a significant impact, but the campaign has cost tens of millions of dollars, and about one-quarter of Americans still smoke.

Congress does not regulate to remedy the effects of every inequity. Sometimes the costs are seen as greater than the gains; in other cases, resistance by politically powerful groups—the banking and telecommunications industries, for instance—is stronger than lobbying by potential beneficiaries of regulation.

Kinds of Regulation

There are several types of regulation:

1. *Requiring information.* Government may regulate by requiring that an employer, lender, or other entity provide certain kinds of information to employees or consumers. For example, credit card companies must provide cardholders with information about interest rates and how to appeal charges they think are not really theirs. Manufacturers of many food products must list ingredients on the label and give their nutritional content. This requirement allows consumers to see whether their peppermint ice cream, for example, is colored with beet juice or red dye number 2, a potentially dangerous additive, and how many calories come from fat and sugar. This requirement is called **truth in labeling.** Manufacturers sometimes oppose labeling the contents of their goods because, as one said, "If you label, you're telling consumers there is something wrong with this product."[16]

    The FDA also requires that when information *is* provided, it should be accurate. Many manufacturers have taken advantage of a new public awareness of the relationship between health and nutrition by labeling their products as "health" foods. The FDA has forced manufacturers to remove words such as *fresh* from processed juices and *no cholesterol* from food products that are high in vegetable fats that could contribute to heart disease. It is also demanding that manufacturers remove false claims that their products are "organic," "biodegradable," or in other ways "environmentally safe." Such consumer come-ons are called *green fraud*.

2. *Licensing.* Government may regulate by requiring people to obtain licenses to practice certain trades or professions or to operate certain businesses. For example, the federal government licenses radio and television stations, and states license doctors, beauticians, dentists, and many others. This reassures clients and patients that those providing the services have met minimum qualifications for their professions. But licensing is also valuable for those receiving a license because it allows them to make money while keeping others out.

3. *Setting standards.* Manufacturers must meet certain standards for content, quality, environmental cleanliness, workplace safety, and employee wages and working conditions. A product called chicken soup must have a minimum amount of chicken in it, and hot dogs cannot include more than a certain proportion of bone, hair, insects, and other extraneous material. The FDA requires manufacturers of condoms to test them for leaks and to destroy an entire batch of one thousand if more than four are defective. Failure to maintain the standards can result in fines or other legal penalties, if convicted.

4. *Providing economic incentives.* Higher taxes may be imposed on goods or activities viewed as less beneficial than on those deemed more beneficial.

Examples are a tax on cars that use fuel inefficiently or on an industry that emits toxic chemicals into the air. Some people, particularly conservatives, believe taxation is a better way to achieve regulatory goals than setting mandatory standards because it gives individuals or businesses an incentive to comply and the choice not to.

5. *Limiting liability.* Some regulations are designed to discourage legal actions against individuals or firms. Congress has passed laws limiting the ability of patients to sue their HMOs and exempting manufacturers of the smallpox vaccine from liability for any side effects suffered from receiving the vaccine. Federal law also prohibits citizens from filing suits against nuclear power plants for personal or property losses resulting from a nuclear accident. In these cases, individuals or taxpayers, not the industry, assume the burden. Similarly, drafters of the Homeland Security bill sneaked in a provision exempting drug manufacturers from liability for the mercury content of vaccines, a provision having nothing to do with homeland security but a lot to do with protecting the financial interests of campaign donors. Government also provides individuals who live on the banks of rivers with flood insurance because private insurers will not insure homes in places that frequently flood. Opponents of such policies argue that this simply encourages individuals to engage in dangerous or risky behavior.

To save lives, federal regulations mandate testing autos for safety. These dummies allow simulation of the impact of crashes on humans. No doubt these crash test dummies were the inspiration for the rock group of the same name.

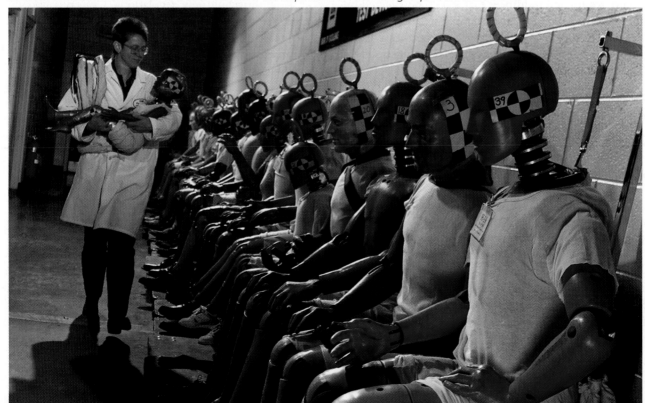

Brad Trent

The Regulatory Process

Many Americans blame federal bureaucrats when they are stymied by Byzantine rules or endless paperwork to get government approval for some activity. But regulation is a many-layered process with at least five different aspects: passing the legislation that defines regulatory goals, writing rules to achieve those goals, overseeing the rule writers, implementing and enforcing the rules, and keeping pace with change after the standards are set and rules are written. Here we discuss rule writing, oversight, and implementation, leaving to the next section the discussion of reforming rules to keep pace with change.

Writing Regulations

Most regulatory activity stems from very general, even vaguely stated, mandates because passing legislation, especially in a divided government, requires compromise. If bill writers were too specific, legislation would probably never get passed. When a bill is passed establishing some regulatory goal, such as driver safety, child labor protection, safe food, or clean air, its content rarely includes specifics on how the goals are to be achieved. Instead, as discussed in Chapter 12, after a bill becomes law, it is up to executive branch specialists to write the rules necessary to achieve these goals. Because most regulations are implemented at the state level, federal regulators often work with their state counterparts in writing these rules.

Laws granting regulatory authority often require public input, so citizens and interest groups also get involved in rule writing. This has been true since the beginning of the twentieth century for areas of regulatory policy such as food safety and fair labor practices. But historically, much of the public's input came from the interest groups and industries that would be affected by the rules being written. In fact, interest groups and industry lobbyists work so closely with regulators in writing rules that there is always concern, as discussed in Chapter 12, that agencies can be "captured" by those they are supposed to be regulating. Kenneth Lay, CEO of Enron, had a direct hand in selecting the man George W. Bush named to replace the head of the Federal Energy Regulatory Commission (FERC), the agency that was supposed to regulate Enron. Lay opposed the reappointment of the former head after he set limits on power prices and refused Enron greater access to the national power grid.[17] But congressional investigators found that FERC knew for at least a year that energy companies were withholding electricity supplies to drive up prices, yet FERC took no action against them.

In the 1960s, when the participation and procedural "revolutions" swept through government, Congress began placing more emphasis on citizen participation in rule writing. The Consumer Product Safety Act even authorized nongovernmental groups and organizations to submit their own versions of rules to agencies.[18] This movement to democratize the process by providing more public hearings and extended periods for public comment on regulations had advocates among both pro- and antiregulatory groups in Congress. On the one hand, it was a way to open up the process and make it more accountable, but it was also a way of slowing down the issuance of new rules by allowing many opportunities for rule opponents to impede the process. Where citizens see an immediate impact of rules, such as those on handling toxic waste in their communities, ensuring clean drinking water, defining safe foods, or placing restrictions on the use of public lands, a surprising number of people attend hearings or submit written comments. Using the Web sites of regulatory agencies to solicit comments has also greatly increased the public's role in writing rules.

Standards of Evaluation

No matter how many individuals and groups get involved in the process, writing effective regulations requires guidelines beyond the policies and goals stated in the authorizing legislation. One of the standards by which the effectiveness of any regulation is judged is whether it results in a net benefit for society. It is easy for both the average citizen and the bureaucrat to see that it is not cost-effective to enforce a rule requiring all workplace toilet seats to be horseshoe shaped. No one fought to prevent the rule's abolition. But in most cases, it is far more difficult to decide whether a rule has more negative than positive effects. How do we decide whether the risk involved in using a particular chemical or product, or working in a hazardous environment, is great enough to regulate? There is no agreement on which standard of evaluation should be used.

In authorizing new regulations, Congress uses different standards of risk. One is the "no-risk" standard: If a substance is found to cause cancer or present any life-threatening risk, it cannot be used—even in amounts well below the danger level. Sometimes called the better-safe-than-sorry rule, it is often applied to regulations on food and drug safety.

In other cases, the "margin of safety" criterion is used. The regulatory agency establishes a reasonable standard and then allows an extra margin of safety. For example, standards for clean air mandate the Environmental Protection Agency to declare how much lead, sulfur, and other materials can be in the air before it is judged unsafe. Then the agency is supposed to set the standards a little higher to allow the extra margin of safety.[19]

Sometimes Congress mandates a standard whereby cost of the regulation is to be weighed against the risk. The process of making this evaluation is called **cost–benefit analysis.** Today any rule that will have an economic impact greater than $100 million must be submitted to

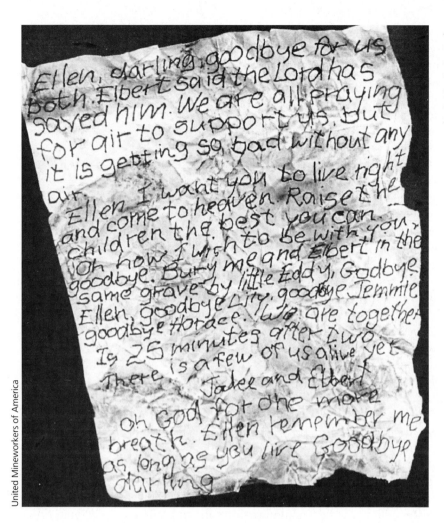

United Mineworkers of America

Jacob Vowell wrote this letter shortly before dying of suffocation in a mine disaster in Fraterville, Tennessee, in 1902. Such disasters eventually prompted government regulation of mining, which has since saved many lives, including the Pennsylvania miners rescued in summer 2002.

cost–benefit analysis. A rule governing consumer product safety, for example, would not be adopted unless the benefits outweigh the costs to business of complying with the rule. Generally, proregulation groups prefer the no-risk or extra margin standards, while antiregulation forces prefer cost–benefit analysis.

Deciding which standard to apply and assigning values to these standards inevitably involve both science and politics. For example, critics of cost–benefit analyses have charged that these analyses are not done fairly or competently.[20] They believe that costs are concrete and easily calculated, while benefits are often more difficult to put in dollar terms. How do you quantify saving human lives? If a particular rule is likely to save five lives per year at a cost of $5 million, does the regulation offer a net cost or a net benefit? It ultimately depends on a value judgment, which, critics charge, can be obscured by a cost-accountant mentality.

There was a time in the 1980s when the value placed on human life varied from $2 million at Occupational Safety and Health Administration (OSHA) to $1 million at the CPSC and $650,000 at the FAA.[21] One of the measures used to set values is lifetime earning power, so, for example, the life of a man with a college degree

would be worth more than that of a woman with a high school degree, and either life would be worth more than a child's. The ugliness of this type of calculation was brought home when private charities were making decisions on how much to compensate families of victims lost in the World Trade Center collapse. Because of their greater earning power, the lives of stockbrokers were deemed worthy of far more compensation than those of the fire fighters who died trying to save them. This is everyday decision making for insurance companies, but many citizens believe government should value lives equally and, where lives are at risk, should not use cost–benefit analysis in writing rules.

A more stringent variation of cost–benefit analysis called *risk assessment* was put in place in 1995 when the Gingrich Republicans assumed control of Congress. This standard for determining whether a rule is needed requires that the risks to the public of a particular product or act be assessed using rigid standards of scientific proof. In essence, risk assessment requires that the methods and data an agency presents to show proof of risk must be replicable in independent research by outside scientists. Risk assessment is the standard currently applied by regulatory overseers in the Bush administration.

Once in final form, rules are published in the *Code of Federal Regulations* and updated each year. Divided into more than three hundred categories, or titles, each representing a regulatory area, they total tens of thousands of pages. Title 40 alone—environmental protection rules—required twenty-seven volumes by 2002. But rule writing is just the beginning of the process.

Regulatory Oversight

Rule writing is overseen primarily by Congress and the president, but the federal courts have a role when an aggrieved party challenges the legality of rules or the interpretation of congressional intent. And the public has an oversight role that has been steadily increasing over the past thirty years.

The president has several ways to exercise oversight. Since the Carter administration, a principal means has been to issue executive orders that identify an overall rationale for rule writing that is in keeping with the political philosophy and goals of the administration. With Carter it was rational management and public participation; with Reagan and George H. Bush, it was cost–benefit analysis or, more specifically, eliminating rules whose implementation was costly to business. Clinton's executive orders stressed public participation and openness as well as cost-effectiveness.

Presidents also exercise oversight through their appointment powers, since all agency heads are presidential appointees. Most are selected on the basis of policy agreement with the president, but the head of the EPA is under more pressure to follow presidential preferences than ones on fixed-term appointments. In addition, a presidential appointee heads the Office of Management and Budget (OMB), which is the principal oversight agency for the executive branch, and which must approve agency budget requests.

The OMB authority to review agency rules derives from an executive order issued by President Reagan as part of his efforts in administrative deregulation. This innovation was designed to give the OMB the authority to identify and eliminate duplicate rules and to develop procedures for cost–benefit analyses. Reagan gave OMB the job of reviewing rules from more than fifty federal agencies. Many argued that giving this power to the OMB would erode the independence of regulatory agencies. This was, no doubt, partly the intent of the change. Regulations developed by agencies under formal rules and according to due process could be killed by the OMB without any public hearings or advance notification. This violated the spirit of the Administrative Procedure Act, which requires openness in rule making, and it diminished governmental responsiveness to the general public. For example, EPA rules for limiting the amount of toxic chemicals that industries could dump in municipal sewage systems were killed three months after they were issued. This undoing of the rules followed extensive lobbying of the OMB by chemical manufacturers and other producers of toxic wastes.[22]

In the first Bush administration, much of the president's oversight function was assigned to a new group, the Council on Competitiveness, headed by the vice president and devoted to making American business more competitive. Known for their devotion to deregulation, council members were often asked to review new rules, especially environmental regulations, opposed by business. Although Bush supported passage of the Clean Air Act of 1990, he allowed the council to gut one of its main provisions when it killed a rule that required industries to inform the EPA whenever they exceeded permitted pollution levels.[23]

One of the first regulatory reforms initiated by the Clinton administration was to abolish the Council on Competitiveness. And Clinton limited OIRA's ability to kill rules by requiring OMB approval only for rules whose economic impact was $100 million or greater. However, in an attempt to further diminish the rule-writing authority of agencies, Congress passed the Congressional Review Act, which requires agencies to submit proposed regulations to Congress and the GAO and gives them fast-track authority to reject new rules.[24]

These examples illustrate some of the difficulties the oversight function presents to regulatory agencies. Each new administration can send different guidelines, often by executive order, for writing rules or for the standards of evaluation written into rules. Just as an agency starts carrying out a directive—sometimes even before it has had the chance—administrations change, or control of Congress changes hands, and all the proceeding guidelines are overridden by new legislation or executive orders. Just as regulatory policy changed when George H. Bush left office and Clinton entered, there were also sharp differences between Clinton's last directives to regulatory agencies and those sent by George W. Bush, as will be discussed later in the chapter. Although regulatory agencies are frequently criticized for waste and inefficiency, they have to work under this burden of constantly shifting directions.

Ultimately, it is Congress that has the broadest powers of oversight because, at the beginning of the process, it can influence the ways rules are written by the clarity of direction it writes into the enabling legislation. Congress can also amend the original law, change budget authorization for agencies, or attach riders to appropriations bills that effectively kill agency-written rules.

Like presidents, members of Congress also try to impose their political agendas on regulatory agencies. The Gingrich Republicans were zealously committed to deregulation and insisted on the use of the risk assessment standard to determine whether a rule was necessary. They also supported opening the process of rule writing further to peer and judicial review, hoping proposed regulations would die while tied up in administrative and court challenges. Critics called the Gingrich policy the paralysis approach to deregulation: "Its cleverness lies not in streamlining the regulatory process but in adding 31 new steps, two additional years of review, and $700,000 in additional cost to every rule issued by the [EPA] and other federal agencies. . . . In case that doesn't work, [it] also creates 267 new opportunities to sue at every step of agency rulemaking." The process was likened to injecting Arnold Schwarzenegger with steroids, "in hopes he soon will be so musclebound he can't move at all."[25]

Congressional oversight can also affect the regulatory process when committees become captured by lobbyists. The recent wave of corporate corruption scandals, for example, had as much to do with the failure of congressional oversight as it did with the laxness of regulatory agencies. Taking just one aspect of the scandal, the misrepresentation of corporate earnings, it is clear that Congress prevented regulatory agencies from doing their job. In the late 1990s, the Financial Accounting Standards Board (FASBE, pronounced "fasby") proposed a new rule that would prohibit corporations from giving their employees stock options without counting them as a business expense. These options cost companies hundreds of millions of dollars, yet corporations were not required to subtract them from their earnings. The effect of this was to greatly inflate the annual earnings reports and mislead investors into thinking the companies were in much better shape than they were.

FASBE's proposed rule had the support of the chairman of the Securities and Exchange Commission, but it did not go over well among powerful members of Congress who collectively had received millions of dollars in campaign contributions from accounting firms. Senators Christopher Dodd and Joseph Lieberman, both Democrats from Connecticut (the site of many corporate headquarters), led a successful fight for a Senate resolution repudiating FASBE's proposed rule. FASBE retreated, as did the SEC chair, Arthur Levitt, who later said it was the worst decision he made at the SEC.[26]

Congress also balked when Levitt proposed a new SEC rule to restrict accounting firms from acting as consultants to the corporations they audited. House Energy and Commerce Committee chair, Billy Tauzin (R-La.), sent Levitt a four-page list of detailed questions about the rule and also told him that an appearance of conflict of interest was not enough; he must provide proof that auditors' objectivity was undermined by serving in the dual role of consultant. Soon Levitt received similar letters of objection from forty-six other congressmen. And, at the request of industry lobbyists,

Henry Bonilla, (R-Tex.), a member of the House Appropriations Committee, threatened to cut the SEC's budget. Levitt fought back by organizing a nationwide series of public hearings, but Congress delayed the rule on procedural grounds, knowing Levitt's term was near an end.[27] (Chapter 9's "You Are There" discusses more of this episode.)

These abuses of the oversight function to win concessions for political supporters and campaign contributors are a huge challenge to effective rule writing and enforcement, and they are not likely to go away. There are seventy-five lobbyists in Washington for every member of Congress; many have deep pockets.[28] The defeat of the FASBE and SEC rules contributed to investor losses in excess of $60 billion, the bankruptcy of Enron and other corporations, and the collapse of the accounting firm Arthur Anderson. And the corporate malpractice that led to these failures was then investigated by the very oversight committees whose members thwarted the rules that might have prevented it.

Implementing and Enforcing Regulations

Federal and state regulatory agencies share the responsibility for the implementation and enforcement of those rules not killed in the oversight process. After standards and general rules are set by federal agencies, the specific plans for implementing them are designed by state regulators. Because state bureaucracies often divide functional authority differently than the federal government, responsibility for implementing rules on worker safety, fair labor practices, toxic emissions into the air and water, or disposal of hazardous waste may be spread over multiple agencies, each of which may have played some role in writing or refining rules as well as in their enforcement. The challenges to effective implementation are enormous due to the number of agencies, scientists, legislators, and regulated parties involved and the political and technical differences among them. Moreover, divided government, court challenges, and federal and state disagreement over jurisdiction also present obstacles to effective implementation.

We have already seen how divided government can impede implementation of rules if the president and the majority in Congress have different views on regulation. But the regulators themselves are often divided on policy issues. The directors of federal agencies might be from a different party than the heads of state agencies, and their views on regulation and commitment to enforcement can vary considerably. Furthermore, the scientists and technicians who staff regulatory agencies may well be guided more by professional competence than by the policy preferences of an agency head or elected official.

Regulated industries or other affected parties often refuse to comply with rules or the standards on which they are based. They frequently challenge the jurisdiction of the agencies, the constitutionality of rules, and the reasonableness of standards in federal courts. Every health standard ever issued by OSHA has been challenged in court. And each year hundreds of EPA rules are subjects of lawsuits.[29] Federal regulators also find that, in practice, some rules are nitpicking and not worth enforcing or that enforcement costs more than any benefit that might be gained. Other rules are based on standards that end up not working well to achieve the goal. In the current era of rapid technological change, some rules, and the standards they are based on, become obsolete soon after they are written. This is especially true for the regulation of telecommunications and biotechnology.

Then there are the inevitable disagreements over jurisdiction between federal and state rule makers. For example, some states have resisted implementing rules that they think will endanger their ability to attract industry or that they believe give federal authorities too much say over their state resources (for example, conservation of wetlands and wilderness areas, or protection of animals on the endangered species list). Governors and other state officials are far closer to the electorate in their states than Washington bureaucrats are and more likely to listen to them than to an EPA, OSHA, or FDA administrator.

One recent example of state regulators resisting federal jurisdiction comes from the deregulation of electric utilities. In the 1990s, twenty-four states deregulated their utilities, leaving them free to buy and sell electricity wherever they could get the best price, from independent companies and peaker plants (companies that generate electricity for sale just during peak periods of use), rather than from in-state plants. This approach required transmitting electricity around the country from generating plants to wherever it was most needed at any point in time. So the deregulated power plants could purchase electricity from sources hundreds and even a thousand miles away. As new plants entered the market, the demand for use of the national grid system to transmit electricity increased, leading to regional electricity shortages and brownouts. Congress ordered monopoly utilities in regulated states to allow other companies to use their grids, but the states believed they should retain the regulatory authority they had always had over utilities. Congress argued that power transmitted across a national grid system is interstate commerce, and only Congress has the authority to regulate it. The result was a tug of war between Congress and the states over regulation of utilities.[30]

Thus, as we have seen, every phase of the regulatory process is open to influence by parties affected by the content of regulations. Those with a direct stake in a particular type of regulation can give testimony and lobby influential legislators while legislation is being written. They can lobby bureaucrats who write the rules mandated by legislation, agency heads responsible for implementation of rules, or members of congressional committees with oversight functions. Rules, and the way they are or are not enforced, can be appealed to the agencies issuing them and in some cases challenged in federal courts. For powerful interest groups, there are opportunities to pressure the White House on the appointment of agency heads and the content of specific rules.

Because regulation does incur costs as it bestows benefits, it is inevitable that those who sustain the costs will compete with those seeking benefits to influence the process of writing and implementing rules. All of this competition between pro- and antiregulation forces, between regulators and the regulated, and among the regulators themselves, slows implementation and enforcement of rules designed to achieve regulatory goals established by Congress. Effective implementation is also slowed by weak enforcement powers. Although agencies are authorized to assess penalties for noncompliance, these punishments are usually negligible. In the face of these obstacles, it is amazing how much federal and state regulators have been able to achieve in protecting lives, safeguarding the environment, and promoting equity and competitiveness in the marketplace. (See the "Regulating to Save Lives" box.)

Cycles of Regulation

Like other government activity, the push for government regulation comes in fits and starts. The first spurt came in the late 1800s, when a poor economy led to charges, especially by farmers, that the large corporations of the day were exploiting the public. In 1890 with the Sherman Antitrust Act, Congress prohibited firms from conspiring to set prices or in other ways to restrain trade. It also declared monopolies illegal and established the Interstate Commerce Commission to regulate the railroads.

The next burst of regulatory activity came after the turn of the century, in the Progressive era. Demands for consumer protection arose largely because industrialization and railroad transportation created national markets for goods formerly produced and consumed locally. In these new national markets, consumers had little recourse if the products they bought from distant companies were not safe or reliable. Consumer fraud became endemic. Business engaged in deceptive advertising, food products often contained harmful substances (Coca-Cola contained cocaine; formaldehyde was used

Most Americans share the belief that the private sector can do many things better than government and have a general distaste for red tape and in-your-face government.

But it was the federal government, not industry, that took the initiative on environmental protection and workplace health and safety. Federal regulations have resulted in a multitude of benefits for the American public. Workers are safer on the job, endangered species have been saved, large-scale reforestation has taken place, and recycling has become commonplace.

Although to some Americans there is no such thing as a good regulation, most would agree that the following federal regulations, many administered by state governments, are examples of what government does right. The benefits have not come cheap, but all have been realized through regulatory activity.

Because of government regulations mandating unleaded and lower leaded gasoline, the lead content of the air has dramatically decreased. Fewer children have brain damage, and fewer adults have high blood pressure from airborne lead.[1] When testing began, measurable levels of lead in children were eight times higher than they are today.[2]

Crib safety standards have reduced infant crib deaths by 44 percent since 1974, and standards for fire-resistant children's sleepwear have reduced serious burns and deaths by 20 percent. A regulation requiring collapsible steering columns on cars and trucks is estimated to have saved twenty-six thousand lives over a twenty-five-year period.[3] Requiring baby seats in cars has saved thousands more.

Industrial accidents and deaths decreased because of OSHA's rules on workplace safety. In one two-year period, these rules prevented an estimated 350 deaths and saved $15 billion in lost time and employee compensation for accidents. In 1999, workplace injuries and illnesses fell to the lowest rate on record.[4]

In 1965, more than 50 percent of men and about 35 percent of women smoked; smoking is linked to one in seven deaths in the United States and costs billions in health care.[5] Restrictions on tobacco use and advertising, and an aggressive public education campaign, have helped reduce the number of Americans who smoke to about a quarter of the adult population.

FDA testing of over-the-counter and prescription drugs has saved an untold number of lives. Although the testing process lengthens the time it takes to get products on the market, American drugs have been safer than those produced in Europe, where the regulatory process is less stringent. Of all the drugs removed from the market as unsafe between 1990 and 1992, only nine were U.S. made, and three involved criminal withholding of evidence of risk by the manufacturers.[6]

Despite the problems in regulating the environment, there have been significant successes. In 1972, the Great Lakes were near cesspools, and Lake Erie was in such a bad state that it caught on fire. Today, 60 percent of all rivers and lakes are safe for swimming and fishing, and 89 percent of Americans have safe drinking water.[7] Although Americans are driving almost two and a half times as many miles as they drove in 1970, their cars are emitting 41 percent fewer pollutants; and since 1988, the health risk from chronic exposure to toxic chemicals has decreased by over two-thirds.[8] Los Angeles has the cleanest air in the forty years air quality has been monitored; it had no smog alerts in 1999, compared to 122 in 1978. While the Superfund program is cleaning up the worst toxic waste sites around the country, the EPA's Brownfields program is helping reclaim abandoned industrial and commercial sites in inner cities (brownfields) by providing tax incentives to private investors to clean them up and start new business. As dangerous waste sites are being reclaimed and neighborhoods made safer for children to play in, new industries and jobs are being brought into neglected urban areas.

If the federal government had not regulated these activities, who would have? Would it have been done better or cheaper?

1. David Bollier and Joan Claybrook, *Freedom from Harm* (Washington, D.C.: Public Citizen and Democracy Project, 1986).
2. "Kids and Chemicals," Bill Moyers's *Now*, PBS, May, 10, 2002. Transcript online at www.pbs.org.
3. *Lincoln Journal,* April 19, 1987, 7.
4. *Budget of the U.S. Government, Fiscal Year 2001* (Washington, D.C.: U.S. Government Printing Office, 2000).
5. "Cigarette Makers Reach $368 Billion Accord to Curb Lawsuits and Curtail Marketing," *New York Times,* June 21, 1997, 8.
6. Peter H. Stone, "Ganging up on the FDA," *National Journal,* February 18, 1995, 412–413.
7. Gregg Easterbrook, "Here Comes the Sun," *New Yorker,* April 10, 1995, 39–40; *Budget of the U.S. Government, Fiscal Year 2001,* 86.
8. *Budget of the United States for Fiscal Year 2003,* 304; Barbara Whitaker, "Los Angeles Loses Distinction: Worst Summer Smog Day," *New York Times,* September 5, 1999, 15.

to preserve milk), and popular patent medicine usually contained alcohol or addictive drugs, such as opium.[31] Reformers also pointed to unsafe and unsanitary conditions in the meat-packing industry. After the media and so-called muckrakers highlighted these scandals, Congress banned certain food additives, prohibited false claims about products, and gave the Department of Agriculture power to inspect meat sold in interstate commerce.

The New Deal era spurred further regulatory activity. After one hundred people died from an unsafe drug, Congress passed an act mandating that the FDA declare a drug safe before it could be marketed. In the activist 1960s and 1970s, reformers were again influential in pressuring Congress to undertake new regulatory activity. Agencies were established to regulate consumer product safety (the CPSC), the environment (the EPA), and industrial safety (OSHA). The powers of older agencies, such as the Federal Trade Commission (FTC),were strengthened.

Deregulation

As long as there has been regulation, there have been demands for **deregulation**—that is, ending or paring back regulation in a particular area. Although deregulation has had broad bipartisan support since the 1970s, there are partisan differences in the nature of this support. Democrats tend to support deregulation to the extent that it makes business activity more efficient and less cumbersome. Republicans are more likely to see this as a starting point and go further by opposing in principle certain kinds of regulation—working conditions, product safety, and a minimum wage, for example—as interference with market competition.

Deregulation can be carried out legislatively—that is, by act of Congress—or administratively—by executive orders, new appointments, and the oversight function of the OMB. One method of administrative deregulation is to strip regulatory agencies of personnel and budgets. This was a favored tactic of President Reagan; it was not until the last year of his administration that regulatory agencies (with the exception of the EPA) recovered to the level of funding they had when he entered office.

Another way to deregulate administratively is to appoint agency heads who favor either little regulation or self-regulation by industry. This will almost ensure that the number of regulations proposed and enacted decreases, and that enforcement slows too. Reagan used this means to deregulate at EPA and OSHA in particular, and George W. Bush has taken this approach to almost every area of rule making. To regulate the energy industry, he appointed a man recommended by leaders of the industries he would be regulating. Similarly, to head the SEC and regulate the stock market, Bush chose Harvey Pitt, a corporate lawyer whose career had been spent representing some of Wall Street's most powerful firms and who immediately said he would make the SEC an "accountant-friendly" place. To deal with possible conflicts of interest created by stock analysts rating stocks in which they had a financial stake, Pitt proposed as an alternative to writing new rules an honor system that would require brokers to sign a statement denying they benefited financially from their ratings.[32] Pitt finally became a liability to the Bush administration and was forced to resign after he named to head a new accounting oversight board a man who had chaired the audit committee of an accounting firm under investigation for fraud.

In addition to his appointment powers, a president can also use executive orders to deregulate—just as he can to regulate—by sending directives to agencies changing evaluation standards or implementation and enforcement procedures. This is one way for a president to bypass Congress—and perhaps a necessary way when Congress is controlled by an opposing party—to pursue some of his objectives. But, as noted earlier, these actions do not have the permanence of legislative measures. The next president can revoke existing guidelines by issuing his own countermanding executive orders.

Types of Deregulation

Legislative and administrative deregulators may cast a narrow net, targeting individual rules, industries, or specific agencies, or a broad net, targeting the entire regulatory apparatus.

Eliminating Rules Presidents Carter, Reagan, and Clinton promoted regulatory reform through the elimination of unnecessary rules. During the Carter administration, OSHA abolished more than 1,100 of its 10,000 rules; many, such as the horseshoe-shaped toilet seat rule, had been severely criticized as nitpicking. OSHA paperwork requirements, particularly for small businesses, were reduced, and safety inspections were concentrated on the industries with the worst safety records. The Reagan administration continued this pattern.

But at the outset of the Clinton administration, federal statutes and formal rules still totaled about 100 mil-

"I've deregulated Arthur, but he still doesn't run very efficiently."

lion words. OSHA's remaining four thousand major regulations specified "everything from the height of railings to how much a plank can stick out from a temporary scaffold," although most of its 140 regulations on wooden ladders were eliminated.[33]

It is easy to see why rule elimination is a logical target for a deregulator: It is not only costly and inefficient to monitor and enforce rules on the grain of wood in ladders; it is also impossible. There are not enough inspectors even to enforce safety rules, and most rules do deal with health and safety issues.

There is a documentable difference between Republican and Democratic administrations in commitment to rule enforcement. During the height of the Reagan–Bush deregulatory push in the 1980s, when the number of OSHA inspectors was cut by 25 percent and one-third of its field offices were closed, there were from 10 to 12 deaths per 100,000 workers each year. By the end of the Clinton administration, which imposed tougher rules and beefed up enforcement, that ratio had fallen to 4.5 per 100,000.[34] Deregulators believe there is no correlation between those figures and federal safety rules; they say the death rate has been falling since 1974 (it has), and any decline is due to employers improving working conditions and becoming more safety-conscious because it is in their interest to do so.

The year 2001 will stand out as an exception in this pattern as the destruction of the World Trade Center sent the number of annual workplace deaths skyrocketing. Clearly, the terrorists bear primary responsibility for the deaths, but faulty fireproofing, stairwell design, and elevator placement have been cited as adding to the number unable to escape the buildings.

Deregulating by Industry Many proponents of deregulation argue that it is not enough to streamline, eliminate the more trivial rules, and make regulators more accountable; in some areas, regulators simply should not be regulating at all.

Deregulating by industry began in the Carter administration with trucking, the railroads, and the airlines, and it had strong bipartisan support. The advantage to industry of less regulation is transparent, but it is also meant to benefit consumers by providing greater choice and lower prices or fares due to increased competition and greater efficiency in the marketplace. Not everyone agrees that these goals have been achieved by wholesale deregulation of industries. Here we look at the example of the airline industry.

From 1938 until 1978, commercial airlines were heavily regulated by the Civil Aeronautics Board (CAB) and needed its approval to select routes and set fares. Originally, regulations were designed to help the struggling airline industry by protecting it from competition.

This worked so well for existing air carriers that after forty years of federal rule making, it was almost impossible for new airlines to enter the industry. By the mid-1970s, however, when the oil crisis had caused fares to skyrocket and several airlines were in economic difficulty, many in Congress felt it was time to deregulate. In 1978, President Carter signed a bill phasing in deregulation. The CAB was abolished, and regulation was left to the Federal Aviation Administration (FAA), which oversees air safety.

By opening up competition among the airlines, proponents of deregulation hoped the airlines would seek ways to become more efficient and then lower fares. Airlines were allowed to fly new routes without CAB approval and were permitted flexibility in setting their fares. But Congress also provided subsidies to carriers serving small communities to ensure they did not abandon unprofitable routes.

In its early years, deregulation did increase competition; the number of airlines nearly tripled between 1978 and 1983, and the number of people choosing to travel by air doubled by the 1990s. But comparatively little money went into expanding airports, upgrading air traffic control equipment, or building new airports. Only six new runways were built at the largest airports during the 1990s, and Denver's International is the only major airport to have been built since 1976. Travelers had more flights to choose from, but planes became more crowded, flying at 70 to 80 percent of capacity compared to 50 percent in the decade before deregulation. Passenger complaints and lost baggage claims skyrocketed. Although average airfares dropped 36 percent after deregulation, passengers had to contend with a Byzantine system for setting fares. On one 1997 United Airlines domestic flight, for example, twenty-nine passengers with identical coach accommodations paid twenty-three different fares, ranging from $87 to $728.[35]

Deregulation had a much stronger downside for small and midsize cities that often were left with a single carrier and monopoly prices. The impact on rural areas has been described as "an unmitigated disaster." Since the lowest fares went to travelers who could plan well ahead or fly stand-by, business travelers with fixed appointments made at short notice were the hardest hit economically; in 2000, they were paying 50 percent more than they had in 1996.[36]

There was also evidence that in the struggle to be competitive and profitable, some airlines shortchanged passenger safety. Due to the higher volume of air traffic, jets built in the 1960s were kept in service beyond their planned life span, and today American carriers have the oldest jet fleet in service in the industrialized world.[37] In addition, the number of experienced mechanics available to service them declined. According to government reports, Valujet had an accident rate fourteen times higher than that of the major airlines before its poor safety record put it out of business.[38] The former inspector general of the Department of Transportation was so alarmed by the FAA's failure to enforce air safety regulations that she resigned and wrote a book about it.[39] Yet for the industry as a whole, the number of fatalities per passenger fell so dramatically that by 2000 the only safer mode of transportation was a city bus.[40]

The problem with deregulating airlines to foster competition is that it requires big capital outlays for a new company to break into the market. The first carriers were protected from competition by the Civil Aeronautics Board, the now-defunct independent regulatory agency, but for the postderegulation startups, there was no such protection. Many airlines folded or sold out during the recession of the early 1980s. By 1990, the eight largest airlines controlled about 90 percent of all commercial air travel in the United States. In the economic recovery of the late 1990s, airlines' business boomed, but their profit margins remained below those of other major industries. To cut costs, airlines began forming strategic alliances; Continental and Northwest, Delta and United, and American and US Airways formed alliances with their major international competitors that gave them control over 82 percent of domestic air travel. Although national security policies prohibit U.S. carriers from merging with foreign airlines, these "proxy mergers" allowed them to share flight codes, coordinate schedules and baggage handling, and honor one another's frequent flyer programs.[41] The major carriers also planned further domestic consolidation, with United Airlines bidding for US Airways, the country's sixth largest carrier. Had Congress not stopped the merger, United would have accounted for about 25 percent of the country's air travel.[42]

Competition was also diminished when the airlines divided up the nation into regional turfs. In ten major cities, two-thirds of the air traffic fell under the control of one airline, such as TWA in St. Louis and Northwest in Minneapolis and Detroit. In the huge hub airports at Chicago and Atlanta, two airlines, United and American, gained control of three-fourths of the traffic.

This domination contributed to the congestion at major airports. The special twenty- to thirty-year leasing arrangements major carriers made with large airports gave a single airline control over much of the traffic and a de facto veto power over airport expansion. The dominant airlines at hub airports were able to stop expansion projects that would provide new gates for potential competitors.[43]

At these airports, the daily number of allowable landings and takeoffs is set by the federal government. When the Department of Transportation allocated those slots, they were divided among all carriers, but since 1986, when carriers were freed to buy, sell, lease, or trade their landing and takeoff slots, the major carriers gained control of 98 percent of airport slots.[44] Not surprisingly, a Government Accounting Office study showed that at concentrated or "fortress" hubs, the fares of the dominant airlines were consistently higher than the fares at other airports.[45] And trying to route most passengers through hub airports to make connecting flights led to enormous inefficiencies. Although the country has 429 airports, 70 percent of all air traffic is routed through just 31 of them.[46] That makes most of the nation's flights dependent on the weather in hub cities, and when flights are grounded there, traffic backs up around the country. By 2000, the busiest airports were plagued by flight delays, canceled flights, and angry passengers.

When deregulation of the airline industry was approved, the government thought it was encouraging more competition, greater efficiency, and lower fares. But by 2000, the growing consolidation in the industry, the explosion of consumer complaints, and heavy lobbying by business travelers for price relief led Congress to consider thirteen passenger bills of rights. The airlines promised to reform themselves and Congress tabled its legislation, but many members were ready to reregulate when they were confronted with the merger proposals. If approved, the industry could have ended up with less competition than it had in 1978, when it had been deregulated precisely to foster competition. "With only three carriers, we'd have to treat them as a utility," one member of Congress said. "Nobody wants to talk about the nasty-R word, but the reality is it may have to happen."[47] Then came the terrorist attacks of 9/11, making 2001 the worst year in American aviation history. (See the "After 9/11" box.)

Reregulation

In politics as in physics, actions usually produce reactions. Actions to deregulate bring cries for a resumption of regulatory activity, or **reregulation.** Airline deregulation is an example of this cycle of action and reaction, as are electric utilities and corporate accounting practices.

Banking is still another example of how industry deregulation led to reregulation, but only after it had cost taxpayers $150 billion. Traditionally, banks and savings and loan (S&L) institutions were heavily regulated and protected from competition. But during the 1970s and early 1980s, interest rates rose rapidly, and banks and S&Ls competed fiercely to retain their depositors and attract new ones. They were also in competition with the federal government for investors' money as interest rates on treasury notes continued to rise. In the bipartisan deregulatory mood of the time, Congress adopted a series of measures, beginning in 1980, to deregulate many aspects of the banking industry. To help S&Ls be more competitive, the cap was lifted on the interest they could pay depositors; at the same time, Congress raised the maximum level of federal deposit insurance allowable on each account. Both banks and S&Ls were given more freedom to decide what financial services to offer. Within days, interest was being paid on checking accounts; credit card companies raised their interest rates; brokerage, insurance firms, and even department stores got into the banking business; and S&Ls offered a new range of services and made new types of investments formerly prohibited.

With the cap removed on interest rates, some S&Ls attracted new depositors by paying interest rates that were more than double the interest rates their mortgage holders were paying. With these policies, it was only a matter of time before the S&Ls would go broke, unless they made windfall profits from their investments. As a result, many S&Ls, big and small, made increasingly risky investments to survive and profit in the now highly competitive atmosphere. Banks, too, made high-risk loans to foreign governments and domestic farmers, while some S&Ls made shaky real estate investments, then saw the bottom drop out of their investments when real estate prices plummeted.

During this period, federal scrutiny of bank and S&L activities fell off drastically, even though the government, through its deposit insurance program, guaranteed each deposit (of up to $100,000) that the banks and S&Ls used for their risky investments. Charles E. Schumer (D-N.Y.) said the government "behaved like a fire insurance company that said to its customers: 'Go ahead, play with matches. We'll cover you if anything goes wrong.'"

The Federal Home Loan Bank Board, which regulates S&Ls, was repeatedly denied its requests for more examiners and auditors. In the last half of the 1980s, one thousand banks failed, including the nation's eighth largest, Continental Illinois. Thanks to the federal deposit insurance program, few individuals lost their savings, but it took an additional $4 billion loan from the government to restore Continental Illinois to solvency.

The S&L crisis proved much more costly; 27 percent of all thrifts failed. Covering the losses, the federal insurance company for S&Ls, the Federal Savings and Loan Insurance Corporation (FSLIC), went broke. As a consequence, the Federal Deposit Insurance Corporation (FDIC), the institution that insures bank deposits, took control of more than two hundred S&Ls, trying to put them on a sounder financial base. By 1996, about $150 billion of taxpayer money had been committed to the bailout.

In short, deregulation in the financial industry led to disaster. Proponents of deregulation argue that a truly free market would be more efficient because consistently bad business decisions would bring failure

The bank failures of the 1930s, which wiped out the life savings of ordinary and wealthy citizens alike, led the government to provide insurance for depositors at banks and savings and loans. This program meant that the taxpayers in general, and not individual depositors, paid the bill when reckless and sometimes illegal actions of banks and savings and loans caused a new round of failures after deregulation in the 1970s.

Paula Nelson/Dallas Morning News

REREGULATING THE AIRLINES

Even before the 9/11 attacks, the government had been trying to find the right balance between regulation and deregulation of the airline industry. In 2001, with major carriers entering into alliances to control huge chunks of the market and passenger dissatisfaction growing, Congress was considering a variety of reregulatory measures. The hijackings and fatalities on September 11 forced Congress to consider far more sweeping legislation. The immediate economic impact on the industry was severe: All air traffic in the United States was temporarily grounded, then restricted; National Guard troops policed airport concourses, emergency security measures were imposed, and passengers stayed away in droves. Within days, Congress was asked to approve a financial bailout for the industry, and it was also faced with the much larger problem of reregulating to prevent future terrorist attacks.

In the year before the attacks, the air passenger and freight industry had revenues of $130 billion, employed 685,000 people, and helped create millions of other jobs in travel, tourism, and aircraft manufacture.[1] Because of its importance to the country's economic health, and because the recession was already cutting into industry revenues when the attacks occurred, government aid provoked little debate or contro-versy. It took Congress just a few weeks to approve a $15 billion bailout package, including $5 billion in grants and $10 billion in guaranteed loans.

Some help was needed, but Congress found itself offering subsidies to an industry whose major players had recently been muscling out competition, exploiting their best customers—business travelers—and whose overexpansion and bad management practices had put them in serious economic difficulties before 9/11 ever happened. United, for example, had lost more than a half billion dollars in the first half of 2001.

Congress delegated authority to decide which airlines would get how much to a new Air Transportation Stabilization Board (ATSB), with Fed Chair Alan Greenspan as chair. The panel was to grant loans to airlines with the strongest business plans and to deny help to any airline that looked as if it was going to fail. In return, airlines receiving aid were asked to give the government an equity stake in their companies.[2]

Congress also tightened regulation to try to prevent future hijackings. The lapses that allowed the terrorists to board the flights that crashed on 9/11 were due both to inadequate federal safety standards and to indifferent airline enforcement. The standard security questions directed at passengers had long since become a joke. At electronic check-ins, passengers were allowed to answer the questions on the whereabouts and packing of their luggage just by pressing options offered on a computer screen. One reporter said it was as if airport security expected travelers to ask one another, "Dear, did we pack the nuclear waste in your suitcase or mine?" or, "Honey, is the plutonium in your purse or the black duffel?"[3]

A study of twenty thousand cases handled by the FAA in the 1990s showed a dismal security record for both the airlines and the agency. The FAA's main enforcement action had been to issue warning letters to airlines; fines were levied in only 25 percent of all cases, including incidents involving weapons infractions. In the year prior to the attacks, government inspectors found that screeners had failed to detect dangerous objects hidden in baggage 20 percent of the time.[4] Passenger and baggage screening had been privatized and contracted out by airport management. The contractors often did not do background checks and hired many workers who knew little English, were poorly educated, and had little training in screening procedures. Although it provoked a furious debate between deregulators and reregulators, Congress decided to end privatization and make all airport screeners federal employees, requiring citizenship and a

without benefit of a taxpayer rescue. But in the case of Continental Illinois and the hundreds of insolvent S&Ls, the government believed the nation could not afford to let them go under. Huge banks defaulting and millions of people losing their savings would send shockwaves throughout the nation, so the federal government stepped in to save them. Thus, critics of banking deregulation argue that since banks have the luxury of Uncle Sam's pocketbook when things go wrong, they should be forced by Uncle Sam to conduct themselves in a prudent manner. The S&L bailout reflected this view by imposing tougher new regulations that S&Ls must now meet.

Deregulation: The Next Round

Reregulation, especially by industry, is often a response to a transparent failure of deregulation, sometimes of crisis proportions, as with S&L failures, power shortages, airline security, and corporate bankruptcies. For the most part, support for reregulation has remained industry-specific. Where there are no crises looming,

high school diploma, upgrading pay and benefits, and imposing more rigorous training standards. But the new job requirements applied only to the eighty-one largest airports. That left security procedures at 348 other airports for the government to tackle later.

Congress also required airports to purchase new, much more sensitive screening equipment, screen all check-in luggage, and thoroughly search all carry-on bags and passengers. As added protection, Congress reinstated the old sky marshal program, putting security guards on passenger flights. Among the most controversial changes were the authorization of pilots to carry guns and limitations on the legal liability of airlines for injuries caused by those pilots.

The success of these measures will depend at least partially on well-trained and motivated personnel. But a year after the attacks, all major airports asked for extensions on deadlines for putting the new policies in effect. There was a shortage of the new screening machines and of money to buy them or to train personnel, despite the new security fees added to passenger fares.

The dire state of the industry after 9/11 led to many operational changes that could improve the efficiency and overall performance of the big airlines. With travel down, airlines permanently eliminated flights to cities already well

served by other carriers. And competition increased as small no-frills airlines stepped into the breach and won over many passengers who had relied on the large carriers. A year after 9/11, low-fare airlines were carrying more than 20 percent of all air passengers in the United States.[5] They fly point to point without connecting flights, avoiding hub airports. Some lines fly only a single type of aircraft, cutting down on training and maintenance costs, and many have no food service or frequent flier plans. Businesses that had begun cutting travel budgets well before 9/11 started flocking to the discount airlines, a big blow to the major carriers, which make most of their profits from business travelers.[6]

But will discount airlines be able to stay in business? The early years of deregulation saw the same flurry of new carriers only to see them disappear within a decade; in fact, since 1978, 137 carriers have filed for bankruptcy. And in the years from the end of World War II until 1994, "the sum of the industry's profits and losses was less than zero." This led investment analyst Warren Buffet to suggest that it might have been "a blessing for shareholders if someone had thought to shoot down Orville Wright at Kitty Hawk."[7]

But four airliners still control two-thirds of the domestic market, and five global alliances control three-quarters of

international travel.[8] Some industry analysts see the continued dominance of megacarriers as inevitable because the industry, like information technology or telecommunications, evolves "toward heavy concentrations among a few players because of the high barriers to entry and heavy capital costs." This is the view of those who see the airline industry as a combination public-private enterprise that should be treated like a controlled monopoly and exempt from antitrust rules. They believe the benefits to consumers (low fares, more routes, standardized service) are worth it. But deregulation advocates say that it should be left to the marketplace to determine which carriers will survive the industry crisis.[9]

1. Alex Berenson," Cry for Help: This Industry Doesn't Fly," *New York Times*, November 18, 2001, Section 4, 5.
2. Laurence Zuckerman, "Do All Airlines Deserve a Taxpayer Rescue?" *New York Times*, October 2, 2001, Section 3, 1, 10.
3. Thomas L. Friedman, "Naked Air," *New York Times*, December 26, 2001, A3.
4. "Few Airlines Pay for Mistakes, *Champaign-Urbana News-Gazette*, September 26, 2001, A3.
5. David Leonhardt and Micheline Maynard, "Troubled Airlines Face Reality: Those Cheap Fares Have a Price," *New York Times*, August 18, 2002, 1.
6. "Bargain Airlines," *News Hour with Jim Lehrer*, PBS, September 17, 2002.
7. Roger Lowenstein, "Into Thin Air," *New York Times Magazine*, February 17, 2002, 40–42.
8. Stephen Labaton, "Airlines and Antitrust: A New World. Or Not," *New York Times*, November 18, 2001, Section 3, 1.
9. Ibid., 13.

the default rhetorical position for most elected officials is to favor deregulation wherever possible.

The principle of deregulation has been gaining momentum ever since the Carter administration. In the Reagan years, it became an ideological position. In the early 1990s, as the country faced huge budget and trade deficits and an economy that was barely growing, there was near unanimous support for reducing the regulatory burden on both private and public entities to see whether it would help speed the economic recovery. During the long period of economic expansion that fol-

lowed, sentiment for deregulation did not decrease but continued to gain momentum.

At least four factors contributed to continued deregulatory zeal. The first stems from the general policy approach of the Clinton administration, which was to find the middle ground in every policy dispute. Although Clinton favored health-based regulations, he opposed overconcentration of rule making in the federal government and was sympathetic to the complaints of both business and state governments about the cost of implementing regulations.

A second factor was the strong deregulatory policy of the Republican leadership that took control of both houses of Congress in 1995. Divided government kept in check, or overrode, Clinton administration tendencies to come down on the side of regulation when a middle ground could not be found.

A third factor sustaining deregulatory momentum was structural change in the global economy. Advances in transportation and telecommunications have changed the "balance between government and international markets" and the terms of business competition.[48] Global competition for market share has allowed businesses, including the heavily regulated banking and utilities industries, to argue that to have the freedom to reorganize on a scale necessary to maintain competitiveness in international markets, they must be deregulated. This argument found broad bipartisan support in Congress and in both the Clinton and second Bush administrations.

In 1999, for example, Congress essentially dismantled the Glass-Steagall Act that had separated the banking, insurance, and securities industries since the Great Depression. Commercial banks, already the second most profitable of all industries, are now free to engage in securities trading and to handle the title insurance of your new home as well as to give you a home mortgage and handle your checking account. Congress even sanctioned the creation of banks for large depositors, where accounts will not be protected by deposit insurance.

Within the new, bigger-companies-for-bigger-markets rationale, the number of mergers mushroomed, with only token opposition from Justice's antitrust division or from the FTC, even though the 1990s saw the twenty largest mergers in U.S. history.[49] Warner-Lambert and Pfizer, two of the country's largest pharmaceuticals, merged; the Seven Sister oil companies became five (the merger of Exxon and Mobil was the largest industrial merger in history); and the seven Baby Bells became four.[50] Proposed mergers would give five cable companies control of forty of fifty-nine cable networks, even though no cable merger has ever resulted in a price decrease for consumers. (In fact, cable prices have increased three times faster than inflation.)[51] The freight and shipping industries have also undergone similar consolidations.

While the number of merger proposals more than tripled between 1991 and 1999, staff size at the FTC, decimated during the Reagan years, grew by only several dozen and has yet to catch up to where it was in 1980. To cut the caseload, Congress, with the support of the FTC and Justice, proposed exempting mergers of smaller companies from regulatory review.

Many in government see the 1990s wave of mergers as inevitable, necessitated by global competition. But critics of "merger mania" argued that too little thought is being given to the consequences of corporate consolidations—namely, that the greater the assets companies acquire through mergers, the more resources they have to buy still other companies. One member of Congress warned, "We've got to have the [antitrust] resources that prevent this society from turning from a capitalist society into an oligarchy."[52]

A fourth stimulus to deregulation is the power of large corporations to influence the political process. Through their key role in financing the campaigns of candidates of both major parties (see Chapter 9), they are guaranteed at least a symbolic hearing for their arguments for deregulation.

Corporate financial power resulting from consolidations—Adelphia and WorldCom, for example—gave political access and protection from congressional oversight. Several regulations of the financial industry, rolled back in the 1990s, allowed CEOs and their auditors to cook their books, and eventually led to a stock market crash. This in turn led to investor (voter) rage and to legislation reregulating accounting firms and the ways corporations compensate their CEOs and report company earnings.

However, at the same time that limited reregulation was taking place, deregulation continued at a stepped-up pace in other sectors of the economy, including energy, mining and logging, telecommunications, worker

scottadams@aol.com; 2002 United Feature Syndicate, Inc.

safety, product liability, and, as we will discuss later, environmental protection. George W. Bush shares the deregulatory fervor of the Gingrich Republicans and, with a divided Congress in his first two years, employed Reagan's approach of appointing antiregulation agency heads and cutting agency budgets. Bush also appointed to head OIRA a major advocate of the risk assessment standard who has vowed to review and eliminate rules that do not meet this standard.

Keeping Pace with Change

A former EPA director once said that the EPA's mission is like trying to give someone an appendectomy while the person is running the hundred-yard dash.[53] The agency is always shooting at a moving target: Just as regulators establish rules for dealing with a pollutant, research reveals new dimensions to the problem or identifies other toxins from new sources.

Today many other regulators must share this sentiment as rapid advances in technology over the past decade have challenged government's regulatory powers. One of the most difficult issues has emerged from advances in biotechnology: Should government or the marketplace decide whether science should engineer human life, and business market it?

Some argue that cloning, for example, could save thousands of lives by providing healthy tissue, bone marrow, or organs needed by people with illnesses that require grafts or transplants from a genetically matched person. Some make a straightforward argument for genetic engineering; they see nothing wrong with procedures that could eliminate the risk of disabling diseases or birth deformities in unborn children. Cloning might also allow infertile couples to have children. In fact, some see cloning as a reproductive freedom issue, and just as they do not want government to regulate whether a woman can terminate a pregnancy, they do not believe government should prevent the cloning of offspring.

To what standard does government look to determine whether cloning is good or bad for the public, and what is the legal basis for this regulatory authority? Typically, government regulates to promote public health and safety and equal access in the marketplace. Should regulatory decisions on cloning be made by committees of scientists, doctors, clergy, and ethicists? If so, who would choose the committee members, and how would they be accountable to the public?

Consumer concern about the safety of genetically engineered foods has also brought demands for new regulation. Lawsuits have been filed against the federal government and biotech companies demanding that the foods grown from genetically altered seeds (called "frankenfoods" by their critics) be more carefully stud-

New scientific developments that affect ecological balances prompt calls for regulation, in this case, of genetically altered food.

ied before being declared safe. In some cases, opponents have demanded the removal of food already on the market. While the FDA insists that genetically altered foods are safe, it has written new rules requiring manufacturers to inform the FDA of their intent to market such products and has drawn up guidelines for those who want to label contents voluntarily. But food safety is not the only issue. About half the soybeans and a third of the corn planted in the United States are grown from genetically altered seed stocks, creating the potential for emergence of pesticide-resistant insects.[54] In this area, too, government has begun to act, ordering farmers to grow at least 20 percent of their corn and soybeans from nongenetically altered seed.

Communications technology is another area where changes are occurring more rapidly than regulators can keep pace. In 2002, more than half of all Americans had access to the Internet, and online commerce was booming. Many of its supporters see the Internet as the model of a free market, open to all and completely unregulated, and they believe it should stay that way. Advocates of greater government oversight believe that excitement over the development of e-commerce, the new ease in rapid global communication, and the emergence of global markets have contributed to the "general ideological drift toward greater respect for the market [and] unwarranted deregulatory zeal."[55] They say an unregulated Internet has resulted in consumer and credit card fraud, illegal online securities trading, criminal solicitation, access of children to pornography, and public dissemination of personal credit and medical histories and other invasions of personal privacy. Congress has yet to adopt measures to regulate in most of these areas, but more than seventy-five bills dealing with issues of privacy, access, and content on the Internet were under consideration before September 11.[56] After the 9/11 terrorist attacks, legislative attention shifted to removing privacy protection, allowing (under the Patriot Act) intelligence and law enforcement agencies unprecedented access to individual email accounts and records of Internet activity.

Regulating high tech requires scientific study and time for assessment and also requires members of Congress to familiarize themselves with the intricacies of a multitude of new technologies and their applications before they write legislation. But changes are occurring with such rapidity it seems impossible that government regulation will be able to keep pace with their application in the market.

Regulatory Politics and Environmental Protection

Government action to safeguard public health through protection of the environment has had broader public and more bipartisan legislative support than almost any area of regulation. For three decades, the importance of this type of regulatory activity has been proclaimed by leaders from Richard Nixon—who called a clean environment the "birthright" of every American—to Al Gore, who wrote a best-selling book based on the notion that safeguarding the environment should be "the central organizing principle for civilization."[57]

A majority of the public supports spending for environmental protection, even when agreeing with the statement that government should regulate less. In 1999, after almost three decades of EPA regulating, more than two-thirds of Americans surveyed were still worried a "great deal" about safe drinking water; toxic waste contamination; pollution of rivers, lakes and reservoirs; and air pollution.[58] Nevertheless, neither widespread support for regulatory activity nor its real achievements were able to prevent a strong backlash from developing against the environmental activism of federal agencies and interest groups. This is reflected in federal funding, which peaked in 1980, fell sharply during Reagan's deregulatory push, and grew by modest increments during the first Bush administration and the Clinton administration before beginning to fall again during the presidency of George W. Bush.

During the years when Republicans had control of both houses of Congress and Clinton was president (1995–2000), we had a hostilely divided government, and environmental protection was one of the battlegrounds. There was so much opposition in Congress to new initiatives on air quality and global warming that

Clinton did not even submit the Kyoto Treaty to the Senate for consideration, an international agreement on global warming that he had signed. Moreover, Congress tried to kill new White House and EPA initiatives on air and water quality and wilderness preservation by attaching riders to appropriations bills to cut off funding for implementation. Why, when there is so much bipartisan support for environmental protection, is there such strong opposition from a minority?

The crucial question in the debate over government's role can be stated simply, but it cannot be answered simply. How can we define standards that protect society's interest in having a clean and healthy environment and at the same time not unreasonably handicap business and individual producers of pollution? Historical and current debates over environmental policy revolve around this issue.

In this section we use the example of environmental protection to illustrate how legislators, regulators, and interest groups have contributed to the politicization of the regulatory process.

Evolution of Government's Role

Eighteenth-century Americans did not worry about harming the environment. The continent, largely unsettled, was graced with resources that seemed almost infinite: "A fertile, widespreading country . . . blessed with a variety of soils . . . and watered . . . with innumerable streams, for the delight and accommodation of its inhabitants."[59]

The Constitution contains no hint of concern about preserving and protecting the environment. Indeed, the Founders' and our own orientation to the environment is rooted in the Western, Judeo-Christian tradition that the physical world exists to serve human needs.[60] This sentiment was reinforced during the eighteenth-century period known as the Enlightenment, which led people to believe that through science and learning, we could conquer almost any obstacle to human progress.[61] Awareness of the negative consequences of science and technology for the environment was a long way away.

But in the nineteenth century, concern grew about the effect that the Industrial Revolution, coupled with rapid population growth, might have on the environment. Late in that century, a conservationist movement to preserve some of the natural environment from farmers, ranchers, and loggers who were clearing the land resulted in the creation of the national forests and a national park system.[62]

Along with concern about saving some forests and other areas of scenic beauty came an awareness of pollution. The first effort to combat water pollution was an 1899 law requiring that individuals dumping waste into navigable waters get a permit from the Army Corps of

Engineers. In 1924, Congress banned oceangoing ships from dumping oil in coastal waters. Neither of these acts was enforced very well, but the legislation did indicate an embryonic concern with pollution.

The modern environmental movement probably stems from a book, *Silent Spring,* published in 1962 by Rachel Carson, a marine biologist. Carson argued that pesticides used in agriculture find their way into the air and water and harm crops, animals, and people. Moreover, she demonstrated that scientists and engineers did not know the extent of these harmful effects, nor did they seem particularly concerned. The chemical industry immediately attacked Carson, accusing her of hysteria and misstatement of facts. The industry's attacks created widespread publicity for her views and raised the environmental consciousness of millions of Americans. President Kennedy cited Carson's work as his reason for ordering a review of government regulation of pesticides.

The decade and a half following the publicity over Carson's book was characterized by a burst of new regulatory activity. Beginning in 1964 and continuing through 1977, Congress passed a series of laws designed to protect the air and water from pollution and to deal with hazardous waste.

Public concern peaked, too. Huge oil spills, rivers catching fire, and the growing impact of the automobile on air quality lent substance to these concerns. By 1970, opinion polls showed that the most frequently cited public problem was protecting the environment, surprising in light of the continuing protest against the Vietnam War.[63] In April 1970, Earth Day was inaugurated, and hundreds of thousands of citizens across the nation demonstrated to show their concern about the environment. Every year since, one day in April has been set aside to celebrate the planet's resources and to heighten environmental awareness.

In 1970, Congress gave citizens a more formal way to affect environmental policy. New legislation (the National Environmental Policy Act, NEPA) mandated government agencies to prepare **environmental impact statements** for internal projects or projects they fund. Impact statements require justification for projects or actions proposed as well as a list of all the people and agencies consulted. Most important, these analyses must detail the effect, including any negative consequences, that a project or other activity would have on the environment. No new buildings, dams, sewers, pipelines, or highways were to be built, nor any research or other government projects initiated, until this statement had been filed.

Not only did the law give federal agencies the power to comment on each other's environmental impact statements, but it also gave citizens access. Early environmental legislation was the first to incorporate the 1960s ethic of public involvement and "full disclosure of the information on which government bases its decisions."[64] These provisions became an important device for organizations interested in protecting the environment, giving them a real opportunity to influence environmental policies. Within a few years, more than four hundred legal suits were filed to force the government to comply with the act's provisions; by 1980, thousands had been filed.[65]

Over the years, impact statements have become a major issue in environmental politics as public agencies and industries have complained that the time required to prepare the analyses, and the power NEPA gives environmental activists to challenge them, has unfairly delayed the implementation of projects. Shortly after his election, George W. Bush issued executive orders exempting certain projects from the requirement and ordering federal agencies to expedite the processing of other impact statements. Environmental activists charge that it is a prelude to elimination of all environmental impact statements.

Another landmark move marking the growing federal involvement in environmental protection was the 1970 creation of the **Environmental Protection Agency (EPA)** by President Nixon.[66] Recognizing that responsibilities for pollution control were spread throughout the executive branch, Nixon, with congressional approval, brought them together in one regulatory agency with a single head who reported to the president.

During the EPA's first years, three foundational pieces of environmental protection legislation were passed by Congress: the Clean Air Act (1970), the Clean Water Act (1972), and the Endangered Species Act (1973). During the 1970s, the EPA received extensive new mandates to regulate hazardous waste, pesticides,

An Earth Day celebrant illustrates a possible future scenario if air pollution is not curbed.

and noise pollution. Today, under the watch of seventy congressional committees and subcommittees, the EPA administers sixteen major environmental statutes and more than ten thousand pages of regulations.[67]

Implementing Environmental Regulations

Passing laws is one thing, enforcing them another. Congress mandated the EPA to achieve certain goals, but the EPA had to write the rules for reaching them and then monitor their implementation by the states. For example, under the Clean Air Act, the EPA was ordered to establish air quality standards for major pollutants, a task the EPA estimated would require writing three hundred to four hundred rules. States were mandated to draw up plans that would bring local air quality into compliance with these new federal standards. In keeping with the commitment to public involvement in the regulatory process, the Clean Air Act also permitted citizens to sue to enforce its provisions.[68] Of course, the industries and public utilities subject to the new rules also had the right to challenge them. Because the process is vulnerable at all stages to influence by affected parties, enforcing air quality standards for industries has been difficult.

Auto manufacturers, which had to reduce auto emissions or face fines, immediately asked for more time to reduce emissions, claiming they could not meet the standards. After the oil price hike brought financial difficulties to auto manufacturers in the mid-1970s, several extensions were granted. However, it became apparent that, counter to U.S. auto manufacturers' claims, the standards *were* technologically feasible since foreign manufacturers were able to meet them. Consequently, by the end of the 1970s, the standards had been restored, only to be partly rolled back during Reagan's deregulation campaign.

Though in theory the EPA can have a noncomplying company closed down, this move is simply not politically feasible or particularly wise. Generally, the agency is reluctant to enforce standards against large companies with political clout or small profit margins, especially industries crucial to the nation's economic health. To take action against a large industry requires significant political will all the way to the White House. That kind of commitment is rarely evident.

The standards approach to rule writing provided few incentives for industry to comply. Penalties were often not assessed, and when they were, the fines were usually far less than the cost of complying with the standards. Also, the practice of specifying methods of compliance for entire industries did not make sense in every instance; a company might achieve compliance more cheaply using methods other than those the regulation specified.

To deal with these objections, the Carter administration adopted the policy of allowing compliance in some industries to be based on the bubble concept. This policy allowed companies to meet an overall standard for emission of pollutants. Imagine that a bubble has been placed over a factory with ten smokestacks, each emitting pollutants. Under the old rules, each smokestack would have to meet EPA standards. Under the bubble concept, one or more smokestacks might exceed the limits on emissions as long as the total emissions within the bubble met the standard. Rather than bringing all ten smokestacks into compliance, the company might find it cheaper to install equipment on five smokestacks if doing so would reduce total emissions to the required level. The bubble concept provided greater flexibility in determining how a standard would be met and reduced the cost of compliance.

From the bubble concept, a more flexible system evolved, allowing for a multifactory bubble. A limit or cap is placed on the amount of a pollutant that can be emitted in a geographic area, and factories within that area are allowed to buy, sell, or trade rights to pollute as long as collective emissions do not exceed the cap. For example, the EPA sets a limit on how much sulfur dioxide (the chemical that causes acid rain) can be emitted into the air in a particular area; then state environmental agencies sell permits to pollute. Each permit is good for one ton of emissions per year. Utility companies, which emit a great deal of sulfur dioxide, can then decide whether it is cheaper for them to buy and install scrubbers to reduce plant emissions or to buy permits that allowed them to pollute. This policy, called **cap-and-trade,** allows industries some flexibility in meeting pollution standards, but if they do pollute, they have to pay in advance.

The bubble concept was hardly a panacea, however. It still required the EPA to set standards for each particular type of pollutant. Since the petrochemical industry was founded during World War II, eighty-five thousand new chemicals have been manufactured, and of the three thousand that are in high production, just over 40 percent have been even minimally tested for health effects.[69] During its first twenty years, the EPA set standards for only seven of the most toxic. Believing that it would be impossible to set standards for each separate chemical, the EPA replaced the pollutant-by-pollutant approach with a more comprehensive industry-by-industry approach.[70] Now limits are set on all toxic emissions combined, and, following the cap-and-trade policy, industries with emission levels below allowable limits earn credits that they can "bank," sell, or trade to other industries whose emission levels are above the standard.

Regulation of air quality is a good illustration of how industry and public responses to the implementation of rules can influence reassessment and revision. The goals of the original Clean Air Act were not weakened but strengthened by subsequent amendments and reauthorizing legislation because the rules to reach goals were revised in ways that make them less cumbersome and more cost-effective to administer.

The cap-and-trade approach has been adopted by international environmental agencies as a means for achieving worldwide reductions in the emission of carbon dioxide and other gases linked to global warming, with nations, rather than businesses, buying and trading permits to pollute.

Water Quality

Before 1972, at least eighteen thousand communities regularly dumped their untreated raw sewage into rivers and lakes. Food, textile, paper, chemical, metal, and other industries discharged 25 trillion gallons of waste water each year.

These activities occurred despite federal attempts to improve water quality. A 1948 law authorized the federal government to give funds to local governments to build sewage treatment plants. Thousands of communities used the grants for this purpose, and the program was seen as a welcome pork barrel project as much as a regulatory one. In 1965, Congress mandated that states establish clean water standards in order to get these sewage treatment grants. But the law was not effective. States did not want to establish stringent quality standards because they were afraid industries would leave.

In 1972, the federal government tried again. It set as goals achieving "fishable and swimmable" waters by 1983 and zero discharges into water by 1985. Industries were to have permits to discharge wastes; they were to use the "best practicable" technology by 1977 and the "best available" technology by 1983 to make sure the pollutants discharged were the smallest amounts possible. The EPA set uniform national standards for discharge control for each type of industry so states did not have to compete to get industries or to keep them from moving away by setting the most lax standards.

It took years to implement water quality standards effectively, for many of the same reasons that confounded air quality enforcement: rules not correctly written, inadequate monitoring, industry resistance, and foot dragging in Congress. A substantial number of industries and municipalities did not meet the standard of technology necessary to clean up waste.[71] Some sewage treatment facilities were built inadequately, and others were operated improperly because they lacked trained technicians. The EPA and state environmental agencies did not have the personnel to monitor carefully how local governments spent their sewage grants. Local governments also resisted the standards set by the Clean Water Act because of the cost to municipal budgets. Most towns and cities, especially during the bad economic times of the 1970s, did not have the resources to pay for what was essentially an unfunded mandate. Even today, one-third of all EPA spending is on grants to the states to build and maintain water and sewage facilities.

Congress yielded to political pressure from local governments and industry. In 1977, it weakened some of the provisions of the 1972 act and granted exemptions and extensions. Thus, polluters had reason to believe they need not comply with standards or deadlines because Congress would come to their rescue.

Congress also dragged its feet on enforcement of the 1974 Safe Drinking Water Act, waiting a dozen years before imposing a timetable on the EPA for issuing safety standards. Finally, in 1991, Congress did pass new and more stringent safety standards for tap water, requiring more frequent testing for lead levels in municipal water supplies, only to see them threatened by a new round of deregulation.

But the difficulty achieving the goals of clean water legislation was not all due to resistance to regulation and its costs. Part of the problem was with the rules themselves: When the first rules were written, not enough was known about the sources of water pollution to determine which sources to target first. Industries and municipal sewage plants account for only part of the water pollution problem. Other contributors were not being regulated. For example, what are called "nonpoint sources" (that is, discharges that do not come from a specific pipe) account for as much as half of all water pollution. Runoff of fertilizer from farmlands is a big source of nonpoint pollution and is difficult to control. So are the sewers connecting drains and grates in city streets. Storm sewers collect gas, oil, fertilizers, pesticides, animal excrement, and other unpleasant substances and then deposit them directly into the nearest waterway.

Current rules written to achieve clean water goals stress pollution from these nonpoint sources. For example, the EPA has told states that they have to develop plans for controlling pesticide runoff from farms and for limiting urban sprawl. This will create a new set of enforcement problems. Cracking down on farmers and construction firms or local land developers is much more difficult politically than attacking huge corporations that dump toxic waste in public waterways. In the Grain Belt states, local politicians may find it hard to tell cash-strapped family farmers that if they do not alter their use of pesticides (changes that could lower production), they may have to help pay for pesticide cleanup.

Despite all of these problems, today's drinking water is much safer than it was before the clean water laws were enacted, and 60 percent of all rivers and lakes are now safe for swimming and fishing.

Hazardous Waste

In the mid-1970s, residents living near Niagara Falls, New York, began to complain about pungent fumes, dead bushes and trees, holes opening in the ground, thick oils fouling their basement pumps, children and pets developing sores and blisters, and high rates of birth defects and miscarriages. Eventually, they realized they were living nearly on top of twenty-one thousand tons of dangerous chemicals dumped in the abandoned Love Canal more than two decades earlier. In the old days, people dumped wastes anywhere, without much thought for the hazards they might create. There was no clear understanding about whose responsibility it was to clean up the sites. After many months of negotiation, the canal was declared a disaster area, the state bought the residents' homes, and the residents were evacuated.[72] But who was responsible for the mess in Love Canal was still unclear.

The Love Canal incident occurred while the EPA was writing new regulations for handling hazardous waste. The rules require hazardous substances to be tracked from generation through disposal. This is called a manifest system or a **cradle-to-grave** procedure.[73] When toxic wastes are produced, treated, transported, or disposed of, the handlers must file a one-page form (a manifest) identifying the type and quantity of waste, where it was produced, who transported it, and to what storage or waste site it was shipped. Copies are filed with all participants in the process.

The Love Canal incident not only put the spotlight on the current regulations the EPA was writing to implement a 1976 law but also revealed that the law had a large loophole: it only dealt with current waste sites, not long abandoned ones like Love Canal.

In 1980, Congress attempted to remedy the problem with new legislation designed to find and clean up existing hazardous waste sites. The bill ordered owners of hazardous waste sites to report them and placed liability for cleaning up the sites with their owners, but it authorized the EPA to clean up leaking sites if the responsible parties could not be located. The bill also imposed a tax on industry to help pay for the cleanup. This revenue, along with federal funds for hazardous waste cleanup, is referred to as the **Superfund.**

To carry out these laws, the EPA began to develop regulations for storage and treatment facilities for hazardous waste and for landfills. It also began to evaluate each of the nation's known hazardous waste sites and to target some for cleanup with the Superfund.

In 1986, Congress amended the Superfund Act to give communities the right to know about chemicals made, used, and stored by local businesses. Citizens themselves now put pressure on industry to clean up unsafe dumps. But they are often not strong enough to face up to large industries.

Like most rule making, the waste regulation process is open to "technical controversy, litigation, and other challenges."[74] The complexity of the problems inherent in defining hazardous waste, setting standards for disposal, and identifying existing dumps are mind-boggling. As a simple example, chemical manufacturers are reluctant to release to the EPA information about new chemical compounds for fear of giving away trade secrets. As with toxic chemicals emitted into the air, the EPA knows little about thousands of chemicals disposed of in industrial and military waste dumps.

Hazardous waste cleanup is among many new duties assigned to the EPA without a substantial increase in staff or budget. Moreover, the EPA has lacked the clout necessary to enforce hazardous waste laws against two of the nation's worst polluters: the government's own Departments of Defense and Energy. (See the box "Who Will Regulate Government?")

The EPA has also had difficulty establishing industry liability for cleanup on sites where several or more companies have dumped wastes. The insurance companies against which claims are made for cleanup of such sites challenge the liability of the industries they cover. A RAND study of Superfund spending claimed that only 10 percent of the money from insurance company settlements went to site cleanup, while 90 percent was spent on legal costs.[75] The fund became so controversial that Congress ordered that taxes for cleanup of toxic waste no longer be collected from chemical and oil companies.

By 2002, the government reported having partially or totally cleaned up eight hundred sites, about 60 percent of those on the priority list.[76] However, several hundred new sites are expected to be added to the list in the coming decade. With the decline in assessments made on the polluters, the taxpayers are being asked to pick up more than half the costs for toxic waste cleanup.[77]

Reforming Environmental Regulations

Everyone breathes the air and drinks the water, and one in four Americans lives or works in proximity to a hazardous waste site.[78] Therefore, environmental protection has a huge constituency. With the information explosion on how exposure to toxic substances in our food, water, land, and air may be linked to cancer and other illnesses, Americans have become increasingly health-conscious. Heightened awareness of environmentally related diseases has led to increased pressure on government to protect us from toxic substances.

Critics say this fact has at times made government too responsive to public pressure and created a politics of panic.[79] For example, in 1989 Congress passed a law in the wake of a public outcry over the littering of East

The Bush administration wants to drill for oil wherever it can be found, including in federal wildlife preserves and on federal land in the west, such as this spot near Moab, Utah.

Robbie McClaran

Coast beaches with medical and human waste and dead sea life that summer. After cities spent billions to comply with the law, some experts said the beaches had been contaminated by overtaxed storm sewer systems, not by toxic waste dumped in the ocean. While limiting the use of oceans as dumping grounds is a good thing in itself, it is extremely expensive to regulate, and the danger it presents is less than that from inadequate sewage systems.

Policies on toxic waste and hazardous substances are singled out by critics as the worst examples of wasteful spending and misguided priorities. They point to studies by the National Cancer Institute that claim that only 1 to 3 percent of the nation's half-million yearly cancer deaths result from exposure to environmental pollutants.[80] Yet regulations to control these pollutants often force businesses and government to spend billions of dollars to restore contaminated sites to a pristine state. Reformers cite as examples the unsafe standard for dioxin presence in water, which is equivalent to one drop in Lake Michigan, and the so-called dirt-eating rules, or standards of safety determined by how much chemical-contaminated soil a child could consume without becoming ill.[81] Opponents of the no-risk standard ask whether it is cost-effective to clean up all toxic waste sites to the point that dirt is safe to eat or the water safe to drink, especially if the amount of chemical contained in that soil or water presents no significant risk through normal exposure.

In too many cases, critics argue, the evidence used to support policy decisions has been unsound. Laws are made and standards mandated, only to have researchers revise the findings on which the laws were based. Scientists studying dioxin and DDT toxicity, for example, have said that early estimates of the danger level for hu-

man exposure were faulty. Much of the research on toxicity has been based on animal studies using the method of administering a "maximum tolerance dose" of the substance being studied. Researchers say that two-thirds of the chemicals such studies showed to be carcinogenic would be benign if ingested at lower levels. In addition, there is not a direct correspondence between rodent and human body chemistry, so we cannot be certain that humans will be affected in the same way rats are when exposed to the same chemicals. Arsenic, for example, is highly toxic to humans but not to rats.[82]

But environmentalists counter by asking whether we really want to risk people's lives by waiting until we get better evidence. They support low- and no-risk standards and believe it is better to err on the side of safety and not wait to regulate until people start dying. They take issue with the National Cancer Institute findings and claim environmental pollutants are responsible for up to 15 percent of all cancer deaths.

The jobs Congress has asked the EPA to do are huge compared to the resources the agency has, and some say, while billions are spent to achieve unrealistic and unnecessary goals, more threatening hazards are ignored. The National Cancer Institute, for example, thinks priority should be given to public education on diet and other behavior that puts people at greater risk for cancer than exposure to environmental pollutants. City governments would rather spend federal grants on repairing sewer systems than on trying to restore contaminated sites to the safety thresholds prescribed by Congress.

Some believe environmental interest groups are partially responsible for a high-pressure approach to regulation by playing on public fears and making unreasonable

While the government legislates, negotiates, and cajoles to get businesses and industries to assume some financial responsibility for environmental cleanup, who will hold the nation's worst polluters—the Departments of Defense and Energy (DoD and DoE)—responsible for unsafe activities? The problems of accountability are even more formidable than for the private sector. The Department of Justice does not want to sue other federal agencies, the EPA can impose fines but has no power to collect them, and citizens' right to sue the federal government has been restricted where national security activities are at issue. Charges can be brought against the private industries that pollute while fulfilling DoD or DoE contracts, but they can claim they were just following orders from federal agencies. States left with huge toxic waste problems by weapons or energy plants have been told by the Supreme Court that they cannot collect civil penalties from a federal agency. How can government be made accountable for damage to the environment and the health of its citizens? Who will regulate the regulators?

Much of the government's polluting is tied to the development of nuclear weapons and nuclear power. These projects have already exacted enormous health costs. No one warned the citizens of Nevada about radioactivity, even though the government exploded more than one thousand bombs in their state. Atomic Energy Commission documents refer to people living in the fallout area as "a low-use

segment of the population."[1] According to a study by the Centers for Disease Control, eleven thousand died because of exposure to radioactive fallout from above-ground weapons testing, and it contributed to a minimum of twenty-two thousand cancers.[2]

Thousands of others suffered health problems as a result of working in or living near weapons industries or serving as subjects in weapons research. Six hundred thousand people in thirty-seven states worked in the nuclear weapons industry during the Cold War. In the 1940s, when government engineers recruited Navajo men and boys living near Cove, Arizona, to mine the uranium necessary for new atomic weapons programs, no one mentioned the dangers of radon exposure. In a government study of how irradiated nutrients are metabolized (paid for by the Quaker Oats Company), boys in a state home were fed oatmeal laced with radioactive isotopes. In other experiments, terminal cancer patients were radiated to toxic levels; hospital patients were injected with plutonium, and at least two hundred thousand military personnel were exposed to radioactive materials to test consequences of exposure to atomic weapons and bomb blasts.

Not until the 1990s did Congress hold hearings on the "human radiation experiments" and appropriate money to compensate for injuries and deaths to uranium miners, participants in nuclear testing, and victims of radioactive fallout.[3] By that time, Congress was also facing the massive cost of cleaning

up toxic waste and other pollution at the nation's military bases and nuclear weapons plants.[4] Plants that built nuclear bombs focused on national security and gave little attention to safety procedures or to the effects their actions might have on surrounding communities. Leaking earthen pits were used as dumps for industrial chemicals and radioactive wastes. Sewage systems, some built when the plants opened, leaked pollutants into the ground. Inadequate or nonexistent air pollution control devices allowed toxic and sometimes radioactive emissions into the air. Other radioactive waste was discharged into streams and rivers.

The nuclear weapons plant in Hanford, Washington, knowingly released into the air massive amounts of radioactive materials, including iodine, for test purposes. Downwind, near Mesa, Washington, in an area known as the "death mile," 14 of 108 residents became ill with or died of cancer, and several children died or were born with disabilities.[5] Researchers from the Centers for Disease Control believe that twenty thousand children in eastern Washington may have been exposed to unhealthy levels of this iodine by drinking milk from cows grazing in contaminated pastures.[6]

In Fernald, Ohio, a red-and-white checkerboard design on a water tower and the name "Feed Materials Production Center" led some residents to believe a local firm produced animal feed. Instead, it made uranium rods and components for warheads. Resi-

demands for safety standards. This creates obstacles to the EPA's planning. Environmentalists have also been criticized for being unwilling to admit their successes for fear of losing financial support for their organizations and momentum for the movement. These successes, coupled with what has been characterized as "compassion fatigue" among the American public, has led to an intense competition among environmental groups for membership and financial support.[83] This, in turn, the

groups' critics argue, has led them to make "apocalyptic prophecies to further their political objectives." One fund-raising letter from the National Audubon Society, for example, claimed that it could "project with some accuracy the eventual end of the natural world as we know it."[84]

Many people have also criticized the command and control approach to regulatory policy that lays down rules and orders people and industries to comply.[85] To

Cheerleaders at Hanford, Washington, High School, whose teams are named the "Bombers," illustrate the civic pride in the nuclear weapons plant located nearby.

Doug Menuez/Reportage

dents were stunned to find out that, for thirty-five years, the plant had dumped radioactive refuse into pits in the ground that regularly overflowed when it rained. The plant also discharged 167,000 pounds of waste into a local river and released about twice that much into the air. Though these actions were taken by the private company that ran the plant, they were approved and even encouraged by the supposed regulators, the Atomic Energy Commission. Senator John Glenn (D-Ohio) said, "We are poisoning our people in the name of national security."[7]

To add insult to injury, the government backed federal contractors challenging the findings of the medical panels who ruled on the eligibility of nuclear weapons workers to receive financial aid for medical care. In 2002, President Bush reversed this policy and told the DoE to help twelve thousand workers file claims for compensation.

But no one has given the EPA, which has the authority to regulate waste disposal at federal weapons plants, the authority to collect fines it assessed against the DoE for delays in implementing a cleanup plan for the Fernald plant or to force the DoE to carry through on plans to clean up the Hanford Nuclear Reservation. However, after receiving some bad press coverage, the DoE agreed to pay a small fine and negotiated a new thirty-year cleanup schedule for Fernald. DoE estimates of the cost of cleaning up after the nuclear weapons program at all 164 sites it is responsible for continue to rise and now stand somewhere near $220 billion.[8]

This does not include costs of restoring DoD sites, which also pose huge cleanup problems. DoD domestic military installations produce more hazardous waste each year than the top U.S. chemical companies. This includes many bases that have been closed to reduce military spending. None can be sold or converted to any civilian use until they are detoxified and made safe from such hazards as unexploded artillery and mortar shells. During the 1980s, these sites were labeled "national sacrifice zones," because they could not be returned to normal use without some danger to human life. A study commissioned by the DoE gave the term new meaning when it concluded that many of the sites used for nuclear weapons development, including Hanford, cannot—for reasons of technology, money, and political will—be fully cleaned up and will remain polluted in perpetuity.[9] The bill for decades of carelessness and neglect has come due.

1. Carole Gallagher, *American Ground Zero: The Secret Nuclear War* (Cambridge, Mass.: MIT Press, 1993), xxiii.
2. "Cold War Testing Could Have Killed 11,000," *Champaign-Urbana News-Gazette*, March 2, 2002, A5.
3. Hearings on *The Human Radiation Experiments* (S.Hrg. 103-1060; S.Hrg. 104-588).
4. Cass Peterson, "A Monumental Cleanup Job," *Washington Post National Weekly Edition*, December 12–18, 1988, 11.
5. "Nuclear Danger and Deceit," *Newsweek*, October 31, 1988, 20–30.
6. "They Lied to Us," *Time*, October 31, 1988, 64.
7. Ibid., 61.
8. *Budget of the U.S. Government, Fiscal Year 2003*, 125.
9. "Nuclear Sites May Be Toxic in Perpetuity, Report Finds," *New York Times*, August 8, 2000, A12. The study was carried out by the National Academy of Science.

force compliance with rules requires monitoring by a large, expensive, and unwanted bureaucracy. When rule breakers are caught, they are assigned penalties that realistically cannot be enforced, even after huge sums are spent on legal fees to force compliance. Reformers stress the need to make greater use of economic incentives to encourage desired behavior and to reduce the cost of enforcing regulations. Instead of trying to control their behavior after the fact, individuals and businesses should be made to "face up to the full costs and consequences" of harmful actions at the time they make their decisions."[86]

The objective of the proposed reforms is to discourage environmentally or other socially harmful behavior by driving up its cost and thereby putting the individual or business engaging in it at a competitive disadvantage in the marketplace. This approach tries to eliminate a negative externality by bringing the polluter's incentives in line with the social costs imposed on the public. Disincentives could take the form of high-cost pollution permits for companies that decide to pollute and taxes on manufacturing or purchasing environmentally harmful products, waste disposal processes, and energy use. Environmental groups support heavy "green" taxes on "products and activities that pollute, deplete or otherwise degrade natural systems."[87] Such taxes would help pay for mounting cleanup costs and at the same time would provide a market incentive to avoid actions that endangered the public.

Market-based incentives have been proposed by those deregulation advocates who, in almost every instance, place individual and private property rights above those of the commons (that is, mineral resources, waterways, and parklands) and the public good. They assume that the marketplace is the only arena for resolving what is rational and appropriate economic behavior. But the marketplace is no more or less than the people who operate within it, precisely because it is a place where individuals and businesses pursue private gain. There is no guarantee that the cumulative effect of these actions will benefit the common good.

Other supporters of regulatory reform believe it is possible for the government to set standards for health and safety and environmental protection while limiting its role in rule writing. This view was expressed in Philip Howard's best-selling book on regulatory law. In *The Death of Common Sense*, much cited by both Republicans and Democrats, Howard argues that the federal government has gone too far in its belief that science and technology make it possible to protect against every public danger. This has led to an excessive number of rules that try to anticipate every eventuality and in the process left the economy suffocating under the weight of law.

Howard's solution is to decentralize the rule-writing process while leaving federal standards in place. This would allow businesses and localities more flexibility in finding ways to meet the mandated standards, greatly reduce the oversight bureaucracy, and result in more cost-effective rules. This was generally in line with the form of deregulation advocated by the Clinton administration.

Clinton, a critic of the confrontational politics of the more militant environmental interest groups, but a supporter of their general goals, gave high priority to achieving consensus between the various parties affected by environmental regulation, such as the timber industry and habitat protectors, or the energy and mining industries and wilderness advocates. In accordance with the Clinton–Gore "reinventing government" policy, EPA administrator Carol Browner advocated a "Common Sense Initiative" (CSI) to revise unrealistic, costly standards and to eliminate unnecessary rules.[88] She said

the issues of risk assessment, property rights, and unfunded mandates "cast a shadow over environmental legislation" and had to be "addressed head-on" before any new regulations could be written.[89]

The EPA's attempts to control pollution and hazardous substances are undermined by fast-changing technology, inconsistent goals of political leaders, and, of course, resistance by regulated groups. Defending environmental protection in principle has remained good politics, but forcing *implementation* of EPA rules is not always seen as good politics. When Congress held hearings in the early 1990s to consider renewing several major pieces of environmental legislation and to evaluate the implementation process, deregulators particularly targeted the Clean Water Act, which is extremely costly to implement, and the Endangered Species Act, which many western farmers and ranchers believe interferes with their property rights. While the Republican-controlled Congress did not revoke the major clean air and water statutes, it did little to compel state governments, which have responsibility for 85 percent of all enforcement cases, to comply with them.

George W. Bush's policy is in basic agreement with that of congressional Republicans. He has called the CSI ineffective because it lacked clear goals and was without legal authority.[90] He has signaled his commitment to rely primarily on voluntary compliance by business and application of the risk assessment standard to spur deregulation. In the case of clean air standards, for example, Bush has argued that the economic demands of meeting standards impedes economic growth and discourages businesses from modernizing. His Clean Skies Initiative lowers compliance standards by allowing industries to modernize or remodel without undergoing inspection to see whether the new facilities have in place the antipollution technology to control emissions from new or remodeled smokestacks.

The public's behavior is also not entirely consistent with the goals it claims to support. We want clean air and water, but we do not want to give up gas-guzzling cars and SUVs, plastic containers, energy-consuming conveniences, and other pollution-causing aspects of our lifestyles. We use far more energy per person than do the people of any other nation except Canada, and with energy use comes pollution. And emissions from vehicles now cause more pollution than emissions from industrial smokestacks. Part of this heavy consumption is due to our level of economic development and to consumer wealth, but part is plain wastefulness. High oil prices in the 1970s curbed energy use for a while, but we have returned to our high-consumption ways, despite a renewed interest in curbing our dependence on Middle Eastern oil. It is unrealistic to expect the EPA to control pollution when we do not police ourselves.

It might be partly OPEC's fault, for using its cartel to limit supplies.

It might be partly the oil companies' fault, for using tight supplies to gouge on profits.

And just possibly it's partly your fault, for buying that ridiculous vehicle that gets what, 12 miles per gallon?

NOTHING IS EVER MY FAULT.

I'M AN AMERICAN MOTORIST.

MY MISTAKE.

Changing human behavior is at the center of the current debate over how much progress has been made in environmental protection and how much remains to be done. The optimists point to real achievements in improving air and water quality, reforestation, and cleaning up toxic waste, and they believe it is possible to control or limit ecological damage through adjustments in human behavior. A different school of optimist believes that science will provide the technology needed to combat the environmental damage that is an inevitable by-product of economic development, and they remind us of the importance to our economic security of continued growth. The pessimists acknowledge the achievements made in rolling back damage from pollution and other consequences of our current lifestyles. But they argue that the major ecological threats cannot be addressed without fundamental change in human behavior. Representing this outlook, Al Gore has said, "The maximum that is politically feasible, even the maximum that is politically *imaginable* right now, still falls short of the minimum that is scientifically and ecologically necessary."[91]

Benefits and Costs of Regulation

Regulation has many acknowledged successes.[92] But they are produced at a cost. Some are trivial, such as depriving hunters of the satisfaction of shooting eagles. But some are significant. Businesses and environmentalists differ wildly about what the net cost of these improvements has been, although it is indisputable that regulation requires industry to increase its costs to relieve the larger community of the burden of pollution, unsafe products, hazards to workers, or other negative aspects of business activity. Most of these costs are passed on to consumers in the form of higher prices. According to Bush's 2003 budget message, consumers pay, mostly through higher prices, $50 to $60 billion each year—one hundred times what the EPA spends—on cleaning up our air.

All dollar estimates of the cost of environmental regulation are controversial because of the disagreement over what monetary value to put on intangibles such as human health, comfort, appreciation of clean air, or loss of individual liberties or over whether it is even possible to put a price on them. The best estimates show that air pollution control, for example, has been a large net benefit not only to the nation's air quality but to its economy. Although industries must pay employees to deal with federal regulations, and some pollution control equipment costs millions, pollution devices improve health and ultimately mean fewer days lost from sickness, reduced medical costs, and longer life for materials less damaged by corrosion.[93] Cleaning up the air also increases agricultural output. Some people are laid off when factories choose to close rather than install pollution control devices, but even more people are employed making, distributing, and educating people about air pollution devices.

In addition, sixty thousand public and private companies are engaged in environmental activities, employing almost one and a half million people and generating annual revenues of $59 billion.[94] Ecotourism is also developing as a major industry, helping revive small towns and rural areas bypassed by development. Today the number of birdwatchers is greater than that of hunters and fishermen combined, and birders spend an estimated $20 billion a year on travel to festivals and on gear and seeds.[95] Whale watching has also become a huge industry.

Yet regulation remains controversial because some believe that its cost is too high and can be counted in decreased productivity, lost jobs, crushing paperwork, endless litigation, and loss of liberties to businesses and individual property owners. It is how these calculations are made that brings values, and therefore politics, into the regulatory process. There is no way for science or accounting alone to place a value on a human life that all will agree on, any more than regulators can put a dollar value that will be acceptable to everyone on preservation of the bald eagle or of wilderness areas within national parks. Many do not even accept the idea that quantitative values can be placed on human life or on the intrinsic satisfactions that exist above and beyond the economic value of protecting endangered species and their habitats.

This argument is increasingly made by environmentalists in legal battles to stop offshore oil drilling and logging in wilderness areas. The basic premise of this approach to cost–benefit analysis is that the cost of preserving a wilderness area must be offset by its "existence value" or "contingent value," the price the public is willing to pay just for the sake of keeping a pristine area in existence. But even those who concede that it is valid to factor existence value into the equation are uncertain how to determine the dollar value people will place on a wilderness area, and some environmentalists worry that putting a dollar value on nature is a bad precedent. Former interior secretary Bruce Babbitt, for example, has said we have reached the point where "[w]e know the cost of everything and the value of nothing . . . you can't just cost this stuff out." He argues that it is dangerous to use contingent value because it may lead to an underestimation of the value of wilderness areas and furthermore that economics should not drive a debate that is about something much deeper.[96]

Americans want government to anticipate problems and to proscribe behavior by businesses and individuals that endangers public health. But we do not want to force unnecessary, costly regulations on business that will drive up prices for consumers, slow the economy, and increase unemployment. Is our national economic condition such that we must pick our poisons and regulate to protect public health and safety only when it is "cost-effective"?

Conclusion: Is Regulatory Policy Responsive?

Americans have called on government to protect them from unsafe workplaces, unclean air and water, fraudulent advertising, hazardous highways and drunk drivers, dangerous drugs, and many of life's other perils. But then we turn around and say we want government "off our backs." We resent the rules, regulations, and red tape. We want government protection, but we are uncertain about how much and what we are willing to give up in return.

Most businesses favor regulation that brings sufficient order in the marketplace to support public confidence because without it business—certainly publicly traded companies—cannot exist. Some may even lobby for the kind of regulation that protects them from domestic or foreign competitors. But business, too, wants government off its back and complains that regulation decreases autonomy while increasing costs of operation.

Complaints about overregulation provoke legislative attempts to deregulate and to cut money for enforcement by both federal and state regulatory agencies. But the subsequent laxness in enforcement can lead to abuses and provoke calls for reregulation. All of these actions and reactions are responsive, in the sense of giving the public and business community at least some of what they want. But elected officials may respond to their political base first and to the larger public only when pressured. For example, George W. Bush's decision to rescind the Clinton rule lowering the amount of arsenic allowable in drinking water provoked such a negative public response that Bush reversed himself and restored the standard. It was one in a series of Clinton rules Bush had overridden, but the sharp reaction to this one caused him to pay more attention to public perception of his deregulatory program, leading one watchdog group to refer to his policies as "before arsenic and after arsenic."[97] In the same way, hostile public reaction to corporate corruption forced Bush to accept publicly, and even to campaign for, regulations he had earlier opposed. Out of the public spotlight, however, he sent a more business-friendly directive to regulatory agencies, telling them how he expected the new rules on auditing corporate finance to be implemented.

Regulators have a hard job because they have to be responsive to the president and his political appointees in their agencies as well as to Congress and the political agendas of its members. In addition, they must be responsive to the thousands of inquiries about, and challenges to, rules posed by the public, including powerful interest groups and lobbyists who may be aligned with members of congressional oversight committees. Theirs is not an easy road to walk.

In forming our opinions about government regulations and regulators, it is sometimes easy to forget that regulators are carrying out presidential orders and congressional acts. While bureaucrats may be overly zealous or overly lax in enforcing laws they are mandated to enforce, ultimately it is Congress that decides what is to be regulated and that calls an agency to heel when they are overregulating or neglecting to regulate.

Regulatory policy is a good example of fluctuations in government responsiveness to the public. In general, regulation exists because influential groups—sometimes representing a majority, other times not—demand government action to protect their interests. At times, regulatory effort is directed primarily toward protecting business. At times of heightened public awareness of finite natural resources and the health risks of environmental degradation, consumer and environmental groups have succeeded in getting government to better regulate business and itself.

The public generally approves of deregulating up to the point it affects them negatively. But a majority has long opposed efforts to get government completely out of the business of protecting health, safety, and the environment.

Nevada Continues to Fight

n July 2002, after the Senate joined the House in approving the proposal for a nuclear waste storage facility at Yucca Mountain, Governor Guinn issued a statement saying he was disappointed but that the state would fight on. The Nevada Protection Fund had already hired two high-powered lobbyists of its own, former chiefs of staff in the Clinton and Reagan administrations, to take on those representing the nuclear industry.

Guinn rejected advice to use the decision as a way to bargain for state benefits. "We will not bargain, we will not negotiate, we will not waver in our determined opposition to Yucca Mountain. Today we lost a battle, but we will win the war."[98] He even threatened to stand in front of trains carrying waste into the state.

The governor also took the only legal recourse left to him: he filed another suit in federal court. Up to this point, he said, politics had pre-vailed over science. But in the courts the "playing field is level and Nevada's factual, scientific arguments will be heard by impartial judges," where there will still be a chance to hold the DoE accountable for its "unsound decisions."[99]

The politics of nuclear waste disposal were put more directly by one of the state's former senators: "The reaction here is that Nevada got screwed because it's a small state with little representation in Congress." The battle over the Yucca facility was just one more blow to the self-esteem of a small state, he lamented.[100]

It would be hard to refute the senator's assessment. With only two votes in the House, Nevada does not have much to bargain with. Its main protection was having a president who was willing to veto the project—and that promise from Clinton helped him carry the Republican state in both 1992 and 1996.

Nevadans were skeptical that Yucca Mountain was the best rather than the most politically acceptable site. In fact, it was the only area the DoE gave serious consideration. They had that "been there, done that" feeling. During the Cold War, virtually all the atomic and nuclear weapons testing carried out within the continental United States was done in Utah and Nevada. Even then, when the states were far less populated than they are today, residents suffered the health effects of fallout for decades afterward—how extensively only came to light with the declassification of documents in the 1980s and 1990s.[101] This revelation is fresh in people's minds. Of course, there is a huge difference in the risk factor of exposure to fallout from atmospheric and underground weapons testing and living in proximity to radioactive waste sealed in casks and cement a thousand feet below ground. But those who live nearby, which is 75 percent of

AP Photo

Yucca Mountain, proposed site of the nuclear waste repository.

Nevada's population, will have to live with the possibility of accidents, terrorist attacks, and earthquakes and hope the DoE studies on the integrity of the site and materials are correct.

Another issue hanging over the Yucca Mountain decision is the federal relationship. No recent president has been a greater rhetorical supporter of ceding power to the states than George W. Bush, nor more critical of how the federal government has exercised its control over public lands in western states. But Bush had no difficulty going against the wishes of Nevada's governor, state legislature, almost every important organization and interest group, and 70 percent of the population when he opposed the Yucca repository.

The nuclear power companies create negative externalities in the process of generating electrical power. Though the federal government can control some of these externalities by regulating the way the power is generated and limiting the number of nuclear power plants licensed, ultimately nuclear waste will be generated. How should the cost of dealing with this waste be shared? The cost is not only financial but includes the potential exposure of communities to radioactive waste.

This set of decisions illustrates a fundamental issue of democracy. When we say "majority rules," what majority do we mean? In the United States, a national majority, as expressed through the wishes of the president and Congress, can usually override a local majority, even on an opinion held as strongly as the Yucca Mountain repository. In many regulatory issues, the national majority does in fact overrule a local majority, whether it is the wishes of westerners to mine or deforest their land rather than having the federal government preserve it for future generations or the desire to settle in areas where development is threatened by preservation of endangered species. In this case, the national majority determined that the Nevada population would take the largest share of the negative externalities of nuclear power generation. But Nevadans said yes to their governor, reelecting him in 2002 with 68 percent of the vote.

 To learn more about the Yucca Mountain controversy, go to this chapter's "You Are There" exercises on the text Web site.

Key Terms

tragedy of the commons

externality

antitrust law

monopoly

truth in labeling

cost–benefit analysis

deregulation

reregulation

environmental impact statement

Environmental Protection Agency (EPA)

cap-and-trade

cradle-to-grave

Superfund

Further Reading

Rachael Carson, *Silent Spring* (New York: Fawcett, 1962). This book, and industry's reaction to it, spurred the development of the modern environmental movement.

Mark Dowie, *Losing Ground: American Environmentalism at the Close of the Twentieth Century* (Cambridge, Mass.: MIT Press, 1995). A former publisher of *Mother Jones* argues that the environmental movement has become weak and irrelevant by catering to Washington and losing touch with its grassroots supporters.

Gregg Easterbrook, *A Moment on the Earth: The Coming Age of Environmental Optimism* (New York: Viking, 1995). An environmental reporter gives an upbeat assessment of the achievements of environmentalism and argues that the movement needs to acknowledge its successes and redefine its priorities and tactics.

Carole Gallagher, *American Ground Zero: The Secret Nuclear War* (Cambridge, Mass.: MIT Press, 1993). A photojournalistic study of the victims of radioactive fallout from nuclear testing in Nevada.

Richard Harris and Sidney Milkis, *The Politics of Regulatory Change* (New York: Oxford University Press, 1989). An even-handed account of the rise and fall of deregulation during the Reagan administration.

Shepard Krech III, *The Ecological Indian: Myth and History* (New York: Norton, 1999). An environmental anthropologist examines the stereotype of the ecologically correct American Indian and shatters some myths about the relationship between Indian cultures and the environment.

Derek Leebaert, *The Fifty-Year Wound: The True Price of America's Cold War Victory* (New York: Little, Brown, 2002) A cost–benefit analysis of the Cold War that looks at both the dollar and human costs of defeating the Soviet Union.

Jonathan D. Moreno, *Undue Risk: Secret State Experiments on Humans* (New York: Freeman, 1999). A biomedical ethicist describes U.S. Department of Defense, Atomic Energy Commission, Public Health Service, and CIA experiments on Americans during World War II and the 1950s, concluding that human rights should never be subordinated to national defense.

Walter Rosenbaum, *Environmental Politics and Policy,* 3d ed. (Washington, D.C.: CQ Press, 1995). Probably the best overview of environmental policy.

Eric Schlosser, *Fast-Food Nation: The Dark Side of the All-American Meal* (Boston: Houghton Mifflin, 2001). An account of how America's indulgence in fast foods can affect health and nutrition. It tells you things you may not want to know about how much fat is in McDonald's French fries and the lax standards regulating the raising and slaughter of the cattle that gave their lives for your hamburger.

 Electronic Resources

www.epa.gov/
The home page of the EPA offers information on issues, organization, and regulations. You can also find a guide to all major environmental protection projects in your state.

www.ftc.gov/
The home page of the Federal Trade Commission. It provides information on antitrust action, consumer credit privacy, and business guidance. You can also file a complaint online.

www.cpsc.gov
The home page of the Consumer Product Safety Commission offers updates on product safety problems and each month posts a list of recalled products, such as a McDonalds's give-away for children, a bobble-headed figurine with high lead content in its paint.

www.hanford.gov
A toxic waste site with its own Web page! You can see photos of the site and get progress reports on cleanup and on the work of the Superfund.

www.sierraclub.org/
The home page of the Sierra Club, one of the largest and most influential environmental interest groups. From this page, you can check on the environmental voting records of your members of Congress and see where they got their campaign contributions.

www.fda.gov/
The Web site of the Food and Drug Administration contains information on all major areas of the agency's work in food and drug safety, reports on current research, and pending regulations and legislation.

 InfoTrac College Edition

Search for the following articles in the InfoTrac database:

Anderson, James E. "The Struggle to Reform Regulatory Procedures, 1978–1998," *Policy Studies Journal* (Autumn 1998).

Easterbrook, Gregg. "Air Condition: Bush, Pollution, and Hysteria," *New Republic,* July 1, 2002.

Kane, Tim D. "Deregulation California Style," *USA Today* (magazine) (July 2001).

Page, Reid, et al. "Environmental Crimes," *American Criminal Law Review* (Summer 1999).

For more articles, enter

"Deregulation" in the Subject Guide;

"George W. Bush" in the Subject Guide, and then go to subdivision "environmental policy";

"Clean Air Act" in the Subject Guide.

 American Government Resources

Visit the Public Policy section of the Wadsworth American Government Resources Web site (politicalscience. wadsworth.com/amgov/) for a variety of tools to help you explore regulation and environmental policy further. Included are simulations, video clips, Microcase exercises, and a wealth of other activities.

FOREIGN POLICY

World trade center survivors. The attacks of September 11, 2001, dramatically altered the foreign policy of the Bush administration and reinforced Bush's determination to topple Saddam Hussein.

Should You Give the President a Blank Check to Invade Iraq?

ou are Richard Lugar, Republican senator from Indiana and senior member of the Foreign Relations Committee.[1] It is September 2002. You are considering a congressional resolution that would give President Bush authority to take whatever action he deems necessary to force Saddam Hussein, president of Iraq, into compliance with the UN resolutions that forbid him to have programs for manufacturing weapons of mass destruction (WMD). Although not spelled out in the resolution, U.S. action in Iraq would almost certainly include removing Saddam from power, a goal Bush set early in his administration.

You were a supporter of the first President Bush when he launched Desert Storm, the military campaign to liberate Kuwait after it had been invaded by Saddam in 1991. But when he had said that as commander in chief he did not need congressional approval, you had advised him that it would be foolhardy to undertake such a mission without congressional support. Under fierce criticism from fifty-four members of Congress who sued him for breach of the War Powers Act, the elder Bush gave in, winning approval of his resolution by just five votes. After the younger Bush announced his intentions to launch a military strike against Iraq, he, too, said that while he was willing to consult Congress, he did not need its approval.

You gave the son the same advice you gave his father: Send a resolution to Congress and build an international coalition. But unlike the elder Bush, George W. has shown little interest in working through the UN or trying to build an international alliance.

You are troubled by Bush's willingness to use military force unilaterally. You are considered one of the Senate's leading foreign policy experts and a "cardinal" of the realist school.[2] Realists are at odds with the Senate's neoconservatives, who want to go it alone and assert America's unmatched military power wherever the president thinks it is in our national interest to do so. One of those neoconservatives, Jesse Helms (R-N.C.), pulled rank of you several years ago to prevent you from becoming chair of the Senate Foreign Relations Committee.

Realists like you also differ, although less frequently, with the "Wilsonians" like current Foreign Relations Committee chair Joseph Biden (D-Del.). They put faith in international law and organizations and believe the United States, wherever possible, should try to work through the UN and other multilateral arrangements. Realists, as the name suggests, are neither ideologues nor idealists. Your group believes the United States must take a hard-nosed view of what it can and cannot accomplish in the world and that it should not undertake what it cannot afford to do or cannot finish. This makes you a sometime ally of the Wilsonians because they are also cautious about committing U.S. resources to achieve goals that are not shared by our allies or others in the international community who could help share the burden.

One reason you think invading Iraq may be overreaching is the unfinished war in Afghanistan. We have not accomplished our objective of eliminating Osama bin Laden and al Qaeda. Though the capital, Kabul, seems relatively peaceful, in other parts of the country, warlords and pockets of al Qaeda sympathizers are still in control, although most of the organization's leaders appear to have escaped into Pakistan or other countries. In addition, although you believe Iraq is an "acute problem," you see it "as one proliferation problem among many."[3]

As the senior Republican on the Foreign Relations Committee, you joined forces with Biden to write an op-ed piece for the *New York Times* urging the president to build public support, seek congressional approval, and try to work through the United Nations before undertaking unilateral action. And Bush did it: He went to the United Nations and made a speech outlining all the reasons Saddam was a danger and why the UN should take action to force compliance with its sanctions. With Biden, you wrote the president commending the speech, urging him to keep the American public informed, and reminding him again that he must seek congressional approval for any military action.[4]

Now congressional hearings have been held, and the president has submitted a resolution. But like many in both parties in Congress, you are worried about its sweeping language: He is asking for authority "to use all means that *he determines* to be appropriate, including force, in order to enforce the United Nations Security Council resolutions . . . defend the national security interests of the United States against the threat posed by Iraq, and *restore international peace and security in the region*"[5] (italics added).

Voting yes on this resolution would be giving the president a blank check to

wage war throughout the entire Middle East and to undertake any measures necessary to ensure stability after a military victory. Almost everyone in Congress agrees with the president that Saddam is a dangerous man willing to use weapons of mass destruction against us, just as he has already used chemical weapons against his own people. Like most members of Congress, you want to support the president on this national security issue. But you are not convinced that a military invasion is the only option.

Yet, with the midterm election just six weeks away, many in Congress, both Democrats and Republicans, are unwilling to speak out on the issue for fear of appearing critical of the president on an issue of national security. So they pussyfoot around the issue, fearful of being labeled unpatriotic. And many Democrats want to pass the resolution quickly and get the campaign focused on the domestic issues important to voters. The public seems divided; opinion polls show a majority supportive of invasion, but support drops significantly when approval is for a war where there might be a significant number of American deaths. Yet Americans do want to strike back at those who attacked on 9/11, and, despite the lack of evidence, the president continues to link Iraq and al Qaeda.

Any president has a huge advantage in getting his way in foreign policy

matters. He represents the country as well as the party, and he has access to information that the public, and even Congress, does not. The president has made Iraq a campaign issue by making support for his policy the main issue at virtually every fund-raiser he has attended. The election is of huge importance to both parties because of the narrow margins of their majorities in both chambers.

You have the stature and the bipartisan respect to question the president's approach. But as a Realist, you want answers to nagging questions. You still have no idea how many troops Bush wants to send to Iraq, how much it will cost, where the money will come from, what the region will look like, and what our commitment will be to a post-Saddam Iraq. You also want to know whether we will be engaging in nation building as we are in Afghanistan, how much that will cost, or how the operation will affect the success of the war against al Qaeda. Many Realists believe that al Qaeda is far more of an immediate threat to the United States than Iraq, which, since the Gulf War in 1991, has shown no appetite for using weapons against other nations. Analysts believe that other countries with a presumed nuclear capability, such as North Korea, are as likely to use them as Iraq. Even if forthcoming evidence convinces you war is necessary, you are not certain Congress should sign the blank check the president has asked for.

No one is going to accuse you of turning this into a partisan issue. Now in your fifth term, you will not be standing for reelection this year, and, anyway, your seat is as safe as any Senate seat. Moreover, you are one of the Senate's experts on terrorism and weapons of mass destruction. After the breakup of the Soviet Union, you took a special interest in reducing stockpiles of nuclear and chemical weapons left over from the Cold War. You were especially concerned about terrorists getting access to the weapons or material to make them and staging an attack on the United States. You even made a series of campaign commercials for television in which you tried to raise public awareness of the dangers.

You must decide: Do you trust the president's judgment as commander in chief and vote to give him the blanket authority he wants to use force in the Middle East? Or should you work with those Democrats and Republicans who think Congress should assert its authority as the only body with constitutional power to declare war and define the terms under which the president can wage a war on Iraq?

The foreign policy of the United States has a substantial impact on the world, yet we are not all-powerful. We are one of many nations; decisions about war and peace and about trade and diplomacy are made by people in all nations. In this sense, public expectations about what we can achieve have often been unrealistically high.

Yet we are the world's most powerful nation in terms of both military and economic strength.[6] Thus, our power, and how we use it, has a tremendous impact on people throughout the world.

In the 1990s, many of the resources that had been devoted to competition with the former Soviet Union were redirected toward other goals. We suffered from a sense of uncertainty because the Cold War with communist countries, which had defined much of our foreign policy since the late 1940s, was over. The nature of international cooperation and competition changed, and we were forced to rethink the means we use to pursue our foreign policy objectives. During the unprecedented period of peace and prosperity at the end of the century, we were more inward looking and less willing to devote as much of our energies and resources to foreign policy as we had in the past. As we shifted from a world divided between East and West to one increasingly linked by the forces of globalization, much of the world seemed to have left behind the great power struggles of the Cold War and immersed itself in trade rivalries and economic competition.

At the outset of the twenty-first century, as the sole remaining superpower, we settled into a kind of triumphalism grounded in a belief that the Western ideals of democracy, capitalism, and free trade had become the world's agenda. In this atmosphere of unrivaled military power, the United States experienced the first attack on its territory since the Japanese bombed Pearl Harbor in 1941 and the first attack on the continental United States since the War of 1812.

In this chapter, we examine past and present foreign policy goals, how foreign policy decisions are made, and how foreign policy concerns have changed over time. Then we describe the major military and economic instruments of foreign policy and the challenges policymakers face in an era of globalization and a post–September 11 world.

Foreign Policy Goals

The goals any nation has and the means it uses to pursue them are influenced by its traditions, core values, ideology, and geopolitical situation (that is, the advantages and limitations imposed by geographic location, size, and wealth relative to other nations). *Foreign policies* are the strategies adopted and actions taken by a government to achieve its goals in its relationships with other nations. These actions range from informal negotiations to waging war, from writing position papers to initiating trade boycotts. They may require economic, political, cultural, or military resources.

The art of foreign policymaking includes choosing means suitable to the objective sought. Due to our size and great wealth, huge diplomatic corps, military forces, and intelligence establishment, we have the fullest possible range of foreign policy instruments at our disposal. Sometimes the possession of so many means of pursuing foreign policy objectives affects the setting of the objectives themselves; that is, the more a country is able to do, the more it may try to do.

Our primary foreign policy goal is, as is every nation's, to protect our physical security. Until the era of long-range bombers and ballistic missiles, achieving this goal meant preventing land invasions, and in this we have been successful. Our success was due largely to our separation from the other major powers by two oceans and being bounded on the north and south by two friendly countries. In the nuclear era, when we could be attacked by air by long-range bombers and intercontinental ballistic missiles launched by land or sea, we had to develop an air as well as a ground defense.

In today's era of terrorist attacks—with conventional weaponry or biological, chemical, or nuclear weapons of mass destruction (WMD)—physical security must be

FIGHTING WAR AT HOME

The United States has not been a theater of war since we fought England in the War of 1812, the last time foreign troops were on U.S. soil. Responsibilities for defending North America have always been divided among various commanders in regional theaters of war such as the Pacific, European, and Southern (South America) commands, for example, or under NORAD, the agency responsible for detecting attacks by air or space. September 11 precipitated two major organizational changes in this arrangement: the establishment of a Homeland Security Department (discussed in Chapter 11) and the creation of a new regional defense theater, the U.S. Northern Command (NorthCom).

NorthCom places under a single command the responsibility for defense against attacks—whether by land, air, space, or sea—on U.S. territory, population, and critical infrastructure. NorthCom is designed to prevent the confusion that arose on 9/11 over who was in charge of what. For example, after the hijacked planes were detected, fighter planes scrambled, but there was confusion over areas of responsibility and the chain of command. Even when fighter planes caught up with the flight over Pennsylvania, there was uncertainty over who had authority to approve shooting down a civilian aircraft.

The establishment of a military command on U.S. soil for the first time in modern history poses a potential threat to the cardinal principles of our democracy: that civilians should control the military and the military should never interfere in domestic politics and governance. The role of the armed forces within U.S. territory has been strictly limited since the passage of the Posse Comitatus Act of 1878. That law, passed during the Reconstruction era to stop federal troops from being used to enforce civilian laws (such as supervising elections in states of the former Confederacy), makes it illegal for the U.S. military to play a role in domestic law enforcement. This also applies to the National Guard when nationalized by the president. National Guard troops that provided security at airports after 9/11, for example, had to do so under state command; if nationalized and under presidential authority, they would have been forbidden by the Posse Comitatus Act from engaging in law enforcement or surveillance work.

With a military command operating on U.S. soil, there is the potential for conflict between civilian and military authorities in their overlapping responsibilities for responding to terrorist attacks. For example, can military officers from NorthCom assume control of civilian functions in future defense emergencies, supplanting local law enforcement, the FBI, and Homeland Security personnel? The specter of military officers in civilian roles has raised concerns among civil libertarians who believe that we must maintain strict boundaries around the military's role, limiting it to national defense and restricting its involvement in civilian affairs.

Thus far, Pentagon officials and NorthCom's commander see no conflict. They say that their role is one of coordination and providing backup to civilian authorities. NorthCom's commander calls

---

defended against both external and internal attacks. (See the "After 9/11" box.) Since September 11, 2001, more emphasis has been placed on how to prevent terrorist attacks from within and how to stop the proliferation of weapons of mass destruction. As we will discuss later, how we provide for our physical security in an age of high technology and globalization is undergoing serious rethinking.

A second goal is to help protect the physical security of our neighbors and major democratic allies. Since World War II, we have committed ourselves, through the North Atlantic Treaty Organization (NATO), to join in the defense of Canada and western, southern, and, now, some eastern European nations. We also have treaty commitments to Japan, South Korea, and the nations of South and Central America.

A third goal is to protect our economic security. Although the United States is blessed with many natural resources, we must purchase abroad such essential resources as oil, manganese, and tin. Safeguarding access to these resources may include stabilizing the governments of producing nations or protecting the sea lanes in which goods are shipped. Our economic well-being is equally dependent on selling our goods abroad, which in turn depends on how cheaply we can manufacture or grow products desired in other parts of the world and how willing our trading partners are to buy them.

Economic self-interest is almost always a factor in foreign policy, even in dealings with our closest allies, because they do not always want to import U.S. goods that will compete with their own. Thus, trade missions and participation in the international organizations that govern trade relations are crucial to achieving our foreign policy goals, even though the public paid scant attention to them before the 1990s. Today the electronic flow of capital into and out of the country is also essential to our economic viability, so ensuring the privacy of

it "one-stop shopping."[1] In the event of an attack, and at the request of local officials or FEMA, NorthCom could supply people trained to respond to chemical, biological, and nuclear attacks; equipment; and supplies. Or it could provide intelligence or other assistance to law enforcement agencies. And NorthCom can do some things no domestic law enforcement can do, such as flying occasional combat air patrols over U.S. cities.

Historically, federal courts have allowed the military to play the indirect role of providing assistance while ruling against their taking a direct or active role in any matter under the jurisdiction of domestic law enforcement. But some are concerned that NorthCom makes it difficult to limit the military's role or keep it subordinate to civilian authority.[2] One reason is that NorthCom's mission is not only to defend against foreign invasion or internal terrorist attacks but to help Homeland Security and FEMA deal better with natural disaster and other civil problems. These new duties may have the potential for the military to supersede civilian control.

Civil libertarians are especially worried about the potential for the kind of domestic surveillance of leftist and anti-war groups the military engaged in during the 1960s. They say that NorthCom's responsibility for defense against terrorist attacks means it will have to be actively engaged in monitoring domestic events and collecting intelligence within the United States. NorthCom will have 150 to 200 people working in intelligence, although the commander says they will only collect intelligence from other agencies, like the FBI, state militia, and the National Guard Bureau, and send it on to the Defense Intelligence Agency for analysis. But NorthCom will have responsibility for passing along intelligence information from one civilian agency to another. And in a not altogether reassuring description, NorthCom's commander said, "We are not going to be out there spying on people. We get information from people who do."[3]

But the Bush administration insists that the military will continue to be "outward looking," as the military always has been, and will not be engaged in domestic spying.[4] Verbal guarantees are not enough for the ACLU, which claims the Posse Comitatus Act has loopholes that with "creative interpretation" would allow the military to be involved in domestic law enforcement.[5] They want Congress to establish guidelines that will guard against any domestic law enforcement role for the military. While the Pentagon has not asked for changes in the Posse Comitatus Act, the White House has asked that the law be reviewed to see whether it interferes with the military's role in homeland security.[6]

1. Interview with General Ralph E. Eberhart, Commander of NorthCom, by Dan Sagalyn. Portions were aired on the *NewsHour with Jim Lehrer*, PBS, September 27, 2002. The full transcript is at www.pbs.org/newshour/terrorism.
2. "Guarding the Homeland," *NewsHour with Jim Lehrer*, PBS, September 27, 2002. The transcript is at pbs.org/newshour/newshour_index.html.
3. Ibid.
4. Donald Rumsfeld, "Special Briefing on the Unified Command Plan," April 27, 2002. The transcript of the news conference is at the Defense Department's Web site, www.dod.gov.
5. "Guarding the Homeland."
6. Eric Schmitt, "Military Role in U.S. Gains Favor," *New York Times*, July 21, 2002, 16.

information transfers, including financial transactions, and securing computer systems against hackers are becoming as important to national security as protecting sea lanes.

A fourth overlapping goal is to extend our sphere of influence. Historically, this has meant keeping foreign powers out of the Caribbean and Latin America. In the 1780s, Thomas Jefferson said he hoped Spain would hold onto its territory in South America until "our population can be sufficiently advanced to gain it from them piece by piece."[7] Since the beginning of the nineteenth century, we have warned off foreign powers from meddling in the affairs of any country in the Americas, and there is still a tendency to see Latin America as our "turf."

Since World War II, our sphere of interest has extended around the world. We have sought to influence security arrangements on all continents. We have more military bases and more troops outside our borders than has any other country in the world. We also try to spread our influence by promoting democracy, capitalism, and Western cultural values. Our State Department maintains a system of public libraries around the world to disseminate information on our government, economy, and popular culture and also funds thousands of cultural and academic exchanges between American and foreign artists and scholars each year. At most, we offer our political and economic systems as models of development, and, at least, we try to foster a favorable attitude toward the United States that will make it easier for us to achieve our foreign policy goals.

Our specific foreign policy objectives, such as protecting access to oil in the Middle East, removing trade barriers, drying up the funding sources for terrorist operations, and aiding the economic restructuring of Russia, are almost always related to achieving one or more of these four general goals.

Making Foreign Policy in a Democracy

Alexis de Tocqueville was one of the first to remark that it is difficult to have a coherent foreign policy in a democracy. His sentiments have been echoed thousands of times since. Why, when there has been basic agreement on the broad goals of our foreign policy, has the United States had such difficulty articulating a coherent and consistent set of objectives?

Some of the confusion in foreign policymaking is because we elect new leaders every four or eight years. Inconsistencies within a single administration can also be partially explained by the sheer number of organizations and individuals who in some way influence the process of making and implementing foreign policy: the president, members of Congress, heads of relevant cabinet departments and independent agencies, chiefs of the armed services, White House staff and other political advisers, interest groups, lobbyists, the media, and the public. Leaders and citizens from other countries may also have some influence when they are crucial to the successful pursuit of an objective. Which of these groups and individuals will actually have some impact on policy varies greatly with the issue and the decision-making style of the president. (See the box "Figuring Out How U.S. Foreign Policy Is Made.")

Historically, inconsistencies in our foreign policy were rarely caused by differences among policymakers over fundamental goals but rather over whether action was necessary in a specific situation and what that action should be. For example, most Americans supported the goal of containing Soviet influence, just as today they support the destruction of al Qaeda's terrorist network. But they do not always agree on how much intervention in the internal affairs of another country is justifiable or on what form that intervention should take (see this chapter's "You Are There").

Between the end of the Cold War and the September 11 attacks, there was disagreement even over the fundamentals. Of course, policymakers still believed that physical and economic security were primary goals, but there was more confusion than at any time in the past over what constituted the primary threats to national security and exactly who and what we should be protecting ourselves from. But the direct attack on U.S. soil crystallized our foreign policy focus, perhaps even more strongly than during the Cold War.

In this section, we will look at some of the groups and individuals who influence the foreign policymaking process and how division and conflict among them can affect the content and execution of U.S. policy.

The Inner Circle

As head of state and commander in chief of the armed forces, the president is in control of the nation's diplomatic and military establishments. In addition, as the nexus of the vast diplomatic and military communications and intelligence networks, he has the most complete and privileged access to information of anyone in the policymaking network. In times of crisis, without immediately available alternative sources of reliable information, members of Congress and the public historically have almost always relied on the president's sources. The Clinton years were a partial exception to this rule. With the presidency weakened by scandals, an especially contentious Congress controlled by conservative Republicans during most of Clinton's administration, and no real foreign policy crises, presidential decisions, even those taken in response to attacks on U.S. facilities and forces abroad, faced constant challenges from Congress.

Given the central role of the president in foreign policymaking, and the fact that most presidents enter the office with very little foreign policy expertise, it is important to know who advises him. No firm rules dictate whom the president must consult on foreign policy, but usually he gives at least a perfunctory hearing to those people who head departments and agencies involved with making or implementing policy. The government officials best positioned to advise the president on foreign policy include the secretaries of defense and state, the national security adviser, and the head of the CIA. The president also frequently consults the Joint Chiefs of Staff, the U.S. ambassador to the United Nations, the secretary of the treasury, the U.S. trade representative, and influential members of Congress.

These individuals represent a wide range of experience and bring different perspectives to the analysis of foreign policy issues. The secretary of state is usually concerned with the nation's diplomatic relations and the use of diplomatic channels to implement the president's policies. The secretary of defense (a civilian) is primarily concerned with military and security issues and the use of the military to pursue foreign policy goals. Members of the Joint Chiefs of Staff are military professionals who give advice to the president on both the readiness of their service arms and the appropriateness of their use in specific situations. Members of Congress may be consulted because they are political allies of the president, because they are in leadership positions crucial for mobilizing support on an issue, or because they have developed expertise in military or foreign policy issues through their committee assignments.

The president may also consult his wife or friends and advisers outside government, not because of their policy expertise but because he trusts in their good judgment and wants the perspective of people close to him who may have no organizational interests or policy agenda to further. In recent years, it has become common for presidents to call on private citizens to negotiate disputes, a practice that has been dubbed the franchising or subcontracting of foreign policy. These freelancers are often retired diplomats, but individuals with little foreign policy experience, such as former presidential candidate Jesse Jackson, have also been used.

The most noted of these private diplomats is former president Jimmy Carter, who heads a center, affiliated with the Carter presidential library, devoted to international mediation. Carter has gone, sometimes at his own initiative, to many trouble spots, including North Korea and Bosnia, where he helped negotiate a short-lived truce. His mission to Haiti with General Colin Powell in 1994 successfully negotiated the departure from Haiti of the military junta, allowing U.S. troops to come ashore unopposed. For his efforts mediating conflicts and monitoring elections in some of the world's newer democracies, Carter received the Nobel Peace Prize in 2002. But sitting presidents have not always been happy with Carter's high-profile visits or his comments about them, believing that the former president has appeared at times to be conducting an independent policy line.

Who the president draws into his inner circle of advisers depends in large part on his experience and decision-making style. President Kennedy, who had almost no foreign policy experience, assembled a committee of cabinet heads and close advisers to help him construct his response to the Soviets during the Cuban missile crisis. But during the Persian Gulf crisis, the first President Bush reportedly made the decision to send troops to Saudi Arabia relying almost exclusively on his own judgment and that of a few close advisers.

Figuring Out How U.S. Foreign Policy Is Made

One insight into U.S. foreign policy-making was offered by Nizar Hamdoon, Iraq's ambassador to the United States from 1983 to 1987, years when we supported Iraq in its war with Iran and before the Persian Gulf War. Hamdoon lived through what he calls "every ambassador's nightmare" when, during his term, the Iraqi Air Force mistakenly attacked a U.S. ship. Dealing with this tragedy, he believed, confirmed several lessons he had learned about how Americans make foreign policy. Though these observations were written in the late 1980s, they are still true today. In the 1990s, Hamdoon returned to the United States as ambassador to the UN, where he became a familiar figure on talk shows during periodic U.S.-Iraqi crises.

1. Washington is driven by crises and expectations of crises. To influence policy, one needs to seize opportunities that arise during these crises.

2. Make contact with media and give them access. Don't be afraid of them. They shape public opinion, and public opinion is what matters, especially during a crisis. Be honest with the media, and when they call, be available.

3. Don't ignore the bureaucracy. A diplomat watches the internal debates of, and listens to gossip about, the middle-level bureaucracy. By the time policy pronouncements are made from the top, it may be too late to influence them.

4. Cultivate good relations with the "desk officer" at the State Department—that is, the official who is in charge of policymaking and information about your particular country. Also cultivate congressional staff. Hamdoon reported that the Iraqi Embassy held a lunch or dinner for congressional staff every few weeks.

5. Never feel secure about any issue. Things can happen quickly in Congress, the executive branch, or the media, and you had better be ready.

6. Take the long-range view of issues.

7. Reach out to all Americans, no matter what their position on issues. Be prepared to debate rationally and refute stereotypes of your country.

8. Get away from Washington. As Hamdoon said, "If you stick too long in the capital, you begin to think that America is a nation of opportunists, and that nobody cares about you unless you are a power broker in a business suit." But, he concluded, people outside Washington are not so influenced by the media and not so caught up in what's happening today.

9. Watch out for checks and balances. Washington is different from other capitals because in Paris, London, or Moscow, there is a central government in charge of foreign policy. In the United States, you may deal with a State Department official today, only to find that the policy has been reversed by Congress tomorrow. The positive side of this approach, however, is that you can affect policy because it is so changeable. "Nothing is ever final in Washington. . . . Everything and everyone is workable."

SOURCE: This box is summarized from Nizar Hamdoon, "The Washington Education of an Arab Diplomat," *Washington Post National Weekly Edition,* September 14, 1987, 24.

If a president comes to office with a foreign policy agenda and expects to make his political reputation and leave his mark on history in this policy area, as Richard Nixon and the first George Bush did, he will surround himself with like-minded people and replace those who disagree with him or ignore their advice. Bush appointed both members of the foreign policy establishment who had held high positions in previous administrations and several associates from his tenure as CIA director, an organizational tie that made many in Congress uncomfortable.

Ex-governors like Carter, Reagan, Clinton, and George W. Bush can compensate for their lack of foreign policy experience when they become president by surrounding themselves with experts. Nevertheless, Carter and Reagan chose foreign policy advisers with limited experience and had difficulty maintaining unity among them. In contrast, Clinton appointed an experienced team of advisers, including a number from the Carter administration, but was himself undecided on policy direction early in his presidency. George W. Bush chose his entire first-tier foreign policy advisers, and part of the second tier, from his those who had served in his father's and earlier Republican administrations. Collectively they were, arguably, the most experienced group of foreign policy advisers assembled by any president since the end of World War II.

Specialists

The process of formulating long-term policy usually involves more people than the number involved in decision making in crisis situations. The State Department, with twenty-six thousand employees, has experts on every region of the globe and on substantive policy issues such as economic assistance, trade, political affairs, and arms control.

Political officers in Washington and in our embassies and consulates abroad write daily summaries of important political and economic events in the countries to which they are assigned. This information is used to provide daily briefings for higher-level officials, but almost none of it ever reaches the president's desk, and only a small portion of it can be read even by the secretary of state. Specialists in other cabinet departments and independent agencies, such as Defense, Treasury, Commerce, Agriculture, and Justice, do research and write reports, and the work of intelligence gatherers is also extremely important.

We should not assume that these experts present neutral information that is somehow mechanically cranked out as public policy. Even if the experts do their best to provide the most accurate information and most comprehensive policy alternatives possible, top policymakers see the information through their own percep-

tual and ideological lenses. Our Vietnam policies failed in part because many of our best Asian experts had been purged from the State Department during the McCarthy era. The Reagan administration ignored advisers who cautioned against its covert policies in Nicaragua and Iran and replaced State Department experts who disagreed with its Central America policies. More than most presidents, Reagan made appointments to key positions in the State Department based on political considerations rather than on career expertise.

High turnover in specialist positions has, at times, put us at a disadvantage relative to our adversaries and allies. Almost all of the policymaking positions within the foreign policy establishment are held by political appointees who usually stay only a few years. This turnover compounds the loss of expertise that comes from maneuvering specialists out of career positions when their recommendations do not support the preferred policies of a particular administration. During the Cold War, for example, the former Soviet Union had much the same team of arms control negotiators for many years. Our negotiating teams changed, on average, every three to four years. Since arms control is an extremely complex field, our negotiators were continually in the process of learning.

There are, however, career specialists in the federal bureaucracy who are not political appointees, such as the staff of intelligence agencies, area specialists in the State and Defense Departments, and almost all members of the Foreign Service. Their briefings may simply be ignored if they do not support policy choices preferred by their superiors. And turf battles can result in incomplete or inaccurate information reaching the highest levels. Agency separation, competition, and even antagonism led to many of the intelligence failures prior to and after the September 11 attacks.

Experts outside government who are associated with various think tanks are also sometimes influential in foreign policymaking. Primarily located in Washington, close to decision makers and the national media, these institutions—such as the Institute for Policy Studies on the left of the political spectrum; the Cato and Heritage Foundations on the right; and the Brookings Institution, the American Enterprise Institute, and the Council on Foreign Relations in the middle—conduct and publish research on policy issues. By writing articles for national newspapers and journals and being interviewed on news and public affairs programs, experts in these institutions "wage perpetual war against each other" trying to determine the course of American foreign policy.[8]

Congress

The leading members of congressional committees on foreign affairs and armed services and of the oversight committees for intelligence agencies play a larger role in foreign policy than does the average member. But Congress as a whole has specific constitutional authority to act as a check on the president's policies through its power to declare and fund wars and the requirement for Senate ratification of treaties and confirmation of ambassadorial and high-level State Department officials. Because Congress appropriates all money for carrying out foreign policy, the president is limited in the actions he can take without congressional approval.

Rivalry between the White House and Congress in foreign policymaking intensifies or diminishes with the issue in question. Nowhere is conflict greater than over the use of the military to achieve foreign policy goals. (This subject is discussed in greater detail in Chapter 11.) Politicians and scholars have been arguing for more than two hundred years about how Congress's constitutional authority to "declare war" limits the president's authority as commander in chief. The Founders, believing it too dangerous to give war powers to the president alone, were also unwilling to accept wording that would have given Congress the power to "make war." Instead, they gave Congress the power to "declare war," leaving the president, according to James Madison's notes on the debate, "the power to repel sudden attacks."[9] This left Congress and the president to struggle over what constitutes an attack on the United States and when a military intervention is a war.

There have been more than two hundred occasions when the president has sent troops into combat situations without congressional approval. In fact, Congress has exercised its power to declare war only five times, and on only one of those occasions, the War of 1812, did it conduct a debate before issuing the declaration. Yet the two undeclared wars in Korea and Vietnam alone produced almost one hundred thousand American deaths, more than the combined losses of all of our declared wars, except World War II.[10]

The War Powers Act, which was intended to curb what Congress believes is presidential usurpation of its authority, has been opposed by every president since Lyndon Johnson. No prior approval was sought for sending troops to Lebanon, Grenada, or Panama, and both Presidents Bush sought it for their actions in Iraq only under pressure (see the "You Are There" for this chapter). During the Clinton administration, Democrats tried to strengthen the act and Republicans to repeal it; neither effort was successful. As one supporter of the act commented, "Every president finds Congress inconvenient, but we're a democracy, not a monarchy."[11]

Whatever their differences with Congress, presidents in the postwar era have usually proclaimed their desire to have a "bipartisan" foreign policy; that is, they want support from both parties in order to present a united front to the world. Presidents will often try to frame policies in a national security context as a way to pressure Congress into accepting their position, but Congress's role is not simply to rubber-stamp executive branch policies.

Presidents especially need bipartisan support when treaties are to be ratified because it is rare for one party to have the necessary two-thirds majority in the Senate or for members of each party to be united in their ranks. Carter, for example, had to woo and win Republican support to secure ratification of the hotly contested Panama Canal treaties, which returned control of the United States–built canal and the Canal Zone to the government of Panama. In contrast, after signing the Kyoto Treaty that laid out measures for dealing with global warming, Clinton did not even submit it to the Senate for confirmation because he knew he could not get the necessary sixty-seven votes.

Presidents like to say that in facing the rest of the world, Americans are all on the same side. But this view is too simplistic. Policies shaping how we deal with the rest of the world are controversial and complex. Party positions do differ on these as on most other issues, as shown in roll call votes.[12] Democrats are more likely than Republicans to favor cuts in military spending, to agree that the United States was partially responsible for the Cold War, and to support military intervention to stop human rights abuses. Republicans are more likely to support unrestricted trade, military intervention to protect U.S. economic interests, and military aid to poor countries rather than aid for development, health, and family planning. They are also more likely than Democrats to oppose placing U.S. troops under foreign command as part of multilateral forces.[13]

Differences between the two major parties on foreign policy are usually apparent in the national platform each party issues in presidential election years. Even so, it often seems that the opposition party has no coherent alternative to the president's policy. This is probably because under normal circumstances, members of Congress spend most of their time on the domestic issues that are so important to their constituents (especially at election time). In times of crisis, as when U.S. troops are committed to combat, the opposition party usually rallies in support of administration policy so that the country can present a united front to the world. Once these troops are actually engaged in battle, those who continue to oppose the president's actions can find themselves in the position of appearing to give higher priority to their policy preferences than to the safety of U.S. troops. At this point, it is very difficult for the opposition party to oppose the president's policy effectively. Despite George H. Bush's narrow margin of congressional support for the use of force in the Persian Gulf, once the air war began there was virtually no criticism of administration policies by members of Congress. There are notable exceptions, such as bipartisan criticism of Johnson's and Nixon's Vietnam policies, but this dissent came late in the course of the fighting, when public opinion was turning against the war and administration policies did not seem to be working. Even then, Congress approved virtually all expenditures requested to wage the war.

In Congress, members of the opposition party are more likely to state policy alternatives on an ad hoc basis, acting as individuals, not for the party. The public may be confused when it hears a half dozen or more policy alternatives presented by members of the same party, and it may even conclude that they are "lone rangers" trying to gain political advantage in a situation that seems to call for national unity. This was evident in the debate over Bush's Iraq policy just prior to the 2002 midterm elections. When campaigning for Republican congressional candidates, Bush suggested that Democrats who dissented from his policy were politicizing the war (though by using this issue in his campaign speeches, the president was also politicizing the war). In the end, most Democrats retreated, leaving the president to make his Iraq policy a key issue in the election.

Interest Groups and Lobbyists

A multiplicity of interest groups are concerned with foreign policy issues: international businesses; public interest groups, such as those that lobby on environmental and human rights issues; veterans' organizations; farmers who grow crops for export; labor unions; and ethnic groups interested in their ancestral lands, such as African, Jewish, Arab, Irish, Cuban, Mexican, and Polish Americans.

In general, it is harder for interest groups to affect foreign policy than domestic policy. Part of the reason for this is that the president and the executive branch have greater weight than Congress in day-to-day foreign policy decision making. But interest group activity has always been effective in some policy areas, especially those related to containing communism, trade, and foreign investment. For example, electronics industries lobby against national security restrictions that keep them from exporting computer equipment and software that have military applications. Farm and business organizations lobby on behalf of import quotas to protect their domestically produced goods and against embargoes that prevent them from selling their products abroad. When Congress placed sanctions on India and Pakistan for conducting nuclear tests, it exempted what could have been the biggest penalty—food exports. Wheat farmers in the Northwest argued that sanctions on food exports would have prevented them from bidding on a $37 million wheat order from Pakistan, their biggest customer.[14]

Americans have a long history of trying to win favorable U.S. policy for their countries of birth or ancestry. Some have even undertaken private action in support of home countries: Irish Americans have sold guns to the Irish Republican Army and Jewish Americans to Jews in Palestine trying to establish an independent Israel, while Cuban Americans have trained a military force on U.S. soil to overthrow the Castro government in Cuba (even though it is illegal to do so under U.S. law).

Perhaps no other nationality group has had as much success in setting the foreign policy agenda for their homeland as Cuban Americans. The strength of their lobby is due in part to a predisposition in Congress for their policy preference and in part to the concentration of their population in one state with a large number of electoral votes. The Cuban American lobby has been the driving force behind preferential treatment for Cuban immigrants and the maintenance of an economic embargo against the Castro government. In recent years, however, the Cuba lobby has seen its influence decline. U.S. farm and business lobbies, afraid of losing export and investment opportunities on the island to Canada and Europe, have succeeded in getting Congress to lift the sanctions on food exports and lighten travel restrictions.

During the past quarter century, three factors have opened up the foreign policy decision-making process to greater influence by interest groups. The first is the growing importance of campaign spending and the rise of political action committees (PACs). Both the president and members of Congress depend on large campaign contributions from interest groups and are thus more vulnerable to a wide range of their demands.

Second, the personal presidency, in combination with the rise of identity politics, has increased the need of presidents to serve a multitude of constituencies and interests. Under pressure from African American interest groups, Clinton gave U.S. policy toward Africa a prominence it never had previously. His twelve-day trip to six African nations in 1998 was the first by a U.S. president for twenty years and the most extensive ever. Women's and religious interest groups have also become important lobbies, affecting policies on foreign aid, family planning, abortion, immigration, and women's rights. Women's groups found an advocate in Madeleine Albright, the first woman to serve as secretary of state; she identified international women's rights as one of the Clinton administration's priority issues.

Third, the globalization of economic activity has intensified interest groups' efforts to influence trade policy because of their concern about its impact on wages, job opportunities, child labor, worker safety, and the environment. This has led to new and very vocal alliances among trade unions and environmental and human rights groups to oppose current trade policy. During a conference of the world's top trade officials in Seattle in 1999, thousands of protestors took to the streets and managed to shut down parts of the city and interrupt the proceedings, and at each succeeding summit meeting, they have launched similarly high-profile attacks on international monetary policy.

Private citizens who are part of Washington's elite also play a role in foreign policy.[15] For example, Henry Kissinger, former secretary of state; Brent Scowcroft, former national security adviser; and Lawrence Eagleburger, former undersecretary of state, formed a consulting business. They advised some of the world's largest corporations about foreign affairs and how international developments might affect the world economic climate in general and their corporations in particular. At the same time, Kissinger and his associates provided advice to government through their service on various influential advisory boards.

Some former members of Congress and high-level political appointees have become registered agents (lobbyists) for foreign governments after leaving office. Some who are public officials one day are private citizens the next and public officials again a few years later.[16] Rules about what constitutes a conflict of interest in such cases are unclear.

Public Opinion

Overall, the views of the public on foreign policy are not that different from those of elected policymakers. When they do vary, public opinion has little direct effect except on high-profile issues that could make a difference at the polls. One reason is that much of our foreign policy is made incrementally over a long period of time and out of public view. Other decisions are made in "crisis" situations or in secrecy for national security reasons. On issues such as invading Grenada or trading arms to Iran in exchange for hostages, public opinion was registered only after the fact; even Congress was not informed in advance of the invasion.

Another factor limiting the public's ability to influence foreign policy decisions is that only a minority of Americans know much about even the most publicly discussed issues, and many have no opinion about them. The public has always been more interested in domestic issues that impinge directly on daily life, such as the availability of jobs and the cost of consumer goods. Although there is growing awareness of the impact of foreign policy, especially trade issues, on daily life, it is difficult for the public to be well informed on the technical problems involved in trade and tariff negotiations.

Network television news programs, responding to their viewers' primary interest in domestic issues, cut back international coverage substantially during the 1990s. Americans who rely on television as their main

President Bush meets with Secretary of State Powell.

news source, as a majority of Americans do, see only a few minutes of foreign coverage each day. After 9/11, when Americans began expressing more interest in foreign policy and information about other countries, especially those with Muslim populations, television news programs increased their coverage of international affairs. But in polls taken one month after the attacks, Americans were saying again that their primary concerns were jobs and the economy.

In general, the public is more likely to concede its ignorance on a wider range of issues in foreign policy than in domestic policy and to accept the judgments of decision makers. Therefore, on most issues, it is easier for the president to influence public opinion on foreign affairs through use of the media than it is for public opinion to change the president's foreign policy. Sometimes, however, public opinion resists attempts to change it. It is more likely to remain firm when the public holds the administration in low repute or when the government is divided, as it was on Vietnam. Deeply held opinions are also more resistant to administration pressure.

In the long term, the public always has the option of voting out of office those who disagree with majority views on foreign policy issues. However, it is difficult to use the vote to mandate that a president take a specific action, since, as we saw in Chapter 8, people vote on the basis of many different issues, most of them involving domestic policy.

Trade policy provides a good illustration of the limits on the ability of public opinion to change the president's position on a foreign policy issue. The many interest groups that have allied to oppose U.S. trade policy constitute a substantial segment of the general public. Interest group opposition to the North American Free Trade Agreement (NAFTA), which eliminated trade

In World War I, government rhetoric and propaganda shaped public opinion by portraying German opponents as bloodthirsty gorillas. This army enlistment poster was printed in 1917.

barriers among Mexico, Canada, and the United States, was so strong that it led most Democrats, who were then the majority in Congress, to openly oppose their own party's president on this issue. One member said, "All of the traditional groups we count on to reelect us [Democrats] are against NAFTA."[17] The only person in his district willing to help get the bill passed was a Republican from the Chamber of Commerce. Despite this opposition from his own party's leadership and from traditional Democratic constituencies, Clinton never wavered in his support for NAFTA because increasing trade was the cornerstone of both his domestic and foreign policies.

Ultimately, without some public support, foreign policy objectives that require substantial commitments of time and resources will prove unsuccessful. The necessity of public support for large-scale undertakings is evident in attempts to manipulate public access to information. This is most common during wartime, when the government can justify press censorship on national security grounds. Withholding negative information (for example, high casualty rates, slow progress, civilian losses) can help keep public support high. The Persian Gulf War was fought with keen attention to public opinion. The short air war preceding the ground attack was calculated not only to minimize military casualties and the length of the ground war but also to maintain public support for the president's policies. Moreover, the restricted press coverage, which did not allow casualties to be shown, enhanced that support.

Sometimes the withholding or manipulating of information can backfire, as it certainly did during the Vietnam War. And Reagan's use of covert action in channeling money from Iran arms' sales to Nicaraguan guerrillas to skirt congressional and public opposition to his policy eventually increased that opposition.

In general, because of the revolution in information technology, it is getting harder for the president, or the president and Congress together, to appeal for public support based on a claim of privileged information. Even though the president and Congress may have more reliable information, and better analysis of it, the press, interest groups, and the general public now have many more sources of information on foreign policy issues than they had a decade ago. More Americans are in e-mail contact with people in other countries and have access to the Web sites of foreign newspapers, governments, and think tanks, as well as to declassified documents in electronic archives. In fact, private firms here and abroad, including former Soviet intelligence operatives, will even sell satellite reconnaissance photography to order.[18]

Changing Approaches to U.S. Foreign Policy

Isolationism

Historically, noninvolvement with other nations outside the Americas was a principal goal of our foreign policy. This policy is called **isolationism.** In the nineteenth and early twentieth centuries, Americans generally stayed aloof from European conflicts and turned inward, busy with domestic expansion and development.

One important exception was our continuing military and political involvement in Latin America, which was justified by the **Monroe Doctrine** of 1823. In articulating this doctrine, President James Monroe warned European powers that were not already in Latin America to stay out. This was a brazen move because we were a minor power challenging the major powers of the time.

As European powers withdrew from the region in the late nineteenth and early twentieth centuries, the United States began to play an increasingly active, and at times interventionist, role. With little regard for national sovereignty, we sent troops to protect U.S. citizens or business interests and to replace existing governments with those more sympathetic to our wishes. Paradoxically, the Monroe Doctrine derived primarily from isolationist, not interventionist, sentiment. By keeping foreign powers on their side of the ocean and out of our hemisphere, we believed we would be less likely to be drawn into conflicts abroad.

During this time, Americans did not think it appropriate to intervene in the problems of Europe or to keep a large standing army at home. This attitude was an offshoot of the predominant mood in domestic affairs: preoccupation with economic growth and fear of a strong central government. Isolationism was also a realistic position in the sense that the United States was not yet a world power. Yet another source of isolationist sentiment were those who believed that the United States was unique and that the more entangling alliances it entered into with foreign countries, the more likely it would "be corrupted and its unique nature . . . subverted."[19]

This isolationist sentiment lapsed briefly in 1917–1919, when America entered World War I on the side of the British and French against Germany, but rapidly revived at its close. Despite the wishes of President Woodrow Wilson, the United States refused to join the League of Nations, the ill-fated precursor to the United Nations. Although we have no public opinion polls from these early years, with hindsight, 70 percent of Americans polled in 1937 thought it had been a mistake to enter World War I.

Yet the United States was never truly isolationist in its actions. Throughout the whole early isolationist era, we frequently intervened diplomatically and militarily in the Caribbean and Central America and consistently sought to expand U.S. commercial and cultural influ-ence throughout the world. Even President McKinley, who was labeled an "imperialist" by Democrats for his military adventures in the Caribbean and the Philippines, was easily reelected. And his successor, Theodore Roosevelt, was closer to an interventionist than an isolationist. Polls from the post–World War I era show that Americans overwhelmingly favored joining an international peacekeeping body like the League of Nations. And historians have pointed out there were enough votes in the Senate to ratify participation in the league had President Wilson been willing to accept amendments to the treaty agreement.[20]

Americans have almost always been willing to participate in world affairs to defend our national interests. But we are often slow to recognize just what is at stake. In 1939, we refused to join Britain in its war to stop Nazi Germany's attempted conquest of Europe. It was not until the December 1941 Japanese attack on Pearl Harbor, Hawaii, that the public was willing to support entry into World War II. When Germany and Italy then declared war on the United States, we fought in Europe alongside Britain, the Soviet Union, and remnant armies from the occupied nations of Europe.

Containment

The Allied victory in 1945 brought a split between the Soviet Union and its Western allies. The Soviet Union lost 20 million people in the war (the United States lost four hundred thousand). Given these losses in a German invasion that was only one of many invasions of Russian territory over the centuries, the Soviet government was determined, especially as a protection against Germany,

Courtesy Tatiana Baltermants and Paul Harbaugh

Millions of Russian civilians as well as soldiers were killed in World War II. Grieving Soviets search for their friends and relatives after Nazi murder squads massacred a village in the Crimea in 1942.

to have friendly neighbors in Europe, just as we wanted them in Latin America. To ensure this, the Soviet Union was willing to use any means, including intervention, to secure communist governments in the ring of nations surrounding it—Poland, Czechoslovakia, Romania, Hungary, and Bulgaria. Our wish for free elections in these nations was seen by the Soviet Union as an attempt to isolate it. The Russians believed we wanted to surround them with anti-Soviet governments, thus making their sacrifices in World War II futile. Many of our policymakers saw the subversion of eastern European governments as the beginning of a Soviet effort to conquer Europe.

As the only major power not decimated by the war, the United States was unable to return to its isolationist prewar stance. In 1947, the Truman administration formulated a policy to limit the spread of communism by meeting any action taken by the Soviet Union to spread its influence with counterforce or a countermove by the United States. Known as **containment** (or the Truman Doctrine), this policy led U.S. decision makers to see most of the world's conflicts in terms of rivalry between the Soviet Union and the United States. The Soviet coup d'état in Czechoslovakia in 1948 and the rise to power of the Chinese communist government of Mao Zedong in 1949 fueled U.S. fears that the communists would try to expand the area under their control as far as possible. Thus, when communist North Korea attacked South Korea in 1950, we intervened as the nucleus of a United Nations force, believing we had to stop the spread of communism in Korea before the Soviets undertook further expansion.

Just as isolationism began as a defensive posture to keep European conflicts out of the Americas, so containment was aimed at limiting the Russians to their post–World War II reach and out of our sphere of influence. Instead of trying to roll back Soviet power, containment was designed to keep it from expanding to a point that changed the global power balance or dragged the United States into unwanted conflicts. The chief instruments of containment policy were economic and military aid to developing countries, cultural exchanges, covert activity, alliance building, nuclear deterrence, and, as in Korea and Vietnam, limited war fought with conventional weaponry.

Containment philosophy was at work in the Marshall Plan, which provided economic relief to the nations of western Europe in 1947 (aid was offered to some eastern European governments, but they refused). In addition, the United States entered into military alliances with friendly nations in Europe and Asia to stop the spread of, or to roll back, Soviet influence. The most important of these was **NATO, the North Atlantic Treaty Organization,** which in 1949 joined the United States, Canada, and their western European al-lies in a mutual defense pact against Soviet aggression in Europe. Building these military alliances to compete with the Soviet Union and its eastern European allies reflected the **Cold War** era that we had now entered. We were not in military battle with the Russians, but the deep hostility between the two nations threatened to turn any conflict into a major armed confrontation.

Nuclear Deterrence

The nuclear era began in 1945, when the United States dropped atomic bombs on the Japanese cities of Hiroshima and Nagasaki. Although the debate on the necessity and ethics of dropping these bombs still continues, Japan surrendered, bringing the war in the Pacific to an end.

At the close of the war, the United States was the only nuclear power. The Soviet Union exploded its first bomb in 1949, but it did not have an operational warhead until the mid-1950s and for a while thereafter had no intercontinental bombers or missiles to deliver the bombs. Despite our nuclear superiority, we found our power limited. Nuclear weapons were of little use in the pursuit of most foreign policy objectives because the threat of inflicting mass destruction to achieve a nonvital objective was not credible to opponents. Thus, during the period of nuclear superiority, the United States saw its Chinese Nationalist allies lose to communists in China, its French allies lose to Ho Chi Minh in Indochina, and an anticommunist uprising in Hungary in 1956 crushed by Soviet tanks.

In 1955, the Soviet Union and its eastern European satellites formed the Warsaw Pact, a military alliance to counter NATO. People began to see international relations as a bipolar competition between a Western bloc of countries united under the U.S. nuclear umbrella and an Eastern bloc of nations operating under the protection of the Soviet nuclear umbrella.

American nuclear dominance began to erode in the late 1950s. *Sputnik* (the Soviet satellite that was the first to orbit the Earth) showed that the Soviet Union had successfully built large rockets capable of firing missiles that could reach the United States. The fear of Soviet rocketry advances led to a program to build and deploy nuclear-tipped intercontinental ballistic missiles (ICBMs) to supplement our bomber force.

Even with Soviet advances, American nuclear superiority was maintained for another decade. Yet everyone agreed that neither side could attack the other without the certain knowledge that the attacker as well as the attacked would suffer enormous damage. No sane leader would risk so much damage by striking first.[21] This capability, with the appropriate acronym of **MAD,** is called **mutual assured destruction.**

Despite public frustration with the Cold War—being neither totally at war nor at peace—successive adminis-

Fifty years after the bombing of Hiroshima, the city appears fully restored, but the U.S. decision to use atomic weapons is still so controversial that the Smithsonian Institution had to withdraw a planned fiftieth anniversary exhibit that presented arguments against as well as for the bomb's use. Other assaults on cities, such as the firebombing of Tokyo and Japan's "Rape of Nanjing," caused as many or more deaths, but the use of the atomic bomb stands out in public memory because it opened the door to a new kind of warfare.

Both photos from Sygma

trations found that "rolling back" communism in the nuclear age was not possible without the kind of risk and commitment of resources most Americans were unwilling to assume. While the Kennedy administration did risk nuclear war over Soviet placement of nuclear weapons in Cuba, ninety miles from our shores, we stood by and avoided such risks when the Soviet Union invaded Hungary in 1956, Czechoslovakia in 1968, and Afghanistan in 1979. And the Soviet Union stood by and avoided confrontation with the United States when we sent military forces to Vietnam.

One of the basic premises of containment was that all communist nations were controlled by the Soviet Union. But as the 1950s progressed, it became clear that this was not true. Both Albania and Yugoslavia spurned Moscow's control. The Chinese became increasingly independent and in the early 1960s broke with the Soviet Union, declaring "there are many paths to socialism." Despite this, we continued to define most international events in terms of communists versus anticommunists, no matter how poorly such a characterization fit. This conviction formed the basis of the **domino theory,** the proposition that if one country fell to communist rule, it would set off a chain reaction in neighboring countries, just as a long line of dominoes standing on end will fall in sequence when the first one is toppled. If U.S. intervention could prevent the first country to come under attack from falling, others would stand firm. This rationale led us into Vietnam, our longest war.

Vietnam

Early Period If one were ranking the landmark events of the twentieth century, surely World War II would rank at the top. We live in a completely different world than would have existed had Hitler not been defeated. Fighting alongside Britain and the Soviet Union, the United States achieved its greatest military victory and forged the alliance with western Europe that led to our most important treaty relationship. Yet the Vietnam War has had a far greater impact on U.S. foreign and military policy in the last quarter of the century. In this section we try to explain why.

When we became involved in Vietnam, it was still part of the French colonial territory of Indochina. After the defeat of the Japanese occupying forces in World War II, the Indochinese Communist Party, led by Ho Chi Minh, engaged the returning French forces in a war for independence. Ho appealed several times to the United States—a critic of both British and French colonial policies—for support in this effort but was rebuffed. As the war in Indochina dragged on, the Cold War settled in, and containment became the organizing concept in American foreign policy. By 1954, when Ho's troops defeated the French in a major battle, the United States was underwriting 80 percent of the cost of the French effort in Vietnam. But after considerable deliberation, the Eisenhower administration refused to provide troops or air support to save the French because Eisenhower believed this could bog us down in a long war requiring many troops.

At a conference in Geneva in 1954, a temporary boundary was established separating the territory of Ho's government in the North from that of the French- and U.S.-backed government in the South until elections could be held to choose leaders for all of Vietnam. The new prime minister in the South, Ngo Dinh Diem, was a staunch anticommunist Catholic with influential friends in the U.S. Catholic community and Congress. Diem's government refused to participate in the elections scheduled for 1956, and the United States backed him because it believed Ho's communist government would win the election. The temporary partition between the North and South continued, and after the assassination of Diem in 1963, it soon became clear that the South Vietnamese government would collapse without more U.S. intervention.

Armed Intervention In 1964, President Johnson won congressional approval for massive intervention in Vietnam. In an August television address to the American public, Johnson claimed that two U.S. destroyers had been attacked by North Vietnamese torpedo boats while on routine patrol in international waters near the Gulf of Tonkin. He announced his intention to retaliate by bombing sites in North Vietnam. The next day, after presenting misleading information about the role of the U.S. destroyers in initiating the attack, he asked Congress to endorse the Gulf of Tonkin Resolution authorizing him "to take all necessary measures to repel any armed attack against the forces of the U.S. and to prevent further aggression."

Presidents Johnson and Nixon used the Tonkin Resolution to justify each act of escalation in the war. This

President Johnson listens in anguish to a tape sent by his son-in-law (Charles Robb, then an officer in Vietnam, later a U.S. senator from Virginia), talking about the men lost in battle in Vietnam.

deception laid the groundwork for the gradual erosion of congressional support for the war effort.

In early 1965, Johnson sent in U.S. troops in the belief that the war would be over "in a matter of months." After all, the United States had sophisticated equipment and training and complete air superiority. But three years later, after half a million U.S. troops had been committed to combat, the Vietcong—North Vietnam's southern allies—were able to launch a major offensive that demonstrated that all our military efforts had not made one square foot of Vietnam truly secure. When the Joint Chiefs of Staff requested more than two hundred thousand additional troops, a stunned President Johnson decided to undertake a review of Vietnam policy. Even the Joint Chiefs were not sure how many years and troops it might take to win. As public opposition to the war grew, Johnson called for peace talks and announced that he would not run for reelection in 1968. The talks began in May 1968 and dragged on through the administration of Johnson's successor, Richard Nixon.

President Nixon wanted to leave Vietnam without appearing to have lost the war. To accomplish this, he tried "Vietnamizing" the war by forcing the South Vietnamese government to give more responsibility to its own army. He authorized the massive bombing of Hanoi and began withdrawing U.S. troops.

In a march on Washington, antiwar protesters put flowers in the guns of military police to symbolize peace.

Nixon's most controversial war policy was his decision to expand the war into neighboring Cambodia, supposedly to destroy a huge underground headquarters of the North Vietnamese army near the Vietnamese border. In addition to igniting the largest public protests of the war, the invasion finally led to significant congressional opposition. The Gulf of Tonkin Resolution was repealed, and a resolution passed prohibiting the president from using budgeted funds to wage a ground war in Cambodia. Nixon had planned to withdraw the troops from Cambodia anyway and did so quickly. But bombing in Cambodia continued until 1973, when Congress forbade the use of funds for this purpose. This was the only time Congress actually blocked presidential policies in the war.

In 1973, the United States and North Vietnam signed a peace agreement. We might have reached the same agreement in 1969, but President Nixon had believed this would jeopardize his reelection chances in 1972 and perhaps other foreign policy goals, too.[22] The victory of the Vietcong and North Vietnamese finally occurred in 1975 as the South Vietnamese army disintegrated in the face of a communist attack.

Lessons from Vietnam Much of our thinking about the use of the military today is still informed by the lessons of policy failures in Vietnam.[23] Even though at its peak in 1968–1969 our military force in Vietnam exceeded half a million, had sophisticated equipment and training, and had complete air superiority, we were eventually defeated. Why did we fail?

■ *We did not have clear goals.* Policymakers never agreed on whether we were fighting China, the Soviet Union, North Vietnam, or rebels in the South (the Vietcong). It was not clear what or whom we were trying to defend or what Vietnam was supposed to look like after the North was defeated.

■ *We did not understand the political aspects of the war.* Supporting a series of unpopular South Vietnamese governments, we were at first oblivious to the vast indigenous opposition to the South Vietnamese government from communists, other nationalists, and Buddhists. Our inability to construct an effective policy for "winning the hearts and minds" of the domestic opposition to the South Vietnamese government appears to have been a fatal weakness of policymakers from Eisenhower through Nixon.

In 1995, on the twentieth anniversary of the war's end, Robert McNamara, secretary of defense in the Kennedy and Johnson administrations and a principal architect of early Vietnam policy, wrote a book publicly stating for the first time that by 1967 he had come to the conclusion that the war was a mistake and could not be won. Principal among his eleven reasons for the loss were the incompetence of the South Vietnamese government and armed forces and American underestimation of the North Vietnamese.[24] President Johnson's refusal to accept this conclusion led McNamara to leave—or be made to leave—the cabinet in 1968. But as recently revealed, at the very time he was making large troop commitments, Johnson was saying, "I don't see any way of winning."[25]

■ *We did not understand the nature of guerrilla warfare.* For much of the war, we did not fight against a standing army dressed in the uniform of an enemy

AP/Wide World Photos

Joe McNally/*Life* magazine © Time Inc.

This photo of a naked South Vietnamese girl screaming after a napalm attack by "friendly" forces was one of the most famous photographs of the war and one that fueled antiwar protest. The girl, Kim Phue, survived, although in pain and under long-term treatment for her wounds. Now living in Canada, she is pictured here with her son, Huan. (His name means "prospects.") She notes, "I know my picture did something to help stop the war. I have to show [my son] what happened to his mom, to her country, and that there should never be war again."

Mobs of South Vietnamese civilians scale the walls of the U.S. embassy in Saigon, trying to hitch a ride on the evacuation helicopters as the North Vietnamese enter the city and the last Americans leave in 1975.

force. It was often impossible for our troops to tell soldier from civilian or enemy from ally. Although we inflicted heavy casualties on the Vietcong and North Vietnamese forces, we killed thousands of civilians in the process. Our opponents were able to demonstrate to the people of the South that their government and its ally, the United States, could not protect them or their villages. In fact, the Vietcong were able to dominate much of the rural South. Our policies—to "destroy villages in order to save them" and to take people from their own villages to "strategic hamlets," where presumably they were safe from the Vietcong—were bitterly resented by many South Vietnamese.

■ *We were impatient with the war and were unwilling to devote unending resources to winning it.* We knew from the British experience in defeating communist guerrillas in Malaysia that we would need at least ten soldiers to the guerrillas' one and that we might need ten years to win the war, but no leader dared tell the public that we must commit ourselves for that long. We were unwilling to invest the resources or time needed to defeat a guerrilla enemy. Since the goals were unclear, few wanted to risk use of the ultimate weaponry that could have destroyed the North. Although this stance was rational, it did not seem to lead to the obvious question of whether our objectives were worth the effort we were making.

■ *We did not have public support.* Although public opinion was generally supportive during the first years of the war, support eroded as it appeared we were bogged down in an interminable and indeci-

sive conflict. Only about 20 percent of the public favored an immediate withdrawal in 1965, but by mid-1969, support for withdrawal began to increase and reached 50 percent by 1970. By 1971, public support for withdrawal grew to overwhelming proportions.[26]

The United States persisted in Vietnam for nearly eleven years because most policymakers believed in standing firm against what they saw as communist aggression and because no president wanted to be responsible for losing a war. But Vietnam shattered the belief in containment and U.S. illusions that it could serve as the world's police force. Many Americans believed both our aims and tactics in Vietnam were immoral. Others believed our aims were just but unachievable. Still others believed we should have stayed until we won. All these sentiments led to a good deal of public self-examination about the war.

The failure of our Vietnam policy produced the **Vietnam syndrome,** an attitude among the public and officials of uncertainty about our foreign policy goals and our ability to achieve them through military means. Decision makers became more reluctant to commit troops to combat situations or to threaten military action to pursue containment goals. Some people believed this new caution was a positive development that would keep us from becoming involved in new military entanglements we could not win. But many others believed this national self-doubt tied the hands of decision makers and prevented them from using the full range of our capabilities to pursue national interests abroad.

These differences persist among principal policymakers today. Colin Powell, former chairman of the Joint Chiefs of Staff and current secretary of state, served in Vietnam and came away with a reluctance to commit U.S. forces to combat abroad without clear goals and exit plans. It led to his early opposition to committing troops to Operation Desert Storm in 1991 and to unilateral military action against Iraq in 2002. In considering whether to vote for the congressional resolution giving George W. Bush a free hand in Iraq, Senator Robert Byrd (D-W.V.), drew a parallel with the Gulf of Tonkin Resolution and lamented his own vote in favor of the resolution that gave Lyndon Johnson a free hand in Vietnam.

Detente

Richard Nixon came to office after public opinion had begun to turn against the war. Perhaps partly for this reason and partly because his central interest was in foreign and not domestic policy, he immediately began looking for ways to shape international relations in the post–Vietnam War era.

As a man whose career was built on making political hay out of his staunch anticommunism, President Nixon was well placed to make diplomatic overtures to the Soviet Union without fear of being attacked by any but the most die-hard Cold Warriors. Thus, Nixon and his national security adviser and later secretary of state, Henry Kissinger, developed a policy called **detente,** which was designed to deescalate Cold War rhetoric and to promote the notion that relations with the Soviet Union could be conducted in ways other than confrontation.

With a policy of detente, we could reward the Soviet Union for "good behavior" on the international scene and at the same time reduce our own military expenditures, slow the arms race, and perhaps step back from the brink of war. The detente doctrine recognized that although the Soviet Union would remain our adversary, it, too, had legitimate interests in the world. Detente also recognized the growing military strength of the Soviet Union and that it was in our interests to pursue bilateral agreements, such as on arms control, that would try to limit this strength.

Among the most notable achievements of the detente policy were the Strategic Arms Limitation Talks, which produced a treaty (SALT I), signed by President Nixon and Soviet leader Leonid Brezhnev in 1972. SALT I limited the number of ABM (antiballistic missile—a defensive missile) launchers that each side could possess and put a five-year freeze on the number of offensive missiles in each side's stockpile.

During this era of new diplomacy with the Soviet Union, President Nixon also sent out feelers to see whether China was interested in reestablishing diplomatic ties. Even though it was home to one-fifth of the world's population, China had been shut out of the mainstream diplomatic community, largely due to U.S. pressure, since the communist victory in 1949. After two years of negotiations through third parties, the first cultural exchange (a visit by the U.S. Ping-Pong team) was arranged in 1971. By the time of President Nixon's visit in 1972, many nations had resumed diplomatic relations with China, and it had regained its seat in the United Nations Security Council. (Full diplomatic recognition by the United States did not come until the Carter administration.)

The resumption of diplomatic relations between China and the United States was one of the most remarkable achievements of the Nixon–Kissinger attempts to make a breakthrough in the Cold War stalemate. Nonetheless, it was consistent with their balance-of-power approach to foreign policy. By making this effort during a period of hostility in relations between the Soviet Union and China, Nixon was probably hoping to gain leverage in dealings with the Soviet Union (what some referred to as "playing the China card").

The Nixon–Kissinger visits to China were all the more remarkable because they occurred while U.S. troops were still fighting in Vietnam. It had been the specter of a Sino-Soviet-led communist bloc and a near paranoid fear of "yellow hordes" (in the racist parlance of the time) advancing throughout Asia that led us to fight in Korea and Vietnam. Within a few short years, China's image was recast from dreaded enemy to friendly ally, and Cold War fears of world communist domination were greatly diminished.

One of the first major achievements of the Nixon–Kissinger policy of detente was to reestablish normal relationships with the People's Republic of China, governed by the Communist Party since 1949. Here Nixon attends a state banquet in Beijing with then premier Zhou Enlai.

The doctrine of detente complemented the mood of isolationism and weariness that grew in the wake of the Vietnam War. Public and elite opinion after the war was divided. Isolationist, go-it-alone sentiment peaked immediately after the war but then declined.

A new spirit of cooperative internationalism characterized the early Carter administration.[27] Carter and his advisers saw the world as far more complex than Cold War rhetoric suggested. They believed problems of global poverty, inequitable distribution of wealth, abuse of human rights, and regional competitiveness were substantial threats to world order and that the United States should work with other nations to solve these problems.

Carter continued the negotiations begun during the Ford administration on a follow-up treaty to SALT I, and in 1979, he and President Brezhnev signed SALT II, which placed limitations on offensive missiles. But the stunning invasion of Afghanistan by the Soviets in 1979 ended the chance of gaining Senate approval for the treaty. Public and elite opinion shifted; Cold War views, never completely dead, became much more respectable again.

Cold War Revival and Death

The Reagan administration took office in 1981 determined to challenge the Soviet Union in every way possible. During his first term, Reagan totally renounced the Nixon–Kissinger principle of detente and labeled the Soviet Union an "evil empire." He and his advisers continued to view the world largely in light of a U.S.-Soviet competition. They painted a simple picture of an aggressive and reckless Soviet Union and a peace-loving and virtuous United States. Despite the rhetoric, however, the administration did not risk direct confrontation.

Reagan's approach differed from containment because it was more ideologically than strategically driven; he sought not just to contain the Soviets but to undo the status quo. One method Reagan endorsed was stepping up the arms race and, by forcing them to keep pace, drive the Soviets into economic ruin. The centerpiece of this policy was his plan to build an antimissile defense system, the Strategic Defense Initiative (SDI), or Star Wars program. The plan was based on a laser technology that did not yet exist but that was supposed to intercept and destroy nuclear-tipped ballistic missiles before they reached their targets in the United States. Its projected cost was tens of billions of dollars. Reagan's SDI and military buildup programs increased military spending to record peacetime levels.

Though the election of Reagan put a Cold Warrior in the White House, the public was not willing to buy Cold War arguments wholeheartedly. By Reagan's sec-

To comply with the SALT treaty, the air force chopped up B-52 airplanes. Each plane got four chops from a huge guillotine blade, and the pieces were sold as scrap for 16 cents a pound. The planes were left in their dismembered state for ninety days so that Russia could confirm their destruction by satellite photography.

ond term, a dramatic drop in public support for increased military spending and growing public pressure for progress on arms control helped push the administration toward a less belligerent stance. Violent rhetoric was toned down and conciliatory gestures multiplied.[28] Washingtonians believed President Reagan wanted to reach some agreement with the Soviets in order to be remembered as a peacemaking president.

The moderation in Reagan's rhetoric was also a response to changes in the Soviet Union. In 1985, Mikhail Gorbachev, the new general secretary of the Communist Party of the Soviet Union, called for "new thinking" and began to shake up Soviet society as it had not been shaken since the Russian Revolution in 1917.[29] Faced with a stagnating economy and an antireform Soviet leadership, Gorbachev encouraged competition in the economy, criticism of corruption and inefficiencies by government agencies, and free elections of some government legislative bodies.

In addition to shaking up Soviet society, Gorbachev challenged the status quo in the international community with his policy of *glasnost,* or opening to the outside world. He encouraged foreign investment and requested foreign aid to help rebuild the Soviet economy; he made it easier for Soviet citizens to emigrate, pulled

Soviet troops out of Afghanistan, and reduced aid to Soviet-backed governments in Nicaragua and Cuba.

Gorbachev also took the initiative in resuming arms control negotiations with President Reagan. In 1987, the two men reached an agreement on intermediate-range nuclear forces (INF). To ensure compliance, the United States sent inspectors or monitors to the Soviet Union, and the Soviets sent them to western Europe and the United States to observe production facilities and the dismantling and removal of the missiles.

During the first two years of George H. Bush's administration, the Soviet empire in eastern Europe disintegrated with such rapidity that all policymakers were caught off guard. The Soviet-dominated governments were dismantled, Communist Parties changed their names, opposition parties formed, and free multiparty elections were held.

In late 1989, demonstrators assaulted the most visible symbol of the Cold War, the Berlin Wall (built by the Soviets in 1961 to divide Soviet-occupied East Berlin from NATO-occupied West Berlin), and began tearing it down. A year later, the reunification of Germany marked the end of the post–World War II power alliance in Europe.

Then, in 1991, after a brief, unsuccessful coup against him, Gorbachev resigned as head of the Communist Party and stripped the party of its role in government. Faced with massive restructuring problems and the possibility of food shortages, he made major foreign policy concessions to Western governments in order to obtain economic aid. Among them was an agreement to remove Soviet military forces from Cuba, the last vestige of Cold War competition in the Western Hemisphere.

With no strong center left in Moscow, the non-Russian states of the Soviet Union declared their independence or announced their intent to redefine their relationship with the national government inside a reformulated federal structure. Gorbachev was left with no country to lead, his power supplanted by the presidents of the independent republics. As the Soviet Union passed from the scene, replaced by new republics, all nations were groping to figure out what the new alignment of the world order would be.

Early in the 1990s, President George H. Bush referred to a "new world order," although no one was quite certain what it meant in terms of concrete foreign policies, other than the absence of U.S.–Soviet military competition. In the new order, foreign policies would presumably be less dependent on military capabilities. Still, some feared that, as the world's sole remaining military superpower, the United States would feel freer to use its military advantage in pursuit of its foreign policy goals; however, without the Soviet threat to justify expenditures, the United States began to shrink its military. There was also strong public pressure to avoid new foreign entanglements. With the Cold War over, Americans seemed weary of trying to understand and change the world. They were more impressed by the failures of foreign aid, military intervention, and diplomacy than by foreign policy successes, more weighed down by problems at home than by those in other countries. Bush found he could justify intervention in the Persian Gulf, and later in the civil war in Somalia, only through cost sharing and participation in an international force under UN auspices.

Merchant Diplomacy and Multilateralism

Bill Clinton took office as the first president born after World War II and one of the few never to have served in the military. He was a self-described child of the Cold War, an opponent of the Vietnam War, and more shaped by the skepticism of that era than by memories of the Allied victory in World War II. In his campaign, he reminded voters that we had not defeated the Soviet Union in battle but that it had collapsed from within due to "economic, political and spiritual failure." The lesson, Clinton said, was, "Given the problems we face at home, we must first take care of our own people and their needs." He believed that the best foreign policy is to have a strong economy.[30]

With this as his theme, Clinton signaled a change in approach to foreign policy. Befitting the end of the Cold War, greater emphasis would be given to economic than to military instruments of foreign policy, and more attention would be paid to using our economic strength to achieve political goals, such as promotion of democracy and human rights, which Clinton said we had neglected in our pursuit of strategic interests.

Clinton's foreign policy was so rooted in the pursuit of national economic interests that almost all issues were discussed in terms of their value to U.S. trade relations. (Clinton's second-term national security adviser was an international trade lawyer.) This led some observers to label his foreign policy "merchant diplomacy."[31] Deemphasizing military in favor of economic diplomacy suited Clinton's approach to foreign policy, according to one presidential aide, because the president saw force as a zero-sum (winner-take-all) game. "He is not a zero-sum kind of guy—he is a positive-sum guy; he likes situations in which everyone can come out a winner."[32] This approach was also compatible with the public mood, which, although not one of withdrawal from world affairs, was leery of new political entanglements.

Despite the deemphasis on use of military force, there were many occasions during Clinton's administration when its use was necessary. But unlike previous presidents, he was reluctant to rely on the unilateral use of force. He sent troops to Haiti in 1994 to oust a military dictatorship and restore the elected president, but only after gaining UN backing. It marked the first time an American president had sought prior international approval for a military intervention in the Caribbean. To some, it was a radical departure from, or even an end to, the Monroe Doctrine.[33] But it was compatible with Clinton's view of the post–Cold War world as a community of nations becoming increasingly linked through the forces of globalization and where every country should assume part of the burden for maintaining international peace and security. Avoiding costly military entanglements also helped end budget deficits run up by the huge military spending of the 1980s.

The difficulty with a multilateral approach to achieving foreign policy goals is that the national interests (and therefore the motivation for intervening) that each country has at stake in any international dispute vary. This can paralyze the policy process and make military cooperation to resolve a conflict impossible to achieve.

Homeland Security and Preemption

When he campaigned for the presidency, George W. Bush advocated a foreign policy that was less interventionist than Clinton's had been. He opposed any long-term or open-ended commitment of U.S. troops to international combat units or peacekeeping missions. He said we had to be "humble" about our role in the world and that we should not be engaged in nation building in countries where our troops were committed. Naming Colin Powell, a man famously reluctant to commit U.S. troops to combat, to be secretary of state suggested that Bush might follow a very cautious approach to American military involvement around the world.

Bush's early actions also indicated a shrinking back from diplomatic engagement, and he was soon labeled as someone who preferred going it alone. The United States did not withdraw from international organizations, but Bush's rhetoric suggested that he would only consult with other countries, not deal with them as equals. He announced his opposition to a number of treaty arrangements. He withdrew U.S. involvement in the Kyoto agreements on global warming, which Clinton had signed, because he thought it placed unreasonable burdens on American businesses; he refused to renew the Anti–Ballistic Missile Treaty because it would keep him from pursuing the development of a space-based antimissile defense system (SDI); and he refused to agree to U.S. participation in an international court to try war crimes and human rights abuses because he thought it would make American peacekeeping troops subject to false accusations.

These early actions contributed to the view that his foreign policy approach would shift the U.S. stance from multilateralism to unilateralism. The September 11 attacks reinforced certain aspects of this approach while changing others. He did organize a multinational force before taking military action in Afghanistan, suggesting a retreat from unilateralism. But he also identified a group of nations—Iraq, Iran, and North Korea—as forming an "axis of evil" acting as agents of state-sponsored terrorism. The conviction that an international ring of terrorists was lying in wait to launch other attacks led to a major redefinition of U.S. defense policy. Whereas historically the United States has maintained a posture of defensive response, striking only after being attacked, the Bush national security team endorsed a strategy of *preemption,* or striking first.[34] In a much-quoted speech delivered at West Point after 9/11, Bush said, "The war on terrorism will not be won on the defensive. . . . We must take the battle to the enemy, disrupt its plans, and confront the worst threats before they emerge." Said Vice President Cheney, "We have enemies with nothing to defend. . . . For that reason, this struggle will not end with a treaty or accommodation of terrorists [but] with complete and utter destruction" of terrorist networks.[35]

Preemption is not a new idea in U.S. foreign policy; it has always been there as an option in defense policy. John Kennedy, for example, had General Maxwell Taylor write a paper outlining a strategy for a nuclear first strike against the Soviet Union.[36] And a Clinton defense secretary coauthored a book on preventive defense, although his emphasis was on preemptive diplomatic action to prevent military assaults[37] It is not likely that any president would fail to strike first in a situation where it was certain it would prevent a lethal attack on the United States. The distinctive aspect of the Bush position is having preemption as a guiding principle of defensive strategy rather than as a policy option.

Bush put his policy into effect shortly after announcing it by calling for a preemptive strike against Iraq. If the administration had argued that it had proof that an attack on the United States was imminent, probably few would have seen preemption as a policy shift. But Bush's Iraq policy was based not on known capabilities or actual plans but on intent. And it was unclear whether it was just the first in a series of strikes against the "axis of evil." Congressional critics argued that invoking the policy to invade a sovereign nation with thousands of combat troops encroached on Congress's constitutional prerogative to declare war.

After less than two years in office, Bush's approach to foreign policy had been drastically revised from a passive unilateralism to an interventionist unilateralism. For reasons of both principle and cost (human and economic), many in Congress expressed a reluctance to accept preemption as a principle of foreign policy, if not rejecting is as a necessary option in specific situations. Its opponents believe that the idea of attacking a country only to prevent the possibility that it might attack us sets a frightening precedent for international rules of engagement, legitimizing military or nuclear preemption by other countries, such as India against Pakistan, or vice versa.

Instruments of Foreign Policy

The United States, because of its size and wealth, has enormous capabilities for pursuing its foreign policy objectives. In this section, we describe some of them, beginning with diplomacy, the universal means for the conduct of state-to-state relationships.

Diplomacy

As head of state, the president serves as chief diplomat. The principal office for carrying out his foreign policy is the State Department. The United States has relations with 180 nations but does not recognize the remainder. Unlike many other countries that automatically recognize every government accepted by its own people, the United States' decisions on formal recognition are made on political grounds. Thus, it was years before we recognized the governments of the Soviet Union and the People's Republic of China, and we still do not recognize the Cuban government established by Fidel Castro in 1959.

In addition to its permanent Washington-based civil service bureaucracy, the State Department maintains 260 embassies, consulates, and missions to international organizations in countries around the world. They are staffed by nine thousand Foreign Service officers and about thirty thousand local nationals.

Directing each embassy is the president's personally appointed emissary, or ambassador. Ambassadors are often career Foreign Service officers, but in some of the largest and most important embassies, and in some of the smaller but very desirable posts, the ambassador may be a political appointee chosen from among the president's friends or campaign contributors. Ambassadors not only represent the president's policy to officials in the countries where they are posted but also act as intermediaries, carrying policy messages back to the president or secretary of state from their host countries.[38] The United States also has ambassadors or emissaries attached to regional and international organizations such as the UN, NATO, and the World Trade Organization.

The work of other Foreign Service officers is divided by function—cultural and military attachés, trade representatives, aid specialists, and consular and political officers, for example. It is common in the most strategically important countries for one or more of these individuals to be an undercover CIA officer. The staff carry out country-specific policies and programs (such as development aid, trade policy, arms control, illegal drug suppression, and cultural exchanges), expend a good deal of effort burnishing the image of the United States, and tend to the needs of American business interests, U.S. citizens traveling abroad, and foreign nationals seeking entry visas to the United States.

Political officers track in-country political, economic, and social events that could affect state-to-state relations and write daily briefings, a very tiny portion of which ever reaches the secretary of state, let alone the president. But they form part of the basis for country reports that may influence the content of the president's intelligence briefing. The State Department also maintains its own Washington-based intelligence agency, as will be discussed in the next section.

For the huge tasks assigned it, the State Department is a very small organization, tenth in size among cabinet departments. And it must make do with a very small budget—about 1 percent of total spending, which, when adjusted for inflation, is about 50 percent less than we spent twenty years ago.[39]

Intelligence Gathering

One of the important components in formulating foreign and military policy is economic, military, and diplomatic information gathered by operatives of the government's fourteen intelligence agencies. The best known of these is, of course, the Central Intelligence Agency (CIA), but several cabinet departments (Treasury, State, and Energy) also have intelligence-gathering offices, and Justice has the FBI. Although historically devoted mainly to domestic law enforcement, the FBI does have a counterterrorism division and a role in policing international drug trafficking. In addition to the Pentagon's Central Defense Intelligence Agency (DIA), which is more involved in analysis than gathering information, each of the service arms (army, navy, air force, marines) has its own intelligence office. And there are three separate agencies for high-tech intelligence gathering such as satellite reconnaissance and aerial mapping. The National Security Agency is so secret that its employees cannot be photographed; its funding is part of the "black budget," unknown to the public and to much of Congress. In fact, total annual spending on intelligence gathering and analysis—about $30 billion— is a guesstimate, since some part of it is not included in the published budget.

The CIA also has a covert operations division, about whose activities little is ever made public. Agents sign lifetime agreements prohibiting them from public discussion of their work; manuscripts must be vetted by the agency prior to publication, and publication can be prevented or book royalties impounded if material is published without agency permission. However, most of the work done by intelligence agencies, including the CIA, involves routine fact collecting, research, and report writing rather than covert operations. And the scope of action for covert operations, such as assassinations of foreign heads of government (now illegal without presidential authorization) and recruiting local collaborators of dubious character, was drastically curtailed in the 1970s.

It is difficult for the public to assess the overall contributions of intelligence agencies. Over the past several decades, we have heard of many failures, some spectacular, but we rarely hear about successes, so it is hard to put the failures in context. But for the past twenty-five years, public accounts of our intelligence-gathering capability have revealed increasing ineptness: years of overestimating Soviet military and economic strength, counterproductive undercover activities in Vietnam, and failure to detect moles working in our agencies. During NATO's bombing of Yugoslavia, U.S. intelligence was unable to provide a fighter pilot with the correct location of the Chinese embassy in Belgrade (a publicly listed building), leading to its bombing, the deaths of Chinese civilians, and a huge international incident. The Chinese accused us—and many Chinese continue to believe—that the bombing was deliberate because they could not accept that our intelligence operatives were that incompetent.

Of the fourteen agencies responsible for intelligence work, almost all criticism has fallen on the CIA and the FBI. It may not be a coincidence that these two are often headed by political appointees rather than career professionals.

The failures surrounding the September 11 attacks were so great that they led to the first major reassessment of our intelligence-gathering capabilities since the 1970s. Evidence from the joint inquiry of the House and Senate suggests that our intelligence agencies are very good at gathering information but very poor at timely translations and analysis, and disastrous at interagency information sharing.[40] The rivalry and turf wars between the FBI and CIA in particular contributed to inefficiencies in data sharing and analysis. Although the FBI has been reorganized, the principal foreign intelligence agencies remain untouched by post-9/11 reforms, except for improvements in interagency coordination, renewed efforts at recruiting more highly skilled area specialists, and greater flexibility for covert operations.

Some critics of the post-9/11 reorganization believe that by leaving the FBI and CIA outside the Homeland Security department, intelligence gathering and analysis will become even more decentralized. Some are even concerned that policymakers will be able to go "analysis shopping," choosing whichever agency's data best support their policy preferences. This kind of competition between agencies, critics charge, will further politicize intelligence work.[41]

Military Instruments

Defense policy evolves in rough correspondence with changing approaches to foreign policy and perception of security threats. Formulating policy on how to use the country's military capabilities is the work of the secretary of defense, the president's national security team, and the Joint Chiefs of Staff. A private group of unpaid consultants, the National Defense Council, also advises the president on occasion. Many are former cabinet secretaries or members of Congress.

For more than forty years, we thought our military strength was our most important asset in our effort to keep the world "free." Relying on the strategy of mutually assured destruction, we built up an arsenal of nuclear-tipped missiles and bombers capable of delivering nuclear warheads. But the effectiveness of nuclear weapons as an instrument of foreign policy depended on their *not* being used. The nuclear arsenal helped to achieve the ultimate goal of avoiding defeat or destruction by a foreign power, but it was not a flexible instrument of policy. In the first decades of the Cold War, we relied so heavily on nuclear deterrence that we neglected other aspects of our military capability, including the capacity to fight limited wars with conventional weaponry. Yet conventional fighting forces have always been more important than nuclear weapons in pursuing containment and other foreign policy goals.

In the 1960s, our military planners thought we should be strong enough to fight two and a half wars at the same time. As the Vietnam War demonstrated what a drain on our economic and military resources a limited war could be, the Nixon administration lowered our goal to waging one major and one smaller war. Our defeat in Vietnam, combined with the growing likelihood that containment would be more dependent on conventional limited wars than on strategic nuclear warfare, led the Carter and Reagan administrations to place greater emphasis on improving combat readiness and building a new arsenal of high-tech weaponry.

Spending on nuclear preparedness itself became an instrument of foreign policy in the 1980s, as Reagan vowed to crush the Soviets economically by forcing them into a spending war in a race to acquire an antiballistic missile system. The arms race added to the Soviets' economic woes but also endangered our own economic security by contributing to huge budget deficits and robbing the civilian economy of many of our best scientists and engineers. In total, an estimated $5.1 trillion (not counting cleanup costs) was spent on nuclear preparedness, consuming from one-fourth to one-third of all military spending and producing about seventy thousand warheads and weapons.[42]

The end of the Cold War removed the need to prepare for a major nuclear conflagration with the Soviet Union. The arsenal of warheads, ICBMs, and nuclear bombers was drastically cut, and many domestic and foreign bases closed. After the Gulf War, the size of the military was cut by a third, and base closings continued. We also reached tentative agreement with Russia to reduce our stockpile of 10,400 operable nuclear weapons to 3,000. (By later agreement between George W. Bush and Russian president Vladimir Putin, this number was lowered to 2,000.) By the turn of the century, military spending was at its lowest level—3 percent of GDP—since before World War II.

But questions were being raised about whether military training and armaments were appropriate for twenty-first-century warfare. The Clinton administration determined that the major security threats, such as terrorism, could not be dealt with by traditional warfare. And early in the Bush administration, military planners called for a shift to give the military a "richer set of military options."[43]

Today, the primary objective of reform is to make the military more mobile, capable of quick response and armed with lighter, more flexible high-tech weaponry. A major showdown over this change came when some of the army leadership went against the secretary of defense to lobby Congress for funding for the forty-ton Crusader cannon that the army wanted for land battles. The Crusader is so large that just transporting it to the scene of battle is a major problem. Secretary Donald Rumsfeld wanted this weapon program killed and the money transferred to weapons to outfit a mobile light infantry more suitable to counterterrorism. Because the Crusader's manufacture brings dollars to many districts, Congress was inclined to go against the secretary of defense, but after 9/11, the majority agreed that old concepts of military preparedness had to be transformed. None of these changes will reduce defense spending. In fact, the 2003 defense budget saw the largest one-year increase since the Reagan years.

In 2001, the Pentagon began to prepare the armed forces for **asymmetrical warfare**—that is, conflict between combatants of very unequal strength. In this type of warfare, the weaker antagonist, knowing that direct military confrontation would lead to certain defeat, identifies and attacks a weak spot in the armor of the stronger opponent. The 9/11 attacks are an example. The perpetrators used openness and access in American society to their advantage in organizing, training, and eventually gaining control of commercial airliners to use as weapons against American citizens.

Given the traditions and career paths established in the service arms over the decades, it has not been easy for civilian leadership to win acceptance among the military leadership of big changes in strategies, weaponry, and training. But the success of any training program is also dependent on the recruitment of personnel capable of carrying out the new missions. Americans have not been pushing to enlist. The armed services are so short of people with foreign language skills and knowledge of other countries that they are considering recruiting foreigners to serve in their elite Special Forces.

In Afghanistan, Bosnia, Nigeria, and other countries, the Pentagon is already using military contractors—private citizens—to help train recruits and do other combat-related work. In Bosnia in 1996, one of every ten Americans in the peacekeeping force was a civilian under contract to the Pentagon.[44] These civilians are not subject to the same rules, discipline, or chain of command as regular military personnel.

Major defense changes are also complicated by the tension between civilian and military leadership, which was especially strong during the Clinton administration. Part of this tension stems from the Vietnam experience, and some undoubtedly comes from the end of the draft and the conversion to an all-volunteer armed services more than thirty years ago. Few politicians under the age of fifty have served in any branch of the armed forces. Since the end of the Vietnam War, the proportion of members of Congress who have had military training has fallen from 77 percent to 33 percent.[45] As a veteran, Al Gore was an exception among the highest-ranking civilian decision makers in the Clinton administration. George W. Bush served in the Texas Air National Guard but was never on active duty, and Vice President Cheney, one of the administration's principal defense strategists, avoided the draft during the Vietnam War. However, the professional military was enthusiastically supportive of Bush's candidacy, and he has had far better relationships with the high command than Clinton did.

Nevertheless, serious disagreements persist over national security policy. Some officers objected to spending priorities, and others were leery of Bush's first-strike policy and announced intention to invade Iraq. The lessons of Vietnam still linger: Do not commit U.S. troops where no clear objectives or timetable can be established.

Military Intervention

Over the course of American history, the military has been used less often to wage total or limited warfare than to intervene in small countries whose affairs have been seen as linked to U.S. economic or security interests. Through much of the Cold War, we were somewhat more reluctant to intervene with U.S. troops for fear of escalation to a nuclear conflict. But the Reagan and Bush administrations demonstrated a renewed willingness to pursue U.S. objectives with military force, especially in situations where we had unrivaled military superiority. Still, there were strong indicators that the military was ill prepared to carry out an interventionist role to achieve primarily political objectives. For example, the seven thousand troops the elder President Bush sent into Panama in 1989 had mixed success. We did remove Panamanian president Manuel Noriega from power and install a new government, but we killed more Panamanian civilians than soldiers.

The military performed better in the Persian Gulf War. This war was short, fought largely from the air with high-tech weaponry, well planned from the standpoint of minimizing American casualties, and the troops functioned according to or above expectations. From the standpoint of personnel (training and morale), the military appeared to be more battle-ready in the early 1990s than it had been in the 1970s and early 1980s. While some of the much-vaunted weaponry did not perform as well as initially claimed, it did serve to limit American casualties.

To judge the success of a military intervention, we have to be able to identify its objectives. In many cases, these are not made clear, or the real goals are hidden behind more palatable objectives. For example, the Persian Gulf War was fought, according to the president, to make the world unsafe for dictators and to restore Kuwaiti independence. After the deaths of thousands of Iraqis, Kuwait did regain its independence, but the Gulf region had no fewer dictators than it had before the war. The intervention was also successful in achieving the less openly stated goal of keeping a large part of the world's oil supply in the hands of governments sympathetic to the United States and other wealthy, oil-dependent countries.

While military intervention can be effective in achieving an immediate or limited goal, it may be detrimental to long-range objectives. In Panama, we ousted an unpopular government no longer serving U.S. interests, but Panamanians, who were originally supportive of the U.S. invasion, then became distrustful of the U.S.-installed government (even though it had been popularly elected). Many became hostile to the United States, and some sued for compensation for damage to homes or businesses or for relatives killed in the fighting. By the mid-1990s, some of the same politicians who had been prominent in the Noriega era returned to power.

Intervention can also give rise to new expectations and demands. Our intervention with European allies in Bosnia and Kosovo helped save lives and keep those conflicts from spreading to other countries, but it did little to solve the underlying political problems. The defeat of the Taliban in Afghanistan liberated many people, women especially, but in the midst of political instability, the United States has created a demand for nation building that it may not be able to satisfy.

Direct intervention is a high-risk (and in some cases unlawful) tool of foreign policy; it requires great planning and skill, as well as luck and good timing, to be militarily successful. It is even more difficult to make intervention work politically. When intervention does not achieve what it was supposed to, either from the standpoint of U.S. policymakers or in the eyes of the populace of the target country, everyone knows whom to hold accountable.

However, due to the size and capabilities of our military establishment, our desire to play a world leadership role, and the expectations of other world leaders about our role in world peacekeeping, it is impossible for any American president to ignore the uses of the military in the pursuit of foreign policy goals.

Military Alliances

For decades, the United States gave highest priority to security relationships with Great Britain and the nations of western Europe. This was due in large part to shared heritage, commitment to democratic government, and, in the postwar years, common membership in NATO.

Since its beginnings in 1949, NATO has grown to nineteen members and acquired a much broader strategic focus than its original purpose of deterring Soviet aggression in Europe. Despite the unity of purpose among the founding members, there were always internal differences. In the early years of the alliance, the United States was by far the strongest power in the West. Britain and France had been shattered by World War II, but as the years passed, these nations regained their economic power. West Germany also recovered and joined the alliance in 1954. As these states became stronger, they wanted to assume a more powerful role in the alliance. They feared that the United States, with its Asian

"With the whole world in NATO, we won't have to take any more crap from Mars."

TABLE 1	NATO	
Belgium*	Hungary	Turkey
Canada*	Iceland*	United Kingdom*
Czech Republic	Italy*	United States*
Denmark*	Poland	Luxembourg*
France*	Portugal*	Netherlands*
Germany	Spain	Norway*
Greece		
May join NATO in 2004		
Albania	Latvia	Slovakia
Bulgaria	Lithuania	Slovenia
Estonia	Romania	
Applicants		
Croatia		
Macedonia		

*Original member. NATO was established in 1949.

interests and adventures, could drag them into wars they did not wish to fight. They also worried that they might be vulnerable to Soviet military power because the United States would not think it worthwhile to risk all-out war. France, which never accepted U.S. domination of NATO, withdrew from some military aspects of the alliance.

The end of the Cold War defused the long-standing differences of the alliance partners over the nature of the Soviet threat and the control and use of American nuclear weapons deployed in Europe. The United States agreed to remove its nuclear weapons from European soil and to reduce the number of troops stationed in Germany.

In the post–Cold War years, the alliance has continued to address problems of stability in Europe, including ethnic warfare in the disintegrating Yugoslavia and separatist movements in the successor states of the Soviet Union. In NATO's earlier years, military force was the principal deterrent to aggression in western Europe, but today the principal strategy for maintaining regional political stability is integrating new states militarily and politically into the Western alliance. Thus, in 1999, three former Warsaw Pact states joined NATO, seven more will be admitted in 2004, and two others are applicants. (For a complete list of members, see Table 1.) What this expanded membership will mean to NATO's unity remains to be seen. But NATO's original singularity of purpose no longer exists.

The United States' relationships with the countries of Asia also have had a strong military component, including military agreements with China and Taiwan, defense treaties with both Japan and South Korea, and large military contingents in both countries. With the end of the Soviet threat, China lost its role in our con-

tainment policy and is now seen by some as a potential threat to the security of smaller nations in the region. North Korea, a Marxist system ruled by the same family since the end of World War II, remains the only power in the area openly hostile to the United States, one of three countries Bush included in his "axis of evil." But the Clinton administration launched a diplomatic offensive to normalize relations, resulting, in 2000, in the first meeting of high-level officials since the Korean War. Because North Korea has a nuclear capability and is an invasion threat to the South, U.S. troop strength has been maintained in South Korea.

Since the end of the Allied occupation of Japan, we have assumed a large part of the responsibility for Japan's defense by including Japan under our "nuclear umbrella." Under Japan's constitution, which was authored by U.S. occupation forces after World War II, Japan is prohibited from using war as an instrument of national policy and forbidden from creating an "offensive" military establishment. Many younger politicians now support a stronger military role for Japan, including participation in international peacekeeping forces. And leaders appear to be considering development of a nuclear arsenal, partially in response to growing Chinese military power.

To protect U.S. security and trade routes, the Seventh Fleet has been based in Japan since the end of World War II, and the United States continues to maintain military bases extending from the southern to the northernmost sections of the island. The forty-five thousand U.S. military personnel stationed in Japan have aroused continuous opposition among the Japanese public. To understand why, imagine that Japan maintained military bases from Florida to Alaska and had stationed thousands of soldiers on U.S. soil. One former Japanese prime minister referred to his island country as the United States' "unsinkable aircraft carrier in the Pacific."[46]

Military Aid

Another means of pursuing foreign policy goals is to provide grants, credits, or loans to countries with whom we have common defense interests to enable them to purchase armaments and other military equipment. In addition, we often send American forces abroad to train soldiers or bring foreign officers to the United States to study in our military schools. One-third to two-thirds of all U.S. foreign aid is spent on military support. We extend aid in the hope that greater military preparedness of allies will reduce the likelihood of our having to intervene to defend mutual security interests. Aid also supports U.S. defense industries and arms dealers, since "virtually all military assistance is spent on U.S. goods and services."[47] (The United States is the world's largest arms dealer, accounting for 49 percent of all arms delivered to other countries in 1999.[48])

Since the 1960s, one of the principal recipients of military aid has been Israel, a country that shares many of our political and cultural values and has been our strongest ally in the Middle East. However, a great deal of our military aid has gone to countries like Egypt and Jordan, whose ties to us are far less stable and whose governments are not democracies. Aid is a kind of reward for actions taken under pressure from the United States (such as making peace with Israel) and a way of tying these military establishments to our own.

We have also built up the armed forces of countries that, after a change in leadership or foreign policy, have used those forces to work against our national interests. The most spectacular case in recent years was our support for the military buildup in Iraq when it was at war with Iran (which we had also armed). When Iraq threatened our interests by seizing oil-rich Kuwait, we went to war against an army that we and our allies had helped supply and train.

In intelligence work, this phenomenon of an unintended spillover is called *blowback*.[49] For example, some of the leaders of the Taliban, the militant Islamic group that gained control of Afghanistan after the Soviet exit and gave shelter to those who planned the 9/11 attack on the United States, received military training and equipment from U.S. intelligence operations in the country while it was under Soviet occupation.

These examples illustrate the risks of trying to achieve foreign policy goals through the use of military aid. When it goes, as it often has, to unstable governments, or to those with whom we have little in common besides a temporarily shared enemy, we can find our weapons and training used against our interests.

Economic Instruments

In this section, we discuss several economic instruments of foreign policy: trade, economic sanctions, and foreign aid. Much of our economic diplomacy is carried out by the State Department and its Agency for International Development (USAID). Other cabinet departments devote increasing amounts of time to the pursuit of international economic goals. American ambassadors now receive training in how to promote American businesses,[50] and the Treasury Department has become so involved in economic diplomacy that former secretary Lloyd Bentsen said that his role had "virtually merged with the job of Secretary of State."[51]

Achieving the economic goals of foreign policy is not simply a matter of negotiating the technical details of trade or aid agreements. Their pursuit often involves pressuring the governments of other countries to change internal policies. For example, when the United States

demands that Japan remove trade barriers on certain products that we want to export, such as rice, meat, or auto parts, we are asking Japan to negate long-standing political agreements between their government and domestic producers. And when we make loans or give aid, the agreements are often conditional on the recipient countries adopting domestic policies that we dictate. Thus, the aggressive pursuit of economic goals can lead to extensive intervention in the affairs of other countries.

Trade

Negotiating sound trade agreements is essential to the economic health of a large importing and exporting country such as the United States. At the end of World War II, the United States was the world's greatest trading power; half of all world trade passed through our ports. Today that figure has fallen to 14 percent, and we have lost much of the power we once had to regulate the flow of trade.[52] This is especially significant because trade now accounts for about a quarter of our GDP and one-third of our economic growth.[53]

Maintaining old markets and finding new ones for our exports are major preoccupations of foreign policy. And Americans increasingly see the competition for jobs as a problem in foreign policy. There is widespread disagreement, however, on the extent to which trade relations should be used to protect American producers and consumers and whether they should be used at all to pursue political goals.

We import far more goods from other countries than they import from us, creating a trade deficit. For years our trade deficit has been climbing, reaching a new high with virtually each successive quarter of financial reporting. Business and labor leaders want government protection from imports, and as a result, political support for protectionist policies grows. **Protectionism** is government intervention to protect domestic producers and their employees against competition from foreign producers of manufactured and agricultural goods. Protectionist policies can take the form of a ban on goods from abroad, quotas on imports, or taxes (tariffs) on imports to make them more expensive and therefore less competitive in the United States. We have used protectionist policies to help American farmers and the manufacturers of automobiles, textiles, steel, clothing, computer chips, and other goods. For example, in 1983, President Reagan put a four-year tariff on large Japanese motorcycles to make them so expensive that Americans would buy American-made Harley-Davidsons.

Protecting American industries sounds patriotic. Supporters of protectionism argue that these policies protect new industries until they can get established and support old industries essential to our defense and basic self-sufficiency. They also say that protectionist policies can save American jobs and maintain our standard of living by placing tariffs on imported goods manufactured by foreign workers who are paid subsistence wages. They even claim protection can help make domestic industries more efficient and competitive. They point to Harley-Davidson, which, with tariff protection, raised its product quality, productivity, and profits.

Protectionist policies usually mean higher consumer prices, however. Auto quotas added about $1,300 to the price of each new Japanese car and $650 to each new American car sold here. Each job saved by the import quotas on Japanese cars cost American consumers more than $100,000.[54] It would have been much cheaper to compensate the auto workers thrown out of work and retrain them for other jobs. And tariffs on computer chips doubled the price of chips within a year, increasing the price U.S. computer firms paid for chips imported from Japan. Thus, the tariff ended up helping the Japanese computer industry more than our own.

Higher prices for consumer products are just one of the criticisms of protectionism made by advocates of **free trade.** Free trade is a policy of minimum intervention by governments in trade relations. Its advocates, or free traders, believe government regulation of trade, for economic or political reasons, reduces the efficiency of the world economy, thus preventing countries from maximizing their income.[55] Free trade, like capitalism, is a relative term; all countries place some restrictions on trade to protect domestic labor and business interests. In fact, forms of protection historically applied to 30 to 40 percent of all trade.

Free traders claim that, in addition to increasing prices, protectionism also discourages industry efficiency and competitiveness. They say the success of a Harley-Davidson is an exception and point to the benefits to the U.S. auto industry of international competition. Opening U.S. markets to Japanese cars gave Americans the choice of a superior product, and they deserted self-satisfied U.S. manufacturers in droves. The American auto industry was forced to improve its efficiency and its cars. By the 1990s, American auto workers were able to turn out a car for significantly less money than Japanese workers, and they had a product much superior to their 1970s models. By 1993, almost half of all Americans thought U.S. cars were a better value than Japanese-made cars.[56]

Finally, critics of protectionism say that it invites other nations to aim their own protectionist policies at goods we want to export to them. Retaliatory measures can spiral into a trade war, and trade wars have the potential to expand into military competition to protect market access.

Despite these dangers, pressure for protectionist legislation continues because job retention and creation are major issues in all industrialized countries. But the ability of the U.S. government to adopt protectionist measures is limited by membership in the World Trade Orga-

A Beijing bicyclist delivers computer monitors.

nization (WTO). The WTO, headquartered in Geneva, Switzerland, was founded in 1995 to remove barriers to free trade and to mediate trade disputes between member countries. WTO policies are set primarily by consensus of its 136 member countries, represented by their trade ministers. All members belong to the general council, which is empowered to resolve trade disputes. However, there is an appellate body, and countries can be sanctioned for not abiding by WTO decisions.[57]

The near-universal membership of the WTO includes many smaller and poorer countries that do not have the legal infrastructure or the political freedoms that exist in the United States. This has created concern among U.S. interest groups that membership in the WTO will cause a rollback in regulatory standards to the lowest level existing in any member country. Unions worry they will lose well-paying jobs with benefits to nonunionized workers in poorer countries who will work for low wages, no benefits or safety protections, and who perhaps lack the freedom to unionize. And environmental activists fear that none of the regulations applied to food production and distribution in the United States will be enforced for foodstuffs imported from countries without a commitment to environmental protection. They claim that globalization and free trade are hastening the relocation of industry to countries where there are no limitations on toxic emissions into the air and water or regulation of the dumping and storing of hazardous waste. Human rights groups claim free trade is adding to the already widespread abuse of child labor, unequal pay for women, and the exploitation of prison labor. They oppose the removal of barriers to trade and investment in countries controlled by dictatorships, fearing that by helping build up their

A demonstrator refuses to give way to a police horse during protests against economic policies toward developing nations.

economies, we will strengthen the governments and contribute to even greater human rights abuses.

When free trade advocates in developing countries hear attacks on "environmental" or "human rights" abuses by their governments, they often take them as code words for protectionism and dismiss the substance of the complaints. But free trade opponents point to the impact of NAFTA. This agreement among the United States, Canada (our leading trade partner), and Mexico phases out tariffs, duties, and other trade barriers and creates near total market access for agricultural products. In the first six years after NAFTA was passed, trade between Mexico and the United States increased from $82 billion to more than $200 billion by 1999. But more than two-thirds of Mexicans still live in poverty, according to UN statistics.[58]

The NAFTA law has become an example of the loss of regulatory control that critics of globalization fear. It provided for the establishment of a tribunal (the International Center for Settlement of Investment Disputes) to rule on charges of unfair trade practices brought by a business in one NAFTA country against a business in another member country. The rulings of the tribunal, which meets in secret, can supersede rulings of U.S. courts, including the Supreme Court. The provision for establishing the tribunal was unknown to most lawmakers, because almost none had read the whole bill before voting on it. Ralph Nader once offered $10,000 to any senator who had read NAFTA legislation in its entirety;

he had one taker, who read the law only after hearing Nader's challenge. He said if he had read it, he would not have voted for it.[59]

There is no doubt that NAFTA, which created the world's second largest and richest trading bloc, was a response to the **European Union (EU).** Formerly called the European Economic Community, or Common Market, the EU was formed in 1957 to foster political and economic integration in Europe. The very countries that have served as our staunchest military allies are at the same time among our strongest economic competitors. In 1992, the EU removed all internal economic barriers and customs posts for member nations. The membership of the EU has expanded to fifteen from its original six members, with ten more waiting entry (Table 2). The EU, with a single trade policy, a single agricultural policy, and a single market of 340 million people, is the world's biggest importer and exporter. The EU took another step toward the economic integration of Europe in 2002 when twelve of its fifteen members began phasing in a common currency (the euro).

The United States is particularly concerned about EU competition in the export of agricultural goods. U.S. farmers are highly subsidized, but European farmers are even more so, making it very difficult for us to export our agricultural products to Europe. In the late 1990s, the food war escalated as U.S. farmers fought to ban imports of European beef after the outbreak of "mad cow" disease in England, and European farmers waged a campaign to ban the import of genetically altered foods ("frankenfoods") and hormone-fed beef and poultry into European markets. The rift was widened when the EU successfully appealed to the WTO to force an end to U.S. government subsidies (in the form of a tax break) for American exporters.

TABLE 2	European Union	
Austria	Germany*	Netherlands*
Belgium*	Greece	Portugal
Denmark	Ireland	Spain
Finland	Italy*	Sweden
France*	Luxembourg*	United Kingdom
Will join the EU in 2004		
Cyprus	Latvia	Poland
Czech Republic	Lithuania	Slovakia
Estonia	Malta	Slovenia
Hungary		
Will join the EU in 2007		
Bulgaria		
Romania		

*Original member. The European Union was established in 1957.

George W. Bush, in an apparent bid to win votes of American steelworkers, escalated war with the EU by imposing tariffs on steel imports to diminish competition to the declining steel industry. Yet his administration took a proposal to the WTO just months later, calling for the total elimination of tariffs on all manufactured goods over the next thirteen years. The U.S. trade representative claims it would save the average family $1,600 a year.

Trade problems in East Asia also loom large in our foreign policy. Until 1997, this region had some of the fastest-growing economies in the world, including China, Taiwan, South Korea, Indonesia, and Singapore. In 1997, when major recessions hit South Korea and Indonesia, we faced one of those paradoxical problems in foreign policy—providing aid to our trade competitors (see "Foreign Aid" later in the chapter).

The U.S. business community has long coveted access to China's consumer market of 1.3 billion people, and developing export and investment opportunities in that massive market will continue to receive priority in our relations with China. That was evidenced by the token actions taken against that government for its brutal repression of the prodemocracy movement in 1989 and Clinton's decision in 2000 to grant China permanent normal trade relations. We have pressured China far more on the issue of protecting the copyrights of American artists, musicians, and writers than on human rights. Jeopardizing access to Chinese consumers in a period of high trade deficits to defend a principle is a bigger risk than U.S. policymakers are willing to take, even though imports from China account for much of our trade deficit.

Economic Sanctions

Economic sanctions are policies designed to get a state to change its behavior, or to take some action or set of actions, by refusing to engage with it in the conventional range of international economic relations (for example, trade, aid, loans) or by denying it access to specific economic goods or services. Economic sanctions are generally regarded as middle-of-the-road measures.[60] They are stronger than talking diplomacy but weaker than military confrontation. No country in the world has imposed them as often as the United States; in 1998, we had sanctions in place against twenty-six countries that held half of the world's population.[61]

When the United Nations voted to place economic sanctions on Iraq for its invasion of Kuwait in August 1990, it set off another round in an old debate on the usefulness of such measures. There is a widespread belief that economic sanctions are not effective in getting governments to change their behavior. Opponents argue that sanctions require unrealistic amounts of time and international cooperation to bring about the desired results. The longer the sanctions are in effect, the argument continues, the greater the temptation for nations

Ronald McDonald is flattened by protesters in Cavaillon, France. Many Europeans are opposed to the importation of American genetically altered food. The French in particular are angry about the increasing popularity of American fast foods.

Reuters/STR/Archive Photos

to pursue their own economic interests by trading or selling prohibited goods to the targeted nation.

Those who believe that under the right circumstances economic sanctions can work point to their use against the government of South Africa. South Africa, one of the largest countries in Africa, was governed by a white minority of 5 million in a nation of about 30 million. Due to the system of apartheid, the huge black majority had no say in government and lacked basic civil rights, including the right to vote, the right to marry a person of another race, equal opportunities for good jobs and pay, and the right to live in most areas of the country. All black adults had to carry identification cards, and thousands were arrested each year for not having proper identification. Most public facilities were segregated. Both black and white critics of the regime were subject to arbitrary arrest and indefinite imprisonment.

After rising public protests in the United States had pressured corporations to remove their businesses from South Africa, and colleges, churches, cities, and foundations to "divest"—sell stocks in companies that had investments in South Africa—and refuse to do business with companies that operated in South Africa, the United States imposed mild economic sanctions. In this case, it might be said that government policy was co-opted by the private sector. Divestiture occurred on an international scale, with corporations from all parts of the world pulling out of South Africa. These actions, coupled with sanctions placed on South Africa by the United Nations, undoubtedly played a role in the elimination of all remaining apartheid laws and the end of white minority rule.

In situations where the international community cannot achieve such widespread consensus as it did on South Africa, economic sanctions have not been as effective in attaining their objectives. One study of 103 instances of economic sanctions dating from World War I found a success rate of 36 percent. Sanctions were most effective when the goals were modest or when the sanctions were used to destabilize a government; they were least effective in damaging a country's military capacity or in effecting some major change in a state's behavior.[62] Sanctions are much more likely to be successful when a large state targets a much smaller, weaker state, but even then there is not a high likelihood of success if the goals are too ambitious.

Rarely does the United States target a large or powerful country, unless it is to achieve a very limited objective, such as by using trade sanctions to force the former Soviet Union to allow the emigration of Jews. The United States elects not to impose an embargo on China, even though democracy and human rights are at the very least as scarce as in Cuba, against which we have had a trade embargo for forty years. China is a large and economically powerful country, and the last two administrations decided that sanctions would achieve nothing while hurting the United States economically.

The Cuba example shows that even against a much smaller country, which was once quite dependent on the United States as a trading partner, sanctions will not necessarily be effective. Even the most severe form of sanction, a trade embargo, has not achieved its goal of effecting significant political and economic reform or destabilizing the Castro government. Sanctions likely contributed to a lower standard of living for Cubans, but they did little to change the leadership's policies (or lifestyle). Many other countries are willing to trade with Cuba, and meanwhile, the Cuban government was able to use the U.S. embargo to deflect criticism from its own economic failures. As the influence of the Cuban American lobby declined in comparison to that of the American farm and business lobbies, Congress voted to lift restrictions on the sale of food and medicine to Cuba. For the first time since Castro came to power, American business fairs were held in Cuba in 2002, and the government signed agreements to buy almost $90 million of foodstuffs.

The international sanctions imposed on Iraq after it invaded Kuwait were the toughest imposed on any nation in modern times and cost Iraq an estimated $120 billion in the first decade. Yet they did virtually nothing to change the behavior of the Iraqi government. The first team of UN arms inspectors were not even able to carry out their weapons-monitoring program. An estimated 1 million Iraqi children have died from malnutrition or disease since the sanctions have been in place, even though concessions were made allowing Iraq to sell oil to buy food and medicine for children. While we pressured the world to continue the sanctions, Iraq remained one of our largest suppliers of oil. Few countries were interested in enforcing the sanctions, and some dealt with Iraq on the black market. Only with the certain option of military invasion did Iraq allow UN inspectors back into the country in 2002. Iraq is another case where economic sanctions were completely ineffective in achieving their objective of forcing an aggressor state to disarm.

Sanctions may be continued despite evidence of their ineffectiveness simply as a way to exact punishment for behavior other states cannot change, or, as a congressional aide said, "We all know they don't work. But they make us feel good." The downside has been compared to the chicken soup remedy: "Chicken soup keeps you from going to the doctor and taking the corrective measures you really need. Worse yet, it really does a job on the chicken."[63]

Foreign Aid

Extending economic assistance to other countries is another tool of American foreign policy. Aid can take the form of grants, technical assistance, or guaranteed loans, for example. The primary object of the aid is to promote development and stability, but indirectly it is a means for influencing the direction of other countries' development, expanding export markets for U.S. goods, and in general spreading our sphere of influence. Most of the money earmarked for economic assistance has been channeled through USAID, and 80 percent of its contracts and grants are used to purchase American goods.[64]

Since the end of World War II, the United States has spent more than a half trillion dollars on foreign aid, about two-thirds of which was given in military assistance. Whereas economic sanctions operate by *denying* a state goods or services until it changes its behavior, foreign aid is used as an *incentive* to change behavior or as a reward for actions taken. In recent years, for example, the United States has paid millions of dollars in aid to the Ukraine and Russian Republics to destroy nuclear weapons inherited from the Soviet arsenal and promised $4.6 billion to North Korea to pay for denuclearization and the development of alternative energy sources. And in each year after 1976, when they

In an unusual delivery of foreign aid, the United States dropped packets of food during the early weeks of military action in Afghanistan. In addition to providing some modest humanitarian relief, this aid drop was designed to influence public opinion in the United States, Afghanistan, and around the world.

signed the U.S.-brokered peace treaty, until 2001, Israel and Egypt have received at least 40 percent of our annual aid budget. Today the second-highest recipient of foreign aid is Afghanistan.

The greatest success ever achieved with foreign aid was the rebuilding of Europe after World War II under the Marshall Plan. Since that time, major successes have been rare, and in recent years there has been great disillusionment with economic aid as an effective means for achieving our goals. Too often the money ended up in the bank accounts of corrupt leaders—as in Haiti, Zaire, and Panama, for example—or was spent on showy construction projects that did little to further development.

Such failures have led to congressional and public disillusionment with the effectiveness of foreign aid, both as a tool of foreign policy and as a spur to economic development. In response to criticism, USAID closed its missions in twenty-three countries, and Congress cut its budget in 1995 and threatened to eliminate it before moving it to the State Department. The attack on foreign aid was rationalized as budget cutting, but the program accounts for a tiny portion (less than 1 percent) of the federal budget and costs the average taxpaying family just $32 per year.[65] Our aid to the world's poorest countries costs about $6 per U.S. citizen annually.[66]

Loans and credits to help bail out countries suffering from recession or financial collapse are an increasingly common form of foreign aid. Though Congress and the public have been reluctant to help pay for the financial failings of other countries, especially when they are strong trade competitors, in the global economy we are all swimming in the same financial sea, and a regional economic crisis can quickly become a world crisis. If it foments political instability, such an economic crisis may even lead to larger security crises. The technology that has allowed money to move almost instantaneously from one country to another has also, Fed chair Alan Greenspan warns, "enhanced the ability of the system to rapidly transmit problems in one part of the globe to another."[67] To prevent or minimize the impact on our economy, we have to help pay for other governments' mistakes.

One of our most perplexing foreign policy problems is how to use aid to help the world's poorest countries. Our relations with developing countries are important, yet in most cases, military aid, military intervention, and economic aid have not worked very well in promoting economic progress, democratic government, or positive attitudes toward the United States.

One major reason is that we often target aid to countries that are politically important but not necessarily democratic or stable. We also tend to give poorer

Aid from America and other industrialized nations helps keep these Sudanese children alive, but some experts believe that such aid can prolong civil wars such as the one in the Sudan.

countries too little aid to accomplish anything. In Sub-Saharan Africa, one of the world's poorest regions, we spread $700 million in development aid among forty-eight countries in 1998.[68]

About a quarter of the world's population live in "extreme poverty" (defined as living on less than $1 per day), while the world's richest three billionaires own more of the world's wealth than the poorest 600 million people combined.[69] The fear is that globalization will exacerbate this already lopsided division of the world's wealth, leaving behind anyone without educational or technological resources. The only significant gain in living standards in recent decades has been for East Asians.

Why do we aid governments with poor human rights records that are sometimes militantly anti-American in their foreign policy rhetoric and corrupt governments that have made little effort to improve the lot of the average person? In terms of our national interests, it is not good that half of the world's population is unable to buy the agricultural and industrial goods we export. Aid can be seen as an investment that will pay off in stability and friendly governments, which will translate into more exports and reduced military spending for us. The countries of Africa, for example, have a combined market of 700 million people but accounted for only 1 percent of all U.S. trade in 1997.[70]

The Clinton administration, not surprisingly, put most of its effort into trade policy, believing "that open markets and rules-based trade are the best engine we know to lift living standards, reduce environmental destruction and build shared prosperity. This is true whether you're in Detroit, Davos, Dacca, or Dakar."[71] In other words, increasing trade with Africa creates jobs in the United States and raises living standards in Africa, while costing the American taxpayer virtually nothing in aid.

The Bush administration has placed an equally strong emphasis on trade, elevating free trade to a "moral principle."[72] Bush has used his newly restored fast-track trade authority to continue the free trade negotiations with Morocco and countries in Central and South America begun by Clinton. But Bush has also proposed increasing foreign aid by 50 percent and has urged international agencies to give more grants and fewer loans to poorer countries. However, Bush plans to attach strings to any new U.S. aid, giving it only to the poorest countries, and only if they commit to democracy, free trade, open markets, and deregulation.[73]

The irony of the reliance on trade, and free trade at that, is that American and European protectionist policies on agricultural products are some of the most economically damaging policies that farmers in poorer countries face. As one World Bank official noted, "The average cow is supported by three times the level of income of a poor person in Africa."[74] For many years, the world's largest economies have been one another's principal trading partners. With the populations of these countries stabilizing, can their economies continue to grow without parallel growth in developing economies?

Defining Security in the Global Age

We began this chapter by stating that the first and most transparent foreign policy goal of any country is protecting its security. Globalization and the end of the Cold War have required a redefinition of national security and a reassessment of how prepared we are to meet the new challenges. At the end of the century, one-third of the world's nations were waging war, many of them conflicts that the Cold War had kept from erupting. In addition, new threats have arisen from independent or state-sponsored terrorism. This has made the threat from weapons of mass destruction much more uncertain.

Today, the most difficult security challenge is preventing terrorist groups, acting alone or in concert with a state hostile to the United States, from gaining access to missile technology and to the materials needed to make biological, chemical, or nuclear weapons. During the Cold War, only five nations (the United States, the Soviet Union, Britain, France, and China) produced and stockpiled nuclear weapons. Two of those powers were our allies in NATO, and with the Soviet Union, we at least had diplomatic relations and the capacity to negotiate treaties on testing, stockpiling, and even use (as in the no-first-strike agreements). The MAD (mutual assured destruction) strategy was rooted in, and dependent on, the conviction that the fairly small number of people who were in a position to make decisions about the use of nuclear weapons were sane and rational, and had something to lose if their countries were destroyed, and that the threat of mutual destruction would keep any leader from launching a first strike.

As the number of states that have or are trying to gain nuclear capability has increased, the materials and technology to make nuclear weapons have proliferated across the globe. When India and Pakistan conducted tests in 1998, the number of nuclear-ready countries increased to seven. Another thirteen nations probably have the capacity to produce warheads.

Argentina, Brazil, Algeria, and South Africa have renounced nuclear weapons and put their programs under the supervision of the International Atomic Energy Commission, but North Korea reactivated its program in 2002. After its defeat in the Gulf War, Iraq was forced to renounce its weapons program and submit to United Nations monitoring, but this process broke down before it could dismantle Iraq's chemical and biological weapons programs.

The largest stores of enriched uranium and plutonium needed to make nuclear weapons are in the United States and the successor states of the Soviet Union, mainly Russia. In addition to the amounts produced for research and continuing weapons production, large reservoirs are accumulating from the dismantling of thousands of warheads as required by disarmament agreements between the United States and Russia. All of this material has to be disposed of or stored, and Russian storage sites are scattered and poorly secured. A major aspect of the U.S. response to the new security threat has been to assist Russia and its neighbors with transporting, storing, and safeguarding these materials.

The production and storage of enriched uranium and plutonium are supposed to be carefully recorded and monitored, but record keeping has been so inadequate, especially at Russian sites, that no one is sure exactly how much material is missing. Substantial black market trafficking in these materials is well documented.[75] Once the material is acquired, the assembly is not especially difficult; the technology necessary to build a simple uranium bomb like the one dropped on Hiroshima in 1945 is available to "anyone with a personal computer."[76]

The black market activity in weapons-grade material encourages the proliferation of missile technology and increases the likelihood that governments that acquire nuclear warheads will be able to develop short- or medium-range delivery capabilities much faster than would be expected through the normal research and development process. Businesses are eager to sell even high-tech equipment with military applications to foreigners. With technology and expertise moving across borders and available in books or on the Internet, the breakdown of security measures in Russia, and the deliberate dissemination of restricted technology by states interested in increasing the

"I miss the Commies."

number of nuclear powers, the likelihood that nuclear weapons will fall into the hands of "rogue" states or terrorist groups continues to grow.

A few years ago it was hard to imagine that we might look back at the Cold War as a simpler and even safer time, yet today's world is more complex than it was in the days of MAD. Nuclear proliferation makes defense against nuclear strikes exceedingly difficult because it is no longer sufficient just to monitor national defense establishments. It is less certain from where or from whom a strike might come. The CIA's failure to predict India's nuclear tests, despite years of surveillance of its arms program, is not reassuring about our ability to determine when independent actors have gained access to nuclear, chemical, and biological weapons or missile technology.

There are few left who are not convinced of the seriousness of the new threats, but disagreement still exists on how to protect against them. One idea has been the development of an antimissile defense system, not for defense against a massive nuclear attack but to intercept and destroy a single missile, or at most, a few missiles launched by a rogue state or a terrorist group. Opponents argue that the technology does not work and that the strategy itself has a dangerous premise. The assumption, antimissile defense system critics say, is that nuclear weapons *will* be used and that we will be able to defend ourselves against them. This premise, they argue, is both misleading and destabilizing and "represents a fundamental shift in how the nation thinks about nuclear war."[77] In addition, many military experts believe there is far greater danger that terrorists would use biological rather than nuclear weapons, in part because dangerous germs are cheap and easy to come by and do not require expensive missile delivery systems.

Globalization has intensified the threat from terrorist attack. International exchanges of people and goods are ubiquitous, and there are so many points of vulnerability, including the computer systems on which international business and finance, as well as national security systems, are now completely dependent. Globalization means that foreign problems left unattended find their way to our door, not only armed conflicts but also financial and environmental crises and epidemic diseases that can spread rapidly from one country to another.

For this reason, the Clinton administration declared health, education, and environmental protection in developing countries as primary U.S. foreign policy goals, linking them to U.S. national security. Almost everyone can see the worldwide AIDS epidemic as an urgent humanitarian and health issue, but many in Congress were stunned by Clinton's characterization of the AIDS epidemic in Africa as a national security issue. However, given international health organizations' death projections for some African countries, where as many as a third of the population may be infected, it is not difficult to see the epidemic as a potentially destabilizing force. A CIA report released two years into the Bush administration reinforced this view; it identified five "major regional or global players," including China and Russia, whose political and economic stability are endangered by surging rates of HIV and AIDS.[78]

Adding to the potential for instability is the rising incidence of AIDS in the armies of some African nations. One in four South African soldiers is reportedly infected with HIV/AIDS.[79] Money to teach AIDS prevention and pay for health care is now an important aspect of foreign aid. This is just one of the new meanings of security in a very interdependent world.

Conclusion: Is Our Foreign Policy Responsive?

As the head of the world's largest military and economic power and a partner in major military and trade alliances, the president has a constituency larger than the American public. He is often called upon to be responsive to the needs of other people or countries: victims of famines, civil wars, natural disasters, and human rights abuses, or countries in need of military and economic assistance.

But is the direction of our foreign policy responsive to the American public? Public attitudes can constrain the general policy directions of the president and Congress, but presidents can do a lot to shape these attitudes. Over the long term, as in Vietnam, the administration must be somewhat responsive to public sentiment that intensely opposes administration policy. But it is far harder for the public to have a short-term impact on military policy. Because everyone agrees on the general goal of protecting the nation from external attack, the public is far less inclined to be critical of military policy than it is of other areas of foreign policy. But this free rein has led to excessive secrecy, inefficiencies, and extravagant spending that are surely not in the public interest.

After 9/11, there was no need to convince the public that a threat existed, and the public gave the president unprecedented levels of support for military action against al Qaeda. However, when he used this support to move the United States into a more aggressive or preemptive defense posture against other targets, public support was less firm, and Bush had to explore diplomatic and multinational options to quiet criticism. But it is unusual for foreign policy decisions such as that on invading Iraq to be the subject of weeks of open debate in Congress and the UN. And while individual Democrats spoke out against the Bush policy, the party as a whole—reflecting the difficulties of parties out of power—offered no alternative. Thus, it is difficult to know how well public opinion was translated into policy.

In other areas of foreign policy, the public has more opportunity for influence than in the past, even on more technical issues like trade, immigration, and human rights. The rise of powerful lobbies on trade issues and the voting blocs of "hyphenated" Americans, for example, can have a significant impact on policy decisions. In the day-to-day world of diplomacy, foreign service officers work tirelessly to promote American agricultural and other exports and American business interests in general. The State Department's own description of its work cites creating jobs and opening markets as central to its mission. Representing American policy as a vehicle for the promotion of individual economic interests is in itself an indication of how necessary policymakers feel it is to at least have the appearance of being responsive to the public.

EPILOGUE

Lugar Votes to Fill in the Blanks

Lugar did not vote for the resolution as worded by the White House. He wanted to vote for some resolution in support of action against Iraq but did not want to give the president a blank check to make war. Lugar made several suggestions for compromise wording, but the president resisted them all, including one circulated by Lugar and Biden that would have required that any use of force be approved by the UN Security Council.[80]

Bush said that weakening the original language would "tie his hands." He also chided the Democrat-controlled Senate by saying they were putting special interests above national security and that if they waited to vote until they knew what action the UN was going to take, the American people would think they were signing off the country's most pressing national security interests to international organizations.

While Congress continued to negotiate compromise wording, Iraq agreed to let UN inspectors back into the country to search for weapons of mass destruction. This took some steam out of the urgency for military action and helped convinced Bush he would

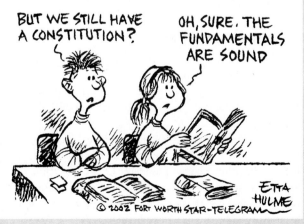

have to accept a much more specifically worded resolution.

A bipartisan group in the House, led by Richard Gephardt, drafted its own version of the resolution and got White House support. The members of Congress wanted to get the issue out of the way so they could get out on the campaign trail and without leaving the president empty-handed or looking like they had avoided the issue.

This left the Biden–Lugar resolution, which required a UN resolution approving use of force before troops were committed to Iraq, dead in the water. They offered their terms as an amendment to the House resolution. With the momentum all in the direction of the House version already accepted by Bush, the Biden–Lugar amendment was defeated. Bush called Lugar and promised to "push diplomacy to the maximum degree," and Lugar voted for the resolution.[81] Only one Republican defected from the party, but twenty-one Democrats voted no.

The House version accomplished much of what Lugar wanted, including restricting the use of military force to Iraq, requiring the president to exhaust all diplomatic means before turning to force, setting a schedule for congressional briefings, and making it clear that all of the authority being given the president was limited to his powers as defined in the War Powers Resolution. Bush got his check, but many of the blanks had been filled in.

By refusing to do what its predecessors had done for Lyndon Johnson—passing the Gulf of Tonkin Resolution with little debate or dissent—Congress exercised its checking power on the president's role as commander in chief. The time that elapsed during the committee hearings and debate allowed the United Nations, which had been doing nothing to enforce the sanctions against Iraq, to rally and provide an alternative to immediate invasion. However, if UN inspections fail to disarm Iraq and the Bush administration launches a military attack, Congress might well yet become a bystander on Iraqi policy. Once troops are in combat, the conduct of war rests in the hands of the president and the military.

Senator Lugar, however, will be in a position of greater leverage with respect to the White House. When the Republicans retook control of the Senate in 2003, he finally got the chair of the Foreign Relations Committee that he had been seeking for years.

 To learn more about this important vote and its implications, go to this chapter's "You Are There" exercises on the text Web site.

Key Terms

isolationism

Monroe Doctrine

containment

North Atlantic Treaty Organization (NATO)

Cold War

mutual assured destruction (MAD)

domino theory

Vietnam syndrome

detente

asymmetrical warfare

protectionism

free trade

European Union (EU)

Further Reading

Robert Baer, *See No Evil: The True Story of a Ground Soldier in the CIA's War on Terrorism* (New York: Crown, 2002). An ex-CIA agent gives an account of his years aiding Afghan rebels fighting the Soviet occupation of their country.

Louis Fisher, *Presidential War Power* (Lawrence: University of Kansas Press, 1995). A staff member of the Congressional Research Service reviews presidential use of the military from the first days of the republic to the present and concludes that congressional war-making powers have been usurped by the executive branch.

Robert S. McNamara, *In Retrospect: The Tragedy and Lessons of Vietnam* (New York: Times Books, 1995). The former secretary of defense and a principal architect of Vietnam War policy gives eleven reasons why he thinks the Vietnam War was a mistake, rejecting the domino theory and placing a preponderance of blame on the incompetence of South Vietnamese forces and U.S. underestimation of the North Vietnamese.

Joseph Nye, *The Paradox of American Power: Why the World's Only Superpower Can't Go It Alone* (New York: Oxford University Press, 2002). A political science professor and former Clinton Defense Department official explains why he believes that unilateralism cannot work in the era of globalization.

David Remnick, *Lenin's Tomb: The Last Days of the Soviet Empire* (New York: Random House, 1993). A chronicle of the demise of the Soviet Union.

Neil Sheehan, *A Bright Shining Lie* (New York: Random House, 1988). The Vietnam War as seen through its effect on a young American officer.

Joseph Stiglitz, *Globalization and Its Discontents* (New York: W. W. Norton, 2002). A Nobel Prize–winning economist and supporter of globalization argues there are too many inequities in trade relations between rich and poor countries and criticizes the IMF for forcing policies on poorer countries that undermine democracy.

Kenneth Timmerman, *The Death Lobby: How the West Armed Iraq* (New York: Houghton Mifflin, 1992). An account of how the United States and its allies built up the war machine of Saddam Hussein during the Iran–Iraq War. The author accuses intelligence agencies of being so focused on preventing an Iranian victory that they overlooked or ignored Iraq's nuclear weapons program.

 ## Electronic Resources

usinfo.state.gov
This site has the United States Information Agency's daily briefings and news on a variety of international issues from the official U.S. government perspective. Includes links to several foreign language sources and a searchable database from archived material.

www.state.gov/
The home page of the State Department. Links to information on the department itself and on a variety of international issues, organized by region and by issue.

www.nytimes.com/
The home page of the New York Times. *The* Times *provides the most thorough coverage of international news by any U.S. newspaper.*

www.economist.com/
The home page of the international magazine The Economist. *The* Economist *specializes in in-depth articles on important international and political issues and provides a foreign perspective on the news.*

www.cwihp.si.edu/
The Cold War International History Project at the Smithsonian's Woodrow Wilson Center makes available new information and perspectives on the history of the Cold War, in particular, findings from previously inaccessible sources from former communist countries.

www.loc.gov/rr/international/portals.html
Portals to the world, a site managed by the Library of Congress area studies division with in-depth information and annotated Internet resources for selected countries of Europe, Africa, North and South America, and Asia.

www.gwu.edu/~nsarchiv
A site maintained by an independent research institute at George Washington University to make available declassified international affairs and national security documents obtained through FOIA.

 ## InfoTrac College Edition

Search for the following articles in the InfoTrac database:

Brooks, Stephen G., and William C. Wohlforth. "American Primacy in Perspective," *Foreign Affairs* (July–August 2002).

Hirsh, Michael. "Bush and the World," *Foreign Affairs* (September–October 2002).

Johnson, Dan. "The World in 2015," *The Futurist* (May 2001).

Meilinger, Phillip S. "Force Divider: How Military Technology Makes the United States Even More Unilateral," *Foreign Policy* (January–February 2002).

For more articles, enter

"International relations" in the Subject Guide;

"National security" in the Subject Guide;

"Terrorism" in the Subject Guide.

 ## American Government Resources

Visit the Public Policy section of the Wadsworth American Government Resources Web site (politicalscience.wadsworth.com/amgov/) for a variety of tools to help you explore foreign policy further. Included are simulations, video clips, Microcase exercises, and a wealth of other activities.

THE DECLARATION OF INDEPENDENCE*

In Congress, July 4, 1776.

A Declaration by the Representatives of the United States of America, in General Congress assembled.

When in the Course of human Events, it becomes necessary for one People to dissolve the Political Bonds which have connected them with another, and to assume among the Powers of the Earth, the separate and equal Station to which the Laws of Nature and of Nature's God entitle them, a decent Respect to the Opinions of Mankind requires that they should declare the causes which impel them to the Separation.

We hold these Truths to be self-evident, that all Men are created equal, that they are endowed by their Creator with certain unalienable Rights, that among these are Life, Liberty, and the Pursuit of Happiness—That to secure these Rights, Governments are instituted among Men, deriving their just Powers from the Consent of the Governed, that whenever any Form of Government becomes destructive of these Ends, it is the Right of the People to alter or to abolish it, and to institute new Government, laying its Foundation on such Principles, and organizing its Powers in such Forms, as to them shall seem most likely to effect their Safety and Happiness. Prudence, indeed, will dictate that Governments long established should not be changed for light and transient Causes; and accordingly all Experience hath shewn, that Mankind are more disposed to suffer, while Evils are sufferable, than to right themselves by abolishing the Forms to which they are accustomed. But when a long Train of Abuses and Usurpations, pursuing invariably the same Object, evinces a Design to reduce them under absolute Despotism, it is their Right, it is their Duty, to throw off such Government, and to provide new Guards for their future Security. Such has been the patient Sufferance of these Colonies; and such is now the Necessity which constrains them to alter their former Systems of Government. The History of the present King of Great Britain is a History of repeated Injuries and Usurpations, all having in direct Object the Establishment of an absolute Tyranny over these States. To prove this, let facts be submitted to a candid World.

He has refused his Assent to Laws, the most wholesome and necessary for the public Good.

He has forbidden his Governors to pass Laws of immediate and pressing Importance, unless suspended in their Operation till his Assent should be obtained; and when so suspended, he has utterly neglected to attend to them.

He has refused to pass other Laws for the Accommodation of large Districts of People, unless those People would relinquish the Right of Representation in the Legislature, a Right inestimable to them, and formidable to Tyrants only.

He has called together Legislative Bodies at Places unusual, uncomfortable, and distant from the Depository of their Public Records, for the sole Purpose of fatiguing them into Compliance with his Measures.

He has dissolved Representative Houses repeatedly, for opposing with manly Firmness his Invasions on the Rights of the People.

He has refused for a long Time, after such Dissolutions, to cause others to be elected; whereby the Legislative Powers, incapable of Annihilation, have returned to the People at large for their exercise; the State remaining in the mean time exposed to all the Dangers of Invasion from without, and Convulsions within.

He has endeavoured to prevent the Population of these States; for that Purpose obstructing the Laws for Naturalization of Foreigners; refusing to pass others to encourage their Migration hither, and raising the Conditions of new Appropriations of Lands.

He has obstructed the Administration of Justice, by refusing his Assent to Laws for establishing Judiciary Powers.

He has made Judges dependent on his Will alone, for the Tenure of their offices, and the Amount and payments of their Salaries.

He has erected a Multitude of new Offices, and sent hither Swarms of Officers to harass our People, and eat out their Substance.

He has kept among us, in times of Peace, Standing Armies, without the consent of our Legislatures.

He has affected to render the Military independent of, and superior to the Civil Power.

He has combined with others to subject us to a Jurisdiction foreign to our Constitution, and unacknowledged by our Laws; giving his Assent to their Acts of pretended Legislation:

For quartering large Bodies of Armed Troops among us:

For protecting them, by a mock Trial, from Punishment for any Murders which they should commit on the Inhabitants of these States:

---

*The spelling, capitalization, and punctuation of the original have been retained here.

For cutting off our Trade with all Parts of the World:

For imposing Taxes on us without our Consent:

For depriving us, in many cases, of the Benefits of Trial by Jury:

For transporting us beyond Seas to be tried for pretended Offences:

For abolishing the free System of English Laws in a neighbouring Province, establishing therein an arbitrary Government, and enlarging its Boundaries, so as to render it at once an Example and fit Instrument for introducing the same absolute Rule into these Colonies:

For taking away our Charters, abolishing our most valuable Laws, and altering fundamentally the Forms of our Governments:

For suspending our own Legislatures, and declaring themselves invested with Power to legislate for us in all Cases whatsoever.

He has abdicated Government here, by declaring us out of his Protection and waging War against us.

He has plundered our Seas, ravaged our Coasts, burnt our towns, and destroyed the Lives of our People.

He is, at this Time, transporting large Armies of foreign Mercenaries to compleat the works of Death, Desolation, and Tyranny, already begun with circumstances of Cruelty and Perfidy, scarcely paralleled in the most barbarous Ages, and totally unworthy the Head of a civilized Nation.

He has constrained our fellow Citizens taken Captive on the high Seas to bear Arms against their Country, to become the Executioners of their Friends and Brethren, or to fall themselves by their Hands.

He has excited domestic Insurrections amongst us, and has endeavoured to bring on the Inhabitants of our Frontiers, the merciless Indian Savages, whose known Rule of Warfare is an undistinguished Destruction, of all Ages, Sexes and Conditions.

In every state of these Oppressions we have Petitioned for Redress in the most humble Terms: Our repeated Petitions have been answered only by repeated Injury. A Prince, whose Character is thus marked by every act which may define a Tyrant, is unfit to be the Ruler of a free People.

Nor have we been wanting in Attentions to our British Brethren. We have warned them from Time to Time of Attempts by their Legislature to extend an unwarrantable Jurisdiction over us. We have reminded them of the Circumstances of our Emigration and Settlement here. We have appealed to their native Justice and Magnanimity, and we have conjured them by the Ties of our common Kindred to disavow these Usurpations, which would inevitably interrupt our Connections and Correspondence. They too have been deaf to the Voice of Justice and of Consanguinity. We must, therefore, acquiesce in the Necessity, which denounces our Separation, and hold them, as we hold the rest of Mankind, Enemies in War, in Peace, Friends.

We, therefore, the Representatives of the UNITED STATES OF AMERICA, in General Congress Assembled, appealing to the Supreme Judge of the World for the Rectitude of our Intentions, do, in the Name, and by Authority of the good People of these Colonies, solemnly Publish and Declare, That these United Colonies are, and of Right ought to be, Free and Independent States; that they are absolved from all Allegiance to the British Crown, and that all political Connection between them and the State of Great Britain, is and ought to be totally dissolved; and that as Free and Independent States, they have full Power to levy War, conclude Peace, contract Alliances, establish Commerce, and to do all other Acts and Things which Independent States may of right do. And for the support of this declaration, with a firm Reliance on the Protection of divine Providence, we mutually pledge to each other our Lives, our Fortunes, and our sacred Honor.

CONSTITUTION OF THE UNITED STATES OF AMERICA*

We the people of the United States, in Order to form a more perfect Union, establish Justice, insure domestic Tranquility, provide for the common defence, promote the general Welfare, and secure the Blessings of Liberty to ourselves and our posterity, do ordain and establish this Constitution for the United States of America.

Article I

Section 1. All legislative Powers herein granted shall be vested in a Congress of the United States, which shall consist of a Senate and House of Representatives.

Section 2. The House of Representatives shall be composed of Members chosen every second Year by the People of the several States, and the Electors in each State shall have the Qualifications requisite for Electors of the most numerous Branch of the State Legislature.

No person shall be a Representative who shall not have attained to the Age of twenty-five Years, and been seven Years a Citizen of the United States, and who shall not, when elected, be an Inhabitant of that State in which he shall be chosen.

Representatives and direct [Taxes]^1 shall be apportioned among the several States which may be included within this Union, according to their respective Numbers [which shall be determined by adding to the whole Number of free Persons, including those bound to Service for a Term of Years, and excluding Indians not taxed, three fifths of all other Persons].^{2} The actual Enumeration shall be made within three Years after the first Meeting of the Congress of the United States, and within every subsequent Term of ten Years, in such Manner as they shall by Law direct. The Number of Representatives shall not exceed one for every thirty Thousand, but each State shall have at Least one Representative; and until such enumeration shall be made, the State of New Hampshire shall be entitled to chuse three, Massachusetts eight, Rhode Island and Providence Plantations one, Connecticut five, New-York six, New Jersy four, Pennsylvania eight, Delaware one, Maryland six, Virginia ten, North Carolina five, South Carolina five, and Georgia three.

When vacancies happen in the Representation from any State, the Executive Authority thereof shall issue Writs of Election to fill such Vacancies.

The House of Representatives shall chuse their Speaker and other Officers; and shall have the sole Power of Impeachment.

Section 3. The Senate of the United States shall be composed of two Senators from each State [chosen by the Legislature thereof],^{3} for six Years; and each Senator shall have one Vote.

Immediately after they shall be assembled in Consequence of the first Election, they shall be divided as equally as may be into three Classes. The Seats of the Senators of the first Class shall be vacated at the Expiration of the second year, of the second Class at the Expiration of the fourth Year, and of the third Class at the Expiration of the sixth Year, so that one third may be chosen every second Year [and if Vacancies happen by Resignation, or otherwise, during the Recess of the Legislature of any State, the Executive thereof may make temporary Appointments until the next Meeting of the Legislature, which shall then fill such Vacancies.]^4

No Person shall be a Senator who shall not have attained to the Age of thirty Years, and been nine Years a Citizen of the United States, and who shall not, when elected, be an Inhabitant of that State for which he shall be chosen.

The Vice President of the United States shall be President of the Senate, but shall have no Vote, unless they be equally divided.

The Senate shall chuse their other Officers, and also a President pro tempore, in the Absence of the Vice President, or when he shall exercise the Office of President of the United States.

The Senate shall have the sole Power to try all Impeachments. When sitting for that Purpose, they shall be on Oath or Affirmation. When the President of the United States is tried, the Chief Justice shall preside: And no Person shall be convicted without the Concurrence of two thirds of the Members present.

Judgment in Cases of Impeachment shall not extend further than to removal from Office, and disqualification to hold and enjoy any Office of honor, Trust or Profit under the United States; but the Party convicted shall nevertheless be liable and subject to Indictment, Trial, Judgment and Punishment, according to Law.

---

*The spelling, capitalization, and punctuation of the original have been retained here. Brackets indicate passages that have been altered by amendments to the Constitution.
1. Modified by the Sixteenth Amendment.
2. Modified by the Fourteenth Amendment.
3. Repealed by the Seventeenth Amendment.
4. Modified by the Seventeenth Amendment.

Section 4. The Times, Places and Manner of holding Elections for Senators and Representatives, shall be prescribed in each State by the Legislature thereof; but the Congress may at any time by Law make or alter such Regulations, except as to the Places of chusing Senators.

[The Congress shall assemble at least once in every Year, and such Meeting shall be on the first Monday in December, unless they shall by Law appoint a different Day.][5]

Section 5. Each House shall be the Judge of the Elections, Returns and Qualifications of its own Members, and a Majority of each shall constitute a Quorum to do Business; but a smaller Number may adjourn from day to day, and may be authorized to compel the Attendance of absent Members, in such Manner, and under such Penalties as each House may provide.

Each House may determine the Rules of its Proceedings, punish its Members for disorderly Behaviour, and, with the Concurrence of two thirds, expel a Member.

Each House shall keep a Journal of its Proceedings, and from time to time publish the same, excepting such Parts as may in their Judgment require Secrecy; and the Yeas and Nays of the Members of either House on any question shall, at the Desire of one fifth of those present, be entered on the Journal.

Neither House, during the Session of Congress, shall, without the Consent of the other, adjourn for more than three days, nor to any other Place than that in which the two Houses shall be sitting.

Section 6. The Senators and Representatives shall receive a Compensation for their Services, to be ascertained by Law, and paid out of the Treasury of the United States. They shall in all Cases, except Treason, Felony and Breach of the Peace, be privileged from Arrest during their Attendance at the Session of their respective Houses, and in going to and returning from the same; and for any Speech or Debate in either House, they shall not be questioned in any other Place.

No Senator or Representative shall, during the Time for which he was elected, be appointed to any civil Office under the Authority of the United States, which shall have been created, or the Emoluments whereof shall have been encreased during such time; and no Person holding any Office under the United States, shall be a Member of either House during his Continuance in Office.

Section 7. All Bills for raising Revenue shall originate in the House of Representatives; but the Senate may propose or concur with Amendments as on other Bills.

Every Bill which shall have passed the House of Representatives and the Senate, shall, before it become a Law, be presented to the President of the United States; If he approves he shall sign it, but if not he shall return it, with his objections to that House in which it shall have originated, who shall enter the Objections at large on their Journal, and proceed to reconsider it. If after such Reconsideration two thirds of that House shall agree to pass the Bill, it shall be sent, together with the Objections, to the other House, by which it shall likewise be reconsidered, and if approved by two thirds of that House, it shall become a Law. But in all such Cases the Votes of both Houses shall be determined by yeas and Nays, and the Names of the Persons voting for and against the Bill shall be entered on the Journal of each House respectively. If any Bill shall not be returned by the President within ten Days (Sundays excepted) after it shall have been presented to him, the Same shall be a Law, in like Manner as if he had signed it, unless the Congress by their Adjournment prevent its Return, in which Case it shall not be a Law.

Every Order, Resolution, or Vote to which the Concurrence of the Senate and House of Representatives may be necessary (except on a question of Adjournment) shall be presented to the President of the United States; and before the Same shall take Effect, shall be approved by him, or being disapproved by him, shall be repassed by two thirds of the Senate and House of Representatives, according to the Rules and Limitations prescribed in the Case of a Bill.

Section 8. The Congress shall have Power To lay and collect Taxes, Duties, Imposts and Excises, to pay the Debts and provide for the common Defence and general Welfare of the United States; but all Duties, Imposts and Excises shall be uniform throughout the United States;

To borrow Money on the credit of the United States;

To regulate Commerce with foreign Nations, and among the several States, and with the Indian Tribes;

To establish a uniform Rule of Naturalization, and uniform Laws on the subject of Bankruptcies throughout the United States;

To coin Money, regulate the Value thereof, and of foreign Coin, and fix the Standard of Weights and Measures;

To provide for the Punishment of counterfeiting the Securities and current Coin of the United States.

To establish Post Offices and post Roads;

To promote the Progress of Science and useful Arts, by securing for limited Times to Authors and Inventors the exclusive Right to their respective Writings and Discoveries;

To constitute Tribunals inferior to the supreme Court;

To define and punish Piracies and Felonies committed on the high Seas, and Offences against the Law of Nations;

To declare War, grant Letters of Marque and Reprisal, and make Rules concerning Captures on Land and Water;

To raise and support Armies, but no Appropriation of Money to that Use shall be for a longer Term than two Years;

To provide and maintain a Navy;

To make Rules for the Government and Regulation of the land and naval Forces;

To provide for calling forth the Militia to execute the Laws of the Union, suppress Insurrections and repel Invasions;

To provide for organizing, arming, and disciplining the Militia, and for governing such Part of them as may be employed in the Service of the United States, reserving to the

---

5. Changed by the Twentieth Amendment.

States respectively, the Appointment of the Officers, and the Authority of training the Militia according to the discipline prescribed by Congress;

To exercise exclusive Legislation in all Cases whatsoever, over such District (not exceeding ten Miles square) as may, by Cession of particular States, and the Acceptance of Congress, become the Seat of the Government of the United States, and to exercise like Authority over all Places purchased by the Consent of the Legislature of the State in which the Same shall be, for the Erection of forts, Magazines, Arsenals, dock-Yards, and other needful Buildings;—And

To make all Laws which shall be necessary and proper for carrying into Execution the foregoing Powers, and all other Powers vested by this Constitution in the Government of the United States, or in any Department or Officer thereof.

Section 9. The Migration or Importation of such Persons as any of the States now existing shall think proper to admit, shall not be prohibited by the Congress prior to the Year one thousand eight hundred and eight, but a Tax or duty may be imposed on such Importation, not exceeding ten dollars for each Person.

The Privilege of the Writ of Habeas Corpus shall not be suspended, unless when in Cases of Rebellion or Invasion the public Safety may require it.

No Bill of Attainder or ex post facto Law shall be passed.

[No Capitation, or other direct, Tax shall be laid, unless in Proportion to the Census or Enumeration herein before directed to be taken.][6]

No Tax or Duty shall be laid on Articles exported from any State.

No Preference shall be given by any Regulation of Commerce or Revenue to the Ports of one State over those of another; nor shall Vessels bound to, or from, one State, be obliged to enter, clear, or pay Duties in another.

No Money shall be drawn from the Treasury, but in Consequence of Appropriations made by Law; and a regular Statement and Account of the Receipts and Expenditures of all public Money shall be published from time to time.

No Title of Nobility shall be granted by the United States; and no Person holding any Office or Profit or Trust under them, shall, without the Consent of the Congress, accept of any present, Emolument, Office, or Title, of any kind whatever, from any King, Prince, or foreign State.

Section 10. No state shall enter into any Treaty, Alliance, or Confederation; grant Letters of Marque and Reprisal; coin Money; emit Bills of Credit; make any Thing but gold and silver Coin a Tender in Payment of Debts; pass any Bill of Attainder, ex post facto Law, or Law impairing the Obligation of Contracts, or grant any Title of Nobility.

No State shall, without the Consent of the Congress, lay any Imposts or Duties on Imports or Exports, except what may be absolutely necessary for executing its inspection Laws; and the net Produce of all Duties and Imposts, laid by any State on Imports or Exports, shall be for the Use of the Treasury of the United States; and all such Laws shall be subject to the Revision and Controul of the Congress.

No State shall, without the Consent of Congress, lay any duty of Tonnage, keep Troops, or Ships of War in time of Peace, enter into any Agreement or Compact with another State, or with a foreign Power or engage in War, unless actually invaded, or in such imminent Danger as will not admit of delay.

Article II

Section 1. The executive Power shall be vested in a President of the United States of America. He shall hold his Office during the Term of four Years, and, together with the Vice President, chosen for the Same Term, be elected, as follows.

Each State shall appoint, in such Manner as the Legislature thereof may direct, a Number of Electors, equal to the whole Number of Senators and Representatives to which the State may be entitled in the Congress; but no Senator or Representative, or Person holding an Office of Trust or Profit under the United States, shall be appointed an Elector.

[The Electors shall meet in their respective States, and vote by Ballot for two Persons of whom one at least shall not be an Inhabitant of the same State with themselves. And they shall make a List of all the Persons voted for, and of the Number of Votes for each; which List they shall sign and certify, and transmit sealed to the Seat of the Government of the United States, directed to the President of the Senate. The President of the Senate shall, in the Presence of the Senate and House of Representatives, open all the Certificates, and the Votes shall then be counted. The Person having the greatest Number of Votes shall be the President, if such Number be a Majority of the whole Number of Electors appointed; and if there be more than one who have such Majority, and have an equal Number of Votes, then the House of Representatives shall immediately chuse by Ballot one of them for President; and if no Person have a Majority, then from the five highest on the List the said House shall in like Manner chuse the President. But in chusing the President, the Votes shall be taken by States, the Representation from each State having one Vote; A quorum for this Purpose shall consist of a Member or Members from two thirds of the States, and a Majority of all the states shall be necessary to a Choice. In every Case, after the Choice of the President, the Person having the greatest Number of Votes of the Electors shall be the Vice President. But if there should remain two or more who have equal Votes, the Senate shall chuse from them by Ballot the Vice President.][7]

The Congress may determine the Time of chusing the Electors, and the Day on which they shall give their Votes; which Day shall be the same throughout the United States.

No person except a natural born Citizen, or a Citizen of the United States, at the time of the Adoption of this Constitution, shall be eligible to the Office of President; neither shall

6. Modified by the Sixteenth Amendment.

7. Changed by the Twelfth Amendment.

any Person be eligible to that Office who shall not have attained to the Age of thirty five Years, and been fourteen Years a Resident within the United States.

[In Case of the Removal of the President from Office, or of his Death, Resignation, or Inability to discharge the Powers and Duties of the said Office, the same shall devolve on the Vice President, and the Congress may by Law provide for the Case of Removal, Death, Resignation or Inability, both of the President and Vice President, declaring what Officer shall then act as President, and such Officer shall act accordingly, until the Disability be removed, or a President shall be elected.][8]

The President shall, at stated Times, receive for his Services, a Compensation, which shall neither be encreased nor diminished during the Period for which he shall have been elected, and he shall not receive within that Period any other Emolument from the United States, or any of them.

Before he enter on the Execution of his Office, he shall take the following Oath or Affirmation:—"I do solemnly swear (or affirm) that I will faithfully execute the Office of President of the United States, and will to the best of my Ability, preserve, protect and defend the constitution of the United States."

Section 2. The President shall be Commander in Chief of the Army and Navy of the United States, and of the Militia of the several States, when called into the actual Service of the United States; he may require the Opinion, in writing, of the principal Officer in each of the executive Departments, upon any Subject relating to the Duties of their respective Offices, and he shall have Power to grant Reprieves and Pardons for Offences against the United States, except in Cases of Impeachment.

He shall have Power, by and with the Advice and Consent of the Senate, to make Treaties, provided two thirds of the Senators present concur; and he shall nominate, and by and with the Advice and Consent of the Senate, shall appoint Ambassadors, other public Ministers and Consuls, Judges of the supreme Court, and all other Officers of the United States, whose Appointments are not herein otherwise provided for, and which shall be established by Law; but the Congress may by Law vest the Appointment of such inferior Officers, as they think proper, in the President alone, in the Courts of Law, or in the Heads of Departments.

The President shall have Power to fill up all Vacancies that may happen during the Recess of the Senate, by granting Commissions which shall expire at the end of their next Session.

Section 3. He shall from time to time give to the Congress Information of the State of the Union, and recommend to their Consideration such Measures as he shall judge necessary and expedient; he may, on extraordinary Occasions, convene both Houses, or either of them, and in Case of Disagreement between them, with Respect to the Time of Adjournment, he may adjourn them to such Time as he shall think proper; he shall receive Ambassadors and other public Ministers; he shall take Care that the Laws be faithfully executed, and shall Commission all the Officers of the United States.

Section 4. The President, Vice President and all civil Officers of the United States, shall be removed from Office on Impeachment for, and Conviction of, Treason, Bribery, or other high Crimes and Misdemeanors.

Article III

Section 1. The judicial Power of the United States, shall be vested in one supreme Court, and in such inferior Courts as the Congress may from time to time ordain and establish. The Judges, both of the supreme and inferior Courts, shall hold their Offices during good Behaviour, and shall, at stated Times, receive for their Services, a Compensation, which shall not be diminished during their Continuance in Office.

Section 2. The judicial Power shall extend to all Cases, in Law and Equity, arising under this Constitution, the Laws of the United States, and Treaties made, or which shall be made, under their Authority;—to all Cases affecting Ambassadors, other public Ministers and Consuls;—to all Cases of admiralty and maritime Jurisdiction;—to Controversies to which the United States shall be a Party;—to Controversies between two or more States;—[between a State and Citizens of another State;][9]—between Citizens of different States,—between Citizens of the same State claiming Lands under Grants of different States, [and between a state, or the Citizens thereof, and foreign States, Citizens or Subjects.][10]

In all cases affecting Ambassadors, other public Ministers and Consuls, and those in which a State shall be Party, the supreme Court shall have original Jurisdiction. In all the other Cases before mentioned, the supreme Court shall have appellate Jurisdiction, both as to Law and Fact, with such Exceptions, and under such Regulations as the Congress shall make.

The Trial of all Crimes, except in Cases of Impeachment, shall be by Jury; and such Trial shall be held in the State where the said Crimes shall have been committed; but when not committed within any State, the Trial shall be at such Place or Places as the Congress may by Law have directed.

Section 3. Treason against the United States, shall consist only in levying War against them, or in adhering to their Enemies, giving them Aid and Comfort. No Person shall be convicted of Treason unless on the Testimony of two Witnesses to the same overt Act, or on Confession in open Court.

The Congress shall have Power to declare the Punishment of Treason, but no Attainder of Treason shall work Corruption of Blood, or Forfeiture except during the Life of the Person attainted.

8. Modified by the Twenty-fifth Amendment.

9. Modified by the Eleventh Amendment.
10. Modified by the Eleventh Amendment.

Article IV

Section 1. Full Faith and Credit shall be given in each State to the public Acts, Records, and judicial Proceedings of every other State. And the Congress may by general Laws prescribe the Manner in which such Acts, Records and Proceedings shall be proved, and the Effect thereof.

Section 2. The Citizens of each State shall be entitled to all Privileges and Immunities of Citizens in the several States.

A Person charged in any State with Treason, Felony, or other Crime, who shall flee from Justice, and be found in another State, shall on Demand of the executive Authority of the State from which he fled, be delivered up, to be removed to the State having Jurisdiction of the Crime.

[No Person held to Service or Labour in one State under the Laws thereof, escaping into another, shall, in Consequence of any Law or Regulation therein, be discharged from such Service or Labour, but shall be delivered up on Claim of the Party to whom such Service or Labour may be due.][11]

Section 3. New States may be admitted by the Congress into this Union; but no new State shall be formed or erected within the Jurisdiction of any other State; nor any State be formed by the Junction of two or more States, or Parts of States, without the Consent of the Legislatures of the States concerned as well as of the Congress.

The Congress shall have Power to dispose of and make all needful Rules and Regulations respecting the Territory or other Property belonging to the United States; and nothing in this Constitution shall be so construed as to Prejudice any Claimes of the United States, or of any particular State.

Section 4. The United States shall guarantee to every State in this Union a Republican Form of Government, and shall protect each of them against Invasion, and on Application of the Legislature, or of the Executive (when the Legislature cannot be convened) against domestic Violence.

Article V

The Congress, whenever two thirds of both Houses shall deem it necessary, shall propose Amendments to this Constitution, or on the Application of the Legislatures of two thirds of the several States, shall call a Convention for proposing Amendments, which, in either Case, shall be valid to all Intents and Purposes, as Part of this Constitution, when ratified by the Legislatures of three fourths of the several States, or by Conventions in three fourths thereof, as the one or the other Mode of Ratification may be proposed by the Congress; Provided that no Amendment which may be made prior to the Year One thousand eight hundred and eight shall in any Manner affect the first and fourth Clauses in the Ninth Section of the first Article; and that no State, without its Consent, shall be deprived of its equal Suffrage in the Senate.

11. Repealed by the Thirteenth Amendment.

Article VI

All Debts contracted and Engagements entered into, before the Adoption of this Constitution, shall be as valid against the United States under this Constitution, as under the Confederation.

This Constitution, and the laws of the United States which shall be made in Pursuance thereof; and all Treaties made, or which shall be made, under the Authority of the United States, shall be the supreme Law of the Land; and the Judges in every State shall be bound thereby, any Thing in the Constitution or Laws of any State to the Contrary notwithstanding.

The Senators and Representatives before mentioned, and the Members of the several State Legislatures, and all executive and judicial Officers, both of the United States and of the several States, shall be bound by Oath or Affirmation, to support this Constitution; but no religious Text shall ever be required as a Qualification to any Office or public Trust under the United States.

Article VII

The Ratification of the Conventions of nine States, shall be sufficient for the Establishment of this constitution between the States so ratifying the Same.

Done in Convention by the Unanimous Consent of the States present the Seventeenth Day of September in the Year of our Lord one thousand seven hundred and Eighty seven and of the Independence of the United States of America the Twelfth. IN WITNESS whereof we have hereunto subscribed our Names.

Go. WASHINGTON
Presid't. and deputy from Virginia

Attest
William Jackson
Secretary

Delaware
Geo. Read
Gunning Bedford jun
John Dickinson
Richard Basset
Jaco. Broon

Massachusetts
Nathaniel Gorham
Rufus King

Connecticut
Wm. Saml. Johnson
Roger Sherman

New York
Alexander Hamilton

New Jersey
Wh. Livingston
David Brearley

Wm. Paterson
Jona. Dayton

Pennsylvania
B. Franklin
Thomas Mifflin
Robt. Morris
Geo. Clymer
Thos. FitzSimons
Jared Ingersoll
James Wilson
Gouv. Morris

Virginia
John Blair
James Madison Jr.

North Carolina
Wm. Blount
Richd. Dobbs Spaight
Hu. Williamson

South Carolina
J. Rutledge
Charles Cotesworth Pinckney
Charles Pinckney
Pierce Butler

Georgia
William Few
Abr. Baldwin

New Hampshire
John Langdon
Nicholas Gilman

Maryland
James McHenry
Dan of St. Thos. Jenifer
Danl. Carroll

Amendment I[12]

Congress shall make no law respecting an establishment of religion, or prohibiting the free exercise thereof; or abridging the freedom of speech, or of the press; or the right of the people peaceably to assemble, and to petition the Government for a redress of grievances.

Amendment II

A well regulated militia, being necessary to the security of a free State, the right of the people to keep and bear arms, shall not be infringed.

Amendment III

No Soldier shall, in time of peace be quartered in any house, without the consent of the owner, nor in time of war, but in a manner to be prescribed by law.

Amendment IV

The right of the people to be secure in their persons, houses, papers, and effects, against unreasonable searches and seizures, shall not be violated, and no warrants shall issue, but upon probable cause, supported by oath or affirmation, and particularly describing the place to be searched, and the persons or things to be seized.

Amendment V

No person shall be held to answer for a capital, or otherwise infamous crime, unless on a presentment or indictment of a Grand Jury, except in cases arising in the land or naval forces, or in the militia, when in actual service in time of war or public danger; nor shall any person be subject for the same offence to be twice put in jeopardy of life or limb; nor shall be compelled in any criminal case to be a witness against himself, nor be deprived of life, liberty, or property, without due process of law; nor shall private property be taken for public use, without just compensation.

Amendment VI

In all criminal prosecutions, the accused shall enjoy the right to a speedy and public trial, by an impartial jury of the State

and district wherein the crime shall have been committed, which district shall have been previously ascertained by law, and to be informed of the nature and cause of the accusation; to be confronted with the witnesses against him; to have compulsory process for obtaining witnesses in his favor, and to have the assistance of counsel for his defence.

Amendment VII

In Suits at common law, where the value in controversy shall exceed twenty dollars, the right of trial by jury shall be preserved, and no fact tried by a jury, shall be otherwise reexamined in any Court of the United States, than according to the rules of the common law.

Amendment VIII

Excessive bail shall not be required, nor excessive fines imposed, nor cruel and unusual punishments inflicted.

Amendment IX

The enumeration in the Constitution, of certain rights, shall not be construed to deny or disparage others retained by the people.

Amendment X

The powers not delegated to the United States by the Constitution, nor prohibited by it to the States, are reserved to the States respectively, or to the people.

Amendment XI
(Ratified February 7, 1795)

The Judicial power of the United States shall not be construed to extend to any suit in law or equity, commenced or prosecuted against one of the United States by Citizens of another State, or by Citizens or Subjects of any Foreign State.

Amendment XII
(Ratified June 15, 1804)

The Electors shall meet in their respective states, and vote by ballot for President and Vice-President, one of whom, at least, shall not be an inhabitant of the same state with themselves; they shall name in their ballots the person voted for as President, and in distinct ballots the person voted for as Vice President, and they shall make distinct lists of all persons voted for as President, and of all persons voted for as Vice-President, and of the number of votes for each, which lists they shall sign and certify, and transmit sealed to the seat of the government of the United States, directed to the President of the Senate;—The President of the Senate shall, in the presence of the Senate and House of Representatives, open all the certificates and the votes shall then be counted;—The person having the greatest number of votes for President, shall be the President, if such number be a ma-

---

12. The first ten amendments were passed by Congress on September 25, 1789, and were ratified on December 15, 1791.

jority of the whole number of Electors appointed; and if no person have such majority, then from the persons having the highest numbers not exceeding three on the list of those voted for as President, the House of Representatives shall choose immediately, by ballot, the President. But in choosing the President, the votes shall be taken by states, the representation from each state having one vote; a quorum for this purpose shall consist of a member or members from two-thirds of the states, and a majority of all the states shall be necessary to a choice. [And if the House of Representatives shall not choose a President whenever the right of choice shall devolve upon them, before the fourth day of March next following, then the Vice-President shall act as President, as in the case of the death or other constitutional disability of the President.][13]—The person having the greatest number of votes as Vice-President, shall be the Vice-President, if such number be a majority of the whole number of Electors appointed, and if no person have a majority, then from the two highest numbers on the list, the Senate shall choose the Vice-President; a quorum for the purpose shall consist of two-thirds of the whole number of Senators, and a majority of the whole number shall be necessary to a choice. But no person constitutionally ineligible to the office of President shall be eligible to that of Vice-President of the United States.

Amendment XIII
(Ratified on December 6, 1865)

Section 1. Neither slavery nor involuntary servitude, except as a punishment for crime whereof the party shall have been duly convicted, shall exist within the United States, or any place subject to their jurisdiction.

Section 2. Congress shall have power to enforce this article by appropriate legislation.

Amendment XIV
(Ratified on July 9, 1868)

Section 1. All persons born or naturalized in the United States, and subject to the jurisdiction thereof, are citizens of the United States and of the State wherein they reside. No State shall make or enforce any law which shall abridge the privileges or immunities of citizens of the United States; nor shall any State deprive any person of life, liberty, or property, without due process of law; nor deny to any person within its jurisdiction the equal protection of the laws.

Section 2. Representatives shall be apportioned among the several States according to their respective numbers, counting the whole number of persons in each State, excluding Indians not taxed. But when the right to vote at any election for the choice of electors for President and Vice President

dent of the United States, Representatives in Congress, the Executive and Judicial officers of a State, or the members of the Legislature thereof, is denied to any of the male inhabitants of such State, being [twenty-one][14] years of age, and citizens of the United States, or in any way abridged, except for participation in rebellion, or other crime, the basis of representation therein shall be reduced in the proportion which the number of such male citizens shall bear to the whole number of male citizens twenty-one years of age in such State.

Section 3. No person shall be a Senator or Representative in Congress, or elector of President and Vice President, or hold any office, civil or military, under the United States, or under any State, who having previously taken an oath, as a member of Congress, or as an officer of the United States, or as a member of any State legislature, or as an executive or judicial officer of any State, to support the Constitution of the United States, shall have engaged in insurrection or rebellion against the same, or given aid or comfort to the enemies thereof. But Congress may by a vote of two-thirds of each House, remove such disability.

Section 4. The validity of the public debt of the United States, authorized by law, including debts incurred for payment of pensions and bounties for services in suppressing insurrection or rebellion, shall not be questioned. But neither the United States nor any State shall assume or pay any debt or obligation incurred in aid of insurrection or rebellion against the United States, or any claim for the loss or emancipation of any slave, but all such debts, obligations and claims shall be held illegal and void.

Section 5. The Congress shall have power to enforce, by appropriate legislation, the provisions of this article.

Amendment XV
(Ratified on February 3, 1870)

Section 1. The right of citizens of the United States to vote shall not be denied or abridged by the United States or by any State on account of race, color, or previous condition of servitude.

Section 2. The Congress shall have power to enforce this article by appropriate legislation.

Amendment XVI
(Ratified on February 3, 1913)

The Congress shall have power to lay and collect taxes on incomes, from whatever source derived, without apportionment among the several States, and without regard to any census or enumeration.

13. Changed by the Twentieth Amendment.

14. Changed by the Twenty-sixth Amendment.

Amendment XVII
(Ratified on April 8, 1913)

The Senate of the United States shall be composed of two Senators from each State, elected by the people thereof, for six years; and each Senator shall have one vote. The electors in each State shall have the qualifications requisite for electors of the most numerous branch of the State legislatures.

When vacancies happen in the representation of any State in the Senate, the executive authority of such State shall issue writs of election to fill such vacancies: *Provided,* That the legislature of any State may empower the executive thereof to make temporary appointments until the people fill the vacancies by election as the legislature may direct.

This amendment shall not be so construed as to affect the election or term of any Senator chosen before it becomes valid as part of the Constitution.

Amendment XVIII
(Ratified on January 16, 1919)

Section 1. After one year from the ratification of this article the manufacture, sale, or transportation of intoxicating liquors within, the importation thereof into, or the exportation thereof from the United States and all territory subject to the jurisdiction thereof for beverage purposes is hereby prohibited.

Section 2. The Congress and the several States shall have concurrent power to enforce this article by appropriate legislation.

Section 3. This article shall be inoperative unless it shall have been ratified as an amendment to the Constitution by the legislatures of the several States, as provided in the Constitution, within seven years from the date of the submission hereof to the States by the Congress.[15]

Amendment XIX
(Ratified on August 18, 1920)

The right of citizens of the United States to vote shall not be denied or abridged by the United States or by any State on account of sex.

Congress shall have power to enforce this article by appropriate legislation.

Amendment XX
(Ratified on January 23, 1933)

Section 1. The terms of the President and Vice President shall end at noon on the 20th day of January, and the terms of Senators and Representatives at noon on the 3rd day of January, of the years in which such terms would have ended if this article had not been ratified, and the terms of their successors shall then begin.

Section 2. The Congress shall assemble at least once in every year, and such meeting shall begin at noon on the 3rd day of January, unless they shall by law appoint a different day.

Section 3. If, at the time fixed for the beginning of the term of the President, the President elect shall have died, the Vice President elect shall become President. If a President shall not have been chosen before the time fixed for the beginning of his term, or if the President elect shall have failed to qualify, then the Vice President elect shall act as President until a President shall have qualified; and the Congress may by law provide for the case wherein neither a President elect nor a Vice President elect shall have qualified, declaring who shall then act as President, or the manner in which one who is to act shall be selected, and such person shall act accordingly until a President or Vice President shall have qualified.

Section 4. The Congress may by law provide for the case of the death of any of the persons from whom the House of Representatives may choose a President whenever the rights of choice shall have devolved upon them, and for the case of the death of any of the persons from whom the Senate may choose a Vice President whenever the right of choice shall have devolved upon them.

Section 5. Sections 1 and 2 shall take effect on the 15th day of October following the ratification of this article.

Section 6. This article shall be inoperative unless it shall have been ratified as an amendment to the Constitution by the legislatures of three-fourths of the several States within seven years from the date of its submission.

Amendment XXI
(Ratified on December 5, 1933)

Section 1. The eighteenth article of amendment to the Constitution of the United States is hereby repealed.

Section 2. The transportation or importation into any State, Territory, or possession of the United States for delivery or use therein of intoxicating liquors, in violation of the laws thereof, is hereby prohibited.

Section 3. This article shall be inoperative unless it shall have been ratified as an amendment to the Constitution by conventions in the several States, as provided in the Constitution, within seven years from the date of the submission hereof to the States by the Congress.

Amendment XXII
(Ratified on February 27, 1951)

No person shall be elected to the office of the President more than twice, and no person who has held the office of President, or acted as President, for more than two years of a term to which some other person was elected President shall be

---

15. The Eighteenth Amendment was repealed by the Twenty-first Amendment.

elected to the office of the President more than once. But this Article shall not apply to any person holding the office of President when this Article was proposed by the Congress, and shall not prevent any person who may be holding the office of President, or acting as President, during the term within which this Article becomes operative from holding the office of President or acting as President during the remainder of such term.

Amendment XXIII
(Ratified on March 29, 1961)

Section 1. The District constituting the seat of Government of the United States shall appoint in such manner as the Congress may direct:

A number of electors of President and Vice President equal to the whole number of Senators and Representatives in Congress to which the District would be entitled if it were a State, but in no event more than the least populous State; they shall be in addition to those appointed by the States, but they shall be considered, for the purposes of the election of President and Vice President, to be electors appointed by a State; and they shall meet in the District and perform such duties as provided by the twelfth article of amendment.

Section 2. The Congress shall have power to enforce this article by appropriate legislation.

Amendment XXIV
(Ratified on January 23, 1964)

Section 1. The right of citizens of the United States to vote in any primary or other election for President or Vice President, for electors for President or Vice President, or for Senator or Representative in Congress, shall not be denied or abridged by the United States or any State by reason of failure to pay any poll tax or other tax.

Section 2. The Congress shall have power to enforce this article by appropriate legislation.

Amendment XXV
(Ratified on February 10, 1967)

Section 1. In case of the removal of the President from office or of his death or resignation, the Vice President shall become President.

Section 2. Whenever there is a vacancy in the office of the Vice President, the President shall nominate a Vice President who shall take office upon confirmation by a majority vote of both Houses of Congress.

Section 3. Whenever the President transmits to the President pro tempore of the Senate and the Speaker of the House of Representatives his written declaration that he is unable to discharge the powers and duties of his office, and until he transmits to them a written declaration to the contrary, such powers and duties shall be discharged by the Vice President as Acting President.

Section 4. Whenever the Vice President and a majority of either the principal officers of the executive departments or of such other body as Congress may by law provide, transmit to the President pro tempore of the Senate and the Speaker of the House of Representatives their written declaration that the President is unable to discharge the powers and duties of his office, the Vice President shall immediately assume the powers and duties of the offices as Acting President.

Thereafter, when the President transmits to the President pro tempore of the Senate and the Speaker of the House of Representatives his written declaration that no inability exists, he shall resume the powers and duties of his office unless the Vice President and a majority of either the principal officers of the executive department or of such other body as Congress may by law provide, transmit within four days to the President pro tempore of the Senate and the Speaker of the House of Representatives their written declaration that the President is unable to discharge the powers and duties of his office. Thereupon Congress shall decide the issue, assembling within forty-eight hours for that purpose if not in session. If the Congress, within twenty-one days after receipt of the latter written declaration, or, if Congress is not in session, within twenty-one days after Congress is required to assemble, determines by two-thirds vote of both Houses that the President is unable to discharge the powers and duties of his office, the Vice President shall continue to discharge the same as Acting President; otherwise; the President shall resume the powers and duties of his office.

Amendment XXVI
(Ratified on July 1, 1971)

Section 1. The right of citizens of the United States, who are eighteen years of age or older, to vote shall not be denied or abridged by the United States or by any State on account of age.

Section 2. The Congress shall have the power to enforce this article by appropriate legislation.

Amendment XXVII
(Ratified on May 7, 1992)

No law, varying the compensation for the services of the Senators and Representatives, shall take effect, until an election of Representatives shall have intervened.

FEDERALIST PAPER 10

Among the numerous advantages promised by a well-constructed Union, none deserves to be more accurately developed than its tendency to break and control the violence of faction. The friend of popular governments never finds himself so much alarmed for their character and fate as when he contemplates their propensity to this dangerous vice. He will not fail, therefore, to set a due value on any plan which, without violating the principles to which he is attached, provides a proper cure for it. The instability, injustice, and confusion introduced into the public councils have, in truth, been the mortal diseases under which popular governments have everywhere perished, as they continue to be the favorite and fruitful topics from which the adversaries to liberty derive their most specious declamations. The valuable improvements made by the American constitutions on the popular models, both ancient and modern, cannot certainly be too much admired; but it would be an unwarrantable partiality to contend that they have as effectually obviated the danger on this side, as was wished and expected. Complaints are everywhere heard from our most considerate and virtuous citizens, equally the friends of public and private faith and of public and personal liberty, that our governments are too unstable, that the public good is disregarded in the conflicts of rival parties, and that measures are too often decided, not according to the rules of justice and the rights of the minor party, but by the superior force of an interested and overbearing majority. However anxiously we may wish that these complaints had no foundation, the evidence of known facts will not permit us to deny that they are in some degree true. It will be found, indeed, on a candid review of our situation, that some of the distresses under which we labor have been erroneously charged on the operation of our governments; but it will be found, at the same time, that other causes will not alone account for many of our heaviest misfortunes; and, particularly, for that prevailing and increasing distrust of public engagements and alarm for private rights which are echoed from one end of the continent to the other. These must be chiefly, if not wholly, effects of the unsteadiness and injustice with which a factious spirit has tainted our public administration.

By a faction I understand a number of citizens, whether amounting to a majority or minority of the whole, who are united and actuated by some common impulse of passion, or of interest, adverse to the rights of other citizens, or the permanent and aggregate interests of the community.

There are two methods of curing the mischiefs of faction: the one, by removing its causes; the other, by controlling its effects.

There are again two methods of removing the causes of faction: the one, by destroying the liberty which is essential to its existence; the other, by giving to every citizen the same opinions, the same passions, and the same interests.

It could never be more truly said than of the first remedy that it was worse than the disease. Liberty is to faction what air is to fire, an aliment without which it instantly expires. But it could not be a less folly to abolish liberty, which is essential to political life, because it nourishes faction than it would be to wish the annihilation of air, which is essential to animal life, because it imparts to fire its destructive agency.

The second expedient is as impracticable as the first would be unwise. As long as the reason of man continues fallible, and his is at liberty to exercise it, different opinions will be formed. As long as the connection subsists between his reason and his self-love, his opinions and his passions will have a reciprocal influence on each other; and the former will be objects to which the latter will attach themselves. The diversity in the faculties of men, from which the rights of property originate, is not less an insuperable obstacle to a uniformity of interests. The protection of these faculties is the first object of government. From the protection of different and unequal faculties of acquiring property, the possession of different degrees and kinds of property immediately results; and from the influence of these on the sentiments and views of the respective proprietors ensues a division of the society into different interests and parties.

The latent causes of faction are thus sown in the nature of man; and we see them everywhere brought into different degrees of activity, according to the different circumstances of civil society. A zeal for different opinions concerning religion, concerning government, and many other points, as well of speculation as of practice; an attachment to different leaders ambitiously contending for pre-eminence and power; or to persons of other descriptions whose fortunes have been interesting to the human passions, have, in turn, divided mankind into parties, inflamed them with mutual animosity, and rendered them much more disposed to vex and oppress each other than to cooperate for their common good. So strong is this propensity of mankind to fall into mutual animosities that where no substantial occasion presents itself the most frivolous and fanciful distinctions have been sufficient to kindle their unfriendly passions and excite their most violent conflicts. But the most common and durable source of factions has been the various and unequal distribution of property. Those who hold and those who are without property have ever formed distinct interests in society. Those who are creditors, and those who are debtors, fall under a like discrimination. A landed interest, a manufacturing interest, a mercantile interest, a moneyed interest, with many lesser interests, grow up of necessity in civilized nations, and divide them into different classes, actuated by different sentiments and views. The regulation of these various and interfering interests forms the principal task of modern legislation and involves the spirit of party and faction in the necessary and ordinary operations of government.

No man is allowed to be a judge in his own cause, because his interest would certainly bias his judgment, and, not improbably, corrupt his integrity. With equal, nay with greater reason, a body of men are unfit to be both judges and parties at the same time; yet what are many of the most important acts of legislation but so many judicial determinations, not indeed concerning the rights of single persons, but concerning the rights of large bodies of citizens? And what are the different classes of legislators but advocates and parties to the causes which they determine? Is a law proposed concerning private debts? It is a question to which the creditors are parties on one side and the debtors on the other. Justice ought to hold the balance between them. Yet the parties are, and must be, themselves the judges; and the most numerous party, or in other words, the most powerful faction must be expected to prevail. Shall domestic manufacturers be encouraged, and in what degree, by restrictions on foreign manufacturers? are questions which would be differently decided by the landed and the manufacturing classes, and probably by neither with a sole regard to justice and the public good. The apportionment of taxes on the various descriptions of property is an act which seems to require the most exact impartiality; yet there is, perhaps, no legislative act in which greater opportunity and temptation are given to a predominant party to trample on the rules of justice. Every shilling with which they overburden the inferior number is a shilling saved to their own pockets. It is in vain to say that enlightened statesmen will be able to adjust these clashing interests and render them all subservient to the public good. Enlightened statesmen will not always be at the helm. Nor, in many cases, can such an adjustment be made at all without taking into view indirect and remote considerations, which will rarely prevail over the immediate interest which one party may find in disregarding the rights of another or the good of the whole.

The inference to which we are brought is that the *causes* of faction cannot be removed and that relief is only to be sought in the means of controlling its *effects.*

If a faction consists of less than a majority, relief is supplied by the republican principle, which enables the majority to defeat its sinister views by regular vote. It may clog the administration, it may convulse the society; but it will be unable to execute and mask its violence under the forms of the Constitution. When a majority is included in a faction, the form of popular government, on the other hand, enables it to sacrifice to its ruling passion or interest both the public good and the rights of other citizens. To secure the public good and private rights against the danger of such a faction, and at the same time to preserve the spirit and the form of popular government, is then the great object to which our inquiries are directed. Let me add that it is the great desideratum by which alone this form of government can be rescued from the opprobrium under which it has so long labored and be recommended to the esteem and adoption of mankind.

By what means is this object attainable? Evidently by one of two only. Either the existence of the same passion or interest in a majority at the same time must be prevented, or the majority, having such coexistent passion or interest, must be rendered, by their number and local situation, unable to concert and carry into effect schemes of oppression. If the impulse and the opportunity be suffered to coincide, we well know that neither moral nor religious motives can be relied on as an adequate control. They are not found to be such on the injustice and violence of individuals, and lose their efficacy in proportion to the number combined together, that is, in proportion as their efficacy becomes needful.

From this view of the subject it may be concluded that a pure democracy, by which I mean a society consisting of a small number of citizens, who assemble and administer the government in person, can admit of no cure for the mischiefs of faction. A common passion or interest will, in almost every case, be felt by a majority of the whole; a communication and concert results from the form of government itself; and there is nothing to check the inducements to sacrifice the weaker party or an obnoxious individual. Hence it is that such democracies have ever been spectacles of turbulence and contention; have ever been found incompatible with personal security or the rights of property; and have in general been as short in their lives as they have been violent in their deaths. Theoretic politicians, who have patronized this species of government, have erroneously supposed that by reducing mankind to a perfect equality in their political rights, they would at the same time be perfectly equalized and assimilated in their possessions, their opinions, and their passions.

A republic, by which I mean a government in which the scheme of representation takes place, opens a different prospect and promises the cure for which we are seeking. Let us examine the points in which it varies from pure democracy, and we shall comprehend both the nature of the cure and the efficacy which it must derive from the Union.

The two great points of difference between a democracy and a republic are: first, the delegation of the government, in the latter, to a small number of citizens elected by the rest; secondly, the greater number of citizens and greater sphere of country over which the latter may be extended.

The effect of the first difference is, on the one hand, to refine and enlarge the public views by passing them through the medium of a chosen body of citizens, whose wisdom may best discern the true interest of their country and whose patriotism and love of justice will be least likely to sacrifice it to temporary or partial considerations. Under such a regulation it may well happen that the public voice, pronounced by the representatives of the people, will be more consonant to the public good than if pronounced by the people themselves, convened for the purpose. On the other hand, the effect may be inverted. Men of factious tempers, of local prejudices, or of sinister designs, may, by intrigue, by corruption, or by other means, first obtain the suffrages, and then betray the interests of the people. The question resulting is, whether small or extensive republics are most favorable to the election of proper guardians of the public weal; and it is clearly decided in favor of the latter by two obvious considerations.

In the first place it is to be remarked that however small the republic may be the representatives must be raised to a certain number in order to guard against the cabals of a few; and that however large it may be they must be limited to a certain number in order to guard against the confusion of a multitude. Hence, the number of representatives in the two cases not being in proportion to that of the constituents, and being proportionally greatest in the small republic, it follows that if the proportion of fit characters be not less in the large than in the small republic, the former will present a greater option, and consequently a greater probability of a fit choice.

In the next place, as each representative will be chosen by a greater number of citizens in the large than in the small republic, it will be more difficult for unworthy candidates to practice with success the vicious arts by which elections are too often carried; and the suffrages of the people being more free, will be more likely to center on men who possess the most attractive merit and the most diffusive and established characters.

It must be confessed that in this, as in most other cases, there is a mean, on both sides of which inconveniencies will be found to lie. By enlarging too much the number of electors, you render the representative too little acquainted with all their local circumstances and lesser interests; as by reducing it too much, you render him unduly attached to these, and too little fit to comprehend and pursue great and national objects. The federal Constitution forms a happy combination in this respect; the great and aggregate interests being referred to the national, the local and particular to the State legislatures.

The other point of difference is the greater number of citizens and extent of territory which may be brought within the compass of republican than of democratic government; and it is this circumstance principally which renders factious combinations less to be dreaded in the former than in the latter. The smaller the society, the fewer probably will be the distinct parties and interests composing it; the fewer the distinct parties and interests, the more frequently will a majority be found of the same party; and the smaller the number of individuals composing a majority, and the smaller the compass within which they are placed, the more easily will they concert and execute their plans of oppression. Extend the sphere and you take in a greater variety of parties and interests; you make it less probable that a majority of the whole will have a common motive to invade the rights of other citizens; or if such a common motive exists, it will be more difficult for all who feel it to discover their own strength and to act in unison with each other. Besides other impediments, it may be remarked that, where there is a consciousness of unjust or dishonorable purposes, communication is always checked by distrust in proportion to the number whose concurrence is necessary.

Hence, it clearly appears that the same advantage which a republic has over a democracy in controlling the effects of faction is enjoyed by a large over a small republic—is enjoyed by the Union over the States composing it. Does this advantage consist in the substitution of representatives whose enlightened views and virtuous sentiments render them superior to local prejudices and to schemes of injustice? It will not be denied that the representation of the Union will be most likely to possess these requisite endowments. Does it consist in the greater security afforded by a greater variety of parties, against the event of any one party being able to outnumber and oppress the rest? In an equal degree does the increased variety of parties comprised within the Union increase this security. Does it, in fine, consist in the greater obstacles opposed to the concert and accomplishment of the secret wishes of an unjust and interested majority? Here again the extent of the Union gives it the most palpable advantage.

The influence of factious leaders may kindle a flame within their particular States but will be unable to spread a general conflagration through the other States. A religious sect may degenerate into a political faction in a part of the Confederacy; but the variety of sects dispersed over the entire face of it must secure the national councils against any danger from that source. A rage for paper money, for an abolition of debts, for an equal division of property, or for any other improper or wicked project, will be less apt to pervade the whole body of the Union than a particular member of it, in the same proportion as such a malady is more likely to taint a particular county or district than an entire State.

In the extent and proper structure of the Union, therefore, we behold a republican remedy for the diseases most incident to republican government. And according to the degree of pleasure and pride we feel in being republicans ought to be our zeal in cherishing the spirit and supporting the character of federalists.

To what expedient, then, shall we finally resort, for maintaining in practice the necessary partition of power among the several departments as laid down in the Constitution? The only answer that can be given is that as all these exterior provisions are found to be inadequate the defect must be supplied, by so contriving the interior structure of the government as that its several constituent parts may, by their mutual relations, be the means of keeping each other in their proper places. Without presuming to undertake a full development of this important idea I will hazard a few general observations which may perhaps place it in a clearer light, and enable us to form a more correct judgment of the principles and structure of the government planned by the convention.

In order to lay a due foundation for that separate and distinct exercise of the different powers of government, which to a certain extent is admitted on all hands to be essential to the preservation of liberty, it is evident that each department should have a will of its own; and consequently should be so constituted that the members of each should have as little agency as possible in the appointment of the members of the others. Were this principle rigorously adhered to, it would require that all the appointments for the supreme executive, legislative, and judiciary magistracies should be drawn from the same fountain of authority, the people, through channels having no communication whatever with one another. Perhaps such a plan of constructing the several departments would be less difficult in practice than it may in contemplation appear. Some difficulties, however, and some additional expense would attend the execution of it. Some deviations, therefore, from the principle must be admitted. In the constitution of the judiciary department in particular, it might be inexpedient to insist rigorously on the principle: first, because peculiar qualifications being essential in the members, the primary consideration ought to be to select that mode of choice which best secures these qualifications; second, because the permanent tenure by which the appointments are held in that department must soon destroy all sense of dependence on the authority conferring them.

It is equally evident that the members of each department should be as little dependent as possible on those of the others for the emoluments annexed to their offices. Were the executive magistrate, or the judges, not independent of the legislature in this particular, their independence in every other would be merely nominal.

But the great security against a gradual concentration of the several powers in the same department consists in giving to those who administer each department the necessary constitutional means and personal motives to resist encroachments of the others. The provision for defense must in this, as in all other cases, be made commensurate to the danger of attack. Ambition must be made to counteract ambition. The interest of the man must be connected with the constitutional rights of the place. It may be a reflection on human nature that such devices should be necessary to control the abuses of government. But what is government itself but the greatest of all reflections on human nature? If men were angels, no government would be necessary. If angels were to govern men, neither external nor internal controls on government would be necessary. In framing a government which is to be administered by men over men, the great difficulty lies in this: you must first enable the government to control the governed; and in the next place oblige it to control itself. A dependence on the people is, no doubt, the primary control on the government; but experience has taught mankind the necessity of auxiliary precautions.

This policy of supplying, by opposite and rival interests, the defect of better motives, might be traced through the whole system of human affairs, private as well as public. We see it particularly displayed in all the subordinate distributions of power, where the constant aim is to divide and arrange the several offices in such a manner as that each may be a check on the other—that the private interest of every individual may be a sentinel over the public rights. These inventions of prudence cannot be less requisite in the distribution of the supreme powers of the State.

But it is not possible to give to each department an equal power of self-defense. In republican government, the legislative authority necessarily predominates. The remedy for this inconveniency is to divide the legislature into different branches; and to render them, by different modes of election and different principles of action, as little connected with each other as the nature of their common functions and their common dependence on the society will admit. It may even be necessary to guard against dangerous encroachments by still further precautions. As the weight of the legislative authority requires that it should be thus divided, the weakness of the executive may require, on the other hand, that it should be fortified. An absolute negative on the legislature appears, at first view, to be the natural defense with which the executive magistrate should be armed. But perhaps it would be neither altogether safe nor alone sufficient. On ordinary occasions it might not be exerted with the requisite firmness, and on extraordinary occasions it might be perfidiously abused. May not this defect of an absolute negative be supplied by some qualified connection between this weaker department and the weaker branch of the stronger department, by which the latter may be led to support the constitutional rights of the former, without being too much detached from the rights of its own department?

If the principles on which these observations are found be just, as I persuade myself they are, and they be applied as a criterion to the several State constitutions, and the federal Constitution, it will be found that if the latter does not perfectly correspond with them, the former are infinitely less able to bear such a test.

There are, moreover, two considerations particularly applicable to the federal system of America, which place that system in a very interesting point of view.

First. In a single republic, all the power surrendered by the people is submitted to the administration of a single government; and the usurpations are guarded against by a division of the government into distinct and separate departments. In the compound republic of America, the power surrendered by the people is first divided between two distinct governments, and then the portion allotted to each subdivided among distinct and separate departments. Hence a double security arises to the rights of the people. The different governments will control each other, at the same time that each will be controlled by itself.

Second. It is of great importance in a republic not only to guard the society against the oppression of its rulers, but to guard one part of the society against the injustice of the other part. Different interests necessarily exist in different classes of citizens. If a majority be united by a common interest, the rights of the minority will be insecure. There are but two methods of providing against this evil: the one by creating a will in the community independent of the majority—that is, of the society itself; the other, by comprehending in the society so many separate descriptions of citizens as will render an unjust combination of a majority of the whole very improbable, if not impracticable. The first method prevails in all governments possessing an hereditary or self-appointed authority. This, at best, is but a precarious security; because a power independent of the society may as well espouse the unjust views of the major as the rightful interests of the minor party, and may possibly be turned against both parties. The second method will be exemplified in the federal republic of the United States. Whilst all authority in it will be derived from and dependent on the society, the society itself will be broken into so many parts, interests and classes of citizens, that the rights of individuals, or of the minority, will be in little danger from interested combinations of the majority. In a free government the security for civil rights must be the same as that for religious rights. It consists in the one case in the multiplicity of interests, and in the other in the multiplicity of sects. The degree of security in both cases will depend on the number of interests and sects; and this may be presumed to depend on the extent of country and number of people comprehended under the same government. This view of the subject must particularly recommend a proper federal system to all the sincere and considerate friends of republican government, since it shows that in exact proportion as the territory of the Union may be formed into more circumscribed Confederacies, or States, oppressive combinations of a majority will be facilitated; the best security, under the republican forms, for the rights of every class of citizen, will be diminished; and consequently the stability and independence of some member of the government, the only other security, must be proportionally increased. Justice is the end of government. It is the end of civil society. It ever has been and ever will be pursued until it be obtained, or until liberty be lost in the pursuit. In a society under the forms of which the stronger faction can readily unite and oppress the weaker, anarchy may as truly be said to reign as in a state of nature, where the weaker individual is not secured against the violence of the stronger; and as, in the latter state, even the stronger individuals are prompted, by the uncertainty of their condition, to submit to a government which may protect the weak as well as themselves; so, in the former state, will the more powerful factions or parties be gradually induced, by a like motive, to wish for a government which will protect all parties, the weaker as well as the more powerful. It can be little doubted that if the State of Rhode Island was separated from the Confederacy and left to itself, the insecurity of rights under the popular form of government within such narrow limits would be displayed by such reiterate oppressions of factious majorities that some power altogether independent of the people would soon be called for by the voice of the very factions whose misrule had proved the necessity of it. In the extended republic of the United States, and among the great variety of interests, parties, and sects which it embraces, a coalition of a majority of the whole society could seldom take place on any other principles than those of justice and the general good; whilst there being thus less danger to a minor from the will of a major party, there must be less pretext, also, to provide for the security of the former, by introducing into the government a will not dependent on the latter, or, in other words, a will independent of the society itself. It is no less certain than it is important, notwithstanding the contrary opinions which have been entertained, that the larger the society, provided it lie within a practicable sphere, the more duly capable it will be of self-government. And happily for the *republican cause,* the practicable sphere may be carried to a very great extent by a judicious modification and mixture of the *federal principle.*

ABRAHAM LINCOLN'S GETTYSBURG ADDRESS

Four score and seven years ago our fathers brought forth on this continent a new nation, conceived in liberty and dedicated to the proposition that all men are created equal. Now we are engaged in a great Civil War, testing whether that nation or any nation so conceived and so dedicated can long endure. We are met on a great battlefield of that war. We have come to dedicate a portion of that field as a final resting place for those who here gave their lives that that nation might live. It is altogether fitting and proper that we should do this. But in a larger sense, we cannot dedicate—we cannot consecrate—we cannot hallow this ground. The brave men, living and dead, who struggled here have consecrated it far above our poor power to add or detract. The world will little note nor long remember what we say here, but it can never forget what they did here. It is for us the living, rather, to be dedicated here to the unfinished work which they who fought here have thus far so nobly advanced. It is rather for us to be here dedicated to the great task remaining before us—that from these honored dead we take increased devotion to that cause for which they gave the last full measure of devotion—that we here highly resolve that these dead shall not have died in vain, that this nation, under God, shall have a new birth of freedom, and that government of the people, by the people, for the people shall not perish from the earth.

Chapter 1

1. *Federalist Paper 2* (any edition).
2. Gore Vidal, "Coached by Camelot," *New Yorker* (December 1, 1997): 88.
3. See John Hibbing and Beth Theiss-Morse, *Congress as Public Enemy: Public Attitudes toward American Political Institutions* (Cambridge: Cambridge University Press, 1995); Hibbing and Theiss-Morse, "Civics Is Not Enough; Teaching Barbarics in K–12," *PS* (March 1996): 57–62.
4. Hibbing and Theiss-Morse, *Congress.*
5. Walt Whitman, *Leaves of Grass and Selected Prose,* ed. Lawrence Buell (New York: Random House, 1981), 449.
6. Edward Countryman, *Americans: A Collision of Histories* (New York: Hill & Wang, 1996), 3–22.
7. John Sugden, *Tecumseh: A Life* (New York: Holt, 1998).
8. INS Statistics, emigration tables (www.ins.gov/ graphics.aboutins/statistics/300.htm).
9. Ibid.
10. U.S. Census Bureau, "The Foreign-Born Population in the United States," March 2000, 1 (www.census.gov).
11. Ibid.
12. "Immigrants," *2000 INS Statistical Abstract* (www.census.gov).
13. *U.S. Statistical Abstract, 2000,* Table 54.
14. Michael Lind, "The Beige and the Black," *New York Times Magazine* (August 16, 1998): 38.
15. George F. Will, "Buchanan Takes Aim," *Washington Post National Weekly Edition,* December 16–22, 1991, 28.
16. The *Christian American,* quoted in Dick Kirschten, "Building Blocs," *National Journal,* September 26, 1993, 2173.
17. "Religion and the Founding of the American Republic, Part I: America as a Religious Refuge: The Seventeenth Century," Library of Congress exhibit (lcweb.loc.gov/exhibits/religion).
18. Nicholas von Hoffman, "God was Present at the Founding," *Civilization* (April/May 1998).
19. Michael J. Sandel, *Democracy's Discontent: America in Search of a Public Philosophy* (Cambridge, Mass.: Belknap, Harvard University Press, 1997), 56–57.
20. Sarah Mondale and Sarah B. Patton, eds., *School: The Story of American Public Education* (Boston: Beacon, 2001), 36.
21. Elizabeth Becker, "All White, All Christian and Divided by Diversity," *New York Times,* June 10, 2001, Section 4, 7. Becker was writing about her hometown.
22. "Belief by the Numbers," *New York Times Magazine* (December 7, 1997): 60–61; Gustav Niebur, "Makeup of American Religion Is Looking More Like Mosaic, Data Say," *New York Times,* April 12, 1998, 12. The census does not collect data on religious affiliation, so most numbers, such as those in the annual *Statistical Abstract,* come from self-report of religious denominations.
23. Quoted by James Q. Wilson in "The History and Future of Democracy," lecture delivered at the Reagan presidential library November 15, 1999 (reprinted by School of Public Policy, Pepperdine University), 3.
24. On identity politics, see Walter Benn Michaels, *Our America: Nativism, Modernism, and Pluralism* (Durham, N.C.: Duke University Press, 1997).
25. U.S. Bureau of the Census, *General Social and Economic Characteristics: U.S. Summary* (Washington, D.C.: U.S. Government Printing Office, 1990), Part 1, Table 12.
26. The origins of governmental systems are discussed by John Jay in *Federalist Paper 2.*
27. Garry Wills, *Lincoln at Gettysburg: The Words That Remade America* (New York: Simon & Schuster, 1992), 145.
28. Mondale and Patton, eds., *School,* 13.
29. Ibid., 4.
30. Carl F. Kaestle, "Introduction," in *School,* ed. Mondale and Patton, 16.
31. "The Educated Citizen," in *School,* ed. Mondale and Patton, 22.
32. Robert Reinhold, "Resentment against New Immigrants," *New York Times,* October 26, 1986, 6E.
33. Michael Thompson, Richard Ellis, and Aaron Wildavsky, *Cultural Theory* (Boulder, Colo.: Westview, 1990), 216.
34. For a discussion of the Declaration of Independence's origins in pragmatism versus the political philosophy of the Founders, see Pauline Maier, *American Scripture: Making the Declaration of Independence* (New York: Knopf, 1997).
35. Wilfred M. McClay, "Communitarianism and the Federal Idea," in *Community and Political Thought Today,* ed. Peter Augustine Lawler and Dale McConkey (Westport, Conn.: Praeger, 1998), 102.
36. Alexis De Tocqueville, *Democracy in America* (New York: Knopf, 1945; first published 1835).
37. For a discussion of this point, see Mark Warren, "Democratic Theory and Self-Transformation," *American Political Science Review* 86 (March 1992): 8–23.
38. This discussion draws on Sidney Verba and Norman Nie, *Participation in America* (New York: Harper & Row, 1972), and Stephen Earl Bennett and Linda L. M. Bennett, "Political Participation," in *Annual Review of Political Science,* ed. Samuel Long (Norwood, N.J.: Ablex, 1986).
39. E. J. Dionne Jr., *Why Americans Hate Politics* (New York: Simon & Schuster, 1991).
40. Robert A. Dahl, *A Preface to Democratic Theory* (Chicago: University of Chicago Press, 1956), 142.
41. See Arthur F. Bentley, *The Process of Government* (Chicago: University of Chicago Press, 1908), and David Truman, *The Governmental Process* (New York: Knopf, 1951).
42. Robert Michels, *Political Parties* (New York: Collier, 1915).
43. The classic work is C. Wright Mills, *The Power Elite* (New York: Oxford University Press, 1956).
44. Thomas R. Dye, *Who's Running America? Institutional Leadership in the United States* (Englewood Cliffs, N.J.: Prentice Hall, 1976), 11–15. Since completing his original study, Dye has updated it for each administration through Clinton's.
45. Michael Parenti, *Democracy for the Few,* 6th ed. (New York: St. Martin's, 1996).
46. John B. Judis, *The Paradox of American Democracy: Elites, Special Interests, and the Betrayal of Public Trust* (New York: Pantheon, 1999). Judis is senior editor of *The New Republic.*
47. University of Michigan National Election Studies (www.umich.edu/,nes/).
48. Reported in Robert Wright, "Hyper Democracy," *Time,* January 23, 1995, 18.
49. David S. Broder, "Can We Govern?" *Washington Post National Weekly Edition,* January 31–February 6 1994, 23.
50. Hedrick Smith, *The Power Game: How Washington Works* (New York: Random House, 1988), Chapter 17.
51. For example, see Theodore J. Lowi, *The End of Liberalism,* 2d ed. (New York: Norton, 1979).
52. *New York Times* columnist Russell Baker, reprinted in the *Champaign-Urbana News-Gazette,* August 29, 1997, A4.
53. League of Conservative Voters poll, March 2002. Roper Center, University of Connecticut Public Opinion Online.
54. E. J. Dionne Jr., "Preferring Policies over Politics," *Washington Post National Weekly Edition,* February 7, 2000, 22.
55. This was the headline on an op-ed piece by the sociologist Alan Wolfe in the *New York Times,* March 15, 1998, Section 4, 17. He was summarizing the results of a survey of middle-class opinion he published in *One Nation, After All* (New York: Viking, 1997).
56. Polls conducted by the Harwood Institute and by *Time* and the Cable News Network, January 2002; Public Opinion Online, Roper Center, University of Connecticut.

Chapter 2

1. Nixon thought he might be considered an American Disraeli. (Benjamin Disraeli, a British prime minister in the nineteenth century, was a Tory who had progressive ideas.) Nixon praised Robert Blake's biography of Disraeli, and one cabinet secretary remarked in 1971, "The similarities are great, Mr. President, but what a pity that Blake could not quote Disraeli's conversations." Nixon did not destroy the tapes, even after they became a liability, apparently for this reason. Sidney Blumenthal, "The Longest Campaign," *New Yorker* (August 8, 1994): 37.
2. *United States v. Reynolds,* 345 U.S. 1 (1953).
3. The Indians, of course, had their own governments, and the Spanish may have established St. Augustine, Florida, or Santa Fe, New Mexico, before the English established Jamestown. These Spanish settlements were extensions of Spanish colonization of Mexico and were governed by Spanish officials in Mexico City.
4. This is not to suggest that the Pilgrims believed in democracy. Apparently, they were motivated to draft the compact by threats from some on the *Mayflower* that when the ship landed they would "use their owne libertie; for none had power to command them." Thus, the compact was designed to bind them to the laws of the colony. Richard Shenkman, *"I Love Paul Revere, Whether He Rode or Not"* (New York: HarperCollins, 1991), 141–142.
5. David Hawke, *A Transaction of Free Men* (New York: Scribner's, 1964), 209.
6. William H. Riker, *Federalism* (Boston: Little, Brown, 1964), 18–20.
7. For an account of the foreign affairs problems of the Articles, see Frederick W. Marks III, *Independence on Trial: Foreign Affairs and the Making of the Constitution* (Baton Rouge: Louisiana State University Press, 1973).
8. Louis Fisher, *President and Congress* (New York: Free Press, 1972), 14.
9. The government under the Articles, however, could boast one major accomplishment. The Northwest Ordinance, adopted in 1787, provided for the government and future statehood of the land west of Pennsylvania (land that would become most of the Great Lakes states). The law also banned slavery in this territory.
10. Gordon S. Wood, "The Origins of the Constitution," *This Constitution: A Bicentennial Chronicle* (summer 1987): 10–11.
11. Eric Black, *Our Constitution* (Boulder, Colo.: Westview, 1988), 6. Shays, eventually pardoned by Massachusetts, settled in New York and became a staunch Federalist (8).
12. For development of this idea, see Kenneth M. Dolbeare and Linda J. Medcalf, "The Political

Economy of the Constitution," *This Constitution: A Bicentennial Chronicle* (spring 1987): 4–10.

13. Black, *Our Constitution,* 59.

14. The Constitution, however, would reflect numerous aspects of the Articles. See Donald S. Lutz, "The Articles of Confederation as the Background to the Federal Republic," *Publius* 20 (winter 1990): 55–70.

15. Robert McCloskey, *The American Supreme Court* (Chicago: University of Chicago Press, 1960), 29.

16. Fred Barbash, "James Madison: A Man for the '80s," *Washington Post National Weekly Edition,* March 30, 1987, 23.

17. Robert A. Dahl, *A Preface to Democratic Theory* (Chicago: University of Chicago Press, 1956), 5. Yet, according to a poll in 1987, the bicentennial of the Constitution, only 1 percent of the public identified Madison as the one who played the biggest role in creating the Constitution. Most—31 percent—said Thomas Jefferson, who was a diplomat in France during the convention. Black, *Our Constitution,* 15.

18. Paul Finkelman, "Slavery at the Philadelphia Convention," *This Constitution: A Bicentennial Chronicle* (1987): 25–30.

19. Ibid., 29.

20. Ibid., 18.

21. Thomas G. West, *Vindicating the Founders: Race, Sex, Class, and Justice in the Origins of America* (Lanham, Md.: Rowman & Littlefield, 1997), 15.

22. Theodore J. Lowi, *American Government* (Hinsdale, Ill.: Dryden, 1976), 97.

23. C. Herman Pritchett, *Constitutional Law of the Federal System* (Englewood Cliffs, N.J.: Prentice Hall, 1984), xi.

24. Richard Hofstadter, *The American Political Tradition and the Men Who Made It* (New York: Random House, 1948), 13.

25. *Federalist Paper* 51.

26. *Federalist Paper* 47.

27. Max Farrand, *The Framing of the Constitution of the United States* (New Haven, Conn.: Yale University Press, 1913).

28. *Federalist Paper* 51.

29. Richard E. Neustadt, *Presidential Power and the Modern Presidents* (New York: Macmillan, 1990), 29.

30. Seymour Martin Lipset, "Why No Socialism in the United States?" in *Sources of Contemporary Radicalism,* ed. Seweryn Bialer and Sophis Sluzar (Boulder, Colo.: Westview, 1977), 86.

31. These were not the only reasons people migrated to America, of course, but these were the primary ones. For development of this idea, see John W. Kingdon, *America the Unusual* (Boston: Bedford/St. Martin's, 1999), 58–63. After the Revolutionary War, many Americans who were sympathetic to England, and more comfortable with authority, moved to Canada. At the same time, some Canadians who were more individualistic moved to the United States, thus reinforcing the original migration pattern.

32. For elaboration, see West, *Vindicating the Founders,* 43–54.

33. Donald S. Lutz, "The Relative Influence of European Writers on Later Eighteenth-Century American Political Thought," *American Political Science Review* 78 (March 1984): 139–197.

34. Alpheus T. Mason and Richard H. Leach, *In Quest of Freedom: American Political Thought and Practice,* 2d ed. (Englewood Cliffs, N.J.: Prentice Hall, 1973), 51.

35. For development of this idea, see Martin Landau, "A Self-Correcting System: The Constitution of the United States," *This Constitution: A Bicentennial Chronicle* (summer 1986): 4–10.

36. John P. Roche, "The Founding Fathers: A Reform Caucus in Action," *American Political Science Review* 56 (March 1962): 799–816.

37. Benjamin F. Wright Jr., "The Origins of the Separation of Powers in America," in *Origins of American Political Thought,* ed. John P. Roche (New York: Harper & Row, 1967), 139–162.

38. Ibid.

39. Charles Beard, *An Economic Interpretation of the Constitution* (New York: Macmillan, 1913).

40. Ellen Nore, "Charles A. Beard's Economic Interpretation of the Origins of the Constitution," *This Constitution* (winter 1987): 39.

41. R. E. Brown, *Charles Beard and the Constitution* (Princeton, N.J.: Princeton University Press, 1956); Forrest MacDonald, *We the People* (Chicago: University of Chicago Press, 1976).

42. James MacGregor Burns, *The Vineyard of Liberty* (New York: Knopf, 1982), 33.

43. Bernard Bailyn, *Voyagers to the West* (New York: Knopf, 1982), 20.

44. The Boston Tea Party, contrary to myth, was not prompted by higher taxes on British tea. Parliament lowered the taxes to give the British East India Company, facing bankruptcy, an advantage in the colonial market. This threatened American shippers who smuggled tea from Holland and controlled about three-fourths of the market. The shippers resented Parliament's attempt to manipulate the economy from thousands of miles away. Shenkman, *"I Love Paul Revere, Whether He Rode or Not,"* 155.

45. *Federalist Paper* 10.

46. Black, *Our Constitution,* 21.

47. Calvin C. Jillson and Cecil L. Eubanks, "The Political Structure of Constitution Making," *American Journal of Political Science* 29 (August 1984): 435–458.

48. Jonathan Elliot, *The Debates in the Several State Conventions on the Adoption of the Federal Constitution as Recommended by the General Convention at Philadelphia, in 1787,* 2d ed., 5 vols. (Philadelphia: n.p., 1896), 2: 102; as quoted in Cecilia M. Kenyon, "Men of Little Faith," in *Origins of American Political Thought,* ed. Roche, 197–198.

49. For Anti-Federalist thinking, see William B. Allen and Gordon Lloyd, eds., *The Essential Antifederalist,* 2d ed. (Lanham, Md.: University Press of America, 2002); John F. Manley and Kenneth M. Dolbeare, *The Case against the Constitution* (Armonk, N.Y.: Sharpe, 1987).

50. "A Fundamental Contentment," *This Constitution: A Bicentennial Chronicle* (fall 1984): 44.

51. Charles Warren, *The Making of the Constitution* (Boston: Little, Brown, 1928), xiv. Jefferson made this observation from afar, as he was ambassador to France during the Constitutional Convention.

52. Alan P. Grimes, *Democracy and the Amendments to the Constitution* (Lexington, Mass.: Lexington, 1978). Grimes also shows how the adoption of new amendments reflects the rise of new power blocs in society.

53. This section borrows heavily from George P. Fletcher, *Our Secret Constitution: How Lincoln Redefined American Democracy* (New York: Oxford University Press, 2001); Bruce Ackerman, *We the People, 2: Transformations* (Cambridge, Mass.: Belknap, 1998); and Garry Wills, *Lincoln at Gettysburg* (New York: Simon & Schuster, 1992). For a complementary view, see Charles Black, *A New Birth of Freedom: Human Rights, Named and Unnamed* (New York: Grosset/Putnam, 1997). For a somewhat different view about the impact of the New Deal, see G. Edward White, *The Constitution and the New Deal* (Cambridge, Mass.: Harvard University Press, 2001).

54. Historian James McPherson, quoted in Fletcher, *Our Secret Constitution,* 57; Ackerman, *We the People,* 10.

55. Many of Lincoln's prejudicial comments came in response to more blatant racist remarks by his opponents. Lincoln abandoned his support for black emigration before he was elected to a second term as president. For a critical perspective on Lincoln's racial views, see Lerone Bennett Jr., *Forced into Glory: Abraham Lincoln's White Dream* (Chicago: Johnson, 2000). For a positive perspective, see William Lee Miller, *Lincoln's Virtues: An Ethical Biography* (New York: Knopf, 2002).

56. Fletcher, *Our Secret Constitution,* 24.

57. John Hope Franklin, *From Slavery to Freedom,* 3d ed. (New York: Vintage, 1969), 283.

58. The proclamation also prompted European workers, who were attracted to the idea of laborers around the world gaining more freedom, to rally to the Union's cause. Ibid., 283.

59. These paragraphs rely on the interpretations from Wills, *Lincoln at Gettysburg,* and Fletcher, *Our Secret Constitution.*

60. Fletcher, *Our Secret Constitution,* 53.

61. A precursor of this view was the era of Jacksonian democracy in the 1830s.

62. A contemporaneous celebration of the nation as an entity can be seen in the poetry of Walt Whitman.

63. Wills, *Lincoln at Gettysburg,* 38. Wills insists that this was not a coincidence, and he debunks the notion that Lincoln hastily dashed off his remarks while on his way to the town or to the speech itself (27–31).

64. Fletcher, *Our Secret Constitution,* 35, 4. Others might put forth Lincoln's second inaugural address, in which he offered reconciliation to the South, or Martin Luther King's "I Have a Dream" speech.

65. The *Dred Scott* case is explained in Chapters 13 and 15.

66. The equal protection clause is covered fully in Chapter 15, and the due process clause is covered fully in Chapter 14.

67. Fletcher, *Our Secret Constitution,* 25.

68. In this vein, Congress first experimented with an income tax during the war. It would return to this tax in the decades after the war.

69. There was a debate about the validity of the Thirteenth and, especially, the Fourteenth Amendment, as there had been about the validity of the Constitutional Convention and Constitution for bypassing the procedures for amendment established by the Articles of Confederation. Congress conditioned the slave states' reentry into the Union upon their ratification of the Fourteenth Amendment. Otherwise, not enough states would have ratified the amendment. Yet one legal scholar argues that Congress served as a quasi–constitutional convention in which members, as Lincoln before them, sensed that they were reinventing rather than following the Constitution. Their actions would have been thwarted if the public had opposed them. Ackerman, *We the People,* Chapters 6–8.

70. For example, the abolitionist movement and the Fifteenth Amendment would fuel the drive for women's suffrage, as explained in Chapter 15.

71. This section borrows heavily from Ackerman, *We the People,* and Theodore J. Lowi, *The Personal President* (Ithaca, N.Y.: Cornell University Press, 1985).

72. We never had a pure laissez-faire approach—there always was some governmental regulation—but this is the term most associated with the attitudes of the time.

73. At least one legal scholar dismisses the notion that the Court's old men were reactionaries or fools. Although today people consider them mistaken, at the time they were following established doctrine. Ackerman, *We the People.*

74. Elaboration of and sources for these statements are included in Chapter 13.

75. The Court said he did affect the market slightly because he did not buy the twelve acres worth of wheat that he would have needed if he had obeyed the order. The Court's main point, however, was that Congress has the authority to pass such laws. *Wickard v. Filburn,* 317 U.S. 111 (1942).

76. Lowi, *The Personal President,* 49. Writers during the Depression and in the decades after it also recognized this as a revolution. Ernest K. Lindley, *The Roosevelt Revolution, First Phase* (New York: Viking, 1933); Mario Einaudi, *The Roosevelt Revolution* (New York: Harcourt, Brace & World, 1959).

77. Karl Vick, "A President Who Woke Up Washington," *Washington Post National Weekly Edition,* April 28, 1997, 8.

78. Ibid., 9.

79. Lowi, *The Personal President,* 44.

80. Ibid., xi.

81. This era also saw a shift to a more presidential centered government that persists to a significant degree today. Lowi, *Personal President*.

82. President Ronald Reagan in the 1980s and congressional Republicans in the early 1990s mounted the biggest challenges to the changes initiated by the Depression and the New Deal, as will be discussed in later chapters.

83. Of course, the process was evolutionary; the changes did not spring solely from these two crises. Moreover, some might maintain that the Supreme Court under the leadership of Chief Justice Earl Warren in the 1950s and 1960s also remade the Constitution because of its rulings expanding the Bill of Rights. Yet the changes brought about by the Warren Court probably had less impact overall than those wrought by Reconstruction or the New Deal.

84. For a discussion of the role played by the philosophy of pragmatism in resolving these conflicts, see Fletcher, *Our Secret Constitution*, Chapter 11.

85. West, *Vindicating the Founders*, xi.

86. "South Africa Looks at U.S. Constitution," *Lincoln Journal-Star*, October 7, 1990; David Remnick, " 'We, the People,' from the Russian," *Washington Post National Weekly Edition*, September 10–16, 1990, 11.

87. William O. Douglas, *The Record of the Association of the Bar of the City of New York*, 4 (1949): 152.

88. Harold J. Spaeth, *Supreme Court Policy Making* (San Francisco: Freeman, 1979), 13.

89. Kingdon, *America the Unusual*, 7–22. Exceptions include education and regulation of civil rights and the environment. Exceptions also include a massive national defense establishment and an extensive criminal justice system. In these ways we have bigger government than many other advanced industrialized countries.

90. Richard Morin, "Happy Days Are Here Again," *Washington Post National Weekly Edition*, August 25, 1997, 35.

91. About 25 percent split their ticket between candidates for president and representative. In addition, others split their vote between candidates for president and senator or between candidates for representative and senator. For an examination of the research about divided government, see Morris Fiorina, *Divided Government*, 2d ed. (Boston: Allyn & Bacon, 1996), 153.

92. Lewis Lapham, "Get Me Rewrite!" *New York Times Book Review* (February 4, 1996): 11.

93. 418 U.S. 683 (1974).

94. Jeffrey Toobin, *A Vast Conspiracy* (New York: Touchstone, 1999), 333–334.

95. Tip O'Neill with William Novak, *Man of the House* (New York: Random House, 1987). The tapes did contain some useful advice for future presidents. Unfortunately, this advice, on tapes not released until 1999, came too late for President Clinton: "Frankly, we shouldn't have had those interns. They're a pain in the ass." "Verbatim," *Time* (October 18, 1999): 35.

96. Bob Woodward and Carl Bernstein, *The Final Days* (New York: Simon & Schuster, 1976), 343, 403–404, 423.

97. "Tapes Confirm Nixon Approved Hush Money," *Lincoln Journal-Star*, June 5, 1991. For a survey of presidents' efforts to record their conversations, see William Doyle, *Inside the Oval Office: White House Tapes from FDR to Clinton* (New York: Kodansha, 1999).

Chapter 3

1. This segment is based in part on Timothy Egan, "Putting Some Space between His Presidency and History," *New York Times*, January 16, 2000, Section 4, 3; "President Expands Protection of Sequoias," *New York Times*, April 16, 2000, 25; Michael Janofsky, "U.S. Readies a Major Land Protection Initiative," *New York Times*, November 21, 1999, 17; Barbara Whitaker, "A Plan to Preserve Giant Sequoias, World's Biggest Trees," *New York Times*, April 9, 2000, 18; "President Gives Land in Four Areas New Status," *Champaign-Urbana News-Gazette*, January 12, 2000, A3.

2. 1999 figures, latest available. *Statistical Abstract of the United States, 2001* (Washington, D.C.: U.S. Government Printing Office, 2001), Table 344.

3. Christopher John Farley, "The West Is Wild Again," *Time* (March 20, 1995): 46.

4. Erik Larson, "Unrest in the West," *Time* (October 23, 1995): 54.

5. William H. Riker, *The Development of American Federalism* (Boston: Kluwer Academic, 1987), 6.

6. The delegate was George Read of Delaware. See William H. Riker, *Democracy in America*, 2d ed. (New York: Macmillan, 1965).

7. *Federalist Paper 39* (any edition).

8. Vernon L. Parrington, *Main Currents in American Thought* (New York: Harcourt, Brace, 1927).

9. David Truman, "Federalism and the Party System," in *Federalism: Mature and Emergent*, ed. Arthur W. MacMahon (New York: Russell & Russell, 1962), 123.

10. Daniel Elazar, *American Federalism: A View from the States*, 3d ed. (New York: Harper & Row, 1984).

11. All figures in this paragraph from the *Statistical Abstract of the United States, 2001*, Tables 20, 23, 24, and 652. Income figures in current dollars.

12. Robert S. Erikson, Gerald C. Wright, and John McIver, *Statehouse Democracy: Public Opinion and Policy in the American States* (New York: Cambridge University Press, 1993).

13. See Madison's discussion of this in *Federalist Paper 39*.

14. See Forrest McDonald, *States Rights and the Union: Imperium in Imperio* (Lawrence: University Press of Kansas, 2001).

15. A 1976 Supreme Court decision used the Tenth Amendment as a reason to forbid the federal government to extend minimum wage and hour laws to state and local government employees. See *National League of Cities v. Usery*, 426 U.S. 833 (1976). This decision was partially overruled in 1985. See *Garcia v. San Antonio Metropolitan Transit Authority*, 469 U.S. 528 (1985).

16. Political scientist Howard Gillman, quoted in Linda Greenhouse, "At the Court, Dissent over States' Rights Is Now War," *New York Times*, June 10, 2002, Section 4, 3.

17. Part of this discussion is drawn from Richard Leach, *American Federalism* (New York: Norton, 1970), Chapter 1. See also Christopher Hamilton and Donald Wells, *Federalism, Power and Political Economy: A New Theory of Federalism's Impact on American Life* (Englewood Cliffs, N.J.: Prentice Hall, 1990).

18. *McCulloch v. Maryland*, 4 Wheat. 316 (1819).

19. Alfred Kelly and Winfred Harbeson, *The American Constitution: Its Origins and Development* (New York: Norton, 1976).

20. Daniel Elazar, *The American Partnership* (Chicago: University of Chicago Press, 1962).

21. Perhaps because he is a sociologist (!), Theodore Caplan did not fully appreciate the extent of federal involvement in Muncie, even in 1924—the support of veterans, schools, roads, and hospitals by federal land grants. Nevertheless, his major point is valid: The federal presence was low-profile in the 1920s. Caplan is quoted in Daniel Walker, *Toward a Functioning Federalism* (Cambridge, Mass.: Winthrop, 1981), 3–4.

22. Theodore Lowi, *The Personal President* (Ithaca, N.Y.: Cornell University Press, 1985).

23. Timothy Conlan, *From Federalism to Devolution: Twenty-five Years of Intergovernmental Reform* (Washington, D.C.: Brookings Institution, 1998), 6.

24. On Nixon's managerial approach to federalism, see Lawrence D. Brown, *New Policies, New Politics: Government's Response to Government's Growth* (Washington, D.C.: Brookings Institution, 1983). The comparative discussion of Lyndon Johnson's, Richard Nixon's, and Ronald Reagan's federalism policies draws on Conlon, *From New Federalism to Devolution*, Chapters 1, 6, and 13.

25. Conlon, *From New Federalism to Devolution*, 109.

26. Quoted in ibid., 11.

27. Quoted in ibid., 1.

28. See, for example, William J. Clinton, "Federalism," Executive Order 13132, *Federal Register* 54, no. 163 (August 10, 1999): 43255–43259. Clinton discussed his views on state activism and federalism in general with the historian Gary Wills in "The War between the States and Washington," *New York Times Magazine* (July 5, 1998): 26–29.

29. "Bush Order Would Give States More Power," *Champaign-Urbana News-Gazette*, September 3, 2001, A3.

30. Dan Carney, "Latest Supreme Court Rulings Reinforce the Federalist Trend," *Congressional Quarterly*, June 26, 1999, 1528; Linda Greenhouse, "High Court Faces Moment of Truth in Federalism Cases," *New York Times*, March 28, 1999, 20.

31. Linda Greenhouse, "At the Court, Dissent over States' Rights Is Now War," *New York Times*, June 10, 2002, Section 4, 3.

32. David Broder, "Take Back the Initiative," *Washington Post National Weekly Edition*, April 10, 2000, 6.

33. James W. Brosnan, "Not Taxing Internet Sales Hurts," *Champaign-Urbana News-Gazette*, February 21, 2000, A6.

34. Barney Frank (D-Mass.) quoted in Michael Grunwald, "Everybody Talks about State's Rights," *Washington Post National Weekly Edition*, November 1, 1999, 29. Frank was referring to Republicans only, but the quote fits Democrats as well.

35. Wills, "The War between the States and Washington," 26.

36. Sheryl Gay Stolberg, "As Congress Stalls, States Pursue Cloning Debate," *New York Times*, May 26, 2002, 1, 19.

37. Stephen Labaton, "Washington's Deregulatory Mood Finds Its Opposite in Vexed States," *New York Times*, January 13, 2002, 1.

38. Kirsten Downley Grimsley, "Where Congress Fears to Tread," *Washington Post National Weekly Edition*, August 21, 2000, 18.

39. Ibid., 19.

40. *Statistical Abstract of the United States, 2001*, Tables 449 and 640.

41. Alice Rivlin, *Reviving the American Dream: The Economy, the States and the Federal Government* (Washington, D.C.: Brookings Institute, 1992).

42. See Mary Ann Glendon, *Abortion and Divorce in Western Law* (Cambridge, Mass.: Harvard University Press, 1987), 87–88; see also Susan Welch, Sue Thomas, and Margery Ambrosius, "Family Policy," in *State Politics and Policy*, 5th ed., ed. Virginia Gray and Herbert Jacob (Boston: Little, Brown, 1995).

43. For a review of the politics surrounding the law, its provisions, and limitations, see Conlon, *From New Federalism to Devolution*, Chapter 13, 257–292.

44. Neil Berch, "Why Do Some States Play the Federal Aid Game Better Than Others?" *American Politics Quarterly* 20 (July 1992): 366–377.

45. Enid F. Beaumont and Harold Hovey, "State, Local and Federal Development Policies: New Federalism Patterns, Chaos, or What?" *Public Administration Review* 45 (March/April 1985): 327–332; Barry Rubin and C. Kurt Zorn, "Sensible State and Local Development," *Public Administration Review* 45 (March/April 1985): 333–339.

46. Thomas Hargrove, "How Taxes Affect Population Growth," *Champaign-Urbana News-Gazette*, March 24, 2002, B1.

47. Broder, "Take Back the Initiative," 6; John Maggs, "Ballot Boxing," *National Journal*, July 1, 2000, 2147.

48. Wills, "The War between the States and Washington," 27.

49. Richard Cohen, "States Aren't Saints Either," *Washington Post National Weekly Edition*, April 3–9, 1995, 28; R. W. Apple, "You Say You Want a Devolution," *New York Times*, January 29, 1995, Section 4, 1; "Study: Legislators Mix Personal, State Affairs," *Champaign-Urbana News-Gazette*, A–9.

50. B. Drummond Ayres Jr., "Louisiana Apathy: The Ebb and Flow," *New York Times,* November 18, 2001, A20.

51. Katherine Sullivan, "In Defense of Federal Power," *New York Times Magazine* (August 18, 1996): 36.

52. Richard Neustadt, *American Presidency* series, Episode 5 (PBS broadcast, April 2000).

53. Eliza Newlin Carney, "Power Grab," *National Journal,* April 11, 1998, 798–800.

54. NBC News poll, January 2002.

55. ABC News poll, January 2002.

56. NBC News/*Wall Street Journal* poll, December 2001; both CBS and Gallup polls in June 2002 showed declining approval levels for Congress and the Supreme Court.

57. Egan, "Putting Some Space between His Presidency and History," 3.

58. William Booth, "The Green President," *Washington Post National Weekly Edition,* January 22–28, 2001, 6. The "not a bird-watcher" quote was from Clinton's interior secretary Bruce Babbit.

Chapter 4

1. Richard Moran and Claudia Deae, "Thumbs Up for the USA," *Washington Post National Weekly Edition,* December 3–9, 2001, 34.

2. Richard Moran and Dana Milbank, "Bush and the GOP Enjoy Record Popularity," *Washington Post,* January 29, 2002, A01.

3. Mike Allen, "A War Strategy at Home," *Washington Post National Weekly Edition,* January 14–20, 2002, 15.

4. Moran and Milbank, "Bush and the GOP."

5. Mike Allen, "A War Strategy at Home," *Washington Post National Weekly Edition,* January 14–20, 2002, 15.

6. Richard Morin, "The Ups and Downs of Political Poll-Taking," *Washington Post National Weekly Edition,* October 5, 1992, 37.

7. Gallup Poll, "Bush Continues to Enjoy Single-Digit Lead over Gore in Presidential Race," May 3, 2000.

8. T. E. Cook, "The Bear Market in Political Socialization and the Costs of Misunderstood Psychological Theories," *American Political Science Review* 79 (December 1985): 1079–1093.

9. S. W. Moore et al., "The Civic Awareness of Five- and Six-Year-Olds," *Western Political Quarterly* 29 (August 1976): 418.

10. R. W. Connell, *The Child's Construction of Politics* (Carlton: Melbourne University Press, 1971).

11. F. I. Greenstein, *Children and Politics* (New Haven, Conn.: Yale University Press, 1965), 122; see also F. I. Greenstein, "The Benevolent Leader Revisited: Children's Images of Political Leaders in Three Democracies," *American Political Science Review* 69 (December 1975): 1317–1398; R. D. Hess and J. V. Torney, *The Development of Attitudes in Children* (Chicago: Aldine, 1967).

12. Hess and Torney, *Development of Attitudes in Children;* Connell, *Child's Construction of Politics.*

13. Greenstein, *Children and Politics;* Greenstein, "The Benevolent Leader"; and Hess and Torney, *Development of Attitudes in Children.*

14. Connell, *Child's Construction of Politics.*

15. F. C. Arterton, "The Impact of Watergate on Children's Attitudes toward the President," *Political Science Quarterly* 89 (June 1974): 269–288; also F. Haratwig and C. Tidmarch, "Children and Political Reality: Changing Images of the President," paper presented at the 1974 Annual Meeting of the Southern Political Science Association; J. Dennis and C. Webster, "Children's Images of the President and Government in 1962 and 1974," *American Politics Quarterly* 4 (October 1975): 386–405; R. Hawkins, S. Pingree, and D. Roberts, "Watergate and Political Socialization," *American Politics Quarterly* 4 (October 1975): 406–436.

16. Gallup Poll, "Public Trust in Federal Government Remains High," January 8, 1999.

17. M. A. Delli Carpini, *Stability and Change in American Politics: The Coming of Age of the Generation of the 1960s* (New York: New York University Press, 1986), 86–89.

18. R. Merelman, *Political Socialization and Educational Climates* (New York: Holt, Rinehart & Winston, 1971), 54.

19. R. Sigel and M. Hoskin, *The Political Involvement of Adolescents* (New Brunswick, N.J.: Rutgers University Press, 1981).

20. John Hibbing and Elizabeth Theiss-Morse, *Congress as Public Enemy: Public Attitudes toward American Political Institutions* (Cambridge: Cambridge University Press, 1995). It is plausible to assume that the content of early political socialization influences what is learned later, but the assumption has not been adequately tested. Thus, we might expect the positive opinions toward government and politics developed early in childhood to condition the impact of traumatic events later in life. D. Easton and J. Dennis, *Children and the Political System: Origins of Regime Legitimacy* (New York: McGraw-Hill, 1969); R. Weissberg, *Political Learning, Political Choice and Democratic Citizenship* (Englewood Cliffs, N.J.: Prentice Hall, 1974). See also D. D. Searing, J. J. Schwartz, and A. E. Line, "The Structuring Principle: Political Socialization and Belief System," *American Political Science Review* 67 (June 1973): 414–432.

21. J. Citrin, "Comment: The Political Relevance of Trust in Government," *American Political Science Review* 68 (September 1974): 973–1001; J. Citrin and D. Green, "Presidential Leadership and the Resurgence of Trust in Government," *British Journal of Political Science* 16 (1986): 431–453.

22. D. Jaros, H. Hirsch, and F. Fleron Jr., "The Malevolent Leader: Political Socialization in an American Subculture," *American Political Science Review* 62 (June 1968): 564–575.

23. K. Tedin, "The Influence of Parents on the Political Attitudes of Adolescents," *American Political Science Review* 68 (December 1974): 1579–1592.

24. M. Kent Jennings, *Generations and Politics* (Princeton, N.J.: Princeton University Press, 1981).

25. K. Dolan, "Attitudes, Behaviors, and the Influence of the Family: A Reexamination of the Role of Family Structure," *Political Behavior* 17 (September 1995): 251–264.

26. On the impact of the public schools and teachers on political socialization, particularly in the area of loyalty and patriotism, see Hess and Torney, *Development of Attitudes in Children.*

27. G. Almond and S. Verba, *Civic Culture* (Boston: Little, Brown, 1965); John R. Hibbing and Elizabeth Theiss-Morse, "Civics Is Not Enough: Teaching Barbarics in K–12," *PS: Political Science and Politics* (March 1996): 12; Norman Nie, Jane June, and Kenneth Stehlik-Barry, *Educations and Democratic Citizenship in America* (Chicago: University of Chicago Press, 1996).

28. Nie et al., *Educations and Democratic Citizenship in America.*

29. Alfonso Damico, M. Margaret Conway, and Sandra Damico, "Patterns of Political Trust and Mistrust: Three Moments in the Lives of Democratic Citizens," *Polity* 32 (spring 2000): 377–400.

30. Hibbing and Theiss-Morse, *Congress as Public Enemy.*

31. Richard G. Niemi and Jane Junn, *Civic Education: What Makes Students Learn* (New Haven, Conn.: Yale University Press, 1998). See also Richard Niemi and Julia Smith, "Enrollments in High School Government Classes: Are We Shortchanging Both Citizenship and Political Science Training?" *PS: Political Science and Politics* 34 (June 2001): 281–288.

32. Julia Smith and Richard G. Niemi, "Learning History in School: The Impact of Course Work and Instructional Practices of Achievement," *Theory and Practice in Social Research* 29 (winter 2001): 18–42.

33. Stephen Bennett, Staci Rhine, and Richard Flickinger, "Reading's Impact on Democratic Citi-

zenship in America," *Political Behavior* 22 (September 2000): 167–195.

34. Nie et al., *Educations and Democratic Citizenship in America.*

35. R. Merelman, "Democratic Politics and the Culture of American Education," *American Political Science Review* 74 (June 1980): 319–332; Almond and Verba, *Civic Culture;* Hibbing and Theiss-Morse, "Civics Is Not Enough"; Nie et al., *Educations and Democratic Citizenship in America.*

36. Material for this section is drawn from E. C. Ladd and S. M. Lipset, *The Divided Academy* (New York: McGraw-Hill, 1975); C. Kesler, "The Movement of Student Opinion," *National Review,* November 23, 1979, 29; E. L. Boyer, *College: The Undergraduate Experience in America* (New York: Harper & Row, 1986); "Fact File: Attitudes and Characteristics of This Year's Freshman," *Chronicle of Higher Education,* January 11, 1989, A33–A34; General Social Survey, National Opinion Research Center, 1984, 87.

37. Alexander W. Astin, W. S. Korn, and Linda Sax, *The American Freshman: Thirty Year Trends* (Los Angeles: Higher Education Research Institute, Graduate School of Education and Information Studies, 1997).

38. Thomas Bartlett, "Evaluating Student Attitudes Is More Difficult This Year," *Chronicle of Higher Education,* February 1, 2002, A35–A38. See also Linda Sax, Alexander W. Astin, and W. S. Korn, *The American Freshman: National Norms for Fall 1998* (Los Angeles: Higher Education Research Institute, Graduate School of Education and Information Studies, 1998).

39. "College Freshman More Politically Liberal Than in the Past, UCLA Survey Reveals," 2001 CIRP Press Release: CIRP Freshman Survey, January 28, 2001.

40. Linda Sax, Alexander W. Astin, William S. Korn, and Kathryn M. Mahoney, *The American Freshman: National Norms for Fall 1999* (Los Angeles: Higher Education Research Institute, Graduate School of Education and Information Studies, 1999).

41. "College Freshman More Politically Liberal Than in the Past."

42. M. Kent Jennings and Richard G. Niemi, *The Political Character of Adolescence* (Princeton, N.J.: Princeton University Press, 1974), 243.

43. M. McCombs and D. Shaw, "The Agenda Setting Function of the Media," *Public Opinion Quarterly* 36 (summer 1972): 176–187.

44. B. I. Page, R. Shapiro, and G. R. Dempsey, "What Moves Public Opinion?" *American Political Science Review* 81 (March 1987): 23–44.

45. Herbert Weissberg, "Marital Differences in Voting," *Public Opinion Quarterly* 51 (1987): 335–343.

46. Michael A. Fletcher, "On Campus, a Patriotic Surge," *Washington Post National Weekly Edition,* December 10–16, 2001, 31.

47. R. Abramson, *Political Attitudes in America* (San Francisco: Freeman, 1983), 150, 213; see also Paul R. Abramson, *The Political Socialization of Black Americans* (New York: Free Press, 1977).

48. E. Converse, A. R. Clausen, and W. Miller, "Electoral Myth and Reality," *American Political Science Review* 59 (1965): 321–326.

49. J. Robinson, "The Press as Kingmaker: What Surveys Show from the Last Five Campaigns," *Journalism Quarterly* 49 (summer 1974): 592.

50. Susan Herbst, *Numbered Voices: How Opinion Polling Has Shaped American Politics* (Chicago: University of Chicago Press, 1993); Benjamin Ginsberg, "How Polling Changes Public Opinion" in *Manipulating Public Opinion,* ed. Michael Margolis and Gary Mauser (Pacific Grove, Calif.: Brooks/Cole, 1989).

51. For a review of the history of polling, see Bernard Hennessy, *Public Opinion,* 4th ed. (Monterey, Calif.: Brooks/Cole, 1983), 42–44, 46–50. See also C. Roll and A. Cantril, *Polls: Their Use and Misuse in Politics* (New York: Basic Books, 1972), 3–16.

52. "The 1936 Literary Digest Poll," *Public Opinion Quarterly* 52 (1988): 125–133; see also Don Cahalan,

"The Digest Poll Rides Again," *Public Opinion Quarterly* 53 (1989): 107–113.

53. Hennessy, *Public Opinion,* 46.

54. "Consulting the Oracle," *U.S. News and World Report,* December 4, 1995, 52–55; Joshua Green, "The Other War Room," *Washington Monthly* (April 2002): 11–16.

55. Green, "The Other War Room."

56. John F. Harris, "Presidency by Poll," *Washington Post National Weekly Edition,* January 8–14, 2001, 9–10.

57. Green, "The Other War Room."

58. Harris, "Presidency by Poll."

59. Steven Mufson and John F. Harris, "Clinton's Global Growth," *Washington Post National Weekly Edition,* January 22–28, 2001, 8–9.

60. Green, "The Other War Room."

61. Ibid., 11.

62. Ibid., 12.

63. Lawrence Jacobs and Robert Shapiro, *Politicians Don't Pander: Political Manipulation and the Loss of Democratic Responsiveness* (Chicago: University of Chicago Press, 2000).

64. Bill Kovack and Tom Rosensteil, "Campaign Lite," *Washington Monthly* (January/February 2001): 31–38.

65. Claudia Deane, "And Why Haven't You Been Polled?" *Washington Post National Weekly Edition,* January 18–25, 1999, 34; Richard Morin, "The Election Post-Mortem," *Washington Post National Weekly Edition,* January 13–20, 1997, 34; Richard Morin, "Standing on the Record," *Washington Post National Weekly Edition,* September 30–October 6, 1996, 37.

66. *All Things Considered,* National Public Radio, October 30, 1992.

67. "Consulting the Oracle," 53.

68. Ibid.

69. R. Morin, "Surveying the Surveyors," *Washington Post National Weekly Edition,* March 2–9, 1992, 37.

70. David Broder, "Push Polls Plunge Politics to a New Low," *Lincoln Star,* October 9, 1994, 5E.

71. *New Yorker* (March 20, 1999): 18.

72. Richard Morin, "When the Method Becomes the Message," *Washington Post National Weekly Edition,* December 19–25, 1994, 33.

73. Richard Morin, "Tuned Out, Turned Off," *Washington Post National Weekly Edition,* February 5–11, 1996, 6–8.

74. Ibid.

75. Ibid.

76. Richard Morin, "They Know Only What They Don't Like," *Washington Post National Weekly Edition,* October 3–9, 1994, 37.

77. 1986 National Election Study, Center for Political Studies, University of Michigan; "Wapner Top Judge in Recognition Poll," *Lincoln Star,* June 23, 1989, 1.

78. Michael X. Delli Carpini and Scott Keeter, "U.S. Public Knowledge of Politics," *Public Opinion Quarterly* (winter 1991): 583–612.

79. Richard Morin, "We Love It—What We Know of It," *Washington Post National Weekly Edition,* September 22–29, 1997, 35.

80. Morin, "They Know Only What They Don't Like."

81. Morin, "Tuned Out, Turned Off."

82. Ibid.

83. Richard Morin, "Foreign Aid: Mired in Misunderstanding," *Washington Post National Weekly Edition,* March 20–27, 1995, 37.

84. Richard Morin, "What Informed Public Opinion?" *Washington Post National Weekly Edition,* April 10–16, 1995, 36.

85. V. O. Key, *The Responsible Electorate* (Cambridge, Mass.: Harvard University Press, 1966); N. Nie, S. Verba, and J. R. Petrocik, *The Changing American Voter* (Cambridge, Mass.: Harvard University Press, 1976), Chapter 18; Samuel L. Popkin, *The Reasoning Voter: Communication and Persuasion in Presidential Campaigns* (Chicago: University of Chicago Press, 1994).

86. Morin, "Tuned Out, Turned Off."

87. B. Sussman, "When Politicians Talk about Issues People Listen," *Washington Post National Weekly Edition,* August 18–25, 1986, 37.

88. Jacobs and Shapiro, *Politicians Don't Pander.*

89. John Zaller, "Monica Lewinsky's Contribution to Political Science," *PS: Political Science and Politics* (June 1998): 182–189.

90. 2000 General Social Survey.

91. Ibid.

92. Herbert Gans, *The War against the Poor* (New York: Basic Books, 1995).

93. 2000 General Social Survey.

94. Ibid.

95. Data here are from Peter Hart Research Associates Survey for the Council for Excellence in Government, March 16–18, 1995.

96. Poll, Pew Research Center, March 7, 2002.

97. David Broder and Richard Morin, "A Question of Values," *Washington Post National Weekly Edition,* January 11–18, 1999, 6–7.

98. Richard L. Berke, "Chasing the Polls on Gay Rights," *New York Times,* August 2, 1998, 3.

99. This section draws heavily on H. Schuman, C. Steeh, and L. Bobo, *Racial Attitudes in America* (Cambridge, Mass.: Harvard University Press, 1985); H. Schuman, C. Steeh, L. Bobo, and Maria Krysan, *Racial Attitudes in America,* rev. ed. (1997); data summaries are drawn from the General Social Surveys of the National Opinion Research Center, University of Chicago, and National Elections Studies of CPS, University of Michigan; see also L. Sigelman and S. Welch, *Black Americans' Views of Racial Inequality* (Cambridge, Mass.: Cambridge University Press, 1991).

100. General Social Survey, 1996; *Washington Post National Weekly Edition,* October 30–November 6, 1989, 37.

101. General Social Surveys, 1996; "Whites Retain Negative Views of Minorities, a Survey Finds," *New York Times,* January 10, 1991, C19; M. Jackman, "General and Applied Tolerance: Does Education Increase Commitment to Racial Inequality?" *American Journal of Political Science* 22 (1978): 302–324; M. Jackman, "Education and Policy Commitment to Racial Equality," *American Journal of Political Science* 25 (1981): 256–269; D. Kinder and D. Sears, "Prejudice and Politics," *Journal of Personality and Social Psychology* 40 (1981): 414–431.

102. Richard Morin, "We've Moved Forward, but We Haven't," *Washington Post National Weekly Edition,* October 5–12, 1998, 34.

103. "Whites Retain Negative Views."

104. General Social Survey, 1998; see also Donald Kinder and Lynn Saunders, *Divided by Color: Racial Politics and Democratic Ideals* (Chicago: University of Chicago Press, 1996); H. Schuman and L. Bobo, "Survey-Based Experiments on White Attitudes toward Residential Integration," *American Journal of Sociology* 94 (1988): 272–294; W. R. Merriman and E. Carmines, "The Limits of Liberal Tolerance: The Case of Racial Politics," *Polity* 20 (1988): 519–526; see also Schuman et al., *Racial Attitudes.*

105. General Social Survey, 1998.

106. Richard Morin, "It's Not as It Seems," *Washington Post National Weekly Edition,* July 16–22, 2001, 34.

107. Ibid.

108. Richard Morin, "No Place for Calm and Quiet Opinions," *Washington Post National Weekly Edition,* April 24–30, 1994, 34.

109. Martin Gilens and Paul Sniderman, "Affirmative Action and the Politics of Realignment," paper presented at the Midwest Political Science Association Meeting, Chicago, 1995.

110. "It's Not as It Seems"; ABC/*Washington Post* poll, 1981 and 1986.

111. General Social Survey, 1998.

112. Robert Putnam, "Bowling Together," *American Prospect* 13 (February 11, 2002) (online article).

113. Ibid.

114. J. Sullivan, G. Marcus, S. Feldman, and J. Pierson, "Sources of Political Tolerance: A Multivariate Analysis," *American Political Science Review* 75 (March 1981): 92–106.

115. S. Stouffer, *Communism, Conformity, and Civil Liberties* (New York: Wiley, 1954).

116. R. W. Jackman, "Political Elites, Mass Publics, and Support for Democratic Principles," *Journal of Politics* 34 (August 1972): 753.

117. H. McClosky and J. Zaller, *The American Ethos: Public Attitudes toward Capitalism and Democracy* (Cambridge, Mass.: Harvard University Press, 1986).

118. C. Z. Nunn, H. H. Crockett Jr., and J. A. Williams, *Tolerance for Nonconformity* (San Francisco: Jossey-Bass, 1976).

119. "Polls Find Americans Angry, Anxious, Less Altruistic," *Lincoln Journal,* September 21, 1994, 9.

120. Richard Morin and Claudia Deane, "A Thumbs Up for the U.S.A.," *Washington Post National Weekly Edition,* December 3–9, 2001, 34.

121. Judith Shklar, quoted in Paul Taylor, "In Watergate's Wake: The Good, the Bad, and the Ugly," *Washington Post National Weekly Edition,* June 22–29, 1992, 25.

122. Almond and Verba, *Civic Culture,* 64–68.

123. A. Miller, "Political Issues and Trust in Government, 1964–1970," *American Political Science Review* 68 (September 1974): 951–972.

124. A. Miller and S. Borrelli, "Confidence in Government during the 1980s," *American Politics Quarterly* 19 (April 1991): 147–173.

125. "Clinton's High Victory Rate Conceals Disappointments," *Congressional Quarterly Weekly Reports,* December 31, 1994, 3619–3623.

126. David Broder and Dan Balz, "Who Wins?" *Washington Post National Weekly Edition,* February 15–22, 1999, 6–7.

127. Alexander Stille, "Suddenly, Americans Trust Uncle Sam," *New York Times,* November 3, 2001.

128. T. J. Lowi, *The Personal President* (Ithaca, N.Y.: Cornell University Press, 1995).

129. S. M. Lipset and W. Schneider, *The Confidence Gap* (New York: Free Press, 1983).

130. A. Miller, "Political Issues and Trust in Government, 1964–1970," *American Political Science Review* 68 (September 1974): 951–972.

131. Richard Morin, "Less Than Meets the Eye," *Washington Post National Weekly Edition,* March 16–23, 1998, 35.

132. Hibbing and Theiss-Morse, *Congress as Public Enemy.*

133. Richard Morin, "Is Anyone Listening?" *Washington Post National Weekly Edition,* February 15–22, 1999, 34.

134. Benjamin Page and Robert Shapiro, "Effects of Public Opinion on Policy," *American Political Science Review* 77 (March 1983): 175–190.

135. Sidney Verba and Norman H. Nie, *Participation in America: Political Democracy and Social Equality* (New York: Harper & Row, 1972), Chapter 15.

136. State of the Union Address, *New York Times,* January 30, 2002.

137. Ibid.

138. Lawrence L. Knutson, "Bush Ties Arctic Drilling to Security," *Lincoln Journal-Star,* February 24, 2002, 2A.

Chapter 5

1. The source for information in this "You Are There" is Nick Kotz, "Breaking Point," *The Washingtonian* (December 1996): 94–121.

2. James David Barber, *The Pulse of Politics* (New York: Norton, 1980), 9.

3. Kevin Phillips, "A Matter of Privilege," *Harper's* (January 1977): 95–97.

4. Richard Harwood, "So Many Media, So Little Time," *Washington Post National Weekly Edition,* September 7–13, 1992, 28.

5. Thomas R. Dye and L. Hannon Zeigler, *American Politics in the Media Age* (Monterey, Calif.: Brooks/Cole, 1983), 123–124.

6. Edwin Diamond, *The Tin Kazoo* (Cambridge, Mass.: MIT Press, 1975), 13.

7. According to the first nationally representative study, conducted by the Henry J. Kaiser Family Foundation in 1999. "Media Use Almost a Full-time Job for American Youth, Study Finds," *Lincoln Journal-Star,* November 18, 1999.

8. Doris A. Graber, *Mass Media and American Politics* (Washington, D.C.: Congressional Quarterly, 1980), 2.

9. William Lutz, *Doublespeak* (New York: Harper & Row, 1989), 73–74.

10. Shanto Iyengar, *Is Anyone Responsible? How Television Frames Political Issues* (Chicago: University of Chicago Press, 1991), 1.

11. "Ticker," *Brill's Content* (May 1999): 128.

12. Elizabeth Gleick, "Read All about It," *Time* (October 21, 1998): 66.

13. "Ticker," 128.

14. Scott Althaus, "American News Consumption during Times of National Crisis," *PS: Political Science & Politics* (September 2002): 517–521.

15. Thomas E. Patterson, *The Mass Media Election* (New York: Praeger, 1980), 58–60, 62–63.

16. Michael J. Wolf and Geoffrey Sands, "Fearless Predictions," *Brill's Content* (July/August 1999): 110.

17. Eve Gerber, "Divided We Watch," *Brill's Content* (February 2001) 110–111.

18. Harwood, "So Many Media, So Little Time."

19. Donald Kaul, "Effects of Merger between AOL, Time Warner Will Be Inescapable," *Lincoln Journal-Star,* January 18, 2000; Ken Auletta, "Leviathan," *New Yorker* (October 29, 2001): 50.

20. For examination of this development, see Lawrence Lessing, *The Future of Ideas* (New York: Random House, 2001).

21. Otto Friedrich, "Edging the Government Out of TV," *Time* (August 17, 1987): 58; Edmund L. Andrews, "A New Tune for Radio: Hard Times," *New York Times,* March 1992; Sydney H. Schanberg, "The News You Don't Read," *Washington Post National Weekly Edition,* September 6–12, 1999, 21.

22. Benjamin M. Compaine, *Who Owns the Media?* (White Plains, N.Y.: Knowledge Industry Publications, 1979), 11, 76–77; Michael Parenti, *Inventing Reality* (New York: St. Martin's, 1986), 27; Paul Farhi, "You Can't Tell a Book by Its Cover," *Washington Post National Weekly Edition,* December 5–11, 1988, 21; Andrews, "A New Tune for Radio."

23. Robert McChesney, "AOL–Time Warner Merger Is Dangerous and Undemocratic," *Lincoln Journal-Star,* January 17, 2000.

24. Elizabeth Lesly Stevens, "Mouse.Ke.Fear," *Brill's Content* (December 1998/January 1999): 95. For other examples, see Jane Mayer, "Bad News," *New Yorker* (August 14, 2000): 30–36.

25. Jim Hightower, *There's Nothing in the Middle of the Road but Yellow Stripes and Dead Armadillos* (New York: HarperCollins, 1997), 121.

26. Rifka Rosenwein, "Why Media Mergers Matter," *Brill's Content* (December 1999/January 2000): 94.

27. Dean Alger, *Megamedia: How Giant Corporations Dominate Mass Media, Distort Competition, and Endanger Democracy* (Lanham, Md.: Rowman & Littlefield, 1998).

28. Neil Hickey, "Money Lust," *Columbia Journalism Review* (July/August 1998): 28.

29. Victor Navasky, "Is Big Really Bad? Well, Yes," *Time* (January 24, 2000).

30. Howard Kurtz, "Welcome to Spin City," *Washington Post National Weekly Edition,* March 16, 1998, 6.

31. Elizabeth Kolbert, "For Talk Shows, Less News Is Good News," *New York Times,* June 28, 1992, E–2.

32. "The Vocal Minority in American Politics," Times Mirror Center for the People and the Press, Washington, D.C., July 1993.

33. In addition, she received $50,000 for a book elaborating on her story, $250,000 for posing nude for *Penthouse* magazine, and about $20,000 for ap-

pearing on German and Spanish television shows. "Flowers Says She Made Half Million from Story," *Lincoln Journal-Star,* March 21, 1998.

34. Ernest Tollerson, "Politicians Try to Balance Risk against Rewards of Reaching Talk-Radio Audiences," *New York Times,* March 31, 1996, 12.

35. Richard Harwood, "The Growing Irrelevance of Journalists," *Washington Post National Weekly Edition,* November 2–8, 1992, 29.

36. David Halberstam, "Preface" in Bill Kovach and Tom Rosenstiel, *Warp Speed: American in the Age of Mixed Media* (New York: Century Foundation Press, 1999), x.

37. Tom Rosenstiel, *The Beat Goes On: President Clinton's First Year with the Media* (New York: Twentieth Century Fund, 1994), 35. For an extensive examination of this incident, see Dan E. Moldea, *A Washington Tragedy* (New York: Regnery, 1998).

38. Howard Kurtz, "The Story That Wouldn't Stay Buried," *Washington Post National Weekly Edition,* December 1, 1997, 12.

39. Kurtz, "Welcome to Spin City."

40. Richard Corliss, "Look Who's Talking," *Time* (January 23, 1995): 25.

41. Kurt Anderson, "The Age of Unreason," *New Yorker* (February 3, 1997): 42.

42. Dom Bonafede, "Press Paying More Heed to Substance in Covering 1984 Presidential Election," *National Journal,* October 13, 1984, 1923.

43. Seth Mnookin, "Advice to Ari," *Brill's Content* (March 2001): 97.

44. Thomas M. DeFrank, "Playing the Media Game," *Newsweek* (April 17, 1989): 21.

45. Charles Peters, *How Washington Really Works* (Redding, Mass.: Addison-Wesley, 1980), 18.

46. William Greider, "Reporters and Their Sources," *Washington Monthly* (October 1982): 13–15.

47. See, for example, Jeffrey Toobin, *A Vast Conspiracy: The Real Story of the Sex Scandal That Nearly Brought Down a President* (New York: Simon & Schuster, 1999), 310.

48. Howard Kurtz, "Lying Down on This Job Was Just Fine," *Washington Post National Weekly Edition,* April 19–25, 1999, 13.

49. Ann Devroy, "The Republicans, It Turns Out, Are a Veritable Fount of Leaks," *Washington Post National Weekly Edition,* November 18–24, 1991, 23.

50. Daniel Schorr, "A Fact of Political Life," *Washington Post National Weekly Edition,* October 28–November 3, 1991, 32.

51. Howard Kurtz, "How Sources and Reporters Play the Game of Leaks," *Washington Post National Weekly Edition,* March 15–21, 1993, 25.

52. Steven Brill, "Pressgate," *Brill's Content* (July/August 1998): 123–151; Steven Brill, "At Last, a Leakless Investigation," *Brill's Content* (December 1998/January 1999): 31–34.

53. Brill, "Pressgate," 149.

54. James Poniewozik, "Down by Law," *Time* (December 25, 2000–January 1, 2001): 79.

55. Samuel Kernell, *Going Public: New Strategies of Presidential Leadership* (Washington, D.C.: Congressional Quarterly, 1986), 59. Woodrow Wilson also tried to cultivate correspondents and host frequent sessions, but he did not have the knack for this activity and he scaled back the sessions. Kernell, *Going Public,* 60–61. He did perceive that "[s]ome men of brilliant ability were in the group, but I soon discovered that the interest of the majority was in the personal and the trivial rather than in principles and policies." James Bennet, "The Flack Pack," *Washington Monthly* (November 1991): 27.

56. Dwight Eisenhower was actually the first president to let the networks televise his press conferences, but he did not do so to reach the public. When he wanted to reach the public, he made a formal speech. The networks found his conferences so untelegenic that they stopped covering the entire session each time. Kernell, *Going Public,* 68.

57. Kernell, *Going Public,* 104.

58. Bennet, "The Flack Pack," 19.

59. Dom Bonafede, " 'Mr. President,' " *National Journal,* October 29, 1988, 2756.

60. Garry Wills, "But Don't Treat It as a Game," *Lincoln Journal,* March 26, 1993.

61. James Fallows, *Breaking the News: How the Media Undermine American Democracy* (New York: Pantheon, 1996), 196.

62. Charles Hagen, "The Photo Op: Making Icons or Playing Politics?" *New York Times,* February 9, 1992, H28.

63. "The Man behind the Curtain Award," *Mother Jones* (September/October 2002): 67.

64. Kiku Adatto, cited in Howard Kurtz, "Networks Adapt to Changed Campaign Role," *Washington Post,* June 21, 1992, A19. Also, Diana Owen, "Media Mayhem: Performance of the Press in Election 2000," in *Overtime! The Election 2000 Thriller,* ed. Larry J. Sabato (New York: Longman, 2002), 123–156.

65. Lance Morrow, "Time Essay," *Time* (August 18, 1980): 78.

66. David Halberstam, "How Television Failed the American Voter," *Parade,* January 11, 1981, 8.

67. George E. Reedy, *The Twilight of the Presidency* (New York: New American Library, 1970), 112.

68. Thomas Griffith, "Winging It on Television," *Time* (March 14, 1983): 71.

69. "Talking about the Media Circus," *New York Times Magazine* (June 26, 1994): 63.

70. W. Lance Bennett, *News: The Politics of Illusion,* 2d ed. (New York: Longman, 1988).

71. Larry J. Sabato, *Feeding Frenzy: How Attack Journalism Has Transformed American Politics* (New York: Free Press, 1991).

72. Deborah Tannen, *The Argument Culture* (New York: Ballantine, 1998), 81.

73. Ibid., 55.

74. Robert J. Bennett, "We Should Scuttle the Partisanship," *Washington Post National Weekly Edition,* March 24–30, 1997, 21.

75. Fallows, *Breaking the News,* 62–63.

76. Joan Konner, "Diane 'Got' Gore. But What Did We Get?" *Brill's Content* (September 1999): 59–60.

77. Joseph N. Cappella and Kathleen Hall Jamieson, *Spiral of Cynicism* (New York: Oxford University Press, 1997), 31.

78. Mary Matalin and James Carville, *All's Fair* (New York: Random House, 1994), 184–185.

79. See Sabato, *Feeding Frenzy,* for additional reasons for this increase.

80. "Ticker," *Brill's Content* (July/August 1998): 152, citing the Project for Excellence in Journalism, "Changing Definitions of News: A Look at the Mainstream Press over 20 Years," March 6, 1998.

81. Fallows, *Breaking the News,* 196.

82. John David Rausch Jr., "The Pathology of Politics: Government, Press, and Scandal," *Extensions* (University of Oklahoma) (fall 1990): 11–12.

83. Tannen, *The Argument Culture,* 124.

84. Brill, "Pressgate," 134.

85. William Rivers, "The Correspondents after 25 Years," *Columbia Journalism Review* 1 (spring 1962): 5.

86. James David Barber, *Presidential Character* (Englewood Cliffs, N.J.: Prentice Hall, 1992), 238.

87. As a young sportscaster in Des Moines, Iowa, Reagan announced Major League baseball games "live." He got the barest of details—who was at bat, whether the pitch was a strike or a ball or a hit—from the wireless, and he made up the rest to create a commentary that sounded as though he were watching in person.

88. Hedrick Smith, *The Power Game* (New York: Random House, 1988), 403.

89. Timothy J. Russert, "For '92, the Networks Have to Do Better," *New York Times,* March 4, 1990.

90. Smith, *Power Game,* 420.

91. Steven K. Weisman, "The President and the Press," *New York Times Magazine* (October 14,

1984): 71–72; Dick Kirschten, "Communications Reshuffling Intended to Help Reagan Do What He Does Best," *National Journal,* January 28, 1984, 154.

92. Sidney Blumenthal, "The Syndicated Presidency," *New Yorker* (April 5, 1993): 45.

93. Brit Hume (NBC News).

94. For an extensive examination of this phenomenon, see Toobin, *A Vast Conspiracy.*

95. John F. Harris, "Bush's Lucky Break," *Washington Post National Weekly Edition,* May 14–20, 2001, 23.

96. For examination of coverage during Clinton's early time in office, see William Glaberson, "The Capitol Press vs. the President: Fair Coverage or Unreined Adversity?" *New York Times,* June 17, 1993, A11; Christopher Georges, "Bad News Bearers," *Washington Monthly* (July/August 1993): 28–34; and Toobin, *A Vast Conspiracy,* 247–248.

97. Tannen, *The Argument Culture,* 54.

98. Howard Kurtz, "Assessing—and Controlling—the Damage to the Presidency," *Washington Post National Weekly Edition,* February 2–8, 1998, 21.

99. John F. Harris, "On the World Stage, Bush Shuns the Spotlight," *Washington Post National Weekly Edition,* April 23–29, 2001, 11; Ronald Brownstein, "Bush Forced into Role He May Not Want: Communicator," *Lincoln Journal-Star,* September 15, 2001.

100. John F. Harris and Dan Balz, "A Well-Oiled Machine," *Washington Post National Weekly Edition,* May 14–20, 2001, 6.

101. James Carville, quoted in John F. Harris, "Bush's Lucky Break," *Washington Post National Weekly Edition,* May 14–20, 2001, 23.

102. Aides claimed that Air Force One was a target, but it was revealed that this claim was an exaggeration to parry the criticism that Bush received. Eric Pooley and Karen Tumulty, "Bush in the Crucible," *Time* (September 24, 2001): 49.

103. Calvin Woodward, "Warrior Bush: It Doesn't Come Naturally," *Lincoln Journal-Star,* October 6, 2002.

104. Michael Duffy, "Marching Alone," *Time* (September 9, 2002): 42.

105. According to presidential historian Henry Graff, cited in Ron Fourier, "President Stumbles with Mideast Rhetoric," *Lincoln Journal-Star,* April 20, 2002.

106. David L. Greene, "Bush Often Great Miscommunicator," *Lincoln Journal-Star,* October 6, 2002.

107. For a reporter's perspective on the difference this makes, see Harris, "Bush's Lucky Break." As Harris observes, imagine the reaction if Clinton had been in office when the surveillance plane was forced down in China. Could he have gotten away with insisting that the detained personnel were not actually hostages, and then cutting a deal to get them, but not our plane, back by apologizing for being in international airspace?

108. Stephen Hess, *Live from Capitol Hill!* (Washington, D.C.: Brookings Institution, 1991), 62; Timothy E. Cook, *Making Laws & Making News: Media Strategies in the U.S. House of Representatives* (Washington, D.C.: Brookings Institution, 1989), 2.

109. Hess, *Live from Capitol Hill!* 102.

110. Hendrik Hertzberg, "Comment: The Pot Perplex," *New Yorker* (January 6, 1997): 4–5. For an interesting article about medical uses of marijuana and about a club of marijuana users, see Evelyn Nieves, "Half an Ounce of Healing," *Mother Jones* (January/February 2001): 49–53.

111. Robert Schmidt, "May It Please the Court," *Brill's Content* (October 1999): 74.

112. Ibid., 73.

113. Ibid.

114. Edward Jay Epstein, *News from Nowhere* (New York: Random House, 1973), 13.

115. Graber, *Mass Media and American Politics,* 62.

116. Milton Coleman, "When the Candidate Is Black Like Me," *Washington Post National Weekly Edition,* April 23, 1984, 9.

117. Roper Organization, "A Big Concern about the Media: Intruding on Grieving Families," *Washington Post National Weekly Edition,* June 6, 1984. Also, see Cappella and Jamieson, *Spiral of Cynicism,* 210. This phenomenon occurs even when individuals are judging the same newspaper, and the pattern holds regardless of the extent to which the paper is slanted in one direction. Russell J. Dalton, Paul A. Beck, and Robert Huckfeldt, "Partisan Cues and the Media: Information Flows in the 1992 Election," *American Political Science Review* 92 (March 1998): 120–121.

118. John Cassidy, "Striking It Rich: The Rise and Fall of Popular Capitalism," *New Yorker* (January 14, 2002): 63–73.

119. Parenti, *Inventing Reality,* Chapters 7–11; Charles E. Lindblom, *Politics and Markets* (New York: Basic Books, 1977); MacDonald, *One Nation under Television;* Dan Nimmo and James E. Combs, *Mediated Political Realities* (New York: Longman, 1983), 135.

120. John R. MacArthur, *Second Front: Censorship and Propaganda in the Gulf War* (New York: Hill & Wang, 1992); James Bennet, "How They Missed That Story," *Washington Monthly* (December 1990): 8–16; Christopher Dickey, "Not Their Finest Hour," *Newsweek* (June 8, 1992): 66.

121. In the 1950s and early 1960s, newspapers, magazines, and television networks sent few correspondents to Vietnam, so most accepted the government's account of the conflict. Susan Welch, "The American Press and Indochina, 1950–1956," in *Communication in International Politics,* ed. Richard L. Merritt (Urbana: University of Illinois Press, 1972), 207–231; Edward J. Epstein, "The Selection of Reality," in *What's News?* ed. Elie Abel (San Francisco: Institute for Contemporary Studies, 1981), 124. When they did dispatch correspondents, many filed pessimistic reports, but their editors believed the government rather than the correspondents and refused to print these reports. Instead, they ran articles that quoted optimistic statements by government officials. See David Halberstam, *The Powers That Be* (New York: Dell, 1980), 642–647. In 1968, the media did turn against the war, but rather than sharply criticize it, they conveyed the impression that it was futile. Daniel C. Hallin, *The "Uncensored War": The Media and Vietnam* (New York: Oxford University Press, 1986).

122. "Return of Talk Show Is Healthy Sign," *Lincoln Journal Star* (October 6, 2001).

123. Anthony Collings, "The BBC: How to Be Impartial in Wartime," *Chronicle of Higher Education,* December 21, 2001, B14.

124. Leon V. Sigal, *Reporters and Officials* (Lexington, Mass.: Heath, 1973), 120–121; Lucy Howard, "Slanted 'Line'?" *Newsweek* (February 13, 1989): 6. See also Hess, *Live from Capitol Hill!* 50. Trivia buffs might also ask who has been the subject of the most cover articles in *Time* magazine—Richard Nixon (fifty-five). "Numbers," *Time* (March 9, 1998): 189.

125. Cook, *Making Laws & Making News,* 8.

126. Lichter et al., *The Media Elite,* 21–25. See also Hess, *Live from Capitol Hill!* Appendix A, 110–130.

127. John Johnstone, Edward Slawski, and William Bowman, *The Newspeople* (Urbana: University of Illinois Press, 1976), 225–226.

128. Stanley Rothman and S. Robert Lichter, "Media and Business Elites: Two Classes in Conflict?" *The Public Interest* 69 (1982): 111–125; S. Robert Lichter and Stanley Rothman, "Media and Business Elites," *Public Opinion* (October/November 1981): 44.

129. Stephen Hess, *The Washington Reporters* (Washington, D.C.: Brookings Institution, 1981), 89; Lichter et al., *The Media Elite,* 127–128.

130. James Fallows, "The Stoning of Donald Regan," *Washington Monthly* (June 1984): 57. Most individual reporters also probably care more about their career than ideology, but this could lead to bias. In 1976, one media analyst ran into an old friend, an NBC correspondent. When the analyst asked how she was doing, she answered, "Not so great. My candidate lost." That is, the candidate she had covered during the presidential primaries lost his bid for the nomination. Because reporters often follow "their" presidential candidate into office, she lost her chance to become NBC's White House correspondent. Graeme Browning, "Too Close for Comfort?" *National Journal,* October 3, 1992, 2243.

131. A Pittsburgh publisher interjects his views into news stories. Kimberly Conniff, "All the Views Fit to Print," *Brill's Content* (March 2001): 105.

132. Russell J. Dalton, Paul A. Beck, and Robert Huckfeldt, "Partisan Cues and the Media: Information Flows in the 1992 Presidential Election," *American Political Science Review* 92 (March 1998): 118. Other studies reached similar conclusions. C. Richard Hofstetter, *Bias in the News* (Columbus: Ohio State University Press, 1976); Graber, *Mass Media and Politics,* 167–168; Michael J. Robinson, "Just How Liberal Is the News?" *Public Opinion* (February/March 1983): 55–60; Maura Clancy and Michael J. Robinson, "General Election Coverage: Part I," *Public Opinion* 7 (December/January 1985): 49–54, 59; Michael J. Robinson, "The Media Campaign, '84; Part II," *Public Opinion* 8 (February/March 1985): 43–48.

133. Clancy and Robinson, "General Election Coverage"; Robinson, "The Media Campaign '84"; Michael J. Robinson, "Where's the Beef? Media and Media Elites in 1984," in *The American Elections of 1984,* ed. Austin Ranney (Durham, N.C.: Duke University Press, 1985), 184; Michael J. Robinson, "News Media Myths and Realities: What Network News Did and Didn't Do in the 1984 General Campaign," in *Elections in America,* ed. Kay Lehman Schlozman (Boston: Allen & Unwin, 1987), 143–170; Kim Fridkin Kahn and Patrick J. Kenney, *The Spectacle of U.S. Senate Campaigns* (Princeton, N.J.: Princeton University, 1999), 126–129.

134. Ken Auletta, "Inside Story," *New Yorker* (November 18, 1996): 55. Most journalists—89 percent, according to one poll—voted for Clinton over Bush, but after the election, the media gave Clinton more negative coverage than they had given Bush in his first eighteen months. "Dealing with Bias in the Press," *Civilization* (February/March 1997): 24–27.

135. It helped the Democrat Carter in 1976 but hurt him in 1980. It helped the Republican Bush in 1988 but hurt him in 1992. Thomas E. Patterson, *Out of Order* (New York: Vintage, 1994), 131.

136. Ibid., 100–107. Another reason was the slump in the economy, which resulted in coverage of the Bush administration trying to defend its economic policies against various critics of these policies. Dalton et al., "Partisan Cues and the Media," 116.

137. For example, Seth Mnookin, "Live but Not in Person," *Brill's Content* (November 2000): 104; Charles Peters, "Tilting at Windmills," *Washington Monthly* (November 2000): 8; Robert Shogan, *Bad News: Where the Press Goes Wrong in the Making of the President* (Chicago: Dee, 2001), Chapter 11; Adam Clymer, "Better Campaign Reporting: A View from the Major Leagues," *PS: Political Science & Politics* (December 2001): 779-784.

138. Bill Kovach and Tom Rosenstiel, "Campaign Lite," *Washington Monthly* (January/February 2001): 31–36; Shogan, *Bad News,* 245.

139. Seth Mnookin, "The Charm Offensive," *Brill's Content* (September 2000): 129.

140. Shogan, *Bad News,* 231.

141. Shogan, *Bad News,* 204–245; Clymer, "Better Campaign Reporting."

142. Robert Parry, "He's No Pinocchio: How the Press Has Exaggerated Al Gore's Exaggerations," *Washington Monthly* (April 2001): 23–28.

143. However, he never used this word.

144. Shogan, *Bad News,* 237–245; Hendrik Hertzberg, "Comment: They've Got Personality," *New Yorker* (November 6, 2000): 38.

145. Clymer, "Better Campaign Reporting," 781.
146. Less than one in ten stories on the 2000 debates focused on policy differences; seven in ten focused on candidates' performance or strategy. Kovach and Rosenstiel, "Campaign Lite," 31–32.
147. Shogan, *Bad News,* 234.
148. For a perceptive analysis, see Clymer, "Better Campaign Reporting."
149. Shogan, *Bad News,* 245.
150. The media, however, did pay a lot of attention to Ross Perot's presidential bid in 1992 because he said he would spend $100 million on his campaign and because polls showed he could compete with Bush and Clinton.
151. For a recounting of his campaign, see Ralph Nader, "My Untold Story," *Brill's Content* (February 2001): 100.
152. "Clinton Gains More Support from Big Papers," *Lincoln Journal-Star,* October 25, 1992. Newspapers insist that there is little relationship between their editorial endorsements and their news coverage or even their political columns. An endorsement for one candidate does not mean more positive coverage or columns for that candidate, because American media have established a tradition of autonomy in the newsroom. Dalton et al., "Partisan Cues and the Media," 118. However, some research shows that when papers endorse candidates, the papers show a small bias toward the candidates in their news stories (if the candidates are incumbents). Kim Fridkin Kahn and Patrick J. Kenney, "The Slant of the News: How Editorial Endorsements Influence Campaign Coverage and Citizen's Views of Candidates," *American Political Science Review* (June 2002): 381–394.
153. Stanley Rothman and S. Robert Lichter, "The Nuclear Energy Debate," *Public Opinion* 5 (August/September 1982): 47–48; Stanley Rothman and S. Robert Lichter, "Elite Ideology and Risk Perception in Nuclear Energy Policy," *American Political Science Review* 81 (June 1987): 383–404; Lichter et al., *The Media Elite,* Chapter 7; Sabato, *Feeding Frenzy,* 87, and sources cited therein.
154. Bernard Goldberg, *Bias: A CBS Insider Exposes How the Media Distort the News* (New York: Regnery, 2002).
155. Robinson, "Just How Liberal Is the News?" 59.
156. Jeff Cohen and Jonah Goldberg, "Face-off: Beyond Belief," *Brill's Content* (December 1999/ January 2000): 54.
157. Genever Overholser, "It's Time for News Networks to Take Sides," *Lincoln Journal-Star* (August 26, 2001).
158. Ibid.; David Plotz, "Fox News Channel," *Slate* (November 22, 2000). Available at slate.msn.com.
159. Cohen and Goldberg, "Face-off."
160. Bruce Nussbaum, "The Myth of the Liberal Media," *Business Week,* November 11, 1996; Paul Starobin, "Bias Basics," *National Review,* October 28, 1996; Fallows, *Breaking the News,* 49.
161. Hofstetter, *Bias in the News;* Hess, *Live from Capitol Hill!* 12–13.
162. Robinson, "Just How Liberal Is the News?" 58; Arthur H. Miller, Edie N. Goldenberg, and Lutz Erbring, "Type-Set Politics," *American Political Science Review* 73 (1979): 69; Patterson, *Out of Order,* 6; Charles M. Tidmarch and John J. Pitney Jr., "Covering Congress," *Polity* 17 (spring 1985): 463–483.
163. Richard Morin, "The Big Picture Is Out of Focus," *Washington Post National Weekly Edition,* March 6–13, 2000, 21.
164. Steven Brill, "Quality Control," *Brill's Content* (July/August 1998): 19–20.
165. Patterson, *Out of Order,* 25, 245.
166. "Anchorwoman Verdict Raises Mixed Opinions," *New York Times,* August 9, 1983.
167. Theodore H. White, *America in Search of Itself* (New York: Harper & Row, 1982), 186.
168. Kovach and Rosenstiel, *Warp Speed,* 64.
169. Hess, *Live from Capitol Hill!* 34.

170. Molly Ivins, "Media Conglomerates Profit at Expense of News, Public," *Lincoln Journal-Star,* October 26, 2001.
171. James Fallows, "On That Chart," *Nation,* June 3, 1996, 15.
172. Maureen Dowd, "Flintstone Futurama," *New York Times,* August 19, 2001, WK 13.
173. "Poll: Reporters Avoid, Soften Stories," *Lincoln Journal-Star,* May 1, 2000; David Owen, "The Cigarette Companies: How They Get Away with Murder, Part II," *Washington Monthly* (March 1985): 48–54. Also see Daniel Hellinger and Dennis R. Judd, *The Democratic Facade,* 2d ed. (Belmont, Calif.: Wadsworth, 1994), 59. Through the 1920s, newspapers refrained from pointing out that popular "patent medicines" were usually useless and occasionally dangerous, because the purveyors bought more advertising than any other business. Mark Crispin Miller, "Free the Media," *Nation,* June 3, 1996, 10.
174. Roger Mudd, quoted in Martin A. Linsky, ed., *Television and the Presidential Elections* (Lexington, Mass.: Heath, 1983).
175. "Q & A: Dan Rather on Fear, Money, and the News," *Brill's Content* (October 1998): 117.
176. Barry Sussman, "News on TV: Mixed Reviews," *Washington Post National Weekly Edition,* September 3, 1984, 37.
177. Bill Carter, "Networks Fight Public's Shrinking Attention Span," *Lincoln Journal-Star,* September 30, 1990.
178. Epstein, *News from Nowhere,* 4.
179. William A. Henry III, "Requiem for TV's Gender Gap," *Time* (August 22, 1983): 57.
180. Richard Morin, "The Nation's Mood? Calm," *Washington Post National Weekly Edition,* November 5–11, 2001, 35.
181. Ibid.
182. For an examination of how the media exaggerated the Whitewater scandal, see Gene Lyons, *Fools for Scandal* (New York: Franklin Square Press, 1996).
183. The third and final special prosecutor concluded that there might be some evidence of wrongdoing in the law firm records of Hillary Clinton but that there was not enough evidence to justify prosecution.
184. Fallows, *Breaking the News,* 133.
185. Peggy Noonan, quoted in Jeffrey Klein, "News Value, Not Values," *Brill's Content* (July/ August 2000): 54.
186. "Naked News Program Taken Off Air," *Lincoln Journal-Star,* January 15, 2002.
187. The pope was making an historic visit to Cuba. The networks had considered this so important that they had sent their anchors to Havana. At the same time, renewed violence in Northern Ireland threatened to scuttle the peace talks between Catholics and Protestants, and continued refusal from Iraq to cooperate with United Nations biological and chemical weapons inspectors threatened to escalate to military conflict.
188. Eric Pooley, "Monica's World," *Time* (March 2, 1998): 40.
189. Fallows, *Breaking the News,* 201.
190. Samuel G. Freedman, "Fighting to Balance Honor and Profit on the Local News," *New York Times,* September 30, 2001, Section 2, 26.
191. Lawrie Mifflin, "Crime Falls, but Not on TV," *New York Times,* July 6, 1997, E3. According to one researcher, crime coverage is also "the easiest, cheapest, laziest news to cover" because stations just listen to the police radio and then send a camera crew to shoot the story.
192. Heather Maher, "Eleven O'Clock Blues," *Brill's Content* (February 2001): 99.
193. Molly Ivins, "Don't Moan about the Media, Do Something," *Lincoln Journal-Star,* November 1999.
194. David S. Broder, "Can We Govern?" *Washington Post National Weekly Edition,* January 31–February 6, 1994, 23.

195. Newspaper ads were placed in college papers by deniers, claiming that there is no proof that gas chambers actually existed. The editor of one paper justified accepting the ad by saying, "There are two sides to every issue and both have a place on the pages of any open-minded paper's editorial page." Tannen, *The Argument Culture,* 38. For examination of this phenomenon, see Deborah E. Lipstadt, *Denying the Holocaust: The Growing Assault on Truth and Memory* (New York: Plume, 1993).
196. Kathleen Hall Jamieson, *Dirty Politics: Deception, Distraction, Democracy* (New York: Oxford University Press, 1992), 184–185.
197. Kathleen Hall Jamieson, quoted in Fallows, *Breaking the News,* 224.
198. Cappella and Jamieson, *Spiral of Cynicism.*
199. Tannen, *The Argument Culture,* 286.
200. Howard Kurtz, quoted in Tannen, *The Argument Culture,* 29.
201. Patterson, *Out of Order,* 53–59 and generally.
202. For the 1976 presidential campaign: Thomas E. Patterson, *The Mass Media Election* (New York: Praeger, 1980), 24. For the 1984 presidential campaign: Henry E. Brady and Richard Johnson, "What's the Primary Message: Horse Race or Issue Journalism?" in *Media and Momentum,* ed. Gary R. Orren and Nelson W. Polsby (Chatham, N.J.: Chatham House, 1987), 127–186. For the 1988 presidential primaries: S. Robert Lichter, Daniel Amundson, and Richard Noyes, "The Video Campaign: Network Coverage of the 1988 Primaries" (Washington, D.C.: American Enterprise Institute for Public Policy Research, 1988), 65. For the 1988 presidential campaign: Stephen Ansolabehere, Roy Behr, and Shanto Iyengar, "Mass Media and Elections: An Overview," *American Politics Quarterly* 19 (January 1991): 119. For the 1992 presidential campaign and in general: Patterson, *Out of Order.* For the 1992 congressional campaigns: Charles M. Tidmarch, Lisa J. Hyman, and Jill E. Sorkin, "Press Issue Agendas in the 1982 Congressional and Gubernatorial Election Campaigns," *Journal of Politics* 46 (November 1984): 1231.
203. Lee Sigelman and David Bullock, "Candidates, Issues, Horse Races, and Hoopla: Presidential Campaign Coverage, 1888–1988," *American Politics Quarterly* 19 (January 1991): 5–32. So was emphasis on human interest. In 1846, the *New York Tribune* described the culinary habits of Representative William "Sausage" Sawyer (D-Ohio), who ate a sausage on the floor of the House every afternoon: "What little grease is left on his hands he wipes on his almost bald head which saves any outlay for Pomatum. His mouth sometimes serves as a finger glass, his shirtsleeves and pantaloons being called into requisition as a napkin. He uses a jackknife for a toothpick, and then he goes on the floor again to abuse the Whigs as the British party." Cook, *Making Laws & Making News,* 18–19.
204. Thomas E. Patterson, *Out of Order* (New York: Vintage, 1994), 74; Marion R. Just, Ann N. Crigler, Dean E. Alger, Timothy E. Cook, Montague Kern, and Darrell M. West, *Crosstalk: Citizens, Candidates and the Media in a Presidential Campaign* (Chicago: University of Chicago Press, 1996); Mathew Robert Kerbel, *Remote and Controlled* (Boulder, Colo.: Westview, 1995); Bruce Buchanan, *Electing a President* (Austin: University of Texas Press, 1991).
205. Owen, "Media Mayhem," 127.
206. Richard Morin, "Toward the Millennium, by the Numbers," *Washington Post National Weekly Edition,* July 7, 1997, 35.
207. Patterson, *Out of Order,* 81–82.
208. Fallows, *Breaking the News,* 162, 27.
209. Epstein, *News from Nowhere,* 179, 195.
210. John Horn, "Campaign Coverage Avoids Issues," *Lincoln Journal-Star,* September 25, 1988. Another survey found that 28 percent of women change channels every time during commercial breaks, while 40 percent of men do. "Ticker," *Brill's Content* (September 1999): 128.

211. John Eisendrath, "An Eyewitness Account of Local TV News," *Washington Monthly* (September 1986): 21.

212. Michael Deaver, "Sound-Bite Campaigning: TV Made Us Do It," *Washington Post National Weekly Edition,* November 7–13, 1988, 34.

213. Fred Friendly, quoted on *All Things Considered,* National Public Radio, March 4, 1998.

214. Donald L. Shaw and Maxwell E. McCombs, *The Emergence of American Political Issues: The Agenda-Setting Function of the Press* (St. Paul, Minn.: West, 1977). For a review of agenda-setting research, see Everett M. Rogers and James W. Dearing, "Agenda-Setting Research: Where Has It Been, Where Is It Going?" *Communication Yearbook* 11 (Newbury Park, Calif.: Sage, 1988), 555–594.

215. Lutz Erbring, Edie N. Goldenberg, and Arthur H. Miller, "Front-Page News and Real-World Clues: A New Look at Agenda-Setting by the Media," *American Journal of Political Science* 24 (February 1980): 16–49.

216. Michael Bruce MacKuen and Steven Lane Coombs, *More Than News* (Beverly Hills: Sage, 1981), 140; Rogers and Dearing, "Agenda-Setting Research," 572–576; G. E. Lang and K. Lang, *The Battle for Public Opinion* (New York: Columbia University Press, 1983), 58–59.

217. Richard Morin, "Public Enemy No. 1: Crime," *Washington Post National Weekly Edition,* January 24–30, 1994, 37; Molly Ivins, "Hard Questions, Easy Answers," *Lincoln Journal,* July 7, 1994; Richard Morin, "A Public Paradox on the Drug War," *Washington Post National Weekly Edition,* March 23–29, 1998, 35.

218. Shanto Iyengar and Donald R. Kinder, *News That Matters* (Chicago: University of Chicago Press, 1987), 42–45.

219. Erbring et al., "Front-Page News," 38; MacKuen and Coombs, *More Than News,* 128–137.

220. Rogers and Dearing, "Agenda-Setting Research," 569; MacKuen and Coombs, *More Than News,* 101; Erbring et al., "Front-Page News," 38.

221. Rogers and Dearing, "Agenda-Setting Research," 577, citing Jack L. Walker, "Setting the Agenda in the U.S. Senate," *British Journal of Political Science* 7 (October 1977): 423–445. See also Cook, *Making Laws & Making News,* 116, 130–131.

222. Michael J. Robinson and Margaret A. Sheehan, *Over the Wire and on TV* (New York: Russell Sage Foundation and Basic Books, 1983); Robinson, "The Media Campaign, '84," 45–47.

223. Thomas Griffith, "Leave Off the Label," *Time* (September 19, 1984): 63.

224. He did own property in the district, so he did satisfy the residency requirement.

225. Doris A. Graber, "Kind Pictures and Harsh Words: How Television Presents the Candidates," in *Elections in America,* ed. Kay Lehman Schlozman (Boston: Allen & Unwin, 1987), 141.

226. Ibid., 116.

227. Anthony Lewis, quoted in Larry J. Sabato, "Open Season: How the News Media Cover Presidential Campaigns in the Age of Attack Journalism," in *Under the Watchful Eye,* ed. Mathew D. McCubbins (Washington, D.C.: CQ Press, 1992), 146.

228. Tannen, *The Argument Culture,* 79–83.

229. See the excellent summary found in Stephen Ansolabehere, Roy Behr, and Shanto Iyengar, "Mass Media and Elections," *American Politics Quarterly* 19 (January 1991): 109–139.

230. Bruce Buchanan, *Electing a President: The Markle Commission Report on Campaign '88* (Austin: University of Texas Press, 1990); Montague Kean, *30-Second Politics* (New York: Praeger, 1989). Marion Just, Lori Wallach, and Ann Crigler, "Thirty Seconds or Thirty Minutes: Political Learning in an Election," paper presented at the Midwest Political Science Association Meeting, April 1987, Chicago.

231. In the Democratic race in 1976, Carter finished second to "uncommitted" in the Iowa caucuses. This was enough to give him twenty-three

times more coverage in *Time* and *Newsweek,* and five times more coverage on network television, than any of his rivals. Finishing first by just 4 percent in the New Hampshire primary landed him on the covers of *Time* and *Newsweek* and brought him twenty-five times more coverage on network television than the runner-up. David Paletz and Robert Entrum, *Media—Power—Politics* (New York: Macmillan, 1981), 35ff.

232. Patterson, *Out of Order,* 44.

233. Ansolabehere et al., "Mass Media and Elections," 128–129; Christine F. Ridout, "The Role of Media Coverage of Iowa and New Hampshire in the 1988 Democratic Nomination," *American Politics Quarterly* 19 (January 1991): 45–46, 53–54; Marc Howard Ross, "Television News and Candidate Fortunes in Presidential Nomination Campaigns," *American Politics Quarterly* 20 (January 1992): 69–98.

234. Henry Brady, "Chances, Utilities, and Voting in Presidential Primaries," paper delivered at the Annual Meeting of the Public Choice Society, Phoenix, Arizona, cited in Ansolabehere et al., "Mass Media and Elections"; Bartels, *Presidential Primaries and the Dynamics of Public Choice* (Princeton, N.J.: Princeton University Press, 1988).

235. Lee Sigelman and Carol K. Sigelman, "Judgments of the Carter-Reagan Debate," *Public Opinion Quarterly* 48 (1984): 624–628.

236. Theodore H. White, *The Making of the President 1960* (New York: Atheneum, 1961), 333.

237. The clearest examples occurred in 1976 and 1984. In 1976, Gerald Ford erroneously said there was "no Soviet domination of Eastern Europe." People surveyed within twelve hours of the debate said they thought Ford won. But the media zeroed in on this slip, and people surveyed later said they thought Carter had won. In the first debate in 1984, Reagan appeared tired and confused. By a modest margin, people polled immediately after the debate said they thought Walter Mondale had won. But the media focused on Reagan's age and abilities, and by increasingly large margins, people polled in the days after the debate said Mondale had won. Perhaps viewers did not catch Ford's statement or, due to selective perception, notice Reagan's doddering, but the media called attention to them, which prompted many viewers to reconsider and reverse their verdict.

238. John R. Zaller, "Monica Lewinsky's Contribution to Political Science," *PS: Political Science & Politics* (June 1998): 182–189.

239. MacKuen and Coombs, *More Than News,* 222.

240. For a review, see MacKuen and Coombs, *More Than News,* 147–161.

241. Robert S. Erickson, "The Influence of Newspaper Endorsements in Presidential Elections," *American Journal of Political Science* 20 (May 1976): 207–233; Dalton et al., "Partisan Cues and the Media." Also see Kahn and Kenney, "The Slant of the News."

242. David Barker, "The Talk Radio Community," *Social Science Quarterly* 79 (June 1998): 261–272; C. Richard Hofstetter, "Political Talk Radio, Situational Involvement, and Political Mobilization," *Social Science Quarterly* 79 (June 1998): 273–286.

243. There is speculation that the earlier call for Gore cost Bush some votes in Florida, as polling places were still open in the western panhandle. However, the earlier call was just ten minutes before the polling places were scheduled to close, so it is doubtful that it caused many voters to turn around and go home without voting.

244. Shogan, *Bad News,* 266–268.

245. Benjamin I. Page, Robert Y. Shapiro, and Glenn R. Dempsey, "What Moves Public Opinion?" *American Political Science Review* 81 (March 1987): 23–43. Critical news and commentaries about presidents seem to lower their popularity. Darrell M. West, "Television and Presidential Popularity in America," *British Journal of Political Science* 21 (April 1991): 199–214. Even television's "framing" of events, as isolated incidents or parts of pat-

terns, affects viewers' opinions about these events. Shanto Iyengar, *Is Anyone Responsible? How Television Frames Political Issues* (Chicago: University of Chicago Press, 1991).

246. Iyengar, *Is Anyone Responsible?* Chapters 6 and 8.

247. Kathleen Hall Jamieson, quoted in Howard Kurtz, "Tuning Out the News," *Washington Post National Weekly Edition,* May 29–June 4, 1995, 6; William Raspberry, "Blow-by-Blow Coverage," *Washington Post National Weekly Edition,* November 6–12, 1995, 29.

248. Michael J. Robinson, "Public Affairs Television and the Growth of Political Malaise," *American Political Science Review* 70 (1976): 409–432; Miller et al., "Type-Set Politics."

249. "Study: Public More Cynical Than Media," *Champaign-Urbana News-Gazette,* May 22, 1995.

250. Fallows, *Breaking the News,* 202–203.

251. Also, see Cappella and Jamieson, *Spiral of Cynicism.*

252. Fallows, *Breaking the News,* 247.

253. Graber, *Mass Media,* 244; Doris Graber, *Processing News: How People Tame the Information Tide* (New York: Longman, 1984). A 1993 survey concluded that almost half of Americans over sixteen have such limited reading and math skills that they are unfit for most jobs. One task the survey included was to paraphrase a newspaper story. Many people could scan the story but not paraphrase it when they finished it. Paul Gray, "Adding Up the Under-Skilled," *Time* (September 20, 1993): 75.

254. Reuven Frank, quoted in Neil Hickey, "Money Lust," *Columbia Journalism Review* (July/August 1998): 35.

255. The idea for this paragraph came from James Fallows, "Did You Have a Good Week?" *Atlantic Monthly* (December 1994): 32, 34.

256. Iyengar, *Is Anyone Responsible?*

257. "The New Political Landscape," *Times Mirror Center for the People & the Press* (October 1994): 4.

258. Joe Klein, "Dizzy Days," *New Yorker* (October 5, 1998): 45.

259. Marta W. Aldrich, "Support for Media Freedoms Waning," *Lincoln Journal-Star,* July 4, 1999.

260. Stephen Earl Bennett, "Trends in Americans' Political Information," *American Politics Quarterly* 17 (October 1989): 422–435; Richard Zoglin, "The Tuned-Out Generation," *Time* (July 9, 1990): 64.

261. Peters, *How Washington Really Works,* 32.

262. The source for the epilogue, except where noted otherwise, is Kotz, "Breaking Point."

263. Tannen, *The Argument Culture,* 82.

264. Ibid., 74.

265. Yet when journalists themselves come under occasional attack from other media, they do not like it any more than officials do. They are just as "thin-skinned" as officials are. Issues of *Brill's Content* provide numerous examples. Another example comes from Toobin, *A Vast Conspiracy,* 268. After the 1992 election, Linda Bloodworth-Thomason, a Hollywood supporter of Bill Clinton, produced a short film for the inauguration. The film included a series of sound bites from Washington journalists during the campaign, dismissing Clinton as "unelectable" and "dead meat." Although Thomason apparently regarded the film as "a harmless needle at some puffed up egos," some of the journalists regarded it as "an act of war." In Toobin's view, the controversy over the film, which poisoned the relationship between the president and the press from the beginning, reflected the thin skins of the press corps.

Chapter 6

1. Jeffrey Goldberg, "Big Tobacco's Endgame," *New York Times Magazine* (June 21, 1998): 36. Information on Gingrich's father is also from this source. Other sources include Ceci Connolly and John Mintz, "How Big Tobacco Got Smoked," *Washington Post National Weekly Edition,* April 6, 1998, 6–7; Ceci Connolly and John Mintz, "The Mississippi

Connection," *Washington Post National Weekly Edition,* April 6, 1998, 8–9; Saundra Tory and John Schwartz, "Making Nice to Make a Deal," *Washington Post National Weekly Edition,* March 9, 1998, 29; James Carney, "McCain's Big Deal," *Time* (April 13, 1998): 62–64; John Bresnahan, "Tobacco Lobbyists Prepare for Fight," *Roll Call* (May 1998): 1, 13; Alan Greenblatt, "Tobacco Debate Rages on, Keeping Bill Alive, If Unwieldy," *Congressional Quarterly Weekly Report,* June 13, 1998, 1605–1607.

2. Jeffrey Birnbaum, *The Lobbyists* (New York: Times Books, 1992), 32.

3. M. A. Peterson and J. L.Walker, "Interest Group Responses to Partisan Change: The Impact of the Reagan Administration upon the National Interest Group System," in *Interest Group Politics,* 2d ed., eds. A. J. Cigler and B. A. Loomis (Washington, D.C.: CQ Press, 1987), 162.

4. A. de Tocqueville, *Democracy in America* (New York: Knopf, 1945), 191.

5. G. Almond and S. Verba, *Civil Culture* (Boston: Little, Brown, 1965), 266–306.

6. David Truman, *The Governmental Process* (New York: Knopf, 1964), 25–26.

7. Ibid., 59.

8. Ibid., 26–33.

9. James Q. Wilson, *Political Organizations* (New York: Basic Books, 1973), 198.

10. Graham. K. Wilson, *Interest Groups in America* (Oxford: Oxford University Press, 1981), Chapter 5; see also Graham K. Wilson, "American Business and Politics," in *Interest Group Politics,* 2d ed., ed. Cigler and Loomis, 221–235.

11. K. L. Schlozman and J. T. Tierney, "More of the Same: Washington Pressure Group Activity in a Decade of Change," *Journal of Politics* 45 (May 1983): 335–356.

12. Christopher H. Foreman Jr., "Grassroots Victim Organizations: Mobilizing for Personal and Public Health," in *Interest Group Politics,* 4th ed., ed. A. J. Cigler and B. A. Loomis (Washington, D.C.: CQ Press, 1994), 33–53.

13. William Brown, "Exchange Theory and the Institutional Impetus for Interest Group Formation," in *Interest Group Politics,* 6th ed., ed. A. J. Cigler and B. A. Loomis (Washington, D.C.: CQ Press, 2002), 313–329; William Brown, "Benefits and Membership: A Reappraisal of Interest Group Activity," *Western Political Quarterly* 29 (1976): 258–273; Terry M. Moe, *The Organization of Interests: Incentives and the Internal Dynamics of Political Interest Groups* (Chicago: University of Chicago Press, 1980).

14. Jack L. Walker, "The Origins and Maintenance of Interest Groups in America," *American Political Science Review* 77 (June 1983): 398–400; see also *National Journal* (August 1981): 1376.

15. R. H. Salisbury, "An Exchange Theory of Interest Groups," *Midwest Journal of Political Science* 13 (February 1969): 1–32.

16. J. M. Berry, *The Interest Group Society* (Boston: Little Brown, 1984), 26–28.

17. Ibid.

18. Wilson, *Political Organizations,* Chapter 3.

19. Alex Kuczynski, "New AARP Magazine Courting Younger Readers," *New York Times,* January 22, 2001, C1.

20. C. Brown, "Explanations of Interest Group Membership over Time," *American Politics Quarterly* 17 (January 1989): 32–53.

21. N. Babchuk and R. Thompson, "The Voluntary Associations of Negroes," *American Sociological Review* 27 (October 1962): 662–665; see also J. Klobus-Edwards, J Edwards, and D. Klemmach, "Differences in Social Participation of Blacks and Whites," *Social Forces* 56 (1978): 1035–1052.

22. Robert Putnam, *Bowling Alone* (New York: Simon & Schuster, 2000); Robert D. Putnam, "Bowling Alone: America's Declining Social Capital," *Journal of Democracy* (January 1995): 65–78; see also Robert J. Samuelson, "Join the Club," *Washington Post National Weekly Edition,* April 15–21, 1996, 5.

23. Samuelson, "Join the Club."

24. Richard Stengel, "Bowling Together," *Time* (July 22, 1996): 35.

25. Theda Skocpol, "Associations Without Members," *American Prospect* (July/August, 1999), 66–73.

26. M. T. Hayes, "The New Group Universe," in *Interest Group Politics,* 2d ed., ed. Cigler and Loomis, 133–145.

27. Tomkins, "A Sense of Urgency," *New Yorker* (March 27, 1989): 48–74.

28. Walker, "The Origins and Maintenance of Interest Groups in America"; E. E. Schattschneider, *Semi-Sovereign People* (New York: Holt, Rinehart, & Winston, 1960), 118.

29. David Broder and Michael Weisskopf, "Finding New Friends on the Hill," *Washington Post National Weekly Edition,* October 3–9, 1994, 11.

30. Charles E. Lindblom, "The Market as Prison," *Journal of Politics* 44 (May, 1982): 324–336; Michael Genovese, *The Presidential Dilemma: Leadership in the American System* (New York: Haper-Collins, 1995).

31. Steven Greenhouse, "AFL-CIO Plans $40 Million Political Drive," *New York Times,* February 18, 1999, A19.

32. Steven Greenhouse, "Michigan Unions Push Hard for Gore," *New York Times,* October 13, 2000, A22.

33. Seven Greenhouse, "Bush Is Moving to Reduce Labor's Political Coffers," *New York Times,* February 16, 2001.

34. Steven Greenhouse, "Union Membership Rose in '98, but Unions' Percentage of Workforce Fell," *New York Times,* January 20, 1999, A22; E. Johnson, "Organized Labor in an Era of Blue Collar Decline," in *Interest Group Politics,* 3d ed., ed. A. J. Cigler and B. A. Loomis (Washington, D.C.: CQ Press, 1991), 33–62.

35. Steven Greenhouse, "Report Faults Laws for Slowing Growth in Unions," *New York Times,* October 24, 2000, A14.

36. Steven Greenhouse, "Union Membership Slides Despite Increased Organizing," *New York Times,* March 22, 1998, A8.

37. Frank Swoboda, "A Healthy Outcome for Organized Labor," *Washington Post National Weekly Edition,* March 8, 1999, 18; Steven Greenhouse, "In Biggest Drive since 1937, Union Gains a Victory," *New York Times,* February 26, 1999, A1.

38. Steven Greenhouse, "The Most Innovative Figure in Silicon Valley? Maybe This Labor Organizer," *New York Times,* November 14, 1999, 26.

39. Steven Greenhouse, "Angered by HMO's Treatment, More Doctors Are Joining Unions," *New York Times,* February 4, 1999, A1, A25.

40. Steven Greenhouse, "Graduate Students Push for Union Membership," *New York Times,* May 15, 2001.

41. Richard Corliss, "RAs of the World Unite!," *Time* (March 17, 2002); Daniel J. Fitzgibbons, "Administration Opposes Union Bid by RAs," *The Campus Chronicle,* April 13, 2001.

42. A. J. Cigler and J. M. Hansen, "Group Formation through Protest: The American Agriculture Movement," in *Interest Group Politics,* ed. A. J. Cigler and B. A. Loomis (Washington, D.C.: CQ Press, 1983), Chapter 4; A. J. Cigler, "Organizational Maintenance and Political Activity on the Cheap: The American Agriculture Movement," in *Interest Group Politics,* ed. Cigler and Loomis, 81–108.

43. Dick Lugar, "The Farm Bill Charade," *New York Times,* January 21, 2002.

44. A. S. McFarland, *Common Cause* (Chatham, N.J.: Chatham House, 1984); see also A. S. McFarland, *Public Interest Lobbies: Decision Making on Energy* (Washington, D.C.: American Enterprise Institute, 1976).

45. R. G. Shaiko, "More Bang for the Buck: The New Era of Full Service Public Interest Groups," in *Interest Group Politics,* 3d ed., ed. Cigler and Loomis, 109.

46. Ibid., 120.

47. For a discussion of the evolution of NOW and its success in lobbying Congress, see A. N. Costain and W. D. Costain, "The Women's Lobby: Impact of a Movement on Congress," in *Interest Group Politics,* ed. Cigler and Loomis.

48. EMILY's List home page, www.emilyslist.org; Birnbaum and Pooley, "New Party Bosses."

49. "Gender Rights: Helping Men, Women, Etc.," *Time* (June 18, 2001): 72.

50. Ibid.

51. Richard Morin and Claudia Deane, "The Administration's Right-Hand Women" *Washington Post National Weekly,* May 7–13, 2001, 12.

52. E. M. Uslaner, "A Tower of Babel on Foreign Policy," in *Interest Group Politics,* 3d ed., ed. Cigler and Loomis, 309.

53. K. Wald, *Religion and Politics* (New York: St. Martin's, 1985), 182–212.

54. James L. Guth, John C. Green, Lyman A. Jellstedt, and Corwin E. Smidt, "Onward Christian Soldiers: Religious Activist Groups in American Politics," in *Interest Group Politics,* 3d ed., ed. Cigler and Loomis, 57.

55. Michael Lind, "The Right Still Has Religion," *New York Times,* December 9, 2001, A13.

56. Sidney Blumenthal, "Christian Soldiers," *New Yorker* (July 18, 1994): 36.

57. Ibid., 37.

58. David Von Drehle and Thomas B. Edsall, "The Religious Right Returns," *Washington Post National Weekly Edition,* August 29–September 4, 1994, 6; "Prodding Voters to the Right," *Time* (November 21, 1994): 62.

59. Laura Goodstein, "Church Debate over Voter Guides," *New York Times,* October 29, 1998, A21.

60. "Citing 'Moral Crisis,' a Call to Oust Clinton," *New York Times,* October 23, 1998, A18.

61. Hanna Rosin, "Aiming at the Mainstream," *Washington Post National Weekly Edition,* April 17, 2000, 17.

62. Drehle and Edsall, "The Religious Right Returns," 6.

63. Lind, "The Right Still Has Religion."

64. Ibid.

65. Richard Berke, "Falwell Is Raising Money to Press Conservative Family Agenda," *New York Times,* December 14, 2001, A19.

66. Charles Levendosky, "Alternative Religious Voice Finally Being Raised," *Lincoln Journal-Star,* March 3, 1996, 7B.

67. The source for most of the next paragraphs is Eric Marcus, *Making History: The Struggle for Gay and Lesbian Equal Rights 1945–1990* (New York: HarperCollins, 1992). Also see Jeffrey Schmalz, "Gay Politics Goes Mainstream," *New York Times Magazine* (October 11, 1992): 18ff.

68. Shawn Zeller, "Marching On, but Apart," *National Journal,* Januay 12, 2002, 98–103.

69. Richard Lacayo, "The New Gay Struggle," *Time* (October 26, 1998): 33–36.

70. Zeller, "Marching On, but Apart."

71. "Gray Power," *Time* (January 4, 1988): 36.

72. "Our Footloose Correspondents," *New Yorker* (August 8, 1988): 70.

73. C. J. Bosso, "Adaption and Change in the Environmental Movement," in *Interest Group Politics,* 3d ed., ed. Cigler and Loomis, 155–156.

74. Ibid., 162.

75. Ibid., 169.

76. Katharine Q. Seelye, "Bush Team Still Reversing Environmental Policies," *New York Times,* November 18, 2001, A20.

77. "Echoes of Tobacco Battle in Gun Suits," *New York Times,* February 21, 1999, 18.

78. Thomas B. Edsall, "Targeting Al Gore with $10 Million," *Washington Post National Weekly Edition,* May 29, 2000, 11; John Mintx, "Would Bush Be the NRA's Point Man in the White House?" *Washington Post National Weekly Edition,* May 8, 2000, 14; Mike Dorning, "NRA Promises an All-out Assault on Al Gore's Presidential Campaign," *Lincoln Journal-Star,* May 21, 2000, 2A.

79. Linda Greenhouse, "U.S. in a Shift, Tells Justices Citizens Have a Right to Guns," *New York Times,* May 8, 2002.

80. Ibid.

81. Ibid.

82. Sam Howe Verhovek, "Creators of Anti-abortion Web Site Told to Pay Millions," *New York Times,* February 3, 1999, A11.

83. Charles Lane, "Ruling Curbs Abortion Foes: Tactics: Court Says 'Wanted' Posters and Web Site Are Intimidation," *Washington Post,* May 17, 2002, A2.

84. Kevin Sack and Gustav Niebuhr, "After Stem-Cell Rift, Groups Unite for Anti-abortion Push," *New York Times,* September 4, 2001.

85. A. Rubin, "Interest Groups and Abortion Politics in the Post-Webster Era," in *Interest Group Politics,* 3d ed., ed. Cigler and Loomis, 249–251; *Congressional Quarterly Weekly Report,* March 27, 1993, 755–757.

86. David Broder, "Let 100 Single-Issue Groups Bloom," *Washington Post,* January 7, 1979, C1–C2; see also David Broder, *The Party's Over: The Failure of Politics in America* (New York: Harper & Row, 1972).

87. Wilson, *Interest Groups,* Chapter 4.

88. M. Evans, "Lobbying the Committee: Interest Groups and the House Public Works and Transportation Committee, in the Post-Webster Era," in *Interest Group Politics,* 3d ed., ed. Cigler and Loomis, 257–276.

89. Berry, *Interest Group Society,* 188.

90. Jeffrey Birnbaum, *The Lobbyists* (New York: Times Books, 1992), 40.

91. Leslie Wayne and Michael Moss, "A Nation Challenged: The Airlines; Bailout for Airlines Showed the Weight of Mighty Lobby," *New York Times,* October 19, 2001, A1, B10.

92. Ibid.

93. Ibid.

94. Ibid.

95. Robert Pear, "Lobbyists Seek Special Spin on Federal Bioterrorism Bill," *New York Times,* December 11, 2001, A1, A18.

96. Wittenberg and Wittenberg, *How to Win in Washington,* 24.

97. David Broder and Spencer Rich, "The Health Care Battle Begins," *Washington Post National Weekly Edition,* September 27–October 3, 1993, 6.

98. E. Drew, *Politics and Money: The New Road to Corruption* (New York: Macmillan, 1983), 78.

99. Ibid.

100. Lowell Bergman and Jeff Gerth, "Power Trader Tied to Bush Finds Wasington All Ears," *New York Times,* May 25, 2001.

101. Ibid.

102. Eric Schmitt, "Nomination for FDA Post Nears Approval in Senate," *New York Times,* October 21, 1998, A13.

103. Rebecca Adams, "Harvard Professor Faces Tough Questions but Is Expected to Win Confirmation as Head of Regulatory Affairs Office," *CQ Weekly,* May 19, 2001, 1166.

104. Sheryl Gay Stolberg, "Bush in Political Hot Spot in Picking an F.D.A. Chief," *New York Times,* February 8, 2002, A17; Sheryl Gay Stolberg, "Deputy Is Appointed to Direct Food and Drug Agency as Impasse Continues," *New York Times,* February 26, 2002.

105. Evelyn Nieves, "Civil Rights Groups Suing Berkeley over Admissions Policy," *New York Times,* February 3, 1999, A11.

106. William Glaberson, "Groups Gird for Long Legal Fight On New Bush Anti-terror Powers," *New York Times,* November 30, 2001, A1, B7.

107. James Dao, "Environmental Groups to File Suit Over Missile Defenses," *New York Times,* August 28, 2001.

108. For an article dealing with the success of interest group litigation at the district court level, see L. Epstein and C. K. Rowland, "Debunking the Myth of Interest Group Invincibility in the Courts," *American Political Science Review* 85 (March 1991): 205–220.

109. S. Kernell, *Going Public* (Washington, D.C.: CQ Press, 1986), 34.

110. R. Harris, "If You Love Your Grass," *New Yorker* (April 20, 1968): 57.

111. Alison Mitchell, "A New Form of Lobbying Puts Public Face on Private Interest," *New York Times,* September 30, 1998, A1, A14.

112. Ibid.

113. Evans, "Lobbying the Committee," 269.

114. Michael Weisskopf, "Letting No Grass Roots Grow under Their Feet," *Washington Post National Weekly Edition,* October 24, 1993, 20–21.

115. Sandra Boodman, "Health Care's Power Player," *Washington Post National Weekly Edition,* February 14–20, 1994, 6–7.

116. Ibid.

117. Ibid.

118. Ibid.

119. Ibid.

120. James Dao, "The 2000 Campaign: The Grass Roots," *New York Times,* October 22, 2000.

121. Ibid.

122. Ibid.

123. Ibid.

124. Michael Towle, "Ad for Fighter Plane Aimed at Congress," *Lincoln Journal-Star,* May 2, 1997, 7A.

125. Greenpeace, "Denial and Deception: A Chronicle of ExxonMobil's Efforts to Corrupt the Debate on Global Warming" (Washington, D.C.: Author, May 2002).

126. Birnbaum, *The Lobbyists,* 40.

127. Dan Balz and David Broder, "Take Two Lobbyists and Call Me in the Morning," *Washington Post National Weekly Edition,* October 18–24, 1993, 10–11.

128. Rebecca Adams, "Intense Lobbying Gets Under Way Over Whether to Block Ergonomics Rules," *CQ Weekly,* February 10, 2001), 328.

129. R. Kenneth Godwin and Barry J. Seldon, "What Corporations Really Want from Government: The Public Provision of Private Goods," in *Interest Group Politics,* 6th ed., eds. A. J. Cigler and B. A. Loomis (Washington, D.C.: CQ Press, 2002), 205–224.

130. Much of the information in this section is taken from B. A. Loomis, "Coalitions of Interests: Building Bridges in the Balkanized State," in *Interest Group Politics,* 2d ed., ed. Cigler and Loomis, 258–274.

131. Birnbaum, *The Lobbyists,* 83.

132. Steven Greenhouse, "Carnival of Derision to Greet the Princes of Global Trade," *New York Times,* November 11, 1999, A12.

133. Ibid.

134. Cary Goldberg, "How Political Theater Lost Its Audience," *New York Times,* September 21, 1997, 6.

135. "Greenpeace Protest Shipload of Newsprint," *Lincoln Journal-Star,* October 21, 1999, 3.

136. "15 Antimissile Protesters Face Felony Charges," *New York Times,* August 12, 2001, A16.

137. David Segal, "Bob Dole Leads the Cast of Rainmakers," *Washington Post National Weekly Edition,* September 22, 1997, 20.

138. Deborah L. Acomb, "Poll Track," *National Journal,* January 5, 2002, 58.

139. Godwin and Seldon, "What Corporations Really Want from Government."

140. Dan Clawson, Alan Neustadt, and Denise Scott, *Money Talks* (New York: Basic Books, 1992), 91.

141. Schattschneider, *Semi-Sovereign People,* Chapter 2.

142. Ibid., 35.

143. Kevin Phillips, "Fat City," *Time* (September 26, 1995): 51.

144. Goldberg, "Big Tobacco's Endgame," 67.

145. Ibid.

146. Saundra Torry, "One for the Record," *Washington Post National Weekly Edition,* May 25, 1998, 10.

147. "Confidential Tobacco PR Memo," at www.citizen.org/tobacco/premo.htm.

148. Michael Scherer, "Up in Smoke," *Mother Jones* (November/December, 2002): 15.

149. Ibid.

150. Ibid.

Chapter 7

1. Materials have been drawn from the following: Mike Christensen, "Anguished Transformation from Maverick to Outcast," *CQ Weekly,* May 26, 2001, 1242; Amy Goodstein and Dana Milbank, "Now, Real Bipartisanship?" *Washington Post National Weekly Edition,* May 28–June 3, 2001, 6; Mike Allen and Ruth Marcus, "GOP Missteps Helped Prompt Jeffords to Leave the Party," *Washington Post National Weekly Edition,* May 28–June 3, 2001, 7; Douglas Waller, "How Jeffords Got Away," *Time* (June 4, 2001): 36–38; Alson Mitchell and Adam Clymer, "GOP Senator Is Considering a Party Switch," *New York Times,* May 23, 2001; Richard L. Berke, "A Question of Governing from the Right," *New York Times,* May 25, 2001.

2. Christensen, "Anguished Transformation from Maverick to Outcast."

3. Congressional Quarterly, *CQ's Politics in America 2002: The 107th Congress,* ed. Brian Nutting and H. Amy Stern (Washington, D.C.: Congressional Quarterly Press, 2001), 1031.

4. Christensen, "Anguished Transformation from Maverick to Outcast."

5. Milbank, "Now, Real Bipartisanship?"

6. Clymer, "GOP Senator Is Considering a Party Switch."

7. Waller, "How Jeffords Got Away."

8. E. E. Schattschneider, *Party Government* (New York: Holt, Rinehart, & Winston, 1960), 1.

9. Jack Dennis, "Trends in Public Support for the American Party System," in *Parties and Elections in an Anti-Party Age,* ed. Jeff Fishel (Bloomington: Indiana University Press, 1978).

10. Frank Sorauf, *Political Parties in the American System,* 4th ed. (Boston: Little, Brown, 1980).

11. Richard Hofstadter, *The Idea of Party System: The Rise of Legitimate Opposition in the United States, 1780–1840* (Berkeley: University of California Press, 1969).

12. Theodore J. Lowi, *The Personal President: Power Invested, Promise Unfulfilled* (Ithaca, N.Y.: Cornell University Press, 1985).

13. James MacGregor Burns, *The Vineyard of Liberty* (New York: Knopf, 1982).

14. Kevin Phillips, *The Emerging Republican Majority* (New York: Doubleday, 1969).

15. James L. Sundquist, *Dynamics of the Party System: Alignment and Realignment of Political Parties in the United States* (Washington, D.C.: Brookings Institution, 1973).

16. Thomas B. Edsall, "The Fissure Running through the Democratic Party," *Washington Post National Weekly Edition,* June 6–12, 1994, 11.

17. J. R. Petrocik and F. T. Steeper, "The Political Landscape in 1988," *Public Opinion Magazine* (September/October 1987): 41–44; H. Norpoth, "Party Realignment in the 1980s," *Public Opinion Quarterly* 51 (fall 1987): 376–390.

18. Thomas Edsall, "The Democrats' Class and Gender Gap," *Washington Post National Weekly Edition,* June 6, 1994, 12.

19. Ibid.

20. Edsall, "The Fissure Running through the Democratic Party," 11.

21. Thomas B. Edsall, "The Shifting Sands of America's Political Parties," *Washington Post National Weekly Edition,* April 9–15, 2001, 11.

22. Ibid.

23. Thomas B. Edsall, "What Is the 2000 Census Telling Us?" *Washington Post National Weekly Edition,* July 16–22, 2001, 11.

24. Ibid.

25. Ibid.

26. Everett Carll Ladd, *Where Have All the Voters Gone?* (New York: Norton, 1982), 78; 1984 and

1988 data are from the 1984 and 1988 CPS National Election Study.

27. Martin P. Wallenberg, *The Rise of Candidate-Centered Politics* (Cambridge, Mass.: Harvard University Press, 1991).

28. Walter Dean Burnham, *Critical Elections and the Mainstream of American Politics* (New York: Norton, 1970); Helmut Norpoth and Jerrold Rusk, "Partisan Dealignment in the American Electorate," *American Political Science Review* 76 (September 1982): 522–537; David W. Rhode, "The Fall Elections: Realignment and Dealignment," *Chronicle of Higher Education,* December 14, 1994, B1–B2.

29. John Petrocik, "Realignment," *Journal of Politics* 49 (May 1987): 347–375; George Rabinowitz, Paul-Henri Gurian, and Stuart MacDonald, "The Structure of Presidential Elections and the Process of Realignment," *American Journal of Political Science* 28 (November 1984): 611–635; D. Broder, "The GOP Plays Dixie," *Washington Post National Weekly Edition,* September 12–18, 1988, 4; T. B. Edsall, "A Serious Case of White Flight," *Washington Post National Weekly Edition,* September 10–16, 1990, 13

30. Maurice Duverger, *Political Parties* (New York: Wiley, 1963). See also Edward R. Tufte, "The Relationship between Seats and Votes in Two-Party Systems," *American Political Science Review* 67 (1973): 540–554.

31. See also Lowi, *Personal President.* He makes the point that two parties survived in the United States despite the use of multimember districts in elections for Congress in the nineteenth century.

32. *CQ Weekly,* January 12, 2002, 136.

33. Robert S. Erikson, Gerald C. Wright, and John P. McIver, *Statehouse Democracy: Public Opinion and Policy in the American States* (Cambridge: Cambridge University Press, 1993), Chapter 5.

34. Frank Bruni, "Bush Signaling Readiness to Go His Own Way," *New York Times,* April 3, 2000, A1–A15.

35. Robert G. Kaiser, "Hindsight Is 20/20," *Washington Post National Weekly Edition,* February 19–28, 2001, 11.

36. Barbara Ehrenreich, "Don't Blame Me," *Time* (November 20, 2000): 69.

37. Ralph Nader, "My Untold Story," *The Presidency and the Press* (February 2001).

38. D. Sarasohn, "Wall Falls on Reagan Coalition," *Lincoln Sunday Journal-Star,* February 18, 1990, 1C.

39. Steven Roberts, "Near Death Experience," *U.S. News and World Report,* November 6, 1996, 28.

40. *CQ Weekly,* January 12, 2002, 136.

41. For a discussion of party influence on voting in Congress, see William R. Shaffer, *Party and Ideology in the United States Congress* (Lanham, Md.: University Press of America, 1980).

42. Bruce I. Oppenheimer, "The Importance of Elections in a Strong Congressional Era," in *Do Elections Matter?* ed. Benjamin Ginsberg and Alan Stone (Armonk, N.Y.: Sharpe, 1996), 120–138.

43. David Broder, "Polarization Growing Force for Political Parties," *Lincoln Journal-Star,* January 22, 1995, 4B.

44. Dan Carney, "As Hostilities Rage on the Hill, Partisan-Vote Rate Soars," *Congressional Quarterly Weekly Report,* January 27, 1996, 199–200.

45. *Congressional Quarterly Weekly Report,* December 11, 1999, 2993–2994.

46. Lloyd Grove, "A Good Ol' Boy Going in for the Kill," *Washington Post National Weekly Edition,* August 22–28, 1994, 13–14, 32.

47. Thomas B. Edsall, "The Lobbyist and RNC Chairman," *Washington Post National Weekly Edition,* December 24, 2001–January 6, 2002, 15.

48. Frank J. Sorauf, *Money in American Elections* (Glenview, Ill.: Scott, Foresman, 1988), 121–153; Paul Herrnson, *Party Campaigning in the 1980s* (Cambridge, Mass.: Harvard University Press, 1988).

49. Frank Bruni, "G.O.P. Tries to Counter Lack of Support Among Women," *New York Times,* August 1, 2001.

50. Neil Munro, "The New Wired Politics," *National Journal,* April 22, 2000, 1260–1263.

51. Xandra Kayden, "The Nationalization of the Party System," in *Parties, Interest Groups, and Campaign Finance Laws,* ed. Michael Malbin (Washington, D.C.: American Enterprise Institute, 1980).

52. Milton L. Rakove, *Don't Make No Waves, Don't Back No Losers* (Bloomington: Indiana University Press, 1975).

53. Austin Ranney, *Participation in American Presidential Nominations, 1976* (Washington, D.C.: American Enterprise Institute, 1977). See also Austin Ranney, "Parties in State Politics," in *Politics in the American States,* 3d ed., ed. Herbert Jacob and Kenneth Vines (Boston: Little, Brown, 1980), 61– 99.

54. Oppenheimer, "The Importance of Elections."

55. Waller, "How Jeffords Got Away."

56. Ibid.

57. Ibid.

58. Berke, "A Question of Governing from the Right"

59. Ibid.

Chapter 8

1. One might advantage you and disadvantage your opponent. The networks' first projection, that you were the winner, occurred after the polls closed in the eastern time zone but ten minutes before those in Florida's panhandle (on central time) closed. A Bush stronghold, it is possible that some Republican supporters did not go to the polls because the election had been declared. Although it seems unlikely that this affected many voters, because it could only have affected those already in their car nearing the polls or even at them already, even a few are crucial in such a close race.

2. Quoted in Alan M. Dershowitz, *Supreme Injustice: How the High Court Hijacked Election 2000* (New York: Oxford University Press, 2001), 25.

3. Tom Fiedler, "The Perfect Storm," in *Overtime!* ed. Larry Sabato (New York: Longmans, 2002), 9.

4. William Flanigan and Nancy H. Zingale, *Political Behavior of the American Electorate* (Boston: Allyn & Bacon, 1972), 13. See also Chilton Williamson, *American Suffrage from Property to Democracy* (Princeton, N.J.: Princeton University Press, 1960).

5. James MacGregor Burns, *Vineyard of Liberty* (New York: Knopf, 1982), 363.

6. August Meier and Elliot Rudwick, *From Plantation to Ghetto* (New York: Hill & Wang, 1966), 69.

7. Robert Darcy, Susan Welch, and Janet Clark, *Women, Elections, and Representation* (Lincoln: University of Nebraska Press, 1995).

8. Grandfather clause: *Guinn v. United States,* 238 U.S. 347 (1915); white primary: *Smith v. Allwright,* 321 U.S. 649 (1944).

9. Data on black and white voter registration in the southern states are from the *Statistical Abstract of the United States* (Washington, D.C.: U.S. Bureau of the Census, various years).

10. Richard Limpne, "Mass Mobilization or Government Intervention? The Growth of Black Registration in the South," *Journal of Politics* 57 (May 1995): 425–442.

11. *City of Mobile v. Bolden,* 446 U.S. 55 (1980).

12. *Thornburg v. Gingles,* 478 U.S. 301 (1986).

13. Bob Benenson, "Arduous Ritual of Redistricting Ensures More Racial Diversity," *Congressional Quarterly Weekly Report,* October 24, 1992, 3385. For a very thorough review of the legal and behavioral impact of the Voting Rights Act, see Joseph Viteritti, "Unapportioned Justice: Local Elections Social Science and the Evolution of the Voting Rights Act," *Cornell Journal of Law and Public Policy* (fall 1994): 210–270.

14. *Shaw v. Reno,* 125 L.Ed.2d 511, 113 S.Ct. 2816 (1993); *Miller v. Johnson,* 132 L.Ed.2d 762, 115 S.Ct. 2475 (1995); *Bush v. Vera,* 135 L.Ed.2d 248, 116 S.Ct. 1941 (1996).

15. Darcy et al., *Women, Elections, and Representation.*

16. The discussion in this paragraph is drawn largely from Lois Banner, *Women in Modern America* (New York: Harcourt Brace Jovanovich, 1974), 88–90; Glenn Firebaugh and Kevin Chen, "Vote Turnout of Nineteenth Amendment Women," *American Journal of Sociology* 100 (January 1995): 972–996.

17. Nicholas Thompson, "Locking Up the Vote," *Washington Monthly* (January 2001): 17–21; see also "Barred from the Ballot," *Time* (January 21, 2001): 63.

18. Ibid., 18.

19. Ibid, 20. Data cited are from a forthcoming book by Jeff Manza and Christopher Uggen.

20. Richard Jensen, "American Election Campaigns: A Theoretical and Historical Typology," paper delivered at the 1968 Midwest Political Science Association Meeting, quoted in Walter Dean Burnham, *Critical Elections and the Mainsprings of American Politics* (New York: Norton, 1970), 73.

21. Frances Fox Piven and Richard A. Cloward, *Why Americans Don't Vote* (New York: Pantheon, 1988), 30.

22. Part of the explanation for declining voting rates is that the number of citizens who are ineligible to vote has increased, which depresses voting turnout statistics. Immigrants, other noncitizens, and in some states convicted felons are not eligible to vote. When those individuals are removed from the calculation of proportion voting, the proportion voting is increased by about five points, and most of the turnout decline occurs in the 1960s. See Michael McDonald and Samuel Popkin, "The Myth of the Vanishing Voter," *American Political Science Review* 95 (December 2001): 963–974.

23. *Statistical Abstract of the United States 2001,* Table 401. This self-report is probably an overestimate.

24. *Statistical Abstract of the United States 2001,* Table 404.

25. Daniel Elazar, *American Federalism: A View from the States* (New York: Crowell, 1972); *Statistical Abstract 1997,* Table 465.

26. Piven and Cloward, *Why Americans Don't Vote,* 162; *Statistical Abstract of the United States 2001,* Table 401; Piven and Cloward, *Why Americans Still Don't Vote* (Boston: Beacon, 2001).

27. Powell, "American Voter Turnout," 30; Piven and Cloward, *Why Americans Don't Vote,* 119; Arend Lijphart, "Unequal Participation: Democracy's Unresolved Dilemma," *American Political Science Review* 91 (March 1997): 1–14.

28. Eric Plutzer, "Becoming a Habitual Voter: Inertia, Resources, and Growth in Young Adulthood," *American Political Science Review* 96 (March 2002): 41–56.

29. See http://projects.edtech.sandi.net/lewis/rock/.

30. See www.vote-smart.org/ce/.

31. George Will, "In Defense of Nonvoting," *Newsweek* (October 10, 1983): 96.

32. Richard Morin, "The Dog Ate My Forms, and, Well, I Couldn't Find a Pen," *Washington Post National Weekly Edition,* November 5–11, 1990, 38.

33. Curtis Gans, quoted in Jack Germond and Jules Witcover, "Listen to the Voters—and Nonvoters," *Minneapolis Star Tribune,* November 26, 1988. This effect was foreshadowed by Michael J. Robinson, "American Political Legitimacy in an Era of Electronic Journalism," in *Television as a Social Force,* ed. Douglass Cater and Richard Adler (New York: Praeger, 1975).

34. Priscilla Southwell, "Voter Turnout in the 1986 Congressional Elections," *American Politics Quarterly* 19 (January 1991): 96–108; Stephen Ansolabehere, Shanto Iyengar, Adam Simon, and Nicholas Valentino, "Does Attack Advertising Demobilize the Electorate?" *American Political Science Review* 88 (December 1994): 829–838.

35. Richard Lau, Lee Sigelman, Caroline Heldman, and Paul Babbitt, "The Effects of Negative Political Advertisements," *American Political Science Review* 93 (December 1999): 851–875; Steven E. Finkel and John Geer, "A Spot Check: Casting Doubt on the Demobilizing Effect of Attack Advertising," *Ameri-*

can Journal of Politics 42 (April 1998): 573–595. Research on turnout is found in Ansolabehere and Iyengar, Going Negative. In her book Packaging the Presidency (New York: Oxford University Press, 1984), Kathleen Jamieson also argues that there are checks on misleading advertising, but later ("Is the Truth Now Irrelevant in Presidential Campaigns?"), she notes that these checks do not always work well. See Jamieson, Dirty Politics: Deception, Distraction and Democracy (New York: Oxford University Press, 1992).

36. Curtis B. Gans, "The Empty Ballot Box," Public Opinion 1 (September/October 1978): 54–57. See also Austin Ranney, Channels of Power (New York: Basic Books, 1983); and Richard Boyd, "The Effect of Election Calendars on Voter Turnout," paper presented at the Annual Meeting of the Midwest Political Science Association, April 1987, Chicago.

37. Boyd, "The Effect of Election Calendars."

38. Ibid.

39. Ruy Teixeira, Why Americans Don't Vote: Turnout Decline in the United States 1960–1984 (Boulder, Colo.: Greenwood, 1987); Teixeira, The Disappearing American Voter (Washington, D.C.: Brookings Institute, 1992); and Peverill Squire, Raymond Wolfinger, and David Glass, "Residential Mobility and Voter Turnout," American Political Science Review 81 (March 1987): 45–66.

40. For a review of these studies, see Bill Winders, "The Roller Coaster of Class Conflict: Class Segments, Mass Mobilization, and Voter Turnout in the U.S., 1840–1996," Social Forces 77 (1999): 833–860.

41. Piven and Cloward, Why Americans Don't Vote, 17.

42. More recent studies of turnout include Richard J. Timpone, "Structure, Behavior and Voter Turnout in the United States," American Political Science Review 92 (March 1998): 145–158; Henry Brady, Sidney Verba, and Kay Lehman Schlozman, "Beyond SES: A Resource Model of Political Participation," American Political Science Review 89 (June 1995): 271–294.

43. See Piven and Cloward, Why Americans Don't Vote, 196–197, for illustrations of these kinds of informal barriers, and Piven and Cloward, Why Americans Still Don't Vote, for further examples.

44. Kim Quaile Hill and Jan E. Leighley, "Racial Diversity, Voter Turnout, and Mobilizing Institutions in the United States," American Politics Quarterly 27 (July 1999): 275–295.

45. Piven and Cloward, Why Americans Still Don't Vote, 245.

46. Raymond Wolfinger and Steven Rosenstone, Who Votes? (New Haven, Conn.: Yale University Press, 1980), Table 6.1.

47. James A. Barnes, "In Person: Marsha Nye Adler," National Journal, February 18, 1989, 420.

48. Piven and Cloward, Why Americans Don't Vote, 230–231.

49. Stephen Knack, "Does 'Motor Voter' Work?" Journal of Politics 57 (August 1995): 796–811.

50. Michael Martinez and David Hill, "Did Motor Voter Work?" American Political Quarterly 27 (July 1999): 296–315; Piven and Cloward, Why Americans Still Don't Vote.

51. Squire et al., "Residential Mobility and Voter Turnout." See also Samuel C. Patterson and Gregory A. Caldeira, "Mailing in the Vote: Correlates and Consequences of Absentee Voting," American Journal of Political Science 29 (November 1985): 766–788.

52. Winders, "The Roller Coaster of Class Conflict."

53. For a review of this literature, see John Petrocik, "Voter Turnout and Electoral Preference," in Elections in America, ed. Kay Schlozman (Boston: Allyn & Unwin, 1987). See also Bernard Grofman, Guillermo Owen, and Christian Collet, "Rethinking the Partisan Effects of Higher Turnout," Public Choice 99 (1999): 357–376.

54. Kim Quaile Hill, Jan Leighley, and Angela Hinton-Anderson, "Lower-Class Mobilization and Policy Linkage in the U.S. States," American Journal of Political Science 39 (February 1995): 75–86.

55. Anthony Downs, An Economic Theory of Democracy (New York: Harper & Row, 1957).

56. Morin, "The Dog Ate My Forms."

57. Kay Lehman Schlozman, Sidney Verba, and Henry Brady, "Participation's Not a Paradox: The View from American Activists," British Journal of Political Science 25 (January 1995): 1–36.

58. Norman H. Nie, Sidney Verba, Henry Brady, Kay Lehman Schlozman, and Jane Junn, "Participation in America." The standard work, though now dated, on American political participation is Sidney Verba and Norman Nie, Participation in America (New York: Harper & Row, 1972).

59. Brady et al., "Beyond SES."

60. Nie et al., "Participation in America"; Verba and Nie, Participation in America.

61. Paul Allen Beck and M. Kent Jennings, "Political Periods and Political Participation," American Political Science Review 73 (1979): 737–750; Nie et al., "Participation in America."

62. The following discussion draws heavily upon John Aldrich, Before the Convention (Chicago: University of Chicago Press, 1980).

63. Ibid. See also David Rohde, "Risk Bearing and Progressive Ambition: The Case of Members of the United States House of Representatives," American Journal of Political Science 23 (February 1979): 1–26.

64. Quoted in Audrey A. Haynes, Paul-Henri Gurian, Stephen M. Nichols, "The Role of Candidate Spending in Presidential Nomination Campaigns," Journal of Politics 59 (February 1997): 213–225.

65. "Political Grapevine," Time (February 8, 1988): 30.

66. Hendrick Hertzberg, "This Must Be the Place," New Yorker (January 31, 2000): 36–39.

67. Ibid., 39.

68. "The Fall Campaign," Newsweek Election Extra (November/December 1984): 88.

69. Bruce Babbitt, "Bruce Babbitt's View from the Wayside," Washington Post National Weekly Edition, February 24–March 6, 1988, 24. The 999 days figure is from the Congressional Quarterly Weekly Report, February 1, 1992, 257.

70. B. Drummond Ayres Jr., "He's Taking Care of Political Business," New York Times, July 18, 1999, 12.

71. Gerald Pomper and Susan Lederman, Elections in America (New York: Longman, 1980), Chapter 7.

72. Lee Sigelman and Paul Wahlbeck, "The Veepstakes: Strategic Choice in Presidential Running Mate Selection," American Political Science Review 94 (December 1997): 855–864.

73. Ibid.

74. Ibid.

75. Robert L. Dudley and Ronald B. Rapaport, "Vice-Presidential Candidates and the Home State Advantage: Playing Second Banana at Home and on the Road," American Journal of Political Science 33 (May 1989): 537–540.

76. "Squall in New Orleans," Newsweek (November 21, 1988): 103.

77. "Conventional Wisdom Watch," Newsweek (November 21, 1988): 18.

78. See Congressional Quarterly, July 23, 1988, 2015; Thomas Holbrook, "Campaigns, National Conventions and U.S. Presidential Elections," American Journal of Political Science 38 (November 1994): 973–998.

79. Benjamin Page and Richard Brody, "Policy Voting and the Electoral Process," American Political Review 66 (1972): 979–995.

80. Thomas F. Patterson, Mass Media Elections (New York: Praeger, 1980), 3.

81. The discussion of the functions of the media relies heavily on the excellent summary found in Stephen Ansolabehere, Roy Behr, and Shanto Iyengar, "Mass Media and Elections," American Politics Quarterly 19 (January 1991): 109–139.

82. Martin Schram, The Great American Video Game: Presidential Politics in the Television Age (New York: Morrow, 1987).

83. Martin Schram, The Great American Video Game: Presidential Politics in the Television Age (New York: Morrow, 1987).

84. Robert McNeil, The Influence of Television on American Politics (New York: Harper & Row, 1968), 182.

85. Elisabeth Bumiller, "Selling Soup, Wine and Reagan," Washington Post National Weekly Edition, November 5, 1984, 6–8.

86. John Theilmann and Allen Wilhite, "Campaign Tactics and the Decision to Attack," Journal of Politics 60 (November, 1998): 1050–1062.

87. Paul Taylor, "Pigsty Politics," Washington Post National Weekly Edition, February 13–19, 1989, 6.

88. Theilmann and Wilhite, "Campaign Tactics and the Decision to Attack."

89. Eileen Shields West, "Give 'Em Hell These Days Is a Figure of Speech," Smithsonian (October 1988): 149–151. The editorial was from the Connecticut Courant.

90. Charles Paul Freund, "But Then, Truth Has Never Been Important," Washington Post National Weekly Edition, November 7–13, 1988, 29.

91. Quoted in Freund, "But Then, Truth Has Never Been Important," 29.

92. Stephen Ansolabehere and Shanto Iyengar, Going Negative (New York: Free Press, 1996).

93. The study of negative advertising research was done by Richard Lau, Lee Sigelman, Caroline Heldman, and Paul Babbitt, "The Effects of Negative Political Advertisements," American Political Science Review 93 (December 1999): 851–875.

94. Ibid.

95. Kathleen Hall Jamieson, Packaging the Presidency (New York: Oxford University Press, 1984).

96. "Some Big Glitches in E-Campaigning," New York Times, November 7, 1999.

97. See Thomas E. Mann, "Elections and Change in Congress," in The New Congress, ed. Thomas Mann and Norman Ornstein (Washington, D.C.: American Enterprise Institute, 1981), 32–54; David Mayhew, The Electoral Connection (New Haven, Conn.: Yale University Press, 1974); Glenn Parker and Roger Davidson, "Why Do Americans Love Their Congressmen So Much?" Legislative Studies Quarterly (February 1979): 53–62.

98. See Paul Feldman and James Jondrow, "Congressional Elections and Local Federal Spending," American Journal of Political Science 28 (1984): 152; Glenn R. Parker and Suzanne Parker, "The Correlates and Effects of Attention to District by U.S. House Members," Legislative Studies Quarterly 10 (1985): 239.

99. Christopher Buckley, "Hangin' with the House-boyz," Washington Monthly (June 1992): 44.

100. Linda L. Fowler, Who Decides to Run for Congress? (New Haven, Conn.: Yale University Press, 1989), 47. Hibbing and Brandes, "State Population." See also Glenn Parker, "Stylistic Change in the U.S. Senate," Journal of Politics 47 (November 1985): 1190–1202.

101. Thomas Mann, Unsafe at Any Margin: Interpreting Congressional Elections (Washington, D.C.: American Enterprise Institute, 1978).

102. "Women, Minorities Join Senate," CQ Almanac (1992): 8A–14A: "Wave of Diversity Spared Many Incumbents," CQ Almanac (1992): 15A–21A, 24A; "The Elections," CQ, November 12, 1994, 3237.

103. Gary Jacobson, The Politics of Congressional Elections, 2d ed. (Boston: Little, Brown, 1987), 51.

104. Ibid.

105. Barbara Hinckley, "The American Voter in Congressional Elections," American Political Science Review 74 (September 1980): 641–650; Hinckley, "House Reelections and Senate Defeats: The Role of the Challenger," British Journal of Political Science 10 (October 1980): 441–460; Mann and Wolfinger, "Candidates and Parties"; Alan I. Abramowitz, "A Comparison of Voting of U.S. Senators and Representatives in 1978," American Political Science Review 74 (September 1980): 633–640.

106. Alford and Hibbing, "The Disparate Electoral Security of House and Senate Incumbents."

107. A good review of these arguments is found in John R. Hibbing and Sara L. Brandes, "State Population and the Electoral Success of U.S. Senators," *American Journal of Political Science* 27 (November 1983): 808–819. See also Eric Uslaner, "The Case of the Vanishing Liberal Senators: The House Did It," *British Journal of Political Science* 11 (January 1981): 105–113; Abramowitz, "A Comparison."

108. Hibbing and Brandes, "State Population." See also Glenn Parker, "Stylistic Change in the U.S. Senate," *Journal of Politics* 47 (November 1985): 1190–1202.

109. Edie Goldenberg and Michael Traugott, *Campaigning for Congress* (Washington, D.C.: CQ Press, 1984); Gary Jacobson and Samuel Kernell, *Strategy and Choice in Congressional Elections,* 2d ed. (New Haven, Conn.: Yale University Press, 1983).

110. Edward Walsh, "Wanted: Candidates for Congress," *Washington Post National Weekly Edition,* November 25, 1985, 9.

111. Ceci Connolly, "GOP Hold on House Hazier," *Washington Post,* June 8, 1998, A1.

112. Alan Ehrenhalt, "Technology, Strategy Bring New Campaign Era," *Congressional Quarterly Weekly Report,* December 7, 1985, 2561; Mann, "Elections and Change in Congress"; Jacobson, *The Politics of Congressional Elections.*

113. Paul Hernson, *Party Campaigning in the 1980s* (Cambridge, Mass.: Harvard University Press, 1988).

114. Stanley Kelley Jr., *Interpreting Elections* (Princeton, N.J.: Princeton University Press, 1983); Stanley Kelley Jr., Richard Ayres, and William G. Bower, "Registration and Voting: Putting First Things First," *American Political Science Review* 61 (June 1967): 359–379.

115. Marjorie Connelly, "Who Voted," *New York Times,* November 12, 2000, 4.

116. These data are from "Portrait of an Electorate," *New York Times,* November 10, 1996, 28. Lee Sigelman, "If You Prick Us, Do We Not Bleed? If You Tickle Us, Do We Not Laugh? Jews and Pocketbook Voting," paper prepared for presentation at the 1990 American Political Science Meeting: Susan Welch and Lee Sigelman, "The Politics of Hispanic Americans," *Social Science Quarterly* (1991); *New York Times,* November 5, 1992, B9.

117. Paul Abramson, John H. Aldrich, and David Rohde, *Change and Continuity in the 1996 Elections,* rev. ed. (Washington, D.C.: CQ Press, 1998), 121.

118. Ibid, 131.

119. Ibid., 135.

120. Ibid.

121. Ibid., 140.

122. Ibid.

123. Morris Fiorina, *Retrospective Voting in American National Elections* (New Haven, Conn.: Yale University Press, 1981).

124. Edward Tufte, *Political Control of the Economy* (Princeton, N.J.: Princeton University Press, 1978); Douglas Hibbs, "The Mass Public and Macroeconomic Performance," *American Journal of Political Science* 23 (November 1979): 705–731; John Hibbing and John Alford, "The Electoral Impact of Economic Conditions: Who Is Held Responsible," *American Journal of Political Science* 25 (1981): 423–439.

125. Robert Kaiser, "Deeply Divided We Stand—And That's No Surprise," *Washington Post National Weekly Edition* (November 20, 2000): 22.

126. See Gerald Wright Jr. and Michael Berkman, "Candidates and Policy in United States Senate Elections," *American Political Science Review* 80 (June 1986): 567–588; Erikson and Wright, "Voters, Candidates, and Issues in Congressional Elections."

127. See James Campbell, "Explaining Presidential Losses in Midterm Elections," *Journal of Politics* 47 (November 1985): 1140–1157. See also Barbara Hinckley, "Interpreting House Midterm Elections," *American Political Science Review* 61 (1967): 694–700;

Samuel Kernell, "Presidential Popularity and Negative Voting," *American Political Science Review* 71 (1977): 44–66; Edward Tufte, "Determinants of the Outcomes of Midterm Congressional Elections," *American Political Science Review* 69 (1975): 812–826; Alan Abramowitz, "Economic Conditions, Presidential Popularity and Voting Behavior in Midterm Elections," *Journal of Politics* 47 (February 1985): 31–43.

128. Benjamin I. Page and Robert Shapiro, "Effects of Public Opinion on Policy," *American Political Science Review* 77 (March 1983): 175–190.

129. Arthur Schlesinger Jr., *Wall Street Journal,* December 5, 1986.

130. Hendrik Hertzberg, "Up for the Count," *New Yorker,* December 18, 2000, 41.

131. Kosuke Imai and Gary King, "Did Illegally Counted Overseas Absentee Ballots Decide the 2000 U.S. Presidential Election?" available at gking.Harvard.edu.

132. Ibid.

133. David Barstow and Don Van Natta, "How Bush Took Florida: Mining the Overseas Absentee Vote," *New York Times,* July 15, 2001, available at www.nytimes.com/2001/07/15/national/15ball.html?pagewanted5all.

134. Ibid.

135. Jonathan Wand, Kenneth Shotts, Jasjeet Sekhon, Walter Mebane, Michael Herron, and Henry Brady, "The Butterfly Did It: The Aberrant Vote for Buchanan in Palm Beach," *American Political Science Review* 95 (December 2001): 793–809. They examined the Palm Beach Buchanan vote in relation to all other counties in the United States, to the absentee ballots (which did not use the butterfly format) in Palm Beach County, precinct-level data, and individual ballots.

136. Fiedler, "The Perfect Storm," 8.

137. Ibid.

138. Ibid., 13.

139. Quotes from National Public Radio, *All Things Considered,* November 13, 2000.

140. Quoted in Fiedler, "The Perfect Storm," 11.

141. Ibid., 11.

Chapter 9

1. www.senate.gov/,schumer/; and Michael Barone with Richard Cohen and Grant Ujifusa, *The Almanac of American Politics 2002* (Washington D.C.: National Journal, 2001), 1038.

2. Barone et al., *The Almanac of American Politics 2002,* 1038.

3. Kenneth Jost, "Accountants under Fire," *CQ Researcher* (March 22, 2002): 255.

4. Richard Dunham, "The Vindication of Arthur Levitt," *Business WeekOnline,* February 18, 2002.

5. Jost, "Accountants under Fire," 255.

6. Daniel J. Parks, "Fuzzy Battle Lines Complicate Effort to Overhaul Financial Services," *Congressional Quarterly Weekly,* February 27, 1999, 491.

7. Jimmy Breslin, *How the Good Guys Finally Won: Notes from an Impeachment Summer* (New York: Ballantine, 1974), 14.

8. Robert E. Mutch, "Three Centuries of Campaign Finance Law," in *A User's Guide to Campaign Finance Reform,* ed. Gerald C. Lubenow (New York: Rowman & Littlefield, 2001).

9. Congressional Quarterly, *Dollar Politics,* 3d ed. (Washington, D.C.: CQ Press, 1982), 3.

10. Ibid.

11. James Madison, *Federalist 10.*

12. Haynes Johnson, "Turning Government Jobs into Gold," *Washington Post National Weekly Edition,* May 12, 1986, 6–7.

13. Quoted in Richard Hofstadter, *The American Political Tradition* (New York: Vintage, 1958), 165.

14. Congressional Quarterly, *Dollar Politics,* 3.

15. Larry J. Sabato, *Feeding Frenzy* (New York: Free Press, 1991).

16. Elizabeth Drew, *Politics and Money* (New York: Collier, 1983), 9.

17. *Buckley v. Valeo,* 424 U.S. 1 (1976).

18. Federal Election Commission, reported in Harold Stanley and Richard Niemi, *Vital Statistics in American Politics, 2001–2002* (Washington, D.C.: CQ Press, 2001), Table 2–4.

19. See Larry Sabato and Glenn Simpson, *Dirty Little Secrets: The Persistence of Corruption in American Politics* (New York: Times Books, 1996); Marick Masters and Gerald Keim, "Determinants of PAC Participation among Large Corporations," *Journal of Politics* 47 (November 1985): 1158–1173; J. David Gopoian, "What Makes PACs Tick?" *American Journal of Political Science* 28 (May 1984): 259–281.

20. *Federal Election Commission v. National Conservative PAC,* 470 U.S. 480 (1985).

21. Ruth Marcus, "Taking Issue with Advocacy," *Washington Post National Weekly Edition,* April 15–21, 1996, 13.

22. David Broder, "Both Major Parties Abuse Soft Money Loophole," *Centre Daily Times,* May 30, 2000, 6A.

23. Ibid.

24. Ruth Marcus, "Off the Ballot but in the Contest," *Washington Post National Weekly Edition,* July 6, 1998, 13.

25. Alison Mitchell, "Time Passes, Money Flows," *New York Times,* June 16, 1996, E5.

26. Mike Allen, "Does an Embassy Trump the Lincoln Bedroom?" *Washington Post National Weekly Edition,* May 7–13, 2001, 14.

27. Mike Allen, "The Mother of All Fundraisers," *Washington Post National Weekly Edition,* May 20–26, 2002, 13.

28. Alan C. Miller, "Diaper Donors: Study Shows Children Giving to Candidates," *Lincoln Journal-Star,* February 28, 1999; David Rosenbaum, "Soft Money and Some Not-So-Hard Promises," *New York Times,* April 11, 1999, 19.

29. Drew, *Politics and Money,* 68; Thomas B. Edsall, "More Than Enough Is Not Enough," *Washington Post National Weekly Edition,* February 9, 1987, 13. See also Edward Handler and John Mulkern, *Business in Politics* (Lexington, Mass.: Heath, 1982), 1–34.

30. Nancy Gibbs and Karen Tumulty, "A New Day Dawning," *Time* (April 9, 2001): 50.

31. "Stop Opening Loopholes," *Washington Post,* June 22, 2002, A18.

32. Thomas B. Edsall, "Leaders of the PAC," *Washington Post National Weekly Edition,* April 15–21, 2002, 12.

33. Paul Taylor, "TV's Political Profits," *Mother Jones* (May/June 2000): 32.

34. David S. Broder, "Where the Money Goes," *Washington Post National Weekly Edition,* March 26–April 1, 2001, 4.

35. Jeff Leeds, "TV Stations Balk at Free Air Time for Candidates," *Lincoln Journal-Star,* May 14, 2000, 3A.

36. Ibid.

37. Ibid.

38. *Statistical Abstract of the United States 2001,* Table 406.

39. Michael Weisskopf, "To the Victors Belong the PAC Checks," *Washington Post National Weekly Edition,* January 2–5, 1995, 13. The remainder of the paragraph is also drawn from this source.

40. *Statistical Abstract of the United States 2001,* Table 411.

41. See Kevin Grier and Michael Mangy, "Comparing Interest Group PAC Contributions to House and Senate Incumbents," *Journal of Politics* 55 (August 1993): 615–643.

42. J. David Gopoian, "Change and Continuity in Defense PAC Behavior," *American Politics Quarterly* 13 (July 1985): 297–322; Richard Morin and Charles Babcock, "Off Year, Schmoff Year," *Washington Post National Weekly Edition,* May 14–20, 1990, 15.

43. Thomas Romer and James M. Snyder, "An Empirical Investigation of the Dynamics of PAC Con-

tributions," *American Journal of Political Science* 38 (August 1994): 745–769.

44. Gary Wasserman, "The Uses of Influence," *Washington Post National Weekly Edition,* January 11–17, 1993, 35.

45. Larry Makinson and Joshua Goldstein, *Open Secrets: The Cash Constituents of Congress,* 2d ed. (Washington, D.C.: Congressional Quarterly, 1994), 23.

46. Amy Dockser, "Nice PAC You've Got There . . . A Pity If Anything Should Happen to It," *Washington Monthly* (January 1984): 21.

47. Juliet Eilperin, " 'The Hammer' De Lay Whips Lobbyists into Shape," *Washington Post National Weekly Edition,* October 25–31, 1999, 8.

48. Jeff Leeds, "TV Stations Balk at Free Air Time for Candidates," *Lincoln Journal-Star,* May 14, 2000, 3A; Paul Taylor, "TV's Political Profits," *Mother Jones* (May/June 2000): 31–33.

49. Meg Greenfield, "The Political Debt Bomb," *Newsweek* (April 1987): 76.

50. Quoted in the *New York Times,* June 13, 1998, A7.

51. "Numbers," *Time* (February 28, 2000): 27.

52. Gary Jacobson, *Money in Congressional Elections* (New Haven, Conn.: Yale University Press, 1980), 61.

53. David Broder, "The High Road to Lower Finance?" *Washington Post National Weekly Edition,* June 29, 1987, 4; Diane Granat, "Parties' Schools for Politicians or Grooming Troops for Election," *Congressional Quarterly Weekly Report,* May 5, 1984, 1036.

54. Diana C. Mutz, "Effects of Horse-Race Coverage on Campaign Coffers: Strategic Contributing in Presidential Primaries," *Journal of Politics* 57 (November 1995): 1015–1042.

55. Audrey A. Haynes, Paul-Henri Gurian, and Stephen M. Nichols, "The Role of Candidate Spending in Presidential Nomination Campaigns," *Journal of Politics* 59 (February 1997): 213–225; see 220. See also Gary Orren, "The Nomination Process," in *The Elections of 1984,* ed. Michael Nelson (Washington, D.C.: CQ Press, 1986), Chapter 2; Wayne Parent, Calvin Jillson, and Ronald E. Weber, "Voting Outcomes in the 1984 Democratic Primaries and Caucuses," *American Political Science Review* 81 (1987): 67–84.

56. Haynes et al., "The Role of Candidate Spending," 223.

57. Nelson Polsby and Aaron Wildavsky, *Presidential Elections* (New York: Scribner's, 1984), 56.

58. David Nice, "Campaign Spending and Presidential Election Results," *Polity* 19 (spring 1987): 464–476, shows that presidential campaign spending is more productive for Republicans than Democrats.

59. John Alford and David Brady, "Person and Partisan Advantages in U.S. Congressional Elections, 1846–1990," in *Congress Reconsidered,* ed. Larry Dodd and Bruce Oppenheimer, 5th ed. (Washington, D.C.: Congressional Quarterly, 1993).

60. David Epstein and Peter Zemsky, "Money Talks: Deterring Quality Challengers in Congressional Elections," *American Political Science Review* 89 (June 1995): 295–308.

61. Robert S. Erickson and Thomas R. Palfrey, "Campaign Spending and Incumbency: An Alternative Simultaneous Equations Approach," *Journal of Politics* 60 (May 1998): 355–373; Alan Gerber, "Estimating the Effect of Campaign Spending on Senate Election Outcomes Using Instrumental Variables," *American Political Science Review* 92 (June 1998): 401–411.

62. Gary Jacobson, *Money in Congressional Elections;* Jacobson, "The Effects of Campaign Spending in House Elections," *American Journal of Political Science* 34 (May 1990): 334–362; Christopher Kenny and Michael McBurnett, "A Dynamic Model of the Effect of Campaign Spending on Congressional Vote Choice," *American Journal of Political Science* 36 (November 1992): 923–937; Donald Green and Jonathan Krasno, "Salvation for the Spendthrift Incumbent," *American Journal of Political Science* 32 (November 1988): 884–907; Jacobson, *The Politics of Congressional Elections,* 2d ed. (Boston: Little,

Brown, 1987), Chapter 4; Stephen Ansolabehere and Alan Gerber, "The Mismeasure of Campaign Spending," *Journal of Politics* 56 (November, 1994): 1106–1118; Gerber, "Estimating the Effect of Campaign Spending."

63. Leslie Wayne, "If No Guarantee of Victory, Money Sure Makes It Easier," *New York Times,* November 6, 1998, A23.

64. Data on these Senate races are from the National Election Commission's *Campaign Finance Reports and Data* found on the commission's Web pages: www.fec.gov/finance_reports.html.

65. "Scandal Shocks Even Those Who Helped It Along," *New York Times,* February 3, 2002, 7.

66. The survey of donors is reported in Bob Hebert, "The Donor Class," *New York Times,* July 19, 1998, 15; Woodrow Jones and K. Robert Keiser, "Issue Visibility and the Effects of PAC Money," *Social Science Quarterly* 68 (March 1987): 170–176; Janet Grenzke, "PACs and the Congressional Supermarket," *American Journal of Political Science* 33 (February 1989): 1–24, found little effect of PAC money on a series of votes that were not obscure. Laura Langbein, "Money and Access," *Journal of Politics* 48 (November 1986): 1052–1064, shows that those who received more PAC money spend more time with interest group representatives.

67. Jean Reith Schroedel, "Campaign Contributions and Legislative Outcomes," *Western Political Quarterly* 39 (September 1986): 371–389; Richard L. Hall and Frank Wayman, "Buying Time: Moneyed Interests and the Mobilization of Bias in Congressional Committees," *American Political Science Review* 84 (September 1990): 797–820.

68. "Running with the PACs," *Time* (October 25, 1982): 20. The quotation is from Representative Thomas Downey (D-N.Y.).

69. "Congress Study Links Funds and Votes," *New York Times,* December 30, 1987, 7.

70. John Frendreis and Richard Waterman, "PAC Contributions and Legislative Behavior: Senate Voting on Trucking Deregulation," *Social Science Quarterly* 66 (June 1985): 401–412. See also W. P. Welch, "Campaign Contributions and Legislative Voting," *Western Political Quarterly* 25 (December 1982): 478–495; Jonathan Silberman and Garey Durden, "Determining Legislative Preferences on the Minimum Wage," *Journal of Political Economy* 84 (April 1976): 317–329.

71. Diana Evans, "Policy and Pork: The Use of Pork Barrel Projects to Build Policy Coalitions in the House of Representatives," *American Journal of Political Science* 38 (November 1994): 894–917; Laura Langbein, "PACs, Lobbies and Political Conflict: The Case of Gun Control," *Public Choice* 75 (1993): 254–271; Laura Langbein and Mark Lotwis, "The Political Efficacy of Lobbying and Money: Gun Control in the House, 1986," *Legislative Studies Quarterly* 15 (1990): 413–440; Jean Schroedel, "Campaign Contributions and Legislative Outcomes," *Western Political Quarterly* 39 (1986): 371–389.

72. Adam Clymer, " '84 PACs Gave More to Senate Winners," *New York Times,* January 6, 1985, 13.

73. Kirk Brown, "Campaign Contributions and Congressional Voting," paper prepared for the annual meeting of the American Political Science Association, 1983, cited in Malbin, *Money and Politics,* 134.

74. Drew, *Politics and Money,* 79.

75. See Grenzke, "PACs and the Congressional Supermarket"; also see Frank Sorauf, *Money in American Elections* (Glenview, Ill.: Scott, Foresman, 1988).

76. Janet Grenzke, "Political Action Committees and the Congressional Supermarket"; John Wright, "Contributions, Lobbying and Committee Voting in the US House of Representatives," *American Political Science Review* 84 (1990): 417–438; Henry Chappel Jr., "Campaign Contributions and Voting on the Cargo Preference Bill," *Public Choice* 36, no. 2 (1981): 301–312.

77. Jasper Shannon, *Money and Politics* (New York: Random House, 1959).

78. "How to Be a Top Banana," *Time* (February 7, 2000) 42*ff.*

79. "Study: Bush Donors Get Government Favors," *Lincoln Journal-Star,* May 28, 1992.

80. "Clinton Regrets Rich Pardon," CBSNEWS. com/stories/2002/03/31/politics/main505042. shtml; "Rich's '$450,000' for Clinton Library," news.bbc.co.uk/hi/English/world/Americas/ newid_1163000/1163917.stm. George H. Bush's last-minute pardon of a convicted $1.5 million heroin trafficker got much less publicity ("George Bush's Heroin Connection," www.gwbush.com/ pressrollstone.htm).

81. Charles Lewis quoted in "Book Details Candidates' Extensive Financial Alignments," *Lincoln Journal-Star,* January 12, 1996, 5A.

82. Tom Kenworthy, "The Color of Money," *Washington Post National Weekly Edition,* November 6–12, 1989, 13.

83. Susan Welch and John Peters, "Private Interests in the U.S. Congress," *Legislative Studies Quarterly* 7 (November 1982): 547–555. See also John Peters and Susan Welch, "Private Interests and Public Interests," *Journal of Politics* 45 (May 1983): 378–396.

84. "Having It All, Then Throwing It Away," *Time* (May 25, 1987): 22.

85. Elizabeth Drew, "Letter from Washington," *New Yorker* (May 1, 1989): 99–108; see also Dan Balz, "Tales of Power and Money," *Washington Post National Weekly Edition,* May 1–7, 1989, 11–12.

86. "Having It All, Then Throwing It Away," 22.

87. Hank Paulson, the CEO of Goldman Sachs, quoted in Joseph Nocera, "System Failure," *Fortune* (June 24, 2002).

88. Keith Bradsher, "How to Pooh-Pooh $70 Million War Chests," *New York Times,* April 30, 2000, 6.

89. Richard Stevenson and Jeff Gerth, "Web of Safeguards Failed as Enron Fell," *New York Times,* January 20, 2002, 1.

90. Paul Krugman, "A System Corrupted," *New York Times,* February 18, 2002, A25.

91. Ibid.

92. Jonathan Alter, "Which Boot Will Drop Next?" *Newsweek* (February 4, 2002): 25.

93. "Enron and Other 'Bumps,' " *Washington Post,* June 23, 2002, B6.

94. "An 'Accounting Opportunity,' " *Washington Post,* June 18, 2002, A18; "System Failure."

95. Michael Kinsley, "Blame the Accountants for Crooked Companies," *Lincoln Journal-Star,* June 4, 2002, 4B; Molly Ivins, "A Story That's Been Neglected Too Long," *Centre Daily Times,* June 12, 2002, A8.

96. Alter, "Which Boot Will Drop Next?" 25.

97. Paul Krugman, "Fool Me Once," *New York Times,* October 8, 2002, online at www.nytimes.com/ 2002/10/08/opinion/08krug.html.

Chapter 10

1. Biographical material on Snowe from "Olympia I. Snowe," *Congressional Quarterly,* October 30, 1999. In Special edition, "Fifty Ways to Run Congress, 58–59; Michael Barone, Richard E. Cohen, and Charles E. Cook Jr., *Almanac of American Politics 2002* (Washington D.C.: National Journal, 2002), 692–693.

2. "Olympia I. Snowe," 59.

3. Ibid.

4. Dan Carney, "Impeachment's Long Shadow," *Congressional Quarterly Weekly Review,* January 2, 1999, 10.

5. James R. Chiles, "Congress Couldn't Have Been This Bad, or Could It?" *Smithsonian* (November 1995): 70–80.

6. Ibid. Per diem and travel allowances for the first members were verified in 2002 when Senate custodial staff found a ledger with payment accounts.

7. David Broder, "Dumbing Down Democracy," *Lincoln Journal-Star,* April 5, 1995, 18.

8. Quoted in Kenneth J. Cooper and Helen Dewar, "No Limits on the Term Limits Crusade," *Washington Post National Weekly Edition,* May 29–June 4, 1995, 14.

9. Brad Cain, "Oregon Lawmakers Take Aim at Term Limit Restrictions," *Champaign-Urbana News-Gazette,* April 1, 2000, B1.

10. Richard Pérez-Peña, "Lawyers Abandon Legislatures for Greener Pastures," *New York Times,* February 2, 1999, Section 4, 3.

11. Jim Abrams, "The Son Also Runs," *Champaign-Urbana News-Gazette,* November 7, 1999, B1.

12. Daniel Gross, "Trends Giving Rise to American Aristocracy," *Lincoln Journal-Star,* February 25, 2001.

13. "Congress of Relative Newcomers Poses Challenge to Bush, Leadership," *Congressional Quarterly Weekly Review,* January 20, 2001, 179–181.

14. "$100,000 Pension Set for Some Lawmakers," *Champaign-Urbana News-Gazette,* December 31, 1997, C–8.

15. Robert Erikson and Gerald Wright Jr., "Policy Representation of Constituency Interests," *Political Behavior* 2 (1980): 91–106; Erikson and Wright, "Voters, Candidates, and Issues in Congressional Elections," in *Congress Reconsidered,* 3d ed., ed. Lawrence Dodd and Bruce Oppenheimer (Washington, D.C.: CQ Press); Wright, "Policy Voting in the U.S. Senate: Who Is Represented?" *Legislative Studies Quarterly* 14 (November 1989): 465–486.

16. Wright, "Policy Voting in the U.S. Senate."

17. 369 U.S. 186 (1962).

18. *Wesberry v. Sanders,* 376 U.S. 1 (1964).

19. Bruce Cain and Janet Campagna, "Predicting Partisan Redistricting Disputes," *Legislative Studies Quarterly* 12 (1987): 265–274.

20. See the report on *Miller v. Johnson,* 515 U.S. 900 (1995), in *New York Times,* July 2, 1995, E1, E4.

21. Steven A. Holmes, "Did Racial Redistricting Undermine Democrats?" *New York Times,* November 13, 1994, 32.

22. These figures from a July 13, 2001, Census Bureau press release. For reports on all aspects of data collection in the 2000 Census, go to the Census Bureau Web site at www.census.gov/.

23. Bob Beneson, Gregory L. Giroux, and Jonathan Allen, "Safe House: Incumbents Face Worry-Free Election," *Congressional Quarterly Weekly Review,* May 18, 2002, 1274.

24. Roger H. Davidson and Walter J. Olezsak, *Congress and Its Members,* 7th ed. (Washington, D.C.: CQ Press, 2000), 114.

25. John Alford and John Hibbing, "The Disparate Electoral Security of House and Senate Incumbents," paper presented at the American Political Science meetings, Atlanta, September 1989.

26. Richard Fenno, *Home Style* (Boston: Little, Brown, 1978).

27. *CQ Daily Monitor,* August 23, 2002. Availale at www.CQ.com. For a brief history of the franking privilege, see *Congress from A to Z* (Washington, D.C.: Congressional Quarterly, 1999), 171–173.

28. "House Members Ready to Boost Office Funds," *Champaign-Urbana News-Gazette,* June 4, 1999, C–11.

29. Tim Miller, "Frankly Free Mail Seems to Help Incumbents," *Washington Post National Weekly Edition,* August 8, 1985, 13–14. For an investigation of the impact of franked mail, see Albert Cover, "The Electoral Impact of Franked Congressional Mail," *Polity* 17 (summer 1985): 649–663.

30. Miller, "Frankly Free Mail Seems to Help Incumbents." See Glenn Parker, "Sources of Change in Congressional District Attentiveness," *American Journal of Political Science* (February 1980): 115–124.

31. Carol Matlack, "Live from Capitol Hill," *National Journal,* February 18, 1989, 390.

32. *Setting Course: A Congressional Management Guide* (Washington, D.C.: American University Congressional Management Program, 1984); Norman Ornstein, Thomas E. Mann, and Michael Malbin, *Vital Statistics on Congress, 1991–1992* (Washington, D.C.: American Enterprise Institute, 1992), 161.

33. See C-SPAN's Web site on Congress: www.c-span.org/congress/.

34. Norman J. Ornstein, Thomas E. Mann, and Michael J. Malbin, *Vital Statistics on Congress, 1997–1998* (Washington D.C.: Congressional Quarterly, 1998), 129.

35. Morris Fiorina, "Congressional Control of the Bureaucracy: A Mismatch of Incentives and Capabilities," in *Congress Reconsidered,* 2d ed., ed. Lawrence C. Dodd and Bruce I. Oppenheimer (Washington, D.C.: CQ Press, 1981), 341.

36. Morris Fiorina, *Congress: Keystone of the Washington Establishment* (New Haven, Conn.: Yale University Press, 1977), especially 48–49.

37. Robert Sherill, "Squealing on Porcine Politics," *Washington Post National Weekly Edition,* September 7–12, 1992, 35; the quote is by Alan Schick from Brian Kelly, "Pigging Out at the White House," *Washington Post National Weekly Edition,* September 14–20, 1992, 23.

38. Jeffrey Brainard and Ron Southwick, "A Record Year at the Federal Trough: Colleges Feast on $1.67 Billion in Earmarks," *Chronicle of Higher Education,* August 10, 2001, A20.

39. "Introduction," in *The 2002 Pig Book* (http://cagw.org). This is a Web site maintained by the public interest group Citizens against Government Waste. It contains an archive of Pig Books, a state ranking of pork per capita, and a list of the "oinker of the month" and other pork award winners in Congress. Also see Deroy Murdock, "An Unchecked Appetite for Pork," *Champaign-Urbana News-Gazette,* October 7, 2001, B1.

40. Quoted in Kenneth Shepsle, "The Failures of Congressional Budgeting," *Social Science and Modern Society* 20 (1983): 4–10. See also Howard Kurtz, "Pork Barrel Politics," *Washington Post,* January 25, 1982. Reported in Randall Ripley, *Congress,* 3d ed. (New York: Norton, 1983).

41. Herbert Asher, "Learning of Legislative Norms," *American Political Science Review* 67 (June 1973): 499–513. Michael Berkman points out that those freshmen who have had state legislative experience—now more than half of all House members—adapt to the job faster than other members. See "Former State Legislators in the U.S. House of Representatives: Institutional and Policy Mastery," *Legislative Studies Quarterly* 18 (February 1993): 77–104.

42. Minot (N.D.) *Daily News,* June 17, 1976. Quoted in Ripley, *Congress.*

43. Samuel Kernell, *Going Public* (Washington, D.C.: CQ Press, 1986).

44. Viewer statistics are available at C-SPAN's Web site (www.c-span.org). These are from July 2002.

45. Katharine Q. Seelye, "Gingrich Used TV Skills to Be King of the Hill," *New York Times,* December 14, 1994, A14.

46. Diane Duston, "They're Angry, Conservative, and They're Dialing Right Now," *Centre Daily Times* (State College, Pa.), July 16, 1993, 1. The study was done by the Times-Mirror Center for the People and the Press.

47. Adriel Bettelheim, "Votes Belie Partisan Intensity," *Congressional Quarterly Weekly Review,* January 6, 2001, 56.

48. Ibid.

49. Derek Wills, "Pattern of Partisanship Persists," *Congressional Quarterly Weekly Review,* January 12, 2002, 114.

50. Richard Fenno, "U.S. House Members and Their Constituencies: An Exploration," *American Political Science Review* 71 (1977): 883–917; and Fenno, *Home Style.*

51. Benjamin Page et al., "Constituency, Party and Representation in Congress," *Public Opinion Quarterly* 48 (winter 1984): 741–756; Jerrold E. Schneider, *Ideological Coalitions in Congress* (Westport, Conn.: Greenwood, 1979).

52. Mark Hankerson, "Participation Hits Record," *Congressional Quarterly Weekly Review,* December 11, 1999, 2979.

53. John Kingdon, *Congressmen's Voting Decisions* (New York: Harper & Row, 1973).

54. Congressional Quarterly, *The Origins and Development of Congress* (Washington, D.C.: CQ Press, 1976).

55. Neil McNeil, *Forge of Democracy* (New York: McKay, 1963), 306–309.

56. Mark Hankerson, "Participation Hits Record," 2979.

57. Jackie Koszczuk, "Master of the Mechanics Has Kept the House Running," *Congressional Quarterly Weekly Review,* December 11, 1999, 2963.

58. Michael Barone, Richard E. Cohen, and Charles E. Cook Jr., *Almanac of American Politics 2002* (Washington D.C.: National Journal, 2002), 46.

59. Ibid.

60. For a review of all congressional committees and subcommittees, see the *Congressional Quarterly* special edition *CQ Guide to the Committees,* March 16, 2002.

61. Davidson and Oleszek, *Congress and Its Members,* 198.

62. See Roger Davidson, "Subcommittee Government," in Mann and Ornstein, *The New Congress,* 110–111. Some of this occurs because members of Congress tend to be wealthy, and the wealthy make investments in corporations. It also occurs because members' financial interests are often similar to the interests in their districts (for example, representatives of farm districts are likely to be involved in farming or agribusiness).

63. Alan Ehrenhalt, "Media, Power Shifts to Dominate O'Neill's House," *Congressional Quarterly Weekly Review,* September 13, 1986, 2131–2136; Stephen Hess, "Live from Capitol Hill, It's," *Washington Monthly* (June 1986): 41–43. The Biden quotation is from this article. See also Steven Smith and Christopher Deering, *Committees in Congress* (Washington, D.C.: CQ Press, 1984), 67.

64. Eric Planin, "David Obey Appropriates a New Fiefdom," *Washington Post National Weekly Edition,* May 9–15, 1994, 11.

65. John Hibbing and Sara Brandes-Crook, "Congressional Reform and Party Discipline: The Effects of Changes in the Seniority System on Party Loyalty in the U.S. House of Representatives," *British Journal of Political Science* 15 (April 1985).

66. Richard E. Cohen, "Hastert's Hidden Hand," *National Journal,* January 20, 2001, 174.

67. *Congress from A to Z,* 378.

68. *Congress and Its Members,* 204.

69. Richard E. Cohen, "Best Seats in the House," *National Journal,* March 4, 2000, 682; Karen Foerstel, "House Offers Mixed Reviews for Committee Term Limits," *Congressional Quarterly Weekly Review,* June 22, 2002, 1653–1655.

70. For a review of how the task force has been used, see Walter Oleszek, "The Use of Task Forces in the House" (CRS Report for Congress, # 96-843 GOV, 1996). The text can be found at www.house.gov/rules/96-843.htm.

71. John Fairhall, quoting Thomas Downey (D-N.Y.), "Bureaucratic Bloat Crippling Congress," *Lincoln Journal-Star,* June 7, 1992, 7B.

72. *Analytical Perspective: Budget of the United States Government Fiscal Year 2003* (Washington, D.C.: Government Printing Office, 2002), 497–505.

73. Michael J. Malbin, "Delegation, Deliberation, and the New Role of Congressional Staff," in Mann and Ornstein, *The New Congress,* 135.

74. Ibid.; *Congress A to Z,* 416.

75. Jeffrey Biggs, "Political Knowledge: Confessions of a Staffer," *Civilization* (April/May 2000): 65. The author was an assistant to former House Speaker Tom Foley.

76. Ibid.

77. Alan Ehrenhalt, "In the Senate of the '80s, Team Spirit Has Given Way to the Rule of Individuals," *Congressional Quarterly Weekly Review,* September 4, 1982, 2175.

78. Ronald Moe and Steven Teel, "Congress as a Policy-Maker: A Necessary Reappraisal," *Political Science Quarterly* 85 (September 1970): 443–470.

79. Bruce Oppenheimer, "The Rules Committee," in *Congress Reconsidered,* ed. Lawrence Dodd and Bruce Oppenheimer (New York: Praeger, 1977), 96–116.

80. Thomas Geoghegan, "Bust the Filibuster," *Washington Post National Weekly Edition,* July 12–18, 1994, 25.

81. Quoted in Sarah A. Binder and Steven S. Smith, "The Politics and Principle of the Senate Filibuster," in *Extensions* (Norman: University of Oklahoma, Carl A. Albert Center, Fall 1997), 15–16.

82. Michael Malbin, "Leading a Filibustered Senate," in *Extensions* (Norman: University of Oklahoma, Carl A. Albert Center, Spring 1985), 3.

83. Richard E. Cohen, "The Third House Rises," *National Journal,* July 28, 2001, 2395, quoting Clinton aide Chuck Brain.

84. David J. Vogler, *The Third House: Conference Committees in the United States Congress* (Evanston, Ill.: Northwestern University Press, 1971); see also Lawrence D. Longley and Walter J. Oleszek, *Bicameral Politics* (New Haven, Conn.: Yale University Press, 1989).

85. Morris Ogul, "Congressional Oversight: Structures and Incentives," in *Congress Reconsidered;* see also Loch Johnson, "The U.S. Congress and the CIA: Monitoring the Dark Side of Government," *Legislative Studies Quarterly* 5 (November 1980): 477–501.

86. Joseph Califano, "Imperial Congress," *New York Times Magazine,* January 23, 1994, 41.

87. *Congress and Its Members,* 365.

88. D. Roderick Kiewiet and Matthew McCubbins, "Congressional Appropriations and the Electoral Connection," *Journal of Politics* 47 (February 1985): 59–82.

89. John Hibbing, "The Liberal Hour: Electoral Pressures and Transfer Payment Voting in the United States Congress," *Journal of Politics* 46 (August 1984): 846–865.

90. Michael Wines, "Washington Really Is in Touch. We're the Problem," *New York Times,* October 16, 1994, Section 4, 2.

91. Richard Fenno, "U.S. House Members and Their Constituencies: An Exploration," *American Political Science Review* 71 (September 1977): 883–917.

92. Ibid.

93. CNN/Gallup/*USA Today* poll, May 2002. Poll data are available at the *National Journal*'s "Poll Track" the Western Hemisphere link (www.nationaljournal.com/).

94. "Poll Track," *National Journal,* January 5, 2002, 58.

95. The information in this paragraph comes from Karen Foerstel, "Grass Greener after Congress," *Congressional Quarterly Weekly Review,* March 11, 2000, 515–519.

96. This paragraph is drawn from Jeffrey L. Katz, "Exit Strategies Divide Senate," *Congressional Quarterly Weekly Review,* January 30, 1999, 249.

97. Ibid.

98. Ibid.

99. Carroll J. Doherty, "Senate Acquits Clinton," *Congressional Quarterly Weekly Review,* February 13, 1999, 363.

100. Carroll J. Doherty, "Senate Acquits Clinton," *Congressional Quarterly Weekly Review,* February 13, 1999, 361–362.

101. Barone et al., *Almanac of American Politics 2002,* 693.

Chapter 11

1. This section is based on information at Congresswoman Jane Harman's Web site, which can be linked through www.loc.gov/thomas, as well as in Michael Barone, Richard E. Cohen, with Charles E. Cook Jr., *The Almanac of American Politics 2002* (Washington, D.C.: National Journal, 2001), 254–256; Chuck McCutcheon, "Defining Homeland Security," *Congressional Quarterly Weekly Review,* September 29, 2001, 2252–2254; Thomas E. Ricks, "A Mega-Department Proposal," *Washington Post National Weekly Edition,* June 10–16, 2002, 11; Bob Williams and David Nather, "Homeland Security Debate: Balancing Swift and Sure," *Congressional Quarterly Weekly Review,* June 22, 2002, 1642–1650; Alexander Simendinger, Sydney J. Freedberg Jr., and Siobhan Gorman, "Bush's Homeland Gambit" and "The Experiment Begins," *National Journal,* June 15, 2002, 1766–1769, and 1775–1787.

2. Jane Harman, "Securing American Homeland Requires a Strategy," *The Hill,* June 4, 2002. This is an op-ed piece posted at the Congresswoman's Web site.

3. Gebe Martínez, "GOP Pick: An Armey of One," *Congressional Quarterly Weekly Review,* June 22, 2002, 1650.

4. Williams and Nather, "Homeland Security Debate," 1643.

5. Woodrow Wilson, *Congressional Government: A Study in American Politics* (New Brunswick, N.J.: Transaction, 2002).

6. Theodore J. Lowi, *The Personal President* (Ithaca, N.Y.: Cornell University Press, 1985).

7. Arthur M. Schlesinger Jr., *The Imperial Presidency* (Boston: Houghton Mifflin, 1973).

8. Harold M. Barger, *The Impossible Presidency* (Glenview, Ill.: Scott Foresman, 1984).

9. Richard Morin, "A Pollster's Worst Nightmare: Declining Response Rates," *Washington Post National Weekly Edition,* July 5–11, 1993, 37; John Hibbing and Elizabeth Theiss-Morse, *Congress as Public Enemy* (Cambridge: Cambridge University Press, 1995).

10. Jefferson's management of the presidency is described in Joseph J. Ellis, *American Sphinx: The Character of Thomas Jefferson* (New York: Knopf, 1997), 186–228.

11. David Stout, "Presidential Candidates Seem Indifferent to a Salary Rise," *New York Times,* May 30, 1999, 16; Daniel J. Parks, "Prospective Presidential Pay Raise, First in 30 Years, Would Also Ease Other Officials' Salary 'Compression,' " *Congressional Quarterly Weekly Review,* May 29, 1999, 1264.

12. "Datafile," *Congressional Quarterly Weekly Review,* February 2, 2001, 256.

13. Quoted in Allen Cowell, "Impeachment: What a Royal Pain," *New York Times,* February 7, 1999, Section 4, 5.

14. "George Mason: Forgotten Founder," *Smithsonian* (May 2000): 145.

15. The full text of Starr's report to Congress appeared in the *New York Times,* September 12, 1998, B1–B18. The transcript of Clinton's grand jury testimony was reprinted in the *New York Times,* September 22, 1998, B1–B8. You can review impeachment documents, hear sound bites from trial testimony, and look at the principal participants at www.pbs.org/newshour/impeachment.

16. *The Presidency A to Z: A Ready Reference Encyclopedia* (Washington, D.C.: Congressional Quarterly, 1992), 12.

17. For discussion of the president's removal powers in light of a 1988 Supreme Court decision regarding independent counsels, see John A. Rohr, "Public Administration, Executive Power, and Constitutional Confusion," and Rosemary O'Leary, "Response to John Rohr," *Public Administrative Review* 49 (March/April 1989): 108–115.

18. Charles O. Jones, *The Presidency in a Separated System* (Washington, D.C.: Brookings Institution, 1994), 53.

19. Alexander Simendinger, Sydney J. Freedberg Jr., and Siobhan Gorman, "The Experiment Begins," *National Journal,* June 15, 2002, 1775–1787.

20. *The Presidency A to Z,* 169.

21. The Bush White House provides a link to all executive orders issued by the president at the White House home page (www.whitehouse.gov/).

22. *The Presidency A to Z,* 170.

23. Marc Lacey, "Resurrecting Ghosts of Pardons Past," *New York Times,* March 4, 2001, 21.

24. *United States v. Curtiss-Wright Export Corporation,* 299 U.S. 304 (1936).

25. See the discussion in *Federalist Paper* 69, written by Alexander Hamilton.

26. Quoted in "Notes and Comment," *New Yorker* (June 1, 1987): 23.

27. Ibid.

28. John Barry, "What Schwarzkopf's Book Leaves Out," *Newsweek* (September 28, 1992): 68.

29. *Youngstown Sheet and Tube Co. v. Sawyer,* 343 U.S. 579 (1952).

30. Thomas F. Cronin, *The State of the Presidency* (Boston: Little, Brown, 1975), 118.

31. The source of the anger was Roosevelt's court-packing scheme; see Chapter 13.

32. James Reston, "Cut the Public Relations Budget," *Lincoln Star,* February 7, 1989, 6.

33. Jones, *The Presidency,* 56–57.

34. For more on Bush's White House staff and method of making appointments, see G. Calvin Mackenzie, "The Real Invisible Hand: Presidential Appointees in the Administration of George W. Bush" and Martha Joynt Kumar, "Recruiting and Organizing the White House Staff," *PS* 1 (March 2002): 27–40.

35. "Hell from the Chief: Hot Tempers and Presidential Timber," *New York Times,* November 7, 1999, Section 4, 7.

36. Fred I. Greenstein, *The Hidden-Hand Presidency* (New York: Basic Books, 1982).

37. Quoted in Richard Pious, *The American Presidency* (New York: Basic Books, 1979), 244.

38. *The American President,* episode 10 (PBS). Series text appears in Kunhardt et al., *The American President,* cited in "Further Reading" earlier.

39. Ann Reilly Dowd, "What Managers Can Learn from Manager Reagan," *Fortune* (September 15, 1986): 32–41.

40. See John H. Kessel, "The Structures of the Reagan White House," *American Journal of Political Science* 28 (May 1984): 231–258.

41. Hillary Rodham Clinton quoted in Carol Gelderman, *All the Presidents' Words: The Bully Pulpit and the Creation of the Virtual Presidency* (New York: Walker, 1997), 160.

42. A good description of Clinton's relationship to his White House staff can be found in Joe Klein, *The Natural: The Misunderstood Presidency of Bill Clinton* (New York: Doubleday, 2002).

43. For more on Bush's management style, see the several articles in the special section "C.E.O. U.S.A.," *New York Times Magazine* (January 14, 2001): 24–58.

44. "The White House Office," in *U.S. Government Manual, 1997–1998* (Washington, D.C.: U.S. Government Printing Office, 1997), 90–93.

45. Edith Mayo, ed., *The Smithsonian Book of First Ladies* (Washington, D.C.: Smithsonian Institution, 1996), 11.

46. Gil Troy, *Affairs of State: The Rise and Rejection of the First Couple since World War II* (New York: Free Press, 1997), 250. Troy also discusses attempts at re-organizing the first lady's office. See especially 178–188 and 248–258.

47. Michael Nelson, ed., *The Presidency A to Z* (Washington D.C.: CQ Press, 1998), 487–488.

48. For a review of the backgrounds of men who have served in the vice presidency and the roles they have played, see Purcell, *The Vice Presidents;* Michael Nelson, *A Heartbeat Away* (New York: Priority, 1988); Paul C. Light, *Vice-Presidential Power: Advice and Influence in the White House* (Baltimore: Johns Hopkins University Press, 1984); and George Sirgiovanni, "The 'Van Buren Jinx': Vice Presidents Need Not Beware," *Presidential Studies Quarterly* 18 (winter 1988): 61–76.

49. Purcell, *The Vice Presidents,* 380.

50. *CQ Daily Monitor,* June 25, 2002. Available at: www.CQ.com.

51. Jeffrey K. Tulis, *The Rhetorical Presidency* (Princeton, N.J.: Princeton University Press, 1987).

52. Garry Wills, *Lincoln at Gettysburg* (New York: Simon & Schuster, 1992), 31.

53. David Halberstam, *The Powers That Be* (New York: Dell, 1980), 30.

54. These figures are from Clinton's former chief speechwriter, Michael Waldman, during an interview on *Morning Edition,* National Public Radio, January 1, 2002.

55. Lowi, *The Personal President.*

56. Associated Press, "Poll Shows Americans Want a Strong Leader," *Lincoln Journal-Star,* June 16, 1992, 5.

57. "A Talk with Clinton," *Newsweek* (January 25, 1993): 37.

58. Carl M. Cannon, "Judging Clinton," *National Journal,* January 1, 2000, 23.

59. Klein, *The Natural,* 208.

60. Richard E. Neustadt, *Presidential Power: The Politics of Leadership from FDR to Carter* (New York: Wiley, 1980).

61. Samuel Kernell, *Going Public: New Strategies of Presidential Leadership* (Washington, D.C.: CQ Press, 1986), 15.

62. Ibid.

63. Ibid., 38–42.

64. Ibid., 120.

65. "Notes and Comments," *New Yorker* (November 7, 1988): 29.

66. "The Presidency," *Newsweek* (December 20, 1993): 46.

67. George C. Edwards III, *The Public Presidency* (New York: St. Martin's, 1983), 253.

68. John Mueller, *War, Presidents and Public Opinion* (New York: Wiley, 1970).

69. For example, see Edwards, *The Public Presidency,* 239–247.

70. Poll scores reported here are from the following *National Journal* issues: December 8, 1990, 2993; January 19, 1991, 185; and February 16, 1991, 412.

71. For more on the Gulf War's impact on Bush's ratings, see John A. Krosnick and Laura A. Brannon, "The Impact of the Gulf War on the Ingredients of Presidential Evaluations: Multidimensional Effects of Political Involvement," *American Political Science Review* 87 (December 1993): 963–975.

72. These survey results are from "Opinion Outlook," *National Journal,* February 18, 1995, 452.

73. M. Fiorina, *Divided Government* (New York: Macmillan, 1992), 7.

74. D. R. Mayhew, "Divided Party Control: Does It Make a Difference?" *PS* (December 1991): 637–640.

75. Reported in George C. Edwards III, *Presidential Influence in Congress* (San Francisco: Freeman, 1980), 125.

76. Quoted in Dick Kirschten, "Reagan Warms Up for Political Hardball," *National Journal,* February 9, 1985, 328.

77. Edwards, *Presidential Influence,* 127.

78. Richard E. Cohen, "Checking and Balancing," *National Journal,* April 20, 2002, 1134–1139.

79. Nicholas Lemann, "The Quiet Man," *New Yorker* (May 7, 2001): 68.

80. "Bush Starts a Strong Record of Success With the Hill," *Congressional Quarterly Weekly Review,* January 12, 2002, 112.

81. "A Furor over the Secret War," *Newsweek* (April 23, 1984): 22.

82. Charles W. Ostrom Jr. and Brian I. Job, "The President and the Political Use of Force," *American Political Science Review* 80 (June 1986): 541–566.

83. Elizabeth Drew, "Letter From Washington," *New Yorker* (February 4, 1991): 83.

84. Charlie Cook, "Why Kosovo Fails to Stir Public Passion," *National Journal,* April 3, 1999, 908.

85. Richard J. Stoll, "The Sound of the Guns," *American Politics Quarterly* 15 (April 1987): 223–237.

86. Richard J. Barnet, *The Rockets' Red Glare: When America Goes to War—The Presidents and the People* (New York: Simon & Schuster, 1990).

87. Karen Toombs Parsons, "Exploring the 'Two Presidents' Phenomenon: New Evidence from the Truman Administration," *Presidential Studies Quarterly* 24 (summer 1994): 495–514.

88. See, for example, the comments of Arthur Schlesinger in "Judging Clinton," 22; Steven A. Holmes, "Losers in Clinton–Starr Bouts May Be Future U.S. Presidents," *New York Times,* August 23, 1998, 18; Adam Clymer, "The Presidency Is Still There, Not Quite the Same," *New York Times,* February 14, 1999, Section 4, 1.

89. See, for example, David Broder and Dan Balz, "Who Wins?" *Washington Post National Weekly Edition,* January 15, 1999, 6–7; "Judging Clinton," 22–23.

90. Richard E. Neustadt, *Presidential Power: The Politics of Leadership from FDR to Carter* (New York: Wiley, 1980).

91. Quoted in Arthur M. Schlesinger Jr., "The Ultimate Approval Rating," *New York Times Magazine* (December 18, 1996): 50.

92. Ibid.

93. Ibid.

94. Statement posted on Congresswoman Harman's Web site.

95. Quoted in *CQ Daily Monitor* (July 11, 2002). Available at www.CQ.com.

96. *CQ Daily Monitor,* July 30, 2002. Available at www.CQ.com.

97. Adriel Bettelheim, "Gauntlet of House Committees Greets Homeland Security Plan," *Congressional Quarterly Weekly Review,* July 13, 2002, 1858.

Chapter 12

1. Nancy Gibbs, "Botching the Big Case," *Time* (May 21, 2001): 36.

2. George Lardner Jr., "The Rest of the Ruby Ridge Story," *Washington Post National Weekly Edition,* August 13–19, 2001, 30; Dan Eggen, "More FBI Blunders in the Lee Probe, *Washington Post National Weekly Edition,* September 3–9, 2001, 29. In 2001, the press revealed that numerous FBI offices did not turn over relevant evidence and paperwork for the Oklahoma city bombing prosecution; and in 2002, there were more humiliations as hundreds of FBI computers and guns were found to be missing and the agency could not account for them.

3. Steve Fainaru and Dan Eggen, "Chief among the Charges," *Washington Post National Weekly Edition,* June 10–16, 2002, 30.

4. All quotes and remarks attributed to Robert Mueller in this section are from press releases and statements to Congress made by Mueller and posted at the FBI's Web site (www.fbi.gov).

5. Taken from Bruce Adams, "The Frustrations of Government Service," *Public Administration Review* 44 (January/February 1984): 5. For more discussion of public attitudes about the civil service, see Herbert Kaufman, "Fear of Bureaucracy: A Raging Pandemic," *Public Administration Review* 41 (January/February 1981): 1.

6. For a description of Weber's view of bureaucracy, see H. H. Gerth and C. Wright Mills, trans., *From Max Weber: Essays on Sociology* (New York: Oxford University Press, 1946), 196–239.

7. Barry Bozeman, *All Organizations Are Public: Bridging Public and Private Organizational Theories* (San Francisco: Jossey-Bass, 1987).

8. "Federal Executives' Bonuses Scrutinized," *Champaign-Urbana News-Gazette,* January 23, 2002, A4.

9. From a letter to W. T. Barry, quoted in "A Citizen's Guide on Using the Freedom of Information Act and the Privacy Act of 1974 to Request Government Records," report to the U.S. House of Representatives 50 (1999), 2.

10. Ibid.

11. Reported in Sam Archibald, "The Early Years of the Freedom of Information Act—1955–1974," *PS: Political Science & Politics* (December 1993): 730.

12. Debra Gersh Hernandez, "Many Promises, Little Action," *Editor & Publisher* (March 26, 1994): 15.

13. General Accounting Office, *Freedom of Information Act: State Department Request Processing* (Washington, D.C.: U.S. Government Printing Office, January 23, 1989).

14. "President Declassifies Old Papers," *Omaha World-Herald,* April 18, 1995, 1.

15. Evan Hendricks, *Former Secrets: Government Records Made Public through the Freedom of Information Act* (Washington, D.C.: Campaign for Political Rights, 1982); "Behind the Freedom of Information Act," *Now with Bill Moyers,* PBS, April 5, 2002.

16. Joyce Appleby, "That's General Washington to You," *New York Times Book Review* (February 14, 1993): 11. This is a review of Richard Norton Smith, *Patriarch* (Boston: Houghton Mifflin, 1993). See also James Q. Wilson, "The Rise of the Bureaucratic State," *Public Interest* 41 (fall 1975): 77–103.

17. Karl Vick, "The President Who Woke Up Washington," *Washington Post National Weekly Edition,* April 28, 1997, 8.

18. Wilson, "The Rise of the Bureaucratic State."

19. Leonard D. White, *Introduction to the Study of Public Administration,* 4th ed. (New York: Macmillan, 1955), 4.

20. David H. Rosenbloom, " 'Whose Bureaucracy Is This, Anyway?' Congress 1946 Answer," *PS: Political Science & Politics* (December 2001): 773.

21. Paul C. Light, *Thickening Government: Federal Hierarchy and the Diffusion of Accountability* (Washington, D.C.: Brookings Institution, 1995).

22. Office of Management and Budget, *Special Analyses: Budget of the United States: Fiscal Year 1990* (Washington, D.C.: U.S. Government Printing Office, 1989), 1–13; *Historical Tables: Budget of the United States: Fiscal Year 1996* (Washington, D.C.: U.S. Government Printing Office, 1995), 245.

23. *2001 Statistical Abstract of the United States,* Table 450.

24. Richard E, Stevenson, "Bush Budget Links Dollars to Deeds with New Ratings," *New York Times,* February 3, 2002, 1, 23; Eric Schmitt, "Is This Any Way to Run a Nation?" *New York Times,* April 14, 2002, WK4. Agency evaluations can be viewed at the OMB Web site (www.omb.gov).

25. Paul C. Light, "What Federal Employees Want from Reform: Reform Watch Brief #5" (Washington, D.C.: Brookings Institution, March 2002), 2. The report is posted at www.brookings.edu.

26. "Datafile," *Congressional Quarterly Weekly Review,* January 12, 2002, 92.

27. For a discussion of these issues, see Peter T. Kilborn, "Big Change Likely as Law Bans Bias toward Disabled," *New York Times,* July 19, 1992, 1, 16.

28. Jill Smolows, "Noble Aims, Mixed Results," *Time* (July 31, 1995): 54.

29. Theodore Lowi, *The End of Liberalism* (New York: Norton, 1969).

30. Woodrow Wilson, "The Study of Administration," *Political Science Quarterly* 56 (December 1941): 481–506. This was reprinted from the article's original publication in *The Academy of Political Science* in 1887.

31. See David H. Rosenbloom, "Editorial: Have an Administrative Rx? Don't Forget the Politics!" *Public Administration Review* (November/December 1993): 503–507.

32. "Hatch Act Revamped," *PA Times,* November 1, 1993, 3; "Hatch Act Political Curbs Retained for Some Workers," *Lincoln Journal-Star,* July 16, 1993, 3.

33. Charles Peters, *How Washington Really Works* (Reading, Mass.: Addison-Wesley, 1980), 46–47.

34. Terry Moe, "Regulators' Performance and Presidential Administrations," *American Journal of Political Science* 26 (May 1982): 197–224; Terry Moe, "Control and Feedback in Economic Regulation," *American Political Science Review* 79 (December 1985): 1094–1116.

35. Joan Biskupic, "Asking the Court to Read between the Lines," *Washington Post National Weekly Edition,* May 9–15, 1994, 32.

36. Moe, "Control and Feedback."

37. The term *capture* is widely used, but its use by political scientists studying regulation seems to have originated with Samuel Huntington, "The Marasmus of the ICC," *Yale Law Journal* 61 (April 1952): 467–509; it was later popularized by Marver Bernstein, *Regulating Business by Independent Commission* (Princeton, N.J.: Princeton University Press, 1955).

38. See "C-5As with Wing Modifications Planned for September Delivery," *Aviation Week & Space Technology* (December 22, 1969): 13; "Whatever Happened to the C-5A 'White Elephant'?" *U.S. News and World Report,* June 19, 1972, 63.

39. David C. Morrison, "Extracting a Thorn, Air Force–Style," *National Journal,* March 7, 1987, 567. For more on Fitzgerald's experiences, see A. Ernest Fitzgerald, *The Pentagonists: An Insider's View of Waste, Mismanagement, and Fraud in Defense Spending* (Boston: Houghton Mifflin, 1989).

40. W. John Moore, "Citizen Prosecutors," *National Journal,* August 18, 1990, 2006–2010.

41. Merit Systems Protection Board, Office of Policy and Evaluation, "Whistleblowing in the Federal Government: An Update" (Washington, D.C.: U.S. Government Printing Office, 1993).

42. Marci Alboher Nusbaum, "Blowing the Whistle: Not for the Fainthearted," *New York Times,* February 10, 2002, Section 3, 10.

43. Ibid.

44. Eric Schmitt, "The Rube Goldberg Agency," *New York Times,* March 24, 2002, WK5.

45. Charles T. Goodsell, *The Case for Bureaucracy: A Public Administration Polemic,* 2d ed. (Chatham, N.J.: Chatham House, 1985), 140.

46. "Is This Any Way to Run a Nation?"

47. Statement of Robert S. Mueller at FBI press conference, May 29, 2002.

48. The FBI restructuring plan is posted at the agency's Web site.

Chapter 13

1. The vote tallies here are approximate numbers rather than actual numbers.

2. Harris tried to capitalize on her newfound fame by running for the House of Representatives in 2002. But when she failed to follow the election laws that she was responsible for enforcing, she was forced to resign her position as secretary of state. *CQ Daily Monitor,* August 14, 2002. Available at www.CQ.com.

3. Of ballots for which the machines did not detect a vote—that is, the "undervotes." The order did not include ballots for which the machines detected more than one vote, disqualifying them—that is, the "overvotes."

4. Samual Issacharoff, "Political Judgments," in *The Vote: Bush, Gore, and the Supreme Court,* ed. Cass R. Sunstein and Richard A. Epstein (Chicago: University of Chicago, 2001), 64.

5. Richard A. Epstein, " 'In Such Manner as the Legislature Thereof May Direct': The Outcome in *Bush v. Gore* Defended," in *The Vote,* ed. Sunstein and Epstein, 13–37; Michael W. McConnell, "Two-and-a-Half Cheers for *Bush v. Gore,*" in ibid., 98–122.

6. David A. Strauss, "*Bush v. Gore:* What Were They Thinking?" in *The Vote,* ed. Sunstein and Epstein, 203.

7. For example, it did not force Miami–Dade County to resume the recount it had stopped; it did not force Republican counties where officials improperly treated absentee ballots to reassess them; and it did not declare the infamous butterfly ballot of Palm Beach County unlawful. For further discussion, see Strauss, "*Bush v. Gore,*" 202–203.

8. Six were Democratic appointees; one was a compromise choice.

9. This is not to say that they were clearly nonpartisan. We do not know. They issued a mixed bag of rulings, with more going against Gore's campaign than for it.

10. Justice Frankfurter in *Colegrove v. Green,* 328 U.S. 549, 556 (1946).

11. The liberal is Justice Stevens, who some consider a moderate liberal. In any event, he is not an arch liberal such as Justices Douglas, Brennan, or Marshall, or even a less consistent liberal such as Chief Justice Warren.

12. Jeffrey Rosen, "A Majority of One," *New York Times Magazine* (June 3, 2001): 34.

13. *Planned Parenthood v. Casey,* 505 U.S. 833.

14. The Court could declare the case a "political question," though this term is normally used for cases involving separation of powers on the federal level.

15. Issacharoff, "Political Judgments," 56.

16. Rosen, "A Majority of One," 64.

17. Bush's lawyers considered this their weakest argument, though it would attract the most justices. Another argument could be based on an interpretation of Article II, Section 1 of the Constitution. According to this interpretation, the Florida court cannot exercise judicial review of any Florida legislation affecting the presidential election. Discussion of this interpretation gets quite complex for an introductory text, and ultimately this interpretation attracted only three justices.

18. The Rehnquist Court has also used it in cases addressing racial legislative redistricting. For an intriguing argument that the Court is altering equal protection doctrine in these cases, see Pamela S. Karlan, "The Newest Equal Protection: Regressive Doctrine on a Changeable Court," in *The Vote,* ed. Sunstein and Epstein, 77–97.

19. Cass R. Sunstein, "Order without Law," in *The Vote,* ed. Sunstein and Epstein, 213.

20. Ibid., 218.

21. Frank I. Michelman, "Suspicion, or the New Prince," in *The Vote,* ed. Sunstein and Epstein, 130; 136, n. 34.

22. *McCleskey v. Kemp,* 481 U.S. 279 (1987). All of the justices in the majority in *Bush v. Gore* were in the majority in *McCleskey,* except Thomas, who was not on the Court yet.

23. Alan M. Dershowitz, *Supreme Injustice: How the High Court Hijacked Election 2000* (New York: Oxford University Press, 2001), 133–134.

24. John Hibbing and Elizabeth Theiss-Morse, *Congress as Public Enemy: Public Attitudes toward American Political Institutions* (New York: Cambridge University Press, 1995), Chapters 2 and 3.

25. John R. Schmidhauser, *Justices and Judges* (Boston: Little, Brown, 1979), 11.

26. *Federalist Paper 78.*

27. Henry J. Abraham, *Justices and Presidents* (New York: Oxford University Press, 1974), 74.

28. Henry J. Abraham, *The Judicial Process,* 3d ed. (New York: Oxford University Press, 1975), 309.

29. Drew Pearson and Robert S. Allen, *The Nine Old Men* (New York: Doubleday, Doren, 1937), 7; Barbara A. Perry, *The Priestly Tribe: The Supreme Court's Image in the American Mind* (Westport, Conn.: Praeger, 1999): 8–9.

30. *Federalist Paper 78.*

31. 1 Cranch 137 (1803). Technically, *Marbury* was not the first use of judicial review, but it was the first clear articulation of judicial review by the Court.

32. Jefferson was also angry at the nature of the appointees. One had led troops loyal to England during the Revolutionary War. Eric Black, *Our Constitution: The Myth That Binds Us* (Boulder, Colo.: Westview, 1988), 66.

33. Debate arose over whether the four should be considered appointed. Their commissions had been signed by the president, and the seal of the United States had been affixed by Marshall, as secretary of state. Yet it was customary to require commissions

to be delivered, perhaps because of less reliable record keeping by government or less reliable communications at the time.

34. One, Oliver Ellsworth, had been coauthor of the bill and then chief justice of the Supreme Court before Marshall.

35. Walter F. Murphy and C. Herman Pritchett, *Courts, Judges, and Politics,* 3d ed. (New York: Random House, 1979), 4.

36. John A. Garraty, "The Case of the Missing Commissions," in *Quarrels That Have Shaped the Constitution,* ed. John A. Garraty (New York: Harper & Row, 1962), 13.

37. *Fletcher v. Peck,* 6 Cranch 87 (1810); *Martin v. Hunter's Lessee,* 1 Wheaton 304 (1816); *Cohens v. Virginia,* 6 Wheaton 264 (1821).

38. *Gibbons v. Ogden,* 9 Wheaton 1 (1824).

39. *Scott v. Sandford,* 19 Howard 393 (1857).

40. *Ex parte Merryman,* 17 Federal Cases 9487 (1861).

41. *Ex parte McCardle,* 7 Wallace 506 (1869).

42. For examination of the ways in which the Civil War and Reconstruction fomented a constitutional "revolution," see Bruce Ackerman, *We the People: Transformations* (Cambridge, Mass.: Harvard University Press, 1998). Ackerman offers a similar examination of the significance of the New Deal period.

43. *Hammer v. Dagenhart,* 247 U.S. 251 (1918).

44. *Lochner v. New York,* 198 U.S. 45 (1905).

45. *Adkins v. Children's Hospital,* 261 U.S. 525 (1923).

46. *Adair v. United States,* 208 U.S. 161 (1908); *In re Delis,* 158 U.S. 564 (1895).

47. *United States v. E. C. Knight Co.,* 156 U.S. 1 (1895).

48. Lawrence Baum, *The Supreme Court,* 2d ed. (Washington, D.C.: CQ Press, 1985), 177.

49. C. Herman Pritchett, *The American Constitution,* 2d ed. (New York: McGraw-Hill, 1968), 166.

50. One legal scholar says the most striking feature about Supreme Court decision making in the 1990s was the effort by five justices to resolve most issues as narrowly as possible, shunning sweeping pronouncements for case-by-case examination. Cass R. Sunstein, *One Case at a Time: Judicial Minimalism on the Supreme Court* (Cambridge, Mass.: Harvard University, 2001).

51. With the possible exception of freedom of speech, which will be addressed in Chapter 14.

52. Ray Kurzweil, quoted in Joel Garreau, "The Second Evolution of the Species," *Washington Post National Weekly Edition,* May 6–12, 2002, 11.

53. Occasionally for important cases the entire group of judges in one circuit will sit "en banc." (Or, in the large Ninth Circuit, eleven judges will sit.)

54. If at least $75,000 is at stake, according to congressional law.

55. Henry Abraham, "A Bench Happily Filled," *Judicature* 66 (February 1983): 284.

56. Harry P. Stumpf, *American Judicial Politics,* 2d ed. (Upper Saddle River, N.J.: Prentice Hall, 1998), 175. After Taft nominated a Catholic to be chief justice, the Speaker of the House cracked, "If Taft were Pope, he'd want to appoint some Protestants to the College of Cardinals." Henry J. Abraham, *Justices and Presidents: A Political History of Appointments to the Supreme Court,* 2d ed. (New York: Oxford University Press, 1985), 168.

57. Victor Navasky, *Kennedy Justice* (New York: Atheneum, 1971), 245–246.

58. Although some previous presidents sought judges who agreed with them on one or two controversial issues, Reagan and Bush made a systematic effort to identify candidates who agreed with their administrations' views on many issues. Reagan pioneered this process, Bush followed, and so far it appears that George W. Bush also is following it. For an analysis of internal documents that established this process in the Reagan administration, see Dawn Johnsen, "Tipping the Scale," *Washington Monthly* (July/August 2002): 1–18.

59. M. Nejelski, *Women in the Judiciary: A Status Report* (Washington, D.C.: National Women's Political Caucus, June 1984).

60. Sheldon Goldman, "Reagan's Second Term Judicial Appointments," *Judicature* 70 (April/May 1987): 324–339.

61. David Byrd, "Clinton's Untilting Federal Bench," *National Journal,* February 19, 2000, 555–557.

62. One of President Reagan's nominees, Douglas Ginsburg, withdrew his nomination due to widespread opposition in the Senate, so officially his nomination was not denied.

63. Qualifications include conflicts of interest or the appearance of conflicts of interest as well as other indicators of merit. Charles M. Cameron, Albert D. Cover, and Jeffrey A. Segal, "Senate Voting on Supreme Court Nominees: A Neoinstitutional Model," *American Political Science Review* 84 (June 1990): 525–534.

64. Abraham, *Justices and Presidents,* 6–7.

65. The heat of the battle obscured the fact that when the vacancy occurred, President Reagan was spoiling for a fight. His reputation had been tarnished by the Iran-Contra affair, and he wanted a fight to demonstrate that he could still dominate Congress as he had during his first term. Aides gave the Senate Judiciary Committee a list of possible nominees and asked if any would pose problems. The Democrats said Bork would pose the greatest problem.

66. Thomas even insisted that he had no position on abortion and, in fact, had never discussed the issue with anyone. Yet both Souter and Thomas freely acknowledged their support for capital punishment. For this issue, their position coincided with the views of the majority of the public.

67. Jeffrey Segal and Harold Spaeth, "If a Supreme Court Vacancy Occurs, Will the Senate Confirm a Reagan Nominee?" *Judicature* 69 (1986): 188–189.

68. Al Kamen, "Switching Sides to Court Victory," *Washington Post National Weekly Edition,* July 14, 1997, 15.

69. Neil A. Lewis, "Impeach Those Liberal Judges! Where Are They?" *New York Times,* May 18, 1997, E5.

70. Lewis, "Impeach Those Federal Judges!" Neil A. Lewis, "Stalled Judicial Nominee Feels the Personal Pain of Politics," *New York Times,* November 16, 1997, 22. One nonpartisan research center—the Miller Center of Public Affairs at the University of Virginia—has attributed these tactics, in general, to the Republicans' reliance on conservative interest groups that focus primarily on the judiciary. Garland W. Allison, "Delay in Senate Confirmation of Federal Judicial Nominees," *Judicature* 80 (July/August 1996): 14.

71. Sheldon Goldman. Biskupic, "Objecting to Judicial Activism."

72. All but Kennedy and Thomas.

73. Schmidhauser, *Justice and Judges,* 55–57.

74. Merle Miller, *Plain Speaking* (New York: Berkeley/Putnam's, 1974), 121.

75. Harold W. Chase, *Federal Judges* (Minneapolis: University of Minnesota Press, 1972), 189.

76. *Morrison v. Olson,* 487 U.S. 654 (1988).

77. Martin Shapiro, "The Supreme Court: From Warren to Burger," in *The New American Political System,* ed. Anthony King (Washington, D.C.: American Enterprise Institute, 1978), 180–181.

78. Robert Seigliano, *The Supreme Court and the Presidency* (New York: Free Press, 1971), 147–148.

79. Abraham, *Justices and Presidents,* 62.

80. Earl Warren, *The Memoirs of Earl Warren* (Garden City, N.Y.: Doubleday, 1977), 5.

81. Abraham, *Justices and Presidents,* 63.

82. "How Much Do Lawyers Charge?" *Parade,* March 23, 1997, 14.

83. Lois G. Forer, *Money and Justice* (New York: Norton, 1984), 9, 15, 102.

84. Karen O'Connor and Lee Epstein, "The Rise of Conservative Interest Group Litigation," *Journal of Politics* 45 (May 1983): 481. See also Richard C. Cortner, *The Supreme Court and the Second Bill of Rights* (Madison: University of Wisconsin Press, 1981), 282.

85. *Tileston v. Ullman,* 318 U.S. 44 (1943).

86. *Poe v. Ullman,* 367 U.S. 497 (1961).

87. *Griswold v. Connecticut,* 381 U.S. 479 (1965).

88. C. K. Rowland and Bridget Jeffery Todd, "Where You Stand Depends on Who Sits," *Journal of Politics* 53 (February 1991): 175–185.

89. Fred Barbash and Al Kamen, "Supreme Court, 'A Rotten Way to Earn a Living,'" *Washington Post National Weekly Edition,* October 1, 1984, 33.

90. The dentist agreed to fill the cavity only in a hospital, where the procedure would be far more expensive. *Bragdon v. Abbott,* 141 L.Ed.2d 540 (1998).

91. *Sutton v. United Air Lines,* 144 L.Ed.2d 450 (1999).

92. The Court ruled the same in a case involving a man with high blood pressure who could not get a job driving trucks. *Murphy v. United Parcel Service,* 144 L.Ed.2d 484 (1999).

93. *Toyota Motor Manufacturing v. Williams,* 151 L.Ed.2d 615 (2001).

94. Robert Bork, *The Tempting of America* (New York: Touchstone/Simon & Schuster, 1990).

95. Lawrence Tribe, *On Reading the Constitution* (Cambridge, Mass.: Harvard University Press, 1992).

96. *Osborn v. U.S. Bank,* 9 Wheaton 738 (1824), at 866.

97. Abraham, *Judicial Process,* 324.

98. *U.S. v. Butler,* 297 U.S. 1, at 94.

99. Murphy and Pritchett, *Courts, Judges, and Politics,* 586.

100. Alexander Bickel, *The Morality of Consent* (New Haven, Conn.: Yale University Press, 1975), 120.

101. "Judicial Authority Moves Growing Issue," *Lincoln Journal,* April 24, 1977.

102. *Furman v. Georgia,* 408 U.S. 238 (1972). Blackmun did vote against the death penalty later in his career.

103. Jeffrey A. Segal and Albert D. Cover, "Ideological Values and the Votes of U.S. Supreme Court Justices," *American Political Science Review* 83 (June 1989): 557–564. For different findings for state supreme court justices, see John M. Scheb II, Terry Bowen, and Gary Anderson, "Ideology, Role Orientations, and Behavior in the State Courts of Last Resort," *American Politics Quarterly* 19 (July 1991): 324–335.

104. Harold Spaeth and Stuart Teger, "Activism and Restraint: A Cloak for the Justices' Policy Preferences," in *Supreme Court Activism and Restraint,* ed. Stephen P. Halpern and Clark M. Lamb (Lexington, Mass.: Lexington, 1982), 277.

105. *Engel v. Vitale,* 370 U.S. 421 (1962).

106. *Abington School District v. Schempp,* 374 U.S. 203 (1963).

107. *Stone v. Graham,* 449 U.S. 39 (1980).

108. *Lee v. Weisman,* 120 L.Ed.2d 467 (1992).

109. *Santa Fe Independent School District v. Doe,* 147 L.Ed.2d 295 (2000).

110. *Burnet v. Coronado Oil and Gas,* 285 U.S. 293 (1932), at 406.

111. Abraham, *Judicial Process,* 13.

112. *Denver Area Educational Telecommunications Consortium v. Federal Communications Commission,* 116 S.Ct. 2374 (1996).

113. *U.S. v. Butler,* 297 U.S. 1 (1936), at 79.

114. Some might say that judges, rather than make law, mediate among various ideas that rise to the surface, killing off some and allowing others to survive. Robert Cover, "Nomos and Narrative," *Harvard Law Review* 97 (1983): 4.

115. Murphy and Pritchett, *Courts, Judges and Politics,* 25.

116. The formal term is *amicus curiae* briefs. The Latin phrase roughly translates to "friend of the court."

117. *Webster v. Reproductive Health Services,* 492 U.S. 445 (1989).

118. David J. Garrow, "The Rehnquist Reins," *New York Times Magazine* (October 6, 1996): 70.

119. Robert Wernick, "Chief Justice Marshall Takes the Law in Hand," *Smithsonian* (November 1998): 162.

120. Joan Biskupic, "Here Comes the Judge? Maybe Not," *Washington Post National Weekly Edition,* February 14, 2000, 30.

121. Jeffrey A. Segal and Harold J. Spaeth, *The Supreme Court and the Attitudinal Model* (New York: Cambridge University Press, 1993), 262–264.

122. Jeffrey Rosen, "Rehnquist's Choice," *New Yorker* (January 11, 1999): 31.

123. Michael S. Serrill, "The Power of William Brennan," *Time* (July 22, 1985): 62.

124. Ibid.

125. David J. Garrow, "One Angry Man," *New York Times Magazine* (October 6, 1996): 68–69.

126. *Webster v. Reproductive Health Services.*

127. *U.S. v. Virginia,* 135 L.Ed.2d 735, 787–789 (1996).

128. Alpheus T. Mason, *Harlan Fiske Stone* (New York: Viking, 1956), 308.

129. Interview with Justice Ginsburg, *Morning Edition,* NPR, May 2, 2002. Ginsburg said foreign jurists admit they disagree with each other but do not make it public.

130. Linda Greenhouse, "The High Court and the Triumph of Discord," *New York Times,* July 15, 2001, Section 4, 1.

131. Baum, *The Supreme Court,* 4.

132. 410 U.S. 113.

133. Craig R. Ducat and Robert L. Dudley, "Federal Appellate Judges and Presidential Power," paper presented at the Midwest Political Science Association Meeting, April 1987.

134. Baum, *The Supreme Court,* 158.

135. Sheldon Goldman, "How Long the Legacy?" *Judicature* 76 (April/May 1993): 295.

136. The Eleventh Amendment overturned *Chisholm v. Georgia* (1793), which had permitted the federal courts to hear suits against a state by citizens of another state. The Fourteenth overturned the Dred Scott case, *Scott v. Sandford* (1857), which had held that blacks were not citizens. The Sixteenth overturned *Pollock v. Farmers' Loan and Trust* (1895), which had negated a congressional law authorizing a federal income tax. The Twenty-sixth overturned *Oregon v. Mitchell* (1970), which had negated a congressional law allowing eighteen-year-olds to vote in state elections.

137. *Goldman v. Weinberger,* 475 U.S. 503 (1986).

138. William N. Eskridge Jr., "Overriding Supreme Court Statutory Interpretation Decisions," *Yale Law Journal* 101 (1991): 338.

139. Thomas R. Marshall, "Public Opinion, Representation, and the Modern Supreme Court," *American Politics Quarterly* 16 (July 1988): 296–316.

140. Richard Morin, "A Nation of Stooges," *Washington Post,* October 8, 1995, C5.

141. Gregory A. Caldeira, "Neither the Purse nor the Sword," paper presented at the American Political Science Association Meeting, August 1987.

142. Abraham, *Justices and Presidents,* 342–343.

143. Robert G. McCloskey, *The American Supreme Court* (Chicago: University of Chicago Press, 1960), 225.

144. *Bush v. Gore,* 121 S.Ct. 512 (2000). Five days earlier, the Court had asked the Florida Supreme Court to clarify the legal basis of its order. This was a narrow ruling that did not address the substance of the dispute.

145. *Bush v. Gore,* 121 S.Ct. 525 (2000).

146. Two dissenting justices did express concerns about the absence of statewide standards, but in all other respects they disagreed with the majority.

147. Three justices in the majority also objected to the Florida Supreme Court's interpretation of Florida law. They said Article II of the Constitution allows the U.S. Supreme Court to invalidate a state supreme court's interpretation of its own law that applies to presidential elections.

148. The majority misconstrued the "safe harbor" provision of federal electoral law as an actual deadline. McConnell, "Two-and-a-half Cheers for *Bush v. Gore*," 118. In fact, twenty states failed to submit their electors by this supposed deadline in 2000. "Numbers," *Time* (December 25, 2000); (January 1, 2001): 53.

149. And by preventing the state from trying specific standards, the Court disregarded its customary practice of announcing the law and then allowing the losing litigant to fix the problem.

150. Dershowitz, *Supreme Injustice*, 37; George P. Fletcher, *Our Secret Constitution* (New York: Oxford University, 2001), 247; Strauss, "*Bush v. Gore*," 193; Sunstein, "Order without Law," 209.

151. Jeffrey Toobin, *Too Close to Call* (New York: Random House, 2001), 184. The minority apparently was just as stunned as the legal scholars. Ibid., 249.

152. Sunstein, "Order without Law," 207.

153. Quoted in Dershowitz, *Supreme Injustice*, 83.

154. A. E. Dick Howard, quoted in David G. Savage, "The Vote Case Fallout," *ABA Journal* 87 (February 2001): 32.

155. Elizabeth Garrett, "Leaving the Decision to Congress," in *The Vote*, ed. Sunstein and Epstein, 46; Michelman, "Suspicion, or the New Prince," 129–130; Sunstein, "Order without Law," 212. There was no identifiable group singled out for discriminatory treatment, and there was no intentional discrimination.

156. Karlan, "The Newest Equal Protection," 95.

157. Dershowitz, *Supreme Injustice*, 230, n. 34.

158. Karlan, "The Newest Equal Protection," 90–91. The older, punch-card machines are more likely to fail to detect a vote on some ballots *and* on other ballots mistakenly detect more than one vote, causing these ballots to be disqualified. Thus, these machines have a poorer record for both undervotes and overvotes.

159. Dershowitz, *Supreme Injustice*, 82.

160. For an extended examination, see Dershowitz, *Supreme Injustice*, Chapter 4. Also see Michelman, "Suspicion, or the New Prince," 126–137.

161. Strauss, "*Bush v. Gore*," 187.

162. Ibid., 189–191; Bruce Ackerman, quoted in Dershowitz, *Supreme Injustice*, 175; Jamin B. Raskin, "Bandits in Black Robes," *Washington Monthly* (March 2001): 25–28.

163. Terrance Sandalow, quoted in Linda Greenhouse, "Collision with Politics Risks Court's Legal Credibility," *New York Times*, December 11, 2000, A1.

164. Quoted in Dershowitz, *Supreme Injustice*, 94. For an extended discussion, see 95–120.

165. Strauss, *Bush v. Gore*, 194.

166. Dershowitz, *Supreme Injustice*, 8.

167. Evan Thomas and Michael Isikoff, "The Truth behind the Pillars," *Newsweek* (December 25, 2000).

168. Dershowitz, *Supreme Injustice*, 162–163; Rosen, "A Majority of One," 73.

169. "Book: Justice Might Have Changed Mind," *Lincoln Journal-Star*, September 10, 2001.

170. Sunstein, "Order without Law," 205–222; McConnell, "Two-and-a-half Cheers for *Bush v. Gore*," 107.

171. For a discussion, see Garrett, "Leaving the Decision to Congress," 38–54.

172. For development of this idea, see Sunstein, "Order without Law," 205–222.

173. John F. Harris, "A Muddled Outcome," *Washington Post National Weekly Edition*, November 19–25, 2001, 11.

174. Unpublished study by James L. Gibson, Gregory A. Caldera, and Lester K. Spence, cited in John C. Yoo, "In Defense of the Court's Legitimacy," in *The Vote*, ed. Sunstein and Epstein, 226–227, no. 21.

175. Study by Wendy W. Simmons, cited in Yoo, "In Defense of the Court's Legitimacy," 226, no. 19.

176. Rosen, "A Majority of One," 37.

Chapter 14

1. John Cloud, "Can a Scout Be Gay?" *Time* (May 1, 2000): 34–36. Girl Scout policy forbids discrimination against lesbians.

2. It had opposed homosexuality in one prior lawsuit. It did adopt policies opposing homosexuality after expelling Dale, but these were inconsistent and, as a result, unclear, perhaps reflecting the schism in the organization. These are discussed at length in Justice Stevens's opinion in this case.

3. Phrase from Justice Souter's opinion in this case.

4. *Roberts v. U.S. Jaycees,* 468 U.S. 609 (1984); *Board of Directors of Rotary International v. Rotary Club of Duarte,* 481 U.S. 537 (1987).

5. The Court has also invalidated racial discrimination in labor unions and private schools and sexual discrimination in law firms because it concluded that there was a compelling reason to do so, despite the claims of freedom of association. *Railway Mail Association v. Corsi,* 326 U.S. 88 (1945); *Runyon v. McCrary,* 427 U.S. 160 (1976); *Hison v. King & Spalding,* 467 U.S. 69 (1984).

6. *Hurley v. Irish-American Gay, Lesbian and Bisexual Group of Boston,* 515 U.S. 557 (1995).

7. Richard Morin, "The High Price of Free Speech," *Washington Post National Weekly Edition,* January 8–14, 2001, 34.

8. Poll for the First Amendment Center and the *American Journalism Review,* conducted by the Center for Survey Research and Analysis at the University of Connecticut, June and July 2002. Reported in the *American Journalism Review* (September 2002). Available at: www.ajr.org, September 30, 2002.

9. The states did not ratify a proposed amendment that would have required at least one representative in Congress for every fifty thousand people. That amendment would have put about five thousand members in today's Congress. The states did not ratify, until 1992, another proposed amendment that would have prohibited a salary raise for members of Congress from taking effect until after the next election to Congress.

10. *Reid v. Covert,* 354 U.S. 1 (1957).

11. *Barron v. Baltimore,* 32 U.S. 243 (1833).

12. *Gitlow v. New York,* 268 U.S. 652 (1925). *Gitlow* is usually cited as the first, because it initiated the twentieth-century trend. However, *Chicago, Burlington and Quincy R. Co. v. Chicago,* 166 U.S. 266 (1897), actually was the first. It applied the Fifth Amendment's just compensation clause, requiring government to pay owners "just compensation" for taking their property.

13. *Argersinger v. Hamlin,* 407 U.S. 25 (1972).

14. Freedom of association is not listed in the First Amendment, but the Court has interpreted freedom of speech and assembly to imply such a right.

15. *Milk Wagon Drivers Union v. Meadowmoor Dairies,* 312 U.S. 287 (1941).

16. Deborah Tannen, *The Argument Culture* (New York: Ballantine, 1998), 25.

17. Thomas I. Emerson, *The System of Freedom of Expression* (New York: Random House/Vintage, 1971), 6–8.

18. For a history of early speech cases, between the Civil War and World War I, see David M. Rabban, *Free Speech in Its Forgotten Years* (New York: Cambridge University Press, 1997).

19. Zechariah Chafee Jr., *Free Speech in the United States* (Cambridge, Mass.: Harvard University Press, 1941), 51–52.

20. *Schenk v. United States,* 249 U.S. 47 (1919); *Frohwerk v. United States,* 249 U.S. 204 (1919); *Debs v. United States,* 249 U.S. 211 (1919); *Abrams v. United States,* 250 U.S. 616 (1919); *Gitlow v. New York,* 268 U.S. 652 (1925); *Whitney v. California,* 274 U.S. 357 (1927).

21. *Gitlow v. New York.*

22. *Dennis v. United States,* 341 U.S. 494 (1951).

23. *Yates v. United States,* 354 U.S. 298 (1957); *Scales v. United States,* 367 U.S. 203 (1961).

24. Earl Warren, *The Memoirs of Earl Warren* (Garden City, N.Y.: Doubleday, 1977), 6.

25. *Brandenburg v. Ohio,* 395 U.S. 444 (1969).

26. Ibid.

27. *Esquire* (November 1974).

28. Jean E. Jackson, "ACTA Report Criticizes Professors," *Anthropology News* (March 2002): 7.

29. Gia Fenoglio, "Is It 'Blacklisting' or Mere Criticism?" *National Journal,* January 19, 2002, 188.

30. The university president acted with the support of Governor Jeb Bush. In 2003, this professor was arrested for his involvement in an organization that funneled money to Palestinian terrorists. When he was indicted, the university fired him. He has not yet been tried. Tim Padgett and Rochelle Renfor, "Fighting Words," *Time* (February 4, 2002): 56.

31. *Jeannette Rankin Brigade v. Chief of Capital Police,* 409 U.S. 972 (1972); *Edwards v. South Carolina,* 372 U.S. 229 (1963).

32. *United States v. Grace,* 75 L.Ed.2d 736 (1983).

33. *Grayned v. Rockford,* 408 U.S. 104 (1972); *Tinker v. Des Moines School District,* 393 U.S. 503 (1969).

34. *Brown v. Louisiana,* 383 U.S. 131 (1966).

35. *Southeastern Promotions v. Conrad,* 420 U.S. 546 (1975).

36. *Adderley v. Florida,* 385 U.S. 39 (1966).

37. *Greer v. Spock,* 424 U.S. 828 (1976).

38. *Amalgamated Food Employees v. Logan Valley Plaza,* 391 U.S. 308 (1968).

39. *Lloyd v. Tanner,* 407 U.S. 551 (1972); *Hudgens v. NLRB,* 424 U.S. 507 (1976).

40. *Gooding v. Wilson,* 405 U.S. 518 (1972); *Lewis v. New Orleans,* 408 U.S. 913 (1972).

41. C. Herman Pritchett, *The American Constitution,* 2d ed. (New York: McGraw-Hill, 1968), 476, no. 2. However, police in some places continue to arrest for swearing. Judy Lin, "ACLU Fights Police on Profanity Arrests in Pittsburgh Area," *Lincoln Journal-Star,* July 11, 2002.

42. *Rosenfeld v. New Jersey,* 408 U.S. 901 (1972); *Brown v. Oklahoma,* 408 U.S. 914 (1972).

43. *Cohen v. California,* 403 U.S. 15 (1971).

44. *FCC v. Pacifica Foundation,* 438 U.S. 726 (1968). In response, Congress and the FCC have considered several proposals to ban offensive speech except for hours when children are not likely to be listening. In 1993, a federal court of appeals ruled that a ban except from midnight until 6 A.M. was too broad. The court said it infringed on the rights of adults.

45. *Wilkinson v. Jones,* No. 86-1125, 1987.

46. *Cox v. Louisiana,* 379 U.S. 536 (1965).

47. *Schenk v. Pro-Choice Network,* 137 L.Ed.2d 1 (1997).

48. *Collin v. Smith,* 447 F.Supp. 676 (N.D. Ill., 1978); *Collin v. Smith,* 578 F.2d 1197 (7th Cir., 1978).

49. *U.S. v. Schwimmer,* 279 U.S. 644 (1929).

50. *Frisby v. Schultz,* 101 L.Ed.2d 420 (1988).

51. *United States v. O'Brien,* 391 U.S. 367 (1968).

52. *Tinker v. Des Moines School District.*

53. *Smith v. Goguen,* 415 U.S. 566 (1974); *Spence v. Washington,* 418 U.S. 405 (1974).

54. *Texas v. Johnson,* 105 L.Ed.2d 342 (1989).

55. Walter Isaacson, "O'er the Land of the Free," *Time* (July 3, 1989): 15; "What Price Old Glory?" *Time* (July 10, 1989): 23.

56. *U.S. v. Eichman,* 110 L.Ed.2d 287 (1990).

57. David Halbertstam, *The Best and the Brightest* (Greenwich, Conn.: Fawcett, 1969), 769.

58. From Watergate tapes released in 1996. For transcripts of tapes made public in 1996, see Stanley Kutler, ed., *Abuse of Power: The New Nixon Tapes* (New York: Free Press, 1998).

59. *New York Times v. United States,* 403 U.S. 713 (1971). In addition to seeking injunctions, the Nixon administration sent a telegram to the *New York Times* demanding that it cease publication of the excerpts, but the FBI had the wrong telex number for the newspaper, so the telegram went first to a fish company in Brooklyn. R. W. Apple, "Lessons from the Pentagon Papers," *New York Times,* June 23, 1996, E5.

60. Actually, the Pentagon Papers did include some current information, regarding ongoing negotiations and the names of CIA agents in Vietnam, but Ellsberg had not passed this information to the newspapers. However, the government and the Court were unaware of this, so the government argued that publication could affect national security, and the Court decided the case with this prospect in mind. Thus, the Court's ruling was stronger than legal analysts realized at the time. Erwin N. Griswold, " 'No Harm Was Done,' " *New York Times,* June 30, 1991, E15.

61. *U.S. v. Progressive,* 467 F.Supp. 990 (W.D., Wis., 1979).

62. *Hazelwood School District v. Kuhlmeier,* 98 L.Ed.2d 592 (1988).

63. William Glaberson, "Censors and Finances Curb Student Press, Report Says," *New York Times,* May 1, 1994, 19. However, a bigger problem for city schools has been a lack of money to publish a paper at all.

64. Then radio and television stations used actors with Irish accents to dub the comments made by IRA members. In 1994, the government lifted the ban.

65. *Branzburg v. Hayes,* 408 U.S. 665 (1972).

66. *Cox Broadcasting v. Cohn,* 420 U.S. 469 (1975).

67. This was not a Supreme Court case.

68. *Time v. Hill,* 385 U.S. 374 (1967).

69. 376 U.S. 254.

70. Harry Kalven, "The *New York Times* Case: A Note on 'the Central Meaning of the First Amendment,' " *Supreme Court Review* (1964): 221.

71. *Monitor Patriot v. Roy,* 401 U.S. 265 (1971).

72. *Associated Press v. Walker,* 388 U.S. 130 (1967).

73. *Greenbelt Cooperative Publishing v. Bresler,* 398 U.S. 6 (1970).

74. *Curtis Publishing v. Butts,* 388 U.S. 130 (1967).

75. *Gertz v. Robert Welch,* 418 U.S. 323 (1974), and *Time v. Firestone,* 424 U.S. 448 (1976).

76. Eric Press, "Westmoreland Takes on CBS," *Newsweek* (October 22, 1984): 62.

77. William A. Henry III, "Libel Law: Good Intentions Gone Awry," *Time* (March 4, 1985): 94.

78. Ibid., 71.

79. D. D. Guttenplan, "The Holocaust on Trial," *Atlantic Monthly* (February 2000): 45–66.

80. *Roth v. United States,* 354 U.S. 476 (1957); *Manual Enterprises v. Day,* 370 U.S. 478 (1962); *Jacobellis v. Ohio,* 378 U.S. 184 (1964); *A Book Named "John Cleland's Memoirs of a Woman of Pleasure" v. Attorney General of Massachusetts,* 383 U.S. 413 (1966).

81. *Miller v. California,* 413 U.S. 15 (1973).

82. *Jenkins v. Georgia,* 418 U.S. 153 (1974).

83. "Project—An Empirical Inquiry into the Effects of *Miller v. California* on the Control of Obscenity," *New York University Law Review* 52 (October 1977): 810–939.

84. *Hudnut v. American Booksellers Association,* 89 L.Ed.2d 291 (1986).

85. *Young v. American Mini Theaters,* 427 U.S. 50 (1976); *Renton v. Playtime Theaters,* 89 L.Ed.2d 29 (1986).

86. The Pilgrims, who had experienced religious toleration in Holland (after persecution in England), left Holland because they wanted a place of their own—not because they could not worship as they pleased. The Dutch were so tolerant that the Pilgrims' children had begun to adopt Dutch manners and ideas. Richard Shenkman, *"I Love Paul Revere, Whether He Rode or Not"* (New York: Harper-Collins, 1991), 20–21.

87. Gary Wills, quoted on "Thomas Jefferson," PBS, February 18, 1997.

88. *Torcaso v. Watkins,* 367 U.S. 488 (1961).

89. *Pierce v. Society of Sisters,* 268 U.S. 510 (1925).

90. *Cooper v. Pate,* 378 U.S. 546 (1963); *Cruz v. Beto,* 405 U.S. 319 (1972).

91. *Church of the Lukumi Babalu Aye v. Hialeah,* 124 L.Ed.2d 472 (1993).

92. *Reynolds v. United States,* 98 U.S. 145 (1879). Most Mormons, however, did not approve of polygamy. Even when polygamy was most popular, perhaps only 10 percent of Mormons practiced it. Shenkman, *"I Love Paul Revere, Whether He Rode or Not,"* 31. Yet today reports indicate that polygamy is still flourishing among Mormons, perhaps more than ever. Lawrence Wright, "Lives of the Saints," *New Yorker* (January 21, 2002): 43.

93. *Sherbert v. Verner,* 374 U.S. 398 (1963).

94. Although a congressional statute mandates "reasonable accommodation," the Court interpreted it so narrowly that it essentially requires only minimal accommodation. *T.W.A. v. Hardison,* 432 U.S. 63 (1977). For analysis, see Gloria T. Beckley and Paul Burstein, "Religious Pluralism, Equal Opportunity, and the State," *Western Political Quarterly* 44 (March 1991): 185–208. For a related case, see *Thornton v. Caldor,* 86 L.Ed.2d 557 (1985).

95. *Wisconsin v. Yoder,* 406 U.S. 205 (1972).

96. *United States v. Lee,* 455 U.S. 252 (1982).

97. *United States v. American Friends Service Committee,* 419 U.S. 7 (1974).

98. *Goldman v. Weinberger,* 475 U.S. 503 (1986); and *O'Lone v. Shabazz,* 482 U.S. 342 (1986).

99. *Employment Division v. Smith,* 108 L.Ed.2d 876 (1990).

100. American Indian Religious Freedom Act of 1994.

101. Ruth Marcus, "One Nation, under Court Rulings," *Washington Post National Weekly Edition,* March 18–24, 1991, 33.

102. *Boerne v. Flores,* 138 L.Ed.2d 624 (1997).

103. William Lee Miller, "The Ghost of Freedoms Past," *Washington Post National Weekly Edition,* October 13, 1986, 23–24.

104. *Church of Holy Trinity v. United States,* 143 U.S. 457 (1892).

105. *Engel v. Vitale,* 370 U.S. 421 (1962); *Abington School District v. Schempp,* 374 U.S. 203 (1963).

106. *Stone v. Graham,* 449 U.S. 39 (1980). The Ten Commandments themselves have been divisive. In 1844, six people were killed in a riot in Philadelphia over which version of the Ten Commandments to post in the public schools. E. J. Dionne Jr., "Bridging the Church–State Divide," *Washington Post National Weekly Edition,* October 11, 1999, 21.

107. C. Herman Pritchett, *The American Constitution,* 3d ed. (New York: McGraw-Hill, 1977), 406.

108. Kenneth M. Dolbeare and Phillip E. Hammond, *The School Prayer Decisions* (Chicago: University of Chicago Press, 1971).

109. Robert H. Birkby, "The Supreme Court and the Bible Belt," *Midwest Journal of Political Science* 10 (1966): 304–315.

110. Julia Lieblich and Richard N. Ostling, "Despite Rulings, Prayer in School Still Sparks Debate, Still Practiced," *Lincoln Journal-Star,* January 16, 2000.

111. "Five Schools Get Ten Commandments," *Lincoln Journal-Star,* August 12, 1999.

112. J. Gordon Melton, quoted in Jon D. Hull, "The State of the Union," *Time* (January 30, 1995): 55.

113. Peter Cushnie, "Letters," *Time* (October 15, 1984): 21.

114. The Supreme Court invalidated Alabama's law that authorized a moment of silence "for meditation or voluntary prayer" because the wording of the law endorsed and promoted prayer. But most justices signaled approval of a moment of silence without such wording. *Wallace v. Jaffree,* 86 L.Ed.2d 29 (1985).

115. *Lee v. Weisman,* 120 L.Ed.2d 467 (1992).

116. *Jones v. Clear Creek,* 977 F.2d 965 (5th Cir., 1992).

117. *Moore v. Ingebretsen,* 88 F.3d 274 (1996).

118. *Santa Fe Independent School District v. Doe,* 530 U.S. 290 (2000).

119. Anna Quindlen, "School Prayer: Substitutes for Substance," *Lincoln Journal-Star,* December 8, 1994.

120. Ibid.

121. James M. Wall, "Keep Faith Voluntarily," *Lincoln Journal-Star,* January 29, 1995.

122. A current guide for public school teachers, addressing practices that are permissible and those that are advisable in various situations, is Charles C. Haynes, ed., *Finding Common Ground* (Nashville, Tenn.: Vanderbilt University, 1997).

123. *Widmar v. Vincent,* 454 U.S. 263 (1981). The law requires high schools that receive federal funds to allow meetings of students' religious, philosophical, or political groups if the schools permit meetings of any "noncurriculum" groups. Schools could prohibit meetings of all noncurriculum groups. Thus, a Salt Lake City high school banned all nonacademic clubs rather than let students form a homosexual organization in 1996. Interviews with teachers and students two years later indicated that as a result of the ban on clubs, school spirit declined and class and racial rifts expanded. Clubs no longer brought students together, and clubs such as Polynesian Pride and the Aztec Club, for Latinos, no longer provided a link between these students and their school. "Club Ban Aimed at Gays Backfires," *Lincoln Journal-Star,* December 6, 1998.

124. *Board of Education v. Mergens,* 110 S.Ct. 2356 (1990).

125. David Van Biema, "Spiriting Prayer into School," *Time* (April 27, 1998): 28–31.

126. Harriet Barovick, "Fear of a Gay School," *Time* (February 21, 2000): 52.

127. *Rosenberger v. University of Virginia,* 132 L.Ed.2d 700 (1995).

128. *Lynch v. Donnelly,* 79 L.Ed.2d 604 (1984).

129. *Allegheny County v. ACLU,* 106 L.Ed.2d 472 (1989). Organizations that want to post the Ten Commandments in public buildings have tried to capitalize on these rulings. The organizations have gotten some states to consider posting the Ten Commandments in displays with other "historical" documents, such as the Declaration of Independence.

130. *Epperson v. Arkansas,* 393 U.S. 97 (1968).

131. Some groups use the more sophisticated-sounding term *creation science.* Although these groups do address the science of evolutionary theory, the courts consider creation science to be religion in the guise of science.

132. *Edwards v. Aguillard,* 482 U.S. 578 (1987). The Kansas Board of Education tried to circumvent these rulings by simply deleting evolution from the state's science curriculum in 1999. A lower court also invalidated a Louisiana school district's policy that evolution be taught only with a disclaimer mentioning the biblical version of creation, and the Supreme Court denied certiorari over the objections of Justices Scalia and Thomas. *Tangipahoa Board of Education v. Freiler,* 147 L.Ed.2d 974 (2000).

133. Peter Applebome, "Seventy Years after Scopes Trial, Creation Debate Lives," *New York Times,* March 10, 1996, 1, 12.

134. For examination of these trends, see Jeffrey Rosen, "Is Nothing Secular?" *New York Times Magazine,* January 30, 2000, 40–45.

135. *Everson v. Board of Education of Ewing Township,* 330 U.S. 1 (1947); *Board of Education v. Allen,* 392 U.S. 236 (1968); *Meek v. Pittinger,* 421 U.S. 349 (1975).

136. *Lemon v. Kurtzman,* 403 U.S. 602 (1971); *Committee for Public Education and Religious Liberty v. Nyquist,* 413 U.S. 756 (1973).

137. For example, striking down tax credits but upholding tax deductions to reduce tuition costs for parents. *Lemon v. Kurtzman; Committee for Public Education and Religious Liberty v. Nyquist, Mueller v. Allen,* 463 U.S. 388 (1983).

138. *Zelman v. Simmons-Harris,* 153 L.Ed.2s 604 (2002).

139. Milwaukee and the state of Florida also had voucher programs at this time.

140. *Rochin v. California,* 342 U.S. 165 (1952).

141. Seymour Wishman, *Confessions of a Criminal Lawyer* (New York: Penguin, 1981), 16.

142. *Stein v. New York,* 346 U.S. 156 (1953).

143. Wendy Kaminer, *It's All the Rage* (Reading, Mass.: Addison-Wesley, 1995), 78.

144. *Weeks v. United States,* 232 U.S. 383 (1914).
145. 367 U.S. 643 (1961).
146. This exception applies when police use a search warrant that, unbeknownst to them, is invalid. *United States v. Leon,* 82 L.Ed.2d 677 (1984); *Massachusetts v. Sheppard,* 82 L.Ed.2d 737 (1984).
147. *Olmstead v. United States,* 277 U.S. 438 (1928).
148. *Katz v. United States,* 389 U.S. 347 (1967).
149. "Numbers," *Time* (June 14, 1999): 41.
150. *Brown v. Mississippi,* 297 U.S. 278 (1936).
151. *McNabb v. United States,* 318 U.S. 332 (1943); *Mallory v. United States,* 354 U.S. 449 (1957); *Spano v. New York,* 360 U.S. 315 (1959).
152. *Ashcraft v. Tennessee,* 322 U.S. 143 (1944).
153. *Rogers v. Richmond,* 365 U.S. 534 (1961); *Lynumn v. Illinois,* 372 U.S. 528 (1963).
154. 384 U.S. 436 (1966).
155. *Dickerson v. U.S.,* 530 U.S. 428 (2000).
156. Jan Hoffman, "Police Tactics Chipping Away at Suspects' Rights," *New York Times,* March 29, 1998, 35.
157. *Johnson v. Zerbst,* 304 U.S. 458 (1938).
158. *Powell v. Alabama,* 287 U.S. 45 (1932).
159. *Gideon v. Wainwright,* 372 U.S. 335 (1963).
160. *Argersinger v. Hamlin,* 407 U.S. 25 (1972); *Scott v. Illinois,* 440 U.S. 367 (1974).
161. *Alabama v. Shelton,* 152 L.Ed. 2d 888 (2002).
162. *Douglas v. California,* 372 U.S. 353 (1953).
163. Wendy Cole, "Death Takes a Holiday," *Time* (February 14, 2000): 68.
164. *Time* (April 29, 1991).
165. Peter Applebome, "Indigent Defendants, Overworked Lawyers," *New York Times,* May 17, 1992, E18.
166. Alan Berlow, "Texas, Take Heed," *Washington Post National Weekly Edition,* February 21, 2000, 22.
167. Richard Carelli, "Death Rows Grow, Legal Help Shrinks," *Lincoln Journal-Star,* October 7, 1995.
168. The Burger Court did rule that the right to counsel entails the right to "effective" counsel, but the Court set such stringent standards for establishing the existence of ineffective counsel that few defendants can take advantage of this right. See *Strickland v. Washington,* 466 U.S. 668 (1984); *U.S. v. Cronic,* 466 U.S. 640 (1984).
169. *Baldwin v. New York,* 339 U.S. 66 (1970); *Blanton v. North Las Vegas,* 489 U.S. 538 (1989).
170. *Duncan v. Louisiana,* 391 U.S. 145 (1968).
171. *Taylor v. Louisiana,* 419 U.S. 522 (1975).
172. *Swain v. Alabama,* 380 U.S. 202 (1965).
173. The Court implicitly upheld the death penalty in *Wilkerson v. Utah,* 99 U.S. 130 (1878); *In re Kemmler,* 136 U.S. 436 (1890).
174. *Furman v. Georgia,* 408 U.S. 238 (1972).
175. *Gregg v. Georgia,* 428 U.S. 153 (1976).
176. *Woodson v. North Carolina,* 428 U.S. 289 (1976).
177. *Coker v. Georgia,* 433 U.S. 584 (1977).
178. *McCleskey v. Kemp,* 95 L.Ed.2d 262 (1987). Studies of Florida, Illinois, Mississippi, and North Carolina have found similar results. Fox Butterfield, "Blacks More Likely to Get Death Penalty, Study Says," *New York Times,* June 7, 1998, 16.
179. Leonard Pitts Jr., "Fate of 100 Innocent Men Casts Doubt on Capital Punishment," *Lincoln Journal-Star,* April 13, 2002.
180. *Atkins v. Virginia,* 153 L.Ed. 2d 335 (2002).
181. *Brady v. United States,* 397 U.S. 742 (1970).
182. *Griswold v. Connecticut,* 38 U.S. 479 (1965).
183. For a rare exception, see *Time v. Hill,* 385 U.S. 374 (1967).
184. *Griswold v. Connecticut.*
185. *Eisenstadt v. Baird,* 405 U.S. 438 (1972); *Carey v. Population Services International,* 431 U.S. 678 (1977).
186. *Eisenstadt v. Baird.*
187. Lloyd Shearer, "This Woman and This Man Made History," *Parade* (1983).
188. 410 U.S. 113 (1973).
189. Bob Woodward, "The Abortion Papers," *Washington Post National Weekly Edition,* January 30–February 5, 1989, 24–25.

190. All but New York's. Three other states allowed abortion on demand though not quite as extensively as *Roe,* so the ruling also invalidated their laws. Jeffrey A. Segal and Harold J. Spaeth, *The Supreme Court and the Attitudinal Model* (New York: Cambridge University Press, 1993), 333.
191. *Akron v. Akron Center for Reproductive Health,* 76 L.Ed.2d 687 (1983).
192. "The Supreme Court Ignites a Fiery Abortion Debate," *Time* (July 4, 1977): 6–8.
193. *Beal v. Doe,* 432 U.S. 438 (1977); *Maher v. Roe,* 432 U.S. 464 (1977); *Poelker v. Doe,* 432 U.S. 519 (1977); *Harris v. McRae* 448 U.S. 297 (1980).
194. Benjamin Weiser, "The Abortion Dilemma Come to Life," *Washington Post National Weekly Edition,* December 25–31, 1989, 10–11.
195. *Facts in Brief: Abortion in the United States* (New York: Alan Guttmacher Institute, 1992); Stephanie Mencimer, "Ending Illegitimacy as We Know It," *Washington Post National Weekly Edition,* January 17–23, 1994, 24.
196. *Webster v. Reproductive Health Services,* 106 L.Ed.2d 410 (1989).
197. *Planned Parenthood of Southeastern Pennsylvania v. Casey,* 120 L.Ed.2d 674 (1992).
198. William Booth, "The Difference a Day Makes," *Washington Post National Weekly Edition,* November 23–29, 1992, 31.
199. *Hodgson v. Minnesota,* 111 L.Ed.2d 344 (1990); *Ohio v. Akron Center for Reproductive Health,* 111 L.Ed.2d 405 (1990); *Planned Parenthood Association of Kansas City v. Ashcroft,* 462 U.S. 476 (1983).
200. Carlson, "Abortion's Hardest Cases," 24.
201. Butch Mabin, "Supreme Court Says Teen Seeking Abortion Too Immature," *Lincoln Journal-Star,* December 13, 1997.
202. *Stenberg v. Carhart,* 530 U.S. 914 (2000).
203. Barry Yeoman, "The Quiet War on Abortion," *Mother Jones* (September/October 2001): 46–51.
204. "Survey Reveals U.S. Views on Abortion to be Contradictory," *Lincoln Journal-Star,* June 19, 2000.
205. Alissa Rubin, "The Abortion Wars Are Far from Over," *Washington Post National Weekly Edition,* December 21–27, 1992, 25.
206. Sandra G. Boodman, "Bringing Abortion Home," *Washington Post National Weekly Edition,* April 19–25, 1993, 7.
207. Richard Lacayo, "One Doctor Down, How Many More?" *Time* (March 22, 1993): 47.
208. Rebecca Mead, "Return to Sender the Usual Hate Mail," *New Yorker* (October 29, 2001): 34.
209. Douglas Frantz, "The Rhetoric of Terror," *Time* (March 27, 1995): 48–51.
210. Dan Sewell, "Abortion War Requires Guns, Bulletproof Vests," *Lincoln Journal-Star,* January 8, 1995.
211. "Blasts Reawaken Fear of Domestic Terrorism," *Lincoln Journal-Star,* January 17, 1997.
212. Richard Lacayo, "Abortion: The Future Is Already Here," *Time* (May 4, 1992): 29; Jack Hitt, "Who Will Do Abortions Here?" *New York Times Magazine* (January 18, 1998): 20.
213. Randall Terry, quoted in Anthony Lewis, "Pro-Life Zealots 'Outside the Bargain,'" *Lincoln Journal-Star,* March 14, 1993; Joseph Scheidler, quoted in Boodman, "Bringing Abortion Home," 6.
214. Stanley K. Henshaw, "Abortion Incidence and Services in the United States, 1995–1996," *Family Planning Perspectives* (November/December 1998).
215. For further analysis of the role of abortion in our legal and political debates since *Roe,* see Alan M. Dershowitz, *Supreme Injustice* (New York: Oxford University Press, 2001), 191–194; 201.
216. E. J. Graff, "In the Bedroom," *The American Prospect,* March, 2003, A22.
217. The laws of five states—Arkansas, Kansas, Missouri, Oklahoma, and Texas—target homosexuals. "Two Men Fined for Sodomy Appeal to Challenge Texas Law," *Lincoln Journal-Star,* November 21, 1998. The laws are also criticized by advocates for people with disabilities, who say the laws forbid one kind of sex that people who must use wheelchairs can have.

218. *Bowers v. Hardwick,* 92 L.Ed.2d 140 (1986); see also *Doe v. Commonwealth's Attorney,* 425 U.S. 901 (1976).
219. "Ex-Justice's Second Thoughts to Make Heated Debate Hotter," *Lincoln Journal-Star,* October 28, 1990. The Texas law has been enforced against homosexuals as recently as 1998. "Two Men Fined for Sodomy Appeal to Challenge Texas Law."
220. *Romer v. Evans,* 134 L.Ed.2d 855 (1996).
221. The House sponsor of the act, Robert Barr (R-Ga.), said the act was necessary because "[t]he flames of hedonism, the flames of narcissism, the flames of self-centered morality are licking at the very foundation of our society, the family unit." At the time he was protecting the family unit, he was in his third marriage. Margaret Carlson, "The Marrying Kind," *Time* (September 16, 1996): 26.
222. As of March 2000. "Californians Approve Proposition Rejecting Gay Marriage," *Lincoln Journal-Star,* March 8, 2000.
223. The civil unions also allow the rights to make medical decisions for a partner who is ill, visit a partner who is in the hospital, choose the final resting place for a partner who dies, and receive wrongful death benefits for a partner who dies.
224. President Clinton also ordered the FBI to end its policy that made it difficult for homosexuals to be hired.
225. The policy originally was based on psychoanalytic theory, which considered homosexuality a mental illness. This conclusion was rejected by the American Psychiatric Association some years later.
226. Randy Shilts, "What's Fair in Love and War," *Newsweek* (February 1, 1993): 58–59.
227. Israel drafts every eighteen-year-old man and woman. It does consider homosexuality in the assignment of jobs. Gays who admit their orientation to their superiors confidentially are restricted from security-sensitive jobs for fear they are susceptible to blackmail. But gays who acknowledge their orientation openly could not be blackmailed, so they are treated the same as straights. Shilts, "What's Fair in Love and War," 58–59; Eric Konigsberg, "Gays in Arms," *Washington Monthly,* November 1992, 10–13; "Canada Had No Problems Lifting Its Military Gay Ban," *Lincoln Journal-Star,* January 31, 1993. See also Randy Shilts, *Conduct Unbecoming: Gays and Lesbians in the U.S. Military* (New York: St. Martin's, 1993).
228. Philip Shenon, "New Study Faults Pentagon's Gay Policy," *New York Times,* February 26, 1997, A8.
229. "Group Says Gays Worse Off in Military since New Policy," *Lincoln Journal-Star,* February 28, 1996; Shenon, "New Study Faults Pentagon's Gay Policy." Pentagon officials say many discharges result from recruits who decide that they do not like the military and who then volunteer that they are homosexual as a way of getting discharged. Dana Priest, "The Impact of the 'Don't Ask, Don't Tell' Policy," *Washington Post National Weekly Edition,* February 1, 1999, 35. As a result of the increase in discharges, the Clinton administration tried to bolster the policy by having the services discourage harassment, from threats to derogatory jokes aimed at gays, and by requiring low-ranking officers to consult with senior legal advisers before beginning an investigation into alleged homosexual conduct.
230. Al Kamen, "When Exactly Does Life End?" *Washington Post National Weekly Edition,* September 18–24, 1989, 31; Alain L. Sanders, "Whose Right to Die?" *Time* (December 11, 1989): 80.
231. *Cruzan v. Missouri Health Department,* 111 L.Ed.2d 224 (1990).
232. Otto Friedrich, "A Limited Right to Die," *Time* (July 9, 1990): 59.
233. Tamar Lewin, "Ignoring 'Right to Die' Directives, Medical Community Is Being Sued," *New York Times,* June 2, 1996, 1.
234. *Washington v. Glucksberg,* 138 L.Ed.2d 772 (1997); *Vacco v. Quill,* 138 L.Ed.2d 834 (1997).

235. David E. Rosenbaum, "Americans Want a Right to Die. Or So They Think," *New York Times,* June 8, 1997, E3.

236. Ibid.

237. Dershowitz, *Supreme Injustice,* 189.

238. *Boy Scouts of America v. Dale,* 147 L.Ed.2d 554 (2000).

Chapter 15

1. John W. Dower, *War without Mercy* (New York: Pantheon, 1986), 112.

2. Peter Irons, *Justice at War* (New York: Oxford University Press, 1983), 269.

3. Dower, *War without Mercy,* 92.

4. John Hersey, "Behind Barbed Wire," *New York Times Magazine,* September 11, 1988, 120.

5. Russell Nye, *Fettered Freedom* (Lansing: Michigan State University Press, 1963), 187, 227–229.

6. *Scott v. Sandford,* 19 How. 393 (1857).

7. Despite the ruling, Taney considered slavery "a blot on our national character." Three decades before the case, he had freed his own slaves, whom he had inherited from his parents. When the South seceded, Taney remained with the Union. Richard Shenkman, *"I Love Paul Revere, Whether He Rode or Not"* (New York: HarperCollins, 1991), 168.

8. Slavery became so much a part of the southern economy that the paper money of some Confederate states featured pictures of slaves harvesting cotton. *Fresh Air Weekend,* National Public Radio, August 18, 2002.

9. The Emancipation Proclamation apparently was a tactical move to discourage European countries from aiding the Confederacy. It gave the Civil War a moral purpose, making foreign intervention less likely. The proclamation could not free southern slaves at the time because the Union did not control southern states then.

10. Bruce Ackerman, *We the People: Transformations* (Cambridge, Mass.: Harvard University Press, 1998); George Fletcher, "Unsound Constitution: Oklahoma City and the Founding Fathers," *New Republic,* June 23, 1997, 14–18. These conclusions make dubious the arguments that judges should be guided only by the intentions of the original Founders as they resolve contemporary cases. Ignoring the transformation that occurred as a result of the Civil War and these amendments amounts to using a highly selective and self-serving version of history.

11. Civil Rights Act of 1866; Civil Rights Act of 1871; Civil Rights Act of 1875.

12. See generally Eric Foner, *Reconstruction: America's Unfinished Revolution* (New York: Harper & Row, 1988).

13. The name "Jim Crow" came from a white performer in the 1820s who had a vaudeville routine in which he blackened his face with burnt cork and mimicked black men. He sang "Wheel About and Turn About and Jump, Jim Crow." This routine led to minstrel shows in high schools and colleges, with students portraying and satirizing blacks. The shows were popular into the 1960s.

14. Kenneth Karst, "Equality, Law, and Belonging: An Introduction," in *Before the Law,* 5th ed., ed. John J. Bonsignore, Ethan Katsh, Peter d'Errico, Ronald M. Pipkin, Stephen Arons, and Janet Rifkin (Geneva, Ill.: Houghton Mifflin, 1994), 429.

15. C. Vann Woodward, *The Strange Career of Jim Crow,* 2d ed. (London: Oxford University Press, 1966), 44.

16. *Civil Rights Cases,* 109 U.S. 3 (1883).

17. C. Herman Pritchett, *The American Constitution,* 3d ed. (New York: McGraw-Hill, 1977), 486.

18. *Plessy v. Ferguson,* 163 U.S. 537 (1896). The Court's ruling prompted states to expand their Jim Crow laws. Before *Plessy,* states segregated just trains and schools.

19. *Cumming v. Richmond County Board of Education,* 175 U.S. 528 (1899). Then the Court enforced seg-regation in colleges. It upheld a criminal conviction against a private college for teaching blacks together with whites. *Berea College v. Kentucky,* 211 U.S. 45 (1908).

20. Woodward, *Strange Career of Jim Crow,* 113. Before the Civil War, northern states had passed some Jim Crow laws, which foreshadowed the more pervasive laws in southern states after the war. Leon F. Litwack, *Trouble in Mind: Black Southerners in the Age of Jim Crow* (New York: Knopf, 1998).

21. Jacqueline Jones, *The Dispossessed: America's Underclasses from the Civil War to the Present* (New York: Basic Books, 1992), 83. And they were still being cheated. One sharecropper went to the landowner at the end of the season to settle up but was told he would not receive any money that year because the landowner needed it to send his son to college. The sharecropper moved North. Interview with sharecropper's son, "The Best of Discovery," Discovery television channel, June 11, 1995.

22. Richard Kluger, *Simple Justice* (New York: Knopf, 1976), 89–90.

23. Philip Dray, *At the Hands of Persons Unknown* (New York: Random House, 2002).

24. Ibid.

25. Woodward, *Strange Career of Jim Crow,* 114.

26. Yet talk of the riot was banished from newspapers, textbooks, and everyday conversations. After some years, most Oklahomans were unaware of it, except those who lived through it. In the 1990s, newspaper articles prompted the state to establish a commission to investigate the riot, leading to more awareness. Jonathan Z. Larsen, "Tulsa Burning," *Civilization* (February/March 1997): 46–55; Brent Staples, "Unearthing a Riot," *New York Times Magazine* (December 19, 1999): 64–69. For an examination, see James S. Hirsch, *Riot and Remembrance: The Tulsa Race War and Its Legacy* (New York: Houghton Mifflin, 2002).

27. "Torn from the Land," Associated Press, http://wire.ap.org. The Web site offers an investigative report with numerous stories.

28. Wilson apparently opposed segregation in government but still allowed it to appease southerners who were a major portion of his Democratic Party and whose support was essential for his economic reforms.

29. *Guinn v. United States,* 238 U.S. 347 (1915).

30. *Buchanan v. Warley,* 245 U.S. 60 (1917).

31. In 1939, the NAACP established the NAACP Legal Defense and Educational Fund as its litigation arm. In 1957, the IRS, pressured by southern members of Congress, ordered the two branches of the NAACP to break their connection or lose their tax-exempt status. Since then, they have been separate organizations, and chapter references to the "NAACP" are to the NAACP Legal Defense and Educational Fund.

32. Juan Williams, "The Case for Thurgood Marshall," *Washington Post,* February 15, 1999.

33. Kluger, *Simple Justice,* 134.

34. *Missouri ex rel. Gaines v. Canada,* 305 U.S. 337 (1938).

35. *Sweatt v. Painter,* 339 U.S. 629 (1950).

36. *McLaurin v. Oklahoma State Regents,* 339 U.S. 637 (1950).

37. Esther Brown, a white woman from a Kansas City suburb, had a black maid who lived in nearby South Park. In 1948, when Brown saw the decrepit school for black students in South Park, she complained to the board of education in the town. At a meeting, she said, "Look, I don't represent these people. One of them works for me, and I've seen the conditions of their school. I know none of you would want your children educated under such circumstances. They're not asking for integration—just a fair shake." From the audience Brown received catcalls and demands to go back where she came from. A woman behind her tried to hit her. The school board responded by gerrymandering the black neighborhood out of the South Park school district. Kluger, *Simple Justice,* 388–389.

38. Earl Warren, *The Memoirs of Earl Warren* (Garden City, N.Y.: Doubleday, 1977), 291.

39. 347 U.S. 483 (1954).

40. *Holmes v. Atlanta,* 350 U.S. 879 (1955); *Baltimore v. Dawson,* 350 U.S. 877 (1955); *Schiro v. Bynum,* 375 U.S. 395 (1964); *Johnson v. Virginia,* 373 U.S. 61 (1963); *Lee v. Washington,* 390 U.S. 333 (1968).

41. *Brown v. Board of Education II,* 349 U.S. 294 (1955).

42. Justice Tom Clark later told a political science conference that one justice had proposed desegregating one grade a year, beginning with kindergarten or first grade, but this concrete standard was rejected because the other justices felt it would take too long. In retrospect, it might have been quicker, and easier, than the vague standard used.

43. *Griffin v. Prince Edward County School Board,* 377 U.S. 218 (1964); *Norwood v. Harrison,* 413 U.S. 455 (1973); *Gilmore v. Montgomery,* 417 U.S. 556 (1974); *Green v. New Kent County School Board,* 391 U.S. 430 (1968).

44. James F. Simon, *In His Own Image* (New York: McKay, 1974), 70.

45. William Cohen and John Kaplan, *Bill of Rights* (Mineola, N.Y.: Foundation, 1976), 622.

46. *Swann v. Charlotte-Mecklenburg Board of Education,* 402 U.S. 1 (1971); *Columbus Board of Education v. Penick,* 443 U.S. 449 (1979); *Dayton Board of Education v. Brinkman,* 443 U.S. 526 (1979); *Keyes v. School District 1, Denver,* 413 U.S. 921 (1973).

47. *Milliken v. Bradley,* 418 U.S. 717 (1974).

48. For example, some suburbs of Kansas City, Missouri, did not allow black students to attend high schools. Some black families, then, moved back to the city, aggravating both school segregation and residential segregation. James S. Kunen, "The End of Integration," *Time* (April 29, 1996): 41.

49. Lee A. Daniels, "In Defense of Busing," *New York Times Magazine* (April 17, 1983): 36–37.

50. Rob Gurwitt, "Getting off the Bus," *Governing* (May 1992): 30–36.

51. *Board of Education of Oklahoma City v. Dowell,* 112 L.Ed.2d 715 (1991). The Court said school districts could stop busing when "the vestiges of past discrimination had been eliminated to the extent practicable." See also *Freeman v. Pitts,* 118 L.Ed.2d 108 (1992).

52. *Missouri v. Jenkins,* 132 L.Ed.2d 63 (1995).

53. Anjetta McQueen, "Desegregation Waning," *Lincoln Journal-Star,* May 16, 1999.

54. FBI director J. Edgar Hoover ordered wiretaps that he hoped would link King with communists. When the taps failed to reveal any connection, Hoover had agents bug a hotel room, where they heard King having extramarital sex. Taylor Branch, *Pillar of Fire: America in the King Years 1963–65* (New York: Simon & Schuster, 1998).

55. Woodward, *Strange Career of Jim Crow,* 186.

56. *Norris v. Alabama,* 294 U.S. 587 (1935); *Smith v. Texas,* 311 U.S. 128 (1940); *Avery v. Georgia,* 345 U.S. 559 (1952).

57. Henry Louis Gates Jr., "After the Revolution," *New Yorker* (April 29; May 6, 1996): 60.

58. Patrick Reddy, "Why It's Got to Be All or Nothing," *Washington Post National Weekly Edition,* October 18, 1999, 23.

59. This point held true for national elections. The transformation took longer for state and local elections.

60. *Heart of Atlanta Motel v. United States,* 379 U.S. 421 (1964).

61. For discussion of organized labor's ambivalence toward enactment and enforcement of the employment provisions of the act, see Herbert Hill, "Black Workers, Organized Labor, and Title VII of the 1964 Civil Rights Act: Legislative History and Litigation Record," in *Race in America,* ed. Herbert Hill and James E. Jones (Madison: University of Wisconsin Press, 1993), 263–341.

62. *Griggs v. Duke Power,* 401 U.S. 424 (1971).

63. *Washington v. Davis,* 426 U.S. 229 (1976). When the Burger Court held that standards must relate to the job, it placed the burden of proof on employers. (They had to show that their requirements were necessary.) In *Wards Cove Packing v. Atonio,* 490 U.S. 642 (1989), the Rehnquist Court shifted the burden of proof to workers. This technical change had a substantial impact; it made it hard for victims to win in court. In 1991, Congress passed new legislation to override the ruling and clarify its intent that employers should bear the burden of proof.

64. *Firefighters Local Union v. Stotts,* 81 L.Ed.2d 483 (1984).

65. *Shelley v. Kraemer,* 334 U.S. 1 (1948).

66. Less directly, the numerous national and state policies that encouraged urban sprawl provided the opportunity for middle-class whites to flock to the suburbs—and leave the cities disproportionately black.

67. For more extensive examination, see Andrew Hacker, *Two Nations: Black and White, Separate, Hostile, Unequal* (New York: Scribner's, 1992).

68. Richard Morin, "Southern Discomfort," *Washington Post National Weekly Edition,* July 15–21, 1996, 35.

69. Gary Orfield, quoted in Mary Jordan, "Separating the Country from the *Brown* Decision," *Washington Post National Weekly Edition,* December 20–26, 1993, 33.

70. Mary Jordan, "On Track toward Two-Tier Schools," *Washington Post National Weekly Edition,* May 31–June 6, 1993, 31.

71. Jordan, "Separating the Country from the *Brown* Decision."

72. J. Harvie Wilkinson, *From Brown to Bakke* (New York: Oxford University Press, 1979), 118–125; "School Segregation Worsens, Study Says," *Lincoln Journal,* December 14, 1993; illiam Celis III, "Forty Years after *Brown,* Segregation Persists," *New York Times,* May 18, 1994, A1.

73. Kunen, "The End of Integration," 39.

74. Jonathan Kozol, *Savage Inequalities: Children in America's Schools* (New York: HarperPerennial, 1992), 4.

75. Ibid., 3.

76. Ibid., 35. However, only three public schools in Alabama are named after King, a native of the state. "Numbers," *Time* (January 24, 2000): 23.

77. Gurwitt, "Getting off the Bus"; Jervis Anderson, "Black and Blue," *New Yorker* (April 29; May 6, 1996): 64.

78. "That's Quite a Range," *Lincoln Journal,* January 21, 1993.

79. In addition, cities have numerous nonprofit institutions—colleges, museums, hospitals—that benefit the entire urban area but do not pay property taxes. According to one estimate, 3 percent of the cities' potential tax base is tax exempt, compared with 3 percent of the suburbs'. Kozol, *Savage Inequalities,* 55.

80. Ibid., 198, 137, 236, 57. There are a few exceptions, such as Newark, New Jersey, which spent more than $9,000 per pupil in recent years. Jordan, "On Track toward Two-Tier Schools," 31.

81. Kozol, *Savage Inequalities,* 140, 36, 23–24.

82. Ibid., 155–156.

83. Ibid., 53, 84.

84. Ibid., 123–124. Researchers debate the extent to which more resources lead to more learning. The results are mixed, though most show that resources do improve learning. Larry V. Hedges, Richard D. Laine, and Rob Greenwald, "Does Money Matter? A Metaanalysis of Studies of the Effects of Differential School Inputs on Student Outcomes," *Educational Researcher* 23 (1994): 5–14; Kevin B. Smith and Kenneth J. Meier, "Politics, Bureaucrats, and Schools," *Public Administration Review* 54 (1994): 551–558; David Card and Alan B. Krueger, "Does School Quality Matter?" *Journal of Political Economy* 100 (1992): 1–40; Ronald F. Ferguson, "Paying for Public Education: New Evidence on How and Why Money Matters," *Harvard Journal of Legislation* 28 (1991): 465–498; Keith Baker, "Yes, Throw Money at the Schools," *Phi Delta Kappan* 72, no. 8 (1991): 628–631. For an earlier, contrary view, see Eric A. Hanushek, "The Economics of Public Schooling: Production and Efficiency in Public Schools," *Journal of Economic Literature* 24, no. 3 (1986): 1141–1177.

85. Steve Lopez, "Money for Stadiums but Not for Schools," *Time* (June 14, 1999): 54.

86. Jay Mathews, "A Confirmation of Bias," *Washington Post National Weekly Edition,* March 19–25, 2001, 34; Robert England and Kenneth Meier, "From Desegregation to Integration: Second Generation School Discrimination as an Institutional Impediment," *American Politics Quarterly* 13 (April 1985): 227–247; Charles Bullock and Joseph Stewart, "Incidence and Correlates of Second-Generation Discrimination," *Race, Sex, and Policy Problems,* eds. Marian Palley and Michael Preston (Lexington, Mass.: Lexington Books, 1979); Stephen Wainscott and J. David Woodard, "Second Thoughts on Second Generation Discrimination," *American Politics Quarterly* 16 (April 1988): 171–192.

87. Kenneth Meier and Robert England, "Black Representation and Educational Policy," *American Political Science Review* 78 (June 1984): 392–403; Kenneth Meier, Joseph Stewart, and Robert England, *Race, Class, and Education: The Politics of Second-Generation Discrimination* (Madison: University of Wisconsin Press, 1989).

88. Beverly Cross, quoted in Jodie Morse, "Learning While Black," *Time* (May 27, 2002): 50.

89. Suits claiming discrimination fell 51 percent from 1975 to 1984. Marc Galanter, "Beyond the Litigation Panic," in *New Directions in Liability Law: Proceedings of the Academy of Political Science* 37 (New York: Academy of Political Science, 1988): 21, 23.

90. Gary Boulard, "Jim Crow Said Alive in the South," *Lincoln Journal,* October 3, 1991.

91. Richard Morin and Michael H. Cottman, "The Invisible Slap," *Washington Post National Weekly Edition,* July 2–8, 2001, 7.

92. Edward Barnes, "Can't Get There from Here," *Time* (February 19, 1996): 33.

93. Hacker, *Two Nations,* 48–49.

94. William A. Henry III, "The Last Bastions of Bigotry," *Time* (July 22, 1991): 66–67.

95. "Study Demonstrates Hiring Discrimination against Blacks," *Lincoln Star,* May 15, 1991.

96. "Deciphering a Racist Business Code," *Time* (October 19, 1992): 21–22.

97. Earl G. Graves, *How to Succeed in Business without Being White* (New York: HarperBusiness, 1997).

98. Reed Abelson, "Anti-Bias Agency Is Short of Will and Cash," *New York Times,* July 1, 2001, BU1.

99. Jerry DeMuth, "Fair-Housing Suits: Color Them Gold," *Washington Post National Weekly Edition,* August 11, 1986, 34.

100. "Hispanics Face More Bias in Housing," *Lincoln Journal-Star,* November 8, 2002. Another study found similar discrimination in fairly progressive northern cities. "Professional Should Address Discrimination," *Lincoln Journal-Star,* April 24, 2002.

101. *All Things Considered,* National Public Radio, August 5, 2001.

102. Jerry Knight, "Coloring the Chances of Getting a Mortgage," *Washington Post National Weekly Edition,* October 28–November 3, 1991, 26; "Racial Disparities Seen in Home Lending," *Lincoln Journal,* October 22, 1991.

103. Nina Burleigh, "The Suburbs Won't Vouch for This," *Time* (May 13, 1996): 43. Yet Presidents Nixon and Ford instituted a small-scale program for housing vouchers, and President Reagan also supported the idea.

104. Sarah Cohen and D'Vera Cohn, "Continental Shift," *Washington Post National Weekly Edition,* April 9–15, 2001, 6.

105. James Traub, "The Year in Ideas," *New York Times Magazine* (December 9, 2001): 94.

106. Hacker, *Two Nations,* 35–38.

107. "Study Says EPA Penalties Smaller in Minority Areas," *Lincoln Journal,* September 14, 1992. President Clinton issued an executive order intended to prevent minority neighborhoods from being burdened with an unfair share of dumps, incinerators, and other sources of pollution, but state governments and industrial groups challenged the order.

108. David Dante Troutt, "Behind the Court's Civil Rights Ruling," *New York Times,* April 29, 2001, WK4.

109. According to Supreme Court interpretation of Fourth Amendment search and seizure law, police can stop and frisk individuals who officers have "reasonable suspicion" to believe are committing a crime. But officers must have more than a hunch to meet the standard of "reasonable suspicion" (though less than the "probable cause" required to obtain a search warrant). A person's race is not a valid criterion, except when the person's race and physical description match those of the suspect being sought.

110. John Lamberth, "DWB Is Not a Crime," *Washington Post National Weekly Edition,* August 24, 1998, 23.

111. Michael A. Fletcher, "May the Driver Beware," *Washington Post National Weekly Edition,* April 8–14, 1996, 29.

112. Jeffrey Goldberg, "The Color of Suspicion," *New York Times Magazine* (June 20, 1999): 53.

113. David Cole and John Lamberth, "The Fallacy of Racial Profiling," *New York Times,* May 13, 2001.

114. Pierre Thomas, "Bias and the Badge," *Washington Post National Weekly Edition,* December 18–24, 1995, 6–9.

115. Henry Louis Gates Jr., "Thirteen Ways of Looking at a Black Man," *New Yorker* (October 23, 1995): 59; Anderson, "Black and Blue," 64.

116. Tammerlin Drummond, "Coping with Cops," *Time* (April 3, 2000): 72–73.

117. Laura M. Markowitz, "Walking the Walk," *Networker* (July/August 1993): 22.

118. William Raspberry, "The Little Things That Hurt," *Washington Post National Weekly Edition,* April 18–24, 1994, 29. And see Ellis Cose, *The Rage of a Privileged Class* (New York: HarperCollins, 1993).

119. Morin and Cottman, "The Invisible Slap," 6.

120. Kozol, *Savage Inequalities,* 179–180.

121. Juan Williams, "Why Segregation Seems So Seductive," *Washington Post National Weekly Edition,* January 24–30, 1994, 24. For an extended examination, see Derrick Bell, *Faces at the Bottom of the Well: The Permanence of Racism* (New York: Basic Books, 1992).

122. Stephan Thernstrom and Abigail Thernstrom, *America in Black and White: One Nation, Indivisible* (New York: Simon & Schuster, 1997), especially Part 3. Some improvement began before the civil rights movement—when southern blacks migrated to northern cities in the 1940s.

123. Andrew Tobias, "Now the Good News about Your Money," *Parade,* April 4, 1993, 5.

124. James Smith and Finis Welch, "Race and Poverty: A 40-Year Record," *American Economic Review* 77 (1987): 152–158.

125. Joel Garreau, "Candidates Take Note: It's a Mall World after All," *Washington Post National Weekly Edition,* August 10–16, 1992, 25.

126. However, their rate of home ownership—48 percent—is the same as the national rate was in the 1940s. Whites' rate is 74 percent now. Deborah Kong, "Strides Made, but Still Much Disparity between Blacks, Whites," *Lincoln Journal-Star,* July 22, 2002.

127. Thernstrom and Thernstrom, *America in Black and White,* 500.

128. Ibid., 507.

129. Ibid., 506.

130. Orlando Patterson, quoted in ibid., 507.

131. Orlando Patterson, quoted in Anderson, "Black and Blue," 62.

132. From 1967 to 1987, according to calculations by William Julius Wilson. David Remnick, "Dr. Wilson's Neighborhood," *New Yorker* (April 29; May 6, 1996): 98.

133. Sociologist William Julius Wilson develops this idea extensively in *The Truly Disadvantaged* (Chicago: University of Chicago Press, 1987).

134. U.S. Department of Commerce, *Statistical Abstract of the United States 2001* (Washington, D.C.: U.S. Government Printing Office, 2001), Table 38.

135. Wilson, *The Truly Disadvantaged.*

136. Remnick, "Dr. Wilson's Neighborhood," 98.

137. Samuel Walker, *Sense and Nonsense about Crime and Drugs,* 3d ed. (Belmont, Calif.: Wadsworth, 1994), xviii, 3.

138. Thernstrom and Thernstrom, *America in Black and White,* 533.

139. Peter Reuter, "Why Can't We Make Prohibition Work Better: Some Consequences of Ignoring the Unattractive," in *Perspectives on Crime and Justice: 1996–1997 Lecture Series* (Washington, D.C.: National Institute of Justice, 1997), 30–31.

140. "Doctor: Harlem's Death Rate Worse Than Bangladesh's," *Lincoln Journal,* January 18, 1990.

141. Connie Cass, "More Young Black Men in Trouble with Law," *Lincoln Journal-Star,* October 5, 1995.

142. Donald Kaul, "Only Surprise Is That Riots Didn't Happen Sooner," *Lincoln Journal,* May 19, 1992.

143. *New York Times,* April 2, 1978.

144. Although Hispanics commonly are spoken of as though they are a separate race, they really are not. Most are an amalgam of European, African, and/or Indian ancestry that makes it impossible to identify a race. On the 1990 census forms, where individuals indicate their own race, half of the Hispanics left this line blank. Hacker, *Two Nations,* 6.

145. According to the most recent research, in 2002, Hispanics might face somewhat more discrimination in housing than blacks. Hispanics who tried to buy a house faced discrimination 20 percent of the time, and those who tried to rent an apartment did so 25 percent of the time. "Hispanics Face More Bias in Housing."

146. Tammerlin Drummond, "It's Not Just in New Jersey," *Time* (June 14, 1999): 61.

147. Guadaloupe San Miguel, "Mexican American Organizations and the Changing Politics of School Desegregation in Texas, 1945–1980," *Social Science Quarterly* 63 (1982): 701–715. See also Luis R. Fraga, Kenneth J. Meier, and Robert E. England, "Hispanic Americans and Educational Policy: Structural Limits to Equal Access and Opportunities for Upward Mobility," unpublished paper, University of Oklahoma, 1985.

148. San Miguel, "Mexican American Organizations," 710.

149. Leo Grebler, Joan W. Moore, and Ralph C. Guzman, *The Mexican-American People* (New York: Free Press, 1970), 157.

150. Even children of illegal aliens have been given the right to attend public schools by the Supreme Court. The majority assumed that most of these children, although subject to deportation, would remain in the United States, given the large number of illegal aliens who do remain here. Denying them an education would deprive them of the opportunity to fulfill their potential and would deprive society of the benefit of their contribution. *Plyler v. Doe,* 457 U.S. 202 (1982).

151. Fraga et al., "Hispanic Americans," 6.

152. Luis Ricardo Fraga, Kenneth Meier, and Robert England, "Hispanic Americans and Educational Policy: Limits to Equal Access," *Journal of Politics* 48 (November 1986): 850–873.

153. *San Antonio Independent School District v. Rodriguez,* 411 U.S. 1 (1973).

154. Anjetta McQueen, "Dual-Language Schools Sought," *Lincoln Journal-Star,* March 16, 2000.

155. *Lau v. Nichols,* 414 U.S. 563 (1974).

156. McQueen, "Dual-Language Schools Sought."

157. Lynne Duke, "English Spoken Here," *Washington Post National Weekly Edition,* December 21–27, 1992, 37.

158. Eloise Salholz, "Say It in English," *Newsweek* (February 20, 1989): 23.

159. Joel Kotkin, "Can the Melting Pot Be Reheated?" *Washington Post National Weekly Edition,* July 11–17, 1994, 23.

160. James Traub, "The Bilingual Barrier," *New York Times Magazine* (January 31, 1999): 34–35.

161. Ibid., 33–34.

162. Margot Hornblower, "No Habla Espanol," *Time* (January 26, 1998): 63.

163. "Bilingualism's End Means a Different Kind of Change," *Champaign-Urbana News-Gazette,* June 7, 1998.

164. Hornblower, "No Habla Espanol."

165. Jacques Steinberg, "Test Scores Rise, Surprising Critics of Bilingual Ban," *New York Times,* August 20, 2000, Y1.

166. 1990 Census of the Population, Social and Economic Characteristics, Part I, Table 13. Less than 5 percent of Asian language speakers and less than 2 percent of other-language speakers do not speak English.

167. Nancy Landale and R. S. Oropesa, "Schooling, Work and Idleness among Mexican and Non-Latino White Adolescents," Pennsylvania State University, Population Research Institute, working paper, 1997.

168. Thomas Boswell and James Curtis, *The Cuban American Experience* (Totowa, N.J.: Rowman & Allanheld, 1983), 191.

169. Kevin F. McCarthy and R. Burciaga Valdez, *Current and Future Effects of Mexican Immigration in California—Executive Summary* (Santa Monica, Calif.: RAND Corporation, 1985), 27.

170. Gregory Rodriguez, "Finding a Political Voice," *Washington Post National Weekly Edition,* February 1, 1999, 23.

171. "Survey: Hispanics Reject Cohesive Group Identity," *Lincoln Journal,* December 15, 1992.

172. Lynne Duke, "English Spoken Here," *Washington Post National Weekly Edition,* December 21–27, 1992, 37.

173. Rodriguez, "Finding a Political Voice," 22–23.

174. Karen Tumulty, "Courting a Sleeping Giant," *Time* (June 11, 2001): 74.

175. *Cherokee Nation v. Georgia,* 5 Peters 1 (1831); *Worcester v. Georgia,* 6 Peters 515 (1832).

176. Alfonso Ortiz, *The Pueblo* (New York: Chelsea House, 1994), 10.

177. Vine Deloria Jr. and Clifford M. Lytle, *American Indians, American Justice* (Austin: University of Texas Press, 1983), 221.

178. Ibid., 222–225.

179. Michael Lieder and Jake Page, *Wild Justice* (New York: Random House, 1997).

180. Indian Self-determination Act (1975).

181. Harvey Arden, "Who Owns Our Past?" *National Geographic* (March 1989): 383, 388, 393.

182. Ellen Nakashima and Neely Tucker, "A Fight over Lost Lands, Money Owed," *Washington Post National Weekly Edition,* April 29–May 6, 2002, 30.

183. According to the Indian Gaming Regulatory Act (1988), tribes can establish casinos if their reservation lies in a state that allows virtually any gambling, including charitable "Las Vegas nights."

184. Kathleen Schmidt, "Gambling a Bonanza for Indians," *Lincoln Journal-Star,* March 23, 1998.

185. Felicity Barringer, "Ethnic Pride Confounds the Census," *New York Times,* May 9, 1993, E3.

186. W. John Moore, "Tribal Imperatives," *National Journal,* June 9, 1990, 1396.

187. Ruth B. Ginsburg, *Constitutional Aspects of Sex-Based Discrimination* (St. Paul, Minn.: West, 1974), 2.

188. Karen DeCrow, *Sexist Justice* (New York: Vintage, 1975), 12.

189. Nadine Taub and Elizabeth M. Schneider, "Women's Subordination and the Role of Law," in *The Politics of Law: A Progressive Critique,* rev. ed., ed. David Kairys (New York: Pantheon, 1990), 160–162.

190. *Bradwell v. Illinois,* 16 Wall. 130 (1873).

191. From an amicus curiae (friend of the court) brief by 281 historians filed in the Supreme Court case, *Webster v. Reproductive Health Services,* 106 L.Ed.2d 410 (1989).

192. Donna M. Moore, "Editor's Introduction" in *Battered Women,* ed. Donna M. Moore (Beverly Hills: Sage, 1979), 8.

193. Barbara Sinclair Deckard, *The Women's Movement,* 2d ed. (New York: Harper & Row, 1979), 303.

194. In the early 1960s, a board game for girls—"What Shall I Be?"—offered these options: teacher, nurse, stewardess, actress, ballerina, and beauty queen. David Owen, "The Sultan of Stuff," *New Yorker* (July 19, 1999): 60.

195. Reprinted in "Regrets, We Have a Few," *Time, Special Issue: 75 Years of Time,* 1998, 192.

196. For an examination of Betty Friedan's role in the movement and the political dynamics among the various factions in the movement, see Judith Hennessee, *Betty Friedan: Her Life* (New York: Random House, 1999). For an examination of women's views toward feminism, see Elinor Burkett, *The Right Women* (New York: Scribner's, 1998).

197. Robert Alan Goldberg, *Enemies Within* (New Haven: Yale, 2002), cited in Mark Rozzo, "Book Currents," *New Yorker* (January 14, 2002): 21.

198. DeCrow, *Sexist Justice,* 119.

199. Thus, Betty Friedan later felt compelled to write a book espousing the concept of motherhood: *The Second Stage* (New York: Summit, 1981).

200. For a discussion of these points, see Jane Mansbridge, *Why We Lost the ERA* (Chicago: University of Chicago Press, 1986); Mary Frances Berry, *Why ERA Failed* (Bloomington: Indiana University Press, 1986); Janet Boles, "Building Support for the ERA: A Case of 'Too Much, Too Late,'" *PS* 15 (fall 1982): 575–592.

201. Shenkman, *"I Love Paul Revere Whether He Rode or Not,"* 136–137.

202. *Reed v. Reed,* 404 U.S. 71 (1971).

203. *Hoyt v. Florida,* 368 U.S. 57 (1961).

204. *Taylor v. Louisiana,* 419 U.S. 522 (1975).

205. *Stanton v. Stanton,* 421 U.S. 7 (1975).

206. "White Men Still First," *Lincoln Journal-Star,* April 1, 1995.

207. "Gender Wage Gap Still an Issue," *Champaign-Urbana News-Gazette,* April 3, 2001.

208. Lisa McLaughlin, "In Brief," *Time* (October 9, 2000): G12.

209. U.S. Department of Commerce, *Statistical Abstract of the United States, 1997* (Washington, D.C.: U.S. Government Printing Office, 1997), Table 645.

210. This view is according to a survey of women in three countries. Women in Canada and Great Britain had these same complaints. Carol Kleiman, "Study Examines Barriers to Women Climbing Ladder," *Lincoln Journal-Star,* April 2, 2001.

211. Susan Benesch, "The Birth of a Nation," *Washington Post National Weekly Edition,* August 4, 1986, 12.

212. The act also requires employers to continue health insurance coverage during the leave and to give the employee the same job or a comparable one upon her or his return.

213. Lisa Genasci, "Many Workers Resist Family Benefit Offers," *Lincoln Journal-Star,* June 28, 1995.

214. *Time* (June 28, 1993): 55–56.

215. From a personal conversation with a business professor in attendance at a conference.

216. Joyce Gelb and Marian Lief Palley, *Women and Public Policies* (Princeton, N.J.: Princeton University Press, 1982), 102. The author of Title IX, Representative Patsy Mink (D.-Haw.), had applied to medical schools but was not considered because she was a woman. Mink intended Title IX to open the doors. She said it was "never intended to mean

equal numbers or equal money" in athletics. Susan Reimer, "Title IX Has Unintended Consequences," *Lincoln Journal-Star,* April 9, 2000.

217. Steve Wulf, "A Level Playing Field for Women," *Time* (May 5, 1997): 80.

218. Jeremy L. Milk, "Women's Soccer on a Roll," *Chronicle of Higher Education,* November 3, 1993, A39.

219. Welch Suggs, "Uneven Progress for Women's Sports," *Chronicle of Higher Education,* April 7, 2000, A52–A56; Bill Pennington, "More Men's Teams Benched as Colleges Level the Field," *New York Times,* May 9, 2002, A1.

220. Suggs, "Uneven Progress for Women's Sports," A52.

221. Mary Duffy, quoted in E. J. Dionne Jr., "Nothing Wacky about Title IX," *Washington Post National Weekly Edition,* May 19, 1997, 26.

222. *Mississippi University for Women v. Hogan,* 458 U.S. 718 (1982).

223. *Orr v. Orr,* 440 U.S. 268 (1979).

224. *Michael M. v. Sonoma County,* 450 U.S. 464 (1981).

225. *Rostker v. Goldberg,* 453 U.S. 57 (1981).

226. A simplified version of this scenario was used by President Johnson in support of affirmative action.

227. Early decisions include *University of California Regents v. Bakke,* 438 U.S. 265 (1978); *United Steelworkers v. Weber,* 443 U.S. 193 (1979); *Fullilove v. Klutznick,* 448 U.S. 448 (1980).

228. Robert J. Samuelson, "End Affirmative Action," *Washington Post National Weekly Edition,* March 6–12, 1995, 5.

229. Two critics include Thomas Sowell, *Preferential Policies: An International Perspective* (New York: Morrow, 1990), and Dinesh D'Souza, *Illiberal Education* (New York: Free Press, 1991).

230. *United Steelworkers v. Weber; Sheet Metal Workers v. EEOC,* 92 L.Ed.2d 344 (1986); *Firefighters v. Cleveland,* 92 L.Ed.2d 405 (1986); *United States v. Paradise Local Union,* 94 L.Ed.2d 203 (1987).

231. *Firefighters v. Stotts,* 467 U.S. 561 (1985); *Wygant v. Jackson Board of Education,* 90 L.Ed.2d 260 (1986).

232. *Richmond v. Croson,* 102 L.Ed.2d 854 (1989); *Adarand Constructors v. Pena,* 132 L.Ed.2d 158 (1995). The perception that minorities are taking over is also reflected in a peculiar poll finding: The average American estimated that 32 percent of the U.S. population was black and 21 percent was Hispanic at a time when they were just 12 percent and 9 percent. Richard Nadeau, Richard G. Niemi, and Jeffrey Levine, "Innumeracy about Minority Populations," *Public Opinion Quarterly* 57 (1993): 332–347.

233. James E. Jones, "The Genesis and Present Status of Affirmative Action in Employment," paper presented at the American Political Science Association Annual Meeting, 1984; Robert Pear, *New York Times,* June 19, 1983; Nelson C. Dometrius and Lee Sigelman, "Assessing Progress toward Affirmative Action Goals in State and Local Government," *Public Administration Review* 44 (May/June 1984): 241–247; Peter Eisinger, *Black Employment in City Government* (Washington, D.C.: Joint Center for Political Studies, 1983); Milton Coleman, "Uncle Sam Has Stopped Running Interference for Blacks," *Washington Post National Weekly Edition,* December 19, 1983.

234. Gertrude Ezorsky, *Racism and Justice: The Case for Affirmative Action* (Ithaca, N.Y.: Cornell University Press, 1991), 48–49, 63–65.

235. Wilson, *The Truly Disadvantaged.*

236. Donald Kaul, "Privilege in Workplace Invisible to White Men Who Enjoy It," *Lincoln Journal-Star,* April 9, 1995; Richard Morin and Lynne Duke, "A Look at the Bigger Picture," *Washington Post National Weekly Edition,* March 16–22, 1992, 9.

237. Eisinger, *Black Employment in City Government.*

238. James Traub, "The Class of Prop. 209," *New York Times Magazine* (May 2, 1999): 51.

239. John Larew, "Why Are Droves of Unqualified, Unprepared Kids Getting into Our Top Colleges?" *Washington Monthly,* June 1991, 10–14; Theodore Cross, "Suppose There Was No Affirmative Action

at the Most Prestigious Colleges and Graduate Schools," *Journal of Blacks in Higher Education* (spring 1994): 47, 50.

240. For an examination of the *Bakke* ruling and its impact on graduate schools, see Susan Welch and John Gruhl, *Affirmative Action and Minority Enrollments in Medical and Law Schools* (Ann Arbor: University of Michigan Press, 1998).

241. Thomas J. Kane, "Racial and Ethnic Preference in College Admissions," paper presented at Ohio State University College of Law Conference, "Twenty Years after *Bakke,*" April 1998.

242. Richard Lacayo, "A New Push for Blind Justice," *Time* (February 20, 1995): 39.

243. Richard Morin and Sharon Warden, "Poll Says Americans Angry about Affirmative Action," *Washington Post,* March 24, 1995, A4. There appears to be majority support for the vague concept of "affirmative action," undefined, but the support evaporates when the questions use language indicating or implying any preference for minorities or women. Richard Morin, "No Place for Calm and Quiet Opinions," *Washington Post National Weekly Edition,* April 24–30, 1995, 34. Public opinion about affirmative action divides largely along racial lines. Although 81 percent of whites oppose affirmative action for minorities, 46 percent of blacks do.

244. So far the primary effect on the University of California system has been "cascading," with minority enrollments dropping at the most competitive UC campuses but increasing at the less competitive ones. Minorities have been cascading from the top tier to the next tiers, where their academic records more closely match other students' records. Traub, "The Class of Prop. 209."

245. This "is one of the better kept secrets of the debate." Alan Wolfe, "Affirmative Action, Inc.," *New Yorker* (November 25, 1996): 107. See also numerous sources cited therein.

246. Kluger, *Simple Justice,* 90.

247. Dick Kirschten, "Not Black-and-White," *National Journal,* March 2, 1991, 496–500.

248. 323 U.S. 214 (1944).

249. Peter Irons, "Race and the Constitution: The Case of the Japanese American Internment," *This Constitution* (winter 1986), 23.

250. William O. Douglas, *The Court Years* (New York: Random House, 1980), 279.

251. Irons, *Justice at War,* vii–ix, 186–218.

252. Ibid., vii, 367; Hersey, "Behind Barbed Wire," 73.

253. *Korematsu v. United States,* 584 F.Supp. 1406 (1983).

254. In 1948, Congress passed a law providing $37 million to settle damage claims by internees, but this was less than one-tenth of the amount that the government estimates internees had lost.

255. Tom Zeller, "In Every Mind the Memory, in Every Building a Threat," *New York Times,* September 30, 2001, WK4.

Chapter 16

1. Richard W. Stevenson, "House Approves a Bill to Repeal the Estate Tax," *New York Times,* June 10, 2000, A12.

2. "Statement by Senator Patty Murray in Favor of the Estate Tax Elimination Act (S. 1128)."

3. John Godfrey, "Though Tax Writers Are Busy, House and Senate Far Apart in Follow-Up to Last Year's Cut," *Congressional Quarterly Weekly Review,* May 25, 2002, 1384.

4. Michael Barone, Grant Ujifusa, and Charles E. Cook Jr., *The Almanac of American Politics 2000* (Washington, D.C.: National Journal, 1999).

5. Richard W. Stevenson, "House Approves a Bill to Repeal the Estate Tax," *New York Times,* June 10, 2000, A12; Joel Friedman and Andrew Lee, "Permanent Repeal of the Estate Tax Would be Costly, yet Would Benefit Only a Few, Very Large Estates," report of the Center on Budget and Policy Priorities, June 20, 2002, 1 (www.cbpp.org).

6. John Godfrey and Jeremy Torobin, "Senate Thwarting of Estate Tax Repeal Blunts GOP's Legislative Offensive," *Congressional Quarterly Weekly Review,* June 15, 2002, 1592.

7. "Statement by Senator Patty Murray on Marriage Penalty Tax Relief." Murray's Web site maintains an archive of press releases.

8. Mancur Olson, *The Logic of Collective Action* (New York: Schocken, 1971).

9. Adam Smith, *An Inquiry into the Wealth of Nations* (1776; reprinted in several editions, including Indianapolis: Bobbs-Merrill, 1961).

10. James Galbraith, *Balancing Acts* (New York: Basic Books, 1988); Robert Heilbroner and Lester Thurow, *Five Economic Challenges* (Englewood Cliffs, N.J.: Prentice Hall, 1981), 62.

11. Quoted in *Time* (January 30, 1989): 46.

12. John Maynard Keynes, *The General Theory of Employment, Interest and Money* (1936).

13. The FOMC is made up of a board of governors including five Federal Reserve Bank heads.

14. Ben Wildavsky, "Atlas Schmoozes," *National Journal,* May 17, 1997, 974–977.

15. For a brief review of the Fed's work, see James L. Rowe Jr., "Holding the Purse Strings," *Washington Post National Weekly Edition,* June 28, 1999, 6–8.

16. William Grieder, *Secrets of the Temple* (New York: Simon & Schuster, 1988), 461. Grieder's analyses of the Reserve Board's anti-inflation policies in the early 1980s are revealing and compelling.

17. Robert D. Auerbach, "That Shreddin' Fed," *Barrons,* December 10, 2001, 36. Auerbach was an economist for the House Banking Committee for eleven years.

18. Louis Uchitelle, "He Didn't Say It. But He Knew It," *New York Times,* April 30, 2000, Section 3, 1.

19. Douglas Hibbs, "Political Parties and Macroeconomic Policy," *American Political Science Review* 71 (December 1977); Paul Peretz, *The Political Economy of Inflation* (Chicago: University of Chicago Press, 1983).

20. Henry Chappell and William Keech, "The Economic Conservations of the Reagan Administration," paper presented at the conference on the Resurgence of Conservatism in the Anglo-American Democracies, May 1986; Douglas Hibbs, *The American Political Economy: Macroeconomics and Electoral Politics* (Cambridge, Mass.: Harvard University Press, 1987).

21. "Spoils to GOP Victors," *Champaign-Urbana News-Gazette,* August 6, 2002, 1.

22. Edward Tufte, *Political Control of the Economy* (Princeton, N.J.: Princeton University Press, 1978).

23. *National Journal,* November 7, 1992, 2544.

24. Steven Greenhouse, "Brady Sought Greenspan Policy Pledge," *International Herald Tribune,* September 25, 1992, 13.

25. "Poll: Citizens OK about Money, Glum on Future," *Champaign-Urbana News-Gazette,* April 12, 1995, B8.

26. Paul Krugman, "Dynamo and Microchip," *New York Times,* February 20, 2000, Section 4, 13.

27. The government raises small amounts of revenue by taxing consumption through the levies it places on the sale or manufacture of some luxury and nonessential items such as liquor and cigarettes, as well as on a few essential products such as gasoline. These excise taxes are designed not only to raise revenue but to limit or discourage use of scarce or dangerous products, which is why they are sometimes called "sin taxes."

28. Isaac Shapiro, "Overall Federal Tax Burden on Most Families—Including Middle-Income Families—at Lowest Levels in More Than Two Decades." Center on Budget and Policy Priorities report, April 10, 2002, 2 (www.cbpp.org).

29. Data are from the Center on Budget and Policy Priorities, quoted in "Middle-Class Tax Blow Hits Lowest Level since 1957," *Champaign-Urbana News-Gazette,* April 15, 2002, A8.

30. Isaac Shapiro, "Are We Soaking the Rich?" Center on Budget Policy and Priorities Report, April 16, 2002, 1 (www.cbpp.org).

31. Shapiro, "Overall Federal Tax Burden," 3–4.

32. Donald L. Barlett and James B. Steele, *The Great American Tax Debate: How Spiraling Fraud and Avoidance Are Killing Fairness, Distorting the Income Tax, and Costing You* (Boston: Little, Brown, 2000), 242–243.

33. Donald L. Barlett and James B. Steele, *America: What Went Wrong?* (Kansas City, Mo.: Andrews & McMeel, 1992), 41; Robert D. Hershey Jr., "A Hard Look at Corporate 'Welfare,' " *New York Times*, March 7, 1995, C1–C2.

34. David Cay Johnston, "I.R.S. Is Bolstering Efforts to Make Cheaters Pay Up," *New York Times*, February 13, 2000, 28.

35. "Service Check Shows Woes of IRS in Dealing with Public," *Champaign-Urbana News-Gazette*, July 16, 2001, A3.

36. "PAYGO Goes by the Wayside," *Congressional Quarterly Weekly Review*, January 13, 2001, 96.

37. David Stockman, *Triumph of Politics* (New York: Harper & Row, 1986).

38. Robert Greenstein, "President's Budget Uses Accounting Devices and Implausible Assumptions to Hide Hundreds of Billions of Dollars in Costs," Center for Budget and Policy Priorities, February 5, 2002, 2 (www.cbpp.org).

39. Mark Murray, John Maggs, et al., "The Deficit Difference," *National Journal*, February 9, 2002, 384, quoting Brookings analyst William G. Gale.

40. Thomas K. McCraw, "Deficit Lessons: Hamilton the Hero," *New York Times*, February 21, 1995, C1.

41. See John Schwartz, *America's Hidden Success*, rev. ed. (New York: Norton, 1988), and Bennett Harrison and Barry Bluestone, *The Great U-Turn* (New York: Basic Books, 1988), for analyses of the economy in the 1970s.

42. Paul Peretz and Raymond Ring, "Variability of Inflation and Income across Income Classes," *Social Science Quarterly* 66 (March 1985): 203–209.

43. *New York Times*, April 18, 1991, C18.

44. George Will, "Good Roads, Robust Economy Linked," *Lincoln Star*, March 12, 1990.

45. Paul Krugman, *Age of Diminished Expectations: U.S. Economic Policy in the 1990s* (Cambridge, Mass.: MIT Press, 1992), x.

46. John Berry, "The Legacy of Reaganomics," *Washington Post National Weekly Edition*, December 19–25, 1988; Spencer Rich, "Are You Really Better Off Than You Were Thirteen Years Ago?" *Washington Post National Weekly Edition*, September 8, 1986, 20; Levy, "We're Running Out of Gimmicks to Sustain Our Prosperity," *Washington Post National Weekly Edition*, December 29, 1986, 18–19.

47. "Two Trillion Dollars Is Missing," *New York Times*, January 8, 1989, E28.

48. Barbara Vobejda, "Class, Color, and College," *Washington Post National Weekly Edition*, May 15–21, 1989, 6.

49. Lester C. Thurow, "Companies Merge; Families Break Up," *New York Times*, September 3, 1995, E11.

50. Louis Uchitelle, "For Employee Benefits, It Pays to Wear Union Label," *New York Times*, July 16, 1995, 10.

51. Louis Uchitelle, "Fewer Jobs Filled as Factories Rely on Overtime Pay," *New York Times*, May 16, 1993, 15.

52. In 1982, 49 percent of low-wage employees had health insurance, but only 26 percent did in 1996. Peter Passell, "Benefits Dwindle Along with Wages for the Unskilled," *New York Times*, June 14, 1998, 23.

53. "Study Finds Uninsured Poor Parents on Rise," *Champaign-Urbana News-Gazette*, April 25, 2000, 1.

54. "Personal Bankruptcies Continue to Grow," *Congressional Quarterly Weekly Review*, August 3, 2002, 2117; Richard W. Stevenson, "Cheap Mortgage, Expensive Debt," *New York Times*, October 20, 2002, Section 4, 5.

55. "Family Wealth Down for 1st Time in 55 Years," *Champaign-Urbana News-Gazette*, March 14, 2001, A8.

56. Stephanie Aronson, "The Rise in Lifetime Earnings Inequality among Men," Federal Reserve Board Staff Report, March 2002, 4 (www.frb.gov).

57. David Leonhardt, "Executive Pay Drops Off the Political Radar," *New York Times*, April 6, 2000, Section 4, 5. For a survey of executive salaries, see "Will Today's Huge Rewards Devour Tomorrow's Earnings?" *New York Times*, April 2, 2000, Section 3, 1, 14–17.

58. Michael Lind, *The Next American Nation: The New Nationalism and the Fourth American Revolution* (New York: The Free Press, 1995), 139–216.

59. Keith Bradsher, "Gap in Wealth in U.S. Called Widest in West," *New York Times*, April 17, 1995, C4; Kevin Phillips, *Wealth and Democracy* (New York: Broadway Books, 2002), 123.

60. "College Grants Found Increasingly Going to Wealthier," *Champaign-Urbana News-Gazette*, February 18, 2000, A3.

61. "Study: Tuition Taking Bigger Bite of Family Income," *Champaign-Urbana News-Gazette*, May 2, 2002, A4.

62. Lance Gay, "Labor Leader: We Need a U.S. Industrial Base," *Champaign-Urbana News-Gazette*, September 1, 2002, B1.

63. See, for example, Charles F. Cnudde and Deane E. Neubauer, eds., *Empirical Democratic Theory* (Chicago: Markham, 1969); Phillips, *Wealth and Democracy*.

64. According to United Nations statistics.

65. David E. Sanger, "Look Who's Carping about Capitalism," *New York Times*, April 6, 1997, E5. This estimate has been accepted by the former chair of the Council of Economic Advisers, Laura D. Tyson.

66. One proponent of this view is former labor secretary Robert Reich. See his *Work of Nations: Preparing Ourselves for the Twenty-first Century* (New York: Vintage, 1992).

67. "A National Call to Action to Close the Digital Divide," White House press release, April 4, 2000 (www.whitehouse.gov/ WH/New/html/20000404.htm).

68. Peterson, "Net Dreams," 767.

69. Murray's press release explaining her vote against repeal of estate tax, June 12, 2002.

70. "Senate Thwarting Estate Tax Repeal," 1592.

Chapter 17

1. Gebe Martinez, "Playing the Blame Game on Farm-Friendly Politics," *Congressional Quarterly Weekly Review*, April 20, 2002, 1010.

2. Press release from the office of Senator Tim Hutchinson, May 13, 2002.

3. *Statistical Abstract of the United States, 2001*, Table 801.

4. Elizabeth Becker, "As House Prepares Farm Bill, Question of Who Needs Help, and How Much," *New York Times*, September 9, 2001, 22.

5. John Kelly, "Ag Subsidies; Rich Get Richer, Rest Get By," *Champaign-Urbana News-Gazette*, September 23, 2001, A1.

6. Becker, "As House Prepares Farm Bill."

7. "Spoils to GOP Victors," *Champaign-Urbana News-Gazette*, August 6, 2002, A7.

8. Gebe Martinez, "Free Spending Farm Bill a Triumph of Politics," *Congressional Quarterly Weekly Review*, May 4, 2002, 114. The first quote is from John Boehner (R-Ohio) and Cal Dooley (D-Calif.), and the second from Patrick Toomey (R-Pa.).

9. Press release from Senator Hutchinson's office, February 13, 2002. An archive of statements to the press can be found at the senator's Web site.

10. Philip Brasher, "Big Farms Hog Much of Subsidies," *Champaign-Urbana News-Gazette*, August 2, 2001, C6.

11. Martinez, "Playing the Blame Game On Farm-Friendly Politics," 1008.

12. Donald Barlett and James B. Steele, "Corporate Welfare," *Time* (November 9, 1998): 35.

13. Patricia Dunn, "The Reagan Solution for Aiding Families with Dependent Children: Reflections of an Earlier Era," in *The Attack on the Welfare State*, ed. Anthony Champagne and Edward Harpham (Prospect Heights, Ill.: Waveland, 1984), 87–110.

14. Melinda Upp, "Relative Importance of Various Income Sources of the Aged, 1980," *Social Security Bulletin* 46 (January 1983): 5.

15. "A Brief History of Social Security," *Basic Social Security Fact Sheet*, SSA Publication No. 21–059, August 2000 (www.ssa.gov).

16. *Women and Social Security Fact Sheet*, Social Security Administration (www.ssa.gov).

17. Press briefing on 2000 income and poverty estimates, Chart 9, U.S. Census Bureau (www.census.gov).

18. *Basic Social Security Fact Sheet* (www.ssa.gov).

19. Martin Anderson, *Welfare: The Political Economy of Welfare Reform in the U.S.* (Stanford, Calif.: Hoover Institution, 1978); Richard Margolis, "The Arithmetic of Poverty," *New Leader*, April 16, 1990, 14–15; Julie Kosterlitz, "Measuring Misery," *National Journal*, August 4, 1990, 1892–1896; Jason De Parle, "In Debate over Who Is Poor, Fairness Becomes the Issue," *New York Times*, September 3, 1990, 1, 10.

20. Greg J. Duncan, *Years of Poverty, Years of Plenty: The Changing Economic Fortunes of American Workers and Families* (Ann Arbor: Survey Research Center, Institute for Social Research, University of Michigan, 1984); Spencer Rich, "Who Gets Help and How," *Washington Post National Weekly Edition*, May 15–19, 1989, 37.

21. *Temporary Assistance for Needy Families (TANF) Program*, Administration for Children and Families, Department of Health and Human Services, final rule summary at www.acf.dhhs.gov/programs/ofa/exsumcl.htm; Liz Schott, Ed Lazere, Heidi Goldberg, and Eileen Sweeney, "Highlights of the Final TANF Regulations," Center on Budget and Policy Priorities, April 29, 1999.

22. Jack Tweedie, "Eight Questions to Ask about Welfare Reforms," *State Legislatures* (January 1999), at www.ncsl.org/statefed/ welfare/8quest.htm.

23. Pamela Loprest, "Long Ride from Welfare to Work," *Washington Post*, August 30, 1999, at www.urban.org/news/press/ loprest083099.html.

24. For a view of welfare reform from the states, see the report issued by the National Conference of State Legislatures' Executive Committee Task Force on Welfare Reform Reauthorization, July 2002 (www.ncsl.org).

25. E. J. Dionne Jr., "Welfare Reform's Clues Are in Wisconsin," *Washington Post National Weekly Edition*, September 29, 1997, 26.

26. Mark Murray, Marilyn Werber Serafini, and Megan Twohey, "Untested Safety Net," *National Journal*, March 10, 2001, 690.

27. Richard B. Freeman, "Labor Market Institutions and Earnings Inequality," *New England Economic Review* (May/June 1996): 158; U.S. Census Bureau, Current Population Survey, March 1960 to 2001 (www.census.gov).

28. John Kelly, "Lion's Share of Farm Subsidies Going to a Select Few," *Centre Daily Times*, September 10, 2001, 1.

29. "Farm Subsidies That Kill," A21.

30. John Lancaster, "Our Farm-Friendly Lawmakers," *Washington Post National Weekly Edition*, September 10–16, 2001, 11.

31. Ibid.

32. Becker, "As House Prepares Farm Bill."

33. John Beckerman, "Stockman Is Right: Military Pensions Are a Scandal," *Washington Post National Weekly Edition*, April 1985, 25; *Statistical Abstract of the United States, 1999*, Table 618; *Fact Sheet on TANF*, Administration for Children and Families, Department of Health and Human Services, February 17, 2000, at www.acf.dhhs.gov/programs/opa/facts/tanfpr.htm.

34. Murray et al., "Untested Safety Net," 691.

35. Clarke E. Cochran et al., *American Public Policy* (New York: St. Martin's, 1982), 262. See also Spencer Rich, "Look Again: The Anti-Poverty Programs Do Work," *Washington Post National Weekly Edition,* May 21, 1984, 24.
36. Matthew Miller, "Where It May Really Hurt," *Time* (December 18, 1995): 29.
37. Murray et al., "Untested Safety Net," 687.
38. Jay Mathews, "Study Shows Early Head Start Gains," *Centre Daily Times,* June 5, 2002, 1.
39. Alison Leigh Cowan, "Big-City Paydays at 'Farmer Mac,' " *New York Times,* August 28, 2002, Section 3, 10.
40. Sharon LaFraniere, "Though They Owe, Still They Reap," *Washington Post National Weekly Edition,* February 28–March 6, 1994, 10–11.
41. "Nature Humbles a State of Mind," *New York Times,* February 10, 1991, E3; Marc Reisner, "The Emerald Desert," *Greenpeace* (July/August 1989): 7.
42. Barlett and Steele, "Corporate Welfare," 38.
43. Donald L. Barlett and James B. Steele, "Fantasy Island," *Time* (November 16, 1998): 84.
44. Ibid., 87.
45. Donald L. Barlett and James B. Steele, "The Empire of the Pigs," *Time* (November 30, 2002): 53–54.
46. These figures are from the *Time* magazine series by Barlett and Steele on corporate welfare. "Paying a Price for Polluters," (November 23, 1998): 77; and "Corporate Welfare," 39.
47. For some sample costs of cleanup of industrial waste, see "Paying a Price for Polluters," 72–80.
48. Robert Samuelson, "Why Medical Costs Keep Soaring," *Washington Post National Weekly Edition,* December 5–11, 1988.
49. Erik Eckholm, "Those Who Pay Health Costs Think of Drawing Lines," *New York Times,* March 28, 1993, 1.
50. Watzman, "Socialized Medicine." In Canada, doctors cannot collect as much per caesarean if the frequency with which they do the procedure exceeds the percentage considered reasonable. Thus, the economic incentive to do caesareans disappears.
51. Richard Rich, quoted in "Access vs. Equity: The Real Health Care Reform Issue," *LAS Newsletter* (University of Illinois) (winter 1994): 6.
52. "While Congress Remains Silent, Health Care Reforms Itself," *New York Times,* December 18, 1994, 1.
53. Lauren Neergaard, "U.S. Health Care Costs Rank High," *Centre Daily Times,* June 21, 2000, 11A.
54. Cited in Gina Kolata, "Research Suggests More Health Care May Not Be Better," *New York Times,* July 21, 2002, 1, 20.
55. Harrell R. Rodgers Jr., *The Cost of Human Neglect: America's Welfare Failure* (Armonk, N.Y.: Sharpe, 1982), 91. Recent studies show that this continues to be true. See Peter Kilborn, "Racial Health Gap Remaining a Reality," *Lincoln Journal-Star,* January 26, 1998, 3A.
56. Robert Shapiro, Lawrence Jacobs, and Lynn Harvey, "Influences on Public Opinion toward Health Policy," paper prepared for the 1995 Midwest Political Science Association, Chicago.
57. *Basic Social Security Fact Sheet* (www.ssa.gov).
58. Richard Stevenson, "House Social-Security Bill Shows Trade-Offs for Bush," *New York Times,* July 29, 2001, 17.
59. *Basic Social Security Fact Sheet.*
60. Nina Bernstein, "Side Effect of Welfare Law: The No-Parent Family," *New York Times,* July 29, 2002, 1, 14.
61. Murray et al., "Untested Safety Net," 687.
62. Ibid.
63. Somini Sengupta, "Living on Welfare: A Clock Is Ticking," *New York Times,* April 29, 2001, 26.
64. Eileen Sweeney, *Recent Studies Indicate That Many Parents Who Are Current or Former Welfare Recipients Have Disabilities,* Center on Budget and Policy Priorities, February 29, 2000, at www.cbpp.org; Erica Goode, "Childhood Abuse and Adult Stress,"

New York Times, August 2, 2000, at www.nytimes.com/library/national/science/health/080200hth-stress-women.html.
65. Press release from Hutchinson's office, February 13, 2002.
66. Elizabeth Becker, "Accord Reached on a Bill Raising Farm Subsidies," *New York Times,* April 2, 2002, 11.
67. Press release from Hutchinson's office, May 13, 2002.
68. "Farm Subsidies That Kill," A21.

Chapter 18

1. The summary of Guinn's career is from Michael Barone, Richard E. Cohen, Charles E. Cook, and National Journal Group, *Almanac of American Politics 2002* (Washington, D.C.: National Journal Group, 2001), 943–944.
2. Shawn Zeller, "Gambling Millions on Anti-Yucca Lobbying," *National Journal,* June 15, 2002, 1797.
3. Ibid.
4. Statement of Kenny C. Guinn before the U.S. Senate Energy and Natural Resources Committee, May 22, 2002 (www.state.nv.us/nucwate/news2002), 6.
5. Ibid., 3–4.
6. Barone et al., *Almanac of American Politics 2002,* 940.
7. Ibid., 1797.
8. From a position paper issued by the state of Nevada, "Why Does the State Oppose Yucca Mountain?" (www.state.nv.us/nucwaste).
9. Adam Smith, *An Inquiry into the Wealth of Nations* (1776; any edition).
10. See discussion in William Ophuls, *Ecology and the Politics of Scarcity* (San Francisco: Freeman, 1977).
11. NBC News Special Report on the 20th Anniversary of Earth Day, April 22, 1991.
12. *Environmental Encyclopedia* (Detroit: Gale Research, 1993), 320–321; Ruth A. Eblen and William R. Eblen, eds., *The Encyclopedia of the Environment* (New York: Houghton Mifflin, 1994), 243.
13. Steven Pearlstein, "The Disaster of Deregulation," *Washington Post National Weekly Edition,* September 10–16, 2001, 6.
14. Kirk Victor and Michael Posner, "Merger Mania," *National Journal,* July 15, 2000, 2282; Stephan Labaton, "Oligopoly," *New York Times,* June 11, 2000, Section 4, 1.
15. Steve Lohr, "The New Math of Monopoly," *New York Times,* April 9, 2000, Section 4, 1. Excerpts from the federal court ruling against Microsoft appeared in *New York Times,* April 4, 2000, C14–C15.
16. Margaret Kriz, "Global Food Fight," *National Journal,* March 4, 2000, 689.
17. Neela Banerjee, "Who Will Needle Regulators Now That Enron's Muzzled?" *New York Times,* January 20, 2002, Section 3, 12.
18. Cornelius M. Kerwin, *Rulemaking: How Government Agencies Write Law and Make Policy* (Washington, D.C.: CQ Press, 1994), 171.
19. See the discussion in Walter A. Rosenbaum, *Environmental Politics and Policy* (Washington, D.C.: CQ Press, 1985), 90–95.
20. See Susan Tolchin and Martin Tolchin, *Dismantling America* (Boston: Houghton Mifflin, 1983), especially Chapter 4. See George C. Eads and Michael Fix, *Relief or Reform?* (Washington, D.C.: Urban Institute Press, 1984), 241–245, for an assessment of cost savings under Reagan's regulatory policies.
21. *Fortune* (February 3, 1986); Michael Reagan, *Regulation* (Boston: Little, Brown, 1987), 126.
22. Tolchin and Tolchin, *Dismantling America.*
23. "A New Rule Clouds the Clean Air Act," *New York Times,* June 28, 1992, E6.
24. Rebecca Adams, "GOP, Businesses Rewrite the Regulatory Playbook," *Congressional Quarterly Weekly Review,* May 5, 2001, 994.
25. Denis Hayes, "Earth Day Plus 25 Years: Things Are Looking Up for the Earth," *Champaign-Urbana News-Gazette,* April 23, 1995, B1.

26. Interview with Arthur Levitt Jr., SEC chair during the Clinton administration. Bill Moyers's *Now,* PBS, June 20, 2002.
27. Jane Mayer, "The Accountants' War," *New Yorker* (April 22 and 29, 2002): 70.
28. Ibid., 68.
29. Kerwin, *Rulemaking,* 264.
30. Margaret Kriz, "Electric Power Play," *National Journal,* June 3, 2000, 1744–1748.
31. Kenneth J. Meier, *Regulation* (New York: St. Martin's, 1985), 78–80.
32. Joseph Nocera, "System Failure," *Fortune* (June 24, 2002, 3) (www.fortune.com).
33. Philip K. Howard, *The Death of Common Sense: How Law Is Suffocating America* (New York: Random House, 1994), 26, 12.
34. Greg Gordon, "AFL-CIO Worries about Worker Safety under Bush," *Champaign-Urbana News-Gazette,* January 14, 2002, D4.
35. Matthew L. Wald, "So, How Much Did You Pay for Your Ticket?" *New York Times,* April 12, 1998, Section 4, 1.
36. Kathy Koch, "Can Congress Prevent Aviation Gridlock?" *Congressional Quarterly* Outlook, October 16, 1999, 7; Jeff Plungis, "Lawmakers Wary of Unfriendly Skies Weigh Revisiting Airline Regulation," *Congressional Quarterly Weekly Report,* July 8, 2000, 1675.
37. Koch, "Can Congress Prevent Aviation Gridlock?" 9.
38. Figure cited on the PBS show "Surviving the Bottom Line," Part 1, January 16, 1998.
39. Mary Schiavo, with Sabra Chartrand, *Flying Blind, Flying Safe* (New York: Avon, 1997), excerpted in *Time* (March 31, 1997): 52–62.
40. Wald, "Getting There: A Reality Check," Section 5, 14.
41. "Demise of 'Regs' Threw Airlines into Tailspin," *Congressional Quarterly Outlook,* October 16, 1999, 14.
42. Laurence Zuckerman, "Rising Tide of Passengers Fume over Delays at Nation's Airports," *New York Times,* July 16, 2000, 1.
43. Kirk Victor, "Hub Cap," *National Journal,* May 12, 1990, 1145.
44. "Demise of 'Regs' Threw Airlines into Tailspin," 15.
45. Koch, "Can Congress Prevent Aviation Gridlock?" 7.
46. James C. Benton, "Hill Ready to Wrest Control in America's Frustrated Skies," *Congressional Quarterly Weekly Review,* June 23, 2001, 1488.
47. Plungis, "Lawmakers Wary of Unfriendly Skies," 1671.
48. Daniel Yergin and Joseph Stanislaw, *Commanding Heights: The New Relationship between Government and the Marketplace* (New York: Simon & Schuster, 1998), 11.
49. Victor and Posner, "Merger Mania," 2281.
50. Labaton, "Oligopoly," 1, 4.
51. "Media Mergers," Bill Moyers's *Now,* PBS, April 26, 2002. Transcripts are online at www.pbs.org.
52. Victor and Posner, "Merger Mania," 2289.
53. Quoted in David Bollier and Joan Claybrook, *Freedom from Harm* (Washington, D.C.: Public Citizen and Democracy Project, 1986), 95.
54. Kriz, "Global Food Fight," 688.
55. Richard W. Stevenson, "Playing Catch-up with Monopolies," *New York Times,* November 14, 1999, Section 4, 16.
56. "Internet Bills Multiply," *Congressional Quarterly Weekly Report,* September 4, 1999, 2033.
57. Albert Gore Jr., *Earth in the Balance* (Boston: Houghton Mifflin, 1992), 294.
58. Mary H. Cooper, "Setting Priorities and Paying the Tab," *Congressional Quarterly Outlook,* June 5, 1999, 9.
59. John Jay, "The Federalist #2," in *The Federalist: A Commentary on the Constitution of the United States* (New York: Modern Library), 8–9.
60. Lynn White Jr., "The Historical Roots of Our Ecological Crisis," *Science* 155 (March 10, 1967).

61. See Robert Nisbet, *The History of the Idea of Progress* (New York: Basic Books, 1980), for an interesting examination of the idea of progress from antiquity to the present.

62. See Meier, *Regulation,* Chapter 6, for an overview of early attempts by the federal government to protect the environment.

63. James Anderson, David Brady, and Charles Bullock, *Public Policy and Politics in America* (North Scituate, Mass.: Duxbury, 1977), 74.

64. Kerwin, *Rulemaking,* 171.

65. Meier, *Regulation,* 145; Norman Vig and Michael Kraft, "Environmental Policy from the Seventies to the Eighties," in *Environmental Policy in the 1980s,* ed. Vig and Kraft (Washington, D.C.: CQ Press, 1984), 16.

66. Information about the founding of the EPA is drawn from Steven A. Cohen, "EPA: A Qualified Success," in *Controversies in Environmental Policy,* ed. Sheldon Kamienecki, Robert O'Brien, and Michael Clarke (Albany: State University of New York Press, 1986), 174–199; Meier, *Regulation,* 142–146.

67. Easterbrook, "Here Comes the Sun," 38–42; Margaret Kriz, "A New Shade of Green," *National Journal,* March 18, 1995, 662; Howard, *The Death of Common Sense,* 26.

68. Meier, *Regulation,* 147.

69. "Kids and Chemicals," Bill Moyers's *Now,* PBS broadcast, May 10, 2002.

70. Quoted from the EPA's 2000 long-term mission statement, "Preparing for a New Era of Environmental Protection," at www.epa.gov/.

71. Helen Ingram and Dean Mann, "Preserving the Clean Water Act," in *Environmental Policy in the 1980s,* ed. Vig and Kraft, 260.

72. See Lois Gibbs, *Love Canal* (Albany: State University of New York Press, 1983), for the Love Canal story from the perspective of the woman who organized the neighborhood to demand that government do something. Andrew Danzo, "The Big Sleazy," *Washington Monthly* (September 1988): 11–17, describes bureaucratic delay in helping the residents of Love Canal. See also Adeline Gordon Levine, *Love Canal: Science, Politics, and People* (Lexington, Mass.: Heath, 1982).

73. The Resource Conservation and Recovery Act of 1976 and the Toxic Substances Control Act of 1976; also see the EPA's dictionary of terms at www.epa.gov/.

74. Rosenbaum, *Environmental Politics,* 215.

75. "Little of Superfund Settlements Go to Cleanup," *New York Times,* April 26, 1992, 16.

76. *Budget of the U.S. Government, Fiscal Year 1999* (Washington, D.C.: U.S. Government Printing Office, 1998), 178.

77. Katharine Q. Seelye, "Bush to Shift Toxic Cleanups to Taxpayers," *New York Times,* February 24, 2002, 22; Margaret Kriz, "Superfund Slowdown," *National Journal,* June 1, 2002, 1623–1625.

78. Albert Gore Jr., "Earth Days Have Become Earth Years," *New York Times,* April 23, 1995, E16.

79. Much of the discussion in this section is based on a series of articles on environmental policy written by Keith Schneider, Michael Spector, and Joel Brinkley that ran in the *New York Times* from March 21 to March 26, 1993.

80. Keith Schneider, "Second Chance on Environment," *New York Times,* March 26, 1993, A17.

81. Keith Schneider, "New View Calls Environmental Policy Misguided," *New York Times,* March 21, 1993, 16.

82. Joel Brinkley, "Many Say Lab-Animal Tests Fail to Measure Human Risk," *New York Times,* March 23, 1993, A16.

83. Keith Schneider, "For the Environment, Compassion Fatigue," *New York Times,* November 6, 1994, E3.

84. National Audubon Society fund-raising letter cited by Keith Schneider, "Big Environment Hits a Recession," *New York Times,* January 1, 1995. F4.

Other critical assessments of the environmental movement's pessimistic outlook can be found in Martin W. Lewis, *Green Delusions* (Durham, N.C.: Duke University Press, 1992); Bill McKibben, "An Explosion of Green," *Atlantic Monthly* (April 1995): 61–83; Evan J. Ringquist, "Is 'Effective Regulation' Always Oxymoronic? The States and Ambient Air Quality," *Social Science Quarterly* 76, no. 1 (March 1995): 69–87.

85. David Osborne and Ted Gaebler, *Reinventing Government: How the Entrepreneurial Spirit Is Transforming the Public Sector* (New York: Penguin [Plume], 1992), 299–305.

86. Ibid., 302.

87. Philip Shabecoff, "Tax Proposed on Products and Activities That Harm Environment," *New York Times,* February 10, 1991, 1.

88. *Budget of the U.S. Government, Fiscal Year 1996* (Washington, D.C.: U.S. Government Printing Office, 1995), 81–90.

89. Carol Browner, quoted by Margaret Kriz, "The Conquered Coalition," *National Journal,* December 3, 1994, 2827.

90. *U.S. Budget for Fiscal Year 2003* (Washington, D.C.: U.S. Government Printing Office, 2002), 305.

91. Quoted by Bill McKibben, "Not So Fast," *New York Times Magazine* (July 23, 1995): 25.

92. See research by Nicholas Ashford reported in U.S. Senate Governmental Affairs Committee, 96th Congress, "Benefits of Environmental, Health, and Safety Regulation" (Washington, D.C.: U.S. Government Printing Office, March 25, 1980); Gregg Easterbrook, *A Moment on the Earth: The Coming Age of Environmental Optimism* (New York: Viking, 1995).

93. See Rosenbaum, *Environmental Politics,* 126–127; Bollier and Claybrook, *Freedom from Harm,* 116.

94. *Statistical Abstract of the United States, 1999,* Table 415.

95. Jonathan Rosen, "Birding at the End of Nature," *New York Times Magazine* (May 21, 2000): 66.

96. Sam Howe Verhovek, "They Exist: Therefore They Are. But, Do You Care?" *New York Times,* October 17, 1999, Section 4, 5.

97. "GOP, Businesses Rewrite the Regulatory Playbook," 995.

98. Interview on the *NewsHour with Jim Lehrer,* PBS, July 10, 2002.

99. Statement issued by the office of the governor of Nevada, July 9, 2002.

100. "Gambling Millions on Anti-Yucca Lobbying," 1797.

101. See, for example, Carole Gallagher, *American Ground Zero: The Secret Nuclear War* (Cambridge, Mass.: MIT Press, 1993).

Chapter 19

1. The representation of Senator Lugar's views is based on press releases and biographical material posted at his Senate Web site and interviews on the *NewsHour with Jim Lehrer,* PBS, August 1, 2002, and September 19, 2002.

2. Miles A. Pomper, "Philosophical Conflicts Complicate Iraq Debate," *Congressional Quarterly Weekly Review,* August 3, 2002, 2096–2100.

3. "Lugar Statement on '10110 over 10' at Senate Foreign Relation Committee Hearing," press release from Lugar's office, October 9, 2002.

4. The September 10, 2002, Lugar–Biden letter to President Bush can be found at Lugar's Web site under the "press releases" link (lugar.senate.gov/091202.htm). Their op-ed letter can be linked at Biden's Web site (biden.senate.gov).

5. Joint resolution submitted to Congress September 19, 2002.

6. *U.S. Budget for Fiscal 1996* (Washington, D.C.: U.S. Government Printing Office, 1995), 121.

7. Walter LaFeber, *New York Times,* July 3, 1983; "Diplomatic Subcontracting's Fine If You Get Good Help," *New York Times,* September 25, 1994, E6.

8. I. M. Destler, Leslie H. Gelb, and Anthony Lake, *Our Own Worst Enemy: The Unmaking of American Foreign Policy* (New York: Simon & Schuster, 1984), 115–116.

9. Joan Biskupic, "Constitution's Conflicting Clauses Underscored by Iraqi Crisis," *Congressional Quarterly Weekly,* January 5, 1991, 34; Madison's notes from *Documents Illustrative of the Formation of the Union of the American States,* quoted in "Framers Were Wary of War Powers," in the same source.

10. Ronald D. Elving, "America's Most Frequent Fight Has Been the Undeclared War," *Congressional Quarterly,* January 5, 1991, 37.

11. Representative Toby Roth (R–Wis.), quoted in Katharine Q. Seelye, "House Defeats Bid to Repeal 'War Powers,' " *New York Times,* June 11, 1995, A7.

12. Barry B. Hughes, *The Domestic Context of American Foreign Policy* (San Francisco: Freeman, 1978), Chapter 5.

13. Robert Weissberg, *Public Opinion and Popular Government* (New York: Prentice Hall, 1976).

14. Eric Schmitt, "How to Bypass Sanctions and Do Business," *New York Times,* August 9, 1998, Section 4, 4.

15. Information in this paragraph is based on Jeff Gerth with Sarah Bartlett, "Kissinger and Friends and Revolving Doors," *New York Times,* April 30, 1989, 1ff.

16. For a discussion of the foreign policy establishment, see Walter Isaacson and Evan Thomas, *The Wise Men: Six Friends and the World They Made* (New York: Simon & Schuster, 1986).

17. Carl M. Cannon, "Judging Clinton," *National Journal,* January 1, 2000, 21.

18. Robert Wright, "Private Eyes," *New York Times Magazine* (September 5, 1999): 50–54; William J. Broad, "Snooping's Not Just for Spies Any More," *New York Times,* April 23, 2000, Section 4, 6.

19. Historian Michael Hogan quoted in John M. Broder, "Gentler Look at the U.S. World Role," *New York Times,* October 31, 1999, 14.

20. Paul Johnson, "The Myth of American Isolationism," *Foreign Affairs* 74, no. 3 (May/June 1995): 162.

21. Bruce Russett, *The Prisoners of Insecurity* (San Francisco: Freeman, 1983).

22. See James Nathan and James Oliver, *United States Foreign Policy and World Order,* 2d ed. (Boston: Little, Brown, 1981), 359–361.

23. For one view of the impact of Vietnam on the thinking of today's high-ranking officers, see (Major) H. R. McMaster, *Dereliction of Duty* (New York: HarperCollins, 1997).

24. Robert S. McNamara, *In Retrospect: The Tragedy and Lessons of Vietnam* (New York: Times Books, 1995).

25. Michael Beschloss, *Reaching for Glory: Lyndon Johnson's Secret White House Tapes, 1964–1965* (New York: Simon & Schuster, 2001), 166.

26. Weissberg, *Public Opinion and Popular Government,* 144–148.

27. Ole Holsti, "The Three-Headed Eagle," *International Studies Quarterly* 23 (September 1979): 339–359; Michael Mandelbaum and William Schneider, "The New Internationalisms," in *The Eagle Entangled: U.S. Foreign Policy in a Complex World,* ed. Kenneth Oye, Donald Rothchild, and Robert J. Lieber (New York: Longman, 1979), 34–88.

28. For an analysis of U.S.–Soviet relations in the Reagan era, see Alexander Dallin and Gail Lapidus, "Reagan and the Russians," and Kenneth Oye, "Constrained Confidence and the Evolution of Reagan Foreign Policy," in *Eagle Resurgent?* ed. Kenneth Oye, Robert Lieber, and Donald Rothchild (Boston: Little, Brown, 1987); John Newhouse, "The Abolitionist," Parts 1 and 2, *New Yorker* (January 2 and 9): 1989.

29. See George F. Kennan, "After the Cold War," *New York Times Magazine* (February 5, 1989): 32ff.

30. Bill Clinton, "A Democrat Lays Out His Plan," *Harvard International Review* (summer 1992).

31. Quoted in Thomas Friedman, "What Big Stick? Just Sell," *New York Times,* October 2, 1995, E3.

32. Ibid.

33. Elaine Sciolino, "Monroe's Doctrine Takes Another Knock," *New York Times,* August 7, 1994, E6. For a discussion of the U.S. turn to multilateralism see Stanley Hoffmann, "The Crisis of Liberal Internationalism," *Foreign Policy* 98 (spring 1995): 159–177.

34. *The National Security Strategy of the United States* (September 2002). The president's annual report to Congress is posted at www.whitehouse.gov/.

35. "Bush Plans 'Strike First' Military Policy," *Champaign-Urbana News-Gazette,* June 10, 2002, A-3.

36. Fred Kaplan, "JFK's First-Strike Plan," *Atlantic Monthly* (October 2001): 81–86.

37. Ashton B. Carter and William J. Perry, *Preventive Defense: A New Security Strategy for America* (Washington, D.C.: Brookings Institution, 1999).

38. To get an idea of an ambassador's work, look at "Ambassador: Under Fire Overseas" at www.pbs.org/.

39. U.S. State Department, "Diplomacy: The State Department at Work," 2 (www.state.gov/).

40. The findings of the congressional investigation into intelligence failures prior to and after 9/11 can be read at the Web site for the Senate Select Intelligence Committee. See transcripts of the testimony of Eleanor Hill, director of the Joint Inquiry staff.

41. James Bamford, "How to (De-)Centralize Intelligence," *New York Times,* November 24, 2002, Section 4, 3.

42. Brookings Institute estimate, cited in Tom Cohen, "The NATO Connection," *Champaign-Urbana News-Gazette,* March 14, 1999, B5. A lower estimate of the costs of nuclear preparedness can be found in David C. Morrison, "Putting a Price Tag on the Arms Race," *National Journal,* May 13, 1995, 1171.

43. United States Department of Defense, *Quadrennial Defense Review Report* (2001), 17. The full report is at the Pentagon's Web site (www.dod.gov).

44. Leslie Wayne, "America's For-Profit Secret Army," *New York Times,* October 13, 2002, Section 3, 10.

45. James Kitfield, "Standing Apart," *National Journal,* June 13, 1998, 1351; Charles Pope, "New Congress Is Older, More Politically Seasoned," *Congressional Quarterly Weekly Report,* January 9, 1999, 60.

46. Quoted in David E. Sanger, "Corrosion at the Core of Pax Pacifica," *New York Times,* May 14, 1995, Section 4, 1; Nicholas D. Kristof, "Drawing a Line in the Pacific," *New York Times,* July 16, 1995, E4; James Sterngold, "Some Leaders in Japan Begin to Question U.S. Bases," *New York Times,* August 28, 1994, 7.

47. "Diplomacy: The State Department at Work," 2.

48. Cited in "Still No Policy on Arms Sales," *New York Times,* April 3, 1994, op-ed page. The world's primary arms suppliers are the five permanent members of the UN Security Council: the United States, Russia, the United Kingdom, France, and China; Michael R. Gordon, "Russia Is Pushing to Increase Share in Weapons Trade," *New York Times,* July 16, 2000, 4.

49. Jim Hoagland, "What Goes Around . . . ," *Washington Post National Weekly Edition,* January 24, 2000, 5.

50. Joan Spero, an undersecretary of state, quoted in David E. Sanger, "How Washington Inc. Makes a Sale," *New York Times,* February 19, 1995, Section 3, 1.

51. David E. Sanger, "Foreign Relations: Money Talks, Policy Walks," *New York Times,* January 15, 1995, Section 4, 1.

52. "Diplomacy's New Hit Man: The Free-market Dollar," *New York Times,* May 24, 1998, Section 4, 5.

53. Julie Kosterlitz, "Trade Crusade," *National Journal,* May 9, 1998, 1054–1055.

54. Alan Blinder, *Hard Heads, Soft Hearts* (New York: Addison-Wesley, 1988), 118–119.

55. For a concise summary of the advantages and disadvantages of protectionism and free trade, see Paul Krugman, *The Age of Diminished Expectations* (Cambridge, Mass.: MIT Press, 1992), 101–113.

56. David E. Sanger, "64% of Japanese Say U.S. Relations Are 'Unfriendly,'" *New York Times,* July 6, 1993, 1, 6.

57. For a description of WTO structure, membership, and activities, see "WTO: Special Report," *Congressional Quarterly Weekly Review,* November 27, 1999, 2826–2838.

58. Mark Schapiro, "Revenge on the Nerds," *Civilization* (June/July 2000): 59.

59. Interview of Ralph Nader by Bill Moyers, *Now,* PBS, June 2002; Anthony DePalma, "Nafta's Powerful Little Secret," *New York Times,* March 11, 2001, Section 3, 1, 13.

60. Gary Clyde Hufbauer and Jeffrey J. Schott, with Kimberly Ann Elliot, *Economic Sanctions Reconsidered: History and Current Policy* (Washington, D.C.: Institute for International Economics, 1985), 10.

61. Gary Hufbauer, "Foreign Policy on the Cheap," *Washington Post National Weekly Edition,* July 20–27, 1998, 22.

62. Ibid, 80.

63. Dick Kirschten, "Chicken Soup Diplomacy," *National Journal,* January 4, 1997, 13.

64. "Diplomacy: The State Department at Work," 2.

65. Joseph Kahn, "The World's Bankers Try Giving Money, Not Lessons," *New York Times,* October 1, 2000, Section 4, 5.

66. Missy Ryan, "Arrested Development," *National Journal,* June 10, 2000, 1822.

67. David E. Sanger, "Strategies in a Market Era," *New York Times,* January 4, 1998, Section 4, 4.

68. James Bennet, "Africa Gets the Clinton Treatment," *New York Times,* March 29, 1998, Section 4, 4.

69. Tom Walker, "Planet of Riches Still Blighted by Poverty," *Sunday Times* (London), January 2, 2000, 16.

70. March 23, 1998, 1.

71. Clinton quoted in Jane Perlez, "At Conference on Trade, Clinton Makes Pitch for Poor," *New York Times,* January 30, 2000, 6.

72. "The National Security Strategy of the United States," 18.

73. David E. Sanger, "Bush Plan Ties Foreign Aid to Free Market and Civic Rule," *New York Times,* November 26, 2002, A12.

74. *CQ Daily Monitor,* August 28, 2002 (www.CQ.com).

75. Material in this section is drawn from Michael Gordon, "A Whole New World of Arms Races to Contain," *New York Times,* May 3, 1998, Section 4, 1; John Kifner and Jo Thomas, "Singular Difficulty in Stopping Terrorism," *New York Times,* January 18, 1998, 16; Keith Easthouse, "The Stewardship Debate," *Champaign-Urbana News-Gazette,* June 14, 1998, B1, B4–B5; Michael R. Gordon, "Russian Thwarting U.S. Bid to Secure a Nuclear Cache," *New York Times,* January 5, 1997, 1, 4.

76. Quoted from PBS's *Frontline* Web site at www.pbs.org/wgbh/pages/frontline.

77. Ibid.

78. "AIDS Threatens Global Security," report on the *News Hour with Jim Lehrer,* PBS, October 1, 2002. The transcript is at www.pbs.org/newshour/newshour_index.

79. Henri E. Couvin, "Stability of Africa Is Threatened as AIDS Gains Foothold in Armies," *New York Times,* November 24, 2002, 11.

80. *CQ Daily Monitor,* October 1, 2002 (www.CQ.com).

81. "Lugar Statement on Iraq Resolution," press release from Senator Lugar's office, October 3, 2002 (lugar.senate.gov/100302a.htm).

Abscam A 1981 FBI undercover operation in which six House members and one senator were convicted of taking bribes.

Activist judges Judges who are not reluctant to overrule the other branches of government by declaring laws or actions of government officials unconstitutional.

Adversarial relationship A relationship in which the parties are constantly in conflict with each other.

Affirmative action A policy in job hiring or university admissions that gives special consideration to members of traditionally disadvantaged groups.

Agents of political socialization Sources of information about politics; include parents, peers, schools, the media, political leaders, and the community.

Aid to Families with Dependent Children (AFDC) A program that provides income support for the poor.

American Civil Liberties Union (ACLU) A nonpartisan organization that seeks to protect the civil liberties of all Americans.

Amicus curiae In Latin, "friend of the court." A third party that gives advice in a legal case to which it is not a party.

Antifederalists Those who opposed the ratification of the U.S. Constitution.

Antitrust legislation Laws that prohibit **monopolies**.

Appropriations Budget legislation that specifies the amount of authorized funds that will actually be allocated for agencies and departments to spend.

Articles of Confederation The first constitution of the United States; in effect from 1781 to 1789.

Authorizations Budget legislation that provides agencies and departments with the legal authority to operate; may specify funding levels but do not actually provide the funding (the funding is provided by **appropriations**).

Baker v. Carr A 1962 Supreme Court decision giving voters the right to use the courts to rectify the malapportionment of legislative districts.

Balanced budget amendment A proposed constitutional amendment that would require balancing the federal budget.

Balanced government Refers to the idea that the different branches of government all represent different interests, forcing the various factions to work out compromises acceptable to all.

Bandwagon effect The tendency of voters to follow the lead of the media, which declare some candidates winners and others losers, and vote for the perceived winner. The extent of this effect is unknown.

Bay of Pigs invasion The disastrous CIA-backed invasion of Cuba in 1961, mounted by Cuban exiles and intended to overthrow the government of Fidel Castro.

Behavioral approach The study of politics by looking at the behavior of public officials,
voters, and other participants in politics, rather than by focusing on institutions or law.

Bible Belt A term used to describe portions of the South and Midwest that were strongly influenced by Protestant fundamentalists.

Bilingual education Programs where students whose native language is not English receive instruction in substantive subjects such as math in their native language.

Bill of Rights The first 10 amendments to the U.S. Constitution.

Bills of attainder Legislative acts that pronounce specific persons guilty of crimes.

Black Codes Laws passed by Southern states following the **Civil War** that denied most legal rights to the newly freed slaves.

Blockbusting The practice in which realtors would frighten whites in a neighborhood where a black family had moved by telling the whites that their houses would decline in value. The whites in panic would then sell their houses to the realtors at low prices, and the realtors would resell the houses to blacks, thereby resegregating the area from white to black.

Block grants A system of giving federal funds to states and localities under which the federal government designates the purpose for which the funds are to be used but allows the states some discretion in spending.

Boll Weevils Conservative Democratic members of Congress, mainly from the South, who vote more often with the Republicans than with their own party.

Brownlow Committee Appointed by Franklin Roosevelt in 1935, the committee recommended ways of improving the management of the federal bureaucracy and increasing the president's influence over it.

Brown v. Board of Education The 1954 case in which the U.S. Supreme Court overturned the **separate-but-equal doctrine** and ruled unanimously that segregated schools violated the Fourteenth Amendment.

Bubble concept A policy that permits flexibility in meeting pollution standards by allowing a company to meet an emissions standard if total emissions from all smokestacks at a factory or from all factories in a given area (under an imaginary bubble) meet the standard, even though emissions from individual smokestacks or factories fail to comply.

Budget and Accounting Act of 1921 This act gives the president the power to propose a budget and led to presidential dominance in the budget process. It also created the **Bureau of the Budget,** changed to the **Office of Management and Budget** in 1970.

Bureaucratic continuity The stability provided by career-oriented civil servants, who remain in government for many years while presidents, legislators, and political appointees come and go.

Bureau of the Budget Established in 1921 and later changed to the **Office of Management and Budget,** the BOB was designed as the president's primary means of developing federal budget policy.

Burger Court The U.S. Supreme Court under Chief Justice Warren Burger (1969–1986). Though not as activist as the **Warren Court,** the Burger Court maintained most of the rights expanded by its predecessor and issued important rulings on abortion and sexual discrimination.

Canadian health care plan A single-payer system in which individuals choose their own doctors and the province pays the doctors for services performed; fees are strictly regulated.

Capitalist economy An economic system in which prices, wages, working conditions, and profits are determined solely by the market.

Captured agencies Refers to the theory that regulatory agencies often end up working on behalf of the interests they are supposed to regulate.

Casework The assistance members of Congress provide to their constituents; includes answering questions and doing personal favors for those who ask for help. Also called **constituency service**.

Caucus Today, a meeting of local residents who select delegates to attend county, state, and national conventions where the delegates nominate candidates for public office. Originally, caucuses were limited to party leaders and officeholders who selected the candidates.

Central Intelligence Agency (CIA) Created after World War II, the CIA is a federal agency charged with coordinating overseas intelligence activities for the United States.

Checks and balances The principle of government that holds that the powers of the various branches should overlap to avoid power becoming overly concentrated in one branch.

City-state In ancient Greece, a self-governing state such as Athens or Sparta, consisting of an independent city and its surrounding territory.

Civil case A case in which individuals sue others for denying their rights and causing them harm.

Civil Rights Act of 1964 Major civil rights legislation that prohibits discrimination on the basis of race, color, religion, or national origin in public accommodations.

Civil Rights Act of 1968 Civil rights legislation that prohibits discrimination in the sale or rental of housing on the basis of race, color, religion, or national origin; also prohibits **blockbusting, steering,** and **redlining.**

Civil Service Commission An agency established by the **Pendleton Act of 1883** to curb **patronage** in the federal bureaucracy and replace it with a merit system.

Civil War The war between the Union and the Confederacy (1861–1865), fought mainly over the question of whether the national or state governments were to exercise ultimate political power. Slavery was the issue that precipitated this great conflict.

Classical democracy A system of government that emphasizes citizen participation through debating, voting, and holding office.

Closed primary A primary election where participation is limited to those who are registered with a party or declare a preference for a party.

Cloture A method of stopping a **filibuster** by limiting debate to only 20 more hours; requires a vote of three-fifths of the members of the Senate.

Coalition A network of **interest groups** with similar concerns that combine forces to pursue a common goal; may be short-lived or permanent.

Coalition building The union of **pressure groups** that share similar concerns.

Cold War The era of hostility between the United States and the Soviet Union that existed between the end of World War II and the collapse of the Soviet Union.

Commercial bias A slant in news coverage to please or avoid offending advertisers.

Committee of the Whole Refers to the informal entity the House of Representatives makes itself into to debate a bill.

Commodity groups Interest groups that represent producers of specific products, such as cattle, tobacco, or milk producers.

Comparable worth The principle that comparable jobs should pay comparable wages.

Concurrent resolutions Special resolutions expressing the sentiment of Congress, passed by one house with the other concurring, but not requiring the president's signature.

Confederal system A system in which the central government has only the powers given to it by the subnational governments.

Conference committee A committee composed of members of both houses of Congress that is formed to try to resolve the differences when the two houses pass different versions of the same bill.

Conflict of interest The situation when government officials make decisions that directly affect their own personal livelihoods or interests.

Conscientious objectors Persons who oppose all wars and refuse military service on the basis of religious or moral principles.

Conservative A person who believes that the domestic role of government should be minimized and that individuals are responsible for their own well-being.

Constituencies The persons a member of Congress represents. For a senator, all the residents of the state; for a member of the House, all the residents of the member's district.

Constituency service The assistance members of Congress provide to residents in their districts (states, if senators); includes answering questions and doing personal favors for those who ask for help. Also called **casework.**

Constitution The body of basic rules and principles that establish the functions, limits, and nature of a government.

Constitutional Convention The gathering in Philadelphia in 1787 that wrote the U.S. Constitution; met initially to revise the **Articles of Confederation** but produced a new national **constitution** instead.

Containment A policy formulated by the Truman administration that aimed to limit the spread of communism by meeting any action taken by the Soviet Union with a counter-move; led U.S. decision makers to see most conflicts in terms of U.S.-Soviet rivalry.

Contras Rebels who fought to overthrow the Sandinista government of Nicaragua.

Cooperative federalism The continuing cooperation among federal, state, and local officials in carrying out the business of government.

Cost-benefit analysis The process of evaluating a **regulation** by weighing its cost against the risk of harm if it is not implemented.

Cost overruns The amount by which the cost of a certain project exceeds the expected cost.

Cost-plus project A project for which the contractor is reimbursed for all of its costs in addition to a set, agreed-upon profit rate.

Court-packing plan President Franklin D. Roosevelt's attempt to expand the size of the U.S. Supreme Court in an effort to obtain a Court more likely to uphold his New Deal legislation.

Courts of appeals Intermediate courts between trial courts (**district courts** in the federal system) and the supreme court (the U.S. Supreme Court in the federal system).

Cracking, stacking, and packing Methods of drawing district boundaries that minimize black representation. With cracking, a large concentrated black population is divided among two or more districts so that blacks will not have a majority anywhere; with stacking, a large black population is combined with an even larger white population; with packing, a large black population is put into one district rather than two so that blacks will have a majority in only one district.

Cradle-to-grave regulations for dealing with hazardous wastes that require the wastes to be identified as toxic and handled in an environmentally sound manner from the time of creation until disposition.

Credentials committee A body responsible for examining the credentials of political convention delegates.

Criminal case A case in which a government (national or state) prosecutes a person for violating its laws.

Cruel and unusual punishment Torture or any punishment that is grossly disproportionate to the offense; prohibited by the Eighth Amendment.

Cuban Missile Crisis The 1962 stand-off between the United States and the Soviet Union over an offensive missile buildup in Cuba. The Soviets finally agreed to remove all the missiles from Cuban soil.

Cumulative voting A proposed reform to increase minority representation; calls for members of Congress to be elected from at-large districts that would elect several members at once. Each voter would have as many votes as the district had seats and could apportion the votes among the candidates as he or she wished, such as giving all votes to a single candidate.

De facto segregation Segregation that is based on residential patterns and is not imposed by law; because it cannot be eliminated by striking down a law, it is more intractable than **de jure segregation.**

Deficit A condition in which expenditures exceed revenues.

De jure segregation Segregation imposed by law; outlawed by ***Brown v. Board of Education*** and subsequent court cases.

Delegated legislative authority The power to draft, as well as execute, specific policies; granted by Congress to agencies when a problem requires technical expertise.

Demagogue A leader who obtains political power by appealing to the emotions and biases of the populace.

Democracy A system of government in which authority resides in the people.

Departments Executive divisions of the federal government, such as the Departments of Defense and Labor, each headed by a cabinet officer.

Depression A period of prolonged high unemployment.

Deregulation Ending **regulation** in a particular area.

Detente A policy designed to deescalate **Cold War** rhetoric and promote the notion that relations with the Soviet Union could be conducted in ways other than confrontation; developed by President Richard M. Nixon and Secretary of State Henry Kissinger.

Direct democracy A system of government in which citizens govern themselves directly and vote on most issues; e.g., a New England town meeting.

Direct lobbying Direct personal encounters between lobbyists and the public officials they are attempting to influence.

Direct primary An election in which voters directly choose a party's candidates for office.

Discretionary spending Spending by the federal government where the amount is set by annual **appropriations** bills passed by Congress; includes government operating expenses and salaries of many federal employees.

District courts The trial courts (lower-level courts) in the federal system.

Divided government The situation when one political party controls the presidency and the other party controls one or both houses of Congress.

Dixiecrat A member of a group of southern segregationist Democrats who formed the States' Rights Party in 1948.

Domino theory The idea that if one country fell under communist rule, its neighbors would also fall to communism; contributed to the U.S. decision to intervene in Vietnam.

Dred Scott case An 1857 case in which the U.S. Supreme Court held that blacks, whether slave or free, were not citizens and that Congress had no power to restrict slavery in the territories; contributed to the polarization between North and South and ultimately to the **Civil War.**

Dual federalism The idea that the Constitution created a system in which the national government and the states have separate grants of power with each supreme in its own sphere.

Due process The guarantee that the government will follow fair and just procedures when prosecuting a criminal defendant.

Earned income tax credit (EITC) A negative income tax. Instead of paying tax, persons with low incomes receive a payment from the government or a credit toward their taxes.

Education Amendments of 1972 These forbid discrimination on the basis of sex in schools and colleges that receive federal aid.

Electoral College A group of electors selected by the voters in each state and the District of

Columbia; the electors officially elect the president and vice president.

Environmental impact statement An analysis of a project's effects on the environment; required from government agencies under the National Environment Policy Act of 1970 before any new projects could be carried out.

Environmental Protection Agency (EPA) The regulatory agency with responsibility for pollution control; created in 1970 by President Richard M. Nixon.

Equal Credit Opportunity Act This act forbids discrimination on the basis of sex or marital status in credit transactions.

Equal Employment Opportunity Commission (EEOC) The EEOC enforces the **Civil Rights Act of 1964,** which forbids discrimination on the basis of sex or race in hiring, promotion, and firing.

Equal Pay Act A statute enacted by Congress in 1963 that mandates that women and men should receive equal pay for equal work.

Equal protection clause The Fourteenth Amendment clause that is the Constitution's primary guarantee that government will treat everyone equally.

Equal Rights Amendment (ERA) A proposed amendment to the Constitution that would prohibit government from denying equal rights on the basis of sex; passed by Congress in 1972 but failed to be ratified by a sufficient number of states.

Establishment clause The First Amendment clause that prohibits the establishment of a church officially supported by government.

European Union (EU) A union of European nations formed in 1957 to foster political and economic integration in Europe; formerly called the European Economic Community or Common Market.

Exclusionary rule A rule that prevents evidence obtained in violation of the Fourth Amendment from being used in court against the defendant.

Executive leadership The president's control over the bureaucracy in his capacity as chief executive; achieved through budgeting, appointments, administrative reform, lobbying, and mobilizing public opinion.

Executive orders Rules or regulations issued by the president that have the force of law; issued to implement constitutional provisions or statutes.

Executive privilege The authority of the president to withhold information from the courts and Congress.

Exit polls Election-day poll of voters leaving the polling places, conducted mainly by television networks and major newspapers.

Ex post facto law A statute that makes some behavior illegal that was not illegal when it was done.

Externality A cost or benefit of production that is not reflected in the product's market price. **Regulation** attempts to eliminate negative externalities.

Faithless elector A member of the **Electoral College** who votes on the basis of personal preference rather than the way the majority of voters in his or her state voted.

Farm subsidies Government payments to farmers to raise the price they receive for crops to above-market prices.

Federal Communication Commission (FCC) A regulatory agency that controls interstate and foreign communication via radio, television, telegraph, telephone, and cable. The FCC licenses radio and television stations.

Federal Election Campaign Act A 1974 statute that regulates campaign finance; provided for public financing of presidential campaigns, limited contributions to campaigns for federal offices, and established the **Federal Election Commission,** among other things.

Federal Election Commission Created in 1975, the commission enforces federal laws on campaign financing.

Federalism A system in which power is constitutionally divided between a central government and subnational or local governments.

Federalist Papers A series of essays in support of the U.S. Constitution; written for New York newspapers by Alexander Hamilton, James Madison, and John Jay during the debate over ratification.

Federalists Originally, those who supported the U.S. Constitution and favored its ratification; in the early years of the Republic, those who advocated a strong national government.

Federal Register A government publication describing bureaucratic actions and detailing regulations proposed by government agencies.

Federal Reserve Board Created by Congress in 1913, the board regulates the lending practices of banks and plays a major role in determining **monetary policy.**

Felonies Crimes considered more serious than **misdemeanors** and carrying more stringent punishment.

Feminization of poverty The phenomenon that the majority of families living in poverty are headed by females.

Fifteenth Amendment An amendment to the Constitution, ratified in 1870, that prohibits denying voting rights on the basis of race, color, or previous condition of servitude.

Filibuster A mechanism for delay in the Senate in which one or more members engage in a continuous speech to prevent the Senate from taking action.

Fireside chats Short radio addresses given by President Franklin D. Roosevelt to win support for his policies and reassure the public during the Great Depression.

Fiscal policy Government's actions to regulate the economy through taxing and spending policies.

Fixed-cost project A project that a contractor has agreed to undertake for a specified sum.

Flat tax A tax structured so that all income groups pay the same rate.

Food stamp program A poverty program that gives poor people coupons redeemable in grocery stores for food.

Franking The privilege of members of Congress that allows them to send free mail to their constituents.

Freedom of speech The First Amendment guarantee of a right of free expression.

Free exercise clause The First Amendment clause that guarantees individuals the right to practice their religion without government intervention.

Free trade A policy of minimum intervention by government in trade relations.

Frontrunners Candidates whom political pros and the media have portrayed as likely winners.

Full faith and credit A clause in the U.S. Constitution that requires the states to recognize contracts that are valid in other states.

Fundraiser An event, such as a luncheon or cocktail party, hosted by a legislator or candidate for which participants pay an entrance fee.

Game orientation The assumption in political reporting that politics is a game and that politicians are the players; leads to an emphasis on strategy at the expense of substance in news stories.

Gender gap An observable pattern of modest but consistent differences in opinion between men and women on various public policy issues.

General revenue sharing A Reagan administration policy of giving states and cities federal money to spend as they wished, subject to only a few conditions.

Gerrymander A congressional district whose boundaries are drawn so as to maximize the political advantage of a party or racial group; often such a district has a bizarre shape.

Glasnost Mikhail Gorbachev's policy of opening the Soviet Union to the outside world by encouraging foreign investment, allowing more Soviet citizens to emigrate, and permitting multiparty elections in eastern Europe.

Globalization The international dispersion of economic activity through the networking of companies across national borders.

Going public The process in which Congress or its members carry an issue debate to the public via the media; e.g., televising floor debates or media appearances by individual members.

GOP Grand Old Party or Republican Party, which formed in 1856 after the Whig Party split. The GOP was abolitionist and a supporter of the Union.

Grace Commission A special commission established by President Ronald Reagan to recommend ways of cutting government waste.

Grandfather clause A device used in the South to prevent blacks from voting; such clauses exempted those whose grandfathers had the right to vote before 1867 from having to fulfill various requirements that most people could not meet. Since no blacks could vote before 1867, they could not qualify for the exemption.

Grand jury A jury of citizens who meet in private session to evaluate accusations in a given **criminal case** and to determine if there is enough evidence to warrant a trial.

Grants-in-aid Federal money provided to state and, occasionally, local governments to establish programs to help people such as the aged poor or the unemployed; began during the New Deal.

Grassroots lobbying The mass mobilization of members of an **interest group** to apply pressure to public officials, usually in the form of a mass mailing.

Great Compromise The decision of the **Constitutional Convention** to have a bicameral legislature in which representation in one house would be by population and in the other house, by states; also called the Connecticut Compromise.

Habeas corpus Latin for "have ye the body." A writ of habeas corpus is a means for criminal defendants who have exhausted appeals in state courts to appeal to a federal **district court.**

Hatch Act A statute enacted in 1939 that limits the political activities of federal employees in partisan campaigns.

Head of state The president's role as a national symbol of collective unity and pride.

Health maintenance organization (HMO) A group of doctors who agree to provide full health care for a fixed monthly charge.

Home rule The grant of considerable autonomy to a local government.

Honoraria Legal payments made to legislators who speak before **interest groups** or other groups of citizens.

Hyperpluralism The idea that it is difficult for government to arrive at a solution to problems because **interest groups** have become so numerous and so many groups have a "veto" on issues affecting them.

ICBM Intercontinental ballistic missiles, or land-based missiles.

Identity politics The practice of organizing on the basis of sex, ethnic or racial identity, or sexual orientation to compete for public resources and influence public policy.

Ideology A highly organized and coherent set of opinions.

Impeachment and removal A two-step process by which Congress may remove presidents, judges, and other civil officers accused of malfeasance. The House decides questions of impeachment; if a majority favors impeachment, the Senate decides whether to remove the accused from office.

Imperial presidency A term that came into use at the end of the 1960s to describe the growing power of the presidency.

Implied powers clause The clause in the U.S. Constitution that gives Congress the power to make all laws **"necessary and proper"** for carrying out its specific powers.

Impoundment A refusal by the president to spend money appropriated by Congress for a specific program.

Incrementalism A congressional spending pattern in which budgets usually increase slightly from year to year.

Independent A voter who is not aligned with any political party.

Independent agencies Government bureaus that are not parts of **departments.** Their heads are appointed by and responsible to the president.

Independent counsel See **Special prosecutor.**

Independent expenditures Campaign contributions made on behalf of issues or candidates, but not made directly to candidates or political parties.

Independent spending Spending on political campaigns by groups not under the control of the candidates.

Indirect democracy A system of government in which citizens elect representatives to make decisions for them.

Indirect lobbying Attempts to influence legislators through such nontraditional means as letter-writing campaigns.

Individualistic political culture One of three primary political cultures in the United States. One in which politics is seen as a way of getting ahead, of obtaining benefits for oneself or one's group, and in which corruption is tolerated. See also **moralistic** and **traditionalistic political cultures.**

Inflation The situation in which prices increase but wages and salaries fail to keep pace with the prices of goods.

Influence peddling Using one's access to powerful people to make money, as when former government officials use access to former colleagues to win high-paying jobs in the private sector.

Informal norms Unwritten customs that help keep Congress running smoothly by attempting to diminish friction and competition among the members.

Infotainment Television news stories that, without any sacrifice of probity or responsibility, display the attributes of fiction, of drama.

Injunction A court order demanding that a person or group perform a specific act or refrain from performing a specific act.

Inquisition A medieval institution of the Roman Catholic Church used to identify and punish heretics.

Institutional approach An investigation of government that focuses on institutions, such as Congress or the civil service, and their rules and procedures.

Institutional loyalty An **informal norm** of Congress that calls for members to avoid criticizing their colleagues and to treat each other with mutual respect; eroded in recent decades.

Interest groups Organizations that try to achieve at least some of their goals with government assistance.

Investigative reporting In-depth news reporting, particularly that which exposes corruption and wrongdoing on the part of government officials and big institutions.

Iroquois Confederacy An association of Native Americans in what is now New York State that was based on the principles of **checks and balances** and **federalism,** among other things.

Isolationism A policy of noninvolvement with other nations outside the Americas; generally followed by the United States during the nineteenth and early twentieth centuries.

Issue consistency The extent to which individuals who identify themselves as **"liberal"** or **"conservative"** take issue positions that reflect their professed leanings.

Issue voting Refers to citizens who vote for candidates whose stands on specific issues are consistent with their own.

Jeffersonian Republicans (Jeffersonians) Opponents of a strong national government. They challenged the **Federalists** in the early years of the Republic.

Jim Crow laws Laws enacted in southern states that segregated schools, public accommodations, and almost all other aspects of life.

Joint resolutions Measures that have the force of law and must be approved by both houses of Congress and signed by the president.

Judicial review The authority of the courts to declare laws or actions of government officials unconstitutional.

Junkets Trips by members of Congress to desirable locations with expenses paid by lobbyists; the trips are ostensibly made to fulfill a "speaking engagement" or conduct a "fact-finding tour."

Jurisdiction The authority of a court to hear and decide cases.

Justices of the peace Magistrates at the lowest level of some state court systems, responsible mainly for acting on minor offenses and committing cases to higher courts for trial.

Keating 5 Senators Alan Cranston, John McCain, Donald Riegle, John Glenn, and Dennis DeConcini, who were investigated by the Senate for ethics violations in connection with campaign contributions they received from financier/developer Charles Keating. All later intervened on his behalf with federal regulators.

Keynesian economics The argument by John Maynard Keynes that government should stimulate the economy during periods of high unemployment by increasing spending even if it must run **deficits** to do so; the deficits would be made up by higher employment and thus higher tax revenues during periods of prosperity.

Kitchen cabinet A group of informal advisers, usually longtime associates, who assist the president on public policy questions.

Know-Nothing Party An extreme right-wing party in mid-nineteenth-century America that opposed Catholics and immigrants.

Lame duck An officeholder, legislature, or administration that has lost an election but holds power until the inauguration of a successor.

Landslide An election won by a candidate who receives an overwhelming majority of the votes, such as more than a 10-point gap.

Leaks Disclosures of information that some government officials want kept secret.

Legislative calendar An agenda or calendar containing the names of all bills or resolutions of a particular type to be considered by committees or either legislative chamber.

Legislative veto A congressional **oversight** tool that allows one or both houses to block agency actions. Though the legislative veto was held unconstitutional by the Supreme Court in 1983, legislation with provisions for legislative vetoes continues to be passed, and agencies continue to honor the vetoes.

Libel Printed or broadcast statements that are false and tarnish someone's reputation.

Liberal A person who believes in a national government that is active in domestic policies, providing help to individuals and communities in such areas as health, education, and welfare.

Limited government A government that is strong enough to protect the people's rights but not so strong as to threaten those rights; in the view of John Locke, such a government was established through a **social contract.**

Line-Item veto A proposal that would give a president the power to veto one or more provisions of a bill while allowing the remainder of the bill to become law.

Literacy tests Examinations ostensibly carried out to ensure that voters could read and write but actually a device used in the South to disqualify blacks from voting.

Litigation Legal action.

Lobbying The efforts of **interest groups** to influence government.

Majority leader The member of the majority party in the House of Representatives who is second in command to the **Speaker.** Also, the leader of the Senate, who is chosen by the majority party.

Majority-minority district A congressional district whose boundaries are drawn to give a minority group a majority in the district.

Managed competition An aspect of the Clinton health care plan that involved joining employers and individuals into large groups or cooperatives to purchase health insurance.

Mandamus, writ of A court order demanding government officials or a lower court to perform a specified duty.

Mandate A term used in the media to refer to a president having clear directions from the voters to take a certain course of action; in practice, it is not always clear that a president, even one elected by a large majority, has a mandate or, if so, for what.

Mandatory spending Spending by the federal government that is required by permanent laws; e.g., payments for **Medicare.**

Marble cake federalism The idea that different levels of government work together in carrying out policies; governments are intermixed, as in a marble cake.

Marbury v. Madison The 1803 case in which the U.S. Supreme Court enunciated the doctrine of **judicial review.**

Market share The number of members of an **interest group** compared to its potential membership; having a large market share is an advantage.

Markup The process in which a congressional subcommittee rewrites a bill after holding hearings on it.

McCarthyism Methods of combating communism characterized by irresponsible accusations made on the basis of little or no evidence; named after Senator Joseph McCarthy of Wisconsin who used such tactics in the 1950s.

McCulloch v. Maryland An 1819 U.S. Supreme Court decision that broadly interpreted Congress's powers under the **implied powers clause.**

McGovern-Fraser Commission A commission formed after 1968 by the Democratic Party to consider changes making convention delegates more representative of all Democratic voters.

Means test An eligibility requirement for poverty programs under which participants must demonstrate that they have low income and few assets.

Media event An event, usually consisting of a speech and a photo opportunity, that is staged for television and is intended to convey a particular impression of a politician's position on an issue.

Media malaise A feeling of cynicism and distrust toward government and officials that is fostered by media coverage of politics.

Medicaid A federal-state medical assistance program for the poor.

Medicare A public health insurance program that pays many medical expenses of the elderly and the disabled; funded through **Social Security** taxes, general revenues, and premiums paid by recipients.

Merit system A system of filling bureaucratic jobs on the basis of competence instead of **patronage.**

Minimum tax A proposed tax that would require corporations and individuals with high incomes to pay a certain minimum amount in federal taxes.

Minority leader The leader of the minority party in either the House of Representatives or the Senate.

Miranda rights A means of protecting a criminal suspect's **rights against self-incrimination** during police interrogation. Before interrogation, suspects must be told that they have a right to remain silent; that anything they say can be used against them; that they have a right to an attorney; and that if they cannot afford an attorney, one will be provided for them. The rights are named after the case *Miranda v. Arizona.*

MIRV Stands for multiple independently targeted reentry vehicles; an offensive missile system that uses a single rocket to launch a number of warheads, each of which could be aimed at a different target.

"Mischiefs of faction" A phrase used by James Madison in the *Federalist Papers* to refer to the threat to the nation's stability that factions could pose.

Misdemeanors Crimes of less seriousness than **felonies,** ordinarily punishable by fine or imprisonment in a local rather than a state institution.

Missouri Compromise of 1820 A set of laws by which Congress attempted to control slavery in the territories, maintaining the balance between slave and nonslave states.

Mixed economies Countries that incorporate elements of both capitalist and socialist practices in the workings of their economies.

Monetary policy Actions taken by the **Federal Reserve Board** to regulate the economy through changes in short-term interest rates and the money supply.

Monopoly One or a few firms that control a large share of the market for certain goods and can therefore fix prices.

Monroe Doctrine A doctrine articulated by President James Monroe in 1823 that warned European powers not already involved in Latin America to stay out of that region.

Moralistic political culture One of three political cultures in the United States. One in which people feel obligated to take part in politics to bring about change for the better, and in which corruption is not tolerated. See also **individualistic** and **traditionalistic political cultures.**

Most favored nation (MFN) Trade status granted to a trading partner that permits that nation to export goods to the United States under the most advantageous **tariff** arrangements that the United States allows.

Motor voter law A statute that allows people to register to vote at public offices such as welfare offices and drivers' license bureaus.

Muckrakers Reform-minded journalists in the early twentieth century who exposed corruption in politics and worked to break the financial link between business and politicians.

Mutual assured destruction (MAD) The capability to absorb a nuclear attack and retaliate against the attacker with such force that it would also suffer enormous damage; believed to deter nuclear war during the **Cold War** because both sides would be so devastated that neither would risk striking first.

NAACP (National Association for the Advancement of Colored People) An organization founded in 1909 to fight for black rights; its attorneys challenged segregation in the courts and won many important court cases, most notably, *Brown v. Board of Education.*

Nader's Raiders The name given to people who work in any of the "public interest" organizations founded by consumer advocate and regulatory watchdog Ralph Nader.

National chair The head of a political **party organization,** appointed by the **national committee** of that party, usually at the direction of the party's presidential nominee.

National committee The highest level of **party organization;** chooses the site of the national convention and the formula for determining the number of delegates from each state.

National debt The total amount of money owed by the federal government; the sum of all budget **deficits** over the years.

National Organization for Women (NOW) A group formed in 1966 to fight primarily for political and economic rights for women.

NATO (North Atlantic Treaty Organization) A mutual defense pact established by the United States, Canada, and their western European allies in 1949 to protect against Soviet aggression in Europe; later expanded to include other European nations.

Natural rights Inalienable and inherent rights such as the right to own property (in the view of John Locke).

"Necessary and proper" A phrase in the **implied powers clause** of the U.S. Constitution that gives Congress the power to make all laws needed to carry out its specific powers.

Neutral competence The concept that bureaucrats should be uninvolved or neutral in policymaking and should be chosen only for their expertise—not their political affiliation.

New Deal A program of President Franklin D. Roosevelt's administration in the 1930s aimed at stimulating economic recovery and aiding victims of the Great Depression; led to expansion of the national government's role.

New Deal coalition The broadly based coalition of southern conservatives, northern liberals, and ethnic and religious minorities that sustained the Democratic Party for some 40 years.

New federalism During the Nixon administration, the policy under which unrestricted or minimally restricted federal funds were provided to states and localities; during the Reagan administration, a policy of reducing federal support for the states.

News release A printed handout given by public relations workers to members of the media, offering ideas or information for new stories.

Nineteenth Amendment An amendment to the Constitution, ratified in 1920, guaranteeing women the vote.

Nullification A doctrine advocated by supporters of state-centered federalism, holding that a state could nullify laws of Congress.

Obscenity Sexual material that is patently offensive to the average person in the community and that lacks any serious literary, artistic, or scientific value.

Obstruction of justice A deliberate attempt to impede the progress of a criminal investigation or trial.

Occupational Safety and Health Administration (OSHA) An agency formed in 1970 and charged with ensuring safe and healthful working conditions for all American workers.

Office of Management and Budget (OMB)
A White House agency with primary responsibility for preparing the federal budget.

Open primary A primary election that is not limited to members of a particular party; a voter may vote in either party's primary.

Overlapping membership The term refers to the tendency of individuals to join more than one group. This tends to moderate a group's appeals, since its members also belong to other groups with different interests.

Oversight Congress's responsibility to make sure the bureaucracy is administering federal programs in accordance with congressional intent.

Parliamentary government A system in which voters elect only their representatives in parliament; the chief executive is chosen by parliament, as in Britain.

Party boss The head of a political "machine," a highly disciplined state or local **party organization** that controls power in its area.

Party convention A gathering of party delegates, on the local, state, or national level, to set policy and strategy and to select candidates for elective office.

Party identification A psychological link between individuals and a political party that leads those persons to regard themselves as members of that party.

Party in government Those who are appointed or elected to office as members of a political party.

Party in the electorate Those who identify with a political party.

Party organization The "professionals" who run a political party at the national, state, and local levels.

Patronage A system in which elected officials appoint their supporters to administrative jobs; used by **political machines** to maintain themselves in power.

Pendleton Act of 1883 This act created the **Civil Service Commission,** designed to protect civil servants from arbitrary dismissal for political reasons and to staff bureaucracies with people who have proven their competence by taking competitive examinations.

Pentagon Papers A top-secret study, eventually made public, of how and why the United States became embroiled in the Vietnam War; the study was commissioned by Secretary of Defense Robert McNamara during the Johnson administration.

Permanent campaign The situation in which elected officials are constantly engaged in a campaign; fund-raising for the next election begins as soon as one election is concluded.

Personal presidency A concept proposed by Theodore Lowi that holds that presidents since the 1930s have amassed tremendous personal power directly from the people and, in return, are expected to make sure the people get what they want from government.

Platform committee The group that drafts the policy statement of a political party's convention.

Plea bargain An agreement between the prosecutor, defense attorney, and defendant in which the prosecutor agrees to reduce the charge or sentence in exchange for the defendant's guilty plea.

Plebiscite A direct vote by all the people on a certain public measure. Theodore Lowi has spoken of the "Plebiscitary" presidency, whereby the president makes himself the focus of national government through use of the mass media.

Plessy v. Ferguson The 1896 case in which the U.S. Supreme Court upheld segregation by enunciating the **separate-but-equal doctrine.**

Pluralism The theory that American government is responsive to groups of citizens working together to promote their common interests and that enough people belong to **interest groups** to ensure that government ultimately hears everyone, even though most people do not participate actively in politics.

Pocket veto A legislative bill dies by pocket veto if a president refuses to sign it and Congress adjourns within 10 working days.

Policy implementation The process by which bureaucrats convert laws into rules and activities that have an actual impact on people and things.

Political action committee (PAC) A committee established by corporation, labor union, or **interest group** that raises money and contributes it to a political campaign.

Political bias A preference for candidates of particular parties or for certain stands on issues that affects a journalist's reporting.

Political culture A shared body of values and beliefs that shapes perceptions and attitudes toward politics and government and, in turn, influences political behavior.

Political equality The principle that every citizen of a democracy has an equal opportunity to try to influence government.

Political machines Political organizations based on **patronage** that flourished in big cities in the late nineteenth and early twentieth centuries. The machine relied on the votes of the lower classes and, in exchange, provided jobs and other services.

Political socialization The process of learning about politics by being exposed to information from parents, peers, schools, the media, political leaders, and the community.

Political tolerance The willingness of individuals to extend procedural rights and liberties to people with whom they disagree.

Political trust The extent to which citizens place trust in their government, its institutions, and its officials.

Politics A means by which individuals and **interest groups** compete, via political parties and other extragovernmental organizations, to shape government's impact on society's problems and goals.

Poll tax A tax that must be paid before a person can vote; used in the South to prevent blacks from voting. The Twenty-fourth Amendment now prohibits poll taxes in federal elections.

Popular sovereignty Rule by the people.

Pork barrel Funding for special projects, buildings, and other public works in the district or state of a member of Congress. Members tend to support such projects because they provide jobs for constituents and enhance the members' reelection chances, rather than because the projects are necessarily wise.

Power to persuade The president's informal power to gain support by dispensing favors and penalties and by using the prestige of the office.

Precedents In law, judicial decisions that may be used subsequently as standards in similar cases.

Precinct The basic unit of the American electoral process—in a large city perhaps only a few blocks—designed for the administration of elections. Citizens vote in precinct polling places.

Presidential immunity Immunity of the president from lawsuits for acts that occur during his term in office and are related to his official responsibilities.

Presidential preference primary A **direct primary** where voters select delegates to presidential nominating conventions; voters indicate a preference for a presidential candidate, delegates committed to a candidate, or both.

Presidential press conference A meeting at which the president answers questions from reporters.

Pressure group An organization representing specific interests that seeks some sort of government assistance or attempts to influence public policy. Also known as an **interest group.**

Pretrial hearings Preliminary examinations of the cases of persons accused of a crime.

Prior restraint Censorship by restraining an action before it has actually occurred; e.g., forbidding publication rather than punishing the publisher after publication has occurred.

Private interest groups Interest groups that chiefly pursue economic interests that benefit their members; e.g., business organizations and labor unions.

Probable cause In law, reasonable grounds for belief that a particular person has committed a particular crime.

Productivity The ratio of total hours worked by the labor force to total goods and services produced.

Professional association A **pressure group** that promotes the interests of a professional occupation, such as medicine, law, or teaching.

Progressive reforms Election reforms introduced in the early twentieth century as part of the Progressive movement; included the secret ballot, primary elections, and voter registration laws.

Progressive tax A tax structured so that those with higher incomes pay a higher percentage of their income in taxes than do those with lower incomes.

Prohibition Party A political party founded in 1869 that seeks to ban the sale of liquor in the United States.

Protectionism Government intervention to protect domestic producers from foreign competition; can take the form of **tariffs,** quotas on imports, or a ban on certain imports altogether.

Public forum A public place such as a street, sidewalk, or park where people have a First Amendment right to express their views on public issues.

Public interest A term generally denoting a policy goal, designed to serve the interests of society as a whole, or the largest number of people. Defining the public interest is the subject of intense debate on most issues.

Public interest groups Interest groups that chiefly pursue benefits that cannot be limited or restricted to their members.

Public opinion The collection of individual opinions toward issues or objects of general interest.

Pure speech Speech without any conduct (besides the speech itself).

Quorum calls Often used as a delaying tactic, quorum calls are demands that all members of a legislative body be counted to determine if a quorum exists.

Realignment The transition from one stable party system to another, as occurred when the **New Deal coalition** was formed.

Reapportionment The process of redistributing the 435 seats in the House of Representatives among the states based on population changes; occurs every 10 years based on the most recent census.

Recession Two or more consecutive three-month quarters of falling production.

Reciprocity An **informal norm** of Congress in which members agree to support each other's bills; also called logrolling.

Reconstruction The period after the **Civil War** when black rights were ensured by a northern military presence in the South and by close monitoring of southern politics; ended in 1877.

Redistricting The process of redrawing the boundaries of congressional districts within a state to take account of population shifts.

Redlining The practice in which bankers and other lenders refused to lend money to persons who wanted to buy a house in a racially changing neighborhood.

"Red Scare" Prompted by the Russian Revolution in 1917, this was a large-scale crackdown on so-called seditious activities in the United States.

Reelection constituency Those individuals a member of Congress believes will vote for him or her. Differs from a geographical, loyalist, or personal constituency.

Regressive tax A tax structured so that those with lower incomes pay a larger percentage of their income in tax than do those with higher incomes.

Regulation The actions of regulatory agencies in establishing standards or guidelines conferring benefits or imposing restrictions on business conduct.

Rehnquist Court The U.S. Supreme Court under Chief Justice William Rehnquist (1986–); a conservative Court, but still has not overturned most previous rulings.

Religious tests Tests once used in some states to limit the right to vote or hold office to members of the "established church."

Republic A system of government in which citizens elect representatives to make decisions for them; an **indirect democracy.**

Reregulation The resumption of regulatory activity after a period of **deregulation.**

Responsiveness The extent to which government conforms to the wishes of individuals, groups, or institutions.

Restrained judges Judges who are reluctant to overrule the other branches of government by declaring laws or actions of government officials unconstitutional.

Restrictive covenants Agreements among neighbors in white residential areas not to sell their houses to blacks.

Retrospective voting Voting for or against incumbents on the basis of their past performance.

Right against self-incrimination A right granted by the Fifth Amendment, providing that persons accused of a crime shall not be compelled to be witnesses against themselves.

Right to a jury trial The Sixth Amendment's guarantee of a trial by jury in any **criminal case** that could result in more than six months' incarceration.

Right to counsel The Sixth Amendment's guarantee of the right of a criminal defendant to have an attorney in any **felony or misdemeanor** case that might result in incarceration; if defendants are indigent, the court must appoint an attorney for them.

Right to privacy A right to autonomy—to be left alone—that is not specifically mentioned in the U.S. Constitution, but has been found by the U.S. Supreme Court to be implied through several amendments.

Rules Committee The committee in the House of Representatives that sets the terms of debate on a bill.

Sandinistas The name of the group that overthrew Nicaraguan dictator Anastasio Somoza in 1978 and governed Nicaragua until 1990.

Scientific polls Systematic, probability-based sampling techniques that attempt to gauge public sentiment based on the responses of a small, selected group of individuals.

Scoop To obtain information before another reporter; also the information so obtained.

Seditious speech Speech that encourages rebellion against the government.

Selective perception The tendency to screen out information that contradicts one's beliefs.

Senatorial courtesy The custom of giving senators of the president's party a virtual veto over appointments to jobs, including judicial appointments, in their states.

Senior Executive Service The SES was created in 1978 to attract high-ranking civil servants by offering them challenging jobs and monetary rewards for exceptional achievement.

Seniority rule The custom that the member of the majority party with the longest service on a particular congressional committee becomes its chair; applies most of the time but is occasionally violated.

Separate-but-equal doctrine The principle, enunciated by the U.S. Supreme Court in *Plessy v. Ferguson* in 1896, that allowed separate facilities for blacks and whites as long as the facilities were equal.

Separation of powers The principle of government under which the power to make, administer, and judge the laws is split among three branches—legislative, executive, and judicial.

Setting the agenda Influencing the process by which problems are deemed important and alternative policies are proposed.

Sharecroppers Tenant farmers who lease land and equipment from landowners, turning over a share of their crops in lieu of rent.

Shays's Rebellion A revolt of farmers in western Massachusetts in 1786 and 1787 to protest the state legislature's refusal to grant them relief from debt; helped lead to calls for a new national **constitution.**

Shield laws Laws that protect news reporters from having to identify their sources of information.

Single-issue groups **Interest groups** that pursue a single public interest goal and are characteristically reluctant to compromise.

Social choice An approach to political science based on the assumption that political behavior is determined by costs and benefits.

Social contract An implied agreement between the people and their government in which the people give up part of their liberty to the government in exchange for the government protecting the remainder of their liberty.

Social insurance A social welfare program such as **Social Security** that provides benefits only to those who have contributed to the program and their survivors.

Socialism An economic system in which the government owns the country's productive capacity—industrial plants and farms—and controls wages and the supply of and demand for goods; in theory, the people, rather than the government, collectively own the country's productive capacity.

Social issue An important, noneconomic issue affecting significant numbers of the populace, such as crime, racial conflict, or changing values.

Social Security A social welfare program for the elderly and the disabled.

Soft money Contributions to national party committees that do not have to be reported to the federal government (and sometimes not to the states) because they are used for voter registration drives, educating voters on the issues, and the like, rather than for a particular candidate; the national committees send the funds to the state parties, which operate under less stringent reporting regulations than the federal laws provide.

Sound bite A few key words or phrase included in a speech with the intent that television editors will use the phrase in a brief clip on the news.

Speaker of the House The leader and presiding officer of the House of Representatives; chosen by the majority party.

Special interest caucuses Groups of members of the House of Representatives who are united by some personal interest or characteristic; e.g., the Black Caucus.

Specialization An **informal norm** of Congress that holds that since members cannot be experts in every area, some deference should be given to those who are most knowledgeable about a given subject related to their committee work.

Special prosecutor A prosecutor charged with investigating and prosecuting alleged violations of federal criminal laws by the president, vice president, senior government officials, members of Congress, or the judiciary.

Speech plus conduct Speech combined with conduct that is intended to convey ideas; e.g., a sit-in (conduct) where the protesters chant slogans (speech).

Stagflation The combination of high inflation and economic stagnation with high unemployment that troubled the United States in the 1970s.

Standing committees Permanent congressional committees.

Standing to sue The principle that individuals or groups must themselves have lost rights and suffered harm before they can bring a lawsuit.

Stare decisis Latin for "stand by what has been decided." The rule that judges should follow **precedents** established in previous cases by their court or higher courts.

"Star Wars" The popular name for former President Reagan's proposed space-based nuclear defense system, known officially as the Strategic Defense Initiative.

States' rights The belief that the power of the federal government should not be increased at the expense of the states' power.

Statistical Abstract Annual summary of reports published by the federal government.

Statutes Laws passed by the legislative body of a representative government.

Steering The practice in which realtors promoted segregation by showing blacks houses in black neighborhoods and whites houses in white neighborhoods.

Straw polls Unscientific polls.

Structural unemployment Joblessness that results from the rapidly changing nature of the economy, which displaces, for example, auto and steel industry workers.

Subcommittee bill of rights Measures introduced by Democrats in the House of Representatives in 1973 and 1974 that allowed members of a committee to choose subcommittee chairs and established a fixed jurisdiction and adequate budget and staff for each subcommittee.

Subgovernment A mutually supportive group comprising a **pressure group,** an executive agency, and a congressional committee or subcommittee with common policy interests that makes public policy decisions with little interference from the president or Congress as a whole and little awareness by the public. Also known as an iron triangle.

Subpoena A court order requiring someone to appear in court to give testimony under penalty of punishment.

Suffrage The right to vote.

Superdelegates Democratic delegates, one-fifth of the total sent to the national convention who are appointed by Democratic Party organizations, in order to retain some party control over the convention. Most are public officials, such as members of Congress.

Superfund Revenue from a tax imposed on industry, along with federal funds, that is used for cleaning up hazardous waste sites.

Super Tuesday The day when most southern states hold **presidential preference primaries** simultaneously.

Supplemental Security Income (SSI) A program that provides supplemental income for those who are blind, elderly, or disabled and living in poverty.

Supply-side economics The argument that tax revenues will increase if tax rates are reduced; supposedly, more money will be available for business expansion and modernization, which will stimulate employment and economic growth and result in higher tax revenues.

Supremacy clause A clause in the U.S. Constitution stating that treaties and laws made by the national government are to be supreme over state laws in cases of conflict.

Symbiotic relationship A relationship in which the parties use each other for mutual advantage.

Symbolic speech The use of symbols, rather than words, to convey ideas; e.g., wearing black armbands or burning the U.S. flag to protest government policy.

Tariff A special tax or "duty" imposed on imported or exported goods.

Tax deductions Certain expenses or payments that may be deducted from one's taxable income.

Tax exemptions Certain amounts deductible from one's annual income in calculating income tax.

Teapot Dome scandal A 1921 scandal in which President Warren Harding's secretary of the interior received large contributions from corporations that were then allowed to lease oil reserves (called the Teapot Dome); led to the Federal Corrupt Practices Act of 1925, which required reporting of campaign contributions and expenditures.

Temporary Assistance for Needy Families (TANF) A program that provides income support for the poor; successor to Aid to Families with Dependent Children (AFDC).

Third party A political party made up of independents or dissidents from the major parties, often advocating radical change or pushing single issues.

Three-fifths Compromise The decision of the **Constitutional Convention** that three-fifths of a state's slave population would be counted in apportioning seats in the House of Representatives.

Ticket splitting Voting for a member of one party for a high-level office and a member of another party for a different high-level office.

Trade association An **interest** or **pressure group** that represents a single industry, such as builders.

Traditionalistic political culture One of three political cultures in the United States. One in which politics is left to a small elite and is viewed as a way to maintain the status quo. See **individualistic** and **moralistic political cultures.**

Tragedy of the commons The concept that although individuals benefit when they exploit goods that are common to all such as air and water, the community as a whole suffers from the pollution and depletion of resources that occur; a reason for **regulation.**

Treason The betrayal of one's country by knowingly aiding its enemies.

Truth in labeling The requirement that manufacturers, lenders, and other business entities provide certain kinds of information to consumers or employees.

Turnout The proportion of eligible citizens who vote in an election.

Unanimous consent agreements Procedures by which a legislative body may dispense with standard rules and limit debate and amendments.

Underdogs Candidates for public office who are thought to have little chance of being elected.

Unfunded mandates Federal laws that require the states to do something without providing full funding for the required activity.

Unitary system A system in which the national government is supreme; subnational governments are created by the national government and have only the power it allocates to them.

United Nations An international organization formed in 1945 for the purpose of promoting peace and worldwide cooperation. It is headquartered in New York.

Unreasonable searches and seizures Searches and arrests that are conducted without a warrant or that do not fall into one of the exceptions to the warrant requirement; prohibited by the Fourth Amendment.

Unscientific polls Unsystematic samplings of popular sentiments; also known as **straw polls.**

Vietnam syndrome An attitude of uncertainty about U.S. foreign policy goals and our ability to achieve them by military means; engendered among the public and officials as a result of the U.S. failure in Vietnam.

Voting Rights Act (VRA) A law passed by Congress in 1965 that made it illegal to interfere with anyone's right to vote. The act and its subsequent amendments have been the main vehicles for expanding and protecting minority voting rights.

War Powers Act A 1973 statute enacted by Congress to limit the president's ability to commit troops to combat.

Warren Court The U.S. Supreme Court under Chief Justice Earl Warren (1953–1969); an activist Court that expanded the rights of criminal defendants and racial and religious minorities.

Watergate scandal The attempt to break into Democratic National Committee headquarters in 1972 that ultimately led to President Richard M. Nixon's resignation for his role in attempting to cover up the break-in and other criminal and unethical actions.

Weber, Max German social scientist, author of pioneering studies on the nature of bureaucracies.

Whigs Members of the Whig Party, founded in 1834 by National Republicans and several other factions who opposed Jacksonian Democrats.

Whips Members of the House of Representatives who work to maintain party unity by keeping in contact with party members and attempting to win their support. Both the majority and the minority party have a whip and several assistant whips.

Whistleblower An individual employee who exposes mismanagement and abuse of discretion in an agency.

White primary A device for preventing blacks from voting in the South. Under the pretense that political parties were private clubs, blacks were barred from voting in Democratic primaries, which were the real elections because Democrats always won the general elections.

Whitewater investigation An investigation conducted by a **special prosecutor** into the activities of President Bill Clinton and Hillary Rodham Clinton in connection with an Arkansas land deal and other alleged wrongdoings.

Wire services News-gathering organizations such as the Associated Press and United Press International that provide news stories and other editorial features to the media organizations that are their members.

Writ of certiorari An order issued by a higher court to a lower court to send up the record of a case for review; granting the writ is the usual means by which the U.S. Supreme Court agrees to hear a case.

Yuppies Young upwardly mobile professionals.

Acid rain Lluvia acida
Actionable Procesable, enjuiciable
Action-Reaction syndrome síndrome de
acción y reacción
Actual malice Malicia expresa
Administrative agency Agencia administrativa
Advice and consent Consejo y
consentimiento
Affirm Afirmar
Affirmative action Acción afirmativa
Agenda setting Agenda establecida
**Aid to Families with Dependent Children
(AFDC)** Ayuda para Familias con Niños
Dependientes
Amicus curiae brief Tercer persona o grupo
no involucrado en el caso, admitido en un
juicio para hacer valer el interés público o el
de un grupo social importante
Anarchy Anarquía
Anti-Federalists Anti-Federalistas
Appellate court Corte de apelación
Appointment power Poder de apuntamiento
Appropriation Apropiación
Aristocracy Aristocracia
Attentive public Público atento
Australian ballot Voto Australiano
Authority Autoridad
Authorization Autorización

Bad-tendency rule Regla de tendencia-mala
"Beauty contest" Concurso de belleza
Bicameralism Bicameralismo
Bicameral legislature Legislatura bicameral
Bill of Rights Declaración de Derechos
Blanket primary Primaria comprensiva
Block grants Concesiones de bloque
Bureaucracy Burocracia
Busing Transporte público

Cabinet Gabinete, consejo de ministros
Cabinet department Departamento del
gabinete
Cadre El núcleo de activistas de partidos
políticos encargados de cumplir las funciones
importantes de los partidos políticos
americanos
Canvassing board Consejo encargado con la
encuesta de una violación
Capture Captura, toma
Casework Trabajo de caso
Categorical grants-in-aid Concesiones
categóricas de ayuda
Caucus Reunión de dirigentes
Challenge Reto
Checks and balances Chequeos y equilibrio
Chief diplomat Jefe diplomático
Chief executive Jefe ejecutivo
Chief of staff Jefe de personal
Chief of state Jefe de estado
Civil law Derecho civil
Civil liberties Libertades civiles
Civil rights Derechos civiles
Civil service Servicio civil
Civil Service Commission Comisión de
Servicio Civil
Class-action suit Demanda en representación
de un grupo o clase
Class politics Política de clase

Clear and present danger test Prueba de
peligro claro y presente
Climate control Control de clima
Closed primary Primaria cerrada
Cloture Cierre al voto
Coattail effect Effecto de cola de chaqueta
Cold War Guerra Fría
Commander in chief Comandante en jefe
Commerce clause Cláusula de comercio
Commercial speech Discurso comercial
Common law Ley común, derecho
consuetudinario
Comparable worth Valor comparable
Compliance De acuerdo
Concurrent majority Mayoría concurrente
Concurring opinion Opinión concurrente
Confederal system Sistema confederal
Confederation Confederación
Conference committee Comité de conferencia
Consensus Concenso
Consent of the people Consentimiento de la
gente
Conservatism Calidad de conservador
Conservative coalition Coalición
conservadora
Consolidation Consolidación
Constant dollars Dólares constantes
Constitutional initiative Iniciativa
constitucional
Constitutional power Poder constitucional
Containment Contenimiento
Continuing resolution Resolución contínua
Cooperative federalism Federalismo
cooperativo
Corrupt Practices Acts Leyes Contra Acciones
Corruptas
Council of Economic Advisers (CEA)
Consejo de Asesores Económicos
Council of Government (COG) Consejo de
Gobierno
County Condado
Credentials committee Comité de credenciales
Criminal law Ley criminal

De facto segregation Segregación de hecho
De jure segregation Segregación cotidiana
Defamation of character Defamación de
carácter
Democracy Democracia
Democratic Party Partido Democrático
Détente No Spanish equivalent
Dillon's Rule Regla de Dillon
Diplomacy Diplomácia
Direct democracy Democracia directa
Direct primary Primaria directa
Direct technique Técnica directa
Discharge petition Petición de descargo
Dissenting opinion Opinión disidente
Divisive opinion Opinión divisiva
Domestic policy Principio político doméstico
Dual citizenship Ciudadanía dual
Dual federalism Federalismo dual

Economic aid Ayuda económica
Economic regulation Regulación económica
**Elastic clause, or necessary and proper
clause** Cláusula flexible, o cláusula propia
necesaria

Elector Elector
Electoral College Colegio Electoral
Electronic media Media electronica
Elite Elite (el selecto)
Elite theory Teoría elitista (de lo selecto)
Emergency power Poder de emergencia
Enumerated power Poder enumerado
Environmental impact statement
Afirmación de impacto ambiental
**Equal Employment Opportunity
Commission (EEOC)** Comisión de
Igualdad de Oportunidad en el Empleo
Equality Igualdad
Equalization Igualación
Era of good feelings Era de buen sentimiento
Era of personal politics Era de política
personal
Establishment clause Cláusula de
establecimiento
Euthanasia Eutanasia
Exclusionary rule Regla de exclusión
Executive agreement Acuerdo ejecutivo
Executive budget Presupuesto ejecutivo
Executive Office of the President (EOP)
Oficina Ejecutiva del Presidente
Executive order Orden ejecutivo
Executive privilege Privilegio ejecutivo
Expressed power Poder expresado
Extradite Entregar por extradición

Faction Facción
Fairness doctrine Doctrina de justicia
Fall review Revisión de otoño
Federalist Federalista
Federal mandate Mandato federal
Federal Open Market Committee (FOMC)
Comité Federal de Libre Mercado
Federal Register Registro Federal
Federal system Sistema federal
Federalists Federalistas
Fighting words Palabras de provocación
Filibuster Obstrucción de iniciativas de ley
Fireside chat Charla de hogar
First budget resolution Resolución primera
presupuesta
First Continental Congress Primér Congreso
Continental
Fiscal policy Político fiscal
Fiscal year (FY) Año fiscal
Fluidity Fluidez
Food stamps Estampillas para comida
Foreign policy Política extranjera
Foreign policy process Proceso de política
extranjera
Franking Franqueando
Fraternity Fraternidad
Free exercise clause Cláusula de ejercico
libre
Full faith and credit clause Cláusula de
completa fé y crédito
Functional consolidation Consolidación
funcional

Gag order Orden de silencio
Garbage can model Modelo bote de basura
Gender gap Brecha de género
General law city Regla general urbana
General sales tax Impuesto general de ventas

Generational effect Efecto generacional
Gerrymandering División arbitraria de los distritos electorales con fines políticos
Government Gobierno
Government corporation Corporación gubernamental
Government in the Sunshine Act Gobierno en la Acta: Luz del Sol
Grandfather clause Cláusula del abuelo
Grand jury Gran jurado
Great Compromise Grán Acuerdo de Negociación

Hatch Act (Political Activities Act) Acta Hatch (acta de actividades políticas)
Hecklers' veto Veto de abuchamiento
Home rule city Regla urbana
Horizontal federalism Federalismo horizontal
Hyperpluralism Hiperpluralismo

Ideologue Ideólogo
Ideology Ideología
Image building Construcción de imágen
Impeachment Acción penal contra un funcionario público
Inalienable rights Derechos inalienables
Income transfer Transferencia de ingresos
Incorporation theory Teoría de incorporación
Independent Independiente
Independent candidate Candidato independiente
Independent executive agency Agencia ejecutiva independiente
Independent regulatory agency Agencia regulatoria independiente
Indirect technique Técnica indirecta
Inherent power Poder inherente
Initiative Iniciativa
Injunction Injunción, prohibición judicial
In-kind subsidy Subsidio de clase
Institution Institución
Instructed delegate Delegado con instrucciones
Intelligence community Comunidad de inteligencia
Intensity Intensidad
Interest group Grupo de interés
Interposition Interposición
Interstate compact Compacto interestatal
Iron Curtain Cortina de Acero
Iron triangle Triángulo de acero
Isolationist foreign policy Política extranjera de aislamiento
Issue voting Voto temático
Item veto Artículo de veto

Jim Crow laws No Spanish equivalent
Joint committee Comité mancomunado
Judicial activism Activismo judicial
Judicial implementation Implementación judicial
Judicial restraint Restricción judicial
Judicial review Revisión judicial
Jurisdiction Jurisdicción
Justiciable dispute Disputa judiciaria
Justiciable question Pregunta justiciable

Keynesian economics Economía Keynesiana
Kitchen cabinet Gabinete de cocina

Labor movement Movimiento laboral
Latent public opinion Opinión pública latente
Lawmaking Hacedores de ley
Legislative history Historia legislativa

Legislative initiative Iniciativa de legislación
Legislative veto Veto legislativo
Legislature Legislatura
Legitimacy Legitimidad
Libel Libelo, difamación escrita
Liberalism Liberalismo
Liberty Libertad
Limited government Gobierno limitado
Line organization Organización de linea
Literacy test Exámen de alfabetización
Litigate Litigar
Lobbying Cabildeo
Logrolling Práctica legislativa que consiste en incluir en un mismo proyecto de ley temas de diversa índole
Loophole Hueco legal, escapatoria

Madisonian model Modelo Madisónico
Majority Mayoría
Majority floor leader Líder mayoritario de piso
Majority leader of the House Líder mayoritario de la Casa
Majority opinion Opinión mayoritaria
Majority rule Regla de mayoría
Managed news Noticias manipuladas
Mandatory retirement Retiro mandatorio
Matching funds Fondos combinados
Material incentive Incentivo material
Media Media
Media access Acceso de media
Merit system Sistema de mérito
Military-industrial complex Complejo industriomilitar
Minority floor leader Líder minoritario de piso
Minority leader of the House Líder minorial de la Casa
Monetary policy Política monetaria
Monopolistic model Modelo monopólico
Monroe Doctrine Doctrina Monroe
Moral idealism Idealismo moral
Municipal home rule Regla municipal

Narrow casting Mensaje dirigído
National committee Comité nacional
National convention Convención nacional
National politics Política nacional
National Security Council (NSC) Concilio de Seguridad Nacional
National security policy Política de seguridad nacional
National aristocracy Aristocracia natural
Natural rights Derechos naturales
Necessaries Necesidades
Negative constituents Constituyentes negativos
New England town Pueblo de Nueva Inglaterra
New federalism Federalismo nuevo
Nullification Nulidad, anulación

Office-block (Massachusetts) ballot Cuadro-oficina (Massachusetts), voto
Office of Management and Budget (OMB) Oficina de Administración y Presupuesto
Oligarchy Oligarquía
Ombudsman Funcionario que representa al ciudadano ante el gobierno
Open primary Primaria abierta
Opinion Opinión
Opinion leader Líder de opinión
Opinion poll Encuesta, conjunto de opinión
Oral arguments Argumentos orales
Oversight Inadvertencia, omisión

Paid-for political announcement Anuncios políticos pagados
Pardon Perdón
Party-column (Indiana) ballot Partido-columna (Indiana) voto
Party identification Identificación de partido
Party identifier Identificador de partido
Party-in-electorate Partido electoral
Party-in-government Partido en gobierno
Party organization Organización de partido
Party platform Plataforma de partido
Patronage Patrocinio
Peer group Grupo de contemporáneos
Pendleton Act (Civil Service Reform Act) Acta Pendleton (Acta de Reforma al Servicio Civil)
Personal attack rule Regla de ataque personal
Petit jury Jurado ordinario
Pluralism Pluralismo
Plurality Pluralidad
Pocket veto Veto de bolsillo
Police power Poder policiaco
Policy trade-offs Intercambio de políticas
Political Action Committee (PAC) Comité de acción política
Political consultant Consultante político
Political culture Cultura política
Political party Partido político
Political question Pregunta política
Political realism Realismo político
Political socialization Socialización política
Political tolerance Tolerancia política
Political trust Confianza política
Politico Político
Politics Política
Poll tax Impuesto sobre el sufrágio
Poll watcher Observador de encuesta
Popular sovereignty Soberanía popular
Power Poder
Precedent Precedente
Preferred-position test Prueba de posición preferida
Presidential primary Primaria presidencial
President pro tempore Presidente provisoriamente
Press secretary Secretaría de prensa
Prior restraint Restricción anterior
Privileges and immunities Privilégios e imunidades
Privatization, or contracting out Privatización
Property Propiedad
Property tax Impuesto de propiedad
Public agenda Agenda pública
Public debt financing Financiamiento de deuda pública
Public debt, or national debt Deuda pública o nacional
Public interest Interés público
Public opinion Opinión pública
Purposive incentive Incentivo de propósito

Ratification Ratificación
Rational ignorance effect Efecto de ignorancia racional
Reapportionment Redistribución
Recall Suspender
Recognition power Poder de reconocimiento
Recycling Reciclaje
Redistricting Redistrictificación
Referendum Referéndum
Registration Registración
Regressive tax Impuestos regresivos
Relevance Pertinencia

Remand Reenviar
Representation Representación
Representative assembly Asamblea representativa
Representative democracy Democracia representativa
Reprieve Tregua, suspensión
Republic República
Republican party Partido Republicano
Resulting powers Poderes resultados
Reverse Cambiarse a lo contrario
Reverse discrimination Discriminación reversiva
Rule of four Regla de cuatro
Rules committee Comité regulador
Run-off primary Primaria residual

Safe seat Asiento seguro
Sampling error Error de encuesta
Secession Secesión
Second budget resolution Resolución segunda presupuestal
Second Continental Congress Segundo Congreso Continental
Sectional politics Política seccional
Segregation Segregación
Select committee Comité selecto
Selectperson Persona selecta
Senatorial courtesy Cortesía senatorial
Seniority system Sistema señiorial
Separate-but-equal doctrine Separados pero iguales
Separation of powers Separación de poderes
Service sector Sector de servicio
Sex discrimination Discriminación sexual
Sexual harassment Acosamiento sexual
Slander Difamación oral, calumnia
Sliding-scale test Prueba escalonada
Social movement Movimiento social
Social Security Seguridad Social
Socioeconomic status Estado socioeconómico
Solidary incentive Incentivo de solidaridad
Solid South Súr Sólido
Sound bite Mordida de sonido

Soviet bloc Bloque Soviético
Speaker of the House Vocero de la Casa
Spin Girar/giro
Spin doctor Doctor en giro
Spin-off party Partido estático
Spoils system Sistema de despojos
Spring review Revisión de primavera
Stability Estabilidad
Standing committee Comité de sostenimiento
Stare decisis El principio característico del ley común por el cual los precedentes jurisprudenciales tienen fuerza obligatoria, no sólo entre las partes, sino también para casos sucesivos análogos
State Estado
State central committee Comité central del estado
State of the Union message Mensaje sobre el Estado de la Unión
Statutory power Poder estatorial
Strategic Arms Limitation Treaty (SALT I) Tratado de Limitación de Armas Estratégicas
Subpoena Orden de testificación
Subsidy Subsidio
Suffrage Sufrágio
Sunset legislation Legislación sunset
Superdelegate Líder de partido u oficial elegido quien tiene el derecho de votar
Supplemental Security Income (SSI) Ingresos de Seguridad Suplementaria
Supremacy clause Cláusula de supremacia
Supremacy doctrine Doctrina de supremacia
Symbolic speech Discurso simbólico

Technical assistance Asistencia técnica
Third party Tercer partido
Third-party candidate Candidato de tercer partido
Ticket splitting División de boletos
Totalitarian regime Régimen totalitario
Town manager system Sistema de administrador municipal
Town meeting Junta municipal
Township Municipio

Tracking poll Seguimiento de encuesta
Trial court Tribunal de primera
Truman Doctrine Doctrina Truman
Trustee Depositario
Twelfth Amendment Doceava Enmienda
Twenty-fifth Amendment Veinticincoava Enmienda
Two-party system Sistema de dos partidos

Unanimous opinion Opinión unánime
Underground economy Economía subterráea
Unicameral legislature Legislatura unicameral
Unincorporated area Area no incorporada
Unitary system Sistema unitario
Unit rule Regla de unidad
Universal suffrage Sufrágio universal
U.S. Treasury bond Bono de la Tesoreria de E.U.A.

Veto message Comunicado de veto
Voter turnout Renaimiento de votantes

War Powers Act Acta de Poderes de Guerra
Washington community Comunidad de Washington
Weberian model Modelo Weberiano
Whip Látigo
Whistleblower Privatización o contratista
White House Office Oficina de la Casa Blanca
White House press corps Cuerpo de prensa de la Casa Blanca
White primary Sufrágio en elección primaria/blancos solamente
Writ of certiorari Prueba de certeza; orden emitida por el tribunal de apelaciones para que el tribunal inferior dé lugar a la apelación
Writ of habeas corpus Prueba de evidencia concreta
Writ of mandamus Un mandato por la corte para que un acto se lleve a cabo

Yellow journalism Amarillismo periodístico

interest groups, 157–158
media bias and, 128
New Deal coalition and, 185
in public schools, 9–10
voting choices and, 242, 243
voting rights, religious tests and, 211
Religious Right
conservatism of, 97
gospel grapevine, 165
interest groups, 157
media coverage, 128
Republican Party and, 194
Rendition procedure, 41
Republican Eagles, 258
Republican National Committee
(RNC), 197
Republican Party, 10. *See also*
Realignment
abortion issue, 450
business interests and, 150
characteristics of, 194–195
in Congress, 196, 283
dominance of, 183
economic policy and, 514–517
elephant symbol, 183
Equal Rights Amendment and, 492
on estate taxes, 505–506
ethical lapses in, 273
ethnic voters and, 186
founding of, 182
geographic distribution for, 234–235
media bias, 125
mobilization of voters, 222
moderates in, 178
PAC donations, 262
partisan intensity, 187
party identification and voting,
242–243
platform in 2000, 192
positions of, 179–180
race and, 95
Religious Right and, 194
right, movement to, 178
rise of, 182–183
soft money donations, reward for, 258
trends in, 187
Vietnam War and, 185
Whitewater scandal, 121
Republicans for Clean Air, 259–260
Republics, 16, 28, 30–31
Reregulation, 578–580
of airline industry, 580–581
Research by bureaucracy, 377
Responsible party government, 195
Restrictive covenants, 474
Retrospective voting, 244
Revolutionary Communist Youth
Brigade, 429
Revolutionary War
interest groups and, 147
women veterans of, 27
Riceland Foods, 539
Rice Mill, 539
Rickets, 546
Right to counsel, 444–445, 448
death penalty cases, 445, 448
Right to die, 455–456
Right-to-life groups, 450, 452
"Right Words" (Luntz), 96
Riots, 466–467, 483
Risk assessment, 571–572
RJ Reynolds, 145–146, 174
RJR Nabisco, 145–146
Rock the Vote, MTV, 219
Roe v. Wade, 390, 414, 449–450, 452
RU-486 (abortion pill), 161
Ruby Ridge standoff, 359
Ruckus Society, 168
Rule of four, 407
Rules Committee, 230, 305–306
Rumors, media and, 114–115
Russia. *See also* Soviet Union
foreign aid to, 630
immigration from, 9
nuclear weapons in, 633
Russian Orthodox immigrants, 6
Russian Revolution, 7
Rutherford Institute, 406

Sadomasochism, 433
Safe Drinking Water Act of 1974, 587
Sales tax, national, 520–521

Salon magazine, 113
Same-day voter registration, 222
Same-sex marriages, 454–455
Samples, 89
Santeria religion, 435
Sarbanes-Oxley Act, 276
Saturday Night Massacre, 24
Savings and loan association bailout,
578–580
Schering-Plough, 151
Schindler's List, 89
Schools. *See also* African Americans;
Colleges and universities; Prayer in
schools; Segregation
and affirmative action, 499
as agents of political socialization,
83–86
bilingual education, 485–486
Brown v. Board of Education, 468–469
busing, 470–471
Columbine High School attacks, 132
creationism, teaching of, 440
desegregation of, 467–471
evolution, teaching of, 440
funding, inequality in, 475–476
hidden curriculum in, 85
Hispanics, discrimination against,
484–486
inner-city schools, 476
media coverage, 128
parochial schools, establishment clause
and, 440–441
prayer, decision on, 411
prior restraint and publications of, 430
religious practice in, 9–10
second-generation discrimination,
476–477
separate-but-equal doctrine, 465
Title IX of Education Amendment of
1972, 495–496
women, discrimination against, 490
Scoops, 117
Scurvy, 546
Seabord Corporation, 553
Search and seizure, 441, 443
exclusionary rule and, 443
stop and frisk, 443
Sea Shepherds, 160
Secession, federalism and, 55
Second Amendment
civil liberties in, 424
full text of, 645
gun control and, 442
SEC (Securities and Exchange
Commission), 251–252, 373
accountancy industry and, 384
Congress and, 309
Enron and, 275–276
Financial Accounting Standards Board
(FASBE) and, 573
Pitt, Harvey and, 576
Schumer, Charles and, 274–276
Securities industry, Glass-Steagall Act, 582
Sedition Act of 1798, 112
Sedition Act of 1918, 425
Seditious speech, 425–426
Segregation, 464–465
Brown v. Board of Education, 468–469
de facto segregation, 470–471, 474
de jure segregation, 470, 474
Hispanics, school segregation and, 454
housing, desegregation of, 474
Jim Crow laws, 465
in North, 465
overlapping Constitutional powers
and, 46
persistence of, 479
public accommodations, desegregation
of, 473, 477
public opinion on, 100
residential segregation, 471
separate-but-equal doctrine, 465
Select committees, 300
Selective perception, 137
Self-incrimination, privilege against,
443–444
Senate. *See also* Committees
cabinet nominations, approval of, 325
calendars of, 305
challengers in, 239
cloture vote in, 307
consent agreements in, 306–307

contemporary leadership of, 296
differences from House, 308
direct-election constitutional
amendment, 39
filibusters, 307–308
friendships in, 289
incumbents, security of, 239, 241
judges, criteria for, 402–404
majority leader in, 297–298
presidential campaigns, senators in, 224
presiding officer of, 296
specialization in, 289
terms in, 32
Watergate Committee hearings, 48
Senatorial courtesy, 325
judges, selection of, 400
Seneca Nation, 34
Senior Executive Service (SES), 382
Seniority rule, 299
Sensationalism of news, 131
Separate-but-equal doctrine, 465
Separation of church and state, 435
Separation of powers, 31–32, 46
Separation policy, 487
September 11th attacks, xiii, 2, 4
airline industry and, 580, 581
Al-Jazeera on, 138
American system and, 5
bipartisanship and, 188–189
budgetary issues and, 516–517
Bush, George W. on, 123
executive orders after, 327
FBI (Federal Bureau of Investigation)
and, 359–361
federal budget after, 310
FEMA (Federal Emergency
Management Agency) and NYC,
64–65
Foreign Intelligence Surveillance Court
and, 400
government, views on, 20
human life, value of, 571
Hussein, Saddam and, 598
immigration and, 8–9
imperial presidency and, 328–329
intelligence-gathering failures and, 622
interest groups and, 152–153
leaks about, 117
media bias and, 125
National Guard units and, 72
new issues after, xiv
normalcy after, 82
opinion about government and, 87
partisanship and, 240
political socialization and, 86
presidential succession issue and, 324
public documents, deletion of,
366–367
racial issues and, 102
Religious Right on, 157
workplace deaths and, 577
Sequoia National Forest, California, 51, 76
Service Employees International
Union, 154
Serviceman's Readjustment Act, 550–551
Setting the agenda, 135
Seven Sister oil companies, 582
Seventh Amendment
civil liberties in, 424
full text of, 645
Seventh-Day Adventists, 435
Seventh Fleet
in Japan, 625
Seventeenth Amendment, 32
full text of, 647
Sex discrimination, 489–496
Sex education, 161
Sexual harassment, 496–497
Sharecropping, 465
Shays's Rebellion, 26
Sherman Antitrust Act of 1890, 567, 574
Sierra Club, 160
court access and, 406
protest tactics, 168
Sikh religion, 436, 440
Silent Spring (Carson), 585
Single-member districts, 189
Single parents, welfare for, 545
Sit-ins, 169
Sixth Amendment
civil liberties in, 424
full text of, 645

jury trial, right to, 448
right to counsel, 444–445, 448
Sixteenth Amendment, full text of, 646
60 Minutes, 129, 130
Slavery, 10, 462–463
black slave owners, 464
Continental Congress issue, 29–30
Dred Scott case, 395, 463
Emancipation Proclamation, 41–42, 463
Fourteenth Amendment, 43
Fugitive Slave Act, 73
interest groups and, 147
Lincoln, Abraham and, 41
Reconstruction period, former slaves
in, 464–465
Republican Party and, 184
Senate debates over, 294
slave ships, 29
Thirteenth Amendment abolishing,
39, 43
Three-fifths Compromise, 30
SLOP surveys, 91
Small Business Administration, 553
Small-scale government, 59
Smith Act, 425
Smog, 565
Smoking, 146
Snake handling, 437
Social contract, 36
Social disintegration, 482
Socialism, 507
media bias and, 125
mixed economies, 507–508
Social issues. *See also* Abortion; Gay
issues; Social welfare; Women
campaign finance and, 267
media bias and, 127–128
public opinion on, 98–100
Religious Right on, 157
Socialist Party, 147
Social Security, 62, 541–543
AARP (American Association of
Retired Persons) and, 159
Congress members paying, 283
future of, 556–557
national sales tax and, 521
partisan politics and, 188
polls on, 90
public support for, 97–98
qualification for, 542
restructuring system, 557
same-sex couples, 454–455
as social insurance, 542
taxes, 518, 519
Social Security Administration, 368
role of, 373
Social Security Trust Fund, 523
integrity of, 557
privatization reforms, 557
in Reagan–Bush years, 526
Social welfare policies, 508, 539. *See also*
Medicaid; Medicare; Subsidies;
Welfare
AFDC (Aid to Families with
Dependent Children), 544–545
child-care assistance, 549
corporate welfare, 552–554
direct federal aid, 541
evolution of, 540–541
food stamps, 546–547
future of, 559
for health care, 548–549
liberal-conservative continuum and, 97
political/legal bases of, 539–540
poor, aid to, 543–547
responsiveness of, 559
role of government in, 97–98
TANF (Temporary Assistance to
Needy Families), 545–546
working poor, 546
Sodomy laws, 454
Soft money, 257–258
corporation donations, 262
labor union donations, 262
McCain-Feingold Act, 260
sources of, 261–263
Somalia, troops in, 349
Sound bites, 118–119, 342
South Africa
AIDS in, 634
apartheid era, 167
constitution of, 45

World Trade Center attacks. *See* September 11th attacks
World Trade Organization (WTO), 168, 559
  protectionism and, 627
  U.S. ambassadors to, 621
World War I
  German immigrants and, 7
  isolationism and, 611
  seditious speech and, 425

Wilson, Woodrow and, 320
  women's suffrage and, 214, 215
World War II
  containment policy and, 611–612
  Depression, recovery from, 45
  federalism and, 62
  immigration during, 6
  isolationism and, 611
  Japanese American internment, 7, 329, 332

political socialization and, 86
  Roosevelt, Franklin D. and, 321
  seditious speech and, 425
Writ of certiorari, 407

Xerox, 276

YMCA, 168
Young adults and voting, 216, 219

Yucca Mountain facility, 563–564, 594–596
Yugoslavia, 613
  bombing of, 622
  federalism in, 52, 53

Zaire, 631

Chapter 14

420 Jonathan Barth/Gamma; **425** UPI/Corbis Bettmann; **426** UPI/Corbis Bettmann; **427** Sargent © Universal Press Syndicate. Reprinted with permission. All rights reserved; **428** Hiroji Kubota/Magnum Photos; **429** UPI/Corbis Bettmann; **430** AP Wide World Photos; **431** © 2003 Bob Sacha; **434** Photo by Tom Defoe © 1965, *The Des Moines Register and Tribune Co.* Reprinted with permission; **436** © Phil Schofield; **437** Courtesy of National Archives; **438** © Sylvia Plachy, photographed for *The New Yorker;* **440** Robert Nickelsberg/Timepix; **441** Steve Liss/*Time* magazine; **442** © The New Yorker Collection 1999, Robert Mankoff from cartoonbank.com. All rights reserved; **444** Mark Solomon/*Time* magazine; **445 both** Courtesy of National Archives; **453** Joyce Marshall/*Ft. Worth Star-Telegram*/AP Photo; **454** © *Los Angeles Times.* Reprinted by permission; **455** Steven E. Frischling/Corbis Sygma; **457** Jonathan Barth photography

Chapter 15

460 Justine Parsons; **462** Courtesy of Franklin D. Roosevelt Library, NLR-PHOCO-A-7420 (394); **463** Boston Athenaeum; **466** Tulsa Historical Society; **467** © Bettmann/Corbis; **468** National Archives/Harmon Collection, 200(S)-HS-1-92; **469 both** Will Counts; **470** Stanley J. Forman, Pulitzer Prize, 1977; **471** Charles Moore/Black Star; **472** Fred Blackwell/*Jackson Daily News;* **473** AP Wide World Photos; **476** © David Fields; **478** © Mark Heckman; **485** Stephanie Maze/Corbis; **486** © Mario Pignata–Monti; **487** © The New Yorker Collection 1998, P. C. Vey from cartoonbank.com. All rights reserved; **488 both** Denver Public Library, Western History Collection, J. N. Choate (X-32984, X-32985); **489** © Mug Shots/Corbis; **491 left** Printed by permission of the Norman Rockwell Family Agency © 2003 the Norman Rockwell Family Entities; **491 right** "Fallen Cake" by Stevan Dohanos © 1955 SEPS: Licensed by Curtis Publishing, Indianapolis, IN. All rights reserved. www.curtispublishing.com; **492** © The New Yorker Collection 1996, Liza Donnelly from cartoonbank.com. All rights reserved; **493** Mike Fiala; **494** UPI/Corbis Bettmann; **498** Brent Humphreys; **502** Courtesy of the National Archives, NW-DNS-210-G-A753

Chapter 16

504 © Rich Frishman/frishphoto.com; **506** © The New Yorker Collection 2001, Frank Cotham from cartoonbank.com. All rights reserved; **509** Corbis-Bettmann; **511** UPI/Corbis-Bettmann; **513** Michael O'Neill/Corbis; **514** © The New Yorker Collection 1998, Charles Barsotti from cartoonbank.com. All rights reserved; **515** Robert A. Davis photography; **525 left** Library of Congress; **525 right** Photo by Bill Ganzel from *Dust Bowl Descent,* University of Nebraska Press; **527** © The New Yorker Collection, 1998, Joseph Mirachi from cartoonbank.com. All rights reserved; **530 left** "The Money Tree" © Winston Smith. Reprinted by permission; **530 right** © The New Yorker Collection 1998, Frank Cotham from cartoonbank.com. All rights reserved; **531** Tom Tomorrow © 2001; **533** Toles © *The Buffalo News.* Reprinted with special permission of Universal Press Syndicate. All rights reserved.

Chapter 17

536 Brad Doherty, Brownsville, TX; **540** Jane Addams Memorial Collection (JAMC Neg #5871), Special Collections, Richard J. Daley Library, University of Illinois at Chicago; **542** Mary Ellen Mark; **542** Toles © *The Buffalo News.* Reprinted with permission of Universal Press Syndicate. All rights reserved; **546** Wasserman © 2000 *Los Angeles Times.* Reprinted by permission; **547** Library of Congress; **548** © 1991 Lester Sloan, Woodfin Camp & Associates. All rights reserved; **550** Indiana University Photographic Services; **552** Bebeto Matthews/AP Wide World Photos; **554** © 1995 Mark Alan Stamaty. Excerpted from "Washingtoon" with permission; **555** © The New Yorker Collection 1999, Jack Ziegler from cartoonbank.com. All rights reserved; **558** Reprinted with special permission of North American Syndicate; **560** By permission of Chip Bok and Creators Syndicate, Inc.

Chapter 18

562 © Tom Bean 1997/DRK Photo; **566** Phillippe Diederich, Houston, TX; **567** The Granger Collection, New York; **568** Reprinted with permission of Steve Kelley/*The Times-Picayune,* New Orleans; **569** Brad Trent; **571** United Mineworkers of America; **576** © The New Yorker Collection 1989, J. B. Handelsman from cartoonbank.com. All rights reserved; **579** Paula Nelson/*Dallas Morning News;* **582** scottadams @aol.com. 2002 United Feature Syndicate. Inc.; **583** J. Scott Applewhite/AP Photo; **585** AP/Wide World Photos; **589** Robbie McClaran; **591** Doug Menuez, Reportage; **593** Toles © *The Buffalo News.* Reprinted with permission of Universal Press Syndicate. All rights reserved; **595** AP Photo

Chapter 19

598 © Reuters NewMedia/Corbis; **600** Toles © *The New Republic.* Reprinted with permission of Universal Press Syndicate. All rights reserved; **609** Joyce Naltchayan © AFP/Corbis; **610** Art Collection, Harry Ransom Humanities Research Center. The University of Texas at Austin; **611** Courtesy Tatiana Baltermants and Paul Harbaugh; **613 both** Corbis/Sygma; **614 left** Paul S. Conklin; **614 right** Jack Kightlinger/Lyndon Baynes Johnson Library; **615 left** AP/Wide World Photos; **615 right** Joe McNally/*Life* magazine © Time, Inc./Timepix; **616** AP/Wide World Photos; **617** Courtesy of National Archives; **618** Alex S. MacLean/Landslides; **624** © The New Yorker Collection 1998, J. B. Handelsman from cartoonbank.com. All rights reserved; **627** Greg Baker/AP Photo; **628** Carol Guzy/*The Washington Post.* Reprinted with permission; **629** Reuters/STR/Archive Photos; **631** James Hill/*The New York Times;* **632** Brennan Linsley/AP Photo; **633** © The New Yorker Collection 1999, Jack Ziegler from cartoonbank.com. All rights reserved; **635** Etta Hulme © 2002 *Fort Worth Star-Telegram.* Reprinted by permission of United Media.